1, 2, & 3 JOHN

EVANGELICAL EXEGETICAL COMMENTARY

1, 2, & 3 JOHN

Gary W. Derickson

LEXHAM
ACADEMIC

1, 2, & 3 John
Evangelical Exegetical Commentary

Lexham Academic, an imprint of Lexham Press
1313 Commercial St., Bellingham, WA 98225
LexhamPress.com

English quotations from 1, 2, and 3 John for this commentary are the author's own translation.

Unless otherwise indicated, Bible quotations outside 1, 2, and 3 John are taken from the New King James Version. Copyright 1982 by Thomas Nelson, Inc.

Unless otherwise indicated, NT quotations in Greek are taken from *The Greek New Testament: SBL Edition*. Copyright 2012 by Lexham Press.

All italics added to direct Scripture quotations are the author's emphasis.

ISBN 978-1-57799-575-3

Lexham Editorial Team: Elliot Ritzema, Joel Wilcox
Cover Design: Brittany Schrock
Typsetting: ProjectLuz.com

25 26 27 28 29 30 / IN / 12 11 10 9 8 7 6 5 4 3

For Rebekah, my wife, and Ian, my son,
without whose encouragement and support
I could not have completed this work.

Contents

Commentary Editors

General Editor
H. Wayne House

Old Testament Editor
William D. Barrick

Assistant Old Testament Editor
JoAnna M. Hoyt

New Testament Editor
W. Hall Harris

Assistant New Testament Editor
Andrew W. Pitts

Acknowledgments

I wish to thank the general editor, H. Wayne House, for inviting me to participate in this series. His personal encouragement and help have been invaluable. I have learned much from him as well as from the study of these epistles. Through his encouragement and guidance I have grown as a student of the Scriptures. Through this deeper study, I have grown spiritually as well.

I also wish to thank NT editor W. Hall Harris III for his willingness to work with me and the encouragement he has given throughout the process of writing this commentary. His insights and suggestions have challenged and guided my understanding of key points. He has graciously led me to look more deeply into those points and enabled me to correct and clarify my thinking. I appreciate his extensive knowledge of Johannine literature and the guidance he has willingly provided me.

My greatest desire is that God will be glorified and Christ's church edified, not only through this work, but also through the entire EEC series. As we commit ourselves to the study of his inerrant Word, may he change each of us through it and use us to touch other lives in turn.

Editors' Preface

We are happy to present the Evangelical Exegetical Commentary (EEC) series on the Bible. Though there are many excellent commentaries that have been produced in recent years, the EEC is a needed addition for scholars, pastors, and students of the Bible. As the title of the series indicates, the authors of this series are committed to both the evangelical faith and a careful exegesis of the biblical text. Each of the authors affirms historic, orthodox Christianity and the inspiration and inerrancy of the Holy Scriptures. In this series, the biblical books are studied with the tested tools of biblical scholarship, keeping in mind that these books, produced by human authors, come from the very mouth of God (2 Tim 3:16). The EEC reflects the important interpretative principles of the Reformation, while utilizing historical-grammatical and contextual interpretative methods.

Each part of the biblical text—as reflected in the original reading—has something to teach us about God, his world, and how we should relate to him and to others. Thus in this series, each biblical unit is analyzed and interpreted. Then recommendations for application to everyday life and biblical theology are offered. This last step will aid pastors and teachers in their ministry of God's Word.

We hope that you will have greater appreciation for the Word of God and the ability to better share it because of reading the EEC.

For us, the EEC is an offering of praise to the great Triune God, who is our Creator, Savior, and Sustainer, and who, through Jesus the Messiah and Lord, dwelled among humanity to bring us salvation and gifts of His grace.

ὅτι ἐξ αὐτοῦ καὶ δι' αὐτοῦ καὶ εἰς αὐτὸν τὰ πάντα·
αὐτῷ ἡ δόξα εἰς τοὺς αἰῶνας, ἀμήν. (Rom 11:36)

Because out of him and through him and unto him are all things; To him be the glory unto all the ages, amen. (Rom 11:36)

H. Wayne House, General Editor
William D. Barrick, Old Testament Editor
JoAnna M. Hoyt, Assistant Old Testament Editor
W. Hall Harris, New Testament Editor
Andrew W. Pitts, New Testament Editor

Abbreviations

AB	Anchor Yale Bible Commentary
ACNT	Augsburg Commentaries on the New Testament
AD	anno Domini
ANTC	Abingdon New Testament Commentaries
ASV	American Standard Version
AUSS	*Andrews University Seminary Studies*
BBR	*Bulletin for Biblical Research*
BC	before Christ
BDAG	W. F. Bauer, W. Danker, W. F. Arndt, and F. W. Gingrich, *A Greek-English Lexicon of the New Testament and Other Early Christian Literature.* Rev. and ed. F. W. Danker, 3rd ed. Chicago: University of Chicago Press, 2000.
BDF	Blass, F., A. Debrunner, and R. W. Funk. *A Greek Grammar of the New Testament and Other Early Christian Literature.* Chicago: University of Chicago Press, 1961.
BECNT	Baker Exegetical Commentary on the New Testament
BFCT	Beiträge zur Förderung christlicher Theologie
BGNTL	Baker's Greek New Testament Library
BHS	*Biblia Hebraica Stuttgartensia,* 4th ed.
Bib	*Biblica*
BSac	*Bibliotheca Sacra*
BT	*The Bible Translator*
BTB	*Biblical Theology Bulletin*
Byz.	Byzantine
BZ	*Biblische Zeitschrift*
CBQ	*Catholic Biblical Quarterly*
CGTSC	Cambridge Greek Testament for Schools and Colleges
d.	died
DLNT	*Dictionary of the Later New Testament and Its Developments.* Ed. R. P. Martin and P. H. Davids. Downers Grove, IL: InterVarsity, 2000.
EKKNT	Evangelisch-katholischer Kommentar zum Neuen Testament

ESV	English Standard Version
Etern	*Eternity*
EvJ	*Evangelical Journal*
EvQ	*Evangelical Quarterly*
ExpTim	*Expository Times*
Greg	*Gregorianum*
GTJ	*Grace Theological Journal*
HCSB	Holman Christian Standard Bible
HNT	Handbuch zum Neuen Testament
HNTC	Harper's New Testament Commentaries
HTKNT	Herders theologischer Kommentar zum Neuen Testament
HTR	*Harvard Theological Review*
ICC	International Critical Commentary
Int	*Interpretation*
ISV	International Standard Version
IVPNTC	IVP New Testament Commentary Series
JBL	*Journal of Biblical Literature*
JETS	*Journal of the Evangelical Theological Society*
JOTGES	*Journal of the Grace Evangelical Society*
JOTT	*Journal of Translation and Textlinguistics*
JSNT	*Journal for the Study of the New Testament*
JSOT	*Journal for the Study of the Old Testament*
JTS	*Journal of Theological Studies*
KJV	King James Version
LTP	*Laval théologique et philosophique*
LW	Living Word Commentary
LXX	Septuagint
MACNT	MacArthur New Testament Commentary
MM	*Moulton, J. H., and G. Milligan. The Vocabulary of the Greek Testament.* London, 1930. Repr. Grand Rapids: Eerdmans, 1982.
MNTC	Moffat New Testament Commentary
MSJ	*Master's Seminary Journal*
NAB	New American Bible
NAC	New American Commentary
NASB95	New American Standard Bible (1995 updated ed.)
NBBC	New Beacon Bible Commentary
NCB	New Century Bible Commentary
NCV	New Century Version

NEB	New English Bible
Neot	*Neotestamentica*
NET	New English Translation (NET Bible)
NIBCNT	New International Biblical Commentary on the New Testament
NICNT	New International Commentary on the New Testament
NIDNTT	*New International Dictionary of New Testament Theology*
NIGTC	New International Greek Testament Commentary
NIV84	New International Version (1984 ed.)
NIVAC	NIV Application Commentary
NKJV	New King James Version
NLT	New Living Translation
NovT	*Novum Testamentum*
NovTSup	Novum Testamentum Supplements
NRSV	New Revised Standard Version
NT	New Testament
NTC	New Testament Commentary
NTD	Das Neue Testament Deutsch
NTS	*New Testament Studies*
ODCC	*The Oxford Dictionary of the Christian Church.* F. L. Cross and E. A. Livingstone, eds. 3rd ed. Oxford: Oxford UP, 2005.
OT	Old Testament
PNTC	Pillar New Testament Commentary
Presb	*Presbyterion*
RB	*Revue biblique*
RefR	*Reformation Review*
ResQ	*Restoration Quarterly*
RevExp	*Review and Expositor*
rsv	*Revised Standard Version*
SBJT	*Southern Baptist Journal of Theology*
SBL	Society of Biblical Literature
SBLDS	Society of Biblical Literature Dissertation Series
SJT	*Scottish Journal of Theology*
SP	Sacra Pagina
SPAW	Sitzungsberichte der preussischen Akademie der Wissenschaften
StudBib	Studia Biblica
SwJT	*Southwest Journal of Theology*
TD	*Theology Digest*

TDNT	*Theological Dictionary of the New Testament*. Ed. G. Kittel and G. Friedrich. Trans. G. W. Bromiley. 10 vols. Grand Rapids: Eerdmans, 1964–1976.
TEV	Today's English Version
ThT	*Theologisch tijdschrift*
TJ	*Trinity Journal*
TLNT	*Theological Lexicon of the New Testament*. C. Spicq. Trans. and ed. J. D. Ernest. 3 vols. Peabody, MA: Hendrickson, 1994.
TNTC	Tyndale New Testament Commentary
TR	Textus Receptus
TU	Texte und Untersuchungen
TWOT	*Theological Wordbook of the Old Testament*
TynBul	*Tyndale Bulletin*
UBS[4]	United Bible Society: Greek New Testament, 4th edition
Univ.	University
UP	University Press
Vg.	Vulgate
vol(s).	volume(s)
WBC	Word Biblical Commentary
WesTJ	*Wesleyan Theological Journal*
WTJ	*Westminster Theological Journal*
WUNT	Wissenschaftliche Untersuchungen zum Neuen Testament
ZNW	*Zeitschrift für die neutestamentliche Wissenschaft und die Kunde der älteren Kirche*
ZTK	*Zeitschrift für Theologie und Kirche*

Technical Abbreviations

1	first person
2	second person
3	third person
adj.	adjective/adjectival
adv.	adverb/adverbial
aor.	aorist
ca.	circa
cf.	*confer*, compare
conj.	conjunction
ed(s).	edition; edited by; editor(s)
fem.	feminine

gen.	genitive
gen. ed(s).	general editor(s)
ibid.	*ibidem*, in the same place
impv.	imperative
indic.	indicative
lit.	literally
masc.	masculine
MS(S)	manuscript(s)
n.	note
n.d.	no date
obj.	object
pass.	passive
pf.	perfect
pl.	plural
prep.	preposition
pres.	present
ptc.	participle
repr.	reprint, reprinted
rev.	revised (by)
sg.	singular
trans.	translator; translated by
v(v).	verse(s)
voc.	vocative

Biblical and Extrabiblical Literature

Old Testament

Gen	Genesis
Exod	Exodus
Lev	Leviticus
Num	Numbers
Deut	Deuteronomy
Josh	Joshua
Judg	Judges
1–2 Sam	1–2 Samuel
1–2 Kgs	1–1 Kings
1–2 Chr	1–2 Chronicles
Neh	Nehemiah
Esth	Esther

Psa/Pss	Psalm/Psalms
Prov	Proverbs
Eccl	Ecclesiastes
Song	Song of Songs
Isa	Isaiah
Jer	Jeremiah
Lam	Lamentations
Ezek	Ezekiel
Dan	Daniel
Hos	Hosea
Obad	Obadiah
Mic	Micah
Nah	Nahum
Hab	Habakkuk
Zeph	Zephaniah
Hag	Haggai
Zech	Zechariah
Mal	Malachi

New Testament

Matt	Matthew
GJohn	Gospel of John
Rom	Romans
1–2 Cor	1–2 Corinthians
Gal	Galatians
Eph	Ephesians
Phil	Philippians
Col	Colossians
1–2 Thess	1–2 Thessalonians
1–2 Tim	1–2 Timothy
Phlm	Philemon
Heb	Hebrews
Jas	James
1–2 Pet	1–2 Peter
Rev	Revelation

Apocrypha and Pseudepigrapha

Apoc. Ab.	*Apocalypse of Abraham*
1 En.	*1 Enoch*

Jub.	*Jubilees*
1–4 Macc	1–4 Maccabees
Sir	Sirach
T. Dan	*Testament of Dan*
T. Gad	*Testament of Gad*
T. Iss.	*Testament of Issachar*
T. Reu.	*Testament of Reuben*

Dead Sea Scrolls

1QH	*Thanksgiving Hymns*
1QM	*War Scroll*
1QS	*Community Rule*
CD	*Damascus Document*

Early Christian Writings

Haer.	*Against Heresies*
Hist. eccl.	*Ecclesiastical History*
Pol. Phil.	Polycarp, *To the Philippians*
Pud.	*Modesty*
Strom.	*Miscellanies*

1 John

Introduction

Author

The author of this epistle is John, the beloved apostle. Though he does not identify himself as its author, and so some consider the epistle "technically anonymous," his writing style when compared to the Gospel of John, emphases, and early witness of the church point to John.[1] Much of modern scholarship denies Johannine authorship of the Gospel and Epistles, attributing them to a "Johannine school" or community (Painter, 46–51; Rensberger, 17–19; Schnackenburg, 35; Strecker, xxxv–xlii). Some, while denying the Apostle John's authorship of the Gospel or Epistles, do acknowledge his authorship of Revelation (Williams, 15).[2] Though they deny Johannine authorship of one or more of his works, their arguments have proved inconclusive over the years, as noted repeatedly by Raymond Brown, who represents their views, in terms of both strengths and

1. For example, Stott (17), though he holds to Johannine authorship, notes that the absence of a name on each of the Epistles makes them anonymous, and so "there is no *a priori* need to assign them to the apostle John or to any other John." R. N. Longenecker ("On the Form, Function, and Authority of the New Testament Letters," 112) notes that 1 John probably had cover letters (2 and 3 John) that identified it to its recipients, thereby not requiring John to name himself in it. J. Lieu (7–9) argues that the author of the Epistles (whether a single author or separate) was intentionally anonymous and desired that the Epistles be read from that perspective.

2. R. N. Longenecker ("On the Form, Function, and Authority of the New Testament Letters," 109–10) writes: "While the involvement of amanuenses in the writing of New Testament letters poses no threat to their authority, many view their anonymity (Hebrews, 1 John, and probably Ephesians) and possible pseudonymity (e.g., the Pastoral and General Epistles) as doing just that. With F. E. D. Schleiermacher, J. G. Eichhorn, W. M. L. de Wette, and F. C. Baur, a new literary category of 'canonical Pseudepigrapha' arose in nineteenth-century criticism and has been commonplace in New Testament scholarship ever since."

weaknesses, very well.[3] Rather than attempt to answer their various arguments, it is the position of this commentary that John the Beloved Apostle is the author of these epistles and that the testimony of the church fathers can be trusted, as will be detailed below.

Internal Evidence

Absent from the epistle is any reference to the author's name. However, as Painter (39) points out, no extant copy of the epistle is without a title attributing it to John. He argues though that the title was applied to the work based on the "minor variations" in the Greek MSS. These minor variations do not make the attribution invalid, but indicate its early, even immediate, identification with John from the beginning of its replication by copyists.

Evidence of John's authorship comes from his self-disclosure, writing style, and conceptual connection to the Gospel of John. The two works share key conceptual vocabulary, such as Paraclete (παράκλητος), the only begotten Son (μονογενής), and Jesus as the Word (ὁ λόγος). They share common themes, including light, love, truth, witness, and sonship. Within these common themes, both employ contrasts as a major literary device. These include the themes of light versus darkness, life and death, love and hate, truth and lie (Kistemaker, 197). The author's description of himself in the prologue as an eyewitness who physically saw and touched "the Word of Life," that is, Jesus, places him with Jesus' companions during his earthly ministry. Such a description best fits an apostle rather than some second-generation believer or later church elder. His use of "we" in 1:1–3 and 4:14 places him with the apostolic band as opposed to the false teachers.[4]

3. For a full treatment of the issues addressed by much of modern scholarship, see examples of recent writers who assume the writer(s) were people other than John the apostle, whether disciples of John or members of the theorized "Johannine community" including R. Brown (*The Epistles of John*, 14–35), J. Lieu (*I, II, & III John*), J. Painter (*1, 2, and 3 John*, 44–51), R. Schnackenburg (*Die Johannesbriefe*, 41), S. Smalley (*1, 2, 3 John*, xxii), and G. Strecker (*The Johannine Letters*, xxxii–xlii).

4. Kügler ("Die Belehrung der Unbelehrbaren: Zur Funktion des Traditionsarguments in 1 Joh," 249) argues that 1 John has a non-apostolic actual author who writes as a fictional "implied" Apostle John. Further, he writes to fictional readers as understood by his actual readers. And so he employs fiction in the development of his message, which would have been understood by his readers. Consequently, though the author is not an eyewitness, he writes as one for the sake of argument. The weakness of this view is twofold: First, one cannot demonstrate

Further, the vocabulary of the epistle, along with its grammar and syntax, parallels that of the Gospel of John such that the two must come from the same hand. As Westcott (xxx) notes, "The writing is so closely connected with the Fourth Gospel in vocabulary, style, thought, scope, that the two books cannot but be regarded as works of the same author." Brown (757–59) lists more than ninety shared terms and concepts between John's First Epistle and his Gospel. While rejecting common authorship, he admits that "in the New Testament it is difficult to find two works more similar in expression than GJohn and I John" (Brown, 21). "Overall, then, it seems that the variation of minute stylistic features between GJohn and I John is not much different from the variation that one can find if one compares one part of GJohn to another part" (Brown, 24). He lists the arguments against common authorship based on differences in style, thought, and "life situation," and confesses that none of them is sufficiently convincing to "prove" different authors wrote the works. He sees differences in thought and provides examples of those differences. These include "attribution of important features to God rather than to Christ," "I John stresses aspects of a lower christology in instances where GJohn stresses a higher christology," "the sacrificial and atoning character of the death of Jesus is much clearer in I John ... than in GJohn," "I John offers much less specific reference to the Spirit than does GJohn," the "eschatology of I John differs from that of GJohn," and the absence of "quotations from the Old Testament in I John while there are many in GJohn" (Brown, 21–28). Though he repeatedly affirms that such differences do not demonstrate different authors, Brown still rejects the idea of common authorship between the Gospel and Epistles, while affirming common authorship of the Epistles themselves. His basis for rejecting common authorship is his theory of a "Johannine Community" schism and redactional development of the Gospel over multiple years (Brown, 16–30). Consequently, it seems his assessment is driven by his theory even while admitting that evidence neither proves nor disproves common authorship. That being said, Brown (23) himself points to the example of what he considers "genuinely Pauline"

---

this was a conventional pattern in the Hellenistic world. Second, the church's rejection of other pseudepigraphic literature argues strongly against them accepting this work as apostolic if it were fictional or presented as apostolic, unless it were, in fact, apostolic.

letters to show that differences do naturally occur with an author. The differences between the Gospel and Epistles can easily be explained by their different subjects and themes (just as their similarities can relate to similar themes and concepts). Since the Gospel and Epistles were written at different times of John's life, one would expect his writing style, concepts, and vocabulary to have changed over time.

External Evidence

The early church fathers accepted the Johannine authorship of this first epistle.[5] Their knowledge of the epistle and recognition of its apostolic origin include possible allusions by Ignatius (ca. AD 110), Polycarp in his letter to the Philippian church (ca. AD 120), and Papias. The strongest connection comes from Polycarp. "For everyone who does not confess Jesus Christ to have come in the flesh is Antichrist."[6] This is very close to 1 John 4:2–3 and 2 John 7. Irenaeus, the bishop of Lyons and Vienna around AD 185, referred to Papias as "the hearer of John and a companion of Polycarp" who quoted from 1 John.[7] He links the John who penned Revelation as "the Lord's dis-

5. Brown (7–9) lists several possible allusions to 1 John by early church fathers, while noting that there are no known direct quotations.

6. Pol. *Phil.* 7:1 (from A. Roberts, J. Donaldson, and A. C. Coxe, *The Ante-Nicene Fathers Vol. I : Translations of the Writings of the Fathers Down to A.D. 325* [Oak Harbor: Logos Research Systems, 1997]).

7. Irenaeus, *Haer.* 3.16.5, 8; Eusebius, *Hist. eccl.* 3.29.17. Irenaeus writes: "The Gospel, therefore, knew no other son of man but him who was of Mary, who also suffered; and no Christ who flew away from Jesus before the passion; but him who was born it knew as Jesus Christ the Son of God, and that this same suffered and rose again, as John, the disciple of the Lord, verifies, saying: 'But these are written, that ye might believe that Jesus is the Christ, the Son of God, and that believing ye might have eternal life in His name,'—foreseeing these blasphemous systems which divide the Lord, as far as lies in their power, saying that He was formed of two different substances. For this reason also he has thus testified to us in his Epistle: 'Little children, it is the last time; and as ye have heard that Antichrist doth come, now have many antichrists appeared; whereby we know that it is the last time. They went out from us, but they were not of us; for if they had been of us, they would have continued with us: but [they departed], that they might be made manifest that they are not of us. Know ye therefore, that every lie is from without, and is not of the truth. Who is a liar, but he that denieth that Jesus is the Christ? This is Antichrist.'" Then, with reference to 2 John 7: "These are they against whom the Lord has cautioned us beforehand; and His disciple, in his Epistle already mentioned, commands us to avoid them, when he says: 'For many deceivers are entered

ciple," which term he used often for the author of both the Gospel and this epistle. His references may include 2 John as well (Painter, 39–40).[8] The Muratorian canon (ca. AD 190) also identifies both the Gospel of John and 1 John as Johannine, quoting the first verse of the epistle.[9] It says, "Indeed the Epistle of Jude and two of the above-mentioned John are accepted in the Catholic [church or epistles]" (Bruce, 18–19). All three epistles are included in the earliest Greek codices (Stott, 18). Third-century witnesses include Clement of Alexandria, Dionysius of Alexandria, and Tertullian (Kistemaker, 196).[10]

Recipients and Date

Recipients

The recipients of 1 John were Christians of Asia Minor, where John ended his days in ministry from Ephesus. Though external evidence is insufficient, the internal evidence indicates churches whose membership included more mature converts as well as younger believers (2:13–14). His initial recipients would have been composed of mostly a Gentile audience, evidenced by so few Old Testament references, with the ones used being the kind a Gentile believer would be expected to know from the annual reading of Scripture in church (Kistemaker, 207). Beyond this, theories of the composition of John's audience are speculative at best. For example, Smalley (xxiv) divides

---

into the world, who confess not that Jesus Christ is come in the flesh. This is a deceiver and an antichrist. Take heed to them, that ye lose not what ye have wrought.' And again does he say in the Epistle: 'Many false prophets are gone out into the world. Hereby know ye the Spirit of God: Every spirit that confesseth that Jesus Christ is come in the flesh is of God; and every spirit which separates Jesus Christ is not of God, but is of antichrist.' These words agree with what was said in the Gospel, that 'the Word was made flesh, and dwelt among us.' Wherefore he again exclaims in his Epistle, 'Every one that believeth that Jesus is the Christ, has been born of God.'"

8. Irenaeus, *Haer.* 4.20.11; 4.30.4; 5.26.1; 5.35.2.

9. Some recent scholarship rejects the early date and argues for a fourth-century dating of the fragment (G. M. Hahneman, *The Muratorian Fragment and the Development of the Canon* [1992]; A. C. Sundberg, Jr., "Canon Muratori: A Fourth Century List," 38).

10. Clement of Alexandria, *Strom.* 2.15.66; Eusebius, *Hist. eccl.* 7.25.6–11; Tertullian, *Pud.* 19; F. C. Conybeare, "Dionysius of Alexandria, Newly Discovered Letters to the Popes Stephen and Xystus," 114.

the audience of 1 John into three groups: "(a) Johannine Christians who were committed to the apostolic gospel of Jesus as they had received it; (b) heretically inclined members from a Jewish background; (c) heterodox followers from a Hellenistic (and/or pagan) background." Then he identifies a fourth group: "the secessionists" who were "followers of a Johannine type of Christianity, who had clashed with John... in matters of belief and behavior." Theories based on interpretations of hints from the epistles must remain theories and be recognized as such. Care should also be taken to ensure that interpretations are not based on those theories rather than clear affirmations of the text itself.[11]

Date

No concrete indicators exist for an exact dating of this work. The tone of the author suggests that of an elder addressing a younger generation of readers. Irenaeus placed John's writing to the churches during his stay in Ephesus and prior to his death during the time of Trajan, who ruled Rome from AD 98 to 117.[12] Jerome placed John's death sixty-eight years after Jesus' passion (between AD 98 and 101).[13] Therefore it could not have been written later than the end of the first century since, according to church tradition, John died around the beginning of the second and wrote Revelation last. Further, the epistle is quoted by the early second-century church fathers and so had to be copied and distributed throughout the church prior to their use of it. As Brown (10) notes, "By the end of the second century I John was being cited both in the West and in the East. For instance,

11. D. Guthrie ("Questions of Introduction," 106) notes well, "But many New Testament books have no clear indication of destination (e.g. the Gospels, and such Epistles as James, 1 John, Hebrews and Jude). In some cases our understanding of obscure statements in the text might well be elucidated if more information were available, but the exegete can work only with the data he has."

12. Irenaeus, *Haer.* 3.3.4. Eusebius (*Hist. eccl.* 3.23.3) quotes his claim: "And all the presbyters who had been associated in Asia with John, the disciple of the Lord, bear witness to his tradition, for he remained with them until the times of Trajan."

13. *Vir. ill.* 9. In it Jerome writes that John "returned to Ephesus under Pertinax and continuing there until the tithe of the emperor Trajan, founded and built churches throughout all Asia, and, worn out by old age, died in the sixty-eighth year after our Lord's passion and was buried near the same city" (P. Schaff, *The Nicene and Post-Nicene Fathers Second Series Vol. III* [Oak Harbor: Logos Research Systems, 1997], 364–65.)

Tertullian (d. 215) cites I John some forty or fifty times, referring to it as the work of John. Clement of Alexandria (d. 220) not only cites I John but speaks of it as 'the greater epistle' (*Stromata* 2:14.66; GCS 15, 148), so that he knew at least one other Johannine Epistle."

Thus, a period in the late first century, following the composition of the Gospel and prior to the writing of Revelation is most likely. This would allow for the development of a proto-Gnosticism that would blossom in the next century to have arrived on the scene and been recognized by John as needing to be addressed (Bruce, 48–49). For the Gospel, a date between AD 80 and AD 90[14] seems plausible, while the Revelation was likely written around AD 95.[15] Thus, the First Epistle of John most likely was written around AD 90, a few years before the writing of the Revelation. A date around AD 90 seems to work best for the writing of this epistle.

Theory of a Johannine School

Was there a "Johannine School" that composed the Gospel of John and Epistles? This theory of a Johannine school is given extensive treatment by Brown (108–-12) and influences his interpretation of key passages throughout his work. Kistemaker (1–38) identifies this school with Culpepper.[16] The view is also assumed by Grayston, (6–22), Marshall (*Epistles*, 32), Smalley (xxii), Schnackenburg (41–42), and Strecker (xxxv) among others.[17] They find evidence of a schism between John (or the author) and members of the "Johannine School" in places such as 1 John 2:19; 2 John 7; and 3 John, along with the theological assertion of 1 John 2:22 and 4:3. Others see opponents, but not necessarily arising from a Johannine following as such

---

14. D. A. Carson (*The Gospel according to John*, 82) and A. Köstenberger (*John*, 8) place it around AD 80. Others (K. O. Gangel, *John*, 2; B. F. Westcott, *The Gospel according to St. John*, xxxix) place it closer to the end of the first century, believing that he wrote it just before his death.
15. S. Kistemaker and W. Hendriksen, *Exposition of the Book of Revelation*, 38; G. Osborne, *Revelation*, 9. D. Aune (*Revelation 1–5:14*, lviii) dates it based on a theory of composition that began in the 60s and culminated near the end of Domitian's reign in the 90s.
16. R. A. Culpepper, *The Johannine School*, 1–38.
17. Also C. C. Black ("Christian Ministry in Johannine Perspective," 39).

(Rensberger, 21). Yet others recognize Johannine authorship, but accept the theory of a Johannine school (Yarbrough, 16–21).[18]

The theory is based more on perceived hints from the Gospel and First Epistle than on any concrete external evidence, such as writings of the church fathers. As well, it stands in conflict with John's use of the first person pronoun to refer to himself in the prologue as well as other places throughout the epistle. Though John had opponents, as is clear from his Third Epistle, the theory of a Johannine school, or defectors from a Johannine school, must be seen as speculative since no concrete references occur within any extant literature.[19] The presence of false teachers cannot be questioned. Such is the experience of the church throughout its history from the earliest days. Paul's warning to the Ephesian elders (Acts 20:29–30) makes clear that such would be the normal experience of the church. In his epistle to the church in Colosse, a city in Asia Minor near Ephesus where John would eventually live and write this epistle, Paul addressed a christological error that may have arisen from teachers with a Jewish background. He challenged Timothy to defend the faith, reminding him of the doctrinal error of Hymenaeus and Philetus concerning the resurrection (2 Tim 2:14–19). Titus was to appoint elders who could defend the faith against false teachers (Titus 1:9). Further, Paul wrote both polemical and pastoral instructions, similar to this epistle. Yet, such did not require there be a Pauline school that had elements that broke away from him. Rather, he viewed the church as under his care, became aware of the problem, and wrote to correct the error and encourage the church.

Further, no hard evidence exists for a separate Johannine community even in the area of Asia Minor that received the seven letters of Revelation.

---

18. Thompson (20) is an example of one who chooses to remain neutral on the identity of the author, but assigns to him "his traditional name." She appears unwilling to reject the arguments against Johannine authorship outright despite their inadequacies. Williamson (31–33) also assigns 1 John to a "John," but chooses to refer to the author of 2 and 3 John only as "the elder."

19. As Burge (27) notes, "We have no firsthand information from John's adversaries" in that nothing they have written has survived. This should cause us to pause and ask if these opponents really existed in anything other than an occasional false teacher. Unlike gnostic heretics who did produce literature promoting their teachings, the absence of these opponents' writings argues that they did not form a separate "school" of thought, but were more likely isolated opponents within local congregations.

Though John is more likely addressing a local congregation and has particular false teachers in mind, his warnings apply to the church at large even as Paul's Epistles. It seems best to understand him addressing these issues with the broader church body in mind, knowing that his epistle would be copied and distributed beyond the local congregation he addressed.[20] Yet, he spoke to a particular situation in a local church.

Along with this theory of a Johannine school is the additional theory of a history of the Gospel's composition that involves a process of development. For example, Burge (39) suggests that, though John was the source of the material, his Gospel was circulated in a draft form that was misused or misunderstood. He then followed it with a revision that included the addition of the Gospel's prologue, and he wrote his epistles to correct misunderstandings of the Gospel's message. Burge sees the Farewell Discourse as an "uncertain" additional change to the original Gospel. Then, after John's death, his disciples finished gathering material (including John 21) and editing the Gospel into its present form as well as publishing John's three letters. Again, all of this is speculative, with no external evidence, such as unedited versions of the Gospel, to support it. Moreover, unless there is strong evidence to indicate otherwise, it is best to see the Gospel and Epistles as the early church fathers saw them,[21] namely, coming from the pen of John.

---

20. Peter's two epistles were addressed to a wide range of churches and so indicates he anticipated their copying and distribution. Further, his reference to Paul's writings in 2 Pet 3:14–16 indicates that the practice of copying and distribution of Paul's epistles began early on in the church and was known to the apostle. Further, Paul's instructions to the Colossians (4:16) to trade letters with the Laodiceans indicates Paul incouraged the practice. Additionally, Peter's identifation of Paul's writings with "the rest of the Scriptures" indicates that the apostles, if not the church as a whole, viewed their writings as Scripture. It does not seem that they viewed everything they wrote as such, though, since it can be assumed that each wrote far more than has survived.

21. See comments under "external evidence" above for examples of the early church fathers' views.

Occasion and Setting

Occasion

Based on the internal evidence of 1 and 2 John, a problem had arisen within the church, possibly throughout Asia Minor.[22] We know from church history that near the end of the first century, and in the early second century, proto-Gnosticism, specifically Docetism, arose within the church (Bruce, 16–17; Burdick, 61–63; Williamson, 50).[23] In later years this developed into a theological system known as Gnosticism.[24] Its teachings blended Greek dualism with Eastern mysticism. It adopted the dualistic view that only the nonmaterial, or "spirit," was good while anything material was evil. Along with this came Eastern mysticism's focus on secret knowledge reserved only for the chosen few. Though present in seminal form in the late first century, it blossomed into full expression in the middle and latter second century (Burdick, 54–60). By the middle of the second century its adherents were producing their own gospels and epistles, of which the *Gospel of Thomas* and *Gospel of Judas* are examples.[25]

---

22. P. Perkins (xii–xxiii) proposes that John is simply employing Greek rhetoric rather than addressing an actual group.
23. Haas, de Jonge, and Swellengrebel (4) assume a gnostic background to John's opponents: "There are several allusions to this point of view in the Letter ... John's opponents seem to have boasted of a 'spiritual' fellowship with God and his Son (1:7; 2:6), of their being guided by the Spirit (4:1–6), and of their spiritual knowledge of God (2:3f). And because of these 'spiritual gifts' they felt no need for brotherly love, closely bound to earthly life as it is. On the contrary, they hated their brothers (2:9, 11)."
24. G. L. Borchert, "Gnosticism" in *Baker Encyclopedia of the Bible*, 873–76; P. Perkins, "What Is a Gnostic Gospel?," 104–29; D. M. Scholer, *Dictionary of the Later New Testament & Its Development*, s.v. "Gnosis, Gnosticism"; C. B. Smith, II, *No Longer Jews.*
25. A. D. Deconick, *The Original Gospel of Thomas in Translation: With a Commentaryand New English Translation of the Complete Gospel*; B. D. Ehrman, *The Lost Gospel of Judas Iscariot: A New Look at Betrayer and Betrayed*; C. A. Evans, "Understanding the Gospel of Judas," 561–74; P. Foster, "Polymorphic Christology," 66–99; D. Frankfurter, "A Historian's View of the Gospel of Judas," 174–77; S. Gathercole, "The Gospel of Judas," 209–15; A. Gregory, "The Non-canonical Gospels and the Historical Jesus," 3–22; P. M. Head, "The Gospel of Judas and the Qarara Codices," 1–23; N. Perrin, *Thomas, the Other Gospel* (London: SPCK, 2007); N. T. Wright, *Judas and the Gospel of Jesus: Have We Missed the Truth about Christianity?* (Grand Rapids: Baker, 2006).

John appears to have anticipated Gnosticism's development and threat to the health of the church and wrote to counteract its influence. Based on the Greek dualistic concept that matter is evil and spirit is good, Gnosticism concluded that for God to be truly good, he had to be pure spirit and could not have created a material universe. Therefore, a lesser god, an emanation from the true God, must have created it. The God of the Old Testament was one of these emanations that are called demiurges, and so was a lesser god than the ultimate God.

This form of dualism influenced their view of Jesus. Recognizing his deity, they concluded that Jesus could not have had a physical body. Corporeality would require God to come in contact with the "evil" material world. This teaching was called Docetism (from *dokeo*, "seem" or "have the appearance") and claimed that Jesus only appeared to have a physical body, but in reality was a spirit and so did not suffer and die on the cross. He only appeared to have done so.[26]

A modification of the Docetic view of Jesus was promoted by a false teacher in Ephesus named Cerinthus. His false doctrine, known as Cerinthianism, was an early form of adoptionism, and taught that Jesus was a human upon whom the "Christ spirit" descended at his baptism. It was this spirit of Christ that then empowered Jesus in his ministry. Then, just before Jesus' crucifixion, the Christ spirit departed from the man Jesus, who subsequently died on the cross. So, while Jesus died, the "Christ" neither suffered nor died on the cross, but only appeared to have died.

Such phrases as *what our hands handled* (1:1), *every spirit that confesses that Jesus Christ has come in the flesh* (4:2), and *he who came by water and blood* (5:6) may imply that such a heresy as proto-Gnosticism is being addressed. Each of these references to Jesus uses incarnational language that requires corporeality—a physical existence, and so might indicate an early expression of Gnosticism. These statements served as John's way of affirming the humanity of Jesus, whose deity John had clearly demonstrated in his Gospel. "The issue this epistle addresses is not that the heretics believed Jesus to be someone other than the Christ (and believed in Jesus anyway), but rather that they believed the Christ to be someone other than Jesus" (Akin, 54).

26. BDAG, 254–55; G. Kittel, "δοκέω, δόξα, δοξάζω," *TDNT* 2:233.

Though the evidence is slight, some extrabiblical sources do imply a proto-gnostic issue influenced John's thoughts. For example, Irenaeus writes, "Cerinthus, again, a man who was educated in the wisdom of the Egyptians, taught that the world was not made by the primary God, but by a certain Power far separated from him, and at a distance from that Principality who is supreme over the universe, and ignorant of him who is above all. He represented Jesus as having not been born of a virgin, but as being the son of Joseph and Mary according to the ordinary course of human generation, while he nevertheless was more righteous, prudent, and wise than other men. Moreover, after his baptism, Christ descended upon him in the form of a dove from the Supreme Ruler, and that then he proclaimed the unknown Father, and performed miracles. But at last Christ departed from Jesus, and that then Jesus suffered and rose again, while Christ remained impassible, inasmuch as he was a spiritual being."[27] He quotes Polycarp as recounting an encounter between John and Cerinthus. "There are also those who heard from him that John, the disciple of the Lord, going to bathe at Ephesus, and perceiving Cerinthus within, rushed out of the bath-house without bathing, exclaiming, 'Let us fly, lest even the bath-house fall down, because Cerinthus, the enemy of the truth, is within.'"[28] However, as Burge (30) aptly notes, "It is notoriously difficult to confirm Polycarp's bathhouse story or build any kind of chronology for Cerinthus."

John's "adversaries" were guilty of "an overly high christology" that went beyond what was revealed in the Gospel of John (Brown, 54; Burge, 29).[29] However, an error in Christology need not imply an incipient form of Gnosticism. After listing ten similarities between Gnosticism and statements in 1 John, Brown warns us that "most of the Gnostic material is to be dated from fifty to two hundred years later than the material in I and II John, and some of it has clearly been influenced by GJohn.... Similar ethical

27. Irenaeus, *Haer.* 1.26.1.

28. Irenaeus, *Haer.* 1.3.4. Since Irenaeus is reporting a story and not an eyewitness, the likelihood of this story being true is lessened. No other evidence exists that places Cerinthus in Ephesus with John as contemporaries.

29. C. Black, "Christian Ministry in Johannine Perspective," 39. J. Painter ("The 'Opponents' in 1 John," 49) proposes that the opponents are primarily "pagan" Gentile in origin while the Johannine community was primarily Jewish in origin. But, even as the false teachers of Colossians are difficult to identify, so, too, are the false teachers who are counteracted by John in this first Epistle.

charges directed against both the epistolary adversaries and the Gnostics tell us little about the relation of the two groups, for such charges (neglect of commandments, indifference about behavior, love of the world or money, lack of brotherly love) are standard polemic that one can find over and over again in Christian history" (Brown, 60–62). Even so, these charges should not be viewed as merely polemical rhetoric, but evidence that these problems and issues persisted, and still persist, throughout church history.

Some discern an ethical variance in John's opponents on the basis of statements within the epistle. For them "ethical behavior was of no consequence for the Christian life" (Burge, 31). This view finds evidence of their ethical aberrations in statements by John, such as their claim to be without sin (1:8, 10), or their claim to know and love God while living disobediently and expressing hatred toward brothers (2:4, 9; 4:20). Yet, such statements need not indicate a specific heretical group, since, as Brown noted above, they are standard issues of the day and continue through church history to be an issue within the churches. The same issues can be found in the writings of Paul, Peter, and the author of Hebrews, though their terminology may not be the same. For example, Paul in Rom 12:9–13 connects unhypocritical love with abhorring evil and meeting the needs of the saints. In Gal 5:13–15 he addresses how the Galatians were to express love by their treatment of each other, and that they were not to "bite and devour" each other but to care for one another. When writing to the Ephesians, Paul contrasted walking in love with fornication and covetousness among other sins that his readers were not to practice, even incorporating the concept of walking in light as children of light (Eph 5:1–9). Peter connects love of the brethren with laying aside conduct harmful to others in the body of Christ (1 Pet 1:22–2:1). More importantly, these were issues addressed by Jesus. Furthermore, with John's focus on the person of Jesus, it is natural that he would, in turn, focus on the heart of Jesus' teachings. Just as Matthew recorded Jesus' ethical teachings in the Sermon on the Mount that hateful treatment of others is equivalent to murder (Matt 5:21–26), John recorded his focus on loving one another throughout the evening of the Last Supper (John 13–17). Thus, the internal evidence of this epistle need not describe a specific group, but a common issue throughout the body of Christ throughout its existence, even to this day.

Others connect the issues in 1 John with those of the Gospel of John, seeing its polemic directed against the Jewish synagogues that had expelled the Christians and were persecuting them in the latter years of the first century (Barrett, 134–44; contra Brown, 383, and Dodd, 42).[30]

Yet other scholars believe there may have been more than one error addressed by John, and therefore more than one opponent or group of opponents (Brown, 49–50; Smalley, xxiii–xxv).[31] This can be seen in another quote from Irenaeus. "John, the disciple of the Lord, preaches this faith, and seeks, by the proclamation of the Gospel, to remove that error which by Cerinthus had been disseminated among men, and a long time previously by those termed Nicolaitans, who are an offset of that 'knowledge' falsely so called, that he might confound them, and persuade them."[32] Still, it is not necessary to distinguish groups based on the theological and moral issues raised by John. For example, the absence of Old Testament quotations need not indicate they were Jews who had never converted to Christianity (Brown, 52). John's reference to their departure in 1 John 2 indicates rather that they had at least identified themselves with the Christian community, if not the apostolic circle, at one point. It is more likely that the absence

30. J. Parkes, *Conflict of the Church and the Synagogue*, 60. J. C. O'Neill (*The Puzzle of 1 John*) argues for conceptual connections between 1 John and the Qumran community. This is very unlikely since all of John's conceptual imagery and terminology can be found in the broader Jewish community.

31. Those who see a single group of opponents include P. J. Lalleman ("The Adversaries Envisaged in the Johannine Epistles," 17) and J. Painter ("The 'Opponents' in 1 John," 48–71). The problem of a theory of opponents is that no evidence exists for their presence. After acknowledging that it is difficult to reconstruct the opponents' view, Burge (27) notes, "Writers rarely give a complete hearing to their opponents' views, and we have no firsthand information from John's adversaries. *None of their writings have survived.* Moreover, sometimes John opposes things in his letters that may not be on the agenda of his opponents. For instance, in 1 John 4:18 he says there is no fear in love because perfect love casts out fear. John may be taking an opportunity to chastise his followers, not *necessarily* addressing anyone else." However he pursues a position that one must know the *Sitz im Leben* in order to interpret the epistle. The result is that his interpretations are driven by his theory rather than the affirmations of the text itself. This becomes a circular argument in which the evidences of the text are used to describe the "secessionists" and then their theorized views are imposed on the text to determine its meaning. His conclusion (28): "The secessionists had embraced an aberrant form of Christology that led them to make wrong judgments about Christian living" (italics his).

32. Irenaeus, *Haer.* 3.12.1.

of Old Testament quotations comes from the nature of John's primarily Gentile audience.

All of this having been said, the warning of Judith Lieu must, too, be heeded. She writes, "The dominant model for interpreting the Johannine Epistles over recent decades has been to locate them in a very specific context, to determine their *Sitz im Leben**.[33] Of necessity this external world is reconstructed by reference to the texts themselves… . As often noted, this results in a circular argument—the setting is deduced from the letter and the letter is then interpreted with close reference to the hypothetical situation."[34] Rather than speculating on circumstances, we should allow the text to explain itself and interpret it on the basis of its affirmations rather than based on a theorized split in a hypothetical community. Again, that there were false teachers whose doctrines needed correcting is evident. However, who they were and the full nature of their false teachings will likely never be known. Further, Pieter Lalleman also provides a balanced warning. "One must be careful with pronouncements about the identity of the adversaries mentioned in the Epistles because it would seem that there is no external evidence about them and because the Epistles might be too vague in indicating what or whom exactly they condemn."[35] Thus we can know

33. An asterisk after a word or phrase indicates that it is included in the List of Foreign and Technical Words at the end of this volume.

34. J. M. Lieu, "Us or You? Persuasion and Identity in 1 John," 805.

35. P. J. Lalleman, "The Adversaries Envisaged in the Johannine Epistles," 17. He argues (17–20) that the verses in 1 John that refer to false teachers do not point to Cerinthus or a gnostic group. Based on 2:18–19, he sees the "adversaries" as "formerly part of the Johannine community and, therefore, co-recipients of the Gospel of John. In fact, the adversaries may well have claimed that they were (also) a Johannine community or even the true Johannine Christians." He proposes that the gnostic writing *Acts of John*, though written in "the second quarter of the second century and based on ideas which may have been current in Asia Minor for some time," is a "near-contemporary text which originated among pagan readers of the Gospel of John" and "represents a 'left wing' interpretation of this Gospel and especially of its Christology." The nature of the opponents found in the gnostic *Acts of John* are (1) an emphasis on "the divinity of Christ at the expense of his humanity," (2) an interpretation of the crucifixion "as a glorification and an elevation rather than as a humiliation," and (3) a lack of "distinction between God, the Lord and Christ. There is but one God, the Lord Christ." He describes this as "Christomonism" which is similar to modalism. He utilizes 2 John 7 as evidence of this group and the need to confess Jesus as coming in the flesh. He notes that they did not deny Jesus' coming, but only the mode of His coming. The gnostic

that John addresses both christological and hamartiological errors arising within those churches under his care. Whether these represent an identifiable group or individual elders and pastors scattered among the churches cannot be determined and should not determine our understanding of the text. However, what John says within the context of the message of the Epistles should inform our understanding of each text and does indicate the presence of false teachers and false teachings within his churches. Even so, as John sheds light on the issues confronting the church, we must avoid allowing the fog of a theory to restrict our ability to see what John intends to say to the church of his day and ours.

Setting

The city of Ephesus was visited by Paul between AD 52 and 56 during his third missionary journey.[36] Acts records his evangelistic outreach throughout Asia Minor from his base in Ephesus (Acts 19). Additionally, Timothy was with Paul in the city around AD 63 and again, separate from him, in AD 67 when Paul wrote his second epistle to Timothy from his Roman prison cell.[37] Nothing in the New Testament record or church fathers indicates that John and Timothy were ever together in Ephesus. This implies that John would not have arrived in Ephesus before AD 67 when Timothy likely left to join Paul in Rome. He probably moved to Ephesus just before or soon after the destruction of Jerusalem in AD 70. Irenaeus reported that John wrote to the churches while in Ephesus.[38] The theory that a debate existed between the supposed Johannine community and followers of John the Baptist, some who were converted while Paul was in Ephesus (Acts 19:1–7), is purely speculative. John's recounting of contacts between Jesus and John the Baptist need not "suggest that the Johannine community was in a debate with followers of John the Baptist" (Burge, 41). Rather, the passages that are supposed to hint at a conflict (John 1:35–42; 3:22–4:3; 10:41) instead portray a positive view of John the Baptist and his disciples by John

---

group saw Jesus coming as a spirit, but not corporeally. The prologue's description of John's physical experiences of Jesus was therefore used by him to argue for His corporeal coming as opposed to the gnostics.

36. P. W. Barnett, "Revolutionary Movements," in *Dictionary of Paul and His Letters*, 817; F. F. Bruce, *Paul: Apostle of the Heart Set Free*, 475.

37. G. W. Knight, *The Pastoral Epistles*, 54; W. D. Mounce, *Pastoral Epistles*, xlviii–liv.

38. Irenaeus, *Haer.* 3.3.4.

the apostle, as is true of Luke's portrayal in Acts 19. If anything, John's account should be seen as indicating John the Baptist's endorsement of Jesus as well as Jesus' approval of him.

Order of Composition

No hard evidence exists that establishes without debate the order of composition. Brown provides an excellent discussion of the issue. He begins by listing examples of every combination of epistles being written. He concludes, "Again, if the visit of the Presbyter (II John 12; III John 14) involved only one journey bringing him to several churches, the two letters would have been written in close proximity; but letter format makes it impossible to be sure that such a visit was more than a velleity. No likelihood can be given to the thesis that II John was the previous letter mentioned in III John 9 as having been written to the church" (Brown, 30–31). It seems best to see them written at about the same time. They may have even been sent out from John at the same time, if not the first epistle, at least the second and third. However, whatever the order, the meaning of each is not affected.

Relationship to the Gospel of John

The amount of shared vocabulary and conceptual unity strongly suggests common authorship of the Gospel of John and his First Epistle.[39] The Epistle's relationship to the Fourth Gospel is noted by Bruce, who says, "No one disputes the remarkably close relation between the two compositions in language and outlook; they clearly come from the same circle or school if not from the same individual. It is not easy to speak dogmatically about the common authorship of two anonymous works which, while exhibiting this close relation, belong to different literary genres. This last fact may account in large measure for the differences in vocabulary and style; as for the theological differences, these have been exaggerated" (Bruce, 30–31). Louw notes the both works reflect John's "preference for the perfect tense."[40]

39. Haas, de Jonge, and Swellengrebel (5) adopt a neutral position and take the differences to indicate either that the two works have different authors or their dissimilarities were the result of "different situations" and "different kinds of readers." The Gospel had the Jews as its focus while the epistle was a reaction to gnostics.
40. J. P. Louw, "Verbal Aspect in the First Letter of John," 102.

Painter (127) argues that "overlaps of language and theme between 1:1–4 and the prologue of the Fourth Gospel (John 1:1–18) imply some relationship." He suggests from the similarities found between their prologues that one is likely dependent on the other. Moule argues from a common interplay of futurist and realized eschatology within both the Gospel and Epistle to indicate common authorship.[41] Brown (93) notes that the vast majority of verses in the Epistle clearly reflect both concepts and terminology found in the Gospel, though there does not appear to be any attempt at quoting it.[42] Examples of common language between the Gospel and Epistle include, but are not limited to, a number of items.[43] Both prologues begin with "the beginning," though their intended referents may be different.[44] Early in both works John utilizes the imagery of light, though again with different meanings.[45] The concept of being born of God occurs in both.[46] The truth that no one has ever seen God is repeated identically in both.[47] God's command that we believe in his Son's name is given in John 6:29 and 1 John 3:23.[48] As well as the terms "life" and "eternal life" being common between

41. C. F. D. Moule, "A Neglected Factor in the Interpretation of Johannine Eschatology," 158–59.

42. Akin (28) places the correspondence at 80 percent.

43. See arguments of Brooke (i–ix) for additional comparisons in terms.

44. The Gospel (John 1:1) is introduced with ἐν ἀρχῇ and 1 John (1:1) begins with the relative clause, Ὃ ἦν ἀπ' ἀρχῆς. Though the Gospel refers to the beginning of creation and the Epistle likely refers to the beginning of Jesus' earthly ministry.

45. In John 1:6–9 light is connected with spiritual life (ἡ ζωὴ ἦν τὸ φῶς) while in 1 John 1:5–7 light is descriptive of God's moral purity (ὁ θεὸς φῶς ἐστιν … ἐν τῷ φωτὶ).

46. The concept is introduced in the prologue of the Gospel (John 1:12–13, ἐκ θεοῦ ἐγεννήθησαν) and repeated in Jesus' conversation with Nicodemus in John 3. The same terms (ἐκ τοῦ θεοῦ γεγέννηται) are used in 1 John 5:1 to describe the one who believes in Jesus.

47. In John 1:18 (θεὸν οὐδεὶς ἑώρακεν πώποτε·), this truth is stated in order to emphasize Jesus' role as revealer of the Father. In 1 John 4:12 (θεὸν οὐδεὶς πώποτε τεθέαται), it introduces the reader to the truth of God's abiding in the believer who loves his brother.

48. John 6:29 says, "This is the work of God, that you believe in the one whom He sent" (Τοῦτό ἐστιν τὸ ἔργον τοῦ θεοῦ, ἵνα πιστεύητε εἰς ὃν ἀπέστειλεν ἐκεῖνος.), and 1 John 3:23 says, "And this is his commandment, that we believe in the name of His Son Jesus Christ" (αὕτη ἐστὶν ἡ ἐντολὴ αὐτοῦ, ἵνα πιστεύσωμεν τῷ ὀνόματι τοῦ υἱοῦ αὐτοῦ Ἰησοῦ Χριστοῦ).

them, so, too, John employs the idea of "having" eternal life in both.[49] Jesus is the Savior of the world.[50] In both believers have "passed from death into life."[51] The concept of laying down one's life for one's friends or "sheep" occurs in both works.[52] The "new commandment" to love one another occurs not only in the Gospel and First Epistle, but the Second Epistle as well.[53] The promise and reality of the Paraclete occur in both works.[54] The fact of the world's hatred toward Jesus' followers is first stated by Jesus in the Gospel and repeated by John in the Epistle.[55] Addtionally, both the Gospel and Epistle point to "the water and the blood" as proof of Jesus' incarnation and physical death on our behalf.[56]

---

49. In John 3:16 those who believe in the Son "may have eternal life" (ἔχῃ ζωὴν αἰώνιον), and in 1 John 5:13 John wants his readers to know that they "have eternal life" (ζωὴν ἔχετε αἰώνιον) because they have the Son.

50. In John 4:42 the citizens of Sychar recognize Jesus as "Savior of the world" (οὗτός ἐστιν ἀληθῶς ὁ σωτὴρ τοῦ κόσμου). In 1 John 4:14 John testifies that "the Father sent His Son *to be* the Savior of the world" (σωτῆρα τοῦ κόσμου).

51. In John 5:24 Jesus says this in regard to the one who hears Jesus and believes God (μεταβέβηκεν ἐκ τοῦ θανάτου εἰς τὴν ζωήν). In 1 John 3:14 the believer can assure himself that he has passed from death into life (μεταβεβήκαμεν ἐκ τοῦ θανάτου εἰς τὴν ζωήν) by his love of other believers.

52. In John 10:11 (ὁ ποιμὴν ὁ καλὸς τὴν ψυχὴν αὐτοῦ τίθησιν ὑπὲρ τῶν προβάτων), 15 (τὴν ψυχήν μου τίθημι ὑπὲρ τῶν προβάτων), 17 (ἐγὼ τίθημι τὴν ψυχήν μου), and 18, Jesus applies this concept to himself. He states it as a general principle in John 15:13 (τις τὴν ψυχὴν αὐτοῦ θῇ ὑπὲρ τῶν φίλων αὐτοῦ), though with a view to His own coming death. In 1 John 3:16, John notes that Jesus acted out this truth in giving His life for us (ἐκεῖνος ὑπὲρ ἡμῶν τὴν ψυχὴν αὐτοῦ ἔθηκεν).

53. As Jesus gave His disciples a "new" commandment in John 13:34 (ἐντολὴν καινὴν δίδωμι ὑμῖν, ἵνα ἀγαπᾶτε ἀλλήλους), John reminds his readers of it in 2:7–8 (ἐντολὴν καινὴν γράφω ὑμῖν,) and repeats it to "the elect lady" in 2 John 5–6 (ἐντολὴν καινὴν ... ἵνα ἀγαπῶμεν ἀλλήλους).

54. In the Gospel (John 14:16, 26; 15:26; 16:7) Jesus promises His disciples "another" Paraclete in the person of the Holy Spirit (ἄλλον παράκλητον δώσει ὑμῖν, ὁ δὲ παράκλητος, τὸ πνεῦμα τὸ ἅγιον, Ὅταν ἔλθῃ ὁ παράκλητος). John identifies Jesus as our Paraclete in 2:1 (παράκλητον ἔχομεν πρὸς τὸν πατέρα Ἰησοῦν Χριστὸν), recognizing His primary role as counselor even as the Holy Spirit serves as comforter.

55. In John 15:18–19 Jesus alerts His followers to the reality of the world's hatred because of their identification with him (Εἰ ὁ κόσμος ὑμᾶς μισεῖ, γινώσκετε ὅτι ἐμὲ πρῶτον ὑμῶν μεμίσηκεν.). This same truth is repeated in 3:13 (μὴ θαυμάζετε, ἀδελφοί, εἰ μισεῖ ὑμᾶς ὁ κόσμος.) with the reminder to John's readers not to be amazed at that reality.

56. In John 19:34 John witnesses the flow of blood and water from Jesus' side (καὶ ἐξῆλθεν εὐθὺς αἷμα καὶ ὕδωρ). Then in 1 John 5:6 he points to "water and blood"

Because these two works likely share a common author, John the apostle, the question of their order of composition and relationship also arises. Brown provides a detailed listing of arguments for the priority of both the Gospel of John and his First Epistle. He lists these arguments as support for the priority of First John: (1) "[N]o passage in any of the epistles is a direct or certain quotation from GJohn, a surprising fact if I John was written after GJohn." (2) "A few passages in I John have been judged more 'primitive' than the comparable passages in GJohn." (3) "The theology of I John has also been thought to be earlier or less developed." (4) "Terminology in I John reflective of Jewish apocalyptic… and the warning against idolatry in 5:21" makes the epistle "more 'Jewish' than GJohn." He answers each argument and demonstrates well their subjectivity. He then lists arguments for the priority of the Gospel: (1) Since all the people mentioned in the Epistles have Greco-Roman names, the Epistles are more likely to have been written later when there were "many Gentiles in the Johannine churches." (2) First John reflects a different "life situation" with a community split by theological differences while the Gospel of John reflects a community in conflict with Jewish leadership that led to expulsion from synagogues. (3) And "the thrust of I John is intelligible as a reaction to an *overemphasis* on high christology, on death as glorification, on the activity of the Paraclete-Spirit as teacher, and on final eschatology" (Brown, 33–35). Both sets of arguments are inferential and circumstantial, and so do not adequately point to a definitive answer. For those who view the epistle as a corrective to doctrinal errors arising from misunderstanding John's message, it is natural to posit a Gospel priority (Akin, 28; Brown, 69; Westcott, xxx).[57] Even so, the weight of evidence favors the view that this First Epistle of John was written after the Gospel was completed and distributed (Smalley, xxxii). Brown

---

(δι' ὕδατος καὶ αἵματος) as a testimony of Jesus' incarnational ministry, beginning with His baptism and ending in His crucifixion. C. Black ("Christian Ministry in Johannine Perspective," 40) notes, "Whereas John presupposes Jesus' humanity but elaborates his divinity, First John inverts the emphasis. … Whereas the Fourth Gospel highlights salvation as a present reality, the first epistle underscores the ethical imperatives of eternal life and the future consummation of the elect."

57. P. J. Lalleman, "The Adversaries Envisaged in the Johannine Epistles," 17; D. Rusam, *Die Gemeinschaft der Kinder Gottes,* 10–11. One of his arguments (11) is the observation that 1 John contains more examples of the terms "children of God" and "born of God" than John's Gospel.

sees it being composed during what he viewed as the development of the Fourth Gospel, with neither work being penned by the apostle himself (Brown, 33–35).[58]

Rather than being seen as a corrective to misunderstandings of the Gospel, it would be better to see 1 John more as a reflection on Jesus' teachings in the upper room (see comments below under "Purpose[s]"). John Yarid identifies eight key concepts or themes drawn from the upper room, not all of which occur in the remainder of the Gospel. They include (1) full joy, (2) fellowship with the Father, (3) knowing God by obedience, (4) the mutual abiding relationship, (5) love toward God and other believers, (6) fellowship, (7) believers as beloved little children, (8) and the world in its opposition to believers.[59] The epistle's use of concepts and imagery from the upper room and its focus on Jesus' teachings that evening strengthen the view that the Gospel was prior (Smalley, xxix). Yet, it could just as well be argued that after writing his First Epistle, and reflecting on its background in that evening's instructions from Jesus, he may have chosen to include an account of the evening's discussion in his Gospel afterward.

Relationship to the Other Two Epistles

Though small in comparison to 1 John, John's second and third epistles are important and must never be overlooked. While the basic concept of the three epistles is contained in John's first epistle, each clarifies the question of how love of the brethren is to be expressed. Akin notes well, "If for no

58. Brown posits "five stages in the composition of the Gospel," beginning with material similar to that in the synoptic Gospels, with this material being "sifted" and modified to its GJohn form, followed by its organization, then reediting, and final editing (R. Brown, *The Gospel according to John [I–XII]*, xxxiv–xxxix). As with all redactional theories, no extant MSS have arisen to validate these claims and arguments are necessarily based on theories that divide canonical literature and use interpreted textual data to provide supposed clues to various layers of redaction.

59. J. R. Yarid, Jr., "Reflections of the Upper Room Discourse in 1 John," 66. He notes further (66) that the following terms also appear in both the upper room and John's first epistle: "anointing," "ask," "complete," "the evil one," "give," "hate," "heart," "the Holy Spirit," "keep," "knowledge," "proclaim," and "truth." He concludes his study with these insightful words (76): "Tracing the themes of the Upper Room Discourse throughout 1 John is similar to admiring the many facets of a sparkling diamond. Each time one comes back for an additional glance there is more beauty and intricacy to discover."

other reason than teaching the right (3 John) and wrong (2 John) use of Christian hospitality, these twin epistles have earned their right as part of the canonical Scriptures" (Akin, 22).

Similarities between 1 and 2 John may argue for proximity of writing, but not for order of composition. The idea that 2 John's milder tone may indicate an earlier date is still inconclusive, since the audience of each is different and could as easily explain the difference in tone (Burge, 41). The texts give no indication of dependence on any of the others even though they use the same terms and discuss the same issues. It is more likely that the three epistles were composed about the same time and may have even been carried by the same hand to each of their recipients.

The question of common authorship of the three epistles has been raised in both the early church and among modern critical scholars. Those from the early church who questioned common authorship included Origen, Dionysius of Alexandria, Eusebius, Ambrose, and Jerome. More recent objectors include Balz, Bergmeier, Bousset, Bultmann, Clemen, Ebrard, Harnack, Heinriei, Heise, Hirsch, Langbrandtner, Moffat, Peake, Pfleiderer, Renan, Schleiermacher, Schwartz, Selwyn, Von Dobschütz, von Soden, and J. Weiss. Most objectors attribute the writing of 1 John to one author and the two smaller epistles to a second (Brown, 14). First John's lack of the common epistolary opening and closing contained in both 2 and 3 John is used as an argument against common authorship. Yet they share a significant number of common words along with his Gospel. The speculation of some scholars that the similarities indicate a forger is answered well by Brown. He reasons that the similarity of each message and the absence of verbatim quotations between works serve as clear evidences of a single author. The "minor variants" fit better with an author "rephrasing himself" than a forger attempting to imitate the author (Brown, 15–17).[60] Painter

60. He lists nine "minor dissimilarities" that have raised questions about the common authorship of 1 John and 2 John and responds to each. These include (1) "[t]he sender identifies himself in II John but not in I John"; (2) the different referents of *tekna* in the epistles; (3) "[t]he use of 'Elect' (*eklectos*) in reference to ladies"; (4) 2 John 2 "uses 'truth' as the subject of the verb 'abide in,'" which is not used in any other Johannine literature; (5) the words of 2 John 3, "Jesus Christ, the Son of the Father," are unique to the New Testament; (6) "[t]he expression 'In truth and love' in II John 3 puts together two nouns not found *joined* elsewhere in the Johannine writings"; (7) "[t]he expression 'walk in truth,' which appears in II John 4 and III

(46) provides an excellent analysis of their mutual relatedness: "[First] John shares a close relationship to 2 John in terms of style and vocabulary and 2 John is closely related to 3 John, which is not so closely related to 1 John in terms of language, style, and content." Thus, 2 John serves as a bridge between 1 and 3 John.

Purpose(s)

John states four purposes within his epistle, though they may not exhaust all of his reasons or motives for writing. In 1:3, he writes so that he and his readers may have fellowship with one another and with God. This is immediately followed by a second purpose, that he or they, or better, both, may experience joy (1:4). Then, near the end of his first section of instruction, he writes so that his readers "may not sin" (2:1). Finally, near the end of this epistle, he writes so that his readers might have assurance of their salvation on the basis of their belief in Jesus (5:13).

Interpreters often take either the first or last purpose statement as determining both the purpose and the message of the epistle.[61] Those who interpret 5:13 as the controlling purpose often point to John 20:31, which they see as the stated purpose of the Gospel, as the pattern. The two purpose statements reflect a Johannine practice. "Whereas the Gospel of John is written with an evangelistic purpose, 1 John is penned to provide avenues of assurance whereby a believer can know he has eternal life through the Son" (Akin, 32). Similarly, arguing for the first purpose to be dominant on the basis that it occurs in the epistle's prologue is equally unconvincing. Though one can point to the purpose of the Revelation being stated early (Rev 1:19), such a purpose statement is absent from the Gospel's prologue, and this epistle appears to be more closely patterned after the Gospel than the Revelation (Brown, 90–91; Smalley, xxii).

John 3, occurs nowhere else in the New Testament"; (8) "the dualism which marks (with variations) both GJohn and I John is missing from II John"; and (9) in 2 John the term *truth* "has become equivalent to 'teaching' (II John 9), something that can abide and can belong to a community" (Brown, 17–19).

61. For a full treatment of this subject, see article by author, "What Is the Message of 1 John?," 89–105.

Selecting one or the other purpose statement as controlling the message of the epistle has led to two approaches to the message of 1 John.[62] The first view, and most commonly held, is best described as the "Test of Life" view. The second view, representing a minority of scholars and popular writers, is the "Test of Fellowship" view. In recent years a third approach has developed, taken by this commentary. The interpretation of the epistle should be based on its subject, the experience of eternal life, which is introduced in the prologue, rather than any of the stated purposes.

Both purposes are accomplished along with John's other two stated purposes, and none should be viewed as primary or comprehensive. Rather, the subject of the epistle can be found in its prologue, as with John's Gospel, and should guide one's interpretation of key passages.[63] That being said, what follows is a sketch of the two views.

The Test of Life view identifies three tests in 1 John, which reveal whether the reader is in *union* with God and so has spiritual life. This approach was introduced, and so gained its name, by Robert Law in his commentary, *Tests of Life*. He proposed that John wrote to provide his readers three tests by which they could assure themselves of their salvation.[64] These three tests

---

62. Although it is not the purpose of this commentary to engage in the debate between these two views, they will be touched on as they impact the interpretation of specific passages. It is noted that even the most recent commentaries continue to refer to Law's *Tests of Life*, and so his influence continues to this day (Akin, 87–88; MacArthur, 8–9). Similarly the proponents of these views are often engaged in the so-called Lordship Salvation versus Free Grace debates that characterized much of the 1980s, 1990s, and the first decade of the twenty-first century. Again, it is not the purpose of this work to defend either view or engage in its debate. Rather, both views have positive insights to contribute to the interpretation of this epistle, as well as interpretations that need correction, often the result of assumptions that guide their interpretation of the text more than dealing with the text itself. This debate appears to have arisen mostly because John did not intend to address the issues raised by either view. However there *are* issues dear to John, and it is these that must be addressed.

63. Key themes are introduced in the Gospel's prologue that are then developed throughout the work. In the same way, John introduces key themes in his Epistle's prologue (1:1–4) as well. In both cases, not every theme is included in the prologue. However, those introduced are significant to the central thrust of each work.

64. A. Köstenberger (*A Theology of John's Gospel and Letters*, 481) is an example of a more recent proponent of this view. Though he correctly recognizes that the purpose of the epistle is not to test whether one is saved, he sees its purpose from 5:13 to be to provide "assurance" and "to instill confidence in true believers that

of one's justification include the tests of belief (orthodoxy), righteousness, and love. From then and to this day it has remained the dominant perspective for the purpose of the epistle.[65] Hiebert generally concurs with Law, but modifies his outlook and sees John writing to provide "tests of a vital Christianity, which would promote the assurance of personal salvation in the lives of his readers and would enable them to detect and reject false teachers."[66] More recently, the view is expressed by Akin (115), who sees two primary tests, righteousness (obedience) and love, with perseverance as a third. John is providing tests by which a person can determine if he or she is "saved" and thereby has assurance of salvation. Failure to pass the tests indicates spiritual death, not immaturity. Reflecting Reformed Calvinism, it harmonizes the affirmations of John in the epistle with the Calvinist doctrine of perseverance.[67] Within the Test of Life view, the absence of fruit in the life of a person indicates the absence of spiritual life ("No fruit, no life.").[68]

---

their salvation is assured." He connects this assurance with perseverance in obedience and thus appears to interpret the epistle through the rubric of the Calvinist doctrine of perseverance, that true believers (the elect) will persevere in good works till the end and that the non-elect will fall away or their faith will fail before their deaths.

65. Other more recent representatives include Akin (*1, 2, 3 John*), Burge (*Letters of John*), Kruse (*The Letters of John*), MacArthur (*1, 2, 3 John*), Painter (*1, 2, and 3 John*), and Walls and Anders (*I & II Peter, I, II & III John, Jude*).

66. D. E. Hiebert, "An Expositional Study of 1 John—Part 2: An Exposition of 1 John 1:5–2:6," 330.

67. This doctrine is distinct from the doctrine of eternal security. The Calvinist doctrine of perseverance might be better described as "persevering in good works." By perseverance, the Reformed Calvinist means that a truly regenerate person will continue in good works—will not "fall away" into a life of sin or denial of Christ—from the time of his regeneration until his death. This does not mean sinless perfection, but rather unbroken progressive sanctification with no significant lapse into sin (D. A. Carson, "Reflections on Christian Assurance," 1–29; R. Kearsley, "Perseverance" in *The New Dictionary of Theology*, 506–507).

68. J. F. MacArthur Jr., *The Gospel according to Jesus*, 168; R. Law, *The Tests of Life*, 220; J. E. Rosscup, *Abiding in Christ*, 42; and C. R. Smith, "The Unfruitful Branches in John 15," 13–14. J. C. Laney ("Abiding Is Believing: The Analogy of the Vine in John 15:1–6," 62) is a good example of this understanding of perseverance among those promoting what is termed "Lordship Salvation" when he affirms: "There is no fruit without faith, and there is no faith without fruit."

The Test of Fellowship view also identifies the same three tests in 1 John as did the Test of Life view. However, instead of revealing one's union with God, they test one's relationship—and thus fellowship—with God. There are no tests in the epistle that determine the justification status of anyone. The purpose statement of 1:3 is central to the message of the epistle, and 5:13 relates only to its immediately preceding context. John's use of κοινωνία is relational rather than indicating possession of or joint participation in eternal life. Its key representatives include Anderson, Hodges, King, Mitchell, and Pentecost.[69]

The intermediate view sees neither purpose as dominant and does not see the tests being related to salvation. This is reflected by W. Robert Cook, who sees both purpose statements as controlling.[70] Its two more recent representatives include Steven S. Smalley and Marianne M. Thompson.[71] These two authors are closer to the view of this commentary, though not at every point.

In addition to these two dominant approaches to the purpose of the epistle, biblical scholars also define its purpose as either polemical[72] or pastoral.[73] For example, Akin says that "John's central purpose is to encourage his readers to persevere in their belief in the apostolic proclamation of the Christ as Jesus, the incarnate Son of God" (Akin, 54). However, Brown (48), who builds much of his interpretation on his construction of the supposed "secessionists," acknowledges that "a theory which gives prominence to the role of adversaries in the background does not automatically mean that I John should be classified as a polemical tract." Even so, those statements identified as polemical are aimed at both encouraging the reader to remain true to the faith while, secondarily, refuting the heretical teachings that include both ethical issues as well as christological (Smalley, xxviii).

69. D. R. Anderson, *Maximum Joy: First John—Relationship or Fellowship?*; Z. C. Hodges, *The Epistles of John: Walking in the Light of God's Love*; G. H. King, *The Fellowship*; J. G. Mitchell, *Fellowship*; J. D. Pentecost, *The Joy of Fellowship: A Study of First John*. R. Edwards (*The Johannine Epistles*) appears to hold more of a Test of Fellowship view than of Life, in that she assumes the readers are believers and John is writing to encourage them in their faith (72).

70. W. R. Cook, "Hamartiological Problems in First John," 249.

71. S. Smalley, *1,2,3 John*; and M. Thompson, *1–3 John*.

72. H. Swadling, "Sin and Sinlessness in 1 John," 205.

73. J. M. Lieu ("'Authority to Become Children of God': A Study of 1 John," 210–28) rejects any polemical purpose and sees this as a purely pastoral epistle.

Strecker (33) notes that the issue of false teachings cannot be central to the message of the epistle since John's focus, especially throughout his various dualistic contrasts, is ethical. This is because the "Christian community itself is continually under siege" morally and not just because there are false teachers attempting to influence it.

John's First Epistle appears to have a double purpose, namely, pastoral and polemical, with the pastoral dominant and the polemical brought out only as it relates to pastoral concerns. Westcott describes well John's purposes related to the doctrinal and moral issues: "His object is polemical only so far as the clear unfolding of the essence of right teaching necessarily shews all error in its real character. In other words St John writes to call out a welcome for what he knows to be the Gospel and not to overthrow this or that false opinion" (Westcott, xxxix). Bruce understands it as a pastoral letter in response to the departure of Christians and the subsequent "perplexity" this caused and that he wrote "to state the criteria of truth and life, and to help his readers to see that they, and not the seceders, satisfied these criteria" (Bruce, 27). The polemical element of the epistle cannot be ignored in favor of arguments for a purely pastoral purpose (Smalley, xxxi). The themes of Christ's incarnation and deity clearly indicate theological issues involving Christology that needed to be addressed (Brown, 48). However these issues serve only as secondary to the overall concern of the apostle to encourage his flock. Though John clearly addresses issues raised by false teachers whose salvation he rejects (1 John 2:19), often referred to as the "secessionists," he need not address them constantly throughout his epistle any more than Paul did in his. As will be argued later with particular passages in question, what is often attributed to the secessionists need not be, and, in fact, makes better pastoral sense than polemical when recognized as addressing the faithful rather than responding to the faithless. The two main passages that clearly address the problem of false teachers are 2:18–28 ("they went out from us") and 4:1–6 ("test the spirits").[74] Others, such as 1:6–10 and 2:4–11, which are usually identified as either quotations or allusions to doctrines of the opponents, need not be seen in such a way if a pastoral concern is attributed to them as opposed to a polemical concern. As will

74. Others such as Thompson (14) include 5:5–8 as directly addressing false teachers, but they need not.

be seen in the commentary of those passages, they should be interpreted in light of John's pastoral concern unless clear evidence shows otherwise.

John's pastoral purpose is to promote fellowship within their congregation (1:3) by encouraging them in their faith and walk with God (2:12–17). He does include in his epistle correctives to false doctrines that were appearing and threatening the faith of the church near the end of the first century (2:26). However, he does this as they relate to his pastoral concerns. Deception ultimately degrades unity, which is only possible in the sphere of Christ's love. Though it does appear that some false teachers had arisen within the churches of the recipients of this letter (2:18, 19, and 26), they are neither the reason for his writing nor the focus of this epistle. Nonetheless, when he does turn his attention to them, John is not gentle, as evidenced by the terms he uses to describe them.[75] He addresses them because the churches would be enabled to maintain unity of the faith and love for fellow believers (3:11) by being able to distinguish between true and false teachers. For John, one's behavior springs from one's belief. Also, if a believer believes the wrong things, he or she will act accordingly. All sin results from unbelief. As a result, though behavior may not prove or disprove one's justification (contra Law's tests of life), it certainly indicates the state of one's sanctification (contra Burge, 96).[76]

Several key themes are developed in this epistle. They include eternal life, knowing God, and abiding in faith. Additionally, the author uses contrasts, such as walking in the light and walking in the darkness, being either

75. John introduces the term "antichrist" (2:18, 22) to the church as a descriptor of these false teachers and calls them "liars" (2:22). He uses similarly harsh language to describe disobedient believers, such as referring to them as "children of the devil" and "murderers."

76. Burge (96) says, "In Johannine thought, *knowing, abiding,* and *being* reflect similar meanings, and it is unnecessary to look for a theological progression here. In each case John is acknowledging that men and women might announce their allegiance to Jesus and explain that they have a profoundly intimate relationship with him, and yet there are tests, 'tests of life,' as Robert Law once called them, that signal the authenticity of spiritual vigor." Using Burge's terminology, one may have life without vigor. As a horticulturalist, I know that a sickly plant is still a living plant. In the same sense, lack of vigor does not prove lack of life; it only proves lack of vigor. John's point in this epistle, and a theme he develops in his Gospel, is that it is possible to possess eternal life without experiencing it (in this life) and without expressing it. This idea will be developed more in the commentary on various verses as they relate to this theme.

a child of God or a child of the devil, love or hate, and life or death. These contrasts delineate between true and false teachers and between those believers in fellowship with God and those who are not. However where they bring the salvation of false teachers into question, they never serve as tests of the readers themselves with regard to their salvation, only their sanctification.[77]

This letter includes a call to remain (abide) in the truths they had been taught by John and the other apostles rather than following the new ideas of the false teachers. This is the key to maintaining fellowship with God as well as other believers and is essential to loving others as well. Orthopraxy, biblically correct living, results from orthodoxy, biblically correct thinking. Christlike living results from a correct view of Christ Jesus. One's view of Christ is expressed in a person's conduct of life, particularly in how he or she treats other believers. Thus John exhorts his readers to express their orthodox belief in Jesus by righteous living and practically demonstrated love for others.

Though christological issues are addressed by John, the relational issues are given greater emphasis in his first epistle. How we treat others stems from our view of Christ and God. Even so, John makes it clear that our motivation to love is based on God's actions on our behalf rather than on Christology alone. Thus John connects our actions to a response to God's acts and nature rather than to the Incarnation.

Genre

The literary genre of 1 John continues to puzzle biblical scholars, primarily because of the absence of the normal salutation (Akin, 50; Burge, 43). It may be described as "the least letter-like" of the New Testament epistles. Brown (87–92) lists four proposed literary classifications for 1 John, including (1) a universal religious tract;[78] (2) a circular epistle; (3) a homily, diatribe*, informal tractate, or pastoral epistle; (4) a comment patterned on GJohn. He prefers this last option. Where 2 and 3 John clearly fit in

77. This will be addressed in the body of this commentary when discussing specific verses.

78. Painter (126) rejects this option on the basis that "it deals with issues that have taken place in the community addressed (see 2:18–19)."

the style of Greco-Roman personal letters, 1 John should not be classed as such.[79] Its size and development of its message go beyond the scope of such letters. Painter (37) notes that works such as Romans and Galatians do not reflect the basic format and size of these occasional letters. Characteristics of these "popular" letters include: shorter lengths (can be contained on a single papyrus sheet); an author who identifies himself; identified addressees; and an expression of affection, followed by a "greeting or a prayer for their well being. At the end of each letter the author indicates that he has much to write but would rather communicate in person.... The letters end with a closing greeting." He notes this fits for 3 John. However, it becomes problematic if 2 John is addressed to a church. Being more like the Gospel and Revelation than his other two epistles, 1 John's introduction serves as a prologue rather than a greeting (Westcott, xxxix). It may be better to see 1 John as a tract or as a "written sermon or pastoral address" (Marshall, 14).[80]

Characteristics

First, as noted above, this "epistle" does not begin or end like an epistle. John neither identifies himself at the beginning nor gives any greetings at the end (Bruce, 25). Thus, as noted above, it is stylistically closer to a tract or treatise. Of other New Testament epistles, Galatians comes close to 1 John in terms of the brevity of Paul's greeting and the absence of concluding salutations, though he does end with a blessing.

Second, interpreters find it difficult to identify a clear structure to its argument (Marshall, 49–55). Brown goes so far as to say, "The author's logic is so obscure that one could move around units almost at will and 1 John would read just as well as it does now. ... If at any of a half-dozen places in 1 John the rest of the work had been lost, no subsequent reader would have

79. R. N. Longenecker, "On the Form, Function, and Authority of the New Testament Letters," 106. He proposes that 2 and 3 John may have served as separate cover letters for 1 John.

80. Smalley (xxviii) describes it as equivalent to a modern "paper" designed to further the discussion initiated by John's Gospel. I would not see it this way since the idea of "discussing" issues between opposing views seems absent from the writings of the church fathers. There seems little of the modern "agree to disagree" mentality in the early church. The struggle for truth and orthodoxy was far more dichotomous then than it is today.

had the slightest suspicion that anything was missing" (Brown, 117). John's Semitic thought pattern and writing style are revealed in his use of "and" to connect ideas as well as his interweaving of themes throughout the work. Kistemaker notes well, "Classical Greek sentences show careful structure and balance with numerous subordinate clauses (compare Luke 1:1–4). Semitic Greek has many coordinate clauses that are short and often are connected by the conjunction *and*" (Kistemaker 233). Thus, while writing in Greek, John is often thinking in Hebrew.

Third, John appears to relate purposefully ideas by the use of what Brown (119) aptly coined "hinge verses."[81] These are sentences that contain key terms or concepts both from what precedes and from what follows. For the interpreter, the challenge is to decide if the sentence is the conclusion of the first paragraph, or the introductory sentence of the second. Or could John intend both? It may function as a form of rhetorical double entendre*. As such it would serve a dual purpose and be used thereby to show the interconnectedness of the ideas developed in each unit. This rhetorical device serves well to demonstrate how none of the truths or principles should be viewed in isolation, but as interrelated and interconnected. One is not true apart from the other. Furthermore, the experience of eternal life is not a product of compartmentalization, however must result from a holistic approach to the life of faith.

Fourth, though it *appears* to interact with some aspects of Gnosticism, it does not do so openly. The use of such themes as light versus darkness and truth versus error likely was designed to resonate with the Greek worldview of John's readers. However, at the same time, these concepts were not absent from classic Jewish thought either. So, John's conceptual source for the imagery he chooses and the themes he develops is more likely Jewish in origin than a reaction to an often theorized life situation involving Greek dualistic influences.[82] This is evident as well from his use of similar imagery in his Gospel. Further, since the Old Testament is replete with similar

81. Examples include 2:28 (connects the following discussion with the previous by inclusion of the term "abide") and 3:24 (connects "keeps His commandments" from the previous with "Spirit" from what follows). I do not see 5:12 or 13 serving as a hinge as does Brown (119).

82. G. L. Borchert,"The Fourth Gospel and Its Theological Impact," 256; W. W. Combs, "Nag Hammadi, Gnosticism and New Testament Interpretation," 211; R. L. Giese, Jr., "Dualism in the LXX of Prov 2:17," 295.

imagery, one need not look to Gnosticism to see the literary influences on John.[83]

Finally, none of John's three epistles contain Old Testament quotations. Moreover, of all the New Testament literature, only 2 and 3 John and Philemon lack either quotations from or allusions to the Old Testament.

Theological and Practical Emphases of the Epistle

Eternal life—its significance, source, and enjoyment—stands as the principal focus of this epistle. Beginning with the prologue in which eternal life is a Person rather than an experience, the contingencies of experiencing it through a healthy relationship with Christ are then detailed through the body of the epistle.[84] The experience of eternal life is contingent on the health of one's relationship with Jesus, who is eternal life incarnate and from whom that life flows in the person of the Holy Spirit, who indwells believers. It cannot be experienced apart from honesty with God about sin, obedience to his command to love one another, and orthodox beliefs about Jesus. Eternal life cannot be enjoyed by a believer apart from God's truth and can only be enjoyed on God's terms. Finally, its experience flows from a confidence in one's standing with God, both in terms of one's assurance of salvation as well as acceptance into his presence through prayer.

A second focus, related to the experience of eternal life, is the concept of mutual abiding. It is introduced in the first chapter with the term "fellowship" and then developed in the passages that follow. For the child of God, abiding is experiential and contingent on obedience to God's commands, especially Christ's particular command to love other believers.[85] It

---

83. Beginning with the division of light and darkness in Gen 1, we see light and darkness used in judgment in Exod 10 and the ninth plague. The contrast between light and dark appears in Job 3:4; Eccl 2:13; and Isa 5:20, where they are used to contrast moral spheres much as in 1 John 1.

84. The issue is not one of "possessing" in that John is not questioning his readers' possession of eternal life. Rather, he is explaining what is involved in its expression in their lives.

85. This follows the basic pattern of the term in John's Gospel as well. As E. Malatesta (*Interiority and Covenant*, 28) notes, its use by John and Jesus, besides having the literal sense of staying somewhere (John 1:32–33, 38–39; 2:12; 4:40; 7:9; 9:41 [sin]; 10:40; 11:6, 54; 12:24 [seed]; 14:25; 15:16; 19:31) or continuing in life (12:34; 21:22–23), describes the mutual relationship between God the Father and

is a familial issue within the body of Christ. Disobedience does not cause one to become unregenerate; one remains a child of God. However disobedience can keep one from experiencing the eternal life one possesses.

Christology is a third, and foundational, focus of this epistle. What a person believes about Jesus is critical in his or her experience of eternal life. Because God is true in all he says and does, one must relate to him on the basis of truth. Also, one cannot have a healthy relationship with Jesus unless one knows him as he has defined himself. Christological error in the lives of regenerate saints will not cause them to become unregenerate (cannot lose their salvation). However, it will certainly keep them from abiding in Christ and experiencing the eternal life they possess in the same way that disobedience does. God relates to us on his terms, not ours.

A fourth area of interest to John may be called his ethic of love for other believers. Reflecting on Jesus' instructions in the upper room, John develops the concept of expressed love in the church in his Epistle. In the Gospel of John, Jesus demonstrated his love by washing the disciples' feet. Then, having washed their feet, he commanded them to imitate his love and said that they "also ought to wash one another's feet" (John 13:14). As the discussion progressed, Jesus repeated the command to love one another within the context of his demonstrated love by serving them when he washed their feet (John 13:34–35; 15:12, 17).[86]

Son (John 15:10), the Father and believers (John 14:23 ["home"]), God the Son and believers (John 15:4–7, 9), and the Holy Spirit's indwelling believers (John 14:16–17). Even so, Jesus' use of "abiding" included at times a justification sense or application when he addressed nonbelievers (John 6:27, 56; 8:35). Once John refers to God's wrath "abiding" on nonbelievers (John 3:36).

86. Jesus did not institute an ordinance of footwashing, but demonstrated loving servanthood that is to characterize His followers (L. D. Pettegrew, "Teaching Methods of Christ," 15–16). When He commanded them to imitate him, He was not referring to the act of footwashing, but His acting out love by humble service (W. R. Cook, *The Theology of John*, 110). This same truth is expressed by Paul in Phil 2:5–11, wherein he uses Jesus' humbling himself through incarnation and death demonstrated that we were more important than himself in His mind (Phil 2:4). This is the kind of serving love Jesus had in mind in the Upper Room, and that John has in mind in his epistle. See H. Weiss, "Foot Washing in the Johannine Community," 298–325, for an eschatological interpretation of footwashing. For arguments in its favor as an ordinance, see A. Edgington, "Footwashing as an Ordinance," 425–34.

Literary Design

This epistle guides its readers into an understanding and experience of eternal life (sanctification reality) by: giving the content and purpose of its message (1:1–4); describing the prerequisite for fellowship with God (1:5–2:6); reminding them of the origin of his message (2:7–11); reminding them of the purpose of his message (2:12–14); warning against compromising their relationship with God (2:15–29); contrasting the lifestyles of believers and unbelievers (3:1–10); describing the outworking of the lifestyle of love (3:11–18); reviewing the message he has been delivering (3:19–24); warning them against false prophets (4:1–6); calling upon them to love with God's love (4:7–21); describing the outworking of a relationship with Christ (5:1–12); giving the promise of answered prayer (5:13–17); and, finally, reviewing the major concepts of his epistle (5:18–21).

Themes introduced in the prologue include "Word of Life" (Christ), eternal life, fellowship, and the incarnation. Other themes developed in the epistle include the character of God, Jesus as the Son of God, obedience, and sin.

Johannine Dualism

A characteristic of John's writing style involves his use of antithesis, or dualistic imagery. His dualism is expressed in the themes of light versus darkness, love versus hatred/murder, and children of God versus children of the devil. It is different from the Greek philosophical dualism. Whereas Greek dualism developed from a view that spirit is good and matter is evil, John's dualism is moral in nature. John likes to divide the world into two opposite groups or effects with no intermediate options being offered. "For him there is only light and darkness, and no twilight. He sees only 'life' and 'death'" (Westcott, 108). He offers only opposite categories to his reader with no exceptions or mitigation. Usually the reader will find himself or herself unable to fit honestly into either category. Thus the "either-or" world created forces the reader into introspection and evaluation. That John does not see the world from this perspective is evident in his discussion of sin in the life of the believer. Thus, while he says in 3:6 that an abiding believer does not sin, he affirms the opposite in 1:8–10, reminds his readers of Jesus' work on their behalf when they do sin in 2:1–2, and commends prayer for certain sins in other believers in 5:16. As a result we should recognize that when he writes that a believer is either walking in the light or the darkness, loving or hating his brother, and loving or murdering his brother, he knows that every believer will ultimately fail the test, including himself. This can be seen in his reassurances for his readers of their relationship with God in 2:12–14, their confidence before God even when they feel they have failed the test of love in 3:20, as well as his purpose of their assurance of salvation in 5:13.

Outline

The epistle appears to have both a prologue (1:1–4) and an epilogue (5:18–21). Less clear is the structure of the body of the letter. Rather than following a sequential argument like Paul or Peter, John appears to touch on his themes repeatedly, following what appears more circular or spiral in pattern (Kistemaker, 218; Linski, 367; Marshall, 26; Plummer, liv).[87] This reflects an Eastern way of thinking as contrasted with a Western (Greek) rhetorical approach that tends to be more linear. Bruce notes well, "Attempts to trace a consecutive argument throughout 1 John have never succeeded" (Bruce, 29).

Some, including Brown, Burge, Feuillet, and Smalley, divide the body of the epistle into two main parts (xxxii).[88] For example, Burge (43–45) divides it based on the repeated phrase "this is the message." He argues further that this approach reflects a similar pattern as the Gospel of John. Each has a prologue and epilogue, with a bipartite body of material. Brown (125–28) bases his division on the two statements, "God is light" and "God is love." However, as with the other approaches to the structure of the epistle, these fail to account for all the units of material.

The most common approach, and the one taken in this commentary, is a threefold division reflected in such works as those of Bruce (29),

87. Lenski (402) describes it thus: "This letter is not arranged in blocks that are laid side by side but is built like an inverted cone. John's facts circle upward and outward in a natural inner sequence. Every new circular sweep has its plainly marked center so that every statement is closely integrated. The weave unfolds itself in a perfect pattern and design."
88. A. Feuillet, "The Structure of First John," 202.

Schnackenburg (10), Smit-Sibinga,[89] and Thompson (31).[90] This approach divides the epistle more thematically. I appreciate Burge's honesty in expressing his "reluctance" to defend his twofold division (Burge, 63). I must admit to the same struggle with my own threefold approach.

Absent from this epistle are the usual greetings or closing salutations. This may result from a desire to imitate the Gospel, even to the point of placing a purpose statement at the close of the work (Brown, 91). Or it may be better to see this as John's approach to non-epistolary literature, as reflected in the Gospel, First Epistle, and Revelation.

The following outline has been adopted in this commentary.

1. Prologue: Eternal Life Is a Person (1:1–4)
2. God Is Light (1:5–2:27)
    - a. Walking in the Light (1:5–2:6)
        - i. God's Moral Purity (1:5)
        - ii. Honesty with God about Sin (1:6–2:4)
        - iii. Imitation of Christ (2:5–6)
    - b. Loving Believers, Not the World (2:7–17)
        - i. New Commandment (2:7–11)
        - ii. Assurance (2:12–14)
        - iii. Love God, Not the World (2:15–17)
    - c. Avoid the Antichrists (2:18–27)
3. God Is Righteous (2:28–4:6)
    - a. Expectation of Righteousness (2:28–-3:3)
        - i. Boldness at his Return (2:28–29)
        - ii. Children of God Who Is Pure (3:1–3)
    - b. Expression of Righteousness (3:4–24)
        - i. Expression of Parentage (3:4–10)
        - ii. Murder and Love (3:11–18)
        - iii. Assurance from God (3:19–24)
    - c. Test False Teachers (4:1–6)

89. J. Smit-Sibinga, "A Study in I John," 194.

90. Bruce (29) outlines the epistle in this way: "At best we can distinguish three main courses of thought: the first (1.5–2.27), which has two main themes, ethical (walking in light) and Christological (confessing Jesus as the Christ); the second (2.28–4.6), which repeats the ethical and Christological themes with variations; the third (4.7–5.12), where the same two essential themes are presented as love and faith and shown to be inseparable and indispensable products of life in Christ."

4. God Is Love (4:7–5:21)
   a. God's Love Perfected (4:7–21)
      i. Imitating God's Love (4:7–12)
      ii. Confessing Jesus and Loving Believers (4:13–16a)
      iii. Purpose of Perfected Love (4:16b–19)
      iv. Absence of Love (4:20–21)
   b. God's Love Communicated (5:1–20)
      i. Loving God's Child (5:1–5)
      ii. Believing God's Testimony (5:6–13)
      iii. Praying for Sinning Christians (5:14–17)
      iv. What We Know (Epilogue) (5:18–20)
   c. Avoid Idols (5:21)

Selected Bibliography

Arndt, W., F. W. Danker, and W. Bauer. *A Greek-English Lexicon of the New Testament and Other Early Christian Literature*. 3rd ed. Chicago: University of Chicago Press, 2000.

Aune, D. E. *Revelation 1–5:14*. WBC 52A. Dallas, TX: Word, 2002.

Black, C. C. "Christian Ministry in Johannine Perspective." *Int* 44 (1990): 29–41.

Borchert, G. L. "The Fourth Gospel and Its Theological Impact." *RevExp* 78 (1981): 246–56.

Brown, R. E. *The Gospel according to John (I–XII)*. AB. Garden City, NY: Doubleday, 1966.

Carson, D. A. *The Gospel according to John.* Grand Rapids: Eerdmans, 1991.

———. "Reflections on Christian Assurance." *WTJ* 54 (Spring 1992): 1–29.

Combs, W. W. "Nag Hammadi, Gnosticism and New Testament Interpretation." *GTJ* 8 (1987): 195–212.

Conybeare, F. C. "Dionysius of Alexandria, Newly Discovered Letters to the Popes Stephen and Xystus." *English Historical Review* 25 (1910): 112–14.

Cook, W. R.. "Hamartiological Problems in First John." *BSac* 123, no. 491 (July 1966): 249–60.

———. *The Theology of John*. Chicago: Moody, 1979.

Culpepper, R. A. *The Johannine School: An Evaluation of the Johannine-School Hypothesis Based on an Investigation of the Nature of Ancient Schools.* SBLDS 26. Missoula, MT: Scholars Press, 1975.

Culy, M. M. *1, 2, 3 John: A Handbook on the Greek Text.* Waco, TX: Baylor University Press, 2004.

Deconick, A. D. *The Original Gospel of Thomas in Translation: With a Commentary and New English Translation of the Complete Gospel.* Library of New Testament Studies 287. New York: T & T Clark, 2006.

Derickson, G. W. "What Is the Message of 1 John?" *BSac* 150 (1993): 89–105.

Ehrman, B. D. *The Lost Gospel of Judas Iscariot: A New Look at Betrayer and Betrayed*. Oxford: Oxford University Press, 2006.

Elwell, W. A., gen. ed. *Baker Encyclopedia of the Bible*. Grand Rapids: Baker, 1988.

Evans, C. A. "Understanding the Gospel of Judas." *BBR* 20 (2010): 561–74.

Foster, P. "Polymorphic Christology: Its Origins and Development in Early Christianity." *JTS* 57 (2007): 66–99.

Frankfurter, D. "A Historian's View of the Gospel of Judas." *Near Eastern Archaeology* 70 (2007): 174–77.

Freedman, D. N., A. C. Myers, and A. B. Beck. *Eerdmans Dictionary of the Bible.* Grand Rapids: Eerdmans, 2000.

Feuillet, A. "The Structure of First John: Comparison with the Fourth Gospel; The Pattern of Christian Life." *BTB* 3 (1973): 194–216.

Gangel, K. O. *John*. Holman New Testament Commentary 4. Nashville: Broadman & Holman, 2000.

Gathercole, S. "The Gospel of Judas." *ExpTim* 118 (2007): 209–15.

Giese, R. L., Jr. "Dualism in the LXX of Prov 2:17: A Case Study in the LXX as Revisionary Translation." *JETS* 36 (1993): 286–95

Gregory, A. "The Non-canonical Gospels and the Historical Jesus—Some Reflections on Issues and Methods." *EvQ* 81 (2009): 3–22.

Guthrie, D. "Questions of Introduction." In *New Testament Interpretation: Essays on Principles and Methods*, edited by I. Howard Marshall, 101–14. Milton Keynes, UK: Paternoster, 1977.

Hahneman, G. M. *The Muratorian Fragment and the Development of the Canon*. Oxford: Clarendon, 1992.

Hawthorne, G. F., R. P. Martin, and D. G. Reid, eds. *Dictionary of Paul and His Letters.* Downers Grove, IL: InterVarsity, 1993.

Head, P. M. "The Gospel of Judas and the Qarara Codices." *TynBul* 58 (2007): 1–23.

Hiebert, D. E. "An Expositional Study of 1 John—Part 1: An Exposition of 1 John 1:1–4." *BSac* 145, no. 578 (April 1988): 197–210.

———. "An Expositional Study of 1 John—Part 2: An Exposition of 1 John 1:5–2:6." *BSac* 145, no. 579 (July 1988): 329–42.

Kearsley, R. "Perseverance" in *New Dictionary of Theology*, ed. S. B. Ferguson and J. I. Packer, 506–7. Downers Grove, IL: InterVarsity Press, 2000.

Kistemaker, S. J., and W. Hendriksen. *Exposition of the Book of Revelation.* NTC 20. Grand Rapids: Baker, 1953–2001.

Knight, G. W. *The Pastoral Epistles: A Commentary on the Greek Text.* Grand Rapids: Eerdmans, 1992.

Köstenberger, A. J. *A Theology of John's Gospel and Letters: The Word, the Christ, the Son of God*. Biblical Theology of the New Testament. Grand Rapids: Zondervan, 2009.

Kügler, Joachim. "Die Belehrung der Unbelehrbaren: Zur Funktion des Traditionsarguments in 1 Joh." *BZ* 32 (1988): 249–54.

Lalleman, P. J. "The Adversaries Envisaged in the Johannine Epistles." *ThT* 53 (1999): 17–24.

Laney, J. C. "Abiding Is Believing: The Analogy of the Vine in John 15:1–6." *BSac* 146 (1989): 54–66.

Lieu, J. M. "'Authority to Become Children of God': A Study of 1 John." *NovT* 23 (1981): 210–28.

———. "Us or You? Persuasion and Identity in 1 John." *JBL* 4 (2008): 805–19.

Longenecker, R. N. "On the Form, Function, and Authority of the New Testament Letters." In *Scripture and Truth*, edited by D. A. Carson and J. D. Woodbridge, 97–114. Grand Rapids: Baker, 1992.

Louw, J. P. "Verbal Aspect in the First Letter of John." *Neot* 9 (1975): 98–104.

MacArthur, J. F., Jr. *The Gospel according to Jesus*, Grand Rapids: Academie, 1988.

Malatesta, E. *Interiority and Covenant: A Study of εἶναι ἐν and μένειν ἐν in the First Letter of Saint John*. Rome: Biblical Institute Press, 1978.

Martin, Ralph P., and Peter H. Davids, eds. *Dictionary of the Later New Testament and Its Developments*. Downers Grove, IL: InterVarsity Press, 2000.

Moule, C. F. D. "A Neglected Factor in the Interpretation of Johannine Eschatology." In *Studies in John,* 155–160. NovTSup 24. Leiden: Brill, 1970.

Mounce, W. D. *Pastoral Epistles*. WBC. Vol. 46. Dallas, TX: Word, 2002.

O'Neill, J. C. *The Puzzle of 1 John*. London: SPCK, 1966.

Osborne, G. R. *Revelation*. BECNT. Grand Rapids: Baker Academic, 2002.

Painter, J. "The 'Opponents' in 1 John." *NTS* 32 (1986): 48–71.

Parkes, J. *The Conflict of the Church and the Synagogue: A Study of the Origins of Antisemitism*. London: Soncino, 1934. Reprint, New York: Atheneum, 1969.

Perkins, P. "What Is a Gnostic Gospel?" *CBQ* 71 (2009): 104–29.

Perrin, N. *Thomas: The Other Gospel*. London: SPCK, 2007.

Pettegrew, L. D. "Teaching Methods of Christ." *Central Bible Quarterly* 15 (1972): 3–31.

Roberts, A., J. Donaldson, and A. C. Coxe. *The Ante-Nicene Fathers Vol. 1: Translations of the Writings of the Fathers Down to A.D. 325*. Oak Harbor, WA: Logos Research Systems, 1997.

Rosscup, J. E. *Abiding in Christ*. Grand Rapids: Zondervan, 1973.

Rusam, D. *Gemeinschaft der Kinder Gottes: Das Motiv der Gotteskindschaft und die Gemeinden der johanneischen Briefe*. Stuttgart: Verlag W. Kohlhammer, 1993.

Schaff, P. *The Nicene and Post-Nicene Fathers, Second Series*. Vol. 1. Oak Harbor: Logos Research Systems, 1997.

Sibinga, J. S. "A Study in I John." In *Studies in John,* 194–208. NovTSup 24. Leiden: Brill, 1970.

Smith, C. B., II. *No Longer Jews.* Peabody, MA: Hendrickson, 2004.

Smith, C. R. "The Unfruitful Branches in John 15." *Grace Journal* 9 (1968): 3–20.

Sundberg, A., C., Jr. "Canon Muratori: A Fourth Century List." *HTR* 66 (1973): 1–41.

Swadling, H. C. "Sin and Sinlessness in 1 John." *SJT* 35 (1982): 205–11.

Westcott, B. F. *The Gospel according to St. John.* 1882. Reprint, Grand Rapids: Eerdmans, 1981.

Wright, N. T. *Judas and the Gospel of Jesus: Have We Missed the Truth about Christianity?* Grand Rapids: Baker, 2006.

Yarid, J. R., Jr. "Reflections of the Upper Room Discourse in 1 John." *BSac* 160 (January 2003): 65–76.

Commentary Bibliography

Akin, D. L. *1, 2, 3 John.* NAC 38. Nashville: Broadman & Holman, 2001.

Alexander, W. *The Epistles of St. John: Twenty-One Discourses with Greek Text, Comparative Versions, and Notes Chiefly Exegetical.* 3rd ed. London: Hodder and Stoughton, 1892.

Barker, G. W. "1, 2, 3 John." In *The Expositor's Bible Commentary*, vol. 12. Grand Rapids: Zondervan, 1981.

Boice, J. M. *The Epistles of John*. Grand Rapids: Zondervan, 1979.

Brooke, A. E. *A Critical and Exegetical Commentary on the Johannine Epistles.* ICC. Edinburgh: T & T Clark, 1912.

Brown, R. E. *The Epistles of John: A New Translation with Introduction and Commentary*. AB 30. New York: Doubleday, 1982.

Bruce, F. F. *The Epistles of John*. Grand Rapids: Eerdmans, 1970.

Bultmann, R. *The Johannine Epistles*. Translated by R. P. O'Hara, L. C. McGaughy, and R. W. Funk. Philadelphia: Fortress, 1973.

Burdick, D. W. *The Letters of John the Apostle*. Chicago: Moody, 1985.

Burge, G. M. *Letters of John*. NIVAC. Grand Rapids: Zondervan, 1996.

Culy, M. M. *1, 2, 3 John: A Handbook on the Greek Text.* Waco, TX: Baylor University Press, 2004.

Dodd, C. H. *The Johannine Epistles*. MNTC. New York: Harper and Brothers, 1946.

Edwards, R. B. *The Johannine Epistles.* Sheffield: Sheffield Academic Press, 2001.

Grayston, K. *The Johannine Epistles*. New Century Bible Commentary. Grand Rapids: Eerdmans, 1984.

Haas, C., M. de Jonge, and J. L. Swellengrebel. *A Handbook on the Letters of John.* UBS Handbook Series; Helps for Translators. New York: United Bible Societies, 1994.

Harris, W. H. *1, 2, 3 John: Comfort and Counsel for a Church in Crisis.* Dallas, TX: Biblical Studies Press, 2003.

Hodges, Z. C. *The Epistles of John: Walking in the Light of God's Love.* Irving, TX: Grace Evangelical Society, 1999.

Houlden, J. L. *The Johannine Epistles.* HNTC. New York: Harper & Row, 1973.

Johnson, T. F. *1, 2, and 3 John.* NIBCNT. Peabody, MA: Hendrickson, 1993.

Kistemaker, S. J. *James and I-III John.* NTC. Grand Rapids: Baker, 1986.

Kruse, C. J. *The Letters of John.* PNTC. Grand Rapids: Eerdmans, 2000.

Lenski, R. C. H. *The Interpretation of I and II Epistles of Peter, the Three Epistles of John, and the Epistle of Jude.* Minneapolis: Augsburg, 1966.

Lieu, J. M. *I, II, & III John.* Louisville, KY: Westminster John Knox Press, 2008.

MacArthur, J. *1, 2, 3 John.* MacArthur NT Commentary. Chicago: Moody, 2007.

Marshall, I. H. *The Epistles of John.* NICNT. Grand Rapids: Eerdmans, 1978.

Mitchell, J. G. *Fellowship.* Portland, OR: Multnomah, 1974.

Moody, D. *The Letters of John.* Waco, TX: Word Books, 1970.

Morris, L. "1 John, 2 John, 3 John." In *The New Bible Commentary.* Rev. ed. Grand Rapids: Eerdmans, 1970.

Painter, J. *1, 2, and 3 John.* Sacra Pagina 18. Collegeville, MN: Liturgical Press, 2002.

Perkins, P. *The Johannine Epistles.* New Testament Message 21. Wilmington, DE: Michael Glazier, 1979.

Plummer, A. *The Epistles of St. John.* CGTSC. Cambridge: Cambridge University Press, 1896.

Rensberger, D. *1 John, 2 John, 3 John.* ANTC. Nashville: Abingdon, 1997.

Schnackenburg, R. *Die Johannesbriefe.* HTKNT 13/3. Freiburg: Herder, 1965.

Smalley, S. S. *1, 2, 3 John.* WBC 51. Waco, TX: Word, 1984.

Smith, D. M. *First, Second, and Third John.* Interpretation. Louisville, KY: John Knox, 1991.

Stott, J. R. W. *The Letters of John.* Rev. ed. TNTC. Grand Rapids: Eerdmans, 1964.

Strecker, G. *The Johannine Letters.* Edited by H. Attridge. Translated by L. M. Maloney. Hermeneia. Minneapolis: Fortress Press, 1996.

Thompson, M. M. *1–3 John.* IVPNTC. Downers Grove, IL: InterVarsity Press, 1992.

Walls, D., and M. Anders. *I & II Peter, I, II & III John, Jude.* Holman New Testament Commentary 11. Nashville: Broadman & Holman, 1999.

Westcott, B. F. *The Epistles of St. John.* Grand Rapids: Eerdmans, 1966.

Williams, R. R. *The Letters of John and James.* Cambridge: Cambridge University Press, 1965.

Williamson, R. *1, 2, & 3 John*. New Beacon Bible Commentary. Kansas City, MO: Beacon Hill, 2010.

Yarbrough, R. W. *1–3 John*. BECNT. Grand Rapids: Baker, 2008.

Prologue: Eternal Life Is a Person (1:1–4)

Introduction

John's First Epistle begins with a long, complex sentence that introduces us to the subject of his epistle. These first three verses form a single sentence. Its main clause does not occur until verse 3 of our English Bible. The actual point of this introductory sentence is, "We declare to you that which we have seen and heard." Everything else is parenthetical to this main idea. The sentence, though complex, is not "confused" structurally, but intentionally complex (contra Strecker, 8).[1] As Brown notes, "The initial four verses of 1 John have a good claim to being the most complicated Greek in the Johannine corpus" (Brown, 152). Its complexity, however, reflects John's intention to communicate the nature of his understanding of eternal life as a relationship with the living Savior who *is* himself eternal life and *gives* eternal life to all who believe in him.

These verses serve as the prologue of this epistle in much the same way as the first eighteen verses of the Gospel of John and the first eight verses of the Revelation (Akin, 50; Kruse, 5; Smalley, 4). In all three prologues, Jesus is introduced and described. Yet the emphases of the three prologues are quite different. Whereas the Gospel focuses on Jesus' metaphysical nature as the Word that gives life, and the Revelation focuses on Jesus' deity and sovereignty, the epistle focuses on the personal experience of Jesus as Eternal Life personified, and as the source of life for every believer.[2]

1. Yarbrough (31) similarly describes it as "convoluted."
2. E. Malatesta (*Interiority and Covenant*, 1–2) notes that rather than using an epistolary address, John chose "a solemn and moving Prologue which sets the tone for all that follows."

Literarily, John draws our attention to his subject and message both through repetition and by utilizing familiar imagery from the Gospel. Though he connects his epistle with the Gospel by his references to "the beginning" and "the Word," he does not intend the ideas introduced in the prologues to be parallel, but rather complementary (Westcott, 3). Additionally, from its very first verses the epistle does not follow the pattern or subject matter of the Gospel, though it does reflect on ideas drawn from the Gospel, particularly Jesus' instruction in the upper room (John 13–17).

As with his other prologues, John introduces his readers to the general thrust of his epistle. Smalley notes that some see the prologue as a self-contained literary unit more than an introduction; however, he disagrees with them. He sees three "main themes" being introduced in the prologue that are developed later in the epistle. They are "life in Christ," developed further in 1 John 5:11–12 and 20; "the historical reality of God's revelation in Jesus Christ," developed in 1 John 4:2 and 5:6; and "the idea of 'seeing' in association with witness," developed further in 4:14 and 5:6–12. For him the central message, the gospel, is "life in Jesus Christ" (Smalley, 4). However, that being the case, he rightly avoids falling into the error of making the epistle solely a test of one's salvation (Test of Life view), though this test is applied to the false teachers who had departed from the apostolic circle because they had never possessed the apostolic faith (2:19).

Normally, prologues contain the main themes of their works, as is true in John's Gospel. Yet, the themes of "keeping the commandment(s) and practicing brotherly love, which are major concerns of 1 John," are missing. From this Brown concludes that the prologue is "not well structured" (Brown, 174). Contrary to his conclusion, one must recognize that not every theme need be introduced in the prologue, as was true in both the Gospel and Revelation. For example, Jesus' omniscience, which is a major theme in the Gospel, is unmentioned in the prologue and can only be subsumed under the larger category of Jesus' deity if it is to be seen therein. In 1 John, though the theme of proper confession may be alluded to in the reference to him as Christ and Son of God, the major theme of loving one's brother is absent even by allusion. It is unrealistic to expect John to introduce every theme in his prologues, including major themes. It is more likely that the author has intentionally introduced only those themes he considers foundational to his primary message.

Original Text

1 Ὃ ἦν ἀπ᾽ ἀρχῆς, ὃ ἀκηκόαμεν, ὃ ἑωράκαμεν τοῖς ὀφθαλμοῖς ἡμῶν, ὃ ἐθεασά-
μεθα καὶ αἱ χεῖρες ἡμῶν ἐψηλάφησαν περὶ τοῦ λόγου τῆς ζωῆς— **2** καὶ ἡ ζωὴ
ἐφανερώθη, καὶ ἑωράκαμεν καὶ μαρτυροῦμεν καὶ ἀπαγγέλλομεν ὑμῖν τὴν ζωὴν
τὴν αἰώνιον ἥτις ἦν πρὸς τὸν πατέρα καὶ ἐφανερώθη ἡμῖν **3** ὃ ἑωράκαμεν καὶ
ἀκηκόαμεν, ἀπαγγέλλομεν καὶ ὑμῖν, ἵνα καὶ ὑμεῖς κοινωνίαν ἔχητε μεθ᾽ ἡμῶν.
καὶ ἡ κοινωνία δὲ ἡ ἡμετέρα μετὰ τοῦ πατρὸς καὶ μετὰ τοῦ υἱοῦ αὐτοῦ Ἰησοῦ
Χριστοῦ. **4** καὶ ταῦτα γράφομεν ὑμῖν,a ἵνα ἡ χαρὰ ὑμῶνb ᾖ πεπληρωμένη.

Textual Notes

4.a. UBS^{4} and Metzger prefer γράφομεν ἡμεῖς ("we write") in v. 4 over γράφομεν ὑμῖν ("we write to you"), while recognizing the larger MS support for ὑμῖν, arguing it is more likely a scribe would alter the text to reflect the earlier use of ὑμῖν in the previous sentence.[3] Comparing MS support, in favor of ἡμεῖς is ℵ A* B P Ψ 33 it^{z} cop^{ms}. These MSS do represent a significant early witness. Still, the MS support for ὑμῖν is too great (A^{c} C K L 049 056 0142 81 88 104 181 326 330 436 451 614 629 630 945 1241 1505 1739 1877 1881 2412 2495 *Byz Lect*^{m} it^{ar,e,dem,div,p,t} vg syr^{p,h,pal} cop^{sa,bo} arm eth) with the Alexandrian clearly divided and Byzantine uniformly in favor. A scribe need not always attempt to smooth out readings. It would seem that if John had intended a nominative case pronoun, he would have placed it prior to the main verb, since it would be functioning in an emphatic role in the sentence. Placing it afterward, which would reflect the normal placement of a subject with regard to its verb, would seem to make it a redundant subject rather than emphatic.

4.b. Similarly, support for ἡμῶν ("our joy") has the stronger support of the Alexandrian MS tradition as well as some lectionaries (ℵ B L Ψ 049 88 181 326 436 1241 *Lect*^{m} *l*^{6,59,62} it^{p,t,z} vg^{ww} cop^{sa}). On the other hand, "your joy" (ὑμῶν) is well attested in the Alexandrian as well as uniformly the Byzantine text tradition and various uncials and minuscules (A C^{vid} K P 056 0142 33 81 104 330 451 614 629 630 945 1505 1739 1877 1881 2412 2495 *Byz* it^{ar,c,dem,div} vg^{mss} syr^{h,pal} cop^{bo} arm eth). In both instances either word makes sense in the

3. B. M. Metzger and United Bible Societies, *A Textual Commentary on the Greek New Testament*, 2nd ed., 639.

sentence, and neither changes its basic meaning nor impacts any doctrine.[4] The final arbiter appears to be the focus of the apostle. It seems more likely his focus would be on the heart and hope of his readers rather than his own satisfaction.

Translation

1 That which[5] was from the beginning, which we have heard, which we have seen[6] with our eyes, which we beheld and our hands handled concerning the Word of Life, **2** and[7] the life was manifested, and we have seen and bear witness[8] and announce to you the Eternal Life that was present[9] with the Father and was manifested to us; **3** that which we have seen and heard, we announce also to you, in order that you also may have fellowship with us. And indeed, our fellowship is with the Father and with his Son, Jesus

4. B. Metzger and United Bible Societies, *A Textual Commentary on the Greek New Testament*, 2nd ed., 639.
5. This reflects the neutral role the neuter relative pronoun is expressing and accords with RSV and NKJV. Other translators choose such renderings as "what" (NAB, NASB, NCV, NRSV), "this is what" (NET), and "the one who ... whom" (NLT).
6. The use of "have" with the first two verbs and its absence from the following are designed to reflect John's shift from the perfect to aor., a shift, it is felt, that he intended his readers to note.
7. Most English translations leave the καὶ untranslated (ESV, HCSB, NIV84, NKJV, NLT) while others reflect its role as a coordinating conj. (NASB95, NET) or explanatory conj. (NASB95).
8. John's shift from the perfect, "have seen," to the pres. in the next two verbs should be noted as something intended to be emphasized in the grammar, as will be discussed more fully below.
9. The inclusion of "present" attempts to express the nuance of the preposition that implies here and in John 1 the separate identity of Jesus from God the Father while existing eternally as a coequal member of the Godhead. In GJohn, the use of the preposition communicates to the reader Jesus' deity while similarly affirming His distinction from God the Father in His personhood. Thus He is both God and with God, divine and standing in the presence of divinity. Here, the same truth is affirmed once more, possibly as an allusion back to the prologue of GJohn. The addition of "present" makes this reality more clear in English than the more literal rendering of "with the Father."

Christ. **4** And we write these things to you[10] in order that your[11] joy may be completely[12] full.

Commentary

1:1 Ὃ ἦν ἀπ' ἀρχῆς, "That which was from the beginning." This initial series of relative clauses serves to describe the nature of John's eyewitness understanding of Jesus, who is Eternal Life personified, described initially as "the Word of Life." These clauses describe his understanding as the result of personal experience. Further, they are introduced with an initial relative clause that takes the reader back to the prologue of his Gospel.[13]

John introduces his subject with the repetition of "that which" in a parenthetical statement describing his authority to speak as an eyewitness. The difficulty of determining John's exact meaning results from his choice to use the neuter relative pronoun ὅ rather than the masculine, which might seem more appropriate grammatically. Culy (2) sees this as "a topic (or 'cleft') construction" wherein John introduces his topic through a "series of appositional relative clauses" whose relative pronoun is in the case it would have within the clause that follows it. Whereas the masculine would clearly refer to Jesus, the neuter allows additional referents. Five possible meanings for

---

10. The text-critical choice of "to you" (ὑμῖν; NKJV, NCV) after "write" as opposed to "we" (ἡμεῖς; NASB, ESV, RSV, NET, NIV, HCSB, NLT, NAB, ISV) before "write" is supported by the greater MS evidence as well as the significance of the placement of the pronoun in the sentence. As a dative case pronoun, it would be in a grammatically logical position. As a nominative case pronoun, it would be in a nonemphatic position, which would make it redundant more than meaningful.

11. The text-critical choice of "your" (ὑμῶν) over "our" (ἡμῶν) is reflected also in the NKJV, with others choosing "our joy" (ESV, HCSB, ISV, NAB, NASB, NCV, NET, NIV84, NLT, NRSV). As noted in the text-critical discussion, though the Alexandrian texts favor "our joy," the majority of other witnesses favor "your joy," and this rendering reflects the apostle's focus on his readers rather than himself. Other translations appear to be influenced by John's statement in 3 John 4.

12. The idea of "completely" reflects the continuing results of completed action indicated in the perfect passive participle

13. Hodges (53, n. 1) proposes that this first verse serves as the title for this epistle. He sees it functioning in the same way as the first verse of Matthew, Mark, and Revelation. Such an approach is unlikely, however, because this clause does not stand alone structurally and is clearly linked with the following clause in v. 3 that continues the introductory formula after the parenthesis of v. 2 is complete.

the pronoun translated "that which" have been proposed: (1) John might be referring to revelation about Christ (Painter, 120). This would fit with some of the doctrinal issues raised in the epistle. (2) It could refer to the teachings of Christ, which would fit with some of the ethical issues raised in the epistle. (3) It refers to the eternal life manifested by Christ. (4) It could refer to Christ himself. On one hand, this option may initially appear less likely because it would be much clearer with the masculine pronoun. However, elsewhere John uses the neuter pronoun to refer to people (1 John 5:4) and Christ (John 3:6; 6:37, 39; 17:2 and 24). Finally, (5) it could refer to all of Jesus' life, teachings, as well as his person (Burge, 53; Haas, de Jonge, and Swellengrebel, 11; Strecker, 10). This use of the neuter avoids the confusion of thinking he is referring exclusively to "life," a feminine noun, or "word," a masculine noun. The neuter pronoun focuses the reader on Jesus as both, the "Word" and "Life." Thus it communicates John's comprehensive view of Christ. Further, his use of "heard," "saw with our eyes," "beheld," and "handled" points his readers to the person of Christ. His reference to "the Word of Life" clearly alludes to the prologue of the Gospel, wherein the Word of God is the incarnate Word, Jesus. Finally, it could be that John intended both Jesus as eternal life incarnate and his teachings about eternal life to be in view (Kistemaker, 8). As Akin notes, "The message and the person ultimately cannot be separated. Each explains the other" (Akin, 51).

"The beginning" is equally ambiguous. (1) It could refer to the beginning of time or creation (Brooke, 1; Burge 53; Haas, de Jonge, and Swellengrebel, 11; Smalley, 7; Strecker, 9).[14] This would give it an identical meaning as the term in John 1:1. John would be consciously developing the prologue of his Epistle along the lines of that of the Gospel.[15] However, though John

14. M. de Jonge ("An Analysis of 1 John 1.1–4," 328) says that "it is obvious that 'the beginning' lies much further back than the 'was manifested'" when the "we" come onto the scene. Thus de Jonge argues that "beginning" refers to Gen 1:1. He builds his argument from the various verb tenses and their relative chronological relationships to one another in the flow of thought. I would agree that the verb tenses are significant, as is noted in the commentary that follows. However, he seems to read too much into the first clause.

15. Strecker (9) argues that John's positive (John 1:1; 1 John 1) and negative (John 8:44; 1 John 3:8) uses of the term in both the Gospel and epistle indicates ἀρχή has the same meaning in both texts. Though it is true that the negative uses (referring to the devil) likely do have the same beginning point in mind, that need not follow for the prologues. John's placement of them with different prepositions (ἐν in John

clearly intends to allude to the prologue of the Gospel, his focus on "life" over "Word" in the parenthetical statement militates against its having the same meaning (Harris, 50). (2) It might allude to the beginning of the reader's faith in Christ (Westcott, 6–7). This could only work if "the Word of Life" had referred to the apostolic teachings. However, the context of the other descriptives makes it more likely a reference to Jesus' earthly ministry since John is describing Jesus as eternal life itself, and so "Word of Life" refers to him. (3) It could be the beginning of Jesus' earthly life, his incarnation (Kruse, 50–51; Mitchell, 22). (4) It could mean the beginning of Jesus' ministry (Brown, 158; Walls and Anders, 155). This would accord with his reference at the end of the epistle to Jesus coming "by water and blood" (1 John 5:6). John's use of ἀπό rather than ἐν also strengthens this view (Culy, 2).[16] (5) It could refer to the beginning of the church in Acts 2 (Williams, 17). In this context it would not be a reference to a commonly held tradition whose details were in dispute. Nor does it serve as an allusion to the apostles' true claims about Jesus as opposed to the claims of the heretics (Brown, 71–72). It should, though, be seen as an initial indication of John's continued emphasis on the deity of Christ and the christological focus of this epistle with Jesus' incarnation in view, as will be evidenced in the phrases that follow.

John chooses first person plural verbs throughout this descriptive prologue to describe his experience of the incarnate Christ. His use of "we" is seen by some as a reference to (1) John himself, equivalent to "I," as an "authorial plural" (Schnackenburg, 52; Strecker, 11), (2) including both John and his readers (Dodd, 9–10), (3) referring to the "Johannine school" (Brown, 160), (4) to "all Christians" (Williams, 17), or (5) referring to the apostolic band of eyewitnesses, which includes John (Hodges,

---

1:1 and ἀπό in 1 John 1:1) clearly nuances their meanings differently. And his changing of the preps. must be seen as intending to differentiate his uses of the term while equally intending his readers to recognize his allusion to the Gospel, not in terms of timing, but in terms of Person.

16. Williams' (17) suggestion that it refers to the beginning of the church in Acts 2 cannot be substantiated from any reference of the text or Johannine connections elsewhere. Further, Acts 2 neither reflects the beginning of instruction for the apostles, which occurred early in Jesus' ministry, nor the beginning of the recipients' faith; they represent a second or third generation of Christians. So, neither John nor his readers could be described as receiving revelation about Jesus from the day of Pentecost onward.

47; Kistemaker, 204–5).[17] The last view seems most reasonable since, as Kistemaker says, "[o]nly Jesus' original disciples can say and write that they touched him with their hands, as John states in the introductory verses of his first epistle" (Kistemaker, 205). Further, John uses the first person singular to refer to himself elsewhere in his epistles, and so should be seen as fully capable to doing so here in order to be clear (Harris, 51). John's use of "we" includes himself and most likely the other apostles as eyewitnesses (Haas, de Jonge, and Swellengrebel, 8). This places him within a larger group of eyewitnesses who are testifying to the church (in this case the recipients of this epistle) their experience of Christ. Culy (3) rightly notes that this emphasizes his "status as one of the limited group of eyewitnesses" and strengthens the epistle's authority by his association with them. In this epistle it is very important to note the person of the verbs and pronouns. Both the verbs and pronouns often occupy emphatic positions in their sentences and are critical to understanding both his meaning and emphasis. Thus, his use of "we" is not as an authorial "we" equivalent to "I," but rather as the spokesman for a group of eyewitnesses whose experience matches his own. Later this will become significant as he develops his "we" versus "them" distinctions between the apostles and false teachers.[18]

ὃ ἀκηκόαμεν, ὃ ἑωράκαμεν τοῖς ὀφθαλμοῖς ἡμῶν, "which we have heard, which we have seen with our eyes." John describes his experience of Christ as eternal life incarnate through the perfect tense verbs ἀκηκόαμεν and ἑωράκαμεν. By these he indicates the continuing impact of his having heard and seen Jesus.[19] The significance of his having seen Jesus is made through what would at first seem a redundant reference to having seen "with our eyes" (τοῖς ὀφθαλμοῖς ἡμῶν). This would place him in contrast to the false

17. M. de Jonge ("An Analysis of 1 John 1.1–4," 327) sees these first person plurals to be "used exclusively and not inclusively," thereby distinguishing between the "group" writing and those receiving the epistle.

18. J. M. Lieu sees a "discontinuity" between John's use of the pl. 1 ("we") in the prologue and the remainder of the epistle where he uses the sg. to distinguish between himself and his readers or opponents (J. M. Lieu, "Us or You? Persuasion and Identity in 1 John," 810–11). This need not be viewed as such. His use of the pl. in the prologue is clearly connected to his intention to identify his testimony, and thus authority to speak, with the apostolic circle. In the remainder of the epistle he need not speak from the group, but from himself, since his ability to speak authoritatively has been clearly established.

19. BDF §342 (2).

teachers who might claim revelations but could never claim eyewitness status. It also establishes a different level of authority from those who were merely eyewitnesses of Jesus' resurrection, such as the five hundred who saw the living Jesus following his resurrection (1 Cor 15:6). Additionally, the perfect clarifies that though he saw him in the past, Jesus' impact on him continues to the present, and so his status as an eyewitness remains valid.

ὃ ἐθεασάμεθα καὶ αἱ χεῖρες ἡμῶν ἐψηλάφησαν, "which we beheld and our hands handled." John's deliberate movement from the perfect to aorist in the next two verbs ἐθεασάμεθα and ἐψηλάφησαν to describe his seeing and handling of Jesus clarifies that, though he and the other eyewitnesses had touched and seen Jesus during his earthly ministry, they no longer do at the time of writing.[20] Jesus is no longer with them and John is not claiming any special appearances of Jesus beyond the corporate experience of the apostles. In contrast to the secret knowledge of Gnosticism, what John testifies to is common knowledge, experienced and known by a group that extends beyond him and his followers. Granted, Paul does meet Jesus on the road to Damascus and in subsequent revelations. However, his experience is not being alluded to by John here. Furthermore, John will again experience a personal appearance of Jesus on the Isle of Patmos some years after the writing of this epistle. However, that is a story awaiting its telling!

John's use of ἐθεασάμεθα can simply mean looking intently at something, though it may also be used as a synonym of the more common ὁράω.[21] Contra Hass et al., John's choice seems to be more than to provide variation in the text, but to heighten the significance of his eyewitness status by the distinction created (Haas, de Jonge, and Swellengrebel, 12). He not only saw Jesus (ἑωράκαμεν), but he paid close attention to Jesus (ἐθεασάμεθα). Thus his understanding of Jesus from personal experience could be seen as both thorough and reliable.

Finally, John affirms further that he not only saw Jesus, but he was in personal, physical contact with him during his earthly ministry. He uses

---

20. Contra J. P. Louw ("Verbal Aspect in the First Letter of John," 101) who sees "no distinction in meaning," and considers the aorists to have the same semantic value as the perfects. Rather, B. M. Fanning (*Verbal Aspect in New Testament Greek*, 192–94) is correct when he argues that the changes between aor. and pf. should not be seen as a case of conj. reduction, but that John intended the difference in aspect between the aor. and pf. to be noted.

21. BDAG, 445; W. Michaelis, "ὁράω, βλέπω, θεάομαι, θεωρέω," *TDNT*, 5:317–18.

ἐψηλάφησαν to emphasize the reality of Jesus' corporeality, by noting that his experience of Jesus was physical as well as aural and visual (Haas, de Jonge, and Swellengrebel, 12). Thus, all of these verbs of perceiving serve to verify John's status as an eyewitness with the right to relate his teachings with authority.[22]

περὶ τοῦ λόγου τῆς ζωῆς, "concerning the Word of Life." What John experienced was "the Word of Life." This is best seen as a reference to Jesus, who is the living "Word" of God (John 1:1, 14) and the "Life" (John 14:6), not just the source of that life (Haas, de Jonge, and Swellengrebel, 19).[23] Some see this referring to revelation: Jesus reveals truths about spiritual life.[24]

Just as Jesus is not referred to as "the Word" in the Gospel after the prologue, John's use here seems to follow the same pattern (Haas, de Jonge, and Swellengrebel, 12).[25] However, although in his Gospel he has the preincarnate "Word" in view, here John has the incarnate "Word" in view. This is likely an allusion to the Gospel account, or at least reflects a conceptual connection.[26] In this prologue, Jesus as eternal life incarnate is introduced

22. W. Michaelis, "ὁράω, βλέπω, θεάομαι, θεωρέω," *TDNT* 5:348.

23. Haas, de Jonge, and Swellengrebel (19) note that an alternative view is to see this use of "Word" to refer to "the Christian message." "Beginning" would then mean "since the gospel message began to be preached." "Life" would then refer to the gospel's content. They reject it and provide three arguments against it. "(a) The verses under discussion have similarities with John 1:1 and 4. (b) One expects the direct object of 'to touch' to be a reference to a person or thing, not an event-word like message. (c) If 'word' had been used in the sense of 'message' one would expect it to be construed as the direct object of the verb 'to proclaim' and not with the Greek preposition rendered 'concerning.'"

24. D. Hercsik, "Das 'Wort Gottes' und die Christologie," 373.

25. Λόγος occurs in 1:10; 2:5, 7, 14; and 3:18. The first four instances refers to Scripture or its teachings, and 3:18 is used of literal speech. Strecker (10) argues well that John's use of τὸν ἀπ' ἀρχῆς in 1 John 2:13–14 to describe Jesus connects τοῦ λόγου τῆς ζωῆς with Jesus through the influence of the prologue of the Gospel. Further, the flow of thought in the epistle's prologue is sufficient to indicate "Word of Life" is an allusion to Jesus rather than revelation about Jesus as John moves toward the central description of Jesus as "Eternal Life" himself.

26. Culy (5) rejects the connection of "the word of life" (τοῦ λόγου τῆς ζωῆς) with the prologue of the Gospel of John because "life" is personified and explained further in the following verse. He argues that it does not refer to Jesus elsewhere in the epistle, that "there are no clear examples of a personified λόγος modified by an attributive gen. elsewhere in the NT," and that the verse lacks any other indicator of personification. None of these arguments is convincing. First, life's further

with the movement from "Word of Life" to "Life," and then to "Eternal Life." Just as John's use of "Word" in the Gospel prologue more likely expressed the Old Testament concept of God's Word in creation, revelation, and salvation, here he appears to intend the same connection.[27] Thus, rather than seeing this as an allusion to the gnostic concept of the *logos*, John is still speaking in terms of the Old Testament concept of divine revelation embodied in the person of Jesus. However, as he develops this concept in these three steps, he takes it further, moving from revelation to source.

Jesus is not simply the One who gives life. He is life itself. Yet Scripture also speaks of eternal life as something we possess as a gift from God, freely given and never revoked. This reference may be taken as an objective genitive, referring to the word *concerning* life. This is supported by passages such as 1 John 1:10; 2:5, 7 and 14 where "word" does not refer to Jesus but to biblical revelation. Some take this as a reference to the gospel message rather than the person of Jesus (Brown, 182; Westcott, 6–7). Yet the subject of the prologue is not the *message* about Jesus and eternal life, but *Jesus,* who is eternal life. The subject is better seen as the person of Jesus rather than the topic of life.

1:2 καὶ ἡ ζωὴ ἐφανερώθη, "and the life was manifested." John pauses to make a parenthetical statement in his description of Christ as Eternal Life (Bultmann, 7; Schnackenburg, 62–63; Brown, 166).[28] He introduces it with the conjunction καὶ and then moves from the aorist ἐφανερώθη to the perfect ἑωράκαμεν and then to the pres. μαρτυροῦμεν. In doing this he moves from a past event (aor.) to its impact that continued to the time of writing (pf.), and then to the response of the eyewitnesses (pres.), creating a chronological sense to this statement.

---

explanation argues the opposite—that this is John's intended sense, one that he builds toward artistically. This explains, in part, his choice of neuter pronouns rather than fem., which would have matched ζωὴ better. The lack of "clear examples" where an attributive gen. modifies a "personified logos" need not deny John the ability to do so here since it is neither grammatically nor conceptually impossible. But, that being the case, John is not personifying "Word" so much as he is personifying "Eternal Life," which is what he is building up to conceptually.

27. D. Hercsik, "Das 'Wort Gottes' und die Christologie," 383; P. L. Metzger, *The Gospel of John*, 28–29.

28. S. S. Smalley, "What about 1 John?," 3:338.

This initial καὶ may be (1) an ascensive conjunction (Hodges, 49), with the sense of "and indeed"; (2) a connective conjunction that simply continues the list of ideas, "and"; or (3) an explanatory conjunction introducing a parenthetical statement, "and" (Hass, 13). In this case, the third use describes well the role of καὶ with the parenthetical clause of verse 2. Culy (5) notes well that "while the specific semantic relationship between clauses or sentences linked by καὶ will vary, clause-initial conjunctive uses of καὶ generally highlight both thematic continuity and progression of thought. ... They thus tend to introduce additional comments regarding a theme or idea that has just been introduced," which is certainly true in this case. Moreover, in this case the "resumptive relative clause that follows" in verse 3 indicates John intended this as a parenthetical statement.

The "life" that was personally experienced by John and the apostles was "manifested."[29] By his use of ἐφανερώθη, John focuses his readers' attention on the sensory, visible aspect of Jesus' appearance more than the cognitive.[30] It was the Life made real and visible that he speaks of rather than the life understood or taught. Thus "life" is a metonymy* for Jesus (Williams, 17).[31] This points us again to the person (Jesus) rather than a possession (unending life) or the quality of an abundant life. This is confirmed by what follows.

καὶ ἑωράκαμεν καὶ μαρτυροῦμεν καὶ ἀπαγγέλλομεν ὑμῖν τὴν ζωὴν τὴν αἰώνιον, "and we have seen and bear witness and announce to you the Eternal Life." John moves from the perfect tense, "we have seen" to the pres. tenses "we bear witness" and "announce." With the perfect, he continues to identify himself with the apostolic witnesses whose experiences with Jesus continued to impact their lives until the day of John's writing. This was true even though they were no longer receiving revelation from him, whether in person (as before he ascended) or by visions.[32] Then, with the two present

29. J-P. Batut ("Believing in the Resurrection; or, The Logic of Love," 34) describes Jesus' manifestation as "that Life in person (and not one living being among others) was made manifest, and ... allowed human beings" to become witnesses by hearing, seeing, looking upon, and touching "the Word of life."

30. BDAG, 1048; R. Bultmann and D. Lührmann, "φαίνω, φανερός, φανερόω," *TDNT* 9 (1964) 4–5.

31. A metonymy is "a figure by which one name or noun is used instead of another, to which it stands in a certain relation" (E. W. Bullinger, *Figures of Speech Used in the Bible*, 538). Culy (6) sees this as personification.

32. This in no way implies that the Holy Spirit was not guiding them into all truth or revealing new truth to them (John 16:13), only that they were not experiencing

tense verbs that follow (μαρτυροῦμεν and ἀπαγγέλλομεν), he indicates that the apostolic witnesses continued to testify of their experience to the readers. This present tense verb draws attention to the readers that what he is writing is based on his personal experience of Jesus as Eternal Life and is a description of that Life to them.

John emphasizes the importance of his message by use of a hendiadys*. In this case he combines the synonyms "bear witness" and "announce" to call attention to the significance of his recounting his personal experience of Christ. He and the other apostles bear witness by reporting what they have experienced. The first term, "bear witness," includes a legal nuance and was often used for the testimony given in court.[33] The verb "denotes the activity of a μάρτυς. It is first used in the New Testament for the declaration or confirmation, on the basis of first-hand knowledge, of individual acts or general facts of experience, though it so happens that there is no special use for testifying in court."[34] His choice of ἀπαγγέλλομεν, on the other hand, focuses attention on the descriptive aspect of what they are reporting. Whereas the first term calls attention to the significance of the report, the second describes its mode of delivery. Thus the first verb draws attention to John's knowledge of his subject while the second focuses on his mode of communicating that knowledge (Culy, 6).

Unlike proto-Gnosticism and later Gnosticism, this "Life" was made known openly (announced) rather than being hidden or obscured such that only a few could know. Rather, all of the world could know. Also, as in the prologue of John's Gospel, where the Word was both God and with God (John 1:1), eternal life, the Person, was with the Father prior to his manifestation to the apostles ("us"). This is not a reference to general revelation, God revealing himself to us in nature, but special revelation, God revealing himself to us in the Person of his Son.

John's use of the article clarifies that he is not discussing eternal life as a subject or a concept, but has a specific "eternal life" in view.[35] Westcott sees this use of "eternal life" to refer to eternal life that is possessed by believers,

---

direct revelations of Jesus.

33. BDAG, 617–18; H. Strathmann, "μάρτυς, μαρτυρέω," *TDNT*, 4:476.

34. H. Strathmann, "μάρτυς, μαρτυρέω," *TDNT*, 4:496.

35. D. B. Wallace (*Grammar*, 226) notes that the article with abstract nouns can be used as a "*par excellence*" or "well known" article to define the conceptual term more closely. In this case John is likely using it in the second sense.

as a quality of life as well as unending experience, rather than as the person of Christ (Westcott, 10). Akin on the other hand sees it referring to Jesus, the Word, "who reveals life and is the Source of eternal life ... the revelation of eternal life itself" (Akin, 54). Based on the clauses that preceded this title, it is best to see Jesus as the referent rather than salvation (Strecker, 10). This is strengthened by its relation "with the Father" (πρὸς τὸν πατέρα).

ἥτις ἦν πρὸς τὸν πατέρα, "that was present with the Father." When John describes this "Life" as being "with the Father," his choice of preposition and grammatical construction follows the pattern of the prologue of the Gospel (John 1:1), where "the Word was with God."[36] As Culy (7) notes, "When followed by a familial term or human referent, the preposition frequently carries a relational nuance." There, as here, the preposition served to emphasize the personal presence of Jesus, as well as his existence as a separate person in the presence of God the Father. Eternal life personified was "with the Father" in the same way that the Word was with God while being God in John 1.[37] This is a clear way to indicate that John's subject is a person and not a possession. John is not speaking figuratively in that he is not personifying eternal life as a quality of life. He does this in order to make clear that he is talking about Jesus as the embodiment of eternal life.

Using "Life" as a metonymy for Jesus, who both *is* and *gives* life, John declares that this "Life," Jesus, "was manifested" to the apostles ("we") and is now being announced by them to the readers. The anaphoric* article before "life" connects the subject of this parenthetical statement with the Word of Life of the previous clause. The phrase "the life was manifested" reflects the prologue of John where "the Word became flesh." Thus it serves to declare Jesus' deity as well as ministry in coming to earth from heaven. Of note, too, is the place of the noun "life" in Johannine writings. It is used only of Jesus and never of God the Father.

Why does John not name Jesus in his prologue? It is likely the same reason he does not name Jesus in the prologue of his Gospel. Culy (2) notes

---

36. D. B. Wallace (*Grammar*, 359) sees this as an example of a stative verb used with a transitive prep., with the verb "overriding" the implied motion of the prep. Thus he describes Jesus in the presence of the Father, not approaching him.

37. Of note is John's choice to combine the transitive prep. with a stative verb. This removes the idea of "motion toward" that would normally be contained in the prep., but still communicates the concept of "present with" (D. B. Wallace, *Grammar*, 359).

well, "The writer's coyness in not directly naming the incarnate Jesus as the topic draws the reader into his discourse that follows." Also, by not naming him, John focuses attention on that aspect of his person from which he wishes to develop his message, namely, that he is life incarnate. This also makes *experiencing eternal life* the subject of the epistle rather than Jesus or eternal life as a possession.

καὶ ἐφανερώθη ἡμῖν, "and was manifested to us." John uses φανερόω in his Gospel to describe Jesus' revelation of his deity (glory) at the wedding in Cana (John 2:11), in healing the man born blind (John 9:3), in teaching the disciples (John 17:6), and in appearing alive after his resurrection (John 21:1, 14). In this case, John's choice of aorist tense affirms Jesus' revelation of himself is no longer occurring, but that John's reference is to his "appearance in history" (Haas, de Jonge, and Swellengrebel, 14).

One might ask if John's use of "eternal life" here and in the epilogue (5:20) serves as an instance of inclusio*.[38] It is unlikely because too little remains on either side. Normally an inclusio marks off a section of material within a larger unit, such as those in the Sermon on the Mount. There Jesus uses an inclusio to mark off the Beatitudes with "for theirs is the kingdom of heaven" (Matt 5:3 and 10) and his more extensive discussion of the practice of the letter of the Law as opposed to the spirit of the Law with "the Law and the Prophets" (Matt 5:17 and 7:12). The final occurrence of "eternal life" in the epilogue is preceded by it in verse 13, which is followed by John's discussion of answered prayer and the sin unto death. Neither fits the role of an inclusio since verse 13 does not end the section of discussion and verse 20 occurs within its own delineated section that is clearly unconnected to its previous section. Though the epilogue serves as a conclusion to the epistle, it does so as a series of summary statements rather than a paragraph covering a single topic. Further, here "Eternal Life" is a person, Jesus. There "eternal life" is a quality of life experienced by the obedient orthodox believer as a result of his or her a relationship with eternal life incarnate, Jesus. This is the outflowing life of the Spirit (John 7:37–39), which Jesus promised to all who thirst, at the Feast of Tabernacles.

John repeats "manifested," placing it at both ends of this parenthetical clause for emphasis. This repetition of "manifested" emphasizes God's

38. An *inclusio* is defined as "the repetition of a word or group of words to mark off a unit within the work" (*Eerdmans Dictionary of the Bible*, 1383).

revelation through the person of Christ in the past to the apostles.[39] In this context, John's use of "us" cannot include his readers, who were not present to see Jesus, and thus experience the physical manifestation of eternal life in the person of Christ.[40] Thus, revelation through the physical presence of the person of Christ is not continuing, but stands as a completed event in the past to which John may refer.[41] Eternal life in the person of Jesus was made visible and recognizable to the apostles, who now stand as witnesses to Jesus as life manifested. Thus John's authority to speak is not that of apostolic tradition, but personal experience (Burge, 54), much like Paul's affirmation in Gal 1:11–12.

1:3 We now encounter the first of four purpose statements in John's epistle. His primary reason for writing is to help his readers understand those things a believer must do if he or she wishes to have "fellowship," in the sense of a vital mutual relationship, with both the apostles and God. Experiencing eternal life involves mutual relationship, both between fellow believers and between believers and God (Westcott, 11). John is not affirming at this point that his readers have fellowship, but that such fellowship is possible. By saying he wishes them "to have fellowship," he is moving beyond the fact that it exists to its experience, its "enjoyment." His use of μετὰ indicates that

39. This is a case of repetition as a literary device, not inclusio, even though the term occurs at the beginning and end of the phrase. An inclusio would be expected to bracket a larger unit of material. Still, repetition is a literary device often utilized by John for emphasis. That an inclusio is not intended can be seen in that ἀπαγγέλλομεν occurs twice as well, but once between φανερόω and then once after. Still, the repetition itself may not "strengthen the connection between the parenthesis and the sentence as a whole" (contra Haas, de Jonge, and Swellengrebel, 14), but does emphasize both Jesus' personal presence in revealing himself (ἐφανερώθη) and John's announcement (ἀπαγγέλλομεν) of that revelation.

40. At other times in the epistle "us" and "we" will include the readers with John. Though John uses pronouns and the person of verbs strategically, the 1pl. clearly cannot be read uniformly but must be viewed in each of its contexts to determine the intended referent(s). For example, in 1:5 John and the apostles are in view, while in 1:6 John and his readers are in view.

41. Even so, John has already affirmed in his Gospel (John 14:26) that the Spirit will continue to "teach you all things" and "reveal" new truths to the apostles. Though the false teachers may have been claiming to be recipients of the Spirit's ministry, John makes clear that the revelatory work of Christ is finished. He will clarify later in 4:1–6 that one's teaching reveals the source of one's revelation and that any claim to Spirit revelation must agree with that given through the apostles.

this fellowship involves the conscious action of both parties, whether that is between two believers or between the believer and God (Westcott, 12).

ὃ ἑωράκαμεν καὶ ἀκηκόαμεν, "that which we have seen and heard." John resumes his sentence after the parenthetical clause with a repetition of the phrase he interrupted in verse 1, "that which we have seen and heard."[42] He heads it up with the same neuter pronoun ὃ as he had repeatedly used earlier. This neuter relative clause, by repeating two verbs from the earlier clause, serves to resume the incomplete sentence caused by the parenthetical statement.[43]

ἀπαγγέλλομεν καὶ ὑμῖν, "we announce also to you." His use of the present active indicative verb ἀπαγγέλλομεν in the main clause makes it an assertion of the apostle to his readers. The content of the message is described with perfect tense verbs for seeing and hearing (ἑωράκαμεν καὶ ἀκηκόαμεν), once more, indicating that the revelation of the message is complete and that John is speaking as an eyewitness. He is recounting what he learned in the past and not giving new revelation, possibly in contrast to the false teachers, whose Christology does not arise from apostolic tradition, but their own falsely claimed new revelations. His repetition of these key terms, including their verb tense, emphasizes their significance. Even so, their reversal from their earlier order should not be viewed as significant, but rather as stylistic variation (Culy, 7; Haas, de Jonge, and Swellengrebel, 17). No chiastic structure or other literarily significant intention should be read into their reversal of order. Instead, their repetition reminds us that the authority for what John will affirm in the remainder of his epistle flows from personal experience, not as secondhand knowledge or dependence on others' experiences or knowledge. As Paul claimed authority to speak based on his personal revelations from Christ (Gal 1:11–12) and Peter wrote as a witness of Jesus' transfiguration (2 Pet 1:16–18), so too John points to three and a half years of walking and talking with Jesus as his authority to speak as his representative. John is not speaking on the basis of apostolic tradition; he is creating it.

ἵνα καὶ ὑμεῖς κοινωνίαν ἔχητε μεθ' ἡμῶν, "in order that you also may have fellowship with us." This, the first of four purpose clauses in the epistle

42. This should not be viewed as an inclusio, but as resumptive repetition.

43. These two perfects continue the same emphasis on the continuing impact of his experience as they did earlier (BDF §342 (2)).

introduced by a ἵνα, gives only one of the purposes for John and the other witnesses communicating their experience of Christ, namely, "fellowship." This clause should be seen as a purpose-result ἵνα clause. It is John's purpose in writing and the intended result of what he is communicating about Jesus (Haas, de Jonge, and Swellengrebel, 17).[44] This is not the sole purpose for John's writing, or necessarily the primary purpose either. It is *a* purpose. Since it was stated first, its importance to John and to the development of his message must not be overlooked. However, fellowship need not be the only or even the controlling purpose.

Some interpreters see fellowship as the primary purpose of the epistle. Based on this they see the focus of the epistle on the believer's fellowship as it relates to his or her sanctification (Burge, 55; Hodges, 50; Mitchell, 16–17; Pentecost, 17; Roberts, 20; Ryrie, 1466).[45] Others see it as a secondary purpose with the primary purpose being found in 5:13. For these, the focus of the epistle is on the believer's assurance of salvation as it relates to his or her justification (Boice, 11; Brown, 91; Bruce, 27; Bultmann, 83; Dodd, 313; Law, 405; Lenski, 531; Marshall, 243; Stott, 186–87; Westcott, 188–89).[46] Akin sees the two purpose statements (here and 5:13) as "equivalent," with John writing to encourage his readers to "persevere" in the faith and so demonstrate thereby that they are regenerate saints (Akin, 55). It seems best to see this as one of John's several purposes, with none being primary or secondary. Rather than making this initial purpose statement into a rubric for interpreting the epistle, it is better to look at the subject of the prologue

44. D. B. Wallace, *Grammar*, 473.

45. E. M. Curtis "The Purpose of 1 John," Th.D. dissertation, Dallas Theological Seminary, 1986; J. M. Lieu, "Authority to Become Children of God," 213. She says of 1:3 that it is "an emphatic declaration that its goal is fellowship—firstly between the author and his readers, and, through this, participation in fellowship 'with the Father and with his Son, Jesus Christ' (i 3) with its corollary, the full experience of Christian joy, an eschatological gift made present (i 4)"; C. C. Ryrie ("The First Epistle of John," *The Wycliffe Bible Commentary,* 1466) identifies 1:3 as containing both the purpose and the theme of the epistle, "fellowship," on the basis of its ἵνα clause. He sees 1:4 as subsidiary to 1:3 because he sees fellowship as the "basis of joy. The readers' joy depended on it, and so did the apostle's."

46. A. Feuillet, "The Structure of First John," 211; J. F. MacArthur, Jr. *The Gospel according to Jesus,* 219; I. de la Potterie, "La connaissance de Dieu dans le dualism eschatologique d'après 1 Jn 2, 12–14," 82–83; M. Boismard, "La connaissance de Dieu dans l'Alliance Nouvelle d'après 1 Jo," 365.

as his central focus, namely, Jesus, who is eternal life incarnate. As Johnson explains, "The subject is commonly introduced at the *beginning* of the text or in some shared context with the original readers. For communication to take place, the reader must understand what the author is talking about. If the author fails to introduce his subject somehow, then what he says has no relation to any subject in particular. Communication of a message is thereby thwarted."[47] Though John's purposes do influence the development of his message, his subject must dominate interpretation rather than one of his stated purposes.[48] John's message is going to focus on Jesus, who is the embodiment and source of life. What that means for the believer will be fleshed out in the epistle as he accomplishes his several purposes, including encouraging their mutual relationship (fellowship) with God and with brothers and sisters in Christ.

John introduces us to his first purpose in writing with a ἵνα clause that reminds his readers of their central role in moving him to write. He accomplishes this by placing the coordinating conjunction καὶ with ὑμεῖς, making the nominative case pronoun emphatic (Culy, 8) since it serves as the subject of ἔχητε. Thereby this sentence carries the sense of: "in order that *you* may have fellowship." It draws attention to his readers and how important they are to John and the other apostles. Similarly, he moves the verb's direct object, "fellowship," before the verb in order to emphasize it as well. Thus the literal word order is "and you fellowship may have with us." Both the readers and the issue of fellowship are brought to the fore before either

47. E. E. Johnson, *Expository Hermeneutics: An Introduction*, 83 (italics his).

48. E. E. Johnson (ibid. 83–84) argues for a unifying message that includes a subject ("what the author writes about") and its complement ("what the author wants to communicate in regard to his subject"). The purpose(s) of the author are secondary to his message, though he has a goal to communicate that message for a reason that may or may not be stated and may or may not be discernable from internal evidences. It seems reasonable to say that an author wrote so that his readers would understand his message whether they knew his motive(s) for writing or were aware of only some of his reasons. He wrote so as to achieve his purpose, but did not need to state it or describe it completely. For example, John's stated purpose in John 20:31, unless made very generic, likely only covers one aspect of the Gospel's purpose in that its message is far broader than engendering faith in John's readers, whether it be justifying faith or sanctifying faith in Jesus. Jesus' instructions in the upper room (John 13–17), for example, include issues of community life, witness, and the believer's relationship to the world.

their possession ("may have") or the apostles, those with whom they are to share fellowship, are mentioned.

Is this a fellowship already shared and therefore to be maintained, something available at all times, or yet to be shared? Based on the pres. subjunctive ἔχητε, Brown (185) sees in this an implicit idea that the readers do not yet share this fellowship with the apostolic circle. This fellowship is something that existed eternally within the Godhead and was brought down to mankind through Jesus. Now it can be shared with others. John could have used the aorist subjunctive, which may have better communicated his idea, or he could have used the perfect subjunctive, had he desired to say that they were already experiencing the fellowship. Instead, John chose the present (or customary)subjunctive since its focus is on the progressive (aspect of the mood. It seems better to see John is communicating the idea that his epistle is an invitation to fellowship available to his readers without implying they either have it or lack it.[49] John's desire is that fellowship comes to characterize their lives. It may be going too far to insist that his readers were not yet in fellowship. However, it is clear that they were being invited to partake of that fellowship. This sets the emotional tone of the epistle with regard to its recipients.

John emphasizes the importance his readers are to him by his use of "you" twice in succession (ὑμῖν, ἵνα καὶ ὑμεῖς) to indicate his focus is on them, even as he invites them to share in his and the other apostles' fellowship with God (Strecker, 19–20).

This use of κοινωνία is interpreted by some to reflect the sense of a positive relationship shared by two or more people, a sanctification concept with a focus on the believer's *relationship* with God (Burge, 55; Pentecost, 17; Roberts, 19, 25, 43–44). Brown (170) sees the "difficult to translate" terms as involving "both the dynamic *esprit de corps* that brings people together and the togetherness that is produced by that spirit." Others see it as participation in a common interest or goal, a sharing of something. It is equivalent to possessing eternal life, a justification concept with a focus on the believer's *union* with God (Akin, 57; Boice, 31; Bruce, 28, 39; Dodd, 6; Law, 372–73).

The term κοινωνία is used by John only four times, and all are in the beginning of this epistle (twice in this verse). Since this is the case, his choice

49. B. M. Fanning, *Verbal Aspect in New Testament Greek*, 392–96.

of this term at this time is worth noting and evaluating.[50] It is not that John does not develop the concept elsewhere. He simply uses other terms to express its meaning. Bruce notes well, "The word 'fellowship' (*koinonia*) and its cognates are absent from the Gospel of John, but the idea that they express is not absent." He points to John 13:8; 14:23; 15:1–16; and 17:21–23 as examples of places where the concept is resident (Bruce, 38).[51] Burge (55) likewise sees this as an expression of Jesus' teaching on the believer's abiding relationship with Jesus as a branch on the vine (John 15:1–8).

Jesus' instructions in the upper room help clarify the relationship between fellowship and abiding in Johannine thought. In John 14:23, Jesus promises the obedient believer that he and the Father will mutually "make our home with him." Consequently, obedience leads to an *abiding* relationship in which the believer is enabled to have fellowship with God because God takes up residence in him. Further, Jesus is promising this to men who already have believed in him and have been given to him by God the Father (John 17:6–9). Thus, all that Jesus says about abiding must be recognized as intimately tied to obedience rather than faith in isolation. That this is not a promise of salvation (regeneration) is evident in that Scripture clearly teaches that salvation is not dependent on our works, even of obedience, but is solely a result of faith (Eph 2:8–9). Through his analogy of the vine and the branches (John 15:1–8), Jesus teaches that abiding results in fruitfulness and answered prayer. However, again, this is predicated on an obedient relationship (John 15:9–10). Furthermore, in John 17 he prays for the church's unity and includes in that prayer mutual abiding, "I in them, and you in me" (John 17:23). In each of these instances the description given by Jesus is relational and to be experienced during this life. This is the more

---

50. D. G. Van der Merwe ("'Experiencing Fellowship with God' according to 1 John 1:5–2:28," 232) sees John using the noun in a "chiastic pattern" involving 1:3, 6, and 7. But the double occurrence of *koinonia* in v. 3, along with the imbalance of text and concepts from vv. 4 to 6, argues against a chiasm. It does serve to emphasize the concept in this section through repetition, though.

51. Bruce (38) relates μέρος with κοινωνία and sees them as synonymous. Paul's use of μέρος in synonymous parallelism with κοινωνία in 2 Cor 6:14 might appear to validate Bruce's interpretation (BDAG, 642; H. Hanse, "ἔχω, μετέχω," *TDNT* 2:831). But Jesus' use of μέρος expresses more clearly the justification truth of *union* with Christ, being a part of the body of Christ, than it does the sanctification truth of *fellowship* with Christ, being a participating member of the body of Christ, especially in light of Jesus' statement that not all of them were clean (John 13:10–11).

abundant life he came to give his sheep (John 10:10), a life in the present. This is not a mere possession of life, but an expression of life, an experience of life that is relational. As Jesus said to his Father, "This is eternal life, that they may *know* you" (John 17:3).

Paul's use of κοινωνία is broader than John's. He uses it with a range of meanings and nuances. (1) It describes the sharing of material possessions in the sense of giving (Rom 15:26; 2 Cor 8:3–4). (2) Joint participation is expressed both positively and negatively. Positively, the Philippian church was participating in Paul's ministry financially and so jointly participating with him in the proclamation of the gospel (Phil 1:3–5). Paul's suffering for Jesus was joint participation in his suffering (Phil 3:10). Negatively, the Ephesians could have "fellowship with the unfruitful works of darkness" by participating in sinful conduct with pagans (Eph 5:11–12). (3) It also describes a mutually positive relationship experienced between the believer and Christ (1 Cor 1:9) as well as between believers (Gal 2:9). Negatively, this mutual relationship can be experienced with demons through participation in pagan feasts or knowingly eating meat sacrificed to idols (1 Cor 10:20–21), and can also be experienced with unbelievers through unequal relationships in business and society (2 Cor 6:14).

For John, κοινωνία refers to a healthy relationship with God and others rather than union, possession, or partnership. It is a relational term, with its concept being fleshed out in his discussion of mutual abiding. Though κοινωνία is only repeated twice more by John, its idea is expressed through other terms, as will be seen later in this commentary, including his use of μένω with a similar nuance as was given it in the upper room.[52]

καὶ ἡ κοινωνία δὲ ἡ ἡμετέρα μετὰ τοῦ πατρὸς καὶ μετὰ τοῦ υἱοῦ αὐτοῦ Ἰησοῦ Χριστοῦ, "And indeed, our fellowship is with the Father and with his Son, Jesus Christ." John describes this fellowship his readers may have as "our" fellowship "with the Father and with his Son." He uses the attributive adjective ἡμετέρα to describe his own positive mutual relationship—along with the other apostles—experienced with two members of the Godhead. Bruce (38) notes: "This language is most naturally understood if a surviving member of the first Christian generation is addressing members of a

52. John does use its verb form (κοινωνεῖ) in 2 John 11 with the sense of participation more than mutual relationship. But that does not produce sufficient proof that his understanding of the term was limited to such a nuance.

later Christian generation, who could not have that unmediated contact with the beginning of the gospel that he himself had." Much need not be made over John's choice of ἡμετέρα over ἡμῶν, though, since the two terms are grammatically equivalent, as can be seen by their synonymous use in 2:2. Thus his choice is likely more stylistic than rhetorical (Culy, 8). John's connection back to the previous sentence with the first person plural verbs and pronouns indicates the apostolic witnesses as well, and not the readers. By this he affirms that the apostles have fellowship with the Father and Son. Based on the preceding clause, John is then inviting his readers to participate in that fellowship. What he is writing is designed to enable his readers to join in the close positive relationships that the eyewitnesses share with God the Father and God the Son (Williams, 18; Painter, 128, 138).[53]

Additionally, John says the apostles' fellowship is "with" both members of the Godhead. His use of a μετὰ ... καὶ μετὰ construction should be seen as an allusion to both shared deity and coequality of the Father and Son (Smalley, 13; contra Culy, 8).

This is the first of four occurrences of John linking Ἰησοῦ Χριστοῦ with υἱοῦ αὐτοῦ. In 3:23, he is to be the object of our faith. In 5:20 he is connected once again to God the Father, as his Son and sharing in deity. Finally in 2 John 3 Jesus shares an equal placed with God the Father as the source of blessing for the "elect lady" and her children.[54]

1:4 Another of John's reasons for writing is to bring his readers' joy to its fullness. However, joy, as it is understood in the Bible, cannot be experienced apart from a proper relationship with God as well as others (Pss 16:11; 51:12; John 15:11). Thus his first purpose is a necessary prerequisite to his second.

καὶ ταῦτα γράφομεν ὑμῖν, "And we write these things to you." John begins this second purpose statement with καὶ. The coordinating conjunction may be viewed in one of three ways. (1) It may reflect a Johannine Semitism, at which point it would have little rhetorical significance. The καὶ serves to

---

53. D. Rusam, *Gemeinschaft der Kinder Gottes*, 182. E. Malatesta (*Interiority and Covenant*, 6) says well that "the communion of Christians with each other and their relationship to the world are grounded in their communion with God."

54. M. de Jonge ("The Use of the Word ΧΡΙΣΤΟΣ in the Johannine Epistles," 66–67) sees these four occurrences as christological statements emphasizing the intimate relationship between God the Father and God the Son.

connect this second purpose with the prologue, bringing it to its conclusion as well as stating a second purpose. (2) It may have a "resultative force" with the sense of "therefore" or "so that" (Haas, de Jonge, and Swellengrebel, 18). This would change this from a purpose to a reason for writing. John would be explaining his motivation rather than his goal. (3) It may serve as a causal conjunction producing "thematic continuity" (Culy, 8). This would tend to make it a continuation of the previous purpose, and thus a secondary purpose rather than one of John's primary purposes in writing.

The demonstrative pronoun ταῦτα may be either anaphoric, referring to what precedes (Burdick, 106), or cataphoric*, whether looking at the immediate context of what is about to be said (Brooke, 9) or to the remainder of the epistle (Brown, 172–73; Culy, 8–9; Haas, de Jonge, and Swellengrebel, 18; Painter, 123; Westcott, 13). In 2:1, just seven verses later, John uses a nearly identical construction anaphorically (the only exception being that "write" is singular as opposed to plural). As will be seen later, what he had just written was designed to motivate his readers to avoid sin, not feel free to sin in light of the cleansing available to all who confess. His final use of ταῦτα with "write" is in 5:13, where it is certainly anaphoric since what precedes most logically produces assurance, as opposed to what follows. The cataphoric sense is strongly implied by the pres. tense verb (Painter, 123), as opposed to the aorist in 5:13. Additionally, the cataphoric sense of 1:4 might be argued on the basis that it forms a kind of inclusio with 5:13 and γράφομεν in 1:4, being pres. tense, looking forward to ἔγραψα in 5:13, which looks back to 1:4. First, against this stands the problem of having an inclusio that encompasses the entire epistle, less its prologue and epilogue. The nature of an inclusio is that it marks off a unit of thought within works, but not whole works. Second, the word, phrase, or concept that marks the two limits of an inclusio does not normally appear within it as well. John's pres. tense γράφω with ταῦτα in 2:1 breaks up the possible inclusio of 1:4 and 5:13, and so the likelihood of a possible inclusio is significantly reduced. Also, the full content of the epistle cannot be subsumed under the rubric of "assurance," which is the clear focus of the statement in 5:13, and not in 1:4. Still, the cataphoric sense seems to be supported better by the nature of what is written before and afterward. It would seem difficult to argue that the content of 1:1–3 alone would cause the readers full joy. However, what follows in the epistle can be seen to encourage the joyful experience of John's readers. A third possibility would be to see this first use of ταῦτα to be both anaphoric and cataphoric and have the entire epistle in view (Smalley, 14). Thus everything John writes, from the prologue through the epilogue, was for the benefit of his readers and was designed to ensure their joyful experience of eternal life.

John's choice of the pres. tense first person plural γράφομεν here may be understood as referring to the band of eyewitnesses rather than as an authorial "we" (Dodd, 9–10).[55] This is the sole instance of John using γράφω in the plural pres. tense. The other six times he uses it in the pres., he uses the first person singular (2:1, 7, 8, 12, 13 [twice]) and so clearly has himself in view. He uses the first person singular another six times in the aorist (2:14 [three times], 21, 26; 5:13). So, why does John break from his pattern here in the prologue of his epistle? He continues the pattern of 1 plurals that have identified him with the body of eyewitnesses who had personally experienced Jesus in his humanity (Painter, 45). His use of "we" includes all the eyewitnesses who have testified, whether orally or in writing (Kistemaker, 238).[56] This need not mean that others helped him compose the epistle, as is the case in several of Paul's epistles. Since the previous verses included the apostolic band as eyewitnesses, it would seem natural for John to be indicating their agreement with him by their inclusion in his testimony, though his readers would understand he was speaking as one of the eyewitnesses, not along with them. Moreover, though by this time most of the apostles would have been martyred, John's identification with them implies rather that their testimonies continue to be known and lend validity to his own (contra Schnackenburg, 55).

John's focus on his readers is expressed by their being included as the recipients of his writing and the focus of his attention. One of the more difficult text-critical issues occurs in this verse, actually twice. The first issue is whether the pronoun in this clause should be the first person plural subject (ἡμεῖς) of the verb "we write," or indirect object of the verb (ὑμῖν), indicating the readers. The weight of manuscript evidence favors the second reading. Although ἡμεῖς has some MS support, including some of the oldest Alexandrian MSS, other Alexandrian uncials as well as the majority

55. See comments on 1:1 for a more complete discussion.
56. Contra BDF (§280).

of minuscules favor ὑμῖν.[57] The Alexandrian tradition is split fairly evenly (once the value of various texts is weighed) while the Byzantine and Western texts favor ὑμῖν uniformly. Thus the weight of external evidence seems to favor ὑμῖν. Furthermore, as Culy (9) notes, if ἡμεῖς were chosen, it would serve a stylistic role "rather than emphatic, given its unmarked position following the verb." Strecker (20) notes that ὑμῖν would fit better the "conclusion of a prescript" but does not see 1 John fitting into the genre of an epistle. He then argues that the author's intention to identify himself with his readers makes ἡμεῖς the better reading. However, John's identification with his readers would not be served best by an emphatic subject (ἡμεῖς), but by a reminder that he has his readers in view (ὑμῖν). Thus, placed as the direct object of the verb, ὑμῖν reminds his readers that they are his.

ἵνα ἡ χαρὰ ὑμῶν ᾖ πεπληρωμένη, "in order that your joy may be completely full." Similar to the problem in the previous clause, a second textual variant calls for a choice between "our joy" (ἡ χαρὰ ἡμῶν) and "your joy" (ἡ χαρὰ ὑμῶν). The majority of interpreters follow Metzger in supporting "our," including Haas, de Jonge, and Swellengrebel (19), Kistemaker (238), Painter (123), Schnackenburg (49), Strecker (8), and Williamson (61). He argues: "As regards intrinsic probability, ἡμῶν seems to suit best the generous solicitude of the author, whose own joy would be incomplete unless his readers shared it; whereas copyists, insensitive to such a nuance, would have been likely to alter ἡμῶν to the more expected 2 ὑμῶν."[58] Hodges (52) favors "our" as representing "the apostolic circle" with the result that the "theme of joy" serves as another "expression of apostolic love for Christian believers." On the other hand, Culy (9) notes that "faulty hearing could have led to unintentional changes in either direction." Also, taking the preceding pronoun to be first person plural, he sees ἡμεῖς as possibly influencing the copyists to change the second person plural to 1 here. However, he argues well: "The fact that the purpose of the letter is clearly to benefit the readers … suggests that ὑμῶν may well have been the original reading, which was accidentally changed early in the text's transmission history." Walls and Anders

57. In support of ἡμεῖς are א A* B P Ψ 33 it^{z} cop^{ms}. Supporting ὑμῖν are A^{c} C K L 049 056 0142 81 88 104 181 326 330 436 451 614 629 630 945 1241 1505 1739 1877 1881 2412 2495 *Byz* *Lect*^{m} $it^{ar,e,dem,div,p,t}$ vg $syr^{p,h,pal}$ $cop^{sa,bo}$ arm eth.

58. B. M. Metzger and United Bible Societies, *A Textual Commentary on the Greek New Testament*, 2nd ed., 649.

(156) also see "your" as the best reading while noting that John's joy could not be complete unless his readers' was. Though the stronger Alexandrian texts support "our" as the best option, they remain split, with other MS evidence favoring "your."[59] Though it is possible that John's joy at hearing of the faith of the church's members (or the Elect Lady's children) in 2 John 4 and Gaius' walking in truth in 3 John 3 points to his joy being included here, the contexts of those two letters indicate he is responding to reports he had received, not expressing a desired response to a letter he had sent. Thus, by recognizing "your" as the better reading, one notes the focus of the epistle is the readers rather than the apostle. Even in this section, though John, along with the other apostles, serves as an eyewitness, his concern as author is the readers. It is they whom John writes to edify and whose walk with God is his concern. Thus, it would be their joy that concerns him most. Akin (60) opts to see the joy as both, "ours" and "yours." In a sense this is the end result of John's readers responding positively to his instruction. However, the word itself cannot be both, but must be one or the other.[60]

The joy John desires for his readers to experience is joy that has reached its goal in their lives, joy to its fullest.[61] This is a distinctly Johannine phrase, which is expressed in his Second Epistle (2 John 12) as well as four times in his Gospel (John 3:29; 15:11; 16:24; 17:13).[62] When he says he wants their joy to be "completely full," he expresses the idea that they have already experienced a measure of joy, but that his desire is that their joy reaches its goal in their lives and they experience it to its "full measure."[63] As Haas, de Jonge,

---

59. In support of ἡμῶν: ℵ B L Ψ 049 88 181 326 436 1241 *Lect*^{m} *l*^{6,59,62} it^{p,t,z} vg^{ww} cop^{sa}. In support of ὑμῶν: A C^{vid} K P 056 0142 33 81 104 330 451 614 629 630 945 1505 1739 1877 1881 2412 2495 *Byz* it^{ar,c,dem,div,} vg^{mss} syr^{h,pal} cop^{bo} arm eth.

60. Yet for those who consider ἡμῶν the better reading, "our" could include John and his readers rather than John and the other apostles. This would be a break from his pattern of identifying himself with the apostolic witnesses in this section, unless one sees this as a transition to the next series of first-person plurals that do include the readers along with John.

61. BDAG, 1077; H. Conzelmann, "χαρά," *TDNT* 9:370. The concept of joy as a personal experience stood in contrast to pagan beliefs about life during the first century (C. Spicq, "χαρά," 498–99).

62. Strecker (20) suggests that the phrase ἡ χαρὰ ὑμῶν ᾖ πεπληρωμένη may be dependent on 2 John 12 (ἡ χαρὰ ἡμῶν πεπληρωμένη ᾖ). Rather than dependence of one author on another, one should see this as reflecting the literary style of a single author.

63. BDAG, 828; G. Delling, "πληρόω," *TDNT* 6:297.

and Swellengrebel (19) beautifully say, this participial construction, which John uses similarly in 2 John 12, "expresses that the joy will lack nothing, that it will fill their hearts to the brim. The term refers to the highest degree: they will be as glad as they possibly can be."

Biblical Theology Comments

Eternal life is more than a possession; it is a person with whom we relate (have fellowship). This is the first and primary theme of this epistle. For John, eternal life has a qualitative aspect that is tied to one's relationship with Jesus, who not only gives that life but also is that life incarnate. That is not to deny its quantitative aspect. However, John's focus will be on this qualitative sense.

John introduces us to the theme of fellowship in his prologue and will develop it further in the epistle, though utilizing synonyms and related concepts, as we will see. As noted above in the commentary, his concept of fellowship is more narrow than Paul's use of the term. Here already fellowship as mutual relationship is expressed by John's invitation to his readers to participate in the fellowship enjoyed by the apostolic witnesses to Christ. The fellowship envisioned is with God the Father and Son, a vertical fellowship, that presupposes a horizontal one as well. Implied already, and clarified later, is the truth that this fellowship will depend on one's relationship with Jesus who is life incarnate. Furthermore, one cannot have fellowship with him apart from having a proper understanding of who he is, as well as living one's life in God's presence with the same obedient love that characterized Jesus. Yet, this fellowship flows from a life experienced as a result of having a healthy relationship with the source of that life, Eternal Life himself, Jesus.

Application and Devotional Implications

We will see in this epistle that it matters what we believe about Jesus. Here we have been introduced to him as life incarnate. A part of mature faith in Christ is recognition of him as our life, not just life giver. At the same time, we remember we are not eyewitnesses, but among those more blessed than Thomas who believe without seeing (John 20:29). We are dependent on the eyewitness accounts to know in whom our faith is placed and to know the right things to believe. Thereby our faith is in the real Jesus, who saves, and not the invention of our minds or of the minds of others who would create a Jesus in their own image.

Selected Bibliography

Batut, J. "Believing in the Resurrection; or, The Logic of Love." *Communio: International Catholic Review* 37 (2010): 34–46.

Boismard, M.. "La connaissance de Dieu dans l'Alliance Nouvelle d'après 1 Jo." *RB* 50 (1949): 365–91.

Bullinger, E. W. *Figures of Speech Used in the Bible.* New York: Eyre & Spottiswoode, 1898. Reprint, Grand Rapids: Baker, 1968.

Curtis, E. M. "The Purpose of 1 John." Th.D. dissertation, Dallas Theological Seminary, 1986.

de Jonge, M. "An Analysis of 1 John 1.1–4." *BT* 29 (1978): 322–30.

———. "The Use of the Word ΧΡΙΣΤΟΣ in the Johannine Epistles." In *Studies in John*, 67–74. NovTSup 24. Leiden: Brill, 1970.

de la Potterie, I. "La connaissance de Dieu dans le dualism eschatolgique d'après 1 Jn 2, 12–14." In *Au service de la parole de Dieu,* 77–99. Gembloux, Belgium: Mélanges Andre-Marie Charue, 1969.

Fanning, B. M. *Verbal Aspect in New Testament Greek*. Oxford: Clarendon, 1990.

Feuillet, A. "The Structure of First John. Comparison with the Fourth Gospel. The Pattern of Christian Life." *BTB* 3 (1973): 194–216.

Hercsik, D. "Das 'Wort Gotte' und die Christologie." *Greg* 89 (2008): 368–95.

Johnson, E. E. *Expository Hermeneutics: An Introduction.* Grand Rapids: Zondervan, 1990.

Lieu, J. M. "'Authority to Become Children of God': A Study of 1 John." *NovT* 23 (1981): 210–28.

Lieu, J. M. "Us or You? Persuasion and Identity in 1 John." *JBL* 4 (2008): 805–19.

Louw, J. P. "Verbal Aspect in the First Letter of John." *Neot* 9 (1975): 98–104.

MacArthur, J. F., Jr. *The Gospel according to Jesus*, Grand Rapids: Academie, 1988.

Malatesta, E. *Interiority and Covenant: A Study of* εἶναι ἐν *and* μένειν ἐν *In the First Letter of Saint John*. Rome: Biblical Institute Press, 1978.

Metzger, B. M., and United Bible Societies. *A Textual Commentary on the Greek New Testament.* 2nd ed. New York: United Bible Societies, 1994.

Metzger, P. L. *The Gospel of John: When Love Comes to Town*. Downers Grove, IL: InterVarsity, 2010.

Rusam, D. *Gemeinschaft der Kinder Gottes: Das Motiv der Gotteskindschaft und die Gemeinden der johanneischen Briefe*. Stuttgart: Verlag W. Kohlhammer, 1993.

Ryrie, C. C. "I, II, and III John." In *The Wycliffe Bible Commentary*, edited by C. F. Pfeiffer and E. F. Harrison. Chicago: Moody, 1962.

Smalley, S. S. "What about 1 John?" In *StudBib 1978, Vol. 3: Papers on Paul and Other New Testament Authors*, edited by E. A. Livingstone, 337–43. Sheffield: JSOT Press, 1980.

Spicq, C. *Theological Lexicon of the New Testament*. Translated and edited by J. D. Ernest. 3 vols. Peabody, MA: Hendrickson, 1994.

Van der Merwe, D. G. "'Experiencing Fellowship with God' according to 1 John 1:5–2:28: Dealing with the Change in Social Behavior." *Acta Patristica et Byzantina* 18 (2007): 231–62.

Wallace, D. B. *Greek Grammar beyond the Basics*. Grand Rapids: Zondervan, 1996.

Additional Exegetical Comments

1:1 John's use of τοῖς ὀφθαλμοῖς ἡμῶν along with the perfect of ὁράω (ἑωράκαμεν) might seem unnecessary. However, rather than seeing this as a synecdoche*, it should be viewed as a dative of reference that emphasizes the physically experiential nature of his personally seeing Jesus (Culy, 3–4). As a synecdoche, John would be using "eyes" for the whole person. However, his following statement, "our hands handled" (αἱ χεῖρες ἡμῶν ἐψηλάφησαν), in the same context indicates that he intended to focus attention on these two specific modes of contact rather than a whole range of experiences. Thus this argues against John's use of the part (eyes) for the whole ("all our senses"). Thus it is better to see this as a dative of reference. Ultimately, either interpretive option leads to the same conclusion. John is emphasizing his role as an eyewitness, a role the false teachers cannot claim.

The genitive noun τῆς ζωῆς may function as (1) an epexegetical genitive, "the Word, namely, that which is life"; (2) as a qualifying genitive, "the life-giving word"; (3) as an object genitive, "the Word concerning or about life"; or (4) with all three senses without distinction (Brown, 165–66). Culy (5) rejects the notion that it is a functioning appositionally to τοῦ λόγου, and thus a second title for Jesus, as Burdick (101) understands it. Since λόγος *is* personified in the very next verse, which is the next clause in the same sentence, it should be allowed to be understood or implied in this verse as well. The two uses are part of the same thought. The wording would be better seen to imply and then make explicit the truth as John wakens us to the Incarnation as a major theme of his epistle.

1:2 The first transitive verb ἐφανερώθη is aorist, followed by a perfect (ἑωράκαμεν) and then two presents (μαρτυροῦμεν καὶ ἀπαγγέλλομεν) and a final aorist (ἐφανερώθη) that repeats the first verb in the statement. The article (ἡ) with life (ζωὴ) is anaphoric, connecting the subject of this parenthetical statement with the previous statement's content. The preposition πρὸς preceding τὸν πατέρα indicates "being in company with someone" and carries the sense of "close relationship."[64] The same preposition. and construction were used in John 1:1 of the Word.

64. BDAG, 875; T. Friberg, B. Friberg, and N. F. Miller, *Analytical Lexicon of the Greek New Testament*, §. 330; B. Reicke, "πρὸς," *TDNT*, 6:721.

God Is Light (1:5–2:27)

Introduction

This first major section of the epistle focuses our attention on the experience of eternal life in terms of God's moral purity. Herein John writes that experiencing eternal life results from an honest, obedient relationship that produces love for the brethren and rejection of the world's thinking.

A portion of this section appears to be chiastically arranged with 1:9, confession of sin, at its center. When a chiasm is used by an author, its focus is the central point, though it may include a climaxing statement at its end as well. Chiasms are recognized by the pattern of repeated terms, concepts, or activities, often parallel but sometimes contrastive, that progress to and from the central point(s). Still, that being said, one must caution against finding chiasms where they do not exist, nor extending them beyond that which the author intends. Larger chiasms would include such works as the Pentateuch, Lamentations, and Matthew's Gospel.[1] Similarly, a chiasm is evident in the letters to the seven churches in Rev 2–3. In these chapters, both Ephesus and Laodicea share in their failure to be what they were at first. Smyrna and Philadelphia both have to deal with a "synagogue of Satan" and neither face criticism from Jesus. Pergamum and Sardis seem to break the pattern of sharing problems or issues, though they both share with Thyatira, which occupies the center of the chiasm. It is in Thyatira that "Jezebel" holds sway, leading the church in spiritual compromise. Of note, too, is the promise of reigning with Christ, to the overcomers of both

1. See G. Derickson, "Matthew's Chiastic Structure and Its Dispensational Implications," 423–37, for a full discussion and defense of Matthew's use of chiasm to structure his Gospel.

Thyatira and Laodicea, indicating that the right to reign with Christ is the central focus of the letters, as well as the danger of spiritual compromise.

In this epistle, John appears to have begun his message with a chiasm, even as he did the Revelation.[2] The chiasm appears as follows:

A (1:6) – Walking in darkness invalidates a claim to fellowship with God.

B (1:7) – Jesus' blood cleanses us if we walk in light.

C (1:8) – Claim of sinlessness is self-deception.

D (1:9) – Confession brings cleansing.

C′ (1:10) – Claim of no sins to confess calls God a liar.

B′ (2:1–2) – Jesus is our Advocate and Propitiation if we sin.

A′ (2:3–4) – Walking in disobedience invalidates a claim to know God (relationally).

Central to John's message is the need to confess our sins if we wish to have fellowship with God by walking in his moral purity, called here "the light." Around this central point is the problem of the false claims (vv. 8, 10) that impede fellowship as well as walking in his light. Around them stands the provision of God: Jesus' blood cleanses us and Jesus assists us. Then, at the outer edges the problem is stated: the false claim of fellowship apart from obedience. The point of the chiasm is that without honesty with God about our sin, we cannot experience the forgiveness that results from Christ's work on our behalf that enables us to have fellowship with God and thereby experience a quality of life that John describes as "eternal life."

---

2. The letters to the seven churches (Rev 2–3) are chiastically arranged with the letters to Ephesus and Laodicea being parallel, forming the A and A′ units. Smyrna and Philadelphia are the praised churches and form the B and B′ units. Pergamum and Sardis form the C and C′ units. The central church (D unit) is Thyatira. See G. K. Beale, *The Book of Revelation,* 32–33, for a fuller discussion of the chiastic structure of Rev 2–3.

Walking in the Light (1:5–2:6)

Introduction

Experiencing eternal life as fellowship with God requires honesty with him concerning sin. When John describes God as "light," is this a reference to his essential or moral nature? Does "darkness" refer to salvation or moral spheres? These questions highlight the challenge of interpreting this section.

Light and darkness refer to moral spheres. Though in his Gospel, John uses this imagery to describe two spheres of existence, regenerate and unregenerate, he changes the referent of the imagery in his epistle, as will be seen in what follows.[3] In the Gospel of John, both John and Jesus use "light" to refer to the sphere of spiritual life resulting from justification. For example, in John 3:14–21 John uses the light-darkness imagery in his explanation of what Jesus meant by "the Son of Man be lifted up, that whoever believes in him should not perish but have eternal life." In this case, light refers to spiritual life and darkness to spiritual death. This same sense can be seen in the prologue of his Gospel (John 1:5). Similarly, the two spheres are that of spiritual life and death in John 8:12 ("He who follows me shall not walk in darkness, but have the light of life."). When Jesus calls himself the light of the world in John 8, he is referring to himself as the source of spiritual life, the world's Savior. However, when he uses "light" in John 9:3–5, he changes the referent since he speaks of his departure from the world and people being unable to work with the departure of his light. When Jesus says, "As long as I am in the world, I am the light of the world," he cannot be talking about being its Savior, for he remains such following his temporary departure from this world and will continue to be such after his return. In John 11:9 Jesus uses light in its literal sense with relation to day and night while speaking metaphorically about his return to Judea to raise Lazarus from the dead. In John 12:35–36 he uses light and darkness in their literal and spiritual senses, but with a view to him as the source of light and darkness being a reference to his absence. Then in John 12:46–50, Jesus again uses light and

3. That he need not keep the same referent for an image can be illustrated by the example of Jesus in the parables of the soils and the wheat and tares (Matt 13). In the parable of the soils, the seed sown is identified by Jesus as "the word of the kingdom" (Matt 13:19). In the parable of the wheat and tares, seed is changed to people (Matt 13:38).

darkness as justification realities, as clarified by his warning of judgment in the last day. Thus even in the Gospel the imagery of light and darkness has two senses. Thus, with this possibility in mind, John's use of the imagery in what follows need not carry a justification sense, though that was its primary use in his Gospel.

Those reflecting the Test of Life view understand this section to describe two spheres of existence for humanity. A person is either regenerate and therefore walking in light, or unregenerate and therefore walking in darkness. Those within the Test of Fellowship view, on the other hand, say believers can move between the two spheres. When John says a believer may walk in light or darkness, he is referring to one's sphere of operation, not one's justification-salvation status. To determine which view is correct, or if both err, the meaning of light and darkness as John uses it here will be explored. Additionally, how this imagery fits within Johannine dualism must be explored in order to clarify the meaning of these two spheres of existence.

In this section there are four confessions (or claims). In verse 6 is the claim of fellowship by someone walking in moral darkness. Verse 8 contains the claim of no present sins (sinless perfection). Verse 9 is a confession of sin. Finally, verse 10 is a denial of one's sin nature, a claim not to need confession because no sin exists to confess with the resultant need for forgiveness.

The key to interpretation is John's use of "we" throughout these verses and in 2:1. He includes himself in the possibility of making the false claims and experiencing the various realities. Though it is common to take these series of claims to be that of John's opponents, as will be discussed below (1:6), such a theory is dependent on John's use of "we" throughout this section to be an authorial "we" rather than continuing the pattern of 1:1–4, or shifting to a "we" that includes John and his readers. The possibility of an authorial "we" or his use of the first person plural as a rhetorical device is weakened by his following use of ὁ λέγων in 2:4 and 6, where he will state claims that may be made by anybody, believer or unbeliever. When he does not wish to necessarily include himself, he moves to the third person. It seems better to see John making these distinctions in person specifically to clarify who he is addressing, describing, or identifying with in each instance. Additionally, if 1:7, 9, are literally true for John, and 2:1–2 includes John with his readers, as I propose they are and do, then it does not follow that his use of "we" in 1:6, 8, and 10 should only be hypothetical or related to opponents. As will be seen in what follows, it makes more sense to see John including himself with his readers as capable of wrong thinking as well as right.

God's Moral Purity (1:5)

Original Text

5 Καὶ ἔστιν αὕτη ἡ ἀγγελία ἣν ἀκηκόαμεν ἀπ' αὐτοῦ καὶ ἀναγγέλλομεν ὑμῖν, ὅτι ὁ θεὸς φῶς ἐστιν καὶ σκοτία ἐν αὐτῷ οὐκ ἔστιν οὐδεμία.

Translation

1:5 And this is the message that we heard from him and announce to you:[4] "God is light, and in him there is absolutely[5] no darkness."

Commentary

John introduces the body of his epistle with a declaration of God's moral nature. This forms the basis of all human relationships with him. Using poetic dualistic imagery, he affirms the moral nature of God in no uncertain terms. The absoluteness of God's purity will raise the problem of human failure, resolved by God, but calling for an honest self-assessment by every human who would seek fellowship with him.

1:5 Painter (128) sees this verse forming "a transition from the Prologue to the first group of assertions made by the opponents." Rather than a transition to his opponents, it is better seen as introducing his first main topic, God's moral purity as it relates to experiencing a healthy relationship with God (experiencing eternal life) through his Son, Jesus, who enables that relationship. First, the assertions of 1:6–10 are not those of opponents, but claims any Christian can make, including John (thus his use of "we" to include himself). Second, this affirmation of the character of God is the basis of all that is said in this section, which includes more than possible claims of false teachers. John's call to imitate Jesus' obedience (2:5–6) and to love God rather than the world (2:15–17) are pastoral issues, not polemical, and so unrelated to false teachers.

---

4. This ὅτι clause is translated as a direct rather than indirect quotation. The direct quotation is reflected in English translations such as HCSB, NAB, NIV84, NCV, NET, and NLT, while the indirect is found in ESV, NASB95, and NKJV.

5. The choice of "absolutely" in translation reflects the emphatic role of the double negative (οὐκ ... οὐδεμία) in Greek.

John begins the main body of his epistle with the clause "And this is the message." With this he moves his readers from the introduction of the prologue to those truths that are foundational to having fellowship with God through Jesus, who is eternal life incarnate. Some see this, along with the same phrase in 3:11, marking off the major sections of John's argument (Brown, 124–28; Burge, 63; Harris, 152). However, as noted earlier, the epistle may be divided thematically (as in this commentary).

Καὶ ἔστιν αὕτη ἡ ἀγγελία, "And this is the message." This introductory sentence is begun with a καὶ that is often left untranslated because of English style, but should be included as a part of John's formula for introducing various themes, in this case God's morally pure nature (Culy, 10). We see the formula, whether as καὶ ἐστὶν αὕτη or καὶ αὕτη ἐστὶν, repeatedly used by John to introduce new material, with the cataphoric* demonstrative pronoun pointing to the epexegetical construction that follows (Brown, 192; Culy, 10–11).[6] This formula serves to alert the readers to key themes John is developing. The change in word order may in this instance primarily serve to mark the transition from prologue to the main body of the epistle. This seems to follow the pattern of John's Gospel, wherein his transition from the prologue to the body of the narrative is marked by the phrase Καὶ αὕτη ἐστὶν ἡ μαρτυρία τοῦ Ἰωάννου. Culy (11) rightly notes, "Where the order καὶ αὕτη ἐστὶν is used, the conjunction carries its usual sentence-initial function of marking thematic continuity.... If the same is true here, this would provide further evidence that the letter is all about having fellowship with the Father and Son ... which can only take place within 'the light.'"[7] Grammatically, this could be serving as a resumptive καί, which would link the following material with the "message" of the prologue. John introduces his readers to the central truth of this first section by connecting what he is

---

6. This formula occurs at 1 John 2:25; 3:23; 5:4, 11, 14; and 2 John 6 with the fem. pronoun. Without the καὶ, the formula αὕτη ἐστὶν occurs in 3:11; 5:3, 9, 11; and 2 John 7, 9. It also occurs with the masc. pronoun in 2:22; 5:6, 20; 2 John 7.

7. Painter (123–24), after noting John's use of both fem. and masc. pronouns with this formula, observes that "the statements using the feminine are wholly positive while those using the masculine are a mixed bag." This should be viewed as incidental since the gender of the pronoun is dependent on its antecedent and carries no special significance beyond that. This may be a good example of modern scholars, in reporting their observations, making "much ado about nothing."

about to say with what he has experienced. As a witness of the eternal life incarnate, Jesus, he now describes what was revealed to him.

ἣν ἀκηκόαμεν ἀπ' αὐτοῦ καὶ ἀναγγέλλομεν ὑμῖν, "that we heard from him and announce to you." John reminds his readers of his eyewitness status by repeating "we have heard" for the third time. What he is saying is the product of personal instruction from Jesus. This truth was taught him by Jesus during his ministry to the apostolic witnesses.[8] John's use of "we" here has been understood in four ways. (1) This "we" distinguishes between John and his readers once again (Haas, de Jonge, and Swellengrebel, 22). It connects John with "the tradition bearers" and thereby goes "directly to Jesus" (Kruse, 61; Painter, 124; also Strecker, 25).[9] (2) This may be a "prophetic plural" used by the disciples of the apostles, who considered themselves their "successors" as tradition bearers (Schnackenburg, 56–57). Brown follows this, seeing it reflecting a combination of the original witnesses who transmitted the message orally and then the following generation, the "Johannine Community," who wrote it (Brown, 172). (3) This "we" represents all believers in the sense that all share a connection with the eyewitnesses (Dodd, 13–16). As with the prologue, John continues to identify himself with the apostolic eyewitnesses as he expresses the truths learned from Jesus regarding the nature of God and his relationship with his children; thus view (1) is preferred.

Further, his use of the perfect tense ἀκηκόαμεν indicates that what was heard is in the past and no longer continues to be heard, though its truth still stands to the present. He follows this with the pres. tense ἀναγγέλλομεν (we announce) to emphasize the present significance of the message being delivered to them in the epistle.

John anticipates his first description of the basis of relationship with God by alerting his readers to what he is about to announce. He has a message to give them, a message from Jesus that carries the authority of Christ through his eyewitness, John. John emphasizes the importance of his message by using the same root word for both the message itself (ἀγγελία) and the communication of that message by him (ἀναγγέλλομεν). Brown (193) notes that this term is used only by John in the New Testament, here and in 3:11. He sees it equivalent to εὐαγγέλιον in the Gospel. Though Painter

8. Z. C. Hodges, "Fellowship and Confession in 1 John 1:5–10," 48–49.

9. A. von Harnack ("'Das Wir' in den Johanneischen Schriften," 104) sees it as an authorial pl.

gives ἀγγελία the sense of "good news" as well and sees it as a technical term for "gospel" (εὐαγγέλιον) in John, it is better to see this as a communication from Christ to his followers rather than an invitation to faith (Painter, 124). Drawing from the Gospels, John's use of the term identifies this more with Jesus' private instruction of the Twelve than his public preaching to the multitudes (John 15:11; 16:1–4). So, this is not the good news of salvation, but the instruction Jesus wanted transmitted to his followers by his representatives. Westcott (15) distinguishes ἀναγγέλλω from its synonym, ἀπαγγέλλω, seeing the former focusing on *who* is receiving the message while the latter focuses attention on the message's *origin*. However, as Culy (11) notes well, such a nuance between the two prefixes (ἀνά and ἀπό) is not supported by usage. It is more likely that John selected the different prefixes for stylistic reasons rather than to change meaning. Here, John's point is that this message sums up what has been heard by the apostles (Painter, 124).

Though John says the message was heard "from him" (ἀπ' αὐτοῦ), he clearly is referring to Christ rather than God the Father (contra Brooke, 11). Both the nearest referent is Christ, and the focus of the previous verses has been on him rather than God the Father.

John does two things grammatically to alert his readers to the importance of what he is saying. He includes both ἔστιν in his sentence as well as its subject, the pronoun αὕτη, neither ἔστιν nor αὕτη being necessary in a Greek sentence. Though the verb ἐστιν need not even be included in the sentence to be understood, its presence and change in location from what would be expected indicate emphasis. John wants his readers to know how important his message is. So he says, "This *is* the message." By adding the pronoun subject, following the verb, which had been moved to the fore of the clause, he is able to include the article with the predicate nominative "message" without it being mistaken for the subject of the clause. By this article with the noun, he alerts his readers that he is speaking of a specific and known message.[10]

ὅτι ὁ θεὸς φῶς ἐστιν, "God is light." John relates his message with an epexegetical ὅτι clause that contains a quotation of "the message" (ἡ ἀγγελία).[11] The content of their message (ἀναγγέλλομεν), given John and the other

10. D. B. Wallace, *Grammar*, 225.

11. D. B. Wallace (*Grammar*, 458–59) identifies this as an appositional ὅτι clause. Though ἀγγελία and ὁ θεὸς φῶς ἐστιν may be substituted for each other without

eyewitnesses by Jesus, is that God is absolutely pure and holy. He accomplishes this with a form of antithetic parallelism normally found in Hebrew poetry, though what he says here is neither poetic nor an attempt at poetry. Antithetic parallelism makes its point by stating opposites. In this case there is the contrast between light and darkness, but with the negation. John describes God's moral nature with both a positive affirmation and a negative. He then affirms in absolute terms what is likewise not true of him. God's purity is so absolute that no hint of anything other than moral purity exists within his being.

First, "God is light."[12] When he describes God as light, he is not describing God's essential being, but his moral nature. This metaphor refers to his character and is one of the bases of his dealings with mankind. The statement appears broad on the surface, which has led to various interpretations:

(1) Some see this as a description of God's essential nature as light (Brooke, 11; Haas, de Jonge, and Swellengrebel, 23). For example, Kistemaker sees this describing God's essential nature in that he "does not have light as one of his characteristics, but he is light; and although he created light (Gen. 1:3), he himself is uncreated light" (Kistemaker, 242). This emphasizes the role of the anarthrous noun, φῶς, indicating quality.[13] However, this misses the metaphorical nature of this statement, and the following negative statement makes less sense. Brown counters this approach and describes this statement as a "Johannine formula" that "is not an abstract definition but portrays God's identity revealed in terms of function" (Brown, 229).

---

changing the meaning of the sentence, this need not require it be appositional, but as direct discourse, and thus a declaration of their message, contra Blass-Debruner (BDF §387 [3]), who identifies this as indirect discourse.

12. Painter (142) sees an inclusion "formed by the statement of the message that God is light (1:5) and the sixth slogan of the opponents who claimed to be in the light (2:9)." This is unlikely since John uses φῶς ("light") in v. 10 to describe the loving Christian as the paragraph continues. The context is such that 2:9 should not be viewed as the end of a unit of thought. Following its use in 2:10, the term does not appear again in the epistle. It does not make sense that an inclusio should end in the middle of a paragraph.

13. D. B. Wallace (*Grammar*, 264) identifies this as a "qualitative predicate nominative," which then allows for the metaphor.

(2) Some see this describing God as the source of spiritual life (Akin, 62, 69).[14] Those in the light are saved (regenerate) while those in darkness are unsaved (unregenerate). Strecker (25–26) says that "God being light means the fulfillment of meaning in human life," which ultimately makes him "the giver of eschatological salvation." This view is consistent with other uses of the light-darkness imagery in the Gospel of John. However, to see this as a description of God as life giver is to read Gospel of John imagery into the epistle. There life and light are interconnected in the prologue and that imagery is developed throughout the narrative of the Gospel, though not in the Upper Room. In the Gospel the focus is on the possession or attainment of spiritual life or continuance in spiritual death. However, here, the text that follows focuses on ethical issues solely, and so the question of life, or lack of life, is not developed further, as will be seen in the commentary that follows.

(3) This is seen as a reference to God's revelatory nature and thus revelation of life (Bultmann, 16; Hodges, 57–58; Williamson, 66; Yarbrough, 48–50). God reveals himself or truths about himself. Painter (128–29) affirms that "God is self-revealing" and that what he reveals is "God's self. Light reveals light; it is self-revealing." This involves expressing his love, and so "the exposition goes on to affirm that the light excludes the darkness of hatred and is to be understood in terms of love (cf. 4:8, 16). Thus the dual theological affirmations 'God is light' and 'God is love' appear to be overlapping and mutually illuminating."[15] However, again, the imagery of the following description would then only be affirming that God does

14. C. P. Baylis, "The Meaning of Walking 'in the Darkness' (1 John 1:6)," 220.

15. Painter (124) sees this statement about God as "the foundation of the love command" because of the "parallel saying, 'God is love' (4:8, 16) and the connection between the love of God and the love command in 4:7–11." He points to several OT passages (Painter, 138–39) to demonstrate this. In Psalm 27:1 God is the psalmist's light. In Psalm 36:9 the psalmist affirms, "In your light we see light." In Psalm 80, the psalmist calls upon God to "shine forth" and to cause His "face to shine" on them. Habakkuk 3:3–4 describes God as having a brightness "like the light." The first two psalms do refer to God's revelation and possibly His revelatory nature. However, John does not appear to be alluding to them or building off their affirmations.

not fail to keep revealing. Furthermore, the descriptions of God and his relationship to his children that follow do not fit such an image or meaning.

(4) This is a picture of his moral purity and holiness (Kruse, 62; Marshall, 109; Schnackenburg, 77; Dodd, 19–20; Smalley, 20).[16] This is based on what John says in 3:3 (2:28–3:3). Therefore, he is talking about spheres of existence rather than states of being. Culy (12) argues well, "Given the following context, which speaks of 'walking' in the light or 'walking' in darkness, the metaphor φῶς almost certainly focuses on moral purity, while σκοτία points to the opposite. It is likely that the lack of article is not intended to point to 'light' as a quality (contra most scholars), something that is already clear from the fact that it functions as a metaphor here, but simply serves to function syntactically to mark φῶς as the predicate of the equative clause." This makes best sense of the issues that follow and the need for confession and cleansing as well as the later statement of Jesus' purity being the motivation for our own pursuit of purity (3:3).

(5) Williamson (66) sees John using gnostic dualistic concepts to distinguish between the Johannine community (those in the light) and the secessionists (those in darkness).[17] This interpretation depends too much on the theory of communities and influence of proto-Gnosticism on the church in the mid to late first century. As noted earlier, light-dark imagery is not the sole propriety of Gnosticism, but may be found in Judaism as well as most any other culture. Further, John's use of the imagery, especially because it is introduced with regard to God's nature or character, relates two kinds of people (those walking in the light and those walking in darkness) in terms of how they reflect God's character. Some like to combine aspects of these views (Smalley, 20). Consequently,

16. E. R. Achtemeier, "Jesus Christ, the Light of the World," 448; S. A. Hunt, "Light and Darkness," *Dictionary of the Later New Testament and Its Developments*; Z. C. Hodges, "Fellowship and Confession in 1 John 1:5–10," 50.

17. Williams (20) sees John being "very bold" and choosing a phrase used by his opponents. But then he notes that Philo used the exact words (*Dreams* 1.75), which demonstrates that John is more likely utilizing a Jewish concept than a gnostic one.

> one might argue for a combination of life and holiness, but would still need to demonstrate how God, being the source of life, relates to the need for holy and loving living in his children, who already have life.

John's use of "light" and "darkness" does not reflect a Greek dualistic worldview. Rather, this terminology was a standard literary image used throughout the ancient world, and one that is used in modern literature as well.[18] Conventional imagery sees light as symbolic of good and darkness as symbolic of evil. Reflected in first century BC and AD literature, this imagery would be recognized by John's readers without reverting to a Greek philosophical worldview even for those who had come out of such a mindset.[19] For example, Qumran literature, reflecting a Jewish worldview, employed this imagery.[20] Painter (139) sees this in terms of light representing "spiritual illumination" and "identification with the divine reality," which he sees as the viewpoint of John's "opponents," though not John's intended sense.[21] Haas, de Jonge, and Swellengrebel (23) similarly identify John's opponents with a Hellenistic dualism that led to "indifference" toward the unenlightened, with light and darkness representing wisdom and knowledge. Similar to Painter, they correctly recognize that John's use of the imagery is ethical rather than metaphysical.

This metaphor introduces John's light-darkness imagery for this epistle. Whereas in the Gospel, light is spiritual life and darkness is spiritual death, here it is moral purity with darkness being its opposite (Williams, 20). As Strecker (33) notes well, the "dualism" of light and darkness are "paralleled and interpreted by the contrast of 'truth and falsehood'" in verses

---

18. R. D. Patterson, "Deliverance from Darkness," 75–78; R. Youngblood, "Qoheleth's 'Dark House' (Eccl 12:5)," 401.

19. E. H. Merrill, "The Odes of Solomon and the Acts of Thomas," 230–33; C. A. Newsom, "Knowing as Doing," 148.

20. 1QS 1:9–10; 3:13–4:26, and underlying the whole of 1QM (see especially 13:10–12).

21. "In such Hellenistic religious texts light carries the sense of spiritual illumination where the mind is the point of identification with the divine reality. While this is not the sense of 1 John 1:5, it may well be precisely what is meant in the assertion made by the opponents, 2:9. ... Even if the author of 1 John and his opponents were both working from the Johannine Gospel tradition, we need to allow for the different ways the Johannine language might be understood." (Painter, 139).

6–10. For the believer who either walks in light or in darkness, it is not a question of spiritual life or death (contra Akin, 69), but of how much of God's moral nature is being expressed in his or her life. Akin (70) acknowledges that the referents of light differ between the Gospel and Epistle, but errs when he sees the "essential content" being the same in both uses. This results primarily because he sees the Epistle's focus being on justification realities—tests of whether the readers are regenerate or not (Test of Life view). Instead, this imagery should be seen as raising the issue of purity or sin. God's light expressed in the life of the believer will be characterized by truthfulness, righteousness, and love for one's fellow Christian (Smalley, 19–20). Darkness, on the other hand, expresses itself in deception, lawlessness, and hatred of one's brother.

Further, this need not be seen as a slogan of John's opponents (contra Burge, 67). This is a fundamental truth held within Judaism. For example, Philo affirmed God's nature as light. In his treatise on dreams, he writes, "And it is easy otherwise by means of argument to perceive this, since God is the first light, 'For the Lord is my light and my Saviour,' is the language of the Psalms; and not only the light, but he is also the archetypal pattern of every other light, or rather he is more ancient and more sublime than even the archetypal model, though he is spoken of as the model; for the real model was his own most perfect word, the light, and he himself is like to no created thing."[22] The apocryphal book of Sirach affirms, "He appointed a ruler for every nation, but Israel is the Lord's own portion. All their works are as clear as the sun before him, and his eyes are ever upon their ways. Their iniquities are not hidden from him, and all their sins are before the Lord."[23] Similar imagery is found in Qumran literature: "In the hand of the Prince of Lights is dominion over all the sons of justice; they walk on paths of light. And in the hand of the Angel of Darkness is total dominion over the sons of deceit; they walk on paths of darkness."[24] The apocryphal Wisdom of Solomon says, "So it was we who strayed from the way of truth, and the light of righteousness did not shine on us, and the sun did not rise upon us. We took our fill of the paths of lawlessness and destruction, and

22. Philo, *De Somniis*, 1.75, titled "on dreams" in C. D. Yonge, *The Works of Philo*, 372.

23. Sir 17:17–20, NRSV.

24. 1QS 3:20–21, as quoted by D. L. Bock and G. J. Herrick in *Jesus in Context*, 225.

we journeyed through trackless deserts, but the way of the Lord we have not known."[25] Thus it seems better to see John affirming a truth recognized by all rather than claimed by proto-gnostics or some other heretical group.

καὶ σκοτία ἐν αὐτῷ οὐκ ἔστιν οὐδεμία, "and in him there is absolutely no darkness." John now affirms with the opposite what he has just said positively about God. This use of antithetic parallelism heightens his affirmation of God's purity. It reaffirms in different language what he means by *God is light*. He reiterates that truth by affirming that there is not the slightest degree of deficiency with God. His use of a double negative makes this emphatic statement as absolute as the first one, heightening its absoluteness (Culy, 13; Haas, de Jonge, and Swellengrebel, 24).[26] Further, such an affirmation makes clear not only God's pure nature, but also his inability to tolerate any darkness in those who come into his presence. This truth then serves as the basis of discussion in what follows. It raises the question of how one who is not capable of absolute moral purity may yet commune with the One who is absolutely morally pure, absolutely holy (Pentecost, 21–22). Because of God's absolutely moral purity, those who would have fellowship with him must likewise be morally pure. As Westcott says, "It follows that all that is in darkness, all that is darkness, is excluded from fellowship with God by his very nature" (Westcott, 17). To answer this, John points to God's work and our attitude.

Burge (65) wrongly connects *in him* in verse 5 with Jesus rather than with God the Father. The weakness of his interpretation is evident in his own question, "Why has John not gone on here to urge that Jesus is the light?" (Burge, 66). Though he correctly notes John's depiction of Jesus as the light in his Gospel, it need not follow that he must use the same image in the same way. In the Gospel, the light-darkness motif involves Jesus' role as revealer of the Father and giver of life. Here it is connected to the moral nature of God, and thus the same image communicates a different concept. Therefore, it is best to see the antecedent of *in him* as *God* in the previous

---

25. Wis 5:6–7, NRSV.

26. Darkness as a metaphor is almost solely Johannine (Painter, 126). He uses it eight times in his Gospel (John 1:5 [x2]; 6:17; 8:12; 12:35 [x2], 46; and 20:1). It occurs six times in this epistle (here and 2:8, 9, and 11 [x3]). The non-Johannine occurrences of darkness in its metaphoric sense are Matt 4:16 (quoting Isa 42:7); 10:27 (Jesus with the sense of "in secrecy"); and Luke 11:34–36 (Jesus describing the condition of the soul).

clause as well as in the immediately following context. This is made evident, not by the light-darkness imagery, but by the role Jesus his *Son* plays in enabling God's children to walk in his light in the verses that follow.

In this first movement of his epistle, John addresses the issue of how sinful people can have fellowship with a holy God. He focuses his readers' attention on their need to confess their sins and God's promise to cleanse them and thereby enable them to commune with him on his terms. An absolutely pure God cannot commune with anyone who is not absolutely pure. However, mankind by nature, being fallen, is not and cannot become perfectly pure apart from a work of God on its behalf. This truth is communicated by John in this following section. He accomplishes this by addressing both false claims and the proper response. He alerts us to the problem we face as sinful people trying to commune with a holy God, and focuses our attention on its solution by means of a chiasm, beginning with verse 6.

Biblical Theology Comments

John's doctrine of God, revealed throughout his writings, reflects that of the rest of the New Testament, but additionally gives us insights into God's character and nature.[27] Here John's emphasis is on the holiness of God.[28] His use of the imagery of light, rather than stating openly that God is holy, introduces his light-darkness contrast (theme) and draws one's attention to the ethical aspect of God's holiness rather than the ontological.[29]

---

27. For example, in John 1:18 we are told that no one has seen God. This truth is repeated in 1 John 4:12 and 20. Jesus told the woman at the well that God is Spirit (John 4:24). However, John revealed further that the invisible God has revealed himself in His Son (R. Reymond, *John, Beloved Disciple*, 121). This same truth is taught by Paul (Col 1:15; 1 Tim 1:17; 6:16) and the author of Hebrews (Heb 11:27). With regard to Jesus' words to the woman at the well, W. R. Cook (*The Theology of John*, 40) notes that the anarthrous noun πνεῦμα expresses God's nature rather than indicating that He is "a" spirit. Paul confirms this in 2 Cor 3:17.

28. W. R. Cook (*The Theology of John*, 40–41) provides an excellent summary of the views on the meaning of "God is light." These include (1) God is "holy love," (2) God is "self-revealed," (3) "God is redeemer," and (4) "God is holy."

29. W. R. Cook (*The Theology of John*, 41) notes well that "the light that makes fellowship possible must be construed as the absence of sin (light is the absence of darkness...)." Though Stevens (*Johannine Theology*, 5) initially identifies this statement with God's ethical nature, he later (61) interprets it "to define the principle or impulse of self-revelation and self-impartation in God." He argues that "light" in 1 John "is little more than a figurative designation for life" based on the context of

Thus, when John speaks of God the Father as light, he is focusing on his moral purity that forms the basis of his relationship with humankind. No sinful man may enter his presence nor experience fellowship with him.[30] Thus, even for believing Israelites, the sacrificial system of Leviticus was established in order to provide a way of restoring a relationship broken by sin. Those sacrifices did not lessen the demand for daily holiness, as evidenced by God's repeated demand (Lev 11:44, 45; 19:2), "Be holy, for I am holy!"[31] This truth forms the basis of believers' relationships with God and becomes the absolute standard that must be met, and can only be met through the work of Jesus, as clarified in the verses that follow.

Application and Devotional Implications

We often sing of God's holiness and read of it in Scripture, but seldom comprehend the full significance of it in our own lives. It forms the basis of God's relationship with us every moment of our existence, whether we are aware of it or not. Our lack of innate holiness makes it impossible for us to comprehend the extent of God's moral purity. Yet, we must never lose sight of this reality, if for no other reason than that it will drive us to the work of Christ on our behalf. We must realize just how dependent we are on our morally pure God to make us pure enough to relate to him and he with us. How many people think they are praying without ceasing, when in reality they are, as Paul put it, only "speaking into the air" (1 Cor 14:9)? What I mean by that is that though we may mouth many words, God hears nothing when sin bars our words from making a sound in heaven. God demanded holiness from Israel, because he is holy. He demands the same from us.

Additional Exegetical Comments

1:5 The formula Καὶ ἔστιν αὕτη is repeated six times in John's epistles (2:25; 3:23; 5:4, 11, 14; and 2 John 6) with the exception that the word order is καὶ

---

the prologue's emphasis on Jesus as eternal life. His discussion seems better suited to the "God is redeemer" view than "self-revealed."

30. Sinful angels do come into God's presence, as evidenced by Job 1–2 and Rev 12:1–10. Even so, a day is coming when no sinful angel will again be allowed in God's presence. This does not invalidate the point made by John in 1:5, for there he speaks with regard to human relations with God.

31. God further says to them (Lev 20:7–8), "consecrate yourselves therefore, and be holy, for I *am* the LORD your God. And you shall keep My statutes, and perform them: I *am* the LORD who sanctifies you."

αὕτη ἐστὶν, moving "this" to a more emphatic position. In the case of 1:5, ἐστὶν becomes emphatic, with *haute* in a nonemphatic role but serving to identify the following nominative case noun as the predicate nominative within the equative construction.[32] This use of αὕτη (αὕτη) enables ἡ ἀγγελία to be recognized as the predicate nominative while being definite, thereby referring to a particular message.

The presence and placement of the first ἔστιν are emphatic, though not its second and third occurrences. The participle ὅτι may be (1) adverb and translated "because," (2) substantival to αὕτη and translated "that," or (3) substantival to ἀναγγέλλομεν and also translated "that." It is best to see it as substantival to ἀναγγέλλομεν and therefore giving the content of the message that was announced to John's readers.

Selected Bibliography

Achtemeier, E. R. "Jesus Christ, the Light of the World: The Biblical Understanding of Light and Darkness." *Int* 17 (1963): 439–49.

Baylis, C. P. "The Meaning of Walking 'in the Darkness' (1 John 1:6)." *BSac* 149 (1992): 214–22.

Bock, D. L., and G. J. Herrick. *Jesus in Context: Background Readings for Gospel Study.* Grand Rapids: Baker, 2005.

Cook, W. R. *The Theology of John*. Chicago: Moody, 1979.

Hodges, Z. C. "Fellowship and Confession in 1 John 1:5–10." *BSac* 129 (1972): 48–60.

Hunt, S. A. "Light and Darkness." In *Dictionary of the Later New Testament and Its Developments*, edited by R. P. Martin and P. H. Davids. Downers Grove, IL: InterVarsity, 2000.

Merrill, E. H. "The Odes of Solomon and the Acts of Thomas: A Comparative Study." *JETS* 17, no. 4 (1992): 230–33.

Newsom, C. A. "Knowing as Doing: The Social Symbolics of Knowledge at Qumran." *Semeia 59*, edited by D. Jobling and T. Pippin. Atlanta: SBL, 1992.

Patterson, R. D. "Deliverance from Darkness." *SBJT* 8, no. 1 (2004): 70–85.

Reymond, R. L. *John, Beloved Disciple: A Survey of His Theology*. Geanies House, Great Britain: Christian Focus Publications, 2001.

von Harnack, A.,"'Das Wir' in den Johanneischen Schriften." *SPAW* (1923): 96–113.

Wallace, D. B. *Greek Grammar beyond the Basics*. Grand Rapids: Zondervan, 1996.

32. D. B. Wallace, *Grammar*, 40.

Yonge, C. D. *The Works of Philo: Complete and Unabridged.* New updated ed. Peabody, MA: Hendrickson, 1996.
Youngblood, R. "Qoheleth's 'Dark House' (Eccl 12:5)." *JETS* 29, no. 4 (1986): 396–417.

Honesty with God about Sin (1:6–2:4)

Original Text

6 Ἐὰν εἴπωμεν ὅτι κοινωνίαν ἔχομεν μετ' αὐτοῦ καὶ ἐν τῷ σκότει περιπατῶμεν,
ψευδόμεθα καὶ οὐ ποιοῦμεν τὴν ἀλήθειαν· **7** ἐὰν δὲ ἐν τῷ φωτὶ περιπατῶμεν ὡς
αὐτός ἐστιν ἐν τῷ φωτί, κοινωνίαν ἔχομεν μετ' ἀλλήλων καὶ τὸ αἷμα Ἰησοῦ τοῦ
υἱοῦ αὐτοῦ καθαρίζει ἡμᾶς ἀπὸ πάσης ἁμαρτίας. **8** ἐὰν εἴπωμεν ὅτι ἁμαρτίαν οὐκ
ἔχομεν, ἑαυτοὺς πλανῶμεν καὶ ἡ ἀλήθεια οὐκ ἔστιν ἐν ἡμῖν. **9** ἐὰν ὁμολογῶμεν
τὰς ἁμαρτίας ἡμῶν, πιστός ἐστιν καὶ δίκαιος, ἵνα ἀφῇ ἡμῖν τὰς ἁμαρτίας καὶ κα-
θαρίσῃ ἡμᾶς ἀπὸ πάσης ἀδικίας. **10** ἐὰν εἴπωμεν ὅτι οὐχ ἡμαρτήκαμεν, ψεύστην
ποιοῦμεν αὐτὸν καὶ ὁ λόγος αὐτοῦ οὐκ ἔστιν ἐν ἡμῖν.

2:1 Τεκνία μου, ταῦτα γράφω ὑμῖν ἵνα μὴ ἁμάρτητε. καὶ ἐάν τις ἁμάρτῃ, πα-
ράκλητον ἔχομεν πρὸς τὸν πατέρα Ἰησοῦν Χριστὸν δίκαιον· **2** καὶ αὐτὸς ἱλασμός
ἐστιν περὶ τῶν ἁμαρτιῶν ἡμῶν, οὐ περὶ τῶν ἡμετέρων δὲ μόνον ἀλλὰ καὶ περὶ
ὅλου τοῦ κόσμου. **3** Καὶ ἐν τούτῳ γινώσκομεν ὅτι ἐγνώκαμεν αὐτόν, ἐὰν τὰς
ἐντολὰς αὐτοῦ τηρῶμεν. **4** ὁ λέγων ὅτι Ἔγνωκα αὐτὸν καὶ τὰς ἐντολὰς αὐτοῦ
μὴ τηρῶν, ψεύστης ἐστὶν καὶ ἐν τούτῳ ἡ ἀλήθεια οὐκ ἔστιν·

Translation

6 If we should say that we have fellowship with him and we are walking in
the darkness, we are lying and not doing the truth. **7** But[33] if we are walk-
ing in the light as he himself[34] is in the light, we have fellowship with one
another,[35] and the blood of Jesus his Son cleanses us from every sin. **8** If we

---

33. This reflects the adversative role of δὲ (HCSB, ISV, NAB, NASB95, NCV, NET, NIV84, NKJV, NLT) and the contrast between walking in darkness and light.

34. Though αὐτός *could* function simply as the subject of this clause, in this instance it is functioning as an intensive pronoun with the verb ἐστιν (D. Wallace, *Grammar*, 349).

35. Strecker (29–30) prefers the alternate reading μετ' αὐτοῦ ("with him"), while recognizing the weight of textual evidence favors μετ' ἀλλήλων ("with one another"). He argues that it is stronger grammatically and agrees with John's choice of αὐτός and τοῦ υἱοῦ αὐτοῦ in the surrounding context. However, the textual evidence is far too complete in favor of ἀλλήλων. Also, ἀλλήλων is to be preferred as the more

should say that we do not have sin, we are deceiving ourselves and the truth
is not in us. **9** If we confess our sins, he is faithful and just to forgive our sins
and to cleanse us from every unrighteousness. **10** If we should say we have
not sinned, we make him a liar and his word is not influencing us.

2:1 My little children, I am writing these things to you in order that you
may not sin. However,[36] if anyone does sin, we have an Advocate[37] in the
presence[38] of the Father, Jesus Christ, the Righteous One.[39] **2** And he him-
self[40] is the atonement[41] for our sins, and not for ours only, but also for *the
sins*[42] of the whole world. **3** And by means of this[43] we know that we have

---

difficult reading, since it would be more expected that copyists would smooth a reading rather than make it more grammatically difficult.

36. "However" reflects the contrastive conj. role of καὶ in this sentence (D. B. Wallace, *Grammar*, 671). This translation sees the relationship of the following conditional clause with the preceding purpose clause, and thereby serving in the context as a transition into the following discussion on obedience as evidence of fellowship with God (knowing him relationally).

37. The term "Advocate" (ESV, HCSB, ISV, NAB, NASB, NET, NLT, NKJV) is chosen over the transliterated "Paraclete" since this communicates more clearly Jesus' activity as well as role in our defense before God the Father. Other translations use "one who speaks to the Father" (NIV84) and "helper" (NCV).

38. John's use of πρὸς τὸν πατέρα is translated here as "in the presence of the Father" in order to communicate the special/relational sense of πρὸς as used in this context. This again is a similar use as in the prologue of the Gospel (John 1:1) as well as the prologue of this epistle (1:2).

39. Literally "the righteous" (ESV, NAB, NASB95, NKJV) as expressed through the anarthrous δίκαιον, defining further "Jesus Christ." The choice of adding "One" to the descriptive title is to recognize John's emphasis on Jesus' moral character as well as His role and title (HCSB, NIV84). He is "the One who is righteous" (ISV). NLT translates it as "the one who is truly righteous" and NCV as "the One who does what is right."

40. The inclusion of the reflexive idea for αὐτὸς is reflected by HCSB, NASB95, NET, NKJV, NLT; but not ASV, ESV, NIV84.

41. See commentary for decision to translate "atonement" as opposed to "propitiation" (ESV, HCSB, NASB95, NKJV), "expiation" (NAB, RSV, NEB), "atoning sacrifice" (ISV, NIV84), or "sacrifice that atones" (NLT).

42. The words "the sins" are not contained in the original text but are implied in the Greek construction and so are included but italicized in this translation.

43. The more cumbersome "by means of" was chosen to ensure the role of ἐν τούτῳ as a dative of means be communicated. Other translations use "by this" (ESV, NASB95, NET, NKJV) or by omitting ἐν τούτῳ altogether (NCV, NIV84, NLT). Other renderings include "this is how" (HCSB, ISV) and "the way we may be sure" (NAB).

come to know him, if we keep his commandments. **4** He who says, "I have come to know him," and does not keep his commandments, is a liar and the truth is not *abiding*[44] in him.

Commentary

The verses following the declaration of God's moral nature contain three contrasts between what one says and does. Each contrast is followed by a result.

1:6 John begins this section with the first of three false claims that any person may make. This first verse, forming the "A" portion of the chiasm, is composed of the false claim, the actual practice, and the reality that results regardless of the person's perception. This first protasis* has two parts: a claim and a practice.

Beginning with this verse, the Johannine ethic of love is introduced through the theme of fellowship, shared with God and with fellow believers. Strecker (28) says well, "The communion that unites persons with God and that is presupposed as fundamental for all Christians implies an ethical obligation: it must lead to *κοινωνία* with one another."

Ἐὰν εἴπωμεν ὅτι κοινωνίαν ἔχομεν μετ' αὐτοῦ, "If we should say that we have fellowship with him." John begins with a third-class conditional clause (Ἐὰν εἴπωμεν), which will be followed by two more (vv. 8, 10), asserting that the protasis may or may not be true. These conditional statements may be viewed in one of three ways. (1) It may be considered "exceptional" and "introduces something which under certain circumstances and from a given standpoint in the present is expected to occur" (Haas, de Jonge, and Swellengrebel, 25). Yet, John is not saying he expects his readers to make this claim while walking in darkness. Additionally, it does not indicate that he expects it of his opponents only. It is only something possible of both groups. For if he expected it of his opponents only, it would seem he would follow the pattern of reassuring his readers. Though in a sense 2:1–2 serves in part to reassure, its place in the structure of this section indicates it serves

44. "Abiding" (μένω) is not contained in the Greek text but is implied in the context and later used in the epistle as well as the Gospel (John 15). Most translations leave "abiding" out and render it simply "in him" (ESV, NCV, NET, NIV84, NKJV). NLT renders it as "that person ... is not living in the truth," which reverses the thrust of the text.

a different role, as will be explained below. (2) John may be developing a hypothetical situation rather than indicating this is something he would expect his readers to say (Williamson, 67). This would again imply it is something true of his opponents but not himself. This solves a possible problem of John calling God a liar and so would necessitate the "we" be authorial or also hypothetical. Yet, John uses the same third-class conditional construction in verse 9, only with ὁμολογῶμεν replacing εἴπωμεν. To be consistent one must also make this hypothetical, which would rob it of its power and belie the point being made. (3) This should be viewed simply as simple conditional clauses that may or may not be true of John and his readers. This third option seems best and would fit the pastoral aspect of his purpose in writing as opposed to a polemical purpose for this segment of the epistle.

This first false claim is not just the claims of false teachers, often described as secessionists, opponents, or revisionists (Brown, 197; Burge, 68; Hodges, 59). John includes himself and his readers in this third-class conditional sentence (Strecker, 28–29; Westcott, 19).[45] By his use of ἐὰν in the protasis of this conditional sentence, he is not saying that every believer does or will make this claim. Rather, it is possible for one to make the claim, including John the apostle.[46] That he intends to include himself is evident in that elsewhere he will use a third person designation to describe those with whom he does not identify. For example, in 1 John 2:4, when stating a principle, he says "he who says" rather than "if *we* say." Thus John introduces us to a claim that may be made by any believer as well as unbelievers or false teachers.

Some scholars take this use of "we" as an authorial "we" and see John quoting his opponents but not really including himself. This is argued based on its connection conceptually to the three impersonal singular pronouns

45. Painter (173) sees this implying "that the lies are within the community, perhaps even among its leaders." He will locate the second set of "claims" (2:4, 6, 9) outside the community similarly because of the nominative masc. sg. participle construction there.

46. Painter (173) does not see this conditional clause in this instance indicating uncertainty, since the apodosis is always true if the protasis is true. Thus it carries more a sense of "when we say" than "if we should say." Though it is true that the apodosis is true whenever the protasis is found true, it would seem better to allow the possibility that some believers would never affirm these things; thus the "if" element should be maintained.

("he who" statements) that follow in 2:4–6 (Williamson, 67).[47] A second approach is to see this "we" having an "inclusive force" and including John with his readers (Haas, de Jonge, and Swellengrebel, 25, Painter, 173). In this case "we" means "someone."[48] This second view is better since John is careful in his selection of person in verbs and pronouns, and those distinctions must never be overlooked. If he did not wish to include himself, he could easily have used something other than a first person plural designation, as he does elsewhere in the epistle. His use of "we" here includes his readers with John as those who could make such a claim, with the false teachers included as well. At this point is would be better to see him not necessarily including the other eyewitnesses from the previous verses, though they could just as easily be included without changing the force of the assertions.

This ὅτι, along with those following, introduces indirect discourse (Brown, 197) rather than direct discourse. Painter (143) disagrees with Brown and argues, "While *hoti* is also used to introduce indirect discourse, to do so the verb would need to be in the third person. Here it is in the first person in the first four claims." However, Brown (197) correctly points to the third antecedent, who is God, to understand this ὅτι construction.

The first half of the false claim is one of fellowship. This is John's third use of κοινωνία in the epistle and continues the thought introduced in the previous verses. He wants his readers to share in fellowship with God that he and the other eyewitnesses have. However, experiencing that fellowship is contingent, not only for the readers, but for the apostle as well.[49] John says this claimed fellowship is with God, and in this case, God the Father. When he says "with him" he is referring to God the Father in that αὐτοῦ has God as its near referent in verse 5.

καὶ ἐν τῷ σκότει περιπατῶμεν, "and we are walking in the darkness." This second part of the condition accompanies the claim in the protasis. It is the reality that determines the validity of the claim, or its lack thereof.

47. J. Houlden, "Salvation Proclaimed II. 1 John 1.5–2.6," 132.

48. J. Bogart, *Orthodox and Heretical Perfectionism in the Johannine Community,* 28.

49. This is reflective of Jesus' instructions to the apostles in the upper room (John 15:1–6) that they must abide in him in order to be fruitful. Addressing the Eleven, clearly regenerate saints (John 17:6, 12), Jesus indicates that both abiding and fruitfulness were contingent experiences that they themselves could miss apart from obedience. Thus it would be wrong to see the apostle failing to include himself in this statement.

This darkness is the opposite of God's moral nature and realm of existence. John's inclusion of the article with "darkness" identifies this with the darkness of verse 5, which is the opposite of God's moral nature. Thus is it not just darkness, but that very darkness that is completely absent from God.

John's use of "walk" here denotes how a believer conducts his or her lifestyle (Haas, de Jonge, and Swellengrebel, 25).[50] John's use of the imagery reflects Jesus' use of the same in his teaching. Jesus intertwines the light-darkness motif with the conceptual use of "walk." Examples include John 8:12 and John 11:9–10 (using the literal sense of "walk" and "darkness" to illustrate spiritual truth). The light-darkness concept is further developed by Jesus in John 3:19–21 and 9:4–5. Similar terminology connecting light and darkness with "walking" is found in the Qumran literature (1Qs III, 20–21; 1Qs IV, 11). [51]

This is a common use of the term throughout the New Testament.[52] Furthermore, just as light and darkness are common elements of Jewish imagery, "walking," as it is used to denote lifestyle, also reflects the Semitic background of its author (Brown, 233).[53] He is affirming that he and his readers could carry on a lifestyle different from God's morally pure existence. His life could be characterized by sin. Also, this use of the pres. tense implies that the claim is being made while the conduct is occurring (Williamson, 67). So the claim is made while someone is in actuality operating in the realm of darkness. He or she is in the process of failing to be morally pure. The nature of the sinful conduct that John has in mind here will be clarified later in the epistle.[54] However, at this point, the principle of the possibility of moral impurity in the life of a believer is affirmed. Later in this chiasm, John will change that theoretical possibility into an actuality by affirming that no one can claim sinless perfection at any point in time.

---

50. BDAG, 803; H. Seesemann, " πατέω, ... περιπατέω," *TDNT* 5:941.

51. G. K. Beale and D. A. Carson, *Commentary on the New Testament Use of the Old Testament*, 476.

52. Περιπατέω occurs ninety-two times in the NT, with seventeen occurences in John's Gospel and ten in his epistles, Though it most often referred to literal walking, it was used by Jesus with the conceptual sense of conducting one's life in John 8:12.

53. Rom 8:1; 2 Cor 5:7; Gal 5:16; Eph 2:2; Col 1:10; 1 Pet 4:3; Jude 16 are just a sampling of its use.

54. This will be seen in passages such as 2:9–11 (hating one's brother), 2:15–17 (loving the world), and 3:17–18 (failure to help a brother in need).

ψευδόμεθα καὶ οὐ ποιοῦμεν τὴν ἀλήθειαν, "we are lying and not doing the truth." John uses the first person plural form of the pres. tense verbs and thereby includes himself. If John had intended to quote or describe his opponents, it would have been more appropriate to use third-person verbs as opposed to first-person (Strecker, 29). Thus John is affirming that it is possible for him to lie. It is possible for his life not to be characterized by truth. Westcott sees this as a conscious and deliberate lie (Westcott, 19). However, that is not required by the grammar or context. Addtionally, the following two false claims with the subsequent results (he tells a lie and calls God a liar) would tend to favor self-deception more than conscious deception on the part of the claimant.

Though the verb ποιοῦμεν is translated by some as "to practice" and sees it denoting conduct over a period of time, it seems best to translate it as "to do." It reflects the Hebrew concept of lifestyle. The same concept can be found in the Old Testament, expressed in terms of doing what "is good and right and true" (2 Chr 31:20), and its opposite, doing wickedly (Neh 9:33). Doing the truth indicates that one is acting "consistently with the truth." Walking in darkness, on the other hand, is conduct that is "contrary to the truth about God, especially the truth about his holiness" (Hodges, 60). Painter relates this to his theory of Johannine opponents whose failure was "not a matter of inconsistency" but "at the heart of the conflict" between them and John in terms of their "understanding of God, of Jesus, and of the life of the believer in relation to them," ultimately expressed in terms of their love ethic (Painter, 144–45).

Some take this to mean that the one making such a claim is unregenerate (Akin, 62; Marshall, 111). They identify the claim with the false teachers, secessionists, rather than with John (Kistemaker, 210–11). Also, for them, not doing truth means the claimant is unsaved. Rather, practicing or doing truth is not a reference to one's salvation, but to one's character (King, 17). The person who does not live out the truth is living a lie. Why? God cannot and will not compromise his moral purity to accommodate a sinful person. There is no shadow in him, and he does not welcome shadows into his presence.

The idea of "doing truth" is unique to John among the New Testament writers. Though the verb ποιέω is commonly used throughout the New Testament with a wide range of meanings, when John uses it conceptually he describes a quality of conduct. For example, he uses the same term with δικαιοσύνη to describe righteous conduct. In both cases what the person does is consistent with either truth or righteousness. So, here in his epistle, doing truth means acting out truth's demands and implications by what one says and does about sin. This same thought is evident in his second epistle when he rejoices that the "Elect Lady's" children are "walking in the truth," which involves "doing" those things connected with truth as a normal part of daily living. The particular content of that truth that is being "done" is never fully fleshed out by him.

The Johannine concept of truth is understood in three different ways among students of his writings. (1) Truth may refer to something one believes or seeks. This can be seen in the response of people to Jesus in the Gospel. (2) Truth is something known and acted on (Brown, 199; Marshall, 111; Smalley, 22). It "conforms to a standard, namely, the standard of God's will" (Haas, de Jonge, and Swellengrebel, 26). This would be the nature of truth presented here. (3) In his second epistle, and by the implications of what follows in this epistle, doing truth includes loving other Christians (Smalley, 320).

This lie may be a conscious lie or self-deception (Akin, 62). Based on what is said here and following, it is best to see this as self-deception. The person is not consciously lying, but his assertion is still just as false. Though this person thinks he can have fellowship with God, as Pentecost rightly observes, "God cannot fellowship with one who is redeemed unless that person is walking in holiness" (Pentecost, 21). Westcott describes the condition of the self-deceived believer as well: "The darkness ... is the absolute opposite of 'the light.' To choose this as our sphere of movement is necessarily to shun fellowship with God" (Westcott, 19). Even today this truth is not understood by many Christians. The problem of God having fellowship with sinful people is that he would then be operating in the sphere of darkness, which violates his character and being. He would thereby be involving himself in our sin (Pentecost, 24). "To be children of the light and to continue to walk in darkness is, therefore, truly a lie because the behavior does not match the reality (and *alētheia* is both 'truth' and 'reality')" (Brown, 236).

1:7 In this conditional sentence, John moves from the condition of walking in the light to its impact in the life of the believer: fellowship and cleansing. John begins this first key statement about fellowship with God with a conditional clause, introduced by "if." As a third-class conditional clause, John is affirming that the *if* clause (the protasis) may or may not be true. However, if it is true, then the *then* clause (apodosis*) that follows will similarly be true. When the *if* clause proves false, then the *then* will similarly be false. This "if" is a claim to be "walking in the light," to be conducting one's life within the sphere of God's moral purity.

ἐὰν δὲ ἐν τῷ φωτὶ περιπατῶμεν, "However, if we are walking in the light." John's use of "we" means that he is included among those who may or may not walk in the light.[55] Because he included himself among those who may claim to walk in the light, the "then" clauses cannot refer to the absence of union (Test of Life view), but must refer to an absence of fellowship.

John is likely alluding to the Old Testament imagery of walking in light from such places as the Psalms and Isa 2:5 ("O house of Jacob, come and let us walk in the light of the LORD").[56] Jesus used this same imagery in John 8:12, saying, "I am the light of the world. He who follows Me shall not walk in darkness, but have the light of life." This same concept was evident in the first-century milieu, reflected in the Essenes' view that walking in light proved one was a "son of righteousness."[57]

John's use of the pres. tense (gnomic) indicates that he describes a present experience, a lifestyle issue. Since "walking" is in the subjunctive mood, John is not making a statement about time. Though a pres. tense verb, it need not be rendered as a pres. progressive with the sense of "if we are in the process of walking in the light." Rather, a more gnomic nuance makes better sense with the continuous aspect in view. In this way John is emphasizing life conduct, lifestyle, over a temporal momentary experience. Even so, it does follow that the apodosis occurs at the time of the "walking."

The light referred to in this verse is that same light that characterizes God's nature and the sphere in which he lives and interacts with us. It is moral purity. By this John does not mean that one walks in sinless

---

55. As noted earlier, though this use of "we" may be interpreted as an authorial "we" or used hypothetically as a rhetorical device, the pattern of John's use of pronouns and verbal subjects indicates he intends that his readers take it literally and include him with them in the possibility of the experience.

56. Examples would include Pss 56:13 ("For You have delivered my soul from death. *Have You* not *kept* my feet from falling, that I may walk before God in the light of the living?") and 89:15 ("Blessed *are* the people who know the joyful sound! They walk, O LORD, in the light of Your countenance").

57. 1QS III, 20.

perfection, but in the sphere of sinlessness that God indwells, so that one is able to share fellowship with God in his presence (Hodges, 60–61). By John's use of "we" to include himself and his readers, and because he clarifies in passages such as 2:12–14 that they are believers, this should not be seen as a question of justification, but sanctification (Westcott, 21). Walking in the light is not describing the possession of spiritual life, but the conduct of life within a sphere of existence. That sphere is moral purity, not spiritual life as opposed to spiritual death. Granted, one must be spiritually alive to walk in the realm of light. However, Paul makes clear that a regenerate child of God who has been transferred from Satan's power into Christ's kingdom (Col 1:13) and delivered from the power of sin may still be a slave of sin (Rom 6:12–14) rather than righteousness based on choices he makes. This is the sense being communicated by John in this passage. Even John can step out of fellowship with God if he fails to walk in God's moral sphere.

ὡς αὐτός ἐστιν ἐν τῷ φωτί, "as he himself is in the light." John's use of ὡς, a comparative conjunction, to complete the protasis draws a comparison between the believer and God.[58] This use of ὡς focuses attention on the character of God and calls for action (walking) from that perspective.[59] The kind of life conduct being described by "walk" is the same kind as God's. "Walking in the light" means being in the light. One cannot walk in it without being in it. So as God is both characterized by and exists in "the light" of moral purity, we also exist and operate in that same "light" at that point in time when we are conducting our lives in moral purity. When we are sinning or living with unconfessed sins, we are operating in the darkness and are subsequently unable to fellowship with God. It is when we then confess our known sins (see discussion on 1:9) that we are able to return to and conduct our lives within the sphere of God's moral purity once again. The spheres of light and darkness are realms related to God's presence. An unbeliever can function only within the sphere of darkness because he or she is excluded from God's presence, being spiritually dead. A believer, on the other hand, may be in or out of fellowship with God, and so functioning in either of the spheres. The spheres of light and darkness are not equivalent

58. G. Schneider, "ὡς," *Exegetical Dictionary of the New Testament,* 3:509; D. B. Wallace, *Grammar*, 675.
59. BDAG, 1104.

to "regenerate" and "unregenerate," or spiritually "alive" or "dead." Rather, they are equivalent to holy or unholy, righteous or unrighteous.

John's use of αὐτός along with ἐστιν to refer to God in this clause is emphatic; thus the translation "he himself." We are pointed back to God as the Christian's model as well as goal. When combined with the affirmation of verse 5, we see a similar pattern as John's declaration of Jesus' deity in the prologue of his Gospel. The Word is both God and with God (John 1:1–2), thereby affirming Jesus' deity along with his personhood distinct from God the Father. Combined with verse 5, these two statements affirm God's moral nature as well as his separateness from others who share in that nature. Moral purity is not God. We do not become divine the instant we are morally pure. We do not become one with the divine essence when we are morally pure. We only come into his presence and share fellowship with him. We only do that by conducting our lives in accordance with his moral purity.

κοινωνίαν ἔχομεν μετ' ἀλλήλων, "we have fellowship with one another." The first benefit of walking in the light is fellowship with God. Since light refers to God's moral nature, to walk in the light is to walk in the realm of his holiness, his moral purity. This is where fellowship occurs. However, with whom is this fellowship? John's choice of the reciprocal pronoun ἀλλήλων appears to be purposefully unclear whether he is referring to fellowship with God or with other believers.[60] Primarily, though, its emphasis is on the mutuality of the relationship. This fellowship is two directional rather than one directional. Both parties involved are experiencing it and contributing to it. John may intend one of three possible senses. (1) By "one another" he may intend to include both God the Father and God the Son (Akin, 62; Hodges, 61, Pentecost, 24). (2) It may refer to fellowship between believers. Haas, de Jonge, and Swellengrebel argue for this on the basis that where "God" would be expected from the flow of thought, based on his view of the epistle as polemical and John quoting his opponents, he is alluding to "fellowship with men" (Haas, de Jonge, and Swellengrebel, 27). (3) It is likely that he intends to refer to both by use of a double entendre.[61] This fel-

60. BDAG, 46; H. Krämer, "ἀλλήλων" in *Exegetical Dictionary of the New Testament*, 1:63.

61. D. Wead ("The Johannine Double Meaning," 106–20) has written a helpful article on John's use of the double entendre throughout his literature. Wead has

lowship is with both God and other believers (Bruce, 43; Marshall, 111–12; Westcott, 12). Because of the singular "him" before this, John is clearly referring to God the Father and not including Jesus at this point. Though by this he is not denying that the Christian does have fellowship with Jesus, in this instance the focus is on the Christian's relationship with God the Father. This is further evident in that Jesus' role in this verse, and later in 2:1–2 as our Paraclete, is that of enabling us to commune with the Father.

Fellowship with God depends on our walking in the light—his moral purity—as God lives only in moral purity. Similarly, mutual fellowship among believers, members of God's family, cannot occur apart from lives characterized by God's moral purity as well. Fellowship requires sharing in something. In this case it is sharing in moral purity.

The pres. tense, "we have," either carries a gnomic sense, describing a general state of being, or an ongoing condition as a customary present. Just as the conduct of life is in the light, so too is the experience of the resulting fellowship. In this case, both senses say essentially the same thing. Still, the use of the pres. here is significant. John points the reader to the moment-by-moment reality of fellowship and links it temporally to the action of conducting one's life (walking) in moral purity (in the light).

καὶ τὸ αἷμα Ἰησοῦ τοῦ υἱοῦ αὐτοῦ καθαρίζει ἡμᾶς ἀπὸ πάσης ἁμαρτίας, "and the blood of Jesus his Son cleanses us from every sin." As the first clause, connected to this one by *καί*, expressed the result of walking in the light, this second clause notes a second result. The believer who conducts his life in the sphere of God's moral purity ("the light") experiences the benefits of Jesus' cleansing work on the cross. By the use of metonymy*, in which "blood" is substituted for crucifixion and the giving of one's life, John makes clear that the benefits of Jesus' work on the cross are a necessary element in our fellowship with God.[62]

A prerequisite to having fellowship is experiencing cleansing. John's use of *καθαρίζει* may allude back to the upper room, though the concept was common enough that it may just be a natural figure of speech to use. In the

---

identified five approaches to communicating dual ideas within a passage, beginning with a normal double entendre within the Greek word itself. Additionally John might utilize the double sense created by the Greek word and its Hebrew equivalent, the Aramaic word translated by a Greek word, a parabolic saying that conveys a double sense, and verb forms such as the 2 pl. (may be either indic. or impv.).

62. E. W. Bullinger, *Figures of Speech Used in the Bible*, 609.

upper room, Jesus uses this same term in John 13:10 to describe the eleven disciples as "clean" in contrast to Judas, who was about to depart their number and betray Jesus. Again, in John 15:2–3 he states that the fruitful branches are "cleansed" by the vinedresser, God the Father, and that the Eleven had already been "cleansed" because they were fruitful branches.

Though καθαρίζω has the literal sense of being cleansed from dirt or filth, it was commonly used figuratively. In the LXX the noun form is often used for both ceremonial and ethical cleanness.[63] Throughout the New Testament it carries a similar sense. Though it can mean the mundane cleaning of dishes (Matt 23:25), it is usually used to refer to spiritual or ceremonial cleansing. For example lepers are cleansed (Matt 8:2; 10:8; Luke 4:27; 17:14, 17) by the removal of their leprosy. The human heart may be cleansed by faith (Acts 15:9), and a person may be pure, "clean," in heart (Matt 5:8). Using this same term, the author of Hebrews affirms the necessity of the shedding of blood for spiritual/ceremonial cleansing from sin to occur before declaring that heaven itself was cleansed of the stain of man's sin by the blood of Christ (Heb 9:22–23). This same concept is evident in John's Gospel (John 3:25; 13:10; 15:2–3). So, here John is using familiar terminology to describe the spiritual and ceremonial cleansing that had been accomplished through the Old Testament sacrificial system, a sanctifying cleansing that restored fellowship with God. Now in the New Testament economy that same fellowship is restored on the basis of Jesus' sacrificial death, his shed blood.

John's use of the present tense "cleanses" describes a principle of life (gnomic sense) and an active process (Haas, de Jonge, and Swellengrebel, 28; Williamson, 69). He is not referring to Christ's work in our justification, but his daily, moment-by-moment ministry in our sanctification. It is a work of God the Father in the life of the believer through his Son (Williamson, 70).

The apostle John's mention of "every sin" refers to sinful deeds rather than the sin nature or original sin. Later, John will define sin, but here he indicates both the presence of sin in the life of the believer as well as each person's responsibility for sins committed (Haas, de Jonge, and Swellengrebel, 28).

63. F. Hauck, "καθαρός, καθαρίζω," *TDNT* 3:414.

Having revealed Jesus' role in the believer's being enabled to commune with God by being made morally pure, John then turns to the believer's role in the process. The Christian can either hinder or help the process, depending on his or her honesty with both God and self about sin.

1:8 John expresses first the false claim and then its cause in the life of the believer. Using another third class conditional sentence, John presents another danger that could hinder fellowship with God. Having declared God's moral purity and the danger of a Christian being able to live outside of that purity, John now posits the first error a believer *might* make. A believer might deny the presence, and therefore guilt, of sin in his or her life.

ἐὰν εἴπωμεν ὅτι ἁμαρτίαν οὐκ ἔχομεν, "If we should say that we do not have sin." This third-class conditional sentence with a first person plural verb again serves to identify John with those capable of expressing this attitude toward sin. The protasis may or may not be true.

The anarthrous noun ἁμαρτίαν is a qualitative rather than indefinite noun because the verb, "to have," when followed by an abstract noun such as ἁμαρτία, indicates a "general quality" (Burge, 81). Thus John is looking at sin as a principle rather than a specific act. Uniquely Johannine, the other three occurrences of these words are spoken by Jesus to describe the Jewish leadership's guilt following its denial of blindness (John 9:41), the world's guilt following his advent (John 15:22, 24), and the Jewish leadership's greater guilt than Pilate's for Jesus' crucifixion (John 19:11). Thus the sense given by Jesus is guilt and accountability for wrongdoing, and so this supports the concept of sinfulness and guilt rather than any specific sinful act (Haas, de Jonge, and Swellengrebel, 29; Williamson, 72).[64] Though it

---

64. Haas, de Jonge, and Swellengrebel (29) concur with Burge (81), who argues that this pattern can be seen in similar constructions in 1 John with conceptual nouns such as "fellowship" (1:3, 6), "life" (3:15; 5:12), "love" (4:16), "joy" (3 John 4), and "confidence" (2:28; 3:21; 4:17; 5:14). He says that when the verb ἔχω occurs with these conceptual nouns that it "then refers to inner possession, and shows a person to be in a certain condition, or to have a certain emotion, which influences him continually." But he errs when he says that the person described such is therefore "dominated by" that sinful attitude. For again, he ignores the reality that John, too, may become guilty of such a claim and therefore attitude. For this to indicate an attitude of the unregenerate, he must be able to demonstrate that the 1 pl. is purely authorial and in no way includes John or his readers within its conceptual realm.

indicates a sinful "disposition of heart," the present tense need not imply one that "constantly exhibits evil deeds" (contra Burge, 81).

Some see John quoting his opponents, who were claiming a form of sinless perfection (Akin, 74; Bogart; Williamson, 72).[65] For example, Brown calls both this and verse 10 "slogans" of the "secessionists," who had misinterpreted John (Brown, 81–82). Kistemaker (247) takes both verses 8 and 10 to be claims of the unregenerate. Though noting that John is included in this statement, he still says such a claim "means that we are unbelievers who have rejected the gospel of salvation" (Kistemaker, 247). However, by John's use of "we" and his subsequent inclusion of himself in the group who could make such an error as this claim, it seems best to conclude otherwise. He is not quoting the false teachers, or secessionists. He is not saying these are the words of unbelievers. Rather, he is addressing a misunderstanding a believer might have that could lead to a denial of the need for Christ's cleansing work on a daily basis. These two statements are similar to Paul's questions in Rom 6:1 and 15, being used by him to clarify possible misunderstandings of what he had just said about the effects of justification. In the same way, these are not just false doctrines promoted by false teachers, but attitudes John and his readers could express as well. Here ἔχομεν, as a present tense verb retained in indirect discourse, is functioning as an instantaneous present and emphasizes an attitude that could be true of a person at any point in time

Interpreters vary in their understanding of what John means here, and later in verse 10. Some see this as a denial of a sin nature (Brooke, 18; Findlay, 106; Painter, 145; Schnackenburg, 83; Smalley, 28; Smith, "Epistles," 172; Stott, 81–82; Westcott, 22; Yarbrough, 60; contra Hauck, 122).[66] This would seem indicated by the anarthrous noun taking on a more indefinite conceptual sense. It is not "a" specific sin that is denied, but sinfulness in general. Others see it as a denial of guilt (Brown, 205–6; Dodd, 22; Hodges, 73, n. 5; Law, 130). In John 9:41; 15:22–24; and 19:11 this same construction is used in which Jesus combines "sin" and "have" to indicate a state of sinfulness resulting from sin, whether admitted or denied.[67] Thus, this use of

65. J. Bogart, *Orthodox and Heretical Perfectionism*, 47–49.
66. W. R. Cook, "Hamartiological Problems in First John," 252.
67. BDAG, 51; W. Grundmann, "ἁμαρτάνω, ἁμάρτημα, ἁμαρτία," *TDNT* 1:305–308; C. Haas, M. de Jonge, and J. Swellengrebel, 29.

the anarthrous noun "sin," though including denial of a single sin, focuses attention on the guilt aspect that would call for confession and admit to the need of Jesus' cleansing work in the previous verse. This latter meaning would seem the better of the two choices in light of what follows, though the second is implied by the first.

ἑαυτοὺς πλανῶμεν, "we are deceiving ourselves." The result of denying guilt is self-deception. John's use of the reflexive pronoun ἑαυτοὺς places the guilt of deception on the believer denying guilt as well as on deceivers who might teach them to do so. Furthermore, he includes himself in the group that could be self-deceived. So this is not an attack on opponents, but a warning to fellow believers.

John's choice of πλανάω with the reflexive pronoun communicates both the cause and the significance of the error in thought. The verb can have one of two nuances. The first would be that of someone trying to deceive another person. The second is the idea of someone lacking a sense of proper direction, wandering off from the truth.[68] John uses the first sense, but places the guilt of deception on the believer, not the false teachers, by use of the reflexive pronoun. He then reinforces the significance of such a denial with synonymous parallelism in which the following clause is equivalent to the first.

καὶ ἡ ἀλήθεια οὐκ ἔστιν ἐν ἡμῖν, "and the truth is not in us." The conjunction καὶ coordinates the two clauses in this case and makes the two clauses parallel. In other words, the absence of truth is expressed through self-deception. The inclusion of ἔστιν in the final clause is emphatic, indicating the seriousness of the error and the completeness of the self-deception.

When John says literally, "The truth is not in us," he is saying that truth is not influencing the believer who denies guilt. The article with ἀλήθεια indicates either a body of "truth" known to the readers or truth as a concept. "Truth in us" is *not* a different way of saying "regenerate" (contra Strecker, 31).[69] Truth here is not a synonym for the gospel either. Rather, it is an ant-

68. BDAG, 821; H. Braun, "πλανάω," *TDNT* 6:242–49.

69. For example, Burge (82) relates "truth" to God's essential nature and thereby personifies it in Jesus Christ on the basis of John 14:6. He then argues that since "truth describes God himself," anyone lacking it lacks "an essential characteristic of God's presence" and therefore may not be regenerate. The problem with this is that Scripture clearly teaches that believers can and do lie, to others if not themselves (Eph 4:25; Col 3:9; Jas 3:14). Further, John contrasts the "lie" with "the truth" in 1

onym for deception. This idea was already introduced in 1:6, as Painter (145) notes well, "Where not doing the truth means not telling the truth, but lying. If the truth is not in us, we do not tell the truth." In this case, the believer making the false claim is lying to himself or herself.[70] Additionally, there is an implied verb, "abiding," in this clause, missing because of elision. Thus John is saying that the truth is not abiding, in the sense of residing in and influencing, in the believer in the same way Jesus said that God's Word "abides" in the believer who experiences answered prayer (John 15:7). In this case, John is saying that when we are self-deceived, the truth is not shaping "our thoughts and attitudes" (Hodges, 63). Bruce notes that this phrase may be "reminiscent" of Jesus' description of the devil in John 8:44 (Bruce, 44). However, this need not mean such a person is unregenerate. Otherwise John would not have included himself in the group that could be deceived. Rather, the theologically confused believer is missing the truth of God's Word and thereby leading himself astray in his attitude toward sin. Those who have no sin have no need of an Intercessor. Thus a self-deceived believer would not know to confess his or her sins.

1:9 This centerpiece to the chiasm begins with another third-class condition—confession may or may not occur—followed by two things that would be true if confession does occur, but would not be true if confession does not occur. This confession involves admitting to specific sins.

ἐὰν ὁμολογῶμεν τὰς ἁμαρτίας ἡμῶν, "If we confess our sins." John once again uses the first person plural to include himself along with the readers and the other apostles (Pentecost, 30). All believers must acknowledge their sin to God, the meaning of "confess," in order to experience Jesus' cleansing work. The idea behind "confess" is that this is an admission to the truthfulness of something, often of one's guilt before a judge. The popular adage that confession means "saying the same thing" as God says about sin

---

John 2:21, where truth is a body of truth rather than an essential characteristic of God or His presence. Thus, being deceived need not imply being unregenerate.

70. Haas, de Jonge, and Swellengrebel (29) wrongly attribute a durative force to this clause and conclude that the absence of truth "will remain so." This need not be a permanent state. Rather, the point John makes is that while someone claims sinlessness, he or she is self-deceived. To make such a claim need not indicate a permanent state or attitude. Indeed, since John includes himself as able to say such a thing, and since any believer may make such an error, the durative sense is untenable.

is also contained in the basic meaning of this verb, though it implies more than just agreement with God.[71] It indicates here taking responsibility for those sins as well. Thus, instead of denying guilt (1:8) or disagreeing with God about the presence of sin (1:10), or instead of asking for forgiveness in a generic or ceremonial sense (because we were commanded to), the person goes to God and says, "I stand guilty before You because I have sinned and it is my nature to sin as expressed by my willful acts." Those willful acts are then recounted to God. This form of confession is heartfelt and consciously specific.

John changes "if we say" (εἴπωμεν) of verses 8 and 10 to "if we confess" (ὁμολογῶμεν). Positioned between two false claims is an honest admission of guilt. John's choice of this term over repeating "say" indicates his desire to draw a striking contrast between the attitudes. Also, as opposed to the self-serving claims in verses 8 and 10, this term indicates a humble as well as honest assessment by the one confessing.

Is this confession private or public (Strecker, 32)? Since the passage does not indicate public worship is in view, but rather daily living, it seems best to see this confession as personal (contra Brown, 208). In 5:16–17, where John addresses praying for others' sins and the problem of the "sin unto death," private prayer is more in view than public prayer or confession. Nowhere else in the epistle is the question of public worship an issue. Similarly, James' call for confession (Jas 5:16) has the elders who have come to minister to the sick member in view rather than the church as a whole. Thus, here it seems best to see this form of confession as private rather than within the public assembly.

John notes that we must confess, literally, "the sins" (pl.) as opposed to sin in a generic sense.[72] This is not a confession where we say, "I am a sinner." Rather, it is the confession involving naming particular sins (Lenski, 392; Marshall, 113). This construction of the article with the plural "sins" is repeated for emphasis. John's point is that we are to confess known sins.[73] We admit to God that we have transgressed specific commands. Again, this

71. BDAG, 708; O. Michel, "ὁμολογέω," *TDNT* 5:207–12.

72. Strecker (32) does not see any significance to the change from sg. to pl. But he still sees the sins confessed as individual sins that "are the expression of sinful existence."

73. B. Bryant, "Confession of Sins in the Spirit-Filled Life," 57. Contra Lenski (392), who includes unknown sins in this confession as well.

can occur only when someone has an honest assessment and sees himself or herself in the light of God's moral purity. Of note also is the absence of "every" in this condition. Moreover, what follows in the apodosis indicates clearly that we are called to confess known sins, not every sin.[74]

πιστός ἐστιν καὶ δίκαιος, "He is faithful and just." We can confess with certainty of forgiveness because God is faithful to keep his promises. We know this because God is both faithful and just.

Most would see this first statement as a description of God's character. He is just, and his forgiveness does not compromise his justice because Jesus satisfied its requirements on the cross (Akin, 75; Burge, 82–83; Hodges, 65; Painter, 155–56; Schnackenburg, 87; Strecker, 32; Thompson, 47–48; Yarbrough, 64–65). Though this is true, John's focus seems to be more on God's response to us rather than a reference to the theological implications of Jesus' work on the cross. When John affirms that God is both faithful and just, he is likely using a hendiadys*, a figure of speech in which two related words are used to communicate an idea incorporating their combined meanings. Both are true of God. God is faithful. God is just. Thus, what John is affirming with this combination is that God is faithful to be just all the time. His justice is faithfully carried out. This serves as a powerful assurance that God's response to our confession of known sins will occur each time and will always be just. We do not confess to a capricious God or an unpredictable God. We can know exactly how he is going to respond each time we come to him and are honest with him about those sins of which we are aware.

---

74. Hodges (63) notes that "repentance" is not mentioned in this context, or the epistle as a whole. He says of this: "In John's usage, Christian repentance is appropriate when a pattern of sin is persisted in and needs to be changed (see Rev 2:5, 16, 21, 22; 3:3, 19)." He sees this as a believer's response to "discovered" sin as a product of communing with God. This may be an accurate observation, but not one that is especially relevant to this passage. In fact, repentance is implied in this verse in that a person confesses in order to receive forgiveness, which necessarily implies a desire to avoid that sin further. Repentance does normally imply a pattern of sin from which the repentant person wishes to depart. But it is equally appropriate for a single act of sin for which that person desires forgiveness and wishes to avoid in the future. And though one might argue that repentance is not necessary for one's justification, it is necessary in one's sanctification if a sin or a pattern of sin hinders one's walk with God.

ἵνα ἀφῇ ἡμῖν τὰς ἁμαρτίας καὶ καθαρίσῃ ἡμᾶς ἀπὸ πάσης ἀδικίας, "to forgive our sins and to cleanse us from every unrighteousness." The ἵνα clause that follows John's description of God's faithfully just character provides two promises from God to the believer who comes to honestly confess his or her sins. This may be a rare use of the "result clause" introduced by ἵνα, but is more likely a "purpose-result" clause, indicating that both are intended and accomplished by God.[75] This would seem to fit the Jewish (Semitic) concept of God's sovereign intent being accomplished such that John may not have drawn "a sharp dividing-line between purpose and consequences."[76]

John again includes himself as one of the recipients of God's faithfully just treatment by the inclusion of ἡμῖν. This is a truth on which John the apostle himself is dependent for walking in the light and having fellowship with God.

When we speak honestly to God about our sins through confession, the first thing we receive from him is forgiveness. The term John uses here (ἀφίημι) has a range of meanings that go from dismissing someone from one's presence, to causing someone to separate from another, distancing oneself from another, to releasing someone from a moral obligation or debt.[77] It is this final sense John intends here. God pardons us by releasing us from that debt (Burge, 83). This same term is used by Jesus when he taught the disciples to pray, "Forgive me of my debts as I have forgiven my debtors" (Matt 6:12). Even so, that release does not set aside God's just character in that Jesus' death (His "blood" in v. 7) is the basis of that release. We are forgiven because Jesus took our guilt upon himself and paid the full price for its punishment. It is on the basis of his completed work on the cross that a believer experiences not only the positional forgiveness (justification reality), but also daily forgiveness (sanctification reality), which is John's focus here.

God's response is twofold. First, he forgives the sins confessed. The aorist tense "forgive" points to the completeness of God's act with regard to the sins confessed and indicates that his response is in regard to specific acts (Haas, de Jonge, and Swellengrebel, 31). John's repetition of "the sins" (τὰς ἁμαρτίας) indicates that the promised forgiveness from God includes

75. F. Blass sees this ἵνα being substituted for infinitives of result (BDF §391 [5]) while D. B. Wallace (*Grammar*, 473) sees it combining both purpose and result.
76. C. F. D. Moule, *An Idiom-book of New Testament Greek*, 142.
77. BDAG, 157; R. Bultmann, "ἀφίημι," *TDNT* 1:511–12.

all sins confessed. This first promise covers only those confessed. This is equivalent to the role of the guilt offering in the Old Testament sacrificial system. The repentant sinner confessed his guilt and offered a sacrifice, following restitution, in order to renew fellowship with God. In the same way, when we come to God and admit to our guilt for specific sins, he promises to forgive them. We know they are forgiven on the basis of Jesus' shed blood in verse 7.

Second, God cleanses us, makes us morally pure. John uses καθαρίζω for the second time to describe the cleansing we receive (see comments on 1:7). By this repetition he connects the two statements together. The cleansing God gives the confessor is accomplished through cleansing by Jesus' blood, his death on the cross on our behalf.

1:10 This conditional sentence contains a protasis with a compound apodosis. It stands as a second denial, parallel to the first denial in the chiasm. Through it John describes once more the wrong attitude about sin any believer, including him, might have while claiming to have fellowship with God.

ἐὰν εἴπωμεν ὅτι οὐχ ἡμαρτήκαμεν, "If we should say we have not sinned." Once again John recounts an attitude toward sin that any believer, including him, could fall into and thereby do harm to their fellowship with God (see comments in 1:6).

One may admit to having sinned in the past or to having a sin nature, but still deny any need to confess sin in the present. John changes the present tense verb of verse 8 to a perfect tense here, indicating a denial that there is a sin in the past whose guilt must be dealt with in the present.[78] Some see this verse as a denial of a sin nature, rather than seeing verse 8 as a denial of sin nature (Bruce, 45). Others see this as a claim to sinlessness, the eradication of the sin nature (Akin, 74; Westcott, 26). This would be a claim that one has ceased sinning, at least for a season. Still others see it as a denial that there is any sin causing guilt before God (Haas, de Jonge, and Swellengrebel, 32; Hodges, 74, n. 8; Williamson, 74). In this way it is parallel to the denial

---

78. B. M. Fanning (*Verbal Aspect in New Testament Greek*, 297) sees this use of the pf., placing "emphasis on the *completion* (or actual occurrence) of the action, with any result of the occurrence referred to only secondarily." Thus he sees it functioning more like an aor. It is a denial of a past sin more than a denial of guilt. Thus if nothing has happened in the past, there is no need for confession in the present.

of verse 8, and in a sense intensifies that denial.[79] It is then the claim that might be made by one who admits to a sin nature, but sees it as no longer affecting him or her. This person claims that there remains no sin that needs forgiving. he or she has nothing to confess. Forgiveness and cleansing are complete and now uninterrupted. However, that is not what God says.

ψεύστην ποιοῦμεν αὐτὸν, "we make him a liar." What John affirms first and foremost, is that if he were to make such an assertion, he would be calling God a liar. Whereas the denial of verse 8 means we are self-deceived, here the parallel effect of such a denial is to say God, who cannot be deceived, has been intentionally dishonest about our spiritual condition. John's use of *ποιέω* does not mean that we cause God to become a liar, but that we depict God as a liar who is falsely accusing us. Though *ποιέω* normally means to do or accomplish something, John often uses it to communicate the idea of someone making a claim. This is evident in John 5:18; 8:53; 10:33; 19:7 and 12, where this term is used by Jesus' opponents as they reject things Jesus has just said about himself. This moves from a mere denial to an accusation and is far more serious than the consequences of the first two denials (Haas, de Jonge, and Swellengrebel, 32).

καὶ ὁ λόγος αὐτοῦ οὐκ ἔστιν ἐν ἡμῖν, "and his word is not influencing us." When John says that "God's word is not in us," this is not a denial of salvation, but recognition that God's Word is not impacting that person's life. It is not "influencing" the one who denies sin in the face of what God has said. John literally says that God's Word is not *in* us.[80] This is likely an ellipsis with the verb *μένω* purposefully left out for emphasis. Thus he is saying

79. Strecker (33) sees this statement as a "rejection of God's offer of forgiveness" rather than a restatement in any form of the false claim of v. 8. He also does not see v. 9 as the center of John's argument here, but rather the "confessional statement" of v. 7 ("the blood of Jesus his Son cleanses us from sin").

80. In John's Gospel, the concept of God's word not being "in" someone is expressed by Jesus with respect to those who do not believe in him such as in John 5:37–40. There Jesus tells the Jews who do not believe in him that God's word, the Scriptures that testify of him, is not "abiding" in them. By this he certainly does not mean that they do not know those Scriptures. They could likely quote each one of them. Rather, he is saying that those Scriptures have not helped them to recognize Jesus for who he is because they have not impacted their thinking. They have not influenced the Jews. Further, Jesus notes that their unresponsiveness to the Scriptures is willful. They are "not willing" to come to Jesus and so are unresponsive to God's revelation in his word.

that God's Word is not abiding in the person who denies sin. This reflects Jesus' teaching in the upper room, where he promised answered prayer to those in whom his Word abides and who are abiding in him (John 15:7). In both instances the meaning of abiding is not just "to exist in." It is not that a person knows Jesus' words. But rather, abiding carries the double sense of presence and influence (Brown, 259–60).[81] Jesus' words are at the forefront of that person's mind and memory and thereby influencing him or her. In this same way, John is saying here that the one who denies sin, and thereby a need to confess sin, is not being influenced by the Word of God. This explains why he or she is denying what God has said about his or her sinfulness.

Since, as Jesus says, God's Word *is* truth (John 17:17), the absence of truth in verse 8 and of God's Word in verse 10 really mean the same thing (Bruce, 45; Haas, de Jonge, and Swellengrebel, 32; Williamson, 75). Burge notes that "it may be an intentionally ambiguous reference to Jesus, who in John's writing is called 'the Word'" (Burge, 84). The clear parallel between verses 8 and 10 makes this unlikely. Rather, John is affirming that the believer who denies a need to confess sin is not thinking truthfully. He or she is self-deceived and not believing God's Word.

Again, though some would see these statements more equivalent to saying the person is unregenerate, John's inclusion of himself throughout the discussion makes such an option untenable. These are not the errors of the false teachers, though they would certainly say such things. These are errors any believer can make. John is not attacking the false teachers here in some gentle way by using an authorial "we" that does not really include him. He clearly distinguishes himself from the false teachers elsewhere in this epistle and certainly would not want to risk confusion here. Rather, his inclusion of himself must be seen as intentional and confessional. His concern here is more pastoral than polemical. Consequently, he again turns to the work of Christ that is the basis of our confession of sin.

2:1 In this verse we have one of the purposes for John's writing.[82] He does not want his readers to sin, though he has already reminded them that they

81. See excursus "Johannine Concept of Abiding" for a full discussion of John's use of *μένω* in his Gospel and epistles.

82. P. Balla ("Child-Parent Imagery in the Catholic Epistles," 71) sees this as the purpose of the epistle rather than 1:3 or 5:13.

are sinful and do have sin that needs to be confessed (1:8, 10). However, he has said these things about sin, not to ignore the issue, but to make them aware of its danger in their lives and so to put them on guard against it. These next two verses describe anew God's provision for our sin. Whereas it comes through Jesus' blood in verse 7, in these next two verses we are told it is through Jesus' propitiation on the cross and advocacy in heaven that we are enabled to walk in the light as he is in the light.

Some see this verse as a "parenthesis" or an interruption of the flow of thought (Burge, 84; Smalley, 35). This indicated by the change from his use of "we" throughout the rest of the passage to the voc. and "you" in this verse (Haas, de Jonge, and Swellengrebel, 33). However, recognizing its role within the chiasm, thus being parallel to 1:7, it should not be mistaken as having a parenthetical role.[83] Rather, it is intended to serve as a parallel concept to 1:7 as it relates to the issue of Jesus' work of continuously cleansing those who walk in the light.[84]

John changes his address from plural to singular. By this he makes the exhortation more personal. Without relinquishing his authority as a member of the apostolic band, he changes the tone of his message to speak personally and lovingly to his readers.[85]

---

83. The chiasm begins in 1:6 and concludes in 2:4, with the following structure. The connection of 2:1–2 with 1:7 is in terms of Jesus' role at Paraclete in 2:1–2 and His role as cleanser in 1:7.

A (1:6) – Walking in darkness invalidates a claim to fellowship with God.
  B (1:7) – Jesus' blood cleanses us if we walk in light.
    C (1:8) – Claim of sinlessness is self-deception.
      D (1:9) – Confession results in moral purity.
    C′ (1:10) – Claim of no sins to confess calls God a liar.
  B′ (2:1–2) – Jesus is our Advocate and Propitiation if we sin.
A′ (2:3–4) – Walking in disobedience invalidates a claim to know God (relationally).

84. The connection with v. 7 can be seen in John's use of ἔχομεν in v. 1 along with ἡμῶν and ἡμετέρων in v 2 to include himself with his readers. As these uses of the 1 pl. is not rhetorical, but intended to be understood literally, so, too, is his use of "we" in v. 7.

85. Haas, de Jonge, and Swellengrebel (33) see this change somewhat differently. "In these cases he does not view himself as representative of the eyewitnesses, as he does when using 'we' (with exclusive force) in 1:1–4, nor does he include himself with his readers, as he does when using 'we' (inclusive) in 1:5–10, and again in the last clause of the present verse."

Τεκνία μου, ταῦτα γράφω ὑμῖν, "My little children, I am writing these things to you." This first use of the vocative τεκνία to address his readers reflects his deep affection for them as well as his spiritual relationship to them (Yarbrough, 71).[86] This may also be reflected in his change from the plural "we" to the singular "I write" (Painter, 145).[87] This term is used ten times in the New Testament, once by Jesus (John 13:33), eight times by John (1 John 2:1, 12, 14, 28; 3:7, 18; 4:4; 5:12), and once by Paul (Gal 4:19). Here, and in this epistle, John writes as an elderly apostle who sees his relationship to his readers as that of a loving father with his beloved children.[88] His instruction flows from his deep concern for them and is coming to them as gentle instruction, not harsh correction.

John states another purpose for his writing. "These things" (ταῦτα) looks back on what he has just written rather than forward either to the purpose (ἵνα μὴ ἁμάρτητε) clause that follows or to the epistle as a whole (Akin, 76; Haas, de Jonge, and Swellengrebel, 34; Yarbrough, 72).[89] What he has said about confessing sin instead of denying it was said in order to encourage them to avoid sin, not to give permission to commit it.

John has likely chosen to remind his readers at this point because he recognizes that some might misunderstand the promise of full forgiveness and cleansing in response to confession and fail to see how evil sin is (Westcott, 41–42) and, as a result, see it as a license to sin (Burge, 84–85;

86. The diminutive voc. expresses "affection" (Marshall, 115, n. 19), "intimacy rather than age" (Haas, de Jonge, and Swellengrebel, 33). Schnackenburg (89, n. 3) rejects the idea of intimacy, but rather argues that it reflects the terminology used of rabbis addressing their disciples and indicates that John is implying that his readers have already been instructed by him. Thus it still carries a sense of authority rather than intimacy between John and his readers. This argument is especially weakened when one considers the other addresses John uses with his readers, particularly when he calls them "beloved" in 3:2, 21; 4:1, 7, 11.

87. J. P. Louw ("Verbal Aspect in the First Letter of John," 100) notes that the pres. tense of γράφω has no significance beyond a statement of fact.

88. P. Balla ("Child-Parent Imagery in the Catholic Epistles," 71) sees this term not only communicating the loving relationship John has with his readers, but also his expectation of their obedience to his instruction.

89. Brooke (23), Schnackenburg (89), Marshall (116, n. 21), and Westcott (42) see ταῦτα referring to both what John has just said and the remainder of the epistle. It seems better, though, to see this use of ταῦτα referring to the previous context since it focuses solely on the issue of sin while the remainder of the epistle addresses additional issues, such as Christology and assurance.

Marshall, 116). They might approach sinning nonchalantly, thinking they can sin and walk in the light so long as they keep confessing. They might fail to see the gravity of sin since its cleansing is so "easily" acquired. They might think that God does not take sin as seriously as he actually does since he is so faithful to forgive and cleanse. This attitude is often attributed to John's "opponents," the "secessionists," rather than his readership as a whole (Brown, 48–68; Smalley, 35). However, John is addressing an attitude that could arise among his readers just as Paul saw it as necessary in his Epistle to the Romans to address a possible misunderstanding of God's grace as a license to sin (Rom 6:1) without having a particular licentious sect in view.[90] Thus, to attribute this attitude to his opponents alone would lead one to miss his pastoral concern by relegating this to a polemic against postulated opponents. Brown (48) acknowledges this before delving into a complex discussion of his theory of opponents. Smalley (xxxii) also connects the behavior of the secessionists with an unloving attitude based on 1 John 2:18–19 and 2 John 7. Again, this need not result from sectarianism, but, as James (2:1–13) indicates clearly, can be characteristic of any church community. Like Paul in Rom 6:1, John moves quickly to clarify his concern for sin lest anyone mistakenly misapply what he has already written.[91]

John changes from the plural to the first-person singular as he addresses his readers directly. He has moved from identifying himself with them or the other apostles (first person singular) to addressing them directly. It is instructive to attend to John's use of person and number in his verbs and pronouns. he is careful to distinguish himself, his readers, the other apostles, and the false teachers in the things he says. In this case, as throughout the epistle, John is not chiding his readers, but is expressing his deep

90. Though Paul uses diatribe in Rom 6 (C. Cranfield, *Romans*, 297; E. Käsemann, *Romans*, 165; D. Moo, *Romans 1–8*, 372), it need not indicate the actual presence of a sectarian group opposing him (K. Boa and W. Kruidenier, *Romans*, 185). Some see this as a response to a mixture of objectors and those who misunderstood Paul's teaching to indicate permissiveness toward sin (Hendriksen, *Exposition of Paul's Epistle to the Romans,* 194, Mounce, *Romans*, 148). Paul is certainly using this rhetorical device, but rather raising questions that his readers, especially those from a Jewish background, might have if they misunderstood his instruction in Rom 5 on the greatness of God's grace (Schreiner, *Romans*, 33).

91. These two verses serve much the same corrective function as Paul's instructions in Rom 6 in response to possible misunderstanding of the fullness of God's grace in forgiving sins as taught in Rom 5.

concern for them by addressing them directly. By moving to the singular he is making it clear that he is personally concerned for them and is addressing them from that concern. He is not just speaking as a representative of the larger apostolic group to which he has referred earlier.

ἵνα μὴ ἁμάρτητε, "in order that you may not sin." The reason for John's writing is so that (in order that) his readers may live morally pure lives (stated positively).[92] The aorist subjunctive with this ἵνα communicates John's desire rather than emphasizing the possibility of sin, with the subjunctive mood resulting from its role in a ἵνα clause as part of a negative command. The sense of this aorist subjunctive is not that they have been sinning and need to stop. Rather, it is that they should not start to sin and should reject it as a matter of practice (Painter, 146).[93]

Yarbrough (72–73) identifies two "lines" or "axes" of sin that John develops in this epistle. These "axes" relate the issue of sin to the person's failure to express his or her faith actively. The first results from a lack of justifying faith, which he identifies as "believing in Christ." He then clarifies this kind of faith. "Belief in the sense of personal trust resulting in reciprocal love is the key to knowing God in a saving way." He correctly points to 5:10 and 13 as John's clarification of justifying faith. As will be seen later, these verses do indeed define John's understanding of the relationship of faith in Christ to justification, and therefore assurance for the child of God. The second axis is related to sanctifying faith. He identifies key passages such as 1:8 and 10, as well as 2:3–5, as evidencing a second "line" that involves "obedience to his commands." However, after noting that John addresses those he knows to be believers, he wrongly says John "has in mind not only the (pistic) belief-unbelief issue but also the (ethical) obedience-disobedience issue." Yet, if John has just made clear that he is addressing believers, whom he has

---

92. Henderson (D. W. Henderson, *Culture Shift: Communicating God's Truth in Our Changing World*, 156–66) discusses the postmodern denial of sin as a reality. This is different from the denial of a sin nature or personal sin discussed earlier in 1:8 and 10. Rather, this is a problem of a modernist view that does not see sin as existing. Thus, such a concern by the apostle would make little sense to the postmodernist. For them it becomes important to first establish the reality of sin before moving to the issue of personal sin.

93. This could also be functioning as a purpose-result ἵνα clause (D.B. Wallace, *Grammar*, 472–73). In this case it would imply that it is John's intention and that he expects his warning to be effective and that his readers will indeed choose not to sin.

called "little children," he cannot have the justifying faith aspect in mind. They are already justified. They cannot be in danger of sinning in that way. He cannot be writing to say, "I want you to stop failing to believe in Jesus." Rather, he has only the ethical expression of faith in view. Furthermore, since the verses preceding and following this statement have to do with the ethical issue, sin of disobedience, his statement necessarily should be limited to his readers as justified saints, and his concern be seen as pastoral and related to issues affecting their fellowship with God, not entrance into his family. Granted, justifying faith and sanctifying faith are related and in some sense integral.[94] One cannot have sanctifying faith without justifying faith having preceded it. But sanctifying faith does not necessarily follow (contra Kistemaker, 89–90).[95] Every time a justified saint sins, his or her "sanctifying faith" has failed. Sin is never an act of faith, but unbelief, even in the life of a believer.

94. This is the principle behind the issue of the Galatians' return to the law for their "perfection." As R. N. Longenecker (*Galatians*, 103–104) notes, the Galatian Christians were failing to maintain their spiritual lives on the same basis that they began them, by faith in God rather than the works of the law. M. Silva (*Philippians*, 46) argues that as one's justification is a work of God rather than being dependent on their own works, one's "growth in sanctification" is also.

95. These would argue that justifying faith continues to express itself permanently and so necessarily produces works: W. Barclay, *The Letters of James and Peter*, 74; J. Adamson, *The Epistle of James*, 124; R. Jamieson, et al., *A Commentary, Critical and Explanatory, on the Old and New Testaments*, Jas 2:17; S. Kistemaker, "The Theological Message of James," 58; W. MacDonald and A. Farstad, *Believer's Bible Commentary*, Jas 2:17; R. P. Martin, *James*, 85; W. Wessel, *The Wycliffe Bible Commentary: New Testament*, Jas 2:15; J. Walvoord, "Series in Christology, Part 4: The Preincarnate Son of God," 423; C. C. Ryrie, *So Great Salvation,* 133; J. R. Blue, "James," *BKC* 2:825; J. M. Boice, *Christ's Call to Discipleship*, 17; P. Davids, *James*, 119; R. B. Hughes and J. C. Laney, *Tyndale Concise Bible Commentary*, 682; J. D. Stevens, "James," *KJV Bible Commentary*, 2590; K. A. Richardson, *James*, 133; W. Wiersbe, *Bible Exposition Commentary*, Jas 2:14; L. S. Chafer, "The Eternal Security of the Believer, Part 2," 401. J. F. Walvoord modifies Chafer's position slightly and says that "while works are not the ground or justification for salvation, they can be the fruit or evidence of it" ("Christ's Olivet Discourse on the End of the Age, Part VII," 312). J. F. MacArthur, Jr. ("Faith according to the Apostle James," 32), states it this way: "Workless faith is dead faith, and dead faith is no faith at all. Real faith cannot die, but if you have a so-called faith that is devoid of works, it is not living faith, and it cannot save."

καὶ ἐάν τις ἁμάρτῃ, "However, if anyone does sin." What John says next stands in contrast to his desire for his readers that they not sin. Thus his use of καὶ as an adversative is contrastive rather than continuative as it introduces a third-class condition (Painter, 146; Yarbrough, 75). Akin (142) rejects this translation on the basis that John does not use καὶ as a contrastive conjunction anywhere else in the epistle, preferring both δὲ and ἀλλά instead. However, context makes this the best sense within the flow of thought.[96]

When John says "if anyone sins," he is communicating that we all may sin, but need not. In this case he is using a third-class conditional clause to describe a hypothetical situation.[97] He is saying that, for the sake of argument, one might be able not to sin. However, in the event that a person does happen to sin there is provision. That sinlessness is a hypothetical situation is evident in that he has just affirmed that to deny the presence of sin in one's life is to call God a liar and that every believer must be honest about his or her sinfulness as well as about particular sins. Moreover, he has just stated his purpose in discussing the confession of sin. He is trying to motivate them not to sin.

Still, his statement is vague by design. Some interpreters take this to mean a lapse rather than a lifestyle of sin (Brown, 215; Bruce, 48; Painter, 158). However, such an interpretation involves reading one's theology into the verse and determining grammar on the basis of theology. Pentecost (34), on the other hand, sees this referring to someone "still in the act of sinning." That may be too specific as well. John is speaking more generally rather than emphasizing one aspect or the other.

The aorist subjunctive is best seen in its undefined sense indicating more a potential for sin than an expression of it (Kistemaker, 254). Often, when the context is not clear, deciding whether it is being used ingressively, consumatively, or any other way can be more a by-product of theology than of grammar. John's statement is sufficiently vague that he likely intends it to mean either a lapse or a pattern of sin. He wants his readers neither to practice sin, nor to commit even a single sin. His focus is not on whether it

96. Painter (146) notes well that "*kai* has an adversative force because 2:1b stands against 1:10." It is within this very clear contrast that the sense of καὶ must be discerned. And John's use of δὲ and ἀλλά elsewhere does not limit him to those terms here.

97. John's use of ἐάν may, in fact, imply an expectation that his readers will sin at some point (M. Zerwick, *Biblical Greek: Illustrated*, §320).

is a single act or a pattern. His point is what follows. God has provided for sin through Christ's work on our behalf. Thus John is focusing on the potential for sin. That he is not intending to imply that they are sinning is evident from his choice of the aorist (undefined) over the present subjunctive, which would have implied that sin was in process (contra Pentecost above).

His use of τις ("anyone") in the protasis is clarified in the apodosis. The "anyone" being described here does not mean "everyone" in the world. Rather, it is any from among "us believers," as is revealed by John's return to the first person plural from this indistinct 3 singular pronoun.

παράκλητον ἔχομεν πρὸς τὸν πατέρα Ἰησοῦν Χριστὸν δίκαιον·, "we have an advocate in the presence of the Father, Jesus Christ, the Righteous One." John now returns to the plural 1 (ἔχομεν) in the apodosis and includes himself among the beneficiaries of Jesus' ministry.

For the believer who finds himself or herself falling into an individual sin or a pattern of sin, God has not left us to our own devices. Rather, he has provided an Advocate. John opens the protasis with the solution to the problem created by sin. Using the same title as Jesus uses to describe the Holy Spirit in John 14:16, given by God in order to help the apostles understand his word, John now applies that title to Jesus. The term "Advocate" (παράκλητον) describes the intercessory work of Jesus on our behalf (Brooke, 23–27; Painter, 146; Yarbrough, 76). When we sin, Jesus acts as our "Advocate" before the Father in heaven's court. Satan, in contrast, stands in heaven as our accuser (Zech 3; Rev 12:10) and is answered by Jesus. Satan's accusations will end one day, though, when he is once and for all cast out of heaven (Rev 12:10). In John this Advocate is someone who assists, comes alongside, and gives aid in accomplishing a task or carrying a burden. This term communicates the idea of concern as well as help.[98] Here the imagery is of someone who goes to court with and serves as one's defense attorney. This sense of advocacy is seen in extrabiblical literature such as Philo (*Moses* 2.134; *Flaccus* 3.4).[99]

---

98. BDAG, 766; J. Behm, "παράκλητος," *TDNT* 5:804, 13.

99. In *Moses* 2.134 Philo writes, "For it was indispensable that the man who was consecrated to the Father of the world, should have as a paraclete [παρακλήτῳ], his son, the being most perfect in all virtue, to procure forgiveness of sins, and a supply of unlimited blessings." And in *Flaccus* 3.4 he writes, "And Tiberius, being deceived by all these representations, without being aware of what he was doing, left behind him a most irreconcilable enemy, to himself, and his grandson, and his

Though the term is used only here and in the Gospel of John (14:6, 26; 15:26; 16:7, all referring to the Holy Spirit), the concept of the Advocate (Paraclete) is not absent elsewhere in the New Testament. The Holy Spirit's ministry as our Advocate is described in detail in Rom 8. Jesus intercedes for Peter in Luke 22:32 when Satan wants to "sift" him "like wheat." Finally, the author of Hebrews describes Jesus' high priestly ministry, as both our intercessor (high priest) as well as our sacrifice.

John changes the indistinct τις of the protasis to include himself in those who benefit from the solution provided by God (Westcott, 43). His choice of ἔχομεν purposely includes himself and carries with it the gnomic sense, that this is continually true for the believer. Furthermore, with this present tense verb he emphasizes the present reality and continuous aspect of Jesus' ministry (Haas, de Jonge, and Swellengrebel, 34).

His choice of the preposition πρὸς to communicate Jesus' role as our Advocate emphasizes the fact that he is standing in God's "presence."[100] This is the same preposition used by John in his Gospel (John 1:1) to describe Jesus' deity as the Word who is both God and "with" (πρὸς) God. Where in the Gospel the Word is in the presence of God, John chooses to say that Jesus, as Advocate, stands before "the Father," thereby reminding his readers of their participation in the family of God (a concept to be developed later in the epistle). This same construction is also used in the prologue of this epistle (1:2) to describe the relationship of eternal life (Jesus) to the Father. As Brown insightfully notes, "The expression connotes both presence with and relationship toward; it can be used to describe both a preincarnational and postresurrectional relationship between Jesus the Word and God the Father. Such a relationship makes Jesus effective as a Paraclete" (Brown, 216).

As Jesus represents us, he petitions the Father on our behalf (Rom 8:34; Heb 7:25). Furthermore, just as he promised the disciples answered prayer when prayed on the basis of God's character and will (John 14:13–14; 16:23–26), so, too, his prayers on our behalf are sure to be heard (John

---

whole family, and to Macro, who was his chief adviser and comforter [παρακλήτῳ], and to all mankind." C. D. Yonge, *The Works of Philo: Complete and Unabridged*, 502, 727.

100. N. H. Young, "'Hilaskesthai' and Related Words in the New Testament," 173. Yarbrough (76) notes that this verse provides "indirect evidence" that John believed in Jesus' resurrection. It seems better to see this as an outgrowth of John's understanding of Jesus' exaltation.

11:42). Jesus' intercession is efficacious because his will is identical to the Father's will (John 8:29).[101]

Kistemaker misses the point when he describes Jesus' action as our Advocate as involving the presentation of *our* prayers to the Father (Kistemaker, 254). This would make his role more of a mediator than an advocate. Rather, he is pleading our case on the basis of his accomplished work on the cross in much the same way as he prayed for Peter in Luke 22 and functions as our high priest in Hebrews. The Holy Spirit, on the other hand, does assist our prayers (Rom 8:27–28) in his intercessory role.

In describing Jesus, John includes his office, the Christ (Messiah), as well as his character, "the Righteous One." Akin (80) sees John's use of "Christ" here to be better read as "Jesus the Christ," and sees this serving as an affirmation of his office as Messiah.[102] That it should be seen as his proper title is evident, but the issue of his messiahship does not fit with the development of John's message. His deity is of greater importance. Consequently, this title would be better seen as affirming Jesus' deity. Following his title is John's affirmation of Jesus' moral standing before God the Father. He is not just righteous (predicate adjective), but is righteousness incarnate, thus the title, "the Righteous One"(contra Haas, de Jonge, and Swellengrebel, 34).[103] The Hebrew root most often translated by δίκαιος in the LXX is צָדֵק and normally refers to "conformity to an ethical or moral standard.[104] In the LXX, δίκαιος is not used to express the Greek concept of conformity to social standards, but rather expresses the Hebrew concept of conformity

101. Just as the Holy Spirit intercedes "according to the will of God" (Rom 8:27), so too does Jesus, though in a different role. The Holy Spirit as Paraclete is aiding us in a nonjudicial role while Jesus' advocacy is within a judicial setting (J. Behm, "παράκλητος," *TDNT* 5:804–13).

102. I. de Jonge ("The Use of the Word ΧΡΙΣΤΟΣ in the Johannine Epistles," 67) also sees δίκαιος as a "messianic' designation" in Acts 3:14, 7:52; and 22:14, but questions whether such is intended by John here. He notes that God the Father is also called "just" in 1:9, and Jesus is called righteous twice more (2:29 and 3:7) in the epistle without any messianic overtones.

103. The attribution of "the Righteous One" was applied to Jesus from the earliest days of the church. Examples include Peter in Acts 3:14 (ὑμεῖς δὲ τὸν ἅγιον καὶ δίκαιον ἠρνήσασθε); Stephen in Acts 7:52 (περὶ τῆς ἐλεύσεως τοῦ δικαίου); and Ananias in Acts 22:14 (καὶ ἰδεῖν τὸν δίκαιον). In his First Epistle (1 Pet 3:18), Peter uses the adjective to contrast Jesus' character with ours as he describes his suffering for our sins, his role as a substitutionary sacrifice, "the just for the unjust" (δίκαιος ὑπὲρ ἀδίκων).

104. H. G. Stiggers, "צָדֵק," *TWOT*, 2:752.

to God's standards. Further the descriptions of God as righteous indicate that the Hebrew concept was that God *is* the standard of righteousness, not that he meets any standard. Righteousness is defined by God's character or nature, rather than as a standard separate from his being. Further, human righteousness is expressed in the social setting by what one does, but has God as its focus rather than one's culture.[105] In this context then, Jesus' designation as "the Righteous One" communicates the idea that he expresses God's ethical standard of moral purity as he acts as our Advocate. He, being righteousness itself, therefore abides in the light with God the Father, and can stand in his presence with a relationship uninterrupted by sin, always making intercession for those whose failure, having moved them from the light of God's presence, desire to be restored.[106] "Jesus is now in the Father's presence as the eternal High Priest, who, having atoned for the sins of his people, now stands as their effective Advocate to ensure that their sins do not disqualify them from fellowship with the Father" (Akin, 82).

2:2 John describes Jesus' propitiatory ministry in the life of the believer. This, along with the previous verse, is parallel to verse 7 in the chiasm (see earlier discussion). Thus Jesus as our propitiation is parallel to his blood cleansing (present tense) us from every sin. So John now describes Jesus' work on the cross, first in terms of its benefit to the child of God, and then of its availability for all of mankind.[107]

καὶ αὐτὸς ἱλασμός ἐστιν περὶ τῶν ἁμαρτιῶν ἡμῶν, "And he himself is the atonement for our sins." John begins this sentence with the coordinate connective καὶ and connects Jesus' work on the cross with his ministry in heaven. Jesus is not only our Advocate. He is also the sacrifice that cleanses us (1:7) and satisfies God's just wrath (2:2).

---

105. G. Schrenk, "δίκαιος," *TDNT* 2:185.

106. Δίκαιος is used by John only three times in his Gospel. (1) In John 5:30 Jesus describes His judgment as "just" (ἡ κρίσις ἡ ἐμὴ δικαία ἐστίν) and argues that His judgment is just particularly because He did not "seek My own will but the will of the Father who sent Me." As God is just, and Jesus acts according to His will, Jesus' judgment thereby conforms to God's justness as well. (2) In John 7:24 Jesus calls upon His detractors to "judge with righteous judgment" (τὴν δικαίαν κρίσιν κρίνετε.), which, again, indicates meeting the standard of God's character. (3) In John 17:25 Jesus uses the voc. form (πάτερ δίκαιε) to address God the Father.

107. The triple repetition of περὶ with the coordinating conj. καὶ serves to heighten John's emphasis on Jesus' universal ministry.

John's use of αὐτὸς here should be seen as emphatic, best translated as "he himself" (Brown, 217; Westcott, 44).[108] This reflexive use of the personal pronoun focuses our attention on Jesus' personal involvement in our cleansing. Αὐτὸς is doing more than functioning as the subject of the sentence since it need not have been included with the predicate nominative ἱλασμός and the verb εἰμί, which is also included for emphasis.[109] Thus John is stressing his point. Jesus *is* the propitiation! Further, the inclusion of the pronoun in this construction serves to ensure that the anarthrous predicate nominative ἱλασμός is not mistaken for an indefinite subject of the verb εἰμί.

The term ἱλασμός occurs in the New Testament only here and in 4:10. Its use may allude to John the Baptist's declaration of Jesus as "the Lamb of God" (John 1:29) and indicates Jesus' role as a substitute (Morris, 130). Furthermore, as Beale and Carson note, his blood would be viewed in light of the Old Testament sacrifices where "the shed blood of the substitute covered the sins of others and appeased the divine wrath by way of atonement."[110] This term is understood in one of three ways.[111]

(1) It is translated as "propitiation," focusing on the satisfaction of God's just wrath (Akin, 82–84; Brooke, 28; Burge, 85–6; Kruse, 75–76; Marshall, 118–19; Stott, 87–88).[112]

(2) It means "expiation," the merciful forgiveness and removal of guilt by God, who is the offended party (Bultmann, 23; Dodd, 25–27; Painter, 159; Westcott, 87; Williams, 21).[113]

---

108. D. B. Wallace (*Grammar*, 322–23) identifies a use of αὐτὸς as the "subject focus." Though his examples do not employ the more reflexive "himself," his point is that the subject is not redundant, but intended to be emphasized. In this context, the more reflexive sense seems best for clarity, though it might be considered a rare use. This is recognized by some translators as well (HCSB, NASB95, NET, NKJV, NLT; but not ASV, ESV, NIV84).

109. This is an instance of the definite predicate nominative (D. B. Wallace, *Grammar*, 263–64). Further, its placement before ἐστιν makes it emphatic as well.

110. G. K. Beale and D. A. Carson, *Commentary on the New Testament Use of the Old Testament*, 428.

111. Of note is the similar debate over the meaning of ἱλάσκεσθαι in Heb 2:17 (B. C. Joslin, "Christ Bore the Sins of Many," 93–94).

112. L. Morris, *The Apostolic Preaching of the Cross*, 144–213.

113. Z. C. Hodges, "What Do We Mean by Propitiation?" 36. Painter (146–47) argues that this appears to be the sense of the LXX use in Zech 7:2 and Mal 1:9, where the verb form is used in each case to indicate entreating God's favor through prayer

(3) The more ambiguous "atonement" is used to indicate that both aspects may be intended by John (Schnackenburg, 92–93; Strecker, 39–40; Yarbrough, 78–79).[114]

Brown (218–20) provides several significant arguments for propitiation:[115]

(1) In both classical Greek and the pagan religions of the first century, the term ἱλασμός meant "placating or propitiating."

(2) "In the LXX of Zech 7:2 and Mal 1:9, *hilaskesthai* is used with God as an object to express the pagan idea of placating God, an idea of which the author disapproves."[116]

(ἐξιλάσασθαι in Zech 7:2 and ἐξιλάσκεσθε in Mal 1:9). N. H. Young ("C. H. Dodd, 'Hilaskesthai' and His Critics," 67–78) provides an excellent summary of the development of the debate on the meaning of ἱλασμός since C. H. Dodd's first proposal ("*Hilaskesthai*, Its Cognates, Derivatives, and Synonyms, in the Septuagint," 352–60). His arguments proved so convincing at the time that "expiation" replaces "propitiation" as the understood meaning in the NT. His conclusions are challenged by L. Morris (L. Morris, "The Use of *hilaskesthai* etc. in Biblical Greek," 227–33; "The Wrath of God," 142–45), R. Nicole ("C. H. Dodd and the Doctrine of Propitiation," 117–57), D. Hill (*Greek Words and Hebrew Meanings*, 23–48), and K. Koch (*Die israelitische Sühneanschauung und ihre historischeen Wandlungen*, Habilitationsschrift, Erlangen, 1956). He concludes (78), "The debate over the translation of *hilaskomai* is in some ways sterile, simply because the proffered alternatives both need to be understood in ways other than their dictionary meanings. If we use 'expiation' we must enrich it to include the idea that the cancelling of sin also causes the God-willed effect—which the NT calls *orgē*—to cease, and at the same time introduces the forgiven sinner to a new relationship with God. . . . If one advocates 'propitiation', the word must be radically applied in the first instance to the removal of pollution and only secondarily to the cessation of wrath."

114. Brown (218–22) provides an extensive and helpful discussion of the arguments for both major views. His choice of the less clear "atonement" is worthy of consideration in that both aspects of Jesus' work may be in intended by John.

115. These arguments need to be seen in the light of his also acknowledging that "expiation" has as strong a defense as "propitiation," and so chooses to see both senses intended by John.

116. Zechariah 7:2 reads, οἱ ἄνδρες αὐτοῦ τοῦ ἐξιλάσασθαι τὸν κύριον. Malachi 1:9 reads, καὶ νῦν ἐξιλάσκεσθε τὸ πρόσωπον τοῦ θεοῦ ὑμῶν καὶ δεήθητε αὐτοῦ.

(3) Passages that use ἱλασμός with the sense of propitiation include Psa 106:30 and Zech 8:22, as well as Sir 45:23.[117] (3) The LXX frequently utilizes forms of the ἱλασμός root in the context of God's wrath. [118]

(4) Micah 7:18–19 provides the rationale for ἱλασμός referring to propitiation.[119]

(5) "The imagery that sacrifices have a pleasing smell to God cannot be separated from propitiation."

(6) The apostolic fathers attributed the sense of propitiation to the term. Akin (83) provides two additional arguments.

(7) The epistle develops the theme of God's coming judgment when Christ returns, and so a coming wrath is in view.[120]

---

117. Psalm 106:30 does not have ἐξιλάσκεσθαι or any related words, but Psa 105:30 does, and reads, καὶ ἔστη Φινεες καὶ ἐξιλάσατο, καὶ ἐκόπασεν ἡ θραῦσις. Sir 45:16 reads, ἐξελέξατο αὐτὸν ἀπὸ παντὸς ζῶντος προσαγαγεῖν κάρπωσιν κυρίῳ, θυμίαμα καὶ εὐωδίαν εἰς μνημόσυνον, ἐξιλάσκεσθαι περὶ τοῦ λαοῦ σου. Sir 45:23 reads, Καὶ Φινεες υἱὸς Ελεαζαρ τρίτος εἰς δόξαν ἐν τῷ ζηλῶσαι αὐτὸν ἐν φόβῳ κυρίου καὶ στῆναι αὐτὸν ἐν τροπῇ λαοῦ ἐν ἀγαθότητι προθυμίας ψυχῆς αὐτοῦ, καὶ ἐξιλάσατο περὶ τοῦ Ισραηλ.

118. For example, Zech 8:22 reads, καὶ ἥξουσιν λαοὶ πολλοὶ καὶ ἔθνη πολλὰ ἐκζητῆσαι τὸ πρόσωπον κυρίου παντοκράτορος ἐν Ιερουσαλημ καὶ τοῦ ἐξιλάσκεσθαι τὸ πρόσωπον κυρίου. Dodd proposed this idea, which has since been challenged and defended. For the fuller discussion of Dodd's proposal (C. H. Dodd, "ἱλάσκομαι, Its Cognates, Derivatives, and Synonyms, in the Septuagint," 352–60), see R. R. Nicole, "C. H. Dodd and the Doctrine of Propitiation," 116–57; L. Morris, *The Apostolic Preaching of the Cross*, 144–213; N. H. Young, "C. H. Dodd, 'Hilaskesthai' and His Critics," 67–78; and R. R. Nicole, "'Hilaskesthai' Revisited," 173–77; N. H. Young, "'Hilaskesthai' and Related Words in the New Testament." 169–76.

119. Micah 7:18–19 reads, τίς θεὸς ὥσπερ σύ; ἐξαίρων ἀδικίας καὶ ὑπερβαίνων ἀσεβείας τοῖς καταλοίποις τῆς κληρονομίας αὐτοῦ καὶ οὐ συνέσχεν εἰς μαρτύριον ὀργὴν αὐτοῦ, ὅτι θελητὴς ἐλέους ἐστίν. [19] αὐτὸς ἐπιστρέψει καὶ οἰκτιρήσει ἡμᾶς, καταδύσει τὰς ἀδικίας ἡμῶν καὶ ἀπορριφήσονται εἰς τὰ βάθη τῆς θαλάσσης, πάσας τὰς ἁμαρτίας ἡμῶν. ("Who *is* a God like You, pardoning iniquity and passing over the transgression of the remnant of His heritage? He does not retain His anger forever, because He delights *in* mercy. He will again have compassion on us, and will subdue our iniquities. You will cast all our sins into the depths of the sea.")

120. He notes 2:28 and 4:17–18 as examples of this coming wrath in 1 John. But both passages relate to believers, not unbelievers. The judgment believers face is from Christ at the Bema Seat (2 Cor 5:10; also Matt 5:11; 19:25–27; 1 Cor 3:10–15; Eph 6:8; Rev 2–3), a judgment wherein a child of God may face loss of rewards, but not loss of eternal life. The judgment unbelievers face is at the Great White Throne, a judgment of punishments (Rev 20:11–15). Both judgments are based on

(8) The immediate context indicates "sins are not only an impersonal barrier to fellowship but include the aspect of personal favor and disfavor."

In favor of "expiation" is the immediate context of chapter 1. There we are introduced to Jesus' work on our behalf in 1:7, with his continual cleansing of believers by his blood (death on the cross). John then turns to the issue of unconfessed sin and the denial of guilt in 1:8 and 10. The promise of cleansing in 1:9 again focuses attention more on the removal of guilt than the satisfaction of wrath. His use of the preposition περὶ with ἁμαρτία gives it the sense of "taking away" or "atoning for."[121] This idea is expressed by the same construction in passages such as 1 Pet 3:18 and Heb 10:18 and 13:11, as well as Num 8:8 in the LXX.[122] Further, its use throughout the New Testament and here, with regard to Jesus presenting himself as the sacrifice, better fits the idea of the payment for sin and its removal than that of satisfying God's wrath. Painter (147) argues that in the LXX it has the sense of "propitiation" when God is the object. However, when he is the agent, it has the sense of "expiation." He then points to Jesus as the active agent in this verse and so gives ἱλασμός the sense of expiation as a result. Westcott (85–87) argues for "expiation" on the basis that the extensive LXX usage of ἱλασμός and ἐξιλασμός to represent כִּפֻּרִים (8 times) and כִּפֶּר (18 times) and that it had the sin as its object rather than God. He concludes from these examples: "They shew that the scriptural conception of ἱλάσκεσθαι is not that of appeasing one who is angry, with a personal feeling, against the offender; but of altering the character of that which from without occasions a necessary alienation, and interposes an inevitable obstacle to fellowship" (Westcott, 87). Young develops an argument for expiation first from Paul's pattern of using the term to indicate removal of guilt over satisfaction of wrath and then with John's argument in 1:6–2:2. He provides a chart with 1:6, 8, and 10 in the left column and 1:7, 9; and 2:1–2 in the right. He argues that while the columns contrast each other, the verses in each column parallel one another with the result that "ἱλασμός parallels καθερίζει, ἀφῇ, καθαρίσῃ and means again

deeds (Matt 16:27; Rev 11:18; 22:12 addresses both). Neither determines destiny, just conditions experienced within those destinies.

121. BDAG, 798; E. H. Riesenfeld, "περὶ," *TDNT* 6:54–55.

122. Numbers 8:8 reads, καὶ λήμψονται μόσχον ἕνα ἐκ βοῶν καὶ τούτου θυσίαν σεμιδάλεως ἀναπεποιημένην ἐν ἐλαίῳ, καὶ μόσχον ἐνιαύσιον ἐκ βοῶν λήμψῃ περὶ ἁμαρτίας.

cleanse from sin, forgive sin by the death (τὸ αἷμα) of Christ."[123] Though he does not recognize the chiasm within this pericope, he does identify the parallel relationship between 1:7 and 2:1–2. So he correctly notes that Jesus' blood cleansing in 1:7 is parallel with Jesus' role as Advocate in 2:1–2.

The LXX also uses the term to describe the mercy seat above the ark of the covenant, on which the high priest sprinkled blood once a year on the Day of Atonement, first for his own sins and then for the sins of the nation (Exod 25:17–22; 1 Chr 28:2). The Day of Atonement brought cleansing, the removal of sin's stain from the tabernacle and temple, and enabled access to God for a nation.[124] Also pictured within this term is the Old Testament practice in which the offerer laid hands on the sacrificial animal and transferred his guilt to that animal, which in turn died in place of the person (Hartley, 20). John's use of the term in 1 John 4:10 alludes to this Old Testament practice in that he describes Jesus' purpose in coming to be that we might "live through him." Our living results because of his dying our justly deserved death on our behalf, not just by the removal of guilt.[125]

---

123. N. H. Young, "'Hilaskesthai' and Related Words in the New Testament," 172–73.

124. J. E. Brenneman, "Atonement, Day of," *Eerdmans Dictionary of the Bible*, 128; J. E. Hartley, *Leviticus*, 237; "Atonement, Day of," *ODCC*, 125.

125. Conversely, Jesus used the verb form of this word in the prayer of the sinner in Luke 18:13, often translated "be merciful to me," but usually understood as "be propitiated toward me" (Marshall, *Luke*, 680). The sinner was asking God to apply the benefits of the sin sacrifice to his sinful life and so accept him (D. L. Bock, *Luke*, 2:1464; J. Reiling and J. L. Swellengrebel, *A Handbook on the Gospel of Luke*, 602). N. H. Young ("'Hilaskesthai' and Related Words in the New Testament," 169) suggests the sinner's cry alludes to Psa 51:1, which in the LXX reads, Ἐλέησόν με, ὁ θεός, but he says "conveys" the same sense of ἱλάσθητι (verb form from the same root as ἱλασμός). Jesus described him as going home "justified," which would fit the idea of expiation better, though he was asking God to hold back his just wrath. N. H. Young ("Hilaskesthai," 170) notes well, "There is no hint of the prayer propitiating God, or God propitiating himself, it is solely a matter of divine forgiveness and acquittal for mercy's sake." Paul uses this term in Rom 3:25 to describe Jesus as the propitiating sacrifice sent by God on our behalf. He further affirms that God reconciled himself to the world through Jesus' death and has given us the ministry of reconciliation (2 Cor 5:18–21)—because His wrath has been satisfied by Jesus' death! The author of Hebrews (2:17) describes Jesus' high priestly role as "making propitiation for the sins of the people." Again, though this does involve the removal of guilt, it also includes the payment for the sin accomplished through the sacrifice.

It seems, though, that John's use of the term in this verse at least includes the sense of propitiation along with expiation. Though what he has said in the first chapter might fit the idea of expiation more than propitiation, John's description of Jesus as our Advocate before the Father in 2:1 has brought the issue of wrath in view. We are facing a justly angry Judge and stand guilty before him. Jesus' role as our defender is not that of proving our innocence. Rather, he intercedes on our behalf before the righteous judge of the universe and turns back his wrath by satisfying his righteous demand for punishment. He is both our defender and our sacrifice. This may be another instance of a Johannine double entendre in which he intends ἱλασμός to include both senses. Jesus' ministry in heaven provides both expiation and propitiation. Thus Brown's choice of "atonement" allows for the ambiguity desired by John that communicates the full scope of Jesus' work to be included.[126]

Of note is John's choice of the plural "sins." He is looking at the individual transgressions, not at the sin nature or sin as a concept (Smalley, 40).[127] Further, he includes himself among the beneficiaries, in that he is included when he says "our sins" (τῶν ἁμαρτιῶν ἡμῶν).[128] Having said that Jesus' work extends to believers, he next turns to the universal impact of Jesus' work on the cross.

οὐ περὶ τῶν ἡμετέρων δὲ μόνον ἀλλὰ καὶ περὶ ὅλου τοῦ κόσμου, "and not for ours only but also for *the sins* of the whole world." John's repetition of περὶ ties these phrases together and emphasizes the universal work of Christ. His use of ἡμετέρων rather than repeating τῶν ἁμαρτιῶν ἡμῶν serves to direct the

126. Brown (219) relates the two concepts well and says: "Is there an angry God who is placated by having sacrifices offered to him by the offender (propitiation), or is the offender made pleasing in God's eyes by the wiping away of the sin and impurity that had made him offensive (expiation)? Even though the same action might be involved, propitiation is primarily directed toward the offended person, while expiation is directed toward removing what has caused the breakdown."

127. Though this might be viewed as an example of the generic article with a concrete noun, thus making sins a broad category (D. B. Wallace, *Grammar*, 227), its contrast with the anarthrous "sin" in the near context of 1:8 and 10 argues against such a use here.

128. Though others see the "community" of faith included in ἡμῶν (Johnson, 35; Westcott, 44; Rensberger, 57), John's inclusion of himself with his readers appears to communicate the more personal aspect of "yours and mine" than the less personal "our community of faith which includes more people than just you and me."

focus to John and his readers with the emphasis on their shared experience (Marshall, 119). Where in the earlier phrase the stress was on "sins," here it is on "ours" (Westcott, 44). He uses a series of contrasts to communicate the extent of Jesus' work on the cross. Through these he makes it clear that Jesus' propitiatory work is not limited just to believers. He does this by moving from a more mild contrast (οὐ ... δὲ), to what would normally be a strong adversative conjunction, ἀλλὰ.[129] Here, it draws two groups together rather than emphasizing their differences.[130] Jesus employs the same construction in John 17:20, where he uses ἀλλὰ to include the apostles' future converts with them.[131] Though the intention is not to contrast the two groups (as noted by Brown, 222), it is also a double περὶ construction and is structurally identical.[132] Additionally, the repetition of περὶ with ὅλου τοῦ κόσμου indicates John has the world's "sins" in view, not the world itself (Smalley, 40; contra Westcott, 45).[133]

This is one of the clearest statements of Scripture that Jesus' propitiatory work on the cross is universal and not limited only to the elect (Strecker, 40). When Jesus gave his perfectly sinless life to satisfy the just wrath of our righteous and holy God, it was sufficient to provide forgiveness for the whole world (John 3:16; 2 Cor 5:14, 15, 19; 1 Tim 2:4; Titus 2:11; Heb 2:9). John's use of ὅλου emphasizes the totality of humanity that is included in the concept of "world" (Johnson, 35).[134] His death was not for the world,

---

129. D. B. Wallace, *Grammar*, 671–72.

130. This construction reflects Jesus' influence on John as an author. The placement of δὲ late in the clause could be considered emphatic, though in this case it appears more out of necessity in order to emphasize the preposition phrase over the coordinating conj. (BDF §475 [(2]).

131. Οὐ περὶ τούτων δὲ ἐρωτῶ μόνον, ἀλλὰ καὶ περὶ τῶν πιστευόντων διὰ τοῦ λόγου αὐτῶν εἰς ἐμέ.

132. Both share οὐ περὶ ... δὲ ... μόνον, ἀλλὰ καὶ περὶ.

133. The term κόσμος occurs 185 in the NT, with 78 occurrences in John's literature, 24 in his epistles. Only once (1 Pet 3:3) does it not refer to either the planet, its people, or its mode of operation (system). This represents John's first use of the term in this epistle.

134. Kistemaker (255) notes that "John chooses the adjective ὅλος (whole) instead of πᾶς (every, all) to communicate the idea of universality." Even so, he does not see Jesus dying for every human being, but limits Jesus' death to "all the people who believe in him" (253). He defines κόσμος, then, in terms of "the world in its totality, not necessarily in its individuality." This demonstrates the difficulty those who would hold to limited atonement face. The text is clear, but their theological

but, as said earlier, for its sins (Lenski, 400).[135] This is emphasized by John's use an ellipsis in the final clause (Kistemaker, 252; Marshall, 119, n. 31; RSV; Stott, 89; contra Westcott, 45). However, dying for sins does not remove them from the unrepentant soul.

2:3 We can know God in one of two ways. Everyone who has trusted Christ, and so is a child of God, knows him (John 17:3). However, that "knowing" is less personal than an intimate relationship.

Καὶ ἐν τούτῳ γινώσκομεν ὅτι ἐγνώκαμεν αὐτόν, "And by means of this we know that we have come to know him." In this and the following verses we see that a healthy relationship with God is contingent on obedience to his commands and imitation of Christ (2:3–6) and that personal proof of a relationship with God is obedience.[136]

John now addresses the issue of fellowship with God by invoking Jesus' descriptive terminology from the upper room. There he talked to the Eleven about knowing him and knowing the Father. he finished in his High Priestly Prayer by defining eternal life as "knowing God." Thus, as John describes the experience of eternal life, he addresses the question of what it means to "know God." He introduces this idea with an instrumental dative to describe how his readers can assure themselves of their fellowship with God, described here as "knowing" him.[137] Bruce (51) sees this as "a practical

---

system forces them to limit its meaning, and so Jesus' work on the cross, to the elect alone.

135. Yarbrough (80) sees Jesus' work being both unlimited and limited at the same time. This may be another way of saying "sufficient for all, but efficient only for the elect."

136. *Καὶ* may be resumptive in parallel with the *καὶ* introducing 1:5 (Harris, 74), or (more likely) a simple logical connective tying this statement to the chiasm of 1:6–2:4. Akin (83) and Rensberger (58–60) see this *καὶ* as a "transitional" marker and that it introduces a new section. Schnackenburg (101) sees it placing the focus on what follows rather than what precedes, thus beginning a new paragraph. Strecker (40, n. 21) sees it connecting back to the preceding verses even while *ἐν τούτῳ* looks to what follows, and so continuing the paragraph.

137. John uses this instrumental dative (*ἐν τούτῳ*) fourteen times in this epistle (1 John 2:3, 4, 5 [twice]; 3:10, 16, 19, 24; 4:2, 9, 10, 13, 17; and 5:2). It is absent from both the Gospel of John and his following two epistles. Generally it refers to what follows when followed by *ὅτι*, *ἵνα*, *ἐὰν*, *ὅταν*, *ἐκ*, or an *ἐν* clause. It need not though, and can refer to what has just been said (Brown, 248–49; Westcott, 46). In this case it seems best to see it pointing to what follows (Brooke, 30; Schnackenburg,

test of verbal profession" while others refer to this as a Test of Life or proof of one's salvation (Akin, 91; Boice, 55; Brooke, 29; Burge, 96; Culpepper, 25; Houlden, 66; Johnson, 40; MacArthur, 55; Marshall, 123; Painter, 174; D. Smith, 53; Stott, 53; Thompson, 52).[138] This is a claim to salvation that is validated by the fruit of good works (Smalley, 43).[139] Others, on the other hand, see this as a test of fellowship, that a healthy relationship with God manifests itself in obedience (King, 33; Mitchell, 54–55; Pentecost, 37). This should be seen as addressing believers since John includes himself in the group that can know (Burge, 95; contra Bultmann, 24).[140]

John's first use of "know" (γινώσκομεν) carries an experiential nuance and should be seen as a relational term (Boice, 57; Burge, 97; Lenski, 404; Westcott, 46).[141] This is the same sense given the term in the upper room. In John 14:9, responding to Philip's request to be shown the Father, Jesus says, "Have I been with you so long, and yet you have not known Me, Philip?" As Jesus had come to "explain" (lit. exegete) the Father (John 1:18) and had "manifested" him to his disciples (John 12:45; 17:6), knowing God was

---

101; Yarbrough; 82). Lenski (408) does not see it as instrumental but meaning "in connection with this."

138. The idea that there are three "tests" of whether a person is regenerate or not was introduced by Law (208–78) and continues to influence interpreters to this day.

139. Smalley balances this (45) by saying, "Obedience is not the *condition* for knowing God; but 'obeying orders' should *characterize* that knowledge (normally, if not without exception), and may be the means of testing it" (italics his).

140. Burge (95) notes three "assertions" in 2:4, 6, 9 that "may be affirmed by believers ('I know him,' 'I live in him,' 'I am in the light') if they are rightly understood." Marshall (121) sees this as John stating "his own belief" before addressing false claims again.

141. Brown (248–50) rejects the nuanced difference between γινώσκω and οἶδα and argues that they are used interchangeably by John with essentially the same meaning. Context and usage, for him, determine their meaning. He argues that there are too many exceptions to the nuances and that there are examples of their being true synonyms. Burge (96) concurs and says that "in Johannine thought, *knowing, abiding,* and *being* reflect similar meanings." Though there is a measure of truth to Brown's point, the nuances are apparent in enough places to make the distinction legitimate. Williams (22) sees this as an allusion to the gnostic false teachers' claims of knowledge, but its connection to the language of Jesus in the upper room argues against this. Brooke (29) sees "fellowship" and "acquaintance" as "cognate ideas" and rightly says that with John "'knowledge' is never a purely intellectual process. It is acquired by the exercise of all the faculties of intellect, heart, and will."

personal and experiential. Thus with Philip the issue was not believing in God, but what he believed about God and how he related to God. Thus, here the sense of the first "know" is relational, another way of saying "in fellowship with." "Fellowship with God and knowledge of God are the two sides of the same coin" (Kistemaker, 255).

His second use of "know" (ἐγνώκαμεν), as a perfect tense, implies knowledge gained in the past that should be influencing the present.[142] Additionally, as Jesus used the same tense in John 14:9 to challenge Philip's request, so too, here John brings up the issue of a claimed relationship. The claim to "have known" God over time may be made at any time (the present tense).[143]

This issue of knowing God need not be a reference to Gnosticism (contra Marshall, 121), but more likely grows out of the Old Testament concept of knowing God.[144] Sin resulted from a failure to know God (Jer 9:6; Hos 4:1–2). Knowledge of God that was personal was revealed by, and obtained through, obedience to God, which was expressed through righteous living (Jer 9:23–24; Hos 6:1–3; Dodd, 30; Grayston, 61). God promised a personal, relational knowledge of himself to the nation as part of the coming messianic age (Isa 11:9; 54:13; Jer 24:7; 31:31–34; Ezek 36:16–38; 37:26; Hab 2:14). This same principle is taught by Jesus in the Gospel of John (John 8:54–55; 15:21–24).

ἐὰν τὰς ἐντολὰς αὐτοῦ τηρῶμεν, "if we keep his commandments." Again John includes himself in the group that must evaluate whether it is in

---

142. The ὅτι clause gives the content of γινώσκομεν and the tense of the verb changes from pres. to pf. I concur with Harris (76), who sees some significance to this change in tenses, contra Brown (249–50). It seems better to see John making a distinction between present experience, the pres. tense "know," and the affects of a past experience that influence the present experience, the pf. tense "know." And, as noted by Harris, J. Louw's article ("Verbal Aspect in the First Letter of John," 98–104) does not address this issue.

143. Painter (174) sees this instance of knowing "him" could refer to either Jesus or God the Father. If Jesus, it would have to be "the heavenly Christ" since many readers could not claim to have known him personally. However, the context seems to make it clear that God the Father is in view here.

144. It was also characteristic of rabbinic Judaism. For example, Rabbi Hananiah ben Teradion (*m. 'Abot* 3.2), martyred in the second century, is quoted as saying, "If two sit together and no words of the Law [are spoken] between them, there is the seat of the scornful. ... But if two sit together and words of the Law [are spoken] between them, the Divine Presence rests between them" (H. Danby, *Mishnah*, 450).

fellowship with God, whether its "knowledge" of God is personal and experiential, or only imagined.

John's First Epistle appears to have the pattern of using ἐὰν to state assumed facts, while using ὅτι for actual facts.[145] By this he is saying that he views this as true of his readers, though he knows there may be exceptions. His readers are characterized by this, though not perfectly.

The referent of αὐτοῦ is best seen as God rather than Jesus based on context and the discussion that follows.[146] King notes well, "It is the fact that in our relationship with him, as that between us and others, there are degrees of acquaintance" (King, 32–33). However, what affects that relationship? It is affected by obedience or the lack thereof. The apodosis of the third-class condition is related to the main clause, not the subordinate ὅτι clause. The present subjective τηρῶμεν reflects either a customary or gnomic sense rather than progressive. In other words, we do not know *while* we are keeping his commandments, but as we see that keeping his commandments characterizes our lives.

This phrase occurs, in one form or another, six times in this epistle (2:3, 4; 3:22, 24; 5:2, 3), as well as twelve times in the Gospel[147] and another six times in Revelation.[148] Thus its importance to John should never be under-

145. BDF §394.

146. Here and in 1 John 2:4; 3:22, 23, 24; 5:2, 3 (2x). Additionally, 4:21 uses τὴν ἐντολὴν ἔχομεν ἀπ' αὐτοῦ. In 3:23 and 4:21, the referent is clearly God the Father. And it seems best to see the Father as the referent of the plural commandments throughout 1 John. Of note is that at one point R. Bultmann saw the referent of αὐτὸς to be Jesus ("Analyse des 1 Joh," in *Festgabe für A. Jülicher*, 138–58). He was challenged by Schnackenburg (75, n. 1) and subsequently responded by changing his view (Bultmann, 24, n. 2). Also, Culy (xx) notes well: "One of the most difficult challenges of the letters of John relates to the writer's use of the pronoun αὐτός and third person verbs without an explicit subject. In 1 John in particular, it is frequently difficult to determine whether he intended to refer to the Father or the Son."

147. John 8:51 (τὸν ἐμὸν λόγον τηρήσῃ), 52 (τὸν λόγον μου τηρήσῃ), 55 (τὸν λόγον αὐτοῦ τηρῶ); 14:15 (τὰς ἐντολὰς τὰς ἐμὰς τηρήσετε), 21 (ὁ ἔχων τὰς ἐντολάς μου καὶ τηρῶν αὐτὰς), 23 (τὸν λόγον μου τηρήσει), 24 (ὁ μὴ ἀγαπῶν με τοὺς λόγους μου οὐ τηρεῖ); 15:10 (x2) (τὰς ἐντολάς μου τηρήσητε ... ἐγὼ τὰς ἐντολὰς τοῦ πατρός μου τετήρηκα), 20 (x2) (εἰ τὸν λόγον μου ἐτήρησαν, καὶ τὸν ὑμέτερον τηρήσουσιν); and 17:6 (τὸν λόγον σου τετήρηκαν). In John 17:12 the verb is used by Jesus to describe His action of preservation of the disciples (ἐγὼ ἐτήρουν αὐτοὺς ἐν τῷ ὀνόματί σου).

148. Revelation 3:8 (ἐτήρησάς μου τὸν λόγον), 10 (ἐτήρησας τὸν λόγον); 12:17 (τῶν τηρούντων τὰς ἐντολὰς τοῦ θεοῦ); 14:12 (οἱ τηροῦντες τὰς ἐντολὰς τοῦ θεοῦ); 22:7 (ὁ τηρῶν

rated. Here again John includes himself. He does not know that he knows God apart from obedience. This third-class condition implies the possibility of John not keeping the commandments. Consequently, if he should fail to do so, by implication, he cannot then know by experience that he has known God.

John's choice of τηρέω throughout this epistle is instructive.[149] First, it reflects Jesus' words in the Upper Room, "If you love me you will keep my commandments" (John 14:15). Second, the sense of "keeping" is more than just obedience, but implies commitment over time and may be described as "watchful" (Brown, 252; Westcott, 47, Stott, 95).[150] As Burge (98) aptly explains, "Its use in the LXX and elsewhere implies duration and perseverance: to observe diligently, to guard carefully, to suddenly realize a truth—and to protect it. In other words, 'to keep God's word' goes far beyond mere conformity to law. It expresses a zealous desire to adhere to God's will."[151] Jesus applied this to his disciples in the upper room and told them that their love for him was proved or disproved by whether they kept his word (John 14:23–24). Thus, even for his disciples, disobedience was possible, and obedience was the proof of love, of relationship. It was not an evidence of their justification, because Jesus did not question that. In fact, he affirmed their salvation and security in his prayer to his Father (John 17:9–12). Obedience proves nothing to God. It serves as evidence to the world of our status as Jesus' disciples (John 13:34–35).

What is kept is God's "commandments" (τὰς ἐντολὰς). This is a common term in both the Gospel (ten times) and John's three epistles (eighteen times).[152] It is also a common term in the LXX, occurring more than

---

τοὺς λόγους τῆς προφητείας), and 9 (τῶν τηρούντων τοὺς λόγους τοῦ βιβλίου τούτου). Outside of John's literature, it may be found in Matt 14:17 and 1 Tim 6:14.

149. Paul's preferred term is φυλάσσω (Rom 2:26; Gal 6:13; 1 Tim 5:21; 6:20; 2 Tim 1:14; 2 Thess 3:3), though he does use τηρέω (1 Tim 6:14) as well. John does use φυλάσσω (1 John 5:21), and quotes Jesus' use of it in John 12:25 and 17:12 (juxtaposed with τηρέω).

150. Brooke (30) contrasts it with φυλάσσω in that he says it "denotes sympathetic obedience to the spirit of a command, rather than the rigid carrying out of its letter."

151. In thE LXXLXX, Prov 19:16, uses both φυλάσσω and τηρέω to say: "He who keeps [φυλάσσει] the commandment [ἐντολήν] keeps [τηρεῖ] his soul."

152. In the Gospel these include commandments from the Father to Jesus (John 10:18; 12:49, 50), to believers (John 15:10); from Jesus to the disciples (John 13:34; 14:15, 21; 15:10, 12); and from the Pharisees to the people (John 11:57). First John 2:3,

two hundred times, most often translating the Hebrew מִצְוָה ("commandment").[153] Its use indicates the general body of precepts most often rather than specific commands, whether singular or plural (Yarbrough, 82–83; contra Schnackenburg, 102, n. 3).[154]

Is John giving us a description of knowing God or a condition? Many see the two ideas as interchangeable (Boice, 57–58; Grayston, 60–61; Stott, 95).[155] For example, Kistemaker (255) says, "To know God is to keep his commands, and to keep his commands is to know God."[156] Others distinguish the two (Akin, 91; Burge 97). For example, Strecker (40) notes, "Keeping the commandments is not a condition but rather a sign of knowing God."[157]

4, 7 (x3), 8; 3:22, 23 (x2), 24; 4:21; 5:2, 3 (x2); 2 John 4, 5, 6 (x2). It also occurs twice in Revelation (Rev 12:17; 14:12).

153. Other terms translated by ἐντολή include פִּקּוּדִים ("commandments"), חֻקָּה ("enactment"), דָּבָר ("word"), חֹק ("statute"), and תּוֹרָה ("instruction, law"). G. Schrenk, "ἐντέλλομαι, ἐντολή," *TDNT* 2:546. Examples include Exod 12:17 (καὶ φυλάξεσθε τὴν ἐντολὴν ταύτην); 16:28, where it is synonymous with the Law ("Εως τίνος οὐ βούλεσθε εἰσακούειν τὰς ἐντολάς μου καὶ τὸν νόμον μου;); 24:12 (τὸν νόμον καὶ τὰς ἐντολάς); Lev 4:22 (πασῶν τῶν ἐντολῶν κυρίου τοῦ θεοῦ αὐτῶν); 22:31 (Καὶ φυλάξετε τὰς ἐντολάς μου καὶ ποιήσετε αὐτάς); Deut 4:2 (φυλάσσεσθε τὰς ἐντολὰς κυρίου τοῦ θεοῦ ὑμῶν); 5:29 (φοβεῖσθαί με καὶ φυλάσσεσθαι τὰς ἐντολάς μοι πάσας τὰς ἡμέρας); and 6:17 (φυλάσσων φυλάξῃ τὰς ἐντολὰς κυρίου τοῦ θεοῦ σου).

154. With the exception of Jesus' obedience to His Father, where the sg. is used, and His command to love one another in John 13:34 and 15:12 (as well as later in this epistle), the pl. form is used to indicate general obedience to God's revealed will, a body of commands. Brown (250–51) raises the question whether there is any significance between the sg. and pl. forms of ἐντολή, arguing that there is not. In one sense he is correct in that Jesus' following his Father's "command" involved many actions. Yet, he does distinguish between a specific command, to love one another, and his body of commands ("If you love me, you will keep my commandments"). That the Gospel does not spell out a body of commands or instructions like we see in Matt 8–9 and 18–23 does not mean that the disciples failed to remember His instructions. Those commands are repeated in their NT epistles as well as the other Gospel accounts. Additionally, Brown (281) suggests that John may be referring or alluding to the Ten Commandments.

155. Stott (95) calls this "the test of moral obedience."

156. Grayston (60–61) says much the same thing in that "a condition for knowing God is actually a description of knowing him: to know God is to obey him and to obey him is to know him."

157. Strecker (40) differs from Schnackenburg (98), rejecting his view that there is a synergistic relationship between knowing God and obedience. I would concur with Schnackenburg, that there is an element of human cooperation because John is describing issues effecting the sanctification of his readers, not their justification.

John is affirming that it is possible for a regenerate person not to know God personally, relationally. He is not saying a disobedient Christian is unregenerate, but only that he or she does not really know the God who has saved him or her in a personal way.[158]

2:4 We know by keeping. This verse explains this truth more clearly. This is communicated by a complex subject that exposes the claim and conduct of someone making a false claim to know God relationally with the resultant reality. This is the first of three claims or statements (2:4, 6, 9) that have corresponding realities in terms of what is or should be true of the person making the claim. Though they may initially appear to be parallel to the three "if" statements in the first chapter, they are not all false statements (Bruce, 51). Also, John does not directly include himself in these three. Thus it is better to see these as describing principles rather than the words of an individual.

ὁ λέγων ὅτι Ἔγνωκα αὐτὸν, "He who says, 'I have come to know him.'" John addresses the first of three false claims by one "who says" and "does not keep." He combines the claim and practice to describe a "liar."[159] His use of a present participle focuses on the person's state of being, his character, rather than focusing on the time element (*while* he is saying and not keeping).[160]

And whereas there is no human action involved in justification, the faith of sanctification is always expressed through works (Jas 2:14). On the more popular level, B. Bryant ("Confession of Sins in the Spirit-Filled Life," 62) is an example of one who distinguishes between having fellowship with and knowing God. He writes, "John tells us that fellowship with God is not identical to knowing God. Fellowship with God is based on confession of sins while knowing God is based on keeping His commandments." He makes a distinction between what are actually synonyms with John in his epistle. It is better to see fellowship and knowing God as describing the same experience for the believer.

158. See my analysis of John 17:3 in *The Disciplemaker* for a full discussion of the relationship of eternal life and relational knowledge of God. Additionally, see my analysis of Jesus' words to Thomas and Philip in John 14:5–11.

159. Brown (464) considers the person described with the articular pres. participle to "personify the true secessionist and Johannine spokesman." This is similar to the view taken here, although secessionists are not in view, simply false teachers who may or may not have been associated with John. Marshall (124) sees these as a restatement of the same false claim in 1:6, as does Brooke (31).

160. Lenski (406) calls these "descriptive" participle As B. M. Fanning (*Verbal Aspects*, 408) describes the pres. ptc as focusing "on the internal make-up of the occurrence and views it in its course (or in its repetition or its continuing existence,

Thus, it carries more of a gnomic sense than progressive. Rather than being adverb, "while not keeping," the second participle functions with the first as a compound subject, describing the person, not indicating the activity of the claimant. This is someone claiming to know God whose lifestyle is one of disobedience.

The subject of the sentence has shifted from first person plural to third person singular. Most scholars see these as the words of John's opponents, the false teachers (Brown, 281; Grayston, 64; Harris, 77; Houlden, 66; Johnson, 40; Marshall, 124; Schnackenburg, 102).[161] The weakness of this is the second and third claims (2:6, 9). In 2:6 John states the obligation that *whoever* makes these claims experiences, and in 2:9 the claimant is hating a Christian brother, and so must be a believer in order to do so.[162] So these are not just things a false teacher would say and do, or fail to do, but are possible of any believer.[163] Rather than seeing this as John responding to opponents, it is better to see him making universal statements to introduce principles by which the spiritual world functions. Though the false teachers could say this, so, too, could any Christian.

καὶ τὰς ἐντολὰς αὐτοῦ μὴ τηρῶν, "and does not keep his commandments." This is the same person as "he who says." This is an example of the Granville Sharp Rule in which two substantives, in this case present participle, are joined by *καὶ* and the first is articular and second anarthrous. They are

---

etc., whatever the specific make-up may be), without regard for the beginning or end-point." It is this aspect of the articular pres. participle that I see in focus with John. He is viewing them in terms of their being, their nature, rather than their activity (though their activity flows out of their nature). This is not to deny that the pres. participle can, as Fanning (409) says, denote "a specific occurrence viewed as it is taking place and thus emphasizing either the simultaneity of the participial occurrence with the main verbal occurrence or portraying it with greater vividness in description" whether in an adv. or substantival role. However, in this case John is describing a kind of person, and so it seems best to see its focus on character rather than activity.

161. Brooke (31) describes this as "the direct and definite statement of the writer conscious of the fact that he is dealing with a real danger, and probably with a statement that has been actually made, by men against whose influence he is trying to guard his *τεκνία*."

162. See the discussion on 2:6 and 9.

163. Perkins (21) sees this as expressing a "Johannine tradition," and thus something that believers could claim. She correctly sees John alluding to 1:5–7, based on the reappearance of the term "walk" in 2:6.

closely related, whether as synonymous or sharing some aspect of meaning.[164] So we have profession and conduct brought together. This is someone claiming knowledge of God while being characterized by a failure to live obediently.[165]

ψεύστης ἐστὶν καὶ ἐν τούτῳ ἡ ἀλήθεια οὐκ ἔστιν·, "is a liar and the truth is not *abiding* in him." This statement reflects back on what he has just said about how we can know if we have come to know God in a relational sense. He is clarifying that just because one claims to know God relationally, that claim may not be true. Its validity is determined by actions. As Houlden (66) aptly says, "Knowledge of God is not speculative and abstract, but practical and experiential." Additionally, someone claiming that knowledge while disobeying him is a liar; he is demonstrating practically that what he claims theoretically is not reality.

John now speaks to the character of the person making a false claim of knowing God relationally.[166] Using a hendiadys, he emphasizes the extent of the deception by the repetition of synonymous ideas. A liar does not have truth resident within him.[167] When John calls him a liar here, he is making a judgment statement about the person's character. He is not just lying to himself.[168] He is a kind of person, a liar.[169]

---

164. D. B. Wallace, *Grammar*, 270–75.

165. The OT concept of keeping God's commandments simply meant a life of obedience. This is evident in such passages as Deut 4:40; 7:11; 8:6; 13:4; 29:9; 30:20; 32:46; Lev 22:31; Num 15:40.

166. Brown rejects the idea that John is describing character (naming Brooke and Westcott as examples he rejects) and sees only "stylistic variation" in John's choice of a ptc. over a verb (Brown, 253).

167. Lenski (407) does not note the hendiadys and so concludes from this that the person must be a conscious deceiver rather than self-deceived because he recognizes the synonymy of the two terms and sees it as "a mere tautology since every liar lacks truthfulness."

168. Boice (58) sees this person as knowing his profession is false rather than being deceived or inconsistent. I am not certain we can make such a strong statement in that John's language indicates the truth is not in this person and so one might imply from this a lack of understanding more than a determined rejection of truth. However, the comparison later to the devil would tend to support Boice's view.

169. Grayston (64), on the other hand, sees this as a person who is only self-deceived and "not necessarily someone who makes false statements with intent to deceive ... but maybe someone who deceives by stating what he falsely believes to be the truth."

John's point in these two recent verses is that a person can claim knowledge (relationship), but the reality of that relationship is measured by obedience. Notice what John says about the person making such false claims. He is both a liar and a person who is not being influenced by the truth (Marshall, 124; Strecker, 41).[170] John is not saying he is unregenerate (contra Burge, 98; Schnackenburg, 102), an unbeliever, but just a liar. Though the article does not necessarily make conceptual nouns definite, in this instance it seems best to see it serving to indicate a specific body of truth rather than truth in general or as a concept. "Truth" is not equivalent to "salvation" or "gospel message."[171] Rather, John uses it often and, in this case, to indicate the body of orthodox teachings that impact one's lifestyle. It is important that we not read every description of a person soteriologically. We must remember that not all saints are saintly in their behavior. Disobedience reveals the lack of a personal knowledge of Jesus in the same way that the apostles, who accompanied Jesus for three and a half years, lacked that knowledge in the upper room. Thus, claiming to know him while disobeying his word is to live a lie, described here by John as "the truth is not in him." What he means by this is that truth is not a controlling influence in the believer's life as was possible for John in 1:6, 8, and 10.

Biblical Theology Comments

This section of John's epistle contributes significantly to our understanding of Jesus' person and work. Though we see him as the Lamb of God who is worthy to break the seals and judge the world in Rev 4–5, here we are

170. Bultmann (25) goes too far when he says that the phrase "he is a liar" indicates more than that "such a person says something untrue, but that he is nothing, since ἀλήθεια ('truth') is reality."

171. Burge (98) observes well that the concept of "truth" is central to Johannine thought. He notes that it "describes Jesus (John 14:6), the Holy Spirit (14:17), and the word (17:17)." And he says well that this "truth ... should accompany all worship that is empowered by God's Spirit (4:24)." But he follows this by saying that "John is here *not* simply saying that someone who fails to obey has missed the point, instead, such people are seriously disconnected from God." By "disconnected" he seems to mean that the disobedient person is unregenerate. But that need not even be the implication. The same thing was said in 1:8 and there connected with self-deception that believers may experience. Thus here it can have the same sense. Though the deceived individual is described with the third person rather than the first person, and so John does not identify himself with him, this need not imply John considers him unregenerate, just deceived.

taught about his ministry on our behalf in heaven. As Jesus was introduced as eternal life incarnate in the prologue, we now see him as our Advocate in heaven, enabling us to walk in God's moral purity ("the light") through the moment-by-moment application of his death on our behalf. Our inability to measure up to God's holiness (in terms of moral purity) is provided for by God, but made contingent on our honesty with him about our need. In John 14:16–17 Jesus promised to send the indwelling Holy Spirit, who would be our earthy help (Paraclete). We learn in 1 John that Jesus ascended to heaven and ministers there as our heavenly help (Advocate, Paraclete). We see also that Jesus' death on the cross was not applied just once, at our justification (Col 2:11–14), but constantly in our sanctification (1:7). Unlike justification, we participate in our sanctification (through faith expressing itself in obedience), though in complete dependence on God to accomplish it.

God's forgiveness and cleansing extend beyond those sins we know to confess. The final clause in 1 John 1:9 promises that God's response to our confession makes us morally pure like him. God "cleanses" us from "every unrighteousness." The inclusion of the adjective πάσης, best translated as "every," expresses the full extent of God's work on our behalf.[172] We cannot be as pure as God unless every shred of darkness, every shadow is removed from our being. We cannot walk in the light apart from being purified light as well. Thus as the plural article and noun of *sins* clarify that it is not just sin in general, the addition of πάσης clarifies that everything else is included in God's work of making us as morally pure as he is. When we confess what we know, God forgives not only the sins we see, but also the sins of which we remain unaware.

This confession impacts the New Testament saint in the same way the Old Testament sacrifices worked in the lives of Old Testament saints. The sacrificial system was designed to restore fellowship with a holy God, not

172. Haas, de Jonge, and Swellengrebel (31) suggest the καὶ that joins the "forgive" and "cleanse" clauses may have a "resultative or explanatory force," preferring the explanatory. It would be better seeing this as a simple coordinating conj. that connects two acts of God in response to confession. This is evident in the distinction brought about by his use of πάσης to modify unrighteousness while only identifying "the sins" with the article. It necessarily includes more than just those sins confessed. To make it a clarification of what he means by sins weakens the promise to the one who confesses.

gain the offerer salvation. They assumed the worshiper coming into God's presence was a redeemed saint, was a believer in God.

John has placed this promise at the center of his chiasm to emphasize the believer's part in walking in the light and communing with God. Though Jesus' work on the cross is the basis of all cleansing, "we must be willing to confess our sins. God's provision and man's responsibility go hand in hand" (Kistemaker, 247).

That God has said we are sinful creatures is evident throughout Scripture. The clearest examples come from the requirements of the Mosaic law's sacrificial system, beginning with the consecration of Aaron and his sons to the priesthood, and the annual provision of the Day of Atonement for the nation. Psalm 14, quoted by Paul in Rom 3:9–18, along with many other passages throughout the Old Testament and New Testament, declares the sinfulness of all of mankind. Only Jesus is sinless. For one of us to claim similar sinlessness is to say that God erred when he inspired the prophets and authors of Scripture to assert man's sinful guilt.

Though his death provides propitiation for every human being, this does not mean everyone is automatically justified.[173] It is not Jesus' death that saves. It is God the Father, the righteous judge, applying the benefits of Jesus' death to a person and declaring that person justified that saves. Without Jesus' death there is no salvation. Christ's death is *sufficient* for all, but *efficient* only for those who believe in him (Kistemaker, 253). Adam, Abraham, and Moses could not be forgiven their sins apart from Jesus satisfying God's just wrath toward each of them. Thus, though salvation is offered to all (Rev 22:17), not all are saved. Only those redeemed by his blood benefit from his work on their behalf. "Christ is a universal propitiation for sins; and he is an advocate for the Christian. He has accomplished a work on earth for all: He is accomplishing a work in heaven for those who are united with him" (Westcott, 41). Paul affirms this same truth in 2 Cor 5:18–19. Even so, though God has reconciled himself toward the whole world, not every person in the world chooses to be reconciled to him. The nonelect will always choose to reject his offer of forgiveness and salvation.

---

173. As Stott (89) notes well, "This cannot be pressed into meaning that all sins are automatically pardoned through the propitiation of Christ, but that a universal pardon is offered for (the sins of) the whole world and is enjoyed by those who embrace it."

Thus, we see that Jesus' propitiatory work does not automatically justify anyone, but provides the means of justification for those who seek reconciliation through faith. Furthermore, though one day the planet itself, along with the rest of creation, will be restored as a result of Jesus' work (Rom 8:22), here it is humanity that John intends.[174]

However, what about the elect? Even the elect are not saved by his death alone, or apart from faith in him. For example, the Ephesian Christians, while being "chosen" by God "before the foundation of the world" (Eph 1:4) were still "dead in trespasses and sins" (Eph 2:1–7) until God "made us alive" in Christ. It was this act of God, not the death of Jesus, that made them alive. Jesus' death does not benefit a person until the Father declares him justified and imputes his sin to Christ and his righteousness to him, regenerates him, transfers him from Satan's kingdom to Christ's, and makes him his child. Again, the elect are not justified before or apart from faith in Christ.

Application and Devotional Implications

1:6–8 All of us have aspects of our attitudes and of our being that differ from God. Furthermore, everywhere we are different from God, we are wicked. Most of us will not pursue God as a lifestyle, and few of us will achieve a level of godliness that results from dealing with the sin in our lives. We love our sin too much. When we recognize an area that is different from God, we have to admit that it is sin, and we have to go to him in prayer and seek his forgiveness in that area. If we do not deal with it, we move into the darkness; we are further from fellowship with God. If we do deal with it, we draw closer to God. We never cease being justified saints, but we can cease being in fellowship even while we are busy acting spiritual. Sanctification is a process of growth that begins with regeneration and ends with glorification (whether following resurrection or rapture). It is never static or continual, but results from obedience over time, and may express itself in varying "rates" of spiritual growth at different times of one's life. Even so, it is as much by grace through faith, and a work of the Spirit, as is

174. Brown (222) notes the κόσμος is "the object of redemption in passages like Mark 16:15; Rom 11:15; 2 Cor 5:19; 1 Tim 1:15; and Rev 11:15. But there are other passages where, even after Christ's coming, the world is regarded as unfriendly, hostile, and destined for damnation, e.g., Matt 18:7; 1 Cor 2:12; 7:31; 11:32; Gal 4:3–4; 6:14; Col 2:8; and Jas 4:4."

justification (Eph 2:8–9). It is not the result of works in our own strength (Gal 3:2–3), though it does include works that express a "living" (effectual) faith (Jas 2:14–17).

1:9 Confession involves genuine honesty with God. Moreover, what we find is that God responds to honesty, "truthfulness," even when approached by a sinful creature. Psalm 18:25–27 says, "With the merciful You will show Yourself merciful; with a blameless man You will show Yourself blameless; with the pure You will show Yourself pure; and with the devious You will show Yourself shrewd." This was such a significant truth that it was included in the epilogue of David's life in 2 Sam 22. God deals with men in accordance with their character. Consequently, here in 1 John, we see that our morally pure God cleanses those honest enough to admit their need.

There are a lot of areas where we are blind to our own sinfulness and will remain such until the day we die. God knows those areas, even though we may remain completely blind to them until the day we meet Jesus and become like him. When we admit to what we do know, God takes care of the rest. He cleanses every area in his relationship with us. When my son comes to me about something he has done wrong, I know plenty of other areas as well. I can list his flaws. When he comes to me, he does not have to admit to everything that is wrong with him. He can't because he does not know! The result is we deal only with the issue at hand. In the same way, God says that he will take care of the other things when we approach him about what we know to be wrong. This is salvation as deliverance, being a process experienced in the present (a sanctification reality). God is continually in the process of delivering us from the very sin we are about to confess (the progressive aspect of salvation). Salvation is a process as well as an event. Knowing these things should free us up to focus on those sins we see rather than trying to find those sins we are yet to discover in our own lives. This gives us confidence before God, but should also motivate us to confess as soon as we become aware of a sin. Why? Though we have far more sins we *could* confess, we need not because God remembers them all and has promised to remove each unknown sin along with the confessed known sin. Furthermore, God keeps his promises.

2:1–4 Though our sins are provided for by the work of Jesus, we still stand in need of his advocacy. We may have the goal of sinlessness, but we have seen that we can never be that this side of eternity. Yet, it does not become an excuse to sin, but a reason to be thankful that Jesus intercedes on our behalf. Rather than lapsing into sin, we should each be motivated to obey. This is not just to prove we know God, but that our knowledge is personal, relational, real. In this section the theme of fellowship is developed under the concept of knowing God. Just as the disciples did not "know" the God they believed in, so we, too, could be guilty of believing in but not personally relating to God. This needs to be a lifelong goal of every believer, that we will persevere in our pursuit of having fellowship with our God and Father through our Lord and Savior, who serves as our Advocate to enable us the access only a moral pure person deserves.

Selected Bibliography

Adamson, J. *The Epistle of James*. NICNT. Grand Rapids: Eerdmans, 1976.

Balla, P. "Child-Parent Imagery in the Catholic Epistles." *Southern Baptist Journal of Theology* 6 (2002): 66–77.

Barclay, W. *The Letters of James and Peter*. Rev. ed. The Daily Study Bible Series. Philadelphia: Westminster, 2000.

Blue, J. Ronald. "James." In *The Bible Knowledge Commentary: An Exposition of the Scriptures*, edited by J. F. Walvoord and R. B. Zuck. Wheaton, IL: Victor, 1983–1985.

Boa, K., and W. Kruidenier. *Romans*. Holman New Testament Commentary 6. Nashville: Broadman & Holman, 2000.

Bock, D. L. *Luke Vol 2: 9:51–24:53*. BECNT. Grand Rapids: Baker, 1996.

Bogart, J. *Orthodox and Heretical Perfectionism in the Johannine Community as Evident in the First Epistle of John*. SBLDS 33. Missoula, MT: Scholars Press, 1977.

Boice, J. M. *Christ's Call to Discipleship*. Chicago: Moody, 1986.

Brenneman, J. E. "Atonement, Day of." In *Eerdmans Dictionary of the Bible*, edited by D. N. Freedman, A. C. Myers, and A. B. Beck. Grand Rapids: Eerdmans, 2000.

Bryant, B. "Confession of Sins in the Spirit-Filled Life." *JOTGES* 14 (2001): 53–62.

Bultmann, R. "Analyse des 1 Joh." In *Festgabe für A. Jülicher zum 70v*, 138–58. Tübingen: J. C. B. Mohr, 1927.

Carson, D. A. "1–3 John." In *Commentary on the New Testament Use of the Old Testament,* edited by G. K. Beale and D. A. Carson, 1063–67. Grand Rapids: Baker Academic, 2007.

Chafer, L. S. "The Eternal Security of the Believer, Part 2." *BSac* 106 (1949): 391–419.

Cook, W. R. "Hamartiological Problems in First John." *BSac* 123 (1966): 249–60.

Cranfield, C. E. B. *A Critical and Exegetical Commentary on the Epistle to the Romans*. ICC. Edinburgh: T & T Clark, 1975.

Danby, H. *Mishnah: Translated from the Hebrew with Introduction and Brief Explanatory Notes*. Oxford: Oxford University Press, 1933.

Davids, P. *Commentary on James*. NIGTC. Grand Rapids: Eerdmans, 1982.

de Jonge, M. "The Use of the Word ΧΡΙΣΤΟΣ in the Johannine Epistles." In *Studies in John*, 67–74. NovTSup 24. Leiden: E. J. Brill, 1970.

Derickson, G. W., and E. D. Radmacher. *The Disciplemaker: What Matters Most to Jesus*. Salem, OR: Charis, 2001.

Dodd, C. H. "*Hilaskesthai*, Its Cognates, Derivatives, and Synonyms, in the Septuagint." *JTS* 32 (1931): 352–60.

Fanning, B. M. *Verbal Aspect in New Testament Greek*. Oxford: Clarendon, 1990.

Hartley, J. E. *Leviticus*. WBC 4. Dallas: Word, 2002.

Henderson, D. W. *Culture Shift: Communicating God's Truth in Our Changing World.* Grand Rapids: Baker, 1998.

Hill, D. *Greek Words and Hebrew Meanings.* Eugene, OR: Wipf & Stock, 2001.

Hodges, Z. C. "What Do We Mean by Propitiation? Does It Only Count If We Accept It?" *JOTGES* 19 (2006): 35–42.

Houlden, J. L. "Salvation Proclaimed II: 1 John 1.5–2.6: Belief and Growth." *ExpTim* 93 (1982): 132–36.

Hughes, R. B., and J. C. Laney. *Tyndale Concise Bible Commentary*. Wheaton, IL: Tyndale House, 2001.

Jamieson, R., A. R. Fausset, and D. Brown. *A Commentary, Critical and Explanatory, on the Old and New Testaments.* Oak Harbor, WA: Logos Research Systems, Inc., 1997.

Joslin, Barry C. "Christ Bore the Sins of Many: Substitution and the Atonement in Hebrews." *SBJT* 11 (2007): 72–96.

Käsemann, E. *Commentary on Romans*. Translated and edited by Geoffrey W. Bromiley. Grand Rapids: Eerdmans, 1980.

Kistemaker, S. J. "The Theological Message of James." *JETS* 29 (1986): 54–61.

Koch, K. *Die israelitische Sühneanschauung und ihre historischeen Wandlungen*. Erlangen: Habilitationsschrift, 1956.

Krämer, H. "ἀλλήλων." In *Exegetical Dictionary of the New Testament.* Edited by H. R. Balz and G. Schneider. Translated by V. P. Howard and J. W. Thompson. Edinburgh: T & T Clark, 1990.

Longenecker, R. N. *Galatians*. WBC 41. Dallas: Word, 2002.

Louw, J. P. "Verbal Aspect in the First Letter of John." *Neot* 9 (1975): 98–104.

MacArthur, J. F., Jr. "Faith according to the Apostle James." *JETS* 33 (March 1990): 11–47.

MacDonald, W., and A. Farstad. *Believer's Bible Commentary: Old and New Testaments.* Nashville: Thomas Nelson, 1997.

Marshall, I. H. *The Gospel of Luke: A Commentary on the Greek Text.* NIGTC. Exeter, England: Paternoster, 1978.

Martin, R. P. *James.* WBC 48. Dallas: Word, 2002.

Moo, D. J. *Romans 1–8.* Wycliffe Exegetical Commentary. Chicago: Moody, 1991.

Morris, L. "The Use of *hilaskesthai* etc. in Biblical Greek." *ExpTim* 62 (1950): 227–33.

Morris, L. "The Wrath of God." *ExpTim* 63 (1951): 142–45.

Morris, L. *The Apostolic Preaching of the Cross.* Rev. ed. Grand Rapids: Eerdmans, 1965.

Moule, C. F. D. *An Idiom-book of New Testament Greek.* 2nd ed. New York: Cambridge University Press, 1959.

Mounce, R. H. *Romans.* NAC 27. Electronic ed. Nashville: Broadman & Holman, 2001.

Nicole, R. R. "C. H. Dodd and the Doctrine of Propitiation." *WTJ 17* (1954): 116–57.

Nicole, R. R. "'Hilaskesthai' Revisited." *EvQ* 49 (1977): 173–77.

The Oxford Dictionary of the Christian Church. 3rd ed. Revised and edited by F. L. Cross and E. A. Livingstone. Oxford: Oxford University Press, 2005.

Reiling J., and J. L. Swellengrebel. *A Handbook on the Gospel of Luke.* UBS. New York: United Bible Societies, 1993.

Richardson, K. A. *James.* NAC 36. Nashville: Broadman & Holman, 2001.

Ryrie, C. C. *So Great Salvation.* Wheaton, IL: Victor, 1989.

Schneider, G. "ὡς," In *Exegetical Dictionary of the New Testament.* Edited by H. R. Balz and G. Schneider. Translated by V. P. Howard and J. W. Thompson. Edinburgh: T & T Clark, 1990.

Schreiner, T. R. *Romans.* BECNT 6. Grand Rapids: Baker, 1998.

Silva, M. *Philippians.* 2nd ed. BECNT 11. Grand Rapids: Baker, 2005.

Stevens, J. D. "James." In *KJV Bible Commentary.* Nashville: Thomas Nelson, 1997.

Stiggers, H. G. "צָדֵק." In *Theological Wordbook of the Old Testament*, edited by R. L. Harris, G. L. Archer, and B. K. Waltke, 2:752. Electronic ed. Chicago: Moody, 1999

Wallace, D. B. *Greek Grammar beyond the Basics.* Grand Rapids: Zondervan, 1996.

Walvoord, J. F. "Christ's Olivet Discourse on the End of the Age, Part VII: The Judgment of the Nations." *BSac* 129 (1972): 306–15.

Walvoord, J. F. "Series in Christology, Part 4: The Preincarnate Son of God." *BSac* 104 (1947): 414–40.

Wead, D. W. "The Johannine Double Meaning." *ResQ* 13 (1970): 106–20.

Wessel, W. W. "James 2:14." In *The Wycliffe Bible Commentary: New Testament.* Edited by C. F. Pfeiffer and E. F. Harrison. Chicago: Moody, 1962.

Wiersbe, W. W. *The Bible Exposition Commentary.* Wheaton, IL: Victor, 1996.

Yonge, C. D. *The Works of Philo: Complete and Unabridged.* New updated ed. Peabody, MA: Hendrickson, 1996.

Young, N. H. "C. H. Dodd, 'Hilaskesthai' and His Critics." *EvQ* 48 (1976): 67–78.

Young, N. H. "'Hilaskesthai' and Related Words in the New Testament." *EvQ* 55 (1983): 169–76.

Zerwick, M. *Biblical Greek: Illustrated by Examples*. Scripta Pontificii Instituti Biblici; 114. English ed. adapted from the 4th Latin ed. by Joseph Smith. Rome: Tipografia P.U.G., 1963.

Imitation of Christ (2:5–6)

Original Text

5 ὃς δ᾽ ἂν τηρῇ αὐτοῦ τὸν λόγον, ἀληθῶς ἐν τούτῳ ἡ ἀγάπη τοῦ θεοῦ τετελείωται. ἐν τούτῳ γινώσκομεν ὅτι ἐν αὐτῷ ἐσμεν· **6** ὁ λέγων ἐν αὐτῷ μένειν ὀφείλει καθὼς ἐκεῖνος περιεπάτησεν καὶ αὐτὸς οὕτως^a περιπατεῖν.

Textual Notes

6.a. Though the external evidence for οὕτως is mixed, it seems best to include it in the text because (1) it has the support of the Byzantine texts, and (2) would be more likely to be dropped from the text through scribal error than to be added. Those texts containing οὕτως include ℵ C Ψ 81 *Byz*; while those omitting it are A B 33 2464. Metzger proposes its omission could have resulted from a scribal error, or it may have been added "as an emphatic correlative with the preceding καθώς"[175]

Translation

5 But whoever keeps his word, truly in him the love of God has been made complete, by means of this[176] we know that we are *abiding*[177] in him. **6** He

175. B. Metzger and United Bible Societies, *A Textual Commentary on the Greek New Testament*, 2d ed., 639–40.

176. Other translations include "by this" (ESV, NASB95, NKJV, Net), "this/that is how" (HCSB, NIV84, NLT), "hereby" (ASV).

177. "Abiding" is understood in the context (abiding follows in the immediate context) and appears to make his point more clear. It is left out of most translations (ASV, ESV, HCSB, NET, NIV84, NKJV). "Living" is added in NLT.

who says he abides in him is obligated, just as he[178] walked, he also should walk in the same way.[179]

Commentary

2:5 In contrast to the liar is the one who "keeps his word." Reflecting Jesus' words in the upper room (John 14:21), John tells us that in such a person (literally: "in this one") God's love has been brought to its full expression.[180]

ὃς δ' ἂν τηρῇ αὐτοῦ τὸν λόγον, "But whoever keeps his word." Using a third person relative clause as the pendent nominative describing ἐν τούτῳ in the clause that follows, John draws a contrast (δὲ) with the liar of v. 4.[181] In contrast with the one who "does not keep his commandments" is the one who "keeps his word."[182] Yet this clause utilizes the conditional particle ἂν and implies by this that someone may yet choose not to keep his word (Williamson, 84).

Here "word" (λόγον) is synonymous with "commandments" (ἐντολὰς) in vv. 3 and 4 (Brown, 252; Burge, 98; Strecker, 41).[183] As well as using the

178. This reflects the use of ἐκεῖνος to designate Jesus throughout this epistle. Literally it means "that one." But it makes better English to express the idea with "he" (ASV, ESV, HCSB, NASB95). Others translate it as "Jesus" (NET, NIV84, NLT).

179. FollowinG ESV. This reflects the sense of οὕτως. Others translate it as "just as" (HCSB, NET, NKJV), "even as" (ASV), "as" (NIV84, NLT), or "in the same manner" (NASB95).

180. Though Marshall (124) connects this verse with v. 3, seeing an ABA construction in vv. 3–5, I differ in that this verse begins a new unit of thought and vv. 3 and 4 are connected to the previous section's chiasmus. On a different note, Moody (34) says, "True knowledge of God is obedience to God, and obedience to God is love for God. This is the logical connection between 2:4 and 2:5."

181. D. Wallace, *Grammar*, 51–52. Akin (92), following R. L. Thomas ("Exegetical Digest of 1 John," 108), wrongly identifies this nominative case relative clause as a nominative absolute construction.

182. See 2:3 for a full discussion of the meaning of "keep." The pronoun ὃς with ἂν introduces an indefinite relative clause. This same construction occurs in 3:17, 22; 4:15; 5:15; 3 John 5.

183. Burge (98) notes also that this fits John's pattern of preferring variation in wording by utilizing synonyms and employing their common meanings. This is not always the case, though, for sufficient examples occur where he intends the nuanced differences to be noted. This is also the case with οἶδα and γινώσκω with John, as will be seen in discussions of the terms in this commentary. Law (212) says "the unity of the 'word' is substituted for the multiplicity of the 'commandments.'" John's point in changing terms, especially in light of its allusion to Jesus' words in the upper room, makes this distinction unlikely. Rather, "word" is understood

two as synonyms, John appears to be consciously reflecting Jesus' use of the two terms in the upper room (John 14:21 "commandments" and 14:23 "word") as well.[184] He may also have chosen the term because it is conceptually more inclusive than commandments in that it reflects the full revelation of God's word as opposed to the 613 commandments of the law (Stott, 96).[185] Further, he has moved the pronoun from after "commandments" to before "word" to emphasize that what is being kept is *God's* Word, *God's* commands (Westcott, 48).[186] Additionally, his use of the present subjunctive emphasizes the ongoing aspect of keeping his word. The person described "keeps on keeping" his word.[187]

ἀληθῶς ἐν τούτῳ ἡ ἀγάπη τοῦ θεοῦ τετελείωται, "truly in him the love of God has been made complete." John begins his description of the obedient man with the adverb "truly" (ἀληθῶς), placed in an emphatic position in its

---

conceptually to include all of God's words, or commandments, and is better seen as a pure synonym rather than a nuanced change of terms as Law is taking it.

184. Brown (252) notes well the pattern of John in his Gospel that develops this synonymy. He describes it as "a chain of thought" in which "Jesus keeps the Father's word (8:55); and the disciples keep Jesus' word (8:51; 14:23; 15:20; and 14:24 [pl.]). However, the disciples also keep God's word (17:6), and other people are challenged to keep the disciples' word (15:20)." He also reminds us of the possible connection with the LXX because "in the OT (Hebrew and Greek) the technical name for the Ten Commandments was the 'Ten Words' (*Decalogue*)."

185. Strecker (41–42) sees in this an "eschatological claim" along with the ethical, that one must believe that Jesus as the Son of God has been sent into the world based on John's words in 5:4–5 ("Because everyone who has been born from God overcomes the world; and this is the victory that has overcome the world, our faith. And who is the one who overcomes the world, if not the one believing that Jesus is the Son of God?") and that John is using apocalyptic terminology. The context of imitating Jesus' walk and the clear ethical focus of this passage mitigates this connection. Further, the fact that τετελείωται shares a common root with τέλος need not indicate an eschatological focus or apocalyptic terminology, even though τέλος is often used in its eschatological sense (Matt 24:6, 14; 1 Cor 15:24; 1 Pet 4:7). It is also used without any eschatological nuance throughout the NT (Matt 26:58; Rom 6:22; 10:4; 1 Tim 1:5; Jas 5:11). It is used by John in its noneschatological sense in John 13:1. And in Rev 2:26, Jesus uses it in the sense of the end of one's life, until death.

186. The possessive pronoun has been moved before τὸν λόγον for emphasis, where it followed τὰς ἐντολὰς in v. 3. Both uses of ἐν τούτῳ may point back to what has just been said or forward to what will follow immediately.

187. D. B. Wallace, *Grammar*, 518. This is an example of a progressive present in an oblique mood (subjunctive).

clause (Brooke, 32).[188] From the same root as *truth*, it appears that John is emphasizing this concept by repetition of its root as well as its position. Just as the false claimant lacks the truth, the true claimant exists in its reality. John's use of ἐν τούτῳ is not a dative of means ("by means of this"), but a dative of sphere ("in the realm/sphere of this person"), with τούτῳ being used in its pronominal sense with its antecedent being the conceptual subject of the clause, "whoever keeps his word," though not its grammatical subject.

The love of God has four possible meanings in this context. (1) It could describe God's love objectively in that man's love is directed toward God (Akin, 93; Brooke, 32; Bruce, 51; Burge, 98; Johnson, 62; Jones, 54; Lenski, 408; Rensberger, 62). This would be based on the context of devotion to God in this paragraph. (2) It could describe God's love subjectively in that man is the object of God's love (Bultmann, 25; Williamson, 84; Yarbrough, 86).[189] Westcott (48–49) argues for the subjective sense: "Generally the genitive after ἀγάπη in the N. T. is *subj.* and defines those who feel or shew love." He then says, "The Christian 'knows the love of God' and it becomes in him a spring of love, attaining its complete development in human life through vital obedience. ... The perfection of love is conditioned by the completeness of obedience." Kistemaker (257) argues for the subjunctive sense from the parallel concepts in vv. 4 and 5, created by the contrast between God's truth not being in the false claimant and God's love being in the obedient one. He sees both truth and love originating in God rather than man. Also, he says further that the broader context of 4:7, John's statement that love comes from God, should inform the meaning of this passage. (3) It could be a "qualitative genitive," (Schnackenburg, 103, n. 2) being used

188. This is the single use of this adv. in 1 John, or anywhere else solely by him. The seven other uses all occur in quotations of others in his Gospel. John 1:47 (Jesus); 4:42 (men of Sychar); 6:14 (people who witnessed the feeding of the five thousand); 7:26 (people of Jerusalem), 40 (visitors to Jerusalem who heard Jesus); 8:31 (Jesus); 17:8 (Jesus praying to the Father).

189. G. Delling, "τέλος, τελειόω," *TDNT*, 8:81–82. Bultmann (25) argues for the subjective gen. on the basis that "man's love cannot be directly oriented toward God." His references to 4:20 ("If anyone says, 'I love God' and hates his brother, he is a liar; for the one who does not love his brother whom he has seen is not able to love God whom he has not seen.") and 5:2–3 ("By this we know that we love the children of God when we love God and keep his commandments. For this is our love for God, that we should keep his commandments; and his commandments are not burdensome.")

descriptively as the "love that is particular to God himself," a divine kind of love (Kistemaker, 257; Marshall, 125).[190] Or, (4) it could be a plenary genitive and so be intentionally ambiguous, combining both senses of the subjective and objective: God's love for us *and* our love for God (Strecker, 42; Thomas, 98).[191] This final sense seems best.

John's use of "made complete" carries the sense of completeness and maturity, but may also look to the future (Strecker, 42).[192] God's love has been brought to its goal, though not to a flawless expression in the person (Thompson, 56).[193] God's love being perfected, or "made complete," can have one of two senses. (1) It may indicate that our love for God grows to the extent that we keep his word. Or, (2) it may indicate that God's love directed toward a believer grows as that person pursues fellowship with God and obedience to his Word. This second sense seems more appropriate to John's use here. The passive τετελείωται indicates that this is a work of God in the believer (Lenski, 408; Schnackenburg, 104; Williamson, 84–85).[194] The believer can "know" experientially that he or she is "in him" only to the extent that he or she is pursuing fellowship with God through obedience. Fellowship with God is not automatic but contingent. Fellowship with God is not a fruit of salvation; it is one of its benefits that may or may not be experienced. Jesus himself tells us that his experience of the Father's love was contingent on his obedience (John 15:10). If such is true of God's Son, it can be no less true of his children.

---

190. Yarbrough (86) leaves this as a possibility.

191. A. C. Thiselton, "Semantics and New Testament Interpretation," 97.

192. B. M. Fanning (*Verbal Aspect in New Testament Greek*, 304) notes that a "proleptic perfect occurs after a conditional element of some kind which throws the entire statement into the future. The sense of the perfect is again reflected, but the 'result of the antecedent occurrence' is foreseen to be valid not now but in the future, when the condition is fulfilled." Blass sees this as an example of a perfect with a "futuristic" thrust when used in a general assertion in accordance with Classical usage (BDF §344). John's focus on present experience seems to mitigate against this (Yarbrough, 86, n. 29).

193. A. T. Robertson (*A Grammar of the Greek New Testament*, 897) earlier saw this as a "customary truth." But this seems to take John's use of the perfect here in too narrow a sense.

194. This is the same term used by Jesus on the cross when His work was complete and He was ready to die (John 19:30, Τετέλεσται, "It is finished!").

ἐν τούτῳ γινώσκομεν ὅτι ἐν αὐτῷ ἐσμεν. "by means of this we know that we are *abiding* in him." This time ἐν τούτῳ looks back on what has just been said (contra Akin, 93). We know we are in him because we see that God's love has been brought to completion in and through us.[195]

John next says that what we know by experience is that "we are in him." Again, interpreters differ with regard to the referent of ἐν αὐτῷ, whether the believer abides in Christ (Brooke, 32–33), or in God the Father (Bruce, 52; Bultmann, 26; Burdick, 159; Lenski, 409–10; Marshall, 127). In the following verse ἐν αὐτῷ refers to Jesus, and so it would seem to do the same here. However, the previous clause of this same sentence has God the Father (τοῦ θεοῦ) in view. So it seems best here to see John referring to abiding in God rather than in Christ.

"In him" is brought forward in the clause for emphasis. John's use of "in him" here indicates an abiding relationship and could be translated as "*abiding* in him."[196] Though no ellipsis is intended, the (synonymous) parallelism with what follows, in which he does use the word "abide," defines what John means by "in him."[197] Further, this phrase alludes to Jesus' words in the upper room in John 14:20–24. There he says being in him (God the Father) is equivalent to God the Father and Son abiding in the believer by making him or her their "abode." Thus this phrase is equivalent to "abiding in him" (Brown, 259–60). What follows in the upper room is the parable of the vine and the branches (John 15:1–7) in which being in Christ is further described as an abiding relationship that makes the believer fruitful

---

195. Various interpreters see ἐν τούτῳ looking forward, backward, both, or either way, with Brown (258) and Marshall (126) deciding that the meaning is about the same either way one sees it. This is an example where the grammar is not always helpful or determinate in translation or interpretation of a passage.

196. Lenski (409) and Stott (96) see "in him" as synonymous with knowing him in vv. 3, 4 and loving him in v. 5. They are related, but not the same thing. Loving him is the cause; abiding in him is the effect, with knowing him the result of the other two. Johnson (42) correctly notes John's use of fellowship, walking in the light, knowing him, and being in him as synonymous concepts, and thus developing the same theme.

197. Contra Williams (22) who understands "to be 'in him' means to be united with him, to belong to him, to trust in him, to be one of his true disciples." He sees this similar to John 15:4, which he sees as union with Christ rather than fellowship. Rather, Jesus is talking to His regenerate disciples (OT saints awaiting the NT era) in the upper room about *their* need to abide, and so could not be discussing justification truths. This has been discussed in detail in *The Disciplemaker*.

(Bruce, 52–53). Thus, abiding in the Father and Son are in actuality the same experience.

2:6 Abiding involves habitual obedience. It is a life lived like Christ lived his. Though habitual obedience is not automatic in the life of the believer, it is an obligation.

ὁ λέγων ἐν αὐτῷ μένειν, "He who says he abides in him." John begins this next statement of a general principle in the same manner as his first one with the articular present participle describing a kind of person.[198] This is a person who claims to abide in God the Father (Akin, 94; Edwards, 72; Grayston, 66; Painter, 175).[199]

John uses the verb *μένω* for the first time in this epistle, and by it he describes the nature of what it means to be "in him" in the previous verse (Bultmann, 26).[200] This term is a relational term describing the mutual fellowship between the believer and God (contra Burdick, 239).[201] It is used

198. Again, this is better seen as a gnomic rather than progressive present participle.

199. Painter (170) considers this an instance of "indirect reporting" of the "opponents" words. He continues to follow the theory of opponents. Yet it seems better to see a principle applying to all rather than an indirect reference to opponents.

200. Μένω occurs 39 times in the Gospel (John 1:33, 38, 39 [2x]; 2:12; 3:36; 4:40 [2x]; 5:38; 6:27, 57: 7:9; 8:31, 35 [2x]; 9:41; 10:40; 11:6, 54; 12:24, 34, 46; 14:10, 17, 25; 15:4 [3x], 5, 6, 7 [2x], 9, 10 [2x], 16; 19:31; 21:22, 23) and 27 times in the three epistles (1 John 2:6, 10, 14, 17, 19, 24 [3x], 27 [2x], 28; 3:6, 9, 14, 15, 17, 24 [2x]; 4:12, 13, 15, 16 [3x]; 2 John 2, 9 [2x]), and once in Rev (17:10).

Burge (99) sees John's use of the term to indicate something "beyond merely imitating Christ in lifestyle or 'living as Jesus lived.'" Rather, it is used to "the indwelling of the Christian in God (1 John 3:24; 4:13ff) or in Jesus (John 6:56; 15:4ff.; 1 John 2:27–28; 3:6). It may even depict God indwelling us (1 John 3:24; 4:12–13, 15–16)." Thus it is used by both Jesus and John in a range of meanings.

Brooke (33) sees it as equivalent to Paul's "to be in Christ" (ἐν Χριστῷ εἶναι).

Painter (44–45) provides an excellent discussion on the Johannine use of *μένω* as a conceptual term to describe the mutual relationship between God and men.

201. Burdick (239) says, "The discussion in these passages has shown that the distinction between dwelling in Christ and not dwelling in him is the distinction between being saved and not being saved. It is not a distinction between two levels of Christian experience." He is referring to 2:6, 24, 27, and 28. Yet what follows in 2:7–14, especially vv. 12–14, clearly indicate that John views his readers as believers and speaks to them as such in these passages. It is not until 2:18 that the false teachers are brought into view and any question of one's justification status is raised.

Grayston (65) describes the range of possible meanings for *μένω* as "to stay where you are, to remain in your present situation, to continue in an allegiance or

by Jesus in both the promise of the Holy Spirit as Paraclete in place of him (John 14:15–21), the parable of the vine and the branches (John 15:1–6), and all that follows. Through the choice of μένω, John is continuing to develop his theme of fellowship with God by describing it in terms of mutual abiding. Furthermore, as in the upper room (John 13–17), where mutual abiding was conditioned on the disciples' obedience, so, too, it is here and in the verses that follow.

In the epistle, as in the Gospel, the concept of abiding is described as the believer in God (2:24, 27, 28; 3:6), God in the believer (4:12), and the mutual abiding of the believer and God (3:2–3; 4:13, 15, 16).[202] John's use of μένω includes both a locative sense as well as durative (Rensberger, 62–63).[203] When used of God or his word, it focuses on the immutability of God, and thus the durative sense.[204]

ὀφείλει καθὼς ἐκεῖνος περιεπάτησεν. "is obligated, just as he walked." What John says is that the claim of abiding carries with it an obligation. His use of ὀφείλω as opposed to δεῖ is instructive (Brown, 262; Westcott, 50). Whereas δεῖ connotes a need and may involve needing to do something because it is appropriate or necessary, ὀφείλω implies a greater sense of moral obligation and thus an inner desire to act.[205]

---

relationship." He applies this final definition to this verse. He says further (66) that "the means by which God remains in us is indicated by passages where something of the divine being is or remains in those who are unshaken in their allegiance to him..." He then applies this to the supposed "dissident group who had not remained members of the community but had left it." This "loyalty over time" sense is absent from any contemporary literature or any other NT usage of μένω (see discussions in BDAG 630–31 and F. Hauck, "μένω," *TDNT* 574–76).

202. Rensberger (62) notes that this conceptual use of μένω is "virtually unique" to John, not only among NT authors, but also in Hellenistic literature as well. He says further (63) that whereas "in the Gospel of John, Jesus always stands as intermediary between Christians and God ... in 1 John, however, they can abide (or simply "be") directly in God and God in them." This was promised by Jesus in John 14:16–17 and 23 and fulfilled with the coming of the Holy Spirit at Pentecost.

203. BDAG 630–31. Painter (170) sees these passages suggesting that "God abides in those who abide in God, so that even when only one aspect of abiding is mentioned, as here the claim to abide in God, mutual abiding is implied if the claim is true."

204. F. Hauck, "μένω," *TDNT* 4:574–75.

205. BDAG, 214, 743; W. Grundmann, "δεῖ," *TDNT* 2:21–25; F. Hauck, "ὀφείλω," *TDNT* 5:559–63.

John uses a καθὼς ... οὕτως construction to emphasize the extent of a Christian's imitation of Christ.[206] Though καθὼς can mean "since" or "just as," either rendering calls for imitation of Christ (Strecker, 43).[207] Switching from the usual pronouns, John's use of the demonstrative pronoun ἐκεῖνος to refer to Jesus is emphatic (Painter, 170). He is pointing to Jesus as the example, much like John the Baptist pointed out Jesus to his disciples when he cried out, "Behold the Lamb of God who takes away the sins of the world!" (John 1:29). This is the first of six times (here and 3:3, 5, 7, 16; 4:17) John will use this term to refer to Jesus (Brooke, 33; Bultmann, 26; Marshall, 127–28; Schnackenburg, 104–5; Stott, 97; Westcott, 51; Williams, 23).

καὶ αὐτὸς οὕτως περιπατεῖν. "he also should walk in the same way." John repeats "walk" to emphasize the believer's imitation of Christ's life in his incarnation (Strecker, 45).[208] Using a constative aorist to refer to Jesus' life while on earth, John pairs it with a present infinitive. The aorist notes Jesus' life while on earth, while the present infinitive focuses on the believer's present ongoing conduct of life.[209]

This same concept of "walk" as conduct of life is seen in the Old Testament. Beginning with Deut 5:33, we see the connection made between conduct of life and obedience using the metaphor of "walk."[210] It contin-

---

206. Painter (170) identifies a Johannine "*kathōs ethic*." Of those passages he sees reflecting it, John 13:15 (he had identified 13:14) is Jesus' command to imitate his serving the disciples. Then in John 13:34 and 15:12 they are to imitate his love toward each of them by loving one another in the same way. The passages in this epistle (here, 2:27; 3:3, 7; 4:17) follow the same pattern. The point of these is that imitation of Christ is to be exact, done in the same way he loved and served. I am not certain that John would have ever thought of these in terms of a "*kathōs ethic*," but simply in terms of imitating Christ.

207. BDF §453 (1,2). Johnson (42) describes this sense as "ongoing."

208. Strecker (45) observes the general non-use of ἀκολουθέω outside of the Gospels where one might expect it, such as here. Schnackenburg (105, n. 2) notes that John uses it either as a "literal following" or "a following in faith." He provides John 8:12; 10:4, 5, 27; and 13:36 as examples. He defines well John's use of "walk" as "active human behavior in a particular realm."

209. Bultmann (26) sees περιπατεῖν as equivalent to the earlier "keeps His commandments." However, the life of Christ to be imitated is far more than his obedience to the Father. It includes Jesus' love of the disciples, demonstrated in his serving them and ultimately giving his life for them.

210. "You shall walk in all the ways which the Lord your God has commanded you." This renders הָלַךְ (*hālak*), "to go or walk," which can be used positively for "walking" with God or in the way of righteousness, or negatively for worshipping

ues throughout Deut (Deut 10:12; 11:22; 26:17) and then continues with Josh (Josh 22:5) and into later literature (Psa 15:2; 84:11; Isa 2:3, 5; 57:2 Mic 6:8), especially the wisdom literature (Prov 2:7, 20; 3:23; 4:12; 6:22; 8:20; 10:9; 14:2).[211]

John is not saying by this that imitation of Christ proves union with him (Westcott, 50; contra Burge, 99; Marshall, 129, and Stott, 97).[212] Rather, the moral obligation that fellowship with Jesus produces is an obligation to imitate his lifestyle. It should lead to the "what would Jesus do?" mindset.[213] Yarbrough (88) notes well that this imitation is "far more profound than merely mimicking externals or even obeying Christ's expressed will in a formal way." It should include imitating Jesus' *motivation* for his conduct as well, the unlimited devotion to the Father's will that characterized his every action, attitude, and word (Pentecost, 57).

Biblical Theology Comments

These verses develop John's teaching on the spiritual life in the realm of the believer's sanctification. Believers have "fellowship" and contribute to this mutual abiding relationship by obeying God. It is the human element in mutual fellowship, defined now as mutual abiding. Believers are actively fellowshipping with God, experiencing a healthy, vital relationship with him when they consciously obey him. Conscious obedience *is* actively relating with God just as with prayer. Just as prayer is not an intellectual exercise but active communication, so, too, obedience is not an activity done apart from God. It is how we interact with him on a personal, one-to-one, level.

---

pagan gods (Ex 32:1), walking in darkness (Isa 9:2), or following one's own counsel (Jer 7:24; Psa 1:1). It is described in terms of keeping God's commandments in places such as 1 Kings 3:14 and Psa 119 (L. Coppes, "498 הָלַךְ," *TWOT,* §498, 216). A second term translated as "walk" is דֶּרֶךְ (*derek*), lit. "way, road, manner, work," which is used metaphorically for "the actions and behavior of men," whether positive and godly, or negative and ungodly (H. Wolf, "דֶּרֶךְ," *TWOT*, §453, 197).

211. Psalm 1:1 provides an example of the concept used negatively. "Blessed *is* the man who walks not in the counsel of the ungodly."

212. Burge calls this a second "test of spiritual vigor and life." I would agree with it being a test of vigor, how healthy one's walk fellowship with Jesus is, but not of whether union with Christ has occurred.

213. D. Smith (54) and Rensberger (63) see Jesus' walk characterized by love; and so imitating His walk means to love other believers.

Application and Devotional Implications

We cannot imitate Jesus' obedience without knowing what God wants and then doing it. To be able to walk as Jesus walked, in obedience, we must read the New Testament with a view to its moral demands. We must choose to order our lives on the basis of New Testament commandments without dismissing them as culturally bound or inapplicable to our situation. This is not legalism. It is obedience. Legalism is when we add rules to God's commands and connect personal righteousness with obeying our man-made rules. Obedience is just that, obeying the clear commands of Scripture. That is God's will. We cannot do that if we do not know what God's will is. We cannot know his will unless we listen to him through his word.

Selected Bibliography

Coppes, L. J. "הָלַךְ," In *Theological Wordbook of the Old Testament*, edited by R. L. Harris, G. L. Archer, and B. K. Waltke, §498. Electronic ed. Chicago: Moody, 1999

Fanning, B. M. *Verbal Aspect in New Testament Greek*. Oxford: Clarendon, 1990.

Metzger, B. M., and United Bible Societies. *A Textual Commentary on the Greek New Testament*. 2nd ed. New York: United Bible Societies, 1994.

Robertson, A. T. *A Grammar of the Greek New Testament in the Light of Historical Research*. Nashville: Broadman, 1931.

Thiselton, A. C. "Semantics and New Testament Interpretation." In *New Testament Interpretation: Essays on Principles and Methods*, edited by I. H. Marshall, 74–100. Milton Keynes, UK: Paternoster, 1977.

Thomas, R. L. *Exegetical Digest of 1 John*. Self-published, 1984.

Wolf, H. "דֶּרֶךְ," In *Theological Wordbook of the Old Testament*, edited by R. L. Harris, G. L. Archer, and B. K. Waltke, §453. Electronic ed. Chicago: Moody, 1999.

Loving Believers, Not the World (2:7–17)

Introduction

John now enters the second movement of this first section of instruction. Having introduced his readers to the importance of obedience in the life of the believer, John moves to the specifics of what is to be obeyed. He takes them to what Jesus focused on with the disciples on the night of his betrayal. What he calls the "new commandment" (2:8) has been God's heart's desire for his people through all of history, sharing a place with the command to love God with all our heart, soul, and strength.[214] In the Old Testament, the second greatest commandment was the command to love one's neighbor as oneself. In the New Testament era, it is the command to love fellow believers. John will eventually explain the practical outworking of this command in terms of meeting needs. As he introduces the concept to his readers here, he lays the foundation that we cannot love one another if we love the world. A choice must be made. That choice is described.

New Commandment (2:7–11)

Original Text

7 Ἀγαπητοί,[a] οὐκ ἐντολὴν καινὴν γράφω ὑμῖν, ἀλλ' ἐντολὴν παλαιὰν ἣν εἴχετε
ἀπ' ἀρχῆς· ἡ ἐντολὴ ἡ παλαιά ἐστιν ὁ λόγος ὃν ἠκούσατε.[b] **8** πάλιν ἐντολὴν
καινὴν γράφω ὑμῖν, ὅ ἐστιν ἀληθὲς ἐν αὐτῷ καὶ ἐν ὑμῖν, ὅτι ἡ σκοτία παράγεται
καὶ τὸ φῶς τὸ ἀληθινὸν ἤδη φαίνει. **9** ὁ λέγων ἐν τῷ φωτὶ εἶναι καὶ τὸν ἀδελφὸν
αὐτοῦ μισῶν ἐν τῇ σκοτίᾳ ἐστὶν ἕως ἄρτι. **10** ὁ ἀγαπῶν τὸν ἀδελφὸν αὐτοῦ ἐν τῷ
φωτὶ μένει, καὶ σκάνδαλον ἐν αὐτῷ οὐκ ἔστιν· **11** ὁ δὲ μισῶν τὸν ἀδελφὸν αὐτοῦ
ἐν τῇ σκοτίᾳ ἐστὶν καὶ ἐν τῇ σκοτίᾳ περιπατεῖ, καὶ οὐκ οἶδεν ποῦ ὑπάγει, ὅτι ἡ
σκοτία ἐτύφλωσεν τοὺς ὀφθαλμοὺς αὐτοῦ.

Textual Notes

7.a. The vocative ἀγαπητοί (supported by א A B C P vg syr^{p} cop^{bo} arm) is preferred over ἀδελφοί (K L 049 69; TR and *The New Testament in the Original Greek: Byzantine Textform 2005*). Metzger sees it appearing in the Byzantine texts "because of its customary usage as the introductory word in lectionary pericopes derived from the apostles."[215]

7.b. The phrase ἀπ' ἀρχῆς should not be included following ἠκούσατε, though it is witnessed in Byzantine and TR, and though it is implied in

214. The Shema of Deut 6:4–5 served as the foundation of the Israelites' relationship with God as their divine King. It was the call to loyalty and devotion that would lead to obedience and worship. Thus to love God with one's whole being meant to obey his law and worship no other god. It was identified by Jesus, and recognized even by his enemies, as the first and foremost of God's commandments (Mark 12:28–33).

215. B. Metzger and United Bible Societies, *A Textual Commentary on the Greek New Testament*, 2d ed., 640.

the context.[216] The majority of witnesses do not include it (א A B C P 33 181 218 322 323 431 453 642 643 vg syr[h] cop[sa] arm eth). Rather it is better to see this as a case where the author's intended ellipsis was amended by a copyist.

Translation

7 Beloved,[217] I am not writing a new commandment to you, but an old commandment which you have had from the beginning; the old commandment is the word that you heard.[218] **8** On the other hand,[219] I am writing a new commandment to you, which is true in him and in you,[220] because the darkness is passing away and the true light is already shining. **9** He who says[221] that he is in the light and hates his brother is in the darkness until now. **10** He who loves his brother abides in the light and there is no cause of stumbling[222] in him. **11** He who hates his brother is in the darkness and is

216. B. Metzger and United Bible Societies, *A Textual Commentary on the Greek New Testament*, 2d ed., 640.
217. Though TR and Byz. texts have ἀδελφοί ("brethren"), the majority of MS evidence favors ἀγαπητοί (beloved). This is reflected in the various translations. Though KJV and NKJV read "brethren," HSCB, NEB, NET, NLT, NIV84, and TEV have "dear friends," and "beloved" is used by ASV, ESV, NASB95, NRSV, and RSV.
218. NKjv repeats "from the beginning" at the end of this sentence, again reflecting the TR and Byz. MS traditions. It is omitted by ASV, NASB95, NIV84, HSCB, and ESV, but implied by NET with the addition of "already," and NLT with "you heard before."
219. Other translations use "again" (ASV, NKjv) or "at the same time" (ESV) to express πάλιν. The choice to reflect the adversative sense of πάλιν, translated by "on the other hand," is represented by NASB95, NET. Others (NIV84, HCSB, NLT) use "yet" to reflect a similar nuance of meaning.
220. Painter (171) notes a variant reading of "in us" (ἡμῖν) as opposed to "in you" (ὑμῖν). He further notes that the weight of MS evidence and the difficulty of reading favor ὑμῖν. UBS4 has ὑμῖν without providing any comments in the apparatus, indicating the confidence in this reading held by the UBS4 translation committee.
221. This verse and the following two all begin with "he who" and reflect an articular pres. participle subject in each case (ὁ λέγων, ὁ ἀγαπῶν, ὁ μισῶν). See commentary below for the significance of this construction.
222. Nlt translates this as "does not cause others to stumble" and so reflects a decision to see John focusing on the impact the believer has on others. Most other translations have the more ambiguous "there is no cause for stumbling in him," which is more likely to reflect John's desired meaning since such a translation allows it to mean either the Christian stumbles or is a cause for others to stumble (a double entendre*).

walking in the darkness and does not know where he is going, because the darkness has blinded his eyes.

Commentary

2:7 Since obedience to Christ's commands is the contingent to personal intimacy with God, one next asks: which commands? John tells his readers that they already know what is expected of them. Repeating key terms and using imperfect and aorist verbs, John reminds his readers that he is not bringing up anything new, but something they have known all along, from the beginning (1 John 1:1; 2:24; 3:11; 2 John 5).

Ἀγαπητοί, οὐκ ἐντολὴν καινὴν γράφω ὑμῖν. "Beloved, I am not writing a new commandment to you." When John addresses his readers as "beloved," he communicates his love and affection for them as well as their status as beloved of God, as believers (Marshall, 128; Moody, 36; Painter, 178; Yarbrough, 96). This is a common term of endearment in the New Testament, occurring sixty-two times (whether singular or plural), including ten times with John (Burge, 100).[223] This is evident especially in light of the pattern of use by other New Testament writers when addressing their readers and describing others in their opening and closing salutations.[224] Thus it is not surprising to find John using the term often with his readers as fellow believers.

223. Outside of John it occurs twenty-four times in its nom. pl. (often voc.) form as ἀγαπητοί (Rom 11:28; 12:19; 1 Cor 10:14; 15:58; 2 Cor 7:1; 12:19; Phil 2:12; 4:1 [x2]; 1 Thess 2:8; 1 Tim 6:2; Heb 6:9; Jas 1:16, 19; 2:5; 1 Pet 2:11, 12; 2 Pet 3:1, 8, 14, 17; Jude 3, 17, 20). It is often used in its sg. form to describe individuals, whether Jesus as God's beloved Son or others as beloved (Matt 3:17; 12:18; 17:5; Mark 1:11; 9:7; 12:6; Luke 3:22; 19:35; 20:13; Rom 16:5, 8, 9, 12; 1 Cor 4:17; Eph 6:21; Col 1:7; 4:7, 9, 14; 2 Tim 1:2; Phlm 1, 2; 2 Pet 1:17; 3:15). Other pl. uses include Act 15:25; Rom 1:7; 1 Cor 4:14; and Eph 5:1. John's use is limited to his First and Third Epistles (1 John 2:7; 3:2, 21; 4:1, 7, 11; 3 John 1, 2, 5, 11). Where it is pl. in 1 John, he uses it in its sg. voc. form with Gaius in 3 John.

224. Paul uses ἀγαπητός in one of its forms twenty-eight times, both to address his readers and to refer to individuals (Rom 1:7; 12:19; 16:5, 8, 9, 12, 14, 16; 1 Cor 4:14, 17; 10:14; 15:58; 2 Cor 7:1; 12:19; Eph 5:1; 6:21; Phil 2:12; 4:1 [x2]; Col 1:7; 4:7, 9, 14; 1 Thess 2:8; 1 Tim 6:2; 2 Tim 1:2; Phlm 1, 16). He also uses the term to describe elect Israel in Rom 11:28. It is used once by the author of Hebrews (6:9) to address his readers. James addresses his reader as "beloved ones" three times (Jas 1:16, 19; 2:5). It is also Peter's preferred term to address his readers as well as describe Paul (1 Pet 2:11; 4:12; 2 Pet 1:17; 3:1, 8, 14, 15, 17).

John reminds his readers that what he is saying is not new, and it is not something new to them. This most likely alludes to Jesus' commandments in John 13:34 and 15:17, thereby making Jesus' "new" commandment to the apostles an "old" one for his readers (Marshall, 129; Rensberger, 64; Schnackenburg, 111). For example, Painter (178) notes that "what was new from the perspective of Jesus' ministry is now deemed old, part of the foundational tradition upon which the life of the community was built." Others see this alluding to the doctrines of the false teachers, or secessionists, who are guilty of progressivism (Brooke, 35; Brown, 26–465; Bultmann, 27; Painter, 178).[225] Grayston (67) sees John's use of "old" to describe the commandment as a rejection of "novelties introduced by the dissidents." However, the play on words between "old" and "new" does not appear to be an allusion to a slogan of the false teachers as much as an allusion to the change brought about by Christ and what he said in the upper room. Others see this as a reference to the new age—the realized eschaton of God's reign through Messiah—that began with Jesus' coming (Rensberger, 64), or as something arising from the Mosaic law (Burge, 100; Williamson, 88; Yarbrough, 97).[226]

Of note is John's movement between "commandments" (plural) and "command" (singular). Bultmann (27) sees no material difference between the singular "commandment" and the earlier plural "commandments." He sees the plural included in the singular use here, but notes that "the singular is probably occasioned by the fact that he has a traditional word in mind" in the following verses. Grayston (67), on the other hand, sees the change to singular to be "looking ahead to 4:21," the commandment to love one's Christian brother. That there is no material difference between the two is evident in the interchange of singular and plural in 3:22–24. The plural does express the idea of a body of commands from God the Father, which however may be expressed with the singular as well. However, John does use the singular, "command," when emphasizing the central command to

---

225. This is rejected by Strecker (49, n. 10) on the basis of his theory that the "newness enthusiasts" opposed in 2 John have been "thoroughly integrated into the Johannine circle" with the result that "their teaching is no longer felt to be a divisive element." Perkins (25) similarly rejects this on the grounds that John is addressing the believing community in this section and does not have the secessionists in view within this context.

226. OT origin is Lev 19:18 and Deut 6:5 (Mark 12:29–31).

love one's Christian brother. This, again, reflects Jesus' use of the singular in the upper room when speaking of his command to love.

John employs an ellipsis of γράφω ὑμῖν in order to focus attention on the contrast between new and old commandments. Using the strong adversative ἀλλὰ, he draws attention to the fact that his readers are not hearing anything new. This is something that has been expected of them all along. He is only reminding them of what they have already been commanded by God. When he refers to the "old" commandment, he may mean either: (1) they had the commandment from the time of their spiritual birth, or (2) the commandment has been around since the beginning of creation (Westcott, 51). The first option seems best in light of Jesus' instructions in the upper room.[227]

ἀλλ' ἐντολὴν παλαιὰν ἣν εἴχετε ἀπ' ἀρχῆς·, "but an old commandment which you have had from the beginning." Having alluded to Jesus' "new" commandment in the upper room, John now refers to it as "old."

His use of the imperfect active εἴχετε along with the aorist ἠκούσατε in the following clause focuses attention on their past instruction. Εἴχετε indicates not only reception of the command in the past, but its continuing force and their continuing need to obey it in the present. Thus it serves as a "progressive imperfect of duration" which indicates "the process as having gone on in past time up to the time denoted by the context" (Kistemaker, 262).

Here, ἀπ' ἀρχῆς either (1) refers to the beginning of their hearing the gospel and responding to its message (Bultmann, 27; Haas, de Jonge and Swellengrebel, 11; Lenski, 412; Marshall, 129; Moody, 36; Perkins, 25; Schnackenburg, 111; Stott, 97; Williamson, 88; Yarbrough, 98), or (2) refers to the beginning of the Johannine community's existence (Grayston, 67; Johnson, 42; Smith, 57; Strecker, 49).[228] This would seem to be supported by John's use of the second person plural to address his readers. It is the community that has heard from the beginning. However, the first option seems best since John's focus is on the individual's fellowship with God and not the life of the community, and the use of the plural is better seen as

227. Schnackenburg (110) says that "the author emphasizes in an intermediate section (vv. 7–8) to show that it involves an old and new commandment. This makes sense only if the opponents in his eyes were 'innovators' (cf. 2 John 9)."

228. Moody (36) additionally sees ἀπ' ἀρχῆς having an "eternal" nuance as well.

including each of his readers individually rather than as a corporate unit. This becomes clearer in the next paragraph when he addresses the three groups within the church.

ἡ ἐντολὴ ἡ παλαιά ἐστιν ὁ λόγος ὃν ἠκούσατε, "the old commandment is the word which you heard." John clarifies that his readers already know the "old commandment." This does not require that it be a reference to when they received the commandment, or when it went into effect, but rather that it was something they had received as part of their instruction in the word. John's use of ὁ λόγος to describe the commandment need not be seen as an allusion to Gnosticism or Greek philosophy. As in the prologue of the Gospel, λόγος refers to God's spoken word embodied in Christ.

Where in the prologue of this epistle, John uses *logos* with much the same sense as the prologue of the Gospel, here λόγος is used differently. Now it refers to the body of instruction given by God rather than the person of Christ (Brown, 265).[229] This is best seen as an allusion to Jesus' use of λόγος in the upper room to refer to his commandments and instructions as well as those of the Father in Scripture (John 14:23–24; 15:3, 20; 17:6, 14, 17). His use of the aorist ἠκούσατε does not specify anything more than that it was heard in the past. Of interest, though, is his choice of terms, since the verb ἀκούω may also imply a heeding of what has been said that leads to obedience.[230] So John may be implying that he knows his readers have heard and obeyed the command to love one another. This is not something they have been failing to do but something they need to continue.[231]

2:8 This verse completes the thought introduced in the previous verse and prepares the readers for what is to follow.

πάλιν ἐντολὴν καινὴν γράφω ὑμῖν, " On the other hand, I am writing a new commandment to you."John begins this statement with the adverb πάλιν, which in some cases is used to introduce a new thought.[232] In this case,

229. Brooke (35), on the other hand, sees this referring to both Jewish and Christian instruction received by John's readers.

230. BDAG, 38; G. Kittel, "ἀκούω," *TDNT* 1:220.

231. This may be similar to Paul's praise of the Thessalonians for their love for one another, which is followed by the command that they "increase more and more" that love for one another (1 Thess 4:9–10).

232. This adv., frequent in the NT (141 occurrences), is regularly used by John (45 times).

though, it basically means "again." It serves to mark a contrast, to introduce an alternative aspect of the discussion, and so can be translated "on the other hand" (Yarbrough, 99).[233]

This commandment is called "new." His choice of καινὴν to describe its newness focuses attention on it being "new in nature," a qualitative newness, and an improvement over the old rather than indicating recent appearance (Moody, 36; Painter, 171). This is in contrast to νέος, which describes something that did not exist before and thus is "new in time or origin" and may have "a suggestion of immaturity or lack of respect for the old."[234] Kistemaker (262) notes that this term "suggests that the old has given birth to the new. The old does not cease to exist but continues along with the new." Further, John places the adjective καινὴν after the noun ἐντολὴν in order to emphasize the command more than its newness. He argues that John's choice of "the adjective καινή (new), not νέα (fresh), is important, for it describes the nature of newness which is superior to the old." Smalley (56) notes that the newness is demonstrated in three ways by God. First, God's "self-giving through Jesus" shows his love for mankind. Second, Jesus fulfilled the Law, which is summed up in its own love commands, by obeying it. Finally, Jesus enabled believers to inherit and experience eternal life and express Christlike love through the ministry of the Spirit. Others see John's choice of "new" to carry an eschatological nuance and be a reference to the new age, "the kingdom of God," which was inaugurated with Jesus' ascension to heaven but has not completely come, thus the coming reference to the darkness "passing away" (Bruce, 54–55; Painter, 179; Rensberger,64; Strecker, 49). Rather than reading an eschatological nuance into this statement, it is better to see it as a deliberate reflection of the words of Jesus in John 13:34, in the upper room (Burge, 100).[235] Here the new commandment, as in John 13:34, is to love one another.[236] The point is not its timing or

233. BDAG, 754; H. Balz, "πάλιν," *Exegetical Dictionary of the New Testament,* 3:9.
234. BDAG, 497; J. Behm, "καινός," *TDNT* 3:447.
235. Painter (171) notes John's use of καινός in Rev (2:17; 3:12 [2x]; 5:9; 14:3; 21:1 [2x], 2, 5) and says this "reveals its distinctive character for 1 John."
236. Grayston (68) sees the interplay between "old" and "new" to indicate changes to the two most important OT commandments: "love for God, is made new by incorporating faith in Jesus; and ... love for neighbour, is made new by practice of love for one another." Thompson (58) sees its newness derived from it being modeled by Jesus and its expression in the "new fellowship" created by His death.

relation to the kingdom but its focus. This newness may also be a reference to its mode of expression in the Christian community (Marshall, 130). Though the command to love others was not new, Jesus' application of the command within the church is distinctly different from that of the Old Testament world.

ὅ ἐστιν ἀληθὲς ἐν αὐτῷ καὶ ἐν ὑμῖν, "which is true in him and in you." This clause is introduced with a neuter relative pronoun. Lacking an apparent antecedent[237]—nouns before and after this clause are feminine—it may have one of the following functions: (1) It introduces "a parenthesis in apposition to the previous clause" (Smalley, 56) and thus refers to the previous statement in vv. 7–8a (Brooke, 36; Marshall, 129 Schnackenburg, 111).[238] (2) It only refers to the immediately preceding relative clause, and so the "newness" of the command being true in Christ and the believer (Strecker, 50).[239] (3) It serves as a postcedent clause modifying the following the ὅτι clause (Baugh, 26). (4) It introduces a clause referring to the "subject matter" of the whole command (Hodges, 9–192, n. 10; Klauck, 120; Westcott, 53; Rensberger, 65).[240] Since John has already used a neuter pronoun in a similar manner (1:1–3) to communicate a comprehensive view of his subject, it is likely that here he again has such a use in mind.[241] Thus it refers to the broader subject matter contained in the command rather than the command alone.

This commandment is described as "true in him," referring to Jesus.[242] This may be an allusion to Jesus' demonstration of his love through washing

237. It implies an ellipsis of a neuter subject and verb (τοῦτο ἐστιν) to fill out the phrase (Kistemaker, 262).

238. Strecker (50) rejects this on the basis of his perception of the author's intention, which he says is not to say that what he writes is "true in him and in you." Of note is his first admitting that ὅ can be used this way and is, in fact, used to refer back to whole sentences in Acts 2:32; Gal 2:20; Col 1:29; 1 Pet 2:8; and Rev 21:8.

239. Yarbrough (101) rejects this on the basis that it is too limited a subject to justify the neuter relative pronoun. Lenski (412) sees it in apposition to ἐντολὴν καινὴν in the previous clause.

240. This last view would see this as an example of *constructio ad sensum** in which the singular relative pronoun has a plural referent that is viewed as a collective unity (BDF §134). Painter (171) identifies this with the gospel message he saw in 1:1, 3 earlier.

241. See comments on 1:1 for a fuller discussion of John's use of the neuter pronoun.

242. Painter (171) sees the meaning of ἀληθὲς here to reflect John's most common use of the adjective in his Gospel. There it means "a true witness" (John 5:31, 32;

the disciples' feet (John 13) as well as his death on our behalf.[243] John is saying that Jesus embodies the new commandment. The idea of "true" is that it is factually true, demonstrably true. Its truthfulness can be verified (Painter, 171).[244]

His inclusion of "in you" with "in him" indicates that it is as true for us as it was for Jesus (Marshall, 129; Rensberger, 65), and should therefore, by implication, be expressed in much the same way. Thus what John would be saying by this is that what was true in Jesus should be true in the believer as well. The change occurring in the spiritual world is the reason it should be true.

ὅτι ἡ σκοτία παράγεται. "because the darkness is passing away." This *ὅτι* clause explains why it is true in Jesus and John's readers. It also continues to develop the light/darkness theme introduced in 1:5.[245]

This "darkness" is likely the same darkness as chapter 1, the darkness the readers were not to walk in, and thus moral darkness rather than spiritual death (Yarbrough, 102).[246] It would make little sense to change the meaning of the image in such a short space.[247] Also, the concept of moral purity will be repeated at the end of chapter 1, thereby tying its contents together under that broad subject. By use of the present progressive, John affirms

---

8:13, 14, 17; 21:24), and so takes it here with the same nuance. He further sees John using it in 3 John 12 in this way as well.

243. The same can be said of God the Father's demonstrated love in Jesus' death on our behalf (John 3:16; Rom 5:8).

244. Bultmann (27, n. 20) describes this adjective as affirming "something verifying itself as real" rather than "correct." Though "correct" is too limiting a sense, the idea of verifiability includes correctness as an assumed aspect of its meaning.

245. This clause may be epexegetical or appositional to *ἐντολὴν*. Strecker (50, n. 21) sees it as causal and related to either *γράφω* or *ἐστιν* (more likely because of proximity).

246. Bultmann (27) identifies the contrast of light and dark as referring to "the antithesis of the epochs" as well as the "divine and nondivine spheres" of 1:5.

247. Painter (171) makes "world" of 2:17 synonymous with "darkness" here because the same verb, *παράγω*, is used in both instances to describe their transitoriness. However, that both are passing away need not make them one and the same. The context of 2:17 makes it clear that "the world" is very different than "the darkness" of 1:5. It is more than its lusts. Though it would be legitimate to say that the world is characterized by moral darkness in 2:17, it is not just its darkness that is transitory. The way the term is used implies that not all of the world is evil, but that all of it is transitory (see comments on 2:17). And so the world should not be seen as synonymous with darkness.

that this "darkness" is in the process of passing away, not that it has passed (aorist or perfect), nor that it will pass (future).[248] The fact of its fading serves as motivation for living in the believer. As Marshall (130) notes: "The light of the world has already dawned in the coming of Jesus ... but it shines like a beacon in the continuing darkness, and will blaze out gloriously at the parousia."

καὶ τὸ φῶς τὸ ἀληθινὸν ἤδη φαίνει, "and the true light is already shining." When he says that the darkness is passing away and the true light is already shining, John is telling us that this command to love belongs to the new era initiated by Christ. John's use of "true light" may refer to (1) Jesus as the "Light of the world" (Painter, 172),[249] (2) the "light" of eternal life Jesus brings (Akin, 70), (3) the idea that obeying the command to love "has the *character of truth*" (Hodges, 85; italics his), or (4) the coming of the eschaton in Christ (Bruce, 54; Stott, 98; Strecker, 51).[250] Schnackenburg (113) sees both Jesus' incarnation and his coming Parousia included in the ἤδη. Brooke (37), on the other hand, sees this as an indication that John considers the Parousia to be imminent.[251] In support of the first option, if this is an allusion back to John 1:9, then it may refer to Jesus, as opposed to the banishment of sin. The second option only works if "light" in chapter 1 refers to spiritual life and "darkness" refers to spiritual death, rather than referring to moral purity (or lack thereof). What John says in the following

---

248. This may be an instance where the transitive verb has a more intransitive sense—darkness is in the state of passing away rather than in the process (BDF §308). B. M. Fanning (*Verbal Aspect in New Testament Greek*, 206–7) notes that the customary or iterative present aspect "denotes a broader time-frame, still regarded as the 'now'. Thus, the *temporal* location is still 'present' or 'simultaneous' with the time of speaking/writing.'" He says further, "The internal viewpoint of the present aspect pictures not a specific occurrence seen as it is taking place, but the continuance of a process or state in a broader time-frame or, more commonly, the repeated occurrence of an action or state over a stretch of time. ... It denotes not a situation which *is occurring* in the immediate environment, but one which *does occur* in a wider time-frame."

249. Painter (172) sees this as an allusion to the prologue of the Gospel, where "the light" (Jesus) shines in the darkness (1:5) and is called "the true Light" (John 1:9).

250. C. Moule, "A Neglected Factor in the Interpretation of Johannine Eschatology," 158.

251. Even so, Brooke (37) does not define that imminence in terms of a bodily return of Christ to earth. Rather is it in "process" and "already at work" in the world and church, being manifested in "the things that are."

verse makes this option untenable. Rather, what we know with certainty is that this light is found in a person, Jesus. Additionally, when John says it is "already shining," he is saying that the new age has begun in the person of Christ.[252] Thus it is best to see this as an allusion to Jesus as the Light of the World, who is dispelling darkness and will one day completely banish it with his appearing and establishment of a kingdom of light, Messiah's kingdom. However, note that darkness and light still coexist. Light is overcoming, but though darkness is in decline, it still exists (Strecker, 51). The significance of this is clarified further in the discussion that follows.

2:9 In this and the following verses, John will affirm that loving one's brother demonstrates that one has a healthy relationship (is in fellowship) with God. In this verse he shows that a person's claim to having fellowship with God is invalidated by an absence of love toward other Christians.[253]

ὁ λέγων ἐν τῷ φωτὶ εἶναι, "He who says that he is in the light." Using the present participle, John describes a kind of person, a gnomic sense, rather than carrying a present progressive nuance, "while making this claim and being in the process of hating his brother" (contra Kistemaker, 264). He is describing a kind of person rather than quoting opponents (contra Bultmann, 28; Johnson, 43). John's focus is not on the present experience, but on the state of being that attitudes produce. He is describing a kind of person whose attitude causes him to operate in one realm or another whether or not he recognizes it as such. This person claims not just fellowship with God, but to be living in God's moral sphere and reflecting his character. This first false claim (made by that kind of person) alludes back to chapter 1 and answers the question raised by the previous verse—namely, "Who is in the light?" (Westcott, 54). It is not just a claim of moral purity, but of fellowship with God (Brown, 289; Johnson, 43; Yarbrough, 103). Being parallel to the false claim of 1:6, loving one's brother in this verse becomes equivalent to walking in the light there (Bruce, 56).

---

252. Yarbrough (102) sees this verse as "both an ethical and Christological note of triumph" on John's part.

253. Burge (101) sees John addressing this to both his unbelieving opponents as well as believers and views vv. 9–11 as a third test of life. As in other places, John's readers are clearly viewed as believers by him and so it seems wrong to see him leading them either to question their salvation or seek to confirm it through works.

καὶ τὸν ἀδελφὸν αὐτοῦ μισῶν, "and hates his brother." This is the first occurrence of μισῶν ("hate") in this epistle as John introduces a new concept to the discussion. This use of the present participle with the coordinating conjunction καὶ makes this a second description of the person claiming to be in the light.[254] This action of hating occurs at the same time the claimant is making the assertion.

By this John is affirming that some individuals in the body of Christ can and do claim to be walking in moral purity, and thus in fellowship with God (in the light), while hating other Christians (Burdick, 162; Lenski, 415; Marshall, 131; Perkins, 26–27; Rensberger, 66; Smith, 56; Yarbrough, 103).[255] Kistemaker (262) sees this as coming from John's religious opponents. He argues that "after John states a spiritual truth, for example in 1:5, 2:3, and here in 2:9, he quotes the words of a religious opponent who makes a claim he cannot substantiate." However, the problem with this view is that John says he hates his "brother," and the religious opponents are not believers based on John's description of them in 2:19.[256] Westcott (55) argues well that this and the other uses of "brother" in the epistle refer to fellow believers.[257] He

254. Though καὶ could be adversative in this context (Yarbrough, 103), it is better understood as coordinating. If it were adversative, then μισῶν would be adv. (being anarthrous). With καὶ functioning as a coordinating conj., the previous article applies to μισῶν and makes it part of the clause's subject (D. B. Wallace, *Grammar*, 671).

255. Strecker (51) notes that along with meaning "fellow Christian," that it is equivalent to "loving one another" as expressed in 1 John 4:11–12; John 13:34; and 15:12, or "loving the children of God" as expressed in 1 John 5:2.

256. Painter (172) sees a problem with John's use of the masculine "brother" without mention of sisters here, or mothers in the following verses when he speaks of "fathers." He does note that John addresses a church using the metaphor of "the elect lady and her children." This indicates that John is not intentionally excluding women from his discussion but using the masculine for both genders. This would be considered the appropriate way of speaking of a generic audience composed of both sexes. His choice of "brother" has a religious association within both the Jewish and Greek societies. His readers would have understood him to mean both Christian men and women (Williamson, 90).

257. Grayston (68), while acknowledging the uniformity of meaning throughout Judaism and paganism, is not willing to "dismiss" it meaning "neighbor." Bultmann (28–29, n. 26) interprets "brother" to mean "neighbor" rather than indicating a fellow believer. His basis is John's failure to use ὁ πλησίον ("neighbor") anywhere in his literature. He acknowledges that both Judaism and paganism used "brother" in the sense of "him with whom one is united in religious fellowship." Thus

notes that "The title occurs significantly in the first record of the action of the Church ... and then throughout the apostolic writings (1 Thess. V. 26; Gal. i. 2: 1 Cor. V. 1; Rom. Xvi. 14 &c.; 1 Tim. Vi. 2; James i. 9; 1 Pet. V. 12 &c; c. iii. 14, 16; 3 John 3, 5, 10). ... The singular is characteristic of this epistle (*vv.* 10, 11, iii. 10, 15, 17, iv. 20 f., v. 16). ... There is, as far as it appears, no case where a fellow-man, as man, is called 'a brother' in the N. T."[258] Others reduce the meaning of *brother* to "those members of the Johannine Community" in theological agreement with the author (Brown, 84).[259] This should not be seen as a reference to mankind (contra Brooke, 38).[260]

Loving one's "brother," in the sense of member of one's religious community, was a major theme within the Essene community, as reflected in Qumran.[261] Rensberger (66) notes also that the Qumran scrolls "also promoted hatred for those outside the sect." Another possibility would be the presence of someone posing as a believer, such as Paul's "so-called brother" of 1 Cor 5:11, whose sexual immorality indicated his unregenerate state and called for removal by the church. Further, John has identified the false teachers as unregenerate and seems to have been careful to exclude the designation of "brother" when referring to them, either referring to

---

he appears to be ignoring the extrabiblical as well as biblical evidence of a similar sense throughout the NT, and therefore with John. F. C. Fensham ("Love in the Writings of Qumrân and John," 72) rejects Bultmann's interpretation on the basis that he is infusing a Gnostic idea into the term and sufficient evidence can be found in Qumrânic material to show that "brother" means fellow-believer as opposed to neighbor.

258. Others who concur include Grayston (67), Painter (172).

259. R. K. J. Tan, "Should We Pray for Straying Brethren?" 602.

260. Brooke (38–39) argues from Jesus being the Light of the World in the John's Gospel and the world's propitiation in the Epistle, along with His teachings about the good Samaritan (defining neighbor) and love of enemies in the Sermon on the Mount to give what seems like a limiting term, "brother," a universal sense. From this he concludes that Jesus "revealed the brotherhood of all men" and so ἀδελφός "includes both classes, neighbours and enemies." This is a case of imposing unrelated ideas from things Jesus said and imposing theological conclusions on the present text. He also ignores the distinction John made in 2:2 between believers and the nonbelieving world with reference to Christ's propitiation. This also ignores the distinction Jesus made between His own and the world in His High Priestly Prayer in John 17. Thus, sufficient examples occur that show John would not be thinking in terms of the universal brotherhood of mankind when he uses the term "brother."

261. Examples include: 1QS 1:9–11; 7:4–9; 10:17–19; *T. Iss.* 5:2; *T. Gad* 6:1–3; and *T. Jos.* 17:2–3.

them as "they" or as antichrists. Though one might argue that the false teachers would have been mistaken for "brothers" and even called such at some point in their association with the apostles, this need not mean that "brother" here is intended to include them. Rather, John's exclusion of the term when describing their departure later in this chapter would seem to argue that he is reserving the term "brother" for those who are the truly regenerate children of God.

John's use of μισέω in his Gospel describes a characteristic of the world that is hostile toward Christ (Painter, 172).[262] What John means by "hate" will be clarified in the chapters that follow.[263] The theme is introduced here and will be defined in stages. These are not mere feelings, but actions. With John there is no neutral position or intermediate state. One either loves or hates his brother (Brooke, 39; Bultmann, 28; Marshall, 131). In this case, he is identifying this person as hating.

ἐν τῇ σκοτίᾳ ἐστὶν ἕως ἄρτι, "is in the darkness until now." Here again "darkness" relates back to chapter 1 and describes a moral state (Westcott, 56).[264] Some see this indicating they are unregenerate (Johnson, 44; Yarbrough, 106), though their hatred is toward fellow Christians (brothers and sisters).[265] Thus it appears Yarbrough is addressing life within the visible church rather than the family of God, which is an inconsistency that follows throughout his discussion.[266]

The use of ἐστὶν in this clause emphasizes a state of being, with the verb included for emphasis. Thus this person is not only out of fellowship with God but is not operating in the same moral sphere as him. When John says

---

262. John 3:20 (those who practice evil hate the light); 7:7 (the world hates Jesus); 15:18 [x2], 19, 23, 24, 25 (the world hates believers along with Jesus); 17:14 (the world hates believers). John 12:25 is the exception in which it is not the world hating, but the person figuratively "hating" his life because of loyalty for Christ. This term appears five times in 1 John (here, 2:11; 3:13, 15; 4:20).

263. Brown (290) sees darkness, falsehood, and hate as equivalents in 1 John, with light, truth, and love being "almost interchangeable." For him "a wrong claim means that one is operating out of falsehood/darkness rather than out of truth/light."

264. Moody (37) sees hate symbolized by darkness here, rather than a continuance of the imagery from 1:5–7.

265. Yarbrough (106) describes these people as "ostensible believers" in the congregation "who were actually strangers to saving grace."

266. The visible church includes both regenerate and unregenerate people, while the family of God is composed only of regenerate saints.

"until now" he indicates that those claiming to be "in the light" while hating others have been living a lie, even if they were ignorant of the consequences of their sin. They can no longer claim such ignorance. They must act *now* to change the reality they now find themselves in.[267]

2:10 This compound sentence now describes the opposite truth from the previous verse. In contrast to a false claim is the man who actually loves his brother. John affirms two truths, one positively and the other negatively, about such a person.

ὁ ἀγαπῶν τὸν ἀδελφὸν αὐτοῦ ἐν τῷ φωτὶ μένει, "He who loves his brother abides in the light." This is John's third instance of an articular present participle (ὁ ἀγαπῶν) used to introduce a principle that is true of all genuine believers.[268] This verse stands as a contrast with v. 9. Instead of hating his brother, this one loves his brother. "His brother" is repeated for emphasis. This repetition also clarifies that the issue John addresses is life within the body of Christ, not just being a generically loving person. Though this has the church body as its focus, John is not implying that it is acceptable to hate nonbelievers. He is simply focused on the relationships within the body of Christ and the love Christ commanded to be expressed between believers.

John now affirms that the person who loves his brother is doing so in the context of God's character. "Abides in the light" is synonymous with "walking in the light" in chapter 1 and "being in the light" (Strecker, 52). This same verb, μένω, is used by Jesus in the upper room, and now by John

---

267. Stählin (G. Stählin, "νῦν," *TDNT* 4:1115) refers to this use of ἄρτι as a "unique present of the New Testament" which focuses attention on the fact that this "darkness" that John is describing is "part of the old aeon" of fallen creation. Lenski (415) sees in this an element of hope on John's part that his opponents will respond to what he has said with repentance.

268. As noted earlier, the articular pres. participle ὁ ἀγαπῶν is best seen as carrying a gnomic force, describing a state of being, more than a progressive idea of a present attitude. Thompson (60) rejects the idea that this clause indicates that "anyone who genuinely loves others is in fact walking in God's light." She translates ὁ ἀγαπῶν as "whoever" and sees this referring only to the Johannine community as opposed to anyone, or the opponents, as this is one of the "tests of life" and cannot be made a single test of salvation. It is clear that John is stating one of several principles that are true and does not intend to make the claim she is avoiding. What he says elsewhere in the Epistle makes it clear that this is just one of several elements in a person's life that impact his or her fellowship with God as well as with other believers.

to describe relationships that impact, or influence, others. Though this present tense verb could carry a progressive sense, it seems better to see it as gnomic. Rather than saying that while he loves he is abiding, John is saying that one who loves is one who abides in a consistent manner (Westcott, 56). The importance of this is seen in John's placement of the verb at the end of its clause for emphasis, as he will do with the following verb, ἔστιν, as well.

Here abiding has the sense of "dwelling" somewhere—in this case in the sphere of light, which is moral purity. This same term is used repeatedly by Jesus in John 15:1–10, where abiding results in mutual relationship (mutual abiding), God's influence in the lives of believers (fruitfulness), and their influence with God in answered prayer.[269]

The believer abides in "the light," which once more describes the sphere of God's moral purity in which he dwells. This is the light that one walks in with the aid of Christ's work on the cross (1:7) and can only result from confession of sin (1:9). Also, along with a loving Christian being able to operate in God's moral sphere, he is protected from the snares that the one blinded by hatred will stumble into.

καὶ σκάνδαλον ἐν αὐτῷ οὐκ ἔστιν.·"and there is no cause of stumbling in him." Literally John says, "and there is not a stumbling block in him." The first problem to resolve is the referent of ἐν αὐτῷ. If αὐτῷ is viewed as a neuter pronoun, the nearest possible antecedent is τῷ φωτὶ (RSV). However, if it is seen as a masculine pronoun, as seems best, then ὁ ἀγαπῶν, the subject

269. In John 6:27 Jesus uses μένω to describe "the food which endures to everlasting life." Then in John 6:53–58 Jesus connects the metaphor of eating his flesh and drinking his blood (for believing in him) with the promise of mutual abiding. With the unbelieving multitude (John 6:64) Jesus uses mutual abiding (*meno*) to describe the connection between him and the possession and experience of eternal life. However, when with his disciples in the upper room, Jesus addresses those who do believe in him and already possess eternal life. Thus, his use of the term in the upper room reflects a different context and emphasis from that by the Sea of Galilee. Moreover, since this epistle is conceptually connected to the upper room instructions of Jesus, John 15 should influence our understanding of John's use here more than John 6. In John 15 the issue is not whether the Eleven will come to believe in him. They already do (John 17:9–12). The issue is whether they will "abide" in the one in whom they believe and thereby "bear much fruit" (John 15:4–5). Thus, where in John 6 the issue is entrance into an abiding relationship, in John 15 it is their need to engage in that abiding relationship.

of the sentence, is its referent (Brown, 274; Perkins, 27; ASV).[270] Thus the person is in view rather than the sphere of light within which that person is walking.

The term *σκάνδαλον* is used to describe a stumbling block or something that causes a person to "stumble," whether morally or physically. This term was used for literal and figurative traps, things that enticed or tempted people to make a wrong decision, and with things that made someone repulsive.[271] Thus in the mind's eye is the picture of something that trips up the person, whether physically or morally. It is this middle sense that John intends. However, with that sense, there are three possible ways John could be using the term.

(1) He may be affirming that nothing in the loving believer is a stumbling block that causes *others* to sin. Smalley (62) argues that in the New Testament, most of the time *σκάνδαλον* refers to something that "trips" others (Kruse, 86; Yarbrough, 108).[272] It is used this way in John 6:61 and 16:1.[273]

(2) While in the light there is no cause for the loving believer to stumble (Schnackenburg, 115; Strecker, 53). This would be indicated if *αὐτῷ* is viewed as a neuter pronoun based on its proximity to the neuter noun φῶς (Painter, 173).[274]

---

270. As Burge (102) notes, the challenge of this verse is that grammatically *ἐν αὐτῷ* can refer just as well to either option. Complicating this is the fact that the clause makes sense both ways as well. It is not likely that John intended this as a double entendre*.

271. BDAG, 926; G. Stählin, "*σκάνδαλον*," *TDNT* 7:356–57.

272. Matt 18:7; Luke 17:1; Rom 14:13; 1 Pet 2:8; and Rev 2:14 are examples of this sense.

273. Burge (102) sees this applying to nonbelievers who are "splitting the church" in that he reads this through the lens of the theorized secessionist community. This may be an instance where one's theory of the epistle's occasion and background influences one's interpretation.

274. In support of this meaning, Painter (173) notes further that this is the use of the synonym *προσκόπτω* in John 11:9 to speak of stumbling in the darkness seems to parallel this verse. However, it would seem that John has chosen a different term, possibly to avoid just such a mistaken connection of referents.

(3) Nothing in the believer himself (including the light) will make him stumble (Brooke, 40; Hodges, 88; Johnson, 45; Moody, 38).[275] The following context makes this third option seem best (Kistemaker, 263–64). Furthermore, John's pattern appears to be to use ἔστιν ἐν with reference to people, whether they are the subject or object of the verb, though not always (Painter, 173). What John is saying by this negation is that hate is a snare, a cause of moral stumbling in the life of a believer. However, one who is characterized by love of the brethren will not have this source of moral failure within him.[276]

2:11 John describes the hater's state and experience in this sentence, giving the reason for his blindness. He continues to distance himself from this person by using the third person articular participle to describe the hating Christian. Having affirmed that one cannot walk in the light while hating his Christian brother, John moves to describe the full consequences of that hatred as it relates to walking in the light. This is what is true of the hating believer whether he is aware of it or not.

ὁ δὲ μισῶν τὸν ἀδελφὸν αὐτοῦ ἐν τῇ σκοτίᾳ ἐστὶν, "He who hates his brother is in the darkness." John again describes the unloving Christian with the same phrase as earlier.[277] As noted before, by this phrase John is describing this person as a fellow believer.[278] Rather than seeing him attacking theolog-

---

275. Lenski (415) sees this stumbling leading to the spiritual death of the person. He bases this on the idea that a σκάνδαλον was a trap that involved a hook and bait.

276. Of interest is the comment by G. Stählin ("σκάνδαλον," *TDNT* 7:345) that may shed light on John's choice of the noun over and against the verb. He says, "The force of the verb σκανδαλίζω is even stronger than that of the noun σκάνδαλον in the New Testament. Whereas σκάνδαλον is only an "occasion of falling" which might lead to a fall or not, σκανδαλίζω is the causing of a fall and σκανδαλίζομαι the actual taking place of the fall."

277. Yarbrough (106) describes this verse as "practically quoting words of Jesus" from John 12:35. Though he correctly denies literary dependence on the Gospel, and it is not a quotation, as he notes, John clearly derives the idea from Jesus' words. Throughout this Epistle, Jesus' teachings, including the way he said things, have clearly been embedded in John's thinking and have evidently influenced his conceptual world. That being said, though, John's writing style is still distinct from Jesus' speaking style as quoted by John in his Gospel and reflected in the other Gospels as well.

278. Articular pres. participle ὁ μισῶν is gnomic, describing a state of being, rather than the progressive idea of a present attitude.

ical opponents, which is the consensus among scholars today, his pastoral concern is more evident when we see later in the epistle how he defines hatred in terms of ignoring needs. Love is helping while hate and murder may be expressed through apathy, inaction, and unconcern, even when outright rejection or antagonism is not visibly or verbally expressed.[279]

John begins this with the contrastive conjunction δὲ, which serves as a contrast, but not of the strength of ἀλλὰ (Yarbrough, 105).[280] With δὲ John is not calling on his readers to focus on the contrast. Rather, he wants them to return to the topic of the unloving Christian and to note the description that follows.

Once again he includes ἐστὶν and moves it to a position after the prepositional phrase and at the end of its clause for emphasis.[281] Further, with this construction he affirms a state of being rather than just a present tense sense. Moreover, the state of being involves a sphere of operation, called "darkness," which has been identified as opposite of God and will be clarified later (3:3) as outside of the sphere of moral purity. This does not mean the hater is not regenerate; otherwise, he could not hate his "brother" (another Christian).[282] This may explain why John chose ἐστὶν over μένει from the previous verse.[283] Though this negative statement is a contrast to the previous positive one, its contrast is between spheres of operation and not states of being.

καὶ ἐν τῇ σκοτίᾳ περιπατεῖ, "and is walking in the darkness." John now moves from the state to its effect in the life of the hater. Note the progression. He is first "in the darkness," then he "walks in darkness," and finally

---

279. John's use of "hate" and "murder" may be viewed as hyperbole. However, as a rhetorical device, John appears to be reflecting Jesus' commentary on murder in the Sermon on the Mount (Matt 5:21–26), which equated unjust anger and degrading verbal attacks on others with murder.

280. Though continuative in one sense, δὲ carries an adversative force. (D. B. Wallace, *Grammar*, 671; BDF §447).

281. This sentence is characterized by all pres. tense verbs and verbals except for the final aor. ἐτύφλωσεν.

282. See commentary on 2:9 for a discussion of the meaning of "brother" in John's literature.

283. John uses εἶναι ἐν and μένειν ἐν as equivalent conceptual terms to describe the mutual relationship between the believer and God as it relates to and expesses the new covenant relationship. The concept is described well by E. Malatesta (*Interiority and Covenant*). As will be noted throughout this commentary, he has much to say about the expression of this mutual relationship in the life of the believer.

"does not know where he is going." Though John uses "walk," the common term figuratively used to denote the conduct of daily life, here he may intend περιπατέω to be taken in a more literal way (Marshall, 133).[284] He is painting a visual picture in the minds of his readers. This use then of the present tense invites the reader (listener) to imagine the hater walking along in darkness. In this analogy the darkness is real, though the image draws from the first chapter to represent the absence of God's moral purity.

καὶ οὐκ οἶδεν ποῦ ὑπάγει, "and does not know where he is going." John next describes the effect of walking in darkness. In life, wandering around in the dark leads to disorientation. People get lost. Here John describes this same phenomenon. He uses οἶδα to describe that knowledge rather than γινώσκω, indicating that the hater's being "lost in the dark" is not the product of experience but lack of instruction.[285] John's point is that the person who hates fellow Christians has lost spiritual perspective, his "sense of direction," and yet remains unaware that he has wandered away from fellowship with God. Brooke (40) sees this indicating not that the unloving believer has stumbled, but is "in danger of falling," thus made susceptible to sin. Schnackenburg (116) describes this phrase as "reminiscent of the gnostic promise to lead to saving knowledge."[286]

ὅτι ἡ σκοτία ἐτύφλωσεν τοὺς ὀφθαλμοὺς αὐτοῦ, "because the darkness has blinded his eyes." This ὅτι clause provides the reason a hating Christian is "lost" (disoriented) in darkness; he or she has been blinded by that darkness.

In the first-century world, barbarians blinded their foes, whether military, political, or social. Subsequently, the helpless wandering of the blind was common knowledge, being used figuratively to describe one's inability to understand things.[287] In his Gospel, John uses the healing of the man born blind (John 9) as the climax of his light/darkness imagery. Therein the one in apparent darkness could "see" spiritually while those with physical sight remained blind because they refused to recognize Jesus as Messiah.

---

284. H. Conzelmann ("σκότος, σκοτία," *TDNT*, 7:444). Moody (38) sees walking in the darkness as a metaphor for sinning and hating. Though John is speaking figuratively, he is describing the spiritual condition of the person that motivates conduct more than the conduct itself.

285. BDAG, 200, 694.

286. "Die Wendung οὐκ οἶδεν ποῦ ὑπάγει erinnert an die gnostische Verheißung, zur rettenden Erkenntnis zu führen."

287. BDAG, 1021; W. Schrage, "τυφλός, τυφλόω," *TDNT*, 8:271–72.

In John 12:40, John quotes Isa 6:10 to explain why so many people did not believe in Jesus after seeing his signs.[288] These connect back to John 3:16–21, where light and darkness describe spheres of existence that men choose to live within and are reflected in their response to Jesus. However, the spheres represented by light and darkness differ between the Gospel and epistles. Where in the Gospel "light" and "darkness" represent spiritual life and spiritual death, in the epistles they symbolize moral purity and sin.[289] Thus darkness personified functions as the agent causing the blindness rather than being an effect of that blindness. The aorist verb, translated "blinded his eyes," indicates a continuing state is created in darkness' victim. Darkness has covered the person's eyes, so he is kept from being able to see where he is going and is caused to stumble. This is a pictorial way of communicating that the hating Christian is unable to understand his condition in that "the darkness" he is experiencing also keeps him from recognizing that he is walking in darkness and out of fellowship with God.

This is the idea that the believer is now in a state of spiritual blindness with regard to truth. He cannot see the reality of his spiritual condition. Thus, this believer is operating in the realm of moral and spiritual darkness, the opposite realm where God dwells. The result is, though he may remain completely unaware of it, he cannot be in fellowship with God.

Biblical Theology Comments

In this section John further develops the concept of light and darkness as moral spheres. Which sphere one operates in is determined by actions, not claims, and those actions arise out of one's character. One may not be aware whether he or she is operating in light or darkness, being completely deceived by his or her own moral state that leads to an inability to discern

---

288. D. A. Carson ("1–3 John," 1064) sees this alluding back to John 12:40 rather than to Isaiah, though it is a quotation of Isa 6:10.

289. Another OT passage that utilizes the same imagery, including the idea of stumbling in the darkness is Isa 59:9–10. Though John was likely familiar with this passage, he does not appear to be directly alluding to it, though he is using its imagery and terminology from the LXX (διὰ τοῦτο ἀπέστη ἡ κρίσις ἀπ᾽ αὐτῶν, καὶ οὐ μὴ καταλάβῃ αὐτοὺς δικαιοσύνη, ὑπομεινάντων αὐτῶν φῶς ἐγένετο αὐτοῖς σκότος, μείναντες αὐγὴν ἐν ἀωρίᾳ περιεπάτησαν. ψηλαφήσουσιν ὡς τυφλοὶ τοῖχον καὶ ὡς οὐχ ὑπαρχόντων ὀφθαλμῶν ψηλαφήσουσιν, καὶ πεσοῦνται ἐν μεσημβρίᾳ ὡς ἐν μεσονυκτίῳ, ὡς ἀποθνήσκοντες στενάξουσιν.).

good and evil. The reality of one's state is not determined by perception but conduct—in particular, one's treatment of others.

Application and Devotional Implications

How do we discern areas of spiritual blindness? Only God can guide us to them and then out of them. John has exposed one key area that impacts the church today. Our lack of love for other Christians is sin that keeps us from fellowship with God as well as God's kind of fellowship with one another, even if we feel good about ourselves. We need to pause regularly and ask ourselves if we are guilty of "hating" Christians around us, especially in our local congregations. Additionally, as is shown by John later in the epistle, this lack of love most often expresses itself, not in anger or conflict but in indifference. How much do we care about the Christians around us? Do we care enough to get involved in their lives, to help them with personal needs? Or are we deceiving ourselves into thinking we are good people while being unengaged in the body of Christ?

Selected Bibliography

Balz, H. R. "πάλιν." In *Exegetical Dictionary of the New Testament*, edited by H. R. Balz and G. Schneider, translated by V. P. Howard and J. W. Thompson. Edinburgh: T. & T. Clark, 1990.

Carson, D. A. "1–3 John." In *Commentary on the New Testament Use of the Old Testament,* edited by G. K. Beale and D. A. Carson, 1063–67. Grand Rapids: Baker Academic, 2007.

Fensham, F. C. "Love in the Writings of Qumrân and John." In *Essays on the Jewish Background of the 4th Gospel,* 66–77. Pretoria: University of South Africa, 1972.

Malatesta, E. *Interiority and Covenant: A Study of* εἶναι ἐν *and* μένειν ἐν *in the First Letter of Saint John*. Rome: Biblical Institute Press, 1978.

Metzger, B. M., and United Bible Societies. *A Textual Commentary on the Greek New Testament.* 2nd ed. New York: United Bible Societies, 1994.

Moule, C. F. D. "A Neglected Factor in the Interpretation of Johannine Eschatology." In *Studies in John,* 155–60. NovTSup 24. Leiden: Brill, 1970.

Tan, R. K. J. "Should We Pray for Straying Brethren? John's Confidence in 1 John 5:16–17." *JETS* 45 (2002): 599–609.

Assurance (2:12–14)

Original Text

12 Γράφω ὑμῖν, τεκνία,

ὅτι ἀφέωνται ὑμῖν αἱ ἁμαρτίαι διὰ τὸ ὄνομα αὐτοῦ·

13 γράφω ὑμῖν, πατέρες,

ὅτι ἐγνώκατε τὸν ἀπ' ἀρχῆς·

γράφω ὑμῖν, νεανίσκοι,

ὅτι νενικήκατε τὸν πονηρόν.

14 ἔγραψα ὑμῖν, παιδία,

ὅτι ἐγνώκατε τὸν πατέρα·

ἔγραψα ὑμῖν, πατέρες,

ὅτι ἐγνώκατε τὸν ἀπ' ἀρχῆς·

ἔγραψα ὑμῖν, νεανίσκοι,

ὅτι ἰσχυροί ἐστε

καὶ ὁ λόγος τοῦ θεοῦ ἐν ὑμῖν μένει καὶ νενικήκατε τὸν πονηρόν.

Translation

12 I am writing[290] to you, little children,[291]

because[292] your sins have been forgiven for his name's sake.

13 I am writing to you, fathers,

because you have known him from the beginning.

I am writing to you, young men,

because you have overcome the evil one.

14 I wrote[293] to you, children,[294]

because you have known the Father.

I wrote to you, fathers,

---

290. This translation is reflected bY ESV, HCSB, NASB95, NET, NIV84, Nlt. Other translations use "I write" (ASV, NKJV).

291. The choice of "little children" expresses the idea of endearment from the diminutive form of τεκνίον (BDAG, 994). This is seen in ASV, ESV, HCSB, NASB95, NET, NKJV. NIV84 expresses the intimacy by the use of "dear children." NLT translates it as "you who are God's children."

292. Causal sense of ὅτι is what most translations follow (ASV, ESV, HCSB, NASB95, NKJV, NLT) rather than content, "that" (NET).

293. ThougH NKjv along witH Kjv leave this in the pres. tense before switching to the past tense with "fathers," the textual evidence favors the aor. sense of "I wrote" or "I have written" (ASV, HCSB, NASB95, NET, NLT). As an epistolary aorist, all six statements could be translated as "I write" or "I am writing" (ESV, NIV84).

294. Some translations repeat "little children" (ASV, NKJV; NIV84 repeats "dear children"; NLT repeats "you who are God's children"), while other follow this translation and change from the diminutive "little children" to simply "children" to reflect the shift in terms by John (ESV, HCSB, NASB95, NET).

because you have known him from the beginning.
I wrote to you, young men,
because you are strong
and the word of God abides in you, and you have overcome the evil one.

Commentary

John now pauses to reassure his readers that he is not questioning their salvation. After what he has just said, it would be natural for some Christians to fall into harmfully self-critical introspection. John writes these next verses to his readers because he is sure of their salvation (justification). The role of these verses in the flow of thought is that they provide assurance for readers who might be questioning themselves after what John has said (Akin, 101; Burge, 110; Schnackenburg, 124). John therefore acts to clarify their salvation and growth in the Lord and thereby assure them of their salvation and standing before God.[295]

These verses describe John's readers in three categories twice over, as little children, fathers, and young men.[296] This has resulted in a range of interpretations regarding the nature of those addressed and their levels of spiritual maturity: (1) They represent three age groups within the church (Windisch, 115–16). However, it is unlikely to be three age groups because the sequence is wrong and what is said of each group does not necessarily reflect one's age as much as one's maturity (Klauck, 132; Smalley, 69). (2) They describe three levels of spiritual maturity within the body of Christ (Bruce, 58; Klauck, 132; Stott, 96).[297] As with the first view, the sequence

295. Smalley (79–80) attempts to find a Trinitarian formula in these verses, with "fathers," "children," and "young men" being equivalent to the Father, Son, and Holy Spirit. It is highly unlikely that John's readers would catch such a subtle analogy. Further, it would distract from the important message of these verses as they provide John's readers assurance of their salvation.

296. Williamson (92) notes that John has the "habit" of addressing his readers with "family terms." Of interest is Bultmann's (31) assessment of these verses. Though he sees the "author" (redactor) using sources for composing the epistle, he views these verses as coming from the hand of the author because they lack the "antithetical division" that he sees characterizing the original source material.

297. Klauck (132) sees the first set of triplets as a general description of all believers and the second set describing them in terms of how long they have been Christians rather than by age.

is wrong. Also, as Smalley (69) notes, one might argue that the traits described should be true of all believers. (3) They describe all of John's readers viewed from each of three perspectives (Dodd, 38–39; Hodges, 94; King 41; Marshall, 138; Rensberger, 71). John's use of *παιδία* to address the whole church at the head of the next section (2:18) a few verses afterward would seem to support this. Their close proximity could argue for a shared sense, and what is said afterward cannot be restricted to just one portion of the church family. When John's readers see themselves as little children, they are reminded of the forgiveness of their sins. When they see themselves as fathers, they have a knowledge and relationship with God that results from obedience to his commands. When they see themselves as young men, they are strong. Yet it seems more natural to see different groups whose experiences come together within the body of the church. John's use of *παιδία* afterward should not prove conclusive since he uses the same term elsewhere to address the church as a whole. Schnackenburg (124, n. 4) rejects this view on the basis that these "apostrophes" are too brief to indicate John intended to "attribute to all Christians the natural vigor of youth and the mature knowledge of old age in their faith experience."[298] (4) They describe two groups, "fathers and young men" with "children" including both groups (Brooke, 43–45; Bultmann, 31; Johnson, 51; Kistemaker, 266; Mitchell, 63; Schnackenburg, 123; Yarbrough, 114).[299] First, this is reflected in the order of the names. If John had intended three groups, he most naturally would have placed "fathers" first. Also, "'children' is commonly used in the Johannine literature for whole communities, while there is no evidence that 'fathers' or 'young men' are ever used in this way" (Burge, 111). These same designations are used by Paul (1 Tim 5:1) and Peter (1 Pet 5:5) to distinguish the two groups of men in the church. The two terms for children (*τεκνία* and *παιδία*) used by John in this epistle are synonyms

---

298. "Wenn 1 Joh allen Christen die natürliche Kraft der Jugend und die reife Erkenntnis des Alters in ihrer Glaubenserfahrung beilegen wollte, dann müßte er dies deutlicher tun als durch diese kurzen Apostraphen."

299. I. de la Potterie, "La connaissance de Dieu dans le dualism eschatolgique d'après 1 Jn 2, 12–14," 91; E. Malatesta, *Interiority and Covenant*, 167. D. Watson ("1 John 2.12–14 as *Distributio, Conduplicatio, and Expolitio*: A Rhetorical Understanding," 99–101) sees this as an example of *distributio* in which the first term (children) refers to the whole while the following (fathers, young men) refers to the parts.

and reflect Jesus' use of them to address his disciples in John 13:33 and 21:5 (Burge, 112). The experiences attributed to the children, namely forgiven sins and knowing the Father, can be said to be true for all believers, whether new or mature. The things said of fathers and young men, on the other hand, need not be the experience of every believer. Finally, it would seem that John's choice to change "children" from τεκνία to παιδία, while keeping "fathers" and "young men" the same, favors this final view as well. Thus this seems the best option for John's recipients.

John's use of ὅτι here and throughout these three verses remains a puzzle to interpreters. It may be causal (Brooke, 43–44; Bultmann, 31; Smith, 63; Rensberger, 71; Westcott, 58; Williamson, 93), declarative/content (Haas, de Jonge, and Swellengrebel, 55; Kruse, 88, n. 62; Painter, 186; Schnackenburg, 123),[300] or both (Smalley, 71).[301] Normally γράφω is followed by a content ὅτι, and so one might argue here.[302] Noack points to 2:8 as an identical construction, once the parenthetical clauses are removed.[303] The three ὅτι clauses of 2:21 follow the same pattern if the sentence is changed to a positive statement (οὐκ removed). He reduces 5:13 to a similar construction. He then notes the role of ταῦτα elsewhere as the object of γράφω and its absence in 2:12–14. Admitting that John "does not trouble himself with stylistics" and that he could have used ταῦτα in the first statement and let it be understood in the five following statements, he still feels that the ὅτι clauses function in the role of ταῦτα and so each should be seen as a content rather than causal ὅτι.[304] However, John uses this construction in a clearly causal manner in both 2:8 and 21 (Strecker, 57; Yarbrough, 121).

Although the absence of ταῦτα may leave open the possibility of ὅτι expressing content, it seems better to see John's choice to be causal. Thus, this use of ὅτι introduces a causal adverb clause rather than a substantive direct object clause. It gives the reason for his writing the epistle as a whole ("why

300. M. Black, "On 1 John II.12–14," 236; E. Malatesta, *Interiority and Covenant*, 166.
301. Marshall (136) sees little or no difference between the two options.
302. As does M. Black ("On 1 John II.12–14," 238) on the basis that ταῦτα is understood (ellipsis) and "it is a misapprehension of the polemical intention of the whole epistle if one says that the author writes to the addressees because of their faith or because of other qualities or experiences of theirs, as if all were well with them and as if their only deficiency consisted in failing to draw the inferences."
303. M. Black, "On 1 John II.12–14," 236–37.
304. M. Black, "On 1 John II.12–14," 237.

I'm writing") rather than the content of what he is writing at the moment ("I'm letting you know your sins are forgiven."). He is not describing his readers, but assuring them. Because their sins have been forgiven, he is writing to them about confessing sin and imitating Christ's obedience to love rather than hating their Christian brothers.

John follows a set pattern in addressing the groups. First, he begins with a statement of the fact of his writing. Second, he gives a description of his readers (children ... fathers ... young men), which is not the order one would expect. Then, third, he states the reason he is addressing them through a ὅτι clause. The first three times he uses the present tense verb for writing, and then the aorist for the following three.[305]

John repeats, as well as develops, his themes in this poetic statement.[306] This repetition would serve to reinforce each point made (Akin, 104). Further, in each stanza John moves from the present or aorist "I am writing" or "I wrote" to perfect tense verbs when describing his readers. The perfect tenses throughout these three verses serve to focus attention on the

305. This is an example of an epistolary aor., in which John places "himself in the place of his readers and from that perspective views the writing of the letter ... as *past*, though from his actual viewpoint these things are *present*" (B. M. Fanning, *Verbal Aspect in New Testament Greek*, 281; italics his).

306. Hodges (98) provides some insightful suggestions for understanding the literary structure of this section. He notes that this second triplet recasts the first triplet. "That this is deliberate is clear when the statements made to 'fathers' and 'young men' in verse fourteen are compared to the previous ones earlier in this verse. What we discover is this: (1) the statement made to 'little children' in verse 12 is *entirely changed* here; (2) the statement made to 'fathers' earlier in this verse is *entirely the same* in verse 14; and (3) the statement made to 'young men' earlier in this verse is *partly changed and partly the same* in verse 14. Such structuring is far from accidental. ... It may be suggested that in two of these categories, statements made in the first set reflect what might be called *minimum experience* in each category, while the second set in the same two categories expresses *more advanced experience* in the category in question. The obvious exception to this is the category of 'fathers' who 'have known him who is from the beginning'" (italics his). What we see then is an implicit understanding on John's part that babes in Christ begin with forgiveness. There is growth (victory) as believers mature into "young men" (and women). And finally, stability comes with full maturity (fathers). That being said, it is not John's purpose to comment on this. Rather, this is an observation of how he viewed his readers as he made his central point to them: he is confident of their status as orthodox and maturing saints.

completion of an action, their faith in Christ, and the resulting state that results from their faith.[307]

And being addressed to his readers, these three descriptors clearly indicate that John views his readers as genuinely regenerate (Strecker, 57). He does not question their salvation. Thus he is not providing "tests of life" by which they should discern whether they are regenerate, or "tests of fellowship" in order to discern if they are enjoying fellowship with God. Rather these are assurances that they as believers need in order to enjoy the eternal life each possesses.[308]

2:12 This first statement is directed to John's spiritual "children." It establishes the pattern of this section: the fact of his writing, whom he addresses, and his reason for writing.

Γράφω ὑμῖν, τεκνία, "I am writing to you, little children." John begins these first three affirmations with the present of γράφω. His repetition of ὑμῖν in this clause and the one to follow appears to be intended to communicate his focus as well as God's focus on them. He appears to have chosen the dative form of ὑμεῖς, a dative of reference, in order to communicate that he is writing these things for his readers' benefit. He follows this with a term of endearment that could indicate one of two things: either (1) he sees himself addressing a younger generation or (2) he sees them as his spiritual children, his own converts (King, 41). His use of the diminutive form of τεκνόν favors the first option in that it expresses the affection of a father to his children (Brooke, 43; Kistemaker, 267).[309]

ὅτι ἀφέωνται ὑμῖν αἱ ἁμαρτίαι διὰ τὸ ὄνομα αὐτοῦ, "because your sins have been forgiven for his name's sake." His use of the perfect passive ἀφέωνται communicates their experience of forgiveness in the past which is still in

307. See B. M. Fanning (*Verbal Aspect in New Testament Greek*, 158–59), for a more complete explanation of this aspect of the perfect.

308. Burge (110) sees vv. 12–14 as a "parenthesis, a pause, designed to reassure John's readers about their own relationship to God ..." and that "a connection with the foregoing verses and those that follow is tenuous at best."

309. Klauck (133), on the other hand, sees this as a reminder that John's readers are believers. He argues that John's use of "forgiveness of sins" and "name" may indicate he is reminding them of their conversion. Further, his use of the term "children" describe those who have "received baptism in the new life and forgiveness as a gift from the hand of the Father" ("Kinder sind jene, die in Taufe und Sündenvergebung das neue Leben als Geschenk aus der Hand des Vaters empfangen.")

effect in the present.[310] They are living in a state of forgiveness. This does not ignore what he said in chapter one.[311] It is not a denial of sin; 2:1–2 makes clear his readers need Jesus' intercession for their sins. However, as in 1:9, he uses the plural articular noun, αἱ ἁμαρτίαι, to indicate specific acts of sin rather than just sin in a generic sense or the sin nature. By implication, he is saying he knows they are those who have confessed their sins and experienced their forgiveness and cleansing.

They are forgiven, not because of their own righteousness, but through Jesus' cleansing work in 1:7, 9, and 2:2. That is the sense of "for his name's sake."[312] Why does he use "name" instead of "Jesus"?[313] It appears he is focusing his readers on the character of Christ more than his purpose (Akin, 104). The ground cause of their forgiveness lies in the character of Christ, who provided it by being both their sacrifice (1:7) and Advocate (2:1). Thus we see that forgiveness of sins depends on Jesus (Smalley, 72). John uses "the name" again in 5:13 and 3 John 7. Its use in these other two instances makes it synonymous with "the faith" (Westcott, 59).

2:13 In this verse John addresses his readers as "fathers" and "young men." He then gives his reasons for writing this epistle based on what is true about them.

γράφω ὑμῖν, πατέρες, "I am writing to you, fathers." John next describes his readers as "fathers." Westcott (60) notes that this term combines the "natural characteristic of age" with "eminence" within the body of Christ. This would seem to argue against John directing it to all of his readers and point to a subgroup within the larger category of his spiritual "children."

---

310. Of interest is John's use of ὑμῖν (dative of reference) following ἀφέωνται where one might have expected ὑμῶν. It appears he may have chosen this in order to produces a repetition of the term in the sentence, which would serve to focus attention on the readers.

311. Smalley (72) notes the distinction between the pres. tense forgiveness of 1:9, suggesting "the *continual* forgiveness" Christians experience, and the perfect tense forgiveness here, "indicating primarily the *initial* experience of forgiveness" one has at conversion. (italics his)

312. Contra Bultmann (31), who takes this to mean "because the readers bear his name."

313. This is an example of *constructio ad sensum** in which the 3 sg. pronoun, in this case αὐτοῦ, lacks a prior referent, but the context is clear enough that one is not needed (BDF §282).

These would be those believers who are spiritually mature (Mitchell, 64) or serve in leadership roles (Williamson, 93). Additionally, in the first-century world "father" was a term of respect, and John's use of it communicates his respect for those mature members of the body of Christ (Yarbrough, 116).

ὅτι ἐγνώκατε τὸν ἀπ' ἀρχῆς. "because you have known him from the beginning." John's second reason for writing his readers is their personal knowledge of God. Stated here and repeated twice in verse 14, John uses the extensive perfect (active) of γινώσκω, knowledge by experience, to communicate they came to know God earlier with a present result of continuing personal knowledge (Schnackenburg, 124; Smalley, 74; Yarbrough, 122). They still know him. Thus they are in fellowship with him.

The lone article τὸν has the prepositional phrase ἀπ' ἀρχῆς, functioning substantively, indicating an ellipsis of either a proper noun, such as God the Father or Jesus, or a verbal making it equivalent to "who was." This is the third use of "from the beginning" in this epistle (1:1, 2:7). Whereas in 1:1 "from the beginning" referred to the beginning of Jesus' ministry, and in 2:7 to the beginning of their Christian experience, here it refers to their Christian experience (Houlden, 72; contra Haas, de Jonge and Swellengrebel, 11).[314] This is indicated by the perfect tense, focusing attention on the experience of the believers rather than the existence of God. Thus, it seems best to see the article referring to God the Father (Bruce, 58; Dodd, 38; Stott, 97; Williamson, 92; Yarbrough, 122) rather than Jesus (Akin, 104; Brooke, 45; Bultmann, 32; Johnson, 50; Westcott, 60).[315] Though knowing Jesus means knowing the Father (John 14:6–7; 17:3), here, as in 2:3, the focus is on one's relationship with God the Father. The "fathers" have known and continue to know God the Father. Thus their lives are characterized by obedience over time. They are sanctified believers whose steady obedience has led to a

---

314. I. de la Potterie, "La connaissance de Dieu dans le dualism eschatolgique d'après 1 Jn 2, 12–14," 94–96; E. Malatesta, *Interiority and Covenant*, 168.

315. Burge (113) remains neutral and says "who is from the beginning" may refer to either God the Father or "Jesus whose preexistence is important to John." Smalley (73) argues for Jesus on the basis that John's "opponents" would not have questioned the Father's eternal existence but would have questioned Jesus'. However, this is only true if "from the beginning" refers to the beginning of time as opposed to the beginning of their spiritual experience, as indicated by "you have known him." The focus is on the readers' experience, not God's existence. Yarbrough (122) notes that "the proximity of this phrase to 'the Father' in the previous clause makes it slightly more possible that John speaks of God here than of Jesus."

steady relationship of fellowship with God. They are experiencing eternal life to its fullest.

γράφω ὑμῖν, νεανίσκοι, "I am writing to you, young men." John now addresses the "young men" among his readers.[316] John changes the expected order: children to young men to old men. This would catch the attention of his first readers even as it puzzles students of Scripture today. His purpose may be to describe his readers in terms of the beginning of their faith, the process of their growth, and the culmination of maturity. Moving from the beginning (children) to the goal (fathers), he emphasizes the struggle they face throughout the process (young men), but in terms of his confidence in them, John would seem to be less concerned about mature believers (fathers) being drawn away by false teachers than by new converts and growing, learning believers who lack the stability that comes from years of instruction and obedience. However, John does not see these "young men" in danger of deception. Rather, he sees them as victorious.

ὅτι νενικήκατε τὸν πονηρόν, "because you have overcome the evil one." John writes this third group precisely because he sees them as overcomers, as victorious Christians. His use of the perfect active indicative *νενικήκατε* describes their spiritual status as a victory over evil or "the evil one," won in the past and enjoyed in the present. "The past remains effective" (Westcott, 60). His readers are overcomers, not struggling to win against evil.[317] His use of the articular noun *πονηρόν* to describe who or what they were victorious over refers to Satan, the devil, rather than to evil in a generic sense (Akin, 105; Schnackenburg, 124; Smalley, 74). This is the same terminology used by Jesus in the disciples' prayer (Matt 6:13) and may also be an allusion to Jesus' prayer after the upper room (John 17:15). This same idea will be

---

316. Burge (113) sees "young men" referring to the youth in the church (age rather than spiritual maturity). Yarbrough (117) essentially concurs but adds those who consider themselves young in spiritual wisdom as well.

317. All but four of the twenty-eight NT uses of *νικάω* are found in John's literature, with "victory" being the central theme of Revelation. Of note, the noun form, *νίκη*, occurs only in 5:4. Thus E. Malatesta (*Interiority and Covenant*, 168–69) sees the theme of victory as a uniquely Johannine concept and communicates the idea of the "eschatological triumph of all Christians by reason of their faith."

repeated in 5:4–19, where the readers are victorious over a world that lies in "the wicked one."[318]

John's reference to "the evil one" need not be viewed as a reference to Gnostic ideas about Satan. Coetzee demonstrates well that John's view of Satan accords with the rest of the apostolic writings (synoptic Gospels). " ...there is in St. John's references to 'the prince of this world' nothing of a Gnostic-deistic dualism, of a good God in heaven and a wicked God of this world, who stand equal in power or alongside each other."[319]

2:14 Though the order remains the same (children, fathers, young men), what is said of them changes. It is these changes that should be noted in that John does so to draw attention to those things said, whether repeated or developed.

ἔγραψα ὑμῖν, παιδία, "I wrote to you, children." John repeats himself and adds to what he has said, changing from the present tense, "I am writing," to the aorist, "I wrote." He does this for literary purposes that remain unclear. Options include: (1) he is referring to an earlier letter or letters.[320] Strecker (54) notes that the aorist form of *γράφω* is often used in other literature to refer to previous letters written by the author. He then suggests that John may be alluding to 2 and 3 John. However, as Schnackenburg (125) notes, there are no passages in either 2 or 3 John that these statements either quote or to which they seem to refer. He also rejects the idea of a "lost" letter. (2) John is referring to something he has written earlier in this epistle (Brooke, 41). However, his repetition of ideas and terminology with the previous verse seems to mitigate against this (Smalley, 77). (3) This represents a change of direction in the epistle (Akin, 102; Smalley, 78). Both Akin (102) and Smalley (78) argue that in this epistle John has a pattern of using *γράφω* to introduce statements and *ἔγραψα* when discussing statements. As a result they see 2:14 as a summary of what will be discussed in the remainder of the epistle. Yet the concepts in 2:13–14 (knowing the Father, knowing Jesus, God's Word abiding, and overcoming Satan) do not

318. John identifies three things that believers overcome: Satan (2:13–14), false teachers (4:4), and the world (5:4–5).

319. J. C. Coetzee, "Christ and the prince of this world in the Gospel and the Epistles of St. John," 117.

320. N. Turner, *A Grammar of New Testament Greek*, 3:73. Plummer (46–47) sees John alluding to things written in his Gospel.

incorporate all that is discussed in what follows. The emphasis on love, for example, is a major focus of the chapters that follow, yet clearly absent from these verses. (4) This indicates a change of perspective (from his to his readers'). (5) It marks a resumption of writing after a pause, viewing the letter as in progress with the present tense and then completed with the aorist (Law, 308–309; Kistemaker, 267; Westcott, 57). (6) This is simply an epistolary aorist (Brown, 295–97; Burge, 111; Schnackenburg, 125; Williamson, 93; Yarbrough, 121). John uses this epistolary aorist in 2:21, 26 and 5:13 to refer to what had just been said in the epistle. It would seem well to see this as the sense here. But then why the present tense just before? Also, this does not explain why John repeats most of what he just said in the verse before using the present tense γράφω (Smalley, 77). The answer seems to be that he did it for purely literary purposes, such as to provide stylistic variation (Bultmann, 31; Johnson, 49).[321] The change in tense serves to structure the six affirmations into a clear doublet and strengthens their connections through repetition. By this the unity of the three classes is affirmed while their distinctness is reinforced as well. Thus, following the same pattern of the previous three statements, John continues to express his confidence in the readers' faith and standing with God.

Using a synonym of τεκνία, John refers to his readers with a second term of endearment, παιδία (Akin, 106; Burge, 112; Rensberger, 70). He may have drawn this from John 21:5, where, following his resurrection, Jesus stands on the shore and calls the disciples who have gone fishing "little children" (παιδία). Along with the change from present, "I write," to past, "I wrote," this distinguishes the second triplet from the first and sets the stage for what John will now affirm and reaffirm.

ὅτι ἐγνώκατε τὸν πατέρα, "because you have known the Father." Whereas before the readers were described as forgiven, now they "have

321. As J. P. Louw ("Verbal Aspect in the First Letter of John," 103) aptly notes, the change from pres. to aor. in these three verses does not involve "aspectual features which are in focus, but temporal alteration for the sake of avoiding stylistic monotony; and consequently the reader should not try to force aspectual distinctions onto γράφω and ἔγραψα. Aspect is a feature of the subtleties of language. In some contexts it may be prominent, in others only latent." Johnson (49) suggests a pattern of variation from John 21:15–17, where Jesus alternates "sheep" and "lambs" as well as utilizes both ἀγαπάω and φιλέω for "love."

known" (perfect tense) the Father.[322] Their present relationship with God is not new but has continued from the past into the present. John's use of this to describe them connects two truths with his readers. Forgiveness of sins and knowing God both describe salvation and may allude to the new covenant blessings of Jer 31:31–33 (Akin, 106; Brown, 320; Culpepper, 261). This shows once again that he is not questioning their salvation or even their fellowship with God, but affirming both (Burge, 112).

ἔγραψα ὑμῖν, πατέρες, ὅτι ἐγνώκατε τὸν ἀπ' ἀρχῆς, "I wrote to you, fathers, because you have known him from the beginning." As with the first group, John includes the "fathers" in the middle part of this address.[323] This is word-for-word identical to the first statement other than the change in verb tense from present to aorist. Saying and meaning the exact same thing as before, John affirms their spiritual stability and maturity.[324] For the spiritually mature, there is the same knowledge of God that the children achieve. Additionally, this description continues to develop John's theme of knowing God. By describing these fathers twice as knowing God the Father (see previous discussion of the referent of τὸν), John is describing a person who lives obediently and thereby experiences fellowship with God. He is also emphasizing two key things: (1) their stability in the faith, and (2) the fact that they have realized the goal of spiritual growth—knowledge of God (Burge, 113).

ἔγραψα ὑμῖν, νεανίσκοι, "I wrote to you, young men." Here for the second time, John addresses the "young men" following the fathers. Now their place in the order of addressees is expected. What is unexpected is that, like the fathers, John continues to describe them the same way, while like the children he has additional things to say about them. Whereas pfs. describe children and fathers, John now uses two present tense and one perfect tense

322. As discussed earlier, these ὅτι clauses are causal rather than substantival (content, indirect discourse).

323. Burge (112–13) notes that normally in the NT "fathers" refers to ancestors. Other than here, the only other instance that "father" refers to an elder member of the church is Acts 22:1. Literal fathers are addressed by Paul in Eph 6:4 and Col 3:21.

324. See discussion on 2:12 for the referent of τὸν ἀπ' ἀρχῆς. D. F. Watson ("1 John 2.12–14 as *Distributio, Conduplicatio, and Expolitio*: A Rhetorical Understanding," 102) sees this as well as his descriptions of the young men as examples of *Conduplicatio* (repetition) in which a word or phrase is repeated for emphasis.

verb describe the young men. The first two describe them as they are. The third, as with children and fathers, describe their present experience resulting from an earlier event.

ὅτι ἰσχυροί ἐστε, "because you are strong." John now says three positive things about the young men he addresses. First, John describes the young men as strong, placing the adjective *ischyroi* (ἰσχυροί, "strong ones") before the verb in word order for emphasis. Their spiritual strength is reflected once more in their victory over Satan, repeating the same words from verse 13 with the perfect tense verb indicating a completed victory still being enjoyed.

καὶ ὁ λόγος τοῦ θεοῦ ἐν ὑμῖν μένει, " and the word of God abides in you." The reason for or means of their victory is now given: God's Word abides in them. This use of λόγος does not have the incarnate Word in view but God's revealed will, as in 1:10 (Akin, 106; Smalley, 79).[325] As before, the sense of μένω here is not just that God's Word is "in" them in the sense that they know it. It is "enduringly and effectively present" in them (Yarbrough, 123). He is saying more than that they have memorized verses and can quote them. Along with them knowing God's Word, it is *influencing* them, guiding them through life. This is in contrast to the one who denies sin in 1:10.[326] Thus victory over Satan comes as one lives according to God's Word. They were living out their lives on the basis of an orthodox biblical worldview.

καὶ νενικήκατε τὸν πονηρόν, "and you have overcome the evil one." As John addresses his readers with these verses, it is clear from his description of them that he does not in any way doubt their salvation. In fact, these words are written following statements that may have led them to question their standing with God. Thus, he writes to assure them of their secure status with God. Recognizing this is important if one is to understand the nature of the "tests" in this epistle. Since John is so certain of the spiritual standing of his readers, it conversely stands against reason to think that any test provided in the epistle would be related to the question of whether

325. Yarbrough (123) says it is "likely a complex combination of God's creational activity and redemptive witness to himself in the many forms attested in salvation history." Johnson (51) sees "word" to indicate "the truth about Jesus" who is "the Word of Life."

326. Schnackenburg (126) sees 1:10 as describing the "heretics" who do not have God's word in them. This verse then serves as a contrast between the young believers and heretics.

they are "saved." The Test of Life view of the epistle cannot be sustained without either ignoring this fact or lessening its significance. This does not mean, though, that the Test of Fellowship view is correct either. John does more than write to give his readers tests of whether they are in fellowship with God. There are other tests in this epistle that *are* tests of life, at least in a sense. They are not tests of the reader's salvation but of the false teachers. Those who do not pass the test are outside of the faith. Further, as a pastor seeking to protect his flock, John will soon alert them to the dangers around them, dangers of false teachers who can pervert their knowledge of God and thereby damage their walk with him as well. However, these are not tests applied to them. These are tests to be applied to teachers and preachers to determine the source of their teaching and, having discerned truth from error, to reject the false teachers while listening to the apostles.

Having assured his readers of their standing with God as his beloved children, John turns to their relationship to the world, not the world of the Gnostics, secessionists, or false teachers, but the world around them, both physical and spiritual, a world that lies under the sway of the evil one.

Biblical Theology Comments

These few verses remind us that God the Father can be known by his children. For John, experiencing eternal life involves a vital relationship with God the Father that is personal and contingent. Spiritual maturity is defined by that relational knowledge rather than mere intellectual acknowledgment.

John also introduces us to the presence of Satan, "the evil one," whom we have victory over even in this world. Jesus overcame Satan at the cross, and even young believers ("young men") experience this victory. Satan is a defeated foe in John's theology, and all believers need to live their lives in light of that reality.

Application and Devotional Implications

Though we are all forgiven and "know" God as his children, we also live in a dynamic world that still lies in the power of Satan. Yet we live as victorious conquerors awaiting the return of our Lord. That should shape the way we think and act. As Paul commands us in Eph 5:1–2, we are to be "imitators of God as beloved children" and "walk in love" as Jesus did while he was on earth. We see this same passionate plea in this epistle, introduced in the first verses of this chapter, and to be developed further in the chapters to come. As the forgiven children of God who are imitating his Son's walk, our goal should be to daily overcome Satan and grow to the stable faith of the "fathers" in these verses.

We need to realize that these goals do not come overnight or quickly, but they are the result of years of learning about God and faithfully obeying him day by day. We can only do this by developing our relationship with God. Every day, read and pray. Every day, learn more about God from his Word. Every day, communicate with him through prayer. None of us can become strong or mature any other way. Spiritual maturity is not automatic. It does not come with time alone. It is the product of a daily decision to walk with God, to get to know him, and to spend time with him. This is not something that is theoretical or existential. It is practical. It is what we do for him, think of him, and say to him in order to relate to him personally.

Selected Bibliography

Black, M. "On 1 John II.12–14." *NTS* 6 (1959): 236–41.

Coetzee, J. C. "Christ and the Prince of This World in the Gospel and the Epistles of St. John." *Neot* 2 (1968) : 104–21.

de la Potterie, I. "La connaissance de Dieu dans le dualism eschatolgique d'après 1 Jn 2, 12–14." In *Au service de la parole de Dieu,* 77–99. Gembloux, Belgium: Mélanges Andre-Marie Charue, 1969.

Fanning, B. M. *Verbal Aspect in New Testament Greek*. Oxford: Clarendon, 1990.

Louw, J. P. "Verbal Aspect in the First Letter of John." *Neot* 9 (1975): 98–104.

Malatesta, E. *Interiority and Covenant: A Study of* εἶναι ἐν *and* μένειν ἐν *in the First Letter of Saint John*. Rome: Biblical Institute Press, 1978.

Moulton, J. H., and N. Turner. *A Grammar of New Testament Greek.* Vol. 3, *Syntax*. London: T & T Clark, 1963.

Spicq, C. *Theological Lexicon of the New Testament.* Translated and edited by J. D. Ernest. 3 vols. Peabody, MA: Hendrickson, 1994.

Watson, D. F. "1 John 2.12–14 as *Distributio, Conduplicatio, and Expolitio*: A Rhetorical Understanding." *JSNT* 35 (1989): 97–110.

Love God, Not the World (2:15–17)

Original Text

15 Μὴ ἀγαπᾶτε τὸν κόσμον μηδὲ τὰ ἐν τῷ κόσμῳ. ἐάν τις ἀγαπᾷ τὸν κόσμον,
οὐκ ἔστιν ἡ ἀγάπη τοῦ πατρὸς ἐν αὐτῷ· **16** ὅτι πᾶν τὸ ἐν τῷ κόσμῳ, ἡ ἐπιθυμία
τῆς σαρκὸς καὶ ἡ ἐπιθυμία τῶν ὀφθαλμῶν καὶ ἡ ἀλαζονεία τοῦ βίου, οὐκ ἔστιν
ἐκ τοῦ πατρός, ἀλλὰ ἐκ τοῦ κόσμου ἐστίν· **17** καὶ ὁ κόσμος παράγεται καὶ ἡ ἐπι-
θυμία αὐτοῦ, ὁ δὲ ποιῶν τὸ θέλημα τοῦ θεοῦ μένει εἰς τὸν αἰῶνα.

Translation

15 Do not love the world or the things in the world. If anyone loves the world, the love of the Father is not in him. **16** Because all that is in the world, the lust of the flesh,[327] and the lust of the eyes,[328] and the boastful pride of life,[329] is not from the Father, but[330] is from the world. **17** Both the world and its lusts[331] are passing away,[332] but he who does the will of God remains forever.

Commentary

John has called on his readers to imitate Jesus' obedient lifestyle, and reminded them of his command to love one another. Then, having reassured them of their standing with God, he expresses his pastoral concern that their walk in light not be hindered by worldliness. His focus on materialism at this point sets the stage for his discussion of love's expression through meeting material needs, which will come in the chapters that follow. However, first John must pause from assuring his readers of his confidence in them to address another hindrance to walking in the light—worldliness.

---

327. ASV, HCSB, NASB95, NKJV translates ἡ ἐπιθυμία as "lust" whilE ESV, Net translates "desire(s)." NIV84 translates this "the cravings of sinful man." NLT translates it as "a craving for physical pleasure."

328. ASV, HCSB, NASB95, NKjv translates the second use of ἡ ἐπιθυμία as "lust(s)" while ESV, NET translates "desire(s)." NLT translates it as "a craving for everything we see."

329. This translates βίος with the sense of those things that make up life, such as possessions, one's occupation, social status. Sometimes it is translated "riches" in that it looks at the material part of one's life and possessions whether one is wealthy or not. NASB95 translates this "boastful pride of life" as well. NKJV says "pride of life." NIV84 translates it "boasting of what he has and does." HCSB translates it as "pride in one's lifestyle." NET says "the arrogance produced by material possessions." ESV says "pride in possessions." NLT says "pride in our achievements and possessions." ASV has "the vain glory of life."

330. As noted in the commentary below, this is the strong adversative ἀλλὰ and emphasizes the contrast between sources with the two ἐκ τοῦ phrases.

331. Though this noun is the sg. ἡ ἐπιθυμία, since three forms of lust were listed, the context calls for a plural "lusts" in accordance with English grammar, which would have been understood in Greek.

332. The variety of translations reflects the challenge of this construction in which the singular ἡ ἐπιθυμία is used once again. ASV says "and the lust thereof." ESV says "along with its desires." HCSB says "with its lust." NASB95 uses "and *also* its lust." NIV84 says "and its desires." NET says, "with all its desires." NKJV says "the lust of it." NLT says "along with everything that people crave."

2:15 John addresses this next hindrance to experiencing eternal life by introducing the topic with its solution. This is accomplished using an imperative followed by a conditional sentence that expresses John's concern for his readers.[333] This is his first mention of the world in this epistle.

Μὴ ἀγαπᾶτε τὸν κόσμον, "Do not love the world." This negative present imperative states a general principle that John's readers were to follow. In this case it communicates the basic idea of "stop loving the world" with the sense that this should characterize their lives (Painter, 190).[334] By this John implies his readers may be guilty of misplaced values. In response, he will quickly explain why such an approach to life is inconsistent with experiencing intimacy with God. Note also, John does not say to abandon the world. Just as Jesus did not ask that his disciples be taken out of the world, only protected from Satan (John 17:15), John is not saying to flee the world or to reject it completely. He is simply saying not to love it.

The term "world" is not evil in itself and John does not always depict it in a bad light.[335] He uses it to designate all of creation in its natural sense (John 1:10). The term also refers to those living on the planet (John 3:17; 1 John 4:14). The world is the sphere wherein God's saving activity occurs (John 1:10; 3:16; 9:5; 13:1; 17:11, 13; 1 John 4:9, 17.[336]

It was the created world (planet) that God declared good and very good in Genesis. Additionally, Jesus did not come to condemn the world's population, but to save it (John 3:17). Yet, this same term at times carries very negative connotations in John's literature.[337] It is this same world from

---

333. D. Love ("Love Not the World," 119) sees this addressing the problem of John's readers "struggling with the tension between loving the world and those who have returned to the world, and loving the family of faith."

334. BDF §336 (3); D. B. Wallace, *Grammar*, 485–87. See also B. M. Fanning, *Verbal Aspect in New Testament Greek*, 327–28.

335. Of the 185 uses of κόσμος in the NT, only once does it *not* refer to the planet, its people, or "the regulation of life in human society" (J. Guhrt, "κόσμος," *NIDNTT*, 1:521) and indicate "the place and object of God's saving activity" (524). It occurs seventy-eight times in John's Gospel and is used by him twenty-four times in his Epistles. The only time in the NT it does not refer to the world or its people, it is translated "adornment" in 1 Pet 3:3 (BDAG, 561).

336. Positive references to κόσμος in his Gospel include John 1:29; 3:16; 4:42; 6:33, 51: 10:36; 12:47; and 17:21.

337. Negative references to κόσμος in his Gospel include John 7:7; 9:39; 12:31; 14:17, 30; 15:18, 19; 16:8, 11, 20, 33; 17:9, 14, 16; and 18:36.

which the disciples have been separated by God (John 15:19; 17:6, 14, 16) and from which Jesus was always separate (17:14, 16). It hated Jesus and hates his followers (John 15:18–20).[338] Often, John's use of the term indicates nonbelievers and those forces opposed to God (John 7:7; 15:18–19; 17:14, 25; 1 John 3:13) as well as the sphere of their activity (1 John 4:1, 3).[339] It is this evil system that Christ and believers have overcome (John 16:33; 1 John 2:13–14; 5:4). Though it is not evil in and of itself, the church does find itself increasingly separated from the world and distinct from it.[340] It makes sense that a child of God should not love it.

μηδὲ τὰ ἐν τῷ κόσμῳ, "or the things in the world." John uses this coordinating conjunction to include the whole (world) with its parts (things). This communicates a comprehensiveness that excludes nothing in this world. "World" may be being used in one of three senses here: (1) Its referent is the people of the world (Rensberger, 73; Grayston, 56; Burdick, 177). This would see "world" as distinct from the things in it, which leaves people as its referent. Yet though Jesus' love ethic is directed toward his own, God's love for the world's people is expressed in places such as John 3:16. Also, this "world" is described as passing away along with its attitudes. This would

338. R. Brown (*The Community of the Beloved Disciple*, 63) suggests a "chronology of relationships" evident in the Gospel that indicates a movement from a primarily Jewish church to Gentile-dominated Johannine community. This comes from John's seeming focus on opposition from "the Jews" in chapters 5–12, while chapters 14–17 shift to "the world," which would include the Gentile believers "encountering Gentile disbelief, even as formerly they faced Jewish disbelief." This is reading too much into the text (a case of eisegesis). We know from the Synoptic Gospels that Jesus' focus in his ministry was the "lost sheep of the house of Israel" (Matt 10:5–6). And since his ministry primarily focused on the Jewish community, it would be natural for any opposition to be primarily Jewish. As he prepares to depart this earth and converses with his disciples in the upper room, Jesus clearly has the world in view. This is evident not only in Jesus' High Priestly Prayer in John 17, but also his three great commissions (Matt 28:18–20; Mark 16:15; Acts 1:8).

339. The world's ruler is Satan (John 12:31; 14:30: 16:11; 1 John 5:19). R. Brown (*The Community of the Beloved Disciple*, 143) argues that John changes the sense of "world" in his Epistle from that of the hostile world of unbelievers in the Gospel to that of the "secessionists who refuse to believe in Christ as proclaimed by the author."

340. R. Brown (*The Community of the Beloved Disciple*, 64) sees this resulting from a "rejection of the Johannine gospel" by both Jews and Gentiles that then produced a sense of "alienation" among the "Johannine Christians" as they discovered that their home was heaven and not this world.

not be true of people. Humanity will exist forever, whether with God or separate from him. (2) It refers to the whole of creation in a neutral sense, though separate from God (Schnackenburg, 133–37).[341] This would be supported by John's later reference to "the world's goods" (3:17) as something useful in expressing love for other believers. However, the immediate context connects lusts and pride with the world referred to here. (3) John's use of "world" here refers to the morally corrupt world system rather than the planet and its material components (Akin, 108; J. Anderson, 67; Brooke, 47; Bruce, 60; Culpepper, 261; Lenski, 424; Lieu, 92; Marshall, 142; Mitchell, 67; Smalley, 115; Smith, 66; Stott, 100; Williams, 28; Williamson, 96; Yarbrough, 127).[342] This system stands opposed to God and everything he values. It is owned and operated by Satan (1 John 3:1; 4:4; 5:19; John 12:31; 15:18; Eph. 6:11, 12; Jas 4:4). This is best seen in light of the author's reference to the world's lusts and pride, which are to be rejected along with it. This evil system will not continue into eternity but will be replaced by Christ's kingdom. Though "things" are not evil in and of themselves, loving them does make one worldly (Bruce, 61).

ἐάν τις ἀγαπᾷ τὸν κόσμον, " If anyone loves the world." This is an example of a fifth class condition—its protasis* may or may not be true of John's readers—which raises the question of their attitude toward the world.[343] Of note, though, is the change from the 2 plural imperative in the previous sentence to the 3 singular pronoun. John is not accusing his readers of loving the world per se, but stating a principle that applies to them as well as anyone else. His choice of τις, a very generic term, appears deliberately to include all humanity, not just believers. Here "world" includes both the

341. H. Sasse, "κοσμέω, κόσμος," *TDNT* 3:867–98; G. Johnston, "'Οἰκουμένη and κόσμος' in the New Testament," 352–360; N. H. Cassen, "A Grammatical and Contextual inventory of the use of κόσμος in the Johannine Corpus," 81–91.

342. E. Malatesta, *Interiority and Covenant*, 178–80. Thompson (68) describes it as a complex web of values, decisions, and directions chosen in life without consideration for knowing or following the will of God. Moody (44) describes it as "that social organism estranged from God and hostile toward those who abide in the *koinonia* of light and love."

343. D. B. Wallace (*Grammar*, 470) describes the "fifth class condition" as "virtually identical" structurally to the third class, but sees the fulfillment of the condition in the present rather than more probable future. Since John is making a statement about reality more than discussing something that may or may not happen, it seems best to see this as a fifth class condition.

system and its "stuff." The "things of the world" are implied and need not be repeated since it has been stated in the immediate context.

οὐκ ἔστιν ἡ ἀγάπη τοῦ πατρὸς ἐν αὐτῷ, "the love of the Father is not in him." John expresses the apodosis* of the conditional sentence with the negative particle and the verb *ἔστιν* moved to the fore of the clause for emphasis. This is not as strong as an *οὐ μὴ* construction, but nearly so.[344] What John is saying is that love of the world reflects a lack of love for God. It is impossible to love both the world and God. Anyone loving the world can be certain, without a doubt, that he or she does not love God.

One may ask what John means by "the love of the Father" (*ἡ ἀγάπη τοῦ πατρὸς*). (1) It could be a subjective genitive with the sense of "the love God is expressing" itself in us. In this case, loving the world would indicate God's love is not being expressed in that person's life (Houlden, 73; Williamson, 96). This may be indicated by John's choice to avoid saying "he who loves God" in verse 17 and says instead, "he who does God's will" (Houlden, 73–74). (2) It could be an objective genitive and so express believers' love directed toward the Father. This would indicate that John intends that one cannot have love toward God when one's love is directed toward the world (Bultmann, 33; Burdick, 178; Lieu, 93; Marshall, 143–44; Moody, 45; Rensberger, 73; Schnackenburg, 127; Stott, 104; Yarbrough, 130). "Love of the Father" would then be parallel to *ἀγαπᾶτε τὸν κόσμον* in the preceding clause and reflect what follows in verse 17 (Kistemaker, 271). John is thus expressing Jesus' teaching in Matt 6:24 (Luke 16:13) that one cannot serve both God and mammon. (3) It may be functioning as a plenary genitive[345] with the sense that God's love expressed within a person is reflected in a love directed toward him by that person rather than loving the world (Smalley, 83; Westcott, 64).[346] Since the same phrase in 2:5 appears to be a plenary genitive, it seems best to see this as such as well. God's love toward us motivates us to love him over the world, as John affirms later: "We love because he loved us first" (4:19).

2:16 "The things of the world" are now related to a triad of sinful attitudes that arise from the world system rather than from God. Of note is that all

344. BDAG, 733–34.

345. D. B. Wallace (*Grammar*, 119) describes a plenary gen. as containing both senses of the subjective and objective gen.s.

346. E. Malatesta, *Interiority and Covenant*, 183.

three areas are described through articular nouns and so draw attention to them as familiar to the readers.

ὅτι πᾶν τὸ ἐν τῷ κόσμῳ, "Because all that is in the world." Introducing this sentence with the causal ὅτι, John explains what he has just said and will show how loving the world excludes the possibility of loving God. Having commanded his readers not to love "the things in the world," John brings those things to the fore in showing their danger to the believer who wishes to walk with the Lord. The world system is inimical to God. Those things characteristic of the world system stand in opposition to God and are to be avoided. When John says "all," he indicates that no aspect of the world system is excluded. Its values and attitudes, even those we do not recognize as evil, stand in opposition to God. That is not to say that every value in every culture is evil. Many of the values of any culture may yet be traced back to divine revelation and parallel God's values. For example, murder is rejected by pagan cultures as well as Christian, even when they have not had even a trace of Christian influence. However, that caveat aside, the values in view do cover every area of life, and so are described in these broad terms.

ἡ ἐπιθυμία τῆς σαρκὸς καὶ ἡ ἐπιθυμία τῶν ὀφθαλμῶν καὶ ἡ ἀλαζονεία τοῦ βίου, "the lust of the flesh, and the lust of the eyes, and the boastful pride of life." "All" is now described in three categories or groups, three areas through which the world influences the believer. Their significance has been viewed differently by interpreters and can be categorized under three views: (1) Some interpreters have connected these three lusts with the temptation of Eve in Gen 3:6 (Morris, 1264; Van Gorder, 81; Williamson, 96). (2) Others have seen these categories as the same three areas in which Jesus was tempted by Satan in Luke 4:1–14 (Westcott, 62). (3) Yet others see Eve's and Jesus' temptations alluded to by these three lusts (Moody, 45; Mitchell, 67–68). There are insufficient correspondences between these and the other temptations to be certain that John meant either of the two (Brooke, 47–48; Brown, 306–7; Burge, 116; Lieu, 94–95; Marshall, 146; Stott, 105).[347] Schnackenburg (128–31) argues that such vice lists can be found in extrabiblical literature of that time and that John "simply coins

347. Burdick (178–81), Painter (191–94), and Rensberger (74–76) ignore the question altogether. Yarbrough (134, n. 29) relegates it to a footnote recounting Augustine's view that it was patterned off of Jesus' temptations.

his own formulation."[348] John was listing areas in which believers could be tempted and their love for God diverted. So what is the significance of the three lusts? They cover every area of life in a broad sense rather than describing Eve's or Jesus' temptations (Westcott, 62).[349]

These three areas are described with genitive constructions that may be seen as subjective gens., showing that these desires arise from the person (Rensberger, 74).[350] Though many see this first "lust" as a generic description with the following two describing aspects of the lust of the flesh (Kruse, 95; Houlden, 74; Marshall, 145–46; Smalley, 83), others see the three lusts covering three different areas of life (Brown, 306–12; Mitchell, 67; Painter, 194; Schnackenburg, 128).[351] The first two areas involve attitudes while the third involves conduct. The first two could be kept hidden, though they normally lead to further sinful conduct. The last one arises from internal motives but expresses itself in external actions (Kistemaker, 271).

This first "thing" of the world is a wrong desire. The term ἐπιθυμία, translated "lust" in most cases, expresses a strong desire for something. It need not be evil; in fact, it may be a healthy or pious desire. But it becomes sinful when directed inappropriately.[352] Here it is lust "of the flesh." "Flesh"

---

348. He provides Philo as an example. He says in *Decalogue* 151, "Is the love of money, or of women, or of glory, or of any one of the other efficient causes of pleasure, the origin of slight and ordinary evils?" and then in *Decalogue* 153, "For, both among the Greeks and barbarians, the wars between one another, and between their own different tribes, which have been so celebrated by tragedians, have all flowed from one source, namely, desire of money, or glory, or pleasure; for it is on such subjects as these that the race of mankind goes mad." In *Creation* (79) he lists other vices and says, "And this would be the case if there were neither irrational pleasures to obtain mastery over the soul raising up a wall of gluttony and lasciviousness, nor desires of glory, or power, or riches, to assume dominion over life, nor pains to contract and warp the intellect, nor that evil councilor—fear, to restrain the natural inclinations towards virtuous actions, nor folly and cowardice, and injustice, and the incalculable multitude of other evils to attack them." (C. D. Yonge, trans., *The Works of Philo*, 531)

349. As Akin (109) notes, they should not be viewed as a comprehensive list, but rather a sampling.

350. The three sins are appositional to πᾶν τὸ ἐν τῷ κόσμῳ (Bultmann, 33; Burdick, 178). Brown (306–12) and Painter (194) see the first two as subjectives and the third as objective.

351. Burge (116) describes them as "a sweeping portrait of what it means to be seduced by worldliness and the allure of sin."

352. BDAG, 372; F. Büchsel, "ἐπιθυμέω, ἐπιθυμητής, ἐπιθυμία," *TDNT* 3:170–71.

(σάρξ) is expressed through a genitive construction. Taken as an attributive genitive, it would communicate the idea that one of the "things of the world" is lusts characterized by the flesh. As an objective genitive, it would communicate the idea of lusts directed toward the flesh. It seems better to see it as a subjective genitive describing the lusts the flesh is producing (Brooke, 48; Brown, 308; Burdick, 178; Rensberger, 74; Schnackenburg, 130; Strecker, 59 n. 22).[353] Further "flesh" is a synecdoche* for the person.[354] This is the first of four uses of the term "flesh" by John in his three epistles. Of the 146 occurrences of σάρξ in the New Testament, it appears twenty times in John's writings. He uses it in the sense of the human body itself (John 1:13; Rev 17:16; 19:18 [5x], 21) and for frail humanity in the sense of a physical being (John 1:14; 6:52). He quotes Jesus' use of the term when he refers to the human as opposed to divine birth (John 3:6) or perspective (John 6:63; 8:15), when he refers to his own body as flesh (John 6:51, 53–56), and to humanity in general (17:2). In his epistles, John's other three uses refer to Jesus' incarnation, that he came as a human being "in the flesh" (4:2, 3; 2 John 7). Thus, from John's use of σάρξ, he views "the flesh" as weak and mortal, but not especially evil.[355] This sense of σάρξ is common throughout the NT writings.[356] Though the term is used by Paul to refer to the sin nature (Rom 8:12; 13:13; Gal 5:16; Eph 2:2), such is not characteristic of John. Even so, in this instance John appears to be using "flesh" in much the

---

353. Yarbrough (132) notes the nuances of either the gen. of quality or subjective gen., but then says it is "simply one more idiomatic rendering of the danger to which John seeks to call attention: things originating in innate human nature regarded as unredeemed by God."

354. Burge (115) notes that "the LXX never uses *sarx* with reference to sensuality but often uses it to refer to humanity in general, particularly as it stands in contrast to God."

355. F. M. Braun, *Jean le théologien*, 31; H. Schneider, "The Word was made Flesh," 344.

356. A. C. Thiselton ("σάρξ," *NIDNTT* 1:671–82) provides an excellent discussion of the meaning and significance of σάρξ throughout the NT. He sees it being used in the sense of meat that is eaten (1 Cor 15:39), temporary relationships as opposed to eternal (Rom 1:3–4; 1 Cor 10:18), human relationships involving physical kinship (1 Cor 1:16; Gal 6:12), the human way of doing things as opposed to divine or spiritual (2 Cor 10:2; 5:16; 11:18), that aspect of human nature that is opposed to God (Rom 13:14; Gal 5:16–17; 1 Pet 2:11), the material portion of the human body (Col 1:22; 2:11), or may represent the whole person (Matt 16:17; Luke 24:39; John 3:6; 7:24; 8:15; Act 2:31; 1 Pet 3:18; Heb 2:14; 5:7).

same sense as Paul when he is referring to the sin nature within the believer (Brooke, 48; Marshall, 145).

Using the same construction, John now adds to those unholy desires arising from the "flesh" other desires related to the eyes. Again, rather than describing eyes that lust (subjective genitive), he is describing desires aroused visually (contra Smalley, 84). Using a metonymy* of the subject, John uses *eyes* to refer to things those eyes see and wrongly desire (Hodges, 103). This "lust" is seen by interpreters to express itself in one of three areas: (1) arrogance, though the following reference to boastful pride makes this unlikely; (2) desire for riches (Houlden, 74; Rensberger, 74; Yarbrough, 133); or (3) sensual desires, whether they be sexual or simply self-indulgent (Bultmann, 34; Brooke, 48; Burge, 115; Marshall, 145).[357] Brown (311) rejects all three of these and sees this simply describing a focus on the "visible" things of life rather than the spiritual.[358]

The boastful pride of life focuses one's attention more on attitudes than desires. The term ἀλαζονεία has more to do with pretension and arrogance than simply "pride" alone (Burdick, 179–80; Grayston, 75).[359] This term was common in the Greco-Roman world as a vice of the wealthy and powerful who abused their social inferiors and whose boastfulness and actions indicated that they thought of themselves as gods in a pejorative sense.[360] However, where this was often applied to the wealthy, John's connection with "life" in general makes it something anyone can do. If he had targeted the wealthy, he would have more likely used πλοῦτος as opposed to βίος, though it could at times be used synonymously. Its reference to "riches" need not refer to the wealthy but to anyone who puts confidence or self-worth in possessions (Williamson, 96; Lenski, 426; Yarbrough, 134).[361] In this case it looks more at an attitude that excludes God (Burge, 116; Schnackenburg, 114). The term βίος focuses more on possessions, occupation, and status—the things that make up life—than on living, breathing, or being alive

357. Burge (115) points to Matt 5:28 ("But I say to you that whoever looks at a woman to lust for her has already committed adultery with her in his heart.") as an example of the eye being used as " a metaphor for sinful passion that corrupts."

358. Also Grayston (75) and Moody (47). Burdick (179) calls this "'feasting' the eyes upon the object in view."

359. BDAG, 40; G. Delling, "ἀλαζών, ἀλαζονεία," *TDNT* 1:226–27.

360. C. Spicq, "ἀλαζονεία, ἀλαζών," *TLNT* 1:63–65.

361. F. M. Braun, *Jean le théologien,* 208.

(Johnson, 53; Rensberger, 74–75; Schnackenburg, 130; Strecker, 59 n. 24).[362] It is not always a negative term in the NT. It was used positively by Jesus in Mark 12:44, and it will be used later by John in this epistle (3:17) with its positive sense. Here "life" is functioning as a subjective genitive (Akin, 111; Brooke, 48; Brown, 312; Schnackenburg, 130)[363] rather than objective (Painter, 192), or a plenary genitive that blends the subjective and objective (Law, 152; Smalley, 85). In combination with its noun, βίος describes pride arising out of one's position and possessions in this world, an ego trip (Burge, 115; Kruse, 96; Schnackenburg, 130). Thus the person guilty of this is focusing on the material things of the world, as well as on self-actualization and accomplishment.[364]

οὐκ ἔστιν ἐκ τοῦ πατρὸς ἀλλ' ἐκ τοῦ κόσμου ἐστίν, "is not from the Father, but is from the world." Though three lusts have been listed, the verb here is singular because the subject is "all that is in the world" rather than the three lusts. Thus everything making up the world system is what is not from the Father. Often translated "of," the Greek preposition ἐκ carries the sense of source or origin (Painter, 194; Smalley, 86).[365] None of the elements of the world system is sourced in God the Father. They do not come from him. As James tells us (Jas 1:13), God does not tempt anyone to do evil nor can he be tempted by evil. In that same light, John has affirmed God's absolute purity in chapter 1, and now he declares that nothing in the impure world system originated with God.

Using the strong adversative ἀλλά, John now reveals the source of those things in the world one might love.[366] He does this by repeating the construction of the previous clause. This heightens the contrast between sources of attitudes. As Brown notes well, John's use of the εἶναι ἐκ construction indicates "origin from and/or adherence to one side or the other" in his literary dualism (Brown, 313). Rather than these evil motives originating

362. R. Bultmann, "ζάω, ζωή (βιόω, βίος)," *TDNT* 2:861–72.
363. E. Malatesta, *Interiority and Covenant*, 184.
364. Lenski (426) provides a humorous aside that John "might have added 'the lust of the ears' since these also reach out far for vile gratification. Add this yourself; John only suggests." He likely was alluding to "worldly" music of his day. And, as we can see, just as human nature remains the same, so, too, the issues. Only the technology and decibels change.
365. BDAG, 296.
366. BDAG, 45.

in God, they arise from the world system wherein John's readers live. Here, once more, "world" looks at the satanically controlled world system and its values. However, what is the proper attitude toward the world and its "things"?

2:17 Using a "both/and" construction, John contrasts all aspects of the world and its system with the believer. Whereas the world is transitory, the obedient believer is eternal. This verse contains all present tense verbs and verbals, drawing our attention to the state of the world wherein we live even today.

καὶ ὁ κόσμος παράγεται καὶ ἡ ἐπιθυμία αὐτοῦ, "Both the world and its lusts are passing away." The double *καὶ* construction offers several alternatives to understanding John's point. (1) The first *καὶ* could be a continuative connective with the second *καὶ* being a coordinate conjunction with an implied ellipsis in its compound subject and verb construction (Bultmann, 34; Strecker, 59 n. 25). However, the contrast is no longer between God and the world as in the previous sentence. It is between transitoriness and eternality. (2) The second *καὶ* may be seen as an explanatory conjunction that could be translated as "namely, its lust." It could be translated as "along with" in order to clarify the sense in English that the world's lust is only one part of what will pass away when the world ends (Brown, 313; Burdick, 180–81; Smalley, 86). (3) It could be a simple "both/and" correlative construction, taken in this commentary. This sees John acknowledging the transitoriness of the world in its entirety, but bringing attention to the heart attitude ("lust") within the world system that is not morally neutral. John's point is that this "world" is transitory, not eternal like God. Consequently, it is in process of "passing away" (present tense), of experiencing its limited existence (Burdick, 181; Kruse, 96; Schnackenburg , 131; Smalley, 87).[367] John is in part reminding his readers of the brevity of life. However, even more so, he points to the brevity of the world and its systems (Brown, 313–14). For in this case, "world" refers to the world system made up of mankind and controlled by Satan (Lieu, 96; Marshall, 146; Schnackenburg, 131; Williamson,

367. As in 2:8, this is an example of the intransitive use of a transitive verb (BDF §308). This same concept is taught by Paul in 1 Cor 7:31.

97) rather than the created world that will be replaced in the eschaton (Akin, 111; Kruse, 96; Painter, 194; Strecker, 60).[368]

Of note is the singular "lust" following the triad of attitudes characteristic of the world system in the previous sentence. Here the singular does not point to a single lust, but lust as a principle that characterizes the passing world system (Lieu, 96).[369] This connects with what John has said about the darkness passing away in 2:8 (Rensberger, 75).[370]

ὁ δὲ ποιῶν τὸ θέλημα τοῦ θεοῦ μένει εἰς τὸν αἰῶνα, "but he who does the will of God remains forever." Though not as strong an adversative as ἀλλὰ in the previous sentence, this clause, introduced with the contrastive conjunction δὲ, draws a contrast between the obedient believer and the passing world system. The articular present participle ὁ ποιῶν describes a kind of person, the obedient Christian who "does" God's will.[371] As Brown (314) notes, this is a Semitism indicating someone who lives or acts according to God's revealed will in his word. Addtionally, this obedient Christian is contrasted with "the world and its lusts."

Whereas the world is "passing away," the one who does God's will "remains." This use of μένω does not carry the same sense as Jesus' use in the upper room where it conveyed the idea of influence, relationship, and mutual indwelling. Here it communicates the idea of continuance, staying around, and so "remaining" (Bultmann, 34; Burdick, 181). With God, the believer

368. Yarbrough (136) chooses a neutral position while rejecting Schnackenburg's arguments. Johnson (54), Rensberger (75), Smalley (87), and Williamson (97) see this in terms of Johannine realized eschatology with Christ's kingdom being experienced in part in the present while yet to come in the future. Burge (116) is not clear. On one hand, he writes in terms of realized eschatology, but appears to leave open the completion of history as well. Schnackenburg (131) does not see John speaking here in terms of realized eschatology.

369. Marshall (146) sees "lusts" as an "abstract noun representing the concrete reality, the person who desires the world." This then draws a contrast between believers and nonbelievers rather than believers and the world system. The context, though, indicates that John has the world system in mind, and so this figure is less likely.

370. John's use of αὐτοῦ here may be subjective, objective, or plenary. Smalley (87) affirms it is at least subjective but may be better seen as plenary.

371. Burdick (181) sees ποιῶν indicating a "continuous practice of God's will." He sees John reflecting the Calvinist doctrine of perseverance as evidence of justifying faith. Rensberger (75) defines "doing the will of God" in terms of "believing in Jesus and loving one another." For him this describes a believer, a possessor of eternal life.

is eternal in contrast to this passing world (Painter, 195; Smith 66).[372] What this does *not* affirm is that an obedient believer will never die. Rather, this is pointing to one's eternal destiny with God in heaven (Moody, 47; Smith, 47), which begins in this life as a quality of life that will be fully expressed in eternity.[373]

Biblical Theology Comments

As noted above, John's view of the world is not always negative, though in this section we learn of the world system's transitory nature. The world system and all it contains stands in contrast to God, both morally and temporally. It is characterized by unholy desires—lusts—that can distract the attention of God's children from him and those things that are of eternal value. This is a call much like Paul's exhortation in Col 3:1–4, to focus on the heavenly things that last rather than the temporal passing world, its possessions, and its values. With John there is no middle state, where one can love the world's things as well as love God. One must choose between the two. Also, with him there are clear consequences to the choice made. Choosing the world is expressed in terms of acceding to its desires, while choosing God is expressed in terms of doing his will. As introduced earlier by John (2:3–6), obedience is the expression of relationship with God. This idea continues to be developed.

Application and Devotional Implications

This is a difficult section, especially for those living in materialistic societies. How do we have God's values and not love the world? Some Christians have mistakenly thought that discarding their material possessions is the answer. For example, Francis of Assisi, upon hearing the reading of Matt 10:7–19, believed he was being personally called to a life of poverty. He discarded his material possessions and began an evangelistic ministry that drew a following of other monks and eventually developed into an order in

372. Schnackenburg (132) sees μένει εἰς τὸν αἰῶνα as equivalent to ζήσει εἰς τὸν αἰῶνα in John 6:51 and 58, both promises of eternal life.

373. Thus, to be consumed with this life and its pleasures and desires leaves the believer unprepared for the next life. Interestingly, C. Hodge (*Systematic Theology*, 3:753) notes, "The early Christians prayed for the souls of apostles and martyrs, whom they assuredly believed were in heaven. It was not, therefore, for any alleviation of their sufferings ... that such prayers were offered, but for the augmentation of their happiness, and the consummation of their blessedness at the last day."

the Catholic Church.[374] Giving all to the poor and living in poverty is not what John had in mind. Poor people can be possessed by their possessions. Wealthy people can have great possessions but not overvalue them because their hearts were in heaven, not bound to earth. They loved God more than anything they possessed.

How do we gain a proper perspective on the passing world? Begin by reading and heeding Ecclesiastes. In it we are reminded about the transitoriness of life and the meaninglessness of things and accomplishments. We are also reminded that God intends that we enjoy this life, while remembering we will give an account to him in the end.

So how do you love God more than the world? First, pause regularly to remind yourself that God does not play second fiddle to anyone or anything. Second, take time regularly to think about the transitoriness of the world and its possessions. Everything on this earth wears out. It is a reminder to us that the world is indeed passing away. Ask yourself whether you are being a steward of God's resources or a consumer of the earth. Only with an eternal perspective will the temporal find its proper place in our values.

Selected Bibliography

Braun, F. *Jean le théologien: sa théologie, le mystère de Jésus-Christ*. Paris: J. Gabalda, 1966.

Brown, R. E. *The Community of the Beloved Disciple*. Mahwah, NJ: Paulist, 1979.

Cassen, N. H. "A Grammatical and Contextual Inventory of the Use of κόσμος in the Johannine Corpus with Some Implications for a Johannine Cosmic Theology." *NTS* 19 (1972): 81–91.

Fanning, B. M. *Verbal Aspect in New Testament Greek*. Oxford: Clarendon, 1990.

Guhrt, J. "κόσμος." In *New International Dictionary of New Testament Theology*, edited by C. Brown, 1:521. 4 vols. Grand Rapids: Zondervan, 1975–1985.

Hodge, C. *Systematic Theology*. 3 vols. Oak Harbor, WA: Logos Research Systems, Inc., 1997.

Love, D. "Love Not the World." *Leaven* 14 (2006): 119–23.

Malatesta, E. *Interiority and Covenant: A Study of* εἶναι ἐν *and* μένειν ἐν *in the First Letter of Saint John*. Rome: Biblical Institute Press, 1978.

Schneider, H. "'The Word Was Made Flesh': An Analysis of the Theology of Revelation in the Fourth Gospel." *CBQ* 31 (1969): 344–56.

The Oxford Dictionary of the Christian Church. 3rd ed. Revised and edited by F. L. Cross and E. A. Livingstone. Oxford: Oxford University Press, 2005.

---

374. "Francis of Assisi," *ODCC*, 635–36

Thiselton, A. C. "σάρξ." In *New International Dictionary of New Testament Theology*, edited by C. Brown, 1:671–82. 4 vols. Grand Rapids: Zondervan, 1975–1985.

Wallace, D. B. *Greek Grammar beyond the Basics*. Grand Rapids: Zondervan, 1996.

Yonge, C. D. *The Works of Philo: Complete and Unabridged*. New updated ed. Peabody, MA: Hendrickson, 1996.

Avoid Antichrists (2:18–27)

Introduction

John, having encouraged his readers to set their hearts on God rather than the world system, turns to the next danger to their spiritual life—false teachers. Believers can think they are rejecting the world and its values yet still fall prey to it through the deception of so-called Christian teachers, who are what Paul called "savage wolves," whose teachings are designed to draw believers away from the flock of God and into their own circles of influence (Acts 20:29–31).[375] Though John has dealt with moral issues to this point, it seems better to see this as the principal issue with the false teachers and the moral issues previously dealt with being a characteristic problem throughout the church. Thus, having dealt with the more common issue affecting one's fellowship with God, John now warns his readers of another, a theological, danger to their relationship with God. He does this by drawing a contrast between believers and antichrists in terms of their confession or rejection of the truth respectively. At the same time, in this polemical section, John's focus is on his readers and their fellowship with God.[376]

375. E. Wendland, "'Dear Children' Versus the 'Antichrists': The Rhetoric of Reassurance in First John," 41. This article appears again as "The Rhetoric of Reassurance in First John: 'Dear Children' versus the 'Antichrists,'" in *Neot* 41 (2007): 173–219. He sees these as false teachers who are incipient Gnostics promoting a "gospel of knowledge" with both christological and moral errors. However, there is no need to connect this error with the moral error corrected previously. This is evidenced by John's including himself in the potential moral errors (his use of "us" and "we") while distancing himself from the christological errors he addresses in this section. This is not to say that false teachers with christological errors did not have moral issues as well. It is just that the ethical issues raised by John are evident throughout the church (found in Paul's Epistles, for example) and need not be identified polemically with the false teachers.

376. D. Van der Merwe ("'Experiencing Fellowship with God' According to 1 John 1:5–2:28: Dealing with the Change in Social Behavior," 246, 260 n. 34) notes that

Among modern interpreters, many see this as the beginning of a new section (Akin, 46; Brown, 124; Burdick, 89; Burge, 45; Painter, 196; Smalley, xxxiii; Stott, 61; Williamson, 98).[377] Even for those who agree on the role of this unit, some still debate whether this section should end with v. 27, 28, or 29. This is likely caused because verses 27 and 28 function as "hinge" verses within 1 John.[378] Others see it marking the beginning of the next major movement (Brooke, 49; Kistemaker, 224; Marshall, 147; Schnackenburg, 138).[379] Where moral error was in view in the epistle up to this point, John now turns from his pastoral concern to address theological error of a christological nature.[380]

This unit is characterized by John's focus on abiding, expressed through the fivefold repetition of *μένω*.[381] As will be seen below, the correct response to false teachers is abiding in the truths taught by the apostles (New Testament Scriptures), which leads to fellowship with God expressed as abiding in the Son and Father.

---

these verses contain "probably the greatest concentration and variety of the experience of fellowship to be found in any part of 1 John." This is based on the "high frequency of personal pronouns and verbs in the second person plural" that "heighten the personalization of the passage."

377. D. Van der Merwe ("'Experiencing Fellowship with God' According to 1 John 1:5–2:28: Dealing with the Change in Social Behavior," 249) sees this as the conclusion of the first major section because it represents "a logical rhetorical building up to an eschatological climax" which began in 1:5 and reaches its conclusion at 2:28. Painter (61) notes that the issue of false teaching is not addressed until this point in the Epistle and argues from the absence of "any polemic posture" in the preceding context that this forms a clear demarcation of emphasis.

378. Harris (103) notes that if verse 28 is allowed to begin a new section, it parallels 2:12 and 2:18.

379. Bruce (31–32) divides this epistle into ten units, with 2:18–27 functioning as an independent unit. Edwards (36) and Strecker (xliv, 61) follow a similar approach with seven units and 2:18–27 functioning independently of the others. Lieu (v–vii) divides the epistle into eleven units, with 2:18 introducing a unit composed of 2:18–28. Johnson (16) breaks it into fourteen sections. Smith (1–2, 23) breaks it into sixteen units without attempting to develop a larger structure. He places 2:18–29 together.

380. Thus this section is best seen as polemical, though it arises from his pastoral concerns.

381. A sixth use occurs in verse 28, which I see beginning the next section. This is another example of a "hinge verse" wherein a key concept from the previous section is related to a key concept in the following section, thereby showing the interconnectedness of the two sections and the concepts developed within them.

Though in recent years a chiastic structure has been proposed for this section, including verses 18 through 28, it seems unlikely that such is the case. Examples of two of these chiasms are illustrated in the chart below. Of note are their similarities and differences. Both are presented in support of translating πᾶς in verse 20 as "all things" (πάντα) as opposed to "all of you" (πάντες). In their favor, both reflect the parallel ideas within the section and acknowledge a Johannine literary device that is increasingly recognized by others. Against them is the problem of the significant variance in determining the divisions and the elements in each chiasm. This reflects the subjective criteria for determining when the author is intending to develop a chiasmus versus when he is simply repeating ideas or drawing contrasts. As one who recognizes at least some Johannine chiasms and has identified one early in the work, I find both doubtful in that they are forced to divide sentences into their clauses in order to create the full parallel and are selective in determining what elements in each unit is to be emphasized. Further, verse 28, though a "hinge verse," functions better as an introduction to what follows than a conclusion to what precedes. Moreover, it would seem that John's choice to change from παιδία (v. 18) to τεκνία (v. 28) mitigates against the terms or verses functioning in parallel with each other in a chiasm.

Proposed Chiastic Structures for 1 John 2:18–28

Ernst R. Wendland:[382]

A (vv. 18–19): "a 'manifestation' of the exit (non-'abiding') of the antichrists."

B (vv. 20–21): "about an 'anointing' from the 'Holy One' so that you know '**all things**'; John 'writes' about the 'truth.'"

C (v. 22): "the liar, antichrist, 'denies' (2 times) that Jesus is the Christ, hence both the Father and the Son."

D (v. 23): "no one who denies the 'Son' has the 'Father'; whoever confesses the 'Son' has the 'Father.'"

E (v. 24a): "as for you—let what *you heard from the beginning abide in you.*"

382. E. Wendland, "'Dear Children' Versus the 'Antichrists': The Rhetoric of Reassurance in First John," 69–71. Italics his.

E′ (v. 24b) "if *in you*—it *abides*, what *from the beginning: you heard.*"

D′ (v. 24c): "you will abide in both the 'Son' and the 'Father.'"

C′ (v. 25): "this is the 'promise' (2 times) which he (Father/Son) gave us, namely, eternal life."

B′ (vv. 26–27d): "about an 'anointing' from him that abide in you and which teaches you '**all things**' concerning what is 'true.'"

A′ (vv. 27e–28): "you must 'abide' in him (Christ), for he will be 'manifested.'" (bold and italics original)

John Breck:[383]

A (v. 18): "*Children*, beware of *antichrist* whom you have heard is *coming*."

B (v. 19): "They have *not abided* with us."

C (vv. 20–21): "Your *anointing from the Holy One* allows you to *know all things*, and that no *lie* is of the *truth*."

D (vv. 22–23): "The *liar* who *denies* the *Christ denies* the *Father* and the *Son*; The one who confesses the Son has the Father."

D′ (vv. 24–26): "*You* who *abide* in what ou heard from the beginning, *abide* in the *Son* and in the *Father*. The promise he promised us is eternal life."

C′ (v. 27): Your *anointing from him* teaches you *all things* and is *true* and is no *lie*."

B′ (v. 27): "*Abide* in him."

A′ (v. 28): *Children*, abide in the *coming Christ*.

Original Text

18 Παιδία, ἐσχάτη ὥρα ἐστίν, καὶ καθὼς ἠκούσατε ὅτι ἀντίχριστος ἔρχεται, καὶ
νῦν ἀντίχριστοι πολλοὶ γεγόνασιν· ὅθεν γινώσκομεν ὅτι ἐσχάτη ὥρα ἐστίν. **19** ἐξ
ἡμῶν ἐξῆλθαν, ἀλλ' οὐκ ἦσαν ἐξ ἡμῶν· εἰ γὰρ ἐξ ἡμῶν ἦσαν, μεμενήκεισαν ἂν
μεθ' ἡμῶν· ἀλλ' ἵνα φανερωθῶσιν ὅτι οὐκ εἰσὶν πάντες ἐξ ἡμῶν. **20** καὶ ὑμεῖς

383. J. Breck, "The Function of ΠΑΣ in 1 John 220," 203–4. Italics his.

χρῖσμα ἔχετε ἀπὸ τοῦ ἁγίου καὶ οἴδατε πάντα.[a] **21** οὐκ ἔγραψα ὑμῖν ὅτι οὐκ
οἴδατε τὴν ἀλήθειαν, ἀλλ᾽ ὅτι οἴδατε αὐτήν, καὶ ὅτι πᾶν ψεῦδος ἐκ τῆς ἀληθείας
οὐκ ἔστιν. **22** τίς ἐστιν ὁ ψεύστης εἰ μὴ ὁ ἀρνούμενος ὅτι Ἰησοῦς οὐκ ἔστιν ὁ χρι-
στός; οὗτός ἐστιν ὁ ἀντίχριστος, ὁ ἀρνούμενος τὸν πατέρα καὶ τὸν υἱόν. **23** πᾶς ὁ
ἀρνούμενος τὸν υἱὸν οὐδὲ τὸν πατέρα ἔχει· aὁ ὁμολογῶν τὸν υἱὸν καὶ τὸν πατέρα
ἔχει.a **24** ὑμεῖς ὃ ἠκούσατε ἀπ᾽ ἀρχῆς, ἐν ὑμῖν μενέτω· ἐὰν ἐν ὑμῖν μείνῃ ὃ ἀπ᾽
ἀρχῆς ἠκούσατε, καὶ ὑμεῖς ἐν τῷ υἱῷ καὶ ἐν τῷ πατρὶ μενεῖτε. **25** καὶ αὕτη ἐστὶν
ἡ ἐπαγγελία ἣν αὐτὸς ἐπηγγείλατο ἡμῖν, τὴν ζωὴν τὴν αἰώνιον.

26 Ταῦτα ἔγραψα ὑμῖν περὶ τῶν πλανώντων ὑμᾶς. **27** καὶ ὑμεῖς τὸ χρῖσμα ὃ
ἐλάβετε ἀπ᾽ αὐτοῦ μένει ἐν ὑμῖν, καὶ οὐ χρείαν ἔχετε ἵνα τις διδάσκῃ ὑμᾶς· ἀλλ᾽
ὡς τὸ αὐτοῦ χρῖσμα διδάσκει ὑμᾶς περὶ πάντων, καὶ ἀληθές ἐστιν καὶ οὐκ ἔστιν
ψεῦδος, καὶ καθὼς ἐδίδαξεν ὑμᾶς, μένετε ἐν αὐτῷ.

Textual Notes

20.a. Stronger support exists for the neuter acc. plural πάντα (A C K 049 056 0142 33 81 88 104 181 326 330 436 451 614 629 630 945 1505 1739 1877 1881 2127 2412 2492 2495 *Byz Lect* it$^{ar,e,dem.div,h,p,z}$ vg syr^{h} cop^{bo} arm eth) rather than the masculine nominative plural πάντες (א B P 398 1838 1852 cop^{sa}).[384] Metzger's choice was more theological than text critical, "understanding the passage to be directed against the claims of a few to possess esoteric knowledge." Thus the committee's choice is based on an assumed *Sitz im Leben** that remains unsubstantiated in the extant literature produced by the church fathers.[385] The use of πάντα reflects John's style of writing in the Gospel.[386] Once the assumed dissenting community is removed from con-

384. Contra D. Black ("An overlooked stylistic argument in favor of πάντα in 1 John 2:20," 206) who asserts that the textual evidence is too divided to determine which reading is best.

385. B. Metzger and United Bible Societies, *A Textual Commentary on the Greek New Testament*, 2d ed., 641.

386. The two examples provided by Black ("An overlooked stylistic argument in favor of πάντα in 1 John 2:20," 206) are John 14:26 (ἐκεῖνος ὑμᾶς διδάξει πάντα καὶ ὑπομνήσει ὑμᾶς πάντα ἃ εἶπον ὑμῖν) and 16:30 (νῦν οἴδαμεν ὅτι οἶδας πάντα). Additional examples might include John 2:24 (ησοῦς οὐκ ἐπίστευεν αὐτὸν αὐτοῖς διὰ τὸ αὐτὸν γινώσκειν πάντας); 5:20 (ὁ γὰρ πατὴρ φιλεῖ τὸν υἱὸν καὶ πάντα δείκνυσιν αὐτῷ ἃ αὐτὸς ποιεῖ); 1 John 3:20 (ὅτι μείζων ἐστὶν ὁ θεὸς τῆς καρδίας ἡμῶν καὶ γινώσκει πάντα). But, the Johannine use of πάντες is not absent. Some examples of these include John 1:7 (ἵνα πάντες πιστεύσωσιν δι᾽ αὐτοῦ); 1:16 (ἐκ τοῦ πληρώματος αὐτοῦ ἡμεῖς πάντες ἐλάβομεν); 5:23 (ἵνα πάντες τιμῶσι τὸν υἱὸν); 7:21 ("Εν ἔργον ἐποίησα καὶ πάντες θαυμάζετε);

sideration, the fact that πάντα fits well within the author's flow of thought, and the preponderance of external evidence in favor of πάντα, it seems reasonable to accept this reading as original.[387] Wendland argues effectively from the rhetorical structure of 2:18–28 that πάντα here is parallel to his use of πάντων in 2:27, where it clearly carries the sense of "all things."[388]

---

and 13:35 (ἐν τούτῳ γνώσονται πάντες ὅτι ἐμοὶ μαθηταί ἐστε). But these examples are not equivalent and so not conclusive to disprove Black's proposal.

387. D. Black's ("An overlooked stylistic argument in favor of πάντα in 1 John 2:20," 208) chiastic arrangement of the material of vv 18–28 around ὑμεῖς in v 24, with πάντα in v 20 parallel to πάντων in v 27 is interesting, but not convincing, since his outline fails to take v 22 into account, thereby breaking up the parallelism he sought to develop. Nonetheless, the parallel concepts between vv 20 and 27, both dealing with the ministry of the "anointing" in their lives, argue for πάντα being the better choice of terms.

388. E. Wendland, "'Dear Children' Versus the 'Antichrists': The Rhetoric of Reassurance in First John," 69–71. His chiasm contains the following proposed divisions: A (vv. 18–19): "a 'manifestation' of the exit (non-'abiding') of the antichrists."; B (vv. 20–21): "about an 'anointing' from the Holy One' so that you know '**all things**'; John 'writes' about the 'truth'."; C (v. 22): "the liar, antichrist, 'denies' (2 times) that Jesus is the Christ, hence both the Father and the Son."; D (v. 23): "no one who denies the 'Son' has the 'Father'; whoever confesses the 'Son' has the 'Father'."; E (v. 24a): "as for you—let what *you heard from the beginning abide in you.*"; E' (v. 24b) "if *in you*—it *abides*, what *from the beginning: you heard.*"; D′ (v. 24c): "you will abide in both the 'Son' and the 'Father'."; C′ (v. 25): "this is the 'promise' (2 times) which he (Father/Son) gave us, namely, eternal life."; B′ (vv. 26–27d): "about an 'anointing' from him that abide in you and which teaches you '**all things**' concerning what is 'true'."; A′ (vv. 27e-28): "you must 'abide' in him (Christ), for he will be 'manifested'." (bold and italics his)

J. Breck ("The Function of ΠΑΣ in 1 John 220," 203–204) proposes a similar chiastic structure and argues similarly for πάντα as opposed to πάντες. His structure appears as follows: A (v. 18): "*Children*, beware of *antichrist* whom you have heard is *coming*"; B (v. 19): "They have *not abided* with us"; C (vv. 20–21): "Your *anointing from the Holy One* allows you to *know all things*, and that no *lie* is of the *truth*"; D (vv. 22–23): "The *liar* who *denies* the *Christ denies* the *Father* and the *Son*; The one who confesses the Son has the Father"; D′ (vv. 24–26): "*You* who *abide* in what ou heard from the beginning, *abide* in the *Son* and in the *Father*. The promise he promised us is eternal life"; C′ (v. 27): Your *anointing from him* teaches you *all things* and is *true* and is no *lie*"; B′ (v. 27): "*Abide* in him"; A′ (v. 28): *Children*, abide in the *coming Christ*. (italics his) As examples of John's intention to develop these parallels, he notes that the only two occurrences of the noun χρῖσμα in the NT occur here and in the parallel v. 27.

23.a...a The second clause (ὁ ὁμολογῶν ... ἔχει) is omitted from some texts, including the Byzantine, but should be included since it has the weight of textual support (Brown, 354; Smalley, 92).[389] This support includes ℵ A B C P, some minuscules, vg syr^{p} cop^{bo} arm eth. Metzger's assessment that this is a case of homoeoteleuton*, its deletion resulting from the repetition of τὸν πατέρα ἔχει with scribes accidently skipping the words between, explains well its absence from such texts as the Byzantine K L and "most minuscules."[390]

Translation

18 Little children, it is the last hour, and just as you heard that Antichrist[391] is coming, even now many antichrists have come,[392] from this we know that it is the last hour. **19** They went out from[393] us,[394] but they were not from us; for if they had been from us, they would have remained with us; but *they went out*[395] with the result that it was made manifest[396] that none of them were from us. **20** But you have an anointing from the Holy One and you know all things.[397] **21** I do not write to you because you do not know the

---

389. B. Metzger and United Bible Societies, *A Textual Commentary on the Greek New Testament*, 2nd ed., 641.

390. B. Metzger and United Bible Societies, *A Textual Commentary on the Greek New Testament*, 2d ed., 641.

391. This is a term unique to John in the NT. Jesus refers to this same person as "the abomination of desolation" (Matt 24:15) and Paul refers to this same individual as "the lawless one" (2 Thes 2:8–9).

392. As noted in the commentary below, this reflects a perfect tense verb, indicating that the false teachers had come onto the scene and were, in fact, still present.

393. The quadruple repetition of ἐξ ἡμῶν ("from us") is reflected in this translation in order to express the intended literary device (repetition). Other translations do not express the repetition, changing the last three from the first one. For example ASV, ESV, NASB95, NKJV has "from us ... of us ... of us ... of us;" HCSB, NIV84 and NET has "from us ... belonged to us ... belonged to us ... belong to us."

394. A critical element to understanding John is to notice the pronouns and the distinction he makes between "they" (the false teachers), "us" (John and the apostolic circle), and "you" (his readers).

395. Though the words are not in the original (elision), their inclusion is understood.

396. So also NKJV, ASV. Other translations say: "would be shown" (NASB95), "showed" (NIV84), "to demonstrate" (NET), "might become plain" (ESV), "proved" (NLT), and "made clear" (HCSB).

397. This reflects the text-critical decision to accept πάντα ("all things," reflected in: ASV, NKJV) as original rather than πάντες ("you all," reflected in: ESV, HCSB, NASB95,

truth, but because you know it and because *you know*[398] that every lie is not from the truth. **22** Who is the liar if not the one who denies, *by saying*,[399] "Jesus is not the Christ"? This is the Antichrist, the one denying the Father and the Son. **23** Everyone who denies the Son does not have the Father; the one confessing the Son also has the Father. **24** Let that which you heard from the beginning abide in you. If what you heard from the beginning abides in you, then you also will abide in the Son and in the Father. **25** And this is the promise which he promised[400] to us,[401] eternal life. **26** I wrote these things to you concerning those who are trying to[402] deceive[403] you. **27** As for you,[404] the anointing which you received from him abides in you and you do not have a need that anyone should teach you, but as his anointing teaches you concerning all things and is true and is not a lie, and just as it taught you, you abide in him.

NET, NIV84, NLT) as is followed in UBS4.

398. These italics recognize John's elision of a third οἴδατε in the sentence, which would serve to heighten the fact that they do indeed know without a doubt that lies do not arise from the truth.

399. This reflects the role of ὅτι preceding the quoted speech. Various translations handle this construction differently. Most translate ὅτι directly as "that" and the content is given as a positive statement, "Jesus is the Christ" (ASV, ESV, NASB95, NET, NIV84, NKJV; HCSB changes "Christ" to "Messiah"). This reflects an attempt to express John's point in a manner consistent with modern English grammar. The more literal sense is reflected in the NLT which follows "that" with the more literal, "Jesus is not the Christ."

400. The choice of "promise ... promised," though redundant in English, reflects John's emphasis through the literary device of pleonasm*. In this case he uses the verb and noun from the same root. This is reflected in ASV and NKJV but removed from other translations (often replaced with "he made") such as ESV, HCSB, NASB95, NET, NIV84, and NLTxxx.

401. This accepts the choice of ἡμῖν over ὑμῖν, which is reflected in UBS4 (see note on 2:25 below) and follows ASV, ESV, HCSB, NET, NIV84, NKJV, NLT.

402. Though the present participle might be translated literally as "deceiving," "trying to deceive" (conative present) reflects the sense of the sentence and context better (D. B. Wallace, *Grammar*, 534). This is reflected in most translations.

403. Translations alternate between "deceive" (ESV, HCSB, NASB95, NET, NKjv) and "lead astray" (ASV, NIV84).

404. This reflects the role of καὶ with the emphatic pronoun ὑμεῖς (lit. "and you") at the head of the sentence and follows ASV, NASB95, NET, and NIV84. ESV, NKJV, and NLT translate this with "but." HCSB drops it altogether.

Commentary

2:18 The four clauses of this verse form a chiasm in which the coming of the antichrist(s) is central and the theme of the "last hour" encloses the coming of the antichrists. It can be structured thus:

A – Little children, it is the last hour,

B – and just as you heard that Antichrist is coming,

B′ – even now many antichrists have come,

A′ – from this we know that it is the last hour.

This serves to focus attention on the central point: John's warning against false teachers.

Παιδία, ἐσχάτη ὥρα ἐστίν, "Little children, it is the last hour." John uses a different term of endearment here (παιδία) than he used in 2:1 (τεκνία), choosing instead his second description of "children" from 2:12–14.[405] This serves to connect all his readers with his previous words of assurance (Smith, 71; Strecker, 62), though John may simply be using this term of endearment for variation (Lieu, 98). Still, he makes clear that he sees himself addressing his beloved spiritual children as a loving father.[406]

He tells them, nearly two thousand years ago, that they are in "the last hour." Though "hour" occurs throughout the Gospel of John, this is the only place "last hour" is used in the New Testament. This is clearly an eschatological term and must be understood within that context. The idea of *hour* is not as much a quantitative term as it is a qualitative term (Lieu, 99).[407]

---

405. Moody (48) observes well, "*Paidia* each time is related to the learning process as *teknia* has to do with the new birth and *agapētoi* with the new brotherhood."

406. Marshall (148) considers this term of endearment to imply his readers "are still like children in their understanding and need his instruction." Schnackenburg (141) sees this statement functioning in much the same way as 1:5 as a "concise statement" that begins a new section (also Strecker [62]), which he sees beginning here and I see beginning in 2:28. It does, though, introduce the discussion of the false teachers and so introduces a new sub-unit within the first section of the epistle.

407. D. E. Hiebert, ("An Expositional Study of 1 John—Part 4: An Exposition of 1 John 2:18–28," 77) notes the lack of an article with "hour" and considers the possibility of it being purposefully indefinite. Thus it should be translated as *a* last hour and denote a quality of the time period in which John's readers lived. Schnackenburg (142) likewise notes the absence of the article and sees this referring to the "eschatological significance" (*eschatologisch bedeutsam*) of the time

Jesus talked about his "hour" coming with respect to his passion (John 2:4; 12:23, 27; 17:1) as did John (John 7:30; 8:20; 13:1). By that he meant the period of his incarnation that included suffering and death, the culmination of his purpose. For John, the presence of false teachers within the Christian community who deny various truths about Jesus serves as evidence that we live in the last days—or more clearly, that the last days are imminent, poised to come at any moment. This "hour" is an eschatological figure of speech indicating the imminence of the Day of the Lord and the end of history without promising its immediateness (Lenski, 430; Strecker, 62–63).[408] It is the "pause before the storm" of God's judgment on wicked mankind before Jesus returns. It is to be followed by the new age of Messiah's kingdom. Ultimately it refers to the period of time from Jesus' ascension to the rapture of the church (Williamson, 99). John is not saying that he thinks there is only a short period of time left to humanity. Even as John the Baptist, and then Jesus, announced to Israel the message, "Repent, for the kingdom is at hand" (Matt 3:1; 4:17), here the idea of nearness is that of imminence rather than immediateness. Though John the Baptist may have thought the kingdom's arrival was chronologically imminent, Jesus knew the kingdom was not coming any time soon when he preached concerning its coming and commanded his disciples to go throughout the nation announcing "the kingdom of heaven is at hand" (Matt 10:7).

Even after his resurrection, as Jesus prepared to depart this earth for the last time, the disciples asked about the imminence of the kingdom, hoping the time was chronologically short (Acts 1:6). Jesus' response (Acts 1:7–8), though ambiguous, indicated otherwise.

---

period they lived in since John clearly sees the Parousia as yet future and separate from his own experience.

408. Lieu (99) and Williamson (99) note well that the term "hour" is used differently in the Gospel as opposed to the epistle. This seems characteristic of John in that he takes an image and infuses different meanings into it. For example, though "hour" is used literally many times, the Gospel of John (and Jesus) use it to refer to the resurrection of the saints and wicked for their judgment before Jesus (John 5:25, 28), the time of Jesus' manifestation of his messiahship (John 2:4), and His passion (John 7:30; 8:20; 12:23, 27; 13:1; 17:1). As was seen earlier, he uses "beginning" (ἀρχή) with clearly different referents. In the Gospel, Genesis 1:1 is in view. In this epistle, the focus moves either to Jesus' ministry or the time of their conversion and instruction in the faith.

Bruce (64–65) sees this term denoting "the terminal phase of the 'last days', like the 'last time' (*kairos eschatos*) of 1 Pet. 1.5 at which the final salvation is to be revealed." John's use of the anarthrous phrase may be used to indicate the "general character" of the period of time rather than the final period of time (Brooke, 51; Lenski, 429). "It was a period of critical change, 'a last hour,' but not definitely 'the last hour'"(Westcott, 69). Burge (126) sees John speaking "theologically rather than chronologically."[409] It is a foretaste of the last hour, though not the hour itself (Burge, 133).[410] Brown rejects the notion that this refers to the period of time from Christ's ascension till his return. Rather, John, according to Brown (330), believes they are in the final days before Jesus' imminent return. This may be indicated by the word order of "last hour," with the emphasis being on "last" and not "hour" (Kistemaker, 276). Yet such passages as Acts 2:17 (Peter's reference to Joel's fulfillment in his day in combination with Acts 10:45) and Heb 1:2 view the "last days" as a present experience of the church in the first century (Lieu, 98).

καὶ καθὼς ἠκούσατε ὅτι ἀντίχριστος ἔρχεται, "and just as you heard that Antichrist is coming." John reminds his readers that Antichrist is coming. Using the comparative conjunction καθὼς, he tells them both what they

---

409. Burge (125) notes that some see the phrase "the last hour" describing "the period of time just before the end and therefore logically, John was wrong. This view suggests that the early Christians believed in the imminent arrival of Christ in power (his second coming) and that his delay brought a major crisis on the church." This view takes Peter's words in 2 Pet 3:3–7 to mean "that people were scoffing at the church because Christ's announced second coming had not happened." This may be implied in the eschatological confusion of the Thessalonians, which would be early. And, in light of the suffering of the church at the end of the first century, one would expect a greater eschatological longing. However, Peter was not describing the condition of his day, but how it would be when the last days of this age were indeed being experienced by the church. He was consciously eschatological, but also clear that he did not consider them in the last days yet. Though 2 Peter is clearly earlier than 1 John, that also need not imply that John thought that mockers had come yet or that Peter's words were being fulfilled.

410. He notes further (133), "He is not so much announcing 'the end' as he is describing the present as bearing features that betray those of the end. ... John is not apocalyptic, saying that the end is coming tomorrow; he is writing and living within an eschatological schema that says there are features present in his day that go along with the end times, and when these features begin to accumulate in history, two things are true: The end *may* break upon us and we must therefore be ready."

already knew and what was happening. They should not be surprised. Why? His readers had already heard what John is telling them (Strecker, 68). John may be referring here to Jesus' warning in Mark 13:22 that "false christs and false prophets will rise and show signs and wonders to deceive, if possible, even the elect" (Burge, 51; Grayston, 77; Lieu, 99).[411] Or John may be referring to other instructions given them by himself and others during the years following Pentecost (Bruce, 66; Schnackenburg, 143).[412]

Using the present tense verb, ἔρχεται, John makes clear that he does not think Antichrist was on the scene in his day.[413] Of note is the lack of an article with Antichrist. This may indicate the term was common in the church and so could be used here as a proper name or title (Smalley, 91; Westcott, 70).[414] Some understand it to indicate not a specific historical person but a kind of false teacher (Grayston, 76; Lenski, 432).[415] It seems best to see

---

411. D. A. Carson ("1–3 John," 1065) correctly observes the connection between Jesus' words and Dan 7:25; 8:12, 23–25; and 11:30–34. He wrongly concludes from this that John was communicating that the "end-time phenomena" Jesus described was also happening at that time. It is clear from John that he sees the heresies being promoted, but not end-time signs and wonders, both true and false.

412. 2 Thess 2:3–4; 2 Pet 2:1.

413. Brooke (52) sees this use of the present tense to indicate that the subject under discussion is commonly held knowledge rather than as a reference to an immediately coming historical event.

414. M. de Jonge ("The Use of the Word ΧΡΙΣΤΟΣ in the Johannine Epistles," 70–71) argues from this that these false teachers do not represent a Christian-Jewish issue of the Messiahship of Jesus. Rather, as a uniquely Christian term, it strengthens the connection between the title Χριστός with the title ὁ υἱὸς τοῦ θεοῦ, and so focuses attention on Jesus' incarnation and relationship to God the Father as God the Son.

415. Burdick (193) notes that the absence of the article could indicate "general character" unless the context indicates otherwise. In this case, he sees the New Testament practice with similar terms indicating that "last hour" here should be definite. However, all of his examples involve prepositional phrases where an article is understood, and so his assertion is not supported by the evidence he provides. The phrase "the last days" (ἐσχάταις ἡμέραις) is used alternately with and without the article in Acts 2:17 (ἐν ταῖς ἐσχάταις ἡμέραις), 2 Tim 3:1 (ἐν ἐσχάταις ἡμέραις), Heb 1:2 (ἐπ' ἐσχάτου τῶν ἡμερῶν τούτων), and 2 Pet 3:3 (ἐπ' ἐσχάτων τῶν ἡμερῶν). "Last times" is used in 1 Pet 1:20 (ἐπ' ἐσχάτου τῶν χρόνων) and Jude 18 ('Επ' ἐσχάτου τοῦ χρόνου), without the article on ἐσχάτου, but serving as the object of the preposition. Thus, none of these examples support the idea of a technical term whose definiteness was established.

this as the same individual whom Jesus identified as "the abomination of desolation" in Matt 24:15 and Paul calls "the lawless one" in 2 Thess 2:8.[416]

The term "Antichrist" combines two Greek words, a preposition and a noun. *Anti*, the preposition, carries the sense of "instead of" or "against."[417] Χριστός, which literally means "anointed one," refers to Jesus' title. Jesus warned the apostles of the coming of "false christs" who would deceive many (Matt 24:24). Jesus' warnings indicated antichrists who claimed to be substitute Christs. This has led some to see this Antichrist in the same vein (Harris, 104; Houlden, 77). However, John's use of "Antichrist" need not indicate false teachers attempting to take the place of Christ in some way. Rather, he is using the term with the emphasis on the "against" aspect of the preposition.[418] His teaching opposes Christ in some way (Burdick, 194).[419]

καὶ νῦν ἀντίχριστοι πολλοὶ γεγόνασιν, "even now many antichrists have come." These many antichrists, whom John already sees in the world in his day, are the false teachers of his epistles (2:22; 4:3; 2 John 7). They serve as forerunners of the ultimate and final Antichrist, called "the beast" by John in Revelation (13:1–18).[420] This ultimate Antichrist will do more than op-

416. Rensberger (78) observes that ἀντίχριστος does not appear in either Jewish or Christian literature before John's use of it in his epistles.

417. MM, sv. "ἀντίχριστος."

418. J. Stott (109) notes that one might argue for "instead of" based on the term *antibasilius* used for "viceroy." He rejects this concept and argues that John could have used the term *pseudochristos* better to describe them if they were presenting themselves as Christ (false christs) rather than being opponents of Christ.

419. S. J. Nichols, "Prophecy Makes Strange Bedfellows: On The History Of Identifying The Antichrist," 76.

420. Bultmann (36) argues that John's connection of the Antichrist with the antichrists of his day indicates that John "historicizes the mythical figure" and considers the "last days" promise as fulfilled. However, John's language clearly indicates that Antichrist is still to come. And, nothing in the text indicates that he sees him as anything other than a coming historical figure, as verified in his depiction of him in Revelation 13. Schnackenburg (143–44) views John's use of antichrist and antichrists as metaphor rather than to be understood in a literal sense and rejects the idea that John really meant to say there were literal antichrists on the scene who were precursors of a future literal antichrist. Brooke (50), too, sees these antichrists as fulfilling the promise of the coming antichrist rather than being an indication that he is coming. Strecker (63), too, sees John demythologizing "the mythological figure of the antichrist" and applying it to the historical situation of his day in the persons of false teachers. Marshall (151) on the other hand rejects the idea of demythologizing. John was anticipating a historical figure who is yet to come. He is

pose Christ. He will claim to be Christ and eventually exalt himself above God (Dan 9:27; 11:31; 12:11; Matt 24:15). For John, a false Christology identifies false teachers with the future false Christ, the antichrist. Thus he calls them antichrists as well.

Though this title is only used by John in his epistles (here and in 2 John 7), the person John designates as Antichrist was clearly taught before these epistles were written.[421] Paul, in 2 Thess 2:1–12, warns of the coming "lawless one." Even before Paul were Jesus' warnings in the Olivet Discourse of "the 'abomination of desolation,' spoken of by Daniel the prophet, standing in the holy place" (Matt 24:15). Additionally, in Rev 13, Jesus will reveal to John the role this beast out of the sea will play in the coming Day of the Lord.[422]

Using the ascensive *καὶ* with *νῦν*, John moves from the fact of Antichrist's coming to the present situation in order to show its significance with regard to the future expectation.[423] Whereas the ultimate one is coming, in the present "many" have appeared. Using the perfect active *γεγόνασιν*, John emphasizes both their appearance in the church, as well as their present influence. They were not a previous problem the church had faced and overcome. They were an ever-present danger from the beginning of the church until that day.

ὅθεν γινώσκομεν ὅτι ἐσχάτη ὥρα ἐστίν, "from this we know that it is the last hour." Repeating "it is the last hour" for emphasis at the end of this long sentence, John creates a short inclusio* to focus his readers on the point of

---

identifying the false teachers with him in that they reflect his "spirit" in the sense of his attitudes and teachings, without mistaking them for him. John still viewed his coming as future.

421. Grayston (76) suggests that John may have coined the word and obtained the idea from ἀντίθεος in Philo's *Dreams* 2.183 (μὴ θαυμάσῃς δέ, ὅτι τοῖς ἐναντίοις ὁ θεὸς καὶ ὁ ἀντίθεος νοῦς εὐφραίνεται, Φαραώ. From Peder Borgen, Kåre Fuglseth and Roald Skarsten, *The Works of Philo: Greek Text With Morphology*).

422. Hodges (108) sees the antichrist as the false prophet of Rev 13. Rather, he is the beast out of the sea with the false prophet serving as a false Elijah, or his "John the Baptist."

423. G. Stählin ("νῦν," *TDNT* 4:1120) sees this use of νῦν to reflect an eschatological concept in John and Paul that reflects Jesus' sense of the "fleeting hours" while for the disciples it reflects the "incompleteness" of their experience, though also the sense that they are making progress toward the end of time. This seems to be reading too much into the term, though what he says about Jesus and the disciples' perspective on time is true.

what is to follow. He is not just saying that Antichrist is coming, but that his forerunners are on the scene threatening the church. Further, though the Day of the Lord will present to the world the ultimate Antichrist, others on the scene in John's day are a reminder that he is coming. Having alerted his readers to that, John is now ready to describe these antichrists.

2:19 For a second time John begins and ends his sentence with the same phrase, in this case employing ἐξ ἡμῶν to emphasize the separation. The quadruple repetition of ἐξ ἡμῶν serves as a powerfully strong emphasis. There is not to be any doubt about the departure, who left, and who did not. Further, using a second class conditional sentence in its center, he describes clearly the fact that these false teachers were never really a part of the apostolic circle, although they may have been identified with it at one point, whether being from Jerusalem or claiming to be their disciples. John's point will be that the antichrists are revealed by their departure.

Verses 18 and 19 contain six uses of the first person plural, and then once again in verse 25. The question is whether these refer to (1) John and his readers (Brown, 338; Bultmann, 36; Schnackenburg, 150; Williamson, 100) or (2) John and the apostolic circle (Hodges, "1 John," 881; Strecker, 63; Yarbrough, 145–46). If it refers to John and his readers, then these verses indicate a church split wherein the false teachers departed and took some of the congregation with them. However, nothing else in the text indicates that their departure was organized or that they formed a sect or separate congregation (Strecker, 36). If they had, this would then make John's warnings in this section unexpected. "If the false teachers have emerged from the church, in what sense were they still a part of it? Furthermore, how could they still constitute a present danger to the congregation? The urgency of John's letter suggests that the danger is not over, but current or imminent."[424] "Us" as the apostolic circle is supported by the first person plural pronouns in the prologue, but not by the use of "we" in 1:6–10.[425] In 2:18–20 there is a clear contrast between "we" (including John) and "you" (the readers). Thus, it could not include John and his readers, but must either be an authorial "we" (John only) or represent John and the apostles, as in the prologue.

424. E. Curtis, "The First Person Plural in 1 John 2:18–27," 28.
425. E. Curtis, "The First Person Plural in 1 John 2:18–27," 28–29.

Therefore, it seems most reasonable to see the false teachers departing from the apostolic community.[426]

ἐξ ἡμῶν ἐξῆλθαν ἀλλ' οὐκ ἦσαν ἐξ ἡμῶν, "They went out from us, but they were not from us." These words have been interpreted widely, often based on theological presuppositions. For example, Bruce (69) relates this to the Calvinist doctrine of perseverance and sees perseverance as evidence of justification and not the cause of its continuance. Marshall (152) concurs and says, "Here is one of the clearest expressions in the New Testament of the way in which we must distinguish between the church visible, composed of those who outwardly belong to it, and the church invisible, composed of those whom the Lord knows to be his (2 Tim 2:19)."[427] We see an example of the error of the doctrine of perseverance in his assertion, "But a person who makes a genuine confession can be expected to persevere in his faith, although elsewhere John warns his readers against the danger of failure to persevere." He points to 2:24 and 2 John 8 as examples of this (n. 14). However, the idea of perseverance proving election is foreign to John, though rejection of Christ does serve such a function, and preservation in one's salvation (eternal security) is accomplished by God (John 6:44 and 10:27–30).[428]

Brown sees this as a reference to the false teachers departing from the "Johannine community" in accordance with his theory of a schism within a group of churches following Johannine Christology (Brown, 338).[429]

426. E. Curtis, "The First Person Plural in 1 John 2:18–27," 30.

427. Bultmann (37) similarly says this verse "permits recognition of the distinction between the empirical and the true congregation: false members are therefore to be found in the empirical congregation." Bruce (70) likewise expresses it clearly. "Membership in a Christian society does not always imply that one belongs to the persevering saints; enrolment in the register of a local church on earth does not necessarily carry with it enrolment in the heavenly book of life." Stott (110) summarizes John's point by saying, "Those who belong to us stay with us. Future and final perseverance is an ultimate test of a past participation in Christ." Burge (127) asks: "Were these people ever Christians? Does this mean that the church is made up of believers and unbelievers today? And if they were and are not now Christians, what does this imply for our understanding of the perseverance of the saints?"

428. Whereas John does not address perseverance, Jesus indicates in John 10:26 that rejection of him demonstrates the fact that a person is not one of His sheep. This provides the setting of the promise of eternal security that follows.

429. Burge (125) follows Brown and sees these as a departure from John's congregations and so "indicates that the antichrist has now laid siege to John's church." Also

However, following the pattern John has established, "us" can only refer to one of two possible groups, the John and the apostles or John and his readers.[430] Lieu (101) notes that John's use of "us" and "you" (vv. 19–20) indicates that the false teachers had not departed from the congregation to whom he wrote but from elsewhere. Though she does not posit the apostolic circle, her example of Judas may imply that she had such in mind here as well. She notes that Judas, too, is described as "going out" in the same way as these false teachers. In this case it seems best to see the departure being from the apostolic circle since John's readers are the ones being warned in this passage.[431] They would already know of the schism and its significance and thus not need such a warning. Further, it would seem that these false teachers are attempting to approach the readers by representing themselves as faithful bearers of Christ's teachings.[432]

John uses the same verb for departure here as he used for Judas' departure in John 13:30. Noting this, Harris (108) says further that it is "probably more than coincidence" and that the "implication is clear—just as Judas betrayed Jesus, so the secessionists have betrayed their fellow members of the community (and indeed, the author himself) and have gone out into the darkness (as Judas went into the night)." Further, as an aorist active, ἐξῆλθαν

M. de Boer, "Jesus the Baptizer: 1 John 5:5–8 and the Gospel of John," 87. Johnson (56) describes this as "the most important verse in the letter of John for understanding the historical setting of these epistles." This is a logical conclusion based on the theory of opponents. But as noted earlier, it lacks external evidence and involves an interpretation of internal evidence that ultimately is circular in nature. It fails completely when "us" in this passage does *not* include John's readers.

430. Rensberger (79) says that "to 'be of' something in Johannine thought means both to originate from it and belong to it, to share both its essence and its characteristics."

431. Contra Burge (127), who reflects his dependence on the Johannine community theory and so sees "us" referring to John and his readers rather than the apostolic witnesses.

432. Having observed that the phrase "they went out from us" is also used in Acts 15:24 to describe Judaizers, Hodges (108–9) connects the Acts passage to this one and speculates that the false teachers of John's day also originated from the Jerusalem church. This must be recognized as speculation in the face of silence among the church fathers, and the clear evidence elsewhere (such as Paul's epistles) that false teachers arose from within congregations throughout the various churches.

indicates their departure was voluntary rather than that they were expelled (Brooke, 53; Burdick, 195) as well as "both definite and final" (Smalley, 102).

Curtis sees the sense of ἐκ to indicate "possession" or "belonging" more than origin (contra Bultmann, 36, n.6; and Burdick, 195).[433] From this he concludes that it was the "false teachers and their ideas" that John had in view that did not represent the apostolic traditions and "were wholly foreign and unauthorized."[434] This would be similar to the words of the church council in Acts 15:24, in which they acknowledged that the Judaizers, who claimed to come from James (Gal 2:12), and who were opposing Paul throughout Galatia, were those "to whom we gave no *such* commandment." However, John's use of ἐξέρχομαι and μένω in conjunction with ἐκ mitigates this. This departure was more than theological or ideological. It was physical and relational.

Utilizing the first of two strong contrasts and the second of four uses of ἐκ in this sentence, John affirms that though their departure was from the midst of the apostolic circle, it did not mean that they were actually part of that circle.[435] John indicates with the imperfect of εἰμι that even before their departure they had not been a part of the apostolic circle (Brooke, 53).

εἰ γὰρ ἐξ ἡμῶν ἦσαν, μεμενήκεισαν ἂν μεθ' ἡμῶν, "for if they had been from us, they would have remained with us." John now moves to explain what he means, introducing this with γὰρ.[436] With this second class conditional construction in which the protasis* is assumed to be false for the sake of argument, John says clearly that he did not consider that the false teachers were ever part of the apostolic circle of faith.[437] The departure of the false teachers from the midst of the apostolic band ("us") revealed they were not true believers; they were never regenerate (Grayston, 77; Smith,

---

433. Burdick (195) argues against the sense of "belonging" by noting, "Whereas the ἐκ speaks of identity of origin, μετά speaks of the mutual relationship of persons in the outward fellowship of the church."Akin (115) and Smalley (102) see it indicating both origin ("out of") and membership ("part of") in the community.

434. E. Curtis, "The First Person Plural in 1 John 2:18–27," 30.

435. Lenski (433) sees this ἀλλὰ as "confirmatory and climacteric" rather than adversative and so "they were either false from the start or became so and then left."

436. Blass (BDF§452) notes that John uses γὰρ "relatively least often" among the NT writers.

437. Impf. ἦσαν is "temporally ambiguous" and keeps its *Actionsart** in this "contrary-to-fact" indicative conditional construction (BDF §360 (3)).

72).[438] Just as John distinguished between "we" and "you" in the first verses of this epistle (1:1, 3), he again distinguishes between "they" and "us." By saying that these false teachers were "not of us," John indicates that they were never identified with the apostolic circle and had never agreed with the teachings of the apostles. If their teachings had agreed with those of the apostles, then they would have remained associated with them.

Using the pluperfect μεμενήκεισαν in the apodosis*, John affirms the completeness of their separation in the past. Further, his switch from past tense verbs to the concluding present tense εἰσὶν following the pluperfect μεμενήκεισαν indicates the continued state of departure. The implication is that their separation in the past involved continued isolation from the apostolic circle. His choice of μένω looks at their revocation of "the close ongoing personal relationship between genuine members of the Christian community" (Harris, 108). Again, John's distinction between "us" and "them" continues to emphasize their nonassociation as demonstrated by the next strong contrast.

ἀλλ' ἵνα φανερωθῶσιν ὅτι οὐκ εἰσὶν πάντες ἐξ ἡμῶν, "but *they went out* with the result that it was made manifest that none of them were from us." The second strong contrast (ἀλλὰ) in this sentence is used to express the significance of their departure by focusing attention on the theoretical possibility of their remaining associated with the apostles as contrasted with the reality of their departure.[439] The ἵνα clause associated with it may be functioning either as a purpose clause ("in order that") or result clause ("with the result that") with an understood ellipsis of ἐξ ἡμῶν ἐξῆλθαν (Harris, 107).[440] As

---

438. Williamson (101) rejects this Calvinist view and posits that John did not mean to "imply" by this that "those who went out were never truly Christian or were never 'saved.'" Yet he admits that John's use of μεμενήκεισαν indicates that "their departure demonstrated that they had never, in John's judgment, been *truly* part of the community" (italics his). Thus, he rejects eternal security while affirming the position of Calvinists that these false teachers had never been regenerate.

439. The ἀλλ' ἵνα construction here indicates an ellipsis from the previous clause and carries the sense of "on the contrary (but) this happened (or a similar verb), on order that ..." (BDF §448 (7)). This is a typical Johannine construction (Harris, 108). It occurs in his Gospel five times. Once it is said by John the Baptist (John 1:31), three times by Jesus (John 9:3; 14:31; 15:25), and only once comes directly from the pen of John (John 1:8). Its only other occurrence in the New Testament also is spoken by Jesus (Mark 14:49).

440. BDF §448(7).

a purpose clause it could be understood in one of two ways: (1) The false teachers intended to show their doctrinal separation by their departure. Or, (2) God revealed their doctrinal departure through their physical separation (Akin, 116; Burdick, 197; Williamson, 101). Even though the second option is attractive, serving as a result clause seems the best option in light of the passive aorist subjunctive φανερωθῶσιν (Williams, 31). Further, the idea behind φανερωθῶσιν ("manifest") is that of bringing into light, making visible, or exposing something.[441] It is not a case of the false teachers having to do something in order to show their departure, but their departure revealed their separation from the apostolic community.[442]

John says literally that what was manifested is that "all are not from us."[443] Westcott (72) notes that "when the πᾶς is separated by the verb from οὐ the negation, according to the usage of the New Testament, is always universal (*all ... not*), and not partial (*not all*)."[444] Thus John is making clear that the false teachers proved their falseness by their departure (Brooke, 54; Schnackenburg, 151; Westcott, 72; Smalley, 104; contra Bultmann, 36–37; Lenski, 434). Further, it would not be the false teachers' purpose to depart. Rather, it was God's purpose in revealing their falseness through their

---

441. BDAG, 1048; R. Bultmann and D. Lührmann, "φαίνω, φανερός, φανερόω," *TDNT* 9:4–5.

442. G. K. Beale and D. A. Carson, *Commentary on the New Testament Use of the Old Testament* (Grand Rapids: Baker Academic, 2007), 1058.

443. This ὅτι clause should be seen as epexegetical to φανερωθῶσιν, describing what has been revealed, contra Lenski (434) who sees it as result ("because" and not "that").

444. E. Curtis ("The First Person Plural in 1 John 2:18–27," 30–31) concurs and says, "First, the clause could mean that none of those who had left belonged to 'us.' In this understanding, the meaning would be all-inclusive. Every person who left was not a part of the apostolic community. The second possibility is that the clause means that not all who so claimed to belong to 'us' actually did belong to 'us.' Then John would be saying that not all those who joined themselves outwardly to the apostolic community truly belonged to it." Brooke (54) concurs and provides as evidence the following verses that utilize a οὐ ... πᾶς construction: Matt 24:22; Mark 13:20; Luke 1:37; John 3:15, 16; 6:39; Acts 10:14; 11:8; 1 Cor 1:29; Gal 2:16; Eph 4:29; 5:5; 1 John 2:21; Rev 7:1, 16; 9:4; 18:22; 21:27; 22:3. He then notes that this verse is the only instance of this construction where the negative is separated from the plural form of πᾶς. Though he has identified the verses that contain both οὐ and a singular form of πᾶς, they do not all reflect the same construction per se (John 3:15 and 16 contain πᾶς but not οὐ, while Acts 11:8 lacks πᾶς). Yet his point is well made that this plural form of πᾶς is unique to John.

departure, thus the passive (Burdick, 196; Williamson, 101). Their departure was the means of making visible their separation from the faith.

John is not saying that every doctrinal deviation is a denial of a person's salvation. Converts have strayed doctrinally throughout church history. However, at the same time, false teachers have infiltrated the church throughout church history and would seek to lead young believers astray. These are the false teachers John has in view. In fact, John will immediately reassure his readers that he is neither describing them nor are they in any danger of departing in the way the false teachers have. Rather, John has told them these things to enable them to discern the true teacher from the false.[445]

This does not mean that everyone who departs from a church over doctrinal issues is an antichrist. As Bruce (69–70) notes well, "John's words are not applicable (although they have sometimes been misapplied) to people who leave one Christian company for another; they are applicable only to people who deliberately abandon the ground of Christianity rightly so called—and one should be quite certain that this is what they have done before speaking or thinking of them in these terms." Sometimes departure is the best option for the orthodox believer when his or her church drifts from truth. However, discernment is needed to determine which issues are worth departure or division within a body of believers. Akin (115) notes well, "It takes wisdom and perception to understand which theological

---

445. Some connect this verse to the doctrine of perseverance and say their departure proved they were never regenerate. They reject the idea that these were simply a sect of believers at variance with John. Rather, they are non-believers whose unbelief manifested itself in their theological and physical departure from the community of faith (Akin, 115; Bruce, 69; Kistemaker, 277; R. A. Peterson, "Apostasy," 30). Rather than the doctrine of perseverance, this reflects more what Jesus taught in the Sermon on the Mount when He warned against following false teachers (Matt 7:15–20). Just as Jesus said, "You will know them by their fruit," John says his readers can "know" the false teachers of their day by the "fruit" of their departure. So, rather than it being his intention to teach a doctrine of perseverance in good works as proof of one's salvation (contra Bruce, 69), John is providing one of the evidences believers can use to discern between true saints and false teachers. To read the doctrine of perseverance into this passage is a case of eisegesis rather than exegesis. It is reading one's theology into the text rather than drawing from the text the author's intended meaning. Of note, Brooke (53–54), who rejects eternal security sees this affirming their departure from faith and spiritual life and responds to Calvinists by saying, "It was natural that the authors of theories of predestination should find in this verse confirmation of their doctrine."

issues are open to discussion and honest disagreement and which ones are so clearly essential that schism must be preferred to compromise." Not every issue is a question of orthodoxy. Not every dissenter is an antichrist, even when his or her dissent leads to division.

2:20 John now moves from discussing the antichrists to reassuring his readers of their standing with God. He accomplishes this by affirming two things that are true about his readers: those to whom John writes know the truth, and this is because of their anointing from God.

καὶ ὑμεῖς χρῖσμα ἔχετε ἀπὸ τοῦ ἁγίου, "But you have an anointing from the Holy One." John begins reassuring his readers by contrasting them with the false teachers. He does this with a contrastive *καὶ* that continues the discussion and introduces his description of the difference between his readers and the false teachers. By changing the person from "they" to "you" with the emphatic use of the pronoun ὑμεῖς, placing it first in the clause, John draws attention to the difference between the false teachers and his readers (Burdick, 196).

The challenge this clause presents the interpreter is to discern what John means by χρῖσμα. This is a term unique to him and used only in this epistle.[446]

(1) It could refer to the Holy Spirit (Akin, 117; Barker, 325; Brooke, 55; Brown, 347; Bruce, 71–72; Burdick, 197; Burge, 128; Johnson, 57; Lenski, 435; Plummer, 59–60; Rensberger, 79; Stott, 111; Thompson, 77; Westcott, 73).[447] The Holy Spirit's descent on Jesus at his baptism uses language similar to this (John 1:32–34). Paul uses the aorist participle form of χρίσας to refer to the Holy Spirit in 2 Cor 1:21–22 (Kistemaker, 279). The anointing's "abiding" and "teaching" is similar to what is said of the Spirit in John 14:17, 26 (Rensberger, 79).[448]

---

446. Many interpreters (Barker, 325; Bultmann, 37; Houlden, 79; Rensberger, 79; Strecker, 65) refer to its possible allusion to a later church practice of anointing people at their baptism which was also practiced in Gnosticism. Additionally, some (Burdick, 196; Marshall, 153; Stott, 111) see this as a play on words with antichrist, since both share the same root.

447. J. C. Coetzee, "The Holy Spirit in 1 John," 53–55.

448. He (Rensberger, 79) sees John using "anointing" in place of Paraclete here (he calls it "displacement") because he had earlier (2:2) used that designation for Jesus.

The noun focuses on the content of the anointing rather than the act of anointing (Brooke, 55; Westcott, 73).[449] This sense of the term would then be a metonymy* of effect for the agent.[450] Thus the Spirit who anoints believers is symbolized by the oil used in anointing (Westcott, 73). Christians are therefore only those who are thus anointed by the Holy Spirit who is the anointing oil as well, being both the agent and the substance.[451] Burge (128) sees the four references to believers as "recipients of the Spirit." Noting the anointing's teaching function, one might argue that, based on Jesus' promise to the apostles in the Upper Room that the Holy Spirit would guide them into all truth (John 16:13), this promise is now being applied to all believers (Hodges, 111).[452] This would be drawing from the OT passages where men were anointed for service and now applied to John's readers (Grayston, 51).[453] The weakness of this view comes in John's subsequent description of the anointing as both "true" and not "a lie" (2:27). If John had said "liar," the referent would be clearly the Holy Spirit.

Moreover, though he is the "Spirit of truth," the Holy Spirit cannot be described as the quality or character of "truth" in a nonpersonal conceptual sense. Further, if John intended the Holy Spirit, it seems more likely he would have named him as he does later in 3:24 and 4:13 (Lieu, 103).

(2) A second possible meaning is that the anointing refers to Scripture and its teaching function (Lieu, 103; Marshall, 153–54; Dodd, 58–64; Yarbrough, 149).[454] This would be a metonymy* of the cause in which

449. J. C. Coetzee, "The Holy Spirit in 1 John," 53. He writes, "Thus the term rather refers to the Spirit as the anointment oil than to the action of anointment." He argues further (54) that "the notion of anointment" in both the OT and NT "always implies an outpouring of and a gift *of the Holy Spirit*" (italics his). Yet he only substantiates the claim with a reference to 2 Cor 1:21–22. Though "anointed" and "Spirit" are in the same verse, they need not be linked even there. The Spirit is not called the agent of element of anointing, but a gift from God that is separate from the anointing.

450. E. W. Bullinger, *Figures of Speech Used in the Bible*, 894.

451. Reflects the same truths as 1 Cor 12:13 and Eph 1:13–14, in that all saints have been baptized and sealed by the Holy Spirit.

452. G. K. Beale and D. A. Carson, *Commentary on the New Testament Use of the Old Testament*, 490.

453. Examples include Aaron (Exod 29:7), Saul (1 Sam 9:15–16; 10:1), David (1 Sam 16:12–13), and Elisha (1 Kgs 19:16), priests (Lev 16:32).

454. Grudmann, TDNT 9:579–80; E. Malatesta (*Interiority and Covenant*, 147) says "the Christian message heard from the beginning is a synonym for the

the cause (the anointing) is used for the effect (having the truth).[455] This anointing is described as "true" and "not a lie," thereby fitting better with something communicated to them rather than the Holy Spirit indwelling them. Further, this anointing protects believers against false teachers, which is something not said of the Holy Spirit. Additionally, Marshall (154) observes that "the anointing remains in his readers in the same way that he speaks about the Word of God or the truth remaining in them." This is rejected by others because Scripture is never described as an anointing (Kistemaker, 279; Stott, 111). This would involve John creating a new image from the Old Testament concept of anointing.[456] However, John's creativity as a writer and willingness to use one image in multiple ways is evidenced by his use of the light/darkness imagery in his Gospel and this epistle. In the Gospel, the light/darkness contrast represents spiritual life and death, while in this epistle it is moral purity and its absence.[457]

(3) A third approach is to combine the two views and see it as the teachings of the apostles (Scripture) as "administered and confirmed by the work of the Spirit" (Marshall, 155). This view was originally promoted by Ignace de la Potterie but has not found wide acceptance.[458] The second view seems the best of the three options. The Holy Spirit's involvement in every believer's life allows the third to be true. However, it is not affirmed by John in this passage, though it may be understood by implication. Still, the absence of any clear teaching on the Holy Spirit's role in protecting believers from false teachers and false teachings mitigates against this third view.

So, then, who is the "Holy One"?[459] The Holy One must be a member of the Godhead: Father, Son, or Holy Spirit. (1) Supporting the Father (Burdick, 197–98; Houlden, 79; Thompson, 78) as its referent is

---

anointing and should remain in the believer."

455. E. W. Bullinger, *Figures of Speech Used in the Bible,* 549.

456. Marshall (155) modifies the view by defining the anointing as "the Word taught to converts before their baptism and apprehended by them through the work of the Spirit in their hearts." However, the text gives no indication that a prebaptismal instruction is in view.

457. See comments on 1:5 for a fuller discussion.

458. I. de la Potterie, "L'onction du chretien par la foi," 12–69.

459. Others (Lieu,104; Rensberger, 80; Williamson, 102) choose to say that either option works (Father or Son).

its common occurrence as a title taken by God in the Old Testament.[460] Further, it is used of God in the LXX (Hab 3:3; Bar 4:22, 37; Sir 23:9; and Psa 77 [78]: 41). Also, in Rev 4:8 and 6:10, God the Father is called holy by angels and martyrs. Grayston (52) argues from "echoes of Isaiah 53:10–11," and the twenty-eight occurrences of "Holy One" in Isaiah to argue that here John also means the Father. However, one objection is that Jesus is referred to as "the Holy One of God" (Houlden, 79; Yarbrough, 150).[461] (2) It could refer to the Son as well (Barker, 325; Bultmann, 37; Johnson, 58; Schnackenburg, 153). It is used to describe Jesus in Mark 1:24; Luke 4:34; John 6:69; Acts 3:14; and later in Rev 3:7.[462] (3) The final, and least likely, possibility is that it refers to the Holy Spirit (Smith, 72). Strecker (64) argues that the occurrence of ἅγιος with πνεῦμα in John 1:33; 14:26; and 20:22 with "the same 'ecclesiastical' notion reflected in 1 John strengthens this option.[463] By his very name, the Holy Spirit may be thought of as "the Holy One." If the "anointing" is interpreted to be a reference to the Holy Spirit, then this "Holy One" cannot be him, but must be either the Father or the Son. Either person of the Trinity would be possible since John has affirmed that both the Father (John 14:16, 26) and the Son (John 15:26; 16:7) have sent the Holy Spirit.[464] However, since the anointing is better seen as teach-

---

460. 2 Ki 19:22; Job 6:10; Pss 71:22; 78:40; 89:17; Prov 9:9; 30:2; Isa 1:4; 5:19; 10:20; 12:5; 17:6; 29:19; 30:11; 31:1; 37:22; 40:24; 41:14; 43:2; 45:10; 47:3; 48:6; 49:6; 54:5; 55:5; 60:9; Jer 50:29; 51:5; Ezek 39:7; Hos 11:9, 12; Hab 1:12; 3:2.

461. Peter calls Jesus that in John 6:65 while demons say the same of him in Mark 1:24 and Luke 4:24.

462. J. C. Coetzee ("The Holy Spirit in 1 John," 53) sees it referring to Jesus.

463. He further acknowledges that either interpretation produces "no contradiction" in interpretations of the remainder of the text. Yarbrough (150) concurs.

464. Schnackenburg (153) says it does not make much difference whether it is the Father or Son being referred to in this case; the end result is the same ("Die Zueignung der Sendung des Parakelten an den Vater (Joh 14, 16. 26) wie an den Sohn (15, 26; 16, 7), ferner der Wechsel zwischen „den Vater erkennen" (1 Joh 2, 14a) und „den Uranfägnlichen (= den Sohn) erkennen" (14b) zeigen aber, daß an dieser Entscheidung nicht viel liegt und nur alles auf die Ausrüstung „von oben", vom göttlichen Bereich her (vgl. 4, 2. 4), ankommt.") Brooke (56) concurs and says, after discussing the various uses of the term in the OT and NT, "The definition of personality which later ages found to be necessary was apparently not present to the consciousness of the writer. Sometimes he distinguishes Father and Son with absolute clearness. At other times he uses language which may be applied indifferently to either."

ing (Scripture), the Holy Spirit may yet be the referent. Jesus' promise that he would teach the apostles "all things" (John 16:26) strengthens this option for those who do not see the anointing as the teaching itself.

Finally, John says this anointing is ἀπὸ, the "Holy One. "Rather than using ἐκ, which he has used to describe the departure and separation of the false teachers from the apostolic circle, he chooses ἀπὸ instead. This preposition is sometimes used synonymously with ἐκ.[465] However, this change of prepositions is not the product of stylistic variation on John's part. Rather, he changes prepositions to alert his readers to the difference. The anointing remains identified with God. It comes "from" God in that it is "sourced in" but not separate from him, whereas the departure of the false teachers separated them from the apostles.

καὶ οἴδατε πάντα, "and you know all things." Some early MSS contain πάντες rather than πάντα. Though the weight of the textual evidence favors πάντα, many scholars prefer πάντες (Bultmann, 32; Burdick, 198; Johnson, 58; Thompson, 79; Williams, 31). For example, Brooke (56–57) and Schnackenburg (154) argue that the emphasis of this passage is on the verb οἴδατε, so that it focuses on the issue of "knowing" as opposed to what is known. The object of that knowledge is elided for emphasis. The result is that they translate this as "you all know" or something equivalent, with the emphasis on "all." Breck counters that this would be the singular instance in 1 John where a transitive verb lacks an object. Further, this construction (οἴδατε πάντες), where the verb is followed by the subject and lacks an object or some other predicate modifier, does not occur anywhere else in the NT.[466] He notes further that the focus on the content of their knowledge in the following verse argues against Schnackenburg's view that the object of οἴδατε is "not obvious" on the basis of the distinction made between "the truth" and "every lie" in v. 21.[467] Thus the immediate context argues for πάντα as opposed to πάντες (Grayston, 78).

465. It can have the sense of "separation from" (synonymous with ἐκ) as well as indicating "source," as it is used here (BDAG, 105).

466. J. Breck, "The Function of ΠΑΣ in 1 John 2:20," 196.

467. J. Breck, "The Function of ΠΑΣ in 1 John 2:20," 198. He notes (199) that of the fifteen instances where John uses οἶδα in his Epistle, eleven are followed by ὅτι clauses. The exceptions are 2:11, where it is used in a negative sense for "radical ignorance," and then here and in v. 21 (twice). In these instances John has πάντα, τὴν ἀλήθειαν, and αὐτὴν serving "as substitutes for the ὅτι clause."

"All things" does not mean "everything." This is not a promise of omniscience, an incommunicable divine attribute. Rather, it describes what one needs to know to resist the false teachers (2:21). The church of John's day was already faced with false doctrines involving the person and work of Christ. Gnosticism was in its early stages of development and would blossom to a major controversy in the following century. Gnostic Christians claimed to receive secret knowledge of the truth. This knowledge was necessary for salvation, and only the élite could know these secret truths and thus have salvation. John opposed this concept by affirming that believers know the truth, everything they need to know. Furthermore, what John is writing is not something new or secret but something known by all.

John changes his word for "know" at this point, using οἶδα rather than γινώσκω. Though the two terms are essentially synonymous,[468] he appears to use them in a nuanced manner throughout his writings. Whereas οἶδα carries the sense of intuitive knowledge or that gained by instruction, γινώσκω may designate knowledge gained by experience and can be used to describe relationship.[469] Thus, in this case, discussing what they have been taught rather than what they have experienced, John switches from γινώσκω to οἶδα.

2:21 John emphasizes his readers' accurate knowledge while affirming that "every lie" is not sourced in truth. Through this he reassures them of his confidence in them, lest they begin to question themselves after what he has just written (Marshall, 156). He accomplishes this with three ὅτι clauses. (1) Some see all three ὅτι clauses expressing content (Brown, 350; Bultmann, 38; Schnackenburg, 155).[470] This allows ἔγραψα to have an objective clause associated with it. (2) Some see them all as causal (Brooke, 57; Marshall, 157). (3) Others see the first two ὅτι clauses as causal with the third being content (Burdick, 199). This would be less awkward grammatically, because of the coordinating adversative conjunction ἀλλ' (Westcott, 74). (4) Rensberger (80) suggests the possibility that the first two ὅτι clauses give content while

468. H. Seesemann, "οἶδα," *TDNT* 5:116.

469. R. Bultmann, "γινώσκω," *TDNT* 1:69c. R. Erickson ("Oida and Ginōskō and Verbal Aspect in Pauline Usage," 109–22) provides an excellent discussion of the verbal aspects involved in the two terms and concludes that they do reflect nuanced differences in meaning.

470. I. de la Potterie, "L'onction du chretien par la foi," 41.

the third is causal. Strecker rightly (67, n. 36) argues for all three uses of ὅτι being identical, whether as content ("that") or causal ("because"). His arguments include the view that if the last ὅτι were content while the first two were causal, it would refer to the second ὅτι and be parallel to αὐτὴν, an "awkward construction." Rather, the verb ἔγραψα naturally calls for the three ὅτι clauses to be parallel. If all three are content, then John is assuring his readers of what they know. If all three are causal, then the third ὅτι follows after what has preceded it and John is affirming the "redeemed nature of his readers.

οὐκ ἔγραψα ὑμῖν ὅτι οὐκ οἴδατε τὴν ἀλήθειαν, "I do not write to you because you do not know the truth." Using the epistolary aorist, John reminds them of one of his purposes in writing (Burdick, 198; Schnackenburg, 154). Lenski (436) links this epistolary aorist to verses 13 and 14 and concludes that this statement refers to all of 1 John, which he sees "the whole of which is directed against 'antichrists,'" and is thus purely polemical in nature. He is followed by others as well (Brown, 349). This ἔγραψα need not refer to the entire epistle but could have only this polemical section of the epistle in view. Even if it does refer to the entire epistle, it need not mean the epistle addresses the antichrists and their false teachings exclusively. As discussed earlier, John's inclusion of himself in certain passages mitigates against this being viewed as a pure polemic and must recognize this epistle's pastoral function, in which polemical elements are included as they relate to his pastoral concerns. What John says here is designed to reassure his readers of his confidence in them. He does not think they have been deceived.

Using οἶδα once again, as contrasted with γινώσκω, John indicates the "truth" they have been taught (Barker, 325).[471] This "truth" is the body of knowledge that accurately describes Jesus (Burge, 129).[472] His use of the article indicates this is a body of truth familiar to his readers and is

---

471. Moody (53) sees John referring to "apostolic truth," those things taught by the apostles. Brown (350) rejects any distinction between γινώσκω and οἶδα here and argues that it is parallel to Jesus' promise in John 8:32 that we would "know the truth" (γνώσεσθε τὴν ἀλήθειαν) and to John's use of γινώσκω in 2 John 1.

472. Bultmann (38) and Schnackenburg (155) both refer to it as "divine reality." Lieu (104), on the other hand, sees this as "a sphere of belonging or place of origin" that stands in contrast to the world. This would connect back to the spheres of light and darkness if that were John's intention. However, the context makes a body of teachings more likely than a sphere of existence.

uniquely Christian rather than new truth (Barker, 325; Burdick, 198; Stott, 112; Thompson, 79). John is not writing to teach his readers something they do not already know accurately. Thus his confident statement that follows.

ἀλλ' ὅτι οἴδατε αὐτὴν, "but because you know it." Moving from the negative, the reason that is *not* motivating John to write, he gives his positive reason for writing.[473] His readers *do* know that truth they have been taught. Moreover, they know more than that.[474]

καὶ ὅτι πᾶν ψεῦδος ἐκ τῆς ἀληθείας οὐκ ἔστιν, "and because *you know* that every lie is not from the truth." John ends his words of encouragement by reminding his readers that they know the source of both truth and deception. He uses once again the prepositional phrase with ἐκ to show that lies are never sourced in truth (Burdick, 199; Williamson, 102; Yarbrough, 152). Further, John's second use of the article with "truth" continues to relate this to the body of Christian doctrines as opposed to truth as a general concept (Burdick, 199). Rensberger (80) sees John using this final clause to affirm that "*this* truth is incompatible with any lie—namely, with the opponents' Christology, the lie that 'Jesus is not the Christ.'" Further, this reminds John's readers and us today that God's revealed truth and deception have opposite origins.

2:22 Using an interrogative transition, John moves from deception to the deceiver and quotes his denial. In both this verse and the following, John will use "Semitic parallelism" to state the truths in both negative and positive terms (Kistemaker, 282). Then in the following verses he will show that the Antichrist is revealed by his denial of Jesus as the Christ that results in denying both the Father and the Son.

Τίς ἐστιν ὁ ψεύστης εἰ μὴ ὁ ἀρνούμενος ὅτι Ἰησοῦς οὐκ ἔστιν ὁ Χριστός, "Who is the liar if not the one who denies, *by saying*, 'Jesus is not the Christ'?" This is the only place ψεύστης occurs with the article in John (Brown, 351).[475]

---

473. As Schnackenburg (155) notes, it is a common Johannine practice to emphasize a point by stating its opposite. This would reflect the antithetic parallelism characteristic of Hebrew literature, especially poetry, as was seen initially in 1:5.

474. Schnackenburg (155) and Strecker (67) rightly see this as another indicator that John views his readers as believers (Strecker: "true Christians").

475. The noun ὁ ψεύστης is the subject rather than the pronoun τίς because articular nouns are more definite than interrogative pronouns (D. B. Wallace, *Grammar*, 40–46). Other instances of ψεύστης without the article include John 8:44, 55; 1

This use would indicate that John is describing a person or personality known to his readers whether from personal contact or from instruction (contra Burdick, 200; Lenski, 436).[476] Brown (351) notes that the epithet "liar" is attached to the devil by Jesus in John 8:44–45 and could indicate the diabolic nature of the Antichrist, who is the eschatological "liar" yet to come. He proposes that seeing this as an "apocalyptic expectation" makes this parallel to verse 20 and so the "the apocalyptic expectation is fulfilled in the secessionists of his own time." Rensberger (80) suggests that this liar "may be an eschatological one" because of his parallel with the antichrist in 2 John 7 and 2 Thess 2:9–10. A better approach is suggested by Stott (116) who sees the use of the article to indicate that John means "the liar *par excellence*" (also Marshall, 126) and so an antichrist, "not the personal antichrist that is to come ... but a living embodiment of the spirit of antichrist." Further, John's use of τίς draws attention to this individual as he raises the question of denial. Having noted that no lie is of the truth, the clear implication is that no liar is either. Thus, the lie of the liar is now quoted (Yarbrough, 156).[477]

With the present articular participle, ὁ ἀρνούμενος, John indicates that this person is one characterized by this denial. The liar's rejection of Jesus is a pattern of teaching, a "continuing practice," not an isolated error (Burdick,

---

John 1:10; 2:4; 4:20; and 5:10. Even so, Schnackenburg (156) sees the use of τίς to indicate *par excellence*.

476. BDF § 252. Lenski (436) sees this as a "generic" article, while Burdick (200) sees the article expressing "the unique character" of the person rather than pointing to a particular person. Brooke (58), on the other hand, rejects the idea of a generic article with "liar," but sees this communicating the idea *par excellence*. Yarbrough (156) sees εἰ μὴ, which is normally translated "except" or "if not," as meaning "verily" according to its LXX usage when "preceding a virtual oath." From this he concludes that John is affirming that "the liar's identity and status are obvious and definite, given a particular indicator," which, in this case, is his or her denial. He further describes this epithet as "bitter language," though it would be better to see this as blunt honesty from John. He does not mince words. This is not the young John of the Gospels who asked permission from Jesus to call down fire from heaven (Luke 9:54). This is the elderly John who is now moved by Christ's command to love (John 13:35), though he can be firm when needed (3 John 10).

477. Though he sees it as coming from the false teachers, Lenski (437–38) considers this to be indirect discourse rather than a direct quote. Yarbrough (156) argues that the substantival participle is being used intransitively with the following ὅτι, which makes it recitative, and thereby makes it a direct quote of the false teachers.

200). John quotes the denial with a direct discourse ὅτι clause (Smalley, 111) and thereby leaves no doubt as to the assertion of the false teachers and the heresy in view.

Denial that Jesus is "the Christ" is ultimately denying that he came in the flesh (1 John 1:1–3; 4:3; 2 John 7). Thus John is affirming that one must acknowledge the full deity of Jesus as well as his full humanity to actually worship God. Brown (352) and Smith (73) argue that the emphasis of this denial is not on ὁ Χριστός because Gnostic heresy never denied Jesus' deity. Rather, the denial focuses on Ἰησοῦς and is thus a denial of the incarnation, that the human Jesus is the divine Christ, as will be addressed further later in the epistle (Brown, 352; Bultmann, 38; Burdick, 200; Burge, 129–30; Lieu, 105–6; Smith, 73).[478] Westcott (75) links this statement to the Gnostic idea that the Christ spirit descended upon Jesus at his baptism and departed from him just before his crucifixion. "A common 'Gnostic' theory was that 'the aeon Christ' descended upon the man Jesus at his Baptism, and left him before the Passion. Those who held such a doctrine denied that 'Jesus was the Christ'; and in so denying, denied the union of the divine and human in one Person."[479] This is not a statement made by Jewish opponents, but Christians. Therefore it cannot be a denial of his messiahship (Burdick, 201; Lieu, 105; Schnackenburg, 157).[480]

οὗτός ἐστιν ὁ ἀντίχριστος, "This is the Antichrist." John now connects "the liar" with "the Antichrist." Some see this as a direct allusion to the coming Antichrist that John has already mentioned and will name again in 2 John 7 (Brown, 351). His use of the article with the title once more indicates a person with whom his readers would have been familiar.[481] We can know

478. Burge (130) rightly says: "Incarnational theology is essential to our understanding of salvation. It is the true union of God and flesh, the complete fusion of divinity and humanity, that makes Christ's sacrificial death potent."

479. P. J. Lalleman ("The Adversaries Envisaged in the Johannine Epistles," 20–21) disagrees. "The denial that Jesus is the Christ has been read as an indication that the adversaries separated the man Jesus from the divine being Christ but that view brings our verse into disharmony with the rest of the Epistle, which gives no indication of any such separation."

480. Schnackenburg (18–19) posits that for the Gentile church "Christ" means "Savior," in parallel with 4:14–15.

481. Williamson (102) notes this but then argues that the context indicates John is speaking generically, focusing not on "a larger-than-life personality but rather doctrinal error."

that early eschatological instruction included a discussion of the coming "abomination of desolation" (Jesus in Matt 24:15; Mark 13:14), "lawless one" (Paul in 2 Thess 2:6–7), and "Antichrist" (John). However, it seems better to see this describing a kind of person, since John's focus is on false teachers of the day more than the coming eschatological antichrist. For example, Westcott (75) sees this reference to "the Antichrist" as expressing "the embodiment of a principle, and is not to be confined to one person."[482] This would seem to fit better with the flow of thought and the context of the first-century world.

ὁ ἀρνούμενος τὸν πατέρα καὶ τὸν υἱόν, "the one denying the Father and the Son." John's reference to denying "the Father and the Son" may be a negative allusion to Jesus' words in John 12:44–45 or 14:10–11 where Jesus and the Father are linked together in terms of faith in one being equivalent to faith in the other. Here John makes clear that denying one member of the Godhead means denying the other.

This is the first use of the title "the Son" in this epistle and serves as another reference to Jesus' relationship to God the Father.[483] It is also an allusion to Jesus' place in the Trinity due to his incarnation. Marshall (157) notes that this use of "the Son" is parallel to "the Christ" and indicates John views the two terms as "virtually equivalent." This shows how the denial of doctrine is equivalent to a denial of the persons of the Godhead to whom the doctrine relates (Brown, 353).

2:23 Using antithetic parallelism (Bultmann, 39), much like in 1:5, John emphasizes the contrast between deceivers and believers. The two clauses are designed to be parallel but opposites.

πᾶς ὁ ἀρνούμενος τὸν υἱὸν οὐδὲ τὸν πατέρα ἔχει, "Everyone who denies the Son does not have the Father." To describe the liar who is an antichrist, John uses an articular present participle with the adjective *πᾶς*.[484] This is

---

482. Brooke (59) concurs when he sees this referring to the spirit of the antichrist rather than the person. However, he goes on to say "The writer is not specially interested in the literal fulfillment of the legend." This reflects his rejection of prophetic knowledge on the apostles' part as well as their inspiration from God who reveals the future precisely because He is God (Isa 42:8–9; 48:5).

483. This reflects a Johannine pattern of referring to "the Father" and "the Son" without modifiers (Brown, 353).

484. BDAG, 782.

the first of thirteen occurrences of πᾶς with an articular noun construction in 1 John (2:23, 29; 3:3, 6 [2x], 9, 10, 15; 4:7; 5:1 [2x], 18). Brown (353) notes that John seems to use this construction to divide people into two opposite groups. He says John's use of πᾶς "emphasizes the individual members of the class denoted by the noun" and so caries the sense of *every, each,* or *any*. However, the pattern of πᾶς serving as a predicate adjective with an articular noun, a participle in this case, is to focus on the whole rather than each part, thus the sense of "all" or the "whole."[485] So rather than identifying "the Antichrist," John is describing a trait true of every antichrist. Using the articular third person singular present participle, John again describes a kind of person. This is more a statement of principle than identifying a specific opponent.[486] This principle, though applying to anyone who denies Jesus' incarnation, will be especially true of the Antichrist when he is revealed in the last of the last days.[487]

What does it mean to *have* the Father? This is the first of three instances where John uses ἔχω with God as its direct object (also 1 John 5:12; 2 John 9). Brown (353–54) observes that this expression is absent in the OT as well as the rest of the NT. However, in his Gospel, John repeatedly expresses the idea of having "divine realities ."[488] Further, no indication exists that John was using this as a Gnostic concept, and so it is more likely his own terminology. Bultmann (39) sees ἔχω as equivalent to γινώσκω. One knows God relationally. Lieu (107) sees the concept of "have" to involve an intended

485. G. Bertram, "πᾶς," *TDNT* 5:887.

486. Burdick (201) rightly calls this πᾶς ... οὐ construction a "universal negative". He says, "The force of οὐδὲ is two-pronged. The οὐ combines with πᾶς to produce a universal negative; the δὲ functions adverbially to mean 'either.' The one who has rejected the Son has rejected the Father as well."

487. P. J. Lalleman ("The Adversaries Envisaged in the Johannine Epistles," 21) appears to understand this denial more in terms of an overemphasis on Christ. "It is difficult to imagine Christians who do not believe in Christ at all, so these words probably mean that they identified Father and Son so closely that the author saw the separate existence of Christ endangered. Thus these verses again refute those who deny Christ's individuality and replace it by Christomonism and also those doubt his abiding significance of the salvation of mankind." His reasoning grows out of a recognition that the false teachers would claim faith in Christ. However, a misapplied Christology that denies the humanity of Christ need not lead to Christomonism and may yet express itself in trinitarian terms.

488. His examples (354) include: John 3:16 and 36 (life); 5:38 (word of God); 5:43 (love of God); 8:12 and 12:35–36 (light); 16:33 (peace); and 17:13 (joy).

"ambiguity between 'being faithful to,' almost synonymous with confessing, and a more subjective experience of divine presence." Rensberger (81) similarly sees "having the Father" as parallel to 1 John 5:12, where having the Son means "believing in and confessing the true Christology," and so here "having the Father" means acknowledging God rightly by rightly acknowledging Jesus." This includes "relationship" with both members of the Godhead by mutual abiding (v. 24). Burdick (201) reflects the family relationship theme in the epistle and so says this means to have God "as father just as it is customary to speak of having a human father or having a friend" and so speaks of "a parent-child relationship." Yarbrough (158) similarly says "to have the Father" means "to be heir of the privileges passed down through a family heritage." He provides the example of John the Baptist's opponents who claimed Abraham as their father (Matt 3:9; Luke 3:8), as did Jesus' opponents (John 8:41). This "having" then results in certain benefits of that relationship, including fellowship (1 John 1:3, 6, 7), Jesus as our advocate (2:1), his anointing (2:20), assurance (2:28; 3:21; 4:17; 5:14), hope (3:3), God's love (4:16), eternal life (5:12–13), and answered prayer (5:15). John also includes as benefits God's command to love (2:7; 4:21) and God's testimony about himself (5:10). These are blessings and privileges forfeited by those who deny Jesus' messiahship. Hodges (113–14) points to the wide range of uses for the verb ἔχω to argue that it need not express a justification sense in this passage. Pointing to 2 John 9, where he does not see salvation as an issue, he views this as a fellowship term. He argues that John is implying more than that the person is out of fellowship with God. God is not having anything to do with him relationally. Thus this person is not in fellowship with God, is not being influenced by God if a believer, or is unconnected to God if an unbeliever. On the other hand, Akin (122) correctly argues that "John's claim that anyone who denies the Son does not have or possess the Father asserts unequivocally that a person who denies the Son has no child-parent relationship with God." John's clear statement, using the same term and language in 5:12, makes it better to see him describing an unbeliever in this passage. This is true even though he will return to issues of fellowship and abiding in the following verses. Additionally, his use of the 3 singular ("he who") indicates he is again stating a principle rather than describing a specific person or group.

Though the Byzantine text omits this last clause, it should be included. It serves to complete the antithetic parallelism being developed by John.

Through repetition, he emphasizes the point being made: confession or denial is directly related to one's relationship with God. As noted above, John's use of the same terminology and constructions in 5:12, which are clearly directed toward assurance of salvation and justification issues, indicates a similar meaning and use here. To have the Father is to be a believer. Moreover, having the Father is contingent on confessing the Son.

ὁ ὁμολογῶν τὸν υἱὸν καὶ τὸν πατέρα ἔχει, "the one confessing the Son also has the Father." "Confession" as John uses it here is not just a public proclamation but the expression of personal belief. This is opposite to the earlier denial that Jesus is the Christ. So those who deny do not confess. Those who acknowledge do so by confession. Consequently, this reveals who is a believer and who is not. Moreover, as a test, this is to be applied to the false teachers, not John's readers, though John speaks in terms of a principle (third person articular present participle).

Lenski (438) notes the absence of a contrastive particle such as δὲ and sees this as heightening the contrast between the false and true confessions. This is made more significant because of the three previous uses of ἀλλὰ in this paragraph preceding this sentence.

Finally, this clarifies that one cannot claim to believe in God while rejecting Jesus because John clearly links confession of One with confession of the Other.[489] This same theme, developed by John in his Gospel (John 5:23; 10:30; 14:6, 7; 15:23), is now made clear here in his epistle (Brown, 355).

2:24 The imperative followed by a third class conditional sentence provides both the instruction and its justification, or need. With this and the following verse, we will see that the believer's abiding in God's Word reveals that he abides in the Son and Father and is experiencing eternal life.[490]

ὑμεῖς ὃ ἠκούσατε ἀπ' ἀρχῆς, ἐν ὑμῖν μενέτω, "Let that which you heard from the beginning abide in you." John begins this command with the emphatic use of second person plural nominative pronoun in a voc. case role (Akin, 123; Lenski, 438; Westcott, 77).[491] Though most translations

489. A. Köstenberger, "The Deity of Christ in John's Letters and the Book of Revelation," 153.

490. Schnackenburg (158) correctly sees these verses as a return to John's theme of fellowship with God.

491. Brown (355) as well as Blass (BDF §466 (1)) see this as a case of anacoluthon*, where the nominative ὑμεῖς has assimilated the following relative pronoun's case

drop the pronoun, it should be translated to show John's emphasis. He is drawing a sharp contrast between his readers and the false teachers (Brooke 60; Burdick, 202; Marshall, 159; Strecker, 68; Schnackenburg, 157; Smalley, 118; Westcott, 77). He has moved from the principle, depicted by the third person plural descriptions of the previous verses, to the application of that principle in the lives of his readers. His movement to the second person plural returns the focus to his readers, going back to the question of what they have been taught and therefore know to be true and not a lie.[492]

John reminds his readers with the constative aorist ἠκούσατε that they need to be acting on what they have been taught consistently in the past (Burdick, 202). Kistemaker (284) suggests that ἠκούσατε "can be translated as a perfect, 'you have heard.'" Though this is true, it is better to see that John is emphasizing their continuing instruction to that point as opposed to earlier instruction that continues to influence them.[493]

John reminds his readers that they must let their previous instruction "abide" in them. The neuter pronoun ὃ points to the content of what they have heard in its entirety rather than separate pieces of instruction (Smalley, 118; Strecker, 68). In this case "abiding" does not mean "continue believing" (contra Burdick, 203), but "continue acting according to" or "continue allowing their instruction to influence." This is reflective of Jesus' command to the Eleven to let his word abide in them (John 15:7). With John the concept of abiding includes more than the relationship between the believer and God. Its meaning includes the idea of influence when referring to things such as God's Word or love as they relate to the individual. Thus, when he says what they heard is "abiding," he means that they continue to

---

because it required an antecedent. Kistemaker (284) suggests that it may be seen as a "suspended subject" utilizing a "nominative independent" construction (also Burdick, 202 and Yarbrough, 160).

492. Strecker (68) sees John's use of the emphatic pronoun designed to distinguish the "attitude of the community from that of the false teachers." Lieu (109) sees this reference to "the beginning" making "its own claim to authority" beyond that of John's apostolic claim from the prologue.

John's repeated use of the 2 pl. throughout these verses indicates that this instruction was to be understood corporately as well as individually (Smalley, 120).

493. Johnson (60) notes that ἀκούω implies that they had heard these truths through someone's preaching, likely John's. It could also include their listening to the reading of Scripture, including epistles from the Apostles.

"listen" to their instruction and be influenced by it. What they heard was the apostolic message (Bruce, 74).[494]

This reference to what they have heard from the beginning influencing them helps clarify the "anointing" of verse 20 and later in verse 27. Rather than seeing the anointing as the Holy Spirit, it is better to see it as the body of truth given them by the Holy Spirit, who does the anointing. This body of truth includes Christology as well as instructions on living, both issues that are addressed in this epistle.

The message that John's readers heard from the beginning[495] has three elements in the epistle: Jesus is the Christ; he is the Son of God; and he has come in the flesh (1:1–3). These truths had been taught from the beginning, and holding them firmly would defend his readers from the false teachings that would hinder them from abiding in fellowship with God the Son and God the Father.

ἐὰν ἐν ὑμῖν μείνῃ ὃ ἀπ' ἀρχῆς ἠκούσατε, "If what you heard from the beginning abides in you." Using a third class conditional construction, John says his readers may let what they heard influence them ("abide in" them), or they may choose to ignore or reject it. His placement of ἐν ὑμῖν at the front of the clause emphasizes the personal nature of Scripture's influence in the life of the believer (Smalley, 119). However, that influence is contingent on each person's willful choices.

Repeating "that which you heard" and "from the beginning" for the second time, John emphasizes the importance of what he is communicating about the place of apostolic teaching in the life of the believer (Akin,

494. Interpreters understand the significance of this verse variously. For example, Bruce (74) sees this as a reference to the new commandment of 2:7 which they had heard from the beginning. Bultmann (40), on the other hand, sees this referring to instruction that "Jesus is the Christ" that has just been spoken of in the previous verses. Schnackenburg (158) understands this to reflect John's concern for their purity in doctrine. He (159) says further, "Christological orthodoxy is the only means of an abiding fellowship with God."

495. See discussion on 2:7 for a detailing of the various views on the referent of "from the beginning" and their proponents. Brooke (60) suggests here that it may have included instruction in synagogues prior to their hearing the gospel as well. This is unlikely since the churches under John's care at the time of the writing of this epistle were composed primarily of Gentile converts and were likely plants from the time of Paul's ministry in Ephesus.

123; Brooke, 60–61; Marshall, 160; Smalley, 119).[496] What they had heard included clear teaching on the incarnation and deity of Jesus (1 John 1:1–3; 4:3; 2 John 7).[497] Further, the repetition of μένω ("abide") throughout these verses drives home the role that sound doctrine plays in the daily experience of life with God. God is a God of truth and, as Jesus told the woman at the well, those who worship him must worship not just in spirit but in spirit *and* in truth (John 4:23). John makes clear by this that the condition of our abiding is God's Word abiding in us. We cannot have fellowship with God apart from the influence of his Word in our lives (Lieu, 110).[498]

καὶ ὑμεῖς ἐν τῷ υἱῷ καὶ ἐν τῷ πατρὶ μενεῖτε, "then you also will abide in the Son and in the Father." Having stated the condition (protasis), he now moves to the experience (apodosis). Abiding in the Son and Father is contingent on the teachings of the apostles abiding in—influencing—the believer (Barker, 326). Schnackenburg (159) sees abiding in God's Word as equivalent to abiding in Christ on the basis of John 15:7, and thus in God the Father as well. This reflects the sense of relationship with God. It is the Johannine sense of fellowship and reciprocal relationship. It is an active abiding on the part of the Christian (Brooke, 61) and a "continuing relationship" with God (Marshall, 161).[499] This is not something that,

---

496. Brown (356) and Smalley (117–18) suggest a small chiasm within the first two clauses of the sentence. However, it is unlikely to be such since it does not include the entire sentence, and the repeated use of μένω in each clause clearly connects them together rhetorically.

497. Westcott (77) notes the change in word order between the two clauses as indicating a change of emphasis. The first clause emphasizes the fact that they heard. This clause emphasizes the beginning.

498. Moody (54–55) says well, "It is in style now to separate abiding in a doctrine from abiding in a person, much as the 'Christ idea' is separated from the 'historical Jesus,' but Johannine theology would classify this as a new form of Gnosticism, as indeed it is."

499. Brooke describes this well when he says, "It is obvious that to the writer μένειν means something more than 'standing still.' It is the 'abiding' of the son who grows up in the house." Lieu (110) argues that the second person plural subject and concludes that what John describes is "not a purely individual experience, nor even the sum of many individuals experiences, but are that which shapes and identifies them as a group." However, though John speaks to them corporately, he clearly intends it to be applied individually in that all previous and following instruction, though it can be obeyed in a corporate setting, must be obeyed individually in order to be effective.

once started, maintains itself. Rather, one's relationship with God must be nurtured and developed even as with human relationships. Additionally, as Van der Merwe notes well, this use of abide "reflects this relationship between the Father, his Son and the children of God in the *familia Dei*. In this reciprocal use, of 'abides in you' (ὑμῖν μένειν) and 'abide in him' (μένετε ἐν αὐτῷ), the latter is not just another way of saying the former."[500] Malatesta describes this relationship as "an inward, enduring personal communion."[501]

Of note in this sentence is the emphasis of John, produced by his placement of key terms and phrases. Abiding is moved from the beginning of the protasis to the end of the apodosis. The repetition of "from the beginning" makes clear the apostolic tradition is intended as opposed to the newer doctrines of the false teachers. Furthermore, fellowship with God depends on the impact those teachings have on them. Thus, the triple repetition of μένω moves the focus from the believer's responsibility to allow the apostolic truths to influence them to the impact of that choice in their relationship with God. If they are not listening to the apostles and living out the truths they know, they cannot fellowship with God (Lieu, 110).[502]

Of further note is John's placement here of the Son before the Father, whereas earlier in verse 22 he listed the Father before the Son. This helps heighten his christological focus in this section (Smalley, 119). However, he also may have changed the word order to indicate that access to the Father is through the Son (Marshall, 77). One cannot come through the Son unless he or she believes the right things about the Son, those things taught from the beginning of their faith.

Finally, he uses the future tense of μένω here at the end. This is not a promise of future abiding but of continuous abiding (Smalley, 120). Additionally, as Malatesta notes, this emphasizes the forward-moving

500. D. G. Van Der Merwe, "'Experiencing Fellowship with God' According to 1 John 1:5–2:28: Dealing with the Change in Social Behavior," 247.

501. E. Malatesta, *Interiority and Covenant*, 25.

502. Lieu (110) notes well, "If what they have heard from the beginning does indeed indwell them—and the wording suggests that this needs positive action on their part and not mere passivity—then they will indwell the Son and the Father; the conditional wording allows for the possibility of the alternative to be avoided. . . . the condition suggests that the indwelling in Son and Father is not simply a reward for faithfulness but in some way is conterminous with it."

nature of abiding in God.[503] It is a "continuing vital relationship with God" (Burdick, 203).[504]

2:25 With this declaration John connects the experience of eternal life with our relationship with God.

καὶ αὕτη ἐστὶν ἡ ἐπαγγελία ἣν αὐτὸς ἐπηγγείλατο ἡμῖν,[505] "And this is the promise which he promised to us." By beginning this sentence with *καὶ*, John connects this promise with abiding in the previous verse (Akin, 123; Burdick, 204; Smalley, 120).[506] Further, his choice of the present tense *ἐστὶν* draws attention to the promise being "continuously present" (Smalley, 121).

Including the relative pronoun *αὕτη* for emphasis, John now directs his readers to the promise of God (Westcott, 78). Using the same root as the message they had received from the beginning, John announces the promise of God to them.[507] The significance of that promise, not yet defined, is emphasized by the Hebrew practice of repeating the noun with its related verb.[508] Both terms come from the same root. The aorist verb reminds the readers that this promise was made in the past. It also connects the promise to that which they had heard from the beginning in the previous verses. John's change from the second person plural (to address his readers) to this first person plural intentionally includes him with the readers. This is not a promise exclusively for the apostles (an allusion to the upper room), but to all believers. It is also a promise made in the past but one that looks to the future for its fulfillment (Lieu, 111).

503. E. Malatesta, *Interiority and Covenant*, 211.

504. Stott (118) says this is "virtually identical" with "having God" in verse 23. Marshall (160) concurs.

505. The first plural *ἡμῖν* is preferred over the second plural *ὑμῖν*. It may have resulted from scribal error or a deliberate change to make the reading match the earlier statement in 1:2 and 3 (*ἀπαγγέλλομεν ὑμῖν*). B. Metzger and United Bible Societies, *A Textual Commentary on the Greek New Testament*, 2d ed., 641.

506. Johnson (60) sees this salvifically and as a promise made to Christians "persevering" in faith "to the end." Rather than imposing a justification sense to the verse, one must recognize that John is writing to justified saints whose salvation he does not question, though their faith can be threatened by false teachings.

507. Bultmann (40) sees this promise as both future and fulfilled at the same time with John based on his statements in 3:2, 14, and 5:12.

508. This is accomplished with a cognate accusative construction (BDF §153) that likely reflects a Semitism on John's part.

The antecedent of αὕτη is ζωὴν, a feminine noun that follows, rather than anything prior (Brooke, 61; Burdick, 204; Law, 381; Westcott, 78; Smalley, 120; Strecker, 69). The accusative case "eternal life" (τὴν ζωὴν τὴν αἰώνιον) functions appositionally to ἣν, which is the direct object of the verb, ἐπηγγείλατο (Brown, 357). Also, John's pattern in this epistle is for αὐτὸς to refer to what follows (Brooke, 61; Marshall, 161). Even so, this makes for an abrupt shift in the flow of thought. However, that is not unusual for John either.

This is the sole use of ἐπαγγελία by John, though a common term in New Testament.[509] Though promise and fulfillment is a significant New Testament theme, it is not so with John (Smalley, 120).[510] Marshall (78) notes that Jesus does not expressly make this promise in the Gospels, though it is evident in Jesus' coming to give men eternal life and in all that he said about it.[511]

The pronoun αὐτὸς is emphatic once again and could refer either to God the Father (Akin, 123; Johnson, 64), or God the Son (Brooke, 61; Brown, 358; Grayston, 92; Harris, 119; Lieu, 111; Westcott, 77), or to both (Houlden, 82; Smalley, 121). It seems best to see it referring to God the Father, especially in light of what is said in chapter 5. Also, what they have heard has to do with truths concerning God the Son and so it is unlikely to refer to Jesus here. Akin (123) and Houlden (82) correctly note that eternal life is something that comes through Jesus Christ but from God the Father.[512]

τὴν ζωὴν τὴν αἰώνιον, "eternal life." Bringing the readers back to the prologue, John now tells them what has been promised. "Eternal life" is more

509. Its noun form occurs fifty-two times in the NT and its verb form another fifteen.

510. Rensberger (82) proposes that the term "may show infiltration into 1 John of ideas from other Christian groups. He also notes that the use of "promise" with "life," as here occurs in later NT literature and identifies 2 Tim 1:1; Titus 1:2; and Jas 1:12 as examples. However, it seems better to see James as an example of earlier Christian literature as opposed to later. John could easily have been informed by Paul's use of the terms and concept. It would be very likely that he had in his possession (or his church's possession) copies of Paul's earlier as well as later epistles, especially since Paul's epistles to Timothy likely would have been sent to Ephesus, John's residence at the time he wrote his own epistles.

511. So, too, Brown (357). Strecker (68) notes well, "The Christ-event has a promissory character, because it opens a redeemed future to those who believe."

512. For them, this allows the double referent for αὐτὸς.

than a quantity of life in John's writings. It is a quality of life, God's life, in the present which will continue to be experienced in eternity (Akin, 124; Burdick, 204; Houlden, 82; Smalley, 121).[513] Bruce (75) describes it as "resurrection life" that is already realized in the life of the believer. We see from the prologue that for John it is a person. We were promised life and found it fulfilled in the person of Jesus. John likely intends this use of eternal life to be understood as a double meaning for both the life possessed and Jesus, who is Life itself. Both Jesus and the life he gives are promised to every believer from God the Father.[514]

For John the relationship between abiding and the experience of eternal life is one of continuity. You cannot have one without the other. Therefore, he is not discussing the issue of one's possession of life, a justification truth, but the question of the *experience* of life, a sanctification truth (contra Stott, 118).[515] This is more than the promise of the resurrection and a future presence in heaven but a present realization of the resurrection life in this life (Akin, 123; Bruce, 75; Marshall, 161).

2:26 Now John addresses his readers concerning another of his reasons for writing. The false teachers are active in the world around them.

Ταῦτα ἔγραψα ὑμῖν, "I wrote these things to you." "These things" with the epistolary aorist, "I wrote," looks back on the previous verses (vv. 18–25) and what John has said about the false teachers (Brooke, 61; Bultmann, 40; Burdick, 204; Lenski, 441; Marshall, 162; Plummer, 115; Smalley, 122;

---

513. Contra Schnackenburg (159) who believes that whereas in the Gospel eternal life was a present possession, here it is a future expectation. Bultmann (40) notes that John's synonymous use of" eternal life" and "life" raises the question whether the term "eternal" has a chronological sense "at all and is not simply a designation of quality."

514. Schnackenburg (159) does not see this use indicating a present possession, as he sees it described in the Gospel. Rather, he sees John's choice of "promise" to indicate eternal life here is a future expectation.

515. Moody (55) describes well this sense of eternal life here as "nothing less than God's life imparted to those who abide in Christ."

Strecker, 76; Westcott, 78; Yarbrough, 162).[516] This indicates John is concluding his discussion.[517]

Many interpreters see this referring to the revisionists/secessionists and providing the occasion for writing the epistle (Bruce, 76; Hodges, 93). Although it should be seen as *a* purpose for writing, it should not be made the dominant purpose. False teachers are a problem and their false teachings must be addressed. One cannot walk with the God of truth apart from walking in the truth. Consequently, false teachers and false teachings must be addressed along with all the other issues impacting one's fellowship with God. However, John is concerned with far more than his readers' Christology. He is concerned with how his readers treat one another and how healthy of a relationship they have with God.

Bruce sees this as an "echo" of Jesus' promise to the apostles in John 14:26 (Bruce, 77). However, other than the use of "these things," there is little connection. What preceded Jesus' statement were calls to obedient living and the promise of the ministry of the Holy Spirit in the lives of the apostles. Here the focus is different.

περὶ τῶν πλανώντων ὑμᾶς, "concerning those who are trying to deceive you." The verb πλανάω means "to deceive," as well as to lead someone astray or to go astray.[518] Though it need not always include deliberate deception, in this case the emphasis is on their intention to influence deliberately. Additionally, when John describes the false teachers as those "deceiving" (present active participle with the article), he does not by this imply their success, thus the translational choice of "trying to deceive you." Their goal is to guide John's readers in a different direction from the apostolic traditions. Still, John is not affirming that his readers are deceived, but that the false teachers are attempting to deceive, are lying to them (Akin, 124; Burdick, 205; Marshall, 78; Smalley, 123; Stott, 118; contra Johnson, 61). Even so, as

516. Other views include Johnson (60) who suggests it could refer to the beginning of the epistle, Harris (120) who sees it referring to the entire epistle, and Williamson (104) who sees it looking back on v. 24 and forward to the promise that follows.

517. A. C. Thiselton, "Semantics and New Testament Interpretation," 78.

518. BDAG, 821; H. Braun, "πλανάω," *TDNT* 6:245–46. As Strecker (76) notes well, its sense of both leading astray and being self-deceived serves as a warning to John's readers of the danger of drifting whether or not they are being influenced by false teachers.

Schnackenburg (160–61) notes well, his use of the present participle indicates that John views the "influence" of the deceivers as "still dangerous" to his readers "despite the outward separation."[519] For Christians then and today, the danger of deception was and continues to be real. For example, Mark 13:6 indicates that one characteristic of the last days is that the false teachers would lead others astray. Thus the warning from John is the same (Lieu, 112). Also, John's reference to "you" as opposed to "us" reminds his readers that he and the apostles are not the ones in danger of being deceived, but the readers (Lieu, 111).

This note from John serves as a reminder that it *is* possible these days for believers to be deceived by false teachers. Some Christians wrongly believe that because the Holy Spirit indwells them they are immune to deception. If that were true, in light of John's affirmation of his readers being "anointed," he would not have needed to warn them of false teachers and their teachings. The warnings themselves prove the danger exists. This is not a theoretical danger but a very real one.

2:27 This long, convoluted sentence serves as an exhortation to abide in the apostolic teachings that would protect John's readers, and therefore all Christians, from the false teachers.[520] With the subject and verb separated by six clauses, his basic command is to abide. However, what are they to abide in?

καὶ ὑμεῖς τὸ χρῖσμα ὃ ἐλάβετε ἀπ' αὐτοῦ μένει ἐν ὑμῖν, "As for you, the anointing which you received from him abides in you." Once again John turns from warning his readers to reassuring them (Lieu, 113). Thus, he instructs his readers with a command encompassed by assurances. He neither questions their salvation nor is he providing a test for them to question their salvation. Rather, he is reminding them of God's provision for them. As in verse 24, John begins with the second-person plural pronoun both to address his readers, like a vocative, and to heighten the contrast between them and the false teachers (Brown, 360–61; Smalley, 125–26; Strecker,

519. Also Plummer (115) and Law (382). Brooke (62) comments that the present participle, while pointing to the present danger of the false teachers "does not determine the extent to which the opponent's efforts had met with success."

520. Rensberger (82) describes it as reflecting the "frustratingly obscure syntax" characteristic of John's epistle.

76; Westcott, 79).[521] Unlike those who are trying to deceive them, God is protecting them. The main verb μένετε in this sentence appears late and is separated from the subject by a long relative clause. This heightens the significance of the subject, "you," as opposed to "them."

He once more refers to the "anointing" that they "received" from God. As before, the possible meanings for this anointing are either the Holy Spirit (Burdick, 205; Harris, 121; Johnson, 61; Schnackenburg, 161; Stott, 118; Strecker, 76),[522] the body of teachings about Jesus delivered by the apostles (Lieu, 112),[523] or both (Akin, 125; Smalley, 123). Pentecost (70) relates this anointing to verse 20 as referring to the ministry of the Holy Spirit in teaching them. Hodges (117–18), on the other hand, sees this anointing referring to those orthodox teachers provided to the church and enabled by the Holy Spirit. He sees these spiritually mature teachers as the ones not needing a teacher. However, John continues to talk about his readers ("you") rather than a separate group of teachers from them.[524] Stott (118), along with Strecker (76), understands this to indicate the Holy Spirit, who leads them to a knowledge of the truth through which the community discerns between what is true and false (also Stott, 118).

"Him" (ἀπ' αὐτοῦ) clearly refers to a member of the Godhead. The nearest antecedent can be found in verses 24 and 25, in which both God the Father and Jesus the Son (Brooke, 62; Harris, 121; Schnackenburg, 161; Stott, 114–15; Westcott, 77) are in view. If the Holy Spirit is understood to be this anointing, then God the Father would be in view (Moody, 56), based on Jesus' promise in John 14:26. If the anointing is a body of doctrine that protects the believers from deceivers, then Jesus would be the referent. This second option is best in light of what follows.[525]

---

521. R. L. Thomas, "Exegetical Digest of 1 John," 217–18. Brooke (62) calls this a nominative absolute construction; Burdick (205), an independent nominative.

522. In this view "receiving" of this anointing occurs at conversion (Acts 2:38) in accordance with Christ's promise in John 14:16–17 (Burdick, 205).

523. E. Malatesta, *Interiority and Covenant*, 147.

524. This is another case of anacoluthon*, where the nominative ὑμεῖς has assimilated the following relative pronoun's case because it required an antecedent (BDF §466 (1)).

525. Regarding the referent of ἐν ὑμῖν, Yarbrough (166) suggests the preposition should be understood to communicate the idea of "among" the readers, a community expression more than being "seen as primarily interior and self-focused." Though this may be allowed, John's use of abiding includes both personal and

καὶ οὐ χρείαν ἔχετε ἵνα τις διδάσκῃ ὑμᾶς, "and you do not have a need that anyone should teach you." No need to be taught? In isolation this statement might be taken to mean that the Holy Spirit teaches us in the same way as Jesus promised the apostles that he would guide them into all truth (John 14:26). Moreover, since we are taught by the Holy Spirit, we do not need any other instructors. However, John cannot mean this (Williamson, 105).[526] As Akin (125) aptly notes, "John is not denying the importance and place of human teachers. The mere fact that he wrote this letter is sufficient proof." Rather, John is reminding his readers that what he is telling them is already known to them and is therefore self-evident (Yarbrough, 167).

Using *ἵνα* to "express a conceived result," John raises the issue of why they would listen to false teachers and then rejects it.[527] What he is assuring them is that they have not missed out on any important information about Jesus. They have been taught everything they need to know. They do not need any "new" instruction about the person of Christ offered by false teachers, or any other teachers for that matter.

ἀλλʼ ὡς τὸ αὐτοῦ χρῖσμα διδάσκει ὑμᾶς περὶ πάντων, "but as his anointing teaches you concerning all things." Beginning with the strong adversative *ἀλλὰ*, John now demonstrates why his readers do not need new instruction about Jesus.[528] Their *anointing* is a fully sufficient source of information about Jesus. Notice that here John describes this anointing in terms

---

corporate experience. Although this phrase could be seen as primarily focused on its corporate experience, the anointing to which John refers should be seen as both individual and corporate.

526. Yarbrough (166) describes this remark as "slight irony" on John's part.

527. R. Hana, *Grammatical Aid*, 435; E. D. Burton, *Syntax of the Moods and Tenses of New Testament Greek*, 218. Brooke (62) sees this as a purely "definitive" *ἵνα* and rejects any other sense.

528. The remainder of this verse is a very complex construction which may be understood structurally in one of two ways. (1) It may consist of a single protasis (*ἀλλʼ ὡς τὸ αὐτοῦ χρῖσμα διδάσκει ὑμᾶς περὶ πάντων … καὶ καθὼς ἐδίδαξεν ὑμᾶς*) with a parenthetical statement (*καὶ ἀληθές ἐστιν καὶ οὐκ ἔστιν ψεῦδος*,) followed by the apodoses (*μένετε ἐν αὐτῷ*). (2) It may consist of two protases (*ἀλλʼ ὡς τὸ αὐτοῦ χρῖσμα διδάσκει ὑμᾶς περὶ πάντων … καὶ καθὼς ἐδίδαξεν ὑμᾶς*) and apodoses (*καὶ ἀληθές ἐστιν καὶ οὐκ ἔστιν ψεῦδος … μένετε ἐν αὐτῷ*). Though both are awkward, the single protasis approach seems the best way to understand it, especially since John does use parenthetical statements elsewhere, including the prologue of this epistle (Burdick, 206–207; Westcott, 80).

of quality rather than character, thereby indicating something inanimate, impersonal.

Some take this "anointing" as a reference to the Holy Spirit, with John using metonymy of the effect (the effect is used for the cause), in this case the anointing for the Holy Spirit (Westcott, 80).[529] However, it seems better to see this as a metonymy of the cause, with the anointing being used for its effect: knowledge. This is made evident in that this anointing "teaches" the readers. Thus apostolic teaching, called "anointing," is personified. Although John is using the simple present active indicative form, it is better to see this as either: (1) gnomic—it continually teaches as a matter of principle; or (2) a perfective sense—its teaching stands true; rather than (3) continuous—it is in the process of teaching (Lenski, 442; Westcott, 80). John is not saying that the anointing is presently teaching them, but that what it has taught stands true to the present (perfective sense). This is clarified by the following clause.

His statement "you do not need anyone to teach you" should not be seen as an allusion to the new covenant of Jeremiah 31 (contra Rensberger, 83).[530] Rather, it is a clarification that John's readers have been taught all there is to learn. Thus, they can know that anyone coming with a claim to new knowledge can be dismissed and they need to continue to hold firmly that which they already know.

Concluding, John now changes the present tense of διδάσκω to an aorist. Some might see this as changing subjects, with the aorist referring to Jesus' teachings in the Upper Room while the present refers to the Holy

---

529. E. W. Bullinger, *Figures of Speech Used in the Bible*, 560.

530. Contra D. A. Carson ("1–3 John," 1065) who sees this as an allusion to Jer 31:31–34. He sees the allusion growing out of the characteristics of the New Covenant which include: "(1) God forgives the sin of his people, concomitantly with God's Torah being written on their hearts, (2) establishing an abiding new-covenant relationship (3) in which all who are under this covenant genuinely know God (4) with genuine knowledge independent of the mediating teachers that characterized the old covenant (e.g., Levites were 'brothers' and 'neighbors' of the rest of the people of God, yet they had peculiar mediatorial teaching roles in this regard, as did the schools of the prophets)." He notes (879) the continued expectation of the New Covenant's fulfillment was expressed by Jesus in John 6:45 when He quoted Isa 54:13, and, based on other allusions to the New Covenant in Isaiah, Micah, and extrabiblical literature, this "expected eschatological blessing probably also lies behind" this verse.

Spirit's ministry. This would be the logical thought if the anointing were seen as the Holy Spirit. However if the anointing is a body of doctrine, then it is what "taught" and "teaches" them. Based on this, he then commands his readers to abide in those truths received.[531]

καὶ ἀληθές ἐστιν καὶ οὐκ ἔστιν ψεῦδος, "and is true and is not a lie." In contrast to the liar (2:22) and to his or her own possible self-deception (1:8), is the assurance of the trustworthiness of God's Word to them (the anointing).[532] Yarbrough (167) understands John to mean by this that their "anointing" is "trustworthy." However, though it is trustworthy, John's point is stronger than that. His use of antithetic parallelism here, similar to what he did in 1:5, seems better to be understood as a statement about the absolute truthfulness of the body of doctrines described as the anointing that "teaches" them. There is not a shred of falseness in them.

καὶ καθὼς ἐδίδαξεν ὑμᾶς, μένετε ἐν αὐτῷ, "and just as it taught you, you abide in him." Westcott (80) notes that John's use of καθὼς indicates "the idea of a definite and fixed standard." The truths contained in the anointing are not changing truths or new theology, but they are true from the day they were taught to the present.

Strecker (77) sees ἐδίδαξεν referring to both the giver and the gift of the χρῖσμα. In this case, he views it as the Holy Spirit (also Harris, 121). Burdick (207), on the other hand sees the subject of ἐδίδαξεν as Jesus. He argues that the present tense διδάσκει had the Holy Spirit as its subject and focused attention on Jesus' continuing ministry. Now the aorist has Jesus' completed teaching ministry in view. This cannot work, however, because the syntax of this complex sentence, with its parenthetical clause, maintains the same subject throughout. In this case, since the anointing is the body of doctrine (my view) in the earlier clause, it continues to be that in this clause. What is affirmed, then, is that what they had been taught in the past continues to stand valid and speaks to their situation as forcefully then as it had earlier.

The verb "abide" in the final clause—the main clause—of the sentence may be either in the indicative (Brooke, 63; Law, 383; Westcott, 81)

531. "All things" does not mean everything, but "everything you need to know" (Marshall, 163).

532. Schnackenburg (161) sees this as a "deliberate dig" at the "wicked lie" of the false teachers. "Diese letzte Wiederholung mit negativem Vorzeichen ist wohl eine bewußte Spitze gegen die boshafte „Lüge" der Irrlehrer." ("This last repetition with a negative form is probably a deliberate dig at the wicked 'lie' of the heretics.")

or imperative (Brown, 361; Kistemaker, 287; Lenski, 443 Smalley, 127; Schnackenburg, 162; Strecker, 76). However, the point made would be quite different. This same word (and spelling) in the preceding verse may be indicative, but in the following verse it is clearly an imperative. With John intentionally relating this paragraph with what follows by the repetition of key words, it should be seen as an imper. here (Strecker, 76–77). It also seems best to see the referent of the pronoun αὐτῷ to follow rather than precede and so be Jesus rather than the anointing (Schnackenburg, 162; Stott, 119; Westcott, 80).[533] Thus John is not simply affirming that they are abiding in the teaching. He is also commanding them to "continue" abiding in Christ as well, the sense of the present imperative, drawing from Jesus' instructions in the Upper Room once more.

Biblical Theology Comments

Other than the book of Revelation, this is John's most extensive development of eschatology. John's use of "the last hour" to describe our present age communicates his understanding of the imminence of Christ's kingdom, a message he preached along with his brother James when Jesus sent them out in pairs (Matt 10; Luke 10:1–24).[534] He recognizes the significance of his day in that many "antichrists" have arisen from their midst whose motives and actions reflect those of the coming Antichrist. John views the Antichrist as a historical figure whose coming is confirmed by those acting according to the spirit that will characterize him. He does not historicize a mythical figure (contra Bultmann, 36), but he reaffirms the reality of Antichrist's coming appearance in world history. His description does not indicate that he expected Jesus' immediate return because of the appearance of the false teachers. Rather, John's instruction serves to remind

533. Burdick (205–206) notes that John does not command his readers to let the anointing abide, but states that it does abide. He sees the significance of both the tense (present) and linear nature of the verb to indicate the permanence of the Spirit's abiding.

534. The sense of "at hand" in the message, "The kingdom of Heaven is at hand," is that of immanence, not chronological nearness. Rather, the perfect active ἤγγικεν indicates the fact that the kingdom was poised to come, but was only near. Though Baur (BDAG, 270) assigns its sense in Matt 10:7 to its temporal nuance (temporally near), it is best to see it spatially. The Kingdom was close at hand (in the person of its king).

his readers of their need to be vigilant in their faith and to recognize the spiritual origin of false teachers. Similarly, the large number of false teachers today is a reminder to our generation that the Antichrist is coming, and also, to our great joy, so is the real Christ!

The test of false teachers is their departure from apostolic truth. As John describes the false teachers in this section, they are unregenerate individuals whose doctrinal departure (more than physical) confirms that they are unregenerate. The false teachers' desire to draw believers after themselves poses an ever-present danger to the church.[535] The believer's defense against false teachers, these antichrists, is not to focus one's study on false teachings and how to refute them, though that is a valuable part of apologetics, but first and foremost to know God's truth, particularly what he says about his Son, Jesus.[536] Orthodox Christology is our only protection against christological heterodoxy. Orthodox Christology is our only protection against heteropraxy as well.

Fellowship with God, described in terms of mutual abiding, is dependent on God's Word having an influence (abiding in) in the believer's life. Moreover, that word in this epistle is christological truth. One cannot fellowship with (abide in) God apart from being rightly related to his Son. Furthermore, one cannot be rightly related to his Son if he believes the wrong things about him. Fellowship with God is as contingent on truth as it is on moral purity. Both are sourced in God. Both are spheres in which a believer must walk in order to abide and thereby experience the eternal life they possess.

Application and Devotional Implications

2:20–21 Our best defense against false teachers is not to study false teachings, but to know God's truth. We can only do that by knowing God's Word. We can only do *that* by reading and studying it. Listening to good preaching is edifying. Reading devotionals or books by Christian authors is edifying as well. However, neither comes close to knowing God's Word. It is through his Scriptures that God has chosen to instruct and protect us. That

---

535. This is especially evident with the woman Jezebel in the church in Thyatira (Rev 2:18–23).

536. Just as Paul's corrective for the church in Colossae was orthodox christology, so too is John's.

is why Paul commanded the Colossians to "let the word of Christ richly dwell within" them (Col 3:16). That is why John speaks of the "anointing" dwelling in us. The idea of dwelling is not just that we are to know God's Word. That is part of it. We are also to be influenced (guided) by God's Word. That is our defense against false teaching today, even as then. The better we know Jesus (have correct Christology), the closer our fellowship can be with him and God the Father. Any congregation that is serious about communing with God must devote themselves to teaching each member about God. Corporate fellowship grows out of each individual's fellowship with God. To the extent a church's believing members know God, the church does. Fellowship does not flow the other direction. Believers do not enjoy fellowship with God as a by-product of being part of a church. They enjoy it only to the extent that God's truth, revealed in his word, shapes their thoughts and actions.

2:23 Unbelieving Jews consciously seek to worship the God of Abraham, Isaac, and Jacob, who revealed himself on Mount Sinai. Muslims claim that Allah is the God of Abraham as well. But do they worship the same God as Christians? Both Jesus (John 5:23; 15:23) and John would say "no!" Jesus stated that he was not only "the way, the truth, and the life," but he followed that by clarifying, "No one comes to the Father except through me" (John 14:6). Jesus limited access to God to himself. As Christians, when we present the gospel of salvation to a lost world we must recognize that there truly is no other way to God except through the gospel of Jesus Christ.

Though ours may be a pluralistic society that views an exclusive gospel as intolerant, we must not retreat from the truth of God's Word. Jesus prayed in the garden of Gethsemane, "O my Father, if it is possible, let this cup pass from me; nevertheless, not as I will, but as you *will*" (Matt 26:39). It was not possible, and so Jesus submitted himself to God's will and died for our sins. God the Father would not have sent Jesus his Son to the cross to die for mankind's sins if there were any other way of salvation. That is why Peter declared to the Jewish multitude who had witnessed his healing of a lame man that "there is no other name under heaven given among men by which we must be saved" (Acts 4:12). These were not unreligious Jews, but men and women who had come to the temple to worship the God of Abraham, Isaac, and Jacob—though they did not recognize Jesus as his Son.

What they did not know, but John now makes clear, is that rejecting the Son is rejecting the Father. No one can worship God except through Jesus. No one can come to God except through Jesus. Let us never forget that. Let us never retreat from clearly communicating that.

Selected Bibliography

Beale, G. K., and D. A. Carson, eds. *Commentary on the New Testament Use of the Old Testament*. Grand Rapids: Baker Academic, 2007.

Black, D. A. "An Overlooked Stylistic Argument in Favor of πάντα in 1 John 2:20." *Filologia Neotestamentaria* 5 (1992): 205–8.

Breck, J. "The Function of ΠΑΣ in 1 John 2:20." *St. Vladimir's Theological Quarterly* 35 (1991): 187–206.

Bullinger, E. W. *Figures of Speech Used in the Bible.* New York: Eyre & Spottiswoode, 1898. Repr., Grand Rapids: Baker 1968.

Burton, E. D. *Syntax of the Moods and Tenses in New Testament Greek*. 3rd ed. Chicago: University of Chicago, 1898.

Carson, D. A. "1–3 John." In *Commentary on the New Testament Use of the Old Testament*, edited by G. K. Beale and D. A. Carson, 1063–67. Grand Rapids: Baker Academic, 2007.

Coetzee, J. C. "Christ and the Prince of This World in the Gospel and the Epistles of St. John." *Neot* 2 (1968): 104–21.

Curtis, E. M. "The First Person Plural in 1 John 2:18–27." *EvJ* 10 (1992): 27–36.

de Jonge, M. "The Use of the Word ΧΡΙΣΤΟΣ in the Johannine Epistles." In *Studies in John*, 67–74. NovTSup 24. Leiden: Brill, 1970.

de la Potterie, I. "L'onction du chretien par la foi." *Biblica* 40 (1959): 12–69.

Erickson, R. J. "Oida and Ginōskō and Verbal Aspect in Pauline Usage." *WTJ* 44 (1982): 109–22.

Hanna, R. *A Grammatical Aid to the Greek New Testament*. Grand Rapids: Baker, 1983.

Hiebert, D. E. "An Expositional Study of 1 John—Part 4: An Exposition of 1 John 2:18–28." *BSac* 146 (1989): 76–93.

Lalleman, P. J. "The Adversaries Envisaged in the Johannine Epistles." *ThT* 53 (1999): 17–24.

Malatesta, E. *Interiority and Covenant: A Study of* εἶναι ἐν *and* μένειν ἐν *in the First Letter of Saint John*. Rome: Biblical Institute Press, 1978.

Metzger, B. M., and United Bible Societies. *A Textual Commentary on the Greek New Testament*. 2nd ed. New York: United Bible Societies, 1994.

Moulton, J. H., and G. Milligan. *The Vocabulary of the Greek Testament.* London, 1930. Repr. Grand Rapids: Eerdmans, 1982.

Nichols, S. J. "Prophecy Makes Strange Bedfellows: On the History of Identifying the Antichrist." *JETS* 44 (2001): 75–85.

Peterson, R. A. "Apostasy." *Presb* 19 (1993): 17–31.

Thiselton, A. C. "Semantics and New Testament Interpretation." In *New Testament Interpretation: Essays on Principles and Methods,* edited by I. H. Marshall, 74–100. Milton Keynes, UK: Paternoster, 1977.

Thomas, R. L. *Exegetical Digest of 1 John.* Self-published, 1984.

Van der Merwe, D. G. "'Experiencing Fellowship with God' according to 1 John 1:5–2:28: Dealing with the Change in Social Behavior." *Acta Patristica et Byzantina* 18 (2007): 231–62.

Wallace, D. B. *Greek Grammar beyond the Basics.* Grand Rapids: Zondervan, 1996.

Wendland, E. R. "'Dear Children' versus the 'Antichrists': The Rhetoric of Reassurance in First John." *JOTT* 11 (1998): 40–84.

God Is Righteous (2:28–4:6)

Introduction

The second major movement in John's epistle focuses on God's character once again. Where his moral purity has been in focus until now, developed in the light/darkness imagery, John moves to the implications of that purity in terms of God's righteous nature and the demands it creates. Jesus has already been identified as "the Righteous One" in 2:2. Now, having been called upon to abide in God, we as finite creatures beset by sin, wonder at times how such a holy and righteous God could ever really accept us. John addresses the impact of one's present attitude toward purity and righteousness in relational terms.

As John continues to develop the concept of fellowship with God in terms of a relationship of mutual abiding, he begins by reminding his readers not only of their place in the family of God, but also of their accountability for the kind of person they choose to be. The implication of those choices is described under the dualistic imagery of love and murder as well as parentage. Those choices involve conduct in the family of God, how Christians treat Christians. It is never separate from faith in Christ and an orthodox understanding of his person and work. Thus John continues to remind his readers of the false teachings and false teachers to avoid. He will end this section once more with words of assurance to his readers, lest they misapply his absolute statements and come to doubt their standing with God their Father.

As before, though the false teachers are addressed and their false teachings dealt with, John's primary concern is pastoral and so the majority of what is written must be viewed in light of its parenetic purpose. We see this in John's inclusion of himself with his readers. We also see by how he addresses them at critical moments to remind them of their standing in the family of God. In this we are also allowed a glance into the very heart of God, a glance that calls for our obedient response in imitation of Christ.

Expectation of Righteousness (2:28–3:3)

Introduction

Our choices have consequences that grow over time. Many of the choices we make today will have a greater impact on our lives ten years from now than they do today or tomorrow. Some of the choices we make today, in fact, will impact us eternally. It is this idea that intertwines these next few verses. John writes knowing that we live and act on the basis of how or what we see ourselves to be as people. Thus he will remind his readers of their privileged position as children of God. However, as we are privileged to be God's children, that position brings with it certain obligations. Additionally, we will be held accountable by our loving Savior for the choices made. That accounting will be given on the day we stand before Jesus, "the Righteous One," who is both our propitiation and advocate. On that day, though, he will be our just and righteous judge, holding us accountable for the choices we have made each day along life's journey. Some of us will be glad to meet Jesus on that day. Others will not be so glad.

Having alerted his readers in the previous section to the significance of the appearance of false teachers—namely, that they were living in "the last hour"—John now addresses the issue of what attitude his readers must have if they are to be prepared for Jesus' second coming.[1] Living with the reality that Jesus may return at any moment should motivate us to pursue his moral purity in anticipation of appearing before him.

Original Text

2:28 Καὶ νῦν, τεκνία, μένετε ἐν αὐτῷ, ἵνα ἐὰν φανερωθῇ σχῶμεν παρρησίαν καὶ μὴ αἰσχυνθῶμεν ἀπ' αὐτοῦ ἐν τῇ παρουσίᾳ αὐτοῦ. **29** ἐὰν εἰδῆτε ὅτι δίκαιός ἐστιν, γινώσκετε ὅτι πᾶς ὁ ποιῶν τὴν δικαιοσύνην ἐξ αὐτοῦ γεγέννηται.

---

1. One characteristic of this section is the nine occurrences of πᾶς ὁ ("everyone who") followed by a participle (Burge, 143). This indicates that John is describing principles that apply to believers and non-believers alike, as will be seen in the discussions that follow.

3:1 ἴδετε ποταπὴν ἀγάπην δέδωκεν ἡμῖν ὁ πατὴρ ἵνα τέκνα θεοῦ κληθῶμεν, aκαὶ ἐσμέν.a διὰ τοῦτο ὁ κόσμος οὐ γινώσκει ἡμᾶς ὅτι οὐκ ἔγνω αὐτόν. **2** ἀγαπητοί, νῦν τέκνα θεοῦ ἐσμεν, καὶ οὔπω ἐφανερώθη τί ἐσόμεθα. οἴδαμεν ὅτι ἐὰν φανερωθῇ ὅμοιοι αὐτῷ ἐσόμεθα, ὅτι ὀψόμεθα αὐτὸν καθώς ἐστιν. **3** καὶ πᾶς ὁ ἔχων τὴν ἐλπίδα ταύτην ἐπ' αὐτῷ ἁγνίζει ἑαυτὸν καθὼς ἐκεῖνος ἁγνός ἐστιν.

Textual Notes

3:1.a...a The phrase, καὶ ἐσμέν, following κληθῶμεν, is likely original as noted by Metzger. Though it lacks solid support in either the Western or Alexandrian texts (P^{74vid} א A B C 33 81 614 1739 it^{h65} vg) and is clearly omitted in the Byzantine and TR, its awkwardness argues for its inclusion since it would be more likely to be omitted by copyists in order to remove the awkwardness of the phrase than to be added for clarity or emphasis.[2]

Translation

2:28 And now, little children, abide in him, in order that when[3] he should appear, we may have confidence and not shrink back in shame[4] from him at his appearing.[5] **29** If you know that he is righteous, you know that everyone

2. B. Metzger and United Bible Societies, *A Textual Commentary on the Greek New Testament*, 2d ed., 642.
3. Most translations (ESV, HCSB, NASB95, NET, NIV84, NKJV) choose to reflect the certainty of Christ's coming and so translate ἐὰν with "when." ASV has "if."
4. The nuance of this verb is translated in a variety of ways, such as: "not be ashamed" (ASV, HCSB, NKJV), "unashamed" (NIV84), "not shrink" (ESV), "not shrink away" (NASB95, NET), and "not shrink back" (NLT). Primarily the difference between the two main thrusts (shame and shrinking back) has to do with whether it is describing emotions or responses.
5. Most translations (ASV, ESV, HCSB, NASB95, NET, NIV84, NKJV) use "coming" (NLT uses "returns") in order to communicate the idea of Jesus' second coming in which He will judge the church. This would be following the rapture of the church and is a reference to the Bema Seat judgment rather than the Great White Throne judgment of Rev 20. "Appearing" was chosen in order to communicate the idea of His presence more than His arrival contained in *parousia*.

who practices[6] righteousness has been born from him. **3:1** Behold[7] what kind of love the Father has given to us that we should be called children of God, and we are.[8] Because of this the world does not know us, because it did not know him. **2** Beloved, now we are children of God, and it has not yet been revealed what we will be. We know that whenever[9] it[10] is revealed, we will be like him, because we shall see him just as he is. **3** And everyone who has this hope in him purifies[11] himself, just as he is pure.

Commentary

2:28 John introduces a new section repeating the command with which he ended the previous section (Rensberger, 84–85).[12] He follows the command by stating its purpose and result, with the double clause stating the same truth both positively and negatively. Thus, having urged his readers to let what they

6. Translations have "practices righteousness" (ESV, NASB95, NET, NKJV) or "does what is right" (HCSB, NIV84, NLT), with the older ASV saying "doeth righteousness." I chose to translate "practices righteousness" in order to reflect John's choice of the present participle of ποιέω as it relates to the fulfillment of moral or social obligations (BDAG, 840).

7. Though NIV84 drops this exclamation from the text, it should be included. It may be expressed in a variety of ways (behold, see, look), all which communicate the call to take note.

8. Though not well attested, this last statement is included because its awkwardness makes it appear the more likely reading. It would not be something added accidentally through scribal error. It is excluded by NKJV but not ASV, ESV, HCSB, NASB95, NET, NIV84, and NLT.

9. This reflects "the more probable future" aspect of the particle and its subjunctive verb. Most translations use "when" (ESV, HCSB, NASB95, NIV84, NKJV, NLT). NET uses "whenever." ASV uses "if."

10. This translation sees the verb related to the previous clause (see discussion below), as does NET. On the other hand, ESV, HCSB, NASB95, NKJV, NIV84 have "when he appears" and see this as a reference to Jesus' return. ASV has "if he shall be manifested."

11. The verb "purifies" and adjective "pure" come from the same root. This translation attempts to achieve John's intention to make that connection.

12. Hodges (124) sees this verse as "a thematic statement for the unit of material which follows (i.e., 2:29—4:19)." Though it is introductory, it should not be seen as thematic. The major theme, God's righteousness, will not be introduced until the next sentence. So, though this paragraph is thematic, its first sentence is not.

have heard from the beginning influence them, he continues to develop the concept of abiding as it relates to Christ and his return to earth.[13]

Καὶ νῦν, τεκνία, μένετε ἐν αὐτῷ, "And now, little children, abide in him." With the use of the transitional conjunctions καὶ νῦν, John moves to a new section while connecting this new movement with what he has just said by repeating the command to abide (Brooke, 64; Burdick, 208; Strecker, 79).[14] This is an example of John's use of "hinge verses."[15] These are verses that "end one section and begin another by having themes of both" (Brown, 119). "The words both complete the previous verses and prepare the reader for an additional but complementary train of thought" (Akin, 128).[16] The challenge is to determine whether the verse belongs with the previous section or the following. In this case, this verse seems best connected to what follows because of the transitional conjunctions and John's use of τεκνία once again to address his readers. It appears that John's purpose in using these transitions is to demonstrate the interrelatedness of the ideas contained in both units of thought. For him, all these truths are interconnected. He does not compartmentalize spiritual truths, but sees them intertwined with each other. One is not true without the other. One cannot be practiced without the other. Orthodoxy and orthopraxy occur simultaneously. It is impossible to have one without the other. As will be shown in the chapters that follow, one cannot walk in the light without loving his brother, which he cannot do without believing the right things about Jesus, which he cannot do without honesty with God, and on and on. Thus these hinge verses communicate John's holistic approach to belief and practice.

John again addresses his readers as "little children" (τεκνία) by using the same term as in 2:1 (and 2:12), which he had changed to παιδία in 2:18 after introducing it in 2:14. This, too, serves to connect what John is about

---

13. Of note is the possible chiastic structure of the ἵνα clause (Brown, 381). It has Christ's appearing at the beginning and end of the clause with "confidence" and "not shrink back in shame" at its center.

14. This use of νῦν is logical, not temporal (BDF §442 (15); Brooke, 64; E. Malatesta, *Interiority and Covenant*, 226; Marshall, 165)

15. Lieu (119) calls 2:28 a "bridge" verse, "bringing one section to an end while provoking some of the ideas of what proves to be a new chain of thought."

16. He sees John's use of τεκνία here and παιδία in v. 18 forming an *inclusio*. However, the similarity of terms in English does not exist in Greek. Though they may be seen as synonyms, to form an *inclusio* would have more likely involved a repetition of the same term.

to say with what he has said up to this point (Akin, 128). Though a new thought is being introduced, it is not disconnected with what was already said. Additionally, this term of endearment expresses John's love and concern for his readers as he leaves a polemical section of his epistle and addresses pastoral concerns once again (Akin, 128; Burge, 143).[17]

John commands his readers to "abide," connecting this verse with what preceded and continuing the thought of verse 27 (Akin, 128; Brown, 379; Strecker, 79).[18] The command to "abide," a relational term, is predicated on obedience (2:4) and imitation of Christ's character and conduct (2:6) which is ultimately summed up in his command to love one another (2:7–8). "In him" again refers to Jesus (Brown, 379; contra Bultmann, 41, n. 31) and takes the readers back to Jesus' command in the Upper Room (John 15:4–10).[19] However, now another issue is introduced. Jesus is coming back.

Following the command to abide, John employs a purpose-result ἵνα clause to say that what follows is both the reason to abide as well as the result of abiding.[20]

ἵνα ἐὰν φανερωθῇ σχῶμεν παρρησίαν, "in order that when he should appear, we may have confidence." He continues his purpose/result clause with the conditional particle ἐὰν which is normally translated by "if." In this case ἐὰν is equivalent to ὅταν and so can be translated by "when" (Bruce 79).[21] The "uncertainty" of this "if" has to do with the timing of Jesus' arrival, not his coming (Akin, 128; Brooke, 65; Brown, 379; Burdick, 208; Lenski, 443; Lieu, 114; Marshall, 165; Plummer, 117; Westcott, 81; Yarbrough, 169).[22]

17. E. Malatesta, *Interiority and Covenant*, 226.

18. This use of μένετε is imperative (Brooke, 64; Westcott, 81) rather than indicative. Strecker (79) sees this imperative addressed to the "community" rather than its individual members.

19. Strecker (79) sees this as equivalent to Paul's "in Christ." However, with Paul being "in Christ" is a positional (justification) truth that impacts one's sanctification, while with John it is a conditional (sanctification) truth involving one's daily relationship with God as Father.

20. D. B. Wallace, *Grammar*, 473–74.

21. BDAG, 268; S. Zodhiates, "ἐάν *eán*," in *The Complete Word Study Dictionary: New Testament*, electronic ed.

22. Jesus uses ἐάν similarly in John 12:32 with regard to his crucifixion and in John 14:3 with regard to his preparing residences in heaven for his followers. In both instances the question was not whether Jesus would die or prepare a place, but the timing.

Thus John is expecting Jesus' return, but not guaranteeing it to his generation—or ours for that matter.

John connects the second coming of Jesus with his first by the repetition of φανερωθῇ, the same verb used in the epistle's prologue to describe Jesus' coming as eternal life incarnate (see comments on 1:3).[23] As a passive, φανερωθῇ may either be translated reflexively, Jesus reveals himself—or passively, he is revealed by the Father (Brown, 380). John doesn't use φανερόω of God the Father, but rather affirms the opposite: we have never seen him (John 1:18). Burdick (208) interprets the aorist to indicate the "suddenness" of Jesus' return, that it "will occur in a moment" rather than as a process. However, this may be a case of reading Paul's description of the rapture of the church and resurrection of believers (1 Cor 15:51–52; 1 Thess 4:15–18) into this passage. Here John does not especially address the suddenness of Jesus' coming but that when he comes he will be visibly present and we will respond to his presence in one of two ways: we may have confidence, or we may not. What determines that will be discussed in what follows.

The first possible response is now described in its positive sense. However, its contingency is seen in the subjunctive mood with ἐὰν. John moves from the second person plural imperative, μένετε ("you abide"), to the first person plural, σχῶμεν ("we may have"), to include himself with his readers and exclude himself and them from those who were trying to deceive them (Bruce, 79). By this he also implies that he *is* abiding and wants them to follow his example. John shows by this that his experience of confidence should be no different from that of his readers. He is inviting them to participate in the fellowship he has with the Father in the same way as he is presently experiencing it—by abiding.

Some take John's movement from second- to first-person plural to distinguish between his readers and the apostles. By this interpretation, John is saying that his confidence at Jesus' return is based on *their* abiding. If they (the apostles) abide, he will have confidence (Bruce, 79; Burdick, 208). Malatesta suggests a possible connection between this and John's purpose in

23. Φανερόω is used of Christ's incarnation within this epistle (1:2; 3:5, 8), John's Gospel (John 1:31; 3:11; 7:4), as well as with Paul (1 Tim 3:16) and Peter (1 Pet 1:20). It is used with respect to Jesus' post-resurrection appearances (John 21:1, 14; 1 John 3:2, 8). It also describes Jesus' return in this epistle (2:28; 3:2) as well as in Paul (Col 3:4).

1:4.[24] This would be similar to what Paul says in 1 Thess 2:19–20, where the Thessalonians are his "crown of rejoicing" in Christ's presence at his return. However, what John is saying by these changes of person should be seen differently. It is not his meeting with Christ that concerns him but theirs.

John is talking about how the believer will feel at the time he or she meets Jesus at his return. Kistemaker (289) sees this confidence being described by a constative aorist and so indicates a state of mind. However, the aorist subjunctive by its nature is undefined. Moreover, the context points to a point in time. The term John chooses, *παρρησία*, expresses the idea of courage and boldness, but in this context it could also be understood in the sense of calm assurance.[25] This same term is used in Heb 4:16 to describe the confidence/boldness we have in approaching God's throne of grace to receive mercy because of what Jesus has accomplished on our behalf. So this is not a brash boldness but a lack of nervousness that results from anticipating or fearing something negative. It is the calm assurance of those who know they will be accepted and treated with kindness by the one in whose presence they are about to stand. As Burdick (209) says well, *παρρησία* "presupposes saving faith, a close spiritual relationship, and faithful obedience to his commands."[26] John next makes clear that this will not be everyone's experience with the negative statement that follows.

καὶ μὴ αἰσχυνθῶμεν ἀπ' αὐτοῦ ἐν τῇ παρουσίᾳ αὐτοῦ, "and not shrink back in shame from him at his appearing." This is Johannine "futurist eschatology" as opposed to "realized eschatology."[27]

---

24. E. Malatesta, *Interiority and Covenant*, 227. He notes that "the plural highlights how the destinies of both [John and his readers] are interwoven."

25. BDAG, 781; H. Schlier, "*παρρησία*," *TDNT* 5:881–82; C. Spicq, "*παρρησία*," *TLNT* 3:62. Spicq notes that the basic sense of *παρρησία* expressed the idea of candor or expressing one's mind openly, whether before friends or superiors. This is the sense used with regard to Jesus' speaking openly (Mark 8:32; John 7:26; 11:14; 16:25, 29). From this the term can also be used to indicate confidence before someone, God, in the case of Heb 4:16 (*προσερχώμεθα οὖν μετὰ παρρησίας τῷ θρόνῳ τῆς χάριτος, ἵνα λάβωμεν ἔλεος καὶ χάριν εὕρωμεν εἰς εὔκαιρον βοήθειαν*) and 10:19 (*Ἔχοντες οὖν, ἀδελφοί, παρρησίαν εἰς τὴν εἴσοδον τῶν ἁγίων ἐν τῷ αἵματι Ἰησοῦ*). With John in his Epistle, *παρρησία* "is always a boldness, consisting of freedom and confidence, that allows one to present oneself before a superior without fear".

26. See also 1 John 3:21, 4:17 and 5:14 for his use of *παρρησία*.

27. C. F. D. Moule, "A Neglected Factor in the Interpretation of Johannine Eschatology," 158.

The opposite of confidence is embarrassment. As in 1:5 of this epistle, where John stated the same truth about God's holiness with antithetic parallelism, here he states the same truth about our appearing before Jesus. So what he is describing by the two is the goal of unashamed confidence in the presence of Jesus.

The term John uses to describe the believer's possible experience in Jesus' presence is αἰσχύνω. Its aorist form, though, can be viewed as either passive or middle voice. As a passive it communicates the sense of feeling shame or being put to shame, being disgraced.[28] As a middle voice verb in combination with ἀπ' αὐτοῦ, it can best be translated by "shrink away in shame" (Brooke, 66; Marshall, 166; Westcott, 83).[29] In Phil 1:20 Paul contrasts αἰσχύνω with παρρησία even as John does here, using them as antonyms (Johnson, 66).[30] This same sense of shame can be found in the OT in regard to the disobedient of the nation of Judah facing God's judgment (Brown, 381).[31]

Of note is John's inclusion of himself with the first person plural (Lieu, 116). He is not warning about losing one's salvation or being declared unregenerate by Christ at his appearing. Rather, he is describing the emotional response a believer will have when brought before Christ at his appearing. Every believer, including John, will have one of two responses to Jesus when they stand in his presence for the first time: the believer either will be comfortable in his presence or will be looking for somewhere to hide in humiliation.

---

28. E. Malatesta, *Interiority and Covenant*, 228.

29. BDAG, 30; R. Bultmann, "αἰσχύνω," *TDNT* 1:190. Harris (125) identifies John 3:17–18 and Rev 6:15–17 as indications that αἰσχύνω does not mean shame of believers, but unbelievers and notes Marshall (166, n.9). However, in neither instance is αἰσχύνω used. Additionally, John 3 describes the state of non-believers in this life. Rev 6 describes the response of rebellious mankind as they are experiencing divine wrath. In neither case are they standing before God as Judge. However, John is speaking of the experience of believers at the Bema seat judgment, and so passages such as 1 Cor 3:10–15 would be more indicative of the embarrassment a believer faces before Jesus. Ultimately, either sense describes a very uncomfortable experience for the disobedient Christian.

30. As Houlden (86) notes, in this passage "confidence" and "not being ashamed" are synonymous ideas.

31. He gives the examples of Isa 1:24, 29 and Jer 2L35–36. He further points to Prov 13:5 to demonstrate the same contrast between boldness and shame as with John here.

This is the only place where John uses the word παρουσία to describe Jesus' return.[32] His lack of explanation indicates his readers would have understood it (Plummer, 117). He may have chosen this word over φανερόω ("manifest"), which he has been using, because of its similarity in sound to παρρησία (Harris, 125; Williamson, 106). The play on sounds (paronomasia*) comes in that he is saying we may have παρρησία at his παρουσία. Παρουσία was originally used to describe "the arrival of a king, ruler, or official with open splendor, dignity, and respect" (Akin, 130). This is the sense of the term as it is used throughout the NT with regard to Christ's return.[33] In using this term here John would seem to have Jesus' return to set up his kingdom in view more than the rapture of the church, our gathering to him in the clouds (1 Thess 4:15–17). Subsequently, the context of this appearing and this judgment is Jesus' return as the righteous judge of the earth at the inauguration of his earthly rule. Still, the judgment alluded to here must be what has been labeled the Bema Seat judgment of Christ, described by Paul in Rom 14:10–13, 1 Cor 3:10–15 and 2 Cor 5:9–11. In this judgment every deed of every believer will be judged. In 1 Cor that judgment will evaluate the quality of their impact in the lives of others, what value they added to the foundation of Christ in each believer's life. Paul warns that some believers will find all of their works burned but will themselves be saved "as through fire," having lost everything. Further, he notes that believers who understand the significance of this judgment from Christ will "fear" him and persuade men to get right with him. John, in describing this same judgment does not distinguish Jesus' two comings (rapture and return), but points to the one judgment believers face. He next explains what will determine how one feels when facing Jesus for the first time as our righteous judge.[34]

32. A. Köstenberger, "The Deity of Christ in John's Letters and the Book of Revelation," 154.

33. A. Oepke, *TDNT* 5:859–61. New Testament uses of παρουσία include the idea of Paul's physical presence or arrival (2 Cor 10:10; Phil 1:26; 2:12), the arrival of Titus (2 Cor 7:6, 7), three of Paul's friends (1 Cor 16:17), the "lawless one" (2 Thess 2:9), the Day of the Lord (2 Pet 3:12), and of Jesus' coming (Matt 24:3, 27, 37, 39; 1 Cor 15:23; 1 Thess 2:19; 3:13; 4:15; 5:23; 2 Thess 2:1, 8; James 5:7, 8; 2 Pet 1:16; 3:4).

34. This is a different judgment from that described by Jesus in John 5:24 and John in John 3:18. In Rev 22:12, Jesus' promise of a sudden return includes the warning that he is coming to judge all men on the basis of their deeds. We see in Rev 1–3 that he stands as the Righteous Judge of the church, and thus all believers. The

2:29 John uses a third class conditional statement to describe the key to boldness and to set the stage for the following paragraph. He also uses this to introduce the theme of this second major movement in the epistle, namely, that God is righteous. Using both terms for "know," John distinguishes between what has been taught and what is experienced.

ἐὰν εἰδῆτε ὅτι δίκαιός ἐστιν, "If you know that he is righteous." John begins by indicating what they should know—not by experience but by instruction—that God is righteous. Using ἐὰν in place of the expected εἰ, John turns what one would expect to be a first class condition into a third class condition and implies that it is possible that they have not come to know the key truth that God is righteous.[35] His use of the second person plural focuses attention on his readers. Additionally, by separating himself from them, he is denying the possibility that he may not know this truth, though some of them may not yet know it. As Brown notes, John's purpose is "not to question the certainty that 'he is just,' but to turn the audience toward self-interrogation: Have they realized that he is just?" (Brown, 382).

Who is being referred to by the "He" in ἐστιν in the first ὅτι clause?[36] Four views are represented by most interpreters:[37]

---

rewards given by him to "overcomers" are based on their works. Paul identifies this same judgement as the Bema Seat judgment of believers wherein each will give an account to Jesus of his or her deeds (2 Cor 5:10). In 1 Cor 3:10–15, this judgment is described as a burning judgment that will evaluate the quality of one's works as they relate to building on the foundation of Christ in people's lives. There a believer may lose reward, but will be saved "as through fire." Thus it is not a judgment of condemnation as described in John 3:18 and 5:24.

35. BDF §372 (1 a) sees this use of ἐὰν as substituting for εἰ with the indicative of reality, and so could be translated with the sense of "just as, as soon as." This seems like a logical theological deduction than a requirement of the grammar. Brown's (382) understanding that it is designed to induce self-evaluation seems better.

36. Harris (127) quotes Brown's (382) complaint, "An occasional use of a proper name by the author would have been very helpful! One wonders whether the author reflects a Jewish reluctance to employ divine names." He then proffers another option, "that our author sees such a close relationship between Jesus Christ and God the Father that he is not always interested in clearly distinguishing between the two." I would add that John appears to employ ambiguity as a rhetorical device, thus his use of double entendre*, and he probably learned it from listening to Jesus.

37. Noting the difficulty posed by this sentence, Bultmann (45) proposes two sources behind the text. If that were the case, this would be an example of poor redacting. With John's pattern of utilizing what we consider awkward grammar elsewhere, and his propensity for ambiguity, we need not look to sources to explain

(1) God the Father is seen as the One who is righteous (Bruce, 79; Lenski, 445; Lieu, 119; Plummer, 119; Stott, 117).[38] The arguments for this follow. He is called "righteous" in 1:9 and John 17:25 (Brown, 382). However, so is Jesus (2:1). God the Father is the focus of the immediate context of the second half of the sentence and so "avoids a harsh transition from the first part of the verse to the latter part, where the antecedent is almost surely God."[39] Houlden (87–88) points to 3:9; 4:7; and 5:1 and 4 as indictors that the final pronoun refers to God the Father. The pattern of αὐτοῦ throughout the epistle indicates God the Father should be in view here (Law, 384). This sense makes the transition to the following verses smoother (Stott, 117). Elsewhere believers are consistently called children of God, never of Christ (Thomas, 224).

(2) John refers to Jesus here as righteous (Brooke, 68–69; Bultmann, 45; Grayston, 97–98; Harris, 127; Johnson, 66–67; Klauck, 172; Marshall, 167; Smith, 75). Several arguments have been given to advance this interpretation.[40] Christ has been called "righteous" in 2:1 (Brown, 382).[41] Christ is the subject in verse 28, and John does not use a personal pronoun in this verse

---

his strategy. As Lieu (119) notes, grammatical "inconsistency is typical of this author's style."

38. D. E. Hiebert, "An Expositional Study of 1 John—Part 5: An Exposition of 1 John 2:29–3:12," 199; U. C. von Wahlde ("The Stereotyped Structure and the Puzzling Pronouns of 1 John 2:28–3:10," 322–29) argues, first, that this section of John's epistle contains four parallel contrasting statements that all describe the individual's relationship with God the Father rather than Jesus. Second, he sees these statements following a pattern of "stereotyped" arguments found in the apocalyptic literature of the Qumran community. The downfall of his argument comes when he notes that this "stereotyped" material that relates to God the Father is interspersed with statements that clearly relate to Christ. This is not the case with the Qumran texts. And, his argument that John "used this common pattern of apocalyptic argument ... but modified it in order to include references to the role of Jesus" is unconvincing. Similarity does not mean sameness. The apparent mixture would argue more for unfamiliarity with Qumran more than intentional alteration of their technique.

39. U. C. von Wahlde, "The Stereotyped Structure and the Puzzling Pronouns of 1 John 2:28–3:10," 320.

40. Those listed by U. C. von Wahlde ("The Stereotyped Structure and the Puzzling Pronouns of 1 John 2:28–3:10," 320) are given without reference, while others are identified by their contributors.

41. U. C. von Wahlde, "The Stereotyped Structure and the Puzzling Pronouns of 1 John 2:28–3:10," 320.

to indicate a change of subjects (Westcott, 83). This verse is similar to 3:7, where ἐκεῖνος clearly refers to Jesus (Brown, 382).[42] The three uses of *αὐτός* in v. 28 all referred to Jesus (Brown, 382; Marshall, 167). The use of *αὐτός* at the end of the verse may indicate a change of antecedents from Jesus to God the Father. A change in subjects is clear in 3:1, where the Father is identified as the subject (Westcott, 83). Later, in 5:1 there is a similar change from Christ to God the Father. However, though Christians are described as being born of the Spirit and born of God, they are never described as being born of Christ (Kistemaker, 288).[43]

(3) John may again be purposefully ambiguous and choosing to refer to both (Smalley, 133; Strecker, 82).

(4) The first refers to Jesus while the second refers to God the Father (Law, 384). John uses a similar change from Christ to God in 5:1.

The righteousness of God is something John's readers know absolutely, by instruction (Brooke, 67–68; Lenski, 446; Plummer, 119; Stott, 117–18; Thomas, 222). John uses *γινώσκω* in the following clause for what they know by experience. "Knowledge which is absolute (εἰδῆτε) becomes the basis of knowledge which is realized in observation (*γινώσκετε*)" (Westcott, 82). Though some recent scholars question the distinction between *οἶδα* and *γινώσκω*, it still seems best to recognize these synonyms are not identical and are often used by John with their nuances intended (Burdick, 227).[44] This use of the two within the same sentence is a good illustration of those nuances being utilized by him.

γινώσκετε ὅτι καὶ πᾶς ὁ ποιῶν τὴν δικαιοσύνην ἐξ αὐτοῦ γεγέννηται, "you also know that everyone who practices righteousness has been born from him." The apodosis* now affirms what can be known by experience. Those who do not conceive that God is righteous do not "know" this either. Those who understand that God is righteous also recognize this truth.

John's use of *γινώσκετε* here again points to experiential knowledge, the content of which is described in the following *ὅτι* clause. By experience

42. U. C. von Wahlde, "The Stereotyped Structure and the Puzzling Pronouns of 1 John 2:28–3:10," 320. The other uses of ἐκεῖνος are 2:7; 3:5, 7, 16; and 4:17.

43. Smith (75) sees the believer described here as being born of Christ rather than God.

44. For example, Harris (126–27) sees the movement from *οἶδα* to *γινώσκω* to be an example of "Johannine stylistic variation" and that he intends "no apparent difference in meaning" between the two.

they have seen that those born of God are characterized by a practice of righteousness.

John may be using γινώσκετε in either of two moods, indicative or imperative:

(1) As an indicative, it states what they know (Brown, 382–83; Harris, 126; Lenski, 446; Plummer, 119). This is supported by the pattern of similar indicatives (though involving οἶδα) in 2:20 and 21 (Plummer, 69; Brown 383). John's depiction of knowledge in this epistle is that it is something already known (Brown, 383). Since 2:28 is an imperative, this verse provides the reason for that command and so would naturally be in the indicative (Westcott, 82).

(2) It is an imperative for the readers to act on what they know (Law, 384; Westcott, 82–83). The presence of impvs. on either side of this argues for it functioning as one in the flow of thought (Brown, 382; Westcott, 82).[45] Thus, it is more logical for John to be instructing them than to pause between impvs. to say they have already done what he is commanding (Westcott, 82–83). The sense of γινώσκω is brought out better with an imperative than an indicative (Law, 384). However, John's repeated reminders to his readers that they already know the truth mitigates against this. Therefore, it is better to see γινώσκετε as an indicative gnomic present that is simply stating a fact.

John moves again from the 1 or 2 to the 3 to describe a kind of person. Using an articular present participle, he describes positively the person who "does" righteousness (πᾶς ὁ ποιῶν τὴν δικαιοσύνην). He includes the adjective πᾶς to indicate that he is stating a principle rather than solely describing his readers or himself. This use of the participle seems best to be viewed with a gnomic or customary sense. This is a kind of person. John is not using it in the progressive sense, in that while someone is doing righteousness he can know. Rather, he is describing the character of the person.

What he affirms is that people exhibit their spiritual parentage by their conduct. Righteous character indicates righteous birth. The righteous person has been "born from him" (ἐξ αὐτοῦ). This is the first of ten references to birth in this epistle and forms a new theme that will be developed by John.

45. Burdick (228) rejects this argument as "purely arbitrary" because "nothing in the text demands a series of imperatives."

Who is the referent of αὐτοῦ? Harris (127) argues for God the Father on the basis that John's other uses of ἐξ αὐτοῦ γεγέννηται clearly refer to the Father and never to Jesus. These include John 1:13; 1 John 3:9, 4:7, 5:1, 5:4, and 5:18. Against this is how it seems to disrupt the transition from Jesus in the first half of the sentence. He then suggests (128) that there is with John a measure of "interchangeability here between the Father and the Son, and this is certainly possible within Johannine Christology." He notes Thomas's confession in John 20:28 as an example of this. Again, here αὐτοῦ has God as its antecedent (Bultmann, 45; Johnson, 66).[46]

This righteousness "is not a condition but the consequence of being God's child" (Brown, 384). Righteous conduct reveals one's spiritual parent is righteous as well. This concept will be the basis of further discussion in chapter 3. John's use of γεγέννηται here does indicate spiritual birth, that the person is born again, but it need not be John's focus.[47] As a perfect of resultant state,[48] it focuses our attention on the continuing experience of that birth rather than the birth itself. In other words, he is not making this a test of life as much as an indication of parentage. This is not a test he is applying to his readers but a principle he is establishing that will be the basis of further discussion in the verses that follow.

John is *not* teaching perfectionism or the impossibility of apostasy in this passage. For example, Akin interprets this statement on the basis of the Calvinist doctrine of perseverance. "This specific righteousness is a distinct characteristic of the one who has been born of God. Likewise, it is a continual, life-characterizing righteousness that comes from having a personal, saving knowledge of him who is absolutely righteous" (Akin, 131). This

---

46. Brown (384) notes, "Grammatically there is no way to know whether *autos* refers to Christ as did the three uses of *autos* in 2:28, or is being used after the preceding reference to Christ ... to change the agency to God. A third possibility is that *autos* refers imprecisely to both Christ and God the Father. ... Since there is never an instance of *gennan* (passive) with the *ek* governing Christ and there are 8 instances with *ek* governing God, almost all scholars take *autos* here to be God."

47. Bultmann (45–46) notes that the concept of "born of God" (γεννηθῆναι ἐκ τοῦ θεοῦ) cannot be located in the writings of any of the mystery religions, and so likely has a Jewish source. In contrast, Schnackenburg (181) still argues for John borrowing his terminology from the mystery religions or from Gnosticism. Burdick (229) notes that it is more likely that the Gnostics borrowed John's terminology than he theirs.

48. B. M. Fanning, *Verbal Aspect in New Testament Greek*, 291–95.

has already been denied in the first chapter. All believers are sinful and in need of continual cleansing by their advocate, Jesus, who is our propitiation. John is *not* saying that every regenerate person always practices righteousness. Rather, he is affirming that "family likeness" is revealed by righteous conduct (Bruce, 79; Westcott, 83). Hodges begins well by noting that reproducing God's righteous nature indicates birth from him. Even so, he misses the point by adding the caveat that reproducing God's righteous nature "to any extent" indicates it (Hodges, 127). John's use of the articular participle, "he who does," does not imply "slightly" or "sometimes." It indicates "is characterized by" and so describes a life characterized by righteousness. This righteousness is identified as something understood by John's readers by his use of the article. He is not talking about righteousness in general, but a particular kind of righteousness, that characteristic of God (Johnson, 66).

Finally, what John has affirmed in the positive, that we can see those born of God from their righteous conduct, need not be true in the reverse. He is not saying by this that those who do not practice righteousness are not born of God. Yes, that could be argued by some as an implication of the text. For those who see 3:10 as prescriptive rather than a part of John's literary dualism, this converse of this statement would then mean that one who does not practice righteousness is unregenerate. However, that implication may not be an intended meaning of the text at this point. Only the positive aspect is intended to be in view, and that negative element is reserved for later in the development of John's argument. Further, as will be noted in 3:10, the issue of failing to love one's "brother" indicates John has loving and unloving believers rather than regenerate (loving) and unregenerate (unloving) people in view.

3:1 This verse uses the metaphor of God being our "Father," as taught by Jesus, to express the privileged position every believer has in his "family." This will serve as the basis of the discussion of righteousness in the following paragraphs.[49]

---

49. Burge (143–44) follows the view of others in seeing four pairs of antithetical descriptions with the "everyone who" construction from 2:29 to 3:10. He posits that 3:1–3 is a parenthetical statement that interrupts the flow but is not part of the symmetry of those four "antithetical pairs." This should warn us against attempting to build arguments from any proposed construct involving those pairs, such as a chiasm or other conceptual framework. We should not miss the antithesis of

ἴδετε ποταπὴν ἀγάπην δέδωκεν ἡμῖν ὁ πατήρ, "Behold what kind of love the Father has given to us." The command to "behold," addressed once again to John's readers, is a call to "take note." In a sense this serves as an exclamation more than a command (Brooke, 80; Schnackenburg, 167). Though present imperatives often carry the nuance of "continuing" to do something, this use is simply a general command, something they should do. Also, his choice of the second person plural over the first person plural consciously excludes John and implies he does it.

John begins his exclamation by replacing the expected interrogative τίς with ποταπὴν.[50] When he says "what kind" or "what manner" (ποταπὴν), he calls attention to more than the presence of God's love but to its expression.[51] This term is used seven times throughout the NT and always communicates a sense of astonishment or surprise (Akin, 132; Brooke, 80; Smalley, 140).[52] This is something "visible" to the believer, in that it can be known and should be seen. That "seeing" will be explained further in what follows. However in the immediate context, it is the privilege of the position that he exults in.

---

each pair, certainly. However, we also should not see more than John intended. This pause in the pairs indicates more than he is not drawing our attention to any special structure composed of those pairs, but rather is still working through his message, wherein these three verses fit in the flow rather than represent a pause that disrupts the flow. Smalley (140) identifies what he views as a chiasm of ideas involving the use of παρουσίᾳ in 2:28 and 3:2 with "new birth" in 2:29 (ἐξ αὐτοῦ γεγέννηται) and 3:1 (τέκνα θεοῦ). As can be seen, various literary structures can be proposed depending on what elements are highlighted by the exegete, and so we must remain suspicious of all unless there is compelling evidence.

50. BDF §298 (3).

51. Burge (145) states that ποταπὴν literally "means 'of what country' and thus implies that God's love is so unusual, so unearthly, so unique to our experience, that we barely expect its result." However, though that may have been its original sense, in Koiné it was simply an exclamation (BDAG, 856). This can be found in A.T. Robertson's *Word Pictures in the New Testament* (1 Jn 3:1). However, as H. A. Virkler (*Hermeneutics*, 100) warns us, there are two disadvantages to studying the etymology of NT words: " (1) the historical roots of words are often conjectural, and (2) the meanings of words often change radically with the passage of time, so that little or no apparent connection remains between the original meaning of the root word and its meaning a few hundred years later."

52. Matt 8:27; Mark 13:1 (2x); Luke 1:29; 7:39; 2 Pet 3:11; 1 John 3:1. Westcott (95) observes that this term is both rare in the NT and absent from the LXX.

The perfect tense δέδωκεν points to an act of God in the past and to the permanence of his love (Akin, 133; Brooke, 80; Williamson, 110).[53] Lieu (123) observes well that this reminds us that our status as God's children "is not earned but is a gift, an act of unmerited and unimaginable generosity, founded not on any obligation felt by God nor on any expectation, but on love." The effects of God's given love continue to the present as a permanent reality in the life of the believer (contra Brown, 387).[54] This privileged position is not passing, whether or not the believer is in fellowship with God. Furthermore, the nature of this relationship is emphasized by John when he reminds us that God is our "Father." By this he draws attention to God as both the giver of this love and as the One who keeps it a permanent experience in the lives of each of his children (Akin, 133). He places ὁ πατήρ at the end of the sentence for emphasis as well as preparing us for what is to follow (Brooke, 80; Burdick, 230; Smalley, 141).

ἵνα τέκνα θεοῦ κληθῶμεν, καὶ ἐσμέν, "that we should be called children of God, and we are." God's love is given in terms of relationship; we are children. This ἵνα clause has been understood as either (1) a purpose clause (Plummer, 120; Westcott, 96; Yarbrough, 175), (2) or an epexegetical clause (Brooke, 80; Brown, 388; Bultmann, 47; Grayston, 100; Harris, 129; Lenski, 449; Smalley, 141). As a purpose clause it would indicate that our being made God's children was the goal of his love. However, nowhere in Scripture is it ever indicated that God loved men so they could be his children (Brooke, 80). As an epexegetical clause, it explains what God's love involves as it relates to us.

To be called God's children indicates a family relationship that is perfect. John is picking up a theme from the prologue of his Gospel (John 1:12–13) and using it to describe his readers.[55] Of note is his change again

53. Brown rejects the idea of permanence and sees this perfect functioning as an aor. This is likely a good example of one's theology impacts one's understanding of the grammar.

54. Thompson (87) concurs.

55. G. K. Beale and D. A. Carson (*Commentary on the New Testament Use of the Old Testament* 421–22) observe: "The reference to believers' right to become 'children of God' in 1:12 clearly builds on the Old Testament characterization of Israel as God's children (Deut. 14:1; see also the reference to Israel as God's son and firstborn in Exod. 4:22; cf. 1 John 3:1–2). On the heels of the oblique reference to the rejection of the Word by 'his own' (i.e., the Jews) in 1:11, however, the reference to children of God 'born not of natural descent ... but born of God' in

from the 2 to the first person plural to include himself in the category of "children."

John uses τέκνα here, repeating the term used in 2:1, 12, and 28 to describe his readers. This reflects his use of the term in John 1:12 and 11:52. Where Paul uses both τέκνα and υἱὸς to describe Christians as God's children, John reserves the designation of υἱὸς solely for Jesus (Brown, 388; Grayston, 100; Harris, 129; Lieu, 123; Moody, 59; Strecker, 86).

The final clause, καὶ ἐσμέν, is separate from the ἵνα, as evidenced by its being in the indicative rather than subjunctive. As a result, it stands as a separate declaration, "and we are."[56] Grayston (100) sees this exclamation by John as polemical. However, the context is pastoral, so this should not be seen as an attack on false teachers but an exclamation designed to excite his readers to the truth of what has just been said.

διὰ τοῦτο ὁ κόσμος οὐ γινώσκει ἡμᾶς, ὅτι οὐκ ἔγνω αὐτόν, "Because of this the world does not know us, because it did not know him." John's use of διὰ τοῦτο with the following ὅτι clause draws our attention to what follows (Brooke, 81; Brown, 392; Smalley, 142) rather than what precedes (Bultmann, 48; Burdick , 231; Law, 386; Marshall, 171, n. 25; Lenski, 450; Plummer, 121; Strecker, 87; Westcott, 96–97; Yarbrough,176),[57] or to both (Grayston, 101). This pattern can be seen in John's six other uses of this construction (John 5:16, 19; 8:47; 10:17; 12:18, 30). When it is not followed by a ὅτι clause, it refers to what precedes (John 1:31; 6:65; 7:222; 9:23; 12:27; 13:11; 15:19; 16:15; 19:11; 1 John 4:5; 3 John 10) (Harris, 130).

What is the impact of being God's child? Being identified with God leads to alienation from the world, just as Jesus told the Eleven in the upper room (John 15:18–25). That is the sense of the world not knowing those who are privileged to be called God's children.[58] It is not that the world

---

1:13 distinguishes between an illegitimate, presumptuous claim of divine sonship based on physical descent and true divine sonship based on faith in the name of God's Messiah (1:12; cf. 8:41–47; 11:51–52)." John takes this idea, introduced in his Gospel, and develops its implications further in these next verses.

56. Brooke (80) notes its awkwardness but then observes that "it is in the author's style." See textual notes on 3:1.

57. Marshall holds his view with the caveat, "there is not a lot of difference in meaning between the two ways of understanding the sentence."

58. Bultmann (48) sees this as a "foil" for the previous statement of our being children of God. Strecker (87) notes well, "The dualism of community and world cannot be more clearly expressed."

does not recognize that we are God's children, but that we, as his children, experience the world's rejection of God in its treatment of us (Lieu, 124). John's choice of γινώσκω for knowledge indicates an experiential, relational knowledge. In short, the world relates to believers in exactly the same way it relates to God: it does not!

John finishes by giving the reason the world does not *know* believers who are privileged to be called children of God. The world does not know them because it has not "known" (aorist) him. The antecedent of αὐτόν is taken one of three ways:

(1) It refers to Jesus (Bultmann, 48; Burdick, 231; Law, 386; Painter, 218; Ryrie, 1018; Stott, 118). John 1:10 uses this same expression to refer to Jesus. The same terminology is used in the immediate context of 3:6 to refer to Jesus. The aorist ἔγνω "points to a particular point in past time when the world did not know him" (Burdick, 231). The pronoun refers to Jesus throughout 1 John prior to this use (Law, 386).[59] Jesus has not yet been manifested to the world, though he was to his disciples (Law, 386).

(2) Its referent is God the Father (Brooke, 81; Brown, 392; Bruce, 87; Lenski, 451, Smalley, 143).[60] This would agree with what Jesus says of the world in John 17:25 (Brown, 392). God the Father is in focus in the immediate context, both before and after (Brown, 392). In these verses John is moving conceptually from God to Jesus as he had from Jesus to God in 2:29 (Smalley, 143). Christians are born from God the Father, not from Christ the Son (Brown, 392).

(3) it may be or either or both (Akin, 132). There appears to be no reason to look beyond its immediate antecedent. John is referring to God the Father toward Whom the world is hostile, and as a result, toward his children as well as his Son.

3:2 Our nature as God's children will be revealed when we see Jesus at his return. This verse moves from the reality of our family identity to its eschatological significance.

Ἀγαπητοί, νῦν τέκνα θεοῦ ἐσμεν, "Beloved, now we are children of God." Addressing his readers as "beloved," as he had in 2:7, John continues his

59. The examples he provides includes 2:8, 12, 27, and 28.
60. Or God in Christ (Westcott, 97).

instruction to the children of God (Brooke, 81).[61] This reminds us that John is now addressing his pastoral concerns rather than continuing his polemic against the false teachers.[62] He has also changed his focus from that of a father instructing his children to a fellow child of God (Smalley, 144).[63]

John begins his declaration with the temporal adverb νῦν. This is the only place he uses it in his epistle without καὶ. This use of νῦν and the present indicative looks at their present state and sets the stage for what is about to be said along with the contrasts to be developed in the following verses (Akin, 135; Burdick, 232; Smalley, 144).[64] Again, including himself, John repeats their privileged status as God's children (τέκνα θεοῦ). This repetition, rather than being an allusion back to his Gospel, should be seen as doubly emphatic.[65] Τέκνα θεοῦ is not only in an emphatic position each time John uses it, but its repetition is equally emphatic. He wants his readers to grasp fully their place in God's family and to realize its significance.

καὶ οὔπω ἐφανερώθη τί ἐσόμεθα, "and it has not yet been revealed what we will be." Using the coordinating conjunction *kai* to join the two clauses, John next reveals the difference between his readers' present condition and their future expectation.[66] The two clauses together express the now-and-not-yet aspect of their status as children of God and states what they "are" while raising the question of what they "will be." This should not be misread as realized eschatology but rather seen as futurist eschatology.[67] John says we are presently "children of God." We will someday be something

---

61. Bultmann (48) sees John's use of "beloved" to "accentuate" the significance of their relationship to God as His children. This is true to an extent, however, John's use of this term to address his readers elsewhere in the epistle (2:7; 3:21; 4:1, 7, 11), and so outside of this conceptual context, would indicate otherwise.

62. Strecker (88) sees this as a "parenetic and paracletic" address.

63. Stott (123) sees this reflecting the sense that John loves those loved by God.

64. BDAG, 681; G. Stählin, "νῦν," *TDNT* 4:1107. Stählin sees this use of νῦν as a "proleptic first stage of the last things." As such there is a "twofold fulfillment" of our participation in the divine life while we wait for its future consummation.

65. W. R. Cook, "Hamartiological Problems in First John," 253.

66. Burdick (232) sees this καὶ as adversative.

67. Barker (330) takes this to mean it is a "'mystery' to be revealed only at the last time." The sense of mystery in the NT has to do with the previously undisclosed plan of God (Rom 16:25–26; 1 Cor 2:7–8; Eph 3:3–9; Col 1:26–27) rather than the future transformation of his children (1 Cor 15:51–54).

more. This something more is yet to be revealed, or made manifest, in the future when we see Jesus face-to-face for the first time.

The aorist passive ἐφανερώθη lacks a clear subject. This same term was used in 2:28 to refer to Jesus. However, it need not here. It seems better to see the phrase τί ἐσόμεθα serving as its subject (Harris, 131; Kistemaker, 296; Smalley, 144–45).[68] However, why the aorist passive, since it looks at what will be revealed in the future? This intensifies the connection with verse 28 and the aorist subjunctive φανερωθῇ. Also, matching the earlier use of the same term in the same aorist tense, the parallel must be intended. His point is that the future arrival of Jesus will reveal what we have become in this life. Akin (135) states this truth well when he says this verb "guarantees that what we will be will be publicly displayed." When Jesus makes himself visibly present as our judge to whom we will give an account, our status as God's children will be visibly demonstrated as well . More will come to light than just that.

οἴδαμεν ὅτι ἐὰν φανερωθῇ, ὅμοιοι αὐτῷ ἐσόμεθα, "We know that whenever it is revealed, we will be like him." John now affirms what he and his readers know by revelation and instruction but cannot yet know by experience, thus his switch to οἶδα with the ὅτι of content.[69] These are things they already know from instruction previously received (Akin, 135; Brooke, 82; Strecker, 88). He also includes himself once again (Yarbrough, 178). This is something John looks forward to, along with his readers.[70]

The referent of the verb φανερόω has been understood variously by modern scholars:

---

68. This is an example of the interrogative pronoun τίς being used as a predicate, in this case utilizing its neuter form, τί (BDF §299), within a subject clause.

69. Bultmann (48) describes this use of οἶδα as "an appeal to the Christian tradition."

70. Rensberger, (88) proposes that the "realized eschatology" of the Gospel of John "does not speak of a future state for believers that will be higher than their present one as God's children." I would propose that his observation is correct, but not because of "realized eschatology." Rather, in the Gospel John focuses primarily on the experience of eternal life in the life of the believer. It is something possessed and experienced in the present (John 7:37–39; 10:10) that is tied to the person of Jesus (John 11:25) in the same way as expressed in the prologue of this epistle. However, where this epistle focuses on the question of how to experience it, the Gospel focuses on the nature of eternal life, what it is we are experiencing. Thus, John's focus is different and one would not expect to find him describing those future realities.

(1) It could refer to be Jesus (Akin, 135; Bultmann, 48; Smalley, 146), and so serves as a reference to his second coming. The context of 2:28 would seem to support this (Bultmann, 48; Schnackenburg, 170; Westcott, 98). Burdick (233) lists these arguments: "The context shows that John is laying stress on the appearances of Christ." Verse three refers "to Christ as the two pronouns αὐτῷ and ἐκεῖνος make clear." Additionally, it is more likely "that John would identify the time of the believer's complete Christ likeness as being the second coming rather than the time when 'it is disclosed.'"

(2) It could refer to God the Father (Bruce, 85–87; Grayston, 101; Strecker, 88).

(3) It refers to the earlier subject, τί ἐσόμεθα, and so should be translated "when it is revealed" (Brown, 394; Rensberger, 88). This is supported by the immediate context of the previous clause, with the subject of the previous φανερόω being τί ἐσόμεθα.[71] The repetition of the verb makes it highly probable, and more logical conceptually, to see its subject as the same (Harris, 132).[72]

Interpreters have taken ὅμοιοι αὐτῷ to refer to God the Father (Brooke, 82–83; Marshall, 172, n. 29; Stott, 124; Westcott, 98) or to God the Son (Akin, 135; Bultmann, 49).[73] However, in the immediate context, τί ἐσόμεθα is the subject of the previous φανερόω (Brown, 394; Lenski, 452; Plummer, 119–20; Rensberger, 88). Additionally, both pronouns used of Christ (αὐτός and ἐκεῖνος) are conspicuously absent (Burdick, 233). With the repetition of the same verb (though a different form), and the absence of a stated subject, initially it seems better to see its implied subject as a continuation of the earlier thought (Harris, 132). However, it is Jesus who is consistently described as appearing rather than God the Father. Additionally, the following clauses and coming use of ἐκεῖνος in verse 3 argues for this being a reference to Jesus.

The believer's future destiny is to be like Jesus. Even so, in what way will we be "like him"? Is this a metaphysical change or moral? The sense of ὅμοιος

71. Brooke (82) observes that this is "the more natural interpretation so far as grammar is concerned."

72. Though he argues for Jesus as its referent, Schnackenburg (170) admits the context favors "it."

73. For example, Bultmann (49) points to John 17:1, 5, and 24 as evidence that Jesus' glorious return is in view. Thompson (89) chooses the generic "God" for the "ambiguous pronoun."

is that of sharing the same nature, but can also indicate similarity. When used with the dative of the person being compared to, it implies a similarity between the two but not especially identicalness (Akin, 137; Smalley, 146; Burdick, 234).[74] Thus Schneider observes that "ὅμοιος is linked with an insight which is important in Johannine theology, namely, that divine sonship is not the highest stage in the being and nature of the Christian. Fulfillment is reached only when Christians are like Christ."[75] Though Scripture does not give all the details of our future existence, it does reveal that our heavenly bodies will be like Jesus' (Phil 3:21). Additionally, we will experience immortality and be free of our sin nature. Westcott speaks of this in terms of a restored divine image (Westcott, 98). This makes sense with what follows. As will be clarified in the next verse, this likeness will be moral rather than metaphysical. What John is *not* saying is that we will become gods or divine in nature. This likeness does not make us identical, just similar to Jesus, and only in certain aspects. Those aspects will be clarified below.

ὅτι ὀψόμεθα αὐτὸν καθώς ἐστιν, "because we shall see him just as he is." John now reveals why the children of God will become like Jesus when he appears.[76] This is Johannine futurist eschatology rather than realized eschatology (Strecker, 88).[77] We will see Jesus. Using the future form of ὁράω, John connects back to the prologue and his own experience of seeing Jesus personally (1:1). He once more includes himself among those who will someday see Jesus.[78] However, now the seeing will be different. As we know from Rev 1, we will see Jesus in his divine glory. However, here John says that we will see him "just as he is." At his appearing, believers will see Jesus in his true nature because their spiritual as well as physical eyes will be fully open. This vision of Christ will change each one. We will become like him

74. BDAG, 706.

75. J. Schneider, "ὅμοιος," *TDNT* 5:188.

76. This second ὅτι clause is causal and so explanatory. It explains further what is meant by ἐσόμεθα (Brooke, 83; Burdick, 234; Law, 388; and Marshall, 172–73; Plummer, 122; Smalley, 147)

77. C. F. D. Moule, "A Neglected Factor in the Interpretation of Johannine Eschatology," 158–59.

78. Passages that use ὁράω to describe seeing Jesus' return include Mark 13:26, Luke 3:6, Heb 9:28 and 12:14, and Rev 22:4. Additionally, Jesus spoke of those in his generation seeing the kingdom (Mark 9:1) or seeing those who enter the kingdom while they are excluded (Luke 13:28).

in terms of what we see in him and in ourselves. What we will come to recognize fully is that Jesus is morally pure, absolutely righteous. At that moment, we too will become so.

3:3 Morally pure living is the response of those who hope to become like Jesus at his return.[79] This description of Jesus must be seen in light of his ministry to believers in 1:7 and 2:2 as well as defining further what "light" means in the first chapter. Now, as John develops his message under the theme of God's righteousness, Jesus' moral purity is brought to the fore as it relates to the believer at his return. As Stott (124) observes well, "John's reason for writing about the return of Christ and our final state is not theological but ethical."

καὶ πᾶς ὁ ἔχων τὴν ἐλπίδα ταύτην ἐπ' αὐτῷ ἁγνίζει ἑαυτόν, "And everyone who has this hope in him purifies himself." John begins this sentence with the continuative conjunction *καὶ*, connecting this following point closely to what was just said about being like Jesus. Thus he is drawing the connection between those eschatological truths and practical living (Akin, 137).

This is the second of fourteen occurrences of *πᾶς ὁ* plus the participle in 1 John (here plus 2:23, 29; 3:3, 4, 6 (twice), 9, 10, 15; 4:7; 5:1 (twice), 4, 18). Returning to the 3, John is stating a truth that applies not only to him and his readers but to all believers (Akin, 137; Strecker, 91).[80] This is a principle that applies to all mankind, in fact, as they respond to revelation about the person and character of Christ.[81]

This is the sole use of "hope" in all of John's literature.[82] Still, it was not an idea foreign to him or the early church. The biblical concept of hope is that it is a positive emotional response to an expectation. With the emphatic

---

79. Marshall (173) aptly reminds us that "doctrine has moral implications."
80. Westcott (100) calls this a "universal form of expression (πᾶς ὁ ἔχων)" rather than "simply descriptive (ὁ ἔχων)." Brooke (83) observes that in the Gospel and epistle, πᾶς "generally sets aside the claims of some party or other who claimed special privileges or exemptions for themselves."
81. Though Hodges (130–31) sees this addressing justification, it is better to see it as an issue of sanctification. The active verb with the reflexive pronoun indicates that this is something accomplished by the believer whereas the holiness imputed to the believer at the time of his or her justification is accomplished by God alone (Rom 4:5–6). Though John ("sanctifies himself") and Paul ("reckon yourself"; Rom 6:11–14) use different terminology, they affirm the same truth.
82. The verb form does occur in John 5:45 with regard to the Jews.

pronoun ταύτην, John indicates that the hope referred to is not Jesus (contra Bruce, 88; Smalley, 149; and Yarbrough, 180), but what has been said in the previous verse (Burdick, 235).[83] The Christian's hope is based on being called a child of God (v. 1). It is the expectation of becoming like Jesus when we see him for the first time (v. 2). This is much like when the author of Hebrews says, "Looking unto Jesus, the author and finisher of our faith" (Heb 12:2). It is the same principle as Paul presents in Col 3:1–4. We are to set our eyes on the things above, where Christ is seated. When one focuses on Jesus, he or she will seek to be more like him. Consequently, since Jesus is absolutely morally pure, so too will the believer whose eyes are fixed on him wish to be. "There is nothing within the believer that creates hope and security for the future. The foundation for hope, now and forever, is Christ alone" (Akin, 138).

The one who expects to become like Christ at his appearing is expecting to become pure like him. The change that will occur is moral and spiritual, not physical. John tells us that the one with hope, who anticipates becoming like Christ, purifies himself. His use of ἁγνίζω with the reflexive pronoun indicates that this is a work done *by* the believer, not *to* the believer. This single use of the term by John likely draws its meaning from the OT background of cultic purification required of every worshipper of God (Strecker, 91–92). Though John has not forgotten that it is Jesus' blood that cleanses and not our works (1:7), he is affirming by this that the believer does participate in his or her sanctification (Akin, 138). Purity is not automatic and does not come by accident. It must be intentional on the part of every Christian. It is impossible apart from Jesus' work on the cross on our behalf (Williamson, 113). However, as was clearly taught in 1:9, experiencing purity requires action on the part of the believer in dependence on God to act in response to confession.[84] Now John affirms that this purity,

---

83. D. E. Hiebert, "An Expositional Study of 1 John—Part 5: An Exposition of 1 John 2:29–3:12," 206. Bultmann (49) sees this use of hope as parenetic rather than eschatological. Strecker (91) sees it as eschatological. Yarbrough (180) identifies a third view by Cassirer (H. W. Cassirer, *God's New Covenant: A New Translation*. Grand Rapids: Eerdmans, 1989) that the sense of "before" from ἐπί with the dative would make this statement equivalent to ἐνώπιον or ἐναντίον, which is supported by BDAG (363).

84. Jesus' words to Peter in the upper room reflect this truth. When He said, "He who is bathed needs only to wash *his* feet, but is completely clean," He was

graciously given by God to those who honestly confess their sins, will only be sought by those whose attention is focused on the character of Christ. The response of hope, the joyful anticipation of being made like Christ, is to act on the basis of that future reality in the present. The one whose hope is in Christ's return pursues purity in the present because he or she recognizes that as our future destiny. The hopeful believer wants to become now what he or she will be then.[85]

καθὼς ἐκεῖνος ἁγνός ἐστιν, "just as he is pure." John's use of καθὼς shows the object of one's focus and goal in seeking purity. He uses the demonstrative pronoun, ἐκεῖνος, to refer to Jesus for the second time. Six times (2:6; 3:3, 5, 7, 16; 4:17) John uses this pronoun in its masculine form in this epistle, always referring to Jesus (Akin, 137; Brown, 397; Bultmann, 49; Smalley, 149). By this he essentially acts as John the Baptist when he pointed out Jesus and cried out, "Behold the Lamb of God who takes away the sins of the world." This pointing out of Jesus demands he be recognized as the only one in view. There is no other. It is Jesus exclusively who is pure. He is not one of many. Rensberger (90) points out that neither ἁγνός nor its cognates are ever used with regard to either Jesus or God the Father anywhere else in the NT or the LXX.[86] He notes well that John's use of it here likely grows out of our call to imitate Jesus.

Biblical Theology Comments

Johannine eschatology anticipates Jesus' return to judge not only the world but also his church. This same theme is repeated in Rev 11:18 and 22:12. Here John reveals opposite responses from believers who are either prepared (confidence) or unprepared (shame) for Jesus' return. That response will result from becoming like him when we see him for the first time.

---

distinguishing between justification and sanctification cleansing. A justified saint stands forgiven before God, the Righteous Judge. However, a justified saint with unconfessed sin stands in need of forgiveness before God, his heavenly Father.

85. Moody (61) summarizes John's teaching in these verses well. "Three steps are noted: (1) the future manifestation of God's children in God's likeness (3:2) is based on (2) the present process of their purification (3:3–4) and (3) the past manifestation of the Son of God to bear away sins (3:5–6)."

86. Rensberger (90) identifies Herm. *Sim.* 5.6.5–6 as the only other place Jesus is called "pure" in early Christian writings.

John develops further our relationship to God as our heavenly Father and we as his children who are born of him. This continues the theme introduced in John's Gospel and reminds us of the exceptional privilege that it involves. Along with that, though, John adds to it the ethical requirement that grows out of our inclusion in the family of God. Being God's children results in certain family obligations, particularly that of God's absolute moral purity which was introduced in 1:5 with the imagery of light and is now stated plainly in relation to Christ.

Application and Devotional Implications

We need to prepare for our future by making the right choices now. To be ready for Jesus' return we must want to be like him now. That means consciously choosing to do those things that are morally pure and to avoid, even purge from our life, anything that is impure. That means not reading certain material or watching certain movies or television programs. That means avoiding conduct that is impure. Yet how do we know what "pure" looks like? We must look to Scripture. We must read the moral commands in Leviticus and Deuteronomy. We must read and memorize the moral commands throughout the New Testament. Then we base our conduct on them. That is what pursuing moral purity looks like. Knowing and doing these things will be freeing, both in terms of the choices made, and in terms of one's conscience, both in the present and in the day we stand before Jesus.

Selected Bibliography

Beale, G. K., and D. A. Carson. *Commentary on the New Testament Use of the Old Testament*. Grand Rapids: Baker Academic, 2007.

Cook, W. R. "Hamartiological Problems in First John." *BSac* 123 (1966): 249–60.

Fanning, B. M. *Verbal Aspect in New Testament Greek*. Oxford: Clarendon, 1990.

Hiebert, D. E. "An Expositional Study of 1 John—Part 5: An Exposition of 1 John 2:29–3:12." *BSac* 146 (1989): 198–216.

Köstenberger, A. J. "The Deity of Christ in John's Letters and the Book of Revelation." In *The Deity of Christ*, edited by C. W. Morgan and R. A. Peterson, 151–67. Wheaton, IL: Crossway, 2011.

Malatesta, E. *Interiority and Covenant: A Study of* εἶναι ἐν *and* μένειν ἐν *in the First Letter of Saint John*. Rome: Biblical Institute Press, 1978.

Metzger, B. M., and United Bible Societies. *A Textual Commentary on the Greek New Testament*. 2nd ed. New York: United Bible Societies, 1994.

Moule, C. F. D. “A Neglected Factor in the Interpretation of Johannine Eschatology.” In *Studies in John*, 155–160. NovTSup 24. Leiden: Brill, 1970.
Robertson, A. T. *Word Pictures in the New Testament*. Jn 2:24. Sunday School Board of the Southern Baptist Convention, 1932–1933. Electronic ed. Oak Harbor, WA: Logos Research Systems, 1997.
Spicq, C. *Theological Lexicon of the New Testament*. Translated and edited by J. D. Ernest. 3 vols. Peabody, MA: Hendrickson, 1994.
Virkler, H. A. *Hermeneutics: Principles and Processes of Biblical Interpretation*. Grand Rapids: Baker, 1981.
von Wahlde, U. C. *The Johannine Commandments: 1 John and the Struggle for the Johannine Tradition*. New York: Paulist, 1990.

Expression of Righteousness (3:4–24)

Original Text

4 Πᾶς ὁ ποιῶν τὴν ἁμαρτίαν καὶ τὴν ἀνομίαν ποιεῖ, καὶ ἡ ἁμαρτία ἐστὶν ἡ ἀνο-
μία. 5 καὶ οἴδατε ὅτι ἐκεῖνος ἐφανερώθη, ἵνα τὰς ἁμαρτίαςa ἄρῃ, καὶ ἁμαρτία ἐν
αὐτῷ οὐκ ἔστιν. 6 πᾶς ὁ ἐν αὐτῷ μένων οὐχ ἁμαρτάνει· πᾶς ὁ ἁμαρτάνων οὐχ
ἑώρακεν αὐτὸν οὐδὲ ἔγνωκεν αὐτόν. 7 Τεκνία, μηδεὶς πλανάτω ὑμᾶς· ὁ ποιῶν
τὴν δικαιοσύνην δίκαιός ἐστιν, καθὼς ἐκεῖνος δίκαιός ἐστιν· 8 ὁ ποιῶν τὴν ἁμαρ-
τίαν ἐκ τοῦ διαβόλου ἐστίν, ὅτι ἀπ’ ἀρχῆς ὁ διάβολος ἁμαρτάνει. εἰς τοῦτο ἐφα-
νερώθη ὁ υἱὸς τοῦ θεοῦ, ἵνα λύσῃ τὰ ἔργα τοῦ διαβόλου. 9 Πᾶς ὁ γεγεννημένος
ἐκ τοῦ θεοῦ ἁμαρτίαν οὐ ποιεῖ, ὅτι σπέρμα αὐτοῦ ἐν αὐτῷ μένει, καὶ οὐ δύναται
ἁμαρτάνειν, ὅτι ἐκ τοῦ θεοῦ γεγέννηται. 10 ἐν τούτῳ φανερά ἐστιν τὰ τέκνα τοῦ
θεοῦ καὶ τὰ τέκνα τοῦ διαβόλου· πᾶς ὁ μὴ ποιῶν δικαιοσύνην οὐκ ἔστιν ἐκ τοῦ
θεοῦ, καὶ ὁ μὴ ἀγαπῶν τὸν ἀδελφὸν αὐτοῦ.

11 Ὅτι αὕτη ἐστὶν ἡ ἀγγελία ἣν ἠκούσατε ἀπ’ ἀρχῆς, ἵνα ἀγαπῶμεν ἀλλήλους,
12 οὐ καθὼς Κάϊν ἐκ τοῦ πονηροῦ ἦν καὶ ἔσφαξεν τὸν ἀδελφὸν αὐτοῦ· καὶ χάριν
τίνος ἔσφαξεν αὐτόν; ὅτι τὰ ἔργα αὐτοῦ πονηρὰ ἦν τὰ δὲ τοῦ ἀδελφοῦ αὐτοῦ
δίκαια. 13 αμὴ θαυμάζετε, ἀδελφοί, εἰ μισεῖ ὑμᾶς ὁ κόσμος. 14 ἡμεῖς οἴδαμεν
ὅτι μεταβεβήκαμεν ἐκ τοῦ θανάτου εἰς τὴν ζωήν, ὅτι ἀγαπῶμεν τοὺς ἀδελφούς·
ὁ μὴ ἀγαπῶν ατὸν ἀδελφόνα μένει ἐν τῷ θανάτῳ. 15 πᾶς ὁ μισῶν τὸν ἀδελφὸν
αὐτοῦ ἀνθρωποκτόνος ἐστίν, καὶ οἴδατε ὅτι πᾶς ἀνθρωποκτόνος οὐκ ἔχει ζωὴν
αἰώνιον ἐν αὐτῷ μένουσαν. 16 ἐν τούτῳ ἐγνώκαμεν τὴν ἀγάπην, ὅτι ἐκεῖνος
ὑπὲρ ἡμῶν τὴν ψυχὴν αὐτοῦ ἔθηκεν· καὶ ἡμεῖς ὀφείλομεν ὑπὲρ τῶν ἀδελφῶν
τὰς ψυχὰς θεῖναι. 17 ὃς δ’ ἂν ἔχῃ τὸν βίον τοῦ κόσμου καὶ θεωρῇ τὸν ἀδελφὸν
αὐτοῦ χρείαν ἔχοντα καὶ κλείσῃ τὰ σπλάγχνα αὐτοῦ ἀπ’ αὐτοῦ, πῶς ἡ ἀγάπη

τοῦ θεοῦ μένει ἐν αὐτῷ; 18 Τεκνία, μὴ ἀγαπῶμεν λόγῳ μηδὲ τῇ γλώσσῃ ἀλλὰ
ἐν ἔργῳ καὶ ἀληθείᾳ.

19 aΚαὶ ἐν τούτῳ γνωσόμεθα ὅτι ἐκ τῆς ἀληθείας ἐσμέν, καὶ ἔμπροσθεν αὐτοῦ
πείσομεν τὴν καρδίαν ἡμῶν, 20 ὅ τι ἐὰν καταγινώσκῃ ἡμῶν ἡ καρδία, ὅτι μείζων
ἐστὶν ὁ θεὸς τῆς καρδίας ἡμῶν καὶ γινώσκει πάντα. 21 Ἀγαπητοί, ἐὰν ἡ καρδία
aἡμῶν μὴ καταγινώσκῃ bἡμῶν, παρρησίαν ἔχομεν πρὸς τὸν θεὸν 22 καὶ ὃ ἐὰν
αἰτῶμεν λαμβάνομεν ἀπ᾽ αὐτοῦ, ὅτι τὰς ἐντολὰς αὐτοῦ τηροῦμεν καὶ τὰ ἀρεστὰ
ἐνώπιον αὐτοῦ ποιοῦμεν. 23 καὶ αὕτη ἐστὶν ἡ ἐντολὴ αὐτοῦ, ἵνα πιστεύσωμεν τῷ
ὀνόματι τοῦ υἱοῦ αὐτοῦ Ἰησοῦ Χριστοῦ καὶ ἀγαπῶμεν ἀλλήλους, καθὼς ἔδωκεν
ἐντολὴν ἡμῖν. 24 καὶ ὁ τηρῶν τὰς ἐντολὰς αὐτοῦ ἐν αὐτῷ μένει καὶ αὐτὸς ἐν
αὐτῷ· καὶ ἐν τούτῳ γινώσκομεν ὅτι μένει ἐν ἡμῖν, ἐκ τοῦ πνεύματος οὗ ἡμῖν
ἔδωκεν.

Textual Notes

5.a. The majority of witnesses (א C K L Ψ 049 056 0142 81 88 104 181 326 330 451 614 630 1505 1877 2127 2412 2492 2495 *Byz Lect* vg syr^{p} cop^{sa,fay}) support inclusion of ἡμῶν following τὰς ἁμαρτίας while only a few (A B P 33 436 945 1241 1739 1881 it^{ar,c,dem,div,h,p,z} syr^{h} cop^{bo} arm eth) support its exclusion. Though it is better supported, it does seem best to see this as an example of scribal assimilation to other passages as argued by Metzger. This would bring it into agreement with "our sins" (τῶν ἁμαρτιῶν ἡμῶν) in 2:2 and 4:10. However, the context of this passage has the world in view while the other two passages have the believer in view. Including ἡμῶν here would bring it into conflict with the affirmation of 2:2 that Jesus' propitiation is not limited to the elect but includes the whole world.[87]

13.a. The καὶ in UBS^{4} has but a few witnesses (א C^{vid} P Ψ 629 945 1241 1739 1881 2492 it^{ar,q,r,z} syr^{p} arm eth). Its absence from the Byzantine and Vulgate as well as a significant number of minuscules (049 056 0142 33 81 88 104 181 326 330 436 451 614 630 1505 1877 2127 2412 2495) and scattering between Alexandrian and Old Latin MSS (A B K L *Lect* it^{c,dem,div,h,p} syr^{h} cop^{sa,bo,fay})

87. B. Metzger and United Bible Societies, *A Textual Commentary on the Greek New Testament*, 2nd ed., 642.

argues for noninclusion. Thus it is more likely that copyists added it rather than removed.[88]

14.a...a Contra Metzger, τὸν ἀδελφόν should follow ὁ μὴ ἀγαπῶν since the Alexandrian and Western are clearly divided and Byzantine united. Though some of the stronger Alexandrian witnesses favor its exclusion (א A B 33 629 945 1241 1739 1881 2127 2492 it^{e,dem,div,h,p,q,r,z} vg cop^{bo,fay} arm), they are not united, with others favoring its inclusion (C K L Ψ 049 81 88 104 181 326 330 451; P 056 0142 436 614 630 1505 1877 2412 2495 add αὐτοῦ following ἀδελφόν). Though, Metzger may be correct in saying that "copyists were more likely to add than to delete an object that completes the thought of the participle," it need not be the case. They were just as likely to follow faithfully the text in their desire to reproduce faithfully the Scriptures, whether it proved awkward or seemed in need of clarification.[89]

19.a. This καί should be included rather than following the pattern of 3:13, contra Metzger, because the weight of MS evidence strongly favors its inclusion and it fits well within the flow of thought. In favor of its inclusion are א C K P Ψ 049 056 0142 81 88 104 181 330 451 614 630 945 1241 1505 1739 1877 1881 2127 2412 2492 2495 *Byz Lect* it^{q} syr^{p} cop^{sa} arm eth. Supporting its exclusion are A B 206 326 429 436 629 it^{ar,c,dem,div,h,p,t} syr^{h} vg cop^{bo,fay}.[90]

21.a, b. This verse has eleven variants that can be summarized into four possible readings based on Metzger's analysis.[91] In each case the question is whether ἡμῶν should be included after both καταγινώσκῃ and καρδία. The vast majority support ἡμῶν following both καδία (א C K 049 056 0142 81 88 104 181 326 330 451 614 629 630 1505 1877 1881 [2127 2495 ὑμῶν] 2412 2492 *Byz Lect* it^{ar,c,dem,div,p,q} vg syr^{p,h} cop arm eth) and καταγινώσκῃ (א K Ψ 049 056 0142 33 81 104 181 326 330 436 451 614 629 630 945 1739 1877 1881 2127 2412 2492 *Byz Lect* it^{ar,c,dem,div,p,q} vg syr^{p,h} cop^{sa,bo,fay} arm eth). The pattern of

88. B. Metzger and United Bible Societies, *A Textual Commentary on the Greek New Testament*, 2nd ed., 642–43.
89. B. Metzger and United Bible Societies, *A Textual Commentary on the Greek New Testament*, 2nd ed., 643
90. B. Metzger and United Bible Societies, *A Textual Commentary on the Greek New Testament*, 2nd ed., 643.
91. B. Metzger and United Bible Societies, *A Textual Commentary on the Greek New Testament*, 2d ed., 643.

Alexandrian copyists' "pruning" the text seems most evident here since the majority of witnesses contain it in both places. Additionally, it is more likely that copyists would remove what they perceive to be redundant words rather than add them from the context. John's penchant for repetition increases the likelihood of their inclusion rather than addition.

Translation

4 Everyone who[92] commits sin also is committing[93] lawlessness, because sin is lawlessness.[94] **5** And you know that he appeared in order that he might take away sins,[95] and *that*[96] in him there is not a *single*[97] sin. **6** Everyone who abides in him does not sin; everyone who sins has neither seen him nor known him. **7** Little children, let no one deceive you; he who does[98] righteousness is righteous, just as he is righteous; **8** he who does[99] sin is from

---

92. This reflects a *pas ho* construction that John will use several times in this section to communicate general principles that apply to believers and non-believers alike.
93. Though the gnomic sense of the present tense could be used both times in this verse (NKJV has "commits ... commits"; ESV, NASB95, and NET has "practices ... practices"; ASV has "doeth ... doeth"; HSCB, NIV84, and NLT remove the parallelism altogether), and would communicate the parallelism reflected in the text, this translation desires to reflect the significance of the statement that I believe John intended. Though it is a principle, it is also a reality in each person's experience.
94. Most translations have "lawlessness" (ASV, ESV, NASB95, NET, NKJV, NIV84), but others say "breaking the law" (HCSB), or "contrary to the law of God" (NLT).
95. Some translations include "our" with sins (NKJV, NIV84, NLt) while others exclude it (ASV, ESV, HCSB, NET). Though the majority of MS support the reading, it appears to be the product of scribal assimilation to passages such as 2:2 and 4:10. However, this passage does not have individual Christians in view as much as the world. Thus, including ἡμῶν here would cause it to conflict with 2:2 and John's affirmation that Jesus' propitiation includes the whole world rather than just the elect.
96. *That* is added to reflect the coordinate relationship of the clauses that are joined by "and."
97. *Single* is added in order to reflect the significance of the anarthrous noun "sin" and to express the absoluteness of the statement as it is intended in the Greek construction.
98. The choice of "does" (ASV, HCSB, NIV84, NLt) over "practices" (ESV, NASB95, NET, NKJV) is designed to reflect John's choice of the present participle of *poieō*, which means "to do."
99. This is again reflecting John's use of the articular participle of *poieō* (ASV). Other translation choices include "he who sins" (NKJV), "the one who practices sin" (NASB95, NET), "whoever makes a practice of sin" (ESV), "when people keep on

the devil, because the devil has sinned from the beginning. For this reason the Son of God appeared,[100] in order that he might destroy the works of the devil. **9** Everyone who has been born from God does not sin, because his seed abides in him, and it is not able to sin, because it has been born from God.[101] **10** By means of this the children of God and the children of the devil are manifest; everyone who does not do righteousness is not from God, also the one not loving his brother. **11** For this is the message which you heard from the beginning, that we should love one another. **12** Not like Cain who was from the evil one and he slaughtered[102] his brother; and again why did he slaughter him? Because his works were evil but those of his brother were righteous. **13** Stop being amazed, brethren, that the world hates you. **14** We know that we have passed out of death into life because we love the brethren; he who does not love his brother abides[103] in death. **15** Everyone who hates his brother is a murderer, and you know that every[104] murderer does not have eternal life abiding in him. **16** By this we have known[105]

---

sinning" (NLT), "he who does what is sinful" (NIV84), and "the one who commits sin" (HCSB). As can be seen by the variance in translations, the nuance of this articular participle can be understood in a variety of ways. Some of the translational choices seem to miss the gnomic sense of the participle, or even a progressive sense, such as HCSB and NIV84.

100. ESV, NASB95, NIV84. Other translations use "was manifested" (ASV, NKjv), "came" (NLT), and "was revealed" (HCSB, NET).

101. Most translations have "of God" rather than "from God." When they translate this prepositional phrase with "of God," it makes it seem to be an intended parallel John's earlier use of "children of God." However, John changes from a gen. construction ("children of God") to a prepositional phrase. I wanted to express the thrust of the preposition (*ek*) which draws attention to source (thus parentage) more than identity.

102. The choice of "slaughtered" attempts to reflect the brutality communicated by John's choice of *sphazō*. Other translations use "murdered" (ESV, HCSB, NIV84, NKJV), "slay/slew" (ASV, NASB95), and "kill" (NLT).

103. This reflects again John's use of *menō* (ASV, ESV, NASB95, NKjv). Other translations use "remains" (HCSB, NET, NIV84), and "is still dead" (NLT).

104. Most translations have "no murderer has" (ASV, ESV, HCSB, NASB95, NET, NIV84, NKJV). Though it is not smooth English, this is an attempt to reflect the Greek construction and what I see as John's emphasis. Others have "murderers don't have" (NLT)

105. This reflects the thrust of the perfect tense verb for "know." Other translations use the more gnomic "know" (ASV, ESV, NASB95, NIV84, NKJV, NLT). The HCSB and NET translation of "we have come to know" reflects the same perfect tense nuance as I am attempting.

love, because that One laid down his life on our behalf;[106] and so we are
obligated to lay down our lives for the brethren. **17** But whoever has the
world's goods and sees his brother having a need and closes his compas-
sions[107] from him, how does the love of God abide in him? **18** Children, let
us neither love in word nor in tongue, but in deed and in truth.[108] **19** And by
this we will know that we are from[109] the truth, and we will persuade[110] our
heart[111] before him **20** in whatever our heart condemns us, because God
is greater than our heart and he knows all things. **21** Beloved, if our heart
does not condemn us, we have confidence before[112] God. **22** And whatever
we ask we receive from him, because we keep his commandments and do
the things that are pleasing before him. **23** And this is his commandment,
that we believe in the name of his Son Jesus Christ, and that we love one

---

106. The standard translation is "for us" (ASV, ESV, NASB95, NET, NIV84, NKJV, NLT). I have chosen "on our behalf" in order to reflect John's use of the preposition *hyper* to describe Jesus' motive in giving his life.

107. The translation choices vary greatly in an attempt to communicate the sense of this term. My own choice is reflected in ASV. Other translations include: "shuts up his heart" (NKJV), "closes his heart" (ESV, NASB95), "shows no compassion" (NLT), "shuts off his compassion" (NET), "has no pity" (NIV84), and "closes his eyes" (HCSB).

108. The translation "in word nor in tongue, but in deed and in truth" attempts to reflect the terms John chose (ASV, NASB95, NET, NKJV). NLT uses "not merely say" and "show the truth." ESV changes "tongue" to "talk." NIV84 changes "deed" to "actions." HCSB uses "word or speech, but with truth and action."

109. This again reflects John use of *ek* to indicate source. Most translations use "of the truth" (ASV, ESV, NASB95, NET, NKJV). Others says "we belong to the truth" (HCSB, NIV84, NLT).

110. The wide range of translations reveals the difficulty of understanding this word. The choice of "persuade" is an attempt to reflect a more literal rendering of the term. I also feel it communicates the person's involvement. This choice is reflected in the footnotes of NKJV and NASB95. "assure" (ASV, NASB95, NKJV) "re-assure" (ESV) "we will be confident" (NLT) "convince" (HCSB, NET) "set our hearts at rest" (NIV84)

111. Some translations make this a plural, "hearts" (NIV84, NKjv). I have chosen to leave it singular because that eliminates any chance of mistaking it for a reference to the church community rather than the individual (ASV, ESV, NASB95). NLT uses "we will be confident." HCSB and NET use "conscience."

112. ESV, HCSB, NIV84, NASB95. Other translations use "toward" (ASV, NKjv), "come to God" (NLT), or "in the presence of" (NET).

another, just as he gave a commandment to us. **24** And[113] he who keeps his commandments abides in him and he in him; and by this we know that he abides in us, from the Spirit whom he gave to us.

Commentary

John moves from the privilege and future of the child of God to show how our privileged position "is incompatible with the practice of sin" (Akin, 139). These following verses are viewed quite differently by the two major approaches to this epistle (Test of Life and Test of Fellowship). Their interpretations will be examined along with a clarification of John's message. Though each view has good things to say and worthy arguments at points, they are incompatible. Only one *can* be right, and neither may be. The problem posed by these following verses comes from missing the literary approach of John and the need to recognize how literally or figuratively, how absolutely or relatively, each statement should be taken.[114] It is the position of this writer that we are delving into the realm of Johannine dualism. If we miss the imagery and intended meaning of John, we are in danger of falling into a bottomless pit of theological pitch. However, if we recognize his imagery and literary devices, we will find a powerful argument for personal purity and loyalty to our Father who has begotten us through a second birth.

The issue that must be addressed before these verses can be analyzed has to do with the nature of the present tense verbs and verbals. Fanning provides a convincing analysis of the problem and its solution, acknowledging the strengths and weaknesses of both the habitual sense and absolute sense.[115] His conclusion is that "the possibility of a habitual sense cannot be ruled out entirely ... , but it seems less likely. On purely grammatical grounds, therefore, the absolute interpretation of 1 John 3:4–10 is to be preferred."[116]

113. Many translations drop this *kai* (ESV, HCSB, NASB95, NIV84, Nlt), however, it should be included (ASV, NET). NKJV reflected its presence with "now."

114. Stott (126) sees John using "generalizations "polemically throughout the epistle, and so this passage should be seen in that light.

115. B. M. Fanning, *Verbal Aspect in New Testament Greek, 212–17.*

116. B. M. Fanning, *Verbal Aspect in New Testament Greek*, 217.

3:4 The practice of sin is the response of the lawless. The two clauses that make up the main statement of this compound sentence are structured so that the terms for "sin" and "lawlessness" are drawn to its center with the verbals (participle and verb) moved to each end. The articles with the nouns in the final clause also serve to concretize what are normally conceptual words.[117]

Πᾶς ὁ ποιῶν τὴν ἁμαρτίαν καὶ τὴν ἀνομίαν ποιεῖ, "Everyone who commits sin also is committing lawlessness." John states another principle, using the 3 construction with an articular present participle to describe a person's practice or character. He uses the same verbal root twice (ποιῶν, ποιεῖ), once as a substantival participle and once as a present indicative, both literally meaning "does." Moody (62) sees this communicating the idea that just as purification is a process, so is sin. With the participle he describes the person in terms of a consistent lifestyle rather than someone guilty of an occasional sin (Burdick, 236; Johnson, 68; Westcott, 102).[118] This is a kind of person who is characterized by sin as a principle. With the present tense verb, he says literally that this person "is doing lawlessness."[119] Again, this is the outward expression of the one whose character is sinful. What he says is that sinful character expresses itself with rebellion against rule. Lawlessness is active rebellion against law, not just the absence of law.

This πᾶς ὁ construction mirrors that which begins the sentence in 3:3 that describes a believer. It makes it a "universal" truth for which "there are no exceptions." His use of this "all-inclusive" πᾶς accentuates "that there is no elite group that is above God's moral standards" (Akin, 139). This also

117. Burge (147) sees 3:4–10 as "a reflection on the tension between sin and perfection in the Christian life."

118. J. P. Louw ("Verbal Aspect in the First Letter of John," 102) reflects the habitual view and says, "The verb ποιέω twice expresses the durative or linear aspect while the event itself is nominalized in surface structure. Two verses further on in 1 Jh. 3:6 we read πᾶς ὁ ἐν αὐτῷ μένων οὐχ ἁμαρτάνει 'everyone who lives in Christ does not live in sin'. In this particular instance ἁμαρτάνει has the same force as ποιεῖν τὴν ἁμαρτίαν being merely its stylistic reduction form already marked for duration by the preceding ποιεῖ in verse 4, and also strengthened aspectually by μένων which lexically signifies a process." Still he (101) notes earlier that a present tense verb, though it can indicate a durative sense, need not be durative unless the context indicates such.

119. The articles make these nouns definite (Lenski, 455), but should not be viewed as par excellence.

indicates that John does not have any particular group in mind (Smalley, 158; Strecker, 93). Through this parallel John contrasts two kinds of people, those who are morally pure and those who are sinful. Because John now connects this πᾶς ὁ to sin, others see him referring to his opponents. This is connected back to John's statement in 2:23 about those who deny the Son (πᾶς ὁ ἀρνούμενος), where the person described is clearly unregenerate. Now they are being identified as "moral indifferentists" (Harris, 134). However, opponents need not be in view since John has left his polemics to engage in paranesis (pastoral concerns). He is drawing a contrast with the one who "does righteousness" (πᾶς ὁ ποιῶν τὴν δικαιοσύνην) in 2:29 (Burdick, 236). As a result, it is better to see John describing a kind of person whether a false teacher or an immoral member of the congregation.

Though καὶ normally functions as a coordinating conjunction, in this instance it is better seen as either emphatic ("indeed") or explanatory ("also").[120] The explanatory function seems best both in terms of the context and construction (Brown, 399; Smalley, 155). This explains why the person whose character is sinful is also lawless. Ultimately, sin is an expression of lawlessness. However, which law is in view? To this question John next turns.

καὶ ἡ ἁμαρτία ἐστὶν ἡ ἀνομία, "because sin is lawlessness." This adverb καὶ should be seen as explanatory (Brown, 399, Smalley 155) rather than coordinating or emphatic (Burdick, 236). Additionally, the article with the singular "sin" indicates that John is referring to sin in a general sense and does not have particular sins in mind (Smalley, 155). As a result, John is using this statement to describe the "essence or character of sin" (Brooke, 84–85; Cook, 250; Stott, 122).[121] Law (133, n. 1) considers the dual use of articles with εἰμί as an indication that John views these two terms as interchangeable, and either could be used to define the other.[122] Smalley (155)

120. D. B. Wallace, *Grammar*, 666–78.

121. Sin is also defined in Rom 14:23 ("whatever is not from faith is sin") and James 4:17 ("to him who knows to do good and does not do it, to him it is sin").

122. He is supported by Westcott (102) who sees this same pattern in Matt 6:22 (ὁ λύχνος τοῦ σώματός ἐστιν ὁ ὀφθαλμός); John 1:4 (ἡ ζωὴ ἦν τὸ φῶς); 15:1 (ἐγώ εἰμι ἡ ἄμπελος ἡ ἀληθινή καὶ ὁ πατήρ μου ὁ γεωργός ἐστιν); 1 Cor 10:4 (ἡ πέτρα δὲ ἦν ὁ Χριστός); 15:56 (τὸ δὲ κέντρον τοῦ θανάτου ἡ ἁμαρτία, ἡ δὲ δύναμις τῆς ἁμαρτίας ὁ νόμος); 2 Cor 3:17 (ὁ δὲ κύριος τὸ πνεῦμά ἐστιν); Phil 3:19 (ὁ θεὸς ἡ κοιλία); and Rev 19:10 (ἡ μαρτυρία Ἰησοῦ ἐστὶν τὸ πνεῦμα τῆς προφητείας).

rejects this and suggests that the presence of the article in this construction indicates that ἀνομία had become a technical term familiar to the readers, and so lawlessness is not a synonym for sin, but "a climactic definition of it."

Lawlessness may be defined as the "state or condition of being disposed to what is lawless," and can include deeds that result from that disposition.[123] This is the sense given by John. However the nature of this lawlessness is debated and can be summarized under two major views:

(1) Lawlessness is rebellion against God's moral law, whether Mosaic or the more general moral law (Houlden, 92; J. Mitchell, 90; Stott, 126; Strauss, 45; Westcott, 102). For example, Strecker (94) says "The relationship of sin to ἀνομία indicates that the divine mandate is to be fundamental for Christians' actions. This is not to be understood as a Jewish or Jewish Christian nomism: rather, it is equated with the 'will of God.'" Lawlessness describes "sin as a wrong act, willfully done. It is doing what is prohibited and omitting what is commanded" (Grayston, 104). Evidence for this is found in such Old Testament passages as Pss 1:4, 32:1–2 (as quoted in Rom 4:7–8) and Jer 31:34 (as quoted in Heb 10:17) where sins and lawless deeds are equated through synonymous parallelism. However, other than these few instances, the Old Testament does not develop a strong "connection" between the two terms (Marshall, 176, n.3; Smalley, 154).[124] John's use of the article with ἀνομία indicates either that it is some known form of rebellion, or it is a technical term familiar to his readers (Haas, de Jonge, and Swellengrebel, 86; Smalley, 155). Also, the absence of interest in the law or lawbreaking in either the Gospel or this epistle mitigates against this view (Marshall, 176; Smalley, 154).

(2) This refers to a form of known eschatological lawlessness related to the "man of lawlessness" in 2 Thess 2:3 (Barker, 331; Brown, 399–400; Bultmann, 50; Marshall, 176–77; Rensberger, 90; Schnackenburg, 186; Smalley, 155; Smith, 83; Thompson, 93; Williamson, 114).[125] This is further seen in the use of ἀνομία in other eschatological passages such as Matt 7:22–23 and 24:11–12 (Haas, de Jonge, and Swellengrebel, 86; Smith, 83; Williamson, 114). It also reflects a connection with the Antichrist, introduced in 2:18,

123. BDAG, 85; W. Gutbrod, "ἀνομία," *TDNT* 4:1085–86.

124. It may be argued that in actuality the OT did not distinguish between sin and lawlessness (Houlden, 92).

125. Schnackenburg (186) suggests ἀνομία be defined as "wickedness" (*Bosheit*).

and Christ's coming in 2:28–29 (Smalley, 155). Thus, it means to participate in rebellion characteristic of the devil (Burge, 148–49; Yarbrough, 181), to sin "like the lawless one" (Haas, de Jonge, and Swellengrebel, 86). This also aligns with 3:8 and the devil sinning from the beginning (Burge, 149). Yarbrough (181) points to Matt 7:23; 13:41; and 24:12 to indicate that the lawless "deserve or receive eschatological punishment."[126] He further points to numerous references in the LXX that relate *ἀνομία* to "utterly despicable transgression" (Gen 19:15; Lev 19:29; 20:14; Deut 31:29; 2 Sam 22:5; Isa 53:8; Zech 5:8; Mal 1:4). Finally, the concept of lawlessness was characteristic of Jewish and Christian apocalyptic literature (Strecker, 94).[127] The greatest weakness of this view is that by its heinousness John's readers would be able to exclude themselves from this danger. Thus it would have to be polemical rather than parenetic in nature, and thus out of line with John's argument in this section. It seems better to see this as every form of rebellion against God that is characterized by any pattern of sin (Bruce, 89).[128] This would fit better with John's pastoral concerns.

126. Yarbrough (182) defines *ἀνομία* as used by John to mean "transgression so weighty that the perpetrator is outside the pale of Christ's followers."

127. S. Kubo ("1 John 3:9: Absolute or Habitual?" 48–49) does not consider Jewish apocalyptic literature as "adequate to explain Christian eschatology, since there is a basic difference between them… . Jewish apocalyptic is still in the future and coincides with the parousia. It is at once complete and final. In Christianity, eschatology begins with the coming of Christ but finds its complete fulfillment at the parousia. In Judaism then, one can speak of sinlessness in the eschatological era, but in Christianity sinlessness cannot yet be considered in that final sense. For the Christian the decisive event has taken place on the cross and in the resurrection, but he lives in a tension between the 'already' and the 'not yet.' … Throughout this epistle the indicatives stand beside the imperatives, the 'already' beside the 'not yet.' The eschatological background of the late Jewish writings does not fully explain the situation in 1 Jn since no absolute perfection is envisaged as in those writings. This means that the absolute view cannot be supported by parallels from Jewish apocalyptic literature."

128. Barker (331) asserts that both John and his opponents agreed that lawlessness was "incompatible with being born of God" while one could sin and still be his child. "What they did not agree on was that sin, defined as transgression of the moral law, was 'lawlessness.'" However, John is not addressing the false teachers in this passage, but his own flock, called "little children" in 2:28 and "beloved" in 3:2. This should be seen as a parenetic section rather than polemical.

3:5 This sentence is composed of a compound ὅτι clause asserting two truths about Jesus. Through this we are taught the purpose of his coming as it relates to sin and contrasts Jesus' response to sin with the lawless person characterized by sin. Its connection to its preceding context is made evident by the repeated statement that they "know" (οἶδα) truths connected to Jesus' manifestation (φανερόω) in the future (v. 2) as well as in the past (here).

καὶ οἴδατε ὅτι ἐκεῖνος ἐφανερώθη, "And you know that he appeared." Using another continuative καὶ, John connects this following statement with what he has just said. He is following the same pattern of verses 2 and 3. There John reminds his readers of what he and they *know* (οἴδαμεν), and then he follows it with an application, connected with καὶ heading up the following sentence.

John has just said that sin is lawlessness. He now reminds them of what they know in regard to that truth. Jesus came to remove it. His use of the demonstrative pronoun ἐκεῖνος without an apparent antecedent refers once again to Jesus (Brown, 401; Lieu, 129; Smalley, 156).

Continuing with the theme of Jesus' manifestation, John uses the aorist passive ἐφανερώθη to describe the historical fact of Jesus' incarnation and earthly ministry (Burdick, 237; Brown, 401; Smalley, 156; Westcott, 103). His choice of its passive form rather than an active or middle indicates that Jesus was made manifest rather than manifested himself. He was not the initiator. This reflects Jesus' words that he had come to do his Father's will, not his own (John 4:33; 6:38; see also Heb 10:5–10 for a heavenly conversation). It also implies Jesus' preexistence prior to his appearance on earth as a human in the incarnation (Akin, 141; Burdick, 237).[129]

ἵνα τὰς ἁμαρτίας ἄρῃ, "in order that he might take away sins." This ἵνα introduces a purpose clause to explain why Jesus appeared (Burdick, 237; Strecker, 95). The purpose of Jesus being manifested was to take away "sins." John's use of αἴρω indicates the removal of sin (Burdick, 237; Westcott, 103;

129. G. Sevenster ("Remarks on the Humanity of Jesus in the Gospel and Letters of John," 189) says ἐφανερώθη suggests the incarnation, and it "possesses a soteriological aspect; the taking away of sins and deliverance from the power of Satan." Harris (136) notes that the verb indicates all of Jesus' earthy life and ministry rather than indicating his self-revelation occurred at the time he began his incarnation.

Williamson, 115). The verb in this context has the sense of taking away without the sense of lifting up.[130]

John's choice of the plural *sins* calls attention to the individual acts of sin, each transgression (Brooke, 85; Bruce, 89; Westcott, 103).[131] His use of the article with "sins" seems intentionally parallel to 2:2, where Jesus is the propitiation, not for sin in general but for each and every sin committed (Bruce, 89). So it is the individual sins, each act of sin, that his manifestation had in view (Smalley, 156). This truth becomes the motivation for purifying ourselves as we anticipate being like Jesus. If we are trying to be like him, we must identify with his purpose in coming. That should be our motivation for removing sin from our lives.

καὶ ἁμαρτία ἐν αὐτῷ οὐκ ἔστιν, "and *that* in him there is not a *single* sin." John affirms a second thing his readers already know, namely, that Jesus is sinless.[132] The pronoun *αὐτῷ* has ἐκεῖνος as its referent, which in this epistle always refers to Jesus (Westcott, 103).[133] Whereas he describes our sins with the article, with Jesus John uses the anarthrous *ἁμαρτία*. In this case, with the negative particle *οὐκ*, it emphasizes the fact that there is not a single sin in Jesus.[134] Just as there is no darkness in God (1:5), there is no sin at all in Jesus, who came to remove it.[135] Also, since εἰμί is a verb that can easily be left out of a sentence without losing its sense, both its inclusion and location at the end of the clause is emphatic along with the movement of *ἁμαρτία* to its beginning (Smalley, 157). Jesus exists in a state of absolute purity. The implication of this use of εἰμί is that this purity has been and will continue to be true of Jesus from eternity past into eternity future (Akin, 141; Brooke,

---

130. BDAG, 28. Bultmann (50), on the other hand, does not see this as related to Jesus' cleansing of sin in 1:7, but that it indicates that Jesus' work "has brought the possibility of freedom from sinning."

131. Examples of this same use of the article to indicate individual sins rather than sin as a principle include Rom 7:5; Col 1:14; and Heb 1:3.

132. This may reflect Jesus' words in John 7:18, where he claimed to be free of any "unrighteousness" or hHis challenge in John 8:46 to hHis opponents.

133. Brooke (85) observes, "The writer apparently sees no difficulty in using ἐκεῖνος and *αὐτός* in the same verse with reference to the same subject."

134. J. Mitchell (92), after defining sin as rebellion, sees this affirming that Jesus has "no trace of rebellion in him."

135. Smalley (157) notes that *ἐν αὐτῷ* could be made to refer to the believer, though it is better to see Jesus as its referent. He provides three "reasons" this might be the case, but then acknowledges that the context favors Christ as its referent.

86; Stott, 127; Westcott, 103).[136] This leads to the application of that truth in what follows.

3:6 John continues his series of "everyone who" statements, setting the stage for what he will say in the next paragraph. He is now describing an obedient believer—not just *a* believer but the opposite of the lawless man.[137] He will accomplish this first with an affirmation of the effect of abiding in Christ. He then will state the principle that sinners have neither seen nor known Jesus. He accomplishes this with a pair of πᾶς ὁ statements that form a contrast and divide the world into two distinct groups (Brown, 402). Though John speaks absolutely, his dualism must be recognized in that what he says must be seen in light of what he has already said. Christians do sin and, in fact, must confess their sins. To deny sin is to be deceived and call God a liar. Therefore, these statements must be seen in light of their rhetorical purpose, as will be discussed below.

πᾶς ὁ ἐν αὐτῷ μένων οὐχ ἁμαρτάνει, "Everyone who abides in him does not sin." John begins again (cf. 3:4) with a πᾶς ὁ construction to describe the abiding believer. Since what he has already said in this epistle denies even the slight possibility of sinless perfection, John cannot be expecting to be understood literally. However, this could be viewed as a "logical deduction" from what was just said (Burdick, 238). The contrast he is drawing here is between abiding and sinning.[138] They are opposites. One cannot sin and abide. One cannot abide and sin.

Lieu (131) notes well that "the theoretical logic of this is easier to follow than its practical application." This ἐν αὐτῷ refers once again to Jesus (Smalley, 158). This is evidenced by the christological focus in the immediate context of the previous verse. Strecker (96) sees abiding in him as the condition for not sinning. He sees the "generalizing" πᾶς indicating "an imperative intention" and says, "this is not the statement of an objectively

136. Strecker (96) observes, "As the sacrificial animal must be unblemished, so also for Christ as the sacrificial lamb the necessary precondition of his atoning efficacy is sinlessness." This is affirmed in such passages as 2 Cor 5:21 and 1 Pet 2:22 (which quotes Isa 53:9). It is alluded to in John 8:46 and 9:16.

137. Westcott (101) observes that whereas the clauses of vv. 4–5 were connected together with καὶ, the next three are not.

138. Harris (137) sees μένων referring to "the permanence of the relationship" and so describes a believer.

discernible fact, but rather, in the parenetic context, it is a warning to the community to draw the necessary conclusions from the liberating indicative of the Christ-event." Houlden says, "Those statements in 3.6, 9 and 5.18, undoubtedly pose a problem; and if eschatology will not solve it (they mean we are on the way to sinlessness soon to be totally achieved), then it may be best to recognize them as hortatory aspiration, as the language of 3.3 implies: the clear sight of the winning post stimulates the race."[139] Marshall (179) notes that the argument that a Christian can live "a life of conscious, complete conformity to the will of God" but be allowed to "commit errors and involuntary sins." He answers it with the fact learned by John Wesley: "even saintly people ... could commit gross, deliberate sins." Thus this verse must be seen as an ideal rather than a universal truth. John must not be talking about a particular sin (he cites the example of the sin unto death in 5:16), but general sins.

John has already talked about God's Word abiding in his readers (2:14) and their need to abide in the apostolic instruction (2:27). Now he describes their fellowship with Christ as an "abiding" relationship. This is reflective of Jesus' instruction to the apostles in the Upper Room (John 15:4–7). There, abiding results in fruitfulness and answered prayer. Jesus continued his discussion of abiding with the issue of obedience as it related to abiding in (experiencing, enjoying) his love. This same relationship to abiding is now being applied by John with regard to sin. Abiding is relational and something the apostles, as believers, had to choose to do. Furthermore, as there, so here, it is something that Jesus' followers can fail to do. Jesus would not have commanded the Eleven to abide in him in order to be fruitful if abiding were automatic and characteristic of a regenerate person. The presence of the command indicates the very real possibility that a believer may not abide. Thus, here, the failure to abide is a possibility. However, then, so is the ability to abide. Of further note is the implication of the active participle. Abiding requires human effort (Brooke, 86). It is not an effortless existence, but the product of choices made and actions taken.

What kind of sin is in view? Many interpreters understand the present tense to indicate habitual sin (Bruce, 90; Westcott, 103; Williamson, 115). Bruce (90) is representative of how many interpreters handle the problem of this absolute statement. He says, "In saying that no one who 'abides' in

139. J. L. Houlden, "Salvation Proclaimed II. 1 John 1.5–2.6: Belief and Growth," 134.

him sins, John is not asserting that it is impossible for a believer to commit an occasional act of sin. He has already pointed to the provision made for such an emergency by means of confession (1.9) and Christ's activity as his people's (2.1 f.), and has warned his readers against unfounded claims to be sinless within or without (1. 8, 10). What he does assert is that a sinful life does not mark a child of God, so that anyone who leads such a life is shown thereby not to be a child of God." Burdick (239) argues for the habitual sin on the basis that the present tense expresses "linear action." If John wanted to depict single acts of sins he would have used the aorist he sees John using Hebrew antithetic parallelism with "the second member of the contrast" providing "added information concerning the first member.[140]

Rensberger (92–93) counters, "The present tense, used in 3:6, 9; 5:18, does generally imply continuous action, so that these verses could mean that Christians do not *habitually* sin, whereas the aorist tense in 2:1 could refer to single acts of sin into which they might lapse. ... However, this does not account for the present tenses of 1:8 and 5:16, or the perfect of 1:10. In general, though few things are completely impossible for this writer, it seems unlikely that so significant a distinction would be expressed solely by this grammatical subtlety." He observes (93), "It is hard to say whether we have here a paradox that is not to be harmonized, a contradiction that represents the contradictoriness of Christian existence ... or simply the work of an author less concerned with clarity and consistency than we might wish." Then he concludes (93), "The author's point is not to derive conduct from origins, but *to demonstrate origins from conduct*." Yarbrough (183) notes, "It is unlikely that John has forgotten what he wrote earlier or changed his mind in the interim. Nor is it advisable to resort to the understandable but unsatisfactory expedient of stressing the alleged continual nature of the sinning John has in mind. ... 5:16 uses the present tense to describe specific sinful acts, not chronic transgression. The present tense cannot bear the weight that the translation 'keeps on sinning' places on it in 3:6, 9."

Marshall's (180) defense of the habitual sin view is:[141] (1) It requires that the continuous aspect of the present tense "in a way which they do

140. Thus "dwelling in him" is explained by "has seen" and "has known."

141. He provides an excellent detailing of various options (180–83) that include "ideal" view (what a Christian should look like), "implicit imperatives" view ("statements of what Christians ought to be"), and the "implicit condition" view ("so

not do elsewhere in the New Testament." (2) John uses the present tense for believers' sins in 5:16. (3) Since John also affirms in this context that believers do not sin because God's seed abides in them (3:9) and Jesus keeps them safe (5:18), "it is hard to see why God preserves him from some sins, but not from all sins."

Marshall's own view (182) may be described as the "eschatological reality" view. He begins with the thought that the early church reflected the Jewish expectation of a sinless life in the coming messianic kingdom. John is describing "the eschatological reality, the possibility that is open to believers, which is both a fact ('he cannot sin') and conditional ('[if he] lives in him'). It is a reality which is continually threatened by the tensions of living in the sinful world, and yet one which is capable of being realized by faith." His arguments for this view include: (1) It "builds on the general understanding of God's eschatological action found in early Christianity." (2) It "avoids limited definitions of the nature of sin." (3) It "fits in which the rest of John's teaching."[142]

Smalley (159–64) provides an extensive and helpful survey of the various approaches to this clause from the grammatical, theological, and situational perspectives. His work need not be repeated here. However his conclusion (164) is that the "Christian can be sinless inasfar as he shares now the life of eternity: by living in Christ, and by being spiritually reborn (vv. 6, 9). But the completion of that process of perfection lies in the future; and this means that sin is still an ongoing habit, and that its necessary concomitant of forgiveness is equally a present experience (1:7, onward)." This is similar to Marshall's eschatological reality view.

The "implicit condition" view seems the best, in that it affirms that abiding results in freedom from sin and that while the Christian abides, he or she does not sin (Brooke, 86; Bruce, 90; Houlden, 94; Plummer, 124). Brooke (86) warns us of the need to remember the context of the entire epistle. "The statements are made absolutely, after the writer's wont. They must, of course, be interpreted in the light of i. 8 ff., where the writer makes

---

long as a person abides in Christ, he will be free from sin"). After discussing the various views, he concludes that habitual sin proves a person is not a believer (183).

142. I appreciate Marshall's insight. In the midst of all this discussion he notes well (183), "Sinlessness is not a negative virtue: it includes full observance of God's positive commands."

it clear that he does not mean that those who have realized their union with Christ have actually attained as yet to a state of complete sinlessness." Lieu (131–32) insightfully observes that abiding in Christ is never complete, and so all believers will still have sins.

πᾶς ὁ ἁμαρτάνων οὐχ ἑώρακεν αὐτὸν οὐδὲ ἔγνωκεν αὐτόν, "everyone who sins has neither seen him nor known him." His use of the present participle with the article should be seen as describing a kind of person once again.[143] This is a person who has fellowship with Christ. Such a person is one who "does not sin." John uses the most basic and unclear forms of the verb to communicate this idea. It appears that he is intentionally speaking absolutely, or choosing to be vague. As Brown observes, "No matter what the author thought, the wording of his affirmations about sinlessness and impeccability is not sufficiently nuanced" (Brown, 430). This is another example of rhetorical or literary dualism characteristic of John but must not be mistaken for the Greek philosophical dualism.[144] He states things in op-

---

143. Burdick (240) sees πᾶς ... οὐκ as a "universal negative construction" that excludes "everyone who fails to pass the test."

144. H. C. Swadling ("Sin and Sinlessness in 1 John," 206–207) sees a gnostic background to this statement on the grounds that ἔγνωκεν is "a gnostic commonplace" and σπέρμα αὐτοῦ in v. 9, "in the sense of a divine indwelling principle, is unheard of elsewhere in the N.T. but it too is a gnostic commonplace." He says of 3:6 and 3:9, "If these verses were discovered today as fragments of an ancient manuscript, there would, no doubt, be considerable debate as to who wrote them. ... Clearly one cannot claim that these two sayings have been taken over from an established gnostic group." He places them "outside the mainstream of Christian thought" and argues that these two verses are "slogans" of the Gnostics because they are unorthodox when taken out of the context and seen in isolation. He posits that in polemical arguments, the practice was to quote one's opponent, then refute him in the next sentence, and that this is exactly what John is doing. "Verses 5 and 8 both contain a Christological reflection: Christ is sinless and forgiveness is to be found in him.... Thus we have two verses, 6 and 9, which demonstrate the form of slogans and have far more in common with Gnosticism than with Christianity. Two of the concepts they contain – those of the sinless believer and the seed of God are, in fact, quite foreign in Christian thought. Nowhere else in the N.T. do we find a connection made between the sinlessness of Christ and that of his followers, despite the commonness of the *imatatio Christi* motif." His reasons for resorting to Gnostic slogans is weak as are all arguments from silence. Additionally, similarity to Gnostic ideas that arose in later church history need not make them Gnostic. This is another case of reading circumstances from church history back into the text. His view that this continues John's polemic against his opponents also ignores the pastoral concerns of John being developed in this parenetic section.

posite and absolute terms. By doing this he forces the reader to choose one or the other, with at least one of the options being impossible, usually the desired option. This heightened contrast makes his statement absolutely clear. In this case, he makes it manifestly obvious that sinning is inconsistent with abiding.

Malatesta (*Interiority and Covenant*, 246) defines sin in terms of love of Jesus rather than acts against others. He says, "If sin for John means refusal to accept the revelation of love which Jesus is, and therefore a refusal to love Jesus, the Father who sent him and the brothers for whom he came, then not sinning means first of all loving devotion to the person of Jesus."

As earlier in this verse, some see this use of this present tense "sins" describing habitual sin rather than a single act (Akin, 142; Burdick, 239; Johnson, 71; Smalley, 164; Westcott, 104; Williamson, 115). This use of the present is best seen in its gnomic sense rather than as a customary (Bruce, 90) or iterative present (Kistemaker, 300). John is not describing habitual sin nor referring to each event of sin. Not only is he not saying "while he is abiding the person is not sinning," he is also not saying that an abiding Christian does not *ever* sin. Thus Schnackenburg (188) overstates it when he says, "Like Christ, the Christian united with him is immune to sin."[145] Otherwise, chapters 1 and 2 make no sense.[146] It is best to see him affirming, rather, that while one is abiding, that person does not sin (Hodges, 134; Lieu, 131–32). Why? He does not sin because he is experiencing a relationship with a sinless Savior.

This next πᾶς ὁ sentence seems on the surface to indicate that habitual sinning indicates an unregenerate person. The two views on John's meaning here is that either he is describing a nonbeliever (Brown, 427; Kistemaker, 300) or a sinning believer (Hodges, 146). Akin interprets the πᾶς ὁ with

145. "Wie Christus so ist auch der mit Christus verbundene Christ von der Sünde geschieden."

146. Brown (431) expresses this truth well. "One is forced, then, to understand the claims to sinlessness and impeccability in 1 John 3:6, 9 in light of the statements on status in 3:1, 2. We are God's children already, and there is a freedom from sin attached to that state. ... But in this last hour he recognizes that we are not yet all that we shall be, and so there is a growth in God's children. The divine seed abides and continues to transform the child of God into the image of God's Son which is the image of God himself, until at the final revelation we are like God himself. The more that this divine seed transforms the Christian, the more impossible it is for the Christian to sin."

the present participle being negated by οὐχ to mean no one who keeps on sinning. He argues that the present tense indicates "character, a prevailing lifestyle" and so "the believer will not live a life characterized by sin" (Akin, 142). This deduction arises from the doctrine of perseverance more than the text of Scripture.

As before, John is describing character, but not someone in the process of sinning. He is stating a principle that applies to all people, regenerate and unregenerate. John has told his readers that he does not want them to sin (2:1), but also that they must confess their sin (1:9) and never deny its presence in them (1:8, 10). Now he states a principle that governs their relationship with Christ. For the unregenerate, sinful conduct demonstrates their lostness. For the regenerate, sinful conduct denies their knowledge of Christ. They are living in conflict with what they should know is true.

Why does John use *see* and *know*, to describe what is not true of the person whose lifestyle is characterized by sin? Akin sees both as justification terms. "The apostle asserts with absolute clarity that those who live in habitual sin have not seen Christ and do not know Christ. This is the same as saying they do not have a saving relationship with Christ" (Akin, 144). Kistemaker understands John's use of *see* to be the equivalent of *believe*, thus a justification term as well. Houlden (94) says "to dwell in him" and "to know him" are "alternative" ways of saying the same thing. A sinful lifestyle proves that a person is unregenerate (Kistemaker, 299–300). Westcott is helpful when he connects the first term to the prologue and the apostolic claim to having seen Christ. Smalley (164) defines this seeing as "the spiritual sense of discerning his real identity and believing in him."

The second term has to do with understanding the truth about Christ (Westcott, 104). Smalley (165) defines it as "denoting a deeply personal and dynamic (spiritual) relationship with him." Thus, ultimately the practice of sin denies an understanding of Jesus. John's use of ἑώρακεν takes his readers back to the prologue of the epistle. His choice of the perfect tense indicates not only that those whose character is sinful have never seen Jesus, but that they have not been impacted by him either. Similarly, his choice of the perfect tense of the relational term for "know" (ἔγνωκεν) implies that sinning indicates they have never known him in a personal way. However, before concluding that this proves they are unbelievers (Williamson, 115), the same was said of the disciples in the upper room (John 14:7–11). When

John uses γινώσκω, his discussion of knowing God is better seen as a sanctification issue rather than justification.[147]

John's use of the perfect with these two verbs draws attention to both the past reality and the resulting state of being (Haas, de Jonge, and Swellengrebel, 89). This is much like what he said of those who do not believe in Jesus in John 3:18. They do not believe in Jesus because they have already been judged and stand in a state of judgment. John is affirming here that a sinful character indicates either these people are not eyewitnesses of Jesus (going back to 1:1–4) or they do not really understand God, much like the disciples whom Jesus chided for their ignorance in the upper room (Smalley, 164). They are out of fellowship with God (Pentecost, 79). This is parallel in thought with 2:9, where one may claim to be in the light while hating his brother but in actuality is in the darkness. Here someone may claim to know God, but a sinful lifestyle indicates that their knowledge is not personal but cursory; they are spiritually blind and ignorant (Hodges, 146). A child can know who their father is without knowing their father. In the same way, a child of God may know of him, and may have placed his or her trust in his Son sufficient to save, without knowing him intimately. None of us knows him fully. When we get to heaven we will come to realize just how little we know him or about him. Yet we can demonstrate a healthy limited knowledge of him by how we relate to him and live for him.

Habitually sinful conduct reveals the lack of fellowship with Christ in the life of a believer. Even so, when someone claims to be a Christian while sin remains the characteristic of his or her lifestyle, their conduct makes it legitimate to question their salvation. However, questioning their salvation is different from declaring that it is impossible for him or her to be a sinful believer. Westcott notes well, "St John speaks of 'abiding' in Christ and not simply of 'being' in Christ, because his argument rests on the efficacy of continuous human effort" (Westcott, 104). When one recognizes John is discussing issues of sanctification within the household of God, it

---

147. BDAG (199) gives this use of γινώσκω the meaning of "to arrive at a knowledge of someone" in the sense of "to know about" or "make the acquaintance of" that person. Another sense identified by BDAG (200) is"to grasp the significance or meaning of something," or "to understand" (R. Bultmann, "γινώσκω," *TDNT* 1:703) In this case I see this second sense applied to one's understanding of God and this is how Jesus used it with Philip (John 14:9) and may be the sense John gives it here with regard to the sinning believer.

is natural to see the issue of human responsibility in sanctification arising from the text.

This now sets the stage for what John is going to discuss in the following verses. With his characteristic dualism, he will offer only two alternatives for one's parentage: God or the devil.

3:7 Verses 7 through 10 involve both parallelism and repetition. In the present verse, parallelism is used to heighten the comparison and connection of the one who lives righteously with Christ, who is the righteous one (2:1).

Τεκνία, μηδεὶς πλανάτω ὑμᾶς·, "Little children, let no one deceive you." John begins this with the same term of endearment (τεκνία) and indicates he views his readers as believers, so what he is about to say will not question their salvation.[148] Smalley (166) describes these τεκνία as the "orthodox members of his community." Though nothing in the epistle warrants the Johannine community theory (see my comments in the introduction), Smalley is right that John's address indicates he views his readers as within the faith. As Westcott (105) notes well, John's use of the term here was "called out by the peril of the situation" his spiritual children were facing. This concern is reflected in his warning.

Some interpreters view John's warning of μηδεὶς πλανάτω as a reference to the antichrists (2:22) who were claiming to know God while denying Christ (Akin, 144; Barker, 332; Houlden, 94; Stott, 128). They were living unrighteous lives (1:6) while making this claim. John counters their claim and practice by affirming that believers practice what Jesus practiced if he dwells within them. Since Jesus is righteous, believers who are in fellowship with him will reflect that righteousness. God's righteousness expresses itself in the lives of his children through their conduct. Righteous character is not produced by righteous conduct, only revealed by it (Westcott, 105). In this approach, these verses continue to reflect a polemic against false teachers, John's opponents. However, while their conclusion is correct with regard to conduct and righteousness, John's pastoral concern, not polemical, is leading him to continue to develop his exhortations as they impact practical living. This will be seen in what he writes in the remainder of the

---

148. Though Hodges (136) suggests that by this John is addressing the church leaders, it is better to see him addressing the congregation as a whole. What he has to say is true for all believers and not restricted to leadership.

epistle. As Strecker (97–98) observes, the warning against deception does not have Christology in view as was characteristic of the false teachers in 2:26, but ethical behavior. Thus μηδεὶς should be taken literally to mean "'no one,' without restriction," not just the false teachers.[149]

Kistemaker (305) identifies three basic approaches to the next few verses: (1) John may be interpreted as presenting an "ideal" rather than a "reality." (2) John is distinguishing between kinds of sin (deliberate versus involuntary, mortal versus insignificant). (3) "John describes the person who persistently sins because he is in the power of the evil one and the Christian who sometimes may fall into sin, but cannot sin persistently (his view). Inman concurs and argues John is affirming, "not that one born of God will never commit a sinful act but that he will not persist in sin."[150]

ὁ ποιῶν τὴν δικαιοσύνην δίκαιός ἐστιν. "he who does righteousness is righteous." Again, stating a principle by using the articular present participle to describe a kind of person, John reveals what determines righteousness in the life of a believer. Righteous conduct and character is what makes a person righteous. Any attempt to reduce the participle *ποιῶν* down to a generic present tense verbal idea (Hodges, 138) ignores the nature of articular participle constructions. Though a time element does exist in every participle, an articular participle focuses more on aspect than time.[151] Even the adverb use's time element is relative to the main verb.[152] Rather, this construction identifies a character trait of the person more than progression of events, especially in light of his attachment of a direct object to the participle that helps define its verbal aspect.

Strecker (98) understands doing righteousness to be a concept common to Judaism and the Hellenistic world.[153] Smalley (167), too, traces this to an OT background. He sees the connection between "acting righteously and being righteous" in such passages as Gen 18:23–26; Psa 1:6; Isa 60:21;

149. Brown (404) notes that this is the single Johannine use of the term and may be emphatic.

150. V. K. Inman, "Distinctive Johannine Vocabulary and the Interpretation of I John 3:9," 142.

151. D. B. Wallace, *Grammar*, 620.

152. D. B. Wallace, *Grammar*, 622.

153. In n. 35 he identifies a multitude of OT and extrabiblical sources that uses the term for ethical behavior. In n. 37 he quotes statements from Plato, Xenophon, and Aristotle to demonstrate the Greek world's concept as well.

and Dan 12:3. The NT examples he provides include Matt 23:28; Luke 18:14; 1 Pet 4:18; and Rev 22:11. However, with regard to Strecker's NT examples, though each uses the term "righteous" or "righteousness," they do not especially make any direct or clear connection between "acting righteously and being righteous."

The article before the noun δικαιοσύνην indicates that a particular kind of righteousness is in view. Akin (145) sees this referring to Christ's righteousness. He quotes Matt 7:16 and says further, "the practice of righteousness is not what makes the individual "righteous" *(dikaios),* but it reveals the inner nature of the one who is practicing righteousness. One practices righteousness because of his righteous character." Burdick (241) notes that John chose ἐστιν over γίνεται because "the practice of righteousness is not said to make one righteous." Rather, "righteous conduct is the sign of righteous character."

Though one might be tempted to relate this to Gnostic antinomianism, it should be remembered that the Nicolaitans, whose antinomianism is strongly suggested in Rev 2 and 3, were also on the scene in John's day. Thus one need not look to supposed secessionists or Gnostics for the source of John's concern. Even today, with neither of these groups on the scene, the same warning is just as valid and contemporary. John's concern is pastoral, not polemical. The relationship of righteous conduct to righteous character is a truth every believer needs to understand at the core of their being.

This statement will be interpreted differently when seen as either justification truth or sanctification truth. For the "tests of life" view this is seen as justification truth, with the present participle describing lifestyle.[154] Additionally, since "fruit proves life," the fruit of unrighteousness would mean a person is an unregenerate nonbeliever while righteous conduct, "fruit," proves regeneration (Bruce, 91). "The individual's conduct is certain evidence of his nature. The one who practices righteousness does so because he has been granted the righteousness of God. In this sense John's regeneration language parallels the New Testament concept of justification. The believer does right because he possesses the imputed righteousness of Christ" (Akin, 145).

154. Hiebert (144–45) says, "The present tense participle makes clear that the test is not the performance of an occasional righteous deed but rather the habitual practice of 'righteousness.'"

With the Test of Fellowship view, or any other view that sees this as sanctification truth, the emphasis usually falls on the present time aspect of the participle Further, this is seen in light of 1:5–10 and the issue of abiding in which "fruit proves influence" rather than life. Pentecost (81) rightly sees this as a reference to the person's "experiential righteousness" (sanctification truth) as opposed to "positional righteousness" (justification truth) and notes that righteous conduct is "positional righteousness translated into experience." Westcott (105), though a representative of the Test of Life view, concurs with Pentecost, in a sense, by seeing this saying that righteous character is revealed by righteous actions.

καθὼς ἐκεῖνος δίκαιός ἐστιν·, "just as he is righteous." Jesus is the ultimate example of one whose righteous character is expressed by his conduct. John refers to Jesus with ἐκεῖνος once more, the pattern of usage well established by now.[155] This, combined with the comparative adverb conjunction καθὼς, points John's readers to Jesus as the example to follow. John is not affirming that the Christian is righteous to the same degree as Jesus, but in the same manner. "In the family of God, the children of God are like the Son of God" (Burdick, 241). Having called him "the righteous one" in 2:1, he reminds his readers of Jesus' character. He is the measure of righteousness, nothing less.

3:8 Verse 8 is parallel in construction to verse 7. Therefore the contrast it creates is between doing righteous deeds or doing sin, between being righteous like Jesus or being wicked like the devil. This Johannine antithesis draws a stark contrast between two kinds of people and leaves no room in the middle. Is this dualism (Strecker, 99) soteriological or otherwise? We shall see below.

ὁ ποιῶν τὴν ἁμαρτίαν ἐκ τοῦ διαβόλου ἐστίν. "he who does sin is from the devil." In contrast to the one who (literally) "does righteousness" is the man who "does sin" (Haas, de Jonge, and Swellengrebel, 89).[156] This present articular participle, once again, should be seen as describing character and thus have a more gnomic sense than "iterative or customary" (Kistemaker, 302).[157] Akin (146) interprets the present participle to indicate "a continual

155. See 3:3 for a full discussion of John's use of ἐκεῖνος. The other uses of ἐκεῖνος are 2:7; 3:3, 5, 16; and 4:17.

156. Smalley (168) sees John's choice of ποιῶν to be emphatic.

157. D. Wallace, *Grammar*, 620, n. 19. B. Fanning (*Verbal Aspect in New Testament Greek*, 165) notes, "The *present* aspect, when used of a truly single situation, denotes

state of sin. One's life is a life of sin. John refers to a habitual life of sin, not just individual acts of sin." However, every believer has habitual sins. The need for daily confession of sins indicates that we all habitually sin, though we confess only known individual acts of sin (Matt 6:12). The distinction made by him ignores 1:8–10 and ignores the reality of every believer's experience. It also ignores John's use of literary dualism to develop absolute antitheses. John is purposefully making a stark contrast between kinds of people. Whereas the one doing righteousness is described as righteous and is identified with Jesus who is righteous, this person is identified with the devil. John's use of ἐκ sees Satan, the devil, as the source of the sin-doer's conduct. Does this necessarily translate into that person being unregenerate? If taken in isolation, this statement might mean such. However, if being used in a purposefully dualistic context, should it not be seen in light of rhetorical license?[158]

This is the first mention of "devil" in this epistle, though John has referred to Satan as "the evil one" earlier (2:13–14). Coetzee argues that John's concept of the devil ("prince of this world") is not dualistic in any sense. Rather, Satan is limited in his power and there is "nothing of a gnostic-deistic dualism, of a good God of heaven and a wicked God of this world,

---

the existence of a state or the continuing progress of an action without beginning or end in view."

158. Hodges (139) argues that appealing to the present tense participle and giving it the iterative or customary sense is an invalid argument that has mostly been abandoned. Yet, it has not been totally abandoned. For example, see V. Inman ("Distinctive Johannine Vocabulary and the Interpretation of I John 3:9," 142) for an example of this approach. Even so, the idea that this is describing someone who practices sin and is therefore unsaved is invalidated by the implication of all New Testament commands. Christians are not given positive and negative commands for things that automatically result from their salvation. For example, we are never commanded to be baptized in the Holy Spirit. Why? It is automatic. We do not baptize ourselves. God baptizes us at the instance of our spiritual birth. Without it there is no spiritual birth (Rom 8:9; 1 Cor 12:13). In the same way, when we are commanded not to do something, it must be possible for believers to do it. Otherwise, the command is nonsensical. Also, if a believer can commit a certain sin once, he or she can obviously do it a second time, a third time, and then habitually. Thus even habitual sin proves nothing. In that light, what John is saying here has to be recognized as rhetorical rather than prescriptive.

who stand equal in power or alongside each other."[159] Strecker (99) sees this reference as anticipating the "opposition between being a child of God or a child of the devil" in verse 10. He further observes that this and verse 10 are the only places in the epistle where the devil is named as God's opponent.

Is this person a child of the devil? Is that the sense of ἐκ? Akin (145) and Bruce (91) both see parentage proven by behavior.[160] They see righteous deeds and sin reflecting character, whether that of Christ or the devil. People act according to their character, which arises out of one "family" or the other.[161] For example, in John 8:44 Jesus says that the unregenerate and unrepentant Jewish leaders were doing the "desires" of their "father" the devil. However, as Harris (140) notes, John does not say the devil is their "father" in this epistle, and ἐκ need not be construed to mean that. Smalley (168) says this indicates that they belong to the devil and "their activities originate from Satan."[162] Williams (37) understands this as indicating that it "reveals a kind of family likeness, to be seen in all those whose behavior is of the sort favoured by 'the devil.'" Based on Jesus' words to Nicodemus in John 3:6, Thompson (95–96) sees Johannine theology affirming that the opposite of being born of God is being "born of the flesh."[163] In John 6:70 Jesus called Judas "a devil," referring to his character. Furthermore, in John 13:2, Judas the betrayer is described as influenced by the devil when he departed to betray Jesus. In each of these instances the ones identified with Satan are clearly not believers. Thus, if John is alluding back to these instances from his Gospel, then what he says here should be understood as describing an unregenerate person. However, nothing in the text at this point indicates he is connecting with anything in the Gospel. However, in most

159. J. C. Coetzee, "Christ and the prince of this world in the Gospel and the Epistles of St. John," 117.

160. Lieu (134) cautions against pushing Johannine dualism too far. She sees John avoiding attributing to Satan generative powers equal to God.

161. Rather than the family imagery, Marshall (184) says, "The person who sins belongs on the devil's side or draws his inspiration from him."

162. He notes Qumran references (1QS 1:10, 18; 2:5, 19; 3:20–23; 1QM 13:12; and CD 12:2) to Belial, the "angel of darkness" and "spirit of hostility" as being a possible background to John's words here about the devil. Haas, de Jonge, and Swellengrebel (90) describes this phrase as meaning "originates from and has the quality of."

163. Jesus says, "That which is born of the flesh is flesh, and that which is born of the Spirit is spirit."

instances, his allusions to the Gospel reflect on the upper room actions and statements by Jesus, more than to the remainder of the Gospel.[164] Rather than the Gospel, what he says next points to a broader picture coming out of the Old Testament and not anything said or done in the Gospel.

ὅτι ἀπ' ἀρχῆς ὁ διάβολος ἁμαρτάνει, "because the devil has sinned from the beginning." There are two possibilities for what ἀπ' ἀρχῆς means in this context:[165]

(1) It looks back to God's creation of the universe prior to the creation of man for the beginning point of Satan's career, not to the fall of man in Gen 3 (Brooke, 88; Haas, de Jonge and Swellengrebel, 11; Houlden, 94; Smalley, 169; Stott, 128–29; Westcott, 106).

(2) It refers to the beginning of human history and Satan's involvement in the fall (Barker, 332; Bultmann, 52; Schnackenburg, 189) and subsequent murder of Abel (Harris, 141; Johnson, 73; Strecker, 100). This connects Jesus' words in John 8:44 that Satan was a "murderer" with John's use of Cain as his illustration of murder in the following verses.[166]

Though translated as a historical past, John uses the present tense to describe the career of the devil. With this "extending-from-past present," John reminds his readers that Satan is characterized by sin, that it is his nature (Smalley, 169).[167] Sin for him is a state of being as much as a practice.[168] However, in contrast to the devil, there is the Son of God.

εἰς τοῦτο ἐφανερώθη ὁ υἱὸς τοῦ θεοῦ, "For this reason the Son of God appeared." Jesus did not just become incarnate. He became incarnate for a reason. So with the prepositional phrase, εἰς τοῦτο, moved to the fore of this

---

164. This can be seen from his focus on loving one another (John 13:34–35), reference to the "new commandment" (John 13:34), the use of the term παράκλητος (John 14:15), their not being of the world but hated by the world (John 15:18–19; 17:14), and the theme of abiding (John 15).

165. Grayston (106) sees John' use of ἀπ' ἀρχῆς as presenting the devil as "the archetype of sinning."

166. Lieu (135) offers both theories without choosing any.

167. B. M. Fanning (*Verbal Aspect in New Testament Greek*, 165) with regard to John's statement here, says, "The *present* views the situation from within, which means portraying the multiple occurrences as continuing, taking place over time, without end-points in view. .... Thus the present gives emphasis to the iterative nature of the occurrence." (italics his)

168. Haas, de Jonge, and Swellengrebel (90) describe it as a "habit" with Satan.

clause for emphasis, and with the verb, ἐφανερώθη, immediately following, John states Jesus' purpose in coming.

To what does εἰς τοῦτο refer? It could either look back on what was just said (the devil's sinning from the beginning) or forward to the ἵνα clause (Harris, 141). When followed by a ἵνα clause, it is best to see it looking forward.

As was noted before (3:5), John's choice of ἐφανερώθη refers to the historical fact of Jesus' incarnation and earthly ministry and alludes to his pre-incarnate existence and his being sent by the Father to achieve the purpose that is about to be described (Smalley, 160).

ἵνα λύσῃ τὰ ἔργα τοῦ διαβόλου, "in order that he might destroy the works of the devil." With the resumptive ἵνα, John describes the purpose of Jesus' incarnation (Harris, 141). He came to destroy the works of the devil. So, what are the "works of the devil" and how does Jesus destroy them?

This is the only place where the phrase "the works of the devil" occurs.[169] The nearest equivalent can be found in John 8:41, where τὰ ἔργα τοῦ πατρὸς ὑμῶν describes the Jews' desire to murder Jesus. Combined with John 8:44, ὑμεῖς ἐκ τοῦ πατρὸς τοῦ διαβόλου ἐστὲ, the same concept can be found from the words of Jesus. It is likely that John remembered Jesus' dispute and how he described those rejecting him.

It is correct, on one hand, to see Jesus' work on the cross as the defeat of Satan and the place where this destruction occurred (Akin, 145). However,

---

169. M. E. Snodderly, "A Socio-Rhetorical Investigation of the Johannine Understanding of 'the Works of the Devil' in 1 John 3:8," 131–38. Snodderly proposes (131) that "the devil's works can be summarized as bringing death—both physical (disease and deformity, social chaos, mental chaos) and spiritual (unbelief, hatred)." She sees the seven signs in John's Gospel as revealing the "spheres" of Jesus' "works" that destroy the works of Satan. These include such things as His power over nature, disease, and death (132–34). She says, "the works of God are clearly seen through Jesus' miraculous and caring good works that were done for the purpose of generating belief in his followers and which had the result of overturning the works of the devil" (135). Finally, she argues that Jesus does his works against the devil now through his followers (137–38). Her observations are helpful, and her conclusion is true to an extent. However, though we may be agents through whom God works (for example, we are God's ambassadors and offer the world reconciliation), it is still the Holy Spirit who is actively convicting the world and drawing men to Jesus. Further, John's focus is on believers, not our ministry to the world. And it is in the realm of our own lives that Satan's works are being destroyed as well as in the world at large.

John is looking at Satan's present works, not his dominion, his initial judgment by Jesus on the cross, or his future judgment.[170] This verse is parallel to 3:5, where Jesus came to take away (αἴρω) sins (Smalley, 170; Strecker, 100; Westcott, 107).[171] Together these two verses indicate that a part of Jesus' destroying the devil's work involves "taking away." However, this "taking away" involves more than forgiveness of individual sins. Satan, who has and continues to sin from the beginning, acted to deceive Adam and Eve into sinning and thereby introduced sin into the human race. He continues to be the tempter of mankind. His goal is clearly to get all men to sin along with him. Jesus' purpose in coming is to stop the cycle, to free men from Satan's power and influence, and to remove sin from their lives (Burdick, 244).[172] By doing this, Jesus "destroys" Satan's work. This is the focus of what John says next. He answers the question of how this is made possible. It is by a spiritual birth and a new parentage.

The impact of Jesus' victory is the removal of sin from the lives of those who look to him for deliverance from the devil and his practices. Jesus came to save men, not just from the fires of hell and eternal damnation but from the power of sin each day of their mortal lives before being translated to glory where sin will forever be removed.

3:9 This sentence is composed of two statements describing the one born of God, with each statement containing an adverb ὅτι clause explaining why each statement is true.[173] Stated as a principle and in absolute terms, it chal-

---

170. Haas, de Jonge, and Swellengrebel (90) sees this referring "both to the Devil's own sinful deeds, and to his instigating others to sin."

171. Schnackenburg (190) relates this to αἴρω as well and describes this as "radical removal" (*radikale Beseitigung*).

172. Marshall (185) describes Jesus work as "to undo whatever the devil had achieved, to thwart whatever he tries to do. No doubt it is his 'work' of temptation and enslaving men that is in view."

173. Williamson (118) identifies a chiasm in this verse composed of five parts:

a – No one who is born of God
  b – will continue to sin
    c – because God's seed remains in him;
  b′ – he cannot go on sinning
a′ – because he has been born of God.

Smalley (171) sees a four part "loose" chiasm:

A No one born of God

lenges the interpreter to understand John's point. In this verse the perfect participle and verb describes the believer while present tense verbs, ποιεῖ and δύναται ἁμαρτάνειν, define his conduct. This verse is similar to what John said in 3:6, so many of the same issues rest with it as will be seen in the discussion that follows. It also builds on what was said in 3:6, moving from affirming that the abiding believer does not sin while he or she is abiding, to state that the believer is "not able to sin." What he means by this must be discerned, once more, in light of 1:8–10, and will be addressed in what follows.

Πᾶς ὁ γεγεννημένος ἐκ τοῦ θεοῦ ἁμαρτίαν οὐ ποιεῖ, "Everyone who has been born from God does not sin." Using another "generalizing" πᾶς ὁ construction, John again addresses the whole community perenetically rather than developing a polemic against opponents (Strecker, 101). This construction in combination with οὐ makes this a "universal negative" meaning "no one" (Burdick, 244). Smalley (171) sees this use of πᾶς highlights the "character" of the believer.

John now employs a perfect participle to describe a regenerate saint. Rather than being an extensive perfect, focusing on the birth itself, this is an intensive perfect that focuses on the results of that birth (Brooke, 89; Smalley, 172; Westcott, 107). The construction identifies God as the source of spiritual birth and looks back to the declaration of 3:1. Though the believer's birth is in the past, their life as children of God (those whose spiritual life is sourced in God) continues to the present (Smalley, 172; Westcott, 107). There is no question of the person's status as a child of God. Brown's observation is noteworthy, that though "God has children and is called their father" and "the devil has children (1 John 3:10) and is called their father (John 8:44)," and though "God's children are said to be begotten by

---

B commits sin;
B′ he cannot sin,
A′ because he has been born of God.

As always, the identification of chiasms tends to be subjective and dependent on what each interpreter "sees" as markers in the text. Thus we have two authors who see a chiasm, but see it differently. What this tells us is that John is repeating himself, and repetition is a significant literary device. By seeing that we will not err, even if we miss a chiasm or two. Finding chiasms where they do not exist, though, is more problematic for interpretation than missing them, since significance is given to a chiasm's structure and the placement of ideas within it.

(from) Him ... nowhere in the Johannine literature are the devil's children said to be begotten by him" (Brown, 404–5).[174]

What John says about this person whose life is sourced in God is that he or she does not sin. Literally he says this person "is not doing a sin." However, this use of the present tense need not be progressive but gnomic. What he is saying is that habitual sin is inconsistent with a Christian's walk. Is John saying that the believer never sins? No. That is impossible in light of 1:8–10. Nor does he say a believer may not fall into persistent sin. That is a theological deduction made by interpreters, not an affirmation anywhere in the New Testament. Even so, 2:1–2 makes it clear that believers should not want to sin and that their sins are dealt with by Jesus when they do occur. It is common for interpreters to take the present tense as continuous action as opposed to single occurrences of sin and thereby to indicate true believers do not "habitually engage in sin" or "practice habitual sin" (Akin, 147; Johnson, 74; Kistemaker, 303; Stott, 130). Dodd (79) identifies the problem and questions "whether the reader could be expected to grasp so subtle a doctrine simply upon the basis of a precise distinction of tenses without further guidance." He also notes (80) that the "apparent contradiction" could not be resolved back then "by grammatical subtlety." However, John makes it very clear in 1:8–10 that no believer can at any time claim an absence of sin in their life. Though one may not knowingly sin, we can be sure that we habitually sin in some area. That is why God provides cleansing from all unrighteousness for the one who confesses known sins (1:9). Kubo, after identifying the absolute and habitual sinning views, defends the absolute view from the "context of the verse" in which the gnostic heretics are in view. He argues that John is drawing a sharp contrast between the two groups and to indicate habitual sin would weaken his argument since the gnostic heretics are not just indifferent toward sin, but does not call the same things sin as the Christian does.[175] For them "sin is ignorance, not

---

174. Schnackenburg (192) concurs.

175. S. Kubo ("1 John 3:9: Absolute or Habitual?" 50) says at length: "The author has isolated in his thinking this one situation and is speaking forcefully to it. The heretic who defines sin as ignorance and not as lawlessness can sin, but the Christian who recognizes sin as lawlessness and that Jesus came to destroy sin and its instigator, the devil, cannot sin. The sharp antithesis is intentional and any qualifications or reservations at this point would undermine the argument. The sharp antithesis must stand. The absoluteness of the statement must remain." After

lawlessness."[176] Brooke (90) concurs and say "the writer speaks, here as elsewhere, in the absolute language of the prophet rather than with the circumspection of the casuist." Windisch (118) argues that the absolute sense was reflected in Jewish literature of that time, such as *1 En.* 5:8–9 and *Jub.* 5:12, as well as Ignatius in *1 Eph* 8:2.[177] Finally, against those who argue for the habitual sense from the present tense, he responds, "If the tense is pressed and one concludes that 3:9 is habitual, then 1:8 must likewise be habitual where a present tense stands."[178] Smalley (172) solves the problem and understands this to indicate "the Christian's *potential* state of sinlessness" (italics his; also Bultmann, 52).

The absence of the article with sin indicates that he is referring to sin as a general principle, a principle true of all believers, rather than a single sin (Brooke, 89). However, this use of the anarthrous noun with the present indicative could be intended to refer to a pattern of sin in a person's life (contra Hodges, 142–43). The problem of this, though, would be its weakening the antithesis between opposites that John is developing. This must be seen as an intentionally absolute statement that is just as intentionally designed to be seen in light of what has already been affirmed in chapters one and two. All believers do sin. All believers must confess their sins in particular

---

reminding the reader that 2:1 affirms Christians *do* sin, he warns that "this possibility must not qualify 3:9, and thus weaken and even destroy the author's argument."

176. S. Kubo, "1 John 3:9: Absolute or Habitual?" 49.

177. *1 En.* 5:8–9 reads: "And then there shall be bestowed upon the elect wisdom, And they shall all live and never again sin, Either through ungodliness or through pride: But they who are wise shall be humble. And they shall not again transgress, Nor shall they sin all the days of their life, Nor shall they die of (the divine) anger or wrath, But they shall complete the number of the days of their life." (R. H. Charles, sv. Enoch 5:8–9, *Pseudepigrapha of the Old Testament*, 2:190)

Jub. 5:12 reads: "And he made for all his works a new and righteous nature, so that they should not sin in their whole nature for ever, but should be all righteous each in his kind alway." (R. H. Charles, sv. *Jub.* 5:12, *Pseudepigrapha of the Old Testament*, 2:20)

1 Eph 8:2 reads: "For when there is no evil desire within you, which might defile and torment you, then do ye live in accordance with the will of God, and are [the servants] of Christ." (As quoted in: A. Roberts, J. Donaldson and A. C. Coxe, *The Ante-Nicene Fathers*, 1:52)

178. S. Kubo, "1 John 3:9: Absolute or Habitual?" 51. Dodd (79) says that "it is not clear why a person of whom the former statement [3:9] is true should not make the latter statement [1:8] about himself. Yet the former is affirmed and the latter is denied."

to be cleansed of their known sins and any that they are unaware of as well. That being said, John makes this blanket statement and then explains why it can theoretically be true.[179]

ὅτι σπέρμα αὐτοῦ ἐν αὐτῷ μένει, "because his seed abides in him." This is the first of two ὅτι clauses that make up this sentence. Both should be seen as causal. They each explain the affirmation that precedes them. In this case, why the one born from God does not sin.

John's use of the present tense μένει indicates both the permanence of the seed's presence and its continuous influence in the life of the believer.[180] Since the seed is from God, it should impact the believer's life with the character of God. Additionally, we know from Jas 1:13 that God neither tempts people to evil nor is tempted by evil. Such is also true of God's seed. So John now explains the significance of God's implanted seed.[181]

What enables a believer not to sin is God's "seed" abiding in him. So, what does John mean by "seed"? The word, σπέρμα, chosen by John is a common term with a range of meanings, both literal and figurative. Along with plant seeds, it often refers to physical descendents of humans (John 7:42; 8:33, 37; Rev 12:17), but not here.[182] Rather this metaphor alludes to

179. Harris (144) describes John's intent well in that "he speaks in theoretical terms which do not discuss the possible occasional exception, because to do so would weaken his argument."

180. Strecker (113) notes that μένω is a "stronger" term that ἐστὶν in that it "describes not only the present situation but its continuing existence."

181. This is an obviously figurative use of "seed" which grows out of its literal sense of "male seed" (BDAG, 761).

182. Brown (408–9) raises this as a possibility and notes that 3 of John's 4 uses of σπέρμα do mean physical descendent or offspring (John 7:42; 8:33, 37). The absence of an article before σπέρμα as well as the double use of αὐτός grammatically allows this possibility. However, he sees the weight of evidence favoring one of the other more common views. Moffat (s.v. 1 John 3:9), on the other hand, does interpret this use of σπέρμα as a reference to the believer himself, described by him as "the offspring of God." He bases this on the other Johannine uses as well as Paul's use in Gal 3:29, where σπέρμα does describe the believer who is the spiritual descendent of Abraham.

something of a spiritual nature (Bruce, 92), though it is not clearly defined.[183] There are four possible meanings of σπέρμα αὐτοῦ:[184]

(1) Seed refers to the Holy Spirit (Brown, 410–11; Burdick, 247; Johnson, 74; Schnackenburg, 190–91; Strecker, 102–3).[185] This is supported from the reference to being born of the Spirit in John 3:5–6 and the Spirit's connection with abiding in the epistle (3:24; 4:13). This would see the Spirit as the "agent of begetting" and so the referent in this verse. However, as Dryden notes, one must distinguish between the sense of a word and the referent, which may be different, and, he affirms, is in this case.[186] Further, the Holy Spirit is never referred to elsewhere as the "seed" of God or as begotten of God. He is sent by God and proceeds from the Father, but he is never described as begotten. His indwelling ministry is described with the metaphors of a flowing spring of "living water" (John 7:37–39), the Comforter (John 14:15–18), and a seal/earnest of our salvation (Eph 1:13). To refer to the Holy Spirit as God's seed would be to confuse him with God the Son.

(2) Seed represents the Word of God (Dodd, 79–80; Hodges, 142; Lenski, 463; Marshall, 187; Moody, 65–66; Westcott, 107).[187] This may be

---

183. Stott (133–34), after detailing the views, chooses to remain neutral and observes that the meaning of the verse remains the same with all of them, "namely that it is the Christian's supernatural birth from God which keeps him from habitual sin."

184. Smalley (173) identifies a fifth view that he refers to as "the divine life principle" view. He argues against this view on the basis that this metaphor is "sandwiched" between two statements about spiritual rebirth and, as an agricultural metaphor, would miss the "relational aspect" of this term in Johannine literature. He then argues for a sixth view which combines the concepts of "word" and "Spirit" from an OT perspective in which God's Word is hidden in their hearts and the NT idea of the word and Spirit's impact in a person's heart leads to "rebirth."

185. Schnackenburg (191) argues that John is using "seed" as a metaphor for the Holy Spirit similarly to Jesus' use of being "born from above" in John 3:6 as a metaphor for spiritual birth (being born of the Spirit). He notes that normally "seed" is used in the NT for the Word of God (Matt 13:3–23, Parable of the Soils; 1 Pet 1:23; James 1:18, 21). Marshall (186) sees it as a combination of both Spirit and Word.

186. J. Dryden, "The Sense of ΣΠΕΡΜΑ in 1 John 3:9," 92.

187. F. Büchsel, *Johannes und der hellenistische Synkretismus*, 59; E. Malatesta (*Interiority and Covenant*, 247–48) sees 1 John 2:14, 24, 27, and 2 John 2 as parallel passages. Marshall (186) allows for both the Spirit and Scripture and says, "There is some doubt whether the seed is intended to signify the Holy Spirit or the Word of God. Probably the two ideas are to be linked together."

indicated by John's statement in 1:10 about God's Word being "in" believers. Strecker (102) rejects this on the basis that word is being contrasted with "lie" and relates more to "truthful speech." Grayston (107) argues that "the Johannine tradition is consciously aware of the generative power of words lodged in the mind and experience of Christians, and regards the Word of God as a projection of the divine being—very similar indeed to the wisdom of God in Jewish tradition." He points to *1 En.* 5:8 as an example.[188] This is based on Scripture being called "the imperishable seed" in 1 Pet 1:23 and the seeds of the sower being called "the word of God" in Luke 8:4–15. However, Jesus (in Luke 8) uses *σπόρος* and Peter uses *σπορά* instead of *σπέρμα* and says they become descendants (are born from that seed) "through the word" (*διὰ λόγου*), not that the word *is* the seed.[189] In John 15:7 Jesus spoke of his words abiding in the believer (*τὰ ῥήματά μου ἐν ὑμῖν μείνῃ*). In 1 John 2:14 God's Word (*ὁ λόγος τοῦ θεοῦ*) abides (*μένει*) in the young men. However, as Harris (145–46) notes, nowhere in the Johannine corpus is the Word of God associated with the "fathering of Christians." This concept is expressed in James 1:18. Also 1 Pet 1:23 connects God's Word with spiritual rebirth.

(3) Seed represents divine offspring (N. Alexander, 86–87; Thompson, 97; Yarbrough, 195).[190] In this view it is argued that since its normal mean-

---

188. "And then there shall be bestowed upon the elect wisdom, And they shall all live and never again sin, Either through ungodliness or through pride: But they who are wise shall be humble." (*Pseudepigrapha of the Old Testament*, ed. R. H. Charles, *1 En.* 5:8)

189. J. Dryden ("The Sense of ΣΠΕΡΜΑ in 1 John 3:9," 93) argues that Matthew's use of *σπέρμα* in the Parable of the Wheat and the Tares while using *σπορά* in the Parable of the Sower strengthens his own view that *σπέρμα* should mean "offspring" as opposed to Scripture. For him, the stronger evidence, though, is the absence elsewhere in the NT or LXX of *σπέρμα* being used for the Word of God in any of its 290 occurrences. Still, that remains an argument from silence in that an author need not follow the conventional meaning of any word and may infuse it with his own meaning for literary purposes.

190. J. A. Bengel, *Gnomon of the New Testament,* 5:128; Dryden, "The Sense of ΣΠΕΡΜΑ in 1 John 3:9," 85, 94; J. M. Lieu, "What was from the Beginning: Scripture and Tradition in the Johannine Epistles," 470–71. She suggests John was responding to "Sethian gnosticism" based on the chapter's dualism and from this concludes that he viewed believers as either carrying "the 'seed' of God's promise" or actually being the "seed" as opposed to non-believers who are children of the devil. This is a case of reading history backward and taking a pastoral section and making it polemical. This may be an example where she is inconsistent with

ing is "offspring" or "children," that should be the sense here, unless the text indicates otherwise.[191] Both the LXX[192] and NT[193] use σπέρμα with this sense. Dryden quotes Joos' Law, which says in a case where the meaning of a word is in question, the word should be defined "in such fashion as to make it contribute least to the total message derivable from the passage where it is at home, rather than, e.g., defining it according to some presumed etymology or semantic history." The anarthrous σπέρμα αὐτοῦ argues against it referring back to πᾶς ὁ γεγεννημένος ἐκ τοῦ θεοῦ (Dodd, 75). Further, for this to mean "offspring," it would form a tautology with πᾶς ὁ γεγεννημένος ἐκ τοῦ θεοῦ, essentially saying that "everyone who has been born of God" does not sin because, as his spiritual offspring, the believer abides in God (Smalley, 173). Of course, John may have intended just such a tautologous construction for emphasis. The argument that John would have chosen τέκνα θεοῦ over σπέρμα θεοῦ is countered with the interchange of John 8:33–39 where they are shown to be synonymously used. Paul also follows this same pattern of synonymy in Rom 9:6–8.[194] J. du Preez rejects this on the basis that if John intended σπέρμα to be a collective noun, then the subject of the following phrase would have been plural, "they cannot sin," rather than singular.[195] He then sees the preceding αὐτοῦ indicating "the individual believer" as well.[196] Dryden argues that "it is likely that John chooses σπέρμα here,

---

her proposal elsewhere that the epistle is primarily pastoral rather than polemical in purpose.

191. M. Joos (Martin Joos, "Semantic Axiom Number One," *Language*, 48 (1972) 257), as quoted by J. Dryden ("The Sense of ΣΠΕΡΜΑ in 1 John 3:9," 94–95).

192. A few LXX examples include Gen 12:7 (Τῷ σπέρματί σου δώσω τὴν γῆν ταύτην), 15:3 (καὶ εἶπεν Αβραμ Ἐπειδὴ ἐμοὶ οὐκ ἔδωκας σπέρμα), 1 Chron 16:13 (σπέρμα Ισραηλ παῖδες αὐτοῦ, υἱοὶ Ιακωβ), and Isa 53:10 (ὄψεται σπέρμα, "he shall see his seed"). In John 8:33 the Jews called themselves "the seed of Abraham" (σπέρμα Ἀβραάμ ἐσμεν) and Jesus agreed with them in 8:37 (σπέρμα Ἀβραάμ ἐστε).

193. NT examples outside of John include Luke 1:55 (τῷ Ἀβραὰμ καὶ τῷ σπέρματι αὐτοῦ), Rom 1:3 (τοῦ γενομένου ἐκ σπέρματος Δαυὶδ κατὰ σάρκα), 11:1 (ἐκ σπέρματος Ἀβραάμ), 1 Cor 11:22 (σπέρμα Ἀβραάμ εἰσιν;), Gal 3:29 (τοῦ Ἀβραὰμ σπέρμα ἐστέ) and others. Yarbrough (195) provides Rom 9:6–8 (... οὐδ' ὅτι εἰσὶν σπέρμα Ἀβραὰμ πάντες τέκνα ... τοῦτ' ἔστιν, οὐ τὰ τέκνα τῆς σαρκὸς ταῦτα τέκνα τοῦ θεοῦ ἀλλὰ τὰ τέκνα τῆς ἐπαγγελίας λογίζεται εἰς σπέρμα.) as an example where Paul "toggles" between σπέρμα and τέκνα in the development of his argument.

194. J. Dryden, "The Sense of ΣΠΕΡΜΑ in 1 John 3:9," 95.

195. J. du Preez, " 'SPERMA AUTOU' in 1 John 3:9," 106.

196. J. du Preez, " 'SPERMA AUTOU' in 1 John 3:9," 107.

instead of τέκνα, to emphasize God's action in begetting his children. ... So it is very possible that John uses σπέρμα, a word with covenantal overtones not associated with τέκνα, to stress the theological point that God's children do not sin because they are born of *God*."[197]

(4) Seed represents the divine nature—the new nature that believers receive at regeneration such as is described in 2 Pet 1:4 (Akin, 147; W. Alexander, 183; Dodd, 77; Law, 389; Smalley, 173; Westcott, 107).[198] Marshall (186) relates this to the seeds in the parable of the sower (Mark 4:3–20). Dryden rejects this on the basis that it would reflect a Gnostic understanding of σπέρμα.[199] Du Preez argues that since this verse begins and ends with being born of God, σπέρμα here is being used in the sense of "life coming from God."[200] Since eternal life ἐν αὐτῷ μένουσαν is used in 3:15, it is "practically the same as the expression ἐν αὐτῷ μένει in 3:9."[201] Since eternal life is the theme of the epistle, σπέρμα will be connected to it closely in this passage.[202] He argues that αὐτοῦ has the believer as its referent rather than God when σπέρμα is made to mean "eternal life."[203] However, in a polemical section of his epistle, one might expect John to use the terminology of his opponents while infusing it with orthodox meaning. This final view seems best and is reflected in what follows.

The absence of the article may indicate that John is thereby focusing attention on the character of God's seed rather than the seed itself (Westcott, 108). However, though that may appear as a grammatical option, the absence of an article does not require such.

καὶ οὐ δύναται ἁμαρτάνειν "and it is not able to sin." The absoluteness of this statement raises a difficulty of interpretation and calls for an

---

197. J. Dryden, "The Sense of ΣΠΕΡΜΑ in 1 John 3:9," 99 (italics his).
198. Westcott (107) describes this as "the ruling principle of the believer's growth. God gives, as it were, of Himself to the Christian. ... The germ of the new life is that out of which the mature man will in due time be developed." He points to John 1:13 ("...who were born, not of blood, nor of the will of the flesh, nor of the will of man, but of God.") to support this. However, little connection can be made between this statement and what John is discussing in this third chapter of his epistle. Bruce (92) favors both this view and the divine offspring interpretation as possibilities.
199. J. Dryden, "The Sense of ΣΠΕΡΜΑ in 1 John 3:9," 94.
200. J. du Preez, " 'SPERMA AUTOU' in 1 John 3:9," 107.
201. J. du Preez, " 'SPERMA AUTOU' in 1 John 3:9," 107.
202. J. du Preez, " 'SPERMA AUTOU' in 1 John 3:9," 107.
203. J. du Preez, " 'SPERMA AUTOU' in 1 John 3:9," 107.

identification of the subject of the verb δύναται. This clause cannot be rendered to say "able not to sin."[204] It clearly says "not able to sin." It also does not say a believer cannot "continue in sin" as some would take it (Akin, 149; Burdick, 248; Burge, 150).[205] This is again reading the doctrine of perseverance into the text along with the rejection of perfectionism. For example, Westcott (108) says, "The ideas of divine sonship and sin are mutually exclusive. As long as the relationship with God is real (ὅτι ἐκ τοῦ θεοῦ γεγένν.) sinful acts are but accidents. They do not touch the essence of the man's being. The impossibility of sinning in such a case lies in the moral nature of things." Hodges (141) counters this view by distinguishing levels of self so that the "regenerate inward self" becomes impeccable because of the presence of "the divine seed." These all are attempts to avoid an absolute statement that flies in the face of Jesus' own teaching of our need for daily confession of sin (Matt 6:12), as well as John's previous affirmations (1 John 1:8–2:1). It also stands in apparent conflict with what he will about praying for sinning brothers in 5:16. Finally, the experience of all redeemed children of God is that we do indeed sin and are daily in need of forgiveness. So is this a part of

---

204. Or as Bultmann (53) interprets it as "the possibility of not sinning," and so might be termed "able not to sin." Harris (146–49) describes eight different approaches to the meaning of "cannot sin." They include (1) an inept redactor, (2) a different group is being addressed than those in 1:8–2:2, (3) this refers to special types of sin rather than sin in general, (4) he is distinguishing between individual acts of sin and a lifestyle of sin, (5) he is distinguishing between "ordinary" and "superior" Christians, (6) he is speaking in different literary contexts, (7) he is writing with differing emphases because of the differing contexts of 1:8–2:2 and 3:1–10, and (8) a specific sin, "failure to love the brethren," is in view.

205. N. Turner, *Grammatical Insights into the New Testament*, 151. Burge (150) provides four arguments for why a believer cannot continue in sin: (1) "The Greek verb 'to sin' appears in the present indicative, and the sense is that we should not have the ongoing, self-endorsing habit of sin. (2) In 3:6b the construction uses a present participle (lit., 'those who sins,' or better, 'the one who continues to sin') to express the same notion. Once again, a participle with a present tense implies ongoing activity. (3) In 3:9a, a different verb is used ('to do sin'), and sin appear as a noun. Again, it appears as a present tense. (4) Finally, in 3:9b John describes Christians as 'not able to sin.' Both the verb ('to be able') and its infinitive ('to sin') appear in the present tense." He notes that some, Marshall in particular, dispute the idea that this describes "habitual sin." He says they argue that "it seems that John may not be diligently following the grammatical function of present and aorist tenses this carefully" and that most of them "see these texts controlled by the theological situation of the Johannine crisis."

Johannine dualism? Is he employing hyperbole? Or is he describing a deep spiritual truth that remains hard to comprehend? A lot may be answered if one determines who or what it is John is discussing.

What remains unclear is the subject of the verb. In this instance John foregoes using a pronoun or other noun as the 3 singular verb's subject in combination with the negative particle οὐ and fleshed out with the infinitive "to sin." The subject of the verb may either be the believer ("he") or the seed ("it"). If the subject is the believer, then John is affirming that anyone who is God's spiritual child, his "seed," cannot sin. Again, this is inconsistent with all that has been written by him so far, especially in 1:8–10. Perfectionism is not an option with John. If the subject is the "seed," referring to the implanted new nature, then John is affirming that the new nature is unable to sin. "The nature that God imparts cannot commit sin because it is God's nature. ... That is, God's seed, God's nature, abides in God's child and the nature cannot sin because it is born of God. ... Thus John is not saying that sin is impossible in the life of the child of God. He traces sin in the life of the child of God to its root—the old fallen nature" (Pentecost, 83). From that divine "seed" being unable to sin Hodges (130) concludes that "at the inward level of his redeemed nature, the believer is every bit as pure as his Savior is. That purity will be totally realized at the coming of the Lord (v. 2), but is ours now at the core of our being" (bold his). Habitual sin is an inconsistency in the life of a Christian though not an impossibility. Thus believers are theoretically able not to sin, but will never achieve that status until the old nature is replaced by a glorified body (Brown 412–16; Smalley 158–64).[206] The old nature, being fallen, naturally and consistently rebels against God. Thus when someone sins, it is the person sinning, but under the influence of their old nature.[207] Even when a believer sins, he or she is acting out of the old nature and being consistent

206. This is especially made clear by Paul in Rom 7 wherein he describes the believer's struggle with sin. Though some theologians attempt to place the struggle in Paul's pre-conversion experience, the location of the chapter in the flow of his argument in Romans cannot describe his unregenerate state. Chapter seven lies at the center of Paul's discussion of sanctification (Rom 6–8) rather than condemnation (Rom 1–3) or justification (Rom 3–5). The attempt of theologians to place Paul's struggle earlier arises from their theology, not the text.

207. This is evident in Paul's experience in Rom 7, with the subsequent solution in Rom 8.

with it. It is the new nature that motivates the believer to obey God, though once again it is the person, not his or her nature, who is doing the obeying.

ὅτι ἐκ τοῦ θεοῦ γεγέννηται, "because it has been born from God." Why does a believer not sin? The absence of sin in a person's life results from his or her spiritual birth, which has a continual impact on his or her being. John's choice of the extensive perfect γεγέννηται (Brown 411; Smalley 175) says more about eternal security than sinlessness. This spiritual birth had a beginning point but continues on with permanent results and implications. The person remains a child of God, and his seed remains in him. Repeating ἐκ τοῦ θεοῦ (1 John 2:29; 4:7; 5:1), John describes this birth as being sourced in God. God is the cause of that birth. John's choice of this phrase reflects Jesus' use of it in the Gospel. In John 7:17 Jesus describes his teachings as being sourced in God. Then in John 8:42 Jesus again uses the phrase to describe his having come "from God" and clarifies its meaning as his having been sent by the Father. It is both of these nuances that are reflected in John's use of the phrase in his epistle.

Hiebert is correct when he says that being born from God causes sinning to be "a moral incompatibility between the believer's old and new nature." However, he wrongly concludes from this that the spiritual birth results in a "believer's inability to continue in the practice of sin" (Hiebert, 148). Akin similarly concludes, "Although the Christian still falls prey to sinful acts, John insists that it is impossible for sin to become a believer's pattern of life" (Akin, 150). However when Paul commands believers not to let sin reign in their mortal bodies (Rom 6:12), by implication such is not only possible but the experience of most. Further, sin does not "reign" through occasional lapses. Paul's warning about becoming enslaved to sin (Rom 6:5–6, 12–14) means that such a believer will habitually sin. Thus, though being born from God gives a person a new nature, that nature does not guarantee immunity to habitual sin any more than occasional sin. The old nature is still resident within and still likes to sin. It has neither been eradicated nor incapacitated. It must still be dealt with in the life of the believer. Thus Paul commands us to "reckon" ourselves "dead to sin" (Rom 6:11). Moreover, he warns that failure to do so results in slavery to sin rather than righteousness.

So, what is the significance of sin in the life of a believer? It speaks to the world. Just as Jesus declared that the world would know his disciples by their love for one another (John 13:35), so too sin denies to the world that same relationship. This is the thrust of what is to follow.

3:10 Christians reveal their new natures by choosing righteous living. The devil's children reveal their unregenerate natures by sinning. So when a Christian sins, he or she fails to express the new nature but reflects the devil's pattern by expressing the old nature.

This is another of John's "hinge" verses and contains concepts from both the previous material and what follows.[208] Key terms such as children of God and doing righteousness are connected to love, which will be the focus in the passage that follows.

ἐν τούτῳ φανερά ἐστιν τὰ τέκνα τοῦ θεοῦ καὶ τὰ τέκνα τοῦ διαβόλου "By means of this the children of God and the children of the devil are manifest." Using an adjective (*φανερά*) from the same root he has been employing to describe Jesus, John now introduces his readers to the concept that conduct makes visible certain realities, in this case, one's spiritual parentage.

John uses the preposition phrase *ἐν τούτῳ* as a dative of means. Though he normally uses this construction to look at what has just been said (Brown 416), he may sometimes refer to what follows (Brooke, 90; Strecker, 104; Westcott, 108). Here it seems best to be understood in light of both what precedes and what follows (Burdick, 248; Schnackenburg, 192, n. 2; Smalley, 179; Yarbrough, 196). The children of God are characterized by what was said in 3:9, while the children of the devil are characterized by what immediately follows. A contrast is being drawn between the children of God and of the devil.

Repeating the root for "manifest," now as an adjective, John continues to develop this theme. Whereas all but one of the prior uses of "manifest" have referred to Jesus, this same term is applied now to believers and nonbelievers.[209] They are divided into two "classes" of people (Westcott, 108). Everyone falls into one or the other. The class they identify with is, in turn, expressed through conduct.

208. For a full explanation of "hinge verses" see the discussion in the introduction under "characteristics."

209. Those uses referring to Jesus include 1 John 1:2 [twice]; 2:19, 28; 3:2 [second use] and 8. In 3:2 the first use of *φανερόω* involves the future nature of believers being revealed at the coming of Christ.

Hodges rejects this as a test of salvation and sees it as a "statement about how God's children do manifest themselves." He argues for this on the basis that the "only test of salvation is faith (cf. 1 John 5:1 and 5:9–13)." To maintain his position he is forced to see "children of the devil" as not describing an unregenerate person, but "a vocal opponent of the truth" (Hodges, 144–45). However, recognizing that John is again employing literary dualism, this should be seen as a description of two kinds of people: saved and unsaved (Smalley, 179), without implying that he questions his readers' salvation. Recognizing that he is using this either-or contrast rhetorically, we should then seek from the larger context of this paragraph to understand it within its flow of thought. That being said, John is affirming that the children of the devil display their basic nature by sinning. Believers who sin are not expressing their nature as children of God; instead, they are following the devil's pattern.

Schnackenburg (193) identifies *Jub.* 15:26, *Apoc. Ab.* 13f, and *T. Dan* 4:7 as examples of literary dualism from Judaism that makes similar contrasts as John's.[210] Strecker (105) identifies this dualism with Jewish apocalyptic literature where similar contrasts are made such as between "the children of darkness" and "the children of light."[211] Thus John is following a conventional pattern that is likely familiar to his readers. Smalley (179) sees John dividing the world into those inside ("orthodox children of God") and outside ("antichristian secessionists") that are characterized either by obedience or heterodoxy. It seems better, based on John's pastoral concerns, to see him dividing the church body into two groups: those who reflect their divine parentage and those who are acting like children of the devil. He accomplishes this by dividing all people, not just the church, into two groups: God's children and the world that does not know God or his children (3:1).

210. *Jub.* 15:26 reads: "And every one that is born, the flesh of whose foreskin is not circumcised on the eighth day, belongs not to the children of the covenant which the Lord made with Abraham, but to the children of destruction" (*Pseudepigrapha of the Old Testament,* 2:36). *T. Dan* 4:7 reads: "Moreover, a twofold mischief is wrath with lying; and they assist one another in order to disturb the heart; and when the soul is continually disturbed, the Lord departeth from it, and Beliar ruleth over it." (*Pseudepigrapha of the Old Testament,* 2:333)

211. Examples he provides include 1QS i.10; 1QH vi.29–30; *Jub.* 15.26–32; *Apoc. Ab.* 13–14; and Dan 4:7.

πᾶς ὁ μὴ ποιῶν δικαιοσύνην οὐκ ἔστιν ἐκ τοῦ θεοῦ "everyone who does not do righteousness is not from God." John now seems to describe the children of the devil negatively, describing what is lacking in them, namely, righteous conduct and being sourced in God. He begins this description with his all inclusive πᾶς ὁ construction (Brooke, 90).

The plain sense is that a person who is unrighteous in character is clearly not regenerate, not "from God." Pentecost, who interprets the epistle from the Test of Fellowship perspective, correctly calls this a "test of sonship" (Pentecost, 83). Yet the clause that follows refers to a believer in that one cannot fail to love one's Christian "brother" without being a Christian as well. What then could John mean by this? Hodges (152) argues that "not of God" does not especially mean "not born of God." He changes the focus of the description to give it the sense that "God is not behind what he is doing" (Hodges, 153). However, John is using this clause to distinguish between τὰ τέκνα τοῦ θεοῦ καὶ τὰ τέκνα τοῦ διαβόλου. Thus his use of ἐκ calls for more than divine purpose and must imply birth. We must allow John to develop his antitheses as dualistically as he desires, even if they make us uncomfortable and creates questions in or minds as to what he actually means. After all, John is only following Jesus' example in that Jesus loved to make his disciples think. This leads to the question of how to understand the next clause.

καὶ ὁ μὴ ἀγαπῶν τὸν ἀδελφὸν αὐτοῦ, "also the one not loving his brother." Again, John's use of the articular present participle describes a kind of person, not just a believer in the process of loving or, in this case, not loving.[212] Here John is not describing what the person does, but what he does not do. This person does not love fellow Christians. John's use of "brother" describes a fellow believer. The Greco-Roman world to which John writes did not use this designation for those outside one's social, political, or religious group. the concept of one's fellow citizen being their "brother" may have been true of Jewish believers, but not of Gentile ones. The Jews called fellow citizens "brother" only because they traced their roots back to the sons of Jacob and so viewed all tribes of Israel as being of the same original family. Though this might be true of Jewish believers, John's audience is at least mixed, if not predominantly Gentile.

---

212. See D. B. Wallace, *Grammar*, 620, including n. 19.

John's point in saying this is that the absence of love is the same as practicing unrighteousness. However, this does not mean the person is unregenerate. He or she is just acting such. Akin (151) correctly points out that the "family of God is marked by the practice of righteousness and love." However, he wrongly concludes from John's statements, "Those who fail to practice righteousness and/or neglect to love other Christians are not of the same spiritual heritage as the child of God." It is better to see John connecting the two, failure to do righteousness and failure to love another Christian, without lumping both in the same group. He is making failure to love other Christians a practice of unrighteousness consistent with a nonbeliever rather than a believer.[213] This last clause serves as both to define righteousness in terms of love of fellow Christians (one's brother), but also serves as an introduction and connection to what will follow (Strecker, 105).

3:11 Loving one another is absolutely necessary, both for living for Jesus and for advancing God's kingdom. This sentence introduces the next paragraph while tying in closely to the previous.[214] In this verse and those that follow John will continue to develop a contrast between two "families," God's and the devil's (Thompson, 100). He will accomplish this using antithesis and absolute terminology designed to heighten the awareness of the significance of one's actions and attitudes.

Ὅτι αὕτη ἐστὶν ἡ ἀγγελία ἣν ἠκούσατε ἀπ' ἀρχῆς, "For this is the message which you heard from the beginning." Using the conjunction ὅτι, John introduces his explanation of what he has just said (Yarbrough, 197). In this case the normally subordinating conjunction is used as an inferential

---

213. Moody (68) relates this to Paul's teaching in Rom 13:9 that love for one's neighbor fulfills the law and sees John communicating the same message, though applying it to Christians.

214. Burge (159) argues for this being the dividing point of the Epistle based on his understanding of a similar division of the Gospel into two parts with this division producing a "balance" in the epistle between its two halves. Further, the Gospel's "emphasis on the light and truth of God in the first half of John is followed by an emphasis on love in the community, a subject found in the second half." Also the phrase "this is the message you heard from the beginning" is "a near copy of 1:5" with both places using *angelia* for message. However, he notes as well the link of this section with the previous by the "intertwining" of love and light. Thus, the weakness of his distinction is made in that the coincidental use of one phrase causes him to ignore other factors that detract from a division at this point.

conjunction equivalent to διότι, thus the translation, "for."[215] This is similar to Paul's use of γὰρ to introduce explanatory sentences. Here ὅτι serves to raise the question in the mind of the reader whether this sentence should introduce the next paragraph or finish the previous one. In this way it again serves as a kind of "hinge" sentence and aids in creating a very tight flow of thought. These two ideas are not to be disjointed but seen holistically.

John continues connecting his ideas to previous statements by the repetition of key terms.[216] "This is the message" (αὕτη ἐστὶν ἡ ἀγγελία) takes the reader back to 1:5 and the declaration that God is light (Brown, 440; Burdick, 260; Marshall, 189; Strecker, 107; Williamson, 121).[217] "From the beginning" (ἀπ' ἀρχῆς) connects with 2:24 and the anointing that abides in them and enables them to abide in the Son and the Father. Rather than referring to the beginning of divine revelation (Pentecost, 85) or creation (Brooke, 91; Haas, de Jonge and Swellengrebel, 11), this connects back to the beginning of their instruction in the faith (Akin, 154; Johnson, 79; Marshall, 189; Yarbrough, 197).[218] What has been announced to them?

ἵνα ἀγαπῶμεν ἀλλήλους, "that we should love one another." The content (ἵνα plus the subjunctive) of what they heard from the beginning is given as the command to love one another (Brooke, 91; Burdick, 261; Lenski, 466; Yarbrough, 197).[219] Strecker (108) considers this ἵνα to be imperative based on what follows in this verse and the verses to come. He points to a similar

215. BDF §456(1).

216. Based on the similarity of this verse to 1:5, some conclude that this begins a new major section in a bipartite outline (Harris, 152–53).

217. Marshall (189, n. 3) says that ἀγγελία is "almost" a command and that the ἵνα clause that follows functions as an indirect command.

218. Harris (152) sees this referring to the beginning of Jesus' ministry rather than creation or their spiritual birth (Harris, 152).

219. Bultmann (54) considers this synonymous with "brother" or "brothers" and interprets it to mean "neighbor" rather than fellow-Christian. However, especially in light of the coming discussion of their alienation from the world, this term must distinguish the readers from the world, and so their "neighbors." Strecker (108) notes that John's discussion here defines the community of believers as "a closed unit separated from the world." And, as ἀλλήλους *is* synonymous with brother(s), ἀδελφός must also refer to fellow believers as opposed to those outside the faith that make up the hostile world.

use in John 13:34 where ἐντολή is used by Jesus.[220] However, it makes better sense as content.[221]

This is the "new commandment" of 2:8, which was defined in terms of love for other believers in 2:9–10. Thus John returns to the issue of obeying the command to love each other within the body of Christ, the church. The present imperative indicates continuous action in this instance. This is something to be doing as a matter of course, something John's readers were doing and he wanted them to keep doing. This same command is repeated in 3:23; 4:7, 11, and 12. In each case John uses a first person plural and thereby includes himself and emphasizes the community expression of this love (Williamson, 121).[222] Lenski (466) sees this connected to John 15:12 and 17 and notes that it is not the Mosaic command to love one's neighbor. This does not preclude love of nonbelievers. Paul's instruction in Gal 5:10 clarifies that. However, he says well, "We love all men as our fellow creatures, but as spiritual brothers we can love only those who are such brothers."

3:12 This verse continues the sentence of the previous verse. The negative comparison clarifies the command to love in terms of how it is *not* to be expressed. Using repetition, John emphasizes the spiritual and moral significance of disobedience to the command to love one another.

οὐ καθὼς Κάϊν ἐκ τοῦ πονηροῦ ἦν, "Not like Cain who was from the evil one." Cain embodies the opposite of loving one's Christian brother. His actions were sourced in Satan and not God, in evil and not righteousness. The negative particle οὐ that heads this clause makes it a stark contrast to the previous clause (Burdick, 261). Thus, Cain's actions are the opposite of loving one another.

This is the fifth time John uses the adverb καθὼς in his epistle.[223] His previous uses provided positive examples following exhortations (Lieu, 143). This is the first instance where it is used to provide a negative example. The

---

220. "A new commandment I give to you, that you love one another" (ἐντολὴν καινὴν δίδωμι ὑμῖν, ἵνα ἀγαπᾶτε ἀλλήλους).

221. Brooke (91) notes that John's use of αὕτη refers to the following material and informs the role of ἵνα as content.

222. Lieu (142) identifies these verses and sees them as a "leitmotif" that governs the next two chapters

223. 2:6 (καθὼς ἐκεῖνος περιεπάτησεν), 27 (καθὼς ἐδίδαξεν ὑμᾶς); 3:3 (καθὼς ἐκεῖνος ἁγνός ἐστιν), 7 (καθὼς ἐκεῖνος δίκαιός ἐστιν).

only other negative use in John's literature comes from the lips of Jesus in John 6:58, where the contrast is between the manna of Israel's wilderness wanderings and Jesus' offer of himself to the multitude.[224]

Using an ἐκ τοῦ construction once again, John identifies the source of Cain's actions with "the evil one," being parallel to "the devil" in verse 8 (Burdick, 262).[225] This echoes Jesus' description of his opponents in John 8:44. Cain demonstrated his spiritual parentage by his actions. Just as the one who loves demonstrates his divine parentage, hate and murder reflect a diabolical and evil source because conduct is consistent with parentage. Strecker (109) connects this to 3:10 so that it means Cain is a child of the devil. According to Strecker, this statement "qualifies not only the deeds but the very existence of Cain as evil."

This is the only clear allusion to the OT in this epistle (Schnackenburg, 195).[226] One might ask why this would be, especially in light of the OT allusions and references in both his Gospel and Revelation. It could result from John's primarily Gentile Christian audience so that he would not feel a need to use it.[227] It is better, though, to see it resulting because the entire epistle is a reflection on Jesus' teachings in the Upper Room. John did not need to quote the OT as his source of authority as did Paul. As an eyewitness, John speaks as someone who learned these truths from Jesus. Additionally, the

224. "This is the bread which came down from heaven—not as your fathers ate the manna, and are dead. He who eats this bread will live forever" (οὐ καθὼς ἔφαγον οἱ πατέρες καὶ ἀπέθανον).

225. Lieu (145) sees John choosing this epithet rather than repeating "devil" from 3:8 because it allows a "smoother transition" to Cain's actions which are described as evil.

226. Strecker (108) identifies this as "the only possible allusion to the OT in 1 John." J. Lieu ("What was from the Beginning: Scripture and Tradition in the Johannine Epistles," 467) describes it as "indisputably OT in origin." Burge (160) agrees with Brown (442–44) that the story of Cain and Abel was "widely discussed in Judaism." Based on his theory of secessionists he then says, "In the Christian church, the envy and revenge harbored by Cain were compared to the feelings of the opponents of Christians, whose sacrificial lives were pleasing to the Lord."

227. Grayston (110) suggests (1) the Johannine school did not value the OT, (2) he did not like the apocalyptic imagery that was used in Revelation, or (3) he had not learned how to use OT symbols with regard to Christ. These assume John was not the author of this Epistle or the Gospel and accept the Johannine school theory. Knowing John authored all the Johannine literature, we can see that none of these speculations carry weight.

issues were such that they could be explained in terms of the readers' world. So why did he choose this one OT example? Stott (144) describes Cain as a "prototype of the world, which still manifests the ugly qualities he first displayed. The 'world' is Cain's posterity. So we should not be surprised if the world hates us."

καὶ ἔσφαξεν τὸν ἀδελφὸν αὐτοῦ·, "and he slaughtered his brother." John's choice of *σφάζω* to describe Abel's murder communicates the brutality of Cain's actions. He did not just kill his brother, but butchered him like one would an animal.[228] In the NT this term is unique to John and occurs only here and in Revelation. There it is used to describe Jesus as the sacrificial Lamb of God (Rev 5:6, 9, 12; 6:4), of tribulation saints who are martyred (Rev 6:9; 18:24), and of the general slaughter of mankind in the second seal judgment (Rev 6:4). It occurs in the LXX with regard to sacrifice, both human (Isaac in Gen 22:10) and animal (Exod 29:11; Lev 1:4, 11; Isa 34:6).[229] It also describes the butchering of animals to eat (Num 11:22).[230] Judges 12:6 describes the slaughter of the Ephraimites by the Gileadites with this same term.[231] Samuel slaughtered Agag after Saul's failure (1 Sam 15:33).[232] John reminds us that it was Cain's "brother," in this case his physical brother, whom he murdered.

Barker (335) notes that in the "sequence of thought" in this passage, Cain does not become a child of the devil by murdering his brother. Rather, he murders his brother because he is already a child of the devil. Lieu (145) does not see John addressing the issue of whether Cain's murder of Abel resulted from his "diabolical affinity" or "established it." However, being "from the evil one" does answer that question. It was his "affinity."

---

228. BDAG, 979; O. Michel, "*σφάζω*," *TDNT* 7:932–35.

229. Gen 22:11 reads *καὶ ἐξέτεινεν Αβρααμ τὴν χεῖρα αὐτοῦ λαβεῖν τὴν μάχαιραν σφάξαι τὸν υἱὸν αὐτοῦ*. Exod 29:11 reads *καὶ σφάξεις τὸν μόσχον ἔναντι κυρίου παρὰ τὰς θύρας τῆς σκηνῆς τοῦ μαρτυρίου*. Lev 1:4 reads *καὶ σφάξουσι τὸν μόσχον ἔναντι κυρίου*; 1:11 reads *καὶ σφάξουσιν αὐτὸ ἐκ πλαγίων τοῦ θυσιαστηρίου πρὸς βορρᾶν ἔναντι κυρίου*. Num 11:22 reads .Isa 34:6 reads *ἡ μάχαιρα κυρίου ἐνεπλήσθη αἵματος, ἐπαχύνθη ἀπὸ στέατος ἀρνῶν καὶ ἀπὸ στέατος τράγων καὶ κριῶν, ὅτι θυσία κυρίῳ ἐν Βοσορ καὶ σφαγὴ μεγάλη ἐν τῇ Ιδουμαίᾳ*.

230. *μὴ πρόβατα καὶ βόες σφαγήσονται αὐτοῖς, καὶ ἀρκέσει αὐτοῖς;*

231. *καὶ εἶπαν αὐτοῖς Εἴπατε δὴ Σύνθημα, καὶ οὐ κατηύθυναν τοῦ λαλῆσαι οὕτως. καὶ ἐπελάβοντο αὐτῶν καὶ ἔσφαξαν αὐτοὺς ἐπὶ τὰς διαβάσεις τοῦ Ιορδάνου, καὶ ἔπεσαν ἐξ Εφραιμ ἐν τῷ καιρῷ ἐκείνῳ δύο τεσσαράκοντα χιλιάδες.*

232. *καὶ ἔσφαξεν Σαμουηλ τὸν Αγαγ ἐνώπιον κυρίου ἐν Γαλγαλ.*

Why does Abel remain the unnamed victim? Strecker (109–10) provides two reasons for John's decision not to name Abel. (1) It indicates "that the focus of the argumentation lies on the negative side of the opposition between good and evil and that the parenetic purpose shapes the thought." (2) John is "not interested in reflecting on the past history of Cain and Abel, but rather on the brotherhood and sisterhood that exist in the present." I would suggest that he did not name Abel in order to repeat "brother" even more, and thereby focus more on their relationship than identities. Since the theme of this section has to do with Christian brotherhood, John seeks to keep his readers' focus on the issue rather than the historical figures.

καὶ χάριν τίνος ἔσφαξεν αὐτόν, " and again why did he slaughter him?" John then raises the question of Cain's motives using an unusual construction with χάριν, in that it precedes the noun it governs only here in the New Testament.[233] This construction, by its uniqueness, would naturally call attention to the question among its readers and hearers. Whereas it normally follows the genitive to which it is related, here John places it before. Yarbrough (206) notes that though this was not practiced in Koiné Greek, it was common in the LXX. He cites 2 Chr 7:21 as the single example of this exact phrase (χάριν τίνος).[234] Its combination with τίνος creates the interrogative, "why?" As Lenski (467) notes well, "The main point is not the *fact* that Cain slew Abel but the *reason* that he did so" (italics his).

Of note is John's repetition of "slaughtered" with this question. It serves to draw attention again to the brutality and moral repugnance of the act and prepares his readers to examine motives.

ὅτι τὰ ἔργα αὐτοῦ πονηρὰ ἦν, "Because his works were evil." John introduces the answer to his question with an adverb ὅτι introducing a causal clause. He repeats key terms for emphasis, including ἦν which he appends on the end of the clause.

The reason for Cain's murder of Abel was that they had different works (lifestyle, attitudes) that came to manifest themselves in their lives. From Genesis we know Cain was sullen because God did not accept his sacrifice while accepting Abel's. The issue in Gen 3 was not that Cain brought the

---

233. BDAG, 1078; BDF §216 (1). This is a case of the use of an "improper preposition" to communicate the idea of "on account of."

234. καὶ ὁ οἶκος οὗτος ὁ ὑψηλός, πᾶς ὁ διαπορευόμενος αὐτὸν ἐκστήσεται καὶ ἐρεῖ Χάριν τίνος ἐποίησεν κύριος τῇ γῇ ταύτῃ καὶ τῷ οἴκῳ τούτῳ;

wrong kind of sacrifice, a grain offering rather than an animal, but that he was not morally prepared to offer a sacrifice to God.[235] Cain's character was further revealed in his response to God's punishment, both his complaint and subsequent rebellious building of a city.[236]

τὰ δὲ τοῦ ἀδελφοῦ αὐτοῦ δίκαια, "but those of his brother were righteous." In contrast to Cain was Abel. Where Cain's works were evil, Able's were righteous.[237] This is another example of John's use of antithesis to communicate the significance of our actions toward other believers that he will develop in later verses. This also connects back to verse 7 where character is revealed by conduct. The contrast made is between the brothers in terms of their works. It was this contrast that provoked Cain to action. His rejection by God led to anger that was then directed toward his accepted brother. This was not jealousy, but anger and resentment that led to murder.

John now moves from the negative illustration of Cain to affirm that love of the brethren reveals the influence of eternal life in a believer. Springing from the concept of hatred by the world, John leads his readers to see the contrast love creates with the unbelieving world around them. This connects to the use of *hate*, which was the motive behind the deed.

3:13 This next paragraph is introduced with an exhortation containing a reminder of what Jesus had taught in the Upper Room, namely, that we will be hated by the world that hated Jesus first.

μὴ θαυμάζετε, ἀδελφοί, "Stop being amazed, brethren." This is the only place John uses *ἀδελφοί* to address the readers. Some see this indicating that he is addressing his readers as equals (Barker, 355; Burdick, 263; Houlden, 98).[238] Rather, as John's choices of *τεκνία* and *παιδία* in 2:12–14 and elsewhere were likely influenced by literary purposes, his choice of *ἀδελφοί* is

---

235. Grain offerings were acceptable sacrifices in the Mosaic Law, but contingent on proper spiritual preparation (Lev 2).
236. We might think of Cain as the first "whiner" in human history.
237. This is the last occurrence of *δίκαια* in the Epistle.
238. Barker (355) says John "appears to step past his relationship to them as 'little children' and to openly proclaim them his peers." He speculates that this may reflect their having experienced persecution or John's anticipation of their coming persecution within the church for identifying with him. This is another example of the theory of a Johannine school influencing one's interpretation.

also.[239] His relationship with his readers is neither changing nor is he in need of winning their acceptance of what he is saying. He wants them to understand the point he is making in this section. Even so, it is correct to see John's choice of "brothers" serving to identify him with his readers as fellow brothers rather than as his flock. This is reiterated in his use of the first person plural with the command to love. This is an issue that is all inclusive, none is exempt from it, none is unaffected by it. Thompson (101) notes Bultmann's view that brother means "neighbor, whether in the world or in the church." She responds to this by reminding us that "this contradicts the epistle's family imagery" in 3:4–10. Additionally, John's changing his address to his readers from τεκνία, παιδία, or ἀγαπητοί to ἀδελφοί *is* significant. Here the term can only refer to fellow believers. His placement of it in this section establishes its sense throughout, even though elsewhere it is in the singular. Lest one argue that the plural disconnects it from the singular uses, the singular emphasizes the individual's responsibility in the community of faith while this plural speaks of that community as a family of faith (Marshall, 190). This shift from his expected terms of endearment, "beloved" or "children," likely arises from the previous illustration and what he is about to say. Cain's murder of his brother was reprehensible and evil. John uses this to remind his readers that they, too, are brothers in Christ. Furthermore, hatred of one another is as evil as Cain's hatred and subsequent murder of his brother.

The present imperative of θαυμάζω implies that John's readers were possibly shocked by the antagonism they had faced as followers of Jesus.[240] Whereas the present imperative is often used to state a principle, in this case the implication from the context is that its primary sense is intended. They need to stop being surprised by it (Burdick, 263). The prohibition, "Stop being amazed" (μὴ θαυμάζετε) does not condemn the initial feeling of surprise when they are the innocent objects of unprovoked hatred. The negative particle (μὴ) with the present imperative, "stop being amazed," calls on

239. Rensberger (98) notes: "The author seems to be playing on the reference to Cain's fratricide in the preceding verse: The readers also are 'brothers and sisters' endangered by treachery."

240. BDAG, 444. This use carries the sense of being disturbed or "extraordinarily impressed" by something, in this case, antagonism or hatred.

them not to give way to a feeling of amazement and self-pity. The prohibition is a direct echo of John 15:18–21.[241]

εἰ μισεῖ ὑμᾶς ὁ κόσμος, "that the world hates you." What was startling his readers was the hatred they were experiencing from "the world," their neighbors and fellow countrymen. The sense here is that John's readers may have been surprised at their changed social standing and removal from accepted society. They were likely social outcasts who were experiencing a pattern of prejudicial treatment and resentment. Literally, John says, "if the world hates you."[242] However, his use of a first class conditional clause implies the actuality of the protasis* and so is best translated as "since" or "that" (Kistemaker, 307; Smalley, 187).[243] Their experience of hated by the world was a fact of life. The same is true for believers today. We should never be surprised by negative reactions from the unbelieving world regardless of our good intentions and actions.

Using the gnomic present μισεῖ John affirms that the world feels a "continuous hatred" toward believers rather than indicating isolated acts of hatred (Smalley, 186). It is the consistent normal response of nonbelieving societies and cultures. John's choice of μισέω likely comes from Jesus' warning in John 15:18–25, as does this warning. That warning followed Jesus' repetition of his command for them to love one another (John 15:12) and so served to contrast them with the world. Here we see John doing much the same thing.

The verb μισέω means more than an absence of love but reflects an active antagonism.[244] When Jesus reminded the disciples of how he had been treated by the world, they would have remembered the myriad

241. D. E. Hiebert, "An Expositional Study of 1 John—Part 6: An Exposition of 1 John 3:13–24," 302.

242. BDF §454 (1) identifies this as an interrogative conditional conjunction and so is not closely connected to θαυμάζω and serving as a replacement for ὅτι as would be expected from other instances of θαυμάζω, such as Mark 15:44.

243. D. B. Wallace (*Grammar*, 690–91) cautions against assigning the idea of "since" to first class conditions on the basis that it only means that thirty-seven percent of the time in the NT. Yet, the context here would indicate that this may be a legitimate instance that certainty is intended. Marshall (190, n. 9) on the other hand considers that the relationship of εἰ to θαυμάζω indicates it should be understood as "if" and imply that the readers may not experience persecution from the world.

244. BDAG, 652. O. Michel, "μισέω," *TDNT* 4:690–94.

confrontations Jesus had experienced from the Jewish leaders and that they were seeking to kill Jesus. Here, John is reminding his readers of what they can expect, the same kind of active antagonism. The world's hatred is not passive.

Here κόσμος carries the same negative connotation as it did in 2:15–16, though where there it described the world system in terms of its values, here it looks at the people who make up that world (Burdick, 264; Schnackenburg, 196–97). This is the world system composed of the non-believing community with values that are influenced by Satan, its master (Yarbrough, 199). Jesus further describes this "world" as the place wherein his disciples will have tribulation and that he had already overcome (John 16:33). Just as the world hates Jesus (John 7:7), it will hate them as well (John 15:18–19; 17:14).

3:14 John states a means for believers to assure themselves of their salvation, using the contrast of two spheres: life and death. Yet that is not the purpose of the statement. Rather, he points to the impact of conduct on our understanding of ourselves and our relationship to Jesus, who is life itself and who exists in the sphere of life. As with his other dualistic imagery (Williamson, 122), the contrast might seem here to be between saved and unsaved. However, as he continues his instruction, it becomes clear that he is not attempting to answer the question of who is saved (Test of Life view) or who is in fellowship with God (Test of Fellowship view), but rather how a believer expresses the life he or she possesses.

ἡμεῖς οἴδαμεν ὅτι μεταβεβήκαμεν ἐκ τοῦ θανάτου εἰς τὴν ζωήν, "We know that we have passed out of death into life." John introduces another contrast with the antithesis of life and death.[245] This theme is introduced here and repeated in 3:15; 5:12, 16. The use of the pronoun ἡμεῖς is emphatic (Bruce,

245. Johnson (82) sees John introducing this as a theme that he develops further in 3:15 and then 5:12 and 16. However, though v. 15 completes the idea introduced in v. 14, 5:12 and 16 focuses on life and does not use the life-death contrast directly enough to indicate a theme is being developed. He is correct that the theme can be found in the Gospel (He provides John 3:16, 36; 5:24–29; 10:17–18, 28; 11:21–25; and 21:22–23 as examples). And we may suspect that John's use of the imagery here relates back to the theme in the Gospel. However, it does not appear that he is focusing the reader's attention on this concept in the epistle beyond its contribution to other issues he is addressing.

96; Burdick, 264; Stott, 145).[246] Here, too, John includes himself with his readers (Rensberger, 99; Strecker, 111). He views his readers as believers, so the idea that he would be providing them "tests" to determine *if* they are believers does not fit the epistle's flow of thought. This indicates that what John has to say about himself and his readers stands in contrast to the hostile world (Schnackenburg, 197).

Hodges (155–57) argues for this use of *we* to include only John and the apostles. He notes that the first person pronoun is not only emphatic, but juxtaposed with κόσμος from the previous sentence.[247] Κόσμος is also in an emphatic position along with the second person plural pronoun, ἡμεῖς. He sees this same "we-you-they" combination developed similarly in 2:19–20 and 4:4–6. However, John's use of "we" in the verses that follow clearly includes his readers. It would make better sense to include them here as well. John does identify himself at times with the apostles in contrast to the false teachers. However, he does not as readily draw this same contrast between his readers and the apostles.

He chooses οἴδα for "know" rather than the experiential γινώσκω, indicating that what is to be known is from instruction, God's Word, not especially from experience (Burdick, 264). It includes the idea of "common" (Marshall, 191, n. 10) or factual knowledge (Stott, 145). Schnackenburg (197) considers it a stronger term over γινώσκω as the reason for John's choice here. The content of what we can know, by faith rather than by experience, is that we exist in a different sphere than we had before.[248]

The ὅτι clause that follows οἴδα explains what is known (Marshall, 191, n. 11). It introduces an indirect discourse clause giving the content of their knowledge (Harris, 156) and so "refers to the nature of the community" (Strecker, 112; contra Lenski, 468).

---

246. Bultmann (55) refers to this use of "we know" as "arrogant."

247. Johnson (82) notes that John's use of "we" in this verse stands in antithesis with "the world" in v. 13.

248. C. F. D. Moule ("A Neglected Factor in the Interpretation of Johannine Eschatology," 158) sees this as another example of "realized eschatology" in the epistle. Harris (156) does not see any significance in the change to οἴδα, seeing it as Johannine stylistic variation.

Rather than the realm of death, we *have passed* into life. This echoes Jesus' words in John 5:24.[249] The perfect tense μεταβεβήκαμεν is a compound verb that is directional in that it means "to move from one place to another" or "to change one's dwelling."[250] The significance of John's choice of the perfect is that he is describing a change of status that occurred in the past and continues to the present in the experience of his readers (Brown 445–46; Burdick, 264; Smalley, 188–89; Strecker, 111).[251] What he will do in the verses that follow is to describe further the contrast between life and death by connecting love and murder, two new opposites, to them. This contrast, and John's description of people's relationship to the two spheres of existence, is equivalent to the light/darkness contrast of chapter 1. However, whereas in chapter 1 the spheres are moral, here they should be seen as soteriological. Thus this is a legitimate means of assurance of salvation, though not a test. Failure does not prove a lack of life, though passing this test can impact one's assurance.

John's use of articles with death and life draws attention to them as spheres of existence rather than death and life in a generic sense (Lenski, 469). These are two spheres into which every human being is divided (Burdick, 264). However, as in the first chapter a believer could "walk" in either sphere (the light of God's moral purity or the darkness of sin), so too here.[252] Though one has passed from the realm of darkness into life, he may choose to operate as if he lived in the realm of darkness. John's point in making this statement is to identify the significance of his readers' choices. Just as failure to love a brother in Christ earlier meant they were not walking in the light, whether they knew they were in darkness or not, failure to love also means they are not living like the "alive" people they are. They are not

---

249. "Most assuredly, I say to you, he who hears my word and believes in him who sent me has everlasting life, and shall not come into judgment, but has passed from death into life." (μεταβέβηκεν ἐκ τοῦ θανάτου εἰς τὴν ζωήν)

250. BDAG, 638; J. Schneider, "βαίνω, μεταβαίνω," 1:523.

251. B. M. Fanning (*Verbal Aspect in New Testament Greek*, 291–94) identifies this as a "perfect of resulting state."

252. That Christians can and do walk in the sphere of sin (darkness) is evident from what John has said in 1:6–7 and 2:9–11. Further, Paul's command in Eph 5:8–11 would not have been written it if walking "as children of light" were automatic or instinctive. That we must choose to do this is evident from his command in Rom 6:11 for believers to "reckon" themselves dead to sin. When one fails to "reckon," they will fall into sin. Conduct follows thinking.

expressing the eternal life they are possessing. How can they know they are walking in the sphere of life, just as they were to walk in light? They know when they see life in action through their love of their Christian brothers.

ὅτι ἀγαπῶμεν τοὺς ἀδελφούς·, "because we love the brethren." The source of our knowledge is our attitude toward fellow Christians. The causal ὅτι that introduces this clause modifies οἴδαμεν rather than μεταβεβήκαμεν (Burdick, 264; Houlden, 98; Marshall, 191, n. 11).[253] He is saying that "we know" by our love. It is not our love of the brethren that caused us to pass from death to life. John "is simply underscoring that *because* such love is already going on, we have a tangible sign of Christ's salvific work in progress" (Burge, 161; italics his). Lenski (469) notes well that "both the physical life and the spiritual life are not seen directly but are apparent only from their evidence, their activity. The plainest activity of the spiritual life is that of loving those who are one with us, are our spiritual brothers."

Love of other Christians has no salvific (justification) value. It is a work. It is a sanctification value. By actively loving other Christians, believers contribute directly to their spiritual growth and walk with the Lord. Additionally, every Christian can experience a measure of assurance of salvation from seeing their life reflecting God's character. Believers can know they are one of those abiding in the realm of life as a direct consequence of conscious, intentional, love of other believers.

Akin (157) says that "the absence of Christian love indicates that one has not passed into the state of spiritual life but remains *(menei)* in the realm of spiritual death." However, this is not a test of life. Yes, assurance may result from actively loving other believers. Yet it remains illegitimate to conclude that one is unregenerate if he or she fails to love other believers. As John has noted already, it is possible for a believer not to love another believer ("brother"). Jesus would not have commanded us to do so if it

253. Brown (446) complains that John's "habit of using *hoti* twice in quick succession, first meaning 'that' and then meaning 'because, for,' is neither elegant nor illuminating." This may serve as an example of John's limitations with the Greek language in terms of grammar, syntax, and vocabulary. However, let no one say he was deficient in his conceptual and philosophical depth, or his use of literary imagery. Strecker (112) offers two possibilities for how John is using this ὅτι. (1) If it modifies the preceding ὅτι clause, then it affirms "the overcoming of death is founded on the community's mutual love." (2) If it is related to οἴδαμεν, then it affirms "the gift of life received in Christ is realized in love."

were automatic for all true believers to love other believers. Thus, though the positive can be concluded by the loving believer, the opposite is not automatically true beyond perception by the person, and that person (the unloving believer) would be wrong in concluding they were unregenerate simply because of their absence of love.

ὁ μὴ ἀγαπῶν τὸν ἀδελφόν μένει ἐν τῷ θανάτῳ, "He who does not love his brother abides in death." Utilizing the articular present active participle, ὁ ἀγαπῶν, to describe a kind of person once again, John states another principle that controls the discussion. The unloving person, believer or not, "abides" in the sphere of death. Just as the self-deceived believer in chapter 1 walks in darkness rather than light without becoming unregenerate, here, too, death is a sphere of existence that a believer may inhabit as well as a nonbeliever. Though some take this to mean the person is spiritually dead (Barker, 335; Bruce, 95–96; Westcott, 111),[254] it is better to see the person is described as operating in the sphere of death, thus the use of "abides" in the present tense. Hodges (157) describes this as "an experience of death" in the life of a believer. He rightly observes that the natural response of most theologians is to see the term "death" and conclude that the person must be unregenerate. However, in literary imagery a term may take on a different significance than what our theological systems assume. Here, with John's pattern of literary dualism to create absolute contrasts, one must place the imagery into its larger context and incorporate all of the data provided by John to discern his use of the imagery and intended meaning. His repeated use of "brethren" serves to remind his readers that he is talking about relationships within the family of God, not with the outside world. Furthermore, with this in mind, one must recognize that he is describing a state that can be true of a believer who fails to obey Christ's command to love that has been discussed in chapter 2.

Death is a sphere of existence that may be associated with separation from fellowship with God. It is a sphere like darkness in chapter 1 wherein one operates outside of God's moral purity. So abiding in death is parallel to walking in darkness in chapter 1. For the unregenerate, it is an absolute separation that is eventually expressed by their eternal relegation to the lake of fire apart from God's presence. For the regenerate, it is the experience

254. D. E. Hiebert, "An Expositional Study of 1 John—Part 6: An Exposition of 1 John 3:13–24," 305.

of social separation from God, a breakdown in fellowship without a loss of family membership. One continues as God's child while being excluded from his presence in the same way a child may be punished by his loving parent by being sent to his room and denied fellowship. This separation from God is not absolute (positional truth) but relative to that day's experience (experiential truth). Thus, this disobedient believer is experiencing a kind of "death" while out of fellowship with God, since spiritual death is not nonexistence but separation.

Strecker (112) describes this last statement as antithetical to the first portion of the verse. Rather than saying they are dead, John again uses *μένω* to describe their experience. He (113) sees this as a stronger term than *ἐστὶν* and notes that John used *μένω* similarly in 3:9 to describe God's seed "abiding" in the believer rather than just "being" in him. Thus they are experiencing death as a "continuing existence. The unloving person is subjected to death and cannot escape that fate."

3:15 John now connects what he has been saying with the earlier analogy of Cain. Believers are no different than Cain when they "hate" their Christian brothers. He uses repetition and word order to emphasize the significance of hating other believers. Just as Jesus said that insulting others was equivalent to murdering them (Matt 5:21–22), John will soon describe murder in terms of treatment as well (Burge, 161).

πᾶς ὁ μισῶν τὸν ἀδελφὸν αὐτοῦ ἀνθρωποκτόνος ἐστίν, "Everyone who hates his brother is a murderer." John begins with another principle, in this case directed at believers. Using the *πᾶς ὁ* construction, John states an all-inclusive truth that arises from the illustration of Cain and Abel.[255] As discussed under previous uses of the present participle, this describes a kind of person (application of the gnomic sense) rather than indicating continuous activity (contra Burdick, 265).

The one who hates is guilty of murder. This is one of three uses of *ἀνθρωποκτόνος* in the NT, two occurring in this verse. The other instance is

255. Brooke (94) considers the *πᾶς* ... *οὐ* construction to be a "Hebraistic" expression one would expect from someone thinking in Hebrew (Aramaic?) and writing in Greek.

John 8:44, where Jesus calls the devil a murderer. It is very likely that John's choice of this term over φονεύς comes from Jesus' use then.[256]

What John says about hate and murder here is as true for believers as unbelievers. However, because he identifies this hatred as directed toward one's fellow believer (contra Bultmann, 54), he is applying this truth to the church community to which he writes (Strecker, 113).[257] Brown (477) sees John using hyperbole. It seems better to see him relating back to Jesus' teaching in the Sermon on the Mount (Matt 5:21–23) and using it as a metonymy* of effect for cause (murder for hatred).[258] His emphasis is on the significance, the heinousness of "hating" other Christians. How one "hates" another Christian will be clarified later in the epistle. For now, though, the contrast is made and the significance is described.

καὶ οἴδατε ὅτι πᾶς ἀνθρωποκτόνος οὐκ ἔχει ζωὴν αἰώνιον ἐν αὐτῷ μένουσαν, "and you know that every murderer does not have eternal life abiding in him." He follows his declaration with a truth that his readers have been taught. This knowledge (οἴδα) once again is that gained by instruction rather than experience. It is "generally accepted, axiomatic, intuitive" (Burdick, 266; Brooke, 94). He reminds his readers that they already have been taught and "know" this truth (Rensberger, 99).[259]

This term for "murderer" (ἀνθρωποκτόνος) is used only twice in Johannine literature, first by Jesus in describing the devil (John 8:44) and now by John in describing a hating believer (1 John 3:15). What he says about this person is equally puzzling on the surface. This murderer does not have eternal life abiding in him. This is understood by some to indicate an unregenerate person (Stott, 146). However, as stated earlier, it is better to see that one cannot hate his Christian "brother" without being a Christian as well. Thus, what John is saying is not an issue of justification. Rather, John is saying that "eternal life," either in the person of Christ or as a

---

256. Φονεύς occurs six times in the NT (Matt 22:7; Acts 7:52; 28:4; 1 Pet 4:15; Rev 21:8; 22:15). John's two uses in Revelation indicates that he could have chosen this term instead of ἀνθρωποκτόνος, but did not.

257. Harris (158) refers back to v. 14 to say that this murderer was never a believer, but has always remained in death. However, as noted before, his hatred is directed toward a Christian "brother," and so by definition he must be one as well.

258. E. W. Bullinger, *Figures of Speech Used in the Bible*, 538.

259. Rensberger (99) says that John is reminding them of something that "was part of the tradition familiar to them."

personification of the quality of life, is not having an influence in the believer's life.[260] Eternal life motivates no one toward hatred, but rather toward love. Here, as in other places with John, μένω is a term describing influence more than presence. Pentecost states John's point well: "John is not saying that a saved man cannot hate. He is not saying even that a saved man cannot kill, because he can and does. What John is saying is that no man who is controlled by the new life of Christ can hate. ... One can be saved and hate, but one cannot be living by the power of the new life of Christ and hate at the same time" (Pentecost, 89).[261]

John places the aorist active participle μένουσαν at the end of this sentence for emphasis. He may be using it as an adjective modifying the direct object of the verb (the abiding eternal life), or as a 2 accusative predicating something about the 1 accusative (eternal life that abides in him). The difference would be (1) a focus on the quality of eternal life or (2) the presence of eternal life. The second option seems best. It fits with John's idea of influence when using μένω with inanimate or conceptual things.

Can a believer be a murderer without killing someone? Murder is going to be further defined by John in the verses that follow. By his definition, many Christians can legitimately call themselves murderers. First, however, he is going to discuss the question of love versus murder positively.

3:16 Our experience of God's love has come by means of the revelation of that love in the action of Jesus Christ on our behalf.[262] Whereas the unloving Christian "murders" his fellow believer, Jesus gives his own life for us. Burge (162) suggests this "might be called John's version of Mark 10:45."[263]

ἐν τούτῳ ἐγνώκαμεν τὴν ἀγάπην, "By this we have known love." Though Westcott (114) sees this use of ἐν τούτῳ looking both forward and backward, it is best to see it referring to what immediately follows with the

---

260. Johnson (83) sees the use of μένω to indicate that eternal life "is not just an eschatological hope; it is a present possession which abides in those who believe in Jesus and love their brothers and sisters."

261. Though John does not address the issue elsewhere, other NT writers make clear that Christians *can and do* commit murder (Gal 5:19–21; Jas, 4:1–2; 1 Pet 4:15).

262. Bultmann (55) understands John's discussion from these next few verses to describe "what genuine love is, or how it is to be tested."

263. He notes Smalley (193) for this idea. C. Maurer ("τίθημι," *TDNT*, 8:156) sees him going "directly back" to Isa 53:10. J. Jeremias ("παῖς θεοῦ," *TDNT*, 5:708) describes it as "reminiscent" of Isa 53:10.

epexegetical ὅτι clause functioning epexegetically (Akin, 158; Brooke, 95; Brown, 448; Haas, de Jonge, and Swellengrebel, 99; Harris, 158).[264]

The truth that is known has been known—the sense of the perfect tense ἐγνώκαμεν—and still affects believers today.[265] This is knowledge the readers had gained by experience, by "contemplation," and was still impacting their lives (Akin, 158; Westcott, 114). In this case, this knowledge came by what they had learned about the life and death of Jesus (Burdick, 267).[266]

John's use of the article without a genitive to define love further indicates John is speaking of love in its "absolute" sense (Brooke, 95; Smalley, 192).[267] He is not saying "we know we are loved" or "we know we are loving others." He is defining love by what follows.

ὅτι ἐκεῖνος ὑπὲρ ἡμῶν τὴν ψυχὴν αὐτοῦ ἔθηκεν, "because that One laid down his life on our behalf." This epexegetical ὅτι resumes the thrust of ἐν τούτῳ in the previous clause (Brown, 448).[268] John is saying that "knowledge of love is found in Christ's self-sacrifice" (Strecker, 114). This is much the same as Paul's affirmation in Rom 5:8 that "God demonstrates his own love toward us, in that while we were still sinners, Christ died for us." There Paul does not say that the purpose of Jesus' death was to demonstrate God's love. Rather, it was the expression of God's love. As God acted in love we could see his love demonstrated by his action. Here John says that the kind of love he is talking about was defined by Jesus' sacrificial death on our behalf.

---

264. Smalley (192) concurs with Westcott, but sees "the chief reference" being to what follows.

265. Strecker (114) describes it as "presupposed."

266. Burdick, (267) describes the sense of γινώσκω here to communicate the idea of "the acquisition of knowledge." Barker (336) sees the significance of the aorist to be that what was known "belongs to the historical event of Jesus."

267. Burdick (266) sees this as showing how genuine love can be recognized, and thereby "the genuineness of one's salvation." However, as has been discussed earlier, John's description of his readers in 2:12–14 and his addressing them as "children," "beloved," and "brothers," makes clear that he not only does not question their salvation, he does not want them to either. Therefore, it is highly improbable that he would want them to start doing that here.

268. Strecker (114, n. 43) describes it as "a typical quirk of Johannine usage" and lists 2:5c; 3:19; 4:9, 10, 13, 17 as examples in this Epistle. It is also used in John 4:37; 9:30; and 16:30. It is seen in combination with ἐὰν in John 13:35 and 1 John 2:3. It is in combination with ἵνα in John 15:8 and 1 John 4:17. It is combined with ὅταν in 5:2 and with ἐκ in 3:24.

The referent of ἐκεῖνος is Jesus once again (Akin, 158; Brooke, 95; Burdick, 267; Brown, 448; Haas, de Jonge, and Swellengrebel, 99; Schnackenburg, 199; Strecker, 115; Rensberger, 100).[269]

This is also the only use of ὑπὲρ in this epistle, though it is common in John's Gospel (6:51; 10:11, 15; 11:50, 51, 52; 13:37, 38; 15:13; 17:19; 18:14) in contrast to περὶ (1 John 1:1; 2:2 (x3), 26, 27; 4:10; 5:9, 10, 16; 3 John 2).[270] This same preposition is used by Jesus four times in John 10:11, 15, 17, and 18 to describe the Good Shepherd's action.[271]

John identifies Jesus' motive for giving his life with the prepositional phrase ὑπὲρ ἡμῶν. Though he says here, "on *our* behalf," John's statement need not be seen as limiting Jesus' death to the elect. What he has said in 2:2 makes clear that, though believers receive the benefit of his death, he gave his life for all of mankind, elect and nonelect.[272] Additionally, his use of ὑπὲρ ἡμῶν to describe the recipients of the benefits of Jesus' death need not imply substitution or be an allusion to the substitutionary atonement of Christ. Burdick (267) sees this as "reminiscent" of Jesus' words in John 10:17–18 and 15:13.[273] He notes that in all the places these terms are used to describe Jesus' death, the focus is on love rather than atonement. It seems better to see it implying "instead of" with regard to death. Jesus' death on our behalf indicates that *instead* of us dying, he died so that we would not.[274] Yet the application John makes in the following sentence indicates that the idea is "for our benefit" more than "in our place." This still fits the practical aspect of John's instruction rather than seeing him pausing to develop Christology. By this John affirms that God's love was demonstrated by Jesus'

---

269. See 3:3 for a full discussion of John's use of ἐκεῖνος. The other uses of ἐκεῖνος are 2:7; 3:3, 5, 7; and 4:17.
270. Schnackenburg (199) describes John 15:13 as a "foil" (*die Folie*) to 1 John 3:16.
271. Bultmann (55) notes that this phrase "contains the insight that active love is based on experienced love: from his love for us we learn what love is."
272. Brown misses the point when he asserts that Jesus' words in John 10:4 and 11 indicates he died only for the "sheep who hear his voice and belong to him." Seeing these as limited to the "Johannine Christians, along with those Christians who are of another fold (10:16)," he limits Jesus' death to only those who respond to the gospel (Brown, 473). This is a case of taking Jesus' words spoken in one context and ignoring clear statements of Scripture elsewhere (John 1:29; 1 John 2:2) that affirm the universal nature of his work.
273. μείζονα ταύτης ἀγάπην οὐδεὶς ἔχει, ἵνα τις τὴν ψυχὴν αὐτοῦ θῇ ὑπὲρ τῶν φίλων αὐτοῦ.
274. Wallace, *Grammar*, 383.

death on our behalf, for our benefit (Akin, 158). Moreover, following this practical pattern, John says we can recognize love in terms of its deeds, with Jesus' giving of his life being the ultimate demonstration of divine love.

John uses the aorist active ἔθηκεν to describe Jesus' death on the cross on our behalf (Haas, de Jonge, and Swellengrebel, 99; Strecker, 115). Though this is the single use of τίθημι in this epistle, John quotes Jesus' use of the word seven times in his Gospel (John 10:11, 15, 17, 18; 13:37, 38; 15:13). It is a common term with a wide range of meanings. However, Jesus' use of it in the Gospel and John's use of it here carries the unusual sense of giving up, or "laying down," especially as it relates to one's life (Haas, de Jonge, and Swellengrebel, 99).[275] Whereas in Greek literature it was used to describe one "risking" his or her life, Jesus changed its sense to include the actual sacrifice of one's life. It is this sense that John adopts in this epistle.

καὶ ἡμεῖς ὀφείλομεν ὑπὲρ τῶν ἀδελφῶν τὰς ψυχὰς θεῖναι, "and so we are obligated to lay down our lives for the brethren." Recognizing what Jesus has done for us necessarily creates a moral obligation. John's use of ἡμεῖς with καὶ makes this more than just a coordinating conjunction (continuative or connecting) or a logical conjunction used to conclude the discussion (Brown, 448).[276] John applies the significance of what he has just said to each person's life (Akin, 159). We have an obligation to follow Christ's example and lay down our lives for other Christians.[277] In this case, this obligation is not universal but limited to fellow believers, to the body of Christ.[278] Additionally, where Jesus gave his actual life, John uses a synecdoche*, where the whole signifies the parts, to say we should give our possessions, time, energy, emotions, or anything else in our lives to meet the

---

275. BDAG, 1003; C. Maurer, "τίθημι," *TDNT* 8:155. Contra Smalley (193) who sees it emphasizing the "laying aside" aspect of the term. However, Jesus' own use of the term, meaning to "lay down" one's life in terms of willingly dying, is evident in the Good Shepherd motif (John 10:11, 15, 17) as well as his call upon his disciples to do the same (John 15:13). It would seem better to see John reflecting Jesus' use here.

276. The pronoun ἡμεῖς is emphatic once again (Lenski, 472).

277. John's repetition of ὑπὲρ emphasizes the sameness of the action (Williamson, 125). Additionally, its placement forward in each of the clauses also makes it emphatic (Johnson, 84).

278. As Lenski (472) notes well, "Ἀδελφοί does not mean neighbors or men in general but 'brothers' who are in the same family with us, begotten from God, God's children."

needs of other Christians. This obligation is a moral debt that demands we meet "certain social or moral expectations."[279] 'Οφείλω focuses on the moral aspect of the obligation whereas δεῖ is related more to the necessity of something without regard to the idea of indebtedness that is conveyed by ὀφείλομεν (Burdick, 268; Law, 391; Smalley, 194).[280] Smalley (194) says well, "The cross is an example to copy, and not simply a revelation of love to admire." The practical nature of this moral obligation is detailed in the sentences that follow.

Strecker (115) sees τὰς ψυχὰς θεῖναι meaning more than to risk one's life, but when combined with ὑπὲρ, it communicates the idea of "sacrificial action."[281] He notes the parallel idea from Mark 10:45 and Matt 20:28 where Jesus uses δοῦναι τὴν ψυχὴν αὐτοῦ to describe his coming death on the cross for mankind (contra Lieu, 151). He notes further that Jesus' example is always intended to be imitated. This can be seen from 2 Cor 5:15; Phil 2:5–11; 1 Tim 6:12–13; 1 Pet 2:21–24; Heb 13:13–14 (Schnackenburg, 182).

3:17 John is not one to create a sense of obligation without suggesting a means of fulfilling it. He moves from the significance of Jesus' action on our behalf to the practical implications of that action. "We lay down our lives" by using our material possessions to meet the physical needs of other believers. This verse represents a lesser-to-greater argument from the world's goods to loving God (Yarbrough, 203).[282]

ὃς δ' ἂν ἔχῃ τὸν βίον τοῦ κόσμου, "But whoever has the world's goods." With the adversative δέ, John now states the same truth from a negative perspective (Akin, 159; Burdick, 268; contra Strecker, 116). This contrast

279. BDAG, 743; F. Hauck, "ὀφείλω," *TDNT* 5:559–64.

280. W. Grundmann, "δεῖ," *TDNT* 2:21–25.

281. BDF §394 notes that θεῖναι is an example of an "explanatory (epexegetical) infinitive" referring to "an actual fact" rather than one that is assumed. The infinitive θεῖναι may be a substantival direct object of a verb (H. E. Dana and J. R.. Mantey, *Manual Grammar*, 217–18) or may function as an adv. (D. B. Wallace, *Grammar*, 598–99). Burge (162) says that this "particular Johannine construction suggests 'divesting oneself of something' that is precious and personally valued."

282. Barker (336) sees this verse as "a practical test of the validity of one's faith." However, as noted before, John does not question the salvation or commitment of his readers (2:12–14). Thus, it is improbable that he would say what follows in order to get his readers to question that which he does not question, namely, their faith.

introduces his idea of how believers express Christ's self-sacrificial love on a daily basis. John is now bringing up "where the rubber meets the road." Rather than pointing a finger, John describes the application of his teaching with a generalization, thus his use of ὃς (Burdick, 268). The person he is describing has the resources to act out love. The ὃς … ἂν construction is best translated as "whoever." It "describes something that is regular and repeated. The author intends to express a principle of general validity" (Haas, de Jonge, and Swellengrebel, 45; Smalley, 196; Strecker, 116). Strecker (116) sees this reflecting the OT (Jewish) practice of the rich giving alms to help the poor. He sees this continuing in the church as well.

John uses the same term for worldly possessions as he had in 2:16 where it was connected with an ungodly attitude. In both instances βίος indicates one's material possessions, or what might be called "the stuff of life." It is not evil in and of itself, but may be desired in an evil way or valued inappropriately, as in 2:16. It is part of the world that is passing away and so should never be viewed as more than a means to an end. So in this passage having the world's goods is not bad. Rather, what one does with them is the issue. In this case John describes the person as "having" (present tense verb). Thus what follows is in the context of his being able to act, having the means of helping at his disposal.

τὸν βίον τοῦ κόσμου "refers to one's means of subsistence—material goods or property" (Burdick, 269; Harris, 160; Schnackenburg, 199; Strecker, 116; Yarbrough, 203). It has a positive connotation. It does not especially imply the person is wealthy (Grayston, 114). For example, Jesus uses βίος to describe the poor widow's money in Mark 12:44.

The τοῦ κόσμου may be an allusion to 2:15–17 ,where the world and its things were passing and not to be loved (Harris, 160; Schnackenburg, 199; Smalley, 196; Strecker,116).[283] Thus Lieu (151) sees John putting his readers "to the test" whether they love the world or God. Others do not see any negative connotation with this use of κόσμος but see that John is simply stating the sphere in which life is lived (Burdick, 269; Rensberger, 101). Yarbrough (203) sees it indicating "material plenty."

καὶ θεωρῇ τὸν ἀδελφὸν αὐτοῦ χρείαν ἔχοντα, "and sees his brother having a need." John's repeated use of "brother" again indicates a situation within the church body in which one member recognizes another member has a

283. Τοῦ κόσμου may be an attributive gen. or partative gen..

need that he is capable of meeting. As elsewhere, ἀδελφὸς refers to a fellow Christian (Brown, 450). John's movement from "brothers" in verse 16 to the singular "brother" here, indicates that he is moving from the principle applicable to all, to the need to apply that principle individually (Akin, 160). In their day the need would be either food, clothing, or shelter. His use of the present participle, ἔχοντα, though part of a double accusative construction which gives it more of an adjective function than adverb, still indicates that the wealthy Christian sees the needy Christian in the process of being in need.[284] This "seeing" a need is not a casual recognition or a passing notice. Rather, the sense of θεωρέω is that of a sustained attentive observation (Akin, 160; Burdick, 269; Lenski, 473; Smalley,196).[285] We "see with our own eyes" (Barker, 336). John's point is that the brother of means is "very much" aware of the need. He sees it over time and has personally noted it. He cannot claim to be unaware and the need continues to exist in his presence.

καὶ κλείσῃ τὰ σπλάγχνα αὐτοῦ ἀπ' αὐτοῦ, "and closes his compassions from him." The phrase *κλείσῃ τὰ σπλάγχνα* cannot be found in any extant literature (biblical or extrabiblical) other than here (Grayston, 114; Strecker, 116). Nonetheless, its meaning is clear. Based on the use of *σπλάγχνα* for "pity" in extrabiblical literature, John's use here would indicate a lack of compassion on the part of the Christian.[286]

Rather than responding to the need and meeting it, this Christian literally shuts up his bowels or emotions from the other believer in need. In Greek and Hebrew thought, the emotions were centered in the bowels more than the heart, with the heart relating more to the will, mind, and inner person, and thus influencing the emotions.[287] Thus John says here that he closes his bowels "from" the believer. In other words he denies the other believer an emotional entrance into his life. He suppresses his natural

---

284. D. B. Wallace, *Grammar*, 182–89. The double accusative includes τὸν ἀδελφὸν and χρείαν ἔχοντα.

285. BDAG, 454; W. Michaelis, "ὁράω, εἶδον, … θεωρέω," *TDNT* 5:345–46.

286. BDAG 938; H. Koester, "σπλάγχνον," *TDNT* 7:550–52. See E. Malatesta (*Interiority and Covenant*, 263–65) for a full discussion of its Jewish intertestimental use.

287. J. Behm, "καρδία," *TDNT* 3:611–13. Heart could refer to emotions and is connected to them. However, it is identified as the seat of emotions rather than the emotion of pity or compassion.

emotions, squelching any pity he may feel toward the one in need. This leads to the real question of God's influence in his life.

πῶς ἡ ἀγάπη τοῦ θεοῦ μένει ἐν αὐτῷ, "how does the love of God abide in him?" John raises the question of God's love having an influence in this person's life. He uses a genitive construction to describe God's love which may be understood in one of four ways: (1) As a subjective genitive, it would describe love coming from God (Brown, 451; Bultmann, 56; Burdick, 270; Houlden, 101; Stott, 144). (2) As an objective genitive, love would be expressed toward God (Brooke, 97; Bruce, 101; Lieu, 152). (3) It may be a plenary genitive (both objective and subjective) and communicate both ideas (Westcott, 115). (4) As a descriptive genitive ("genitive of quality," Schnackenburg, 200), it would express God's kind of love, God-like love (Marshall, 194). It seems the subjective genitive is best because this love received by the believer is supposed to impact him. Further, the parallel between this statement and "eternal life" in 3:15 strengthens this view (Harris, 161).[288]

With this love in view, John asks a rhetorical question that, in this case, expects a negative answer (Haas, de Jonge, and Swellengrebel, 101). This is not a denial of the unloving believer's salvation since it is his Christian "brother" he is failing to love. It is not a question of whether he is loved by God. He has already experienced that love based on previous verses. The question is how much influence God's love has had in his life as one who has received and benefitted from it. This is the sense of *meno*.[289] The point the question is making is that he has not been influenced by the love he has

---

288. Lieu (152) sees this as conceptually parallel to 3:15 where eternal life did not indwell the murderer. Thus here the absence of compassion indicates God's love is not present in them because although "the presence of God's love is itself invisible, ... those who possess it must surely manifest its marks."

289. BDF §366 (4) disagrees with the editors and suggests that the present tense μένει should be recognized as a future instead. They write, "In doubtful; or deliberative questions about what is to take place classical [Greek] employs the subjunctive (deliberative, dubitative) or (less often) the future indicative. ... It is found mostly with the first person, rarely with the third person. ... The present indicative is used very rarely in a deliberative sense in place of the future." Examples they provide are John 11:47 and Matt 12:34. "In 1 Jn 3:17 μενεῖ is to be read instead of μένει." Practically speaking, either tense leads to the same meaning.

received from God. This then leads to the subsequent admonitions and the impact they can have in a believer's life.[290]

Strecker (116–17) says this rhetorical question "shatters the train of thought."[291] This is a good observation in that we see John drawing their attention to the importance of what he is saying. He further understands this question to imply that the gift of life may be lost to the unloving Christian (118). This is not John's point. That John would not think or teach such a thing is evident from his quotations of Jesus' own words where he teaches that he loses none the Father has given him (John 10:28–30; 17:12).

The number of passages that speak to the Christian's responsibility to help his brother or sister in Christ reveals this is a significant issue in the New Testament, and therefore with God. Beginning in the earliest days of the church, its members gave from their possessions to meet the needs of their fellow saints (Acts 2:44–45 and 4:32–37). James (2:15–16) questioned whether one's faith was active or ineffectual if one failed to meet fellow believers' needs when they came to him or her for help. Paul collected monies from the churches to carry to Jerusalem to help the impoverished church there (Rom 15:25–27; 2 Cor 8–9).

3:18 John now challenges his readers to action along with himself.

Τεκνία, μὴ ἀγαπῶμεν λόγῳ μηδὲ τῇ γλώσσῃ, "Children, let us neither love in word nor in tongue." John addresses his readers once more as "little children."[292] By this he is either summarizing what he has just said (Smalley, 198; Strecker, 118) or beginning a new section (Brown, 439; Harris, 162; Rensberger,102). As with other "hinge" sentences, this one seems to serve to do both by linking the two paragraphs. "Love" connects it to the previous paragraph while "truth" ties in with what follows.

The hortatory present subjunctive *ἀγαπῶμεν* with *μὴ* is prohibitive.[293] Strecker (118) recognizes from the subjunctive imperative that this section

---

290. Thompson (104–105) observes well, "Although this may seem far less demanding and heroic than the willingness to sacrifice one's life for another, it is surely difficult enough!"

291. Schnackenburg (200) describes it as an anacoluthon*.

292. Strecker (118) sees John using this term to "distance" himself from his readers and "to use his authority to give emphasis to the apostolic claim" he has been advancing.

293. Burdick (270) interprets the present tense of the subjunctive verb to indicate continuous action. This would give the sense of "let us keep loving," which would

is parenetic rather than a polemic. As a first person plural subjunctive, it expresses a reciprocal force (Haas, de Jonge, and Swellengrebel, 102). It is the gentlest form of a command that by design includes John with his readers and serves more as a summons than a directive. John connects the two related terms by employing a hendiadys* (contra Strecker, 118), the word spoken with the tongue that shapes it, to indicate mere verbalization.[294] Further, since John includes himself in the command, he is not focusing on any particular group but sees this as comprehensive in scope. His point is that love is not expressed by verbalizations. Rather, it is expressed by what follows.

ἀλλὰ ἐν ἔργῳ καὶ ἀληθείᾳ, "but in deed and in truth." John emphasizes the contrast between word and deed with the ellipsis of ἀγαπῶμεν, which is understood through the role of the coordinating adversative conjunction ἀλλὰ.[295] By this he contrasts verbalization with actualization. Love is expressed physically rather than verbally. "In deed and in truth" can be literally translated "in a work" and "in a true thing," though this use of "truth" can be considered more definite within its preposition phrase. John uses "truth" in one of two ways:[296]

(1) He often uses "truth" to indicate sincerity or genuineness (John 1:14; 4:23). This would be its adverb sense. Harris (162) rejects this on the basis that "it is hard to see how the second noun (γλῶσσα) in the first pair can have an adverbial sense." He proposes that the first

---

fit the context.

294. Akin (160) expresses the idea well. "John is not condemning kind or comforting words. The expression of such utterances without an outward manifestation of them, however, is mere noise and therefore worthless (1 Cor 13:1)."

295. Bultmann (56) considers John's use of the μὴ ... ἀλλὰ construction to indicate the "seriousness of the command." C. Collins ("John 4:23–24, 'In Spirit and Truth': An Idiomatic Proposal," 120) sees this ἐν phrase as an idiomatic statement and proposes that it could be interpreted as "'in A, that is to say in B,' when A and B are not synonymous and when the context favors seeing B as a comment on the activity done in manner A, rather than an additional item in a list." He points to John 4:23–24 and 2 Pet 3:7 as examples of this idiomatic way of writing. Extra biblical literature includes Judith 7:25. He says it may possibly also occur in 2 Pet 3:11; 1 Macc 3:51; Ben Sira 45:4.

296. N. Turner,. *Grammatical Insights into the New Testament.*, *9–10*. While "tongue" has the article, "deed" and "truth" do not, being separated by the strong adversative ἀλλὰ. The absence of the article might tempt one to interpret this use of ἀληθείᾳ to mean "sincerely," "genuine, "or "unhypocritically" (Akin, 161; Stott, 148). The hendiadys would communicate the idea of acting in sincerity (Grayston, 114).

noun of each pair is produced by the second noun. Thus as words are produced by the tongue, so righteous deeds are produced by the truth.

(2) At other times, and often as an articular noun, John indicates by "truth" a body of revealed truth that one either responds to or acts on its basis (John 16:13; 17:17; 2 John 1–2, 4; 3 John 3–4, 8). Thus, it is better to recognize the understood article within the prepositional phrase and this use of truth to allude to the apostolic teachings. This hendiadys brings together the two ideas to emphasize the concept of "doing something appropriate to the body of truth delivered by the apostles," or "acting on what you have been taught." Even so, ultimately John is saying, "Instead of talking about it, do what you know ought to be done!"

3:19 John now moves to the practical implications of living out the command to love one another in material ways. Reflective of Jesus' promise of answered prayer as a fruit of abiding (John 15:7), confidence in prayer comes as a fruit of helping other Christians. Though connected to the previous passage by its hinge sentence, this paragraph appears to take a turn in a different direction than what John has been traveling. Kistemaker notes two basic interpretations of the first two verses. Either they are a "digression" about assurance of salvation, or a "warning not to fall into complacency," the view held by the church fathers and Reformers (also Strecker, 122). He then sees what follows being related to them (Kistemaker, 315). Westcott (118) differs and sees this as a word of assurance for believers. John is describing the "fruit of love" as confidence before God, not only in these first two verses, but within the paragraph (Westcott, 115). How they should be understood shall be clarified below.

This and the following verse form a single complex sentence that contains a series of grammatical challenges. The first challenge facing the interpreter is to determine the meaning of πείθω. The second is to determine the role ὅτι is playing in each clause and the relationship of the clauses to each other. The two approaches may be summarized as follows:

(1) Πείσομεν means "to persuade" or convince, and the ὅτι clause is dependent on it (Stott, 150). Burdick (272) notes that this meaning needs further explanation about the content of the persuasion,

whether it is stated or implied. The weakness of this is that ὅτι occurs twice, once before ἐὰν and then before μείζων, in close proximity. Normally resumptive ὅτι clauses are more removed (Brooke, 99–100). This construction is not seen anywhere else in John's literature (Schnackenburg, 202). To solve the problem raised by these ὅτι clauses, they are dismissed as the explanation of πείθω and what we persuade our heart of is left unstated and is to be learned from what was said previously (Brooke, 99; Burdick, 272).

(2) Πείσομεν means "to pacify, quieten, or reassure." This sense is found in Matt 28:14, where the guards from Jesus' tomb are assured by the Jewish leaders that they will appease the governor if he hears of the seal being broken. Instead of ὅτι ἐὰν, the ὅτι is to be divided into the relative construction of ὅ τι combined with ἐὰν.[297] These are seen as equivalent to ὅταν and ἄν. This would give the sense of quieting one's heart in regard to that of which we are accused. The second ὅτι clause is causal. That makes this a generalizing relative clause (Akin, 164; Brooke, 100; Haas, de Jonge, and Swellengrebel, 104; Marshall, 197, n. 4; Schnackenburg, 202; Smalley, 200; Stott, 151). However, the weakness of this approach is that it is "clumsy" grammar (Stott, 151).[298] This second option appears to make the most sense and is adopted herein.[299]

Καὶ ἐν τούτῳ γνωσόμεθα ὅτι ἐκ τῆς ἀληθείας ἐσμέν, "And by this we will know that we are from the truth." With a dative of means, John introduces us

---

297. The MSS that editors rely on to determine the original autograph do not have spaces between words or accent marks. These are editorial choices. The editors of the Greek texts we use today are not inspired, only the author is. Thus either option, ὅτι ἐὰν or ὅ τι ἐὰν, may be chosen by an interpreter of the text without his or her commitment to Scripture's inspiration coming into question.

298. It may be "clumsy grammar" from our perspective. However, if it accomplishes John's purpose, it is the best. Authors are allowed, for rhetorical and literary purposes, to do what they want with grammar in any language. We see John doing that here.

299. W. J. Bradnock ("Questions and Answers," 140) approaches the question from a different perspective and appears to combine elements of both views. He says that to "persuade ourselves" is "an expansion of the idea 'we shall know', and the second 'that' clause refers back to the words 'by this.'"

to an aspect of Christian confidence. We come again to the question of how John is using ἐν τούτῳ. As discussed earlier, normally when ἐν τούτῳ is followed by a ὅτι clause, it looks forward to that clause. If it does not have a ὅτι clause, it is more likely to look backward. With this ἐν τούτῳ we come to the problem that it is followed by two ὅτι clauses with a relative clause between. So to which of them does it refer? The first ὅτι clause gives the content of the verb γνωσόμεθα, and so can be eliminated from consideration (Smalley, 200; Strecker, 121). The second clause should be considered a relative clause (ὅ τι) and relates better with the clause immediately before it. The third ὅτι clause seems to relate better with the same clause as the relative clause (first ὅτι). Thus, none of the three make much sense with ἐν τούτῳ if it refers to them. Therefore, it seems best to see this use of ἐν τούτῳ with the coordinating conjunctive καὶ looking back to what has just been said (Burge, 163; Haas, de Jonge, and Swellengrebel, 103; Johnson, 87; Lieu, 154; Schnackenburg, 201; Smalley, 200; Strecker, 121) and connecting it to the application that follows (Harris, 163).[300]

By loving in deed and according to truth, we will come to know by experience that we are sourced in that same truth. The future tense γνωσόμεθα continues the pattern of ἐν τούτῳ γινώσκομεν used by John in such places as 1 John 2.3; 3.24; 4.2, 13; 5:2. This use of the future tense communicates that this experiential knowledge is dependent on fulfilling specific conditions, in this case, loving practically (Haas, de Jonge, and Swellengrebel, 103; Westcott, 116).[301] Some see this connected to assurance of salvation and that the following section provides a test of one's salvation (Akin, 162; Marshall,

---

300. W. J. Bradnock, "Questions and Answers," 141. C. Jung ("Main Thrust of the Sentence(s) in 1 John 3:19–20: Encouragement or Warning?" 106) notes that if ἐν τούτῳ points forward to the last ὅτι clause, "the meaning of the sentence does not make good sense" because "no clear connection can be suggested between the first clause ('that God….') and the second clause ('by this')." If ἐν τούτῳ points forward to the ὅτι ἐὰν clause (same usage as 1 Jn 2:3), then καὶ is translated as "thus" and makes the first ὅτι in v. 20 unnecessary. He says then that ἐν τούτῳ "more probably points backward to the preceding passage and less probably forward to the last ὅτι clause in v. 20."

301. Burdick (271) sees this use of γινώσκω to "indicate the acquisition of knowledge." This would accord with the experiential nuance of γινώσκω that John appears to apply to it in most instances.

197).[302] For example, Burge (163) agrees with Smalley that "this is how we know," which occurs twice (v. 19, 24) governs the entire section and that this is a section on assurance.[303] Others reject the idea that this involves assurance of salvation but rather involves confidence in one's ability to express Christ's kind of love (Hodges, 163).[304] Since John includes himself by use of the first person plural, assurance of salvation cannot be the issue. John is looking at the source of one's actions and says we can see our actions are sourced in God's truth. Though one must be a believer to be "from the truth," not all believers may be described as doing such. Still, doing truth does indicate parentage just as love and hate did earlier. Doing truth *can* produce assurance of salvation which is integral to confidence before God. However, though this is true, such is not John's focus in this passage. John is not saying he assures himself of his salvation through these works, but that they give him a confidence before God because he recognizes that his actions are sourced in God's truth.

καὶ ἔμπροσθεν αὐτοῦ πείσομεν τὴν καρδίαν ἡμῶν, "and we will persuade our heart before him." John places the preposition ἔμπροσθεν at the beginning of the clause for emphasis. This expresses the idea of being in the presence of someone, as does ἐνώπιον in 3:22.[305] Their meanings are near-

302. Williamson's (126) understanding that the middle voice γνωσόμεθα implies "knowledge that validates the claim of the person" would seem to support such a view. However, though that may be a nuance of the verb in the middle voice, it need not be intended by John here. Rather, based on what follows, it seems to have more the sense of discovery than of validation.

303. Still dependent on his theory of a Johannine school and secessionists, Burge (163) writes, "John's community is a community under siege, and his followers need reassurance that they are indeed on the side of the angels, that they possess the truth."

304. C. Jung ("Main Thrust of the Sentence(s) in 1 John 3:19–20: Encouragement or Warning?" 108) sees the encouragement differently. He says, "Though the whole passage of vv. 19–24 deals with reassurance and encouragement, this does not necessarily suggest that the purpose of the sentence in vv. 19–20 must be to give encouragement, assurance or confidence to believers. The sentence in vv. 19–20 was probably intended to give a warning to believers in order that they may have a true boldness before God." He is correct in one sense. However, assurance seems to be the thrust of these verses, including 19–20 when seen structured differently.

305. BDAG, 325 (ἔμπροσθεν) and 342 (ἐνώπιον). Schnackenburg (202, n. 7) sees this meaning "in the presence of," but not in terms of judgment because the focus of this verse is on God's gracious treatment of His children.

ly identical and they can be used interchangeably.[306] Thus no significance need be sought regarding John's choice of one over the other.

If the future tense *πείσομεν* with *καὶ* indicates that this clause continues the thought of the previous clause rather than referring back to *ἐν τούτῳ* (Bultmann, 56; Burdick, 271), then *πείσομεν* continues the thought of *γινώσκομεν*.[307] With this understanding *καὶ* is functioning as a logical connective instead of coordinating and has the sense of "and so" (Bultmann, 56).

Πείσομεν is translated by "persuade" because the person is pacifying their troubled heart or worried conscience.[308] Though this is future tense and God's judgment is in view, this need not be viewed as an eschatological reference, whether realized eschatology or futurist eschatology. John is not pointing them to a future judgment, though that was in view earlier (2:28–29).

Is this an allusion to the Bema Seat judgment or when one comes "before" God in prayer? The future tense *πείσομεν* would initially seem to indicate the former and so look back on the warning and promise of 2:28–3:3.[309] This would fit with the John's emphasis elsewhere that all mankind will be judged on the basis of works (John 3:19; 14:10; Rev 2:1, 5, 8, 12, 22; 3:1, 7, 14; 14:13; 18:5; 20:12), which fits with what John is discussing here. If this were the case the referent of *ἔμπροσθεν αὐτοῦ* would best be understood as be God the Father as judge (Bultmann, 56; Westcott, 116; Yarbrough, 210), though Christ's judgment may also be in view (Strecker, 121).[310] However,

---

306. BDF §214(6).

307. Burdick (271) says *πείσομεν* and its clause is parallel to *γνωσόμεθα* and its clause. And so John is affirming that active love has two results: "knowledge that people are of the truth" and "assurance before God."

308. BDAG 791 has "conciliate, pacify, set at ease" under the broader sense of "to cause to come to a particular point of view or course of action" when used in its active voice. C. Jung ("Main Thrust of the Sentence(s) in 1 John 3:19–20: Encouragement or Warning?" 101–102) suggests *πείθω* may mean "bribe" rather than "appease" (NKJV), "win him over" (NASB95), or "satisfy" (ESV) based on his rendering of Matt 28:14. He says the verb means "persuade" or "convince" 42 times. It also can mean "trust" (6 times) and "obey" (three times).

309. C. F. D. Moule ("A Neglected Factor in the Interpretation of Johannine Eschatology," 158–59) identifies this as a possible "futurist" eschatology with John rather than "realized eschatology."

310. That we will be judged by Jesus is repeatedly affirmed in passages such as Matt 25:32; 1 Thess 2:19; 1 Cor 3:10–15; 2 Cor 5:10. However, a judgment before God the Father may be implied by Matt 10:32–33 and 1 Thess 3:13.

what follows indicates the second option is best. We may have confidence in prayer. Thus the future tense is better seen to carry a durative force rather than futuristic and so be functioning like a present progressive (Kistemaker, 315).[311]

With "heart" meaning "conscience" rather than emotions (Burdick, 272; Lieu, 154), John says that our conduct impacts our prayer life in terms of the level of confidence we will have when approaching God with our petitions.[312] John's focus is on confidence in prayer, not assurance of salvation or blessing on judgment day.

Of note is the plural possessive pronoun ἡμῶν with the singular heart. This is not unusual in Johannine literature, occurring ten times with various plural possessive pronouns.[313] Johnson (89) interprets it to mean the collective assurance of the community rather than its individual members. Akin (164) describes it as "the oneness of this experience among God's people." However, a better understanding is expressed by Haas, de Jonge, and Swellengrebel (103) who clarify that it has a "distributive force," for which Greek used singulars, unlike English, which uses the plural.

Being a child of God does not necessarily lead to confidence before him any more than being anyone else's child does. Confidence results from relationship—the right kind of relationship. It is also impacted by personality traits and life events that may or may not lead to guilt. It is impacted by one's knowledge and maturity level. On one hand, confidence is available to all on the basis of Christ's work alone (Heb 4:16). On the other, it is contingent on obedience and abiding (John 14:23–24; 15:7–10).

3:20 This is one of the most difficult verses in John's literature to decipher as evidenced by the wide variance between modern translations.[314] It con-

311. A. T. Robertson, *A Grammar of the Greek New Testament*, 871. This fits best under the category of a gnomic future (BDF §349).

312. BDAG 508. Baur et al define "heart" as the "seat of physical, spiritual and mental life" and the "center and source of the whole inner life, with its thinking, feeling, and volition."

313. John 12:40 (αὐτῶν τὴν καρδίαν and νοήσωσιν τῇ καρδίᾳ); 14:1 (ὑμῶν ἡ καρδία), 27 (ὑμῶν ἡ καρδία); 16:6 (ὑμῶν τὴν καρδίαν), 22 (ὑμῶν ἡ καρδία); 1 John 3:19 (τὴν καρδίαν ἡμῶν), 20 (ἡμῶν ἡ καρδία and τῆς καρδίας ἡμῶν), and 21 (ἡ καρδία ἡμῶν).

314. Burdick (273–75) organizes what he views as ten ways to interpret vv. 20–21 under five groupings based on their major characteristics. These include (1) "Love in action (v. 18) persuades (v. 19) that God is greater than the human heart (v. 20)."

tinues the thought of the previous verse and so must be translated and interpreted in light of its immediate context and resulting flow of thought.

ὅ τι ἐὰν καταγινώσκῃ ἡμῶν ἡ καρδία, "in whatever our heart condemns us." The first issue before us is whether this clause begins with a ὅτι or with the relative pronoun ὅ followed by the indefinite pronoun τι and translated "whatever." Jung argues against ὅτι ἐὰν meaning "and if" because it would make the second ὅτι "redundant, even disruptive" (notes Bultmann, 57).[315] This same construction can be found in 3:2 and 5:14. In 3:2 (ὅτι ἐὰν φανερωθῇ) it is a ὅτι of content following οἴδαμεν. In 5:14 (ὅτι ἐάν τι αἰτώμεθα) the ὅτι is epexegetical to the phrase, ἡ παρρησία ἣν ἔχομεν πρὸς αὐτὸν, explaining it further. Therefore, since this ὅτι clause is in a similar construction as 5:14, if it is determined to be ὅτι ἐὰν instead of ὅ τι ἐὰν, it is most likely to be epexegetical as well (Harris, 165). Jung also rejects it being equivalent to ὅταν and meaning "whenever." He rejects this option on the basis that ὅτι ἐὰν is not equivalent to ὅταν, but ὅτε ἐὰν. He does acknowledge that "'whenever' includes the conditional force which properly conveys the phrase."[316] His choice ("more probably") is that it should be translated as "whatever" (ὅ τι) like in the NASB95 (also Smalley, 202). He notes that this use does not occur anywhere else in the NT. However, he does also note that this use does occur in Koiné Greek outside the NT.[317] If the second ὅτι is related to πείθω, then it gives the content of what we assure ourselves with. He notes the possibility of it meaning "because" but then notes that if πείθω means "convince," the ὅτι should mean "that" and give the content of what it believed.[318] It seems best to see John intending the relative clause.[319] This pronoun combination is functioning as a "generalizing relative introducing a relative clause" (Smalley, 202; Schnackenburg, 202). Along with the

(2) "Love in action assures one's heart concerning any guilt feeling." (3) "The *if*-clause is to be viewed as parenthetical." (4) God's greater knowledge is reason to fear rather than to be confident." (5) The statement assumes an ellipsis.

315. Moody (74) interprets this construction to mean "even if."

316. C. Jung, "Main Thrust of the Sentence(s) in 1 John 3:19–20: Encouragement or Warning?" 104.

317. According to BDF §107.

318. C. Jung, "Main Thrust of the Sentence(s) in 1 John 3:19–20: Encouragement or Warning?" 105.

319. See commentary on v. 19 for a full explanation of this choice.

following ὅτι clause, this verse contains two subordinate clauses and continues the sentence begun in the previous verse.

John continues the thought of the previous verse: we can know we are of the truth and persuade our hearts before God. He brings up the reality of self-doubt in the life of a Christian who is serious about obeying God's commands. How do we handle the problem of a lack of confidence before God? We do not look to our works to see if we conform to God's family but to God.[320]

The term καταγινώσκῃ appears to be a play on words with γνωσόμεθα in the previous verse and so the first half of the long sentence (Kistemaker, 316). Looking at the two verses together as a single sentence, one notes the repetition of "heart" (three times) and "know" (twice) with "condemn" sharing the same root as "know" and so repeating the root three times as well. The term καταγινώσκω means to "condemn" or "convict" by bringing an unfavorable judgment against someone.[321] Thus the person is judging themselves and leveling a verdict of guilt. So this is a case of someone entering God's presence with a guilty conscience, certain that he or she has a sin that separates them from fellowship with the holy God.

The third class condition implies that there will be times when our heart does not condemn us, which is what will be addressed in the following sentence. It also implies that we may experience this feeling at times as well. In first century thinking, the heart is the center of conscience rather than emotion. John is thus dealing with the potential insecurity of one who comes to God but is not sure he or she meets God's high standards of loving other believers. In saying that our heart condemns us, John does not imply by this that such feelings result from the convicting ministry of the Holy Spirit. In fact, what follows implies the opposite, that this is strictly a matter of conscience and a question raised by the believer.

ὅτι μείζων ἐστὶν ὁ θεὸς τῆς καρδίας ἡμῶν, "because God is greater than our heart." This last ὅτι in the sentence is causal ("because").[322] Through it John

320. W. M. Aldrich, "Assurance," 311. See Paul's approach in 1 Cor 4:4–5.

321. BDAG, 515; R. Bultmann, "γινώσκω, καταγινώσκω," *TDNT* 1:715. It also has the alternate sense of "despise." The only other use of καταγινώσκω in the New Testament occurs in Gal 2:11 where Paul describes Peter as standing condemned for his hypocrisy.

322. This is the third time John has used ὅτι clauses in close proximity to each other, which is considered rough grammar, but appears to be something he likes to do.

reminds his readers to whom they are coming when they have their doubts. He affirms that God, who is greater than our hearts, is where we look for assurance when we doubt ourselves.

The meaning of this statement may be:

(1) "God is a stricter judge than our conscience is inclined to admit" (Grayston, 115). Grayston's arguments include the following. This is indicated by the "reproach" of verses 17 and 18. In light of the reproach, this verse is an argument from the lesser to the greater ("if our conscious condemns us, how much more will God"). Appealing to God's mercy falls into the opponents' trap of claiming fellowship with God without the need to obey his commandments.

(2) God is more merciful than our hearts (Bultmann, 57; Houlden, 101; Marshall, 198; Schnackenburg, 203; Strecker, 123; Stott, 151–52; Yarbrough, 211) and we can trust in his love for us (Williamson, 127). Strecker (123) understands this to mean "God overcomes the accusations leveled by our consciences against ourselves."

καὶ γινώσκει πάντα. "and he knows all things." Our final assurance is that God is fully aware of our failings and feelings.[323] He is omniscient (Smalley, 203).[324] This truth has been affirmed earlier in 1:9 with his promise to cleanse from all unrighteousness. His point by saying "God knows all things" is that whenever something comes along that impinges upon our confidence before God, he is already aware of it and is greater than our fears.[325] The objector then might raise the question, anticipated by John, concerning the case of a person who does not feel guilt. How does that impact the person's relationship with God?

He does the same in 3:2 and 3:14. Harris (165) sees this last ὅτι as epexegetical and therefore resumptive of the first clause.

323. B. Fanning (*Verbal Aspect in New Testament Greek*, 208) sees γινώσκει as a gnomic present. This aspect expresses "timeless, universal occurrences: the gnomic or proverbial present" that "occurs in proverbial statements or general maxims about what occurs at *all* times."

324. Paul teaches that God knows us (1 Cor 8:2–3; 13:12; and Gal 4:9).

325. Strecker (122) sees John affirming that "God's mercy will have the final word" when we do stand before him in judgment.

3:21 John continues the thought of the previous sentence and answers the question of our expectations from God when we do not feel self-condemned. Using another third class conditional sentence, he affirms the possibility of confidence before God.

Ἀγαπητοί, ἐὰν ἡ καρδία ἡμῶν μὴ καταγινώσκῃ, "Beloved, if our heart does not condemn us." With this address to his readers, John does not move to a new section, but begins his commentary on the previous verses as they relate to his pastoral concerns (Bultmann, 57; Strecker, 123).[326] He likely chooses this term of address because what he has just said might cause concern (Westcott, 118). This reassures them once again of their standing before God as his loved children.

Some Christians may be tempted always to assume their guilt because of 1:8–10, or a background of condemnation or sin that plagues their conscience. Addressing his readers once more with endearment, John reminds them that they need not always feel self-condemned before God. This third class condition once more reminds his readers that they may or may not feel self-condemned. Their conscience will not always be accusing them when they come into God's presence.

That this lack of felt guilt does not in and of itself prove one's innocence is evident from what John has already said earlier in chapters 1 and 2. Those refusing to confess sin still have it and are self-deceived. Those not loving their brothers are walking in darkness whether they know it or not. Similarly, John is not implying by this that those who do not feel guilt do not have guilt. He is simply addressing the question of the person approaching God in prayer. The implication of what he is saying is that when one comes into God's presence and has a clean conscience, it indicates they are not being convicted of any sins by the Holy Spirit. If not convicted, we need not search out sins or stand before God with guilt feelings he has not placed on us.

παρρησίαν ἔχομεν πρὸς τὸν θεὸν, "we have confidence before God." Using the indicative, John makes clear that the one whose conscience does not condemn can have boldness as he or she approaches God.[327] This is the same term for "boldness" that John used in 2:28 with reference to Jesus'

326. Strecker (123) calls this "an emphatic turning toward the readers."

327. *Boldness*, παρρησία, appears four times in 1 John. Here, and in 2:28; 4:17; and 5:14.

judgment at his coming. Again, it is not cockiness, but a feeling of security and calmness in God's presence. As Schnackenburg (204–5) says "Παρρησία describes a friendly relationship which confers a right to speak freely."[328] It is this freedom that enables the child of God to bring any petition before him and to know he or she will gain a hearing.

The sense of πρὸς τὸν θεὸν is that of a personal and relational encounter with God (Akin, 165; Smalley, 204). This same construction is used in John 1:1 to describe Jesus, "the Word," being both God and with God in the sense of being in his presence. "The thought here is of the boldness with which the son appears before the Father, and not of that with which the accused appears before the Judge" (Westcott, 118).

John's point is that we can have confidence before God if, when we look at how we are loving or not loving other Christians, we are convinced that we, in fact, do. We can be confident to the extent that we are obedient to God's command. This is not assurance of salvation, though that is included, but assurance of acceptability in God's presence. We can know God will hear our prayers, as will be seen in what follows.

Bonhoeffer's words summarize these last two verses well. "He knows that God's Word in Jesus Christ pronounces him guilty, even when he does not feel his guilt, and God's Word in Jesus Christ pronounces him not guilty and righteous, even when he does not feel that he is righteous at all."[329]

3:22 This verse completes the sentence begun in the previous verse, providing both the promise of answer and the reason for confidence in prayer. Both present tenses should be seen as gnomic, and so stating principles (Akin, 166; Burdick, 277).[330]

καὶ ὃ ἐὰν αἰτῶμεν λαμβάνομεν ἀπ' αὐτοῦ, "And whatever we ask we receive from him." With the coordinating conjunction *καὶ* John joins this promise with the promise of boldness in the previous verse (Burdick, 277; Strecker, 124).[331] We have both boldness *and* an expectation of answered prayer before God. The third class condition, though, makes reception

328. "Παρρησία setzt ein freundschaftlichnahes Verhältnis voraus, das ein Recht auf freie Rede verleiht."

329. D. Bonhoeffer, *Life Together*, 22.

330. Smalley (205) says they "suggest an ongoing activity and experience."

331. Akin (164) sees it functioning epexegetically and explaining the previous clause. Thus boldness would be defined in terms of answered prayer. It seems better

dependent on the asking.[332] This is similar to James' declaration, "You do not have because you do not ask" (Jas 4:5).

Λαμβάνομεν as a present tense verb is taken by Strecker (124) to communicate the idea of certainty that their prayers will be answered and every "possible kind of concrete wish" will be heard. This explains the nature of the previous παρρησίαν ἔχομεν. Similarly, Westcott (119) sees the promise of "whatever" as absolute. However when John says "whatever" (ὃ) he is not giving a blanket promise of "anything we might think of asking."[333] Rather this must be seen as a synecdoche of the genus (the whole for the part) affirming that no *area* is excluded from God's answer, though individual requests may be denied. For example, God does not give what is evil to his children, even if they ask for it (Matt 7:7–11). So even in the promise of "whatever" there is the understood condition of its being a good and righteous thing requested.

ὅτι τὰς ἐντολὰς αὐτοῦ τηροῦμεν, "because we keep his commandments." Westcott (119) does not see this stating the cause of answered prayer as much its reason. However, John is affirming here that receiving an answer *is* dependent on meeting certain conditions which in this instance includes obedience (Akin, 166; Brown, 462; Hodges, 166; Smalley, 205; contra Schnackenburg, 205). Thus it is better to see it as a causal ὅτι clause (Burdick, 278; Haas, de Jonge, and Swellengrebel, 107; Strecker, 124). The verb is a present progressive in this instance and emphasizes the habitual keeping of God's commandments (Akin, 165; Burdick, 278).[334] Stott (149) says well, "Obedience is the indispensable condition, not the meritorious cause of answered prayer." Bultmann (58) sees this and the next clause forming a hendiadys with this ὅτι clause functioning as "an indirect imperative." Thus we please God by keeping his commandments. Answered prayer is

---

to see this as a second benefit in that boldness has to do with our being in the presence of God more than our asking for things.

332. This is an example of the particle ἐὰν being used instead of ἂν after the relative pronoun ὃ "perhaps in order to underline the conditional aspect" (BDF §107).

333. Strecker (124) translates ὃ ἐὰν as "whatever" and rejects the idea it introduces a conditional clause. Rather, for him it "designates what is ordinary and regular." He sees the clause causing it to be difficult to discern whether this is an iterative or a future statement.

334. B. M. Fanning (*Verbal Aspect in New Testament Greek*, 403) would support this view, noting with regard to the aspect of the subjunctive mood, "In some cases these presents reflect distributive or customary-iterative meaning."

then the expectation of the consistently obedient. However, it would seem better to see it as assurance of answered prayer *while* one is obedient, thus more of the progressive aspect of the present tense coming to the fore in this instance.

Burge (164) notes that this passages "echoes other similar forms of confidence found in passages such as John 14:13–14; 16:23–24." He sees this as similar to 5:14–15, though it is conditioned on asking according to God's will. Conditions are commonly attached to promises of answered prayer as is the case here. "Here John says that we must do 'what pleases him'; this presupposes a quality of intimacy that is in touch with God's very heart." Beale and Carson observe, "The Hebrew Scriptures establish a clear link between a person's righteousness and God's responsiveness to that person's prayers (Job 27:9; Pss 34:15; 66:18; 109:7; 145:19; Prov 15:8, 29; 21:27; 28:9; Isa 1:15; cf. John 14:13–14; 16:23–27; 1 Pet 3:7; 1 John 3:21–22)."[335]

καὶ τὰ ἀρεστὰ ἐνώπιον αὐτοῦ ποιοῦμεν, "and do the things that are pleasing before him." This second part of the ὅτι clause may be viewed as a second condition, but is better seen as the second half of a hendiadys indicating that keeping God's commandments is what pleases him.[336] Ποιοῦμεν as a present progressive focuses our attention on the requirement of having the habit of obedience (Burdick, 278) as a key to answered prayer. Thus it is the carefully obedient Christian who pleases God and can expect answered prayer.

This reflects Jesus' promise in John 15:7 of answered prayer conditioned on abiding in him and his words abiding in us. It also shows the role each child of God plays in their sanctification. Progressive sanctification—spiritual growth—is affected by obedience. Though no work results in justification (spiritual birth is by faith alone) one's sanctification is impacted by works. Though still by faith, it is active faith that sanctifies rather than

---

335. G. K. Beale and D. A. Carson, *Commentary on the New Testament Use of the Old Testament*, 461.

336. Akin (166) is an example of those who distinguish between keeping God's commandments and doing things that please him. He says, "Although the commands appear to be those explicit demands of God's will, the things that please him are those spontaneous acts motivated by love and a desire to honor him above the specified commands."

inoperative faith (Jas 2:14–17).[337] In the same way, confidence that God will answer prayer grows out of a consciously obedient lifestyle. What follows defines further the commitment we are to keep before God.

3:23 This verse is an explanation of the previous verse (Bultmann, 58).[338] John moves from the promise of answered prayer to its basis in the previous verse, and now clarifies God's expectation from us. What God has commanded is faith and love, faith in his Son and love for believers. That these are inseparable—one cannot be done without the other—is made evident by their being described, not as two commands but as a single command (Kistemaker, 318).

καὶ αὕτη ἐστὶν ἡ ἐντολὴ αὐτοῦ, "And this is his commandment." John now summarizes the command that is to be kept by those who wish to experience answered prayer (Strecker, 126). The shift from plural "commandments" to singular may seem to some (Burdick, 279) to be out of place. However, it follows logically. John has said we are to please God by keeping his commandments (plural because there are more than one). Now he relates one of those commandments to us, namely, the one to love one another.

Here αὐτοῦ refers to God the Father once again (Burdick, 279; Johnson, 90), though at least one part of this single command came from the lips of his Son in the upper room. This singular command has two aspects: faith in Christ and love for Christians.

ἵνα πιστεύσωμεν τῷ ὀνόματι τοῦ υἱοῦ αὐτοῦ Ἰησοῦ Χριστοῦ, "that we believe in the name of his Son Jesus Christ." The content of that command is introduced by the epexegetical ἵνα (Brooke, 104) followed by an aorist subjunctive πιστεύσωμεν and then present subjunctive first person plural (ἀγαπῶμεν). Though the ἵνα clause could be epexegetical to αὕτη (Smalley, 207) or be in apposition to ἐντολή, it seems best to see it as epexegetical to ἐντολή and thus communicate the content of God's command. Strecker (126) sees this giving the clause an imperative force, which is true, though these subjunctive verbs should not be viewed as hortatory.

---

337. James uses νεκρός figuratively for "ineffectual" or "inoperative" with the same sense Paul does in Rom 7:8 where he says sin is "dead" (χωρὶς γὰρ νόμου ἁμαρτία νεκρά.) Just as sin is not non-existent apart from the law, just unable to cause death, so too, faith is not non-existent apart from works. It is simply not doing anything.

338. As Bultmann (58) notes, "the indirect imperative of v 22 becomes a direct imperative in v 23."

John includes himself in the recipients of the command to believe. He is expected to keep it as much as his readers. By including himself he is calling upon them to do so without pointing an accusing finger at them. Kistemaker (319) sees the aorist subjunctive as ingressive and pointing to "the moment the Christian accepted Jesus" (Johnson (90) agrees).[339] However, it is better to see it in its more general undefined role and, following the context of the Upper Room and John's inclusion among those receiving the command, to address the continued need for believers to keep believing. So how do they express their faith in Christ in an ongoing manner? They express it by obedience, which is the second half of this singular command from God the Father.

Whereas the verb form of believe dominates the Gospel, this is the first use of the verb πιστεύω in the epistle. It will recur six more times (4:1, 16; 5:1, 5, 10, 13).[340] Though some see this introducing a new section of the epistle (Kistemaker, 319), it is better to see it as a new emphasis in the second half of the epistle.

"Believe in the name" means to believe in the person, Jesus, and his authority (Bultmann, 59; Haas, de Jonge, and Swellengrebel, 108; Lieu, 158; Schnackenburg, 207; Smalley, 208; Strecker, 126).[341] This phrase was used extensively in John's Gospel for justifying faith in Jesus, or the faith of those who were justified as they came to realize that he was their expected Messiah. In John 1:12 it is equivalent to receiving Jesus, in contrast to his own who did not. In John 2:23 the multitudes responded to Jesus' miracles by believing in his name (ἐπίστευσαν εἰς τὸ ὄνομα). We see from John 3:18 that believing "in the name" of Jesus is equivalent to believing "in" (πιστεύω εἰς) Jesus. Later in this epistle (5:13) John will use πιστεύω in combination with εἰς τὸ ὄνομα once more.

---

339. So too, Akin (167) follows Bruce (100) in identifying this as an ingressive aorist.

340. Its noun form, πίστις, also occurs at 5:4.

341. Akin (167) labels this "a dative of personal relationship, which involves a personal commitment of oneself to 'the name' of Jesus Christ." Haas, de Jonge, and Swellengrebel (108) understands this use of the dative to indicate giving credence to in light of its relationship to a "non-personal goal."

Is this an issue of justification or sanctification? Westcott (119–20) sees it as a kind of "work" based on Jesus' statement in John 6:29.[342] However, Jesus' point was just the opposite. There was no actual work the people could do to receive the Bread of Heaven. The only "work" they could do—the only response God would accept—was to believe in his Son, something they were not doing (John 6:61–64) and that did not involve "doing." In this passage, the aorist subjunctive, rather than being viewed as ingressive, could be better seen as a constative imperative (a categorical imperative) with the following present imperative being customary and therefore an ongoing command.[343] This is something believers must do. They must keep on believing in Jesus on the basis of his character.

Finally, John adds Jesus' human name and messianic title, Christ, likely to emphasize both his earthly ministry and exaltation (Kistemaker, 318). This shows that faith in Jesus is not just in him as a historical reality. It involves recognizing him for who he is as both God and Savior. It is recognizing more than that he lived and taught, but that he still lives and it is he who saves those who call upon him. These truths are not just necessary for justifying faith; they are necessary for sanctifying faith as well. Thus John wrote his Gospel so that his readers would continue to believe that Jesus was the Christ and thereby experience eternal life in his name (John 20:31).

καὶ ἀγαπῶμεν ἀλλήλους, "and that we love one another." John follows his aorist *πιστεύσωμεν* with the present subjunctive *ἀγαπῶμεν* ("to keep loving"). By this he is implying that his readers have been loving each other and need to continue to do so.[344] Using the first person plural subjunctive, he includes himself in the need to act out Jesus' command to love once more. This is not something for young believers only. It is something for every believer, beginning with the sole remaining apostle down to the newest convert. His choice of *ἀλλήλους* indicates that this love is to be bidirectional, mutual, among fellow Christians (Akin, 168).

καθὼς ἔδωκεν ἐντολὴν ἡμῖν, "just as he gave a commandment to us." Our love for one another was commanded, but by whom? The subject of the

342. Strecker (127) too refers to it as "a responsible human deed—the single human 'condition' of salvation, but not to be interpreted as something done by the human being in advance, since it is nothing other than the person's own self-surrender."

343. D. B. Wallace, *Grammar*, 720–22.

344. This use of the present has "durative force" (Haas, de Jonge, and Swellengrebel, 108).

verb "command" is not specified and so could be either God the Father or God the Son in this context. Though earlier is it clearly the Father in view since he was commanding we believe in his Son, here it seems better to see the Son as the one giving the command (Lieu, 159). John's choice to give Jesus' two titles serves to make him the antecedent of this verb rather than God the Father. Thus John is alluding once more to the upper room where Jesus commanded his disciples, and so us, to love one another (John 13:34)

Akin (168) concludes that this verse serves as a test of life and says that "John insists that both faith and love stand as essential tests for the true child of God. Right belief and right action reveal the authenticity of one's faith." These are not tests to determine if one is a child of God. John is presupposing that throughout this section. Rather, these are conditions to be met by the child of God in order to experience the benefits of his relationship with God, benefits such as assurance in God's presence and answered prayer.

Lenski (479) summarizes John's point well. "You cannot believe without loving nor love without believing." John has made it clear already and will continue to emphasize the interrelatedness of faith and obedience (including the command to love) along with a correct view of Jesus as they impact a Christian's fellowship with God and other Christians.

3:24 John is stating another principle that governs the believer's relationship with God and connects the Spirit's indwelling with our mutual abiding relationship with God.[345] In this verse he describes the mutual indwelling relationship between the obedient believer and Jesus. This is reminiscent of Jesus' words in the Upper Room (John 15:4–7). The believer abides through obedience and Christ abides in the obedient believer in the person of the Holy Spirit.[346] This use of "abide" is not related to the question of whether one is a believer or not, but whether Jesus is influencing that believer or not.

καὶ ὁ τηρῶν τὰς ἐντολὰς αὐτοῦ ἐν αὐτῷ μένει καὶ αὐτὸς ἐν αὐτῷ·, "And he who keeps his commandments abides in him and he in him." As previously noted, John's use of the articular, third person present active participle *ὁ*

345. Schnackenburg (208) sees this verse recapitulating and summarizing John's argument and his theme of fellowship.

346. Brown (482) observes well, "On our part the abiding is conditioned upon keeping the commandments of God; but on God's part our abiding stems from His giving the Spirit which is not conditioned. The same God who *gave* the commandment (3:23c) *gave* the Spirit that enables us to live out the commandment."

τηρῶν indicates that he is stating a principle that governs man's relationship with God. As such, it is best to see this describing a kind of person (thus the gnomic sense) rather than a lifestyle (customary present) or a momentary condition (present progressive). Bruce (100) sees this obedience as "proof" of dwelling rather than its cause. However, both John's and Jesus' words (John 14:15–18, 23–24) can better be understood as describing the condition that must be met for a believer to have a mutually abiding relationship with God, all three members of the Trinity. What is kept are God's commandments.[347]

To whom does the first ἐν αὐτῷ and αὐτὸς refer? The previous context allows for either Jesus or God the Father (Strecker, 127). Moody (78) argues for God the Father because of the plural "commandments" and his choice of αὐτὸς over ἐκεῖνος. Smalley (201), on the other hand, sees them referring to Jesus on the basis that this sentence is parallel to John 14:23 and 15:3–10. Regardless, αὐτοῦ should be seen as referring to God the Father (Burdick, 281; Johnson, 91). It seems best to see all of the pronouns in this sentence referring to God the Father (Akin, 168; Smalley, 201). It is describing the same mutual relationship resulting from obedience promised by Jesus in the upper room (John 14:16–17, 23–24; 15:4–7). This mutual abiding is accomplished by the indwelling Holy Spirit (John 14:16–17, 26; 15:26; 16:13). However, it is contingent on obedience.

The present tense verb μένει also expresses a gnomic aspect rather than progressive. Thus he is saying that those characterized by obedience experience a mutual abiding relationship with God. He is not saying that while one is obeying he is also abiding.[348] Even so, such is true.

καὶ ἐν τούτῳ γινώσκομεν ὅτι μένει ἐν ἡμῖν, "and by this we know that he abides in us." Using the dative of means with ἐν τούτῳ he describes how we can know we are experiencing Christ's presence within us, which is absolutely necessary for mutual abiding to occur. As with his previous uses of ἐν τούτῳ, some see John pointing back to what he previously said (Burdick, 281; Westcott, 121) or forward to what follows (Akin, 168; Haas, de Jonge, and Swellengrebel, 109). This second option follows John's pattern and so is

347. Strecker (127) does not see any significance to the change from the singular ἡ ἐντολὴ in v. 23 to the plural τὰς ἐντολὰς.

348. C. F. D. Moule ("A Neglected Factor in the Interpretation of Johannine Eschatology," 158) sees this as an example of "realized eschatology" in the epistle.

best.[349] He affirms that this knowledge is experiential with the present tense of γινώσκω, knowledge gained by experience, as opposed to οἴδα, knowledge gained by instruction.[350] This is something we experience, not just believe to be true because we were taught it.

ἐκ τοῦ πνεύματος οὗ ἡμῖν ἔδωκεν, "from the Spirit whom he gave to us." John says we can know by experience that Christ is abiding in us "from" the Spirit. This prepositional phrase completes the idea of ἐν τούτῳ. The preposition ἐκ, in this instance, could convey the sense of cause, and so mean that we know "because of" the Spirit (Strecker, 129).[351] It could communicate the idea of means, and so it is "by means of" the Spirit that we know. It seems best though to see the preposition indicating the source of our assurance being the Spirit ministering to us (Haas, de Jonge, and Swellengrebel, 109).[352]

This is the first use of πνεύμα in the epistle.[353] It appears in two other passages (4:1–6, 13; and 5:6–12). In the first it is used both of the Holy

349. Normally when ἐν τούτῳ is followed by a ὅτι clause, it looks forward to that clause. If it does not have a ὅτι clause, it is more likely to look backward.

350. Akin (169) defines it as "knowledge obtained by drawing a conclusion based on facts." Strecker (129) sees this final use of γινώσκω to be the "end of a chain of criteria for recognition beginning with the perfect ἐγνώκαμεν in v. 16a. Accordingly, Christ's sacrificial surrender represents the criterion of *agapē* relating to the past. Then follows, with the future γνωσόμεθα in v. 19a, the criterion for discerning the truth about the future, which will reveal the believers' triumph in the final judgment. In v. 24 the criterion of recognition related to the present of believers; if it is to be described as μένει ἐν αὐτῷ, it is determined by the gift of the Spirit."

351. Strecker (129) relates this back to χρῖσμα in 2:20 and 27, which he interprets to be the Holy Spirit. Though here the reference is clearly to the Holy Spirit, in discussing those verses I concluded that χρῖσμα referred to those things the readers had been taught, God's word. John's choice of πνεύμα over χρῖσμα indicates that he does not want to make the connection between the anointing there and the Spirit here.

352. Schnackenburg (208–15) sees this probably alluding to the sacraments. It is better to take it plainly. Though John does not emphasize the ministry of the Spirit in his epistle like Jesus does in the Gospel, this can be taken at face value. Of note, though, is his failure to say more. However, since his focus is on relationships within the body of Christ and practical living of one's faith, it is not surprising that he says nothing more. The Spirit's presence implies the Spirit's ministry and therefore expression in the life of every believer. Nothing more need be said at this point, lest it detract from John's flow of thought, which is now to return to the issue of false teachers.

353. Williamson (128) says "the Spirit is an underemphasized presence in 1 John."

Spirit (4:2) as well as false teachers. In the second it refers to the Holy Spirit, who bears witness of Jesus' incarnation. John's mention of the Holy Spirit here "opens the door" to what will follow next, testing the spirits of false teachers (Akin, 169).

Van der Merwe sees this evidence of the Spirit to be "a communal rather than an individual experience."[354] This could be the sense of ἡμῖν. However, it seems better to see this as corporate only in that John is including himself with his readers.

Why is οὗ in the genitive and not a dative direct object since it is clearly the direct object of ἔδωκεν? It is rendered in the genitive because of "attraction" to its antecedent, πνεύματος (Kistemaker, 320; Smalley, 212). Again, the One giving the Spirit in this instance is Jesus who has been the focus throughout this paragraph.

Biblical Theology Comments

Righteousness and sin are opposites, both reflected in conduct. They identify a person either with God or with the devil (3:7–10). At the same time, righteousness is not defined as an absence of sin. Rather, it is an inner reality that expresses itself in activity. In this part of the epistle, that activity is loving other Christians. In the same way, sin is not passive as it springs out of a person's core being.

Love is defined by John as a motive for action in that it expresses itself by acting for the benefit of other brothers and sisters in Christ (3:17). This is exemplified by Jesus' giving himself sacrificially for us. In contrast to love is murderous hatred that can express itself in passivity and a closed heart toward fellow Christians in need. When a Christian stands by and refuses to aid a fellow Christian, then they are not being influenced by the eternal life they possess, they are being influenced by the devil.

Fellowship with God produces confidence in prayer and is contingent on obedience (3:22). Fellowship is experienced through mutual abiding. God dwells within the believer who in turn "abides" with him (3:24). This is enabled through the indwelling Holy Spirit. The effect of the believer abiding in God is that God hears his or her prayers. This expresses the "influence" aspect of μένω. Just as God's Word "abides" in us by our being

354. D. Van der Merwe, "'Experiencing Fellowship with God' According to 1 John 1:5–2:28," 248.

influenced by it, so too, as a believer abides in God, God allows him or her to "influence" him through prayer. That influence results in God listening and responding.

Application and Devotional Implications

3:10 Always think before acting. Ask yourself: is what I am about to do something that reflects well on God? Is it something that would embarrass him if it became public knowledge? Or will it cause people to wonder if my faith is real? If so, why am I doing it? Remember, nothing we do goes unnoticed. Everything we do impacts our reputation and that of both our earthly and divine family. Paul echoes our need to act in accordance with our spiritual parentage and the fact that we are identified with God in Eph 5:1–2 when he commands us to be imitators of God "as beloved children." How do we do that? We imitate God by living righteous lifestyles and walking in love, just as John is saying in this epistle.

3:17 We need to remember that God expects of us those benefits received from him. For example, we are to forgive others as he has forgiven us (Matt 6:14–15). When Jesus told the parable of the unforgiving servant (Matt 18:21–35), he concluded it with the warning, "So My heavenly Father also will do to you if each of you, from his heart, does not forgive his brother his trespasses." We express our appreciation for Christ's self-sacrifice by our own self-sacrifice (3:16). We meet the needs of other Christians. Sometimes this will involve financial help, such as paying bills or purchasing food. Sometimes it will involve time and energy, such as listening to them or helping them work on something around the house. It will always cost us something in terms of money, energy, emotion, or time. If it cost us nothing it would not be a sacrifice. It may mean humble service, even as Jesus demonstrated his love for the disciples by washing their feet (John 13:1–17) and then commanded them to love each other in the same manner he loved them (John 13:34). This is not something "extra" we do for God. This is a minimum expectation he has from us. Yet, even doing our obligation toward God does not go unnoticed or unrewarded (Rev 2–3). We are promised that whatever good we do will receive its appropriate reward (Matt 10:40–42; Heb 6:10). For God, what matters is what we do more than how we feel about doing it. Loving one another must be practical and practiced to be real and blessed by God.

3:18 Am I loving other Christians or murdering them? Am I willing to meet the needs of members of my church? To be able to meet needs I must get to know those around me well enough to know their needs and to be allowed into their lives. That means talking to them about themselves, inviting them to my home, spending time with them, and then doing something when their need becomes visible.

Selected Bibliography

Aldrich, W. M. "Assurance." *BSac* 114 (1957): 308–15.

Beale, G. K., and D. A. Carson. *Commentary on the New Testament Use of the Old Testament*. Grand Rapids: Baker Academic, 2007.

Bengel, J. A. *Gnomon of the New Testament: Vol. 5,* translated by W. Flestcher, 128. Edinburgh: T & T Clark, 1858.

Bonhoeffer, D. *Life Together*. Translated by John W. Doberstein. New York: Harper & Bros., 1954.

Bradnock, W. J. "Questions and Answers." *BT* 5 (1954): 138–44.

Büchsel, F. *Johannes und der Hellenistische Synkretismus*. BFCT 2, 16. Gütersloh, Germany: Bertelsmann, 1928.

Bullinger, E. W. *Figures of Speech Used in the Bible.* New York: Eyre & Spottiswoode, 1898. Repr. Grand Rapids: Baker, 1968.

Charles, R. H., ed. *Pseudepigrapha of the Old Testament.* Bellingham, WA: Logos Bible Software, 2004.

Coetzee, J. C. "Christ and the Prince of This World in the Gospel and the Epistles of St. John." *Neot* 2 (1968): 104–21.

Collins, C. J. "John 4:23–24, 'In Spirit and Truth': An Idomatic Proposal." *Presb* 21 (1995): 118–23.

Dana, H. E., and J. R. Mantey. *A Manual Grammar of the Greek New Testament*. New York: Macmillan, 1957.

Dryden, J. "The Sense of ΣΠΕΡΜΑ in 1 John 3:9." *Filologia Neotestamentaria* 11 (1998): 85–100.

Du Preez, J. "'Sperma Autou' in 1 John 3:9." In *Essays of the General Epistles of the New Testament: 11th Meeting of Die Nuwe-Testamentiese Werkgemeenskap van Suid-Afrika, 1975.* Pretoria: NTWSA, 1975.

Fanning, B. M. *Verbal Aspect in New Testament Greek*. Oxford: Clarendon, 1990.

Hiebert, D. E. "An Expositional Study of 1 John—Part 6: An Exposition of 1 John 3:13–24," *BSac* 146 (1989): 301–19.

Houlden, J. L. "Salvation Proclaimed II. 1 John 1.5–2.6: Belief and Growth." *ExpTim* 93 (1982): 132–36.

Inman, V. K. "Distinctive Johannine Vocabulary and the Interpretation of I John 3:9." *WTJ* 40 (1977): 136–44.

Jung, C. W. "Main Thrust of the Sentence(s) in 1 John 3:19–20: Encouragement or Warning?" *Neot* 41 (2007): 97–111.

Kubo, S. "1 John 3:9; Absolute or Habitual?" *AUSS* 7 (1969): 47–56.

Lieu, J. M. "What Was from the Beginning: Scripture and Tradition in the Johannine Epistles." *NTS* 39 (1993): 458–77.

Louw, J. P. "Verbal Aspect in the First Letter of John." *Neot* 9 (1975): 98–104.

Malatesta, E. *Interiority and Covenant: A Study of* εἶναι ἐν *and* μένειν ἐν *in the First Letter of Saint John*. Rome: Biblical Institute Press, 1978.

Metzger, B. M., and United Bible Societies., *A Textual Commentary on the Greek New Testament.* 2nd ed. New York: United Bible Societies, 1994.

Moule, C. F. D. "A Neglected Factor in the Interpretation of Johannine Eschatology." In *Studies in John,* 155–160. NovTSup 24. Leiden: Brill, 1970.

Roberts, A., J. Donaldson, and A. C. Coxe. *The Ante-Nicene Fathers Vol. I: Translations of the Writings of the Fathers Down to A.D. 325*. Oak Harbor, WA: Logos Research Systems, 1997.

Robertson, A. T. *A Grammar of the Greek New Testament in the Light of Historical Research*. Nashville: Broadman, 1931.

Sevenster, G. "Remarks on the Humanity of Jesus in the Gospel and Letters of John." In *Studies in John,* 185–93. NovTSup 24. Leiden: Brill, 1970.

Snodderly, M. E. C. "A Socio-Rhetorical Investigation of the Johannine Understanding of 'the Works of the Devil' in 1 John 3:8." Ph.D. Diss, University of South Africa, 2008.

Turner, N. *Grammatical Insights into the New Testament.* Edinburgh: T & T Clark, 1965.

Van der Merwe, D. G. "'Experiencing Fellowship with God' according to 1 John 1:5–2:28: Dealing with the Change in Social Behavior." *Acta Patristica et Byzantina* 18 (2007): 231–62.

Wallace, D. B. *Greek Grammar beyond the Basics*. Grand Rapids: Zondervan, 1996.

Test False Teachers (4:1–6)

Introduction

In this next paragraph we learn that experiencing eternal life is contingent on listening to the apostles rather than false teachers (spirits). Some interpreters see this paragraph reflecting the conflict between John and the Gnostic separatists he described earlier (Akin, 170; Westcott, 139).[355] It should be seen as a polemical section that reinforces John's pastoral concerns for the fellowship of those congregations under his care. It does have

355. Lenski (484) sees him referring to them, but also including all false teachers.

the same false teachers in view from 2:18–23, the antichrists, and so shares a common christological theme with that passage.

Though it is a warning against false teachers, nothing here or in chapter 2 requires a separatist group or organized "opponents."[356] As noted earlier, the presence of false teachers must be viewed as a common issue throughout the church. For a full discussion of this issue, see my comments in the introduction ("Theory of a Johannine School"). Having warned of them earlier, John now turns to the root evil behind false teachers, the source of their error.

This paragraph is composed of two movements. Its first half is imperative and descriptive. Warning his readers against the danger of false teachers, John describes the nature of their christological error. The second half of this section is a reminder to his readers that they have overcome the false teachers who are influencing the world that is separate from God. John accomplishes this through a series of antithetical statements that develop his dualistic view of the spiritual world. This is not Greek dualism, but the moral and conceptual dualism already seen in this epistle. Where earlier the antitheses were between light and darkness, love and murder, family of God or the devil, now they are between the Spirit of truth and the spirit of deceit, the Holy Spirit and Satan. As before, whereas the world exists in only one of the two opposite spheres, Christians may walk in either though they belong to only one.

Original Text

1 Ἀγαπητοί, μὴ παντὶ πνεύματι πιστεύετε, ἀλλὰ δοκιμάζετε τὰ πνεύματα εἰ
ἐκ τοῦ θεοῦ ἐστιν, ὅτι πολλοὶ ψευδοπροφῆται ἐξεληλύθασιν εἰς τὸν κόσμον. **2** ἐν
τούτῳ γινώσκετε τὸ πνεῦμα τοῦ θεοῦ· πᾶν πνεῦμα ὃ ὁμολογεῖ Ἰησοῦν Χριστὸν
ἐν σαρκὶ ἐληλυθότα ἐκ τοῦ θεοῦ ἐστιν, **3** καὶ πᾶν πνεῦμα ὃ αμὴ ὁμολογεῖα τὸν
Ἰησοῦνb ἐκ τοῦ θεοῦ οὐκ ἔστιν· καὶ τοῦτό ἐστιν τὸ τοῦ ἀντιχρίστου, ὃ ἀκηκόατε
ὅτι ἔρχεται, καὶ νῦν ἐν τῷ κόσμῳ ἐστὶν ἤδη. **4** ὑμεῖς ἐκ τοῦ θεοῦ ἐστε, τεκνία,
καὶ νενικήκατε αὐτούς, ὅτι μείζων ἐστὶν ὁ ἐν ὑμῖν ἢ ὁ ἐν τῷ κόσμῳ· **5** αὐτοὶ ἐκ
τοῦ κόσμου εἰσίν· διὰ τοῦτο ἐκ τοῦ κόσμου λαλοῦσιν καὶ ὁ κόσμος αὐτῶν ἀκούει.

356. Lieu (163) argues well that "although the appearance of false prophets is the incentive for vigilance, the concern of these verses is entirely with the audience of the letter, and they must be understood not in relation to some external convictions but to those that shape its thought."

6 ἡμεῖς ἐκ τοῦ θεοῦ ἐσμεν· ὁ γινώσκων τὸν θεὸν ἀκούει ἡμῶν, ὃς οὐκ ἔστιν ἐκ τοῦ θεοῦ οὐκ ἀκούει ἡμῶν. ἐκ τούτου γινώσκομεν τὸ πνεῦμα τῆς ἀληθείας καὶ τὸ πνεῦμα τῆς πλάνης.

Textual Notes

3.a…a The SBLGNT reading of *μὴ ὁμολογεῖ* has the support of the clear majority of MSS (א A B K Ψ 029 056 0142 33 81 88 104 181 326 330 436 451 614 629 630 945 1241 1505 1739 1877 1881 2127 2412 2492 2495 *Byz Lect* it[q] syr[p,h] cop[sa,bo] arm favor the reading while a very small minority favor λύει).[357]

3.b. The phrase *ἐν σαρκὶ ἐληλυθότα* should not follow the noun *τὸν Ἰησοῦν*. Metzger's theory that copyists expanded the verse based on the previous verse is supported by the variation in terms used in those expansions.[358] First, significant Alexandrian texts support the shorter reading (A B 945 1241 1739 1881 it[e,div,p,q] vg cop[bo]). Second, too much variation occurs among those that support a longer reading to indicate a clear original text, but rather argues more forcibly for editorial changes occurring in more than one instance.

Translation

1 Beloved, do not believe every spirit, but test the spirits *to see*[359] if they are from God, because many false prophets have gone out into the world. **2** By this we know the Spirit of God; every spirit that confesses Jesus Christ has come in the flesh[360] is from God. **3** But[361] every spirit that does not confess[362]

357. B. Metzger and United Bible Societies, *A Textual Commentary on the Greek New Testament*, 2d ed., 644.
358. B. Metzger and United Bible Societies, *A Textual Commentary on the Greek New Testament*, 2d ed., 645.
359. Italics added because "to see" is understood (ESV, NASB95, Nlt). Other translations either leave it implied and use "whether" (ASV, NIV84, NKJV). HCSB and NET uses "to determine."
360. See discussion about the various options on how to understand the very difficult grammatical construction behind this creedal statement.
361. This reflects an adversative *kai* (HCSB, NET, NIV84, Nlt). Others do not see it as adversative and translate it as "and" (ASV, ESV, NASB95; NKJV).
362. Though a few later MSS substituted a different verb (*luō*, "loose" or "destroy") here, the weight of evidence supports the present translation. This appears to have resulted in part from John's choice to use a negative particle that is not normally used with indic. verbs. However, that actually serves to strengthen the negativeness

Jesus is not from God; and[363] this is the *spirit*[364] of the antichrist that you heard is coming, and now already is in the world. **4** You[365] are from God, little children, and have overcome them, because he who is in you is greater than he who is in the world. **5** They are from the world, because of this they speak from the world and the world hears[366] them. **6** We are from God. He who knows God hears us. Whoever is not from God does not hear us. From this we know the Spirit of truth and the spirit of deception.[367]

Commentary

4:1 Having commanded his readers to "believe" in the name of Jesus (3:23), John now tells them whom not to believe. This first sentence of this next paragraph is composed of a double admonition followed by its justification. It serves as a warning of the danger faced by the church then and in any generation.[368]

Ἀγαπητοί, μὴ παντὶ πνεύματι πιστεύετε, "Beloved, do not believe every spirit." Using ἀγαπητοί as his term of endearment once again, John admonishes his readers as friend to friend more than as parent to child.[369] It is a

---

of the assertion and John, as an author, is free to make use of unusual grammatical constructions to emphasize his points.

363. Some do not translate this *kai* (ESV, HCSB, NASB95, NIV84, Nlt). Others do (ASV, NET, NKJV). Neither option changes the meaning of the text. It is simply a matter of deciding how to relate this use of *kai* to English.

364. The referent of the article (lacking a noun) goes back to the pervious "spirit" and so it is implied here.

365. John began each of the next three vv with emphatic pronouns. In fact, these last three vv reflect several literary devices that make them emphatic. We see from this just how important a truth John is communicating here.

366. "Hears" (ASV, NKjv) translates the verb more literally, though "listens to" (ESV, HCSB, NASB95, NET, NIV84, NLT) is the sense of the verb. This is also the case with the two uses of "hear" in v 6 as well.

367. "Deception" (HCSB, NET, NLT), "error" (ASV, ESV, NASB95, NKjv), or "falsehood" (NIV84).

368. J. C. O'Neill (*The Puzzle of 1 John*, 46) considers 4:1–6 to be sourced in a Jewish document containing a "Christian gloss" in vv 2–3. He argues on the basis of the change to masc. pronouns in vv 4–5 that must refer back to ψευδοπροφῆται in v 1. This is purely speculative and has no basis in extant literature as well as ignoring the cohesion of the paragraph. The changes in pronouns and their referents make perfect sense and need not indicate an addition to the text in any way.

369. Smalley (217) describes this use of ἀγαπητοί as "resumptive."

reminder of both his deep affection and concern for his readers. Included in this is a reminder that they are loved by their heavenly Father as well.[370]

He begins this new movement of thought with a command not to believe every spirit. Πνεῦμα connects what he is about to say with the reference to God's Spirit in 3:24 (Marshall, 203), which serves as another "hinge" verse in this epistle.

It has been the practice through the years to see a present imperative implying that the readers were in the process of believing "spirits." John's prohibition is then against continuing to do so (Burdick, 292). However, though it may be its normal sense, the present imperative here need not have the progressive (iterative) nuance, (contra Brown, 486; Lenski, 486; Yarbrough, 220).[371] Rather, this command functions as a general principle without implying that his readers are guilty of believing the spirits at the time of writing.[372] Thus this serves as a warning rather than an injunction.

Akin (170) feels that it may indicate "in their readiness to hear from God John's readers were unwisely open to what the false prophets had to say." Stott (155) says the present imperative πιστεύετε "suggests that John's readers were tending to accept uncritically all teaching which claimed to be inspired."[373] However, his praise of his readers in 2:12–14 would indicate otherwise.

John's use of πιστεύετε, with the dative πνεύματι, is different than the Gospel's πιστεύειν εἰς, which is justifying faith, faith directed toward Christ.[374] This use indicates trusting what they say, not putting one's faith

370. Yarbrough (220) lists the six uses of ἀγαπητοί in this epistle and notes that each time they "introduce weighty statements of fact." He sees John addressing his readers as a "mentor" that cares about them. I am not sure that "mentor" is an appropriate term to describe either John's view of his relationship to them or theirs to him. The nature of mentorship is closer to that of apprenticeship or discipleship and indicates a more one-to-one process. John's role is more that of a pastor to his congregation, a spiritual leader and authority who is directing those under his care.

371. J. L. Boyer, "A Classification of Imperatives: A Statistical Study," 41. He describes it this way: "Thus the present impv. expresses a command or request that calls for action that is continuing or repeated, often general, universal, habitual; action that characterizes the doer."

372. D. Wallace, *Grammar,* 485, 714–17; B. Fanning, *Verbal Aspects in New Testament Greek*, 325–88.

373. Also Burdick (291) and Johnson (93).

374. Schnackenburg (220) calls this "christological faith" (christologischen Glaubens).

in them (Brooke, 107; Burdick, 292; Smalley, 218; Yarbrough, 220). This sense is reinforced by the following clause. Schnackenburg (220) translates πιστεύετε as "trust" and distinguishes it from justifying faith in Christ. He sees it being used with the dative sense as in John 4:21 when Jesus asked the woman at the well to believe him (πίστευέ μοι) rather than believe *in* him (πιστεύε εἰς ἐμέ). Brown (486) rejects this on the basis that its use two verses earlier clearly means "to commit oneself to" and so should here. However, the fact that this paragraph begins a new movement of thought would seem to indicate the conceptual link between the verbs, in terms of their use, has been broken.

There is one of several tests of false prophets that we find in Scripture (Stott, 155). They include Jesus' instruction to test false prophets by their "fruits" (Matt 7:15–20). John has already applied the moral "test of righteousness" (3:10) and will next apply the "test of love"(4:8). From the OT we find a "lead them astray" test in Deut 13:1–5 and moral test in Jer 23:9–14.

Finally, John's use of παντὶ, "every," does not mean "any," but sets the stage for the second part of this exhortation that reveals their responsibility to be discerning. This is a command to avoid "naive credulity."[375] It is to be a mind-set of vigilance, not paranoia or fear.

ἀλλὰ δοκιμάζετε τὰ πνεύματα εἰ ἐκ τοῦ θεοῦ ἐστιν, "but test the spirits *to see* if they are from God." Instead of believing every "spirit," they are to test them.[376] Δοκιμάζω means to prove something's worth and the testing is evaluative in nature.[377] This is a command for discernment. The nature of

375. E. Malatesta, *Interiority and Covenant*, 284.

376. This is the sole use of δοκιμάζω by John, though it occurs often in the NT.

377. BDAG, 55; W. Grundmann ("δόκιμος ... δοκιμάζω," *TDNT* 2:256–60) links its meaning to "the concept of accreditation" as it is used in the NT with regard to discerning what is of God and what is not. Spicq ("δοκιμάζω," 1:353–57) defines δοκιμάζω as "to prove, test, verify, examine prior to approval, judge, evaluate, discern" (353). He clarifies it by saying this indicates: "Someone makes an examination in order to be able to judge and decide." His examples come from: *P. Oxy*. 2760, 17; Philo, *Moses* 1.263, 306; 2.177. He observes that "the sense of 'put to the proof, examine' is common with precious metals," and provides a long list of examples including Prov 8:10; 17:3; 27:21; Wis 3:6; Sir 2:5; 27:5; Zech 11:13; 13:9; Philo. *Alleg. Interp*. 1.77; 3:168; and *Sacr. Abel and Cain* 80. "In places such as Eph 5:10; Rom 2:18; 14:22; Phil 1:10 δοκιμάζω "means 'discern' what it is important to do, the best course to follow, the best decision to be made" (356). Its use in 1 Thess 2:4 applies to Paul and in 1 Tim 3:10 to deacons.

the test is to see if the teachings are sourced in God (ἐκ τοῦ θεοῦ as before) and is similar to Paul's test in 1 Cor 12:3.[378] This term is found twice in the LXX (Pss 25:2; 138:23), and both times relates to the inner man's motives.[379] Δοκιμάζω is also used by Paul with regard to testing ourselves and potential deacons (1 Cor 11:28; 2 Cor 13:5; Gal 6:4; 1 Tim 3:10). As a present imperative it implies an ongoing practice as was the case with μὴ πιστεύετε in the previous clause (Burdick, 292–93; Williamson, 135). Though this command is corporate, it does not remove the individual's responsibility to be discerning (Lenski, 485).[380]

So what is to be evaluated? Malatesta notes that these are "external criteria, for the divine or evil origin of a spirit can be perceived through an exterior way of acting."[381] Just as Jesus said: their fruits. These "fruits" may be visible conduct, but may also include their teachings.[382] The woman Jezebel of the church in Thyatira (Rev 2:20–22) was identified as a false prophetess because her teachings led men astray into idolatry and sexual immorality. The church was condemned by Jesus for "allowing" her to teach those things. In this epistle (2:22; 4:2, 15; 5:1) and the next (2 John 7), it is their christological confession that reveals the teachers' genuineness or falseness.

What is the meaning or nature of τὰ πνεύματα?

(1) Some see this referring to actual spirits, demonic and angelic (Barker, 340; Culpepper, 267; Smalley, 218). Smalley (214) views John's choice of the

378. In 1 Cor 12:3 Paul identifies a test of whether a person is being led by the Holy Spirit or a false spirit based on whether he or she confesses Jesus as Lord or declares him accursed. He followed this with instructions on spiritual gifts that included evaluating the messages given by prophets (1 Cor 14:29–32). In 1 Thess 5:19–21 Paul instructed the Thessalonians not to quench the Spirit, but to "test all things" (πάντα δὲ δοκιμάζετε). Between the Spirit and the command to test was the command not to despise prophecies. Thus the testing of all things included prophecies that they were to confirm rather than reject out of hand. Both of these instructions are very similar to what John is saying here.

379. Psalm 25:2 (26:1 English text) reads: "Examine me, O Lord, and prove me; try my mind and my heart." (δοκίμασόν με, κύριε, καὶ πείρασόν με, πύρωσον τοὺς νεφρούς μου καὶ τὴν καρδίαν μου.) Psalm 138:23 (139:23 English text) reads: "Search me, O God, and know my heart. Try me, and know my anxieties." (δοκίμασόν με, ὁ θεός, καὶ γνῶθι τὴν καρδίαν μου, ἔτασόν με καὶ γνῶθι τὰς τρίβους μου)

380. E. Malatesta, *Interiority and Covenant*, 283.

381. E. Malatesta, *Interiority and Covenant*, 284.

382. Lenski (487) is correct to identify his "confession" as that which is to be evaluated.

plural πνεύματα to indicate that just as the Holy Spirit can work through many people, so, too, the "spirit" of the antichrist, which he sees as an actual spirit. Schnackenburg (220) acknowledges that Paul had demonic spirits in mind in 1 Tim 4:1 but identifies these as human spirits.

(2) Others see it referring to the Holy Spirit as opposed to Satan (Brown, 486; Bruce, 204; Thompson, 112–13)[383] as the source of the teacher's teachings. This would see the "spirit of truth" and "spirit of error" in verse 6 to refer to the Holy Spirit and Satan (Harris, 174). "The Holy Spirit influences and motivates the human spirits of the believers in the community to which the author is writing, while the evil spirit of deceit influences and motivates the human spirits of the opponents with their false teaching."

(3) It could refer to human spirits, those of orthodox and false teachers (Schnackenburg, 220).[384] This sees πνεύμα as a synecdoche* for "both the prophet and the spirit who inspired him" (Burdick, 292).

(4) It is best to see this as a metonymy* for the teaching or teacher with "spirit" indicating the source behind the teacher or teaching (Akin, 169, n. 70; Haas, de Jonge, and Swellengrebel, 111; Johnson, 96; Kistemaker, 324; Marshall, 204; Smalley, 218).[385] This is indicated by John's use of the masculine (rather than neuter) pronoun αὐτούς in verse 4 (Smith, 98). In other words, it is the false teacher and his teaching that is being evaluated, not the spirits or Spirit influencing him. Granted, one then recognizes the source, but the evaluation is of the person and his or her teachings, not a search for demons or angels within the congregation. John is also in no way implying these false teachers are demonically possessed. They are as likely to be influenced by the "spirit" of this age (the world's values, their culture) as they are by servants of Satan.

Ultimately the evaluation is to identify the source of any teachers' teachings. Are they sourced in God (εἰ ἐκ τοῦ θεοῦ ἐστιν)? Strecker (132, n.

---

383. J. C. Coetzee, "The Holy Spirit in 1 John," 52. "Here the Holy Spirit is clearly preached to be the *inspirator* of true prophesy and the guarantee for sound confession."

384. Grayston (118) offers a fourth definition as "an apparently inspired utterance which may or may not come from God, spoken by persons who seem to be or claim to be prophets."

385. Lenski (485) sees him using "spirit" for the person "with his inner, spiritual character." He says further, "Every person reveals what kind of a personality or spirit he is by his word and his action although he may try to hide what he really is."

7) observes that εἶναι ἐκ is used by John 55 times: 28 times in his Gospel, 19 times in 1 John, and once in 3 John (in contrast to the rest of the NT, where it is used only 28 more times). It is used to describe "descent or origin in a secular sense" in places such as John 1:44; 3:1; and 7:42. It also describes "descent" from a theological perspective "in order to describe, within the dualistic world of ideas, the state of belonging or descent from one of the two sides. Examples of this include 1 John 2:1; 3:8, 12, 19; 4:5; John 3:31; 6:32; 8:23, 44; Acts 5:39; and 1 Cor 11:12. Thus John is calling on his readers to evaluate teachers and teachings in order to discern the source of that teaching, whether it is of God or from elsewhere.

The reason for such concern is the need for discernment in order to avoid those deceptions that convert one's faith into presumption. Faith is only as valid as its object—in this case, the truth it is based on. "True faith examines its object before reposing confidence in it" (Stott, 156), otherwise it is only self-deception.

ὅτι πολλοὶ ψευδοπροφῆται ἐξεληλύθασιν εἰς τὸν κόσμον, "because many false prophets have gone out into the world." John now gives the reason to test the teachings of men to discern their source.[386]

John's change from παντὶ with spirit to πολλοὶ with false prophets indicates that not every spirit tested will fail the test. It also connects back to 2:18 and the many antichrists (ἀντίχριστοι πολλοὶ) who are appearing around them (Rensberger, 111; Williamson, 135). His choice of ἐξεληλύθασιν also parallels the departure of the antichrists in chapter 2. These false prophets came from within the churches and departed from them to align themselves with the world (Williamson, 136).

Why does John describe these men as "false prophets"? Stott (155) sees the issue much the same as the problem Paul addressed in 1 Cor 12 and 14, namely the misuse of prophecy. He likely is alluding to the OT false prophets. In Deut 13:1–3 a false prophet was identified by the attempt to lead Israel into idolatry, not by the ability to predict the future or perform other signs. In the same way, John has been identifying the false teachers in terms of their Christology (2:18–23), which he will do again in verses 2 and 3 (Lieu, 165).

386. Strecker (133) describes their threat well. "They are an enduring and pervasive danger that constantly accompanies the Christian community on its journey through the ages."

How are these false prophets related to the return of Christ? Bultmann (62) says John "historicizes eschatological phenomenon in the same way as the prophecy of the antichrist in 2:18 and immediately below in v. 3." John is then basing these false prophets of the eschaton on what Jesus said of them in Matt 24:11, 24 and Mark 13:22. Strecker (133), on the other hand, sees John connecting to the eschatological expectations of the early church, which saw the arrival of a multitude of false prophets as an integral part of the end times. However, as they were a characteristic of all of Israel's history, so, too, they can be expected to appear throughout church history. John's point earlier (2:18) was not that they were in or were entering the last days, but that those days were imminent. Here, he is continuing the theme and reminding his readers that the presence of false prophets is not limited to the last days, but true throughout church history and serve as a reminder that those days are coming and can come at any time.

Williams (44–45) depicts these false prophets as being identified as such because of their exercise of ecstatic gifts.[387] He says, "When men and women in the Church were carried away in this manner they were said to be 'prophesying'. If they were regularly found to have this gift, they were 'prophets'. The stress was not on any power to foretell the future, though this was sometimes included." He points to 1 Cor 12 and 14 as evidence that the church had difficulty controlling these "pneumatics." Paul in 1 Cor 12:3 indicated that someone could curse Jesus while under the influence of one of these ecstatic spirits, and so their message had to be tested based on their Christology. "Jesus is Lord" comes from the Holy Spirit while "Jesus is cursed" does not. He sees this being the problem John is addressing here.

Lieu (165) rejects the idea that these false prophets were miracle workers or exhibited charismatic gifts. She notes that nothing in the epistle indicates anything out of the ordinary about them beyond their teachings. Burge (173) describes these false prophets as "pneumatics, teachers claiming that their words are inspired by the Spirit of God." He describes well the situation of the early church. "Churches relied on emissaries from their leaders, who relayed information from other communities and taught. Paul sent out Timothy and Silas in this capacity, and John sent out elders as his spokespersons (3 John 5)." "This phenomenon meant that churches could fall prey to unscrupulous itinerant prophets and teachers, and John's

387. Also Barker (340), Smalley (217), and Westcott (140).

churches were no exception (cf. 2 John 7)." Paul's epistles to Colosse, Galatia and Thessalonica are examples of false teachers infiltrating the churches.

John connects back to 2:19 and the departure of the antichrists by his use of ἐξέρχομαι here and reference to the antichrists in verse 2. This shows that what John has in mind are not demons, nor other "spirits," but rather, teachers (Pentecost, 101). This is a similar concept to Paul's in 1 Cor 14:32, where the "spirits" of the prophets are subject to the other prophets when someone wished to prophecy in the church meeting. In this case John is providing a test of false teachers. Though believers are indwelt by the Holy Spirit (3:24), false teachers are not especially demon possessed, but may be influenced by them and are therefore teaching doctrines of demons as Paul described in 1 Tim 4:1–3.

True prophets receive direct revelation from God and communicate it accurately. Thus the tests of Deut 13:1–5 and 18:20–22 still apply today. False prophets claim to receive revelation. However, their predictions fail to be fulfilled and their instruction proves contrary to God's revelation and will. Additionally, as in Deuteronomy where the teachings of a prophet served as evidence of that prophet's source, John affirms the same with regard to the false teachers of his and our day in the verses that follow.

John's use of κόσμος here could either be neutral or negative. (1) If neutral, it refers to the world in which men live, or as Malatesta describes it, "earth and human society as the scene of salvation history."[388] (2) If negative, it refers to the world opposed to God, that John's readers are not to love (2:15–17). This seems the best option, even here. This is seen in its role in the verses that follow. Though John does use "world" at times in a neutral or positive sense, his normal use is negative.[389] In this paragraph the sense here should be informed by its sense in verses 4 through 6.

Stott (156) summarizes this verse well. "So behind every prophet is a spirit and behind each spirit either God or the devil. Before we can trust any spirits, we must test them. It is their origin that matters."

4:2 The test of teachers and their teachings is now given.

---

388. E. Malatesta, *Interiority and Covenant*, 286.

389. See comments on 2:15 for a full description of both the positive and negative senses of κόσμος with John.

ἐν τούτῳ γινώσκετε τὸ πνεῦμα τοῦ θεοῦ·, "By this we know the Spirit of God." "By this" (ἐν τούτῳ) refers to what follows once again (Brooke, 108; Brown, 491; Culy, 101; Schnackenburg, 220).[390] A general characteristic of John's writing style is that when he uses ἐν τούτῳ with a following subordinate clause that is explanatory in nature, it looks forward to that clause and refers to what is contained in it. It may also refer to what follows without such a clause, as here, if the context indicates it is appropriate, which it does in this instance.

John changes from his pattern of following ἐν τούτῳ and with the first person plural γινώσκομεν to the 2 (2:3, 5; 3:16, 19, 24; 4:13; 5:2). This would be noticed by his readers and alert them to the danger of which they are already aware (Lieu, 165).

Is γινώσκετε indicative or imperative? Most interpreters prefer the indicative (Akin, 172; Bultmann, 62; Haas, de Jonge, and Swellengrebel, 115; Lieu, 165; Marshall, 204; Plummer, 95; Smalley, 220; Stott, 157; Strecker, 134, n. 15; Westcott, 140), though some favor the imperative (Kistemaker, 326; Law, 396). The indicative has the better support, such as:

(1) The broader context includes the anointing they have received (2:27), which would give them this knowledge and so it would not seem logical for John to command them to learn what they should already know (Brown, 491).

(2) John does not exhibit a pattern of following ἐν τούτῳ with an imperative (Westcott, 141).

(3) In 3:16, a related text, John reminds his readers of what they know (Strecker, 134, n. 15). Thus, it does seem best to see this as an indicative and John is thereby reminding his readers of what they know (Brooke, 108; Stott, 157, n. 2). They are to test teachers and their teachings on the basis of the truths about Jesus they have been taught. Moreover, though it is based on what they have

390. E. Malatesta, *Interiority and Covenant*, 286. He (284) sees an *inclusio* using ἐν τούτῳ and ἐκ τούτου as its markers. However, the statements that follow each, though initially similar in that each uses γινώσκω, shift from the readers to John and the apostles.

been taught, this is something they can know by experience (thus γινώσκω).[391]

John changes from ἐκ τοῦ θεοῦ to τοῦ θεοῦ, though he will return to ἐκ τοῦ θεοῦ in the next clause. Whereas his use of ἐκ τοῦ θεοῦ is clearly designed to communicate God as the source (Culy, 101), this is a descriptive genitive designed to identify the Holy Spirit.[392] In the clause that follows John clarifies the criterion for passing the discerning test with antithetic parallelism in which he gives the positive confession and then its negative counterpart.

πᾶν πνεῦμα ὃ ὁμολογεῖ Ἰησοῦν Χριστὸν ἐν σαρκὶ ἐληλυθότα ἐκ τοῦ θεοῦ ἐστιν, "every spirit that confesses Jesus Christ has come in the flesh is from God." Orthodox confession is now given. For someone to pass the test of a discerning Christian, they must "confess" Jesus' incarnation. Carson notes that "even confessional formulae must be inspected in this light. In 1 Corinthians 12:3 Paul can affirm that 'no one can say, "Jesus is Lord," except by the Holy Spirit.'"[393] This confession follows the pattern and thought of Paul's confession, though it is not a quotation of it. Bruce (105) sees the difference coming from the changing threat of Gnosticism. However, it seems better to see the difference in writing and rhetorical styles. Both apostles are affirming the same thing, but in their own words.

By "every spirit" John is distinguishing more than a difference between the Holy Spirit and Satan (see comments on verse 1). He is clearly indicating myriad individuals to be tested. Furthermore, since it is the teacher in view, he continues the imagery through a metonymy, naming the source for the one making the confession.

By "confess" John means the teachers' public acknowledgment of something or someone (Akin, 172).[394] This involves more than mere profes-

---

391. Burge (174) sees this statement having two possible meanings. Either "the Spirit of God would equip Johannine believes to recognize God's Spirit in others," or "John's thought may be nothing more mysterious than weighing objectively what was being said by these prophets." His second option makes the most sense of what John has said, and is about to say.

392. John's use of the phrase τὸ πνεῦμα τοῦ θεοῦ to refer to the Holy Spirit is used by Matthew (Matt 3:16) as well as Paul (1 Cor 2:11; 3:16). Paul the anarthrous πνεῦμα θεοῦ as well (Rom 8:9; 1 Cor 7:40).

393. D. A. Carson and J. D. Woodbridge, *Scripture and Truth*, 88.

394. BDAG, 708; O. Michel, "ὁμολογέω," *TDNT* 5:209–10; D. Hiebert, "An Expositional Study of 1 John—Part 7: An Exposition of 1 John 4:1–6," 426.

sion but includes conviction of its truthfulness. It also involves a corpus of facts being acknowledged. That which is openly affirmed as true by those influenced by God's Spirit includes acknowledging the incarnation of Jesus Christ as a historical reality that they are convinced is true.

John's combination of Jesus Christ with the perfect participle ἐληλυθότα can be understood in a number of ways:

(1) It could involve a double accusative with "Jesus Christ" functioning as the subject of the accusative clause and "has come in the flesh" as its complement (Barker, 340; Brooke, 109; Haas, de Jonge, and Swellengrebel, 115; Johnson, 95; Klauck, 228; Marshall, 205; Schnackenburg, 221; Thompson, 115; Williamson, 136; ASV, ESV, HCSB, KJV, NASB95, NEB, NIV84, NKJV, RSV. NLT).[395] This would be a case of a double accusative following a "verb of opinion."[396] Its weakness is that this would be the only place John combines the names "Jesus" and "Christ" with reference to his preincarnate existence (Harris, 176).

(2) It may be a predicate accusative construction with "Jesus Christ" as the One confessed and "has come in the flesh" what is predicated about him, the whole phrase functioning as the direct object of ὁμολογεῖ.[397] This is similar to John's statement in 2 John 7 (Brown, 492; Lenski, 487; KJV, NRSV).[398]

(3) It is a double accusative construction with "Jesus" as the object of "confess," and "Christ come in the flesh" (Christ incarnate) as the predicate (Dodd, 100–1; Harris, 176; Hodges, 177; Houlden, 107; Law, 93–95; Stott, 159; NET).[399] This is similar to the constructions in 2:22 and 5:1.[400] Against this is the absence of the article

395. D. B. Wallace, *Grammar*, 182–89. Nlt renders it "Jesus Christ came in a real body."
396. BDF §416 (3).
397. D. B. Wallace, *Grammar*, 190–92.
398. οἱ μὴ ὁμολογοῦντες Ἰησοῦν Χριστὸν ἐρχόμενον ἐν σαρκί.
399. D. A. Carson and J. D. Woodbridge, *Scripture and Truth*, 88; J. A. R. Moffat (*The Bible, A New Translation*, s.v. 1 John 4:2).
400. 2:22 has ὁ ἀρνούμενος ὅτι Ἰησοῦς οὐκ ἔστιν ὁ Χριστός; 5:1 has ὁ ἀγαπῶν τὸν γεννήσαντα ἀγαπᾷ [καὶ] τὸν γεγεννημένον ἐξ αὐτοῦ.

before Χριστὸν (Harris, 176), though it may have been elided.[401] Schnackenburg (221) rejects this on the basis that "Jesus Christ" is a "fixed expression" in this epistle (1:3; 2:1; 3:23; 5:6a, 20c; John 17:3). Schnackenburg (221) points out that the preposition phrase with the participle should have had an article before it (making it attributive) even if Χριστὸν did not have one.

(4) One could see the whole statement "Jesus Christ, come in the flesh" as a single unit with Jesus Christ being confessed and his incarnation included as part of a description of him more than a focus of the confession (Brooke, 108–9; Brown, 493; Burdick, 296; Lieu, 166; Smalley, 222; Westcott, 141). The parallel clause in verse 3 with τὸν Ἰησοῦν strengthens this view in that the article calls for one to fill in the elision with the use of Ἰησοῦν clarifying that the previous clause is intended (Westcott, 141).

Though little difference in meaning occurs between any of these options, the first option seems the best. When John wishes to separate Jesus' title from his human name he does so (2:22 and 5:1). As a result, the name and title should not be separated when John chooses not to do so (Kistemaker, 327). His use of Jesus Christ together appears to be an intentional statement of the union of both titles in the one person, thus no separation between the body and spirit of Jesus (Akin, 172).

This statement appears to address the teachings of the Docetists, who taught that Jesus, the man, and Christ, the spirit, were two separate beings. Where Jesus had a physical body, the Christ was pure spirit. Rather, this verse is an acknowledgment of the unity of humanity and deity in the one person which is the heart and soul of the incarnation.[402]

John teaches that Jesus came as a human being. He affirms Jesus' incarnation with the anarthrous perfect participle ἐληλυθότα functioning

---

401. Schnackenburg (220) does not see anything strange about the absence of the article before Χριστὸν. ("Das Fehlen des Artikels vor Χριστὸν ware nichts Befremdendes")

402. Schnackenburg (221) rejects the idea that John is addressing any form of Docetism. He sees the theme of the Son of God being sent to redeem sinners as central to the epistle's thought, not a polemic against Docetism. From earlier in the epistle, he sees the false teachers rejecting the need for redemption from sins by Jesus Christ. John was stressing that spiritual life only could come through faith in the incarnate Son of God who gives life.

verbally. Thus he affirms not only that he came but the significance of his coming and its continued impact (Lieu, 167; Rensberger, 112; Yarbrough, 221).[403] "The order (ἐν σαρκὶ ἐλ.) and the tense of the verb (ἐληλ.) lay emphasis on the mode rather than on the fact of Christ's coming" (Westcott, 141; also Burdick, 296). "In the flesh" may allude to John 1:14 (Schnackenburg, 221; Westcott, 141), and so by this he also affirms Jesus' preexistence as he had done in the prologue of his Gospel.[404] His use of the verb ἐληλυθότα along with the noun for "flesh" (σάρξ) indicates that Jesus not only came as a human but continues to be a human to this day. Jesus came in the flesh (ἐν σαρκὶ) and is still in the flesh in heaven (Lenski, 488; Marshall, 205; Stott, 157; Williamson, 136). Jesus' incarnation has not ended.[405] God the Son remains fully God and fully man in his resurrected human body.[406] He has a material body that can be touched and felt, just as he did at his resurrection appearances. Anyone whose teachings involve a denial of Jesus' full humanity proves that he or she is not of God.

Again, some see this indicating that John is responding to incipient Gnosticism.[407] For example, Lalleman sees gnostic doctrine based on his reading of *Acts of John*. He says, "in accordance with 1:1–4 the stress is on the way in which Christ came, viz. ἐν σαρκὶ. I conclude that the 'antichrists' (3b) denied the reality of Jesus' flesh. The perfect form ἐληλυθότα can best

---

403. J. N. Suggit ("1 John 5:21: ΤΕΚΝΙΑ, ΦΥΛΑΞΑΤΕ ΕΑΥΤΑ ΑΠΟ ΤΘΝ ΕΙΔΩΛΩΝ," 388) describes this as "the clearest expression of the faith which the author held and which he sees as the real mark of the true community of faith."

404. John uses ἐν σαρκὶ as a synecdoche for the human body (Culy, 101).

405. D. B. Wallace (*Grammar*, 573–74) notes that the continuing aspect of the perfect tense is only relative to the time of the writer and does not indicate or guarantee continuance beyond that. However, for our purposes Burdick (296) makes an insightful statement. "Although a perfect tense does not guarantee permanence, as some have assumed here, it does indicate that, at the time of writing, Jesus was still incarnate. He still possessed the resurrection body with which he ascended to heaven (Acts 1:9–11) and with which he will return." Thus John's affirmation of Jesus' continued incarnation following his ascension and glorification helps us to envision his continuing humanity at present.

406. The false teachers do not appear to have denied Jesus' deity, only his incarnation. Moreover, as Stott (157) notes well, even demons do that (Mark 1:24; 3:11; 5:7–8; Acts 19:15).

407. D. A. Carson and J. D. Woodbridge, *Scripture and Truth*, 88. M. de Jonge ("The Use of the Word ΧΡΙΣΤΟΣ in the Johannine Epistles," 69) identifies John's "opponents" as Docetists.

be understood by comparison with 1:1–4 and 1:5, which illustrate the author's use of this tense in describing the lasting impact of the coming of Jesus. The author wants his readers to continue confessing their faith in the incarnation."[408]

John's use of *σάρξ* to describe Jesus' coming looks at the mode of his coming and describes his coming into the world (Lieu, 167), that is, "the method rather than the fact" (Brooke, 109). Even though the only other use of *σάρξ* is in a negative context, John's use here is not negative. However, if he is addressing a docetic heresy, *σάρξ* would clearly differentiate between the true Jesus and the Jesus of the false teachers.

The one who acknowledges Jesus' incarnation is described by John as sourced in God (ἐκ τοῦ θεοῦ ἐστιν).[409] This is a positive way of affirming Paul's declaration in Gal 1:8–9, that anyone teaching a different gospel should be anathemized. John says, their source must be recognized. Having stated the principle positively, he now employs antithesis in order to emphasize his point.

4:3 These first verses of chapter 4 provide John's test of teachings. He draws attention to the test in this verse through repetition and elision, connecting the false teachings with their source and eventual champion, the Antichrist. Introduced earlier (2:18), he is now identified with false prophets as well. The triple repetition of *ἔστιν* in this single sentence is emphatic. This is even more evident by the placement of the first and third at the ends of their respective clauses.

καὶ πᾶν πνεῦμα ὃ μὴ ὁμολογεῖ τὸν Ἰησοῦν ἐκ τοῦ θεοῦ οὐκ ἔστιν·, "But every spirit that does not confess Jesus is not from God." Though this use of *καὶ*

---

408. P. J. Lalleman, "The Adversaries Envisaged in the Johannine Epistles," 21.

409. Burge (274) affirms that "incarnational Christology was at the heart of this community's struggles." It seems better to say it was one issue. Their treatment of one another appears to have been of greater concern to John and the major focus of his epistle. As discussed earlier, the subject of the epistle, its central theme is experiencing eternal life in terms of one's relationship with Jesus who is eternal life incarnate. However, that being said, a right view of Jesus is absolutely necessary to have fellowship with him and experience His life. There were false views of Jesus being promoted in the churches of Asia (thus Paul's epistle to Colosse). That it was yet "at the heart of their struggles" cannot be known. Such an assumption, though, will certainly cloud one's interpretation of many passages of this epistle, as well as its overall thrust (polemic or pastoral).

could be thought of as a continuative (Culy, 102), however here it involves a contrast, so is better seen as adversative (Akin, 173; Brown, 494; Haas, de Jonge, and Swellengrebel, 115; HCSB, NET, NIV84, NLT). This is evident not just because the following clause stands in antithesis to the previous, but also because the previous clause fully expressed the idea introduced in the main clause, "By this we know the Spirit of God." What follows this καὶ does not explain how we know the Spirit of God. It explains how we know who is not.

John particularizes the "spirits" with the use of the πᾶν ... ὃ construction. The contrast between the orthodox and heterodox confessions is what they say about Jesus' incarnation. This seems to allude, if not directly refer, to the docetic heresy that denied the incarnation while affirming the deity of "the Christ spirit" apart from the human Jesus. The focus again is in the source of the teaching, whether it is from God. This contrast with the previous statement emphatically denies any connection of the claim with God. John's use of πνεῦμα at the beginning of the sentence and its elision in the second clause (implied second use) again focuses attention on his use of "spirit." Spirit, as used here can be viewed in one of two ways. (1) It may refer to Satan, having the "spirit of deception" in verse 6 (Harris, 178). (2) It refers to the teacher who is being influenced either by God or by Satan (Westcott, 143). This second option seems best and so "spirit" is a metonymy for the teacher or false prophet who claims to speak by the Holy Spirit but is rather being influenced by Satan (demons) or the world system, the spirit of this age.

John's use of repetition, with the injection of the negative particles μὴ and οὐκ, heightens the contrast between the orthodox and heretical confession. His use of μὴ is unusual for the verb ὁμολογέω and so questioned by some.[410] Rather, Smalley (224) and Hiebert see his use of μὴ as a more

410. Blass (BDF §428 (4)) notes that this is one of only two instances in the NT where a relative clause with the indic. uses μὴ to negate rather than οὐ, Tit 1:11 being the other. From this he speculates that an error of dittography may have occurred and the reading should have been ὃ λύει instead. Schnackenburg (222) replaces ὃ μὴ ὁμολογεῖ with ὃ λύει. His reasons include: (1) It is attested in earlier MSS. (2) It represents the more plausible reading since the alternative has the μὴ with the indic. formula. (3) The meaning of λύει is more "pregnant" (prägnante) than ὁμολογεῖ which is "colorless" (farblos) in that context. (4) The replacement of λύει with ὁμολογεῖ is easier to explain than ὁμολογεῖ with λύει. This textual

intense negative than οὐ and so is designed to communicate the absence of exceptions to this statement (Law, 396).[411] Lenski (488) sees this as an example of litotes* in that "'does not confess' is stronger than 'denies' and matches with the phrase, 'is not from God.'"[412]

In this statement the phrase Χριστὸν ἐν σαρκὶ ἐληλυθότα appears to be elided by John (Culy, 102).[413] It is indicated by his use of the article τὸν between ὁμολογεῖ and Ἰησοῦν. The article τὸν before Ἰησοῦν should be seen as an article of previous reference (Lenski, 488) which calls for the understood addition of Χριστὸν ἐν σαρκὶ ἐληλυθότα with Ἰησοῦν.[414]

This warning against false teachers gave John's readers a method to determine if the itinerant preacher was true or false. This is not the only test given in Scripture, just *a* test. For example, Mormons can say that Jesus came in the flesh, as can Jehovah's Witnesses. That does not make them orthodox. They fail other tests, primarily those involving the question of Jesus' deity and eternality. Here John is better understood as giving a sample test rather than limiting this to this single test, though this is an example of how to test the claims and denials of teachers (Bruce, 105).

This test involves discerning, not just what is said but what is *not* said. Of note is John's affirmation that they simply "do not confess" Jesus as

---

choice is supported by Brown (494–96), Bultmann (62), Lieu (*The Theology of the Johannine Epistles,* 46), Painter (258), Perkins (51), and rejected by Brooke (111–14), Burdick (297), Grayston (122), Haas, de Jonge, and Swellengrebel (103), Marshall (207–208), Thompson (115, n.), and Westcott (163–66). Rensberger (113) rejects it and describes it as "created as a vivid expression for use in second-century christological debates."

411. D. E. Hiebert, "An Expositional Study of 1 John—Part 7: An Exposition of 1 John 4:1–6," 429.

412. E. W. Bullinger (*Figures of Speech,* 155) defines litotes as an omission, "not of words, but of sense. One thing is lowered in order to magnify and intensify something else by way of contrast. It is used for the purpose of emphasis; to call our attention, not to the smallness of the thing thus lessened, but to the importance of that which is put in contrast with it." It is also called meiosis.

413. This elision appears to have resulted in a text-critical problem concerning whether Χριστὸν ἐν σαρκὶ ἐληλυθότα should appear a second time after Ἰησοῦν. Strecker (135–36) gives a cogent discussion of the issue which need not be repeated here. The vast majority of MS evidence favors its elision and so that is followed in this commentary.

414. Bruce (105) understands this to imply that John had more than just the earlier confession in mind, though it was in focus, and so this article would be more than one of previous reference.

having come in the flesh. He does not say they deny it. "Heretical teaching can mask the full extent of its deviation from the truth by simply failing to affirm some pivotal biblical truth" (Hodges, 178).

καὶ τοῦτό ἐστιν τὸ τοῦ ἀντιχρίστου, "and this is the *spirit* of the antichrist." John turns to the issue of the Antichrist himself and reminds his readers that he is indeed coming. He is not here yet, but his false teachings are. He has already said in 2:18–23 that the presence of antichrists proves the coming of *the* Antichrist. Here he again alludes back to that previous warning.

The pronominal subject τοῦτό is emphatic. Further, its antecedent is πᾶν πνεῦμα in the previous clause (Brown, 496; Burdick, 299; Houlden, 108, n. 1; Strecker, 136). Brooke (110) relates it to μὴ ὁμολογεῖ τὸν Ἰησοῦν. Law (396) connects it to the antichrist just mentioned. Burdick (299) notes that τὸ and τοῦτό must both refer to the same thing, and since τὸ clearly has πνεῦμα as its antecedent, so, too, must τοῦτό. The article τὸ, being before τοῦ, calls for the presence of πνεῦμα in this clause connecting back to the previous reference in the preceding clause (Lenski, 489; Williamson, 138). Denial of Jesus is the "spirit" of the antichrist in that it is a characteristic attitude, not a demon sent out to influence people (Culy, 103; Smalley, 224). Thus the "spirit of the antichrist" may not refer to a "spirit" as such, but to a doctrine. It is a motivating principle, an ideology, not an entity.[415] We are to discern a teaching or attitude, not the presence of some spirit being, whether angelic or demonic.

ὃ ἀκηκόατε ὅτι ἔρχεται, καὶ νῦν ἐν τῷ κόσμῳ ἐστὶν ἤδη, "that you heard is coming, and now already is in the world." John's use of ἀκηκόατε indicates that this is something they have been taught in the past, their oral traditions (Brown, 496; Strecker, 137).[416] It likely alludes back to 2:18 and the warning of the coming antichrist (Lenski, 489). Even as Paul reminded the Thessalonians that they had been taught end time truths by him earlier (1 Thess 5:1–2; 2 Thess 2:5), John reminds his readers that they know their eschatology as well.

415. Westcott (143) sees the construction indicating "the many forces, which reveal the action of antichrist."

416. Though often misused in higher-critical Gospel studies as a source behind the texts and a denial of eyewitness authorship, here it is a more appropriate term.

Irenaeus recounts a story a story of a false teacher named Cerinthus who lived in Ephesus during John's day and denied the incarnation.[417] He was said to have taught that the divine Christ, an emanation of God, descended upon the human Jesus at his baptism. When Jesus was about to be crucified, the Christ spirit left him and only Jesus the man died on the cross. If the story about Cerinthus is true, John may have him in mind when he writes this instruction. However, it is more likely that he is thinking of false teachers in general who were appearing throughout the church at this time.

John is not describing the antichrist but his spirit (Brown, 496). This was made clear earlier in chapter 2 and so is repeated in this shortened form. The spirit that will inspire and empower the antichrist, namely Satan, is active in the world and influencing it to rebel against God and reject his truth. He is a roaring lion in search of prey (1 Pet 5:8) and the accuser of the saints who awaits expulsion from heaven (Rev 12:7–12). Now, as earlier in chapter 2, John is ready to contrast his readers with the false teachers.

Many interpreters take κόσμος here with a neutral sense as the world of mankind (Haas, de Jonge, and Swellengrebel, 104; Marshall, 209).[418] However, there is no need to see any uses in this section as positive or neutral, especially in light of what he continues to say about the world in verses 4 and 5 (Smalley, 225).[419] This reference is better seen connected with them conceptually rather than introductory to what follows and is neutral.

Smalley (225) notes that the placement of ἤδη at the end of the clause begun with νῦν is emphatic. Stählin sees John's use of νῦν here to indicate that he believed the day of the Lord had come and that as νῦν is used in the New Testament, it expresses "the certainty of eschatology already realized."[420] However, his discussion appears to be more of reading his eschatol-

---

417. For a fuller discussion of Cerinthus, see my comments in the introduction of the commentary under "Occasion and Setting." As noted then, Irenaeus, who reported the story, was not an eyewitness. Thus the likelihood of this story being true is lessened, especially in light of the fact that at this time no other evidence exists that places Cerinthus in Ephesus with John as contemporaries.

418. See S. B. Marrow, "Κόσμος in John" (90–102), for a good summary of John's use of the term in his writings.

419. Though E. Malatesta (*Interiority and Covenant*, 286) recognizes this use of κόσμος as negative, he considers the first reference in v 1 to be "earth and human society as the scene of salvation history," and thus neutral. Rensberger (113) understands "the world" to be neutral in vv 1–3 and opposed to God in vv 4–6.

420. G. Stählin, "νῦν," *TDNT* 4:1118–19.

ogy into the word. Moule correctly identifies this as "futurist" eschatology with John rather than "realized eschatology."[421] This is the same eschatological truth as was expressed in 2:18. The predecessors of Antichrist are present already even though the last days have not begun. We are living in the "last hour" before the last days. John does not affirm that the eschaton has arrived but that it, in fact, is only imminent.

Finally, Burge (176), when comparing 4:1–3 with 2:18–22 observes well, "In the first section, having a right relation with the Father leads to a correct view of the Son. In the second, having a right relation with the Spirit leads to a similarly correct view of the Son. In each case the Son is central in all true contacts with God."[422]

4:4 The reason believers have overcome the false spirits is because God's Spirit is greater. In this second half of the paragraph John uses personal pronouns for his subjects and "be" verbs for emphasis (by redundancy and repetition). This verse and the two that follow all begin with emphatic pronouns and distinguish three groups, "you" the readers, "they" the false teachers, and "we" the apostles (Hodges, 181, Stott, 160). This verse begins its first clause with ὑμεῖς (the readers) and ends it with αὐτούς (the false teachers). The triple repetition of "world" is also worth noting.

ὑμεῖς ἐκ τοῦ θεοῦ ἐστε, τεκνία, "You are from God, little children." The first emphatic pronoun identifies John's readers.[423] It contrasts them with the false teachers of verse 3 (Akin, 173; Brooke, 115; Harris, 179; Smalley, 226). It is combined with the term of endearment, τεκνία and involves the strong affirmation of his readers' relationship with God.

---

421. C. F. D. Moule, "A Neglected Factor in the Interpretation of Johannine Eschatology," 158–59.

422. Schnackenburg (220) also summarizes these verses well. "Thus, in vv 2–3 the Spirit of God and the spirit of the Antichrist, mutually opposing powers, are prompting their human minions on the stage of this world to contrary proclamations of faith." (So sind in VV 2–3 der Gottesgeist und der Geist des Antichrists die einander entgegenwirkenden Mächte, die ihren menschlichen Trabanten auf der Bühne dieser Welt ihre gegenteiligen glaubensproklamationen soufflieren.)

423. Burdick (300) calls this "doubly emphatic" because of its location in the sentence and the fact that ἐστε contains its own subject.

John's use of ἐκ emphasizes source once again (Moody, 84; Smalley, 226).[424] This contrast is with false teachers who separated from the community because they were not "from God" in chapter 2. Schnackenburg (224) identifies εἶναι ἐκ as a Johannine formula for saying someone belongs in one realm, group, or "sphere of being" (Wesensbereich). Strecker (137) sees this introducing "a dualism of God and the world" and indicating they "belong to God." Likewise, Brooke (115) sees it similarly and adds that it "suggests primarily spiritual dependence. A man is said to be 'of God,' 'of the Devil,' who draws all his inspiration, all that dominates and regulates his thought and action, from the sources out of which he is said to be."

John moves the vocative of address, τεκνία, from the beginning of the clause to its end. This heightens the emphatic nature of the pronoun, ὑμεῖς (Brown, 497; Smalley 226).[425] It also serves as a confirmation of their justification. If any doubt may have arisen from earlier statements in the preceding paragraphs, they are removed here. John clearly considers his readers to be believers. What he has been discussing with them in no way is meant to question their salvation or to encourage them to question it.

καὶ νενικήκατε αὐτούς, "and have overcome them." Reflecting Jesus' words in the upper room (John 16:33), John affirms that his readers have "overcome" the false teachers. The perfect tense νενικήκατε in combination (καὶ functioning as a coordinating conjunction) with the present of εἰμί focuses attention on the result (intensive perfect). This is the same term and tense he used of the "young men" of 2:12–14. As there, νενικήκατε indicates that the victory won has effects that continue to the present for John's readers (Akin, 174; Smalley, 226; Williamson, 139). Thus John does not view his readers as in danger of falling victim to false teachings or being influenced

424. Burdick (300) considers ἐκ τοῦ θεοῦ to be a shortening of γεγεννημένος ἐκ τοῦ θεοῦ and so mean "born of God." He points to John's calling his readers τεκνία in v 4 as stressing the fact of their spiritual birth, even as a term of endearment. However, he also calls them "beloved" at the beginning of the discussion and again to begin the next paragraph. If spiritual birth were John's focus rather than source, it would seem that he would have made that clear. However, John is making clear differences between God's people and Satan's, and source better fits the nature of the contrast being made than birth.

425. Culy (103) sees it marking the beginning of a new paragraph. However, its location at the end of the sentence rather than its beginning would indicate otherwise. Additionally, every use of this term need not mean a new paragraph as evidenced in such places as 3:7 and 3:18.

by the false teachers of verses 1–3. Rather, they have already rejected those teachers and their teachings.[426] If not, then John is being proleptic and anticipates their not being overcome by those teachers in the future (Hodges 179). Brooke (115) finds the nature of this victory, not in remaining true to the faith but rather "the expulsion of the false prophets (αὐτούς) from the community."

Of note, too, is the continued contrast between "you," the readers, and "them," the false teachers, thus his use of αὐτούς. The referent of αὐτούς is the false prophets of verse 1, referred to as "spirits" earlier (Brown, 497; Painter, 261; Smalley, 226; Strecker, 137). Harris (179) interprets this to mean John "has shifted the emphasis in 4:4 from the spirits themselves to the people whom they motivate, influence, and control." Actually, he clarifies here that such is what he has meant all along. Bultmann (63) correctly says αὐτούς refers to "the false teachers, and if the antichrist is at work in them, it nevertheless cannot be said of him that he is in them. ... he is not *in* them, but they themselves *are* antichrists (2:18)."[427]

ὅτι μείζων ἐστὶν ὁ ἐν ὑμῖν ἢ ὁ ἐν τῷ κόσμῳ, "because he who is in you is greater than he who is in the world." With this statement we see John rejecting any dualist vision of the universe (Akin, 174). Satan, the spirit of deceit, is not an equal but opposite power to God. Rather, he is the defeated enemy who has likewise been defeated by believers as well. The reason for their victory over deception is now provided. The church's overcoming false teaching, rather than being overcome by it, is ultimately a work of God in its life.

Here the contrast is between two personalities.[428] Using once again the nominative masculine singular article, John contrasts two powers at war over the souls of the saints. The referent of the first ὁ is identified with each member of the Trinity as well as the Trinity.

---

426. D. E. Hiebert, "An Expositional Study of 1 John—Part 7: An Exposition of 1 John 4:1–6," 431.

427. His view that John has "historicized" a mythical figure is certainly incorrect and so was deleted from this quotation. However, in spite of that, what he has to say is insightful.

428. BDF §185 (2) says this use of the particle ἤ was not grammatically necessary, and functions in place of a gen. of comparison. That being the case, John's choice to use it would again heighten the contrast between God's Spirit and the devil.

(1) Some see ὁ referring to God the Father (Brooke, 115; Bultmann, 63; Dodd, 100; Haas, de Jonge, and Swellengrebel, 104; Houlden, 110; Marshall, 208). Lenski (490) sees 2:24 as its referent. Further, God the Father is described as victorious in 1 Cor 15:57. Against this one may observe that God the Father is not described as being in (εἶναι ἐν) believers anywhere else in Scripture, only that he abides (μένω ἐν) in them (Brown, 497).

(2) Others see Jesus (Westcott, 144; Yarbrough, 227).[429] This is supported by John's use of εἶναι ἐν to describe Jesus' abiding in believers in John 14:20, 23; 17:23, 26. Against this is the absence of references to Jesus in this paragraph (Brown, 497).

(3) Most see the Holy Spirit (Akin, 174; Brown, 498; Burdick, 301–2; Bruce, 106; Houlden, 110; Johnson, 97; Stott, 160). This is indicated by the contrast between the Spirit of truth and spirit of deception (Brown, 498). This may reflect Zech 4:6, where the Spirit of God conquers (Brown, 498).

(4) Finally, all three members of the Godhead is a view proposed by Smalley (227), who has been influenced by Malatesta.[430]

John's choice of the second person plural pronoun indicates that he has corporate victory in view rather than personal victory (Westcott, 144). Even so, what is true for the body of Christ is equally true for its members. In fact, if it is not true of its members, it will not be true corporately.

As the first "he who" refers to the Holy Spirit, the second refers to Satan, who rules the world system (Lenski, 490). This is parallel to τὸν πονηρόν in 2:14.[431] Since John uses two masculine articles rather than neuter pronouns, it becomes even clearer that he is contrasting two persons, not impersonal forces (Burdick, 301). His change from neuter to masculine fits Satan well enough but is unusual while keeping the Holy Spirit as his referent. One might point to John 14:26 as another example of a masculine pronoun (ἐκεῖνος) being applied to the Holy Spirit. However, its antecedent is most likely ὁ παράκλητος, the subject of the sentence, rather than the nearer

429. Plummer (98) and Williamson (139) cannot decide between God or Christ.
430. E. Malatesta, *Interiority and Covenant*, 287–89.
431. E. Malatesta, *Interiority and Covenant*, 287.

pronoun ὃ which has τὸ πνεῦμα τὸ ἅγιον as its antecedent. In John 15:26 we find the same pronouns being used once again (ἐκεῖνος and ὃ), but also having similar antecedents (παράκλητος and τὸ πνεῦμα τῆς ἀληθείας). Thus there are no clear Johannine examples of attributing a masculine article or pronoun to the Holy Spirit. That being said, John's point is not lessened whether this verse has two masculine articles or neuter relative pronouns. The two opponents are described in terms of their spheres of operation. The Holy Spirit operates within the sphere of the body of Christ, in the lives of believers. The devil operates within the sphere of the world. As Jesus noted in John 17:14–16, while living in the world, believers are not part of that world.[432]

Schnackenburg (224) notes that whereas God is "in" the Christian, Satan is only "in the world." This avoids attributing direct influence or indwelling to Satan (Strecker, 138). They only reflect his "spirit" in terms of attitudes and doctrines. They are only influenced by him, not controlled or possessed by him. Thus they act as his agents, not as recipients of his spirit as God's children are of his.

4:5 John is now ready to describe further the relationship of false teachers to their source and audience. He affirms further that these false teachers have a hearing from the world. He communicates this by the emphatic inclusion of the pronoun subject of the main clause and by the placement of all three verbs at the ends of their respective clauses.

αὐτοὶ ἐκ τοῦ κόσμου εἰσίν, "They are from the world." John's use of αὐτοὶ may allude to the people who went out from the apostolic band in 2:19. His pronouns are both emphatic and clear (Smalley, 228).[433] These are not the readers, nor are they the apostles.

In contrast to the readers who are from God, these false teachers are not. This is evident from the contrasting parallel of the words in verse 4. Where "they" are sourced in the world (αὐτοὶ ἐκ τοῦ κόσμου εἰσίν) John (ἡμεῖς) and the readers (ὑμεῖς) are sourced in God (Johnson, 98). They arise out of the world and are fully identified with it (Smalley, 228). This use of κόσμος is not of the neutral world of mankind, but the world system characterized by

432. "World" has a negative connotation here, the same as v 3 (Bultmann, 63; Williamson, 139).

433. Burdick (302) identifies this pronoun as "doubly emphatic" in the same way as ὑμεῖς in v 4.

opposition to God (Burdick, 302; Marshall, 209). This indicates that they are not believers as was the case in 2:18–23.

διὰ τοῦτο ἐκ τοῦ κόσμου λαλοῦσιν, "because of this they speak from the world." The preposition phrase διὰ τοῦτο looks back on the previous clause (Culy, 104; Yarbrough, 228). The result of them being "from" the world is that they speak its language. His use of ἐκ τοῦ κόσμου identifies the source of their teachings as the world system rather than God. In this instance also, it is not the devil inspiring or influencing them but their "world." Strecker (138) describes it as "the sphere of the world." We might say that they are speaking according to their world view, the philosophical, cultural, and theological milieu in which they live and breathe (Smith, 100; Williamson, 140).

καὶ ὁ κόσμος αὐτῶν ἀκούει, "and the world hears them." The result of speaking the world's language and values is that a false teacher gains the world's hearing. Though ἀκούω can mean simply "to hear," in this instance it carries the nuance of paying attention in the sense of responding positively to someone and heeding what they say.[434] "It has been true down through the centuries that heterodoxy has a far greater appeal to worldly people than does orthodoxy. Very many religious movements are composed mainly of unsaved people who find the false theology of the movement attractive" (Hodges, 180).

Some see this indicating that the false teachers ("secessionists, opponents") were gathering a greater following than John's followers (Brown, 498; Schnackenburg, 225; Smalley, 228). Strecker (139) rejects this idea and says Schnackenburg "overvalues the possibility of deriving historical, sociological, or psychological data from our text. Instead, what is in the foreground is the dualistic theological statement that wherever the messengers of the world appear they find a hearing among worldly people. This is true no matter what the statistical measure of their success; in turn, it means that wherever God's messengers appear they will also find hearers, namely, those who belong to God." Thus we see the second test of false teachers provided by John: what the world thinks of them (Burge, 176).

4:6 This verse is composed of a series of four statements contrasting the apostolic witnesses from the false teachers of the previous verse in terms of

434. BDAG, 38; G. Kittel, "ἀκούω," *TDNT* 1:216–20.

the response of the world to their word. Beginning with an emphatic claim to divine origin, the focus is turned from the teacher to the hearer. The person's origin is expressed in terms of the one to whom they respond. The contrast moves from that of "you" and "they" now to "we" and "they."

ἡμεῖς ἐκ τοῦ θεοῦ ἐσμεν, "We are from God." John makes the same claim of the apostolic witnesses that he did of his readers in verse 4. The location of the pronoun ἡμεῖς at the beginning with ἐσμεν at the end of the clause both serve to make this an emphatic statement (Burdick, 303). The antecedent of ἡμεῖς has been identified in one of two ways.

(1) It may be limited to the apostles, the "teachers" (Brooke, 115; Burdick, 303; Houlden, 110; Smith, 100; Stott, 157–58; Westcott, 145). This would be consistent with John's contrast between him and the apostles versus the false teachers (Stott, 161).

(2) It refers to all orthodox Christians including John and his readers (Bultmann, 64, n. 15; Haas, de Jonge, and Swellengrebel, 104; Johnson, 98; Kruse, 150; Lieu, 173; Lenski, 491; Marshall, 209; Moody, 86; Schnackenburg, 225; Smalley, 229; Yarbrough, 229).[435] This would follow from the final phrase being applicable to all believers and so the context of the sentence strengthens this option (Akin, 175; Barker, 341; Brown, 499; Marshall, 209; Strecker, 139). Lenski (491) argues that "the spirit of the Antichrist is to be found in the followers as well as in the leaders, and both certainly speak." Thus John would include his readers with himself at this point.[436] Yet, "we" must refer to the apostles from whom the false teachers separated and the contrast in this section is between their teachings and John's.[437]

Even as John reminded his readers that they were sourced in God, he now makes the same claim of himself and the apostles. Within the flow of thought of this paragraph, John is distinguishing three groups: the readers, the false teachers, and now the apostles. He uses the same construction of an emphatic pronoun introducing the clause and the verb concluding it. For him and his readers, the apostles are "from God" (ἐκ τοῦ θεοῦ). In contrast to them are the false teachers who are "from the world" (ἐκ τοῦ κόσμου).

435. E. Malatesta, *Interiority and Covenant*, 288.

436. Barker (341) interprets it to mean "all the faithful" but to have "particular reference to the true teachers."

437. Dodd (100) sees it as indicating both.

The "sameness" of each clause is purposeful, designed to contrast John and the apostles from the false teachers.

In this verse we can hear the words of Jesus echoing from his debate with the Jews in John 8:47. There he explains their rejection of him in that they "do not hear" because they "are not of God."[438] John now says the same for the world. Its people do not hear the apostles because they are not "of God" either.

ὁ γινώσκων τὸν θεὸν ἀκούει ἡμῶν, "He who knows God hears us." Using γινώσκω (experiential and relational knowledge), John now affirms that one's "knowledge" of God is revealed by their response to the apostles. This use of the articular present participle for "know" is seen by some to indicate a person in the process of acquiring knowledge of God (Burdick, 303; Hodges, 181; Kistemaker, 330; Westcott, 145). Schnackenburg (226) sees "knowing God" as equivalent to belonging to him. It also indicates the "continual progress made" in a Christian's life in terms of "the knowledge of him which comes from experience of life in fellowship with him" (also Brooke, 116; Smalley, 229).

It seems best to relate γινώσκω back to 2:3–6 and the upper room so that it describes a person in relationship with God (gnomic rather than progressive). As John noted in his Gospel (John 3:18–21), those of the truth responded positively to Jesus, "came to the light," and those not of the truth rejected him. In the upper room, Jesus told his disciples that the world would respond to them in the same way it had to him (John 15:20–21). John makes that connection here. Whereas in 2:3–6 he affirmed that knowledge of God is demonstrated through an obedient lifestyle, here it is demonstrated by responding positively to apostolic teaching. By his repetition of ἀκούω, his contrast between his readers who listen to the apostles with the world that listens to false teachers is heightened (Burdick, 304).

This serves as another reminder to his readers to remain faithful to what they "had heard from the beginning" rather than new ideas being presented by false teachers (Stott, 161). This theme has been evident already in the epistle (2:7, 24; 3:11) and will be repeated in 2 John (5, 9).

ὃς οὐκ ἔστιν ἐκ τοῦ θεοῦ οὐκ ἀκούει ἡμῶν, "Whoever is not from God does not hear us." Though John makes the point that personal relationship

438. ὁ ὢν ἐκ τοῦ θεοῦ τὰ ῥήματα τοῦ θεοῦ ἀκούει· διὰ τοῦτο ὑμεῖς οὐκ ἀκούετε, ὅτι ἐκ τοῦ θεοῦ οὐκ ἐστέ.

with God is demonstrated by one's response to apostolic teaching, he describes it as the result and not the cause of that relationship. Thus, though this describes the regenerate and unregenerate, John is not providing his readers a "test" of their own salvation as much as an explanation of the significance of one's response to orthodoxy or heterodoxy.

John now turns to the question of salvation and source even though he has not provided a test of one's salvation by what he said in the previous statements. He begins this clause with the nominative singular relative pronoun ὃς that lacks an antecedent in the immediate context. By this he has moved the focus from ἡμεῖς to ὁ, and now to ὃς. Interpreters differ in their assessment of the soteriological status of the person in question. Hodges (181) sees ὃς referring to believer and nonbeliever alike. Others see it referring to nonbelievers only (Kistemaker, 329, Smalley, 229). It seems best to see John using this "generic" pronoun in order to make a general statement of fact with no one in particular in view. This is true of anyone who is operating in the world system. To determine if believers can be included in this *whoever* one must ask whether believers can be drawn into and take part in the world system and its values. The answer comes from John's command and warning in 2:15–17. By implication, believers can and do love the world and the things in it. John would never command someone not to do something if they were incapable of doing it. Thus, believers can love the world in 2:15. That being the case, this principle *could* apply to a believer or a nonbeliever. However, writing from a dualist perspective in which only opposites are allowed to exist, John describes this person as separated from God, as not being sourced in God. What John is saying by this is that failure to *hear* the apostles, in the sense of heed what they say, which is parallel to *hear* as it was used of the world, indicates a person is not *from God*. John's continued repetition of *from God* heightens the contrast between those who are and are not operating on the basis of his character and being. However, is he allowing for this to be true of believers as well? Though one may argue that believers are included (Hodges, 181), John's dualistic approach pushes believers out for the sake of argument. Yes, by implication he would also be saying that believers act like nonbelievers when they fail to listen to the apostles. However, that is just an implication based on the fact that believers do sin and, as we see in 3 John, they did and do rebel against the apostles and their teachings.

In the contrast being made by John in this paragraph, he is describing this person in a way similar to the false teachers of 2:19 who had deserted the apostolic circle and proven by their departure that they were never really part of that circle. John's point that he repeatedly makes in this epistle is that false teachers are *not* believers. Unbelievers follow false teachers. Consequently, believers should not do likewise, though they may, by implication.

ἐκ τούτου γινώσκομεν τὸ πνεῦμα τῆς ἀληθείας καὶ τὸ πνεῦμα τῆς πλάνης, "From this we know the Spirit of truth and the spirit of deception." John now makes an application. Rather than the expected ἐν τούτῳ, he begins this sentence with ἐκ τούτου. This is his sole use of this construction in the epistle.[439] Since nothing follows to which ἐκ τούτου could refer:

(1) It could refer back to ἐν τούτῳ in verse 24 (Brown, 500). This would reflect the unitary nature of verses 1 through 6 as a paragraph and focus attention on the spirits and their relationship to the church and the world.

(2) It could refer to verses 5 and 6.[440] It is parallel in thought to ἐν τούτῳ in verse 2 and both are limited in their reference to "judgments made on the basis of external criteria."[441] (3) It seems best to see it referring to all that preceded in verses 1 through 6 (Harris, 183; Schnackenburg, 226; Strecker, 140). That would serve to make this a summarization and conclusion of this paragraph.

Who is included in this "we know"? (1) It could include John and his readers, or (2) it could refer once more to John and the eyewitnesses. This second option is strengthened by the immediate context where those born of God listen to "us," the apostles.

One can tell by people's responses to the apostolic message what spirit is influencing them. Thus the spirits of truth and deception are revealed by a person's response to the apostolic message (Bultmann, 64). This use of the preposition ἐκ carries the sense of "by means of" in this instance rather than

---

439. He uses it only twice in his Gospel (John 6:66 and 19:12). In both instances it has a temporal sense, rather than logical, and continues the chronological flow of the narrative.

440. E. Malatesta, *Interiority and Covenant*, 286.

441. E. Malatesta, *Interiority and Covenant*, 286.

"out of" or "sourced in" as John has been using it with regard to God and the world.[442] Additionally, his use of γινώσκομεν includes John with his readers (Lieu, 174). He says by this that discernment of truth and error is not limited to the apostles but can be practiced by all believers (Westcott, 146).

John repeats *spirit* and contrasts the two with descriptive gens.: truth and error. Should the first use of spirit be capitalized to refer to the Holy Spirit while the second is not? Or should both be left lowercase? Brown (501) sees this verse clarifying the reference to "spirits" in 4:1, and so refers to the Holy Spirit and Satan. Jesus described the Holy Spirit as the Spirit of truth in John 14:17 with the exact same construction (τὸ πνεῦμα τῆς ἀληθείας). John's pattern of reflecting back on the upper room throughout this epistle makes it seem best to see this as a reference to the Holy Spirit as well (Rensberger, 114). Thus *of truth* is more likely a subjective genitive, carrying the sense that the Holy Spirit speaks the truth in contrast to the spirit that motivates false teachers. Further support for this comes from the reference to the Spirit of God in verse 2 and "he who is in you" in verse 4 (understood as the Holy Spirit or all three members of the Trinity).[443] Others see the spirit of truth in light of extrabiblical Jewish literature.[444] For example the *T. Jud.* speaks of two spirits in the world, truth and error.[445] The *T. Reu.* links the spirit of error with Beliar.[446] The Qumran community thought in

---

442. D. B. Wallace, *Grammar*, 371.

443. Lenski (492–93) sees this as a subjective gen., but interprets it to be a reference to people just as in 4:1.

444. G. Beale and D. Carson, *Commentary on the New Testament Use of the Old Testament*, 489–90.

445. *T. Jud.* 20.1 "Learn therefore, my children, that two spirits wait upon man—the spirit of truth and the spirit of error; and in the midst is the spirit of the understanding of the mind, to which it belongeth to turn whithersoever it will. And the works of truth and the works of error are written upon the breast of men, and each one of them the Lord knoweth. And there is no time at which the works of men can be hid from him; for on the bones of his breast hath he been written down before the Lord. And the spirit of truth testifieth all things, and accuseth all; and he who sinneth is burnt up by his own heart, and cannot raise his face unto the Judge." (From A. Roberts, J. Donaldson and A. C. Coxe, *The Ante-Nicene Fathers Vol. VIII: Translations of the Writings of the Fathers Down to A.D. 325*, 20)

446. *T. Reu.* 2.1 and 3.2 read: "And now hear me, my children, what things I saw in my repentance concerning the seven spirits of error. Seven spirits are given against man from Beliar, and they are chief of the works of youth; and seven spirits are given to him at his creation, that in them should be done every work of man. ... With

such terms as well as evidenced in 1QS.[447] However, "spirit of deceit" is a uniquely Johannine term (Rensberger, 114).

Akin (175–76) summarizes this section well. "The spirits may be tested by first examining their confession, which comes through human instruments, and then by examining the character of their audience, who would give them credence. We can know the true from the false, the Spirit of God from the spirit of the antichrist. It is imperative that we be vigilant in this assignment."

Biblical Theology Comments

Johannine Christology is developed further in these verses. The central place of the incarnation is revealed, as well as the significance of Jesus' flesh and blood life. However, he did not just come and share humanity for a season. He remains fully human to this day in heaven.

God's sovereignty and might is expressed in terms of his power over Satan. Satan stands defeated and only able to influence the population of the world, where God stands victorious and indwells his children, enabling them to experience that same victory over the devil.

Application and Devotional Implications

Discernment only comes with practice. Discernment requires thinking. Only those Christians who know their Bible and can think critically will be able to recognize false teachers and their teachings. This cannot occur without personal study of the Scriptures.

---

these spirits are mingled the spirits of error." (From A. Roberts, J. Donaldson and A. C. Coxe, *The Ante-Nicene Fathers Vol. VIII: Translations of the Writings of the Fathers Down to A.D. 325, 9)*

447. 1QS III, 17–21 reads: "He has created man to govern the world, and has appointed for him two spirits in which to walk until the time of his visitation: the spirits of truth and falsehood. Those born of truth spring from a fountain of light, but those born of falsehood spring from a source of darkness. All the children of righteousness are ruled by the Prince of Light and walk in the ways of light, but all the children of falsehood are ruled by the Angel of Darkness and walk in the ways of darkness. The Angel of Darkness leads all the children of righteousness astray, and until his end, all their sin, iniquities, wickedness, and all their unlawful deeds are caused by his dominion in accordance with the mysteries of God." (Translation from Mitchel G. Reddish, ed. *Apocalyptic Literature: A Reader, 226*)

Confession must arise from conviction and affirm what is true to be biblical confession. A theologian who says, "I believe in the resurrection, but whether it actually happened is immaterial" is not confessing. At best he is confusing. To confess Christ requires a conviction that his life, death, resurrection, ascension, and present ministry in heaven are all actualities of history that are true whether modern historians accede their reality.

These are not individual truths or personal convictions that exist in beliefs but not facts. These are realities of the universe that exist even if no human living were to believe in their existence. Thus, in our day we need to be discerning. Many theologians couch their disbelief in careful language that ultimately denies Christ. They are the modern antichrists. The world is impressed with their theology. We as believers should not be.

Selected Bibliography

Beale, G. K., and D. A. Carson. *Commentary on the New Testament Use of the Old Testament*. Grand Rapids: Baker Academic, 2007.

Boyer, J. L. "A Classification of Imperatives: A Statistical Study." *GTJ* 8 (1987): 35–54.

Bullinger, E. W. *Figures of Speech Used in the Bible.* New York: Eyre & Spottiswoode, 1898. Reprint, Grand Rapids: Baker, 1968.

Carson D. A., and J. D. Woodbridge, eds. *Scripture and Truth*. Grand Rapids: Baker, 1992.

Coetzee, J. C. "The Holy Spirit in 1 John." *Neot* 13 (1979): 43–67.

de Jonge, M. "The Use of the Word ΧΡΙΣΤΟΣ in the Johannine Epistles." In *Studies in John*, 67–74. NovTSup 24. Leiden: Brill, 1970.

Hiebert, D. E. "An Expositional Study of 1 John—Part 7: An Exposition of 1 John 4:1–6." *BSac* 146 (1989): 420–36.

Lalleman, P. J. "The Adversaries Envisaged in the Johannine Epistles." *ThT* 53 (1999): 17–24.

Malatesta, E. *The Epistles of St. John*. Rome: Pontifical Gregorian University, 1973.

Marrow, S. B. "Κόσμος in John." *CBQ* 64 (2002): 90–102.

Metzger, B. M., and United Bible Societies. *A Textual Commentary on the Greek New Testament.* 2nd ed. New York: United Bible Societies, 1994.

Moffatt, J. A. R. *The Bible, A New Translation*. New York: Harper & Row, 1954.

Moule, C. F. D. "A Neglected Factor in the Interpretation of Johannine Eschatology." In *Studies in John*, 155–160. NovTSup 24. Leiden: Brill, 1970.

O'Neill, J. C. *The Puzzle of 1 John*. London: SPCK, 1966.

Reddish, M. G., ed. *Apocalyptic Literature: A Reader*. Nashville: Hendrickson, 1990.

Roberts, A., J. Donaldson, and A. C. Coxe. *The Ante-Nicene Fathers Vol. VIII : Translations of the Writings of the Fathers Down to A.D. 325*. Oak Harbor, WA: Logos Research Systems, 1997.

Suggit, J. N. "1 John 5:21: ΤΕΚΝΙΑ, ΦΥΛΑΞΑΤΕ ΕΑΥΤΑ ΑΠΟ ΤΩΝ ΕΙΔΩΛΩΝ." *JTS* 36 (1985): 386–90.

Wallace, D. B. *Greek Grammar beyond the Basics*. Grand Rapids: Zondervan, 1996.

God Is Love (4:7–5:21)

Introduction

This final section of the body of the epistle develops its message around the third divine attribute that impacts the life of a believer: God's love. This becomes the basis of every believer's assurance that God does indeed desire fellowship with him or her. It also becomes the motivation and model of how every believer should feel and act.

John continues to express pastoral concerns while pausing to address issues raised by false teachings that were appearing across Christendom. Though false teachers are not the focus of his Epistle, he does not neglect them either. However, we should not be distracted by attempts to find false teachers and their false teachings behind the text. Rather, we must address the issues John addresses directly.

John continues through this section to develop his dualism and to express his literary art. One can conclude that John's favorite rhetorical device is antithesis. He loves to offer two options and call on his readers to respond. Rather than finding opponents behind the images he creates, it is better to recognize his message: there are only two choices for every person to make. There are no gray areas in the Christian life. Through many of these contrasts John strips away the false veneer of human righteousness and reveals our need to choose faith and faithfulness to our God, who has acted on our behalf. We must also express his nature through our lives as his children and recognize that anything less than that is a denial of him and his work in us. John has already told us that God is absolutely morally pure, so we need to be. He has told us that God is righteous, and he expects us to be. Now we will learn the depths of God's love and see that believers need to express that as well.

God's Love Perfected (4:7–21)

Introduction

The theme of love dominates this section and is defined fully within it. This is John's final return to the theme of love. He introduced it in 2:7–11 and developed it further in 3:11–18. He now completes it in 4:7–21. This section reviews things already said by John earlier, though in a slightly different vein. Pentecost (107) notes that many critics conclude from the repetition of themes in this third section that John is "rambling." He, on the other hand, correctly sees the literary skill by which John weaves this concept "like a golden thread throughout this epistle" and rather than "being the musings of a senile man, this epistle throbs with the heartbeat of God." This final section begins by describing to us the nature and expression of the God's love, both in terms of his expression of it, and in terms of our expressing it. In this we have the gospel clearly taught, not in terms of a call to faith but in terms of understanding its basis in the love of God.

Original Text

7 Ἀγαπητοί, ἀγαπῶμεν ἀλλήλους, ὅτι ἡ ἀγάπη ἐκ τοῦ θεοῦ ἐστιν, καὶ πᾶς ὁ
ἀγαπῶν ἐκ τοῦ θεοῦ γεγέννηται καὶ γινώσκει τὸν θεόν. **8** ὁ μὴ ἀγαπῶν οὐκ ἔγνω
τὸν θεόν, ὅτι ὁ θεὸς ἀγάπη ἐστίν. **9** ἐν τούτῳ ἐφανερώθη ἡ ἀγάπη τοῦ θεοῦ ἐν
ἡμῖν, ὅτι τὸν υἱὸν αὐτοῦ τὸν μονογενῆ ἀπέσταλκεν ὁ θεὸς εἰς τὸν κόσμον ἵνα
ζήσωμεν δι' αὐτοῦ. **10** ἐν τούτῳ ἐστὶν ἡ ἀγάπη, οὐχ ὅτι ἡμεῖς ἠγαπήκαμεν τὸν
θεόν, ἀλλ' ὅτι αὐτὸς ἠγάπησεν ἡμᾶς καὶ ἀπέστειλεν τὸν υἱὸν αὐτοῦ ἱλασμὸν περὶ
τῶν ἁμαρτιῶν ἡμῶν. **11** ἀγαπητοί, εἰ οὕτως ὁ θεὸς ἠγάπησεν ἡμᾶς, καὶ ἡμεῖς
ὀφείλομεν ἀλλήλους ἀγαπᾶν. **12** θεὸν οὐδεὶς πώποτε τεθέαται· ἐὰν ἀγαπῶμεν
ἀλλήλους, ὁ θεὸς ἐν ἡμῖν μένει καὶ ἡ ἀγάπη αὐτοῦ ἐν ἡμῖν τετελειωμένη ἐστιν.

13 Ἐν τούτῳ γινώσκομεν ὅτι ἐν αὐτῷ μένομεν καὶ αὐτὸς ἐν ἡμῖν, ὅτι ἐκ τοῦ
πνεύματος αὐτοῦ δέδωκεν ἡμῖν. **14** καὶ ἡμεῖς τεθεάμεθα καὶ μαρτυροῦμεν ὅτι ὁ
πατὴρ ἀπέσταλκεν τὸν υἱὸν σωτῆρα τοῦ κόσμου. **15** ὃς ἐὰν ὁμολογήσῃ ὅτι Ἰησοῦς
ἐστιν ὁ υἱὸς τοῦ θεοῦ, ὁ θεὸς ἐν αὐτῷ μένει καὶ αὐτὸς ἐν τῷ θεῷ. **16** καὶ ἡμεῖς
ἐγνώκαμεν καὶ πεπιστεύκαμεν τὴν ἀγάπην ἣν ἔχει ὁ θεὸς ἐν ἡμῖν.

Ὁ θεὸς ἀγάπη ἐστίν, καὶ ὁ μένων ἐν τῇ ἀγάπῃ ἐν τῷ θεῷ μένει καὶ ὁ θεὸς ἐν
αὐτῷ μένει. **17** ἐν τούτῳ τετελείωται ἡ ἀγάπη μεθ' ἡμῶν, ἵνα παρρησίαν ἔχωμεν
ἐν τῇ ἡμέρᾳ τῆς κρίσεως, ὅτι καθὼς ἐκεῖνός ἐστιν καὶ ἡμεῖς ἐσμεν ἐν τῷ κόσμῳ
τούτῳ. **18** φόβος οὐκ ἔστιν ἐν τῇ ἀγάπῃ, ἀλλ' ἡ τελεία ἀγάπη ἔξω βάλλει τὸν

φόβον, ὅτι ὁ φόβος κόλασιν ἔχει, ὁ δὲ φοβούμενος οὐ τετελείωται ἐν τῇ ἀγάπῃ.
19 ἡμεῖς ἀγαπῶμεν,a ὅτι αὐτὸς πρῶτος ἠγάπησεν ἡμᾶς. **20** ἐάν τις εἴπῃ ὅτι
Ἀγαπῶ τὸν θεὸν καὶ τὸν ἀδελφὸν αὐτοῦ μισῇ, ψεύστης ἐστίν· ὁ γὰρ μὴ ἀγαπῶν
τὸν ἀδελφὸν αὐτοῦ ὃν ἑώρακεν, τὸν θεὸν ὃν οὐχ ἑώρακεν αοὐ δύναται ἀγαπᾶν.a
21 καὶ ταύτην τὴν ἐντολὴν ἔχομεν ἀπ' αὐτcῦ, ἵνα ὁ ἀγαπῶν τὸν θεὸν ἀγαπᾷ καὶ
τὸν ἀδελφὸν αὐτοῦ.

Textual Notes

19.a. Though some copyists added *τὸν θεόν* or *αὐτόν* after *ἀγαπῶμεν*, and the MS evidence is quite widespread (א K L Ψ 049 056 0142 33 81 88 104 181 326 330 424 436 451 614 629 630 1505 1877 2127 2412 2492 2495 *Byz Lect*^{m} it^{c,dem,div,p} vg^{cl} syr^{p,h} cop^{bo} arm), it seems best to take it without a direct object[1] There is sufficient early MS support for the shorter reading (A B 5 322 323 424 945 1241 1739 1881 it^{q,vid} vg^{ww} eth^{pp}). Additionally, the variation within the witnesses is sufficiently varied to indicate more than one copyists attempted to correct the grammar and may have indeed mistaken *ἀγαπῶμεν* for a hortatory subjunctive.

20.a...a *Πῶς δύναται ἀγαπᾶν* would seem to reflect John's writing style and has the weight of MS support (A K L 048 049 056 0142 33 81 88 104 181 326 330 436 451 614 629 945 1241 1877 1881 2127 2412 2492 *Byz Lect* it^{ar,c,dem,div,p,q} vg syr^{p} cop^{bo} arm eth), but *οὐ δύναται ἀγαπᾶν* is the better reading because it enables the construction of a small chiasm created by the repetitions noted above (Brown, 533; Smalley, 234).[2]

Translation

7 Beloved, let us love one another, because love is from God, and everyone who loves has been born from God and knows God. **8** The one not loving has not known God because God is love. **9** This is how the love of God was manifested toward us, in that God sent his unique Son[3] into the world in

1. B. Metzger and United Bible Societies, *A Textual Commentary on the Greek New Testament*, 2d ed., 645.
2. B. Metzger and United Bible Societies, *A Textual Commentary on the Greek New Testament*, 2d ed., 645.
3. This expresses the sense of μονογενὴς as only or unique without reference to birth. Other translations include: "only begotten" (ASV, NASB95, NKJV), "only" (ESV, NIV84), and "one and only" (HCSB, NET).

order that we might live through him. **10** In this is love, not that we have loved God, but that he loved us and sent his son *to be* a propitiation[4] for our sins. **11** Beloved, if God loved us in this manner, we also are obligated[5] to love one another. **12** No one has ever seen God. If we love one another, God abides in us and his love has been made perfect in us.

13 By this we know that we are abiding in him and he in us, because he has given to us from his Spirit.[6] **14** And we have seen and are testifying that the Father sent his Son *to be* the Savior of the world. **15** Whoever confesses that Jesus is the Son of God, God abides in him and he in God. **16** And we have known and have believed the love which God has for us.

God is love, and the one abiding in love abides in God and God abides in him. **17** By this love is has been perfected with us, that we may have boldness in the day of judgment, because just as he is we also are in this world. **18** There is no fear in love but perfect love casts out fear, because fear has to do with punishment,[7] and the one fearing has not been perfected in love. **19** We love because he loved us first. **20** If anyone says, "I love God" and hates his brother, he is a liar; for the one who does not love his brother whom he has seen is not able to love God whom he has not seen. **21** And this commandment we have from him, that the one who loves God also should love his brother.

Commentary

This section (4:7–21) moves to pastoral concerns and so should be viewed as parenetic rather than polemic (Strecker, 143). John's use of antithesis in

4. ASV, ESV, HCSB, NASB95, NKJV. Also "atoning sacrifice" (NET, NIV84).

5. The majority of translations (ASV, ESV, NASB95, NET, NIV84, ,NKJV) use "ought." I felt that "obligated" communicates more clearly the seriousness of the response (HCSB).

6. The majority translate it as "of His Spirit" (ASV, ESV, NASB95, NET, NIV84, NKJV). This is a more neutral rendering and does not see the gen. as partitive as I have taken it (along with HCSB). See the commentary below for my reasoning.

7. With ESV, NET, NIV84. Others have: "has punishment" (ASV), "involves torment" (NKJV), and "involves punishment" (HCSB, NASB95).

his literary dualism along with the repeated use of πᾶς and ὅς in this paragraph and the ones to follow shows affinities to wisdom literature (Strecker, 143).[8]

Houlden (112–13) notes the lack of clear connections between verses 6 and 7. From this he deduces evidence that 1 John was composed from a collection of Johannine "pieces" or "homilies" rather than being John's work reflecting his literary style and rhetorical strategy. However, when one sees a new section beginning here, the break is natural and need not imply an editor collecting sayings and piecing them together.

What the broader section teaches is that experiencing eternal life is contingent on our love for one another and that love in action produces assurance of salvation in the loving Christian. John begins this paragraph by reminding us that love for one another demonstrates that we are born of and know (relationally) God. He has been warning his readers about false teachers. He now turns to genuine expression of faith in the life of the believer. What he says is that love for one another demonstrates relationship with God and is the proper response to his manifested love through Christ.

4:7 John begins this section with a command and its justification, or motivation for obedience. He calls out to his fellow brothers and sisters in Christ to obey Jesus' command to love one another.[9] He will explain in the verses that follow why such obedience is the natural and proper response of God's children. These serve as a reminder to us that "fellowship with God and with his Son involves fellowship with one another" (Lenski, 494).

Ἀγαπητοί, ἀγαπῶμεν ἀλλήλους, "Beloved, let us love one another." Addressing his readers once more with one of his characteristic terms, John commands them to love each other. His choice of "beloved" once more reflects his pastoral care and love (Smalley, 236). It may also indicate he may be intending a word play (alliteration) by placing ἀγαπητοί alongside ἀγαπῶμεν (Brown, 513).

---

8. Kistemaker (330) has suggested that these first few verses are poetic. This might be tempting to see, especially in light of the chorus based on vv seven and eight. Strecker (143) correctly rejects this on the basis that no clear parallelisms are apparent. The antitheses do not reflect Hebrew parallelism and the arguments do not evidence any special structural development that would indicate stanzas.

9. Bruce (107) defines love in this passage as "a consuming passion for the well-being of others."

Using the 1 hortatory subjunctive ἀγαπῶμεν, John includes himself and calls on his readers to love one another along with him.[10] The first person plural, beginning here and throughout this section, is inclusive and relates what John says specifically to the Christian community (Haas, de Jonge, and Swellengrebel, 107; Smalley, 237). His use of this form of command communicates his recognition of his own need along with theirs. Moreover, he commits himself to loving them even as he calls for their love. As a present subjunctive, it implies a pattern of action that is continuous and so communicates the idea of "'let us go on loving one another' as we have been doing all along" (Lenski, 495).[11]

Burdick (317) argues that ἀγαπῶμεν should be taken as an indicative rather than imperative because "the main point being expressed in verses 7 through 16 is not an exhortation to love but a declaration that Christians do love because they have been born of God, who is love." However, John's pattern throughout the epistle is to call for proper responses to God's truths. Ἀγαπῶμεν was previously used in 3:18 and will be repeated in 4:19 with the same meaning, though without objects (Bultmann, 65). Thus it is an imperative, not indicative (Strecker, 143). Thus it is better to see him repeating the command rather than switching to a statement.

By his use of the reciprocal pronoun ἀλλήλους John focuses attention on the relationship of fellow believers and the need for love within the family of God more than the need to love all of humanity.[12] Interpreters see the referent of ἀλλήλων in one of three ways. (1) It includes all mankind (Brown, 514; Bultmann, 65–66). (2) It includes both God and nonbelieving neighbor (Schnackenburg, 228–29; Smalley, 234; Stott, 163). (3) It is limited to the Christian community (Burdick, 317; Grayston, 124). This is indicated by the command of verse 11 and the statement that God abides in those who love one another (Thompson, 120, n.).

Further, this use of ἀλλήλους makes this a call to mutual responsibility within the body of Christ, and not a command for "reciprocal love" (contra Bultmann, 66). The command does not assume we receive love in return for our love, but that we are to each love the other regardless.

---

10. D. B. Wallace, *Grammar*, 464–65.

11. Brown (513) allows the possibility that it has a durative force, but does not require it.

12. D. B. Wallace, *Grammar*, 351. BDAG, 46.

Though Scripture is clear that we are to demonstrate God's love by doing good to all men (Rom 12:17–18; Gal 6:10; Phil 4:5; 1 Tim 2:1–4; Titus 3:1–2), this command does not focus on our showing love to nonbelievers. The world's need for God's love and our role in communicating it to that world is not John's focus. Rather, John provides three reasons for believers to exercise mutual love within the family of God.[13]

ὅτι ἡ ἀγάπη ἐκ τοῦ θεοῦ ἐστιν, "because love is from God." The first reason to pursue mutual love within the body of Christ is the source of love, namely, God. John introduces his explanations with ὅτι functioning causally. Where Law (398) sees this ὅτι indicating a test of life, Burdick (318) counters that it introduces "an explanation of why the believer loves" rather than how to determine if one is a believer. John's address of his readers as "beloved" here, as well as the other terms of endearment and his assurance in 2:12–14 makes clear that he regards his readers as believers. Thus providing a "test" for them to discern that runs counter to John's message, especially what he will say in 5:13. John does not want them to question their salvation but to be certain of it. Thus he speaks to them as regenerate saints. Tests to determine if they are spiritually alive would undermine that assurance. However, one would expect him to provide tests of their relationship with God within his family. In that sense the Test of Fellowship view might seem to be in order here. However, it seems best to see him not addressing the question of fellowship within the family of God here as much as communicating the implications and obligations that arise from being a part of that family.

John's repeated use of the article with love particularizes the love he is describing: it is not a generic love but a specific kind of love (Burdick, 317). Using his characteristic construction of the subject forward in the clause and the verb at the end for emphasis, John identifies the source of love once more. Repeating the ἐκ τοῦ θεοῦ formula, John once more identifies love's source. It is sourced in God (Brown, 513; Haas, de Jonge, and Swellengrebel, 120). It arises from his person and values. Marshall (211) sees

---

13. Burdick (317) observes that, though ἀγαπητοί is not limited to passages on love, of its eight uses in this epistle, six are connected to discussions on love (2:7; 3:21; 4:7, 11; 3 John 2; 3 John 5). The two exceptions are 3:2, discussing judgment before Jesus and the need for purity, and 4:1, discussing false teachers and the need to "test the spirits."

this statement meaning that love both "has its origin in God and belongs to the divine sphere."

The inclusion and placement of ἐστιν in the phrase is emphatic. It is also best to see it having a durative force and so communicating the idea that this is an abiding reality.[14] This connects back to 4:6, so we see that "being from God determines the nature of the community" (Strecker, 143). Moreover, this community is expected to be characterized by love for one another.

καὶ πᾶς ὁ ἀγαπῶν ἐκ τοῦ θεοῦ γεγέννηται, "and everyone who loves has been born from God." The second reason for believers pursuing love of fellow believers is that it reflects their spiritual parentage.[15] These words reflect back on 3:7–10, especially verse 10. Just as righteous conduct "manifests" one's spiritual parentage—with God being their heavenly Father (3:1—so, too, does the practice of loving believers. John communicates this truth here with πᾶς ὁ and the present participle ἀγαπῶν used "as a generalization to describe a category of people" (Harris, 184; also Brown, 514).[16] Strecker (144) calls this a "generalizing πᾶς," with love directed either toward God or others. Williamson (142) translates it with a purely progressive nuance and sees this expressing a "lifestyle." Though the πᾶς is generalizing, the articular present participle should still be seen with its gnomic force. John is still describing character that leads to conduct rather than the conduct itself. Thus, the articular present participle with πᾶς carries the sense of "everyone who" and thereby particularizes the statement as another principle impacting John's readers individually more than corporately.[17] This is a reality that, though true of all of humanity, is even more true of them and should motivate each to action. Though it involves the life of the corporate body, this cannot be accomplished apart from individual action. Each of them should

---

14. B. M. Fanning, *Verbal Aspect in New Testament Greek*, 208.

15. Bultmann (66) interprets this as "love of neighbor." Schnackenburg (229) rejects this on the grounds that love of Christian brothers is the theme of this section.

16. Harris (184–85) sees this used in conjunction with John's conceptual dualism ("polar opposites") in order to "categorize" "the opponents on the one hand and the readers, whom the author regards as genuine Christians, on the other." Rather than seeing opponents, the contrast is better seen as being between his readers and the unbelieving world. This was Jesus' concern in the upper room (John 15:18–25). Additionally, as John reflects on Jesus' instructions there, he reflects those themes in this epistle.

17. Burdick (318) focuses on the progressive ("continuing action") nature of the pres. tense when interpreting the sense of ὁ ἀγαπῶν.

be moved to love other believers because this is the natural response of a family member who belongs. Additionally, loving other believers can then become a source of assurance in that one can see he or she is a part of the family of God by his or her conduct within the family.

The words πᾶς ὁ ἀγαπῶν do not look at the cause of spiritual birth but at its effect (Brooke, 118). Birth (γεγέννηται) is the cause, love (ἀγαπῶν) is the effect. As Schnackenburg (228) says, "The true Christian is one who loves."[18] Even so, we must remember that John is focusing on love's relationship to God and regeneration. Love in and of itself does not prove one is spiritually alive (Marshall, 212; Rensberger, 117; Yarbrough, 235). The unregenerate are capable of loving as well. Walls and Anders (209) point to the image of God in all men as evidence that even nonbelievers can express God's nature at times. Thus we need not forget this as John speaks absolutely once again. Thus we need to remember that John is not addressing the question of the presence of love in all men, but its absence in believers and the inconsistency that it represents.

The verb γεννάω as used here "means to be fathered by God and thus a child of God" (Harris, 185). The perfect passive γεγέννηται is the third of five uses by John in this epistle (2:29; 3:9; 4:7; 5:1, 4) and likely a perfect of resulting state, thus focusing on completed results.[19] Burge (186) concurs and sees this perfect "suggesting that divine rebirth is past, yet bearing fruit in the present. A person once converted now demonstrates the fruit of that conversion."[20] It is a birth that occurred in the past and continues to the present (Akin, 178). "Born of God" alludes to Jesus' words to Nicodemus in the upper room (John 3:3–6).[21] However, unlike Jesus' discussion with Nicodemus of the *need* for spiritual rebirth, John uses the intensive perfect to describe the *state* of the person. Those who love believers reveal the source of their spiritual birth. Using the same imagery as earlier (3:10), as God's children they are acting in accordance with their parentage. Lenski (495–96) makes this connection with chapter three and says "The exercise of this love for one another evidences our origin from God ... and proves

18. ... der echte Christ ein Liebender ist.

19. B. M. Fanning, *Verbal Aspect in New Testament Greek*, 291–95.

20. Burdick (318) identifies this as an intensive pf. that communicates the fact that the person has been born into the family of God.

21. John's repeated use of ἐκ τοῦ θεοῦ is emphatic.

that we are no longer 'the children of the devil.'" As Bruce (107) notes, John's point is that "the children of God must reproduce their Father's nature."

καὶ γινώσκει τὸν θεόν, "and knows God." The third thing that mutual love reveals is the individual's knowledge of God.[22] Moving from the perfect tense to describe their state of spiritual birth, John uses the present tense γινώσκει to describe the conditional experience of the believer.[23] This use of the present tense of γινώσκω indicates the believer is continuing to grow in knowledge (Akin, 178) and suggests relationship (Smalley, 238).[24] Reviewing the concept introduced in 2:3–6, John affirms that in loving other Christians the believer can know that he "knows" God experientially.[25] This likely alludes to Jesus' words in John 14:7 once again, words addressed to men whose salvation cannot be questioned. Though we often use the phrase "to know God" to mean "to have exercised justifying faith in God" or "to be a Christian," John teaches that justified believers may not "know" the God in whom they believe (Grayston, 124). This knowledge of God is conditioned on meeting certain criteria, such as obedience and love of other Christians. The disciples were with Jesus more than three years and still did not "know" him. Modern disciples can be in the family of God for decades and still not really know him as well.

---

22. Burdick (318) sees this clause, which he sees as unnecessary to the flow of thought, as "aimed at the Gnostics." However, John employs repetition throughout the epistle for emphasis. The importance of this truth is made clear precisely because it is interjected once more into the flow of thought.

23. Γινώσκει is gnomic rather than progressive or customary. Westcott (148) observes well, "The combination of γεγέννηται with γινώσκει (not ἔγνωκεν) is significant. Living knowledge is regarded only in its present activity."

24. "As the presence of active love is the pledge of advancing knowledge, so the absence of love is the proof that apparent knowledge was not real" (Westcott, 148).

25. Strecker (144) sees "know" to indicate the person "acknowledges God" by their love for him and others. John's focus on relationship with God from the beginning of this epistle indicates that he would have a more relational sense here.

Schnackenburg (228) sees this clause affirming one's salvation. He says, "If the 'begetting of God' refers more to the believer's origin, then 'knowing God' means even more so to have permanent fellowship with God. Only someone who has proven to be one who loves demonstrates - by this love - that he shares God's nature and fellowship." (Wenn sich die "Zeugung aus Gott" mehr auf den Ursprung bezieht, so "Gott erkennen" stärker auf die bleibende Gemeinschaft mit Gott. Nur wer sich als Liebender erweist, zeigt – eben durch seine Liebe --, daß er Gottes Art und Gemeinschaft besitzt.)

Burge (186) after observing John's turn to the present tense notes that this implies "that love is connected to an ongoing awareness of who God is. Why did John select these particular words? Spiritual rebirth and divine knowledge were no doubt promoted among the secessionists (see 3:9)." Though John may have the gnostic heresy in mind as he says this (Kistemaker, 331), it need not be such. Though Gnosticism claimed special knowledge of God, fully developed Gnosticism was still decades away.[26] John's use of γινώσκω varies significantly from later developed gnostic thought, and so too that of incipient Gnosticism. His knowledge of God is relational, not special or mystical.

4:8 This verse provides the contrast to the previous description of the child of God manifested through love for believers (Johnson, 102).[27] It raises the question of whether John's statement describes an essential nature of God or an attribute in focus in this discussion.[28]

ὁ μὴ ἀγαπῶν οὐκ ἔγνω τὸν θεόν, "The one not loving has not known God." In contrast to the believer who loves, there is "the one not loving." John develops his contrast by using the identical words of the previous sentence with the negative particle μὴ replacing πᾶς. No stronger contrast can be made. These are opposites. However, herein lies the problem. The contrast is with someone who loves other Christian brothers and sisters. If this implication is to be continued as part of the discussion, then this is not someone who is simply "unloving" in a general sense but someone who is not showing love to a *fellow believer*.

Hodges (183) argues that John's failure to deny (by stating plainly) this unloving person's birth from God is significant. While the one loving evidences birth from God, this unloving person only evidences a lack of knowledge of God. Hodges (184) concludes, "It is a fact, both of Scripture

26. N. Perrin, "Gnosticism," in *Dictionary for Theological Interpretation of the Bible*, 256–59; D. M. Scholer, s.v."Gnosis, Gnosticism," in *Dictionary of the Later New Testament and Its Developments*.

27. Schnackenburg (229) views this verse as a polemic against the gnostics. However, nothing in this paragraph requires a gnostic background. Rather, John is describing eternal truths that all believers understand regardless of the cause of their unloving conduct.

28. Brown (548) finds in this antithetical statement evidence of a chiasm with what precedes. Strecker (144, n. 14) correctly rejects this on the basis that nothing at the end of v. 7 can be coupled with "God is love" in v. 8.

and of Christian experience, that one Christian *can* hate another" (italics his). However, John provides textual clues that he may not have a believer in mind when he affirms this. His change from the present tense γινώσκει to the aorist ἔγνω seems intended to affirm that failure to love indicates that the person has *not* come to know God (Lenski, 496; Strecker, 144).[29] Though knowledge of God is relational as John uses it, and normally a sanctification reality, it is also a justification reality. One not related to God cannot know him relationally. Additionally, this change to the aorist form of γινώσκω draws a closer parallel to the perfect γεγέννηται in the previous sentence.[30] Interestingly, Jesus uses this same verb and tense (ἔγνων) in Matt 7:23 with those he will refuse entrance into his kingdom.[31] Thus this use of γινώσκω should be viewed as a perfect aorist John is affirming that one characterized by a lack of love has never really known God who is love. This statement appears to be similar to 3:6, which Strecker (144) notes demonstrates that "sin and knowledge of God are mutually exclusive" and that "the one who does not love belongs to the world and has no community with God." Granted, John never actually says that the person who does not love is not born of God (v. 7).[32] However, as a minimum he is affirming that

29. Johnson (102) considers the aor. construction of οὐκ ἔγνω to indicate "the decisive and absolute character" of those who do not know God.

30. Strecker (144) suggests that this may be a rare use of a gnomic aor.

31. Yarbrough (236) observes that γινώσκω is negated five other times in the New Testament (John 1:10; 17:25; 1 Cor 1:21; 1 John 3:1; and Rom 10:19 with Israel) and all six occurrences involve failing to know God. The same negation occurs in the LXX in Isa 1:3 and Jer 8:7. Isa 1:3 reads: ἔγνω βοῦς τὸν κτησάμενον καὶ ὄνος τὴν φάτνην τοῦ κυρίου αὐτοῦ, Ισραηλ δέ με οὐκ ἔγνω, καὶ ὁ λαός με οὐ συνῆκεν. Jer 8:7 reads: καὶ ἡ ασιδα ἐν τῷ οὐρανῷ ἔγνω τὸν καιρὸν αὐτῆς, τρυγὼν καὶ χελιδών, ἀγροῦ στρουθία ἐφύλαξαν καιροὺς εἰσόδων αὐτῶν, ὁ δὲ λαός μου οὐκ ἔγνω τὰ κρίματα κυρίου.

32. Stott (163–64) sees this describing a non-believer since love demonstrates the "authenticity" of his spiritual life and failure to love denies divine parentage. Barker (342) understands this as a test of life and failure means that a person has "not really been born of him, we do not have his nature."Akin (178) interprets this to mean: "The one who does not love is a stranger to God. He never even began to have a relationship with God; that is, there was never a time when this person could have legitimately claimed that he knew God." This would be more possible if the audience were a mixture of believers and unbelievers and John's discussion was of a general nature. However, he is addressing believers and instructing them how to experience the eternal life they possess. Thus, the context of his audience and message must guide our understanding of individual statements. In this case, we should not be seeing a test of life being applied to John's readers.

one cannot have an intimate relationship with God without loving others. Whoever God indwells will reflect his character. Since God is characterized by love, anyone indwelled by him will express his kind of love. So whoever claims to know God personally, experientially and yet does not love other believers is lying, whether to others or to himself or herself.

ὅτι ὁ θεὸς ἀγάπη ἐστίν, "because God is love." This is the second statement in this epistle of God's nature (1:5). Two other places in Scripture we are given similar declarations. In John 4:24 Jesus told the woman at the well, "God is spirit." In Heb 12:29 we learn that "our God is a consuming fire."[33] Introducing this declaration of God's nature with a causal ὅτι (Lenski 498; Strecker, 144), John explains why one cannot know God without loving others. It is in God's nature to love, and those connected to him will reflect his passion.

John's declaration, "God is love," is not an ontological statement and cannot be reversed (Bruce, 107; Harris, 185; Kruse, 157; Strecker, 148). The subject has the article and "love" is anarthrous (Painter, 266).[34] Though "love is of God," love is not God. This is another description of God's character, one of his communicable moral attributes, not his essential being (Bultmann, 66; Smalley, 239–40; Strecker, 148). Brown (195) says of John's "God is" formulas, "While there is emphasis on God's activity, that activity is internally related to what God is before creation." Further, it cannot be made either *a* or *the* most important or controlling of his attributes. However, it is one that believers can, and are expected to, express. God is no more "love" than he is "light," though both describe his character and nature in some sense, light being a metaphor for holiness and purity while love is to be understood literally. Even so, love as defined by John is not so much emotional as volitional. It is God's motive behind what he does more than it is his emotional response or attitude toward his children, though that is understood to be true as well. Rensberger (117) says, "'God is love' is not a speculative statement about the divine nature, but a claim about God's actions. Love is a personal activity, not an abstract quality." Lieu (177) concurs. "Love is not an abstract idea but is known through what

---

33. The text reads ὁ θεὸς ἡμῶν πῦρ καταναλίσκον. Of note is the absence of εἰμι from this declaration as well as Jesus' (John 4:24).

34. B. M. Fanning (*Verbal Aspect in New Testament Greek*, 208) sees "God is love" as a gnomic pres.

God has done toward women and men." Marshall (212) identifies the point of John's affirmation, which will be developed in the verses that follow. He says well, "A person cannot come into a real relationship with a loving God without being transformed into a loving person." Further, we are reminded, "'God is love' means not simply that love is *one* of his activities, but that *all* his activity is loving" (Smalley, 239; italics his).[35]

4:9 In this verse John's focus shifts from God's nature to his actions (Johnson, 102). The manifestation of God's love toward us was his sending his Son to be the propitiation for our sins. John now moves from the theoretical to the practical. These next verses take the truth of verses 7 and 8 and show how it worked itself out in history. This then becomes the Christian's model for action.

ἐν τούτῳ ἐφανερώθη ἡ ἀγάπη τοῦ θεοῦ ἐν ἡμῖν, "This is how the love of God was manifested toward us." John continues his discussion of God's love by describing how it expressed itself.[36] He illustrates to his readers how to express love toward one another practically by describing God's own actions. This is similar to Paul's use of Jesus' incarnation as an illustration of what he meant by considering others more important than oneself in Phil 2:3–11. Thus John begins with the logical connective ἐν τούτῳ. This use of ἐν τούτῳ looks forward once again to the "explanatory" ὅτι clause to complete its idea (Brown, 515; Burdick, 320; Culy, 107; Haas, de Jonge, and Swellengrebel, 121; Strecker, 149; Yarbrough, 237). Though it could be translated literally as "by means of this," the idea of "this is how" expresses the point John is making that God's own action on our behalf shows us how we are to act.

35. Grayston (124–25) does not see this describing God's nature, nor His activity, but "defining the condition on which God may be known." This truth creates a demand just as God is light called for Christians to walk in the light.

36. D. Rusam (*Die Gemeinschaft der Kinder Gottes,* 111) emphasizes that God's fatherhood involves caring love and says, "Thus, in 1 John God's command for brotherly love is not based on God's fatherly authority by which he has the ability to command, but on his fatherly love." (So wird im 1Joh das Gebot der Gottes—und Bruderliebe weniger auf Gottes väterliche Macht zurückgeführt, durch die er die Möglichkeit hat zu gebieten, sondern auf seine väterliche Liebe.)

John uses the aorist form of φανερόω to describe the manifestation, or visible expression, of God's love.[37] Burge (187) describes this as "a word that refers to the disclosure of things formerly hidden." Strecker (149) sees this as a christological term. Though Lieu (180) describes understands the aorist here to indicate "a specific moment," it seems better to see this as a historical aorist (Lenski, 500), similar to the aorist of 1:2 and as a reference to Jesus' coming, not our conversion.[38] His choice of ἐφανερώθη indicates that it was made visible. It was demonstrated.

Love "appearing" indicates that it could be experienced by humans. It is not just theoretical or philosophically present but practically and measurably (Strecker, 149). This same truth is affirmed by Paul in Rom 5:8. Christ died for us, but not because God wanted to demonstrate his love and that was the medium he chose to accomplish his aim. Rather, Christ's dying for us was the response and expression of God's love. When he acted on our behalf we then recognized it as that expression of his love toward us. Jesus' death demonstrated his love though it was not intended as a demonstration of anything.

The genitive construction describing God's love seems best as a subjective genitive, "God's love," rather than divine love as a concept (Burdick, 320; Lieu, 180; Painter, 266; Rensberger, 119; Yarbrough, 237).[39] It is followed by the epexegetical ὅτι clause that explains it (Harris, 186; Lenski, 501). This is not God's kind of love, but the expression of his love.

The sense of ἐν ἡμῖν is interpreted in one of three ways:

---

37. Bultmann (67) defines ἐφανερώθη as "the revelation in the historical event of Jesus' appearance." Schnackenburg (228) defines it as "to become open to experience through God's sending of his only Son into the world." (Darin ist die Liebe Gottes "erschienen", d. H. Erfahrbar geworden, daß er seinen einzigen Sohn in die Welt sandte.)

38. J. P. Louw, ("Verbal Aspect in the First Letter of John," 102) notes: "It is characteristic of the style of the First Letter of John, and likewise of the Gospel of John which is probably by the same author, to alternate the tenses when they repeat each other in the same context." He identifies the series of aor. and perfects in vv 9–14 (ἀπέσταλκεν ... ἠγαπήκαμεν ... ἠγάπησεν ... ἀπέστειλεν ... ἠγάπησεν ... ἀπέσταλκεν) as an example of this. He then notes that the "force of these tenses are that of the perfects, the aor. are reduction forms. To seek for any distinction of meaning between the perfects and aorists in this passage would distort the stylistic effect."

39. Smalley (240) sees this as an objective gen. emphasizing God as the agent.

(1) God's love was directed "toward us," or "for us" (Haas, de Jonge, and Swellengrebel, 122; Schnackenburg, 229, n. 4). Lenski (500) translates this as "in connection with us." In its favor are similar uses found in John 9:3 and in 2 Cor 4:10.[40] However, Brooke (119) counters that John would most likely have used ἡ ἀγάπη τοῦ θεοῦ (ἡ) εἰς ἡμᾶς if he had wanted to communicate this idea.

(2) It can function as a dative of sphere and mean "in our midst" or "among us" (Brown, 516; Burdick, 320; Johnson, 103; Kruse, 158; Lieu, 180; Painter, 266; Smalley 2:40; Stott, 164; Westcott, 149; Smalley, 240; Yarbrough, 238). This follows the special nuance of the preposition (Strecker, 149). Examples of this use include Gal 1:16; Matt 2:6; 1 Cor 2:6; 11:19; 2 Cor 4:3. The preposition can mean "among" when it is followed by a plural noun as here (Burdick, 320): "Thus the manifestation was not an internal experience, 'in us,' but an objective historical event that happened 'among us.'"

(3) Functioning as a dative of sphere, it may mean "within" us (Brooke, 119; Harris, 186; Moody, 91; Thompson, 121–23).[41] Since God dwelling in believers has been mentioned in this context, this third option seems best.

ὅτι τὸν υἱὸν αὐτοῦ τὸν μονογενῆ ἀπέσταλκεν ὁ θεὸς εἰς τὸν κόσμον ἵνα ζήσωμεν δι' αὐτοῦ, "that God sent his unique Son into the world in order that we might live through him." The manner in which God's love was manifested is described in another epexegetical ὅτι clause (Burdick, 320). This clause is emphatic in its construction (Lenski, 501). John has exchanged positions between the subject and verb and moved the verb's direct object to the beginning of the sentence. This serves to emphasize the subject: God.

John uses the same terminology to describe Jesus as he had used in John 3:16, referring to him as God's "unique [μονογενῆ] Son." John is the only biblical author who employs this description of Jesus. This term designates uniqueness rather than physical birth (Grayston, 125; Kruse 159).[42] For example, in Heb 11:17–18 Isaac is described as Abraham's unique

40. BDF §220 (1) sees this use of ἐν ἡμῖν to be ἐν used for "the customary dative" and to carry the sense of "in our case." The prepositional phrase ἐν ἡμῖν is better translated "toward us" (dative of reference) rather than as "among us" (dative of sphere).

John 9:3 reads ἵνα φανερωθῇ τὰ ἔργα τοῦ θεοῦ ἐν αὐτῷ while here it is ἡ ἀγάπη τοῦ θεοῦ ἐν ἡμῖν.

41. Williamson (143) sees it as both "among" and "within."

42. BDAG, 658. F. Büchsel, "μονογενής," *TDNT* 4:739–41. In describing Jesus as God's unique Son, John places the adj. μονογενῆ in a second attributive adj. position

(μονογενῆ) son of promise though he was his second son by birth. Although we are called "sons of God" (Gal 3:26), we are not sons in the same way Jesus is; his sonship is unique. This term is used elsewhere of an only son in Luke 7:12; 9:38 and an only daughter in Luke 8:42. It is used of Isaac in Heb 11:17. It has this same sense in John 1:14, 18; 3:16, 18. In the LXX this term is used to designate Jephthah's daughter as his only child (Judg 11:34).[43] Beale and Carson describe well its use outside the New Testament. "In both Old Testament and Second Temple literature the Son of David and Israel are called God's "firstborn" or even "only" son (cf. Ps. 89:27; *4 Ezra* 6:58; *Pss. Sol.* 18:4; *Jub.* 18:2, 11, 15)." This concept is developed by John to indicate Jesus is "God's 'one-of-a-kind' Son *par excellence*, Jesus (cf. 1:18; 3:16, 18; 1 John 4:9)." It is related to his designation as God's "beloved son."[44]

John's choice of ἀποστέλλω over πέμπω reflects the difference in focus between the two verbs.[45] Πέμπω is more related to sending a messenger or someone for purposes of communication. On the other hand, ἀποστέλλω includes the idea of sending with a commission (Kistemaker, 333).[46] It also implies Jesus' preexistence (Johnson, 103). Further, the perfect tense ἀπέσταλκεν reflects the continuing impact of Christ's accomplished work in his incarnation (Akin, 179; Plummer, 102; Williamson, 144). As an extensive perfect ἀπέσταλκεν ("has sent") focuses on the completed act at the time of writing. The Son is no longer being sent.[47]

---

in order to emphasize both the noun and adj. and thereby both His uniqueness and deity (Akin, 179; Kistemaker, 333).

43. The text refers to her as his only daughter, and clarifies the sense with the following clause. καὶ αὕτη μονογενὴς αὐτῷ ἀγαπητή, καὶ οὐκ ἔστιν αὐτῷ πλὴν αὐτῆς υἱὸς ἢ θυγάτηρ.

44. G. K. Beale and D. A. Carson, *Commentary on the New Testament Use of the Old Testament*, 423.

45. This is the first mention of "sending" in the epistle, though it was a common term in his Gospel (Brown, 517).

46. BDAG, 120; K. Rengstorf, "ἀποστέλλω (πέμπω)," *TDNT* 1:403–405. Rengstorf says, "In John's Gospel ἀποστέλλειν is used by Jesus when His concern is to ground His authority in that of God as the One who is responsible for His words and works and who guarantees their right and truth. On the other hand, He uses the formula ὁ πέμψας με (πατήρ) to affirm the participation of God in His work in the *actio* of His sending."

Moody (91) calls Jesus' coming as "an objective event in history."

47. Haas, de Jonge, and Swellengrebel (108) and Smalley (241) understand the perfect to indicate that the impact of Jesus' coming continues to this day. D. B.

Interpreters are divided on the sense of κόσμος in this verse. (1) Some see it as negative; it is the world in opposition to God (Lieu, 180). Strecker (151) says it is "subjected to the domination of sin and is governed by nothingness and enmity toward God." Moody (92) describes it as "godless." Even so, it is inhabited by the people that are loved by God just as it was in John 3:16. (2) Others see it as neutral. Burdick (322) does not see κόσμος having an "ethical sense" here, but says it should be taken literally as describing "the place where people live" (also Smalley, 242). Brown (517) sees it as positive because it is part of an "incarnational formula," and the pattern is for these formulations to have a positive view of κόσμος. He points to its use in 4:14 where Jesus is sent as "Savior of the world." For him this indicates the sense it should be given here. Either view the meaning intended by John does not change. However, it does seem better to see John's use as neutral here.

This final ἵνα clause gives the purpose of Jesus' incarnation. We are the beneficiaries. This is a clear reference to our justification. As noted before, we were the focus of Jesus' incarnation, not God. God's motivation for sending his son was our need, not his benefit. What he did, he did for us, to give us life. When we listen in on the conversation of his Son in the Garden of Gethsemane, we see that there was no other way for us to have life. If there were any other way, God would have taken it and Jesus would not have gone to the cross. If any other religion could provide salvation, or if it were possible to live a sinless life, or if there were *any* other way that men could receive or achieve forgiveness of sins, the loving Father would not have sacrificed his beloved Son to offer an alternate or additional route. Not only is it not intolerant to say such; it is blasphemous to suggest otherwise. God's love for us compelled him to send his Son. His Son's love for both the Father and us compelled him to willingly obey.

Of interest is John's use of ὁ θεὸς late in its clause. As Lieu (180) notes, since John had already used τοῦ θεοῦ in the previous clause, a pronoun would have been expected. However, his emphasis on God is such that where he has often referred to him with pronouns, even without an antecedent, in

---

Wallace (*Grammar*, 574) cautions against giving the perfect a meaning of eternal or permanent results and "one must be careful not to read his or her theology into the syntax."

Bultmann (67) considers ἀπέσταλκεν here is equivalent to ἔδωκεν in John 3:16.

this paragraph he is emphasizing God's work and less often resorts to the pronoun. This repetition of θεὸς is intentional and emphatic.[48]

With his singular use of the verb ζάω John describes the purpose of God's action.[49] His use of the first person plural includes John with the community of faith (Kruse, 158). Burdick (322) sees John's use of the aorist subjunctive ζήσωμεν to be an ingressive aorist and thus focusing on our spiritual birth (Johnson, 104; Smalley, 242), our acquisition of life more than the experience of it.[50]

John's use of δι' αὐτοῦ could either look at source (Brown, 518) or means (Johnson, 104). Source seems like the sense here in that the thrust of these verses has been on God's work in Christ as the defining expression of his love. John is not describing how God saves people, but why and through whom. As Stott (164) notes well, John is telling us, "While the origin of love is in the being of God, the manifestation of love is in the coming of Christ."

4:10 This verse is both parallel in thought to v 9 and develops its thought further. Where John sends his Son in v 9, we are now told the purpose of his coming and the nature of his mission.

---

48. Smalley (242) and Haas, de Jonge, and Swellengrebel (108) suggest that it is redundant from the previous verse and may indicate this statement is drawn "from a traditional formulation." This is speculative. It seems better to see John using repetition as a literary device to insure his focus on God and His love is unmistakable.
49. The ἵνα may be either purpose or result. The context does not provide enough information to discern which and both senses are true. Smalley (242) opts for both. Painter (269) notes that this does not say God sent His Son to save the world, only those identified as "we." He correctly cautions against taking this to mean "a foreordained group selected" for salvation (election). It does not. However, election is clearly taught in Scripture (Rom 8:29; 9:23; Eph 1:4–5, 11).
50. Williamson (143) sees the subjunctive mood indicating that this "life" is not "irrevocable" but "conditional. One may have life by accepting Christ, but one may forfeit life by rejecting Christ." This is an example of reading one's theology into the grammar. Being in a ἵνα clause, the verb of necessity must be subjunctive. Thus the conditional aspect of the subjunctive is not the point of the clause. That being said, it must be noted that the conditional aspect of the subjunctive mood involves its potentiality more than its continuance unless the context clearly indicates that such is the focus. The idea of "might live" has to do with whether one is enabled to enter into life or not, not whether one can maintain that life. The point being made by John has to do with Jesus' work in giving life, not in maintaining it.

ἐν τούτῳ ἐστὶν ἡ ἀγάπη, "In this is love." Beginning this sentence with the same prepositional phrase and sense, "by means of this," John further clarifies what he has said in the previous verse.[51] This is another instance where ἐν τούτῳ looks forward to an epexegetical ὅτι clause, in this case to two of them (Culy, 108; Haas, de Jonge, and Swellengrebel, 123). By the repetition of ἀποστέλλω John links the purpose of Jesus' coming with its significance. What follows will explain the means by which love was expressed by God.

Love here is the love of God and not love in its absolute sense (Strecker, 152). John's use of the article with love removes it from the abstract conceptual sphere into the concrete world of reality (Lenski, 502). This is an "article of previous reference" (Lenski, 502), whereby John is reminding his readers that he has been talking about this love already and they can understand it from the immediate context.

οὐχ ὅτι ἡμεῖς ἠγαπήκαμεν τὸν θεὸν, "not that we have loved God." Introducing this clause with its negative particle brought forward in the sentence, John emphasizes what is *not* true of God's motives before communicating his reason for sending Jesus (Westcott, 150). With this he introduces us to an antithetical statement that contrast's human love with God's (Strecker, 152). This makes clear that God's love and the actions it initiated were not a response to any love on our part. His actions were motivated purely from his own nature and concern, not ours. To think that God looked into the future and saw anyone's response to him and based his saving action on that person's future attitude or action, would be to place salvation into the hands of men and wrest it from the hands of God. In everyone's salvation God is not the responder, but the initiator (John 1:12–13; Rom 9:11; Eph 1:4–5, 11; 2:8–9; Jas 1:18).

The perfect tense verb ἠγαπήκαμεν in this instance does not focus on the completed results (intensive perfect), that we continue to love God, nor on the past choice to love (extensive perfect) but on the fact that we never did love God prior to his action. One might argue that this is an aorist perfect that parallels the other aorist verbs in the sentence and focuses

---

51. Burdick (322–23) takes this ἐν as locative rather than means. The phrase is then explained by the epexegetical ὅτι clause that follows. For him this sentence is a definition of love. He bases this on the presence of the article and the absence of any other modifier with love, and so is saying: "This is what love 'in and of itself' is."

simply on the fact of our not loving God prior to him sending his Son.[52] That would make the change to the perfect a stylistic variation. However, John's changes in tense are not stylist, but deliberately chosen to communicate ideas. Strecker (152) understands John's choice of the perfect was "to express the endurance of love" while the aorist would have communicated only "its unique occurrence." Thus God was not responding to our love when he acted.

ἀλλ᾽ ὅτι αὐτὸς ἠγάπησεν ἡμᾶς, "but that he loved us." Using the strong adversative ἀλλά, John gives the real reason for God's actions.[53] He was moved by his own love, not ours. Additionally, his inclusion of the pronoun before the verb makes clear that it was he, God, who was doing the loving and we were receiving it. Again, this antithetical statement should not be seen as a response to any opponents but a clear explanation of God's actions on our behalf (Strecker, 152; contra Bultmann, 68).

καὶ ἀπέστειλεν τὸν υἱὸν αὐτοῦ ἱλασμὸν περὶ τῶν ἁμαρτιῶν ἡμῶν, "and sent his son *to be* a propitiation for our sins." John uses the aorist ἀπέστειλεν to speak of God's past action. He sent his Son, but does not continue to do so.[54] Of interest is John's choice of the aorist over and against the perfect. By this he is emphasizing the sending, but not its continuance at the time of his writing. He sees Jesus' coming to be the propitiation for our sins as a completed event.

The term, ἱλασμὸν, may refer to either the "appeasement necessitated by sin" or the "instrument for appeasing," the sacrifice itself.[55] Here John is using it with reference to Jesus serving as the atoning sacrifice, thus as the

---

52. This might be argued from what appears to be an editorial change to the aor. in the majority of MSS. The versions with the aor. ἠγαπήσαμεν appears to be an attempt to align this verb with the other aor. verbs in its immediate context (Burdick, 232; Strecker, 152).

53. This "strong adversative ... expresses sharp contrast between man's love and God's love" (Burdick, 323).

54. Burdick (324) sees ἀπέστειλεν pointing to the incarnation. G. Sevenster ("Remarks on the Humanity of Jesus in the Gospel and Letters of John," 189) adds "in the σὰρξ" as understood in this context and so would seem to support his view. However, with ἱλασμὸς as part of the double acc. construction and clearly the purpose of the sending, incarnation is not in view here.

55. BDAG, 474; F. Büchsel, "ἵλεως, ἱλάσκομαι, ἱλασμός," *TDNT* 3:317–18.

instrument. This connects back to 2:2.[56] In 1:7 we saw the benefits of that sacrifice, our constant cleansing through his blood. Thus we see that Jesus is the satisfaction of God's righteous wrath by being our substitute. Here John spells out what Jesus is propitiating—our sins.

4:11 The proper response to God's demonstrated love is love for one another. We now see the application of the truth just stated.

Ἀγαπητοί, εἰ οὕτως ὁ θεὸς ἠγάπησεν ἡμᾶς, "Beloved, if God loved us in this manner." For the last time in this epistle, John addresses his readers with the endearing "beloved" as he prepares to admonish them once again to action.[57] Rather than seeing this starting a new section or introducing a new thought, it is best to see John softening his command with tender words. This is not a correction but an encouragement. However, before admonishing his readers to love, he reminds them of their motivation for loving.

John reminds his readers of the truth of God's love before addressing the obligation that arises from it. He does this using the first class condition (εἰ followed by the indicative), that assumes the truth of its protasis* (Burdick, 324; Culy, 110; Haas, de Jonge, and Swellengrebel, 124; Johnson, 105)[58] and can often be translated by "since" (Burge, 188). However, it is not just God's love to which he points. It is the manner in which God's love manifested itself, and thus his use of οὕτως.[59] This adverb, often translated "thus" or "so," in this kind of construction points the reader to the preceding material or to the moral of a story that has been concluded.[60] By its placement at the head of its clause, John gives it the same emphatic force

56. Harris (188) sees ἱλασμὸς as "propitiation" with "the idea of turning away the divine wrath." Strecker (153) says it is "a synonym for the soteriological action of Jesus Christ." Moody (92) and Williamson (145) still see it as "expiation." Refer to 2:2 for a full discussion of its meaning and proponents of each view.

57. Where over the course of these first 74 verses, he addresses his readers fifteen times with τεκνία, παιδία, or ἀγαπητοί. In the following 30 verses, he will not repeat any of the three terms until the end (5:21). He uses τεκνία in 2:1, 12, 28; 3:7, 18; 4:4; and 5:21, παιδία in 2:14, 18; and Ἀγαπητοί in 2:7; 3:2, 21; 4:1, 7, 11.

58. BDF §371.

59. Lenski (503) sees John's use here as "aimed at Cerinthus, at his following, and all who are of a similar mind." However, being in a parenetic portion of the epistle, it need not have any different significance than it had in John 3:16.

60. BDAG, 742.

as it had in John 3:16, to which this may allude as well (Brown, 519; Bruce, 109; Kistemaker, 334). Further, it looks back on all that has been said from verse 7 on, with special focus on verse 10 (Strecker, 155).[61] Thus the sense of οὕτως is not that God loved us *so much* that he sent his Son, but that his love expressed itself by the sending of his Son.[62] The point is not the volume or intensity of God's love, but its activity and expression.

καὶ ἡμεῖς ὀφείλομεν ἀλλήλους ἀγαπᾶν, "we also are obligated to love one another." Now the application of the truth of God's demonstrated love is brought home by John.[63] John affirms the importance of the truth stated in the protasis through the apodosis. We have an obligation. He uses the same verb here (ὀφείλω) as he had in 2:6, which expressed our obligation to imitate Jesus' walk.

John once again includes himself in the obligation that results from God's work with ἡμεῖς placed in the emphatic position at the head of the clause (Brown, 520).[64] This is not just a moral obligation John wants his readers to fulfill.[65] It is an obligation he himself senses. Further, he does not use the subjunctive, which might have implied a hortatory command. He uses the indicative instead in order to state a fact. This is not a desire but a reality. This is not a passing obligation or one that is to be fulfilled occasionally. Rather, the present indicative implies it is a "continuous obligation" (Burdick, 324). Thus the application of the truth of God's demonstrated love is that we are obligated to love one another in the same way that he loved us. This is the same truth taught by Jesus in the parable of the unforgiving slave (Matt 18:22–34) and his warning after the disciples' prayer (Matt 6:14–15). To experience the forgiveness of God carries with it the obligation to forgive in like manner. To experience the love of God similarly carries with it the obligation of love in like manner.

---

61. Burdick (324) limits it to vv. 9–10.
62. R. H. Gundry and R. W. Howell, "The Sense and Syntax of John 3:14–17," 35–36.
63. BDF §442. Strecker (155) gives this use of *καὶ* a causal sense and provides examples of similar uses in Matt 5:15; John 12:18; 15:8; and Jas 4:7. Brown (520) sees this *καὶ* as "strongly sequential" and should be translated as "in turn." However, it seems best to see its role as adjunctive (Burdick, 324).
64. Brown (520) sees this forming a contrast with "God" in the previous clause. It would seem better to see it identifying us with God in term of our need to imitate him.
65. BDAG, 743; F. Hauck, "ὀφείλω," *TDNT* 5:559–63.

Here John places ἀλλήλους before ἀγαπᾶν. We see this pattern also with Paul (Rom 13:8) and Peter (1 Pet 1:22). Beyond these three uses, the normal word order places the verb first (John 13:34; 15:12, 17; 1 Thess 4:9; 1 John 3:11, 23; 4:7, 12; 2 John 5). By doing this John draws attention to "one another" as opposed to love in this instance (Brown, 520) and thereby shows the importance of this being applied communally rather than selectively. This also stresses the reciprocal nature of that love. Everyone is to be loving everyone else, and to be the recipient of everyone else's love in turn. This is the body of Christ at its best.

4:12 In this and the next few verses John is going to describe the relationship between love for fellow believers and the abiding relationship one has with God, he abiding in us and we in him. After discussing tests of one's salvation in chapter three, John warned his readers to test the false teachers in 4:1–3. The test was doctrinal. What do they say about Jesus? He then discussed love as it relates to God and said that God's love produces action. In the remainder of this chapter he will address the subject of godly love.[66]

θεὸν οὐδεὶς πώποτε τεθέαται, "No one has ever seen God." John introduces this next thought with the enigmatic statement that God has never been seen.[67] He focuses attention on God by moving his name, the direct object of the verb, to the fore of the clause, thereby making it emphatic (Burdick, 325).[68] This is reminiscent of Exodus 33:18–23, where Moses asked to see God and was told he could not see God and live.[69] It is also reminiscent of Jesus' declaration to the disciple in the upper room (John 14:7–11) and repeats the same concept as John 1:18, 5:37, and 6:46.[70]

---

66. Strecker (156) calls this verse "a piece of proverbial wisdom in harmony with the currents of OT-Jewish and Hellenistic Greek tradition."

67. This same truth is taught elsewhere in the New Testament (1 Tim 1:17; Heb 11:7).

68. Brooke (120) and Westcott (151) state that the absence of the article with θεὸν likely emphasizes the "nature and character of God" (Brooke, 120; Westcott, 151). However, the point of the statement is that no one has seen God physically. Inability to understand His nature or character are not in view anywhere in this passage. It is better to see the absence of the article resulting from John using θεὸν as God's name, which is a definite noun with or without the article.

69. It was God's face he was not allowed to see. God did permit him to see his back (Exod 33:23). I believe this was a theophany, not a christophany, and that it was God the Father who met with Moses and declared his glory.

70. Although, in each of those places Jesus uses ὁράω instead of θεάομαι. John 1:18 reads: θεὸν οὐδεὶς ἑώρακεν πώποτε. John 5:37 reads: οὔτε εἶδος αὐτοῦ ἑωράκατε. John

John makes this an absolute statement by his choice of οὐδεὶς. With this he excludes all of humanity, with no exceptions, from ever seeing God (Burdick, 325). It is not just their generation. It is all of humanity from Adam on.

The term for seeing chosen here by John, θεάομαι, can refer to physical sight, though it can also be used figuratively to indicate "understanding" something. However, even when it means to see physically, it expresses the further nuance of perceptive sight. One sees and comprehends the significance of something.[71] John uses θεάομαι to describe his "seeing" eternal life incarnate in the first verses of this epistle. So now, in contrast to his eyewitness experience with Jesus, John reminds his readers of the presence of God invisible.

Here John uses the perfect τεθέαται to describe men's inability to see God. Burdick (325) describes it as an iterative perfect, which would reflect a sense of "careful examination." Westcott (151) rejects the idea of continuous action because that would make it a "fellowship" term. Williamson (145) on the other hand says it indicates God has not been seen in the past and is still not seen in the present. It seems that this would be seen better as a periphrastic perfect (Lenski, 505). By this John is not only saying that no one has seen God up till this time, but wants to alert the readers to the implication of that truth, which will be addressed in what follows.[72]

Many see this as directed against gnostic claims to visions of God, or those made by John's opponents (Barker, 343; Grayston, 126; Marshall, 216; Schnackenburg, 240; Strecker, 156). However, the discussion that follows focuses on life in the community of faith and develops John's pastoral concern over his readers' need to love each other. It is better to see him returning to Jesus' words in the upper room as the source of his ideas rather than false claims of false teachers or a theorized secessionist group. We must remember that the issue of mutual love and unity was central to Jesus' instructions the night of his betrayal. It is this same concern that now drives John.

6:46 reads: οὐχ ὅτι τὸν πατέρα ἑώρακέν τις.

71. BDAG, 445–46, 719; W. Michaelis, "ὁράω, βλέπω, θεάομαι, θεωρέω," *TDNT,* 5:317–18. On the other hand, ὁράω simply means "to see," with no special emphasis on the intensity of observation.

72. B. M. Fanning (*Verbal Aspect in New Testament Greek*, 319) notes that "most perfect periphrastics in the NT display the sense of the perfect of resulting state, focusing on a condition with an implication of the occurrence which produced it."

Thus he now takes this truth and applies it to the lives of his readers just as Jesus had to the Eleven.

ἐὰν ἀγαπῶμεν ἀλλήλους, "If we love one another." Employing another third class conditional construction, John exposes the reality that fellow Christians may or may not love one another (Akin, 182). Repeating the words from verse 11 but in reverse order, John again includes himself in the group by his choice of the first person plural ἀγαπῶμεν. With the present tense he indicates that this is something that should be continuously practiced. With the reflexive pronoun he affirms that this is a "family" issue. The love under discussion is not what we would exercise toward all men but toward members of the family of God (Burdick, 325). It is a love exercised in the context of community between the members of that community. With the condition given, John now turns to the truth revealed.

ὁ θεὸς ἐν ἡμῖν μένει, "God abides in us." The first part of the apodosis is now stated with the present tense μένει. However, what does John mean by "abides in us"? He is either referring to the individual's experience of God's abiding or to the community's (church body's). If understood as referring to an individual believer it can be understood in one of three ways. The abiding of God in a believer can be seen as referring to justification, sanctification, or both at the same time.

(1) As a justification truth, John would be affirming that only those who exhibit love for other believers are truly born again.[73] Loving other Christians is "evidence" that God is in the person in a justification sense (Marshall, 217; Stott, 167). This takes μένω as a reference to God's presence within the individual believer. Burdick (325) affirms John is saying by this that loving one another is "not the condition or the means of God's indwelling; it is the evidence that God lives in us." Brooke (120) similarly affirms: "What cannot be seen can be known by its fruits. Mutual love is a sign of the indwelling of God in men."

(2) As a sanctification truth, John is affirming that those who exhibit love for other believers evidence God's abiding presence in their lives in terms of the influence he is having in and through them. This is the same truth Jesus taught when he told the disciples, "By this all will know that you are my disciples, if you have love for one another" (John 13:35). He did not say, "If you have love for one another you will be my disciples." They would

73. This is characteristic of the Test of Life view.

be his disciples whether they loved each other or not. It was the world that would recognize them as his disciples by their mutual love.

(3) As an expression of both aspects of salvation in which God both indwells the believer and the believer responds to his presence with obedient living that is enabled through the ministry of the Holy Spirit (God "influences" him). Thus μένει refers to "the permanent relationship which God has with the believer. Here it refers specifically to God's indwelling of the believer in the person of the Holy Spirit, as indicated by 4:13b" (Harris, 190). Thus, bearing fruit not only indicates that one is a child of God but that one is in fellowship with God and being influenced by the Holy Spirit to live obediently.

I believe that this statement can be applied on an individual basis. Even so, as will be demonstrated below, such can only be an implication of the text. John is addressing corporate testimony to the world. The key to applying this individually is to see the implication of the third class condition. This is something that John and his readers are capable of *not* doing. That is the significance of John's choice of the first person plural ἀγαπῶμεν and the reflexive plural ἀλλήλους. So if John fails to love other believers, then God would not abide in him. Furthermore, to say he can be perfectly loving all the time may be theoretically possible, but it is an unrealistic expectation for any human, regenerate or not. Thus, God's abiding, contingent on obedience, must be broken by sin that awaits confession (1:9). Again, as in the upper room, Jesus told the Eleven they could not be fruitful without abiding in him. In John 15:4 Jesus uses this same third class conditional construction and applies it directly to the eleven apostles, who were unquestionably regenerate (John 17:6–10). However, the abiding relationship is presented as contingent. Jesus makes very clear through the vine and branches analogy that, though they are poised to, the apostles would not bear fruit unless they abode in him. Abiding in him, in fact, would result in *much* fruit (John 15:5). Just before this, in John 14:23 Jesus states that God's abiding in a believer is contingent on obedience. Thus Jesus cannot be addressing the question of one's justification. What he teaches is that it is possible for his disciples not to love him. "If anyone loves me" is a third class condition, the fulfillment of which has three parts. The person's part is that he or she will be obedient. The second two fulfillments involve God loving the person who loves him and then both the Father and Son making their abode in him. If this is describing justification, then salvation is contingent on either love or obedience.

He is describing a relationship with God that involves God's influence in the life of the believer. Μένω can refer to indwelling, a metaphysical concept, but is often used by Jesus and John as a relational term that includes within it the relational concept of influence. He is saying by this that it is evident that God is having an influence in the life of the believer who loves other believers. Thus mutual love demonstrates God's presence in the believer through his effect on that person's motives and activities.[74] Strecker (157) says well that a direct vision of God is denied the Christian community; however, "the encounter with God that is promised to them takes place, instead, here and now in love for one another."

The preposition ἐν with the plural pronoun ἡμῖν should be translated "among" rather than "in" (Hodges 189; Smalley, 248; Yarbrough, 245). This is indicated by John's repetition of ἐν ἡμῖν in the following clause that clarifies the community expression of God's love. This would make this a community promise that God will dwell within a congregation that loves its members. As the command is addressed to all, the promise is corporately made rather than individualized as it will be later. If John had not intended a community sense, it seems that he would have used either a πᾶς ὁ formula which he has done as recently as 4:7, or a ὃς ἐὰν formula that he will use in 4:15.

What John has affirmed by this is that God's abiding presence is expressed through the community of believers loving each other which has the effect of causing the world to see God in them. As Burge (188) says well, "Love that is inspired by God, that is a fulfillment of this divine obedience, makes God a tangible reality." Johnson (106) summarizes John's point in that loving one another "brings the unseen God to concrete expression" (Johnson, 106).

καὶ ἡ ἀγάπη αὐτοῦ ἐν ἡμῖν τετελειωμένη ἐστιν, "His love has been made perfect in us." This is the second thing demonstrated by our loving one another (Burdick, 325). As the presence of God is seen in the interrelationships within the body of Christ and it is expressed in the local congregations, so too, is the presence of God's love. It is also the second mention of love being

74. Paul describes this as the fruit of the Spirit (Gal 5:22–26) and a product of being filled with the Spirit (Eph 5:18–21).

perfected, or made complete, in the believer. It was introduced in 2:5, where God's love is perfected in the one who obeys. It will be mentioned twice more in 4:17 and 18 where perfected love brings confidence before God on judgment day.

The genitive construction ἡ ἀγάπη αὐτοῦ ("his love") may be understood in one of three ways:

(1) It may be subjective, describing God's love for us. He is the active agent (Barker, 344; Brooke, 120; Brown 521; Haas, de Jonge, and Swellengrebel, 124; Kistemaker, 335; Kruse, 162, n. 184; Lenski, 505; Stott, 167). Since 4:11 "speaks of believers as the objects of God's love" this makes its role as a subjective genitive more logical (Harris, 190). Since the dominant theme of vv 7–11 has been God's love for the community, the flow of thought argues for it to be the same here (Johnson, 106). Against this an objection is raised on the basis of John's use in 2:15 and 5:3 (Marshall, 217).

(2) It may be objective, describing our love for God (Dodd, 113). This love for God is expressed through loving one another. However, the immediate context does not discuss love for God (Burdick, 326). Further, our love for God can never be described as having reached completion (Lenski, 505).

(3) It may be a genitive of quality or kind, and so this would be God's kind of love (Smalley, 248). This would "reinforce" the theme of this section (Schnackenburg, 241).

Or, better, (4) it is both a subjective and qualitative genitive (Law, 250; Westcott, 152).[75] Marshall (217) sees this saying that "when we love others, God's love for us has reached its full effect in creating the same kind of love as his in us." Burdick (326) concurs and says, "It is God loving through the believer. Of course, when this happens, the love expressed cannot help but be God's kind of love, for God is the source of it."

Τετελειωμένη may be: (1) A periphrastic participle, meaning "his love is perfected in us" (Brooke, 120; Bultmann, 69; Lenski,505). This is supported by the placement of τετελειωμένη next to ἐστιν rather than after ἡ ἀγάπη αὐτοῦ (Burdick, 326). As such it emphasizes the continuance of God's love (Lenski, 505). (2) It could be adjectival, modifying ἀγάπη (Plummer, 104; Westcott, 152) and meaning "his perfected love is in us" (Burdick, 326). The first option is best.

---

75. D. B. Wallace (*Grammar*, 119–21) describes this combination as a plenary gen.

God's love in us attains its goal only as we exercise it within the body of Christ toward fellow believers.[76] "The manifestation of active love by men witnesses to two facts: (1) the abiding of God in them, and (2) the presence of divine love in them in its most complete form. There is both the reality of fellowship and the effectiveness of fellowship" (Westcott, 151). In John 17:23 Jesus prayed for the church's perfection in unity. Here the same term is used by John to describe love's maturity or completeness of expression in the life of the believer (Harris, 190).[77] The concept of perfection is not that of flawlessness but completeness and the reaching of one's goal (Akin, 182; Smith, 110).[78] Thus we see that God's abiding in us is revealed by our love for one another as the love of God is expressed through us in the manner he intends it to be communicated to others. We are the agents through whom God loves his children. To the extent that we express his love fully, its outpouring in our individual and corporate lives achieves God's desires, and so is brought to its full expression, thus "perfected."

Yarbrough (245) summarizes this verse well. "John takes a backseat to no one in Scripture in advancing a lofty view of God the Father's essential being. However, in direct proportion to God's transcendence, for John, is the mandate that believers incarnate God's character, central to which is his love."

John continues the theme of mutual abiding as it relates to experiencing eternal life. In these next verses he will affirm that eternal life expresses itself in mutual abiding between the believer and God. This mutual abiding, and therefore the influence of God in the life of the believer is evidenced by love for other believers. It is not something experienced on an intellectual or spiritual basis alone, but in relationship with God and others. Thus we

76. As a pass. ptc. τετελειωμένη indicates it is a work of God in the believer (Williamson, 146).

77. Love's perfection "refers to what happens when believers love one another" (Harris 190).

78. BDAG, 996; G. Delling, "τέλος, τελέω, ... τελειόω," *TDNT* 8:80–82. As Yarbrough (245) notes, John is not talking about sinless perfection. He should also not be understood as implying a flawless expression of love. Smith (110) recounts, "Candidates for ministry in the Wesleyan tradition are asked whether they expect to be perfected in love in this life and are supposed to be able to give a positive answer." This may be a Wesleyan perspective. However, the Luke 11:2–3 and 1:9 certainly indicate otherwise.

are taken full circle back to the concept of mutual fellowship introduced in the prologue and 1:7.

4:13 John now explains verse 12, how God abides in us. He turns to the question of the metaphysical union of the believer with God in the presence of the indwelling Holy Spirit. What he says here is similar to 3:24 with keeping God's commandments having the same result as loving fellow Christians. So John is now ready to return to the theme of fellowship with God (Kistemaker, 335).

Many begin a new paragraph here while recognizing this is closely linked to what preceded (Brooke, 120; Johnson, 109; Marshall, 218–19; Stott, 168). Stott (169) notes that some interpreters see this new paragraph describing the conditions of our mutual abiding in God. He rejects this and says instead, "Belief and love are not the conditions of the indwelling, however, but the tests and evidences of it." He sees this addressing the issue of assurance of salvation, which he considers the thrust of the epistle.[79]

Ἐν τούτῳ γινώσκομεν ὅτι ἐν αὐτῷ μένομεν καὶ αὐτὸς ἐν ἡμῖν, "By this we know that we are abiding in him and he in us." John's use of *ἐν τούτῳ* with *ὅτι* looks forward (Brown, 521; Burdick, 327; Culy, 111; Lenski, 506; Rensberger, 119; Yarbrough, 245–46) to what he says about the indwelling Holy Spirit rather than backward (Kistemaker, 335) to the evidence of love. It follows the pattern of 4:9 and 4:10 (Yarbrough, 245).

The first *ὅτι* is substantival giving the content of *γινώσκομεν* (Bultmann, 70; Harris, 191; Strecker, 157). What is known is known experientially (Burdick, 327). Though in most ways *γινώσκω* and *οἶδα* are synonyms, with John there does appear to be an intentional distinction made. Whereas with *γινώσκω* he implies an experiential knowledge (Akin, 182–83) and often uses it to further imply relationship, his use of *οἶδα* normally implies knowledge gained by instruction. John once again includes himself in the group. He knows by experience in the same way that his readers will know of the Spirit's presence in their lives. The mutual abiding described here involves relationship and interaction.[80] It includes the fellowship we have with God and the influence God has in our lives.

79. In that light Stott (169) says further, "Christian certainty rests on this combination of the objective and subjective, the historical and experiential, the Son's mission and the Spirit's testimony."

80. The second *meno* (*μένω*) is implied (Brown, 521–22).

ὅτι ἐκ τοῦ πνεύματος αὐτοῦ δέδωκεν ἡμῖν, "because he has given to us from his Spirit." This next ὅτι is either functioning as an adverb (causal) and providing the reason we can know we are experiencing mutual abiding with God (Bultmann, 70; Strecker, 158), or epexegetically, explaining ἐν τούτῳ (Brown, 522; Harris, 191). Harris notes that this would be essentially repeating the final clause of the last section (3:24) and has essentially the same meaning (ἐκ τοῦ πνεύματος οὗ ἡμῖν ἔδωκεν).

The preposition phrase ἐκ τοῦ πνεύματος αὐτοῦ is problematic in that it is not clear how it is functioning.

(1) It may reflect a genitive of source. What God has given us comes "from his Spirit" (Lenski, 506; Westcott, 153). Thus the Spirit is giving us gifts, including the fruit of the Spirit (Gal 5:22). Strecker (158) says this indicates "believers live in the realm of the Spirit who proceeds from God and who determines their very being, hence their knowing." Malatesta applies this by noting "just as in 3,24 the Spirit is the ultimate source of peace of heart (3,19–21) and the answering of our petitions (3,22), so in 4,13 the same Spirit is the source of our confidence on the day of judgment (4,17) and of the absence of fear (18). In each of the respective sections the Spirit is the source of one particular benefit: compassion towards the needy brother (3,17) and the unity of the love of God and the love of the neighbor (4,19–21)."[81]

(2) It may be a partitive genitive indicating that God has given us "some of his Spirit" (Brown, 522; Burdick, 327; Harris, 191; Kistemaker, 336; Lieu, 186). Lenski (506) rejects this on the basis that 3:24 affirms we have been given all of God's Spirit. However, this could be an allusion to Israel's experience in the wilderness. There God took part of his Spirit which was upon Moses and distributed it among seventy elders who would assist him in leading the people (Num 11:24–25). Burdick (327) clarifies this and says it does not mean that believers receive only part of God's Spirit, but that his giving is in "limited measure" as contrasted with Jesus (John 3:34). (3) John may intend both senses. The solution seems to be related to what would be the "missing" direct object of the verb. One would normally expect John to complete the idea of δέδωκεν with a direct object; but he left it out. His use of the perfect tense indicates the permanence of the gift. This accords well

81. E. Malatesta, *Interiority and Covenant*,303.

with the Holy Spirit being given as a pledge of our inheritance (Eph 1:13–14) and with Jesus' promise that he will be in us (John 14:17), as opposed to the fruit of the Spirit, which may or may not be true of a believer's experience at any given time.[82] The source of what God has given us is his Spirit. God's abiding in us is through the presence of the indwelling Holy Spirit, who seals us (his permanent presence) and fills us (his temporal influence and enablement). Furthermore, it is the Holy Spirit's affecting our motives that lead to actions that expresses his presence through our obedience.[83]

John's choice of the perfect δέδωκεν draws attention to the continued results as opposed to using an aorist as he used in 3:24. Where in 3:24 it describes only the giving, here it indicates the "continuing possession in addition to the past reception" (Burdick, 328).[84] As a perfect of resulting state it is looking at the present impact of the Spirit's presence rather than the reception of the Spirit.[85] Thus this describes the "resultant indwelling of the Spirit imparted after regeneration"[86]

The giving of the Spirit does not indicate "magical impartation of purely cognitive data." (Yarbrough, 246) Jesus' promise (John 14:26; 16:13) of the Spirit's giving of special knowledge was limited to the Eleven (Yarbrough, 246). Rather, the Spirit's presence in believers is what enables the reciprocal

82. Paul's command to live by the Spirit in Gal 5:16 precedes his listing of the fruits of the Spirit. Commands of Scripture to believers can be disobeyed by believers with subsequent results. In this case, failure to live by the Spirit will result in the works of the flesh (gal 5:19–21) as opposed to the fruits of the Spirit (Gal 5:22).

83. A fourth option that is given but not developed is that it refers to the Holy Spirit's presence in the believer (Akin, 183, n. 123; Burdick, 328). John's discussion indicates that he would be doing more than just affirming His presence.

84. Schnackenburg (241–42) suggests this may be a "stereotyped formula" from a church catechism because it is nearly identical in wording to 3:24b. (Der fast wörtliche Anklang von 4, 13 an 3, 24b sieht nach einer sterotzpen Wendung aus, die wohl aus dem kirchlichen Unterricht stammt.) This presupposes an author or editor other than John. It has not been found in any extant catechisms. If it were found in any, it is more likely they would be based on this rather than this borrowing from them.

85. B. M. Fanning, *Verbal Aspect in New Testament Greek*, 291–95. Marshall (219, n. 2) does not see a significant difference between this pf. and the previous aor. in 3:24.

86. D. E. Hiebert, "An Expositional Study of 1 John—Part 8: An Exposition of 1 John 4:7–21," 79.

relationship between believers and God.[87] Nor does it refer to the spiritual gifts (contra Marshall, 219). Rather, John is affirming that "it is divine presence and not merely human impulse that moved them to selfless regard for each other" (Yarbrough, 246).[88]

4:14 This and the following verse express the truth that relationship with God is revealed by one's confession that Jesus, the Savior of the world, is the Son of God. This verse exhibits a compound predicate with a shared subordinate clause giving the content of both what was seen and what is being said.

καὶ ἡμεῖς τεθεάμεθα καὶ μαρτυροῦμεν, "And we have seen and are testifying." John affirms the truth by reminding his readers that he is a witness of Jesus, who is eternal life incarnate. He begins this sentence once more with the emphatic placement of *ἡμεῖς* which has been understood in one of three ways: (1) John switches from identifying with his readers to identifying with the apostolic circle of eyewitnesses (Akin, 183; Brooke, 121; Kistemaker, 337; Kruse, 163–64; Lenski, 508; Plummer, 104; Schnackenburg, 242; Stott, 166; Yarbrough, 247). (2) Some see this including the readers on the basis that they have been included in the "we" references beginning from verse 7 (Bruce, 111; Culpepper, 90; Dodd, 115; Hodges, 191; Marshall, 220; Rensberger, 120; Westcott, 153).[89] (3) It includes both the apostolic witnesses and readers (Barker, 345; Bruce, 110–11; Marshall, 220, n. 5).

---

87. Schneider ("The Word was made Flesh," 353) sees this passage teaching: "The Spirit is the fullness of Christ communicated to the believer."

88. Kruse (163) sees this as written to provide the readers assurance of their salvation. As such he sees John implying either "(a) that the Spirit motivates love for fellow believers and the objective practice of love is the basis of their assurance; or (b) that the Spirit teaches the truth about God's sending Jesus as the Saviour of the world and knowing this provides believers with the basis of assurance; or (c) that the very presence of the Spirit himself in believers creates the sense of assurance?" He chooses the second option. Assurance of salvation is not the point John is making, though one may gain it from this, but the nature of the mutual abiding that has expressed itself in the community's love. John is explaining how one knows they are having a mutual relationship (fellowship) with God.

89. Johnson (110) sees this indicating that they would be grounding their assurance in the historical reality of the incarnation. However, as I have said, assurance of salvation is not the point John is making in this section. His readers have already been reassured (2:12–14) and have been identified as God's children (3:1). Thus they do not need reassurance of their justification but clarification of their sanctification.

Each of the last two views would understand τεθεάμεθα to be "the sight of faith" rather than physical seeing (Barker, 345; Smalley, 252; Thompson, 124). However, this need not be the case. John's use of the pronoun and its emphatic placement along with the perfect tense verb argues strongly against an inclusion of the readers (Burdick, 328). Thus neither of the last two views are satisfactory. He has made clear from the beginning that the eyewitness experience of Jesus was not continuing and not something the readers had experienced. It has been John testifying to his readers throughout the epistle, and so here as well. Additionally, John appears to be following the same pattern as the opening verses of his epistle by using the perfect followed by the present μαρτυροῦμεν. However, breaking from the parallel, he uses a different term of perception. Rather than using ὁράω here and making the statements more parallel, he chooses to use θεάομαι instead. Whereas ὁράω focuses on the act of seeing, though it could include the idea of perception, θεάομαι communicates the idea of both an intense and perceptive look.[90] This would not be something his readers could claim.

His choice of the perfect tense for seeing communicates the fact that no new revelation is occurring. Their time with Jesus ended with his ascension. This is not a claim of new revelation or of later appearances of Jesus. Rather, it is a reference to John's previous experience with Jesus as an eyewitness during his incarnation. Present tense of μαρτυροῦμεν indicates that though the vision is past, the telling of it continues to the time of writing (Burdick, 329; Williamson, 147).

ὅτι ὁ πατὴρ ἀπέσταλκεν τὸν υἱὸν σωτῆρα τοῦ κόσμου, "that the Father sent his Son *to be* the Savior of the world." The content of their testimony to John's readers is now given. This ὅτι clause should be viewed as substantival (indirect discourse), giving the content of both τεθεάμεθα and μαρτυροῦμεν rather than one or the other.

Here John uses ἀπέσταλκεν as a perfect of resulting state and so looks at more than Jesus' coming to save.[91] Though he does not continue to be sent, the impact of his coming continues, and he continues to save men and women throughout the world today.

---

90. BDAG, 445; W. Michaelis, "ὁράω, βλέπω, θεάομαι, θεωρέω," *TDNT,* 5:317–18.
91. B. M. Fanning (*Verbal Aspect in New Testament Greek*, 292) describes a pf. of resulting state as having all three elements of the pf. pres. It looks at the completed act in the past, its continuing effect, and present expression.

This title, "Savior of the world," is unique to John.[92] Further, this is the only place σωτήρ is used in the epistle.[93] It is only used once in the Gospel (John 4:42), and that was by the Samaritans! The term was common in the Roman world, but as a title attributed to Caesar in their worship of him as a god.[94] Marshall (220, n. 7) proposes that the apostle's use of this term was a reaction to the emperor cult. However, the subject under discussion makes the words of the woman at the well seem a more likely source. Savior of the world is parallel to "saved through him" in 4:9 (Burdick, 329). Jesus' purpose in coming was to save mankind.[95]

The title focuses our attention on Jesus' purpose in coming and his relationship with the world at this time.[96] So is the sense of κόσμος neutral or evil? Moody (95) defines it everywhere as "the godless mass of humanity estranged and hostile to God." However, it is this mass of humanity Jesus seeks to save, and so here κόσμος should be viewed as neutral (Brown, 523; Burdick, 329; Haas, de Jonge, and Swellengrebel, 126). It is the people of the planet, not the satanically inspired system that Jesus is delivering from their sin and doom.

This title serves as one of the strong evidences for the doctrine of unlimited atonement (Akin, 183; Johnson, 110). "There is no limit to his mission to save, and no limit to its success, excepting man's unwillingness to accept salvation by believing on the Savior" (Plummer, 104). "World" here cannot mean "the elect" or be limited to justified saints, present and future (Burdick, 329). Rather, this continues the concept introduced in 1 John 2:2, with "our sins" and the "whole world" juxtaposed while both experience Jesus' propitiation. Further, John's choice of "the world" and "whoever" in

---

92. Jesus is called "Savior" by Paul (2 Tim 1:10; Titus 1:4; 2:13; 3:6) and Peter (2 Pet 1:1, 11; 2:20; 3:2, 18), but never with this epithet.

93. Westcott (154) notes that neither σώζειν and σωτηρία are found in any of John's three epistles.

94. J. Schneider and C. Brown, *NIDNTT* 3:216; W. Foerster, *TDNT* 7:1003–21. See Schnackenburg (243–44) for a thorough discussion of the use of this term in the Roman emperor worship.

95. Westcott (154) aptly notes that the pf. also indicates that what "is yet partly future in its human application ... is complete in the divine idea."

96. E. Malatesta (*Interiority and Covenant*, 304) says this title indicates: "He is the sign *par excellence* of the Father's love for us (4,9,10,16), and therefore the model and source of our love for each other (3,16; 4,17)."

John 3:16 argues against any limitation of Christ's work to the elect.[97] Both uses of κόσμος are universal in nature. In 1 Tim 2:3–6 Paul describes God as Savior "who desires all men to be saved" and Jesus as mediator between "God and men," not God and believers or the elect.

4:15 How does acknowledging the truth that Jesus is the Savior of the world affect a person? John now answers that question.[98] This sentence is composed of a long relative clause that is epexegetical to the nominative pronoun αὐτὸς in the main clause. It is also justification truth that forms the basis for one's fellowship with God.

ὃς ἐὰν ὁμολογήσῃ ὅτι Ἰησοῦς ἐστιν ὁ υἱὸς τοῦ θεοῦ, "Whoever confesses that Jesus is the Son of God." Though this sentence begins with ἐὰν followed by a subjunctive verb, it is not a conditional clause, but an indefinite relative clause.[99] This ἐὰν introduces an indefinite relative clause, not a conditional clause, because it is connected to and preceded by the relative pronoun ὃς. John's employment of ὃς ἐὰν makes the statements that follow generalities and indicates the opportunity is open to all of mankind (Burdick, 329; Williamson, 147) and is parallel to "the world" in v 14 (Burdick, 329). Thus, John is stating a principle rather than making a claim about either himself or his readers.

The aorist subjunctive ὁμολογήσῃ is different from the present active subjunctive ὁμολογῶμεν of 1:9. The aorist by nature is undefined and so looks at the act of confessing, not as a process, but as an event (Burdick, 330; Johnson, 114). It is not saying when this occurs, but only that it does (Stott, 170; Strecker, 159). Confession is not *claiming* something is true but

97. Schnackenburg (242) sees this as a summary of John 3:17.

98. Bultmann (71) says this verse "interprets ... how 'the savior of the world' is made effective" which is through mutual abiding. However, it seems better that, though this is the basis of communicating Jesus to the world, John's focus here is more foundational. He has already dealt with the question of testimony to the world in vv 11–12.

99. Brown (524) suggests it ὃς ἐὰν could be translated "whenever" instead of "whoever" per BDF 377. In support of this he interprets the perfect tense for confess to mean that the person continues to believe it, not continues to do it. The confession was made at a point in time and continues to be the person's conviction. However, this would make salvation contingent on continued belief rather than a settled issue. Again, assurance of salvation is one of John's focuses in this epistle (as will be seen in chap five), though not its main theme. If John intended the meaning Brown gives it, it would detract from one's assurance rather than acknowledge it.

admitting it to be true. It is something of which someone is convinced to be true. The idea of confession can involve a public acknowledgment of something as true, or a public claim of allegiance to someone as well.[100] So this confession is something stated openly about Jesus. Yarbrough (253) connects a commitment to obedience with the concept of confession. It means "to regard, obey, and commit to Jesus."[101] However, justifying faith is defined most clearly through the example of Abraham in Rom 4:16–22. Abraham understands God's promise in light of the reality of his and Sarah's age and considers God's promise (intellectual). He then responds with hope—a positive emotional response to an expectation—which is the emotional aspect of faith In John 6:28–29, when the unbelieving multitude asked, "What shall we do, that we may work the works of God?" Jesus made clear that there was only one thing they could do to receive the eternal life giving Bread from heaven: "This is the work of God, that you believe in him whom he sent." Thus this confession is not an action, but a conviction, that saves. Granted, it is stated openly. However, it is not the statement that brings justification, but the faith in Jesus that led to the statement.

The content of an orthodox confession includes openly affirming that "Jesus is the Son of God." In the construction of the ὅτι clause, this could be understood as indirect discourse, and therefore describing the nature of the confession. In other words, any teaching that accords with this truth is orthodox. Or it could be understood as direct discourse, with ὅτι being equivalent to quotation marks, and therefore describing what must be stated in order to be an orthodox confession. This may allude back to John's purpose statement in John 20:31, being an exact quotation except for the deletion of ὁ Χριστὸς. It may also look back on Martha's confession of Jesus as both the Christ and Son of God in John 11:27.

The anarthrous 'Ιησοῦς is the subject and the articular ὁ υἱὸς the predicate nominative because 'Ιησοῦς, being a proper name does not need the

---

100. BDAG, 708; O. Michel, "ὁμολογέω," *TDNT* 5:207–12.

101. He (Yarbrough, 253) defines faith as having "pistic, ethical, and agapic" elements. He says of these elements that "the first is primarily doctrinal, the second behavioral, and the third relational." It is on the basis of this behavioral element of faith that he sees the commitment to action. I concur with him that faith has intellectual, volitional and emotional aspects, two which are demonstrated by Abraham in Rom 4:16–22.

article to be definite.[102] The human name, "Jesus," is brought forward to emphasize his humanity (Johnson, 110). His title as Son of God declares his deity.[103] This confession would exclude all gnostics (Burdick, 330; Harris, 193; Johnson, 110; Marshall, 220). It seems better, though, to see John simply clarifying what one must believe about Jesus to have justifying faith in him.

Harris (193) correctly sees this serving as "a confession which constitutes the one who makes it a believer." He points to its similarity to John 20:31 which serves as the purpose statement of the Gospel, which he sees as evangelistic (n. 521). Though I do not see the primary purpose of John's Gospel as evangelistic, I do agree that John 20:31 states John's purpose (see "Excursus on Eternal Life in Johannine Literature" for my reasoning). Furthermore, I concur that this confession is that of a true believer in Jesus.

ὁ θεὸς ἐν αὐτῷ μένει καὶ αὐτὸς ἐν τῷ θεῷ, "God abides in him and he in God." Right confession leads to life with God.[104] Strecker (159) says well: "The reciprocity of God's abiding in believers and believers in God does not refer to any mystical indwelling. What is expressed is a close, personal relationship between believers and God." He thus sees this describing the experience of believers in their sanctification. However, is this justification reality or sanctification? To which abiding does John refer? Akin (183) sees this as a test of life. "John introduces another criterion (hence the use of the conjunction καὶ) for confirmation of the believers' union with God: adherence to the apostolic message." Hodges (193), in contrast, interprets it as a sanctification experience of a "mutual ... relationship" between the believer and God. To this Westcott (155) concurs and describes it as "divine fellowship ... in each direction." Though this is true, and is clearly taught elsewhere, here the impact of the confession seems best to be understood as justification truth, but through confession rather than adherence. Yes, the confession reveals the reality of mutual abiding. However, in the context of the earlier warning against false teachers in 4:1–6, it seems best at least to see the question of union with God included in the idea of mutual fellowship.

---

102. D. B. Wallace, *Grammar*, 45–46.
103. "Son of God" is a common title given to Jesus by John as well as the other writers of Scripture. This phrase is repeated seven times in 1 John (3:8; 5:5,10, 12, 13, 20). He is also called "Son" another ten times (1:3, 7: 2:22, 23, 24; 3:23; 4:9, 10, 14; 5:9).
104. E. Malatesta (*Interiority and Covenant*, 304) sees this as a justifying confession necessary for fellowship with God. He says well, "To confess Jesus is thus to be in communion with the Father."

4:16a Abiding in love is evidence of abiding in God and God abiding in us.

καὶ ἡμεῖς ἐγνώκαμεν καὶ πεπιστεύκαμεν τὴν ἀγάπην ἣν ἔχει ὁ θεὸς ἐν ἡμῖν, "And we have known and have believed the love which God has for us." John continues his discussion with the coordinate conjunction, καὶ. However, rather than connecting back to the immediately preceding sentence, it is likely this continues the thought of verse 14, with verse 15 being a parenthetical statement (Marshall, 221). This is seen in his choice of the perfect tense verbs to describe his experience.

Placing the first person plural pronoun ἡμεῖς once more in an emphatic position at the head of the sentence (Lieu, 191), John affirms a mutual experience. The pronoun can be understood in one of two ways. (1) It could refer to the apostles and John once again (the distinctive use). Thus, ἡμεῖς continues to refer to the apostolic circle of witnesses who came to know and believe in the past and continue to do so to the present. (2) It could include John's readers with him (Akin, 184; Burdick, 330; Harris, 194; Lenski, 508; Rensberger, 121). This is indicated by the change in verbs from those that fit the apostles better in verse 14 to these that are more general (Burdick, 330). The use of ἐν ἡμῖν clearly includes the readers (Burdick, 330). Thus this second option is best.

'Εγνώκαμεν indicates acquisition of knowledge, "have come to know" (Burdick, 330). Lenski (509) says "To know as John speaks of knowing is to believe, and vice versa." Πεπιστεύκαμεν means "one has believed and is now confident" (Burdick, 330). Both verbs are perfect tense and so indicate past experience with present results (Harris, 194). "A knowledge of basic facts must precede belief, for it is necessary to know what is to be believed." Brown (524) likewise sees in the two perfects as a reference to "the basic knowledge and act of faith involved in Christian conversion/initiation/baptism." Yarbrough (254) sees John's use of the perfects to indicate "a reflecting and settled state of knowledge and trust." The object of this knowledge is God's love. Westcott (155) sees John uniting these two verbal ideas into a single concept where "belief qualifies and explains what is in this case the primary and predominant idea, knowledge." As a hendiadys* (Kruse, 165), John is not looking at two separate experiences but a single truth.[105] Harris (195) argues convincingly that John has the pattern in his

---

105. I like Strecker's (160) designation of it as" almost a hendiadys." Further, he says these two words do not describe the relationship between the believer and God,

Gospel of using these two verbs together often enough that he must intend a hendiadys (John 6:69; 8:31–32; 10:38; 14:7–10; 17:8). In this epistle he has already used them together in 4:1–2. He notes from their occurrences in the Gospel, there is no significance to their order or if their order is reversed (contra Burdick, 330). He concludes that John uses them as a hendiadys which makes knowledge and faith "inseparable." The disciples' knowledge of God was integrally linked to their faith in him.[106] In John 6:69 the same words are used by Peter in his declaration of Jesus' deity, only in reverse order. What John is affirming is that both he and his readers have come to recognize and believe that God really does love them. Of note is the change from the perfect to the present. Though the knowledge and faith of the apostles began in the past, God's love is always present. Further, God's love is directed toward the believer.

The phrase ἐν ἡμῖν may be understood in one of two ways. (1) God's love is experienced within the community of believers. Thus it is directed "in us" or "with us." (Brooke, 122; Bruce, 112; Burdick, 331; Culy, 114; Haas, de Jonge, and Swellengrebel, 127; Hodges, 197; Rensberger, 121; Westcott, 155). In favor of this is the repeated use of ἐν with the sense of "in" throughout this passage (Burdick, 331). Better is to see that (2) God's love is expressed toward us. Some might see this as similar to what he said in 3:5 and will again affirm in 5:10 as God's love understood or felt by the believer. Against this is the pattern that the preposition does not normally have the sense of "toward" unless it is with verbs of motion or putting (Rensberger, 121). Also, the present tense "has" argues for it being something happening in the believers rather than something accomplished in the past (Rensberger, 121). Rather, it seems best to see it closer to John 13:35 and the idea of God's love expressed toward us (Smalley, 255). This is a description of God's attitude in this instance, his character, and goes back to what he said in verse 9 about God's manifested love. Harris (195) sees this use has "interiority" in view. He argues that this same phrase is used in 4:9, referring to God's love for us, and 4:12, referring to God indwelling the believer. Thus God's love is "expressed *in* believers." He points to 3:15 and 5:10 where ἔχω is used with ἐν "which literally refer to something 'in' someone." What he sees as his

---

but between the community and the "Christ-event." Thus they are justification truths for him.

106. For a fuller discussion, consult Harris's commentary (194–95).

strongest argument is that this same preposition is used in the following sentence "where interiority is clearly in view."

4:16b Should this sentence begin a new paragraph? The two views are: (1) This should be a continuation of the previous paragraph (Haas, de Jonge, and Swellengrebel, 127; Johnson, 114; Lieu, 192; Marshall, 221; Yarbrough, 255). This is supported by the idea that "the reciprocal concepts of God's love for believers (4:16a) and believers' expression of that love (4:16b) belong together and are complementary" (Smalley, 255). The repetition of mutual abiding reflects similar uses in 4:13 and 15 and so connects this sentence with what preceded. Johnson (114) sees verses 13 through 18 all on Christian confidence. (2) This marks the beginning of a new paragraph (Harris, 195; Perkins, 54; Smith, 113). John's use of ἐν τούτῳ to begin the next sentence most likely refers to what precedes rather than what follows. Thus this sentence would be its referent and makes better sense as an introductory sentence rather than a conclusion (Harris, 195). As an introductory sentence, 4:16b follows the pattern of 4:7 and 11 previous to it. The three themes (love, abiding, perfection) introduced in the previous section (4:11–12) begin this new section (Harris, 195).

Some see it starting a new major section (Brooke, 122; Brown, 545; Kistemaker, 338; Perkins, 54; Westcott, 156) rather than at 4:7 as in this commentary. This is the same construction and statement as 4:8 (see comments there) and so should be included with it when determining the broad movements of John's argument (how to outline the epistle).[107] It further serves as another hinge sentence and connects the thoughts of the opening paragraph of this section with what preceded. Both paragraphs develop the theme of love. Additionally, in this paragraph the theme of the broad section of John's epistle is stated.

John now declares another truth about God's nature and character. This thematic statement, as before, describes God's character but should never be seen as defining him. With that declaration, John shows the importance of living out love for other believers as it impacts one's relationship with

107. Grayston (129) sees the two phrases forming an *inclusio*. However, what follows continues the theme of community love till the end of the chap and so the statements do not enclose his argument. It would be better to see John using repetition for emphasis in order to clarify the importance of this truth about God in all that he has to say in the remainder of his epistle.

God. Mutual abiding does not occur outside of a life of obedience to that command that matters most to God within the context of his family.

Ὁ θεὸς ἀγάπη ἐστίν, "God is love." John makes another thematic statement about God's character as it relates to his dealings with men.[108] This is not a statement of his essential nature any more than 1:5 or 4:8 were (see comments on each). This is the second statement of God's nature as love (4:8), and the only one that is repeated in Scripture (4:8 and here).[109] As before, this statement cannot be reversed. Love is not God any more than light. However, love is one of the bases of God's activity in this world and an expression of another key aspect of his character as it relates to our fellowship with him and his dealings with mankind.

καὶ ὁ μένων ἐν τῇ ἀγάπῃ ἐν τῷ θεῷ μένει καὶ ὁ θεὸς ἐν αὐτῷ μένει, "and the one abiding in love abides in God and God abides in him." Having declared once more the character of God, John turns to its implication. As God being light (moral purity) requires our moral purity for fellowship, and his being righteous demands our righteousness, so, too, his love demands we be loving if we are to commune with him.

John uses μένω with two separate nuances in this sentence. The first use of μένω is as part of the articular present participle construction describing a kind of person (gnomic sense of the present). This person lives or operates within the sphere of God's love (Westcott, 156). This is the same as walking in the sphere of God's moral purity (light) in chapter 1. It is a relational term and indicates that the person operates from a perspective of loving attitudes that reflect the loving character of God. The following uses of μένω look at the relationship that results from being such a person. The verb is both repeated and placed at the end of its respective clauses for emphasis. The two clauses are joined by καὶ and imply the unity of these two ideas against their being parallel concepts (Westcott, 156). Abiding in love

108. Strecker (160) sees this as an "absolute use of ἀγάπη indicates that the author is speaking of love in an unlimited sense. He is thinking not only of God's love for human beings or that of humans for God but also of the love of human beings for one another." However, since John's focus continues to be related to the body of Christ and not the world in general, the sense John is giving it still relates to God and His love for mankind.

109. D. E. Hiebert, "An Expositional Study of 1 John—Part 8: An Exposition of 1 John 4:7–21," 83.

produces mutual abiding which has a "fully interactive character" (Hodges, 198).[110]

The significance of his choice of μένω to describe this relationship and the repetition of the term for emphasis is likely another Johannine double meaning. By this he is stating both justification and sanctification truths. His point is that the one who loves with God's love has God dwelling in him. He is justified. However, he also affirms that the one who loves abides in God as well. As this mutual abiding was a sanctification reality in the upper room, so, too, it is here as well.

What John has said about God's love to this point is that it is both experienced through abiding and expressed through conduct. Loving believers *does* evidence a relationship with God. Only believers can love with God's kind of love, though not all do. Failure to love does not prove one is unregenerate. If it were impossible for a believer to fail to love other believers then we would not have the command to do so. By its very nature, any command, whether positive ("do this") or negative ("don't do that") implies that believers can do the opposite of what is commanded. They can disobey. Thus, believers can and do fail to love other believers with God's love. The consequence is loss of mutual relationship with God (fellowship) as well as with other believers.[111]

4:17 In this and the next two verses John will affirm that love toward one another and from God produces assurance of salvation and results from God's prior love.[112] Here he affirms first that love for one another, as an evidence of abiding, produces assurance of salvation with regard to confidence on judgment day (Johnson, 112). That John is emphasizing issues related

110. Rensberger (123) observes, "Mutual indwelling with God is an 'interior' phenomenon, but two of the three criteria for discerning it in 4:13–16 are external activities: Christological confession and love."

111. C. F. D. Moule ("A Neglected Factor in the Interpretation of Johannine Eschatology," 158) sees this as another example of "realized eschatology" in the epistle. However, though we will indeed love one another perfectly in the eschaton, John's focus is on this side of eternity at this point. The coming eschatological judgment is in view at points and will be in view in the next few verses. However, the expression of love that gives confidence is not future, but pres.

112. Schnackenburg (249) calls 4:17–18 the "Johannine Solomon's Song of Love" (*joh. Hohenliedes der Liebe*).

to believers is evident to the threefold use of "us" and "we" in this verse (Williamson, 149).

ἐν τούτῳ τετελείωται ἡ ἀγάπη μεθ' ἡμῶν, "By this love is has been perfected with us." This use of ἐν τούτῳ is again a dative of means and connects in one of three ways:

(1) It refers to the immediately following ἵνα clause (Brooke, 123–24; Bultmann, 72, n. 1; Burdick, 333; Grayston, 130; Haas, de Jonge, and Swellengrebel, 128; Rensberger, 121; Schnackenburg, 246, n. 3). This would require giving the following ἐν the sense of "about" or "concerning" "with reference to the day of judgment in order to make logical sense" (Harris, 196). It would then make the present perfecting of love in the believer dependent on his future confidence in the day of judgment (Burdick, 333).

(2) It refers to the ὅτι clause in 4:17b (ὅτι καθὼς ἐκεῖνός ἐστιν καὶ ἡμεῖς ἐσμεν ἐν τῷ κόσμῳ τούτῳ). However, the ὅτι is too far removed to function in this way (Burdick, 333). Also, this makes the intervening ἵνα clause awkward (Westcott, 157), "and there is no other instance of the phrase ἐν τούτῳ ... explained by a following *hoti*-clause where a *hina*-clause intervenes between the two in this way (Harris, 196).

(3) It refers to what precedes (Akin, 185; Brown, 527, 560; Burge, 189; Culpepper, 92; Harris, 196; Kistemaker, 339; Lieu, 193; Marshall, 223, n. 17; Smalley, 257; Strecker, 162; Westcott, 157; Yarbrough, 257). This follows the pattern of 3:10 and 19. The "logic in this reading mirrors the statement made in 4:12 (Culy, 115). To refer to what follows causes what is said to make little sense. However, when seen in light of what has just been said, what follows is a logical deduction that does make sense in light of the truth of mutual abiding. The definite article with ἀγάπη is an article of previous reference and connects it with the love already discussed (Lenski, 511; Yarbrough, 257). Against this is that it would "leave the last clause of the verse dangling" (Rensberger, 121). However, that can be resolved and this third option is best.

What John affirms is that the one who operates in the realm of God's kind of love (abides in love), and so experiences a mutually abiding relationship with him, will find that love has achieved its purpose in his or her life (Bultmann, 72). This is the sense of the perfect tense τετελείωται. Love will have achieved its full expression—will have come to "full maturity"—in the person by that person loving others (Boice, 119; Burdick, 333;

Thompson, 126; Williamson, 149).[113] Burge (189) notes well, "God's love is perfected not through our perception of it or our experience of it, *but through our expression of it*. God's love reaches completion by the degree to which it is shared among us" (italics his).

John describes this love as being μεθ' ἡμῶν, "with us" (Culy, 116; Harris, 197; Lieu, 193; Lenski, 510; Smith, 97; Williamson, 149) rather than ἐν ἡμῖν, "in us," which is what he has been using until now.[114] Westcott (157) sees this intending to "place the perfection clearly in the realized fellowship of God and man. Love is not simply perfected in man (ἐν ἡμῖν) by an act of divine power, but in fulfilling this issue God works with man (μεθ' ἡμῶν)." Hiebert, on the other hand says John's use of this preposition "suggests that love not only works in believers but also with them as God's people. Love attains its goal when a believer also communicates his love."[115] Marshall (233, n. 9) sees this as a Hebraism while others see the possibility (Brooke, 124). Burge (189) takes it as "among us" and sees this indicating God's love is perfected "through our expression of it." It "may emphasize the cooperation of men in the realization of fellowship" (Brooke, 124). It is the mutual abiding of God and the believer that leads to loves full expression in the community of faith.

ἵνα παρρησίαν ἔχωμεν ἐν τῇ ἡμέρᾳ τῆς κρίσεως, "that we may have boldness in the day of judgment." The role of ἵνα is understood variously once again. (1) It may be causal and introduce the purpose of God's love being brought to completeness in the believer (Burdick, 334), the divine benefit intended by the full expression of God's love. (2) It may be an epexegetical substantive clause and so describe "the goal to which God's love has been brought" (Lenski, 510). (3) It seems best to see it indicating result (Brown, 528; Culy, 116). The result of God's love being fully expressed is confidence.

113. Schnackenburg (245–46) on the other hand feels that τετελείωται refers to "the interior nature" of the love more than to its degree. "Also τετελείουσθαι referred not so much to degree as to the inner nature of perfection." (Außerdem bezeichnet τετελείοῦσθαι nicht so sehr den Grad wie die innere Art der Vervollkommnung.)

114. It is not modifying ἡ ἀγάπη because if it did it would have the article (Harris, 197).

115. D. E. Hiebert, "An Expositional Study of 1 John—Part 8: An Exposition of 1 John 4:7–21," 84.

John has spoken about boldness already in 2:28 and 3:21.[116] Here, as before, παρρησία indicates boldness or confidence in the sense of calm assurance in the believer who is anticipating Jesus' judgment of the world.[117] It describes that kind of confidence a person has in the presence of a judge when he or she does not anticipate a guilty sentence or a punishment. As Bruce notes well, "Christian confidence and Christian love go together; they find their antithesis in shame and fear" (Bruce, 113). This may look back on 2:28 (see comments there), and so the Bema Seat judgment of Christ, or it may refer to his judgment of the world, which is a condemning judgment (Lenski, 511; Schnackenburg, 246; Smith, 97; Stott, 171; Strecker, 163).[118] In favor of this second option is his choice of κρίσις. Normally κρίσις has more to do with the legal process of a trial, though the idea of the punishment phase of the proceedings is included.[119]

Some prefer to describe God's dealings with his children as "discipline" rather than "judgment." For example, they can point to the author of Hebrews' use of παιδεία to describe God's discipline in the life of a believer as opposed to judgment (Heb 12:4–11). Additionally, God promises in 1 Thess 5:9 that Christians will not experience his wrath (ὀργή) but salvation. Yet κρίμα, the synonym of κρίσις, which carries the same sense and is used much the same way, is used in 1 Pet 4:17 to describe God's judgment "of the house of God"—believers—as a warning to the lost world of its own coming judgment.[120] Paul uses κρίμα in 1 Cor 11:29–32 to describe God's punishment with sickness and death of some members of the church at Corinth for abusing the Lord's Supper. Furthermore, in Heb 10:27, κρίσις is applied to believers who willingly continue sinning. In light of the response of the unprepared believer in 2:28 to Jesus' appearing, it seems best to see this

116. Yarbrough (258) sees these having an eschatological sense, and so too here.
117. Lieu (194) notes that the phrase "day of judgment" does not occur in the Old Testament but is probably related to "the day of the Lord. Brown (528) notes that this is the only instance in the New Testament that both "day" and "judgment" have the article.
118. C. F. D. Moule ("A Neglected Factor in the Interpretation of Johannine Eschatology," 158–59) identifies this as "futurist" eschatology with John rather than "realized eschatology."
119. BDAG, 569; F. Büchsel, "κρίνω, κρίσις." *TDNT* 3:941–42.
120. BDAG, 567; F. Büchsel, "κρίνω, ... κρίμα," *TDNT* 3:942.

referring to the Bema Seat rather than the sheep/goat judgment of Matt 25:31–46 or the Great White Throne judgment of Rev 20.[121]

ὅτι καθὼς ἐκεῖνός ἐστιν καὶ ἡμεῖς ἐσμεν ἐν τῷ κόσμῳ τούτῳ, "because just as he is we also are in this world." John explains why believers can have confidence on judgment day (Schnackenburg, 247; Strecker, 165) with another adverb causal ὅτι clause, thus translated as "because" (Burdick, 335; Lenski, 512).

The demonstrative pronoun ἐκεῖνός has no immediate antecedent and again refers to Jesus, following John's pattern throughout this epistle (Bruce, 113; Bultmann, 72; Burdick, 335; Kruse, 167; Smith, 114; Yarbrough, 259).[122] It seems to be ambiguous by design, but also to serve as another way of indicating Jesus' deity without stating it directly (Hodges, 200–1).

John now uses the enigmatic statement καθὼς ἐκεῖνός ἐστιν. There are at least five views on what John means by "just as he is." (1) This refers to fellowship (relationship) with God (Barker, 346; Brown, 529; Culpepper, 94; Marshall, 223; Smalley, 259; Stott, 171–72). (2) It refers to Christ's perfect confidence that gives the believer boldness with God (Houlden, 119; Thompson, 127). As Jesus abided in God's love during his earthly ministry,

---

121. As can be seen from the examples of John's use of the terms for judgment outside of his epistles, they usually carry a condemning connotation, though not always. Further, when used of God they normally refer to His judgment of the wicked with punishment. In John 5:22–23, Jesus uses κρίνω and κρίσις to describe the judgment given by God the Father to him as Son. Then in John 5:24, that judgment (κρίσις) is parallel to death, and those who believe in Jesus pass from that death into life. So, too, Jesus uses these same terms in John 5:27 and 30 while addressing the unbelieving Jews. In John 7:24 Jesus uses this same verb and noun to describe the Jew's condemning response to his healing on the Sabbath. Nicodemus uses κρίνω (John 7:51) to describe the Law's condemning someone. In John 12:47–48 this judgment (κρίνω) is contrasted with Jesus' purpose of saving the world. In John 18:31 Pilate uses κρίνω when offering Jesus to the Jews so they could "judge him" in order to condemn him. In Rev 6:10 God will judge the wicked (κρίνω) and in that judgment avenge his martyred saints. In Rev 11:18 κρίνω is used to describe God's judgment of saints for reward and of the wicked with destruction. This is the singular instance of κρίνω including a positive result (from the perspective of the recipient). Additional places the term is used with a negative or neutral connotation (in the sense of condemning judgment of the wicked, or of God's right to judge) include John 8:15–16, 26, 50; 12:31; 16:8; Rev 14:7; 15:4; 16:5, 7; 17:1; 18:8, 10; 19:2, 11; 20:4, 12, 13.

122. Other occurrences of this term include 1 John 2:6; 3:3, 5, 7, 16; 4:7; 5:16. Strecker (165) believes the grammar here indicates a reference to God the Father.

and still does, so can Christians (Barker, 346). "Since this relationship is the model of the Christian's relationship with God, and since Jesus can never be thought of as fearing his heavenly Father, his followers should fear him neither" (Haas, de Jonge, and Swellengrebel, 128–29). (3) Christians are God's children in the same way Jesus is his Son, and in that way they are in the world "just as he is" (Brown, 529). (4) It can be viewed as a historical present and so mean "just as he was in the world." (Kruse, 168). Thus believers see that they love the brethren like Jesus loved the disciples when he was here, and thereby have no fear of facing him on judgment day. (5) This is positional truth and describes the believer's standing before God (J. Mitchell, 132; Stott, 171). It probably is a combination of the first two views.

Of interest is John's reference to our similarity to Christ "in this world." This alludes to our future destiny as distinct from "this world." It also reflects what Jesus said of us believers in John 15:19 and 17:14–16, that we are not a part of this world, which is why it hates us along with Jesus. Yet we still live in it for now. So it is in this life that we are to pursue Christlikeness. That John is thinking this way is evident by his choice to describe the present experience of him and his readers in "this" world as distinct from the world to come. Another aspect of this statement is that John is affirming once again, as he did in 2:6, that the product of an abiding relationship with Jesus is imitation.

Strecker (166) sees this as a negative reference to κόσμος. However, John's use of κόσμος here "relates to the natural world in which believers now live (as distinct from being in the heavenly world in which God dwells)" (Kruse, 67). Burdick (335) likewise sees it simply as the location where people live. This use occurs in the context of believers living life and being prepared to face God, their righteous judge. It is not discussing the believer's relationship to the world, but to God.

4:18 In this and the following verse John will affirm that perfect love in us removes fear and results from God's prior love. He repeats the key term φόβος four times as both a noun and a present participle. This sentence is challenging structurally. The second clause, introduced by ἀλλά functions parenthetically to the longer sentence that ends with the third clause. The final clause seems best as its own separate sentence while finishing the thought of the previous sentence. This verse can be viewed as "expanding" on the previous verse (Smith, 114).

φόβος οὐκ ἔστιν ἐν τῇ ἀγάπῃ, "There is no fear in love." John states a principle while moving the predicate nominative φόβος to the head of the clause to make it emphatic.[123] He also includes εἰμι in the clause for emphasis as well. In this case εἰμι should be seen as a gnomic present and thereby make this a universal truth.[124] This, along with its fourfold repetition draws attention to the importance of what John is saying. This first use of φόβος is anarthrous because being moved forward for emphasis (Akin, 186) as the predicate nominative in its sentence, the absence of the article insures it is not mistaken for the subject (Schnackenburg, 247).[125] By this construction John draws our attention to the issue of fear and its relationship to love, with fear being the opposite of confidence (Burdick, 336). This fear is not reverence but dread (Pentecost, 119; Westcott, 159). It represents one of the possible emotions a child of God will experience on the day he or she meets Jesus at the Bema Seat judgment. Just as some will shrink back in shame at his appearing (2:28), so, too, some will experience fear rather than calm assurance when brought into his presence. However, for those who understand God's love, a different expectation rests within them.

John's use of ἀγάπῃ has two possible referents (Marshall, 224): (1) This is God's love for us. We cannot fear if we understand God's love toward us. This seems the best option because "love" has the article of previous reference (Lenski, 513). Even so, though on one hand the article makes love specific, on the other the absence of modifiers makes it more general (Burdick, 336). (2) This is our love for God. We cannot love and fear him at the same time. Our loving God seems a less likely cause of confidence when compared to knowing he loves us. Thus, the first option is best.

---

123. Marshall (224) restates this saying well: "Fear and love cannot coexist." Schnackenburg (248) describes this as a "general statement" which serves as an "admonition." I see it as a truth from which John will develop his discussion about the believer's experience on judgment day.

124. B. M. Fanning, *Verbal Aspect in New Testament Greek*, 208–209.

125. Burdick (336) posits that the absence of article indicates "fear" is an abstract, general idea. However, its lack of an article is better explained by its role in the clause.

ἀλλ' ἡ τελεία ἀγάπη ἔξω βάλλει τὸν φόβον, " but perfect love casts out fear." Introducing this parenthetical statement with the strong adversative ἀλλά makes a sharp contrast between fear and love (Westcott, 159).[126]

Τελεία ἀγάπη ("perfect love") may be understood in various ways: (1) God's love, which is perfect (Williamson, 150). (2) The believer's love for God. (3) The believer's love for other believers. (4) It refers to love in its totality as coming from God and expressing itself in Jesus' sacrifice, which results in believer's expressing it among themselves (Harris, 198).

By τελεία John means the love to which he refers is mature, fully developed, and has achieved its purpose in the life of the believer.[127] This is the love of God fully understood by the Christian. They would understand that God has their highest good in mind and so would recognize this even when facing his judgment (Westcott, 159). However, not all believers understand God's love and so may experience this fear when anticipating his judgment.

This is similar to the idea of walking in the light. John is now talking about the impact of a believer walking in the sphere of God's love. When God's love is fully understood and thereby impacts the life of a believer, it will radically change his or her view of himself or herself. That changed view invokes within each of them a confidence that enables him or her to live in the realm of God's love and not in the realm of fear. As love fully expresses itself in and through the believer, the maturing process that occurs in turn drives out fear (Rensberger, 122; Williamson, 151). Still, for some fear is a proper response, under the circumstances of the choices they are making apart from God's will. However, such choices lead to fear as they anticipate God's response.

ὅτι ὁ φόβος κόλασιν ἔχει, " because fear has to do with punishment."[128] The fear here involves one's anticipation of a future consequence.[129] In this case the consequence is painful and punitive. Brooke (125) says it

126. Haas, de Jonge, and Swellengrebel (129) differ and see ἀλλά indicating a climactic statement follows rather than a contrast.

127. BDAG, 995; G. Delling, "τέλος, ... τέλειος," *TDNT* 8:73–77.

128. Rensberger (122) suggests that John used an obscure way to say "(the prospect of) punishment causes fear."

129. John is not excluding reverential fear by this statement (Marshall, 224). Examples from Scripture include: Luke 1:50; Acts 10:2, 22, 35; 13:16, 26; 2 Cor 7:1; Eph 5:21; 6:5; Col 3:22; 1 Pet 1:17.

"'includes the punishment which it anticipates,' but is in itself of the nature of punishment."

The term κόλασις is better translated as "punishment" rather than "torment," though the idea of suffering is better captured by torment over punishment. It refers to the "infliction of suffering or pain in chastisement" though it can also involve retribution as well.[130] It involves the actual punishment received.[131] Thus Christians in whom God's love has not reached its full mature expression may not understand that they need not fear God's retributive punishment when they meet Jesus. Scripture teaches that believers are disciplined by God (Heb 12) in this life and may even be killed by God for their sins (1 John 5:16–17; 1 Cor 11:29–32). God's children do face a day of judgment when they meet their Lord. However, the purpose of that judgment is not to determine punishment, but reward. It is true that rewards can be lost (2 John 8; 1 Cor 3:10–15), but equally true that punishment cannot be gained. Nowhere in Scripture are believers described as being punished at the Judgment Seat of Christ;[132] only the unregenerate.

Akin (186) interprets this punishment as eternal and that this person is unregenerate. Brown (531) agrees with him seeing it anticipating the "final judgment," which is "the absence of God." He notes that in Hellenistic Greek the meaning and emphasis of κόλασις changed from "harmfully punitive" to "eternal punishment."[133] Thus the affects of that punishment is "already making itself felt" in fear. Likewise, Schnackenburg (248–49) sees κόλασις as a "judicial term for eschatological judgment" (also Williamson,

---

130. BDAG, 555; J. Schneider, "κολάζω, κόλασις," *TDNT* 3:816–17.

131. Bultmann (73) says κόλασις "means the punishment associated with eschatological judgment." It may be understood in one of two ways (74): "Because fear has to do with punishment" or "because fear has punishment (in view)."

132. Christians can, however, suffer loss at the judgment seat of Christ (1 Cor 3:10–15).

133. References to eternal punishment using this term include: *2 Macc.* 4:38, *T. Reu.* 5:5 and *T. Gad* 7:5; and Matt 25:46. Based on these Harris (198–99) sees this meaning fear of eternal punishment. "In other words, in the antithetical ('either/or') categories in which the author presents his arguments, a person is either a genuine believer, who becomes 'perfected' in love a he/she remains/resides in love and in a mutually indwelling relationship with God (cf. 4:16b), or one is not a genuine believer at all, but one who (like the opponents) hates his/her fellow member of the community, is a liar, and does not know God at all."

151).[134] Kruse (168) connects this to Matt 25:46 and sees this meaning eternal punishment for unbelievers.

When seen as a general principle, one could argue such, but would have to ask how this applies to John's readers, whom he clearly considers regenerate believers. That this is not a question of their eternal destiny is clarified by what follows. However, he is introducing the discussion with a general principle that is true of believers and nonbelievers. For the unregenerate, the fear of eternal punishment is legitimate, being outside of the sphere of God's love and walking in the sphere of his wrath (Rom 1:18–19; 2:5; Eph 2:1–3; 1 Thess 1:10; 5:9–10). However, for the regenerate, to the extent that they do not understand the love of God, to the extent that love is not perfected in them, they will experience the same kind of fear. John has already demonstrated that his readers are loved by God. However, one may not feel loved or understand the nature of loving discipline. That one, even as God's child, will fear punishment from him.

Yarbrough (262) understands John to be saying by this that fear "is rooted in the expectation of punishment at God's hands" and "therefore such fear of retribution is a thing of the past for them."

ὁ δὲ φοβούμενος οὐ τετελείωται ἐν τῇ ἀγάπῃ, "and the one fearing has not been perfected in love." So what of the believer who fears Jesus' return? Changing from the noun φόβος to the present articular participle ὁ φοβούμενος, John identifies the fearful Christian. This is a person characterized by fear. It does not mean they deserve punishment. John clarifies this. This person may be earning great reward in heaven, but because of a lack of understanding of the love of God, may still fear meeting Jesus. However, what John says is that when God's love reaches its mature expression in the life of the believer, this fear will be gone. Fear and mature love cannot coexist. Kistemaker (340–41) sees this "complete" love driving out fear because it motivates the believer to "keep God's commands." However, John is not saying that obedience casts out fear. Though love for God expresses itself in obedience, it does not follow that all obedience springs from love. Some obey out of fear, precisely because they are immature spiritually. They may be loved by God, but his love has not reached its mature expression in them.

134. Die Begründung geht davon aus, daß die Furcht noch das Gericht vor sich siehts; ist eschatologischer Gerichtsterminus (The reason for the dread is the anticipation of judgment; κόλασις is a judicial term for eschatological judgment).

However, what is true is that when love's expression in the believer reaches its maturity, it will produce confidence in the Christian anticipating Jesus' judgment of the world and evaluation of his saints. This mature love "involves a love for God which is based upon our sense of God's love for us, and this love relationship is what removes our fear as we face the day of judgment" (Kruse, 168–69).

4:19 We come to another emphatic statement that includes a confession from John. He is no different from his readers as a beneficiary of the love of God. This verse repeats the thoughts of 4:7 and 11 (Rensberger, 125).

ἡμεῖς ἀγαπῶμεν, ὅτι αὐτὸς πρῶτος ἠγάπησεν ἡμᾶς, "We love because he loved us first." John now takes us to the ultimate source and cause of our love for one another and for God. He adds the first-person plural pronoun ἡμεῖς, making it emphatic. Further, his use of the present tense without the expected direct object indicates that the verb is in the indicative rather than subjunctive mood (Westcott, 161). With the indicative, John states a fact. The hortatory subjunctive would have been used for John to invite his readers in joining him in loving. Though this has been commanded earlier, it is not needed now. Rather, John is taking his readers to the source of their ability to love with a love that removes fear.

The pronoun ἡμεῖς is once more emphatically located at the head of the clause. Brooke (125) sees this ἡμεῖς referring to all believers. Strecker (169) sees this use of ἡμεῖς "taking up the first person plurals from vv. 16 and 17." He (169, n. 47) also sees this indicating that this is not a polemical section of John's argument because of his own inclusion in ἡμεῖς. Thus what John has to say is true of him as well as all other believers.

There are two possibilities for the mood of ἀγαπῶμεν: (1) It is the indicative and states a fact (Brooke, 125; Burdick, 338; Haas, de Jonge, and Swellengrebel, 130; Williamson, 151). Though the subject in the immediately prior context is fear in judgment, John is now turning to talk about loving other believers. As an indicative John would be stating a principle on which the discussion that follows is based. Against this is the imperatival nature of what follows as opposed to the declarative nature of what preceded. (2) It is imperative and gives a command (Law, 402; Rensberger, 125; Strecker, 170). Schnackenburg (249) insists that ἀγαπῶμεν must be cohortative (*Kohortativ*) because of its "parenetic application" (*paränetische*

Anwendung). However, it need not be a command to make the following parenetic. Thus the first option seems best.

This absence of a direct object for ἀγαπῶμεν makes that object ambiguous by design.

(1) He could be referring to loving God (Houlden, 120; Rensberger, 125). However, John has talked about God loving us (3:1) and how we recognize his love for us (3:16), and our need to love one another, but not our loving God. So, this would be the first direct statement about us loving God!

(2) It could still include the reciprocal idea of loving fellow believers, loving one another as he had called on us to do in 4:7 (Schnackenburg, 249). This would fit well with what follows and clarify further the nature of the love that cast out fear in the previous verses.

(3) He may intend a double meaning. We are able to love both God and one another (Haas, de Jonge, and Swellengrebel, 130; Harris, 199). John seems to enjoy the double meaning and appears to have used it here in a similar way as in 1:7 concerning mutual fellowship that was equally ambiguous. This double sense fits best with what has been said and will be said in the remainder of this Epistle.

With the adjectival role of πρῶτος John describes the cause-and-effect relationship between God's love demonstrated to us and our response of loving him and others as we imitate him.[135] The emphatic pronoun αὐτὸς refers to God, best seen as God the Father, from the context of the demonstrated love. Thus our motivation for loving one another, as well as God, is God's example in loving us first.

Now it is time to address the issue of personal claims and conduct. Whereas active love produces assurance before God in the life of a believer, an absence of love denies that same relationship with God. This is not to say one is not a child of God, but the relationship is essentially denied by unloving actions. This is similar to what John was saying in 3:7–12, that conduct expresses parentage, so we need to act like our heavenly Father lest we look like we belong with the other.

---

135. BDAG, 892. W. Michaelis,, "πρῶτος," *TDNT* 6:865–66.

4:20 Love of God is demonstrated by loving Christians. In this verse and the one that follows John affirms that an absence of love denies relationship with God. This denial does not mean a person is unregenerate. It just means that the person is not living according to what is true. Their testimony to the world is invalidated and so it will not recognize him or her as a disciple of Jesus (John 13:35). John's explanation of this truth takes the form of a chiasm with ἑώρακεν at its center and ἀγαπῶν and ἀγαπᾶν on both ends.

"The one who does not love"	ὁ μὴ ἀγαπῶν
"his brother whom he has seen"	τὸν ἀδελφὸν αὐτοῦ ὃν ἑώρακεν,
"God whom he has not seen."	τὸν θεὸν ὃν οὐχ ἑώρακεν
"is not able to love"	οὐ δύναται ἀγαπᾶν

So first, John examines the claim and the reality.

ἐάν τις εἴπῃ ὅτι Ἀγαπῶ τὸν θεὸν καὶ τὸν ἀδελφὸν αὐτοῦ μισῇ, "If anyone says, 'I love God' and hates his brother." John employs the same ἐάν construction used in 1 John 1:6, 8, 10; 2:4, 6, 9. Harris (200) sees this statement having John's opponents in view, as he did for the other verses. Others see this suggesting the same and indicating a quotation of the opponents (Brown, 533; Johnson, 117; Rensberger, 126). However, Strecker (170) rejects the idea that this is the "proposition of a false teacher," because "τις has a general significance elsewhere in 1 John as well, and cannot be limited to the emergence of opponents."[136] He notes (171, n. 59) 1 John 2:1, 15 and 5:16 (ἐάν τις), 2 John 10 (εἴ τις), and 1 John 2:27 (τις) as examples. Brooke (125) and Burdick (339) concur, however Brooke allows for the opponents to be in view as well. Burdick (339) interprets this as a hypothetical situation.

John raises the claim that may be made by anyone. His use of τις includes not only his readers but any believer. He is neither describing a nonbeliever nor is he stating a universal principle applicable to believers and nonbelievers alike, as he had earlier with the articular present participle constructions. Rather, this addresses those within the family of God. This is made evident in that he speaks of that person's relationship with *his brother*. The repetition of τὸν ἀδελφὸν αὐτοῦ emphasizes the object of love

136. Jesus uses this ἐάν τις construction three times outside of John's Gospel (Matt 21:3; Mark 11:3; Luke 19:31) and ten times in it (John 6:51; 7:17, 37; 8:51, 52; 10:9; 11:9; 12:26, 47; 14:23). In John 9:22; 11:57 it is used by the Jews. In 9:31 it is used by the man born blind.

or neglect as a fellow believer. So through this John raises the possibility that a Christian may hate another Christian. What he means by "hate" has already been described in terms of neglecting to meet a fellow believer's needs when one is able to do so (3:17). So with that in view, John brings up the logical inconsistency of such an action.

Using a third class condition once again, John raises the possibility that one may claim to love God while hating another Christian. By his use of ἐάν with the subjunctives εἴπῃ and μισῇ, he affirms that this may or may not be said and done by any believer. With the copulative connective καὶ John joins these two together and is speaking of someone making one claim while doing the other. His use of the present tense μισῇ indicates the hating is in process but need not be durative or habitual (contra Haas, de Jonge, and Swellengrebel, 131). Rather than John indicating a lifestyle, he sees any failure to love as invalidating the person's claim while he is hating. Therefore this is something that could be true of a believer. A believer can lie about loving God. However, "The proof of love is seen in action" (Williamson, 152). That lie is exposed by his hateful treatment of his Christian brother. This completes the protasis, the "if" portion of the conditional sentence. He is now ready to talk about the reality that flows from these conditions.

ψεύστης ἐστίν, "he is a liar." John calls the one claiming to love God while hating his fellow Christian a liar.[137] This same term is used to describe the person who claims to know God while not obeying him (2:4), who denies that Jesus is the Christ (2:22)—the first a believer, the second an antichrist. So John does not describe this person as deceived like he had the one making false claims about sin in 1:8. He is also not like the believer who has hated his brother and has been walking in darkness, unaware of his own blindness (2:9–11). Rather, this is a statement of his character. He is not just lying. He *is* a liar.

ὁ γὰρ μὴ ἀγαπῶν τὸν ἀδελφὸν αὐτοῦ ὃν ἑώρακεν, "for the one who does not love his brother whom he has seen." The explanatory clause introduced by γὰρ reflects a chiastic structure as follows:

"the one not loving"	ὁ μὴ ἀγαπῶν
"his brother whom he has seen"	τὸν ἀδελφὸν αὐτοῦ ὃν ἑώρακεν,

137. Burdick (340) defines a liar as someone who "attempts to deceive by conveying misinformation." In this case the misinformation is their claim to love God.

"God whom he has not seen"	τὸν θεὸν ὃν οὐχ ἑώρακεν
"he is not able to love"	οὐ δύναται ἀγαπᾶν

This makes the contrast central to the meaning of the chiasm. The contrast is between who he sees and does not see.

John will now explain why this person is a liar and not just self-deceived. He begins by stating the problem differently. Where he said he "hates" his brother earlier, now that hatred is defined as "not loving." Repeating the articular present participle, ὁ ἀγαπῶν and combining it with the negative particle μὴ John once again describes the character of the person. This is one who by nature does not love his Christian brother. He has already described this lack of love in terms of refusing to meet physical needs (3:17). Thus hating another Christian is not an emotion directed toward someone. It is what we do and can be something as "mild" as unconcern. John's point here is that this lack of love is expressed relationally with fellow believers. This is not a failure to be aware of the need. The aorist ἑώρακεν indicates he has been seeing him for some time (Akin, 187; Haas, de Jonge, and Swellengrebel, 131; Stott, 173). He is personally and visibly aware of that need. There is no excuse.

τὸν θεὸν ὃν οὐχ ἑώρακεν οὐ δύναται ἀγαπᾶν, "is not able to love God whom he has not seen." John now turns to the reality behind a refusal to love one's fellow Christian. The unloving Christian does not love God either. Using the same terms and construction, John now affirms that it is impossible for the believer to love God without loving other believers. The repetition of the perfect tense ἑώρακεν and ἀγαπάω with "his brother" and "God" juxtaposed makes the contrast sharp. Some see this as a rhetorical question: "How is he able to love God whom he has not seen?" (Haas, de Jonge, and Swellengrebel, 114). However, it is better seen as a direct statement because of the role of γὰρ making this statement an explanation of what John means by "he is a liar."[138]

138. Williamson (152) says that either translation means the same thing, which is true. However, the grammar ultimately points to a statement rather than a rhetorical question.

4:21 We are not commanded something in Scripture if it is automatic or could not be done repeatedly. Here John takes us to God's expectation of every recipient of his love.

καὶ ταύτην τὴν ἐντολὴν ἔχομεν ἀπ' αὐτοῦ, "And this commandment we have from him." The logical conjunction *καὶ* ties this sentence with the preceding one (Brown, 534; Smalley 264; Strecker, 173). Strecker (173) sees it also having an epexegetical function as well. Yarbrough (265) says this verse "summarizes and extends" the point John was making in verse 20. It moves from the problem to its solution.

This takes us back to the commandment to love one another, which has now been stated in terms of Christian brothers. Grammatically, "this commandment" (ταύτην τὴν ἐντολὴν) has been moved forward in the sentence for emphasis. The noun ἐντολὴν with its article is functioning as a simple direct object of the verb ἔχομεν like 2 John 10 rather than as some special predicate nominative construction (contra Brown, 513, 524; and Smalley, 264).

In this translation it is similarly moved forward, though grammatically it would normally follow ἔχομεν rather than precede it. This reflects John's literary strategy to call attention to this being the commandment to love. By moving it out of its usual place in English, its significance is similarly communicated. Having done that, John next uses the preposition ἀπὸ to indicate source or origin. Through this he affirms that the command was "spoken" by God; it comes directly from him.

His use of αὐτοῦ seems purposefully ambiguous once again, though the immediate context would indicate God the Father is in view (Akin, 187; Brooke, 127; Haas, de Jonge, and Swellengrebel, 132; Harris, 201; Marshall, 225, n. 28; Schnackenburg, 250, n. 2) rather than Jesus (Barker, 347; Houlden, 120, n. 2; Smith, 116; Stott, 273–74; Thompson, 129) or God's command expressed in Jesus' teachings (Dodd, 123; Grayston, 132; Smalley, 265). If Jesus were in view, John would more likely have used ἐκεῖνος instead, which has been his pattern (2:6; 3:3, 5, 7, 16; 4:17).

ἵνα ὁ ἀγαπῶν τὸν θεὸν ἀγαπᾷ καὶ τὸν ἀδελφὸν αὐτοῦ, "that the one who loves God also should love his brother." This *ἵνα* is again epexegetical to *ταύτην* (Harris, 201; Westcott, 162) rather than expressing purpose or result. The content of the command is now given. This may be an allusion to the two great commands of the Old Testament (Love God, and love your neighbor as yourself). The subjunctive *ἀγαπᾷ* is hortatory as well as, we should realize, obligatory. Here *καὶ* is best rendered "also" and shows the mutual obligation that receiving God's love brings. God's desired response from us is not that we love him. His desire is not selfish. Rather, he desires we love others along with him. He wants to share our love with the rest of our spiritual family as much as he wants to receive it. We see the selflessness of God in this command.

Biblical Theology Comments

We learn more about the person of God in this section. Three truths are developed by John:

(1) God is love. This is not a description of his essential being any more than the earlier declaration, "God is light." Rather, this describes one of his divine attributes. John teaches that the love of God expresses itself in his actions. It is something we can express in our conduct. This obligation we have as a result of his loving action toward us in giving us a Savior and thereby imparting his love to us. As recipients of God's love we are expected to communicate his love to others. This love moves God's children to express their birth by living out his love in their relationships with one another.

(2) God is seen through the love of his children. No living human has seen God. However, God can be seen by this world through the loving actions of his children as they express his love toward each other.

(3) God is relational. He abides with and in his children. This relationship is reciprocal and interior to the child of God. God not only dwells within his children, in the person of the Holy Spirit, but he communes with them as well. This relationship is conditional, predicated on obedience to his command to love one another.

John continues to develop his Christology and we are reminded that Jesus is the Son of God, a title reaffirming his deity. As God's Son, he "was sent" through his incarnation to be the Savior of the world. Thus his relationship to the world is that of its deliverer as well as its Judge. Those who have him as Savior and obey him as Lord by loving their brothers and sisters in the faith, have hope in him rather than fear of him. The lost world and disobedient believers fear his coming judgment, for he is a righteous judge.

The Holy Spirit is a gift from God, both to the individual and the church. He is the agent through whom we experience the mutually abiding relationship with God. John does not develop his pneumatology much at all in this epistle.

With regard to the extent of Jesus' redeeming death, we see John affirm once again its universal efficacy. As Savior of the world, Jesus' death was on behalf of both the elect and nonelect. This does not mean that everyone is automatically saved. However, none can say that God did not provide a means of forgiveness. John does not address the issue of election in this section. He only speaks of the full efficacy of Christ's work on the cross. It was sufficient for all, though not all will benefit from it.

Application and Devotional Implications

4:7–11 How do we go about loving one another, especially when we have some people in our church family that are not particularly easy to love? We have to see ourselves as agents of God's love and recognize that our ability to love that person does not come from our will, but from God's enablement. To understand how to love them we must meditate on God's love until we understand its nature and expression from God to us. Only when we really understand how much and how we are loved by God can we in turn live out this love for others. It is a costly love and will require our time, energy, emotions and money. However, when we do it the world will know we are Christians by our love. They will also know that our God is a loving God. They will see him as he is in the faces and voices of his children.

4:12 The passion narratives of the Gospels give us the most vivid pictures of God's love in action. Though familiar, they are worthy of our lifelong study and meditation. Meditate on how Jesus' death expressed God's love for us. Allow its truth to change you. It was not until I had meditated on Rom 8:9 that I came to comprehend that, whenever I am tempted to question God's love, I have unquestionable proof of his love in Jesus' sacrificial death for me. It changed my view of God from that of an angry Lord to a loving Father. However, this is not the place to stop. As we begin to comprehend God's love, we should also sense the obligation we have to express it to others. To do this we must find ways to show love to others. This kind of love will cost us, just as it cost God his Son and his Son his life. We will not love other Christians without sacrificing time, money, energy, emotions, or public acceptance. However, since loving Christians is an activity rather than an attitude, we will never do it without taking conscious action to act out God's love within the body of Christ.

4:15 This verse serves as a reminder that one must believe in Jesus as he is revealed, not as he is fictionalized by false teachings. It is not just the "name" alone that saves, but the person behind that name when correctly understood. I do not mean to say by this that a person must be conversant in orthodox Christology to be justified, but that whatever he or she knows about Jesus must be true. Muslims believe Jesus was a prophet. However, their denial of his deity and Sonship keeps them from believing in the real Jesus. A Hindu might believe Jesus is a god along with their other gods. Their Jesus is not the real Jesus. The Jesus Seminar believes he was a historical figure. Yet the majority of its participants denied his resurrection and conformed him to their vision of a politically correct Savior. Their redefinition of Jesus certainly keeps them from believing in the real Jesus. In contrast, a five year old child may not understand a whole lot about Jesus. However, when he or she puts faith in Jesus, who rose from the dead and loves the little children of the world, that child of humans becomes a child of God.

"Whoever confesses" is applicable for both believers and nonbelievers. It is true whether one is asking the question of a teacher's salvation or of a fellow believer's fellowship with God. As justification truth, one cannot experience the life of God without believing and confessing the right things about Jesus. As sanctification truth, a believer cannot experience the mutual indwelling he has been granted apart from believing and confessing the right things about Jesus as well. Our walk with the Lord is only as real as it is based on truth. This idea was introduced in 3:24, where mutual abiding was linked to obedience to God's commands.

4:17–18 How do we prepare ourselves for the day we will stand before Jesus as our righteous judge? As we were warned in 2:28 and now here, some Christians will experience fear and shame when brought before Jesus for the first time. However, John tells us how we can avoid the fear and shame. It is in experiencing and expressing the love of God. If we know we are loved by God and his love is expressed through our life, we know Jesus will be pleased to see us when we come before his Bema Seat. We will not be anticipating punishment or disapproval. We will be anticipating reception and acceptance. The love of God we experience now will be the experience we continue to have in his physical presence. So how do we do this? We must let God love us. We must let his love for and in us express itself through us with the children of God he places around me. We must be involved in the life of our church by being positively involved in the life of its members. We must talk to them, pray with them, laugh and cry with them. We must be in their homes and invite them into ours.We must ask them how they are doing and mean it, and then listen attentively as they tell us their story with its sorrows and joys.

4:20–21 Can one love God without loving other Christians? No. We do not express our love for God by saying "I love you" to God. We expess our love for God by doing something loving for a brother or sister in Christ. If we see someone who needs loving and ignore him or her, we are hating him or her. This is not a perspective issue. It is not that I hate him or her from a divine perspective but am okay from a human perspective. God's perspective is absolute reality. He says doing nothing is hating and murdering our brother or sister in Christ. With God there are no degrees of love and hate. So to make our claim to knowing God valid, and to know him as he wants to be known, we must show love for fellow Christians by being honestly concerned about them. Just as in 4:17–18, it is in what we do, not in what we think or feel, that determines whether we love or hate that person.

Selected Bibliography

Beale, G. K., and D. A. Carson. *Commentary on the New Testament Use of the Old Testament*. Grand Rapids: Baker Academic, 2007.

Brown, C., gen. ed. *New International Dictionary of New Testament Theology*. 4 vols. Grand Rapids: Zondervan, 1975–1985.

Fanning, B. M. *Verbal Aspect in New Testament Greek*. Oxford: Clarendon Press, 1990.

Gundry, R. H., and R. W. Howell. "The Sense and Syntax of John 3:14–17 with Special Reference to the Use of Οὕτως … ὥστε in John 3:16." *NovT* 41 (1999): 24–39.

Hiebert, D. E. "An Expositional Study of 1 John—Part 8: An Exposition of 1 John 4:7–21." *BSac* 147 (1990): 69–89.

Louw, J. P. "Verbal Aspect in the First Letter of John." *Neot* 9 (1975): 98–104.

Malatesta, E. *Interiority and Covenant: A Study of* εἶναι ἐν *and* μένειν ἐν *in the First Letter of Saint John*. Rome: Biblical Institute Press, 1978.

Martin, R. P., and P. H. Davids, eds. *Dictionary of the Later New Testament and Its Developments*. Electronic ed. Downers Grove, IL: InterVarsity Press, 2000.

Metzger, B. M., and United Bible Societies. *A Textual Commentary on the Greek New Testament*. 2nd ed. New York: United Bible Societies, 1994.

Moule, C. F. D. "A Neglected Factor in the Interpretation of Johannine Eschatology." In *Studies in John,* 155–160. NovTSup 24. Leiden: Brill, 1970.
.Rusam, D. *Gemeinschaft der Kinder Gottes: Das Motiv der Gotteskindschaft und die Gemeinden der johanneischen Briefe.* Stuttgart: Verlag W. Kohlhammer, 1993.
Sevenster, G. "Remarks on the Humanity of Jesus in the Gospel and Letters of John." In *Studies in John,* 185–93. NovTSup 24. Leiden: Brill, 1970.
Vanhoozer, Kevin J., Craig G. Bartholomew, Daniel J. Treier, and N. T. Wright, eds. *Dictionary for Theological Interpretation of the Bible.* . Grand Rapids: Baker Academic, 2005.
Wallace, D. B. *Greek Grammar beyond the Basics.* Grand Rapids: Zondervan, 1996.

God's Love Communicated (5:1–20)

Introduction

As we continue this third major movement of John's epistle, we see his continued focus on God's love, both flowing from him into his children, and then from his children back to him and to his other children. In 4:8, John declares "God is love." He describes God's love as expressed in history through the sending of his Son as Savior of the world. Further, God's love perfected in his children takes away fear of future judgment at the Bema Seat judgment of Christ. Love of God is impossible apart from love of other believers. The chapter ends with the command, once again, to love other Christians, our "brothers." Now, as we enter chapter 5, he begins by answering the question, "Who is my brother?"

What John teaches in these following verses is that experiencing eternal life is contingent on faith and obedience, leading to active concern for the brethren and confidence in one's position in Christ. This chapter is not without challenges. Furthermore, as will be seen, certain assumptions and theories, such as the Johannine community theory, often exert a powerful influence on the choice of interpretive options. As noted in the introduction and evidenced by the approach taken in interpreting the previous chapters, the theory of a Johannine community and an organized secessionist movement are considered speculative and therefore do not influence how John's message should be understood. As a result, though some of what John says must be recognized as polemical in nature, it must be seen in light of his pastoral concern for his readers and not as a response to an organized movement. He does recognize the presence of false teachers within his churches. He does address christological issues. However, these are secondary to the greater need of his spiritual children to experience the eternal life granted them through a healthy relationship with eternal life incarnate, Jesus Christ, the Son of God.

Original Text

1 Πᾶς ὁ πιστεύων ὅτι Ἰησοῦς ἐστιν ὁ χριστὸς ἐκ τοῦ θεοῦ γεγέννηται, καὶ πᾶς
ὁ ἀγαπῶν τὸν γεννήσαντα ἀγαπᾷ καὶa τὸν γεγεννημένον ἐξ αὐτοῦ. **2** ἐν τούτῳ
γινώσκομεν ὅτι ἀγαπῶμεν τὰ τέκνα τοῦ θεοῦ, ὅταν τὸν θεὸν ἀγαπῶμεν καὶ τὰς
ἐντολὰς αὐτοῦ τηρῶμεν.a **3** αὕτη γάρ ἐστιν ἡ ἀγάπη τοῦ θεοῦ ἵνα τὰς ἐντολὰς
αὐτοῦ τηρῶμεν, καὶ αἱ ἐντολαὶ αὐτοῦ βαρεῖαι οὐκ εἰσίν, **4** ὅτι πᾶν τὸ γεγεννημέ-
νον ἐκ τοῦ θεοῦ νικᾷ τὸν κόσμον. καὶ αὕτη ἐστὶν ἡ νίκη ἡ νικήσασα τὸν κόσμον,
ἡ πίστις ἡμῶν· **5** τίς δέ ἐστιν ὁ νικῶν τὸν κόσμον εἰ μὴ ὁ πιστεύων ὅτι Ἰησοῦς
ἐστιν ὁ υἱὸς τοῦ θεοῦ;

6 Οὗτός ἐστιν ὁ ἐλθὼν δι’ ὕδατος καὶ αἵματος, Ἰησοῦς Χριστός· οὐκ ἐν τῷ ὕδατι
μόνον ἀλλ’ ἐν τῷ ὕδατι καὶ ἐν τῷ αἵματι· καὶ τὸ πνεῦμά ἐστιν τὸ μαρτυροῦν, ὅτι
τὸ πνεῦμά ἐστιν ἡ ἀλήθεια. **7** ὅτι τρεῖς εἰσιν οἱ μαρτυροῦντες,[a] **8** τὸ πνεῦμα καὶ
τὸ ὕδωρ καὶ τὸ αἷμα, καὶ οἱ τρεῖς εἰς τὸ ἕν εἰσιν. **9** εἰ τὴν μαρτυρίαν τῶν ἀνθρώ-
πων λαμβάνομεν, ἡ μαρτυρία τοῦ θεοῦ μείζων ἐστίν, ὅτι αὕτη ἐστὶν ἡ μαρτυρία
τοῦ θεοῦ ὅτι μεμαρτύρηκεν περὶ τοῦ υἱοῦ αὐτοῦ. **10** ὁ πιστεύων εἰς τὸν υἱὸν τοῦ
θεοῦ ἔχει τὴν μαρτυρίαν a ἐν αὐτῷ·a ὁ μὴ πιστεύων bτῷ θεῷb ψεύστην πεποί-
ηκεν αὐτόν, ὅτι οὐ πεπίστευκεν εἰς τὴν μαρτυρίαν ἣν μεμαρτύρηκεν ὁ θεὸς περὶ
τοῦ υἱοῦ αὐτοῦ. **11** καὶ αὕτη ἐστὶν ἡ μαρτυρία, ὅτι ζωὴν αἰώνιον ἔδωκεν ὁ θεὸς
ἡμῖν, καὶ αὕτη ἡ ζωὴ ἐν τῷ υἱῷ αὐτοῦ ἐστιν. **12** ὁ ἔχων τὸν υἱὸν ἔχει τὴν ζωήν· ὁ
μὴ ἔχων τὸν υἱὸν τοῦ θεοῦ τὴν ζωὴν οὐκ ἔχει.

13 Ταῦτα ἔγραψα ὑμῖν ἵνα εἰδῆτε ὅτι ζωὴν ἔχετε αἰώνιον, τοῖς πιστεύουσιν εἰς τὸ
ὄνομα τοῦ υἱοῦ τοῦ θεοῦ, aκαὶ ἵνα πιστεύητε εἰς τὸ ὄνομα τοῦ υἱοῦ τοῦ θεοῦ.a **14**
καὶ αὕτη ἐστὶν ἡ παρρησία ἣν ἔχομεν πρὸς αὐτόν, ὅτι ἐάν τι αἰτώμεθα κατὰ τὸ
θέλημα αὐτοῦ ἀκούει ἡμῶν. **15** καὶ ἐὰν οἴδαμεν ὅτι ἀκούει ἡμῶν ὃ ἐὰν αἰτώμεθα,
οἴδαμεν ὅτι ἔχομεν τὰ αἰτήματα ἃ ᾐτήκαμεν ἀπ’ αὐτοῦ.

16 ἐάν τις ἴδῃ τὸν ἀδελφὸν αὐτοῦ ἁμαρτάνοντα ἁμαρτίαν μὴ πρὸς θάνατον,
αἰτήσει, καὶ δώσει αὐτῷ ζωήν, τοῖς ἁμαρτάνουσιν μὴ πρὸς θάνατον. ἔστιν ἁμαρ-
τία πρὸς θάνατον· οὐ περὶ ἐκείνης λέγω ἵνα ἐρωτήσῃ. **17** πᾶσα ἀδικία ἁμαρτία
ἐστίν, καὶ ἔστιν ἁμαρτία οὐ πρὸς θάνατον.

18 Οἴδαμεν ὅτι πᾶς ὁ γεγεννημένος ἐκ τοῦ θεοῦ οὐχ ἁμαρτάνει, ἀλλ' ὁ γεννηθεὶς
ἐκ τοῦ θεοῦ τηρεῖ αὐτὸν,a καὶ ὁ πονηρὸς οὐχ ἅπτεται αὐτοῦ. **19** οἴδαμεν ὅτι ἐκ
τοῦ θεοῦ ἐσμεν, καὶ ὁ κόσμος ὅλος ἐν τῷ πονηρῷ κεῖται. **20** οἴδαμεν δὲ ὅτι ὁ υἱὸς
τοῦ θεοῦ ἥκει, καὶ δέδωκεν ἡμῖν διάνοιαν ἵνα γινώσκωμεν τὸν ἀληθινόν· καὶ
ἐσμὲν ἐν τῷ ἀληθινῷ, ἐν τῷ υἱῷ αὐτοῦ Ἰησοῦ Χριστῷ. οὗτός ἐστιν ὁ ἀληθινὸς
θεὸς καὶ ζωὴ αἰώνιος.

Textual Notes

1.a. The weight of MS evidence favors the inclusion of the final καὶ (א A K P 049 056 0142 81 88 104 181 330 436 451 614 629 630 945 1241 1505 1739 1877 1881 2127 2412 2492 2495 *Byz Lect* it^{c,p} vg^{cl} syr^{p,h} cop^{bo} arm eth). Metzger's concern over possible scribal emendation is unwarranted and the few MSS that omit it are easier to explain as scribal emendations than keeping the final καὶ (B Ψ 048 33 62 326 2298 it^{ar,dem,div,m,q} vg^{ww} cop^{sa}).[139]

2.a. The better reading is τηρῶμεν over ποιῶμεν, *contra* Metzger, having the broader MS support (א K L P 048 049 056 0142 88 104 181 330 451 629 630 945 1241 1505 1877 1881 2127 2492 *Byz Lect* it^{p}) and being more consistent with John's practice of repetition for emphasis.[140]

7.a. The TR (reflected in NKJV and KJV) includes the words ἐν τῷ οὐρανῷ, ὁ πατήρ, ὁ λόγος, καὶ τὸ ἅγιον πνεῦμα· καὶ οὗτοι οἱ τρεῖς ἕν εἰσι. καὶ τρεῖς εἰσὶν οἱ μαρτυροῦντες ἐν τῇ γῇ, τὸ πνεῦμα, καὶ τὸ ὕδωρ, καὶ τὸ αἷμα, which lacks MS support and should never be included. Metzger's discussion is thorough and conclusive and need not be repeated here.[141]

10.a…a The SBLGNT reading of ἐν αὐτῷ is preferred over the UBS^{4} choice of ἐν ἑαυτῷ, though the meaning of both is identical.[142] First, the majority of support points to some version of αὐτῷ. It is more likely that copyists would change the αὐτῷ to ἑαυτῷ in order to clarify the reflexive idea that is evident

139. B. M. Metzger and United Bible Societies, *A Textual Commentary on the Greek New Testament*, 2d ed., 646.
140. B. M. Metzger and United Bible Societies, *A Textual Commentary on the Greek New Testament*, 2d ed., 646.
141. B. M. Metzger and United Bible Societies, *A Textual Commentary on the Greek New Testament*, 2d ed., 647–48.
142. B. M. Metzger and United Bible Societies, *A Textual Commentary on the Greek New Testament*, 2d ed., 649.

within the context and grammatical construction. Supporting ἑαυτῷ are א Ψ 049 88 181 330 451 614 630 945 1505 1739 1877 1881^{c} 2412 2492 2495 it$^{\text{ar,c,dem,div,m,p,q}}$ vg syr^{p} cop. Though many of these witnesses are significant, the majority of witnesses point to the nonreflexive pronoun. Supporting αυτω (without accenting) are A B P 056 0142 *Lect*, with the accented αὐτῷ supported by K 81 104 326 436 629 1241 1881* 2127 *Byz l*$^{\text{598,603}}$ syr^{h} cop^{bo}. The division of the Alexandrian and uniform support of the Byzantine and Western texts gives greater weight to the nonreflexive pronoun. The one occurrence of a reflexive pronoun in this epistle (3:3) does not argue for a pattern nor reflect a similar grammatical construction that could be used to argue for either option.

10.b…b The vast majority of MS evidence supports τῷ θεῷ over three other readings and one omission (א B K P Ψ 049 056 0142 88 104 181 326 330 451 614 630 945 1505 1739^{c} 1877 1881 2127 2412 2492 2495 *Byz Lect l*$^{\text{598m}}$ it^{p} syr$^{\text{p,h}}$ cop^{bo}) As noted by Metzger, the other changes can be explained as attempts at making this statement more parallel to the previous one structurally. Also, the variation among the changes argues more for them being alterations rather than original.

13.a…a Metzger notes that the TR and some later MSS after ὅτι ζωὴν ἔχετε αἰώνιον add the words: *καὶ ἵνα πιστεύητε εἰς τὸ ὄνομα τοῦ υἱοῦ τοῦ θεοῦ*. This is reflected in the KJV and NKJV. The UBS^{4} omits it on the basis that it reflects "a scribal assimilation to the statement of Jn 20.31."[143] Rather than seeing assimilation from John 20:31, the apparent redundancy it creates should be seen as the more difficult reading and so argues for its inclusion, along with its occurrence in the Byzantine texts along with some Alexandrian texts as well (K L P + most minuscules). Its absence from some "earlier" Alexandrian texts (א* B syr) does not prove its addition since they tended to trim the texts more than add to them.

18.a. The lesser attested reading, αὐτὸν, is preferred over the reflexive pronoun ἑαυτόν. Support for the reflexive pronoun is substantial (א A^{c} K P Ψ 049 056 0142 33 81 88 181 326 436 629 630 945 1241 1739 1877 1881 2127 2492 *Byz Lect l*$^{\text{598m}}$ syr^{p} cop arm). Though few witnesses support αυτον or

143. B. M. Metzger and United Bible Societies, *A Textual Commentary on the Greek New Testament*, 2d ed., 649.

αὐτὸν (A* B 330 451 614 1505 2412 2495 it^{ar,c,dem,div,p,q,t} vg syr^{h} cop^{bo}), it should still be seen as the better reading. The choice of ἑαυτόν can be explained in terms of copyists changing it to reflect their understanding that ὁ γεννηθεὶς ἐκ τοῦ θεοῦ refers to the believer rather than to Christ. Yet, as Metzger aptly argues, the pattern with John is to use the perfect tense of γεννάω to describe believers.[144] The change from the perfect to the aorist participle seems to indicate a change of persons as well. If John had wanted to use repetition for emphasis in this instance, it would seem he would have used the exact same word and spelling to remove all question as to the referent. Thus this aorist form distinguishes from the perfect and fits Christ better. Further, to have the second γεννάω refer to the believer would create an unnecessary redundancy since the same idea could have been communicated with τηρεῖ and the reflexive pronoun ἑαυτόν.

Translation

1 Everyone who believes that Jesus is the Christ has been born from God,[145] and everyone who loves the one who was born also[146] loves the one who has been born from him. **2** By this we know that we love the children of God when we love God and keep[147] his commandments. **3** For this is our love

144. B.M. Metzger and United Bible Societies, *A Textual Commentary on the Greek New Testament*, 2d ed., 650.

145. Most translations use "born of God" (ESV, HCSB, NASB95, NIV84, NKJV, NRSV). The choice of "born from" (ISV) seeks to communicate the idea of source without the idea of being "fathered by God" (*contra* NET). Others use "begotten by" (NAB), "begotten of" (ASV), "is God's child" (NCV), "a child of God" (RSV), "become a child of God" (NLT)

146. This reflects my text-critical choice to retain the *kai* that UBS4 has placed in brackets. The weight of evidence favors its inclusion and it is more likely it would be dropped out of the text by scribal error than that it would be added. Included in ASV, HCSB, ISV, NCV, NKJV. Excluded from ESV, NASB95, NET, NIV84, NRSV, RSV. Included, but in parentheses in NAB. NLT uses "too" at the end of the sentence.

147. "Keep" (ISV, NKjv) reflects the text critical choice of τηρῶμεν over ποιῶμεν *contra* UBS4. Other translations include "obey" (ESV, HCSB, NAB, NCV, NET, NLT, NRSV, RSV), "do" (ASV), "carrying out" (NIV84), and "observe" (NASB95 ["do" in footnote]).

for God,[148] that we should keep his commandments;[149] and his commandments are not burdensome, **4** because[150] everyone who has been born from God overcomes the world; and this is the victory that has overcome the world, our faith. **5** And who is the one who overcomes the world, if not the one believing that Jesus is the Son of God?

6 This is the one coming through water and blood, Jesus Christ, not only by water but by water and by blood; and the Spirit is the one testifying, because the Spirit is the truth. **7** so that there are three who bear witness,[151]
8 the Spirit and the water and the blood, and the three agree as one. **9** If we receive the testimony of men, the testimony of God is greater; because this is the testimony of God that he has testified concerning his Son. **10** He who believes in the Son of God has the testimony in him.[152] He who does not believe God[153] has made him a liar, because he has not believed in the testimony which God has testified concerning his Son. **11** And this is the testimony that God has given to us eternal life, and this life is in his Son. **12** He who has the Son has the life; he who does not have the son of God does not

148. Most use "the love of God" (ASV, ESV, ISV, NAB, NASB95, NET, NKJV, NRSV, RSV). Other translations include: "love for God" (HCSB, NIV84) and "loving God" (NCV, NLT).

149. This reflects my choice to change the punctuation in UBS4 from a comma to a semicolon. I concur with Harris (205) that this begins a separate thought and reflects John's penchant for starting sentences with καὶ. Where he begins a separate sentence, I prefer the use of the semicolon to reflect the connection John intends between the two.

150. The sentence continues from the previous verse (ISV, NAB, NCV, NET, NIV84, NRSV) as a result of the causal role of the ὅτι that heads this clause. Others begin a new sentence with "For" (ASV, ESV, HCSB, NASB95, NKJV, NLT, RSV).

151. Though thE KJV anD NKJV include the words, "in heaven: the Father, the Word, and the Holy Spirit; and these three are one. And there are three that bear witness on earth," between "bear witness" in v 7 and "the Spirit" in v 8, they are not included in this translation because they lack MS support. Known as the Johannine Comma, the overwhelming majority of scholars reject these as part of the original autograph. See my discussion on 5:7 for a full explanation.

152. Based on textual evidence, the pronoun αὐτῷ, translated "him" (ASV, HCsb), is preferred over the reflexive pronoun ἑαυτῷ and translated "himself" (ESV, ISV, NAB, NASB95, NET, NKJV, RSV). The meaning is the same with either word. NIV84, NLT and NRSV translate it as "in his/their heart(s)."

153. The vast majority oF MS evidence supports "believe God" (τῷ θεῷ) over 3 other readings. This is not a Johannine justification formula ("believe in"), but communicates the idea of taking him at His word (see commentary below).

have life. **13** These things I have written to you in order that you may know that you have eternal life, to those believing in the name of the Son of God, [154]and so that you may continue to believe in the name of the Son of God.

14 And this is the confidence which we have before him, that whenever[155] we ask according to his will, he hears us. **15** And if[156] we know that he hears us, whatever we might ask, then we know that we have the requests which we have asked from him. **16** If anyone sees his bother sinning a sin not unto death,[157] let him ask[158] and he will give life to him, to those not sinning unto death. There is a sin unto death; I am not saying he should ask concerning that. **17** Every unrighteous act is sin, but there is a sin not unto death.

---

154. The remainder of this verse is omitted by UBS4 as a scribal assimilation. It is retained in KJV and NKJV. Rather than seeing it as something assimilated from John 20:31, I see it as the more difficult reading that has the support of Byz. texts as well as some Alexandrian. Though it is not assimilated from the Gospel, it does reflect the same concern of John for his readers. The translations that retain it include: ASV, NKJV. Those that exclude it are: ESV, HCSB, ISV, NAB, NASB95, NCV, NET, NIV94, NLT, NRSV, RSV.

155. "Whenever" is represented bY HCSB, NET, Nlt. Other translations use "if" (ASV, ESV, ISV, NAB, NASB95, NCV, NIV84, NKJV, NRSV, RSV). The translation choice arises from a decision about the sense of ἐάν in the sentence. As a third class conditional clause, it could mean if. However, because it is followed by an present indicative in the apodosis, its contingency has to do with the question of "when" the request is made rather than "if" it will be.

156. This use of ἐάν is contingent and includes the possibility that it may or may not be true.

157. The difficulty of rendering *μὴ πρὸς θάνατον* is evident in the range of translations which include: "not unto death" (ASV), "not leading to death" (ESV), "not lead to death" (ISV, NIV84, NKJV, NLT), "not bring death" (HCSB), "not deadly" (NAB), "not lead to eternal death" (NCV), "not resulting in death" (NET), "not *leading* to death" (NASB95), and "not a mortal sin " (NRSV, RSV). In this case I chose not to add words but to leave it as brusque as possible to reflect its harshness.

158. This reflects the impv. role of the fut. tense (HCSB, ISV, NAB, NCV, NET, NIV84, NLT adds "should"). Others reflect the fut. tense, "he will/shall ask" (ASV, ESV, NASB95, NKJV, NRSV, RSV).

18 We know that everyone who has been born from God does not sin, but the One born from God keeps him[159] and the evil one does not grasp[160] him.

19 We know that we are from God and the whole world lies in the power of[161] the evil one.

20 And we know that the Son of God has come and has given us understanding in order that we may know him who is true, and we are in the true One, in his Son, Jesus Christ. He is the true God and Eternal Life.

Commentary

In this section John discusses the believer's relationship with God in terms of both the possession and expression of eternal life.[162] It is evidenced by faith in Christ and obedience to his command to love. This relationship with God is evidenced in one's confession that Jesus is the Christ and one's love for the brethren in obedience to God.[163]

---

159. Though the MS support for the reflexive ἑαυτόν is substantial (ASV, NKjv), the pronoun αὐτὸν is preferred (ESV, HCSB, NASB95, NIV84, NRSV, RSV). Others (ISV, NAB, NET, NLT) translate in such a way as to reflect αὐτὸν but without the use of "him." Textual clues that convince me of this reading is John's change in verb tenses and his choice not to use repetition where it would have communicated a reflexive idea more clearly. It seems to me that the choice of "himself" reflects copyists' attempt to bring the text in line with their recognition that "the One born from God" refers to Jesus. However, they did not see the point John was making regarding Christ's work on behalf of the saint (see commentary below).

160. Though most translations translate ἅπτω with "touch" (ASV, ESV, HCSB, NAB, NASB95, NCV, NET, NKJV, NLT, NRSV, RSV), it can have the nuance of "harm" (ISV, NIV84). I have chosen "grasp" to reflect the intentionality of Satan's act rather than its result (harm).

161. I concur with ESV, NASB95, and NET. Other translations include: "lies *under the sway of*" (NKJV), "is under the sway of" (HCSB), "is under the control of" (NIV84, NLT), "is under/in the power of" (NAB, NRSV, RSV), "the Evil One controls" (NCV), and "lies under the control of" (ISV).

162. M. C. de Boer ("Jesus the Baptizer: 1 John 5:5–8 and the Gospel of John," 96) considers it significant that 5:1–8 and John 3:1–8 "are *the only two passages* in the whole Johannine corpus in which the motif of divine begetting is prominent. One may therefore hypothesize that there is some sort of connection between John 3:5 and 1 John 5:1–8."

163. Akin (188) argues for the first five verses of this section forming another chiasm. Its structure follows a three level pattern with love, of God and His children,

5:1 In this verse we see that relationship with God (in salvation) is revealed by our confession that Jesus is the Christ and our love for him.[164]

Πᾶς ὁ πιστεύων ὅτι Ἰησοῦς ἐστιν ὁ Χριστός, ἐκ τοῦ θεοῦ γεγέννηται, "Everyone who believes that Jesus is the Christ has been born from God." John continues to use a πᾶς ὁ construction with the articular present participle to particularize the stated principle. What he affirms is true of anybody, a general rule, but certainly applicable to John's readers as well as him (Marshall, 227). Here he connects faith in Christ with spiritual birth.[165] The articular present participle describes a kind of person, and so has more of a gnomic force than a progressive sense.[166] Thus, rather than implying continual belief, it describes a kind of person (Culy, 120). The content of his or her faith is connected to the orthodox confession, "Jesus is the Christ," that stands in contrast to the antichrists' denial in 2:22.[167] Their unregenerate

---

at its center. It is marked on either end by the *inclusio* of "he who believes." His chiasm is as follows:

A the one who believes that Jesus is the Christ (5:1a)
  B is born of God (5:1b)
    C love those born of the Father (5:1c)
    C′ love the children of God (5:2)
  B′ everyone born of God (5:4)
A′ the one who believes that Jesus is the Son of God (5:5)

He has certainly identified a pattern. However, his structure fails to take into account v. three, which is not a parenthetical statement. Further, the first half of his chiasm is composed of a single sentence while the second half includes four. It seems better to see the first verse of this paragraph as the theme or summary statement with the remainder of the paragraph developing the ideas introduced in it.

164. Burge (191) prefers to keep 5:1–4 with the previous paragraph. He says that "John does not change his subject, but gives it a different nuance." I see a change here and so have a new paragraph, though I recognize that he has included what was previously discussed in this transitional paragraph that introduces a new topic. As Pentecost (122) observes, this makes a great summary of chaps three and four.

165. Bultmann (59) and Barker (348) say that with John πιστεύω always has an object. The assumed object of faith for this person is Jesus. In a sense they are correct here. However, in this instance John directs the reader to the content (ὅτι) of that faith rather than its object. It is a correct recognition of the deity of Jesus.

166. D. B. Wallace, *Grammar*, 615–16.

167. Related to these is the confession of 4:15 that Jesus is the Son of God. Smalley (266) suggests that the confession, "Jesus is the Christ," "has a creedal flavor."

status was clearly indicated in chapter 2. Now the spiritual birth of those having an orthodox faith is clarified by what follows.[168]

Reflecting back on our privileged position as children of God (3:1), John reminds us of the source of our life. As an extensive perfect, γεγέννηται focuses attention on the person's state as a result of their birth.[169] The perfect tense indicates completed action in the past, spiritual birth, with continuing results in the present, still a child of God (Burdick, 342). Additionally, ἐκ focuses attention on the source of that spiritual birth, which is God, not the individual. All spiritual life results from spiritual birth and is sourced in God who is life itself. Moreover, as God is eternal, so, too, is the life that flows from him.

Those born of God are the ones who have believed the right things about Jesus. In this case it involves believing he is the Christ. What John clearly teaches by this is that "right belief is a necessary condition for being begotten by God" (Brown, 387). It is more than saying, "Believe in the Jesus who lived back then." Mormons believe in a Jesus who is part of creation and was a human who attained deity. Muslims will acknowledge him as a great prophet, but not God. Yet even in evangelicalism there is often a lack of understanding of the person and work of Christ in the call to faith in Jesus. Brown (535) notes the danger of a misfocus that can occur in our understanding of the gospel. "It has been fashionable to affirm that what is demanded is not belief in an intellectual truth about Jesus but belief in a person with whom one enters a relationship. While not denying the latter, I would insist that there is an intellectual content in the Johannine demand for belief, and that one must understand Jesus correctly in order to have a salvific relationship with him."

On one hand it is correct to say that those who have faith in Jesus are "born of" God. However, this need not indicate that faith is the sign or evidence of spiritual birth (*contra* Akin, 189; Kistemaker, 347; Westcott, 176).

168. The confession, "Jesus is the Christ," has the anarthrous Ἰησοῦς moved forward and the articular ὁ Χριστός following ἐστιν. Painter (289) notes that this is the same pattern as 5:5 where Jesus is "the Son of God." He also notes that though it is "tempting" to translate the titles first, "In each case the definite article suggests that 'the Christ' and 'the Son of God' are the important and known titles and Jesus is emphatically being identified with them by placing his name first."

169. B. M. Fanning (*Verbal Aspect in New Testament Greek*, 291–95) calls this a perfect of resulting state.

Rather, it should still be seen as the cause of that birth (Kruse, 171). The condition for being born of God is faith in Jesus. Only those who believe in him are children of God by spiritual birth. Spiritual birth does not precede faith in Christ, but faith in Christ precedes spiritual birth. Those who believe faith is a fruit of regeneration rather than its predecessor miss the point of such passages as Eph 1:13. There Paul indicates with aorist participles that the Ephesians' faith in Jesus preceded their sealing by the Holy Spirit.[170] Prior to being sealed a person cannot be regenerate, because Paul clearly affirms in Rom 8:9 that one does not belong to Christ without the presence of the Holy Spirit within him. Being elect does not make someone automatically regenerate or a child of God either. In Eph 2:1–10 Paul describes the elect Ephesians as being "dead" in sin and "children of wrath" before faith in Christ. In the same way with John, spiritual birth is a work of God in response to belief in Jesus. Until one is regenerate, he or she is *not* a child of God.

Smalley (266) considers the present tense πιστεύων to suggest "the need for continuous faith." As with this same construction earlier, it is better to see this describing a kind of person. Granted, this person's faith is continuous. However, that is not the point of the present participle. This is describing someone who believes, not who is in the process of believing. Otherwise, if continuous faith is necessary to be a child of God, then a person would be maintaining his or her spiritual birth by his or her faith.

---

170. The Ephesians' "hearing the word of truth" (ἀκούσαντες) and then their "believing" (πιστεύσαντες) are both described with aor. adverbial participles that modify ἐσφραγίσθητε, an aor. pass. verb. So they were sealed only "after" hearing and believing. D. B. Wallace (*Grammar*, 614, italics his) states that an aor. adverbial ptcp. "usually denotes *antecedent* time to that of the controlling verb. But if the main verb is also aorist, this participle *may* indicate contemporaneous time." He further comments in a note that, based on a "cursory examination of the data," he has found "the aorist participle is more frequently contemporareous in the epistles than in narrative literature." In the case of Eph 1:13, though, the first aor. participle (ἀκούσαντες) describes them hearing the gospel, which cannot be contemporaneous with the sealing of the Spirit. Similarly, the second aor. participle (πιστεύσαντες), though it could be contemporaneous, seems better to be seen as reflecting the regular understanding of the aorist, and thus following hearing and preceding the sealing of the Holy Spirit. This would agree with Paul's chronology in Rom 10:9–10 where confession and belief (both aor. subjunctives) lead to (and therefore precede) salvation (L. Morris, *The Epistle to the Romans,* 385–86; W. Mounce, *Romans*, 209–10).

It is God who preserves, not the child of God. It is God's faithfulness, not our faith that keeps us securely and eternally saved (John 10:28–30; Rom 8:38–39; Eph 1:13–14; 2 Thess 3:3; 2 Tim 2:13). Passage from death to life is a permanent experience (John 5:24), not contingent on continuous faith. Just as Jesus uses the 3 singular perfect μεταβέβηκεν in John 5:24 to describe the permanent state of the individual who believes in him, so too John uses the first person plural perfect μεταβεβήκαμεν in 3:14 to describe the permanent state of the believer who loves his brother.

There are two approaches to understanding the relationship of believing to spiritual birth as presented in this verse:

(1) Believing is a result of spiritual birth (Brooke, 128). Stott (175) says the perfect tense γεγέννηται in combination with the present tense ὁ πιστεύων shows "believing is the consequence, not the cause of the new birth." Barker (348) sees "believing in Jesus" as a test of life because for him believing is a "direct consequence" of spiritual birth. He describes it as "a 'test' or proof of that birth." Yarbrough (270) concurs and says, "In Johannine theology, spiritual rebirth seems to precede and ultimately create faith: those who believe do so not so much as the result of human volition as of prior divine intention." He cites John 1:12–13. However, those verses do not affirm his chronology. The articular present participle τοῖς πιστεύουσιν is used by John to describe those who received (aorist ἔλαβον) Jesus. The time element in the participle, though diminished by the article, is still contemporaneous with the verb, not subsequent to it. If believing followed receiving, the participle would have been future.[171]

(2) Believing is an evidence of the new birth, not its consequence. Williamson (157) sees the present participle emphasizing continuous believing as proof of life rather than a single event that produces life. Thompson (129) understands 5:1 to be "two expressions of what the child of God does" rather than "commands that one must keep in order to become a child of God." Burdick (343) rejects Stott's statement on the grounds that it misses the significance of the two tenses. Rather, John is saying "anyone who believes in the incarnation is a child of God. The point of the passage is that belief is a sign of new birth, not that belief is a consequence of new birth" (also Westcott, 177). John 1:12 affirms faith as a condition of new birth since it precedes it. Here, with John the perfect passive construction indicates

171. D. B. Wallace, *Grammar*, 498.

the source of spiritual birth–namely, that it is sourced in God. The preposition phrase's location before the verb it modifies makes it emphatic.[172] The passive γεγέννηται shows, too, our dependence on God for spiritual birth. One does not achieve birth by his or her belief. God is the One who causes birth to occur. The believer is completely passive in spiritual birth.

Now, for those who mistake faith as a sign of sonship, it logically follows that they then look to "right behavior" and a departure from "habitual sinning," as well as other signs of obedience as evidence of justifying faith (Akin, 189). Thus Marshall says that proper confession becomes "the evidence which shows that a person stands in the continuing relationship of a child to God his Father: that evidence is that he holds to the true faith about Jesus" (Marshall, 227). So it is not just a lifestyle of obedience but a continuing correct confession. As will be seen later in this chapter, one's assurance of salvation results from believing God's promises and not solely from looking at one's works. Honest self-examination can easily lead to a sense of failure. Yet one can have assurance before God because God is greater than our hearts. Assurance may come from works. We can know we are God's children when we act like it.[173] However, assurance is not based on deeds. It is based on God's faithfulness to his promises. This is true whether that assurance is in regard to salvation or answered prayer.

καὶ πᾶς ὁ ἀγαπῶν τὸν γεννήσαντα ἀγαπᾷ καὶ τὸν γεγεννημένον ἐξ αὐτοῦ, "and everyone who loves the one who was born also loves the one who has been born from him." This statement may be understood in one of three ways: (1) It could be a proverb, applied to parents and now applied spiritually (Brown, 536; Marshall, 227, n. 32; Moody, 102). John's use of πᾶς ὁ to introduce this statement argues for it being a general statement, and so proverbial in nature (Harris, 203). John's use of the present participle indicates that it "happens as a rule" (Burdick, 343; Schnackenburg, 251). (2) This is what one would say about his or her own parent (Brooke, 129; Haas, de Jonge, and Swellengrebel, 132; Westcott, 177). (3) This is a statement about God (Bultmann, 76–77). The theme of God as parent (Father) will continue from this point to the end of the epistle (Strecker, 175). However, such

---

172. D. E. Hiebert, "An Expositional Study of 1 John—Part 9: An Exposition of 1 John 5:1–12," 217.

173. Thompson (130) says well, "Love for the children of God is one criterion by which we test the veracity of the claim to know and to love God."

a statement could have been more clearly made by including θεὸς in the formula. Yet this does appear to be the thrust of the statement (Harris, 203), and John does not mind ambiguity.

While the first "born" clearly is linked to God who gives birth (ἐκ τοῦ θεοῦ γεγέννηται), this second "born" (τὸν γεννήσαντα) may be seen either to refer to Jesus or to believers. The context of loving one's brother in Christ may cause interpreters to think John has other believers in mind (Kruse, 171). However, in favor of Jesus is John's choice of the aorist γεννήσαντα followed by another perfect in the subsequent clause. First, the aorist focuses attention on the simple occurrence of the birth rather than its impact. Second, it is surrounded by perfects that include a reference to God as its source. Third, the absence ἐκ τοῦ θεοῦ or ἐξ αὐτοῦ seems to make a distinction between this One who was "born" *as* God and believers whose birth comes "from" God. Finally, since the preceding and following clauses clearly refer to believers, it makes little logical sense to have a believer in view here as well. John would be saying that the one who loves God's children loves God's children. Furthermore, with the focus on Jesus' incarnation as one of the tests of orthodoxy, this provides another allusion to his incarnation in this epistle.

Our spiritual birth expresses itself in love for other believers, those who have been born into our spiritual family (Kruse, 171). Kistemaker (348) rightly observes that this statement links faith in Christ with love. John is showing the interconnectedness of one's faith and conduct, the interconnectedness of orthodoxy and orthopraxy.

John's use of ἐξ αὐτοῦ breaks from his pattern of ἐκ τοῦ θεοῦ. This αὐτοῦ clearly has θεοῦ (God) as its antecedent. Additionally, though John has been using repetition of ἐκ τοῦ θεοῦ to drive home his contrast between believers and the antichrists, this shift removes the focus from God as the source to the kind of person being loved. Hodges (212) errs when he says that "a Christian is *not defined* by lifestyle, good works, or obedience to God. A Christian is defined only by faith in Christ" (italics his). Rather, John's connection of faith and active love of the brethren indicates that lifestyle can describe or define a Christian in terms of his or her sanctification. When Jesus said that the world would know we are his disciples by our love (John 13:35), he was saying that conduct does indeed define a Christian. It does not create a Christian, but faith leads to regeneration. However, Christian conduct springs from one's faith. It expresses that faith and is colored and shaped by that faith. John's point in this epistle is that love is integral to one's faith as one of its expressions in the life of the believer.

5:2 John now affirms the interconnectedness of love for Christians with love for God and obedience to his commands.[174]

ἐν τούτῳ γινώσκομεν ὅτι ἀγαπῶμεν τὰ τέκνα τοῦ θεοῦ, "By this we know that we love the children of God." Once again John employs the phrase ἐν τούτῳ, a dative of means, to connect assurance with practice. (1) Some see it referring to what precedes (Dodd, 125; Marshall, 227; Painter, 293; Schnackenburg, 252). Strecker (176) rejects this on the basis that it changes this sentence from an explanation of the previous sentence to an "application" of it. Additionally, for him it would make the ὅταν clause that follows unexplainable. (2) Others see it referring both to what precedes and follows (Haas, de Jonge, and Swellengrebel, 178; Painter, 124; Westcott, 178). (3) It is better to see it referring once again only to what follows (Brooke, 129; Bultmann, 77; Burdick, 343; Culy, 121; Harris, 203; Kistemaker, 348; Smalley, 268; Strecker, 176).[175] Though Rensberger (128) holds this view, he admits that "the verse seems to say the exact opposite of what one would expect." Burdick (343) answers the criticism that it is unnatural for τούτῳ to refer to ὅταν by noting that it is no more unusual than John's reference to an ἐὰν clause in 2:3.

Γινώσκομεν has the epexegetical ὅτι clause immediately after. What John affirms is that we can know experientially that we love God's children, our fellow believers. Burdick (344) gives γινώσκω the sense of "examining the evidence and ascertaining thereby that one loves God's people." Of note is John's use of the plural τέκνα rather than τοῦς ἀδελφοῦς (Brooke, 129). It likely results from John's emphasis on spiritual birth (being born of God) in this section (Smalley, 268) and connects the reader with τὸν γεγεννημένον ἐξ αὐτοῦ in the last clause of the previous sentence. Westcott (178) notes that his use of τέκνα here keeps the focus on "the relation of Christians to God and not upon their relation to one another." The focus thus is drawn once more to relationships within the family of God and may allude back to 3:1, our privileged position as children of God.

---

174. Culpepper (271) compares this verse to the *Shema* in Deut 6:4–9 combined with the command of Lev 19:18 to love one's neighbor.

175. Grayston (133) cannot decide.

ὅταν τὸν θεὸν ἀγαπῶμεν καὶ τὰς ἐντολὰς αὐτοῦ τηρῶμεν, "when we love God and keep his commandments."[176] What John says next answers the question raised in 5:1, "How can I know if I love the one born from God?"[177]

The temporal particle ὅταν introduces this dependent clause and is used by John to describe both when and how we may know that we love God's children. This clause is epexegetical to ἐν τούτῳ (Culy, 121; Strecker, 176). It (ὅταν) is a variant of ἐὰν which was used in 2:28 in much this same way (Painter, 290).[178] This indicates that the action of the present tense verbs is contemporaneous with the main verb (ἀγαπῶμεν) of the clause to which it relates. Further, ὅταν with the present subjunctive ἀγαπῶμεν communicates something continually happening (Smalley, 268; Strecker, 176). Thus we love the children of God when we are loving God and keeping his commandments (Brown, 539; Painter, 293).[179]

Loving God and keeping his commandments are once again connected by John.[180] (1) He may be saying by this that there are two ways we can know: by loving God and by keeping his commandments. (2) More likely this is a hendiadys* indicating that loving God and keeping his commandments are two aspects of the same thing (Brown, 539; Perkins, 59; Smalley, 268; Westcott 177). This second option reflects Jesus' words in John 14:15, "If you love Me, you will keep My commandments." "Keeping the commandments is living according to this new law of love" (Moody, 103). It also reflects John's words in 2 John 6, "And this is love, that we should walk

---

176. Some MSS have ποιῶμεν instead of τηρῶμεν. In fact, most would choose ποιῶμεν on the basis that it is the more difficult reading and has significant textual support. The presence of τηρῶμεν is explained then as a scribal change because of its occurrence in the following verse (Culy, 122). However, τηρῶμεν has the broader textual support and fits with John's pattern of repetition. In this case he is emphasizing the significance of keeping God's commandments.

177. Strecker (176–77) correctly says that John is not "polemicizing against false prophets" here nor is he interested in something theoretical. Rather, he is speaking of concrete application of the truths he has been teaching.

178. BDAG, 730. Burdick (344) distinguishes between ὅταν, which "points to every occasion" where ὅτε looks at a "a particular occasion."

179. E. Malatesta (*Interiority and Covenant*, 310) says well: "The love of our brothers is grounded in the love of God ... and in the observance of the commandments, because the love of God consists in the observance of His commandments."

180. Burdick (344) sees the plural ἐντολὰς indicating God's moral commands while the singular ἐντολὴν refers to Jesus' command to love.

according to his commandments." As seen in both Jesus and John's words, they are ultimately two aspects of the same thing.[181]

5:3 John provides another definitional statement, now defining love for God in the following clause. The final clause serves as clarification of any possible objection.

αὕτη γάρ ἐστιν ἡ ἀγάπη τοῦ θεοῦ, ἵνα τὰς ἐντολὰς αὐτοῦ τηρῶμεν, "For this is our love for God, that we should keep his commandments." John begins this next statement with an inferential *γάρ* (Harris, 205; Strecker, 177, n. 28; Yarbrough, 273) that looks back on what he has just said at the end of 5:2 with the hendiadys combining obedience with love (Brown, 539). Our love for God is demonstrated by our keeping his commandments. He is explaining the "essential nature of God's love" (Schnackenburg, 252).

Once again John includes the pronoun *αὕτη* at the head of the sentence, making it emphatic. As an emphatic pronoun it likely points to the *ἵνα* clause rather than the predicate nominative *ἡ ἀγάπη τοῦ θεοῦ* (Haas, de Jonge, and Swellengrebel, 134). Even so, though the referent of *ἵνα* is *αὕτη*, it is epexegetical to the clause preceding it (Culy, 122; Grayston, 133; Harris, 205), thus providing the content of our love for God.[182]

This use of *τοῦ θεοῦ* is an objective genitive and it indicates "our love for God" rather than his for us (Akin, 191; Brown, 540; Burdick, 345; Culy, 122; Grayston, 133; Hodges, 214; Kistemaker, 351; Painter, 291; Smalley, 269; Strecker, 177; Yarbrough, 273).[183] This seems the best interpretation in light of the previous and following verses that all focus on the believer's expression of love, not on God's. This reflects Jesus' words in the upper room that his disciples demonstrate their love for him through obedience (John

---

181. Pentecost (123) sees this as a "second proof of the new birth." Though this may be true, such is not the focus of John at this point. Rather, it is an assurance for the child of God that he or she is properly relating to God by properly relating to His other children. It is the expression of mutual fellowship introduced in chap one.

182. D. B. Wallace, *Grammar*, 661. See also A. T. Robertson, *A Grammar of the Greek New Testament*, 993. BDF §394 says that this is an instance where *ἵνα* is used in place of an epexegetical (explanatory) inf. Brooke (130) says "the definitive *ἵνα* generally introduces an ideal not yet actually attained."

183. J. C. O'Neill, *The Puzzle of 1 John*, 54.

14:23–24).[184] The phrase τὰς ἐντολὰς αὐτοῦ means "God's commandments" (last used by John in 3:22) because the nearest antecedent is θεοῦ.[185]

The present subjunctive τηρῶμεν should be understood with a gnomic sense more than progressive. The keeping of God's commandments characterizes the person who loves God. This brings out the idea of τηρῶμεν which includes in it a sense of persistent obedience more than standing watch over something.[186] Thus τηρῶμεν communicates intentional, consistent observance of God's commandments. Though John is not saying that one loves God only while keeping his commandments, this is true as well. Obedience, especially persistent obedience, is the best way one says to God, "I love you."

καὶ αἱ ἐντολαὶ αὐτοῦ βαρεῖαι οὐκ εἰσίν, "And, his commandments are not burdensome." This *καὶ* provides continuity with what precedes (Culy, 122). However, Harris (205) argues well that this clause makes better sense as a free standing sentence than connected to the previous clause. Thus he differs with the punctuation of the editors of UBS⁴ at this point. He notes that John uses *καὶ* to begin new sentences elsewhere and so is likely doing the same here.[187]

The plural "commandments" clarifies that John has all of God's will in view, not just the command to love one another. The predicate adjective βαρεῖαι is not the same word or from the same root as the "burden" (φορτίον) in Matt 11:30.[188] Whereas βαρύς focuses on the difficulty caused by demands or threats, φορτίον focuses on the burden itself, or the fact of its presence rather than its affect.[189] John's point is that God's commands free us to be

184. Harris (205) notes well that John defines love from God's perspective in 4:10 and from the believer's perspective in 2 John 6. He defines the believer's love for God to be expressed through obedience (John 14:15, 21 and 15:12).

185. Painter (294) considers every plural reference to commandments to be those of God the Father and not Jesus.

186. BDAG, 1002; E. Riesenfeld, "τηρέω," *TDNT* 8:141–45.

187. Bruce (117) sees this clause going with (explained by) what follows. Thus, some punctuation that serves to distinguish it from the preceding statement is helpful.

188. In Matt 23:4 Jesus uses this term to describe the Pharisees placing burdens on the people (φορτία βαρέα).

189. BDAG, 167 (βαρύς), 1064 (φορτίον) ; G. Schrenk, "βάρος, βαρύς," *TDNT* 1:556–58, K. Weiss "φέρω … φορτίον," *TDNT* 9:85–86. Spicq, "βαρύς," *TLNT* 1:252–55. "important, serious, burdensome, grave, dangerous" He quotes Philo (*Spec. Laws* 1.299), who says, "God doesn't ask anything burdensome, complicated, or difficult, but something that is simple and easy: to love him as benefactor, or at least fear him as master and lord."

the people he intended us to be—what Adam and Eve were originally created to be—loving (and holy) creatures reflecting God's character. For the person not rightly related to God, these commands are a burden as they conflict with the rebel's conduct and desires. For the child of God seeking to please him and reflect his character, they prove a help that frees them from sin and its entanglements. This principle is taught by Paul in Rom 6. Freedom in Christ enables the Christian to choose whether he or she will be enslaved by sin or righteousness. It all depends on to which "master" they present themselves. Though Rom 7 takes us through the reality of our struggle with our sin nature, Rom 8 reminds us of the victory available to every believer through the ministry of the Holy Spirit. Similarly here, John moves from the desire to an explanation of how it works in the life of the believer.

Why are the commands not burdensome?[190] God enables us to keep them (Barker, 349; Brown, 541; Bruce, 117; Burge, 192; Culpepper, 100; Dodd, 126; Haas, de Jonge, and Swellengrebel, 135; Houlden, 124; Marshall, 228; Smalley, 269; Stott, 176; Thompson, 131; Yarbrough, 274). "The writer cannot be maintaining that God's commands are not 'exacting'; they are demanding, but the Christian who seeks to live up to God's high moral standards is also given the power to do so" (Smalley, 269). This will be seen in the following verse.

5:4 Bruce (117) is correct that the UBS[4] editor's punctuation at the end of 5:3 is "doubtful" since this verse clarifies the thought of the previous clause and is introduced with a subordinating conjunction. What this and the following verse communicate is that belief that Jesus is the Son of God enables a Christian to overcome the world.

ὅτι πᾶν τὸ γεγεννημένον ἐκ τοῦ θεοῦ νικᾷ τὸν κόσμον·, "Because everyone who has been born from God overcomes the world." As noted earlier, the role of this causal ὅτι should be seen to connect it with the previous clause (Culy, 123; Harris, 206; Hodges, 215; Yarbrough, 275). Some see this referring to victory over the secessionists, John's "opponents"(Harris, 206).

190. Grayston (133) sees this in terms of how few commands we have to keep. Schnackenburg (253) suggests that John may be alluding to a rabbinic teaching about "heavy" and "light" laws.

However, it is explaining why God's commandments are not too heavy to bear (Akin, 192; Yarbrough, 275).

However then, the question may be asked, why is the subject (πᾶν τὸ γεγεννημένον) neuter? John had used the masculine πᾶς ὁ πιστεύων just a few verses earlier in 5:1. His use of the neuter pronoun rather than masculine or feminine may be understood in one of five ways: (1) It serves to make the statement more general (Grayston, 133–34; Marshall, 228, n. 37; Smalley, 270; Westcott, 179; Yarbrough, 275). Blass-Debruner says: "The neuter is sometimes used with respect to persons if it is not the individuals but a general quality that is to be emphasized."[191] He provides the example of John 17:2 where "all flesh" (πάσης σαρκός) is described as "everyone who" (πᾶν ὅ) in the following ἵνα clause. (2) It has a collective sense (Lieu, 203–204; Rensberger, 129).[192] Painter (297) counters that it would have been easier to use the plural. (3) It takes the reader back to the neuter antecedent τέκνα in 5:2 (Marshall, 228, n. 37 raises this possibility; Williamson, 159).[193] (4) Brown (542) understands this to indicate John's "desire to set up a category of what God has begotten over against another category, 'the world.'" (5) It is being used in the same way as the masculine in 5:1 (Painter, 297). The first two options have the greatest merit and together possibly communicate John's intended sense.

The articular perfect participle γεγεννημένον focuses attention on the state of the person who overcomes the world. This one is a child of God by a birth in the past that impacts the present as he or she continues in the new state (Williamson, 158). His repetition of ἐκ τοῦ θεοῦ continues to emphasize source, in this case the birth sourced in God.

For the one who has God as the source of his spiritual birth, there is victory. Using the same term (νικάω) that described the young men in 2:13–14, John now describes the child of God as the one who "conquers" or gains a "victory" over the world. This same term is used in Rev 2–3 to describe those faithful believers in the seven churches who will someday reign with Jesus in his kingdom when he comes victoriously to establish it (Rev 19–20). It

---

191. BDF §138(1).

192. T. W. Manson, "Entry into Membership of the Early Church," 27.

193. Painter (297) raises the possibility that it refers back to σπέρμα in 3:9, but then says it is "difficult to see how 'everything that is begotten of God' can refer to the divine seed."

is in the present tense, showing that victory is a present experience for believers, not something yet future. Even so, it carries the gnomic sense rather than progressive, indicating that this is a characteristic experience of the child of God (Burdick, 346; *contra* Haas, de Jonge, and Swellengrebel, 135; Painter, 298; Smalley, 270).

This victory is over "the world" rather than the devil (*contra* Perkins, 59), though he may be implied. John's use of *κόσμος* in this verse clearly refers to the world that is hostile to God and indicates its "unredeemed humanity" that opposes God (Bultmann, 77; Lieu, 207; Moody, 105; Smalley, 270).[194]

καὶ αὕτη ἐστὶν ἡ νίκη ἡ νικήσασα τὸν κόσμον, ἡ πίστις ἡμῶν, "and this is the victory that has overcome the world, our faith." Beginning again with the emphatic pronoun *αὕτη*, John directs attention to the "overcoming victory" believers have over the world. He accomplishes this by the repetition of the same root for both the noun (*ἡ νίκη*) and articular participle (*ἡ νικήσασα*). This Semitism reflects the practice of combining a noun and verb from the same root in order to make the statement emphatic (Williamson, 159).[195] This use of *ἡ νίκη* is a metonymy* for the means. Therefore John means by this "conquest" or "conquering power" (Brown, 570; Harris, 208; Painter, 298).

John's emphases the conquering role of the believer's victory with the aorist participle *νικήσασα* placed in the second attributive adjective position. The participle may be understood as a simple aorist, thus its implied action is prior to the main verb and the emphasis would be on the past victory over the world that occurred at the time the person became a child of God (Haas, de Jonge, and Swellengrebel, 117; Harris, 209; Smalley, 271). This is the usual sense of an aorist participle with its related verb.[196] This

---

194. Williamson (158–59) sees the secessionists implied. However, this is again reading a theory into the text. It is better to see this as the world of 2:15–17 that believers are not to love, including people and their attitudes and values.

195. John uses this same kind of construction in 5:15 when he speaks of seeing a brother "sinning a sin" (ἁμαρτάνοντα ἁμαρτίαν). E. W. Bullinger (*Figures of Speech*, 275) identifies this as a polyptoton involving a verb and its cognate noun or participle. Other examples include John 6:28 (ἐργαζώμεθα τὰ ἔργα, "we might work the works"), 7:24 (τὴν δικαίαν κρίσιν κρίνετε, "judge with righteous judgment"), 1 Tim 6:10 (ἀγωνίζου τὸν καλὸν ἀγῶνα τῆς πίστεως, "Fight the good fight of faith"), 2 Tim 1:9 (καὶ καλέσαντος κλήσει ἁγίᾳ, "and called *us* with a holy calling"), and 2 Tim 4:7 (τὸν καλὸν ἀγῶνα ἠγώνισμαι, "I have fought the good fight").

196. D. B. Wallace, *Grammar*, 614–15.

sense of the aorist would indicate that he is referring to the power that "has conquered" the world.[197] Thus it is a conquering victory that he has in view.[198] It is not a battle that has been won, but the war. There is finality to this victory with no other battles left to be fought. There is little way to make a stronger statement in Greek than this. The child of God stands as conqueror. Thus John is affirming that the spiritual rebirth of a believer is what provides victory over a world standing in opposition to God. John' use of *κόσμος* here "gathers up the sum of all the limited, transitory powers opposed to God which make obedience difficult" (Westcott, 179).

What conquest is he referring to? This may be viewed in one of five ways: (1) It describes Jesus' victory over the world, death, and the devil (Harris, 209; Marshall, 229; Rensberger, 130; Schnackenburg, 230; Westcott, 180). This is supported by Jesus' words in John 16:33 (Harris, 209; Painter, 298). However, against this is the means of victory, "our faith" (Burdick, 347). (2) This refers to the readers' salvation (Brooke, 131; Burdick, 347; Hiebert).[199] This would then be related to their baptismal confession at the time of their conversion (Harris, 209). (3) It refers to the Johannine community's victory over its opponents, the secessionists, by the readers' rejection of the false teachers (Stott, 177). Against this is the departure of the false teachers being described as voluntary in 2:19, not forced (Harris, 209). (4) John intends all three (Akin, 193). (5) John is intentionally ambiguous.[200] The first option is best as the meaning of "our faith" is clarified.

What leads to victory over the world? Our faith. This is the single use of *πίστις* in all of John's writings, though he regularly uses its verb form.[201]

---

197. Schnackenburg (254) sees this having a pf. sense of final victory, and indicates that in Christ we have victory because of His decisive victory over the world. This is little different from how others understand the aor. For example, Grayston (134) says the aorist "refers to total victory." Kistemaker (351) differs from most and takes this with a gnomic sense, so that the victory that came at birth continues to overcome the world.

198. Aorist ptc. and pres. ptc. that follows is used by John "to portray the victory of faith as a complete action in the first case and as an ongoing process in the second" (Kruse, 174).

199. D. E. Hiebert, "An Expositional Study of 1 John—Part 9: An Exposition of 1 John 5:1–12," 221.

200. Brown (571) cannot decide among the options.

201. Burdick (346) sees *πίστις* as the referent of *αὕτη*, rather than *ἡ νίκη*. However, since we are dealing with an equative sentence, it would seem better to see it

John's use here refers to beliefs, not behavior. It describes doctrines about Jesus rather than practices of the church, traditions of the elders, or faithfulness (Akin, 192; Bultmann, 78; Johnson, 124; Marshall, 229; Rensberger, 130; Smalley, 271; Westcott, 180). This faith has Jesus, the Son of God, as its object (5:5).[202] Harris (209–10) sees this referring to "believers' faith in Jesus, who during his earthly life and ministry conquered the world" by his death, resurrection, and ascension, as will be explained in the next two verses.

5:5 This is another of John's "hinge" verses. Its content could make it the final sentence of the previous paragraph or the beginning of the next. Its role is to show the interconnectedness of the concepts communicated in both paragraphs. One does not happen without the other. They cannot be dichotomized but must occur together for either to be true. Kistemaker sees this verse functioning as a "bridge" between subjects at this point of John's message, but primarily as the beginning of the next (Kistemaker, 351–52). This could be argued on the basis that interrogation is often used to introduce new concepts, such as with Paul in Rom 6:1 and 15. However, again, it need not always.

τίς δέ ἐστιν ὁ νικῶν τὸν κόσμον, "And who is the one who overcomes the world." This question arises from the previous statement that the one born of God overcomes. Now that person is further defined in terms of his or her belief. The sentence begins with the interrogative pronoun *τίς*, and so "individualizes the question" (Akin, 194). John is calling each reader to ask him or herself this question. The articular present participle has often been used by John in this epistle to describe a kind of person.[203]

This is the case here again, though it may be better to see the nuance of this present participle to be more of customary present (Smalley, 270) than gnomic (Hodges, 217). The anaphoric* article connects *ὁ νικῶν* to the previous sentence with the verb form describing the one born of God. This accords better with the previous sentence and explains how someone

---

explaining the entire statement.

202. Brown (571–72) sees "faith" as involving "a public profession" along with commitment to Jesus, though not without its "christological content, specifying who Jesus is." Later, John will define this faith in terms of a confession.

203. See D. B. Wallace (*Grammar*, 614–16) for a discussion of time and aspect with pres. articular participles. He sees the gnomic sense dominating and these substantival participles being used to communicate "generic" ideas.

overcomes as a matter of course. That being said, the customary present is little different from the gnomic, though it should be seen as focusing more on the conduct than the character, as the gnomic would normally be used.[204]

εἰ μὴ ὁ πιστεύων ὅτι Ἰησοῦς ἐστιν ὁ υἱὸς τοῦ θεοῦ; "if not the one believing that Jesus is the Son of God?" The content of our conquering faith is the recognition and confession that Jesus is the Son of God.[205] This use of the articular present participle ὁ πιστεύων again describes a kind of person. He is not saying that victory occurs while someone believes this about Jesus, but that this is the kind of person who overcomes the world. His use of the conditional conjunction εἰ μὴ follows the pattern of 2:22, where he describes the antichrist in his denial of Jesus as the Christ.[206]

Here he describes the believer in terms of his confession with the indirect discourse ὅτι clause (Harris, 210). Thus the content of the person's faith is the confession: "Jesus is the Son of God." So this conquering "faith" is not belief directed toward Jesus, but has as its content the truth about Jesus.[207] This is parallel to 5:1 and so makes believing Jesus is both the Christ and the Son of God equivalent to each other.[208] One cannot be believed apart from the other. Jesus cannot be the Christ if he is not the Son. This belief is the content of "our faith." Why is this so important with John? One cannot act rightly without believing rightly. Thus he is now ready to discuss those significant truths about Jesus and the content of our faith necessary to have assurance.

---

204. D. B. Wallace, *Grammar*, 521–23. The customary pres. expresses the idea of regularly occurring action or a continuing state while the gnomic expresses a "timeless fact."

205. Schnackenburg (256) sees this indicating that victory is dependent on the purity of one's faith and christological confession.

206. Brown (572) translates εἰ μὴ as "none other." The confession, "Jesus is the Son of God," is nearly identical to 2:22 as well as 4:15 (Bultmann, 79).

207. Harris (210) sees this combined with 5:1 forms "the full-orbed Johannine confession 'that Jesus is the Christ, the Son of God' as reflected in the purpose statement of the Fourth Gospel." We thus see the continuity between the two works of John and the expression of his Christology, whether synthesized (Gospel) or detailed (epistle).

208. (Yarbrough, 277) sees ὁ πιστεύων here forming an *inclusio* with ὁ πιστεύων in 5:1. Though an *inclusio* may not be intended, the correlation of ὁ Χριστός with ὁ υἱὸς τοῦ θεοῦ is blatant.

In this next paragraph John affirms that Jesus, the source of eternal life, is witnessed to by the Father in all those who believe in him. Further, it is God's desire that his children know without a doubt their standing with him. That standing is enjoyed by those who depend on God's truthfulness for their confidence.[209]

5:6 Jesus, as the Son of God, came in the flesh. John now moves to describe Jesus in terms of his earthly ministry. This complex sentence introduces truths about Jesus that one must believe as part of the definition of Jesus as the Son of God. It clarifies the truth of Jesus' physical life and ministry on earth and the physical reality of his crucifixion. It is another way of affirming his humanity after clearly affirming his deity in the previous verses.

Οὗτός ἐστιν ὁ ἐλθὼν δι' ὕδατος καὶ αἵματος, Ἰησοῦς Χριστός, "This is the One coming through water and blood, Jesus Christ." Introducing this sentence with the emphatic pronoun οὗτός whose referent is the subject of the last sentence (Painter, 302; Westcott, 181), John uses the now familiar designation for Jesus in this epistle (Brooke, 134; Culy, 124).[210]

He describes Jesus with the articular aorist participle ὁ ἐλθὼν and so focuses attention on his incarnation as a completed historical event (Brooke, 134; Haas, de Jonge, and Swellengrebel, 137; Kistemaker, 355; Lenski, 525; Westcott, 811).[211] He describes Jesus' incarnational ministry as "coming through water and blood." The sequence of nouns is certainly not accidental (Bruce, 118). However, to what do they refer? Both are metonymies in which water and blood symbolize something else to which they are each related.

---

209. J. C. Coetzee ("The Holy Spirit in 1 John," 45) considers 5:6–12 to be the "keystone to the body" of the Epistle. He argues that this forms the climax of the epistle in the same way that John 20:26–29 was the climax preceding John's purpose statement in John 20:30–31. These verses do the same thing preceding the Epistle's purpose statement in 5:13. Seeing that the Holy Spirit is the "central" figure of this climactic paragraph, he then structures the message of the Epistle on that basis. He is correct in affirming that the Holy Spirit's role in the paragraph is as a witness to Jesus. However, his construction of a chiastic arrangement is not convincing, nor his assertion on the central role of the Holy Spirit. If anything, the focus moves from the Holy Spirit in the first few verses to God the Father later in the paragraph.

210. Haas, de Jonge, and Swellengrebel (137) sees οὗτός referring both to Jesus in the previous verse, but also pointing to "Jesus Christ" at the end of this clause.

211. Article with ὁ ἐλθὼν is cataphoric and looks forward to Ἰησοῦς Χριστός. Yarbrough (281–82) suggests the aor. ὁ ἐλθὼν implies Jesus' "heavenly origin."

Six major views on the meaning of "water and blood" have been proposed:

(1) The water and blood refer to the sacraments (Schnackenburg, 257–60).[212] "The chief problem with this view is singular: John's interest is not in church ritual but in historic incarnation" (Burge, 201). Its greatest weaknesses are the complete absence of any mention of either baptism or the Lord's Supper elsewhere in the epistle, as well as the lack of interest in it in John's Gospel. The context does not indicate anywhere that διά should be introducing accompanying circumstances (Brown, 575), which is the only way this view could be correct (Harris, 211). Further, the term "blood" is not used for the bread of the Eucharist anywhere in Scripture or in extrabiblical literature (Brooke, 132; Kistemaker, 353; Smalley, 277). The past tense ὁ ἐλθών indicates it is part of past history, not the continuing experience of the church (Brown, 573; Marshall, 231; Smalley, 277; Stott, 180; Strecker, 182; Westcott, 181).[213] Also, this does not "fit the christological context" (Strecker, 182). Brown (575) also raises the objection that no evidence exists that "the secessionists" did not practice the sacraments. Finally, the role of water and blood as witnesses along with the Holy Spirit in 5:8 argues for historical referents rather than ceremonial. This is the weakest of the four views.

(2) This is a reference to the water and blood that flowed from Jesus' side when thrust through with the spear, and so is symbolic of Jesus' death on the cross (Brown, 578; Culpepper, 272; Grayston, 136–37; Harris, 212–13; Smith, 123–24; Thompson, 133).[214] In support of this is John's inclusion of that fact in his passion account (Westcott, 812).[215] It is less likely, however, in light of the difference in word order in John 19:34 (Akin, 196). There it is blood and then water that flows. This difference makes it less likely that

212. E. Malatesta, *Interiority and Covenant*, 312. This was commonly held by the church fathers. Strecker (182, n. 4) lists Ambrose, Augustine, John Chrysostom, and Cyril of Alexandria as examples.

213. D.E. Hiebert, "An Expositional Study of 1 John—Part 9: An Exposition of 1 John 5:1–12," 223.

214. J. Mitchell (144–45) sees the water and blood referring to Jesus' death on the cross, but then applies the two elements spiritually. He sees water referring to believes "reception of life" and blood to their "judicial cleansing."

215. Thus water and blood refer to the same thing and should be taken literally (Richter, "Blut und Wasser," 5, 20; Brown (573); R. W. Paschal, Jr., "Sacramental symbolism and physical imagery in the Gospel of John," 172–73.

John would be alluding to Jesus' death here. Burge (202) argues that the phrase ὅτι τὸ πνεῦμά ἐστιν ἡ ἀλήθεια at the end of 5:6 indicates that water was the issue, not Jesus' death. John's reference to Jesus' blood cleansing in 1:7 increases the likelihood that he has Jesus' crucifixion in mind with this reference to blood (Brown, 578). He may have changed the word order from his passion account "because for him the precise point of contention with the opponents is over the salvific significance of Jesus' death on the cross" (Harris, 212). Harris (213) sees the second reference to "water only" as alluding to Jesus' baptism with the "water and blood" referring to his crucifixion. Stott (180) rejects this on the basis that "it would be forced to say that in this incident Jesus *came by* (that is, 'through') *water and blood*, when in fact they came out of him" (italics his). Also, "The link between blood, water and testimony, which we have observed in both passages, is not identical."

(3) It is a reference to Jesus' incarnation, with water indicating his birth and blood referring to his crucifixion (Culy, 126).[216] Blood being a metaphor for crucifixion is indicated by John's use of "blood" in 1:7.[217] Lieu (209) rejects this on the basis that "the wording appears to be a very allusive way of emphasizing something that easily could be more clearly expressed." Brown (576) notes that objections to this "centers on the implied thesis of the adversaries." He acknowledges, though, "We do not have evidence that they were true Docetists denying the human body of Jesus. Moreover, none of the many later Docetist documents states that Jesus' body was composed of water only, as opposed to blood."

(4) It is a reference to his incarnation, with water referring to Jesus' baptism and blood again referring to his crucifixion (Akin, 196; Barker, 350; Brooke, 133; Bruce, 118–19; Bultmann, 80; Burdick, 366; Haas, de Jonge, and Swellengrebel, 137–38; Houlden, 127; Kruse, 177; Marshall, 232–33; Moody, 105_6; Perkins, 61; Smalley, 278–79; Smith, 123; Stott, 180–81; Walls and Anders, 223; Yarbrough, 282). The idea of baptism is

---

216. G. Richter, "Blut und Wasser aus der durchgebohrten Seite Jesu (Joh 19,34b)," 134–35; H. Odeberg, *The Fourth Gospel*, 48–71, B. Witherington, ("The Waters of Birth: John 3.5 and 1 John 5.6–8," 158) argues from both the OT and 1QH that water was used to symbolize the amniotic fluids lost in childbirth. He further posits that γεννάω refers to childbirth when used with reference to a woman, and so here it should mean the same thing. The problem, though, is that John does not use γεννάω in this passage and so even if his theory were correct, it would not apply here.

217. M. C. de Boer, "Jesus the Baptizer: 1 John 5:5–8 and the Gospel of John," 93.

strengthened in that the first three references to "water" in the Gospel of John have to do with baptism by John the Baptist ἐν ὕδατι.[218] Burge (201) describes this as a "summing up the totality of Jesus' incarnational ministry." He notes that both the third and this view see the false teachers "demoted the cross." Baptism is both the predominant and best of these last two options (Brown, 576–78; Bruce, 118; Bultmann, 79–80; Hobbs, 126; Marshall, 231–32; Schnackenburg, 257; Smalley, 278). If water is a reference to Jesus' birth, then John is drawing attention to Jesus' humanity. Lalleman gives two arguments against "water" meaning Jesus' baptism: (a) "The Gospel and the epistles do not explicitly mention the baptism of Jesus; in the case of the Gospel this is a deliberate omission." (b) this "would seem to accept the Docetic position that Christ had not been the incarnate son from the beginning, but only from his baptism." Therefore, he takes "water" to be "referring to the very beginning of Christ's life; as such it can be a circumlocution of birth or of that which causes birth, the male seed."[219] Since "'blood' is taken by most to refer to Jesus' death, to believe in his 'coming in water (only)' would amount to a denial of his death."[220] He then argues that "blood" here should be understood in light of John 1:13 and so "represents the corporeal-human side of existence" and concludes "that blood has a physiological sense here, and that in combination with ἔρχομαι it refers to the beginning of life."[221] Lieu (210) rejects this on the basis that it is not polemically effective and might be used by the docetic opponents against John. If it is a reference to his baptism, the focus is on his ministry.

---

218. M. C. de Boer ("Jesus the Baptizer: 1 John 5:5–8 and the Gospel of John," 94, 99) observes this and then wrongly concludes that John is affirming, not that Jesus was baptized but, that Jesus "was a baptizer," though He did it with the Holy Spirit rather than with water like John the Baptist. Jesus came with both baptismal water and the giving of the Holy Spirit in salvation (102). And, arguing that "spirit" is epexegetical to "water" in John 3:5, he concludes that an epexegetical construction occurs in 1 John 5:6 with "blood" being epexegetical to "water" (103). He sees the foot washing water as symbolic of Jesus' blood. He also attempts to explain the different order of water and blood in John 19:34 and 1 John 5:6 on the basis that the Gospel "is seeking to identify Jesus' blood as cleansing water" while 1 John is seeking "to identify water as Jesus' cleansing blood" (104). Thus he ends up with baptismal water symbolizing both the Spirit and the blood of Jesus (105).

219. P. J. Lalleman, "The Adversaries Envisaged in the Johannine Epistles," 22.

220. P. J. Lalleman, "The Adversaries Envisaged in the Johannine Epistles," 22.

221. P. J. Lalleman, "The Adversaries Envisaged in the Johannine Epistles," 22–23.

The birth-death view accords best with John's contention with Cerinthus, who claimed that Jesus, the man, was indwelt by the Christ Spirit at his baptism and deserted by the same Spirit before his death. However, this is a case where context should contribute more to our understanding than a theorized historical background. The baptism-death view connects to Jesus' ministry, starting with his public appearance and ending with his finished work on the cross.

(5) The "water" represents the giving of the Holy Spirit (Grayston, 19–20; Strecker, 186). This is in part based on Jesus' words in John 4:10–14 and 7:37–39 combined with Jesus' words to Nicodemus in John 3:5 ("Unless one is born of water and the Spirit, he cannot enter the kingdom of God."). "Existence 'in spirit and truth' is the condition for genuine worship" according to John 4:23–24 (Strecker, 186).

(6) Kruse (174–80) and de Boer argue for "water" to mean Jesus' baptismal ministry depicted in John's Gospel (John 3:22; 4:1–2).[222] De Boer argues first that John's Gospel says that Jesus baptized in water regularly.[223] John 3:5 combines γεννάω, ὕδωρ, and πνεῦμα, which are also key words in 1 John 5:1–8.[224] Painter (304) counters this by pointing out that in John 4:1, John makes clear that it was not Jesus, but his disciples, doing the physical act of baptizing.

John's use of διὰ may prove helpful in understanding his point. The two best options for how it is being used here are either instrumental (Brooke, 135; Lenski, 525–26) or attendant circumstance.[225] Hodges (218) argues for this being an attendant circumstantial use of the preposition with the resulting sense of "with respect to" or "in relationship to," and so meaning that "he came to be baptized and to die. Not just to be baptized." Thus John would be focusing on the purpose of his coming. However, it is better seen as instrumental, giving the means of his coming, with the resultant translation of "through" (Brown, 573).[226] This is strengthened by John's use of ἐν with the (anaphoric) articular nouns in the following clause to clarify his

222. M. de Boer, "Jesus the Baptizer: 1 John 5:5–8 and the Gospel of John," 95.
223. M. de Boer, "Jesus the Baptizer: 1 John 5:5–8 and the Gospel of John," 95.
224. M. de Boer, "Jesus the Baptizer: 1 John 5:5–8 and the Gospel of John," 96.
225. BDAG, 224; A. Oepke, "διά," *TDNT* 2:66–69.
226. D. B. Wallace, *Grammar*, 369.

meaning here. John is focusing on both the fact of these events and that they were the means by which Jesus accomplished his incarnational ministry.

Of note is John's use of the title, "Jesus Christ." De Jonge sees Χριστός to be interchangeable with the expression ὁ υἱὸς τοῦ θεοῦ in 5:5.[227] However, it is more likely connected to the confession of 5:1 and designed to stress his humanity and deity. As Painter (303) notes well: "The use of the double name affirms the identity of the human Jesus and the divine Christ in one Jesus Christ."

οὐκ ἐν τῷ ὕδατι μόνον ἀλλ' ἐν τῷ ὕδατι καὶ ἐν τῷ αἵματι·, "not only by water but by water and by blood."[228] John changes the preposition from διὰ to ἐν in this following clause. His use of the dative proves as troublesome as his namesake, John the Baptist, when he said that Jesus would baptize "in the Holy Spirit and fire" (ἐν πνεύματι ἁγίῳ καὶ πυρί). Just as in Luke the preposition could have a range of nuances, so too, here with both "water" and "blood." The parenthetical role of this clause, explaining what he means by the previous clause, indicates that he intends ἐν to communicate the same sense as διὰ. Thus, it seems best to see these as datives of means. The means Jesus chose to use in "coming" included water and blood, his baptism and death. John's use of διὰ singularly in the first clause with both nouns while repeating ἐν in the following clause indicates that John saw Jesus' incarnational ministry as a single event, but is emphasizing that Jesus came in both modes and that they are distinct.[229] Painter (303) notes: "The overlapping use of these prepositions confirms a common translation of 'by' indicating agency (*dia*) and instrumentality (*en*)." Culy (126) also sees an intended difference between διὰ and ἐν in this and the previous verse. He says it "may be appropriate ... to maintain that διὰ focuses on the actual vehicle or

227. M. de Jonge, "The Use of the Word ΧΡΙΣΤΟΣ in the Johannine Epistles," 67.
228. Most see John's statement, "not by water only," to be a direct reference to the (Gnostic) false teacher's views (Brown, 574; Burdick, 367; Johnson, 126; Marshall, 232–34; Rensberger, 132). For example, de Boer (M. de Boer, "Jesus the Baptizer: 1 John 5:5–8 and the Gospel of John," 88) sees this as the only instance where John articulates the doctrines of the false teachers. However, though I would like to concur, and I do believe some form of early Docetism is in the background of what John is saying, I must also admit that insufficient evidence is available to say this with certainty.
229. M. C. de Boer, "Jesus the Baptizer: 1 John 5:5–8 and the Gospel of John," 89.

instrument by which the event was carried out, while ἐν focuses more on the circumstances in which the event took place."

Further, his use of the adverb *μόνον* with the correlative conjunctions, *οὐκ ... ἀλλ' ... καὶ*, along with limiting the referent of *ὕδωρ*, clarifies that the two, "water" and "blood" are to be viewed as describing the same event viewed in its entirety.[230] Whereas the nouns *ὕδωρ* and *αἷμα* were anarthrous in the previous clause, they are articular here. However, no significance should be given their articular state since both nouns naturally follow the preposition that makes them definite. These articles are simply anaphoric, clarifying that the water and blood referred to is the same as that described in the previous clause.[231] John's point is that both aspects of Jesus' ministry are in view, its beginning and end, as they relate to his purpose in coming. John's focus is not on just why Jesus came, but that all he did demonstrated his Sonship. This accords with the focus of John's Gospel on Jesus as the Son of God, who came to reveal his Father.

καὶ τὸ πνεῦμά ἐστιν τὸ μαρτυροῦν, ὅτι τὸ πνεῦμά ἐστιν ἡ ἀλήθεια, "and the Spirit is the one testifying, because the Spirit is the truth." John now turns attention to the veracity of what he has said about Jesus. Hodges (219) sees in this clause a reference to Jesus' baptism and the Holy Spirit's descent upon him. Kistemaker (353), on the other hand, sees this alluding to John 15:26 and the Spirit's testimony of Jesus that will be the basis of his disciples' roles as witnesses to the world. Burdick (368) sees the present tense (*ἐστιν*) referring to the Spirit's witness at Jesus' baptism and his continued witness of Jesus' crucifixion through the Gospel accounts (John's eyewitness record in his Gospel) (Haas, de Jonge, and Swellengrebel, 138). Harris (213) understands this statement in light of John 19:34. He notes that in John's description of Jesus' death he recounts how Jesus "handed over" responsibility for his mother to John (John 19:25–27), then he "handed over" the Spirit to the Father (John 10:30). Then in John 19:34 Jesus' side is pierced and blood and water flow. Finally, in John 19:35 John affirms his eyewitness status and the truthfulness of his testimony. Based on his theory of opponents, Harris (213) then sees John appealing "to an even higher witness, the Holy Spirit himself, who offers a present and continuing testimony to the significance of Jesus' coming by 'water and blood,' i.e., his sacrificial death on the cross."

230. BDAG, 659; D. B. Wallace, *Grammar*, 666–78.

231. M. C. de Boer, "Jesus the Baptizer: 1 John 5:5–8 and the Gospel of John," 89.

However, it seems better to see John alluding back to 3:24 and the first verses of chapter 4. There the Spirit, given to those abiding in Christ, confesses Jesus has come in the flesh, much the same truth being affirmed here. John's point is that the Spirit is serving as a witness to Jesus' incarnational ministry just as John claimed of himself in this epistle's prologue (1:1–4). The role of the Holy Spirit at Jesus' baptism is noteworthy in this regard. In John 1:33–34 John the Baptist is enabled to recognize Jesus as the Son of God by the witness of the Holy Spirit who visibly descends upon him, thereby bearing witness about Jesus to John, his forerunner.

John's use of ὅτι to introduce the next clause is causal (Brooke, 136; Brown, 580).[232] With this he provides the reason that the Spirit bears trustworthy testimony about Jesus.

Why does the Spirit bear witness of Jesus? Why can his witness be trusted? Because the Spirit is truth personified (Burdick, 369).[233] This is the same noun used by Jesus to describe himself as "the truth" in John 14:6, and likely alludes back to what Jesus said of the Spirit when he called him "the Spirit of truth" in John 14:17. This is in contrast to the false spirits of 4:1–6, whose testimony was not true and whom they were to evaluate and reject. These false "spirits," the false teachers, were saying the opposite of what is affirmed here.

Some see this alluding to John's testimony as coming from the Spirit rather than the Spirit himself doing the witnessing (Brown, 579; Thompson, 135). However, when John wants to affirm his witness is trustworthy, he does so directly (John 19:35; 21:24). Moreover, the proximity of the "blood and water" flowing from Jesus' side to his first affirmation does not necessitate that in these verses the same proximity can be used to connect the Spirit to John's testimony. When John says the Spirit witnesses along with the water and blood, he intends to mean the Holy Spirit. It should be understood literally.

5:7 In these next two verses John identifies the three witnesses that provide testimony of Jesus' humanity: the Spirit, water, and blood.

---

232. John exhibits similar uses in John 8:14 and 15:27 (Harris, 214). John has used ὅτι in this manner repeatedly (John 1:34; 3:28; 4:39, 44).

233. J. V. Dahms ("The Nature of Truth," 459) defines this use of "truth" to mean that the Holy Spirit is the "ultimate reality."

The added text of the KJV and NKJV, known as the "Johannine Comma" (*Comma Johanneum*), lacks any significant textual evidence. What evidence there is is very late.[234] Therefore, it should not be included as original. No Greek text before the thirteenth century contains these words, and after that only Latin texts until Erasmus' third edition (sixteenth century). It appears in only eight extant Greek MSS, with four of them being marginal notes (Brown, 776).[235] It is also absent from all of the non-Latin or Greek MSS prior to AD 1500 including the Arabic, Armenian, Coptic, Ethiopic, Slavonic, and Syriac translations. As Brown (777) notes, this is "an incredible situation if it were once part of the original Greek text of 1 John." The earliest Latin MSS also lack the Comma.[236] In 1592 it was added into the Catholic edition of the Latin Vulgate (Strecker, 189). It appears to have a Spanish origin in the late fourth century, possibly written by the bishop Instantius, a follower of Priscillian who was martyred around AD 386 (Strecker, 189). The words were clearly added to support Trinitarian theology.[237] For the history of how it was forced into Erasmus' third Greek edition and subsequently into the KJV, Brown's (779–80) summary is worth reading.

ὅτι τρεῖς εἰσιν οἱ μαρτυροῦντες, " so that there are three who bear witness." This clause begins with a consecutive ὅτι and should be seen as continuing

---

234. Brown (775–87) and Strecker (188–91) provide excellent discussions of the history of the Johannine Comma and how it made its way into the KJV and so the details need not be repeated here. An outline seems sufficient. The comma reads: ἐν τῷ οὐρανῷ, ὁ πατήρ, ὁ λόγος, καὶ τὸ ἅγιον πνεῦμα, καὶ οὗτοι οἱ τρεῖς ἕν εἰσι. καὶ τρεῖς εἰσιν οἱ μαρτυροῦντες ἐν τῇ γῇ.

235. The Greek texts are minuscules Gregory 61 (Codex Montfortianus from early sixteenth century), Gregory 629 (Codex Vatic. Ottobonianus, either fourteenth or fifteenth century or later), Gregory 918 (a Spanish MS from the sixteenth century), Gregory 2318 (a Rumanian MS from the eighteenth century), Gregory 88[vl] (a sixteenth century marginal note in Codex Regius, which is a twelfth-century MS), Gregory 221[vl] (a marginal note in a tenth-century MS in Oxford), Gregory 429[vl] (a marginal note in a sixteenth-century MS in Wolfenbüttel), and Gregory 636[vl] (a marginal note in a fifteenth-century MS in Naples). From Strecker (189).

236. The Johannine Comma appears in the Vetus Latina afteR ad 600 and in the Vulgate after AD 750.

237. Luther identified it as a "Catholic" addition in order to combat Arianism. Luther is quoted by Posset ("John Bugenhagen and the *Comma Johanneum*," 246) as saying that the addition should be left out of his translation "because in heaven there will be no need for a testimony ... There, the Trinity will declare himself."

the thought of the previous sentence rather than beginning a new one (Brown, 581; Yarbrough, 284). The Spirit's testimony is added to that of the "water" and "blood," Jesus' baptism and crucifixion. So, rather than there being two witnesses to Jesus' deity as the Son of God (5:5), the veracity of the testimony is strengthened by a third witness. Under the Mosaic Law, one could not be condemned of a capital offense based on a single witness, but only two or more (Deut 17:6; 19:15; Num 35:30).[238] This was practiced in Judaism[239] and formed the backdrop of Jesus' interchange with the Jews (John 8:17) and his instructions to the church (Matt 18:16). Paul invoked that law with regard to his coming visit of the church in Corinth (2 Cor 13:1). The author of Hebrews similarly invokes this law in his warning against willful sin (Heb 10:28). This forms the basis of John's affirmation here.

All of the referents of the masculine plural οἱ μαρτυροῦντες are neuter. However, this is not an "oblique reference to the Spirit's personality" (Culy, 127; contra Plummer, 116). The personality of the Spirit is assumed by John and his readers, and so he is personifying the other two "witnesses" (Akin, 198; Burdick, 370; Haas, de Jonge, and Swellengrebel, 139; Smalley, 281). Brown (581) relates it to "the personal character of the *witnessing* that is underlined by the masculine numeral, as well as by the use of the pres. ptcp" (italics his). Additionally, the present participle indicates that their witness continues to be given.

Schnackenburg (260–63) continues to see the sacraments in these references. In favor of this is the historical nature of the baptism and crucifixion of Jesus. Others (Barker, 353; Brown, 582–85; Dodd, 131; Haas, de Jonge, and Swellengrebel, 120; Houlden, 128–30; Strecker, 182–86) also see the sacraments in this verse though they did not see a reference to them in 5:6.[240] In this view, for Jesus' baptism and death to be continuing to witness today, they must be seen in the sacraments. However, a past event can witness in the present. The idea of the present tense is that its testimony continues to

238. G. K. Beale and D. A. Carson, *Commentary on the New Testament Use of the Old Testament*, 442–43.

239. Josephus (*Ant.* 4.219) writes: "But let not a single witness be credited; but three, or two at the least, and those such whose testimony is confirmed by their good lives." (from W. Whiston, trans.,, *The Works of Josephus: Complete and Unabridged*)

240. See Brown (582–84) for a thorough discussion of the issues involved in the sacramental view. Noteworthy is his choice not to support it.

the present (Burge, 203). For example, in Rom 5:8 God "demonstrates" his love (present tense συνίστησιν) through the past event of Jesus' death (aorist ἀπέθανεν). Heb 11 is filled with people whose past lives still speak to us today.

5:8 The three witnesses to Jesus' deity are named and described as confirming each other's testimony. The Holy Spirit is listed first, and then followed by the two most important historical events of Jesus' incarnational ministry.

τὸ πνεῦμα καὶ τὸ ὕδωρ καὶ τὸ αἷμα, "the Spirit and the water and the blood." "Water" and "blood," as metonymies, are now personified and made witnesses along with the Holy Spirit.[241] Kistemaker (354) asks how the testimony of two historical events could be made equal to the testimony of the Holy Spirit. Jesus answers this question in John 5:31–37. There he first points his opponents to John the Baptist as his witness, then to his works, and finally to his Father. John's use of water and blood fits this same pattern and may, in fact, allude to Jesus' statement there and in John 10:25–38.

There are a range of views on the nature and role of the three witnesses:

(1) They serve as a reference to the Trinity.[242] The Spirit is made to represent the Father based on John 4:24. The water symbolizes the Holy Spirit based on Jesus' words and John's explanation in John 7:38–39. The blood is said to represent Jesus based on the blood that spilled from his side in John 19:34.

(2) They refer to "an early Christian initiation ritual" that involved anointing, baptism, and taking the Eucharist.[243] Schnackenburg (263) gives objections to this view. Though it was practiced in the Syrian churches, no evidence can be found for its practice in New Testament times. It would have made more sense to use "oil of anointing" than the Spirit.

(3) They refer to the sacraments of baptism and the Lord's Supper (Bultmann, 80–81; Dodd, 130–31; Law, 121). Haas, de Jonge, and Swellengrebel (140) see the present tense indicating a present and continuous witness, and so see the sacraments of baptism (water) and the wine of the Eucharist (blood). Harris (217) provides three arguments against this. This view must make a clear reference to the Holy Spirit into a sacrament.

---

241. One may combine more than one figure of speech in a single element. This is not a violation of any literary convention.

242. This view was held by Augustine, but no modern interpreters (Brown, 582).

243. T. W. Manson, "Entry into Membership of the Early Church," 25–33.

"Blood" never refers to the Eucharist anywhere in Scripture. If "water" in 5:6 has Jesus' baptism as its referent, then somehow Christian baptism must become a witness to that. Here again, the argument for water and blood referring to baptism and the Lord's Supper is weakened by their inclusion with the Holy Spirit as witnesses to Jesus' deity. The Holy Spirit cannot be a sacrament (Kistemaker, 354). Yet he bears constant witness to Christ, as do these events.

(4) They refer to the historical event of Jesus' death but allude to the sacraments (Brooke, 137; Bruce, 120–21). The weakness of this view is that of any view including the sacraments. They do not appear in the Johannine writings and do not play any role in the development of the message of this epistle.

(5) They refer to the historical events as they reveal Jesus' incarnation (Stott, 179–82). This fits with the flow of thought in the epistle and takes into account the theory of opponents. It continues the christological polemic and prepares the reader for the discussion of God's testimony about his Son.

(6) They refer to "Jesus' power to make alive (Spirit), cleanse (water) and atone (blood)" (Harris, 215; also Brown, 582). Harris (217) points to the symbolism in John 6:63 and 13:10, along with 1 John 1:7 and 2:2. He further points to Zech 12:10–13:1 which is quoted in John 19:37. Further, this would support John's arguments against his opponents with regard to the "saving significance of what Jesus did during his earthly life and ministry." This last option appears to be the best. This prepares the reader for God's testimony about his Son, specifically in the area of assurance.

καὶ οἱ τρεῖς εἰς τὸ ἕν εἰσιν, "and the three agree as one." Here John uses what appears to be a Semitism (Strecker, 192) in which the preposition εἰς and its object are used substantively as a predicate nominative (Smalley, 282; Brown, 585).[244] This is not the same as Jesus' statement in John 10:30, though there he also uses the adjective ἕν. There Jesus' use of ἕν indicates shared essence, thereby claiming deity. Here the preposition phrase points to the unity of thought resulting from the testimony of the three witnesses (Deut 19:15), thus the idea of agreement between them.[245]

244. BDAG, 230, 291; A. Oepke, " εἰς," *TDNT* 2:420–34; BDF §205, εἰς is being used in place of ἐν, expressing a local sense. D. B. Wallace, *Grammar*, 47–48.
245. Jesus referred to the Deut passage in John 8:17–18.

This phrase uses the masculine numerals to refer to three neuter antecedents: the water, blood, and Spirit. As noted in comments on 4:4, John has used masculine pronouns to refer to the Holy Spirit previously (John 14:26 and 15:26). However, in each of those cases ὁ παράκλητος appears to be the actual referent of ἐκεῖνος. Here John does seem to be implying the personhood of the Spirit but is also likely personifying the water and blood (Marshall, 237, n. 20). He has gone the opposite direction, using neuter pronouns to refer to Jesus (1:1–3). Thus this is not a surprising literary choice with John.

5:9 In these next three verses John will affirm God's witness to Jesus as the source of eternal life and that it is experienced by all who believe in Jesus. He accomplishes this by moving from the testimony of Jesus' works to the testimony of God himself.

εἰ τὴν μαρτυρίαν τῶν ἀνθρώπων λαμβάνομεν, ἡ μαρτυρία τοῦ θεοῦ μείζων ἐστίν·, "if we receive the testimony of men, the testimony of God is greater." John begins with a first class conditional statement (assumes the protasis* is true for the sake of argument) to express something true to life, thus the gnomic present (Burdick, 372). It implies the translation of "since." This is a common practice that stands without question. In courts we accept the testimony of men. This then sets the stage for the most powerful proof of the deity and humanity of Jesus—the testimony of God himself.

What does John mean by testimony of men? (1) It may refer to the three witnesses in 5:8.[246] (2) It could mean human testimony (Schnackenburg, 270). Against this is its seeming disconnect with what precedes. (3) It could refer to John the Baptist's testimony at Jesus' baptism (Brown, 586; Harris, 219). This seems the best option. This could easily be an allusion back to John the Baptist's testimony about Jesus. Though this might be viewed as a polemic against John's opponents, it need not be such. This statement is a deduction drawn from a general principle moving from the lesser to the greater.

John now moves from the lesser to the greater, from the testimony of men to that of God (Akin, 200; Burdick, 372; Kruse, 180; Williamson, 163). We may ask what testimony God gave. John must be referring to God the Father rather than to God the Holy Spirit. In the other Gospels God the

---

246. Brown (586) identifies this view with Bonsirven.

Father is quoted testifying of Jesus at his baptism (Matt 3:17; Mark 1:11; Luke 3:22). However, John does not include his testimony in his account of Jesus' baptism, only the witness of the Holy Spirit. It is also the other Gospels that include the Father's testimony at the Transfiguration (Matt 17:5; Mark 9:7; Luke 9:35). John does not mention it in his Gospel. The resurrection is described in all four Gospels but lacks an oral witness from God the Father. We do hear God's testimony about his Son in John 12:28. In John 5, after pointing to John the Baptist, his works, and God the Father as witnesses to him, Jesus then points to the testimony of Scripture (John 5:39–47). God's witness is going to be described as "within" the believing Christian (v 10) and is described in terms of truths known. Thus, it seems that this reference to a witness from God could be alluding back to the "anointing" of the believer described in 2:27. It would be those propositional truths John's readers had been taught that were ultimately God's revelation bearing witness to his Son.

What is meant by God's testimony "is greater"?

(1) The three testimonies are ultimately God's own testimony (Bruce, 121; Dodd, 132; Houlden, 132; Marshall, 240; Smalley, 284; Stott, 184; Williamson, 163). If these testimonies arise from the community, then God is testifying through them (Harris, 219). God is speaking through the historical events (general revelation) as well through the testifying (convicting) ministry of the Holy Spirit in the world.

(2) His is an additional testimony added to the previous three (Brown, 587; Marshall, 240; Schnackenburg, 270). The context of what follows, in that it describes God's testimony, supports this idea. As they testify to aspects of Jesus' life and ministry, God the Father testifies to the significance of those events and of the Spirit's conviction of the world (John 16:8–11).

ὅτι αὕτη ἐστὶν ἡ μαρτυρία τοῦ θεοῦ ὅτι μεμαρτύρηκεν περὶ τοῦ υἱοῦ αὐτοῦ, "because this is the testimony of God that he has testified concerning his Son." Now God's testimony begins to be described through two ὅτι clauses. Beginning with a causal ὅτι (Harris, 220; Painter, 301; Rensberger, 134), John prepares the reader for the content of God's testimony about his Son by giving the reason his testimony is greater. The significant role of testimony in the life of the believer is seen in the continued repetition of *μαρτυρέω*, and *μαρτυρία*, throughout this paragraph.[247]

Αὕτη follows John's pattern from 1:5; 3:11, and 23 previously. Thus it is cataphoric* and refers to what follows (Culy, 128). It is repeated ("resumptive") in 5:11 and followed by the description of God's testimony which can be read back into this verse as well (Burdick, 376; Harris, 221).[248]

The second ὅτι clause is understood variously. (1) Some see it as an adverbial causal conjunction modifying ἐστίν. However, this would be very awkward in light of the previous causal clause (Harris, 220). (2) It is also a causal ὅτι (Rensberger, 134). In this view the testimony is not identified till 5:11. (3) It is equivalent to or may have been intended to be a relative clause introduced by ὅ τι (Brown, 588; Harris, 220; NET). Objections to this include the problem that the neuter relative pronoun would have the feminine noun ἡ *μαρτυρία* as its antecedent. The presence of the feminine pronoun ἣν in the following verse makes this less likely.[249] As second objection is that it creates a tautology between what was just said and what follows (Rensberger, 134). (4) It serves as a substantival conjunction that is epexegetical (Brooke, 138; Burdick, 374) to either *αὕτη* (Westcott, 186) or ἡ *μαρτυρία* (Painter, 301–2; Smalley, 284). Harris (220) objects that God's testimony is defined in 5:11 and differs significantly from this testimony. Rensberger (134) also objects on the grounds that it creates a "greater tautology" than if it were taken as a relative clause (view two). However, what we see is John creating another polyptoton* with the noun ἡ *μαρτυρία* and the verb *μεμαρτύρηκεν*, thereby highlighting (making emphatically clear) the significance of God's testimony.[250] Thus the ὅτι clause is epexegetical to *μαρτυρία* rather than functioning as a relative clause.

---

247. The subjective gen. τοῦ θεοῦ identifies God the Father as the one making the statement.

248. Schnackenburg (265) sees the pres. tense ἐστὶν arguing against historical events and indicating that this "witness" occurs through the sacraments. However, the following perfect clarifies that God's testimony has been given from the past and continues to stand to this day. It does not indicate especially that he continues to testify, but that his testimony remains in effect.

249. Harris (220) notes these weaknesses but sees this as the best option of the three views.

250. See comment on 5:4 regarding the polyptoton of ἡ *νίκη* ἡ *νικήσασα*.

The content of God's testimony is testimony about his Son, Jesus. The perfect tense μεμαρτύρηκεν indicates that God's testimony was previously given, is complete, and is still in effect and so still stands true (Burdick, 373–74). Thus, though given in the past, it speaks to us today and what was said about his Son is still true. John now gives the content of God's testimony, summarizing the revelation of Scripture about Jesus as well as the testimony of Jesus' life.

5:10 The content of God's testimony will soon be given (5:11).[251] Before giving the content, though, John pauses to make a parenthetical statement about the believer's relationship to this testimony he has been discussing beginning in 5:1 (Rensberger, 134).

ὁ πιστεύων εἰς τὸν υἱὸν τοῦ θεοῦ ἔχει τὴν μαρτυρίαν ἐν αὐτῷ, "He who believes in the Son of God has the testimony in him." Burdick (374) notes well that where John uses the aorist πιστεύσωμεν in 3:24 to refer to initial belief in Christ, here he uses the present πιστεύων to describe "the continuing life of faith." This articular present participle ὁ πιστεύων describes a kind of person (gnomic as opposed to progressive or customary).[252] This description includes the Johannine formula for justifying faith in Jesus (πιστεύω εἰς). Throughout the Gospel and all other Johannine literature, both πιστεύω εἰς and πιστεύω ἐν express the faith of a justified saint, even in passages such as John 2:23, where Jesus did not entrust himself to those believing in him. That need not lead to a false conclusion of spurious or nonjustifying faith as some theologians propose.[253] Rather, it communicates that justifying faith is not always sanctifying faith. What makes justifying faith effective is its object. It is Jesus who saves, not faith. God the Father justifies those whose faith has his Son as its object, not their theology. God justifies them apart from works both at the moment of faith and subsequently (Eph 2:8–9). Furthermore, if justifying faith is workless at salvation, it may remain

---

251. Strecker (193) sees this verse in antithetical parallelism to v 9. Also Schnackenburg (266–67) sees all the verses in this paragraph as antithetical.

252. D. B. Wallace, *Grammar*, 615–16.

253. See the excursus "Johannine Concept of 'Belief'" for a listing of those who do not consider their faith justifying and for my arguments for why it is.

workless and still justify. However, as Jas 2 teaches, apart from works faith will not sanctify, being ineffectual, being "dead" but not nonexistent.[254]

Justifying faith must have the right object, Jesus the Son of God, to be effectual. As a result, theology is important. A person cannot be justified who does not believe in Jesus who is the eternal Son of God and who died and rose again (Acts 4:12; 1 Cor 15:3–8).

What John says about this justified saint is that he "has the witness in him." This witness is related to the anointing discussed earlier (Brown, 589–90; Smalley, 285–86). It is identified, not as "inner testimony" of the indwelling Holy Spirit (Akin, 200–1; Brooke, 139; Law, 125; J. Mitchell, 148; Stott, 182; Williams, 57), but the believers' need to "hold fast" God's testimony about Jesus in Scripture (Bultmann, 82; Kruse, 181; Marshall, 241 n. 39). What follows indicates that John is developing a contrast between those who accept and those who reject what God says about his Son.

ὁ μὴ πιστεύων τῷ θεῷ ψεύστην πεποίηκεν αὐτόν, "He who does not believe God has made him a liar." In contrast to the one who believes *in* the Son of God is the one who does not believe God. John does not include εἰς or ἐν with πιστεύω in this instance. This fits the pattern of Jesus' words in the upper room where he, too, made the distinction with his disciples between believing what he said and believing "in" him (John 14:11–12). The issue here is not the failure to believe that God exists, but to believe God's testimony, what he has said about Jesus (Burdick, 375; Culy, 130). Thus a person may affirm, "I believe in Jesus." However, when that person denies Jesus' resurrection, virgin birth, that he is the only means of salvation, or his humanity or deity, the personhe is calling God a liar. Rejecting Jesus or redefining Jesus to accommodate modern values is an act of choosing not to believe what God has said about his Son. The one who believes in Jesus also possesses God's witness, namely, the truth of God (v. 9) stated about Jesus. The one who rejects God's testimony thereby calls God a liar. People cannot reject Jesus and say they believe God. Like the point made in 2:22–23, denial of one is denial of the other.

---

254. The meaning of Jas 2:17 (ἡ πίστις, ἐὰν μὴ ἔχῃ ἔργα, νεκρά ἐστιν καθ' ἑαυτήν) should be informed by the similar use of νεκρός by Paul in Rom 7:8 (χωρὶς γὰρ νόμου ἁμαρτία νεκρά.). Also, it is not one's justification that Jesus will judge or determine at the Bema Seat, but his subsequent deeds as they express faithfulness or the lack of faithfulness to him following justification.

Harris (221–22) says regarding believing in Jesus (ὁ πιστεύων εἰς τὸν υἱὸν) and believing God (πιστεύων τῷ θεῷ), "there is probably no difference in the significance of these constructions," seeing it as stylistic variation (Haas, de Jonge, and Swellengrebel, 122). In his Gospel, where John uses either εἰς or ἐν to indicate faith placed in the person of Jesus or God the Father, his use of the dative without either of the two prepositions is consistently directed toward believing what Jesus or God has said rather than "in" their persons. For example, in John 2:22, John says they "believed the Scripture and the word" (ἐπίστευσαν τῇ γραφῇ καὶ τῷ λόγῳ), clearly referring to the content of what it said in Scripture and what was said by Jesus. This is immediately followed in the next verse by faith in Jesus (ἐπίστευσαν εἰς τὸ ὄνομα αὐτοῦ). In John 14:1 Jesus uses πιστεύω εἰς for faith placed in both his Father and himself. Yet in John 14:11, when he tells the disciples to believe what he has been saying, Jesus uses πιστεύετέ μοι, the imperative of πιστεύω with the dative pronoun μοι, not either of the two prepositional phrases.[255] Harris is correct that John may sometimes use a dative construction with πιστεύω and communicate the sense of "believe in." For example, this is the sense of 3:23. John's use of πιστεύσωμεν with the dative τῷ ὀνόματι and no preposition still indicates faith placed in the person and character of Christ. However, immediately following this in 4:1 the anarthrous dative παντὶ πνεύματι is placed with πιστεύετε to indicate believing false teachers (spirits), where it refers to their teachings. Thus without the preposition to aid, context will determine its sense, whether it is faith in someone or believing what they have said. The sense of ὁ μὴ πιστεύων τῷ θεῷ should be informed by what is said of that person in the following clauses. The content of this person's rejection is given in the following ὅτι clause where John clarifies that the person is not believing God's testimony. Thus this is the equivalent of Jesus' call on the disciples to believe what he has said, to trust his words, in John 14:11. All this being said, Harris is still correct in that one's trust of God's Word arises from faith in his person and character. The only difference is the nuance of whether that person is responding to God's person or the things God has said about his Son.

---

255. There are also instances, such as John 14:10; 16:27, 31; 17:8, 21, and 20:31 where John uses a ὅτι clause to give the content of what is believed, which is different from believing something said. We see this construction in 5:1 and 5 where John gives the content of faith as well.

ὅτι οὐ πεπίστευκεν εἰς τὴν μαρτυρίαν ἣν μεμαρτύρηκεν ὁ θεὸς περὶ τοῦ υἱοῦ αὐτοῦ. "because he has not believed in the testimony which God has testified concerning his Son." The reason one does not believe God is because he or she has rejected God's testimony. In this case John uses his familiar *πιστεύω εἰς* formula, indicating that believing God involves putting one's trust in what God has said about his Son. Each person must depend on the truthfulness of what God has said for both spiritual birth and life. God's Word, what he has said in Scripture, is a valid object of faith, being revelatory truth from God who is truth. This is different from faith in a doctrine, which is the product of evaluating what God has said. This is also not faith in the Bible as a written record. Rather, this is ultimately faith in God as one believes his testimony (in this sense I agree with Harris's view above). His testimony is contained in Scripture. However, it is God that faith is directed toward in response to what he has said, not the words themselves that makes faith valid.

John uses the perfect tense *πεπίστευκεν* with the negative particle *οὐ* to describe the response of the unbeliever to God's testimony. By this he indicates it was a response to God's testimony in the past that continues beyond the initial decision to reject.[256] This does not imply a change of heart is impossible and that the person will not someday come to faith. Rather, it indicates that a person who does not believe God's testimony rejects it because he or she made a conscious choice. Present unbelief is the product of a choice to reject God's testimony in the past (Brooke, 139; Burdick, 375; Westcott, 187).

What has the rejecter of God rejected? God's established testimony. This second perfect *μεμαρτύρηκεν* indicates that God is no longer testifying. His testimony about his Son is complete. He has nothing more to say. It also indicates that his testimony still stands as true. There is nothing more he needs to say. This leads then to what he has said.

5:11 Continuing the use of repetition, John emphasizes God's testimony about Jesus. He now defines it in terms of two things said by God. This could be seen as the application of the christological truth to the life of a believer. It is not the water and blood that provides the knowledge a believer

256. Brown (590) sees the perfect *πεποίηκεν* as proleptic, indicating the certainty of its future expression.

needs in order to have assurance. Rather, it is God the Father's testimony about his Son, a testimony that clarifies the significance of that which is testified to by the three witnesses.

καὶ αὕτη ἐστὶν ἡ μαρτυρία, "And this is the testimony." The copulative καὶ ties this with what John has been saying about the testimony of the three witnesses and God (Burdick, 376).[257] John again employs an emphatic relative pronoun αὕτη to draw his readers' attention to the importance of what follows in the ὅτι clause (Akin, 201; Burdick, 376; Strecker, 194). He uses the same root word for "testimony" (μαρτυρία) as the verb "witness" in v 9. What God has testified is two truths.

ὅτι ζωὴν αἰώνιον ἔδωκεν ἡμῖν ὁ θεός, "that God has given to us eternal life." The content of God's testimony is introduced with the epexegetical ὅτι clause functioning substantively and defining μαρτυρία more fully (Harris, 222; Strecker, 195).

The first part of God's testimony is that eternal life is a gift from him. It is not something earned, a wage (Rom 4:1–4). The anarthrous use of ζωὴν αἰώνιον by John here points to "eternal life" as a quality of life rather than as a possession (Brooke, 140; Westcott, 187). It is also not a reference to the person of Jesus, though John has identified him as eternal life incarnate in the prologue. The constative aorist ἔδωκεν points to the fact of God's having given eternal life to John and his readers (Brooke, 140; Burdick, 376; Smalley, 287).[258] By this John is reminding his readers that they possess eternal life, freely given them by God. Thus he is not calling upon them to receive that life. Rather, he is reminding them that they have already received it. He is also reminding them of that life's source—God.

---

257. Culpepper (272) sees this marking the end of the body of the epistle even as "this is the message" began it in 1:5. Strecker (194) sees this "beginning something new." However, the role of the copulative καὶ and John's use of ταῦτα ἔγραψα two verses later mitigates against either option. He uses the same construction in 2:25 (αὕτη ἐστὶν ἡ ἐπαγγελία), and 3:23 (αὕτη ἐστὶν ἡ ἐντολὴ αὐτοῦ) without ending or starting a new sections. A new paragraph is begun with this construction in 3:10 (αὕτη ἐστὶν ἡ ἀγγελία). However, as can be seen, this is a regularly used phrase within paragraphs and so should not be seen being used otherwise.

258. Brown (591) warns against pressing the punctiliar aspect of the aor. with regard to Jesus' incarnation. Though it remains possible to see a punctiliar aspect to the aor. its undefined role depicting a past action without regard to specifics (a generic "it happened" sense) is well recognized (D. B. Wallace, *Grammar*, 554–65). And in this case, nothing in the context would have a particular event in view.

Bultmann (83) says that eternal life "belongs to the eschatological time of salvation, but is already present for faith" and is a gift from God to those who have passed from death to life. Strecker (195) sees it as something that "must be grasped continually anew in love for the sisters and brothers." However, in this context, John is about to define this life in terms of one's relationship to its author, Jesus. Its possession and experience is present and related to the person of Jesus, not one's relationship with other believers (though John has made clear how important that is, and he will continue to do so in the verses that follow).

καὶ αὕτη ἡ ζωὴ ἐν τῷ υἱῷ αὐτοῦ ἐστιν, "and this life is in his Son." The second part of God's testimony is that eternal life is found *in* his Son.[259] This takes us back to the prologue wherein eternal life is found to be a person, Jesus, and not a possession. This accords with Jesus' own words wherein he identified himself as "the resurrection and the life" to Martha (John 11:25) and "the way, the truth, and the life" to his disciples (John 14:6). Additionally, though possessing eternal life is an automatic result of regeneration, experiencing eternal life is contingent on one's relationship with Jesus, who is eternal life itself. Thus God's testimony that life is in his Son speaks to two aspects of eternal life. No lost person can receive it apart from believing in his Son. No saved person can enjoy it apart from believing in his Son.

Of note is the addition of the article with *ζωὴ*, both here and in the following verse. These serve as articles of previous reference (Lenski, 530) and point to the anarthrous *ζωὴν αἰώνιον* that God has given. So the focus is on the possession of a quality of life that springs forth from the person of life whom one must believe in to either possess or experience that which is possessed.

5:12 This verse is a great example of antithetic parallelism, where the same truth is stated positively and negatively. This is similar to the statement about God in 1:5. Though much the same words are used in both clauses, their wording is clearly intended to be different rather than parallel.

ὁ ἔχων τὸν υἱὸν ἔχει τὴν ζωήν·, "He who has the Son has the life." The articular present participle ὁ ἔχων with its direct object now describes a

259. This second *αὕτη* takes up the first from the previous clause and thereby includes this clause in *μαρτυρία* at the beginning of the sentence (Strecker, 195).

person in terms of his or her "having" the Son. The participle and its object function as the subject of the clause. However, what does John mean by this? The idea of "having" Jesus is not found anywhere else in John's writings. Parallels to this idea can be found in 2:23 as well as 2 John 9 where one "has" or "does not have" the Father, depending on his or her confession or rejection of his Son (Burdick, 377) or failure to abide in "the doctrine of Christ." Though John is writing to those he knows are regenerate, he still states a principle, a truth that applies to all mankind. Thus this should be seen as clarifying the gospel, though it is addressed to believers and is not being done evangelistically. What John affirms is that eternal life results from "having" the Son of God (Kruse, 182). This "having" means that Jesus "is present in the individual's life," equivalent to John 3:16 and having eternal life (Harris, 224; Kruse, 183). Further, the present tense ἔχει describes this as a state of being and emphasizes that this life is not something future, but a present experience (Akin, 202). Burdick (377) defines its significance as indicating "possession in the sense of being in a vital spiritual relationship with the Father and the Son." "The two occurrences of 'to have' are in the same tense to show that having the Son and having life are contemporaneous. This is to express that during this earthly life already the believer participates in the eternal life, because he has the Son in whom this life is" (Haas, de Jonge, and Swellengrebel, 144). Thus eternal life is not a possession we will enjoy in the future ("pie in the sky when I die") but the life of God expressed in us now and experienced by us now.[260]

ὁ μὴ ἔχων τὸν υἱὸν τοῦ θεοῦ τὴν ζωὴν οὐκ ἔχει, "he who does not have the son of God does not have life." John now states the same truth in terms of its opposite. He adds "of God" after "the Son" in the participial construction that again functions as the subject of its verb. The addition of τοῦ θεοῦ reminds the reader of the inseparable relationship of faith in Christ with faith in God as was seen in 2:23 (Akin, 202). He moves the verb ἔχει to the end of its clause. These shifts serve to emphasize both Jesus' deity and his connection to eternal life. With both "the Son" and "life" at the center

260. Strecker (196), who does not hold to eternal security, defines it as "possessing life, just as, in turn, 'not having' the Son includes loss of life." He sees this reference to τὸν υἱὸν meaning "the Christ-event." This may be defined as "the eternal redemptive work symbolized by the death and Resurrection of Jesus Christ" (G. Kurian, *Nelson's New Christian Dictionary*, s.v. "Christ event") rather than the historical person and resurrection of Jesus.

of the clause and the failure to have both the Son and life on each end, he makes clear that life is found nowhere else.[261] "In the current theological context, John is clearly and convictionally a 'theological exclusivist' with respect to salvation" (Akin, 202).

5:13 Though most commentators see this verse beginning a new paragraph (Akin, 203–4; Barker, 353; Brooke, 141; Brown, 605–8; Bruce, 122; Burdick, 384; Haas, de Jonge, and Swellengrebel, 145–46; Johnson, 133; Kruse, 188; Marshall, 242–43; Rensberger, 129; Strecker, 197; Thompson, 138; Westcott, 188; Williams, 58–59; Williamson, 165; Yarbrough, 296), it seems better to see it concluding the previous one (Bultmann, 85; Lenski, 522–31; Smalley 272; Smith, 121–29; Stott, 186). Several questions are raised by this verse, particularly the referent of *ταῦτα*. It may refer to the whole epistle or only to the immediate context. If it refers to the whole epistle, then John's purpose in describing believers and antichrists is so that his readers can know that they have eternal life. The purpose of the epistle is to provide assurance of salvation (Test of Life view). If it is the purpose statement for the whole epistle, the next question would be to determine if it is also the actual conclusion with the rest of the epistle serving as an epilogue (Smalley, 289, Stott, 186; Westcott, 188), or if it is an introduction to a new section (Brown, 607; NET). If it refers to the immediate context, what John has just written is designed to assure them of their salvation. However, the purpose of the whole epistle goes beyond assurance. Assurance is necessary for experiencing and enjoying the eternal life one possesses. It is an integral part of sanctifying faith, though not justifying faith. Hodges (225) is correct when he says, "It must be remembered here that First John is not an evangelistic tract. It is written to people who 'know the truth,' not to people who 'do not know' it." Even so, that being the case, believers need to be reminded of the truths of the Gospel, otherwise Paul would not have written 1 Cor 15:1–4 to the believers at Corinth, or Rom 1–5 to the church in Rome, much less his Epistle to the Galatians.

Ταῦτα ἔγραψα ὑμῖν ἵνα εἰδῆτε ὅτι ζωὴν ἔχετε αἰώνιον, "These things I have written to you in order that you may know that you have eternal life." The pronoun *ταῦτα* may be understood in one of two ways:

261. Brooke (141) notes that the "negative (*μή*) generalizes the statement. A class of men is described who are distinguished by this characteristic."

(1) It looks back on the entire epistle (Brown, 608; Bultmann, 83; Burge, 213; Culpepper, 107; Culy, 132; Dodd, 133; Haas, de Jonge, and Swellengrebel, 124; Houlden, 137; Johnson, 133; Kruse, 188; Law, 405; Marshall, 243; Painter, 313; Plummer, 120; Stott, 184; Strecker, 198; Westcott, 188).[262] Those who see this verse as a comprehensive purpose statement provide two major arguments. First, they point to John 20:31 as the model for determining the purpose of the epistle (Akin, 203; Brown, 607; Bruce, 122; Burdick, 385 Harris, 225; Johnson, 133; Kistemaker, 359; Painter, 313; Smalley 289; Stott, 186; NET).[263] Brooke (142) rejects this argument on the basis that this verse "does not really present an exact parallel to the conclusion of the Gospel." Also, this argument assumes their assessment of John 20:31 is correct, although it need not be the sole purpose of the Gospel any more than this statement is for this epistle. Moreover, in light of the other three purpose statements in the Epistle (1:3, 4; 2:1), one should be hesitant to make such a claim here. John uses similar phraseology in 2:1 (present tense) and 2:26 (identical aorist) and both very clearly refer to the immediately preceding context. Thus it is best to see him doing the same here.[264]

(2) A second argument is that the purpose statements in 1:4 and 5:13 form an inclusio* with the present tense γράφομεν looking forward and the aorist ἔγραψα looking back (Burdick, 385; Harris, 226; Johnson, 133). Again, the supposed inclusio is broken up by the presence of the other two purpose statements that also use present and aorist tense verbs.

Akin (203–4) is an example of one whose interpretations are guided by his understanding of purpose rather than subject. He provides four arguments for ταῦτα referring to the whole Epistle and this verse serving as the main purpose for writing. (1) John uses the first person singular, which he

---

262. Rensberger (137) sees it both looking back on the entire epistle, but also climaxing the immediate context of 5:1–12.

263. Painter (314) notes that though the two purpose statements have similarities, they are also distinct. John 20:31 says the Gospel was written in order that its readers might believe in Jesus while the epistle is written to people who have already believed in him.

264. This moves the focus of interpretation away from an assumed dominant purpose (fellowship or assurance) to a clearer subject (experiencing eternal life). By focusing on the subject, no purpose is neglected, nor is any interpretation made prisoner of the interpreter's understanding of John's purpose. The focus of interpretation should never be to determine why an author says something, but rather what the author has to say.

has not used since 2:26. (2) The frequency of the appearance of the theme of assurance of salvation in the Epistle. (3) The themes of "know," "eternal life," and "Son of God" are found in 5:13 and are continued in the following verses. (4) He notes the "close parallel" between this verse and John 20:31, which he sees as the purpose statement of John's Gospel. He does note John's purpose statements in 1:4 and 2:1, and see them as giving "some indication of John's purpose for writing this epistle," but appears to pass over the one in 1:3. Yet each of these arguments can be adequately answered: (1) John's use of the first person singular in 2:26 may argue against this being the major purpose precisely because he used it in a context where his purpose was clearly connected to its immediate context (2:18–25). He fails to mention that John had also used the first person singular when addressing his readers in 2:12–14 to assure them of their salvation. (2) The frequency of the theme of assurance in the epistle is related to the issues addressed regarding false teachers and the tests that were to be applied to them. Each of John's assurances (2:12–14; 2:27; 4:4; 5:13) are preceded by discussions that might cause his readers to question their salvation. Additionally, in all but the first instance, the issues are christological and the assurances follow what might be considered polemical sections of his epistle. Thus it would be logical for John to conclude his Epistle with a reminder of the gospel and their security in Christ. (3) The three themes Akin lists are found in the prologue as well where the Test of Fellowship view finds its overarching purpose statement in 1:3. "Eternal life" and "Son of God" are stated directly, with "know" being part of the "abiding" theme that is introduced with "fellowship." (4) Finally, the parallel between 5:13 and John 20:31 is only apparent if one ignores the presence of other purpose statements in the epistle. As noted above, Revelation does not follow the supposed Johannine pattern of a stated purpose at the conclusion of the work, nor does the other two epistles. Further, the purpose statement in the Gospel is made its singular purpose solely because it is the only stated purpose in the Gospel. Yet the Gospel's prologue clearly evidences other purposes behind his writing, such as explaining the Father (John 1:18).

It seems the best answer concerning the relation of this purpose statement to the epistle comes from examining the other purpose statements (1:3, 4; 2:1, 26). In each of the instances where *ταῦτα* and *γράφω* are combined in a stated purpose for writing, the immediately preceding context is clearly in view. He is explaining his reason for writing what was just said. If one wishes to argue from a Johannine pattern, he has established one within the immediate context of this epistle. None of the purpose statements is comprehensive. Thus, John has established a pattern within the epistle. Therefore, (2) the antecedent of ταῦτα in 5:13 must be seen as what he has just written, 5:4–12, and not the entire epistle (Brooke, 142; Lieu, 220–21; Schnackenburg, 273).

John's purpose (ἵνα) for writing about God's testimony in 5:6–12 is that his readers may "know" (εἰδῆτε).[265] This is intuitive knowledge gained by instruction (Brooke, 143; Burdick, 386), not experiential knowledge (γινώσκω). This is something that can be known apart from experience. It is known by believing God's testimony, not looking to one's works for assurance. Moreover, what they know is that they "have."[266] What John has just written was done in order to promote his readers' assurance of salvation. Why? Because believers can lack assurance, and that is not God's will. If we know what we believe, and we know what God expects us to believe, then we can know we are believers whether or not we remember when we believed. The basis of assurance of salvation is belief in God's Word and in his Son, of whom Scripture gives witness. Everyone who has placed his or her faith in Christ can know without a doubt that he or she has eternal life. They know, not because of any fruit in their lives, but because God says they do. Without this confidence, a believer can neither enjoy the gift God has given nor experience the relationship with Christ that is that gift. Westcott (188) observes well: "The eternal life may be present and yet not realized in its inherent power. The fruits may not be referred to their source; and again they may be delayed. However, there is a knowledge of life which is independent of external signs; and this St John seeks to quicken."

τοῖς πιστεύουσιν εἰς τὸ ὄνομα τοῦ υἱοῦ τοῦ θεοῦ, "to those believing in the name of the Son of God." The articular participle τοῖς πιστεύουσιν stands in apposition to ὑμῖν. John is defining his readers as "those who believe." John identifies the recipients of God's assurance as those believing τοῖς πιστεύουσιν

265. Lieu (221) observes well that this use of εἰδῆτε "need not imply that their confidence had been shaken in any way; there is no suggestion that they do not already know this." In fact, John's earlier reassurances that they do know the truth (2:21) would imply he is simply reminding them of what he knows they know.

266. "His present tense implies the enduring, reassuring effects of knowing our eternal destiny. Life is not just a promise, it is an inheritance enjoyed in the present. In Johannine language, it is having fellowship with God"(Burge, 214).

"in the name" of God's Son, thus to justified saints. "In the name of his Son" is a metonymy of adjunct in which "name" is used in place of "person."[267] One's "name" represented his or her character. Thus faith is not just in Jesus, but in him on the basis of whom he is and that he is indeed trustworthy. As always with John, πιστεύω εἰς is a justification formula. This same construction occurs in John 1:12 (ἔδωκεν αὐτοῖς ἐξουσίαν τέκνα θεοῦ γενέσθαι, τοῖς πιστεύουσιν εἰς τὸ ὄνομα αὐτοῦ) where those who believe in Jesus are God's children, a theme developed earlier (3:1–3; 5:1–4) in this epistle as well.

The present participle πιστεύουσιν need not be seen as progressive. If progressive in force it would indicate that assurance occurs only while one believes in Jesus.[268] Though this is likely true, it is still better to see this in a gnomic sense that describes the characteristic of the person.[269] Those who believe in Christ have this assurance. So why did John not choose the perfect participle, which would have indicated someone who had believed in Jesus for justification and was still living in a state of faith? That is clarified by the following clause and John's desire that his readers continue to believe.

καὶ ἵνα πιστεύητε εἰς τὸ ὄνομα τοῦ υἱοῦ τοῦ θεοῦ, "and so that you may continue to believe in the name of the Son of God." The coordinate connective καὶ adds this second clause with the first purpose clause. A second reason he wrote to them about assurance being based on the trustworthiness of God's testimony (in Scripture), was to motivate his readers to continue trusting Christ. In this case, this *is* parallel to the purpose statement of John 20:31. In both places John's point is that believers must keep believing if they are to keep enjoying the eternal life—a quality of life—that Jesus came to give. The present subjunctive with ἵνα not only communicates purpose, but here it is being used as a substitute for the infinitive of result, expressing a desire that may or may not occur.[270] By this John is assuring his readers that he knows they do believe in Jesus. His desire is that they continue to do so, not in order to gain or maintain their salvation but to continue enjoying the eternal life that comes from a healthy relationship with Jesus, who is that life. They cannot do that without continuing to place their faith in him,

267. E. W. Bullinger, *Figures of Speech Used in the Bible*, 587.
268. Williamson (166) sees the pres. participle "stressing the necessity of ongoing faith" as opposed to a single event of belief.
269. D. B. Wallace, *Grammar*, 620.
270. BDAG, 477; E. Stauffer, "ἵνα," *TDNT* 3:323–33.

even as they cannot apart from confession of sin and loving their fellow believer. In the upper room, this relationship was described as "abiding" in the Vine, Jesus (John 15). Here it is to believe in him. Both have the same affect, as is seen in what follows.

5:14 This and the next three verses apply the truth of our assurance as it impacts the life of the church, particularly with regard to sinning brothers. One benefit of a life of faith in Jesus (described as abiding in John 15 and as continuing to believe in his name here in 1 John) is answered prayer. The basis of the believer's confidence in prayer is the knowledge that God answers all prayer according to his will. This will be illustrated with regard to praying for others, though it will be balanced with the question of the sin unto death.[271]

καὶ αὕτη ἐστὶν ἡ παρρησία ἣν ἔχομεν πρὸς αὐτὸν, "And this is the confidence which we have before him."[272] John begins his discussion of the benefit of a lifestyle of faith in Christ with a reminder of the confidence believers may have. This is his fourth and final use of *παρρησία* in his epistle. He used it twice (2:28; 4:17) with regard to the believer's expectations on judgment day. In contrast to the day believers will stand before Jesus as their judge, here he is looking at coming into God's presence with prayer requests as he had in 3:21. This is similar to Heb 4:16: "Let us therefore come boldly to the throne of grace, that we may obtain mercy and find grace to help in time of need." However, whereas in Hebrews the believer comes before his king, here he comes into the presence of his Father with his petitions (John 14:13–14; 15:7–16; 16:23–24). John further defines the believer's boldness with the relative clause (ἣν ἔχομεν πρὸς αὐτὸν ...) functioning substantively as an adjective. That confidence is related to a person, God the Father.

His use of the present tense ἔχομεν describes confidence as a present experience for both John and his readers.[273] John is not referring to that confidence he described earlier, confidence on judgment day when each

271. Bultmann (85) sees vv 14–21 as an appendix with v 13 having concluded the epistle proper.

272. John's penchant for equative sentences can be seen in his seven uses of the equative constructions *αὕτη ἐστὶν* (1:5; 2:25; 3:11, 23; 5:3, 4, 9, 11, 14), *οὗτός ἐστιν* (2:22;), and *τοῦτό ἐστιν* (4:3; 5:6, 20).

273. D. E. Hiebert, "An Expositional Study of 1 John—Part 10: An Exposition of 1 John 5:13–21," 313.

believer gives an account to the Lord Jesus. Rather, this is daily confidence in one's relationship with our heavenly Father.

The referent of *πρὸς αὐτὸν* is God the Father. John's pattern in the epistle is to use *αὐτὸς* to refer most often to God the Father while *ἐκεῖνος* is reserved for Jesus, the Son. In the prologue to his Gospel (John 1:1), he uses the preposition *πρὸς* to communicate Jesus' (the Word's) presence with God the Father and his distinctness from God the Father, while affirming his deity and eternality. Here it is the believer who is described as being in God's presence. Thus John is describing something personal, and relational.

ὅτι ἐάν τι αἰτώμεθα κατὰ τὸ θέλημα αὐτοῦ ἀκούει ἡμῶν, "that whenever we ask according to his will, he hears us." Confidence in God's presence results from knowing that God is listening. John communicates this truth with this substantival (epexegetical) *ὅτι* clause, describing *παρρησία* further (Harris, 226). The sense of *ἐάν* when combined with a present subjunctive verb gives the verb a customary present nuance.[274] Its sense is equivalent to *ὅταν* and so is translated "whenever." The question is not one of "if," but "when."[275] The determining factor is the initiation of the person making the request, not the willingness of God to hear. Thus the uncertainty contained within *ἐάν* is related to the person asking. They may or may not ask according to God's will, but when then do, God hears. This sense of certainty can be seen in similar constructions elsewhere in Scripture. For example, in Luke 19:40 Jesus uses this construction to affirm that if the Pharisees could silence the crowd the stones would cry out his praises.[276] Also in 1 Thess 3:8 Paul uses this construction to say that "now we live, if you stand fast in the Lord."[277] In each case there is a measure of certainty.

The idea of *ἀκούω* is "not merely that he listens but that he listens favorably."[278] God is going to act on the praying saint's behalf. However, this action is conditioned on his hearing. In 3:22, answered prayer was

274. B. M. Fanning, *Verbal Aspect in New Testament Greek*, 403; D. B. Wallace, *Grammar*, 521–22. Haas, de Jonge, and Swellengrebel (125) calls it "expectional." However, it seems better that John is emphasizing its non-exceptionality. This is something believers can expect to happen.

275. BDAG, 268.

276. *Λέγω ὑμῖν, ἐὰν οὗτοι σιωπήσουσιν, οἱ λίθοι κράξουσιν.*

277. *νῦν ζῶμεν ἐὰν ὑμεῖς στήκετε ἐν κυρίῳ.*

278. D. E. Hiebert, "An Expositional Study of 1 John—Part 10: An Exposition of 1 John 5:13–21," 315.

conditioned on doing God's will. Here is it conditioned on asking in accordance with God's will. That is the sense of the preposition *κατὰ*. These requests must fall within the standard of God's will.[279] Still, this "marks an important limitation on one's assurance that his request will be granted."[280] God will not answer prayers that violate his character or his will for the one praying or for those who are the objects of prayer. This leads into the second conditional statement related to answered prayer.

5:15 This sentence varies from the pattern of the previous one while continuing the logical development from cause to effect with regard to answered prayer.[281]

καὶ ἐὰν οἴδαμεν ὅτι ἀκούει ἡμῶν ὃ ἐὰν αἰτώμεθα, "And if we know that he hears us, whatever we might ask." This time *ἐὰν* is used with the indicative where a subjunctive verb would normally be expected or where one would have expected ἐι to be used in a first class conditional clause (Burdick, 388; Culy, 134).[282] Blass-Debruner sees this construction having a causal sense.[283] Schnackenburg (274) sees it functioning as a first class conditional clause

279. BDAG, 512.
280. D. E. Hiebert, "An Expositional Study of 1 John—Part 10: An Exposition of 1 John 5:13–21," 314.
281. Harris (228) suggests a possible chiasm within this and the following verse. Its parts are as follows:

A *αἰτώμεθα* "we ask" (1 pl.)
  B ἀκούει "He hears" (3 sing.)
  B′ ἀκούει "He hears" (3 sing.)
A′ *αἰτώμεθα* "we ask" (1 pl.)

This is an attractive idea that brings out John's focus on the truth that God hears. However, its weakness is that it is formed between only part of two sentences. Though a chiasm can be formed within a long sentence, it does not seem likely that an author would construct one between only parts of two sentences. Certainly this is repetition of ideas by John. And he uses their repetition for emphasis. And I believe Harris is correct in seeing the double repetition and John's purposeful placement of the asking on either side of hearing. However, it seems a chiasm should somehow be a free standing unit with a marked beginning and end rather than its extremities connected to ideas that do not contribute to the development or message of the chiasm.
282. Culy (134) sees this serving as a possible "mild rebuke" from John to his readers by making something they know to be true hypothetical. However, John's point is not that of rebuke, but of the reality that one may or may not know.
283. BDF §372 (1a).

and expressing the consequence of the previous verse and so means "since now" (*da nun* in Schnackenburg's original German). Some see it as a colloquialism (Grayston, 142; Smalley, 296). However, it seems better to see the conditional aspect of ἐὰν still present. Thus ἐὰν still means "if" and still carries the possibility either of being true or false, though it is describing things from the believer's perspective rather than the divine perspective (previous verse). The uncertainty lies in the "presence of the knowledge" in the believer, not in the truth of the statement (Westcott, 190). The believer may or may not know that God hears, even when he does. Also, John uses οἶδα for knowledge in this case rather than γινώσκω. This is intuitive knowledge rather than experiential. What we think is true may not be true even if our experience convinces us it is true. What one perceives to be true, even from his or her experiences, is still impacted by his or her limitations and desires. Perception is not reality. However, what we have been told by God in his Word is true because God is true and he sees everything as it actually is. His perception is reality and so we can trust what he tells us. He tells us that prayer according to his character and will is sure to be heard and answered. So, to the extent that we know our prayers meet these prerequisites we can know with certainty that God hears and will reply favorably.

The limitlessness of the possibilities before us, the power of God to answer whatever prayer we ask, is expressed through the relative clause: ὃ ἐὰν αἰτώμεθα.[284] This relative pronoun gives ἐὰν the sense of "whatever" (Burdick, 389) rather than "whenever" as was its previous use. It also shows that what limits answers to prayer is as much the absence of prayer as it is missing the will of God.[285] So, how do we know our prayers will be answered? We have the promise that follows the condition. If we know we are praying according to God's will, we have certainty.

οἴδαμεν ὅτι ἔχομεν τὰ αἰτήματα ἃ ἠτήκαμεν ἀπ' αὐτοῦ, "then we know that we have the requests which we have asked from him." John repeats οἶδα. This repetition emphasizes what we can know by faith rather than based on experience. This use of οἶδα implies certainty (Burdick, 389). Because God

284. Culy (134) identifies ὃ ἐὰν αἰτώμεθα as a "headless relative clause" because the verb for which it would be the direct object, possibly ἀκούει, is unstated. This makes sense because repeating the same verb in the same short sentence is completely unnecessary and inefficient.

285. This is the same truth is stated negatively in Jas 4:2–3. Unanswered prayer comes from failure to ask or from asking for the wrong reasons.

has made certain promises, we can know those promises are true before we experience them. Our confidence is in God and his promises, not in our experience. Again, John is defining in greater detail what he means by confidence when we enter God's presence to make our requests.

John says that what we can know is that we "have." His use of the present ἔχομεν emphasizes our possession of the answer even as we ask (Akin, 206–7; Burdick, 389; Kistemaker, 361). What we "have" in the present is those things we asked for in the past, thus the perfect tense ᾐτήκαμεν. Rather than seeing this perfect emphasizing a continued prayer offered in the past (Kistemaker, 362), it is used with an aorist sense that the prayer was simply offered in the past. What continues to the present is not the offering of the prayer but its affect on God. God does not forget. Now John will take us to the kinds of prayers we should be praying as an expression of our love of our Christian brothers and sisters.

5:16 Sins for which believers can intercede on behalf of other believers are the nondeadly ones. John's statement comes in the context of confidence in prayer, specifically when the believer knows that God hears his or her prayer. Now he raises the issue of praying for one another, and of whether that prayer will be answered.[286]

Ἐάν τις ἴδῃ τὸν ἀδελφὸν αὐτοῦ ἁμαρτάνοντα ἁμαρτίαν μὴ πρὸς θάνατον, "If anyone sees his brother sinning a sin not unto death." John begins with the question of a believer's intercession for other believers. This third class condition indicates that one may not be aware of another's sin. However, should that be the case, action can sometimes be taken on behalf of the sinning believer by his or her fellow believer. What John says is that believers should intercede for sinning believers. However, lest one thinks that every prayer for a sinning saint will be equally effective, John reminds us that there are conditions to that prayer being answered. First, he must see his brother sinning. This is not a prayer based on suspicion but on firsthand knowledge (Plummer, 121). Second, it must not be a mortal sin. If it is a sin that "leads unto death," there is nothing a believer can do for the one

286. Strecker (202) notes that this and the next verse must be interpreted "as community paranesis, but without reference to any opposing teaching." This is a reminder to us that John's concern in writing this epistle is pastoral first. As he closes out his instruction the false teachers are forgotten. What he has to say now is parenetic rather than corrective.

sinning, as will be clarified by John shortly. Of note is John's use of "brother" to communicate that this is something occurring within the family of God. This statement is similar to Jas 5:20, in which one believer may come to the aid of another in turning him or her from sin and "saving" his or her "soul from death."

John describes the sin observed as in process. Burdick (389) understands the present tense use of ἁμαρτάνοντα to indicate ongoing action. This is not an isolated event but something the believer is persistent in. Thus, the praying Christian sees a brother involved in the practice of sin. However, as in 3:6 and 9, too much should not be made of the present tense. In this case it would be better seeing this as an adverb participle relating to the main verb and so, he sees his brother "while" he is committing the sin. The aorist ἴδῃ as modified by ἁμαρτάνοντα only indicates that the sin was happening when seen. Neither requires the sin be repeated even more than once.

What kind of death does John mean?

(1) He could mean spiritual death.[287] This sin leads to a loss of eternal life and so ends in eternal condemnation (Akin, 208; Brown, 615; Brooke, 146–47; Culpepper, 273; Kistemaker, 363; Kruse, 192; Lenski, 535; Marshall, 247–48; Schnackenburg, 276; Smalley, 298–99; Stott, 191).[288] Bultmann (87) describes this death as "as eternal death, and thus as the nothingness into which the unbeliever has fallen." He does not see the person prayed for as a believer, which fits his pattern of seeing "brother" meaning "neighbor" and so including nonbelievers. Strecker (202) argues that since ζωή means "eternal life" θάνατος should mean "eternal death." It is true that the noun

---

287. Harris (231) points to the church in Sardis that is called "dead" and sees this as spiritual death. However, there Jesus is speaking figuratively and they can revive themselves if they "hold fast and repent" (Rev 3:3).

288. R. K. J. Tan, "Should We Pray For Straying Brethren? John's Confidence In 1 John 5:16–17," 603; I. A. Busenitz, "The Sin unto Death," 30. He says, "The apostle John appears to have in view an unsaved man who professes to be a believer, but who is in actuality in need of salvation. On the one hand, John refers to a man who is sinning but is not doing so to the point of the impossibility of being granted eternal life; he has not yet come to the place where the possibility of divine forgiveness has been revoked. In such cases, as a result of the intercessory prayer of a 'brother,' God would grant spiritual life. On the other hand, the apostle asserts that if a man does sin to such an extent that repentance and forgiveness is impossible, it would be "unto death"' spiritual death, spiritual death in the sense that his condition is irrevocable."

ζωή is used consistently in the Gospel to refer to eternal life and ψυχὴ for human (non-eternal) life.[289] However, it seems that the distinction in the Gospel grows out of his development of the theme of eternal life. He wrote in such as way as to avoid using ζωή to mean anything other than eternal life. At the same time, John did use ζάω in the Gospel for physical life (John 4:50, 51, 53; 5:25; 11:25, 26; 14:19) as well as spiritual/eternal (John 6:51, 57, 58). His use of θάνατος most often referred to physical death (John 8:51, 52; 11:4, 13; 12:33; 18:32; 21:19). Thus, one could as easily argue that θάνατος informs the meaning of ζωή. Additionally, John is free to use words and concepts with different nuances in different works. Such is the case with his light and darkness imagery.[290] Where in his Gospel it represents spiritual life and death, in this epistle it pictures moral purity and sin. Further, the NT provides examples of believers committing sins that lead to their physical deaths, as will be discussed below. So it would seem better to allow θάνατος to inform ζωή.

(2) John could be referring to physical death.[291] John uses this same construction to refer to physical death with regard to Lazarus (John 11:4). His only other use of "death" in the epistle is in 3:14, where it does refer to spiritual death (Moody, 111). However, in that verse John makes clear that believers have passed from death to life permanently, with a life that continues from the time of that passing to the present. Additionally, since the promise that follows is that God will "give him life" in response to the believer's prayer, physical death is the best meaning here as well. The giving of spiritual life has already occurred for the "brother" before his sin. Moreover, if the prayer of a believer for someone else delivered him or her from spiritual death, then John would be affirming that people could be

289. John 10:11, 15, 17; 13:37, 38; and 15:13. In John 12:25 he uses both ζωή and ψυχὴ in the same sentence where the difference can be seen clearly (ὁ φιλῶν τὴν ψυχὴν αὐτοῦ ἀπολλύει αὐτήν, καὶ ὁ μισῶν τὴν ψυχὴν αὐτοῦ ἐν τῷ κόσμῳ τούτῳ εἰς ζωὴν αἰώνιον φυλάξει αὐτήν.)

290. See my discussion of this in the commentary on 1:5.

291. W. R. Cook, "Hamartiological Problems in First John," 258; S. M. Reynolds, "The Sin unto Death and Prayers for the Dead," 133. He says, "John was forbidding prayers for the sin of the dead, a practice which may have been carried into the church from some type of Judaism (cf. 2 Macc. 12:39–46). ... Sin that has not yet continued to physical death is one type of sin, and sin which has continued to death without repentance is another." (from *Pseudepigrapha of the Old Testament*, R. Charles ed., 2:63.

"saved," in the sense of justified, apart from faith on their part. Scripture unquestionably makes this impossible. Also, it is a "brother" who is in the process of sinning the sin, not an ex-brother or a potential brother. John's use of "brother" indicates a fellow believer, not someone who had ceased to be such either (Westcott, 191).[292] Thus the giving of life cannot refer to regeneration, but must refer to their being spared the ultimate consequence of sin for a believer, physical death.

Physical death as a consequence of sin is taught throughout Scripture and was accepted within Judaism. It is a requirement of the Mosaic law that certain sins result in the death of the sinner (Num 18:22; Lev 24:15–16; Deut 22:26). It is reflected in extrabiblical Judaism (*Jub.* 33:12–18).[293] It is seen in the NT with the deaths of Ananias and Sapphira (Acts 5:1–11) and Corinthian believers who were abusing the Lord's Supper by their treatment of fellow believers (1 Cor 11:29–30). In 1 Cor 5:5 Paul threatens a believer with death ("destruction of the flesh") while indicating he would not lose his salvation ("that his spirit may be saved in the day of the Lord").

292. Smith (135) says John never uses "brother" to refer to the one sinning the sin unto death. However, this begs the question. The context of the sentence clearly indicates that both kinds of sins can be committed by Christians.

293. "And again, it is written a second time: 'Cursed be he who lieth with the wife of his father, for he hath uncovered his father's shame'; and all the holy ones of the Lord said 'So be it; so be it.' [13] And do thou, Moses, command the children of Israel that they observe this word; for it (entails) a punishment of death; and it is unclean, and there is no atonement for ever to atone for the man who has committed this, but he is to be put to death and slain, and stoned with stones, and rooted out from the midst of the people of our God. [14] For to no man who does so in Israel is it permitted to remain alive a single day on the earth, for he is abominable and unclean. [15] And let them not say: to Reuben was granted life and forgiveness after he had lain with his father's concubine, and to her also though she had a husband, and her husband Jacob, his father, was still alive. [16] For until that time there had not been revealed the ordinance and judgment and law in its completeness for all, but in thy days (it has been revealed) as a law of seasons and of days, and an everlasting law for the everlasting generations. [17] And for this law there is no consummation of days, and no atonement for it, but they must both be rooted out in the midst of the nation: on the day whereon they committed it they shall slay them. [18] And do thou, Moses, write (it) down for Israel that they may observe it, and do according to these words, and not commit a sin unto death; for the Lord our God is judge, who respects not persons and accepts not gifts."

Which sin is in view? Interpreters have attached a wide range of meanings to this "sin unto death."[294]

(1) It is any sin that is serious enough that God acts to punish the person with physical death. In the Old Testament there were sins that led to death (Num 19:22; Deut 22:26; *T. Gad* 6:6; Isa 22:14). Jewish extrabiblical literature also speak of sins unto death (*Jub.* 21:22; 26:34; 33:13, 18; *T. Iss.* 7:1; 1QS 8). All of these involved physical death. In the New Testament we have examples of people sinning and dying as a consequence (Acts 5:1–11; 1 Cor 5:5; 11:29–30). Other possible examples are 1 Tim 1:20; Jas 5:15; and Rev 2:23.

(2) It is a designation for serious sins in contrast to minor sins. Thus believers can only pray for one another's sins if they are not serious sins. This serious sin is the "unforgiveable sin" of Matt 10:33 (Brooke, 146–47; Smalley, 298).[295]

(3) Some see this as blasphemy against the Holy Spirit (Stott, 191). This is the sin Jesus warned against in Matt 12:32 and Mark 3:29. To the objection that this sin unto death is committed by a "brother" and so cannot refer to the sin of blasphemy against the Holy Spirit, Stott (191) responds that "he who sinned is neither named nor described." Thus the ambiguity of the text allows this one to be a nonbeliever. To answer the objection that John calls this sinner a "brother," Stott (192) responds that in this instance John is giving the term a broader sense than fellow Christian. Schnackenburg (277) rejects both the idea of an unforgiveable sin and blasphemy against the Holy Spirit based on the concept of "mortal" sins being punished by physical death in the OT. He counters, "The phrase 'sin unto death' says nothing about the possibility or impossibility of the repentance of the sinner."[296]

294. Barker (355) considers "conjecture" as "fruitless" and so speculates on none of the options. Walls and Anders (226) review several of the options and then admit they cannot decide.

295. Also Mark 8:28, Luke 9:26, and 12:9.

296. Bei der "Sünde yum Tode" ist über die Möglichkeit oder Unmöglichkeit der Umkehr des Sünders nichts gesagt.

(4) It is apostasy that leads to spiritual death (Bruce, 125; Dodd, 136; Grayston, 60; Johnson, 136; Painter, 318–19; Perkins, 65; Smith, 134–35). This involves a total renunciation of Christ (Moody, 112). Stott (190) rejects this on the basis that a true Christian, according to his understanding of 3:9, cannot continue in sin and so could never apostatize.

(5) It is a sin that believers cannot commit and so John is referring to non-believers who persist in their sin until they die (Akin, 210; Brooke, 147; Plummer, 123; Smalley, 299; Yarbrough, 310–13). Thus it is the continued rejection of the gospel by an unbeliever that includes rejecting Jesus' deity and refusal to love others (Marshall, 248–49).

(6) It "denies the Son" (Lenski, 536) and may mean the rejection of the humanity or deity of Jesus (Kistemaker, 363). Rensberger 140) describes this as a "lack of christological faith." Kruse (194) describes it as the sin of the secessionists.

(7) It is a sin that would lead to excommunication from the Christian community (Westcott, 210).

(8) It may refer to any unconfessed sin (Pentecost, 140).

(9) It results from a life of habitual sin.[297]

(10) John is saying that sinners who have died should not be prayed for following their deaths.[298]

No help is found in extrabiblical literature, though the sin unto death is mentioned.[299] It seems better to see John purposefully leaving it ambigu-

297. I. A. Busenitz, "The Sin unto Death," 25.

298. S. M. Reynolds, "The Sin unto Death and Prayers for the Dead," 132; Augustine reflects this view as well in *Enchiridion*, 110, *City of God*, 21.2.

299. *T. Iss.* 7:1 reads: "I am a hundred and twenty-two years old, and I am not aware of having committed a sin unto death. I have not had intercourse with any woman other than my wife, nor was I promiscuous by lustful look. I did not drink wine to the point of losing self-control. I was not passionately eager for any desireable possession of my neighbor. There was no deceit in my heart; no lie passed through my lips. I joined in lamentation with every oppressed humjan being, and shared my bread with the poor. I did not eat alone; I did not transgress boundaries; I acted in piety and truth all my days." (J. H. Charlesworth, *The Old Testament*

ous.[300] Rather than being a particular sin, it is better to see "sin unto death" as a kind of sin. When we look through the NT for hints as to its nature, we note those believers who died for their sins. In Acts 5:1–11, Ananias and Sapphira lied to the Holy Spirit and it cost them their lives. In 1 Cor 5:1–5 Paul promises to turn the incestuous church member over to Satan "for the destruction of his flesh," likely a reference to either physical illness or death.[301] In 1 Cor 11:27–30 believers died for abusing the Lord's Supper. Whether one wishes to use the terms venial and mortal to describe sins, John makes it clear that there are two kinds of sins. Thus we see that not all sins are equal.

Though we cannot know with certainty what sin leads to death, we do see John teaching the role of every believer is to intercede on behalf of

---

Pseudepigrapha, 1:804). *Jub.* 21:22 reads: "Be careful not to walk in their ways, and to tread in their path, or to commit a mortal sin before God Most High so that he will hide his face from you, and deliver you into the power of your sin, and uproot you from the earth, and your seed from beneath the sky, and your name and seed will perish from all the earth." *Jub.* 26:34 reads: "And it will happen when you become great, and you will remove his yoke from your neck, that then you will surely sin completely unto death, and your seed will be rooted out from under heaven." *Jub.* 33:18–19 reads: "And you, Moses, write for Israel, and let them keep this. And let them do according to these words. And let them not commit a sin worthy of death because the LORD our God is a judge who does not accept persons or gifts." (O. S. Wintermute, *The Old Testament Pseudepigrapha*, 2:96, 107, 120.)

300. And so Bultmann (87) chooses to remain undecided.

301. Paul's punishment on the incestuous church member is one of the strongest arguments for eternal security as well as persistent sin *not* indicating a person is unregenerate. Obviously, if the man had not repented (2 Cor 2:5–11) he would have eventually died in his sins. Yet, Paul had stated clearly that his purpose in handing this one over to Satan was not just the destruction of his flesh, which likely began with a process of physical weakening and could eventually end in death (S. J. Kistemaker, "Deliver this Man to Satan' (1 Cor 5:5): A Case Study in Church Discipline," 41–45), but the salvation of his spirit on judgment day (τὸ πνεῦμα σωθῇ ἐν τῇ ἡμέρᾳ τοῦ κυρίου). He is already a brother, and so is regenerate. This indicates that even when experiencing physical death for personal sin, one's destiny does not change.

Though the majority of interpreters see this passage addressing the discipline of an individual, B. Campbell ("Flesh and Spirit in 1 Cor 5:5: An Exercise in Rhetorical Criticism of the NT," 339–41), following A. Y. Collins ("The Function of 'Excommunication' in Paul," 263) proposes that "flesh" and "spirit" refer to the church community rather than the individual. His arguments are unconvincing in light of the emphasis that Paul places on the individual and his subsequent comments in 2 Cor regarding the individual's restoration. S. Kistemaker's discussion (noted above) adequately answers Campbell's proposal.

other brothers and sisters in Christ. Furthermore, that intercession can be expressed in the context of confident access to a loving Father who is willing to "hear" our prayers and respond positively to them when they accord with his will (Westcott, 190).

The present participle ἁμαρτάνοντα indicates a sin in process.[302] Some see it indicating "a sinful course rather than committing an isolated act of sin" (Bruce, 124; also Williamson, 168). Bruce (125) suggests the possibility that the sin unto death is apostasy and joining the antichrists so that "renunciation of the apostolic witness to Christ and his saving power was indeed a 'sin unto death.'" For him it is possible for a believer to renounce faith in Christ and forfeit his or her salvation. Akin (210), who holds to eternal security, rejects the idea of a believer apostatizing because in his view true believers "cannot continue in sin." For him, then, only a nonbeliever can commit this sin. The false teachers "were never really true believers" and so were not believers continuing in sin. This ignores the fact that this is a "brother" who is seen in the process of sinning as indicated by the anarthrous present active adverbial participle ἁμαρτάνοντα. Further, whether it is a single act of sin that is in progress or a pattern of sin is not clear from the singular noun ἁμαρτίαν. This noun could indicate an actual sin, or a pattern of sin, though not a group of sins. Again, John has chosen to be purposefully ambiguous. He loves to make his readers think. Having said this, he next turns to the role of a believer in the life of the church family.

αἰτήσει καὶ δώσει αὐτῷ ζωήν, τοῖς ἁμαρτάνουσιν μὴ πρὸς θάνατον, "let him ask and he will give life to him, to those not sinning unto death." These two verbs *αἰτήσει* and *δώσει* do not share the same subject or role even though they are joined with *καὶ* in this clause. The one asking is the fellow believer while the One giving life is God. Though the first verb (*αἰτήσει*) is future tense, it should not be viewed as a future but seen to carry an imperatival force, "let him ask" (Painter, 316). In a sense it could still be seen as futuristic, and would imply an inevitable response of one believer on behalf of another (Akin, 207). However, that assumes everyone who sees a brother sinning is a loving Christian and would be concerned. Rather, it is better to see this as a mild imperative addressed to John's readers. Stott (188) rejects the imperative force and says it speaks to "the inevitable and spontaneous reaction" of a Christian who recognizes that he is his brother's keeper.

---

302. W. R. Cook, "Hamartiological Problems in First John," 257.

The referent of δώσει has been understood in one of three ways:

(1) It has the same subject as the verbs on either side of this verb; therefore, the one making the petition gives life to the sinner (Brooke, 146; Bultmann, 87, n. 16; Dodd, 135; Haas, de Jonge, and Swellengrebel, 127; Plummer, 122; Stott, 189; Strecker, 202, n. 23). Stott (189) describes its significance: "It is better to accept the ascription of real efficacy to prayer as in v. 15, so that, under God, he who asks life for a brother may be said not just to gain it for him but actually to 'give' it to him." Jas 5:20 would seem to support this. Though this is grammatically correct, it is theologically out of line with what John has been saying in his epistle and Gospel (Brown, 611; Harris, 229). God the Father and Jesus give life.

(2) God is still the subject, but αὐτῷ is the petitioner receiving life from God rather than the sinner.[303] This is not likely because it is the sinner who has the need for life, not the petitioner (Harris, 230).

(3) God is the understood subject who gives life to the sinning Christian (Akin, 207; Brown, 611–12; Bruce, 124; Burdick, 390; Marshall, 246, n. 17; Schnackenburg, 276; Smalley, 300; Westcott, 192). Though the two verbs are joined by καὶ, it should not be viewed as a continuative or coordinating conjunction, but that it introduces the result ("He will give") that comes from what preceded it ("let him ask").[304] Thus the two verbs can and do have different subjects.

The second verb, (δώσει) is futuristic, the promise that God will act in response to that prayer. He will give the person life in the sense that he will preserve his life. Schnackenburg (276) sees John's use of ζωήν without the article to indicate that God is not giving the person eternal life but that it continues and is being rekindled and increased.[305] Pentecost (135–36) says that the prayer is not for forgiveness for the sinning brother, but ultimately for restoration of fellowship with God. Thus he sees "life" here referring not to physical life, but restored fellowship with God. It seems better to see this referring to physical life just as "death" refers to physical death. To read fellowship into the terms here is to read too much from a too distant context.

303. This option is repeatedly mentioned, but without adherents ever being named (Thompson, 141–42).

304. BDAG, 495 (entry 1,b,ζ).

305. vielmehr daß es in seiner Kraft aufs neue entfacht oder in seinem Umfang vermehrt werden soll. ("Rather, it is rekindled anew in its power and increased in its scope.")

John changes from the single sinner to the plural τοῖς ἁμαρτάνουσιν in order to make this a general principle applicable to all believers (Westcott, 192).[306] This is something that is common in the body of Christ. John has already said we all sin and must confess our sinfulness and our sins (1:8–10). Provision has been provided by Christ (2:1–2). Thus this promise is given by John and serves as a reminder of each believer's responsibility to be praying for one another.

ἔστιν ἁμαρτία πρὸς θάνατον· οὐ περὶ ἐκείνης λέγω ἵνα ἐρωτήσῃ, "There is a sin unto death; I am not saying he should ask concerning that." John now affirms that he is not encouraging a believer to pray concerning a mortal sin. It is a waste of time. Some argue that though we are not commanded to pray for the one sinning a sin unto death, we are not directly forbidden to either (Burge, 215; Hodges, 234). Yet the aorist subjunctive ἐρωτήσῃ is best seen as an indirect command forbidding prayer for a fellow believer when it is known that his or her sin is a deadly sin and they are under God's judgment (Kistemaker, 365). This may explain John's shift from αἰτέω to ἐρωτάω. Though the words are in many ways synonymous, αἰτέω expects an answer more than does ἐρωτάω.[307] Cook proposes that the nuance of inquiry or questioning is contained in ἐρωτάω and the prohibition is against asking God if someone has committed the sin unto death. In his view, John did not have any specific sin in mind but that all sins ultimately lead to physical death if not forgiven by God.[308] He sees John's use of πρὸς having the idea

---

306. Culy (135) sees αὐτῷ as the referent of τοῖς ἁμαρτάνουσιν and so describes it as syntactical "discontinuity." He relates it to a "rhetorical pause that highlights the importance of the writer's clarification."

307. BDAG, 30, 395; G. Stählin, "αἰτέω," *TDNT* 1:192–93. Stählin notes that Jesus' prayers are described with αἰτέω rather than ἐρωτάω. He also observes that αἰτέω expresses a lesser degree of intimacy than ἐρωτάω. H. Greeven, "ἐρωτάω," *TDNT* 2:685–87. Greeven notes that ἐρωτάω "is used almost exclusively of the prayer of Jesus, the one exception being 1 Jn. 5:16. Jesus alone has such inward fellowship with the Father that the word can be used both for the disciples' requests to him (e.g., Jn. 4:31) and for His own petitionary or intercessory prayer to the Father." P. Trudinger ("Concerning Sins, Mortal and Otherwise. A Note on 1 John 5:16–17," 541) argues that ἐρωτάω normally means to ask a question, and only means "to pray" when describing Jesus' petition to the Father on behalf of His disciples and subsequent believers in the Upper Room. He points to John 14:16; 16:26; 17:9 (2x), 15, and 20 as examples. Actually, this is a translational choice, but could have just as accurately been translated "ask" in each instance without changing the meaning.

308. W. R. Cook, "Hamartiological Problems in First John," 258.

of "tending to death not guaranteeing it."[309] These sins are those that, if not dealt with, ultimately bring God's "chastisement" rather than forgiveness in this life with physical death being its "natural consequence."[310]

Here sin lacks the article and so is purposefully indefinite. John may be implying that only one sin leads to this death. However, it seems better to see him stating a principle and generalizing that there is a category of sin that leads to death.

Again, some see this as a sin that Christians cannot commit. Thus when believers pray for other believers they are praying for sins that do not involve spiritual death. Believers possess eternal life and this death is spiritual death, not physical. Unbelievers abide in darkness, which is spiritual death. Against this is John's readers, who are clearly believers. If this were not something they could experience, it would not make sense for John to address it here (Harris, 231). An additional problem with this view, though, is that he sees his "brother" who by definition is another believer. To make this view work one must have John referring to the "church visible" in order to have nonbelieving "brothers" who are dead spiritually, and there is nothing in the epistle to indicate John ever thought in terms of the church visible/invisible model of modern theology.

The final clause is troublesome. It includes an unusual ἵνα clause that indicates the content of what would be asked rather than purpose.[311] Trudinger suggests this final clause might have the sense that John is saying he does not want to discuss the various kinds of sins and translates this ἵνα clause as "in order that one should question or debate it."[312] That is a possible meaning. However, the context does not indicate John's unwillingness to discuss it. It is just that answered prayer is his focus rather than the nature of sin. If he had wanted to, and had the false teachers in mind, this would have been the opportune time to bring them and their teachings to the fore. However, his focus is pastoral, not polemical, so he discusses those things that are of greater importance.

---

309. Lieu (225) agrees and translates πρὸς θάνατον as sin that is "death-bound." Thus she too understands it to imply that the person is moving in that direction but has not arrived yet.

310. W. R. Cook, "Hamartiological Problems in First John," 258.

311. P. Trudinger ,"Concerning Sins, Mortal and Otherwise," 541.

312. P. Trudinger, "Concerning Sins, Mortal and Otherwise," 542.

5:17 This sentence reflects a balanced, though not chiastic, construction with *καὶ* at its center, then *εἰμί* followed by *ἁμαρτία*. What precedes and follows then is the point of the verse, not every sin is unto death.

πᾶσα ἀδικία ἁμαρτία ἐστίν, "Every unrighteous act is sin." Here *πᾶσα ἀδικία* refers to unrighteous acts rather than unrighteousness as a concept or state of being.[313] His inclusion of the adjective *πᾶσα* particularizes *ἀδικία* and moves it from a state of being to each of the transgressions themselves. The gnomic present *ἐστίν* principalizes the statement. Having the same root as the noun "righteous," *ἀδικία* describes that which is opposite to it by the addition of *α* at its fore. This unrighteousness is the opposite of God's character, which is described as *δίκαιος*, righteous. *Δίκαιος* describes God the Father in 1:9 and 2:29. It also describes Jesus in 2:1 and John 7:18.

Though sin and lawlessness are connected in 3:4, this statement is grammatically different and makes a very different point. Where sin was defined in 3:4, unrighteous deeds are categorized under sin in this verse. He is moving each unrighteous act under the umbrella classification of sin which then leads to the further clarification of the following clause.

καὶ ἔστιν ἁμαρτία οὐ πρὸς θάνατον, "but there is a sin not unto death." With the conjunctive *καὶ* being used in a contrastive role, he clarifies that though each unrighteous act may be sin, it is not especially a sin that results in death.[314] This serves as an encouragement for Christians to pray for each other, especially regarding sins when they become aware of them. This is a part of the priesthood of the believer (1 Pet 2:5). Just as Jesus intercedes in 2:2, so too we have the privilege—the responsibility—to go before our Father and intercede for one another.

The final verses of this epistle form its epilogue.[315] They compose three summary statements, each beginning with the affirmation, "we know,"

313. BDAG, 20; G. Schrenk, "ἄδικος, ἀδικία," *TDNT* 1:153–57.

314. BDAG, 496; D. B. Wallace, *Grammar*, 671.

315. Grayston (146) sees them as a polemic against John's opponents. Rather, they should be seen as summary statements for John's readers rather than against John's theorized enemies. This again reflects the influence a theorized *Sitz im Leben* has on one's interpretation of a text. When such theories are set aside, John's parenetic focus becomes much more recognizable. And, with that recognized, the pastoral value of these final words becomes readily recognizable.

using *οἶδα* rather than *γινώσκω*.[316] These are truths that transcend personal experience and are based on the revelation of God in his Word.[317] The basic thrust of this paragraph is that healthy fellowship with God produces confidence in our position in Christ within this hostile world.

5:18 This first concluding statement introduces the formula for each of the three affirmations. Each begins with *οἴδαμεν* followed by the content of that knowledge in a *ὅτι* clause. This is different from the phrase *ἐν τούτῳ γινώσκομεν* that was common with John throughout the epistle (2:3, 5; 3:24; 4:13; 5:2). John changes from knowledge gained by experience to "self-evident" knowledge (Painter, 321).

In each case "we" could either refer to the apostles or to John and his readers. It seems best to see John including his readers as he summarizes his instructions from the epistle. What he affirms in this first of three affirmations is that the believer's security comes from Christ's preservation and protection from Satan.

Οἴδαμεν ὅτι πᾶς ὁ γεγεννημένος ἐκ τοῦ θεοῦ οὐχ ἁμαρτάνει, "We know that everyone who has been born from God does not sin."[318] This is the last of thirteen *πᾶς ὁ* plus participle clauses that focus on the whole while emphasizing the individuals.[319] In this case, the group in focus are those born of God. This class of people is described using the intensive perfect *γεγεννημένος*, which focuses on the present consequences of a past event (Akin, 211–12; Brooke, 148). This is a person who was born of God and continues as a child of God.

This first part of the statement about the believer's security is almost identical to what John affirmed in 3:9. The wording is identical until the last two words, though both are translated the same in English. Where "sin" is a verb (*ἁμαρτάνει*) here, there "sin" is a noun (*ἁμαρτίαν*). As before, John is not claiming sinless perfection. He has not forgotten what he wrote at

---

316. Barker (356) calls them "three certainties." Burge (216) describes them as "three bold statements about Christian certainty."

317. Westcott (193) aptly notes that this "threefold repetition of *οἴδαμεν* (18, 19, 20), gives a rhythmic form to the paragraph."

318. Brown (619) and Burdick (392) say that *οὐχ* should be connected with *πᾶς* and be translated as "no one." However, its proximity to the *ἁμαρτάνει* makes this inappropriate.

319. For further explanation, see comments on 2:23.

the beginning of this epistle and he has just finished writing about seeing a Christian brother in the process of sinning (whether a single sin or repeated sins). Some interpret this to mean a regenerate person does not "continue in sin" or is not "characterized by sin" (Akin, 211; Thompson, 146) or "does not keep on sinning without repentance" (Kistemaker, 365). However, though this verse does accord with the statement of 3:6, neither verse states or implies repentance. Akin (211–12) argues on the basis that "Jesus protects him from the evil one's influence." Stott (194) interprets this to mean: "Sin and the child of God are incompatible. They may occasionally meet; they cannot live together in harmony." Burge (216–17) argues from the present tense of οὐχ ἁμαρτάνει that John implies "ongoing activity." He links it back to the "sin that leads to death" in verses 16 and 17, which in his view are "intentional, willful acts against God." He sees what John says here indicates that Christians "do not engage in this sort of sustained, willful repudiation of God." However, the present tense is better seen carrying a gnomic sense in light of the general nature of the statement as evidenced by the πᾶς ὁ construction that heads it. Even so, this statement is by design more absolute and affords no conditions or exceptions.

Moreover, though the new birth is appropriately described by the perfect tense, it need not imply continuing obedience or immunity to "long-term habitual sinning" (*contra* Akin and Burge). As discussed elsewhere, these are theological deductions being read into the text rather than affirmations of the text. If a believer can commit the same sin twice, he or she can do so habitually; and all Christians do. The idea of immunity to habitual sins is a deduction necessitated by the doctrine of perseverance and its implications rather than a teaching of Scripture. The point of 1:8–10 is that denial of sin is self-deception and cleansing of unknown sins follows confession of known sins.

The implication of Jesus' instructions to confess our sins whenever we pray necessarily means we have sins to confess every time we pray. If we pray every day, which we should, and there are not sins we commit regularly, then either there is a long list of sins we are unconsciously working our way through, or we are just tipping our hats at God and pretending we are sinners. All Christians have habitual sins of which they remain unaware. For that matter, they have habitual sins of which they are aware! For a praying Christian, those repeated sins are repeatedly confessed. God forgives them thousands of times in a lifetime, and cleanses that confessing Christian of the other thousands of sins that he or she remains unaware. John *cannot* be affirming a believer will not persist in some sin as a lifestyle. That becomes equivalent to saying that only intentional sins count in the formula of sinlessness that results from Christ's protection against Satan. That being said, John *is indeed* affirming by this that one born of God is not characterized by sin, but only in the sense that divine birth does not give birth to sin and death, but to life.

What does it mean to be "born from God"? It refers to a Christian whose spiritual birth is sourced in God. Harris (233) identifies this as an anthropomorphism that means "to be fathered by God and thus a child of God. The bold imagery in 1 John is that of God as the male parent who fathers children."

ἀλλ' ὁ γεννηθεὶς ἐκ τοῦ θεοῦ τηρεῖ αὐτὸν "but the One born from God keeps him." With the strong adversative conjunction *ἀλλά*, John now explains why the regenerate person does not sin.[320] There are at least four views on what this means.

(1) It is Christ who keeps him (Brooke, 148–49; Bruce, 126; Bultmann, 88; Burdick, 390; Culpepper, 113; Dodd, 138; Grayston, 145; Haas, de Jonge, and Swellengrebel, 128; Kruse, 195; Marshall, 252; Smalley, 303; Stott, 194; Strecker, 208–209; Westcott, 194). Jesus is the logical choice in light of the mention of "the evil one" in the following clause. Thus we have evidenced again John's literary dualism.

(2) The Christian protects himself against sin (Schnackenburg, 280–81; Thompson, 146; KJV).[321] Since nowhere else in the epistle

---

320. At the end of his commentary, Grayston (147) assesses John's Christology as weak: "Reflection suggests that the writer was not drawing upon a well-articulated Christology, certainly not upon a Gnostic redeemer mythology, but was plugging the gap left by the dissidents with whatever came to hand." The depth and complexity of the themes developed by John in this Epistle belies his assessment. If anything, John exhibits the highest Christology of the NT writers (assuming it is appropriate to compare them). Those who think of John as rambling make a similar error. The multitude of literary devices, beginning with his use of "hinge" verses, literary and conceptual dualism, and powerful imagery should tell us that his epistle is anything but rambling and his Christology is anything but an attempt at "plugging" some gap.

321. Brown (622) remains undecided between the Christian or Jesus.

is Jesus described as "born of God," this is seen as a more likely reference to men who are described as "born of God." This is also based on a textual variant that replaces αὐτὸν with the reflexive ἑαὐτὸν.[322] Against this is Brooke's (149) observation that "τηρεῖν is never used in the Johannine writings with the accusative of the reflex pronoun, or in the N.T. with such an accusative absolutely." Additionally, this does not follow John's thought pattern where God is the source of a believer's strength and life. The idea that a believer keeps himself is not found anywhere else in Scripture either (Burdick, 392).

(3) The Christian "holds on to" God (Houlden, 133). Against this is the problem that αὐτοῦ in the following clause refers to the Christian. Also "holds on to" is not the normal sense given to it by John.[323] However, he does appear to use it with this sense in Rev 3:3.

(4) God is protecting the Christian (Moody, 114). This requires the construction to be a pendent nominative construction "where a description of something within the clause is placed in the nominative case and moved forward ahead of the clause for emphatic reasons" (Harris, 234). The same construction occurs in John 17:2 and appears to be a Semitism.[324]

Though some might see this second articular participle (ὁ γεννηθεὶς) referring to the regenerate saint as well, it seems best to see this as a reference to Christ.[325] John's change from the perfect passive participle to the aorist passive, a phrase unique to John, makes it unlikely that the referent of both would be the same (Akin, 212; Westcott, 194). Thus the pronoun αὐτὸν is not reflexive, "he keeps himself," but is functioning as the direct object of τηρέω which has Jesus as its subject, not the believer. This changes the

---

322. B.M. Metzger and United Bible Societies, *A Textual Commentary on the Greek New Testament*, 2nd ed., 650.

323. This meaning of τηρέω is listed in BDAG (1002) and this verse is noted as an example. However, the sense of "keep watch over" or "guard" fits the context better E. Riesenfeld, "τηρέω," *TDNT* 8:142–43.

324. Harris notes K. Beyer, *Semitische Syntax im Neuen Testament* (Göttingen: Vandenhoeck u. Ruprecht, 1962) 1.216.

325. B. M. Metzger and United Bible Societies, *A Textual Commentary on the Greek New Testament*, 2nd ed., 650.

statement from a sanctification truth (the importance of a believer guarding his soul from temptation) to a justification truth (Jesus guards and keeps every believer). This would especially fit better with the emphasis of the final paragraphs and John's affirmation of our assurance of salvation on the basis of what we affirm and know about God's Son (5:11–13). It also reflects Jesus' High Priestly Prayer wherein he affirmed his preservation of the Eleven during his earthly ministry (John 17:12) and then prayed for their protection from "the evil one" after his departure (John 17:15). This is further reflected in John's choice of τηρέω to describe Jesus' preservation of the saint. The term carries both the nuance of watchful care, but also of preservation and protection.[326]

καὶ ὁ πονηρὸς οὐχ ἅπτεται αὐτοῦ, "and the evil one does not grasp him." The result of Jesus' watchful preservation is that "the evil one" is kept from the believer. Though the term ἅπτω ("grasp") has a wide range of meanings, some quite positive, its use in this context and in light of John 17:15, reflects its more ominous nuance, that of harm (Brooke, 149).[327] Thus John's point is that Jesus' watchcare over believers preserves them from Satan's attempt to lay hold of them in a harmful manner (Painter, 324).[328] The translational choice of "grasp" reflects the sinister nature of Satan's action more clearly than "touch," or "harm" which looks to its desired result.

5:19 This second affirmation of truths taught repeats the statement of the previous verse with the same subject of the apostle and his readers, thus building on the first, but with a view to "positive consequences" (Barker, 356).[329] Also, like the previous sentence, it summarizes another of the teaching points of the epistle.

οἴδαμεν ὅτι ἐκ τοῦ θεοῦ ἐσμεν, "We know that we are from God."[330] John here reminds his readers of their parentage. He and his readers are sourced

---

326. BDAG, 1002; E. Riesenfeld, "τηρέω," *TDNT* 8:140–46.

327. BDAG, 126. Its range of meanings include: to light or kindle; to touch or take hold of; to cling to; to touch in a blessing; to partake of something; to have sexual contact; and to touch in order to harm.

328. M. Wolter ("Der altbose Feind," 25) sees this attempt in terms of the Christian community's suffering persecution.

329. Schnackenburg (288) sees this verse as an application of 3:9. It certainly repeats the teaching point of 3:9.

330. Bultmann (89) sees this as a "repetition" of the last clause of 3:9 (ἐκ τοῦ θεοῦ γεγέννηται) and so is a synonymous idea. Painter (325) sees this as "shorthand" for

in God. Why? God is their Father (3:1). Conspicuously absent is the personal pronoun that had been so prevalent throughout the epistle. This serves to deemphasize John and his readers and focus attention on God in contrast to "the evil one" who is left unnamed (Haas, de Jonge, and Swellengrebel, 152). In this case, also, his use of ἐκ includes both source and possession (Harris, 235). This is similar to 2:16, where the contrast is between being from God (the Father) and from the world. In this instance, though, John's use of ἐσμεν ἐκ τοῦ θεοῦ is parallel to both τέκνα θεοῦ (3:1, 2) and γεγέννηται ἐκ τοῦ θεοῦ (4:4, 6).[331] Thus this is a reaffirmation by John that he sees his readers as regenerate saints. It also reminds them of their privileged status as God's children.

καὶ ὁ κόσμος ὅλος ἐν τῷ πονηρῷ κεῖται, "and the whole world lies in the power of the evil one." Whereas the believer finds his or her source in God, the world does not do the same with "the evil one" but rather finds itself his prisoner. Here κόσμος is a metonymy of subject representing its population (Schnackenburg, 289). Thus humankind finds itself subjected to Satan. John's use of ὅλος with κόσμος might be viewed as hyperbole. However, it is said in light of his already affirming the distinction between believers and the world.[332] Believers are being preserved by Christ. Also, John has just affirmed that Satan cannot touch them (5:18). So ὅλος is best seen as a synecdoche* of the whole for the part. The world system is controlled by Satan.[333] Its populations as a whole, but not every inhabitant, are under his control. Satan claimed this when tempting Jesus (Luke 4:5–7) and Jesus did not dispute that claim. As Schnackenburg (289) reminds us, God gave Satan "dominion over 'the world' as the realm of Satan until the end of this eon."[334] John's use of the passive κεῖται to describe the world "lying" in the

---

"begotten of God."

331. M. Vellanickal, *The Divine Sonship of Christians in the Johannine Writings*, 96.

332. M. Wolter, "Der Altbose Fiend," 23. He describes this distinction as: "Everything that is not part of the Christian community belongs in the sphere of the influence of evil." (Alles, was nicht zur christlichen Gemainde gehört, gehört in den Einflußbereich des Bösen.)

333. John uses the same terms in 2:2 (ὅλου τοῦ κόσμου) with regard to Jesus' relationship to the world as its propitiation.

334. Ein ähnliches Urteil über die "Welt" als Machtbereich Satans, die ihm Gott bis zum Ende dieses Äons überlassen hat.

evil one indicates its helplessness against him and his control.[335] Yet the believer is not helpless, because he is not in Satan's grasp. This is a fulfillment of Jesus' prayer to the Father in John 17:15 that his followers should be kept from "the evil one."

Akin (213) aptly notes, "There are only two possible positions. Everyone is either 'of God' or 'under the control of the evil one.' Neutrality is not possible." Where the nonbeliever has no choice but to be under Satan's sway, Paul teaches us in Rom 6 that believers have a choice. We can make ourselves slaves of sin or righteousness (Rom 6:16–18). However, even as slaves of sin, we are still free from Satan's control, having been transferred from his domain into Christ's kingdom (Col 1:13). However, that being the case, Paul commands us to "reckon" ourselves dead to sin (Rom 6:11). Believers must choose to obey. They must choose not to sin. It is neither automatic nor guaranteed. Yet there is no return to Satan because Jesus keeps us. This then leads to the final affirmation.

5:20 This third closing comment reaffirms John's teaching on the deity and work of Christ.[336] Further, the believer's understanding of his relationship

335. Culy (138) suggests it is possible that the prepositional phrase ἐν τῷ πονηρῷ κεῖται "points to an intimate relationship ... with the verb highlighting the fact that the relationship has been firmly established." Moody (114) sees lying in the evil one as synonymous with abiding in death in 3:14. I would say rather that abiding in death is a consequence of living under Satan's dominion.

336. Following his secessionist theory, Barker (357) describes this verse as "the summary of the epistle" as it addresses the issue with John's opponents. Again, remove the theorized opponents, and we have christological truths that are at the core of a healthy fellowship with God. One cannot fellowship with Christ without an accurate Christology any more than one can have fellowship with another Christian without personal contact that develops into an accurate understanding of that person.

J. Hills, ("'Little children, keep yourselves from idols': 1 John 5:21 Reconsidered," 301–310) sees 5:20–21 forming an *inclusio* with 1:1–3. He argues that "the essential subject matter" of 1:1–3 is Jesus Christ, "that the language of witness and proclamation has a biblical (OT) origin which *explicitly* connects it with the critique of idols; and that 5:21 likewise has a biblical root, in that idols, their manufacturers, and their worshipers are contrasted with God and God's people" (302, italics his). He sees the OT concepts being understood in the prologue and these final words being directed against idolatry. The antithesis between "the true God" of Israel and idols was understood by John's readers. In response, one must note that the role of an *inclusio* is to mark off material within larger works, not to begin and end the

with God is sourced in God the Father and Son. This understanding enables believers to know God in an intimate, personal way.

οἴδαμεν δὲ ὅτι ὁ υἱὸς τοῦ θεοῦ ἥκει καὶ δέδωκεν ἡμῖν διάνοιαν ἵνα γινώσκωμεν τὸν ἀληθινόν, "And we know that the Son of God has come and has given us understanding in order that we may know him who is true." The final truth known to John and his readers is that Jesus, the Son of God, has come. This is a final reference to Jesus' incarnation in this epistle. The present tense verb ἥκει has an intensive perfect tense sense to its basic meaning (Painter, 325) and so very naturally blends its meaning with the verb that follows. Thereby it "denotes a present state or condition" and implies "the occurrence of an action which produced that condition."[337] It joins with the next verb (δέδωκεν) which is also functioning as an intensive perfect (Plummer, 127; Stott, 194; Westcott, 195)[338] to communicate the truths that Jesus "has come,"[339] He is no longer present, he has completed his incarnational ministry, and that its impact continues. Moody (114) describes this use of ἥκει as indicating "the decisive act by which the Son of God entered history."

After affirming Jesus' coming, John reminds his readers that Jesus has given them "understanding." With διάνοιαν, John describes the ability to comprehend and reason with one's mind.[340] This is what God has given us on a permanent basis, thus the perfect tense δέδωκεν. He has given us the ability to understand and know certain truths (Burdick, 394). Paul describes this in terms of the spiritual man appraising all things because he has "the mind of Christ" (1 Cor 2:13–16). This alludes back to the "anointing" of 2:20–21 (Bultmann, 89) and once more alludes to Jesus' instruction of the Eleven in the upper room where he both gave and promised them understanding.

---

work. It would be better to say that vv 20–21 summarize themes introduced in the prologue, if that could be demonstrated. However, idols cannot even be implied in the prologue. His arguments are interesting but unconvincing.

337. B. M. Fanning, *Verbal Aspect in New Testament Greek*, 239.

338. Burdick (394) rejects this and says, "Instead of placing emphasis on Christ's continuing presence, John is stressing the fact that in the past He has come."

339. Bultmann (89) sees ἥκει as synonymous with ἐφανερώθη and so "refers to the appearance of God's Son in history.

340. BDAG, 234; J. Behm, "νοέω ... διάνοια," *TDNT* 4:963–67. "The idea is that the Son of God has awakened in us the mind and given our thinking the orientation to know God, to receive His revelation, to share fellowship with him."

The reason God has given us the ability to understand is so that we can know him experientially.[341] John again uses γινώσκω with the nuance of knowledge by experience. This indicates not knowledge by instruction or intuition, but a personal, relational, knowledge of God who is truth itself.[342] Further the articular adjective ἀληθινόν should be seen in its substantival role as modifying an understood noun and so may be translated literally "the true one" or "him who is true" rather than as "the truth" (would have taken the noun), especially in light of the following clauses. Thus Jesus' coming was not that we would learn truths, but that we would have fellowship with the "true one," namely, God.

καὶ ἐσμὲν ἐν τῷ ἀληθινῷ, ἐν τῷ υἱῷ αὐτοῦ Ἰησοῦ Χριστῷ, "and we are in the true one, in his Son, Jesus Christ." John now affirms that we not only can know God, but that we are "in" him. The referent of τῷ ἀληθινῷ can be understood in one of two ways:

(1) It refers to God the Father (Brooke, 152–53; Dodd, 140; Smalley, 308; Stott, 196; Westcott, 187). In John 17:3 it describes God the Father (Harris, 235) and it has just described him in the previous clause. John's love of repetition for emphasis is exhibited in this construction.

(2) It refers to Jesus (Barker, 357; Brown, 640; Bruce, 128; Bultmann, 90; Marshall, 254; Plummer, 128; Schnackenburg, 290; Thompson, 147; Yarbrough, 320). Culy (139) sees "this prepositional phrase included to clarify that the writer did intend to switch referents in his use of ἐν τῷ ἀληθινῷ, and so it is a reference to Christ. However, the genitive pronoun αὐτοῦ clearly has God the Father in view. Additionally, the antecedent of αὐτοῦ most naturally is ἀληθινῷ in the immediate preceding clause.

Thus the articular adjective ἀληθινῷ once again describes God the Father as is made clear by the following preposition phrase. In this case, being "in his Son" is different from the Pauline concept of being in Christ. Rather it refers back to Jesus' words to the disciples in the upper room (John 14). Just as Jesus is "in the Father" and the Father is "in him" (John 14:11), and the

341. This is a purpose ἵνα clause (Harris, 235) that is dependent on διάνοιαν (Brooke, 151).

342. This once more takes the reader back to Jesus' prayer (John 17:5) after leaving the upper room. "And this is eternal life, that they may know you, the only true God, and Jesus Christ whom you have sent." The parallels are so strong that one must conclude that John had Jesus' prayer in mind as he wrote these concluding words.

disciples share in that relationship (John 14:20), though contingent on a life of obedience (John 14:23), so, too may all believers be "in the true one," God. This has the sense of "abiding," and so refers to fellowship with God. So why did John not use μένω here? Malatesta observes well, "εἶναι is used here instead of μένειν precisely to stress that to be in God and in Jesus is the condition, the way of being, to which the Christian community is called."[343] This also alludes back to 5:13–14 and the connection between having the Son and having life. Thus, though John's use of "in his Son" is more of a sanctification reality (a conditional truth rather than positional truth as with Paul), it presupposes justification as its basis.

οὗτός ἐστιν ὁ ἀληθινὸς θεὸς καὶ ζωὴ αἰώνιος, "He is the true God and eternal life." We now have the strongest and clearest affirmation of the deity of Christ.[344] Malatesta calls this "the author's most profound christological statement."[345] Hills calls this "the highest Christology in the writing."[346] It is the clearest statement in the epistle and serves as the climax of his christological statements throughout. It takes us back to the prologue where eternal life was revealed to be a person. John now clearly restates his theme and says plainly that Jesus is both God and eternal life incarnate.

This use of οὗτός is understood in one of two ways:

(1) It has God the Father as its antecedent (Burdick, 397; Dodd, 140; Grayston, 147; Law, 413; Plummer, 121; Smalley, 308; Stott, 197–98; Westcott, 196).[347] This was said of the Father by Jesus in John 17:3. There eternal life is experiential knowledge (γινώσκω) of God. Painter acknowledges the grammar and that Jesus is the likely antecedent to οὗτός, yet sees this as a reference to God the Father instead. He points to αὐτοῦ in the clause immediately before οὗτός (ἐν τῷ υἱῷ αὐτοῦ Ἰησοῦ Χριστῷ) as referring to God the Father. It is on the basis of this that οὗτός refers to God rather than Jesus for the first time in this epistle.

---

343. E. Malatesta, *Interiority and Covenant*, 321.

344. A. Köstenberger, "The Deity of Christ in John's Letters and the Book of Revelation." 155.

345. E. Malatesta, *Interiority and Covenant*, 322.

346. J. Hills, "'Little children, keep yourselves from idols': 1 John 5:21 Reconsidered," 301.

347. M. J. Harris, *Jesus as God: The New Testament Use of Theos in Reference to Jesus*, 253.

(2) It has Jesus as its antecedent (Barker, 357; Bruce, 128; Haas, de Jonge, and Swellengrebel, 129–30; Marshall, 254, n. 47; Schnackenburg, 291; Thompson, 147).[348] Bultmann (90) says οὗτός cannot refer to God, only Jesus, and that the earlier ἐν τῷ ἀληθινῷ can only refer to God. Since οὗτός normally points to its near antecedent, this use by John has "Jesus Christ" as its antecedent (Brown, 626) and so serves as a final affirmation of the deity of Jesus. If οὗτός refers to God the Father, it makes the clause redundant. Additionally, whenever John uses "life" as a predicate it always refers to Jesus (Thompson, 147).[349] In the Gospel both the "Word" (1:1) and the risen Christ (20:28) are called "God" (Thompson, 147). This statement also looks back on the prologue of the epistle wherein eternal life is a person that the apostles handled, heard, and saw personally. Now we see that experiencing eternal life occurs in *relationship* with the person who is eternal life incarnate. Finally, with the relative pronoun οὗτός John clarifies once more the deity of Christ.

John calls Jesus "true God." Some translate ἀληθινὸς as "real" or "genuine" (Burdick, 395; Culy, 139; Strecker, 210).[350] However, "true" reflects the theme of "truth" in the epistle.[351] Also, "true God" is combined with "eternal life." Jesus as eternal life incarnate was introduced in the prologue as a historical person experienced personally by John. His deity has been repeatedly affirmed. Now the two aspects of Jesus' being are brought together in this final christological affirmation.

Biblical Theology Comments

John's Christology reaches its climax in this final movement of his epistle with the clearest declaration of Jesus' deity. In describing Jesus John has affirmed his humanity and deity. Jesus is the incarnate Son of God (5:20) whom John experienced personally and physically (1:1–3; 4:2). Jesus was

348. D. B. Wallace, *Grammar*, 327; and *Granville Sharp's Canon and Its Kin: Semantics and Significance*, 277; J. Hills, "'Little children, keep yourselves from idols': 1 John 5:21 Reconsidered," 301.

349. John 11:25; 14:6; 1 John 1:2.

350. R. Bultmann, "ἀληθινὸς," *TDNT* 1:249.

351. Truth is related to believers, their conduct and confession (1:7, 8; 2:4; 3:18), to Christ's commandment to love (2:8), to the body of instruction they have received from the apostles (2:21, 27; 3:19), to the Holy Spirit (4:6; 5:6), and finally to God the Father (5:20).

manifested to the world through his baptism and crucifixion (5:6). Through his death he became the propitiation for the sins of mankind (1:7; 2:1–2; 4:10) and, as God's unique Son, sent into the world (4:9), thereby became the Savior of the world (4:14). Jesus is both the Christ and the Son of God (2:22–23; 5:1). Both titles attest to his deity. As such he is also or righteous judge (2:28–29) who is as morally pure as God the Father (3:3). Life, eternal life, is in and through him (4:9; 5:11–12). When these truths are brought together, they declare that he is "true God" and "eternal life."

Eternal life is both a person (Jesus) and a possession. Though the focus of this epistle has been on the relational aspect of eternal life, it is further defined as something possessed by the believer (5:11–13). Even so, that possession is centered in the person of Christ (1:1–3) and only experienced in relation to him (5:12). Our possession of eternal life can be known with certainty (5:13). In fact, it is God's will that we know we have eternal life. That assurance comes from believing God's promise, not from looking at our works. Assurance is God's will for every one of his children because we cannot have fellowship if we are not convinced we are God's children.

Application and Devotional Implications

5:1 On one hand, it *is* Jesus who saves and a person can be very confused in his or her theology and Christology and still become regenerate when they cry out to the authentic Jesus for forgiveness and life. A small child's understanding will be limited. However, what that child knows is still important. His or her faith must be in the real Jesus, not a false Jesus. What his or her parents believe and teach is critical to his or her salvation. Still, even for that child, salvation does not come from just knowing that Jesus is God, believing an "intellectual truth." That child must still direct his or her faith to Jesus. Jesus must still be the object of faith. Then God the Father will declare that child justified and give him or her new life in Jesus. It is not theology that saves; it is Jesus. It is not our information about God that gives life, but God himself. Justifying and sanctifying faith is not valid when it is placed in information, even if true. It is only valid when directed toward a Person, Jesus. Again, it must be the right information that points to the real Jesus. It is only Jesus, who presently resides in heaven at the right hand of the Father in glory, in whom saving faith is placed. Any other Jesus is a fictional character that has no substance and cannot save.

5:5 Begin each day with a commitment to show Jesus that you love him by loving another Christian. Remind yourself that by doing that Jesus will know your love for him. Stop to think about how you feel when people treat your children well or poorly. Then think about how God feels about you and his other children. Let this motivate you to positive action in your church community.

5:13 There are those today who teach that one cannot know they have eternal life with certainty because they do not know whether they are "elect." Their election, and therefore the validity of their faith in Jesus, is proven by their persevering in good works to the end of their life without falling away into a pattern of sin. No one can be sure they will persevere until they have. Therefore, anyone who holds to the doctrine of perseverance (which is distinct from the doctrine of eternal security) cannot know with certainty that they have eternal life. However, here John says that we can *know* we have eternal life. That assurance is God's stated *will* for each of his children. Therefore, any doctrine that robs one of his children of this assurance is a false doctrine.

At the same time, any teaching that one must have assurance of eternal life to have saving faith is equally false.[352] One must believe in God's Son and simply have enough faith to look to him in the same way that the Israelites looked to the bronze serpent to be healed (John 3:14–15). The effectiveness of justifying faith is not found in its volume, strength, maturity, or source. Its effectiveness is found in its object, Jesus Christ our Savior, and in God the Father whose promise to save is unequivocally trustworthy.

Additionally, John's concept of "eternal life" is far more comprehensive than the mere possession of unending life. It is a quality of life resulting from a healthy relationship with Jesus, who is eternal life incarnate. So, John is not writing in order that his readers may possess salvation, but experience and express it.

Whenever you have doubts, and we all do at times, do not look to your works to restore your confidence in your salvation. Remind yourself about God's promises and his faithfulness. Also, go back to the beginning and remember what you believed. Was your faith in Jesus? Then God has

352. Z. Hodges, "We Believe In: Assurance Of Salvation," 15. He says, "Assurance, therefore, is inseparable from—and part of the essence of—saving faith."

promised you life. Let God's promise be your comfort and hope. If anything causes you to wonder if you have the life he promised, remember his will is that you know without a doubt that you are his child. Anything less than certainty is not God's desire, but our error.

Assurance of the experience of eternal life produces confidence in prayer and an active concern for brethren who have sinned. This next section discusses the benefits enjoyed by the believer rightly related by faith to the Son of God. In some ways this may be seen as the anticlimax of the epistle, with the preceding paragraph serving as its climax. What is said here, though, is no less important that what precedes. This is the crux of fellowship with God and its impact in the life of a believer.

5:16–17 Instead of talking to others about someone else's sins, pray for him or her. It is not gossip to talk to God about others' sins as well as your own. He already knows what has happened. However, also remember, this is a real act of love, to care enough to ask God to show him or her mercy. We will only know how great an impact our prayers for others have had when we get to heaven.

5:18–20 Our churches desperately need to know Christology. Only then can "the Christian in the pew" understand the exclusiveness of the gospel in a society that has made pluralism a virtue and exclusivism a vice. Jesus is not a "god" among many (Hinduism, Mormonism), but the God of the universe. He is not a mere prophet (Islam) or good teacher (Liberal theology, humanism), but the Creator and Sustainer of the universe. Evangelical Christians need to be taught this. They need to know why his virgin birth matters, why his death was necessary, and why his resurrection must be a historical reality for our faith to be equally real. Why? As John has made clear, God's life and love flow through us only to the extent we believe the right things about Jesus. The weaker our Christology, the weaker our walks with God. Our churches may grow in numbers apart from a proper understanding of Christ, but they will never grow to spiritual maturity apart from an accurate understanding of the person and work of Christ our Savior. We cannot present him to the world as its Savior if our members don't believe he is and don't live as he is.

Selected Bibliography

Beale, G. K., and D. A. Carson. *Commentary on the New Testament Use of the Old Testament*. Grand Rapids: Baker Academic, 2007.

Bullinger, E. W. *Figures of Speech Used in the Bible*. New York: Eyre & Spottiswoode, 1898. Repr., Grand Rapids: Baker, 1968.

Busenitz, I. A. "The Sin unto Death." *MSJ* 1 (1990): 17–31.

Campbell, B. "Flesh and Spirit in 1 Cor 5:5: An Exercise in Rhetorical Criticism of the NT." *JETS* 36 (1993): 331–42.

Charlesworth, J. H., ed. *The Old Testament Pseudepigrapha*. 2 vols. Garden City, NY: Doubleday, 1983–85.

Coetzee, J. C. "The Holy Spirit in 1 John." *Neot* 13 (1979): 43–67.

Collins, A. Y. "The Function of 'Excommunication' in Paul." *HTR* 73 (1980): 251–63.

Cook, W. R. "Hamartiological Problems in First John." *BSac* 123 (1966): 249–60.

Dahms, J. V. "The Nature of Truth." *JETS* 28 (1985): 455–65.

de Boer, M. C. "Jesus the Baptizer: 1 John 5:5–8 and the Gospel of John." *JBL* 107 (1988): 87–106.

de Jonge, M. "The Use of the Word ΧΡΙΣΤΟΣ in the Johannine Epistles." In *Studies in John,* 67–74. NovTSup 24. Leiden: Brill, 1970.

Fanning, B. M. *Verbal Aspect in New Testament Greek*. Oxford: Clarendon, 1990.

Harris, M. J. *Jesus as God: The New Testament Use of Theos in Reference to Jesus*. Grand Rapids: Baker, 1992.

Hiebert, D. E. "An Expositional Study of 1 John—Part 9: An Exposition of 1 John 5:1–12." *BSac* 147 (1990): 216–30.

———. "An Expositional Study of 1 John—Part 10: An Exposition of 1 John 5:13–21." *BSac* 147 (1990): 309–28.

Hodges, Z. C. "We Believe In: Assurance of Salvation." *JOTGES* 3 (90): 3–17.

Kistemaker, S. J. "'Deliver This Man to Satan' (1 Cor 5:5): A Case Study in Church Discipline." *Master's Seminary Journal* 3 (1992): 32–46.

Kurian, G. T., ed. *Nelson's New Christian Dictionary: The Authoritative Resource on the Christian World.* Nashville: Thomas Nelson, 2001.

Lalleman, P. J. "The Adversaries Envisaged in the Johannine Epistles." *ThT* 53 (1999): 17–24.

Malatesta, E. *Interiority and Covenant: A Study of* εἶναι ἐν *and* μένειν ἐν *in the First Letter of Saint John*. Rome: Biblical Institute Press, 1978.

Manson, T. W. "Entry into Membership of the Early Church." *JTS* 48 (1947): 25–33.

Metzger, B. M., and United Bible Societies. *A Textual Commentary on the Greek New Testament.* 2nd ed. New York: United Bible Societies, 1994.

Morris, L. *The Epistle to the Romans*. PNTC. Grand Rapids: Eerdmans, 1988.

Mounce, R. H. *Romans*. NAC 27. Nashville: Broadman & Holman, 2001.

O'Neill, John C. *The Puzzle of 1 John*. London: SPCK, 1966.

Odeberg, H. *The Fourth Gospel: Interpreted in Its Relation to Contemporaneous Religious Currents in Palestine and the Hellenistic-Oriental World.* Chicago: Argonaut, 1968.

Paschal, R. W., Jr. "Sacramental Symbolism and Physical Imagery in the Gospel of John." *TynBul* 32 (1981): 151–176.

Reynolds, S. M. "The Sin unto Death and Prayers for the Dead." *RefR* 20 (1973): 130–39.

Richter, G. "Blut und Wasser aus der durchgebohrten Seite Jesu (Joh 19,34b)." In *Studien zum Johannesevangelium.* Regensburg: Pustet, 1977.

Robertson, A. T. *A Grammar of the Greek New Testament in the Light of Historical Research.* Nashville: Broadman, 1931.

Tan, R. K. J. "Should We Pray for Straying Brethren? John's Confidence in 1 John 5:16–17." *JETS* 45 (2002): 599–609.

Trudinger, P. "Concerning Sins, Mortal and Otherwise: A Note on 1 John 5:16–17." *Bib* 52 (1971): 541–42.

Vellanickal, M. *The Divine Sonship of Christians in the Johannine Writings.* Rome: Biblical Institute Press, 1977.

Wallace, D. B. *Greek Grammar beyond the Basics.* Grand Rapids: Zondervan, 1996.

W. Whiston, trans. *The Works of Josephus: Complete and Unabridged.* Peabody, MA: Hendrickson, 1996.

Witherington, B. "The Waters of Birth: John 3:5 and 1 John 5:6–8." *NTS* 35 (1989): 155–60.

Wolter, M. "Der altbose Feind." *Glaube und Lernen* 12 (1997): 22–30.

Avoid Idols (5:21)

Original Text

21 Τεκνία, φυλάξατε ἑαυτὰ ἀπὸ τῶν εἰδώλων.[a]

Textual Notes

21.a. The epistle should end with εἰδώλων rather than concluding with ἀμήν.[353]

Translation

21 Children, guard yourselves from idols.[354]

---

353. B. M. Metzger and United Bible Societies, *A Textual Commentary on the Greek New Testament*, 2d ed., 651.

354. Though most translations retain "idols," some do attempt to reflect their understanding of its significance with "false gods" (NCV) and "anything that might

Commentary

This short comment has created a great deal of speculation. It does not appear to have any connection with what has preceded it, other than John's addressing his readers as "children" once again. So why does he close with this command?

John ends his epistle with one more loving reference to his readers, using the diminutive τεκνία one last time. So what he has to say once again flows out of a heart of compassion and is spoken from the perspective of one who loves them.

John begins by charging his readers to "guard" themselves. With this imperative John states a command, a general precept, rather than implying they have not been guarding themselves and need to begin.[355] His use of the reflexive pronoun ἑαυτὰ, with the imperative, focuses attention on the believer's responsibility (Brooke, 154). Though Jesus keeps us from the evil one, we have a responsibility to guard ourselves. The aorist imperative is "urgent, absolute, and final" (Burdick, 397). Contsoumpos believes that the definite article "implies that he sensed danger."[356] Hills notes that φυλάξατε is only one of two aorist impvs. in the epistle, the other being ἴδετε in 3:1.[357] This has the sense of ongoing vigilance. Further, this imperative is modified with the reflexive pronoun ἑαυτὰ. Westcott (197) interprets this to indicate "the duty of personal effort" involved in guarding oneself. However, the choice of a reflexive pronoun often focuses attention on the reflexive aspect of the relationship.[358] Hills notes that the construction includes not

---

take God's place in your hearts" (NLT). The inclusion of "amen" at the end is rare (NKJV), though a few note its presence in some MSS (ISV, NET, NRSV).

355. B. M. Fanning (*Verbal Aspect in New Testament Greek*, 366–69) says "the aorist can be used in general precepts to give an external or summary view of the occurrence commanded. This is used in place of the multiple or customary sense which the present provides in such instances. The aorist in general precepts appears usually to bring out one of the secondary functions of the summary aspect... It is also common to find the *consummative* sense for the aorist in general precepts. In this the aorist is used to emphasize the accomplishment or fulfillment of an effort: a command not merely to work at or attempt the action, as the present may imply, but to do it successfully or actually. The focus is on the end-point of the action even though the command is a general precept."

356. P. Contsoumpos, "The Idolatry Dilemma In 1 John 5:21," 150.

357. J. Hills, "'Little children, keep yourselves from idols': 1 John 5:21 Reconsidered," 289.

358. BDF §310 (2).

only the imperative and reflexive pronoun, but is followed by the preposition ἀπὸ. He traces its use in Attic Greek and the LXX and defines its sense as twofold. If the object is "inanimate" or "immobile," the sense of the imperative is to keep from, avoid. If the object is "mobile" the sense is that of "defending against."[359] In this case, if literal idols are meant, then the sense is "avoid." If the false teachers and their false teachings are meant, then the sense may be "defend yourselves."

So what does John mean by "idols"? Brown (627) identifies ten proposed meanings of "idols" by various writers.[360] This reveals the difficulty interpreters have faced in determining the meaning intended by John. Hills reduces the ten to two main interpretations. The possible meanings that are being proposed by most modern scholars include the following.

(1) John may be referring to literal idols and so may be warning against apostasy involving worship of idols (Dodd, 141; Moody, 116; Strecker, 214; Yarbrough, 323–24).[361] Strecker (214, n. 73) interprets "idols" to mean "false gods" based on Josephus' use of the term.[362] "Simply to walk among the ruins of Ephesus, Sardis, Hierapolis, or Miletus is enough to impress one with the overwhelming reality of pagan worship" (Burdick, 397). Thus it would be natural for John to close with such a warning, especially

---

359. J. Hills, "'Little children, keep yourselves from idols': 1 John 5:21 Reconsidered," 289–91.

360. Brown's (627–28) list includes: (1) Plato's "unreal objects," (2) literal idols of the pagans, (3) food dedicated to idols, (4) compromising with paganism, (5) "the mystery religions and their practices," (6) "gnositc ideologies or philosophies," (7) "Jewish worship in the Jerusalem temple," (8) sins, (9) figurative for "anything that takes the place of God," and (10) a reference to the secessionists.

361. J. Hills, "'Little children, keep yourselves from idols': 1 John 5:21 Reconsidered," 288.

362. Josephus, *Ant.* 9.273 reads: "and when the festival was ended, they went out into the country, and purged it; and cleansed the city of all the pollution of the idols." *Ant.* 10:50 reads: "and when he was twelve years old he gave demonstrations of his religious and righteous behavior; for he brought the people to a sober way of living, and exhorted them to leave off the opinion they had of their idols, because they were not gods, but to worship their own God." (From W. Whiston, trans. *The Works of Josephus: Complete and Unabridged*); *T. Reub.* 4.6 reads: "For a pit unto the soul is the sin of fornication, separating it from God, and bringing it near to idols," (From *Pseudepigrapha of the Old Testament*, ed. Robert Henry Charles, 2:299.

since he had not dealt with the issue previously. Yarbrough (323–34) argues that Zech 13:2 is the background to this statement and that Acts 19:18–19 indicates the Ephesian believers "clung to their occult paraphernalia for some time following their entrance into the church." Paul's instructions in 1 Cor included the issue of idolatry and the Jerusalem Council (Acts 15:20 29) addressed the issue as well. Contsoumpos sees Rev 2:2, 14, 20 and Jezebel referring to participation in banquets at pagan temples, and that the Nicolaitans "agreed with some of the Christians at Corinth that pagan deities did not really exist and that an unscrupulous Christian might fully participate in the social life, commerce, and politics of a great pagan city. John did not specifically describe their doctrine, but focused on their conduct."[363] Hills points to OT and intertestamental parallels for "at least a superficial lexical affinity with 1 John 5:20–21."[364] They include Dan 5:4; 6:27–28; Bel 5; and Tob 14:6.[365] From these similar contrasts, he concludes that they were "conventional" in John's day. Next he quotes two NT texts (Acts 14:15; 1 Thess 1:9) as examples of the same convention.[366] For him this indicates that "conventional language" indicates that

---

363. P. Contsoumpos, "The Idolatry Dilemma In 1 John 5:21," 151.

364. J. Hills, "'Little children, keep yourselves from idols': 1 John 5:21 Reconsidered," 298.

365. Dan 5:4, καὶ ηὐλόγουν τὰ εἴδωλα τὰ χειροποίητα αὐτῶν, καὶ τὸν θεὸν τοῦ αἰῶνος οὐκ εὐλόγησαν τὸν ἔχοντα τὴν ἐξουσίαν τοῦ πνεύματος αὐτῶν.

Dan 6:27–28, Πάντες οἱ ἄνθρωποι οἱ ὄντες ἐν τῇ βασιλείᾳ μου ἔστωσαν προσκυνοῦντες καὶ λατρεύοντες τῷ θεῷ τοῦ Δανιηλ, αὐτὸς γάρ ἐστι θεὸς μένων καὶ ζῶν εἰς γενεὰς γενεῶν ἕως τοῦ αἰῶνος, ἐγὼ Δαρεῖος ἔσομαι αὐτῷ προσκυνῶν καὶ δουλεύων πάσας τὰς ἡμέρας μου, τὰ γὰρ εἴδωλα τὰ χειροποίητα οὐ δύνανται σῶσαι, ὡς ἐλυτρώσατο ὁ θεὸς τοῦ Δανιηλ τὸν Δανιηλ.

Bel 5, καὶ εἶπεν αὐτῷ ὁ βασιλεύς Διὰ τί οὐ προσκυνεῖς τῷ Βηλ; ὁ δὲ εἶπεν Ὅτι οὐ σέβομαι εἴδωλα χειροποίητα, ἀλλὰ τὸν ζῶντα θεὸν τὸν κτίσαντα τὸν οὐρανὸν καὶ τὴν γῆν καὶ ἔχοντα πάσης σαρκὸς κυριείαν.

Tob 14:6, καὶ πάντα τὰ ἔθνη ἐπιστρέψουσιν ἀληθινῶς φοβεῖσθαι κύριον τὸν θεὸν καὶ κατορύξουσιν τὰ εἴδωλα αὐτῶν, καὶ εὐλογήσουσιν πάντα τὰ ἔθνη τὸν κύριον.

366. Acts 14:15, καὶ ἡμεῖς ὁμοιοπαθεῖς ἐσμεν ὑμῖν ἄνθρωποι εὐαγγελιζόμενοι ὑμᾶς ἀπὸ τούτων τῶν ματαίων ἐπιστρέφειν ἐπὶ θεὸν ζῶντα, ὃς ἐποίησεν τὸν οὐρανὸν καὶ τὴν γῆν καὶ τὴν θάλασσαν καὶ πάντα τὰ ἐν αὐτοῖς·.

1 Thess 1:9, αὐτοὶ γὰρ περὶ ἡμῶν ἀπαγγέλλουσιν ὁποίαν εἴσοδον ἔσχομεν πρὸς ὑμᾶς, καὶ πῶς ἐπεστρέψατε πρὸς τὸν θεὸν ἀπὸ τῶν εἰδώλων δουλεύειν θεῷ ζῶντι καὶ ἀληθινῷ.

John would intend idols rather than ideas as his referent, though "with some Johannine coloring."[367]

(2) He uses the term "idols" to refer to foods sacrificed to idols.

(3) They represent all false conceptions of God (Brooke, 154; Marshall, 255–56).

(4) Idols symbolize sin (Nauck, 136–37; Schnackenburg, 292). His view is based on 1QS 2:11 and 1QS 17:4–5.[368]

(5) They are anything that interferes with devotion to God (J. Mitchell, 167; Walls and Anders, 226; Westcott, 197). Lieu (237) sees "idols" as synonymous with "world" in the same way the three lusts in 2:16 are as well.

(6) Idols represent those false ideas about God reflected in the doctrines of the false teachers or secessionists (Akin, 216; Barker, 357; Brown, 628–29; Bruce, 128; Bultmann, 90; Culpepper, 114–15; Grayston, 148; Houlden, 138; Johnson, 141; Kistemaker, 368; Kruse, 202; Lenski, 545; Marshall, 257; Perkins, 65–66; Smalley, 310; Smith, 137 Stott, 197–99; Williamson, 174). Suggit notes that originally the term εἴδωλον meant "ghost" or "phantom" and that this sense continued to be contained in the word.[369] He sees John saying, "Keep yourselves away from ghosts" and sees John meaning by this "the imaginations of Docetics and those who

---

367. J. Hills, "'Little children, keep yourselves from idols': 1 John 5:21 Reconsidered," 300.

368. Nauck (*Die Tradition und der Charakter des ersten Johannesbriefes* , 138, n.2) quotes 1QS 2.11–12, 17. J. Hills quotes vv 11–17. "[11] Further the priests and Levites say: 'Cursed because of the idols of his heart which he worships be [12] he who enters into this covenant and puts the stumbling-block of his sin before him so that he backslides, (stumbling) over it. And if, [13] when he hears the words of this covenant, he blessed himself, thinking: "Peace be with me, [14] for I walk in the stubbornness of my heart"—may his spirit be destroyed, thirst as well as saturation, without [15] forgiveness. May God's wrath and angry judgments flare up against him for everlasting destruction, and may all [16] the curses of this covenant stick to him. May God separate him for evil, that he may be cut off from all the sons of light because of his backsliding [17] from God through his idols and the stumbling-block of his sin. May He put his lot among those who are cursed for ever.'"

369. J. N. Suggit, "1 John 5:21: ΤΕΚΝΙΑ, ΦΥΛΑΞΑΤΕ ΕΑΥΤΑ ΑΠΟ ΤΩΝ ΕΙΔΩΛΩΝ," 387.

deny the reality of the human life and the risen body of Jesus Christ."[370] Further, he argues that the definite article before idols is "necessary" in that it functions anaphorically to refer back to all "the phantoms against which the readers are warned."[371] This is grammatically possible.[372] However, it could also be functioning as a "well-known" or "familiar" article, indicating that he and his readers were familiar with the problem of idols and idolatry in their cities.[373] Thus, he could be referring to a particular idol, such as that of Aphrodite in Ephesus (Brown, 627; Stott, 196). Or there may not be a specific idol in view, but the article is a "generic" article and is meant to include whatever idols happen to be in their city.[374] Hills notes that the other uses in the NT of the plural εἰδώλων, include the article.[375] Therefore it is unlikely that a specific idol was intended but idols in general. This would fit with the letter being intended for a wide audience rather than a specific church.

The meaning of "idol" did not move from that of phantoms to images but retained both senses throughout its history.[376] Judaism within the Greek world seems to have attached the latter sense to the term as its own unique view of Greek idols[377] as reflected in the LXX where γλυπτός ("carved") and εἴδωλον were chosen most often to refer to the wooden or metal idols.[378]

---

370. J. N. Suggit, "1 John 5:21: ΤΕΚΝΙΑ, ΦΥΛΑΞΑΤΕ ΕΑΥΤΑ ΑΠΟ ΤΘΝ ΕΙΔΩΛΩΝ," 389.
371. J. N. Suggit, "1 John 5:21: ΤΕΚΝΙΑ, ΦΥΛΑΞΑΤΕ ΕΑΥΤΑ ΑΠΟ ΤΘΝ ΕΙΔΩΛΩΝ," 389.
372. D. B. Wallace, *Grammar*, 247.
373. D. B. Wallace, *Grammar*, 225.
374. BDF §252 (2).
375. J. Hills, "'Little children, keep yourselves from idols': 1 John 5:21 Reconsidered," 294. These include Acts 15:20; Rom 2:22; 1 Cor 12:2; 1 Thess 1:9; and Rev 9:20.
376. F. Büchsel, "εἴδωλον," *TDNT* 2:375–80.
377. F. Büchsel, "εἴδωλον," *TDNT* 2:377.
378. J. Hills, "'Little children, keep yourselves from idols': 1 John 5:21 Reconsidered," 293–94. He (297) identifies those Qumran readings used to defend the idea of "idols" representing "false teachings" to include 1QS 2.11–12, 17 (Brown, Nauck); 1QS 4.5 (Schnackenburg); 1QH 4.9–11, 15 (Brown); 1QH 4.15, 18–19 (Schnackenburg); CD 20.9–10 (Brown, Schnackenburg). He then points out that when the main text of 1QS 2 includes vv 13–16, the context and sense of idols is symbolic of "sin" and is being used metaphorically for "stubbornness as the willful refusal to answer the call of God." Thus he dismisses the "evidence" from Qumran.

New Testament usage of εἴδωλον consistently refers to the inanimate images of worship rather than concepts or phantoms.[379]

The difficulty of deciding can be illustrated by Painter's assessment (Painter, 328). He sees John referring to something known to his readers that involved a specific issue, thus the article with "idols." He sees it as a warning against John's "opponents." He argues that if the false teachers is not the issue, then John must be introducing a completely different subject in the final verse of his epistle, which would not make sense. He sees the aorist indicating "a specific crisis rather than a perennial problem." Having said that, he notes the issue of idolatry with Paul in 1 Cor 10:7 and 14 and concludes that literal idolatry could be in view.

In light of the fact that John has just reminded his readers that Jesus is the true God, it seems best to see him referring to literal idols as opposed to false ideas or doctrines. Its apparent lack of connection with the remainder of the epistle seems to make this view less attractive. However, one must remember that he is writing from Ephesus, a center of pagan worship, and idolatry surrounded all of the churches under his care. Contsoumpos is correct when he says that idolatry was "one of the more serious problems faced by the early Christians" and so "the issue of idolatry cannot be completely ruled out."[380]

Selected Bibliography

Charles, R. H., ed. *Pseudepigrapha of the Old Testament.* Bellingham, WA: Logos Research Systems, Inc., 2004.

Contsoumpos, P. "The Idolatry Delemma in 1 John 5:21." *DavarLogos* 2 (2003): 147–52.

Fanning, B. M. *Verbal Aspect in New Testament Greek.* Oxford: Clarendon, 1990.

Hills, Julian. "'Little Children, Keep Yourselves from Idols': 1 John 5:21 Reconsidered." *CBQ* 51 (1989): 285–310.

Metzger, B. M., and United Bible Societies. *A Textual Commentary on the Greek New Testament.* 2nd ed. New York: United Bible Societies, 1994.

379. Acts 7:41 (refers to golden calf); 15:21 (pagan idols); Rom 2:22 (pagan idols located in temples); 1 Cor 8:4, 7 (pagan idol as a symbol of the god); 10:19 (pagan idol that sacrifices to which sacrifices are offered); 12:12 (pagan idols worshipped at one time by the Corinthians); 2 Cor 6:16 (pagan idols); 1 Thess 1:9 (pagan idols once worshipped by the Thessalonians); and Rev 9:20 (images of gods made from natural materials).

380. P. Contsoumpos, "The Idolatry Dilemma In 1 John 5:21," 148.

Nauck, W. *Die Tradition und der Charakter des ersten Johannesbriefes, zugleich ein Beitrag zur Taufe im Urchristentum und in der alten Kirche*. WUNT, 3. Tübingen: Mohr, 1957.

Suggit, J. N. "1 John 5:21: TEKNIA, ΦΥΛΑΞΑΤΕ ΕΑΥΤΑ ΑΠΟ ΤΩΝ ΕΙΔΩΛΩΝ." *JTS* 36 (1985): 386–90.

Wallace, D. B. *Greek Grammar beyond the Basics*. Grand Rapids: Zondervan, 1996.

Whiston, W., trans. *The Works of Josephus: Complete and Unabridged*. MA: Hendrickson, 1996.

2 John

Introduction

Author

The apostle John is the author of this epistle. The evidence points to him even though, as in the Gospel, he chose not to name himself. Obviously he did not need to do so then. He certainly does not need to now. It is the general consensus of recent critical scholarship that the apostle John is not the author of any of his epistles (Brooke, i; Brown, 14–35; Bultmann, 1–3; Culpepper, 261–90; Dodd, lxxi; Grayston, 6–9; Johnson, 3; Painter, 23; Perkins, xiii–xiv; Schnackenburg, 295–301; Strecker, xxxvii–xxxix; Williams, 15; Williamson, 33).[1] Among their arguments have been the claim that there were two Johns in the church at Ephesus, though many assume a different author than the supposed "Elder John."[2] By interpreting Papias's statement about the apostles and elders, they posit a John the elder and elect him as the author of this epistle. Or they see it arising from some other leader within the theorized "Johannine community" for which there is no corroborating evidence from external or internal evidence.

John's designation of himself as "the elder" need not point away from apostolic authorship since this was a designation given the apostles in the early centuries of the church. For example, Eusebius quotes Papias as saying, "If, then, any one came, who had been a follower of the elders, I questioned him in regard to the words of the elders,—what Andrew or what Peter said, or what was said by Philip, or by Thomas, or by James, or by John, or by Matthew, or by any other of the disciples of the Lord, and what things

1. J. O'Neill (*The Puzzle of 1 John*) is often noted as influential with modern scholars.
2. For example, Haas, de Jonge, and Swellengrebel (156) identify "elders" as eyewitnesses of Jesus other than the apostles, and so sees this author as one of that group.

Aristion and the presbyter John, the disciples of the Lord, say."[3] Some in turn take his reference to a "presbyter John" in addition to the apostle John to raise the possibility of this one they see as a nonapostle being the author of the epistle (Schnackenburg, 298).[4] Yet both internal and external evidence clarify such a possibility as neither required nor likely.

Various scholars have suggested reasons John may have chosen to refer to himself as "the elder" rather than give his name.

(1) It was a title given him and so used by him because of his age. Brown (*Gospel*, lxxxvii–lxxxix) posits that John lived to a very old age. Thus he would be writing this epistle late in his career and would have, in fact, been quite old. Further, this was a title given leaders in the synagogues, Sanhedrin (Matt 26:27, 59; Acts 22:5), and from among the people (Matt 16:21; 21:23; 26:23; Acts 6:12) within first-century Judaism.[5] The same title was applied to the leadership of the church in Jerusalem (Acts 11:30; 15:2, 4, 6, 22)[6] as well as others (Acts 14:23; 20:17; 1 Tim 5:17, 19; Titus 1:5–9; Jas 5:14). Peter, after introducing himself as an apostle in the introduction of his epistle, took the title of elder as well when he wished to address the elders among his readers (1 Pet 4:19). Thus it should not be surprising for John to do the same.

3. Eusebius, *Hist. eccl.* 3.39.4, in P. Schaff, *The Nicene and Post-Nicene Fathers Second Series Vol. I*, 171.

4. As did Eusebius in the following paragraph of his *Hist. eccl.* 3.39.5–6. But, lest his statement be used to dismiss Johannine authorship, his point was that even the "elder" who was not the apostle was an eyewitness of "the Revelation" that John had witnessed. He was not claiming the elder wrote the epistle, only that he was a witness to Christ.

5. The OT refers to elders within the community of Israel, both from among the people and among the priests, as well (Num 11:16; Deut 19:12; Josh 20:4; Ruth 4:2; 1 Kin. 21:8; Ezra 10:14; Prov. 31:23; Isa 3:14; Jer 19:1).

6. In Acts 15 a distinction is made between apostles and elders, though this need not imply an apostle was not considered an elder as well. In their letter (Acts 15:23) they distinguished between the apostles, elders, and brethren (non-leadership members of the church).

(2) Some argue that "elder" was a title taken by the apostles (Stott, 43; Yarbrough, 330).[7] Again, they point to Peter's use of "fellow elder" in 1 Pet 4:19 as evidence of this.

(3) A third approach notes John's avoidance of self-identification in his Gospel and see him doing the same here and in 3 John as well. John's choice to designate himself as "the disciple whom Jesus loved" (John 13:23; 19:26; 20:2; 21:7, 20, 24) appears to be a humble act designed to keep the focus of his Gospel on Jesus rather than himself, and so would be the same motive for assuming the title of "elder" rather than naming and identifying himself as an apostle (Harris, 240). "John's description of himself reinforces the truth that he wrote this epistle; someone impersonating him would likely have chosen the title "apostle," while a writer not trying to impersonate him would not likely have called himself *the* elder" (MacArthur, 216).

Arguments for "elder" referring to someone other than John include:[8]

(1) Diotrephes would not have attacked him if he were an apostle.[9] This argument is weakened by the apostle Paul's experience of his own apostolic authority being challenged by opponents in Corinth (2 Cor 11:13–15) that Paul called false apostles (Marshall, 44). Schnackenburg (298) responds to Marshall by arguing that Paul had to prove his apostleship while John was recognized as an apostle from the beginning. However, Paul's own comments clarifies that his apostleship was not what was being questioned by them, as they had seen the signs of an apostle in his previous visits. Rather, they were denigrating his status among the apostles and challenging his authority.

---

7. Strecker (218–19), though not holding to Johannine apostleship, provides some insight into the significance of the title "elder." He notes that the term was used of presbyters who "would be a community functionary who—as long as the monarchical episcopate has not yet been established—is acknowledged as having an important share of authority in the community based on an official position." He suggests that some might think Diotrephes was a "bishop" that had excommunicated "the elder" from his church, but that no evidence of that can be found in 3 John.
8. Marshall (42–48) provides an excellent discussion of these issues and objections.
9. E. Käsemann, "Ketzer und Zeuge," *ZTK* 48 (1951) 295.

(2) Because the Gospel of John was slow to be recognized as canonical, and the epistle shares such close affinities in writing style to the Gospel, doubts raised to Johannine authorship of the Gospel are applied to the epistle.[10] As Marshall (44, n. 106) observes that gnostic use of the Gospel may explain its slow acceptance and does not disprove Johannine authorship.

(3) The same author could not have written the Epistles and Revelation. Yet external evidence is strong for Johannine authorship of Revelation, witnessed by Justin Martyr, who wrote, "And further, there was a certain man with us, whose name was John, one of the apostles of Christ, who prophesied, by a revelation that was made to him, that those who believed in our Christ would dwell a thousand years in Jerusalem; and that thereafter the general, and, in short, the eternal resurrection and judgment of all men would likewise take place."[11] Marshall (44), though, posits the possibility that second-century writers might have mistaken a "prophet" named John for the apostle.

(4) The author's choice of "elder" is a claim to authority ("a local authority"), but that less than an apostle (Painter, 331). However, as Marshall (42)

---

10. For example, Painter (46) says: "The Gospel and 1 John make no claims to common authorship. While style and language certainly show there is some relationship between the two works, there is not enough evidence to determine that they are by the same author. The similarities are explicable if the two authors were members of the same school or if the evangelist was the founding teacher of the Johannine school, of which the author of 1 John was a member." Thus doubts of authorship for one is automatically applied to the other, even when external evidence speaks to the contrary. Again, Painter (47) writes: "Because the writings themselves do not identify the author of the Gospel or the Epistles, we must turn to external evidence. Certainly the earliest evidence of authorship attributes both the Gospel and 1 John to John the disciple of the Lord. However the earliest evidence is not very early." He notes (48) that Irenaeus identified both the Gospel and Epistle with John. Yet a date of AD 180 at the latest is viewed by him as too late to be convincing.

11. Justin Martyr, *Dialogue*, 81 (in A. Roberts, J. Donaldson and A. C. Coxe, *The Ante-Nicene Fathers Vol. I: Translations of the Writings of the Fathers Down to A.D. 325*, 240.) Painter (339) notes that since Irenaeus and Papias both speak of a plurality of elders in the churches, "it would have been an easy matter to ensure accurate identification by the use of the full identification 'John the Elder.'" Lieu (*The Second and Third Epistles of John*, 63) says, "That Papias's Elders are relevant to an understanding of the author of 2 and 3 John is therefore highly doubtful."

notes, the epistle implicitly makes a claim that his authority extends beyond his local congregation.

External Evidence

The early church fathers identified John the apostle with this epistle. Irenaeus knew of 2 John and accepted it as written by the apostle John.[12] The Muratorian Fragment mentions two epistles of John, which definitely included 1 John, and probably referred to 2 John as the other (Burdick, 413). Origen identifies the presence of three Johannine epistles, but mentions that not everyone agreed on their authorship.[13] Clement of Alexandria also refers to this epistle.[14] Dionysius of Alexandria attributed both 2 and 3 John to the apostle while recognizing that the title "elder" might seem to indicate

---

12. *Haer.* 1.16.3. "And John, the disciple of the Lord, has intensified their condemnation, when he desires us not even to address to them the salutation of 'good-speed;' for, says he, "He that bids them be of good-speed is a partaker with their evil deeds;" and that with reason, 'for there is no good-speed to the ungodly,' saith the LORD." (in A. Roberts, J. Donaldson and A. C. Coxe, *The Ante-Nicene Fathers Vol. I: Translations of the Writings of the Fathers Down to A.D. 325*, 342.)

Haer. 3.16.8. "and His disciple, in his Epistle already mentioned, commands us to avoid them, when he says: 'For many deceivers are entered into the world, who confess not that Jesus Christ is come in the flesh. This is a deceiver and an antichrist. Take heed to them, that ye lose not what ye have wrought.' And again does he say in the Epistle: 'Many false prophets are gone out into the world. Hereby know ye the Spirit of God: Every spirit that confesseth that Jesus Christ is come in the flesh is of God; and every spirit which separates Jesus Christ is not of God, but is of antichrist." (in A. Roberts, J. Donaldson and A. C. Coxe, *The Ante-Nicene Fathers Vol. I: Translations of the Writings of the Fathers Down to A.D. 325*, 443.)

13. *Hist. eccl.* 6.25.9–10. "Why need we speak of him who reclined upon the bosom of Jesus, John, who has left us one Gospel, though he confessed that he might write so many that the world could not contain them? And he wrote also the Apocalypse, but was commanded to keep silence and not to write the words of the seven thunders. He has left also an epistle of very few lines; perhaps also a second and third; but not all consider them genuine, and together they do not contain hundred lines." (P. Schaff, *The Nicene and Post-Nicene Fathers Second Series Vol. I*, 273)

14. *Strom.* 2.15.66. "John, too, manifestly teaches the differences of sins, in his larger Epistle, in these words: 'If any man see his brother sin a sin that is not unto death, he shall ask, and he shall give him life: for these that sin not unto death,' he says. For 'there is a sin unto death: I do not say that one is to pray for it. All unrighteousness is sin; and there is a sin not unto death.'" (A. Roberts, J. Donaldson and A. Coxe, *The Ante-Nicene Fathers Vol. II : Translations of the Writings of the Fathers Down to A.D. 325*, 362)

otherwise.[15] As late as Eusebius and Jerome, debate remained concerning whether the last two epistles were Johannine or from an elder named John.[16] However, following these men, both were fully accepted into the canon of Scripture as from John the apostle. In summary, the earlier acceptance of the epistle as authentically Johannine argues strongly for his authorship even though there was some later hesitation (Guthrie, 884–86).

Internal Evidence

The similarity of language and authorial passions between 1 and 2 John favors Johannine authorship (Smith, 140). His writing style can be seen in all three epistles and the Gospel, as well as Revelation.[17] The issues at the heart of the author are the same as well.

The Second Epistle claims to have been written by "the elder" (2 John 1). That this need not argue against John is evident in that the term as used by him could be "an affectionate title used of and by the venerable author" and as "a descriptive title indicative of both the age and authority of the author" (Guthrie, 886). It may also reflect John's humility in writing. Rather than assuming the authoritative role of the apostolic office he unquestionably filled, he chose a more gentle title that reflected his concern and affection. His use of the title "would convey this same balance of authority and humility" (Akin, 23). Of note is Papias's reference to the apostles as "elders" (quoted earlier).[18] Also, Eusebius, though he mentions John's burial

15. *Hist. eccl.* 7:25.11 "But neither in the reputed second or third epistle of John, though they are very short, does the name John appear; but there is written the anonymous phrase, 'the elder.'" (Philip Schaff, *The Nicene and Post-Nicene Fathers Second Series Vol. I*, 310)

16. Eusebius, *Hist. eccl.* 3.25.3. "Among the disputed writings, which are nevertheless recognized by many, are extant the so-called epistle of James and that of Jude, also the second epistle of Peter, and those that are called the second and third of John, whether they belong to the evangelist or to another person of the same name." (Philip Schaff, *The Nicene and Post-Nicene Fathers Second Series Vol. I*, 156)

17. Schnackenburg (297–98), while rejecting Johannine authorship, recognizes the same author for all three Johannine epistles based on similar issues, terms, and styles of composition.

18. Eusebius, *Hist. eccl.* 3.39. 3–4 (LCL) (Philip Schaff, *The Nicene and Post-Nicene Fathers Second Series Vol. I,* 170) Yarbrough (331) evaluates Eusebius' reference to an elder John who lived after the apostles say, "Eusebius, like others following Origin's amillenarian lead, needed to find a John of early times to whom to attribute the

in Ephesus, is silent about any other "elder" named John being buried there (Kistemaker, 201).[19]

Recipients and Date

John wrote to "the elect lady and her children" (2 John 1).[20] He either may be referring figuratively to a church community (Barker, 361; Boice, 161; Brooke, 167–70; Brown, 652; Bruce, 137–38; Burge, 233; Culpepper, 276; Culy, 141; Dodd, 144; Grayston, 152; Haas, de Jonge, and Swellengrebel, 158; Houlden, 142; Marshall, 60; Smalley, 318; Smith, 139; Stott, 204; Strecker, 220; Williams, 63; Yarbrough, 334)[21] or may be addressing a literal person (Alexander, 283; Hodges, 251; Kistemaker, 208; MacArthur, 216; Moody, 119; Morris, 1271; Plummer, 57–58).[22] Arguments can be made effectively for either the figurative or literal interpretation.[23] Neither set of arguments can prove conclusively either view. Fortunately, the message of the epistle is the same whether it addresses a person or a congregation.

A number of good arguments favor the figurative interpretation (Brooke, 168–69; Marshall, 60).[24] (1) The universal respect for the lady

---

putatively millenarian book of Revelation. Whereas Dionysius seized on the language of Revelation to do this, Eusebius stretched the language of Papias."

19. Eusebius, *Hist. eccl.* 5.24.2–3. "For in Asia also great lights have fallen asleep, which shall rise again on the day of the Lord's coming, when he shall come with glory from heaven, and shall seek out all the saints. Among these are Philip, one of the twelve apostles, who fell asleep in Hierapolis; and his two aged virgin daughters, and another daughter, who lived in the Holy Spirit and now rests at Ephesus; and, moreover, John, who was both a witness and a teacher, who reclined upon the bosom of the Lord, and, being a priest, wore the sacerdotal plate. He fell asleep at Ephesus." (Philip Schaff, *The Nicene and Post-Nicene Fathers Second Series Vol. I*, 242)

20. Brown (652–55) identifies five options (the lady Electa, the noble Kyria, the dear lady, an elect lady, and an elect lady and her children). He chooses the last option.

21. Stott (204) refers to ἐκλεκτῇ κυρίᾳ as a "personification" of a local church.

22. Some commentators choose not to choose either option (Walls and Anders, 236). Westcott (224) considers the question "insoluble" but leans toward a corporate understanding.

23. E. Wendland ("What is Truth?" 306–307) identifies "elect lady" as an example of "accidental ambiguity" in that John's original readers knew to what or whom he referred while modern interpreters cannot be certain.

24. Grayston (152) makes what appears to be a cynical remark. "The elect lady sounds like the self-conscious language of a pietistic in-group."

by "all who know the truth" argues against an individual (Guthrie, 892). (2) The issues addressed appear to reflect those problems faced by a church more so than by an individual. However, if the woman was accustomed to showing hospitality to visiting preachers, it could apply just as readily to an individual situation (Burdick, 416). (3) The plural pronouns of verses 6, 8, 10, and 12 imply a group rather than an individual (Burdick, 416; Burge, 233; Rensberger, 148). However, they make perfect sense if seen addressing a woman and her children. (4) Neither the lady (unless "Electa" is her proper name) nor her children are named directly whereas in 3 John three names appear (Bruce, 137). (5) If *kyria* (κυρίᾳ) were a proper name, "it is in the highest degree unlikely that St John would have written ἐκλεκτῇ κυρίᾳ and not κυρίᾳ τῇ ἐκλεκτῇ as *v.* 13." Both 3 John 1 and Rom 16:1 evidence this construction with proper names (Westcott, 224). (6) Both Paul and John personify the church as a woman in other passages (2 Cor 11:2; Eph 5:25–27, 31, 32; Rev 21:2, 9; 22:17) (Moody, 119). (7) Peter applies the adjective συνεκλεκτὴ to "she who is in Babylon" in 1 Pet 3:15, which should be taken as referring to a church (Moody, 119; Yarbrough, 334). (8) The closing greeting in verse 13 makes better sense when understood as being sent between congregations rather than from relatives to an aunt (Painter, 334; Rensberger, 148). (9) Cities and countries were personified as a woman in Greek and Jewish culture (Bruce, 137). Similarly, both Israel and the church are often described in Scripture as a woman or a bride (Haas, de Jonge, and Swellengrebel, 158; Smalley, 318; Thompson, 151).[25] Jerusalem was considered the "mother" of the nation by Jews (Marshall, 60).[26] (10) The term κυρίᾳ was used in Koine Greek to refer to "a unit of civic organization comprised of multiple assemblies" (Yarbrough, 334). (11) "Early Christians often endured intense persecution in the second half of the first century. For this reason, writers tried to safeguard the recipients by using innocuous names as designations for the church. In the New Testament, the symbolic representation of the church is often a woman" (Kistemaker, 374). (12) The command to love one another fits a congregation better than a home.

---

25. Examples include: Isa 54:1, 6, 13; Jer 6:2; 31:21, 32; John 3:29; Gal 4:25–26; Eph 5:22; Rev 18–19.

26. He notes Isa 54:1–8 and Bar 4:30–37 as an examples of this.

However, individuals need to obey that command outside their homes and so it would still be appropriate to address a family (Burdick, 416).

Other good arguments favor the view that John wrote to a literal woman (Burdick, 416; Edwards, 29; Plummer, 57–58). (1) Since the literal meaning makes sense, one should not make it figurative unless clear warrant is provided by the author (Guthrie, 891). (2) His reference to her as "elect lady" could reflect a title for a respected woman who was well known. (3) "Kyria" is well attested as an epithet in letters (Lieu, 244; Painter, 340). (4) His describing her children as walking in the truth reasonably applies to literal children who have reached adulthood. This makes sense of the greeting from her sister's children in verse 13. (5) The Greek term translated "elect" can be a proper name with "lady" being a title of respect given her by John or others. However, his use of ἐκλεκτῆς as an adjective in verse 13 argues for ἐκλεκτῇ being an adjective rather than a noun as well (Bultmann, 107; Burdick, 415; Harris, 241; Smith, 139). Edwards (29) responds to this that the adjective in verse 13 does not require that ἐκλεκτῇ be an adjective. In Rom 16:13, the epithet "elect" is attached to the name "Rufus" (Ῥοῦφον τὸν ἐκλεκτὸν). However, Paul uses the article with this adjective, whereas it is absent in 2 John (Painter, 340; Yarbrough, 334). (6) We see Paul passing on greetings from others in his epistles (Rom 16:21, 23; 1 Cor 16:19; Phlm 23–25) and so know that what John does in verse 13 would not be unusual and could thereby indicate a literal person. (7) The four plural references could include the woman and her children rather than indicate a congregation (Burdick, 416). (8) It was not unusual in the Roman world for people to have double names, and ἐκλεκτῇ has been found on Roman inscriptions in combination with other names (Edwards, 29). (9) It is possible that ἐκλεκτῆς in v 13 is a name as well and so it happens that two women have the same name and are Christian sisters rather than relatives (Edwards, 20). (10) As noted above, if the woman were accustomed to showing hospitality to visiting preachers, this epistle could apply just as readily to an individual situation as to a local congregation (Burdick, 416). (11) "It is unnatural that such a simple letter should contain such a lengthy and involved figure of speech" (Burdick, 416).

When viewed as a whole, it seems best to see John addressing a congregation in a more literary manner. The one singular segment of the epistle,verses 4 and 5, quickly transitions back to a corporate address (Burge,

231). As circumstances are changing and more false teachers are appearing on the scene, John feels the need to remind this church of its need to be discerning. Painter (334) considers it likely is that the epistle was intended for a group of house churches and this enabled John "to address each of them individually."

No firm date can be postulated for this epistle. Neither the letter nor church fathers provide any clues as to its dating. However, since it appears to assume an understanding of the meaning of "antichrist" in verse 7 that accords with what John said in his First Epistle, it was likely written in close proximity to 1 John, probably very soon afterward (Burdick, 417). Thus a date in the last two decades of the first century seems best, though no firm date can be posited since no indicators were provided within the letter or from church fathers.

Occasion and Setting

Early church writers located John in Ephesus after Jerusalem fell in AD 70. Thus it is likely that this epistle, along with the others, was written while John ministered there.

Little in the epistle or from church history informs us of the reason for John writing this epistle. From his comments it appears he has met some members of the church to which he writes and that he intends to visit them sometime in the near future. The tenor of his exhortations does not indicate a felt threat to which he is responding. Rather, his warnings seem intended to preempt any future problems while acknowledging the presence of false teachers moving among the churches under his care.[27]

From the data of the epistle, the background seems to be that the false teachers John wrote against in his first Epistle were a potential threat to his readers. These false teachers would then likely be Docetists who needed to be guarded against as they presented themselves as legitimate representatives of the church. The *Didache*, a "Christian manual" compiled near the time of these epistles (Bruce, 142) provides us insight into the nature of the threat that John addresses. Rather than seeing him addressing some

27. Burdick (432), who believes the epistle is written to a lady, proposes she had been failing "to use discernment in the exercise of love" and so had hosted false teachers. This letter was serving as a gentle admonition to exercise discernment.

schismatic group that broke from his fellowship (contra Akin, 29; Brown, 108–12; Smalley, xxiii–xxv), we should recognize the presence of false teachers as a common experience of the church as a whole (Rensberger, 21). As in 1 John 2:18–19, these false teachers had departed from the apostolic fellowship doctrinally. John's reference to their departure, though, need not require they be an organized group that had once been associated with even a given local church. As discussed earlier in the introduction to this commentary, the theory of a Johannine school divided by a secessionist movement is a deduction drawn from passages such as 1 John 2:18–19, 2 John 7, and 3 John as a whole. The theory, though, is not substantiated by external evidence.[28] In fact, it seems that the external evidence that does exist points more toward a general state throughout the churches. After discussing various doctrines and church practices such as baptism, the Lord's Supper, and fasting, the *Didache* addresses the issue of false teachers and says,

> So, if anyone should come and teach you all these things that have just been mentioned above, welcome him. But if the teacher himself goes astray and teaches a different teaching that undermines all this, do not listen to him. However, if his teaching contributes to righteousness and knowledge of the Lord, welcome him as you would the Lord. .... Now concerning the apostles and prophets, deal with them as follows in accordance with the rule of the gospel. Let every apostle who comes to you be welcomed as if he were the Lord. But he is not to stay for more than one day, unless there is need, in which case he may stay another. But if he stays three days, he is a false prophet. And when the apostle leaves, he is to take nothing except bread until he finds his next night's lodging. But if he asks for money, he is a false prophet. ... But if anyone should say in the spirit, "Give me money," or anything else, do not listen to him. But if he tells you to give on behalf of others who are in need, let no one judge him. ... Everyone "who comes in the name of the Lord" is to be welcomed. But then examine him, and you will find out—for you will have insight—what is true and what is false. If the one who comes is merely passing through, assist

28. J. M. Lieu, . "Us or You? Persuasion and Identity in 1 John." 805.

> him as much as you can. But he must not stay with you for more than two or, if necessary, three days.[29]

As can be seen from this lengthy quotation, the early church supported traveling ministers and teachers with monetary gifts as well as providing meals and lodging while they ministered in their city. False teachers similarly relied on this practice of hospitality to support their ministries. This was not a Johannine problem but something found throughout the churches. So John's warning addresses the danger of mistaking a false teacher for a legitimate representative of Christ and calls for discernment.

Purpose

John wrote in order to warn his readers to guard against the false teachers who were trying to infiltrate the church.[30] They were posing as legitimate tradition bearers and seeking entrance to local congregations, including the one or group of churches that were to receive this epistle. Painter (331) sees two issues addressed; the antichrist deceivers and a proper christological confession, and the command to love one another. He is addressing the same issue as 1 John (Williams, 11), but now applying its truths in a practical way with regard to false teachers, as opposed to the practical application of loving one another given in 1 John. His warning addresses the problem of misapplying the command to love to the point of supporting false teachers. Practical love has its boundaries and must be exercised wisely, and thus the warnings of this epistle.[31]

---

29. *Did.* 11.1–12.2. (M. Holmes, *The Apostolic Fathers: Greek Texts and English Translations*, Updated ed., 263–65)

30. E. Wendland ("What is Truth?" 316) sees v 7 providing John's purpose for writing. He was writing to communicate the "truth" as it related to both doctrine ("teaching") and "living."

31. John's motivation for writing is *his* love for these saints. This can be seen in the four-fold occurrence of "love" as either a noun or verb in the first six verses.

Genre

This is a standard Greco-Roman letter.[32] It follows the conventions of first-century letter writing with a salutation that identifies both the author and recipient, the letter proper, and then a closing (Akin, 217–18; Culpepper, 276; Painter, 331; Strecker, 218).[33] Bultmann (107) considers it a fictitious letter because it lacks a named author. Smalley (315) rejects this on the basis of its clear connection with the circumstances and issues evident in both 1 and 3 John. Further, the vocabulary is too Johannine to be that of an imitator (Dodd, lxv; Smalley, 316). Also, "the (slight) external evidence suggests that 2 John received earlier recognition than 3 John ... argues against the view that 2 John was a fictitious imitation" (Smalley, 316). Its size is quite typical as well, being the length that would fit on a single papyrus sheet (Painter, 331).

---

32. E. Wendland ("What is Truth?" 329) differs from others and, while still seeing it as a letter, proposes a chiastic structure for the letter with v 8 at its center. The nine-part chiasm is as follows:

A (1–3) salutation—the elect lady and her children
  B (4) thanksgiving—a cause for 'rejoicing'
    C (5–6) prescription—walk together in love and truth
      D (7) characterization—the 'deceivers' and 'antichrists'
        E (8) admonition—do not disobey the 'command' (i.e. love one another/confess the truth) so you don't lose the 'full reward'
      D′ (9) characterization—those 'who do not abide in the teaching of/about Christ'
    C′ (10–11) proscription—do not show love (fellowship) to those who deny the truth/'teaching'
  B′ (12) wish—to effect an occasion for 'rejoicing'
A′ (13) salutation—'the children of our elect sister'

It is highly unlikely that John would have intended this. Though he does use small chiasms, and some larger ones (such as Rev 2–3 and the seven churches), no indication exists that he would have intended anything more than a letter with 2 John. In fact, its very obvious epistolary format, including following the standard conventions of letter writing, argues against a chiasm.

33. R. Funk, "The Form and Structure of II and III John," 427. Burge (231) contrasts 2 John, which he describes as following the format of a personal letter, with 1 John which he describes as "a public theological document."

Relationship to 1 and 3 John

This epistle came from the same pen about the same time as the other two Epistles.[34] Common vocabulary and writing style between all three Epistles indicates common authorship (Brown, 755–56; Bruce, 136; Haas, de Jonge, and Swellengrebel, 155; Painter, 336; Yarbrough, 329). Common authorship between 2 and 3 John is indicated by his choice in both instances to refer to himself as "the elder" (Painter, 331). Shared subjects indicate common authorship between 1 and 2 John. Thus, depending on one's view of the timing of writing, 1 John may be viewed as an expansion of 2 John (Houlden, 140), a summary of the content of 1 John written after it (Haas, de Jonge, and Swellengrebel, 155), or two separate epistles with different recipients, though similar issues.[35] At any rate, the three epistles are integral to each other and reflect a common concern (love and how it is expressed) that moved John to action (both writing and visiting).

Theological and Practical Emphases of the Book

The focus of this epistle is living according to the body of truth delivered to the church and avoiding support of false teaching. In this way it reflects John's concerns in his first epistle, though not delving into them in great detail. While still emphasizing the central place that love for one another plays in the life of the church, this love is to be tempered when those who are not believers attempt to infiltrate the church, bringing with them false teachings about the person of Christ. Christology is integral to the body of truth that is to guide the Christian's life, especially as it relates to Christian fellowship and God's deep desire that we love one another. We see its importance in the church today, and should recognize that our generation must address false teachings and false teachers even as did John's. Tolerating apostates and their antichristian doctrines is neither Christian

34. Marshall (10) sees it written to the same community as 1 John, but at an earlier date. He bases this on the sense that the false teaches still had access to the churches in 2 John whereas he interprets John's words about their departure to indicate they were no longer allowed access.
35. This would be comparable to Paul's writing of Ephesians and Colossians.

love nor an expression of faith in Christ. What one believes about Jesus matters to God and should matter to us.

Outline

I. Greeting (1–3)
II. Walking in Truth (4–11)
III. Closing Remarks (12–13)

Greeting (1–3)

Introduction

As noted above, this short epistle begins with a standard salutation. John writes the "chosen lady and her children" and offers a greeting of grace, mercy, and peace. His reference to those knowing the truth introduces his recipients to the point of the letter and their need to know and guard the truth in their church. Though this is a standard greeting in many ways, it still raises questions that will be explored below. Even so, we are given a glimpse into the heart of John and are enriched by what he says from the very first words of this epistle.

Original Text

1 Ὁ πρεσβύτερος ἐκλεκτῇ κυρίᾳ καὶ τοῖς τέκνοις αὐτῆς, οὓς ἐγὼ ἀγαπῶ ἐν ἀλη-
θείᾳ, καὶ οὐκ ἐγὼ μόνος ἀλλὰ καὶ πάντες οἱ ἐγνωκότες τὴν ἀλήθειαν, **2** διὰ τὴν
ἀλήθειαν τὴν μένουσαν ἐν ἡμῖν, καὶ μεθ' ἡμῶν ἔσται εἰς τὸν αἰῶνα· **3** ἔσται μεθ'
ἡμῶν χάρις ἔλεος εἰρήνη παρὰ θεοῦ πατρὸς καὶ παρὰ a'Ιησοῦ Χριστοῦ τοῦ υἱοῦ
τοῦ πατρὸς ἐν ἀληθείᾳ καὶ ἀγάπῃ.

Textual Notes

3.a. Though the majority of textual evidence supports including *κυρίου* before 'Ιησοῦ, Metzger's argument that copyists were more likely to add *κυρίου* is substantiated by the absence of this construction in John's other writings.[1] Moreover, the message of this epistle does not indicate that such a

1. B. M. Metzger and United Bible Societies, *A Textual Commentary on the Greek New Testament*, 2d ed., 652.

construction would be called for, nor support the development of his message. Further, the attribution Ἰησοῦ Χριστοῦ is used in the Epistle just a few verses later (v. 7). Supporting κυρίου preceding Ἰησοῦ are ℵ K L P 049 056 0142 33 181 330 451 614 630 945 1877 1881 2412 2492 2495 *Byz Lect* l^{1439} syr^{h} cop^{bo} arm. Supporting Ἰησοῦ only are A B Ψ 048 0232 81 88 326 436 629 1505 1739 2127 $it^{ar,c,dem,div,p}$ vg cop^{sa} eth.

Translation

1 The elder,[2] to the elect lady[3] and her children, whom I love in the truth,[4] and not only I, but also all those who have known the truth, **2** because of the truth which abides in us and will be with us forever. **3** Grace, mercy, peace be with us from God the Father and from[5] Jesus Christ, the Son of the Father, in truth and love.

Commentary

1 This greeting is composed of the identification of its author, his addressees, and a statement of his affection as well as that of the church universal. Unlike modern letter writing, wherein the author normally identifies himself or herself at the end of the letter, in ancient letter writing the practice was for the writer to identify himself first, then the recipient, and then extend a greeting. As we examine this letter along with 3 John, we find John uses a rather standard greeting. Nonetheless, it creates one of the most

---

2. This use of πρεσβύτερος includes the article, indicating John is using it as a title and that he was known by this title among his readers.
3. The words ἐκλεκτῇ κυρίᾳ can be translated in three or more ways that include "the lady Electa," "the noble Kyria," "dear lady," or "elect/chosen lady." However, the consensus of translations is that it should be either "elect lady" (ASV; ESV, HCSB, NET, NKJV, NRSV, RSV) or "chosen lady" (ISV, NAB, NASB95, NCV, NET, NIV84, NLT).
4. See the discussion on whether this should be translated "truly," "in truth" (ASV, ESV, NAB, NASB95, NET, NKJV), or "in the truth" (HCSB, ISV, NCV, NIV84, NLT, NRSV, RSV). This latter sense is best for this use of ἐν ἀληθείᾳ in light of the following uses of ἀληθεία.
5. Some of the better MSS include κυρίου before Ἰησοῦ Χριστοῦ. However, the weight of evidence favors leaving it out. Though the NKJV includes it, most others do not. A few mention the option in a note (ISV, NET, NRSV).

challenging of interpretive problems, namely, identifying both its author and recipient(s).

Ὁ πρεσβύτερος ἐκλεκτῇ κυρίᾳ, "The elder, to the elect lady." The first issue is the identity and meaning of the author.[6] "The elder" (ὁ πρεσβύτερος) refers to the apostle John. This is not "'John the Elder,' whose hypothetical existence rests on a misinterpretation of the witness of Papias" (Smalley, 317). His use of the article with "elder" is the single instance in all the NT. It indicates that he was known by this title by his readers (Akin, 219; Haas, de Jonge, and Swellengrebel, 158; Painter, 340; Schnackenburg, 305–306; Smalley, 317). Hodges (252) sees this as "a self-effacing" term intended to mean nothing more than "the elderly one." However, he is saying more than just that he is old. Although the term can refer to an old man, it also refers to an elderly person who deserves respect (Westcott, 223). It was used by the church to designate its leaders (Acts 14:23; 20:17, 28; 1 Pet 5:1).[7] Thus, it alludes to John's authority in the church, though being a gentler claim to authority than referring to himself as an apostle (Akin, 219). Furthermore, because of what and how he is about to write, it indicates he is more than an elder in a local church, but has responsibilities that extend beyond it (Kistemaker, 372–73). Brown (647–48) understands the significance of

6. Brown (648–51) lists five views on the meaning of elder here and in 3 John. (1) He is "an elderly man with dignity and importance." This would explain the paternal tone of the epistle. Against this is the unlikelihood of his using the title alone in a formal letter, especially when there was a conflict over leadership as evidenced in 3 John. (2) He was a member of a group of elders who sent the letter. Though hints of such groups of elders might be found in the New Testament, especially with James in Jerusalem (Acts 15). Against this is, again, the lack of clear evidence. James is a special case because he gained the role based on his being the brother of Jesus. (3) The title was used by the apostles. This is supported by Peter's designation of himself as a "fellow elder." Against this is Papias' use of the term for both apostles and non-apostles. Thus, it would need further clarification to indicate an apostle. (4) This designated a disciple of Jesus (like Matthias) who was not one of the twelve apostles. This interprets Papias' statement about an elder John to refer to such a person. (5) He was "a disciple of the disciples of Jesus and thus a second-generation figure who served as a transmitter of the tradition that came down from the first generation," to which Brown ascribes (651). See his extensive discussion for all the arguments related to each view. I prefer the third view. Peter's self-designation and the testimony of the church fathers is sufficient proof. The search for other answers arises from presuppositions and a commitment to find another author rather than accept its apostolic origin.

7. See the discussion in the introduction.

his self-designation as "the elder" indicating several things: (1) He had the authority to judge whether someone was walking in truth or not. (2) He could speak authoritatively about the apostolic teachings. (3) Further instruction is desired from his readers (thus his coming visit). (4) He can convey greetings between church congregations and so has authority over more than one congregation, as evidenced in 3 John.

The absence of a name and giving only a title is unusual.[8] The practice of letter writing was that the sender identified himself or herself by name and then sometimes added identifying titles. This is also evident in the other New Testament epistles, and Paul's practice of adding such titles as "apostle," (Rom 1:1; 1 Cor 1:1; 2 Cor 1:1; Gal 1:1; Eph 1:1; Col 1:1; 1 Tim 1:1; 2 Tim 1:1; Titus 1:1) "(bond)servant," (Rom 1:1; Phil 1:1; Titus 1:1), and "prisoner" (Phlm).[9] Peter likewise invoked the title of "apostle" (1 Pet 1:1; 2 Pet 1:1) as well as "bondservant" (2 Pet 1:1). James used "bondservant" as well (Jas 1:1). John's choice to leave off his name may have resulted from his reader's practice of referring to him by "elder" rather than "John" (Brown, 647). Smalley (317) correctly adduces that "his position is more important than his name." He is very obviously known by the congregation(s) receiving this epistle. Moreover, what he has to say is not a personal or private matter. He is not speaking for himself, but for the Lord as his representative.

So, then, why does he not invoke his title, and so authority, as an apostle? Kistemaker (373–74) answers this well. "In the second and third epistles apostolicity is not an issue. We assume that his readers knew that he was an apostle. Especially, in the last decades of the first century, his readers knew John as the only surviving apostle. That is, the apostle John had reached advanced age and bore the honorable title *the elder.*" Further, John takes the title of "elder" to communicate his pastoral role in writing this letter (Yarbrough, 333).

Of note is the absence of a verb for writing in this greeting, whether between "elder" and "lady" or in the sentence itself. This is the standard practice for first-century letter writing (Haas, de Jonge, and Swellengrebel,

---

8. Lieu (241) notes the argument that 2 John is a fictional letter based on the absence of proper names (neither the author or his recipient is named) is invalidated by 3 John where names are used and the author still designates himself as "the elder."

9. Paul did not use any titles when writing 1 and 2 Thess.

157). It can be seen in Paul's epistles as well, whether they were addressed to congregations or individuals.[10]

How should ἐκλεκτῇ κυρίᾳ be translated, and is "she" a person or a church?[11] The translation choice will be influenced by one's decision on the identity of the recipient.[12] The arguments for both views have been provided previously in the introduction and so will not be repeated here. It seems best to see this as corporate and so translated "the elect lady."

καὶ τοῖς τέκνοις αὐτῆς οὓς ἐγὼ ἀγαπῶ ἐν ἀληθείᾳ, "and her children whom I love in the truth." With the corporate view, τοῖς τέκνοις αὐτῆς should be understood to refer figuratively to the members of the local congregation, though it could also allude to daughter churches that remain orthodox (Marshall, 60).

The masculine plural relative pronoun οὓς makes this a corporate address with the preposition phrase ἐν ἀληθείᾳ having two possible senses.[13] (1) If taken adverbially, it would mean "truly love" or he loves them "in integrity and sincerity" (Barker, 366, n. 1; Brooke, 170; Bultmann, 108; Schnackenburg, 307).[14] Burge (232) rejects the adverb use of truth (truly love). For John "the truth is not mere sincerity, but a reality belonging to God (1 John 2:4). ... Truth was not only incarnate in Jesus Christ (John 1:17; 14:6), but it also describes the Holy Spirit ('the Spirit of truth,' 14:15–17). Therefore, the community of love is a community 'in truth,' namely, a community that has embraced Jesus Christ (1 John 5:20) and experienced the

10. 1 Cor 1:1–3; 2 Cor 1:1–2; Gal 1:1–4; Eph 1:1–2; Phil 1:1–2; Col 1:1–2; 1 Thess 1:1; 2 Thess 1:1–2; 1 Tim 1:1–2; 2 Tim 1:1–2; Titus 1:1–4; Phlm 1:1–4.

11. Brown (651–55) provides an extensive discussion of the five ways it could be rendered. They include "the lady Electa," "the noble Kyria," "dear lady," "an elect lady," and "an elect lady and her children."

12. Akin (220) identifies this as a term of "endearment and respect." This is true whether John is addressing an actual lady, or a congregation. We saw this same heart attitude in his first epistle. This also sets the tone for all that he has to say in this letter, which is a loving reminder rather than a reprimand of any kind.

13. Although ἐκλεκτῇ κυρίᾳ is feminine and τοῖς τέκνοις αὐτῆς is neuter, the masculine οὓς is appropriate in that it reflects its compound antecedent's dual genders (BDF §134(2); Culy, 142). This same construction can be found in Gal 4:19 (τέκνα μου, οὓς πάλιν ὠδίνω μέχρις οὗ μορφωθῇ Χριστὸς ἐν ὑμῖν·). It also refers to a group of people, some which will certainly be male.

14. Burdick (420) notes that any notion of "romantic love" is removed by John's use of οὓς, the phrase ἐν ἀληθείᾳ, his inclusion of πάντες οἱ ἐγνωκότες τὴν ἀλήθειαν, and his use of the same terms with Gaius (3 John 1).

indwelling power of the Holy Spirit (3:24)." (2) Seen as a dative of sphere, it would communicate the idea of "sphere of truth" (Brown, 656; Burdick, 420; Dodd, 145; Kruse, 205; Marshall, 62; Smalley, 319; Stott, 205).[15]

That John would use this sense is evident from his practice of linking truth with love elsewhere (1 John 2:4; 3:18–19). The articles with the two following references to truth links this use with them, and they clearly refer to a body of truth (Stott, 205). His reference to knowing "the truth" in the following clause indicates that "truth" is a leitmotif* in this section and so he has the body of truth in mind rather the quality of his love (Brown, 656). Further, when he wants to communicate the idea of "truly" he uses the adverb rather than a prepositional phrase (1 John 2:5). This second option is best and John is intentionally using truth with its full theological sense as will be developed in the statements that follow (Perkins, 82).

John uses the present tense *ἀγαπῶ* to emphasize ongoing love for them (Akin, 220–21). Even so, his placement of the verb in the sentence is not emphatic, though *ἐγὼ* is (Smalley, 319). By including his statement about the sphere of truth wherein his love is expressed, he tells us that "truth is the framework, the principle, that guides and gives genuine meaning to his expression of love" (Akin, 221).

καὶ οὐκ ἐγὼ μόνος ἀλλὰ καὶ πάντες οἱ ἐγνωκότες τὴν ἀλήθειαν "and not only I, but also all those who know the truth." John includes all orthodox believers among those who love this church.[16] This statement accords with his theme of loving the brothers in 1 John. Those who have fellowship with God by walking in his moral purity (the light) express their fellowship with God by loving other believers (1 John 4:7–16). John identifies this group as "those who have known the truth" experientially.[17] This use of "truth" refers to the apostolic teachings, doctrine, that is true in contrast to false teachers

15. Rensberger (149) describes John's use of "truth" as "indeed close to becoming merely a slogan for the group with the 'right' teaching in 2 John. Yet it still retains some of its Johannine connotation of the reality of God." John does not think in terms of slogans. This is a description of a reality his readers walk in that is as significant as the "light" of God's moral purity that introduced his first epistle.
16. "Truth is the ground of reciprocal love" (Stott, 205).
17. Some see this referring to the orthodox members of the Johannine community on the basis of their theory of opponents, as with 1 John (Smalley, 319). However, if the heretics have departed (1 John 2:19), it would not make sense for John to be making such distinctions. This should be seen as a simple designation for believers. It is also reminiscent of Jesus' promise in John 8:32, "And you shall know the truth."

and doctrines. John uses the perfect participle ἐγνωκότες, as opposed to a present participle that might have been expected, based on his practice in 1 John. With John a present participle tends to carry a gnomic nuance that indicates character (1 John 2:9–11, 23–24, 29; 3:6, 8, 15, 24, 29; 4:7, 16; 5:1, 10). However, here the perfect points to the state of the person. This is not someone characterized by a present knowledge of truth, but one whose life has been characterized by his or her knowledge of this body of truth. These are people whose lives from the past and into the present have been characterized by orthodoxy. Thus they are people for whom God's truth is very important. In modern terms we might say that they have lived out a biblical worldview and love those who do likewise.

2 This compound preposition phrase involves an apparent anacoluthon in the second clause. This truth is both in and with John and the recipients of his letter.

διὰ τὴν ἀλήθειαν τὴν μένουσαν ἐν ἡμῖν, "because of the truth which abides in us." With διὰ John relates truth back to "love" and provides the reason for that love. That motivating factor is truth. By this he affirms, "Truth is the motivation as well as the context of all Christian love" (Smalley, 320).

John identifies himself with his readers in regard to the truth abiding in them. Having stated the love of the church universal for its orthodox members, John includes himself among his readers as having this body of orthodox truth. Akin (221) sees truth as abiding corporately in the body of Christ (John is not talking individually) and will remain "an abiding reality" for the church (also Smalley, 320). Though ἐν ἡμῖν may be rendered "among us" (dative of sphere), it is better seen as "in us." This "abiding" relationship is another of John's themes reflected in the upper room. This conceptual term communicates the idea of influence more than presence. It is not that they know the truth, but that it is impacting their lives and influencing their decisions.[18] It is the basis of their conduct.

Rensberger (149) relates this "truth" with the indwelling Holy Spirit of John 14:16–17 and the anointing of 1 John 2:27. Bruce (138) says, "It is through 'the Spirit of truth' that he who is Truth incarnate dwells perpetually in and with his people." Painter (338) connects this with the promise of the Spirit in John 14:16, who would remain forever. Harris (242) likewise

18. Stott (206) describes it as "a present indwelling force."

argues that John's use of "resides in us" indicates that "truth" here does not refer to a body of beliefs or doctrines, but "is personalized and is a manifestation of the Spirit/Paraclete who resides permanently with believers." He points to Jesus' promise in John 14:16–17, and argues that the adjectival participle τὴν μένουσαν indicates that John is referring to "a manifestation of the Spirit of truth himself, and is permanently with the believer, just as the Spirit is." Both are following their understanding of the nature and role of the anointing in 1 John 2:27. However, Jesus has used "abide" with regard to his words abiding in the apostles (John 15:7) as well as John speaking of God's Word abiding in believers (1 John 2:14).[19] In both instances it could be understood to include the body of doctrine, the teachings of Christ, that is now referred to as "truth." Thus it need not be made a reference to the Holy Spirit and, in fact, argues against such an interpretation. Here this "truth" is connected to that which Jesus taught and which is now a part of God's revealed will in his word.

καὶ μεθ' ἡμῶν ἔσται εἰς τὸν αἰῶνα, "and will be with us forever." As John looks forward into the future, he sees this body of truth continuing its influence in the lives of believers, not just in this present world, but into eternity (Stott, 206). John's shift from a participle μένουσαν to the finite verb ἔσται serves to focus attention on the continuing influence of God's truth.[20] These truths have not changed to the present and will not change in the future.[21] As Jesus said in Matt 5:18 that "till heaven and earth pass away, one jot or one tittle will by no means pass from the law till all is fulfilled," so too does John here.

---

19. Truth is "influencing" them in the same way eternal life does in 1 John 3:15.

20. BDF §468(3) says that a participle idea may be "continued by a finite verb" as is the case here. Painter (341) sees the verb tenses as more important than the prepositions. "In the changing of prepositions there is no sense of a developing or greater relationship with the truth." Akin (230) sees ἔσται expressing an eschatological nuance.

21. The body of faith, embodied in the NT Scriptures, is permanent and not subject to cultural shifts. When any culture comes into conflict with God's revelation, God's Word always trumps culture. Those faithful to God's word change their practices to match Scripture. They do not reinterpret Scripture to accommodate culture. In light of its revelatory nature, and the fact that when written it stood in direct conflict with Greek and Hebrew culture, when it conflicts with our cultural practices and values, we need to recognize that it is not just inerrant. It is also normative.

3 John offers a greeting of grace, mercy, and peace in truth and love. This first portion is a fairly standard greeting, seen often in Paul as well. However, not every aspect of this greeting is routine.

ἔσται μεθ' ἡμῶν χάρις ἔλεος εἰρήνη, "Grace, mercy, peace be with us." John begins this salutation with the fut. of εἰμί rather than the present, or its ellipsis as is often true with Paul.[22] Its location at the head of the clause, with its subject following makes it emphatic. He is likely using this as a gnomic future, indicating the certainty that he and his readers will experience these three blessings from God, continuing into the future.[23] As a result, this construction makes this a strong assurance rather than a wish (Haas, de Jonge, and Swellengrebel, 160). If John is intending this as purely future, then it is looking forward to the day of judgment. It may then carry the same blessing expressed by Paul with regard to those believers who had not deserted him in his second Roman imprisonment (2 Tim 1:18). However, it seems better to see this blessing as something not only experienced in this life but as an abiding blessing.

Yarbrough (336) notes that these three terms are not common Johannine terms, though they can be found in Paul (1 Tim 1:2; 2 Tim 1:2).[24] Even so, their similarity to Paul's greetings argues for their conventionality, which would explain in part John's choice to use them here. However, it seems he had other reasons to use them as well. "The blessing combines the Greek 'grace' with the Hebrew 'peace,' *Shalom*, joining West and East, Gentile and Jew" (Painter, 342, italics his; Brooke, 171). "Mercy" is added to make it a threefold blessing. The order of blessings moves from God's past action, to their present need, and then future experience (Westcott, 225).[25] Grace is God's unmerited favor. It can also be described as the "effects produced by divine beneficence which go beyond those associated with a

22. Moody (120) feels John uses the future here because of his use of futuristic pres. in v 2.

23. His use of μεθ' ἡμῶν "includes himself with his readers as a recipients of these blessings to reinforce the sense of their community of love" (Kruse, 206).

24. Grace (χάρις) occurs in John 1:14, 16 [x2], 17; Rev 1:4; 22:21. This is the sole occurrence of mercy (ἔλεος). Peace (εἰρήνη) occurs in John 14:27 [x2], 16:33; 20:19, 21, 26; 3 John 15; Rev 1:4; and 6:4,

25. Westcott (225) says also that the "succession" of these three terms "marks the order from the first motion of God to the final satisfaction of man."

specific Christian's status."[26] Mercy is the compassionate response of God in meeting our needs, which includes withholding deserved punishment.[27] Peace is emotional and spiritual well-being.[28] Unlike the Greek concept of an absence of conflict, the biblical concept of peace (derived from the Hebrew) is that of a state of well-being that is a gift from God and is based on being at peace with God as one anticipates future judgment from God.[29]

παρὰ θεοῦ πατρὸς καὶ παρὰ Ἰησοῦ Χριστοῦ τοῦ υἱοῦ τοῦ πατρὸς, "from God the Father and from Jesus Christ, the Son of the Father." The first source of these blessings is God the Father. With the copulative καὶ John joins Jesus with God the Father as an equal source of blessing. This serves as another reminder of Jesus' equality with the Father and his deity. The repetition of παρὰ indicates that these blessings come "from" Jesus in the same manner as from the Father. Further, it "places the Father and Son on an equal standing and at the same time distinguishes their separate personhood" (Akin, 222).

Finally, John identifies Jesus as "the Son of the Father," a phrase unique to him (Bruce, 138; Painter, 342; Westcott, 226). Jesus is most often designated "the Lord," especially in the Pauline letters (Haas, de Jonge, and Swellengrebel, 162). With this description of Jesus, John looks back again on his incarnation and relationship to God the Father in his earthly ministry. It also serves as second affirmation of his deity. John never refers to believers as "sons" or a "son" of God, only as children. He reserves the designation of Son for Jesus alone (Painter, 343).

ἐν ἀληθείᾳ καὶ ἀγάπῃ, "in truth and love."[30] This phrase forms an inclusio* with ἐγὼ ἀγαπῶ ἐν ἀληθείᾳ in verse 1 in order to mark off the greeting (Akin, 223; Brown, 660). Additionally, it introduces the two themes of the epistle (Barker, 362; Moody, 120) and may function as a small "hinge" like we saw repeatedly in 1 John.

The sphere in which these blessings occur is now given—namely, "truth and love."[31] Just as when Jesus told the woman at the well that those worship-

26. BDAG, 1080.
27. BDAG, 316; R. Bultmann, "ἔλεος," *TDNT* 2:483–85.
28. BDAG, 287–88.
29. W. Foerster, "εἰρήνη," *TDNT* 2:400–402, 411–17.
30. This phrase deviates from the usual introductory remarks of first-century letters (Stott, 207).
31. Stott (207) interprets the preposition ἐν more as a dative of means. "This may mean either that we shall experience grace, mercy and peace from Father and Son

pers God seeks worship "in spirit and truth" (ἐν πνεύματι καὶ ἀληθείᾳ), here also blessing occurs not just in the sphere of God's love, but in accordance with his truth. Of note is the order given by John, with truth preceding love. God's blessings, though motivated by his love, are never given without being in accord with his character. God is the God of truth. Further, the two are conjoined in this prepositional phrase, clearly indicating that neither is a separate reality from the other. There can neither be love apart from truth, nor is truth separate from love. "Truth and love describe an intellectual harmony and a moral harmony; and the two correspond with each other according to their subject matter. Love is truth in human action; and truth is love in regard to the order of things" (Westcott, 226).

Application and Devotional Implications

For the church today "the truth" is the Word of God who is true, as revealed in the commands and teachings of Scripture. Just as John rejoiced to see his spiritual "children" living their lives according to God's truths, handed down to them through the apostles, so, too, God is similarly pleased when we live our lives according to his Word. For every Christian whose desire is to please God, the means of fulfilling that desire is to adopt a biblical worldview and lifestyle. To do that requires two things. First, we must commit ourselves to studying God's Word until we know it thoroughly. Passively waiting to be taught by our pastor or other Bible teachers will never result in more than a cursory knowledge of God's Word and will. Second, we must commit ourselves to acting according to what Scripture says, especially when it comes in conflict with our world's values and beliefs. Along with accepting the Scriptures as revelatory truth from our heavenly Father, we must recognize its commands as his will for our conduct. As Jesus made clear in the Upper Room, if we love God we demonstrate it by obeying him. However, we can only obey that part of his will we know about. Waiting for someone else to tell us about it is spiritual laziness. Thus, if we want to "walk in the truth" we have to know it and then decide to do it every hour of every day. There is no other way.

---

only if we remain in truth and love, or that grace, mercy and peace from Father and Son will express themselves, work themselves out in truth and love" (Stott, 207).

Selected Bibliography

Metzger, B. M., and United Bible Societies. *A Textual Commentary on the Greek New Testament.* 2nd ed. New York: United Bible Societies, 1994.

Walking in Truth (4–11)

Original Text

4 Ἐχάρην λίαν ὅτι εὕρηκα ἐκ τῶν τέκνων σου περιπατοῦντας ἐν ἀληθείᾳ, καθὼς
ἐντολὴν ἐλάβομεν παρὰ τοῦ πατρός. 5 καὶ νῦν ἐρωτῶ σε, κυρία, οὐχ ὡς ἐντολὴν
καινὴν γράφων σοι ἀλλὰ ἣν εἴχομεν ἀπ' ἀρχῆς, ἵνα ἀγαπῶμεν ἀλλήλους. 6 καὶ
αὕτη ἐστὶν ἡ ἀγάπη, ἵνα περιπατῶμεν κατὰ τὰς ἐντολὰς αὐτοῦ· αὕτη ἡ ἐντολή
ἐστιν, καθὼς ἠκούσατε ἀπ' ἀρχῆς, ἵνα ἐν αὐτῇ περιπατῆτε. 7 ὅτι πολλοὶ πλάνοι
ἐξῆλθον εἰς τὸν κόσμον, οἱ μὴ ὁμολογοῦντες Ἰησοῦν Χριστὸν ἐρχόμενον ἐν σαρκί·
οὗτός ἐστιν ὁ πλάνος καὶ ὁ ἀντίχριστος. 8 βλέπετε ἑαυτούς, ἵνα μὴ ἀπολέσητε
ἃ εἰργασάμεθαa ἀλλὰ μισθὸν πλήρη ἀπολάβητε. 9 πᾶς ὁ προάγων καὶ μὴ μένων
ἐν τῇ διδαχῇ τοῦ Χριστοῦ θεὸν οὐκ ἔχει· ὁ μένων ἐν τῇ διδαχῇ ατοῦ Χριστοῦ,a
οὗτος καὶ τὸν πατέρα καὶ τὸν υἱὸν ἔχει. 10 εἴ τις ἔρχεται πρὸς ὑμᾶς καὶ ταύτην
τὴν διδαχὴν οὐ φέρει, μὴ λαμβάνετε αὐτὸν εἰς οἰκίαν καὶ χαίρειν αὐτῷ μὴ λέγε-
τε· 11 ὁ λέγων γὰρ αὐτῷ χαίρειν κοινωνεῖ τοῖς ἔργοις αὐτοῦ τοῖς πονηροῖς.

Textual Notes

8.a. Metzger's argument that the second person plural εἰργασάμεθα was introduced by copyists as a "leveling" process with the other verbs, is not convincing.[1] It should be preferred over εἰργάσασθε. If the weight of textual evidence were not so strong, one might argue this. However, the flow of thought does not call for it. Though the second person plural εἰργάσασθε is supported by some of the earlier MSS (א A Ψ 0232 33 81 88 326 436 630 1241 1505 1739 1881 2495 *l*^{1439} it$^{ar,c,(dem),div,(p)}$ vg syr^{ph,h} cop^{bo} arm eth), support for the first person plural εἰργασάμεθα is equally extensive (B K P 049 056

1. B. M. Metzger and United Bible Societies, *A Textual Commentary on the Greek New Testament*, 2d ed., 652.

0142 104 330 451 629 945 1877 2127 *Byz Lect* syr^{h} cop). It is interesting that Metzger favored the second person plural of ἀπολέσητε and ἀπολάβητε while favoring the first person plural εἰργασάμεθα, though the textual evidence was much the same with both sets of variants. The best option is to see the apostle's concern, not for his reward, which would be selfish, but for that of his audience. The second person plural is supported by the division of witnesses between the use of the second person plurals ἀπολέσητε and ἀπολάβητε as opposed to the 1 pls. ἀπολέσωμεν and ἀπολάβωμεν. The 2 pls. are supported by much the same witnesses as εἰργάσασθε (א A B Ψ 0232 33 81 88 181 326 436 614 630 1241 1505 1739 1881 2412 2492 2495 *l*^{1439} it^{ar,c,dem,div,p} vg syr^{ph,h} cop^{sa,bo} arm eth) while the first person plurals are supported by those choosing εἰργασάμεθα (K P 049 056 0142 104 330 451 629 945 1877 2127 *Byz Lect*).

9.a…a Though the earlier Alexandrian MSS do not favor τοῦ Χριστοῦ after the second διδαχῇ, it is divided and the majority of other MS families favor the reading (against: א A B Ψ 33 81 1739 1881 it^{c} vg syr^{h} cop^{sa} arm; in favor: K L P 049 056 0142 88 104 181 326 330 436 451 614 629 630 945 1241 1505 1877 2127 2412 2492 2495 *Byz Lect l*^{1439} it^{ar} cop^{bo} eth). The more difficult reading need not be chosen and so τοῦ Χριστοῦ is included, *contra* Metzger.[2] This would fit John's pattern of repetition for emphasis.

Translation

4 I rejoiced greatly because I found some of your children walking in truth, just as we received a command from the Father. **5** And now I ask[3] you, lady, not as writing a new commandment[4] to you, but one[5] which we had from the beginning, that we should love one another. **6** And this is love, that we

---

2. B. M. Metzger and United Bible Societies, *A Textual Commentary on the Greek New Testament*, 2d ed., 653.

3. Those that translated with "ask" include ESV, NAB, NASB95, NCV, NET, NIV84, and NRSV. Other translations include "plead" (NKJV), "beg" (RSV), "requesting" (ISV), "urge" (HCSB), "I am writing to remind you" (NLT)

4. John 13:34; 1 John 2:7–8.

5. "One" is not in the Greek text but has been added in order to make the English translation express the idea contained in the relative pronoun ἣν translated by "which" (ESV, ISV, HCSB, NAB, NASB95, NET, NIV84, NLT, NRSV, RSV). Other translations use "that which" (NKJV) or "the same command" (NCV).

should walk according to his commandments; this is the commandment, just as you heard from the beginning, that you should walk in it. **7** For[6] many deceivers have gone out into the world,[7] those who do not confess Jesus Christ as coming in the flesh;[8] this is the deceiver and the antichrist.[9] **8** Watch out for yourselves, that you may not lose those things which you[10] worked for, but that you may receive a full reward. **9** Everyone who goes ahead[11] and does not abide in the teaching of Christ does not have God; he who abides in the teaching[12] of Christ, this one also has the Father and the Son.[13] **10** If anyone comes to you and does not bear this teaching, do not

---

6. This translation reflects the conjunctive role of ὅτι at the head of this sentence. Though some translations include it (ASV, ESV, ISV, NASB95, NET, NKJV, RSV), others have chosen to leave it out (HCSB, NAB, NCV, NIV84, NLT, NRSV).

7. 1 John 2:18–19.

8. Though many (ISV, NAB, NASB95, NIV84, NKJV) have "Jesus Christ *as* coming in the flesh," others vary. For example HCSB says "the coming of Jesus Christ in the flesh," NET translates it as "Jesus as Christ coming in the flesh," ESV has "the coming of Jesus Christ in the flesh," NRSV has "Jesus Christ has come in the flesh," NCV has "Jesus Christ came to earth as a human," and NLT has "Jesus Christ came in a real body."

9. 1 John 2:18, 22.

10. The second pers. pl. εἰργάσασθε ("you worked for," NCV, NIV84, RSV) was chosen over the first pers. pl. εἰργασάμεθα ("we worked for," ASV, ESV, HCSB, ISV, NAB, NASB95, NET, NKJV, NLT, NRSV) based on the overwhelming weight of textual evidence.

11. The difficulty of translating προάγων is apparent in the variety of renderings. These include: "transgresses" (NKJV), "goes too far" (NASB95), "goes beyond" (HCSB, ISV, NCV, NRSV), "is so progressive" (NAB), "runs ahead" (NIV84), "goes on ahead" (ESV, NET, RSV), and "wanders away from" (NLT). The choice of "goes ahead" is an attempt once more to remain as literal as possible without sacrificing understanding for the English reader. That it is explained in what follows is very helpful. Otherwise a less literal rendering would have been necessary to communicate the idea contained in the participle

12. This second "of Christ" (τοῦ Χριστοῦ) is omitted by many (ASV, ESV, HCSB, NAB, NASB95, NET, NIV84, NRSV, RSV) based in part on its omission from some significant Alexandrian texts. However, the Alexandrian is divided, and other MS families favor it. This is reflected in the ISV, NCV, NKJV, and NLT which include it.

13. John 5:23; 1 John 2:22–23; 4:15.

receive him into *your*[14] house and do not say, 'Greetings!' [15] to him. **11** For the one speaking a greeting to him participates[16] in his evil works.

Commentary

John now introduces the body of his letter with words of encouragement, his own. What he is going to say in the verses that follow is that walking in truth means walking according to God's commandments and involves loving the brethren while rejecting deceivers.

Some see verse 4 belonging to the opening of the epistle (Marshall, 81; Mitchell, 176; Rensberger, 147) rather than its body (Barker, 362; Brooke, 171; Bultmann, 110; Houlden, 139; Johnson, 152; Lieu, 39–40; Lenski, 560; Schnackenburg, 310; Smith, 142; Stott, 208; Strecker, 228; Thompson, 152; Williamson, 188; Yarbrough, 339). Others place it as a transitional verse between the greeting and message (Brown, 682; Bruce, 134; Burdick, 418). It is seen by some to be equivalent to Paul's thanksgiving portion of his salutation (Burdick, 422; Marshall, 65; Stott, 208; Yarbrough, 339–40). John's use of ἐρωτάω was a "common way to begin the body of a letter" (Rensberger, 150), and so it seems more appropriate to place it with the body.

---

14. Though the text only has an anarthrous noun after the participle, "your" is understood from the context and so should be supplied (ASV, NASB95). Some versions do not italicize it (ESV, HCSB, ISV, NAB, NCV, NET, NIV84, NKJV, NLT). Others say "into the house," which reflects an understanding of the object of the preposition being definite (NRSV, RSV).

15. I have chosen to follow John as literally as possible and so translated this difficult statement with: "do not say, 'Greetings!' to him." The infinitive χαίρειν was the word used in greetings when friends met (H. Conzelmann, "χαίρω," *TDNT* 9:367). This is difficult to translate into English. Thus the point of the command is used by most translations instead of attempting to achieve the actual statement because of its difficult rendering and the possible problem of being misunderstood. The difficulty of translating this idiomatic statement is reflected in the wide range of renderings. These include: "nor greet him" (NKJV), "or even greet him" (ISV, NAB), "do not give him a greeting" (NASB95), "or welcome him" (NIV84, NRSV), "do not welcome" (NCV), "don't say 'welcome' to him" (HCSB), "do not give him any greeting" (NET), "or give him any greeting" (ESV, RSV), "or give any kind of encouragement" (NLT), and "give him no greeting" (ASV).

16. This is the sole use by John of the verb κοινωνέω to communicate participating. It shares the same root with κοινωνία (fellowship) which occurs only four times in 1 John 1:3 (twice), 6, and 7. Thus neither are typical Johannine terms.

4 This sentence is composed of the main statement and a complex subordinate clause with key terms repeated from the introduction. John constructs it in such a way as to draw attention to his theme of walking in truth.

Ἐχάρην λίαν ὅτι εὕρηκα ἐκ τῶν τέκνων σου περιπατοῦντας ἐν ἀληθείᾳ, "I rejoiced greatly because I found some of your children walking in truth." This expression of joy follows the pattern of first-century letters (Barker, 362; Brooke, 171; Moody, 121) and can be seen in many of Paul's Epistles (Rom 1:8; 1 Cor 1:4; Phil 1:3; Col 1:3; 1 Thess 1:2; 2 Thess 1:3). It serves as "a common epistolary device for moving the letter from the opening formalities into its actual substance or body" (Lieu, 248–49). Though it may be a conventional greeting,[17] it still reflects his sincere emotional response.

John begins by expressing his joy and then providing the reason for it. He makes use of the iterative (Lenski, 561) aorist ἐχάρην to communicate the fact that he continues to experience joy each time he remembers they are walking in truth. Further, his joy is more than satisfaction. To insure his readers understand that, he adds λίαν to describe the intensity of his joy.[18] This serves to emphasize the importance of supporting the truth and avoiding false teachers. The reason for his joy is then given in the following ὅτι clause.

He has seen firsthand (εὕρηκα) the conduct that has led to his joy. His choice of the perfect εὕρηκα indicates he learned it earlier and believes that they continue to walk in truth (Akin, 223; Haas, de Jonge, and Swellengrebel, 163). It is this continued faithfulness that serves as the cause of his joy.

With the partitive preposition ἐκ, he notes that he has seen people from their membership walking in the sphere of truth (Bruce, 139). This use of ἐκ need not indicate that some were not (Barker, 362; Brooke, 172; Haas, de Jonge, and Swellengrebel, 164; Houlden, 143; Kruse, 207),[19] but only tells us that he had not especially seen every member of the church (Bruce, 139; Culy, 144; Harris, 243; Marshall, 65; Stott, 208).[20] What he is saying is

---

17. R. W. Funk, "The Form and Structure of II and III John, 427.
18. This and 3 John 3 are the only occurrences of ἐχάρην λίαν in the New Testament. As Bultmann (110) notes, Paul normally uses either εὐχαριστῶ or εὐλογητὸς in his greetings. Thus the absence can be better explained in terms of writing styles.
19. Brooke and Houlden believe that the majority of the church had followed the false teachers and so see in this a negative situation.
20. Brooke (172) considers it "probable" that the majority of the church addressed had been led astray by the false teachers. However, nothing in the text requires this.

that of those he has seen, they are walking in truth, rather than necessarily indicating that he has seen some who are not.

Some see this as a mild or implied rebuke to those not living in the truth (Barker, 363; Dodd, 147; Houlden, 144; Grayston, 153; Smalley, 323) and that it indicates that some had left (Williamson, 188). Moody (121) sees this as a "note of sadness" and interprets to be indicating John was thinking about those who had departed with the false teachers. Bultmann (111) says those "not walking in the truth" are the "gnosticizing heretics." However, as Brown (661) notes, it is not likely John would have called those who had left the community of faith "your children." He has described them in 1 John as antichrists, and he will do so again in this epistle.

Akin (223) rightly sees this as positive, and nothing negative is implied based on the "positive nature" of the verse and the introduction. Since the pattern of letters is to have a "joy" statement (which Paul often turned into a thanksgiving), it would seem John's focus is on those who are walking, not those who may have left. In fact, his use of the present participle περιπατοῦντας indicates that they are continuing to walk in the truth (Painter, 347), and that it is their continued walk that causes him joy.

John uses the dative of sphere when saying they are "walking in truth" to describe this conduct in the same manner as he had described walking in the light in 1 John 1–2. Though ἀληθείᾳ is anarthrous, its presence with the preposition still makes it definite and a clear reference to the body of truth to which he has already referred (Barker, 363; Lieu, 249).[21] Thus they are not walking truthfully (*contra* Bultmann, 110), but in the realm or sphere of God's truth.[22] "'Walking in the truth' indicates that truth is both what we believe and how we live. It is doctrine and duty, creed and conduct" (Akin,

---

His assessment ignores the positive nature of the salutation and its role in setting the stage for what follows.

21. D. B. Wallace, *Grammar*, 247.

22. Bultmann (110) rejects this as a reference to a body of truth because it lacks the article, and so must be understood to mean "really, in an authentic way." The following καθὼς clause then explains what he means. However, John's use of περιπατοῦντας with ἐν ἀληθείᾳ argues against this. A prepositional phrase need not have the article for the object of the preposition to be definite (Wallace, *Grammar*, 247). The context of the discussion clarifies that he means more than "really." For example, Strecker (228) says the article can be inferred and so it refers to the body of truth and is connected to v 6 where "walking in truth" is clearly "walking according to God's commandments."

225).[23] We can only walk with God according to his Word and based on its teachings. Thus walking in truth can be described as a "habitual commitment (περιπατοῦντας is a present participle) on the part of orthodox believers to the Christian gospel and its moral standards" (Smalley, 323).[24] To have a vital, healthy fellowship with God, we must walk in his truth.

Wendland proposes a conceptual range of the term "truth" within the Johannine writings to include (1) corresponding to facts (John 4:18), (2) reliable or trustworthy (2 John 1; 3 John 1), (3) genuine as opposed to counterfeit (John 4:23–24; 6:55; 15:1), (4) revelation (John 8:32; 14:17; 1 John 4:6), (5) valid, attested (John 5:31–32; 14:6), (6) a body of valid doctrines that may also be called "the faith" (2 John 4; 3 John 3).[25] He sees John infusing it with "love, command, fellowship, and teaching—in order to create a *thematic composite* that communicates on a deeper, more comprehensive and cohesive level than the distinct constituent units would do individually and in simple sequence."[26] It would seem better to see John using "truth" in a variety of ways as its range of meaning allows rather than seeking a unified sense throughout his literature. Here, though, and in this epistle, John's focus is on Wendland's sixth category, that body of doctrines by which we live our lives.[27] As will be seen in the next verse, this truth they were to walk in was God's commandment to "love one another."

---

23. Perkins (83) describes it as "the teaching of the community."
24. Williamson (188) describes walking in truth as "walking in the character of God" and sees it equivalent to walking in the light in 1 John.
25. E. R. Wendland, "What is Truth?" 312. Paul referred to them as "traditions" received from him (the apostles) as well (1 Cor 11:2; 2 Thess 2:15; 3:6), and so represent a body of instructions on Christian living.
26. E. R. Wendland, "What is Truth?" 320.
27. R. R. Nicole ("The Biblical Concept of Truth," 295, italics his) provides an excellent survey of the NT use of truth as a doctrinal basis for living: "The close connection between Satan, darkness, and lying on one hand, and between God, light, and truth on the other hand (cf., e.g., 1 John 1:5–10) is probably the basis for a use of the word *truth* as connoting not merely conformity to fact, but that pattern of living that conforms to the revealed will of God. … Thus in 1 John 1:6 'to live by the truth' (literally 'to do the truth') is the opposite of 'to walk in darkness.' The same contrast is found in John 3:20–21. Some passages speak of 'obeying' (Gal. 5:7; 1 Peter 1:22) or 'disobeying' (Rom. 2:8) the truth. James represents a wayward Christian as 'wandering from the truth' (James 5:19). The 'way of truth' in 2 Peter 2:2 corresponds to 'walking in the truth' (2 John 4; 3 John 3–4). Perhaps the 'belt

καθὼς ἐντολὴν ἐλάβομεν παρὰ τοῦ πατρός, "just as we received a command from the Father." In this clause John clarifies that the truth in which believers walk accords with God's commandment, which will be defined in the following sentence. This is a command received in the past (thus the aorist) and which will be described further in the sentence that follows (Haas, de Jonge, and Swellengrebel, 164). He begins this final clause with καθὼς, indicating that the walk he is describing was based on the commandment (sg.) of God. Thus, "walking in truth" means living in conformity to God's command, particularly to love one another (Hodges, 256). Additionally, καθὼς "suggests that there was a close correspondence between the children's lives and the divine command" (Burdick, 422) which was the reason for his rejoicing greatly. John uses the same term as in 1 John 3:23 for the commandment that comes from God the Father. That commandment will now be repeated.[28]

5 This sentence moves to the body of John's letter and the nature of his appeal. It is composed of a simple statement and its subordinate purpose clause separated by a parenthetical statement that connects it to Jesus' words in the upper room (John 13:34–35) as well as his First Epistle (1 John 2:7). Akin (226) and Yarbrough (341) see this verse and the one following forming a chiasm. It is composed of four parts:

A command (5b)

B love (5d)

B′ love (6a)

A′ commands (6b)

These short chiasms were common in first-century literature and may be more prevalent in New Testament literature than thought earlier.[29] Though

of truth,' mentioned in Ephesians 6:14 as a part of the Christian equipment for spiritual struggle, also fits into this category."

28. Bultmann (110–11) sees this as "the love commandment." Painter (347) also sees this as the command to love one another that Jesus spoke, and so solves the problem of John's reference to the Father by concluding it should be viewed as "the commandment of the Father delivered by Jesus."

29. N. W. Lund, *Chiasmus in the New Testament,* 33, 35. Lund (40–41) proposes seven "laws" of chiastic structures. "(1) *The centre is always the turning point.* ... (2) At the centre there is often a change in the trend of thought, and an antithetic

larger chiasms were more common in Hebrew literature than Greek, both cultures utilized the small chiasm for rhetorical purposes.[30]

καὶ νῦν ἐρωτῶ σε, κυρία, "And now I ask you, lady." John moves to the topic at hand with the conjunction καὶ νῦν. This may be understood as having "a slight adversative force" and so serves as a reminder (Harris 244). Others see it as simply temporal (Brooke, 173; Lenski, 563). It clearly communicates that he is now addressing the issue at hand. Though ἐρωτάω can mean to ask a question, in this instance its second sense, to request something, is intended.[31] It is a "personal request and entreaty" (Painter, 346), at most an indirect command.[32] Lieu (249) says the "author continues to tread carefully" by his use of first person plural verbs that "soften the authoritative request." However, rather than seeing him "tread carefully," it is better to see John speaking lovingly. Lenski (563) describes it well. John's choice of ἐρωτάω expresses both "dignity and due formality." By this choice of words,

---

idea is introduced. After this the original trend is resumed and continued until the system is concluded. ...*the law of the shift at the centre.* (3) Identical ideas are often distributed in such a fashion that *they occur in the extremes and at the centre* of their respective system, and nowhere else in the system. (4) There are also many instances of ideas, occurring at the centre of one system and recurring in the extremes of a corresponding system, the second system evidently having been constructed to match the first. ...*the law of the shift from centre to the extremes.* (5) There is a definite tendency of certain terms to gravitate toward certain positions within a given system... ... (6) Larger units are frequently introduced and concluded by *frame-passages.* (7) There is frequently a mixture of chiastic and alternating lines within one and the same unit."

30. R. E. Mann, "The Value of Chiasm for New Testament Interpretation," 146. D. A. Dorsey (*The Literary Structure of the Old Testament: A Commentary on Genesis-Malachi*) has provided an extended treatment of OT chiasms, arguing for their presence throughout the OT. Many of his proposed chiasms are convincing, though some are not.

31. BDAG, 395; H. Greeven, "ἐρωτάω," *TDNT* 2:685–87. Some (Haas, de Jonge, and Swellengrebel, 165; Smalley, 324) see his use of ἐρωτάω as part of a "common" formula indicating John is beginning the body of his letter. However, as discussed above, I feel he begins the body with v. 4 and this moves from the theme to the issue he is addressing.

32. B. M. Fanning, *Verbal Aspect in New Testament Greek*, 383. He notes that with indirect commands "the *aspectual* distinction is the primary difference between present and aorist forms and the most frequent secondary distinction is the general vs. specific difference." Thus John's point is that he is asking through his letter and is extending this request to his readers.

John softens a command into a request and turns to the reason for his writing (Brown, 663).[33]

Though κυρία can function here as a proper name, it still seems best to see this as a reference to a congregation rather than an individual.[34] As a title of respect in Greek society, John uses it here to communicate a similar respect for the congregation he addresses. Following this singular address, the remainder of John's instruction will address a plural audience until the final verse of the epistle.

οὐχ ὡς ἐντολὴν καινὴν γράφων σοι ἀλλὰ ἣν εἴχομεν ἀπ' ἀρχῆς, "not as writing a new commandment to you, but which we had from the beginning."[35] John clarifies the nature of his request, identifying it now as a commandment. Using the same words as Jesus in the upper room (John 13:34–35), he identifies this command, not with himself but with the Lord Jesus. Though he calls it "new," he will clarify what he means in the next clause.

Beginning with the strong adversative ἀλλὰ, John switches from the singular "you" to the first person plural ("we") of ἔχω. He reminds his readers that this "new commandment" is not new at all.[36] He and they have had it all along, "from the beginning." As in 1 John, this could refer either to the beginning of Jesus' ministry (Harris, 244), or to the beginning of their Christian experience (Brown, 664; Smalley, 325). By including himself with his readers John reminds them that he, like they, is a recipient of the same command (Brooke, 173). Furthermore, since this command was given near the end of Jesus' earthly ministry, it seems best to take "the beginning" to refer to that point in time each of them came to faith and began to receive

---

33. Brown (664) cautions against reading this as begging. It is better to see it as a request between equals. Burdick (423) concurs and prefers "I ask" over "I beg" or "I urge." Though he chooses not to command, John's designation of himself as "the elder" clarifies that he is not speaking from a position of weakness, which would involve begging, but from the strength of a position of love and respect, a love and respect he reciprocates.

34. B. M. Metzger and United Bible Societies, *A Textual Commentary on the Greek New Testament*, 2nd ed., 652.

35. Culy (145) observes that some take ὡς as introducing a parenthetical statement (Haas, de Jonge, and Swellengrebel, 165), but rejects the idea. I concur with Culy. Though it may at times do so, in this case it would break up the thrust of what John is saying.

36. Harris (244) sees "not new" as contrasting John with his opponents who are innovators.

instruction in the faith (Perkins, 84).[37] Burge (235) understands "what was from the beginning" to be "John's appeal to the past, his way of urging that creative theological insights never destroy the groundwork of what we already know about Christ in the Scriptures."

ἵνα ἀγαπῶμεν ἀλλήλους, "that we should love one another." The content of the new commandment is now given once more.[38] The ἵνα is epexegetical, giving the content of the request (Brown, 664; Harris, 244), not causal referring back to ἐντολή (*contra* Brooke, 173; Culy, 145).[39] Using the hortatory subjunctive ἀγαπῶμεν, John includes himself once more with his readers as recipients of the command to love one another.[40] Our walk with God only occurs on the basis of his commandment to love one another, expressed in such places as here and John 13:34–35. This is also parallel to 1 John 2:7 (Bultmann, 111; Burdick, 423; Harris, 244) and repeats the love commandment of John 13:35 (Strecker, 228). After quoting him three times in the Gospel (John 13:34; 15:12, 17), John adds his the sixth repetition of Jesus' command in his epistles (1 John 3:11, 23; 4:7, 11, 12). From this we see that John caught just how important this was to Jesus, and how central it must be to the Christian life.

6 This is another complex sentence, composed of two main statements, each with its own subordinate clause clarifying its meaning. Having reminded his readers that we all are to love one another, John discusses love's expression from the divine perspective. Stott (210) sees this and the following

37. Akin (226) points to Jesus' instructions in the upper room and relates the beginning to that.

38. Strecker (228) interprets the absence of "brothers" in this statement to indicate it is "a less developed version" of the love commandment than that found in 1 John and so 2 John represents an earlier tradition. However, this need not be the case, and is more likely a case of reading too much into the text. Rather, this may only be seen to indicate John is alluding back to the upper room as opposed to 1 John. However, that is not sufficient reason to prove, or even indicate, that one epistle was written prior to the other, or that any significant time separated their writings.

39. Lenski (563) calls this an "accusative appositional clause."

40. Burdick (423–34) considers the first person pl. to indicate John was addressing a single person, the "elect lady," rather than a congregation. However, he consistently used this same first person pl. with similar hortatory commands in 1 John which clearly included a congregation with John, not only individuals. Further, his movement to plural addressees in the body of this epistle argues for more than a single addressee here.

verses alluding to the "three tests (truth, love, and obedience)" from 1 John and says, "The Christian life is here viewed from the standpoint of commands." We do see that walking with God and experiencing his life in this life is integrally connected to a life of obedience. Emphasizing obedience is not legalism. Legalism is adding our own rules on top of God's commands and defining righteousness in terms of man-made religion (Col 2:16–23).

καὶ αὕτη ἐστὶν ἡ ἀγάπη, ἵνα περιπατῶμεν κατὰ τὰς ἐντολὰς αὐτοῦ·, "And this is love, that we should walk according to his commandments." John connects these thoughts with the previous sentence by means of the coordinate conjunctive *καὶ* (Culy, 146). The command to love one another calls for further clarification. However, since he has "requested" rather than commanded compliance, John continues the gentle imperative by explaining why the command to love one another is worthy of obedience. Love is now to be defined further.

This first *αὕτη* either refers to *ἡ ἀγάπη* (Harris, 245) or is cataphoric* and points to the *ἵνα* clause (Culy, 146) which is appositional to *ἡ ἀγάπη* rather than epexegetical to *αὕτη* (Brown, 665; Lenski, 565). Its role in this first clause might not be viewed as emphatic since its grammatical function is to clarify that the articular *ἀγάπη* is the predicate nominative, which will then be explained by the following *ἵνα* clause.[41] However, the repetition of *αὕτη* in this and the following clause does make it emphatic. This "love" is still the same love for one another in verse 5 (Rensberger, 152). Additionally, it seems to "echo" 1 John 5:3 (Lieu, 250). However, where he uses "keep" in 1 John, now he uses "walk."

John begins by describing love in terms of one's walk. However, is this referring to our love for one another (Brown, 665; Marshall, 67), or both love from God and love for others (Akin, 226–27; Barker, 363; Haas, de Jonge, and Swellengrebel, 166; Smalley, 326; Stott, 210). He is decidedly

---

41. Bultmann (111) calls this *ἵνα* clause "strangely pedantic and unnecessary." It would be if John were not stressing the importance of keeping God's commandments, especially His command to love one another. Repetition is a powerful literary device that is characteristic of John. The importance of what he has to say makes this clause anything but pedantic and certainly indicates its necessity. John had very limited space in which to write his thoughts. He knew how little he could say on a single parchment of papyrus. He would not have included this if it were not so important and needed to be emphasized.

ambiguous and most probably intended to mean both. This love is defined by him, though, in terms of God's expectations for one's daily conduct of life.

Love *is* walking according to God's commandments.[42] John describes this "walking" with the first person plural περιπατῶμεν.[43] Lieu (241) correctly sees his use of "we" to be different from many of those in 1 John, thus not the apostolic circle. Whereas in 1 John the contrast was often between the apostolic circle that included John, for example, "us" and "they" in 1 John 2:19, in this verse the false teachers are not in view but Jesus' love command. Rather, this verse has the same thrust as 1 John 4:7–11 wherein John again included himself with his readers. Painter (346) suggests that the "we" in the verb may not include the readers, but others with "the elder." However, this would be alluding, at least, to a contrast between John and his readers, which is not indicated anywhere in the text. Thus it is best to see it including John and his readers. The preposition κατὰ in this instance focuses attention on the standard of conduct to which the readers are expected to conform.[44] The plural "commandments" have all of God's expressed will in Scripture in view, not just the command to love one another (Yarbrough, 342). In this instance John may be using a double meaning in that God's love for us is expressed in his provision of these commands for our benefit while our love for him is expressed in living according to them (Harris, 245). This communicates the idea of 1 John 2:5, God's love is perfected in the obedient Christian. It reflects John 5:3, God's love for us is expressed in his provision of commandments that are not burdens but beneficial. John 15:3 echoes in these words as well. We abide in Jesus' love the same way he abided in his Father's love—through obedience. Thus we see that God's

---

42. Walking in God's commandments and walking in truth are also parallel ideas (Haas, de Jonge, and Swellengrebel, 166) and should be recognized as integral and interdependent for the expression of any of them. One does not happen without the others occurring simultaneously.

43. Present tense περιπατῶμεν is viewed by Akin (227) to indicate "consistency of life." This is a case of reading too much into the pres. It certainly has to do with conduct of life but would be better seen from a gnomic sense. Our lives are to be characterized by obedience. Akin's choice seems motivated by his rubric of perseverance as proof of life that guided his interpretation of 1 John. If consistency is indicated, it should be seen in the nature of the verb itself (BDAG, 803; H. Seesemann, "πατέω, ... περιπατέω," TDNT 5:945), not its tense.

44. BDAG, 512.

love is the motivation for his desire for our obedience. He has revealed his will in the commandments of Scripture in order that we can experience his love through obedience. Moreover, as revealed in 1 John 2:3–11, we obey him by actively loving other believers. "In Johannine thought there is no love of God without love of others, and no love of others without love of God; and neither exists apart from obedience to God's command to love" (Thompson, 152).

αὕτη ἡ ἐντολή ἐστιν, καθὼς ἠκούσατε ἀπ' ἀρχῆς, ἵνα ἐν αὐτῇ περιπατῆτε, "this is the commandment, just as you heard from the beginning, that you should walk in it."[45] This is a challenging series of final clauses that is understood in a variety of ways.[46] What must be determined is the relationship of each of the clauses to one another as well as the previous portion of this long sentence.

John repeats the pronoun αὕτη once again but changes the placement of ἐστιν in order to emphasize "commandment."[47] By his repetition of αὕτη and changing of words he connects "love" and "commandment" in reverse order (Westcott, 228). He also switches from the first person plural, περιπατῶμεν to second person plural, ἠκούσατε and περιπατῆτε. Thus John moves from including himself to applying that truth to his readers. Further, "commandment" is singular whereas the "commandments" we are to walk in are plural This change serves to show the overarching relationship of the command to love one another with all other commands. As Jesus said that all of the law was contained in the two commands—to love God and to love one's neighbor—so too, John posits all commands under the umbrella of loving other believers. This shows the heart of God and the importance of this command in the life of every believer.

45. This is the fourth use of "command" since the letter began. By this repetition John is emphasizing that his message is God's will, not his opinion (Barker, 363).

46. Bultmann (111) calls this "superfluous" with the final ἵνα clause being "completely redundant." He obviously is unaware of the power and significance of repetition (redundancy as a literary device). As noted in my response to his earlier denigration of John's chosen communication style, John clearly must intend for his readers to notice the seemingly redundant or circular argument and thereby to recognize the significance of what John is emphasizing thereby.

47. Rensberger (151) sees the referent of αὕτη ἐστὶν to be the love commandment in v 5. This whole sentence is written in light of that commandment and in order to encourage obedience to it.

John pauses to remind his readers that they have known this truth all along. With the adverb clause introduced by καθὼς, he injects a parenthetical reminder to his readers (Culy, 146). John's familiar "from the beginning" (ἀπ' ἀρχῆς) is expressed once more. By this he could mean one of two things: (1) He could be referring to the beginning of the founding of the church (Strecker, 232). (2) He could be speaking of the beginning of their Christian experience (Akin, 227; Yarbrough, 342). It cannot be the beginning of Jesus' ministry because it is what *they* heard, not what John heard from him. It seems best to see this referring to the beginning of their instruction in the faith since they are the ones doing the hearing.

Some see the second ἵνα clause as epexegetical to αὕτη in the third clause (Brown, 666–67; Culy 145).[48] Others reject this and consider the referent of this second αὕτη to be ἡ ἐντολή, but with αὕτη looking back to what was previously said rather than forward to the ἵνα that follows. Their logic is that it would create a tautology (Brown, 668; Rensberger, 151). However, it seems best to see that the following ἵνα clause gives the purpose (in order that) of the command (Harris, 245). Furthermore, if it creates a tautology, then it is intended. The point John is making along with the role of this final ἵνα clause is expressed well by Barker (363). "The test of love is obedience to God's commands, and the test of obedience is whether one 'walks in love.' The argument is intentionally circular."

John reminds his readers that this love is to be a part of daily conduct by the repetition of "walk." It is to characterize one's lifestyle, not be an occasional event. God's children are to "walk in love" as much as they are to "walk in light" in his first epistle. In fact, the two should be viewed as one and the same.

To what does ἐν αὐτῇ refer? (1) It could refer to ἀγάπη (Bruce, 140; Burdick, 424; Smalley, 326; Marshall, 68, n. 11; Stott, 210; Westcott, 228). However, there are too many feminine nouns between it and αὐτῇ. (2) It could refer to ἐντολή which is the nearest feminine noun (Brooke, 174; Brown, 667; Harris, 246; Rensberger, 151). Harris (246) responds to the objection that John's use of κατὰ earlier in the verse instead of ἐν mitigates against this by noting John's penchant for stylistic variation. However, some reject this on the basis that it creates a tautology (Akin, 227; Marshall, 68, n. 11; Smalley, 326). Lieu (251) argues that though this seems to mean "that the

48. Brooke (174)sees it as resumptive.

heart of the command is to live by it—appears redundant, it would serve the elder's relentless reinforcement of his call to faithfulness to the tradition received." (3) It could refer to ἀληθείᾳ in v 4. It has the same preposition construction and follows the same verb (Akin, 227; Haas, de Jonge, and Swellengrebel, 144; Kruse, 208). This would naturally prepare the reader for the discussion that follows. "In it" could be parallel to "walking in truth" in v 4. However, it is too far removed and has too many other feminine nouns between it and αὐτῇ (Harris, 246).[49] Or, (4) it could be intentionally ambiguous ("semantic density") and refer to "truth," "commandment," and "love" (Kruse, 208–209).[50] The second option is best. As noted earlier, even if it does create a tautology, that tautology is intended and necessary to clarify the importance of obedience to God's command.

7 John now turns his attention to the problem faced by the church of his day, and today.[51] There are false teachers infiltrating the body of Christ. So John now describes the person his readers (and so us) are to guard against.[52]

---

49. Bultmann (111) remained "uncertain" and then said it "makes no difference."
50. E. R. Wendland ("What is Truth?" 309–311) argues that its actual antecedent is ἀληθείᾳ in v 4. Further, he sees John "chaining" concepts lexically in such a way that αὐτῇ "does triple duty by incorporating each of these three seminal ideas into a unified, but multifaceted, conceptual whole which constitutes the thematic core of the entire letter." Weakening his argument is John's pattern in his First Epistle of using the neuter pronoun to encompass a broader conceptual range, where a feminine pronoun might have been expected (see comments 1 John 1:1–3 and 2:8).
51. Lieu (252) notes the similarity of this verse with 1 John 4:1 (ὅτι πολλοὶ ψευδοπροφῆται ἐξεληλύθασιν εἰς τὸν κόσμον.) as well its affinity with 1 John 2:18–19 "suggests that 2 John 7 presupposes and has been formulated in the light of the longer letter." However, similarity argues more for common authorship rather than formulation by an author in light of a previous work. This could still have been penned first by John, who then "fleshed it out" later as he wrote more extensively on the subject in 1 John. Or, if 1 John is prior, it is simply John summarizing the same idea as he communicates it once more, though with more limited space.
52. Bultmann (112) sees vv 7–8 as "identical" with the warning in 1 John 2:18–27 and 4:1–6. Bruce (140) notes its similarity. Lieu (78) says v 7 is difficult to understand apart from those 1 John passages. Painter (351) concludes that the connection between v 7 and the 1 John passages affirms a common author. "Here, as elsewhere, the relationship between 1 John and 2 John does not seem to be the result of a second author copying a first. There is too much freedom taken with the material. More likely the author is revisiting themes treated earlier."

ὅτι πολλοὶ πλάνοι ἐξῆλθον εἰς τὸν κόσμον, "For many deceivers have gone out into the world." Though this sentence begins with ὅτι, it is not structurally connected to the sentence before. Even so, this causal ὅτι still introduces the "grounds for the previous exhortation" (Culy, 147).[53] It stands at the head of a new sentence since its verb is indicative rather than subjunctive (Lenski, 566). It is being used as an explanatory conjunction rather than subordinating (Harris, 247; Schnackenburg, 312).[54] So, though a new movement in the main body of the letter is started here, it is still logically connected with what preceded by the ὅτι (Akin, 228; Kruse, 209; Marshall, 69).[55] This argues against having a paragraph break here (Burdick, 425; Culy, 147; Lieu, 252; *contra* Wendland[56]). Even so, Brown (668) argues for "some break," though not necessarily a paragraph break. He also notes that the ὅτι links back to the previous clause and connects the following Christology with the command to love (Painter, 354). Burdick (425, italics his) says that John is communicating through these connections that "love towards fellow believers ... must not be practiced indiscriminately." Further, "the apostle says that Christians must love one another *because* many false teachers are present in the world. The unity produced by such mutual love enables believers to recognize and resist deceptive error."

The problem is that "many deceivers" are present in the world. The reason believers are to conduct their lives ("walk") according to God's revealed will in his Scriptures ("commandments") is the danger posed by deceivers infiltrating the church. John warns that there are πολλοὶ of these deceivers going out into the world. Whereas in his first epistle (1 John 4:1) these were "false prophets," descriptive of their role, now they are "deceivers," descriptive of the affect. His choice of terms to describe them carries the double sense that they do not just introduce false ideas, but that these false ideas produce wrong conduct (Westcott, 228). Their presence throughout the world is

---

53. Strecker (232) and Yarbrough (343) describe this as an "introductory" causal ὅτι.

54. BDF §456(1) says, "Subordination with ὅτι and διότι is often very loose ... and must be translated 'for.'" See Wallace, *Grammar*, 460. Its function is similar to that of, and is much the same function as, Paul's frequent use of γάρ to string sentences together, with each explaining something that came before.

55. Smith (143) sees the ὅτι referring back to v. 4 and John's joy over those walking in truth. However, it seems best relating to the immediate context since that makes perfect sense with what follows.

56. E. R. Wendland, "'Dear Children' Versus the 'Antichrists,'" 41–42.

reminiscent of what he said of the antichrists in 1 John 2:18–19. This term, πλάνοι, is the same one used by Jesus when describing the last days before his return (Matt 24:4, 11, 24). Perkins (85) sees this as apocalyptic imagery reflective of 1 John 2:18–27 and 4:1–6. Stott (211) suggests that this use of ἐξῆλθον does not relate back to 1 John 2:19, but "as the apostles were sent forth into the world to preach the truth, so these false teachers had gone forth to teach lies." Stott (211) describes the false teachers as "itinerate false prophets, travelling along the great Roman roads of Asia Minor, seeking to insinuate their error into the churches they visited." Smalley (327–28) also sees them "departing" to do missionary work among the churches with the "many" indicating that the heretics were "gaining the upper hand."[57]

John now changes from the previous perfect tense verbs to the aorist ἐξῆλθον. Lieu (252–53) says of this shift in tenses, "Whereas in both those passages the perfect tense put more stress on the fact of their departure and their consequent presence 'out there,' the simple past (aorist) in 2 John 7 would allow more of a focus on the moment of their going, although it may be little more than a stylistic avoidance of the perfect tense." Rather than the moment, that John is remembering some event, the aorist here actually does focus only on the fact of their departure.[58] That is what John wants his readers to focus on here. That will thereby set the stage for the warning that these false teachers will eventually end up on the church's doorstep wanting hospitality and entrance into their fellowship.[59]

---

57. Under the influence of Raymond Brown's work, *The Community of the Beloved Disciple*, many recent scholars see them as the secessionists from the theorized Johannine community (Harris, 247; Kruse, 209; Rensberger, 172; Smalley, 327; Williamson, 191). However, the problem of false teachers was widespread and preceded John's ministry in Ephesus. As noted elsewhere, Paul dealt with false teachers in his epistles (Gal, Col, Titus are the three most obvious) and warned the Ephesian elders that false teachers would arise from their midst. Also, as noted in the introduction, the early church had enough false teachers moving in its midst that it developed rules or principles to help guide them in discerning false teachers and instructing them how to handle them as well.

58. Lenski (566) understood ἐξῆλθον to indicate that the deceivers went out "from their leader Cerinthus, from his headquarters; some take it that they went out from the devil, the archdeceiver." It still seems better to see them departing from the faith rather than churches or a Johannine community. Otherwise they would not be attempting to gain admittance as teachers in the orthodox churches.

59. Painter (352) says that the aor. ἐξῆλθον "suggests a particular crisis, a schism." However, that is reading more into the word than it requires. In fact, the use of the

The departure of these false teachers is into the "world." Many take κόσμος in a neutral sense as the sphere of human existence (Bultmann, 112; Dodd, 148; Marshall, 69, n. 4; Stott, 211). Others see it negatively as the people hostile to Christians and is joined by those who leave the faith (Akin, 228; Culpepper, 122; Johnson, 156), thus the "godless world" (Moody, 123). John's use of κόσμος would appear to be negative here because these false teachers have become a part of it. However, the implication is not so much that they have joined the world, but that they are now moving about in it. As noted in the introduction, this does appear to be the near universal experience of the early church rather than being restricted to Asia Minor or just a few local churches.

οἱ μὴ ὁμολογοῦντες Ἰησοῦν Χριστὸν ἐρχόμενον ἐν σαρκί· "those who do not confess Jesus Christ as coming in the flesh." John now describes the nature of the false teachers' deception. He describes these false teachers as οἱ μὴ ὁμολογοῦντες. John describes these men, not in terms of what they say, but what they fail to say. He then states the truth denied as it relates to Jesus. This is the same confession found in 1 John 4:2 except that the perfect participle is now a present participle. The combination of the name Ἰησοῦν Χριστὸν reminds the readers of Jesus' human and divine natures (Kistemaker, 380). Next, we are faced with the challenging participial construction, Ἰησοῦν Χριστὸν ἐρχόμενον ἐν σαρκί.

This participial construction could be rendered as either "Jesus as Christ coming in the flesh" (Harris, 247–48; Hodges, 259; NET), "Jesus Christ as coming in the flesh" (Smalley, 328–29; Rensberger,153), or as a quote of the confession, "Jesus Christ come in the flesh" (Brown, 492–94; Westcott, 141).[60] This is almost identical to what John said in 1 John 4:2–3 with the exception that the present participle ἐρχόμενον replaces the perfect participle ἐληλυθότα.[61] There is likely little difference in meaning. Here

---

aor. with the very generic, non-technical ἐξέρχομαι would seem to emphasize more the simple idea of departure rather than either a crisis or a schism (BDAG, 348; J. Schneider, "ἔρχομαι ... ἐξέρχομαι," *TDNT* 2:678–79).

60. This is the same problem discussed in 1 John 4:2.

61. D. B. Wallace (*Grammar*, 645–46) says that "an anarthrous participle in the accusative case, in conjunction with an accusative noun or pronoun, sometimes indicates indirect discourse after a verb of perception or communication." He lists this verse as an example. Culy (147) disagrees and says the participle is the

once more "flesh" (σαρκί) is a synecdoche* for his incarnation, including his birth, life, death, and resurrection, his sharing of humanity.

So, why does John use the present participle rather than the perfect as before? Barker (364) notes well that John knew the difference between a present and perfect participle, and so his choice has to be intentional. Various possible reasons have been proposed. (1) The present tense has a futuristic sense here and looks at Jesus' second coming (Strecker; Westcott, 229). This is a possible use of the present tense (called a futuristic present).[62] Strecker (234–36) argues that the New Testament authors exhibited an apocalyptic chiliastic expectation of a thousand-year reign of Christ on earth that included a bodily return of Christ.[63] He also identifies *E. Barn.* 15.4–5 as extrabiblical evidence of a similar eschatological expectation.[64] It is to this John refers. Against this is *E. Barn.* 6:9, which uses a future tense rather than present participle to describe Jesus' second coming (Brown, 669).[65] Also against the future sense is the absence of a similar reference anywhere in Scripture (Moody, 123). This statement is parallel to 1 John 4:2–3 which is silent about a second coming (Williamson, 191). Schnackenburg (313) also rejects this on the grounds that Jesus' coming in glory will not be a bodily return. Against this, Kruse (210) notes that no evidence exists that the secessionists denied Jesus' bodily return. (2) John's use of the present tense alludes to the sacraments and so this is a "denial of the real presence

---

"complement in an object-complement double accusative construction." He points to 1 John 1:10 (ψεύστην) as an example.

62. BDF §339(2).

63. Passages he identifies as indicating this include 1 Cor 15:23–24 and Rev 20:1–3. He cites John 17:2–5, Phil 3:20–21, and Rom 8:17–18 as examples of NT authors that denied the bodily return because they referred to him returning in "glory."

64. *E. Barn.* 15.4–5 reads: "Observe, children, what 'he finished in six days' means. It means this: that in six thousand years the Lord will bring everything to an end, for with him a day signifies a thousand years. And he himself bears me witness when he says, 'Behold, the day of the Lord will be as a thousand years.' Therefore, children, in six days—that is, in six thousand years—everything will be brought to an end. (5) 'And he rested on the seventh day.' This means: when his Son comes, he will destroy the time of the lawless one and will judge the ungodly and will change the sun and the moon and the stars, and then he will truly rest on the seventh day." (M. Holmes, *The Apostolic Fathers: Greek Texts and English Translations*, 315)

65. *E. Barn.* 6:9 reads: "Learn: "Trust," she says, "in him who is to be manifested to you in the flesh—that is, Jesus." (M. W. Holmes, *The Apostolic Fathers: Greek Texts and English Translations*, 140)

of Christ in the sacrament" (Strecker, 233).[66] This view can be rejected on the basis that no evidence exists in either 2 or 3 John that the sacraments were an issue (Painter, 350; Strecker, 234) (3) It emphasizes the truth that Jesus not only came in the flesh, but is still existing in the flesh (Burge, 236). This would be a repudiation of the gnostic teaching that the Christ spirit left Jesus at his crucifixion. (4) The non-Johannine author, "the elder," is "evoking familiar Johannine formulae without being particularly concerned about their precise reference" (Haas, de Jonge, and Swellengrebel, 167; Lieu, 254). (5) It refers to the "process" of Jesus' incarnation (Kruse, 210). (6) It is a "timeless present" indicating that Jesus' coming in the flesh is an "abiding truth" (Akin, 229; Barker, 364; Brooke, 175; Lenski, 566; Marshall, 70–71; Smalley, 329–30; Stott, 212). Burdick concurs (425–26) and lists four arguments in its favor. (a) "No known first century heresy denied Christ's second coming in the flesh." (b) "The Gnostics denied Christ's first coming in the flesh." (c) "The same phrase occurs in 1 John 4:2, where the perfect tense ἐγηθυθότα, 'having come,' clearly refers to Christ's first coming." (d) "Flesh is more naturally used to refer to the present mortal body than to the immortal resurrection body." (7) It refers to Jesus' first coming in the same way the perfect participle had (Schnackenburg, 313). This may be another example of John's love for stylistic variation (Harris, 248). This may reflect the influence of the Gospel's repeated use of ἐρχόμενος (John 1:15, 27; 12:13) to describe Jesus' advent (Lieu, 86–87) and so be a "fixed" or "stereotyped formula" (Brown, 670; Haas, de Jonge, and Swellengrebel, 167; Schnackenburg, 313). Yarbrough (343) concurs. He says "The semantics of the present participle of ἔρξομαι ... are sufficiently elastic to allow application to past activities."[67] Thus it is still a reference to his incarnation (Bruce, 141; Smalley, 329; Thompson, 155). This last view has the strongest support and makes the best sense.

Finally, this confession not only affirms Jesus' coming, but that his coming was "in the flesh." The phrase ἐν σαρκί is a synecdoche meaning "in a human body" (Culy, 148). Lalleman sees this addressing the claim of a gnostic group who composed a document called *Acts of John* and denied

66. Strecker (233) interprets John 6:53–54 as an "extended interpretation of the Lord's Supper" and is reflected here as well.

67. He provides the examples of Luke 16:21; 23:26; John 1:9 and 11:27.

"that Jesus was ever physically on earth."[68] It does seem that John's emphasis on the fleshly aspect of Jesus' incarnation indicates he is addressing a gnostic heresy.

οὗτός ἐστιν ὁ πλάνος καὶ ὁ ἀντίχριστος, "this is the deceiver and the antichrist." John now categorizes the deceptive teacher as an antichrist. His use of οὗτός, which is anaphoric*, moves the attention from the group (πολλοὶ πλάνοι) to any individual who does not confess Jesus (Culy, 148; Yarbrough, 344).

He includes the article with both "deceiver" and "antichrist," using the title of the ultimate antichrist to indicate his followers (by metonymy*). The articles identify a category of people rather than a particular person, thus each and every false teacher who fails this confession is included. (Yarbrough, 344).[69] Why does John combine the two titles? "Deceiver" describes the false teacher's relationship to men while "antichrist" reflects his relationship to Jesus (Westcott, 229). Or we might say, "deceiver" looks at their actions (Akin, 230) while "antichrist" describes their loyalties.[70] Antichrist is a metaphor for the false teachers (Harris, 248), rather than a reference to the actual antichrist. John is describing the character of these false teaches. Thus the two nouns are being used as "collective names" (Kistemaker, 380). The term "Antichrist" occurs only here and in 1 John 2:18, 22, and 4:3. Its use in early patristic literature reflects the influence of 1 John.[71] Brooke (175) says John is taking a "popular expectation" and using it "as the convenient expression of the evil tendencies of his day." However, the antichrist, both as described in 1 John and prophesied in Rev, is far more than a "popular expectation" or a mythical figure (contra Bultmann), but a future historical figure whose attitude and antagonism toward God is expressed in part through these false teachers. John is not using this as a pejorative, but a descriptive term.

---

68. P. J. Lalleman, "The Adversaries Envisaged in the Johannine Epistles," 20.
69. D. B. Wallace, *Grammar*, 227–30.
70. Polycarp says, "For everyone 'who does not confess that Jesus Christ has come in the flesh is antichrist'; and whoever does not acknowledge the testimony of the cross 'is of the devil.'" (in M. Holmes, *The Apostolic Fathers: Greek Texts and English Translations*, 213)
71. Polycarp is an example of John's influence. He writes (Pol. *Phil.* 7.1) "For everyone 'who does not confess that Jesus Christ has come in the flesh is antichrist'; and whoever does not acknowledge the testimony of the cross 'is of the devil.'"

8 John now warns of the danger and the need for diligence.[72] He accomplishes this with a command accompanied by its purpose. Additionally, our motivation for avoiding false teachers is a proper eternal focus.

βλέπετε ἑαυτούς, "Watch out for yourselves." John warns his readers using the imperative with the reflexive pronoun. This is his only use of βλέπω to give a warning (Grayston, 154), though one might have expected it in 1 John as well. His warning serves as a reminder that it is every Christian's own responsibility to guard against false teachers. It is not the pastor or any other teacher that will be held accountable by Christ, but the individual (Culy, 148). The 2 present imperative "emphasizes the duty of personal effort" (Brooke, 176) as well as the need for constant vigilance (Akin, 231). Painter (353) connects this with the warning in 1 John 2:18 of it being the "last hour" which makes this an eschatological warning. He notes the same language and sense from Mark 13:5, 9, and 23, the words of warning from Jesus when telling of the last days and signs of his return. So, too others (Schnackenburg, 314; Smalley, 330). Jesus used this same warning against deceivers.[73] It was also common with Paul and used by the author of hebrews.[74] Thus Yarbrough (344) rightly concludes that John's warning is not unusual. Their reason for vigilance is now given.

ἵνα μὴ ἀπολέσητε ἃ εἰργάσασθε ἀλλὰ μισθὸν πλήρη ἀπολάβητε, "that you may not lose those things which you worked for, but that you may receive a full reward." The purpose for guarding is now given as it relates to their work and reward. John includes himself with his readers in the work that leads to rewards.

There are various views on the meaning of ἃ εἰργασάμεθα.[75]

(1) Some see them ultimately working for salvation, eternal life (Brown, 672; Johnson, 157; Schnackenburg, 314). However, the rewards lost in the following clauses of this sentence cannot refer to whether one goes to heaven or not. The destiny of a believer

72. Culy (148) calls this verse the "peak" of the letter.

73. Matt 24:4; Mark 13:5, 9; Luke 21:8.

74. Acts 13:40; 1 Cor 8:9; Gal 5:15; Eph 5:15; Phil 3:2 [3x]; Col 2:8. Heb 3:12 and 12:25.

75. Yarbrough (346) notes that ἐργάζομαι "frequently denotes the performing or accomplishing of works that meet God's approval." His examples include: Matt 26:10; Acts 10:35; Rom 2:10; 1 Cor 16:10; Gal 6:10; Col 3:23; Heb 11:33; 3 John 5.

is determined and preserved by God, not the believer (1 Pet 1:4–5). Our heavenly destiny is not earned, but a part of the free gift of salvation (Rom 4:1–6; Eph 2:8), and so not something one works to attain or maintain (Stott, 213).[76] Painter (353) rejects this meaning loss of eternal life on the grounds that it "can hardly be had in part" and refers to 1 Cor 3:10–15 as evidence of "the notion of unworthy work (*ergon*) being burned in the fire of judgment, though the person is saved through fire." Additionally, John indicates in 1 John 2:19 that the false teachers were never believers (Harris, 249). He teaches eternal security in John 10:28–29 (believers cannot be taken from God). Also, in John 17 Judas was "lost," but none of the other eleven, because he was never a believer, but a son of perdition.

(2) Others see it as their evangelistic work in this life (Marshall, 72; Smalley, 330). Smalley (330) refers to it as their "pastoral and missionary work." Harris (249–50) refers to it as their evangelistic work in the community that would be lost by false doctrine. Burge (236) makes a different text-critical choice of the first person plural εἰργασάμεθα ("we have worked for") over εἰργάσασθε ("you have worked for") and sees it indicating their work among the churches would be lost.

(3) The reference is to heavenly rewards and not loss of salvation (Hodges, 259; Lenski, 567; Williamson, 192). In contrast to salvation, rewards can be earned and come as a result of works (Rev 2–3). Furthermore, in that light, rewards can be forfeited as well. "While salvation cannot be lost (cf. John 6:37–40; Rom. 5:1; 8:1, 28–39; Heb. 7:25; 1 Peter 1:4), unfaithful believers may forfeit some of the reward that faithfulness to the truth would have gained them" (MacArthur, 234). Paul describes this in such passages as 1 Cor 3:10–15 and John in Rev 2–3. This third view fits best with the context and teaching of Scripture.

With the strong adversative ἀλλὰ once again, John contrasts the loss with its gain. He is not saying they would lose "all" reward, but only that for which

76. Phil 2:12–13, "work out your salvation" has to do with expressing it and living out the implications of it, not attaining or maintaining it.

they had worked. This agrees with passages such as Heb 6:10, where saints are reminded that God does not forget what they have done, though there was the danger of falling away. Another passage is Mark 9:41 where Jesus promises that every kind deed done in his name is sure to be rewarded. Yet, along with these promises are warnings such as Paul's teaching in 1 Cor 3:10–15 of a loss of reward for believers based on their impact in the lives of other believers. John's point here is that falling to false teachers' seduction results in lost rewards for Christians. Just as Jesus warned the members of the church of Philadelphia that they could lose their "crown" if they failed to hold fast (Rev 3:11). Believers can lose rewards by failing to "hold fast" doctrinally. This loss can occur because Christians can be deceived by false teaching about Jesus. Nothing in Scripture even hints at the possibility that Christians are immune to false teaching.

The term, μισθός, refers to a worker's remuneration for work accomplished, his wages.[77] It is used for positive rewards, usually related to heaven.[78] Μισθός is also used for negative rewards or satirically for lost heavenly rewards exchanged for something temporal.[79] In the LXX it referred to pay earned, whether wrongly by Priests (Mic 3:11), Levites for serving in the tabernacle (Num 18:31), or laymen laborers (Exod 2:9; Deut 15:18). Strecker (241–42) interprets this eschatologically and sees it as Christ's rewards given out when he returns, which is "community life" with Christ, and so equivalent to eternal life. Yarbrough (346) sees it as "eschatological reward" in addition to eternal life that is worked for (*contra* Strecker).[80] Marshall

77. BDAG, 653.

78. Matt 5:12; 10:22, 41 [x2], 42; Mark 9:41; 13:13 Luke 6:23, 35; 19:11–27; John 4:36; 1 Cor 3:10–15; 9:17–18; Rev 2:1–3:22; 11:18; 22:12.

79. Matt 5:46; 6:1, 2, 5, 16; Acts 1:18; 2 Pet 2:13, 15; Jude 11.

80. Akin (231) notes that some see vv 9–11 addressing loss of salvation or rewards. He rejects both options and approaches these verses from the doctrine of perseverance. However, he ultimately says that unless one continues faithfully serving the Lord that person will not be saved in the end. Thus this is a test of life once again and ends up little different from someone who does not hold to eternal security. Ultimately there is little difference between either view if neither can assure one that he or she is regenerate and destined for heaven. His view is illustrated well by this statement: "If you remain alert and on guard, you will stay with Christ and receive a full reward. Standing with him proves you truly belong to him. To turn aside and give an ear to false teaching can only result in loss. To walk away and not continue with Christ proves you never received him in the first place."

(72) sees partial loss of rewards indicated. He also notes that vv 8–9 indicate that true Christians can succumb to heresy.

Now, having been warned about the danger of losing reward, the next question John's readers would likely ask is how does one preserve his or her reward? John will explain that in what follows.

9 This verse is a compound sentence and employs repetition to develop its contrast between two kinds of people. The test is whether a person abides in or departs from Christ's teaching. The false teachers reveal they are not God's children by going too far doctrinally.[81]

πᾶς ὁ προάγων καὶ μὴ μένων ἐν τῇ διδαχῇ τοῦ Χριστοῦ θεὸν οὐκ ἔχει·, "everyone who goes ahead and does not abide in the teaching of Christ does not have God."

John introduces this general statement that is not a description of his readers with his characteristic *πᾶς ὁ* construction.[82] With this generalizing statement he identifies a group of which one may or may not be a member. Whereas he was addressing his readers with the second person plural, he now changes to the third person singular In doing this he moves the attention from his readers to the false teachers and focuses on a principle that is true, though not something he sees them doing.

He describes the failure of the false teachers with a hendiadys* composed of the two present participles, *προάγων* and *μένων* governed by a single article.[83] With this "goes ahead" is defined as the failure to "abide in the teaching of Christ."[84] *Προάγων* means "to run ahead"[85] and is normally a positive term. Burge (235) understands "runs ahead" as "a term of superiority

81. Lieu (257) sees vv 9–13 as the purpose of the letter.

82. John uses *πᾶς ὁ* with the participle twelve times in 1 John (2:23, 29; 3;3, 6 [x2], 9, 10, 15; 4:7; 5:1 [x2], 18).

83. The one article with the two participles makes them equivalent (they define each other) (Lenski, 568).

84. Harris (251) sees John's use of *μένω* to be a word-play indicating that not abiding in Christ's teachings means not abiding in Christ and therefore they are not "genuine Christians" as evidenced by John's final clause (also Walls and Anders, 238). This would require the "the teaching of Christ" to be a metonymy for Christ himself. It seems unlikely that John would intend that here since he is emphasizing the need his readers have to walk in the truth, which is a body of teachings received from Christ.

85. BDAG, 864.

and appears only here in the New Testament with a negative connotation. This is not progress *in the faith*, but progress *beyond* it." Some see John borrowing this term from the Gnostics (Akin, 231). Burdick (427) describes this as "professed progress, reflecting the Gnostic claim to have progressed to a higher understanding of God, of the human predicament, and of the secret way of salvation from the predicament." Many modern scholars refer to these false teachers as "progressives" based on this description of them (Brown, 673; Edwards, 31; Harris, 251; Strecker, 242).[86] Yarbrough (350) describes them well as "innovators" who present "something different, faithlessly novel, and supplanting what was former, established, and valid." Lieu (257–58) notes that this use of προάγων does not mean these false teachers were seeking leadership in the churches. The inclusion of μένων for her indicates the problem was their not remaining under the orthodox leadership.

What does John mean by the teaching "of Christ"? This genitive construction may be understood in one of three ways:[87] (1) As an objective genitive he would be referring to the doctrine concerning Christ (Bultmann, 113; Burdick, 427–28; Culy, 150; Marshall, 72–73, n. 13; Painter, 354; Rensberger, 154; Smalley, 332). Thus orthodoxy would be defined as "remaining in the original teaching regarding Jesus."[88] Brown (674) suggests περί would have been more clear. Burdick (427) points to the context and similarity of both vv 7 and 9 to 1 John 2:22–23 and 4:2–3. (2) As a subjective genitive he would mean the doctrines taught by Christ (Alexander, 293; Brooke, 177; Brown, 675; Bruce, 142; Grayston, 154; Haas, de Jonge, and Swellengrebel, 169; Kistemaker, 382; Lenski, 568; Plummer, 138; Schnackenburg, 315; Smalley 332; Stott, 214; Westcott, 230). In favor of this is the pattern of other subjective genitive constructions following the noun διδαχή with John (Brooke, 177; Harris, 251; Westcott, 230).[89] (3) As a plenary genitive he would indicate Christ's teachings about himself.[90] Its

86. Bultmann (113) links this description back to 1 John 2:23 and sees them as the same opponents as John addressed in the epistle.

87. Barker (365) says "it is of little importance ... which alternative is accepted, because the author holds equally to both positions."

88. A. Köstenberger, "The Deity of Christ in John's Letters and the Book of Revelation," 152.

89. Examples include John 7:16, 17 (ἡ ἐμὴ διδαχὴ), 18:19 (τῆς διδαχῆς αὐτοῦ). False teachings are referred to in Rev 2:14–15 (Balaam and Nicolaitans).

90. D. B. Wallace, *Grammar*, 119–121. Culy (150) calls this a "questionable label."

role as a subjective genitive seems best, though the plenary genitive would make sense as well. Thus, the theological deviation in view involves a departure from Jesus' teaching, possibly his command to love, but more likely his instructions about his deity, person, and work. By extension, this "teaching" (διδαχῇ) likely involves more than Jesus' personal instruction of the apostles but includes all the truths delivered to the apostles from the Lord, whether during his earthly ministry or by subsequent revelation. The false teachers, in "going ahead" (προάγων) of the apostolic circle went too far. Theological novelty is not God's ideal. Accuracy in communicating his truth is.

Are these false teachers believers or unbelievers? Hodges (263, italics his) rejects the idea that they are unbelievers on the basis that "going ahead" indicates someone who has held the truth at one time. He argues, "If this person once held the truth that he has now abandoned, then that person is born of God. Contrary to the opinion of some theologians, we are not saved by *continuing* to believe, but by *believing*." However, this "going ahead" does not necessarily mean having "gone along with" at some point. Rather John could be describing them in terms of their view of themselves. His description of false teachers, antichrists, in 1 John 2 indicates he does not consider them misguided believers, but unbelievers whose departure from the apostolic doctrines demonstrates they were never regenerate.

Akin misses the point in interpreting John's words through the grid of the doctrine of perseverance. Though it is true on one hand that "to stay with Christ gives the clearest evidence that one belongs to Christ," it only serves as an external evidence in the eyes of men. He is correct in saying that staying with Christ will cause one to "receive a full reward" (Akin, 231). However, that "reward" is not eternal life. Eternal life is a free gift and never described as a reward of any kind anywhere in Scripture. Herein one sees theology being read into a passage and misapplied. John is not warning his readers that they may prove themselves unsaved or nonelect by failing to persevere in apostolic doctrine. Rather, he is describing unbelieving false teachers who have shown by their fruit that they have always been unbelievers. To hear what John is saying one must discern between what he directs toward his readers and what he directs toward false teachers. Further, one must recognize that John is careful not to confuse what "test" is being applied to whom. Finally, it is an error to think that John ever intended the tests to be interchangeable.

With this John clarifies that those who deviate doctrinally from Christ are not believers. They are not God's children. When Hodges (264) questions whether this must be taken as a denial of their justification he argues that context must "dictate our understanding of the statements in this verse." John's use of ἔχει here, as in 1 John 5:12, must be seen in terms of justification.[91] This use of ἔχει should be seen as a gnomic present because πᾶς ὁ is typically used with gnomic present verbs.[92] Thus John is describing a kind of person and dividing the world into two groups, those who have and those who do not have. Whereas "having" produces assurance in 1 John, here it produces orthodoxy in a teacher of God's Word.[93] There is not an understood "fellowship with" in conjunction with "has." That which is "had" is God (direct object). It is far too much of a stretch to add other ideas in the sentence in order to avoid what appears to be a fairly plain statement. This is another example of reading one's theology into the text.

ὁ μένων ἐν τῇ διδαχῇ τοῦ Χριστοῦ, οὗτος καὶ τὸν πατέρα καὶ τὸν υἱὸν ἔχει, "he who abides in the teaching of Christ, this one also has the Father and the Son." John now states positively what he has just affirmed negatively. Thus the antithesis is completed on a positive note.[94]

---

91. Strecker (242) sees the phrase θεὸν οὐκ ἔχει as Greek and Hellenistic Jewish in origin and only Christianized later. He (n. 55) quotes Epictetus (*Moral Discourses* 2.8.17) as an example of its Greek use. He (n. 56) bases the Hellenistic Jewish origins on H. Hanse's ("ἔχω," *TDNT* 2:823) reference to the LXX and adds to it the examples of 2 Macc 8:36; 11:10; 3 Macc 7:16; *T. Dan* 5; *T. Iss.* 7; Josephus, *Ant.* 8.227.

92. D. B. Wallace, *Grammar*, 532.

93. Barker (365) sees this as implying "not a loss of reward but of God himself, the loss or nonattainment of eternal life as promised in 1 John 2:25." However, rather than seeing a loss of God, thus a loss , of salvation, or reducing it to a loss of fellowship with God, it is best to see this gnomic sense of "has" to indicate the person never "had" God in the sense of any relationship in the past. Lenski (569) is correct. To have the Father and Son is to have salvation.

94. Again, this positive affirmation can be seen to correspond to 1 John 2:24 (Bultmann, 113), though it may or may not be a paraphrase of it. Since we cannot know which epistle was written first, we cannot know whether John alludes to 1 John here, or developed this further in 1 John. What we do know is that John wrote both and the similarity comes from it being the way he says things. He very obviously wanted to communicate the same truth to both sets of recipients (assuming they are not the same) and so would say it much the same way regardless of which he wrote first.

In contrast to the one who goes too far is the one who abides in Christ's teaching. By repeating ἐν τῇ διδαχῇ τοῦ Χριστοῦ John draws the strong contrast between false and orthodox teachers. He places orthodoxy within the realm of Christ's teaching, not the teachings of the apostles. Subsequently, by doing so he identifies the apostles with Christ in that they are teaching what Christ taught them. With the present articular participle μένων John describes the orthodox teachers as individuals who are characterized by their connection with Christ's teaching. They "abide" in it. In other words, they have incorporated it into their lives and are operating in its sphere, being guided and controlled by it. They are not progressing beyond it or deviating from it. This is equivalent to walking in the light in 1 John. Their sphere of activity is Christ's teachings. Today we would describe such a person as living a biblical lifestyle and teaching biblical truth.

The person abiding in Christ's teachings, in contrast to the false teacher, has both God the Father and God the Son. John points to the significance of the one who is characterized by abiding in Christ's teachings with the emphatic pronoun, οὗτος. Though this is true of everyone, John is focusing his attention on the true and false teachers. He clarifies that an orthodox teacher is a believer, thus the formula, "he has." This second ἔχει should be viewed as parallel with the first ἔχει and thus gnomic present as well. However, this time, as in 1 John 2:22–25, having both the Father and Son is connected with sound doctrine about the Son. No one has one without the other. No one communes with one without communing with the other. No one believes the right things about the one without believing the right things about the other. Thus one can say, "I do not believe Jesus is God, but I worship the God of Abraham, Isaac, and Jacob." However, John makes clear that such a person is deceived.

10 John now describes the danger,[95] and our defense against it, with a first class conditional sentence.[96] The protasis* describes the circumstance. The apodosis* is composed of a double imperative that explains the proper response to that circumstance. Deceivers must be rebuffed.[97]

εἴ τις ἔρχεται πρὸς ὑμᾶς καὶ ταύτην τὴν διδαχὴν οὐ φέρει, "If anyone comes to you and does not bear this teaching." The present tense ἔρχεται could have a future look ("in the future, when someone comes") or a gnomic sense ("whenever someone comes").[98] His use of εἴ τις "assumes the case, and does not simply regard it as possible (ἐάν τις). By 'cometh' is to be understood an official 'coming.' St John is not dealing with the casual visit of a stranger but with that of a teacher who claims authority" (Westcott,

95. Schnackenburg (315) sees the danger John addresses is that his readers might lose their salvation if they follow the false teachers (his view of "reward" earlier). However, the danger is deception. And, as seen in 1 John, John makes clear in his First Epistle that his readers are believers and that they have not succumbed to false teachers. Even in this epistle he does not speak in terms of being drawn into their false beliefs, but of endorsing (and thereby supporting) their false teachings as they would impact others. And, the question of "having" God is a test applied to false teachers, not to themselves even as it was in 1 John.

96. Bultmann (114) says that the command to sever or avoid fellowship with the false teachers is the "single original thing" in John's warnings against the false teachers as compared to 1 John. He is correct in his observation. I would take it further, though, and note that this does evidence John's purpose in writing. In 1 John he looked at the issue of false teachers in terms of how their teachings impacted the fellowship of believers in terms of their ability to love one another. His pastoral concern was focused on their need to love each other corporately and practically. Here he is focused on the practical aspect of how to keep the false teachings out of the community of faith more than their need to love each other. Whereas in 1 John the issue is more that of their need to love one another, here it is more their need to keep false teachers out. Brooke (178) does not view this as the unstated purpose of the epistle. I would concur in one sense, but say that it is a fairly clear purpose that need not be stated since it is so obvious the reason John is writing.

97. Stott (215) provides a balanced view of this instruction that should serve as a reminder to every believer and every congregation. "What John writes is relevant both to those who are so tolerant that they will condemn nobody's views and to those who are so intolerant that they condemn everybody's views which diverge from their own. But neither compromise nor separation can find support in this text."

98. D. B. Wallace, *Grammar*, 513–39.

230).[99] It presents the possibility as not just real, but more likely to occur than not (Brooke, 178; Haas, de Jonge, and Swellengrebel, 170; MacArthur, 236). "His statement does not convey possibility or probability, but fact" (Kistemaker, 383).

The first class condition (εἴ plus the indicative in the protasis) presents a scenario that was common in the first century. Someone presenting himself as a teacher arrived and sought an opportunity to minister to a church. This was similar to Paul's missionary journeys in which he would enter synagogues and be afforded an opportunity to teach because of his credentials as a Rabbi. For the first century church, this practice involved itinerant teachers sent out by their home churches to minister to daughter and sister churches. Thus this "coming" would be in an official capacity (Westcott, 230). This issue was addressed in the *Didache*. The churches were warned: "Whosoever then comes and teaches you all these things aforesaid, receive him. But if the teacher himself be perverted and teach another doctrine to destroy these things, do not listen to him, but if his teaching be for the increase of righteousness and knowledge of the Lord, receive him as the Lord."[100] Describing this situation, John used the present tense ἔρχεται most likely with a future look, to communicate the idea that his readers would at some point in time face this issue, "in the future, when someone comes." He might have intended a more gnomic sense in which it would assume that this was a common experience already in the church and so a principle to follow. It would then have the nuance that "whenever someone comes" a certain response was called for.[101] "This teaching" is the incarnational truth that Jesus is not just God, but God who came in the flesh (v. 7).[102] It carries the sense of "this christology" (Painter, 354).

---

99. Painter (354) observes: "That the Elder and his supporters traveled about establishing churches is clear. We now learn that the deceivers also traveled and their appearance among the churches established by the Elder was anticipated." Nothing in the letter implies his first assertion. In fact, based on the testimony of Acts and the evidence of the Pauline letters, the churches to which John ministered were already established when he arrived. They were the product of Paul's missionary work, and possibly that of some of those who returned after Pentecost and the martyrdom of Stephen. However, he is correct that John was anticipating the arrival of false teachers in those churches under his care.

100. *Didache* 11.1–2.

101. D. B. Wallace, *Grammar*, 513–39.

102. Others (Burdick, 428) see it referring to v 9.

μὴ λαμβάνετε αὐτὸν εἰς οἰκίαν καὶ χαίρειν αὐτῷ μὴ λέγετε·, "do not receive him into *your* house and do not say, 'Greetings!' to him." This is the first of two present imperatives John uses to exhort his readers. These present imperatives should be viewed as general prohibitions ("don't do this") rather than taken to indicate his readers were already guilty of doing it and needed to cease ("stop doing this").[103] By this John is warning his readers against something rather than admonishing them to cease something. This fits the same general tenor of 1 John where his discussions of false teachers were followed by assurances that his readers were not guilty of the same things.

This seems to run counter to other New Testament instruction that presupposes a culture of hospitality (Matt 10:11–14) or encourages hospitality (Rom 12:13; 1 Tim 3:2; 5:10; Heb 13:2; 1 Pet 4:9). However, similar instructions can be found in the writings of the early church.[104] We should not see this as forbidding hospitality to strangers or even to fellow Christians with whom we disagree theologically. John is talking about hospitality to false teachers (Kistemaker, 383). "An official coming may have been in view and not just a casual visit from a stranger. A teacher who claims authority is in

---

103. D. B. Wallace, *Grammar*, 713–25.

104. Ignatius is an example of these writings: Ign. *Eph.* 7.1 reads: "For there are some who maliciously and deceitfully are accustomed to carrying about the Name while doing other things unworthy of God. You must avoid them as wild beasts. For they are mad dogs that bite by stealth; you must be on your guard against them, for their bite is hard to heal." Ign. *Eph.* 8:1 reads: "Therefore let no one deceive you, just as you are not now deceived, seeing that you belong entirely to God." *Eph.* 9:1 reads: "But I have learned that certain people from there have passed your way with evil doctrine, but you did not allow them to sow it among you. You covered up your ears in order to avoid receiving the things being sown by them, because you are stones of a temple, prepared beforehand for the building of God the Father, hoisted up to the heights by the crane of Jesus Christ, which is the cross, using as a rope the Holy Spirit; your faith is what lifts you up, and love is the way that leads up to God." Ign. *Smyrn.* 4:1 reads: "Now I am advising you of these things, dear friends, knowing that you are of the same mind. But I am guarding you in advance against wild beasts in human form—men whom you must not only not welcome but, if possible, not even meet. Nevertheless, do pray for them, if somehow they might repent, difficult though it may be." Also, *Did.* 12 reads: "So, if anyone should come and teach you all these things that have just been mentioned above, welcome him. But if the teacher himself goes astray and teaches a different teaching that undermines all this, do not listen to him." (from M. W. Holmes, *The Apostolic Fathers: Greek Texts and English Translations*)

view."[105] "John is not therefore forbidding private hospitality, but rather an official welcome into the congregation, with the wide spread opportunities which would then be available for the heretics to promote their cause" (Smalley, 333).[106] Bruce (142) addresses this well. "It does not mean that (say) one of Jehovah's Witnesses should not be invited into the house for a cup of tea in order to be shown the way of God more perfectly in the sitting-room than would be convenient on the doorstep. Still less does it mean that disagreements on church order should be treated as deviations from 'the teaching of Christ' and used as a ground of exclusion from social as well as ecclesiastical fellowship."

The church is not to "receive" (λαμβάνετε) these false teachers into its "house." John uses the feminine form of οἰκία as a synonym for church, a feminine noun as well. Otherwise no significance should be placed on its gender since both the masculine and feminine forms are used throughout the New Testament. Though every other use of "house" with "church" in the New Testament uses the masculine οἶκος,[107] John appears to have chosen the feminine form because of his reference to "the elect lady" (v 1) and her "sister" (v 13).

As a synonym for the church, it likely refers to its place of meeting, which would be in the home of one of its members (Burge, 238). This could be addressing either the congregation as a whole or to the leadership of the church and the home wherein they met (Smalley, 333). The significance of receiving someone is that those receiving him become identified with him. Acts 17:17 provides a New Testament example when Jason received Paul and became identified with him publicly. Such identification not only threatens the church, but may taint its witness to the lost community around it. "Guilt by association" is a powerful tool in the hands of the enemy of the gospel. Christians should not only refuse to support false teachers when

105. R. Lightner, "False Doctrine and the Child of God," 48.

106. Burge (236, italics his) expresses John's point well. "John's warning is aimed not at those who merely believe these doctrines but especially at those who teach them (who 'bears this teaching')." Further, he notes that the pl. of who comes to you indicates "John is not referring here to a personal visit of one person with another. Rather, this is an audience with the gathered church." And his use of "into your house" "likely has in mind a private residence *used as a primary place of meeting and worship* for the community—a house church."

107. Rom 16:5, 1 Cor 16:19, Col 4:15; Phlm 2.

they come into their community, but they should avoid even appearing to support false teachers as is seen in the instructions that follow.

Along with not welcoming a false teacher into the congregational gathering or the home of one of its members, they are also not to "greet" (χαίρειν) him as well. The infinitive χαίρειν was the customary greeting in Greek society.[108] Thus, John's instruction not to say "greetings" to false teachers communicated clearly to his readers. "Such a greeting would have been regarded as no mere formality but as a positive expression of encouragement" (Marshall, 74). The plural "you" in this imperative indicates that John has the congregation in view and is likely thinking in terms of its being approached on a Sunday as they prepare to worship. This defense of the faith is a congregational responsibility and not to be relegated to the elders. Otherwise John would not have used the generic second person plural verb form rather than something specific to a select group or an individual. Why not even greet a false teacher? That is explained in the next sentence.

11 The reason for avoiding false teachers is now given, with the significance of "greeting" them clarified. When we permit someone to teach in our church, we share responsibility for his or her impact in the lives of our members.

ὁ λέγων γὰρ αὐτῷ χαίρειν κοινωνεῖ τοῖς ἔργοις αὐτοῦ τοῖς πονηροῖς, "For the one speaking a greeting to him participates in his evil works." The logical conjunction γὰρ introduces the explanation for what he has just said (Burdick, 429).[109] John moves from the second person plural in the imperatives to a third person singular articular present participle ὁ λέγων to state another universal principle. This can be applied to believer and unbeliever alike. Because of the singular participle, this likely refers to a personal greeting of an individual, but may be viewed corporately, or by implication would also include a church's public welcome. To greet someone in public meant to identify with him or her. It would serve as a public endorsement of the false teacher, whether within the congregation or in public. The question then is whether this greeting is a welcoming remark (Westcott, 231) or given as parting (Hodges, 266; Smalley, 334). Though χαίρειν can simply mean "to rejoice," it was often used in greetings, normally when meeting

108. H. Conzelmann, "χαίρω," *TDNT* 9:367.

109. D. B. Wallace, *Grammar*, 673.

people (Lenski, 570). It implied "that one is on good terms" with the person addressed.[110] Throughout the remainder of the New Testament χαίρειν is used for greetings at the beginning rather than end of a visit (Westcott, 231). Thus here it means a greeting that welcomes the false teacher into the congregation of gathered believers. This should be seen as more than a casual greeting in passing, but one, whether in public or in private, that communicated public association with that person.

John warns that greeting someone results in participating with him or her in what he or she does, whether good or evil. Some see "participates" (κοινωνεῖ) having a present progressive sense "denoting continuous action" (Akin, 233). However, here it is more the statement of fact, not the focus on the process that John uses the present tense. His point is that greeting is an act of participation with the individual greeted, whether it is a one-time event or over time. agrees with). John chooses the verb κοινωνέω to communicate the significance of this identification with a false teacher.[111] Κοινωνέω "implies more than participation in the definite acts. It suggests fellowship with the character of which they are the outcome" (Westcott, 231).[112] If the person greeted comes with evil intentions, those greeting him share in his intended activity (Brooke, 179; Perkins, 635–37; Rensberger, 155).

False teaching is now described as "evil works" or "deeds." Their evilness is emphasized by the use of the adjective πονηροῖς placed in the second attributive position (with its own article). These "evil works" describe the act of teaching, not immoral conduct (Kruse, 214; Lieu, 262; Painter, 351; Strecker, 244). In this case what is taught is either christological (denial of his incarnation or deity) or ethical (refusal to show love to fellow believers) in nature (Smalley, 334).[113] Identifying with them means participating with them in what they do.

---

110. BDAG, 1075; H. Conzelmann, "χαίρω," *TDNT* 9:366–71.

111. BDAG, 552; F. Hauck, "κοινός ... κοινωνέω," *TDNT* 3:804–807. As with the noun form which occurs only in 1 John, this is the sg. use of the verb form by him as well. It is a synonym with μετέχω and indicates participation or belonging to a group (C. Spicq, "μετέχω," *TLNT* 2:478).

112. R. Lightner, "False Doctrine and the Child of God," 48.

113. Painter (355) notes the significance of the word order and feels it is intended to allude to Satan, "the evil one," and so connect the works back to their ultimate source.

Biblical Theology Comments

This epistle adds little to John's Christology, other than a reminder of its importance and the core of its truth. The incarnation is central to our faith. His use of "Jesus Christ" serves as a reminder that Jesus is both God and man and it is in this Jesus that our faith is placed. The confession of his "coming in the flesh" identifies the central place his incarnation plays in our understanding of Jesus. A flawed Christology keeps one from believing in the real Christ, and so leaves him or her outside the family of God. Furthermore, as we learned in 1 John, that false Christology is a threat to the health of a church in that one cannot commune with Christ apart from an accurate understanding of his person and work.

The orthodox faith, "truth," is not an abstract concept, but a sphere of life that involves more than facts. It is not what we know that matters, but how we live out what we know. Living and conducting our lives within the sphere of truth is contingent on a lifestyle of love for other Christians, obedience to God's revealed will, and an orthodox Christology. We must believe the right things and live according to them if we are to walk with God and have true fellowship with one another.

Application and Devotional Implications

Deceivers do not acknowledge Jesus as "coming in the flesh." They make themselves spiritual stumbling blocks by teaching a different Jesus. The deceivers of John's day were characterized by their view of Jesus' incarnation. Their doctrinal error involved a denial of the incarnation. So, while affirming his deity, they denied his humanity. The question of Jesus' humanity thereby provides one test for identifying false teachers. As those who denied Jesus' physical body in the Gnostic heresies, today anyone who denies the physical reality of the incarnation should be recognized as an antichrist, not a confused saint.

Recognizing this, and remembering what John has said previously, we are reminded that our best defense against false teachers is to walk obediently in the sphere of God's revealed truth. This is a more powerful defense than studying false teachings and false teachers. To know God's Word and to live according to it protects one from deception more than memorizing charts about various cults and cult leaders. That is not to say that studying them is not helpful. It is. However, the study of cults should be secondary to knowing and living by God's Word.

As churches and individuals we are called upon to love one another through actions. However, our love for our fellow Christians must extend to protecting them from the greatest possible harm, namely, deception that will cost them heavenly rewards. Thus we need to investigate and evaluate anyone we invite into our churches. Several years ago I was approached by one of my students to see if I would be willing to speak at her church's upcoming family retreat. When I expressed my willingness, her pastor then contacted me. Though I was a Bible teacher in a conservative Christian college that agreed with his church's theological convictions, I still had to "pass muster." He questioned me extensively on my theology and views of various traditional and current issues. When he was satisfied that I would benefit his congregation, he only then invited me to speak. I was not offended. In fact, I appreciated his pastoral concern and care. When I arrived and met the members of his church, I could see the benefits of his watchcare in the unity and love of that community of faith. I also saw my role, to strengthen the faith of that community by building on the truths their pastor had been teaching them in the years prior, and would continue to teach them in the years following.

Selected Bibliography

Dorsey, D. A. *The Literary Structure of the Old Testament: A Commentary on Genesis-Malachi.* Grand Rapids: Baker, 1999.

Fanning, B. M. *Verbal Aspect in New Testament Greek.* Oxford: Clarendon, 1990.

Funk, R. W. "The Form and Structure of II and III John." *JBL* 86 (1967): 424–30.

Holmes, M. W. *The Apostolic Fathers: Greek Texts and English Translations.* Updated ed. Grand Rapids: Baker, 1999.

Köstenberger, A. J. "The Deity of Christ in John's Letters and the Book of Revelation." In *The Deity of Christ*, edited by C. W. Morgan and R. A. Peterson, 151–67. Wheaton, IL: Crossway, 2011.

Lalleman, P. J. "The Adversaries Envisaged in the Johannine Epistles." *ThT* 53 (1999): 17–24.

Lightner, R. "False Doctrine and the Child of God." *The Journal of Ministry and Theology* 10 (2006): 44–53.

Lund, N. W. *Chiasmus in the New Testament: A Study in the Form and Function of Chiastic Structures.* Peabody, MA: Hendrickson, 1942, 1970.

Mann, R. E. "The Value of Chiasm for New Testament Interpretation." *BSac* 141 (2002): 144–54.

Metzger, B. M., and United Bible Societies. *A Textual Commentary on the Greek New Testament.* 2nd ed. New York: United Bible Societies, 1994.

Nicole, R. R. "The Biblical Concept of Truth." In *Scripture and Truth*, 287–302. Grand Rapids: Zondervan, 1983.

Spicq, C. *Theological Lexicon of the New Testament.* Translated and edited by J. D. Ernest. 3 vols. Peabody, MA: Hendrickson, 1994.

Wallace, D. B. *Greek Grammar beyond the Basics.* Grand Rapids: Zondervan, 1996.

Wendland, E. R. "'Dear Children' versus the 'Antichrists': The Rhetoric of Reassurance in First John." *JOTT* 11 (1998): 40–84.

Closing Remarks (12–13)

Original Text

12 Πολλὰ ἔχων ὑμῖν γράφειν οὐκ ἐβουλήθην διὰ χάρτου καὶ μέλανος, ἀλλὰ ἐλπίζω γενέσθαι πρὸς ὑμᾶς καὶ στόμα πρὸς στόμα λαλῆσαι, ἵνα ἡ χαρὰ ἡμῶνa πεπληρωμένη ᾖ. 13 Ἀσπάζεταί σε τὰ τέκνα τῆς ἀδελφῆς σου τῆς ἐκλεκτῆς.a

Textual Notes

12.a. The majority of MS witnesses favor the UBS4 reading of ἡμῶν rather than the ὑμῶν of SBLGNT. It seems best in light of the context and John's pattern of identifying himself with his readers (א K L P Ψ 049 056 88 104 181 326 330 451 614 629 630 945 1505 1877 2412 2495 Byz Lect l1439 syrph,h arm). Though, as Metzger notes, some of the oldest and best MSS favor ὑμῶν (A B 0142 33 81 436 1739 1881 2127 2492 itar,c,dem,div,p vg copbo eth), it seems best to see this as a scribal change.

13.a. Though MS support for ἀμήν following ἐκλεκτῆς is strong, including some of the lesser Alexandrian texts, its absence from the closing of 3 John argues against its inclusion as original. Thus I concur with Metzger.[1]

1. B. Metzger and United Bible Societies, *A Textual Commentary on the Greek New Testament*, 2nd ed., 654.

Translation

12 Having many things to write to you, I did not wish to write with pen and ink, but I hope to come to you and to speak personally[2] in order that our[3] joy may be made complete.[4] **13** The children of your elect sister greet you.[5]

Commentary

Having communicated his warning, John now closes this epistle, expressing a desire to say more. We all wish he would have written more, but must settle for the limits of the Holy Spirit's inspiration. His wisdom is absolute. We will have to wait for eternity to ask John what else he discussed with them when he did see them face-to-face.

12 John's closing, which is repeated in his epistle to Gaius almost word-for-word, contains both a statement of his desire and a promise to communicate more at a later date.[6] His desire is expressed in terms of shared joy.

Πολλὰ ἔχων ὑμῖν γράφειν οὐκ ἐβουλήθην διὰ χάρτου καὶ μέλανος, "Having many things to write to you, I did not wish to write with pen and ink." John acknowledges that he would like to write a deal more than just this short epistle. He places the pronoun πολλὰ at the fore of this sentence for emphasis.[7] Painter (335) says that the "much more to say" comment was simply a

2. Literally he writes "mouth to mouth" (στόμα πρὸς στόμα) However, the idiom communicates the concept of "personally." Translated into an English figure of speech, we would say "face to face."

3. In the same way as was true of 1 John 1:4, here MS support is mixed between the two readings of "your" (ὑμῶν) or "our" (ἡμῶν). And though the MS support for ὑμῶν is strong, John's pattern of including himself with his readers argues for ἡμῶν being original.

4. 1 John 1:4.

5. Some MSS include "amen" at the end of this sentence. However, it is absent from 3 John and so, in light of the near word-for-word similarity between the two endings, is not likely to be original.

6. Because this closing is "virtually verbally identical" to that of 3 John, Bultmann (115) considers it an "imitation" of 3 John rather than coming from the same author, especially in light of the fact that it is a very "conventional" first-century closing (Kruse, 216; Lieu, 262). As a result we would expect the two endings to be nearly identical since they come from the same pen.

7. Πολλὰ may be serving either epexegetically as the direct obj. of ἔχων or adverbially as the obj. of γράφειν.

conventional way of closing a letter and so need not indicate there was not more that came with it. However, as noted in the greeting, John's use of conventional terminology does not lessen the sincerity of his words. When he says he has more to say, he implies that he has a long list of things he wished to discuss. If he had written them out, it is likely this epistle would have been much longer than 1 John.[8]

He wished to speak directly rather than write more. "Pen and ink" is an obvious metaphor for written correspondence. His choice of the instantaneous (epistolary) aorist indicates that he had thought about writing more and decided on a personal meeting instead (Harris, 254). Painter (356) refers to this statement as "standard in Hellenistic letters."

ἀλλὰ ἐλπίζω γενέσθαι πρὸς ὑμᾶς καὶ στόμα πρὸς στόμα λαλῆσαι, "but I hope to come to you and to speak personally." John moves from the aorist (past) desire not to write too much, to his present desire to come see them.[9] He describes the personal interaction he desired with the figurative *στόμα πρὸς στόμα λαλῆσαι* (literally: "mouth to mouth"), thus verbal communication. Such a visit was their gain and our loss, except that it was by God's design. If John had needed to write more for the benefit of the church, the Holy Spirit would have moved him to write. Perhaps, 1 John is that "many things." At any rate, what we learn of John from this closing that his words to Gaius, is that John valued personal interaction and instruction over correspondence.

ἵνα ἡ χαρὰ ἡμῶν πεπληρωμένη ᾖ, "in order that our joy may be made complete." Why did John wish to see his readers? He had both their and his shared joy in view. With the *ἵνα* of result,[10] John explains why he values a visit over a long letter (Harris, 254). His choice of "our joy" is not so much a reflection of his desire for joy, but his desire for shared joy, fellowship with these saints (Harris, 254; Lieu, 263). The subjunctive *ᾖ*, functioning in this *ἵνα* clause, does not imply only possibility, but the actuality. The completed

---

8. Painter (356) sees this statement as "a reference to the substance of 1 John." Houlden (140) likewise sees 1 John as an "expansion" of 2 John. That would make it a fulfillment of John's wish. I suspect that there was even more he would have liked to say, because even 1 John was limited by the available parchment, I am sure.

9. Both *γενέσθαι* and *λαλῆσαι* are adv. infinitives completing the idea of *ἐλπίζω*. John's use of *γίνομαι* rather than *ἔρχομαι* is not significant since in this context they are synonyms (Bultmann, 115, n. 2; Burdick, 430).

10. D. B. Wallace, *Grammar*, 672.

joy is an expectation, not just a desire. Nonetheless, his desire is a full experience (πεπληρωμένη) of that joy that could only come from a personal visit and the fellowship that follows.

13 Ἀσπάζεταί σε τὰ τέκνα τῆς ἀδελφῆς σου τῆς ἐκλεκτῆς, "The children of your elect sister greet you." John now relays the greetings of his audience's "elect" sister's children. Who is the "elect sister"?

(1) If Lady Electa is a person, this would be an actual person as well, her sister. Then the question arises about why it is her children that send the greeting. The answer could be either that she is deceased, or that she is absent and they happen to be with John at the time of writing (Burdick, 431). (2) If both of these "ladies" refer to churches, then this refers to members of a sister congregation (Smalley, 336). Strecker (250) sees this as the congregation of the author. Moreover, as Westcott (232) notes, though this may sound like a letter to an individual, it also works for the corporate view. These would represent members of the church who are presently with John as he writes (Harris, 255). Thus, σε is a collective singular (Smalley, 336). As noted in the introduction, the corporate interpretation seems best even though the meaning is ultimately the same, regardless of which view is taken.[11]

John begins by using a different term for "greet" than he had earlier in his warning about greeting false teachers (ἀσπάζεταί as opposed to χαίρειν). His reference to an "elect sister" appears to strengthen the argument that "Lady Electa" is a church and not a person (Bruce, 143–44). Thus John is relaying greetings from his local assembly to the congregation receiving this correspondence (Brooke, 180; Stott, 218).

Selected Bibliography

Metzger, B. M., and United Bible Societies. *A Textual Commentary on the Greek New Testament.* 2nd ed. New York: United Bible Societies, 1994.

Wallace, D. B. *Greek Grammar beyond the Basics*. Grand Rapids: Zondervan, 1996.

11. Schnackenburg (306) says Peter uses a similar term in 1 Pet 5:13 (Ἀσπάζεται ὑμᾶς ἡ ἐν Βαβυλῶνι συνεκλεκτὴ), but translates the article ἡ ("she") as "your sister."

3 John

Introduction

Welcome to the shortest book of the Bible! Though it has been assigned fifteen verses (as opposed to 2 John's thirteen), it has only 219 words, while the next shortest book, 2 John, has 245. Both could easily fit on a single papyrus sheet, and most likely did. Additionally, this is the only New Testament book not to have either "Jesus" or "Christ" in it, though he is not absent, much like we see of God in Esther.

By God's design, a personal letter between an apostle and a beloved friend was included in the canon of Scripture.[1] Through it we are granted a glimpse into the life of the church and some of its struggles. We are reminded that the first-century church was little different than what we see today in terms of people's personalities and the problems that often creates in a local congregation. We are also granted another peek into the personality and heart's passion of John as a person, and permitted to see how he handles problems, much like we learn of Paul through his epistles.

Author

The author of this epistle is John the apostle.[2] As with 2 John, John's authorship is attested by early church tradition and stylistic similarities. Though it

1. "The fact that 3 John found its way into the New Testament canon is of itself weighty evidence in favor of the genuineness of the letter. It is not surprising that Romans or 1 Corinthians should be thought worthy of a place in the canon, but the inclusion of such a personal letter as 3 John rules out any possibility that it was a fraud" (Burdick, 441).

2. R. Edwards is an example of the concerns raised by questions of authorship. She asks: "if he is only a local church leader, why does he write so authoritatively to a member of another congregation? Perhaps he is relying on greater seniority in the faith, or presuming on his personal relationship to Diotrephes and Gaius" (Edwards, 25). Accepting Johannine authorship answers the question of authority and explains the confidence with which he writes. However, its technical anonymity need not raise questions of authority since it could as easily follow the pattern

may be questioned by some in recent church history, its content and style matches that of the other two epistles. For a full discussion of authorship, see my discussion in 2 John. Let it suffice to say that no reason compels or tempts me to question apostolic authorship of this epistle.

Recipients and Date

The recipient of this epistle is a believer named "Gaius," though nothing beyond this can be known, either of his location or actual identity. Though there are other men named Gaius in the New Testament (Acts 19:29; 20:4; Rom 16:23; 1 Cor 1:14), the name was so common that it is unlikely he was one of them (Akin, 239; Brooke, 181; Brown, 702; Burdick, 443; Harris, 257; Williams, 67).[3] He was probably the member of one of the churches in Asia Minor to which John's influence had spread during his Ephesian ministry. It is not clear that he was a member of Diotrephes' church (Brooke, 187; Marshall, 88; Stott, 228) or a nearby church (Akin, 246; Brown, 702; Dodd, 161; Kistemaker, 396). His ability to support itinerant preachers indicates that he was a wealthy member of his church, and likely a prominent leader. He was certainly viewed as trustworthy by John, as John entrusts to him the care of Demetrius.

Though nothing within the epistle indicates a date of writing, it was most likely written about the same time as 1 and 2 John, in the latter years of the first century. Some place it as early as AD 85 (Akin, 27) and as late as AD 115 (Rensberger, 30).[4] The majority place it in the last decade of the

---

of Hebrews. In the same way, though Luke was not an apostle, his association with Paul and endorsement by Paul's quotation from his Gospel (1 Tim 5:18 quotes Jesus' words in Luke 10:10) led to the inclusion of Luke's Gospel and Acts in the New Testament canon. Similarly, this epistle's acceptance by the church, and thus canonical status, gives it authority to address the church then and today.

3. L. Marulli, "A Letter of Recommendation? A Closer look at Third John's 'rhetorical' Argumentation," 203. Gaius of Derbe (Acts 19:29) who accompanied Paul on his second missionary journey, Gaius of Macedonia (Acts 20:4), and Gaius of Corinth (Rom 16:23; 1 Cor 1:13) with whom Paul was staying when he wrote Romans are all mentioned by Luke and with Paul early in his ministry. As a result, by the time John was writing this epistle, they would likely have either been quite old or had died. None would likely have been residing in Asia Minor.

4. Marshall (47–48) offers an even wider range, from before the fall of Jerusalem to the last decade of the century, after clarifying that we have no way of dating any

first century (Barker, 301; Brown, 96; Bruce, 31; Burdick, 444; Johnson, 4; Kruse, 27–28; Smalley, xxii; Westcott, xxxii; Williamson, 33).

Occasion and Setting

The background of this epistle is basically the same as John's first two epistles (Houlden, 150–51), though the nature of problems faced in that local church are made clearer from the things said to Gaius. The church had developed a practice of sending out itinerant representatives, possibly as messengers of the apostles or other church leaders (Burdick, 444). This is much like Titus' ministry as Paul's representative to the Corinthians (2 Cor 2:12–13; 7:6–15; and 8:6) and to the churches of Crete (Titus 1:5). These itinerant preachers would spend a period of time in a local church. They would know and teach apostolic doctrines while there, with those benefiting from their instruction, in turn, supporting them. Then, when the church's instruction was complete, they would move on to the next church, being helped along by their church wherein they had just completed their ministry. These men would not only be supported by the churches to which they ministered, but also looked for hospitality and assistance from churches in the towns and villages through which they passed in route to their next ministry destination. This practice is reflected in Titus 3:13 with Paul's command to help Zenas the lawyer and Apollos on their travels. It is also described somewhat in the *Didache*.[5] For example, one set of instructions says,

> Everyone "who comes in the name of the Lord" is to be welcomed. But then examine him, and you will find out—for you will have insight—what is true and what is false. (2) If the one who comes is merely passing through, assist him as much as you can. But he must not stay with you for more than two or, if necessary, three days. (3) However, if he wishes to settle among you and is a craftsman, let him work for his living. (4) But if he is not a craftsman, decide according to your own judgment how he shall live among you as a Christian, yet without being idle. (5) But if he does not wish

---

of John's works with certainty. Strecker (xl-xli) places it in the early second century, as late as AD 125.

5. See T. O'Loughlin, *The Didache: A Window on the Earliest Christians* (Grand Rapids: Baker, 2010), for a fuller discussion of this church practice.

to cooperate in this way, then he is trading on Christ. Beware of such people.[6]

Some men, in this case one named Diotrephes, were attempting to assert their leadership over and against that of the apostles. This was Paul's experience with leaders in the church at Corinth. In the case of Gaius' church, Diotrephes had begun to assert his influence and drive out legitimate representatives of the apostles in order to maintain his personal control, and so had to be corrected.

Letters of introduction were common,[7] and mentioned by Paul (1 Cor 16:3; 2 Cor 3:1; Col 4:7–9; maybe Rom 16:1–2). Though addressing a problem, this epistle would seem to function in just such a role. As with his other epistles, this is likely written from Ephesus where John lived out his days and from which place he ministered to the churches throughout Asia Minor.

Does this indicate a beginning of the monarchical bishopric that developed in the early church? Grayston (161–62) says no. He argues that this could not have been "a successful bishops' revolt" because (1) the Gospel was written after the epistles (his view) and evidences no interest in the issue of monarchical bishopric, (2) the inclusion of 2 John and 3 John in the canon indicates that the elder was successful against Diotrephes. "Therefore either Diotrephes was not a prototype monarchical bishop, or the experiment failed" (Grayston, 62). Painter (363) notes that "Diotrephes was not a bishop excommunicating anyone, but a person who could refuse hospitality to those he did not wish to receive into his own household." Edwards (25) is in agreement and says, "The dispute, then, seems to be about church hospitality rather than doctrine or authority. We are dealing with a pastoral and moral, rather than ecclesiastical, issue." It seems the best answer to this

---

6. *Did* 12.1–5 (Transl. from M. W. Holmes, *The Apostolic Fathers: Greek Texts and English Translations*, 265–67).

7. P.Oxy. I 32.4–15 is an example of a letter of introduction. It reads: "To Julius Domitius, military tribune of the legion, from Aurelius Archelaus, his *benificiarius*, greeting. I have once previously recommended to you my friend Theon, and now again, Sir, I beg you to look upon him as if he were myself. He is indeed a man worthy of your affection. He has left his family, his property and business and followed me, and through all he has shielded me from care. I beg you therefore to grant him admittance to your presence (*ut habeat introitum atte*)." (from A. S. Hunt and C. C. Edgar, *Select Papyri,* 1:320–23)

question is that we cannot know what the issues were other than what is contained in the epistle (Rensberger, 158–59). Moreover, the failure of John to identify theological issues of any kind points to a personality issue over against false teachings of any kind.

Purpose

Though one should never solely base his or her interpretation on an understood purpose of any author of Scripture, internal evidence at times may provide an understanding of the author's major purpose in writing. This would seem especially true in the smaller, more focused personal letters such as this epistle and Paul's letter to Philemon. Larger works, on the other hand, even when they have one or more stated purposes, may not exhaust the author's intentions in that work. As seen in 1 John, no single stated purpose can be made a determinant of meaning or made to exhaust John' intentions in writing, whether stated or implied. In the case of this epistle, though, John's purpose seems primarily to be to encourage Gaius to continue to support the legitimate itinerant representatives of the church and to endorse Demetrius as one of those legitimately sent out (Burdick, 444; Yarbrough, 363).[8] That being his purpose, he has much to say to Gaius about spiritual commitment and participation in ministry. The epistle proves to

8. L. Marulli ("A Letter of Recommendation? A Closer look at Third John's 'rhetorical' Argumentation," 205) rejects the common view that this is a letter of recommendation and argues that it is "an epideictic rhetorical attempt to restore the Elder's honor (discredited by Diotrephes) in Gaius' eyes and persuade him to detach himself from Diotrephes' reprehensible behavior by extending hospitality to the Elder's envoys." He argues that the typical letter of recommendation contained a promise to repay the favor when asking the recipient to welcome someone. Since this "promise" is absent from 3 John, it does not function as a letter of recommendation. Marulli (206–207) does not believe that Demetrius was the actual bearer of the letter because he is named as someone respected by all, but not particularly described as "needing hospitality, carrying out a specific function, or acting as a representative of the Elder." He believes that John was using someone mutually known by him and Gaius as an example to be emulated. This theory is purely speculative and based on his interpretation of one part of the text whereas the overall message makes clear that it is a letter of recommendation.

be, for him and for us, a description of how to and how not to treat fellow believers as well as the significance of our actions.[9]

The influence of theories on interpretation of the purpose and message of a book can be illustrated with Burge's understanding of Diotrephes. He (230) sees Diotrephes as a "secessionist" who is about to lead an entire house church in "defecting entirely" from the "Johannine community."[10] Gaius is not afraid of him or threatened by him. Even so, "John does not ask Gaius to intervene in the controversy by confronting Diotrephes himself" (245). He (245–46) posits, "Christians are called to different roles, and Gaius has done enough if he stand firm for Jesus Christ and provides John and his couriers an entrée into the community." However, nothing in the letter implies a doctrinal rift between Diotrephes and John. Further, as will be seen in the commentary below, John's failure to call him an antichrist or address any doctrinal issues would seem to indicate the issue has more to do with conduct than theology. The theory of secessionists has to do with theological variance (false teachers and false teachings), an issue that does appear in 1 and 2 John, but not in this epistle.

Genre

As with 2 John, this is a second typical Hellenistic letter of the first century (Akin, 237; Painter, 361).[11] These letters contained: "(a) greeting in the third

9. Some (Burdick, 444; Yarbrough, 363) also see a second purpose of warning Gaius about Diotrephes.

10. I do not subscribe to either aspect of the theory of a Johannine school or presence of a secessionist movement to which John responded in any of this epistles. See my introductory remarks for 1 John for a more complete justification of my view.

11. See S. K. Stowers, *Letter Writing in Greco-Roman Antiquity* for examples of letters. He identifies four major kinds of letters: letters of friendship, family letters, letters of praise and blame, and letters of exhortation and advice. The category of exhortation and advice can be divided into letters that are paraenetic, give advice, exhort to a way of life, admonish, rebuke, reproach, and console. Also, see R. L. Funk, "The Form and Structure of II and III John" (424–30) for an excellent explanation of the parts of a letter. An example from the Oxyrhyncus Papyri reads: "Theon to his esteemed Tyrannus, many greetings. Heraclides, the bearer of this letter, is my brother. I therefore entreat you with all my power to treat him as your protégé. I have also written to your brother Hermias asking him to communicate with you about him. You will confer upon me a very great favour if Heraclides

person singular; (b) a wish for good health for the recipient; (c) main body, often containing a request; (d) sometimes a reference to a possible meeting; (e) final greetings and wishes for good health" (Edwards, 22). However, as is true of Paul as well, John varies from the "typical" at points. (1) This letter lacks the author's personal name. That may indicate this is a more formal letter, though the other references in the epistle indicates a close personal relationship between John and Gaius. Paul, on the other hand, identified himself when addressing Philemon. (2) The standard greeting of χαίρειν is missing. This is not unusual for Aramaic letters of the first-century, but would not be absent from a Greek one (Edwards, 23). Also, (3) εἰρήνη σοι ("Peace to you") in v 15 replaces ἔρρωσο ("be strong," or "keep well") in the closing comments. However, these variations do not detract from the originality and factuality of the letter. Rather, they indicate the personal nature of this very personal of letters that God deigned beneficial to the body of Christ across the ages and had it included in the canon of Scripture.

Relationship to 1 and 2 John

Nothing in the epistle enables us to know whether it preceded, followed, or was contemporaneous with either 1 or 2 John (Burdick, 444; Lieu, 163).[12] Painter (361) recounts Dodd's (lxii-lxiii) analysis and details the statistics comparing the vocabulary of the three epistles and the Gospel of John. He concludes that all three epistles come from the same author. Even so, he (361) notes that there is "little overlap between 1 John and 3 John" but concludes (362) concerning 2 and 3 John, "Because there is also freedom to adapt the opening and closing, it is more likely that the two letters were written by the same author. A copyist would have followed the letter he was copying more closely. Further, 3 John overlaps 2 John precisely where 2 John fills a gap in the defense offered by 1 John." Strecker (253) acknowledges common authorship between 2 and 3 John on the basis that "both retain the same Johannine language and style." They share similar vocabulary (ἀλήθεια, τέκνα, ἀγάπη, ἐξέρχεσθαι) and phrases (ἐξάρην λίαν, ἐν ἀληθείᾳ

gains your notice. Before all else you have my good wishes for unbroken health and prosperity. Good-bye." (from B. P. Grenfell and A. S. Hunt, eds. *The Oxyrhynchus Papyri, 2*:292)

12. R. M. Price, "The Sitz-im-Leben of Third John: A New Reconstruction," 109–10.

περιπατεῖν). Both recipients walk in truth. They have nearly identical beginnings and endings. Additionally they share the same "elder" for an author.[13]

There are several notable similarities between 2 and 3 John. In both epistles John identifies himself as "the elder." He loves his recipients "in truth" (2 John 1, 3 John 1), he expresses joy because his readers are "walking in truth" (2 John 4, 3 John 4), and the theme of "truth" dominates both epistles (2 John 1 [2x], 2, 3, 4; 3 John 1, 3 [2x], 4, 8, 12). Both epistles discuss traveling missionaries and their support (2 John 7–10, 3 John 5–8, 10) (Burdick, 442).[14] The concluding remarks evidence the same hand and heart.

Though 3 John has fewer connections with 1 John, it still reflects the heart attitude of that epistle. Both address the expression of God's love in terms of how one treats his fellow Christian (1 John 3:16–18; 3 John 5–8).

In summary, though we do not know the order of writing or the time of writing with any certainty, we do know all three epistles come from the pen (well, reed) of John. They address both similar and different issues and they complement each other.

Theological and Practical Emphases of the Book

This is an epistle about ecclesiology, but also more than ecclesiology. Although John deals with the question of a poor leader, though not a false teacher or antichrist, there is no significant doctrine discussed beyond church order. However, principles are implied by the praises accorded to Gaius and Demetrius as well as John's explanation for his request for help. Thus, much is to be learned from this short epistle, though its contribution to theology is from the implication of things said more than direct command or instruction. Even so, its emphasis on supporting missionaries, and its contrast of Gaius and Diotrephes, speaks volumes about the believer's responsibility to support God's work through God's workers. This letter presupposes Christ's command for mutual love. It also gives us a first-hand example of what hating one's brother by not meeting his needs (1 John

13. Strecker (253) believes that 2 John was the correspondence referred to in v 9 that Diotrephes rejected.

14. Though Burdick (442) points to similar structure as an argument for common authorship, the fact that the epistles conform so closely to Hellenistic letters of their day mitigates against this being a proof. On the other hand, key terminology and deviations from the norm do.

2:9–11 and 3:17) looks like. In this epistle we see the outworking of a biblical lifestyle, called "walking in truth." Thus, we gain a hint of God's purpose in including this shortest of letters in the canon of his Scriptures.

Outline

As with the other two epistles, various options are proposed for outlining this epistle. I have chosen the simplest, which keeps the body as a single unit (Brown, 791–92; Lenski, 579; Rensberger, 161). A basic outline, with a salutation, body of the letter, and closing remarks, reflects the nature of a first-century letter. Others divide up the body of the letter into three or so parts, depending on whether they divide it based on the persons or topics discussed (Akin, 237; Barker, 370; Schnackenburg, 319; Smith, 151–57; Stott, 221; Strecker, 258–66).[15] As with his first epistle, everything said is intertwined and related. Thus it is appropriate to leave the body of the letter as a single thought.

I. Salutation (1–4)
II. Gaius' Responsibility (5–12)
III. Closing Remarks (13–15)

Selected Bibliography

Brand, C., C. Draper, and A. England, eds. *Holman Illustrated Bible Dictionary.* Nashville: Holman, 2003.

Marulli, L. "A Letter of Recommendation? A Closer Look at Third John's 'Rhetorical' Argumentation." *Bib* 90 (2009): 203–23.

Price, R. M. "The Sitz-im-Leben of Third John: A New Reconstruction." *EvQ* 61 (1989): 109–19.

15. Smalley (343) keeps comments about Diotrephes and Demetrius (vv 9–12) together.

Salutation (1–4)

Introduction

These first few verses follow much the same "standard" format of the first-century letter.[1] However, that does not mean that we should skip over them and focus our attention entirely on the body of the epistle. It is in this short introduction that we learn a great deal about John's relationship with Gaius, and the kind of person Gaius was and we should be.

Original Text

1 Ὁ πρεσβύτερος Γαΐῳ τῷ ἀγαπητῷ, ὃν ἐγὼ ἀγαπῶ ἐν ἀληθείᾳ.

2 Ἀγαπητέ, περὶ πάντων εὔχομαί σε εὐοδοῦσθαι καὶ ὑγιαίνειν, καθὼς εὐοδοῦταί
σου ἡ ψυχή. **3** ἐχάρην γὰρ λίαν ἐρχομένων ἀδελφῶν καὶ μαρτυρούντων σου τῇ
ἀληθείᾳ, καθὼς σὺ ἐν ἀληθείᾳ περιπατεῖς. **4** μειζοτέραν τούτων οὐκ ἔχω χαράν,a
ἵνα ἀκούω τὰ ἐμὰ τέκνα ἐν τῇ ἀληθείᾳ περιπατοῦντα.

Textual Notes

4.a. The reading of *χαράν* has greater MS support (א A C K L P Ψ 048 049 056 0142 33 81 88 104 181 326 330 436 451 614 629 630 945 1505 1877 2127 2412 2495 *Byz Lect* l^{1439} it^{p} syr^{ph,h} cop^{sa} arm eth) and is more Johannine than

1. Grayston (160) sees it deviating from normal letters in the introduction because the letter "is in fact both a certificate of approval for Gaius and of disapproval for Diotrephes. That explains two odd features: the elder's failure to give his own name (he is writing formally not personally) and his omission of the standard greeting after v. 1 (he is writing in effect 'to whom it may concern')." It could be that John "missed" the greeting because he was focused on the problem of Diotrephes and his concern for Demetrius' need for hospitality.

χάριν (B 5 57 1891 2143 2298 2492 $it^{ar,e,dem,div}$ vg cop^{bo}).[2] See John 16:20–22; 17:13 for his use.

Translation

1 The elder to the beloved Gaius whom I love in truth.[3] **2** Beloved,[4] I pray that you do well in all things and prosper, just as your soul prospers. **3** For I rejoiced greatly at the coming of brethren and their testifying of your truth, just as you are walking in the truth. **4** I have no greater joy than this, that I may hear of my children walking in the truth.

Commentary

1 John begins this epistle with a standard greeting. However, included in it are a few insights into the person and conduct of the letter's recipient. We also see John's attitude toward Gaius and his joy at how Gaius is living out apostolic instruction. This greeting, though following first century convention, is still very Johannine in its focus on the love felt by John toward this fellow believer.

Ὁ πρεσβύτερος Γαΐῳ τῷ ἀγαπητῷ, "The elder to the beloved Gaius." This self-designation could be part of the title or, simply be serving as the subject with an understood verbal idea of "is writing to."[5] The article is not used for emphasis ("*the* elder") but for identification since John is taking it as a title. Unlike when Jesus called Nicodemus "*the* teacher of Israel" (John 3:10) while rebuking him for failing to understand what he was saying, here it simply serves to identify the subject of the sentence. There may even be an implied "John, the elder." The term "elder" was used in the first century to describe an old man and always contained within it the sense of age, and thus respect. These older persons deserved respect, whether due to

2. B. M. Metzger and United Bible Societies, *A Textual Commentary on the Greek New Testament*, 2d ed., 655.

3. As in 2 John 1, rather than translating this adverbially, "I truly love," the four-fold repetition of ἐν ἀληθείᾳ would indicate all four have the same sense. The other three occurrences reflect datives of sphere and have to do with walking in the realm of truth. So, too, the sense of this use should be seen in that light.

4. 1 John 2:7; 3:2, 21; 4:1, 7. 11; 3 John 5, 11.

5. See the notes for 2 John 1 for a discussion of the significance of the title chosen by John to designate him as "the elder."

the office they occupied or their personal influence in society. Jewish synagogues were led by a board of elders. Subsequently, when the church was born, it followed the Jewish practice of appointing elder leadership from among its members.

Though Gaius is a proper name, and so not in need of an article, the addition of the article with ἀγαπητῷ, which is acting as an attributive adjective, is unusual (Lieu, 267).[6] This makes it emphatic and means more than just "dear friend" (Akin, 239). Painter (367) sees John's reference to him as "beloved" confirming "his Christian status." Johnson (165) sees this designating him a loyal follower of John rather than a close acquaintance or friend. However, no evidence exists in any other use of "beloved" by John that would indicate such a connotation.

John does not want Gaius to miss the point that he loves him. The Gaius to whom John is writing is most likely living in Asia Minor and serving in one of the churches under his care. Because of this, it is very unlikely that he is one of the three men named Gaius mentioned elsewhere in the New Testament and associated with Paul (Gaius of Macedonia in Acts 19:29, of Derbe in Acts 20:4, and of Corinth in Rom 16:23). According to church tradition, he was appointed as the bishop of Pergamum by John, though some modern scholars would reject this (Brooke, 181; Brown, 702).[7] It would be better to see him as he is, a person otherwise unknown to us from the New Testament record or from church history (Bruce, 147; Stott, 222).

ὃν ἐγὼ ἀγαπῶ ἐν ἀληθείᾳ. "whom I love in truth." John's love for Gaius is emphasized through its repetition in this sentence. John's inclusion of ἐγὼ as the subject within this relative clause makes it emphatic (Akin, 240; Barker, 371; Smalley, 345; Yarbrough, 365).[8] By this John is emphasizing that this love is personal and relational. He is speaking for himself, not in an

6. L. Marulli ("A Letter of Recommendation? A Closer look at Third John's 'rhetorical' Argumentation," 203–204) understands the order of names in this greeting indicate either a patron-client relationship or that of two equals since the first name will always be the one with superior social status. Additionally, the presence of "health wishes and third party greetings" argues against Gaius being of a superior social status to John. But, John's requests are indirect enough to indicate that John views Gaius as having equal social status.

7. *Apos. Con.* 7.46.9. Brown (702) considers this account as "dubious" and also rejects the idea that the single-bishop model of church leadership was present at the end of the first century or that the apostles ordained men to the episcopate.

8. D. B. Wallace, *Grammar, 323.*

official capacity, even as he writes this letter to his friend. Even so, his love for Gaius is still connected to his beliefs, and so he loves him in the sphere of truth, as one who is living out God's truth even as Gaius does.

When John says (literally) "in truth" (ἐν ἀληθείᾳ), he may be using a dative of manner to say "whom I *truly* love" (Bultmann, 96; Haas, de Jonge, and Swellengrebel, 176; Painter, 367; Schnackenburg, 320),[9] or of sphere to say "whom I love *within the sphere of* truth" (Burdick, 446–47; Houlden, 151; Kruse, 220; Williams, 68).[10] The dative of sphere seems best because the theme of walking "in (the sphere of) truth" dominates this paragraph. Lieu (268) argues for this on the basis of its "formulaic" use in the other five occurrences in 3 John. Perkins (93) says it forms an inclusio* with the same phrase in v 4. It does not need the article to be definite in light of the later uses of the noun and the example of John 8:45–46 (Burdick, 447).[11] Moreover, as was true in his first epistle, love and truth are interconnected (Akin, 240). One cannot love deceptively or outside of an honest relationship.

What is the nature of this truth? Smalley (345) describes this as "the truth of God which has been made known by Jesus" (so too, Culpepper, 279).[12] Similarly, Hengel sees "in truth" as a figurative way of saying "Christ" and sees this as equivalent to Paul's "in Christ." He argues for this on the basis: "It is the quite personal, private form of the letter which prevents the author from using the title Christ, just as in a private letter a Jew avoids the tetragrammaton by periphrasis."[13] John does not exhibit such a penchant in 2 John, though admittedly it is not to an individual but to a church. It seems more likely that the nature of the request and the problem discussed, being ethical rather than doctrinal, did not require reference to Christ, whether directly or indirectly. This truth is the apostolic teachings about Christ and his commandment to love one another.

9. D. B. Wallace, *Grammar*, 161–62.

10. D. B. Wallace, *Grammar*, 144–45, 153, 161. A few (Akin, 240; Walls and Anders, 248–49) opt for both senses.

11. Verse 45 has the article while v 46 does not. Jesus uses it both ways to refer to the same "truth." ([45]ἐγὼ δὲ ὅτι τὴν ἀλήθειαν λέγω, οὐ πιστεύετέ μοι. [46] τίς ἐξ ὑμῶν ἐλέγχει με περὶ ἁμαρτίας; εἰ ἀλήθειαν λέγω, διὰ τί ὑμεῖς οὐ πιστεύετέ μοι;)

12. Williamson (206) defines it as a relationship with God who is truth.

13. M. Hengel, *The Johannine Question*, 35.

2 This is a fairly standard first century greeting, including the blessing invoked. At the same time, though, it is a sincere wish from John on behalf of Gaius.

Ἀγαπητέ, περὶ πάντων εὔχομαί σε εὐοδοῦσθαι καὶ ὑγιαίνειν, "Beloved, I pray that you do well in all things and prosper."[14] John begins this epistle, following his introduction, with a characteristic Johannine term of endearment, "beloved" (Burdick, 447; Harris, 259).[15] This expresses his deep affection for Gaius in much the same way this same address spoke to the recipients of 1 John.

Some see this as simply expressing a wish rather than indicating that that John actually prayed for these things to be true in Gaius' life. The term εὔχομαί, when used in a Hellenistic letter's introduction, simply meant "I wish this for you" as a courteous greeting or "wish" (Barker, 371; Brown, 790; Bruce, 147; Bultmann, 97; Culy, 156; Haas, de Jonge, and Swellengrebel, 176; Kistemaker, 390; Lieu, 268; Painter, 367; Perkins, 93; Smith, 150; Williamson, 205; Yarbrough, 366).[16] Brown (703) notes that normally, when the verb means "pray," it is followed by a clarifying phrase, which is absent here. "The use of the verb in secular letters as a polite wish for good health means that receivers of a New Testament letter would interpret it the same way unless there was a contextual indication of more profound intent, and that is lacking here."[17] Others read this as "pray" and see John saying that he prays for Gaius (Brooke, 182; Burdick, 447; Lenski, 578; Smalley, 345; Thompson, 159). This is the sense in some first-century

14. The phrase περὶ πάντων may at times be synonymous with πρὸ μὲν πάντων, "above all things," and is commonly found in salutations in letters (BDF §229(2); C. F. D. Moule, *An Idiom-book of New Testament Greek*, 63). If it had that sense here, the clause would be translated "Beloved, above all things I pray that you do well and prosper." However, though the phrase is moved forward in the sentence for emphasis, while still modifying the infinitive εὐοδοῦσθαι.

15. Grayston (159) describes the vocative as "in general a persuasive form of address" and sees a pattern of John's use of the vocative, either "when some feature of religious thought needs explanation (1 Jn 2:7; 3:2, 21), or some action is required (1 Jn 4:1, 7, 11)." For him it is persuasive in vv 5 and 11, but only "formal" in v 2.

16. BDF §392.1c; R. W. Funk, "The Form and Structure of II and III John," 425.

17. Grayston (159) calls this "a neat version of the standard good wishes (which is the meaning of 'I pray') at the beginning of a Hellenistic letter."

letters.[18] John could also intend a double entendre, meaning both senses at once (Akin, 240)[19] or either (Stott, 222; Yarbrough, 366). He would be saying something to the affect of "I both desire to see you doing well materially and physically, and pray to that end as well."

The idea of εὐοδοῦσθαι is that of success in one's activities.[20] Often translated as "prosper," it does not carry the connotation of material prosperity as does the term today (Hodges, 279). On the other hand ὑγιαίνειν means to be in good health. These two terms may be a pleonasm (redundancy), in which John is using two synonyms to say the same thing. Or he may be intending the nuances of their meanings to be noted, thus emphasizing the external aspect of one and the internal aspect of the other. Even so, this need not imply that Gaius was in poor health or suffering economically since it is a standard greeting common in the Greek world (Brooke, 182; Brown, 703; Lieu, 268).[21] This same term is used by Paul in 1 Tim 1:10 (sound teaching), 6:3 (sound words), and Titus 1:9 (sound instruction), 13 (sound faith), and 2:1 (sound instruction).

Some see ὑγιαίνειν hinting at Gaius having health issues (Marshall, 83; Westcott, 236). For example, Moody (127) says "this may indicate some physical frailty or temporary illness." Others reject this option while mentioning it (Barker, 377; Brooke, 182). Barker (377) argues that if Gaius was too ill to confront Diotrephes, then he would likewise be too weak to entertain visitors. Rather, it may simply indicate the more formal nature of this letter of recommendation. Even though John has deep affections for Gaius and does want the best for him, he is still writing to make a request and reflects that purpose in the opening of his letter.

καθὼς εὐοδοῦταί σου ἡ ψυχή, "just as your soul prospers." John's wish for Gaius' success and good health is related to his spiritual life. The conjunction *καθὼς* is often used for comparison or to express the extent or degree to which something is compared.[22] In this case, the implication is that Gaius' "soul" has been prospering.

---

18. Burdick (447) points to *Select Papyri* 1:367, 369, 389 of the Loeb Classical Library as second-century examples where it means "pray" and not "wish."
19. Akin (240) calls it a "prayer-wish."
20. BDAG, 410; W. Michaelis, "ὁδός … εὐοδόω," *TDNT* 5:114.
21. R. W. Funk, "The Form and Structure of II and III John," 425.
22. BDAG, 493.

The noun ψυχή normally means "life" in a generic sense. Some see John using it here to refer to the whole person (Kruse, 221; Thompson, 159; Williamson, 206). Here it is a metonymy*[23] for "your spiritual life" (Culy, 157; Harris, 259; Haas, de Jonge, and Swellengrebel, 176; Houlden, 151; Smalley, 346; Westcott, 236).[24] As such it is "that function of human existence that is concerned with morals and the things of God" (Grayston, 159).[25] Whereas "soul" may be used to designate people in general,[26] in this context, it must be seen in relation to the two infinitives that look at the material aspect of his existence.[27] In other words, John is expressing his desire to see Gaius' daily life express the abundance of his spiritual life (Johnson, 167). This is an indirect way of saying that he is pleased with Gaius' walk with the Lord.

This in no way is a promise of material prosperity as has been taken by some prosperity theologians. It was "a customary concern in Hellenistic letters and constitutes no basis for a 'right to prosperity' among Christians" (Johnson, 167). It "should not be taken as an implicit divine promise of physical health at all times for all God's people" (Williamson, 207). As Yarbrough insightfully notes, the experience of the persecuted church throughout the last century clearly demonstrates otherwise (Yarbrough, 367). Still, Akin (240) asks a haunting question worth pondering. "What if such a prayer was made to God for me and it was answered? What condition would I find myself in physically and spiritually? Compare your bodily

---

23. E. W. Bullinger, *Figures of Speech*, 538.

24. John 10:24, 12:27.

25. Brown (704) calls it "the sentient and most precious aspect of human existence." Schnackenburg (321–22) sees it referring to Gaius' efforts at achieving salvation.

26. Bultmann (97) sees "soul" meaning "the person addressed."

27. Philo (*Heir* 58.285) expresses this concept well. He writes, "Therefore he speaks of him who has lived in peace, who has enjoyed a serene and tranquil life, as a man truly happy and blessed. When then shall this happen? When all external things prosper with me, in such a way as to tend to by abundance and to my glory. When the things relating to the body are in a favourble state, so as to give me good health and strength; and when the things relating to my soul are in a similar state, so as to enable it to enjoy the virtues." (C. Yonge, *The Works of Philo: Complete and Unabridged*, 301.) This translates: μετ' εἰρήνης οὖν τραφεὶς γαληνὸν καὶ εὔδιον κτησάμενος βίον, εὐδαίμον' ὡς ἀληθῶς καὶ μακάριον πότε οὖν τοῦτο συμβήσεται; ὅταν εὐοδῇ μὲν τὰ ἐκτὸς πρὸς εὐπορίαν καὶ εὐδοξίαν, εὐοδῇ δὲ τὰ σώματος πρὸς ὑγίειάν τε καὶ ἰσχύν, εὐοδῇ δὲ τὰ ψυχῆς πρὸς ἀπόλαυσιν ἀρετῶν (from P. Borgen, K. Fuglseth and R. Skarsten, *The Works of Philo: Greek Text With Morphology*).

health to your spiritual health. Dare we hope or pray for ourselves or others in this manner?"

3 John recounts his joy at meeting people who reported seeing Gaius living out his faith consistent with apostolic teachings (Scripture).[28] This expression of joy is a standard part of Hellenistic letters (Bultmann, 97; Kistemaker, 390; Smalley, 346).[29] Even so, it does not lessen the sincerity of John's remarks.

ἐχάρην γὰρ λίαν ἐρχομένων ἀδελφῶν καὶ μαρτυρούντων σου τῇ ἀληθείᾳ, "For I rejoiced greatly at the coming of brethren and their testifying of your truth." John now describes in greater detail what he means by "your soul prospers." He has heard of his conduct from others, namely, that his orthopraxy matches his orthodoxy. Furthermore, using the present participles *ἐρχομένων* and *μαρτυρούντων* with a iterative sense, John indicates that this was a consistent witness of more than one person who had met Gaius (Brown, 704; Burdick, 448), and so they were doing this "often" (Kistemaker, 391; Smalley, 347; Westcott, 236).

He begins by describing his response to the report, he "rejoiced greatly."[30] In other words, John was "very glad" to hear the report about Gaius.[31] This report came from fellow Christians who told John about Gaius. John then relates their report of Gaius' conduct in terms of his walk within the sphere of truth. Thus these were fellow believers who had benefited from his spiritual commitment.[32] John is not clear from this whether these are missionaries that have visited his home church or regular Christians who had traveled through Gaius' town on business (Marshall, 83). If Gaius'

---

28. Painter (369) sees this verse providing evidence of common authorship between 2 and 3 John. He writes, "The prints of the author of 2 John are clearly visible here, confirming common authorship by the Elder." He notes as further evidence, "The slight variations in word order between 'walking in the truth' in 2 John 4 and 3 John 4—the words 'walking in truth' coming after the participle in 2 John and before it in 3 John—manifest an author working freely with his characteristic language. A copier would have replicated the original text."

29. R. W. Funk, "The Form and Structure of II and III John," 425–27.

30. "Joy" (χαρά) occurs once in each of John's epistles (1 John 1:4, 2 John 12, and here). "Rejoice" (χαίρω) occurs twice, 2 John 4 and here.

31. BDAG, 594.

32. For the use of "brothers" to describe the members of one's community of faith, see: BDAG, 18, 2a; J. Guenther, "Brother," *NIDNTT* 1:254–58; H. von Soden, "ἀδελφός," *TDNT* 1:144–46.

home were located along one of the main roads leading to Ephesus, it could very likely include both.

What they were testifying of was Gaius' "truth" (σου τῇ ἀληθείᾳ). This use of truth is interpreted in two ways. (1) It refers to his conduct (Brooke, 183; Bultmann, 97; Haas, de Jonge, and Swellengrebel, 177; Marshall, 84; Westcott, 236; Schnackenburg, 322), though orthodoxy is understood behind that conduct (Akin, 240; Brown, 705–706; Strecker, 258). He was "faithful to the truth of the Christian gospel" (Smalley, 347). As a Johannine term, ἀληθείᾳ often indicates a body of doctrinal (christological) truth (1 John 221–23; 4:2, 6; 5:10, 20; 2 John 7) or ethical behavior (1 John 1:6; 2:4; 3:18–19; 4:20). Based on his comments about Gaius' conduct, it seems here he has ethical truth in mind (Harris, 260). (2) It refers to his orthodox doctrine, and so commitment to the gospel (Burdick, 449).[33] "Truth" here, and in the remainder of the epistle, as in 2 John, refers to the body of truth, the apostolic teachings, received by the church, including Scripture (Lenski, 580). Paul referred to this as the "traditions" of the apostles (1 Cor 11:2; 2 Thess 2:14). Thus, Gaius had a reputation for leading a biblical lifestyle rather than one in conformity with his culture. Here it is less likely to be as specific of an issue as in 1 John. Thus it encompasses more than just Christology. However, John's description of it here as "your" truth would indicate it is more than a body of truth, but the expression of that truth in Gaius' life, thus the first option is better.[34]

Smalley (347) suggests that John's repeated use of "truth" with regard to Gaius indicates that Gaius "had encountered and overcome threats from heretical opponents of the true gospel." This is a case of reading too much into a literary device. Repetition is used for emphasis, and that would seem the implication here. John is saying nothing about Gaius' encounters with those preaching a false gospel. Rather, what John has to say relates to Gaius' positive encounters with those preaching the true gospel.

---

33. Johnson (169) calls it a "spiritual reality as the Elder and his followers understand it."

34. It is functioning as an objective gen. and so means "the truth that belongs to you" (Kistemaker, 391–92). Culy (158) differs from all and sees σου as a subjective gen. and therefore it means "you are truthful" or "you speak the truth." It seems better to see it as a simple possessive or as an objective gen. indicating it is truth expressed in him.

καθὼς σὺ ἐν ἀληθείᾳ περιπατεῖς, "just as you are walking in the truth." This use of καθὼς by John is interpreted as either introducing a comparison (Burdick, 449; Culy, 158) or as introducing indirect discourse (Haas, de Jonge, and Swellengrebel; 177; Smalley, 347). The first option seems best.

With the emphatic 2 singular pronoun σὺ, John focuses attention on Gaius as opposed to others such as Diotrephes (Haas, de Jonge, and Swellengrebel, 177; Smalley, 347; Westcott, 236).[35] Then, using ἐν ἀληθείᾳ as a dative of sphere, John now says that Gaius' commitment to truth (a life of obedience) has led to a lifestyle characterized by adherence to doctrinal truth and ethical conduct that accords with God's revealed will in Scripture. The lack of an article does not make "truth" indefinite because of its close connection to the previous use which was articular (Burdick, 449).[36] Rather, it is describing the basis of his conduct (the previous use of "truth"). What we see by this is that walking "in the truth" "is more than to give assent to it. It means to apply it to one's behavior" (Stott, 224). Additionally, this walking is to be a continuous action (thus the present tense), "you always walk" (Smalley, 347).

4 Having said he rejoices (v 3) when he hears a good report, John explains the basis of his response. He moves from "rejoicing greatly" in verse 3 to "no greater joy" in verse 4.

μειζοτέραν τούτων οὐκ ἔχω χαράν, "I have no greater joy than this." The plural τούτων can mean one of three things. (1) It can be used for the singular sense, which was a common practice (Kistemaker, 392) (2) The plural refers to what follows, which are the things reported at each visit as they relate to John's spiritual children walking in the truth (Brooke, 183; Burdick, 449; Lenski, 581; Smalley, 348; Westcott, 237). In that case, John would be including more than just reports about Gaius' conduct. Since Gaius is the focus, this seems less likely. (3) In this case, John's use of the genitive τούτων is best understood referring to what precedes, namely, the reports (pl.) that John has been receiving from other brethren about Gaius walking in the truth (Brown, 706; Westcott, 237; contra Culy, 159).

---

35. Others see John's use of συ as neither emphatic or polemical (Lenski, 580; Schnackenburg, 322).

36. Lenski (580) sees it expressing a "qualitative" force.

His use of the comparative adjective μειζοτέραν with οὐκ serves to emphasize the central importance of these reports to his life as a spiritual father who is concerned for those under his care.[37] This reflects a similar heart attitude as Paul's in 2 Cor 11:28–29, wherein he relates how his daily concern for the churches consumes him. His concern led him to send Timothy to Thessalonica (1 Thess 3:1–5) to check on their welfare and encourage them in their afflictions. This deep concern explains his reaction to the sinning brother in Corinth who had not been disciplined by the church. First he feels compelled to discipline him by handing him over to Satan (1 Cor 5:4–5). When the sinning brother repents, Paul's response is joyful restoration (2 Cor 2:3–11). In these passages we see Paul's deep concern for each church under his care as well as their individual members. We also see the anguish he goes through on their behalf. In the same way, John is deeply concerned for the churches and individuals under his spiritual care. Consequently, their lives impact his joy.

ἵνα ἀκούω τὰ ἐμὰ τέκνα ἐν τῇ ἀληθείᾳ περιπατοῦντα, "that I may hear of my children walking in the truth."[38] With the epexegetical ἵνα, John now explains what things give him joy (Brown, 706; Burdick, 449–50; Smalley, 348). Nothing else makes him as happy as such good reports concerning his spiritual children. John's use of "child" is metaphor for his own converts and those under his spiritual care (Barker, 372; Haas, de Jonge, and Swellengrebel, 178; Kistemaker, 391; Lieu, 270; Painter, 370).[39] Including Gaius as one of John's "children" may indicate that he was one of John's converts,[40] and thus a spiritual child much like the Corinthian church was to Paul (Smalley, 348).[41] Or, John's use of the term may indicate he was simply under his pastoral care (Brooke, 183; Burdick, 450; Harris, 260; Schnackenburg; 323), as was the case with the recipients of John's first

---

37. "The word μειζοτέραν ('greater') is a 'vulgar' equivalent of μείζων (Bultmann, 98 n.7), and appears only at this point in the NT" (Smalley, 348).
38. This use of "my" is not emphatic (Brown, 707) nor alludes to Diotrephes. It is just a plain statement.
39. M. Hengel, *The Johannine Question*, 35. Johnson (169) notes that Jesus called his disciples τεκνία in the upper room (John 13:33) and παιδία by the seashore (John 21:5).
40. Yarbrough (368) limits the meaning to only John's converts and not those that were the product of Paul's missionary ministry.
41. 1 Cor 4:14–17. Paul also refers similarly to the Galatians (Gal 4:19) and Onesimus (Phlm 10).

epistle (1 John 2:1, 12, 18, 28; 3:7, 18; 4:4; 5:21).[42] This is reflected in his use of "the elder" for his title (Harris, 260) and so seems more likely. This also makes better sense in light of the fact that many in Asia Minor were the product of Paul's missionary activities and the churches had been well established for many years before John's arrival after AD 70.[43]

As noted earlier, "walking in truth" describes a lifestyle based on God's Word, which is true.[44] Thus we see that John was not satisfied with gaining converts only. His heart's passion was their spiritual growth and lifestyle of faith.[45] We see this same passion in his Gospel, where he does not write a gospel tract, but a literary description of what eternal life means to every believer in Jesus, in this life as well as the life to come. We see this in his first epistle's focus on *experiencing* eternal life as well.[46]

Biblical Theology Comments

John continues to express the concept of walking in truth to describe the biblically based lifestyle that expresses God's character. Commitment to God and to his truth is expressed in conduct that can be seen by others. It is much the same concept as was developed in 1 John 4:7–11 with love. Just as God's love in us expresses itself through us and thereby reveals him to the

---

42. His use of the adjective ἐμὰ as opposed to the less emphatic μου gives it the sense of "my own children" (Westcott, 237).

43. See discussion of Occasion and Setting in the Introduction.

44. This phrase, "walking in the truth," does not occur anywhere else in the NT, but the concept of "walking in" something is very Johannine. Thus he speaks of walking in the darkness (1 John 1:6; 2:11), the light (1 John 1:7), and according to God's commandments (2 John 6).

Culy (159) does not see any distinction between ἐν τῇ ἀληθείᾳ (here) or ἐν ἀληθείᾳ (v 3), nor does C. Moule (*An Idiom-book of New Testament Greek*, 112). Culy (also Brown, 707) demonstrates this by noting the synonymous use of the two constructions in John 17:17 (ἁγίασον αὐτοὺς ἐν τῇ ἀληθείᾳ·) and 19 (ἵνα ὦσιν καὶ αὐτοὶ ἡγιασμένοι ἐν ἀληθείᾳ).

45. Smalley (348) interprets this epistle from the theory of a Johannine school in conflict with secessionists. As a result, he reacts to the repetition of being "in truth" or "in the truth" and concludes: "John's emphasis on 'truth' in this letter may indicate that the doctrinal crisis in his community was by now at its most stark."

46. Lieu (270) says of this, "Gaius is reminded of his place among a wider group, and that his appropriate behavior will preserve it."

world, so too, his truth expressed through our lives reveals that we know him who is true.

Application and Devotional Implications

The heart's desire of each of us believers should be to live our lives in such a way that our commitment to truth, especially God's truth, is evident to others. As revealed in the body of this letter, that is best done in the context of how we treat others. We cannot do this if we do not know God's truth as revealed in his Word. We also cannot do this if we do not view his Word as truth. To do this we must see the Scriptures as revelatory truth, inspired by the God of truth. However, to live this kind of life, we must recognize that God's Word is normative and supersedes culture, personal preferences, philosophical agendas, and any excuses we might invent to get around its clear commands. This is not easy. We are blind in so many areas. We are unwilling to change in others. However, if we wish to change, we cannot without a proper view of what it means to walk in God's truth, even as Gaius did.

Selected Bibliography

Borgen, P., K. Fuglseth, and R. Skarsten. *The Works of Philo: Greek Text with Morphology.* Bellingham, WA: Logos Research Systems, Inc., 2005.

Brown, C., gen. ed. *New International Dictionary of New Testament Theology.* 4 vols. Grand Rapids: Zondervan, 1975–1985.

Bullinger, E. W. *Figures of Speech Used in the Bible.* New York: Eyre & Spottiswoode, 1898. Repr., Grand Rapids: Baker, 1968.

Funk, R. W. "The Form and Structure of II and III John." *JBL* 86 (1967): 424–30.

Hengel, M. *The Johannine Question*. London: SCM, 1989.

Marulli, L. "A Letter of Recommendation? A Closer Look at Third John's 'Rhetorical' Argumentation." *Bib* 90 (2009): 203–23.

Metzger, B. M., and United Bible Societies, *A Textual Commentary on the Greek New Testament.* 2nd ed. New York: United Bible Societies, 1994.

Moule, C. F. D. *An Idiom-book of New Testament Greek*. 2nd ed. New York: Cambridge University Press, 1953, 1959.

Yonge, C, D., trans. *The Works of Philo: Complete and Unabridged.* New updated ed. Peabody, MA: Hendrickson, 1996.

Gaius' Responsibility (5–12)

Introduction

Having greeted his friend, John is now ready to address the topic at hand. He is interceding on behalf of missionaries who deserve support in their ministry, the kind of support that Gaius can give.

It is in the body of this letter that we learn a great deal about ecclesiology—not directly, but indirectly. Furthermore, what we learn is not church structure or polity, though many commentators attempt to find such in John's comments (and there are a few hints). Rather, we find what the heart and soul of a church, and a church leader, should and should not be. When the Holy Spirit bore John along in the writing of this letter (2 Pet 1:21), he guided him to discuss those things that matter to God rather than answer some of our curiosity questions. The instruction he has chosen to communicate to us through John's correspondence is not whether a church should have a single bishop or team of elders in its leadership structure. It is not what a local church organization should look like. It is not even about whether churches should be autonomous or subject to a hierarchical organization. It is about how we treat one another and the importance of supporting God's work. It is about how inflated egos do not belong in the body of Christ and hinder his work by hindering his workers. It is about that issue that means the most to God—our need to express God's love by loving one another.

In this section we meet three men, all with Gentile pagan names, all who see themselves as committed Christians. John speaks of each man in terms of his character. He also shows us that character, and one's true spiritual state, is proven by conduct. At the center of this letter is his request for aid. It also contains a promise to intervene in the affairs of a church by confronting the sin and the sinner.

Original Text

5 Ἀγαπητέ, πιστὸν ποιεῖς ὃ ἐὰν ἐργάσῃ εἰς τοὺς ἀδελφοὺς καὶ τοῦτο ξένους, **6**
οἳ ἐμαρτύρησάν σου τῇ ἀγάπῃ ἐνώπιον ἐκκλησίας, οὓς καλῶς ποιήσεις προπέμ-
ψας ἀξίως τοῦ θεοῦ· **7** ὑπὲρ γὰρ τοῦ ὀνόματος ἐξῆλθον μηδὲν λαμβάνοντες ἀπὸ
τῶν ἐθνικῶν. **8** ἡμεῖς οὖν ὀφείλομεν ὑπολαμβάνειν τοὺς τοιούτους, ἵνα συνεργοὶ
γινώμεθα τῇ ἀληθείᾳ. **9** Ἔγραψάα τῇ ἐκκλησίᾳ· ἀλλ' ὁ φιλοπρωτεύων αὐτῶν
Διοτρέφης οὐκ ἐπιδέχεται ἡμᾶς. **10** διὰ τοῦτο, ἐὰν ἔλθω, ὑπομνήσω αὐτοῦ τὰ
ἔργα ἃ ποιεῖ λόγοις πονηροῖς φλυαρῶν ἡμᾶς, καὶ μὴ ἀρκούμενος ἐπὶ τούτοις οὔτε
αὐτὸς ἐπιδέχεται τοὺς ἀδελφοὺς καὶ τοὺς βουλομένους κωλύει καὶ ἐκ τῆς ἐκκλη-
σίας ἐκβάλλει. **11** Ἀγαπητέ, μὴ μιμοῦ τὸ κακὸν ἀλλὰ τὸ ἀγαθόν. ὁ ἀγαθοποιῶν
ἐκ τοῦ θεοῦ ἐστιν· ὁ κακοποιῶν οὐχ ἑώρακεν τὸν θεόν. **12** Δημητρίῳ μεμαρτύ-
ρηται ὑπὸ πάντων καὶ ὑπὸ αὐτῆς τῆς ἀληθείας· καὶ ἡμεῖς δὲ μαρτυροῦμεν, καὶ
οἶδας ὅτι ἡ μαρτυρία ἡμῶν ἀληθής ἐστιν.

Textual Notes

9.a. Though the witnesses vary greatly and no clear majority prevails, the best reading appears to be ἔγραψά without a particle, rather than seeing ἔγραψά τι as leading to the others, as Metzger does.[1] Ἔγραψά without any particle is supported by C K L P Ψ 049 056 0142 88 104 326 330 451 629 1877 2127 2495 *Byz Lect* eth. Ἔγραψά with the particle τι is supported by ℵ* A B 048 1241 1739; with the particle ἄν by ℵ^{c} 33 81 181 436 614 630 945 1505 1881 2412 2492 *l*^{1439} it^{ar,c,dem,div,p} vg; with the particles ἄν τι by 424^{c}. So, even though some of the earliest MS support some particle with ἔγραψά, the majority of witnesses do not. Additionally, the meaning of the passage is not helped or changed by those particles. Rather, it would seem that copyists sought to clarify the text by their addition rather than shortening the text.

Translation

5 Beloved, you are acting faithfully in whatever you do toward the brethren
and at that toward strangers, **6** who bore witness to your love before the
church, which you will do well, having sent them on their way in a manner

1. B. M. Metzger and United Bible Societies, *A Textual Commentary on the Greek New Testament*, 2nd ed., 655.

worthy of God; **7** for they went out on behalf of the Name, receiving noth-
ing from the pagans.[2] **8** Therefore we are obligated to support such men as
these, in order that we may become fellow-workers in the truth. **9** I wrote to
the church; but Diotrephes who loves to be first over them does not receive
us. **10** Because of this, when I come, I will call to attention his works which
he does in evil words disparaging us, and not being satisfied with these, he
does not receive the brethren and those wishing to he hinders and throws
out of the church. **11** Beloved, do not imitate the evil *person*, but the good.
He who does good is from God; he who does evil has not seen God. **12**
Demetrius[3] has received a testimony from all and from the truth itself; and
we are testifying and know that our testimony is true.

Commentary

We now come to the main body of this letter. In it John will communicate to Gaius his responsibility to assist Demetrius in spite of Diotrephes' opposition and attempts to expel those who receive the brethren. Like Paul's letter to Philemon, John is going to make a difficult request of his beloved friend. He will write to convince him. However, unlike Paul with Philemon, he will appeal to other than their personal relationship as a means of persuasion.

5 John begins his instruction with praise. This continues the positive tone of this letter.

Ἀγαπητέ, πιστὸν ποιεῖς ὃ ἐὰν ἐργάσῃ εἰς τοὺς ἀδελφοὺς, "Beloved, you are acting faithfully in whatever you do toward the brethren." With the pause to refer to Gaius as "beloved," John transitions from the introduction to the body of his letter (Culy, 160; Lieu, 270).[4] He is not writing to correct Gaius. He is encouraging him to continue the good he has been doing, in much

2. "Gentiles" (ESV, KJV), "heathen" (RSV), "pagans" (HCSB, NIV84), "those who are not Christians" (NLT), "anyone who was not a follower" (CEV), "non-believers" (NRSV), "unbelievers" (TEV).

3. This is not the same Demetrius as the silversmith at Ephesus who opposed Paul (Acts 19:23–27).

4. The use of the voc., in this case *ἀγαπητέ*, is a literary device that marks the transition from the greetings to the body of the letter. At times in 1 John he did the same thing (1 John 2:1, 7, 18, 28; 4:1, 7; 5:21), though at other times the vocative was used inside the body of a paragraph without a transitional role (1 John 3:2, 7, 13, 18, 21; 4:11).

the same vein as Paul when he told the Thessalonians to "increase more and more" in their love for one another (1 Thess 4:10).

What appears to be an idiomatic statement, πιστὸν ποιεῖς, is commonly used in letters of recommendation (Rensberger, 161) and understood in one of two ways. (1) Some interpret it to mean "act loyally" (Burdick, 450; Haas, de Jonge, and Swellengrebel, 178; Smalley, 349).[5] This is one sense of the phrase and is reflected in some first-century letters. However, the second meaning is better. (2) It expresses the sense of "you are acting faithfully," "you are doing a faithful thing," or "you are careful to consistently act in this manner" (Bruce, 149; Lenski, 582; Schnackenburg, 323; Yarbrough, 370).[6] In this case it refers to his performance of "a Christian duty" (Bruce, 149) and John is noting Gaius' diligence.[7] This lets Gaius know that his faithfulness is at the forefront of John's thinking, even as he writes this letter of recommendation for Demetrius.[8]

Gaius' faithfulness has been expressed in his practice of hospitality. The combination of the subjunctive conjunction ἐὰν with the neuter relative pronoun ὃ is idiomatic for "whatever" rather than communicating contingency. John is drawing attention to a pattern of deeds rather than a single kind of deed (Westcott, 238). In other words, showing hospitality is just one of the many kinds of things Gaius did faithfully. Further, his use of "the brethren" indicates that some of those helped by Gaius were not strangers to him before his welcoming them into his home. This support reflected his faithfulness to God in serving him.

The combination of ἐὰν with the pronoun ὃ communicates either the sense of "whenever" (Haas, de Jonge, and Swellengrebel, 179; Smalley, 349)[9] or "whatever."[10] Its combination with the verb that follows indicates "what-

5. BDAG, 821.

6. Westcott (237–38) translates this as "thou makest sure" in that the deed will not fail to be rewarded.

7. D. E. Hiebert, "An Exposition of 3 John 5–10," 195.

8. Brown (708) suggests the present ποιεῖς may have a future force per BDF §323. However, that need not be the case here. Rather, John is focusing on Gaius' present conduct and will use that as the basis of his coming request.

9. The sense of "whenever" would involve both "the past action ... and the future benefits" (Brooke, 184).

10. BDAG, 268.

ever" is intended in this context because the relative clause is functioning as an "accusative of respect" (Yarbrough, 370).[11]

καὶ τοῦτο ξένους, "and at that toward strangers." John then notes that this hospitality is also extended to "strangers." Culy (160) calls this a "highly elliptical construction" which could mean more or less: καὶ ἐργάζῃ τοῦτο ἐις ξένους. The challenge comes in determining the case (and so sense) of the relative pronoun, the role of the accusative plural ξένους, as well as what other words are elided. Culy's suggestion is helpful as is that of Blass-Debruner who renders it "and at that" or "and especially."[12] The neuter relative pronoun τοῦτο looks back on a particular faithful deed of Gaius that John has in mind, in this case, showing hospitality (Yarbrough, 371). Ξένους is appositional to brethren.[13] Thus, by strangers, John does not mean "anybody who shows up at your doorstep," but other believers that Gaius has not known previously (Hodges, 281; Kistemaker, 392; Yarbrough, 371). Based on what he will say in the next two verses, John is not including unbelievers in the category of "strangers." These strangers-to-Gaius, along with the familiar brethren, have reported his hospitality to John (v 6), and they are also identified with those who do not seek support from "the Gentiles" (v 7). Thus these "strangers" are most likely travelling missionaries that Gaius has assisted (Dodd, 159; Harris, 261; Moody, 129).

Hospitality is not a heart's desire of John alone. It is called for throughout the New Testament and can be seen as a universal need.[14] It continued to be a virtue extolled by the church fathers as well. This is reflected in the

11. John's use of τοὺς ἀδελφοὺς here to indicate "Christian brothers" follows the pattern of his use in the other epistles (Burdick, 450).

12. BDF §290(5) and §442(9).

13. This same term, ξένος, is used by Jesus in the Olivet Discourse (Matt 25:35, 38, 43, 44). Those who show hospitality and "take in" strangers will be invited into His coming kingdom because helping strangers means helping Jesus. Those who do not will be excluded because their refusal will be a rejection of Jesus. In this case the strangers are "the least of these my brethren" and likely will be the Jews facing persecution by the Antichrist.

14. NT passages on hospitality outside of John's literature include Rom 12:13, 1 Tim 3:2 and 5:10, Titus 1:8, Heb 13:2, and 1 Pet 4:9.

writings of Hermas (Herm. *Sim.* 9.27),[15] Justin Martyr (*Apol.* 1.67),[16] and Ignatius (*Smyrn.* 10:1).[17]

6 John now recounts the good reports he has received from those who have benefited from Gaius' hospitality. He follows this with a gentle admonition to continue the practice.

οἵ ἐμαρτύρησάν σου τῇ ἀγάπῃ ἐνώπιον ἐκκλησίας, "who bore witness to your love before the church." John describes the testimony of Gaius' beneficiaries with a relative clause with the aorist ἐμαρτύρησάν. This may refer to

15. "And from the tenth mountain, where were trees which overshadowed certain sheep, they who believed were the following: bishops given to hospitality, who always gladly received into their houses the servants of God, without dissimulation. And the bishops never failed to protect, by their service, the widows, and those who were in want, and always maintained a holy conversation. All these, accordingly, shall be protected by the Lord for ever. They who do these things are honourable before God, and their place is already with the angels, if they remain to the end serving God." (A. Roberts, J. Donaldson and A. C. Coxe, *The Ante-Nicene Fathers Vol. II: Translations of the Writings of the Fathers Down to A.D. 325*, 52)

16. "And the wealthy among us help the needy; and we always keep together; and for all things wherewith we are supplied, we bless the Maker of all through His Son Jesus Christ, and through the Holy Ghost. And on the day called Sunday, all who live in cities or in the country gather together to one place, and the memoirs of the apostles or the writings of the prophets are read, as long as time permits; then, when the reader has ceased, the president verbally instructs, and exhorts to the imitation of these good things. Then we all rise together and pray, and, as we before said, when our prayer is ended, bread and wine and water are brought, and the president in like manner offers prayers and thanksgivings, according to his ability,[147] and the people assent, saying Amen; and there is a distribution to each, and a participation of that over which thanks have been given, and to those who are absent a portion is sent by the deacons. And they who are well to do, and willing, give what each thinks fit; and what is collected is deposited with the president, who succours the orphans and widows, and those who, through sickness or any other cause, are in want, and those who are in bonds, and the strangers sojourning among us, and in a word takes care of all who are in need." (A. Roberts, J. Donaldson and A. C. Coxe, *The Ante-Nicene Fathers Vol. I : Translations of the Writings of the Fathers Down to A.D. 325*, 185–86)

17. "Ye have done well in receiving Philo and Rheus Agathopus as servants of Christ our God, who have followed me for the sake of God, and who give thanks to the Lord in your behalf, because ye have in every way refreshed them. None of these things shall be lost to you. May my spirit be for you, and my bonds, which ye have not despised or been ashamed of; nor shall Jesus Christ, our perfect hope, be ashamed of you." (A. Roberts, J. Donaldson and A. C. Coxe, *The Ante-Nicene Fathers Vol. I : Translations of the Writings of the Fathers Down to A.D. 325*, 91)

a single event (thus its undefined aspect) or to recurring reports in the past, which is more likely because of the present participles in v 3 (Brown, 709). By this John views the many reports as a single act (Burdick, 450), indicating its consistent nature and something his church became used to hearing.

What they have testified to is Gaius' love (σου τῇ ἀγάπῃ) which is expressed through his hospitable treatment of visitors (Brooke, 184). When we speak of someone's hospitality, we normally refer to him or her as a "gracious host." They came away feeling more than welcomed; they knew they had been loved. This love was the kind of love described in 1 John—a love that meets needs. Gaius is the embodiment of a loving Christian. As a result of the testimony of those who have been blessed by him, his love has become known in the subsequent churches they have visited.[18]

Which "church"? His use of the preposition ἐνώπιον and the anarthrous ἐκκλησίας indicates the report came at "a" meeting of the congregation, but does not specify which church (Brooke, 184) but would imply John's local congregation (Harris, 261–62; Smalley, 349; Yarbrough, 371).[19]

οὓς καλῶς ποιήσεις προπέμψας ἀξίως τοῦ θεοῦ, "which you will do well, having sent them on their way in a manner worthy of God." Now John moves to encourage him to continue the practice. He begins this relative clause with the plural relative pronoun οὕς which serves as a generic reference to the coming visitors who will need Gaius' hospitality (Yarbrough, 371–72). Functioning as the object of the participle προπέμψας, it has οἳ as its antecedent, thus the brethren who are strangers to Gaius.

He now repeats the verb ποιέω in the future tense that serves as a mild imperative expressed as an expectation (Culy, 161; Yarbrough, 371).[20] This was a common method of introducing a polite request (Brooke, 184–85; Bruce, 150; Burdick, 451; Haas, de Jonge, and Swellengrebel, 178; Marshall, 85) and is comparable to "please" in English (Akin, 243; Burdick, 451; Marshall, 85; Smalley, 350; Walls and Anders, 249; Yarbrough, 371). It would be considered an indirect request for aid (Marshall, 85; Williamson, 210).[21]

---

18. Smalley (349–50) sees the anarthrous ἐκκλησίας with the preposition ἐνώπιον indicating they had told several Johannine community churches.

19. This is the only place in Johannine literature (other than twenty times in Rev) where ἐκκλησία ("church") is used.

20. Akin (243) identifies this as an idiomatic way of saying "please" and thereby making "a polite request."

21. D. E. Hiebert, "An Exposition of 3 John 5–10," 198.

This is accomplished in that the future tense implies a wish (Westcott, 238) and he is basically saying that he anticipates this pattern of hospitality will continue into the future.[22] Also, by saying this, he is encouraging him to continue doing what he has done in the past (Painter, 371).

The term προπέμπω, while sometimes meaning to "escort" or "accompany" (travel along with)[23] also means to assist by providing food, funds for travel, or a means of travel (Yarbrough, 372).[24] This latter sense is what is intended here (Lieu, 272; Perkins, 95; Strecker, 259).[25] Gaius' hospitality extended beyond the time of their visit and included provision of their needs en route to the next destination. An apparent grammatical problem is John's choice of the aorist participle προπέμψας.[26] Normally the time element of an aorist participle is prior to the main verb.[27] However, as Brown (710–11) notes, the aorist can indicate action occurring at the same time as the main verb and in this use communicates the certainty of the action.

Gaius' provision is described as "worthy of God." Some see this referring both to Gaius' help and the missionaries' activity in the following verse (Akin, 244; Brown, 711). It seems better to see it referring strictly to Gaius. In the Greek world this phrase communicated the idea of doing something that enhanced the public reputation of the gods which was then appreciated by the gods and brought the individual to their attention in a positive light. What John means by this figure of speech then, is that Gaius' loving deeds brought praise to God. Further, being "worthy" conduct, God had noticed and appreciated Gaius as a person. In the Pauline sense, he had "walked worthy" of the Lord (Eph 4:1; Col 1:9; 1 Thess 2:11). This is a reminder that, as the author of Hebrews tells us (Heb 6:10), God does not fail to notice or forget those things we do for one another. Being the loving Father that he is, God appreciates every kind deed done to each of his children, especially by his children.

A second aspect of this is that he is referring to worthy actions that meet God's expectations (Yarbrough, 372). In this case the principle taught

22. This is similar to Jas 2:8 and Ignatius, *Smyrn.* 10.1.
23. Polycarp, *Phil* 1.1.
24. BDAG, 873. I. Lorengin, "Hospitality versus Patronage," 173.
25. The verb προπέμπω is used elsewhere in NT with same sense: Acts 15:3; Rom 15:24; 1 Cor 16:6, 11; 2 Cor 1:16; Titus 3:13.
26. Moody (129–30) sees προπέμπω and ὑπολαμβάνειν in v 8 as equivalent terms.
27. D. B. Wallace, *Grammar*, 624–25; BDF §339.

by the Lord and repeated by Paul that "workers are worthy of their wages" (Matt 10:10; Luke 10:7; 1 Cor 9:7, 14; and I Tim 5:18) indicates that these missionaries "merited assistance from God's people" (Yarbrough, 372). Thus Gaius' actions acknowledge that they merit the assistance of other believers to enable them to serve the Lord. Marshall (86) challenges us to act as Gaius. "Christian ministers and missionaries live in the faith that God will encourage his people to provide for their needs; it is better that such provision err on the side of generosity than stinginess." All indications are that Gaius did.

7 John now explains why Gaius' hospitality was so strategic. He was meeting the needs of saints who were serving Christ and sought to depend on the body of Christ.

ὑπὲρ γὰρ τοῦ ὀνόματος ἐξῆλθον, "for they went out on behalf of the Name." John explains (γὰρ) the significance of Gaius' actions in terms of Christ's reputation. This causal clause (Strecker, 259; Yarbrough, 372) explains what preceded and provides reasons for the requested action of the previous verse (Brooke, 185; Burdick, 451). These brethren and strangers had embarked on their journeys "on behalf of the Name" (ὑπὲρ τοῦ ὀνόματος).

Referring to "the Name," John identifies the purpose of their travels.[28] The use of "name" is an idiomatic expression reflecting the Hebrew use as a more emphatic way of speaking of God, often carrying the sense of "God himself."[29] It serves as a metonymy* for either "God" or "Christ" (Akin, 244; Culy, 161). However, here John does not define what he means by "the name," and interpreters have understood it in one of three ways.[30] (1) It refers to God (Lieu, 272; MacArthur, 248). This is indicated by "the unqualified noun with the definite article" (Harris, 263). "In Rabbinic literature 'the Name' is a frequent substitute for the Tetragrammaton, YHWH, the

28. Westcott (238) interprets this expression to mean they were making "the Name better known." "As applied to God it expresses that which has been made known of him; or, more exactly to distinguish the two factors in the revelation, that which he has made known of himself, and which man can apprehend as addressed to him" (Westcott, 243).

29. E. W. Bullinger, *Figures of Speech Used in the Bible*, 409.

30. The article with "name" particularizes it, and so sets it apart from others (Burdick, 451). However, that alone does not indicate its referent. Houlden (152) differs from all others and sees it indicating "the Christian cause." He does see this as being done in the name "of Christ," though.

name of God, which was too sacred to be pronounced" (Harris, 263). "The call to treat them 'in a manner worthy of God' perhaps suggests that it was for God's name" (Lieu, 272).[31] In response to this Schnackenburg (324–25) objects on the grounds that this designation as "too vague" to be a reference to God the Father. (2) It refers to Jesus (Akin, 244; Barker, 373; Brooke, 185; Bruce, 150; Bultmann, 99; Haas, de Jonge, and Swellengrebel, 180–81; Harris, 262; Kistemaker, 394; Kruse, 223; Lenski, 584; Marshall, 86; Smalley, 351; Painter, 371; Rensberger, 161; Schnackenburg, 325; Stott, 226; Westcott, 238; Williams, 69; Williamson, 211). In its support is Paul's use of this in Rom 1:5 with reference to Jesus. John uses a similar reference in John 1:12, 3:18, and 1 John 2:12 (Williamson, 211). Bruce (150) argues that "as in Jewish parlance, 'The Name' is a surrogate for YHWH, so here 'The Name' is a synonym for Christ." It was used of Christ by the church fathers.[32] (3) It refers to both God the Father and Jesus (Johnson, 172; Yarbrough, 372). Brown (711–12) argues that "in the Johannine tradition the divine name is borne by Jesus who is one with the Father" and this unitary sense is understood in this use (Brown, 711–12). Yarbrough (372–73) points to Jesus' words in John 17:11–12 where both the keeping and the name of Father and Son "is so thoroughly blurred as to be indistinguishable." The second option seems best in this context.[33]

These men have left their homes and churches (ἐξῆλθον) in order to serve Christ and make him known.[34] Their lives are devoted to him. This departure refers to their missionary activities (Barker, 373; Bultmann, 98;

31. She also sees his use of "the name" as indicating "both the motivation for and the content of their activity" (Lieu, 271).

32. Ignatius, *Eph* 3:1 reads: "I do not issue orders to you, as if I were some great person. For though I am bound for the name [of Christ], I am not yet perfect in Jesus Christ." (A. Roberts, J. Donaldson and A. C. Coxe, *The Ante-Nicene Fathers Vol. I: Translations of the Writings of the Fathers Down to A.D. 325*, 50)

33. In the New Testament this use of "name" includes the sense of reflecting God's character or will as well. Thus when Jesus promises answers to prayer "in His name" (John 14:13–14), He is not giving an unconditional promise to answer any and every prayer that concludes with the invocation, "in the Name of Jesus." Rather, He is limiting His promise to include only those prayers that reflect His character and will. God answers prayer, but only on His terms.

34. Brooke (186) suggests that they may have left from Ephesus. However, if John is in Ephesus, the aorist indicates they had already left their homes and were passing through John's church. Harris (264) sees these travelling missionaries being sent out to "counteract the heretical teaching of the opponents."

Harris, 262; Painter, 371; Smalley, 350–51; Strecker, 260) and so provides the reason to support them. This same term is use in Acts 14:20 and 15:40 of Paul's going on missionary journeys (Harris, 262–63). It is used by John of the false teachers in 1 John 2:19, 4:1, and 2 John 7. Even so, there is no indication of an intended contrast between these missionaries and the antichrists of 1 or 2 John (Brown, 712).

Gaius' assistance made him a participant in their ministry, similar to Paul's instruction that support of missionaries means participation in their ministries as co-laborers (Phil 1:3–6, 4:14–17).

μηδὲν λαμβάνοντες ἀπὸ τῶν ἐθνικῶν. "receiving nothing from the pagans." John now describes the actions of the travelers Gaius has been supporting. The present participle λαμβάνοντες indicates this was their practice (Brooke, 186; Haas, de Jonge, and Swellengrebel, 181). This use of the present tense refers to habitual action. "Gentiles," in this case, is not an ethnic designation. John chooses to use ἐθνικῶν to designate the world at large from whom they accept no support. This term is synonymous with ἔθνος and should be viewed as referring to Gentile pagans, but not all Gentiles, especially since the church was populated by Gentile converts (Brown, 713; Harris, 263; Houlden, 152; Kruse, 224).[35] Thus it is a moral designation more than ethnic, and can be translated "heathens" or "pagans" (Burdick, 452; Stott, 226) , non-Christians (Akin 244; Haas, de Jonge, and Swellengrebel, 181; Johnson, 173; Thompson, 161; Williamson, 212), or "unbelievers" (Smalley, 351). The only other New Testament use of ἐθνικῶν is Matt 5:47; 6:7; and 18:17 and in each case it was used in a negative sense. This may be because Matthew was distinguishing between unbelieving Gentiles and Gentile believers (Lieu, 272) and so the more generic term for Gentiles was not used. John may be doing the same here. This contrast between "brothers" and Gentile pagans is evident from Jesus' use in Matt 5:47.[36] The majority of the churches they visited would be composed of mostly, if not all, Gentile saints. Moreover, the missionaries themselves were likely Gentiles, as indicated by Demetrius' name. Thus, they were not willing to be supported by those outside of the household of God. This would be unworthy of Christ.

---

35. Culpepper (280) sees ἐθνικῶν as synonymous with "world" rather than Gentiles because the three names in the epistle are all Gentile names.

36. καὶ ἐὰν ἀσπάσησθε τοὺς ἀδελφοὺς ὑμῶν μόνον, τί περισσὸν ποιεῖτε; οὐχὶ καὶ οἱ ἐθνικοὶ τὸ αὐτὸ ποιοῦσιν;

This also reflects Paul's practice of taking no support from the community to which he was communicating the gospel (Painter, 372; Schnackenburg, 325), even when it brought criticism from his Christian opponents (1 Cor 9:18; 2 Cor 11:7–10).

8 John draws a conclusion that leads to action based on his explanation of the traveling ministers' needs. This conclusion states the obligation, and then its significance.

ἡμεῖς οὖν ὀφείλομεν ὑπολαμβάνειν τοὺς τοιούτους, "Therefore we are obligated to support such men as these." John now draws a conclusion from what he has just said about the commitment of these itinerant ministers. He does this with the conjunction οὖν. Though common in his Gospel, John's use of this conjunction does not occur in his other two epistles, and only occurs in Revelation when he is quoting Jesus (Rev 1:19; 2:5, 16; 3:3 [x2], 19). This may indicate the urgency and seriousness of his coming request. It is on the basis of this conclusion that he will make his request of Gaius in the verses that follow.

John begins his application with the first person plural pronoun ἡμεῖς. Both the use of the pronoun ἡμεῖς and its location are emphatic (Akin 244–45; Bruce, 151; Burdick, 452; Haas, de Jonge, and Swellengrebel, 181; Johnson, 173; Marshall, 87; Smalley, 352; Stott, 227). This use of ἡμεῖς has been understood in one of two ways. (1) It may refer to all Christians (Bruce, 151; Burdick, 452; Harris, 264; Marshall, 87; Schnackenburg, 325). (2) It refers to Johannine believers as opposed (in contrast to) to pagans (Brown, 713; Haas, de Jonge, and Swellengrebel, 181; Johnson, 173; Smalley, 352). The first sense fits the context best. By this he includes himself in the obligation and highlights the universal nature of this obligation. This is not something for just some believers to do. Even the apostles shared in this obligation. This softens the demand he will make on Gaius in the verses that follow. He will not be asking him to do anything he does not see as a personal responsibility and do as well.

He then identifies his request as something every believer is obligated to do. The term he uses (*ὀφείλομεν*) refers to an obligation and may be described as "our dutiful responsibility" (Akin, 245). With the first person plural he includes himself. This is the same sense he gave it in 1 John 4:11. Jesus taught this principle in Luke 10:7 when he instructed his disciples to accept hospitality because "a laborer is worthy of his hire."[37] This responsibility is all inclusive and ongoing, as indicated by the present tense as well.[38]

The Christian's obligation is to "support" those giving themselves fully to God's service. The term John uses to communicate this idea is ὑπολαμβάνειν.[39] This verb has a range of meanings from causing someone to ascend, to assuming or supposing, to replying, and supporting by receiving as a guest.[40] Schnackenburg (325, n. 2) suggests that it means both to "receive as a guest" and "support."[41] Yarbrough (374) suggests the sense of "accommodate," which would include both ideas of Schnackenburg. Lenski (584) proposes it should be translated as "to assist" because they are working along with them. Based on the need of the travelling missionaries, the idea of receiving as a guest seems to be intended here. When anyone received someone into their home, he or she identified himself and herself with that person publically and supplied their needs as long as they remained guests in their home.

When John says Gaius should receive these men as guests, he uses τοὺς τοιούτους to refer to them. In this construction, the article particularizes and points to the self-sacrificing missionaries as a class of people (Yarbrough, 374).[42] As a "qualitative demonstrative pronoun," it "speaks of their character" (Burdick, 452). Thus he is inviting Gaius, and all Christians (previous and emphatic ἡμεῖς) not only to receive this group of men, but others like them who will be coming his way in the future.[43]

ἵνα συνεργοὶ γινώμεθα τῇ ἀληθείᾳ. "in order that we may become fellow-workers in the truth." As second reason for supporting travelling

---

37. Stott (227, italics his) notes a Christian principle in this "ought" of John in that "we Christians should finance Christian enterprises which the world will not, or should not be expected to, support. Indeed, we have an obligation (*ought*) to do so."
38. I. Lorengin, "Hospitality versus Patronage," 166.
39. R. Lightner ("False Doctrine and the Child of God," 49) notes: "This is the exact opposite response that the believer is to have toward false teachers. In 3 John the fellow believer is to welcome and give hospitable support in contrast to the avoidance taught in 2 John."
40. BDAG, 1038; G. Delling, "λαμβάνω ... ὑπολαμβάνω," *TDNT* 4:15.
41. Stott (227) sees John using ὑπολαμβάνειν to create a pun with λαμβάνοντες in v 7.
42. J. H. Moulton and N. Turner, *A Grammar of New Testament Greek*. 3:193–94
43. Moody (130) and Hengel (M. Hengel, *The Johannine Question*, 34.) feel Demetrius had been through Gaius' area on a prior missionary journey and is about to go on a second one. The problem with this, then, is why he would need a letter from John? Gaius would know him already.

ministers of the gospel is now stated by John (Painter, 372). He begins his explanation with a ἵνα of result (Harris, 264) which when combined with γινώμεθα has the sense of "(that) we may prove to be" rather than "become" (Smalley, 352). This is similar to Jesus' words in John 15:8, "By this My Father is glorified, that you bear much fruit; so you will be My disciples" (ἵνα ... γένησθε ἐμοὶ μαθηταί).

What those who support God's workers become are "fellow-workers" (συνεργοὶ). This same term is commonly used by Paul to describe his missionary co-workers (Rom 16:3, 9, 21; 1 Cor 3:9; 2 Cor 1:24; 8:23; Phil 2:25; 4:3; Col 4:11; 1 Thess 3:2; Phlm 1, 24).

Though we have an obligation, we fulfill it with a goal in mind, to participate with them in "the truth." What does John mean by this? Westcott describes this phrase as "ambiguous" (Westcott 239). Once again interpreters understand John's use in one of four ways. (1) Because the noun it modifies has the συν-prefix, this indicates "a sense of cooperation with 'the truth' which is at work through the missionaries" who is "ultimately the Holy Spirit, who works through their efforts. Thus the Christian who supports them, becomes a co-worker with the Spirit of God himself" (Harris, 264). In this use "truth" is personified (Haas, de Jonge, and Swellengrebel, 181). This same "instrumental" construction is found in Jas 2:22 where faith works with deeds (Brooke, 187; Burdick, 453).[44] Brown (715) describes John's point well:

> Jesus is the truth; those who believe have dwelling within them the truth revealed in Jesus; it is not an inert principle; and there is a Spirit of Truth within the believer interpreting the Truth: This Spirit bears witness on behalf of Jesus; and the Spirit does this in and through Christians (John 15:26–27). Missionaries who 'set out for the sake of the Name' are allowing the truth that is within them to find a voice and are the instruments of the Spirit of Truth. By helping them as an act of love, Christians like Gaius are coworkers of the truth.

(2) Culy (162) proposes it should be seen as a dative of reference. The complement of συνεργοὶ is "an implied αὐτοῖς" which would then mean

44. 1 Cor 3:9 has the noun followed by the gen. while Col 4:11 has it used with εἰς.

"fellow-workers with them in the truth." Arguments for this include that (a) "*συνεργοὶ* would more naturally take a personal complement," (b) it does not take a dative object anywhere else in the New Testament or LXX, and (c) "*συνεργοὶ* is not contiguous with *τῇ ἀληθείᾳ*." (3) This could express a dative of advantage[45] and be translated as "for the sake of the truth" (Kistemaker, 395; Lenski, 584; Yarbrough, 375).[46] Some point to Paul's use of *συνεργός* with the preposition *εἰς* in 2 Cor 8:23 (*κοινωνὸς ἐμὸς καὶ εἰς ὑμᾶς συνεργός*) and Col 4:11 (*οὗτοι μόνοι συνεργοὶ εἰς τὴν βασιλείαν τοῦ θεοῦ*) to argue for this (Brooke, 187). (4) Others see it meaning "the reality of God or its revelation," or "the truthfulness of God" (Bultmann, 99; Smalley, 352).

This "truth" must refer to the sphere of truth already mentioned earlier in this epistle and described in his other epistles. Thus it includes revelation from God about Jesus and righteous living. Anyone who supports those promoting God's truth becomes one of their fellow-workers. They join "the team." Thus participating "in the truth" has to do with more than walking in it. It includes identifying with and supporting those who are promoting it within the church. Thus, we participate—become fellow workers—in God's work whenever we support others' ministries, whether that support is public recognition, praise, or financial help.

9 John now turns to the problem at hand. He had attempted to communicate with a church and his communication met opposition from one of its leaders. Whether he was a single elder or simply an influential person in the church is unclear. However, that he dominated his church is evident.

Burge notes two possible issues addressed here. The first is church polity involving the issue of someone wanting singular control. The second possible issue is doctrinal, and Diotrephes is a secessionist heretic. He admits (247–48) "These two views are difficult to defend since 3 John gives us so little information about the struggles in this early period. To suggest that we have a mutiny against apostolic government presses the evidence too far, and to suggest a formal affiliation between Diotrephes and the secessionists is strained when we find virtually no theological argument in the letter concerning right faith in Jesus or obedience." John does not use

45. D. B. Wallace, *Grammar*, 142–44. Also known as *dativus commodi*.
46. Schnackenburg (325) says the dative *τῇ ἀληθείᾳ* indicates personal involvement.

any theologically pejorative language to describe Diotrephes.[47] He sees 2 and 3 John addressing the same context. However, even though 2 John and 3 John were written about the same time, they need not address the same "context" in that they could have been written to address completely different problems. This explains the very different language. That John utilizes the theme of "truth" in each does not require they be addressing the same problem either, even if the themes of "truth" are the same in substance. One cannot get around the fact that John does not take the opportunity afforded him to attack a false doctrine or false teacher if that were the problem. Rather, his silence in 3 John and warning in 2 John tells us that to look for secessionists in the background goes beyond the available evidence in the documents themselves .

"The presbyter begins to discuss the cases of two people, Diotrephes and Demetrius (vv 9–12). Whereas the first was a threat to the unity of the Johannine church, the second added strength to its spiritual life and commitment to the truth" (Smalley, 353).

Ἔγραψά τι τῇ ἐκκλησίᾳ·, "I wrote something to the church." John begins by recounting to Gaius that he had attempted to communicate with Diotrephes' church.

What is the "something" that John wrote? It is likely a letter (Brown, 716). It may be an earlier request for assistance for someone else who had gone out from John and who had been rejected by Diotrephes (Akin, 246; Brooke, 188; Smalley, 353). The aorist indicates a previous letter that is lost, probably destroyed by Diotrephes (Brown, 716; Bruce, 152; Burdick, 453; Haas, de Jonge, and Swellengrebel, 181; Houlden, 153; Johnson, 175; Kruse, 226; Painter, 373; Schnackenburg, 326; Thompson, 161). Some think this previous letter is 2 John (Lenski, 584; Painter, 364; Strecker, 263). However, it could not be because 2 John is not a letter of introduction for orthodox missionaries, but a warning against heterodox ones (Johnson, 175; MacArthur, 256; Williams, 70).

His use of the article with church indicates he had a specific church in mind, and one known to Gaius as well (Brown, 715; Burdick, 454).[48]

47. 1 John 2:18, 3:10, 4:1, and 2 John 7 all describe the false teachers as antichrists or deceivers.

48. Note that this lost letter was written to the church, not to Diotrephes (Akin, 246; Kistemaker, 396).

Some believe that it refers to the church he belongs to (Haas, de Jonge, and Swellengrebel, 181; Kistemaker, 397). This has led to speculation as to Gaius' relationship to that church. (1) Gaius and Diotrephes were members of this same church (Brooke, 187; Hodges, 285–86; Marshall, 88). Stott (228) sees Diotrephes and Gaius as members of the same congregation, but that Diotrephes is a non-believing member of the visible church. Marshall (89) propose two "possibilities" to explain how they could be members of the same church. John's first letter was "suppressed" by Diotrephes and this was a second attempt through Gaius. Gaius lived (sole Christian household) some distance out of town in a village about a day's journey between cities. His health might have been such that he could not travel to Diotrephes' city and confront him personally. These make great theories, but without additional support from the text or church history, they must be seen as primarily conjecture. However, John's use of αὐτῶν (third-person pl.) rather than ὑμῶν indicates different churches (Brown, 717; Dodd, 161; Harris, 265). (2) He was an elder in a sister church (Akin, 246; Dodd, 161; Kistemaker, 396). His use of the third person to refer to Diotrephes' church makes this latter option seem more likely. Further, though John tells Gaius about Diotrephes, what he says should not be construed as a warning, nor should we consider Gaius in danger of expulsion just because John listed that as one of Diotrephes' offenses. Still, the two men had to know each other, based on how John refers to Diotrephes without explanation. The clear impression is that Gaius knows him.

ἀλλ' ὁ φιλοπρωτεύων αὐτῶν Διοτρέφης οὐκ ἐπιδέχεται ἡμᾶς. "but Diotrephes who loves to be first over them does not receive us." Diotrephes' opposition to John is reflected in his refusal to support his messengers and expulsion of those who do.[49] His name means "sustained" or "nurtured by Zeus (Brown, 716; Johnson, 175).[50] Thus he is at least Gentile, and his name may indicate pagan parents.

He is described with a present tense articular participle φιλοπρωτεύων which indicates a continuing ego problem.[51] He is arrogant (Harris,

49. J. Polhill ("An Analysis of II and III John," 468) calls Diotrephes a "sinister figure." Sinister may be a little strong. His role is not that of brooding evil. However, he is not atypical of men in many churches around the world.

50. K. Schmidt, "βασιλεύς," *TDNT* 1:564. Painter (373) prefers "child of Zeus."

51. This term is not found anywhere else in the New Testament or extant extrabiblical literature (Painter, 373). This word may have been coined by John, though we

265) and ambitious (Brooke, 189; Stott, 229). He wants first place, to be in control (Yarbrough, 378),[52] and receiving them would acknowledge that he was under someone else's authority (Westcott, 241).[53] He is doing the opposite of Jesus' instruction in Matt 20:27. This is not an isolated incident, but a pattern that has now affected one of John's messengers. His ego has expressed itself by his continuing to assert his control even when it brings him into opposition with an apostle. Even so, it must be remembered that John does not accuse him of false teaching (Painter, 363). The issue between John and Diotrephes is moral, not theological (Stott, 230).[54]

An incident from John's own life likely has motivated John to address this problem. As Jesus was traveling to Jerusalem in anticipation of his death, the disciples were discussing among themselves who would be greatest in Jesus' kingdom. At this time John's mother approached Jesus with her two sons and asked for seats of prominence when he set up his kingdom (Matt 20:20–28). They were rebuffed by Jesus and then told "whoever desires to be first among you, let him be your slave." Yarbrough (377) suggests that this incident (where his mother asked Jesus to elevate him and James) and Jesus' response was what motivated him to refer to himself as "elder" instead of "apostle" in the opening of this and 2 John. It is also clear that Diotrephes is not serving, but dominating. "Colossians 1:18 states that only Christ rightly deserves the preeminence *(prōteuōn)*. Diotrephes usurped for himself the position only our Lord should hold. He loved being the leader and exercising authority" (Akin, 246).

The present tense ἐπιδέχεται indicates an ongoing activity rather than a single incident (Brown, 718; Burdick, 454). His failure to "receive" people was not an isolated event. John's choice of ἐπιδέχεται has been understood in one of three ways. (1) It means a person does not extend hospitality when someone comes to visit. It is a refusal to accept or welcome someone (Kruse,

---

cannot be certain, based on the small amount of literature discovered to this date.

52. BDAG, 1058.

53. Bruce (152) calls him "a self-promoted demagogue."

54. Painter (364–65) views Diotrephes as one of the false teachers of 2 John. He does this by connecting the evil works (τοῖς ἔργοις αὐτοῦ τοῖς πονηροῖς) of 2 John 11 with the evil words of 3 John 10 (λόγοις πονηροῖς). However, if the issue were doctrinal, it seems that John would have labeled him a deceiver or an antichrist, which he does not (Culpepper, 281; Williamson, 214).

226–27; Rensberger, 162).[55] This is the case in the verse that follows with regard to missionaries he rejected. This concept can be seen in the same root words being used by Paul to describe the welcome and support given by churches (Lieu, 275).[56] Additionally, this is the sense it carried in Greco-Roman diplomacy (Rensberger, 162).[57] (2) It means to reject the apostle's authority. Ignoring a letter from him would be an example of this (Culy, 164; Grayston, 160; Harris, 265). (3) Both senses were intended in that those missionaries rejected had borne a letter from John and their rejection was a rejection of John (Brown, 718; Smalley, 357).

It appears that Diotrephes was neither friendly nor welcoming, but likely expelled John's representative in a brusque manner. Rather than treating him as a brother in Christ, he more likely treated him in the more Greco-Roman custom of a superior to an inferior (patronage).[58] However, in so doing, he has now taken his stand against more than John (*contra* Akin, 246). John does not perceive Diotrephes' refusal as a personal attack, but as an affront against "us" (ἡμᾶς).

The identity of "us" has also been debated. (1) It could refer to the elder only (Johnson, 175; Schnackenburg, 327). In support of this, Haas, de Jonge, and Swellengrebel (183) argue that the use of the first person plural in place of the singular was common in letter writing. However, John consistently uses the 1 singular to refer to himself elsewhere in the epistle (vv 1, 3, 4, 9, 10, 13, 14) (Brown, 717). (2) Schnackenburg (327) sees this use of ἡμᾶς, not as an authorial "we," but a stylistic feature of John's which could then refer to John. (3) The pronoun ἡμᾶς could refer to the elder and his followers and function as an "ecclesial 'we'" (Brown, 717; Burdick, 454; Houlden, 153; Johnson, 175; Kistemaker, 396; Kruse, 227; Smalley, 357;

---

55. BDAG, 370; M. M. Mitchell, "Diotrephes does not receive us," 316–17.
56. She notes: Acts 17:7 (ὑποδέδεκται), Acts 18:27 (ἀποδέξασθαι), Rom 16:2 (προσδέξησθε), and 2 Cor 7:15 (ἐδέξασθε).
57. He notes 1 Macc 10:46; 12:8, 43; 14:23 as examples of this meaning.
58. See I. Lorencin's "Hospitality versus Patronage: An Investigation of Social Dynamics in the Third Epistle of John, (165–74) for a full discussion of patronage in the Greco-Roman world and how it may have impacted the relationships described in this epistle. In Matt 10:40 Jesus uses this same verb (ἐπιδέχεται) to say that when people "received" the apostles, they were receiving Jesus who sent them, and thereby receiving God who sent Jesus.

Strecker, 263).[59] This seems the better option. John is identifying with those in his church and others serving the Lord. He identifies himself with the rejected missionaries and so, though he was not with them in body, he was with them in spirit.

The nature of the conflict has been understood in three ways. (1) It involved the question of ecclesiastical authority, with Diotrephes representing one of the early monarchical bishops. This view was championed by Harnack at the end of the nineteenth century.[60] Brown provides a modification of this view in that he sees Diotrephes caught in the battle between the "Johannine school," the elder, and the secessionists and so closed his church to both sides.[61] Smalley (356) makes a helpful observation even as he rejects this view. He notes that "Diotrephes is better understood as a symptom of the disease which the ministry of monarchical bishops was designed to cure." Thus, rather than seeing Diotrephes as an attempt at monarchical bishopric that John is about to squelch, we should see him as the kind of person that drove the church to that solution. (2) It involved the question of doctrinal orthodoxy.[62] Diotrephes was one of the false teachers identified by John in 1 and 2 John.[63] The opposite view, that Diotrephes was orthodox and "the elder" heterodox was proposed by Käsemann and is noted by most commentators.[64] Nothing in the text or from the church fathers even hints at this as a possibility and so it should not be considered seriously. (3) The conflict results from a misunderstanding.[65] In this theory, Price argues that the order of composition of the epistles is 3 John, 2 John,

59. Yarbrough (378) acknowledges both options but chooses neither. Rensberger (162) rejects the idea that this use of "we" is a reference to the Johannine school.

60. A. von Harnack, "Über den dritten Johannesbrief," *TU* 15 (1897): 3–27.

61. R. Brown, *The Community of the Beloved Disciple*, 160–61.

62. Strecker (262) sees this as a doctrinal issue, that John's view was in the minority, and that orthodoxy was a minority view at that time and until the church of Rome, which was orthodox, gained the upper hand in the controversy. John would have been chiliastic and Diotrephes gnostic, with Gnosticism having the upper hand and John's chiliasm negatively impacting his influence.

63. W. Bauer, *Orthodoxy and Heresy in Earliest Christianity*, 93; also B. Bonsack, "Der Presbyteros des dritten Briefs und der geliebte Jünger des Evangeliums nach Johannes," 45–62.

64. E. Käsemann, "Ketzer und Zeuge: Zum johanneischen Verfasserproblem," 292–311.

65. R. M. Price, "The Sitz-im-Leben of Third John: A New Reconstruction," 109–19.

an then 1 John. These resulted from secret Docetists that John sent out unaware of their theological shift. Diotrephes recognized their heresy when they visited their church and thought mistakenly that they represented a change in theology on John's part. He then began rejecting missionaries from John's church, which upset John, who wrote 3 John and then went to confront him. Learning the truth when they met, John then wrote 2 John (or several letters like it of which 2 John is the sole survivor) to warn other churches against these false teachers. After that he wrote 1 John to clarify his christological view. However, along with being a completely speculative theory with little more evidence than the Johannine school theory, this view of 3 John has to deny its inspiration. It is hard to imagine how the Holy Spirit, who would know what was really happening, would inspire John to write something that was the opposite to reality. (4) We have an instance where Diotrephes, the sponsor of a house church, was "exhibiting patronal behavior."[66] This does fit the cultural practices of the Greco-Roman world and may be evident in such New Testament passages as 1 Cor 11:17–34 and Jas 2:1–9. However, M. Mitchell argues that Diotrephes' actions fit better in the context of rejection than of hospitality. She bases this on the use of the term ἐπιδέχομαι in diplomatic settings. "In rejecting the letter and envoys of the elder and denying them a hospitable reception into his house-church, Diotrephes was rejecting the elder himself and breaking off relations with him. In the first instance (v. 9) the elder named the *implication* of the same act of v 10, that is, in not receiving the brothers whom he sent, Diotrephes did not receive the elder whom they represented."[67] She further argues that both uses of ἐπιδέχομαι means to "receive" or "welcome" rather than "acknowledge authority" based on the use of the term in diplomatic correspondences. She sees John's reference fitting into the Greek view that to receive someone's representative is to receive him.[68] (5) We cannot know from the data we are provided in history or the biblical text in order to be

66. I. Lorencin, "Hospitality versus Patronage," 167.

67. M. M. Mitchell, "'Diotrephes Does not Receive Us': The Lexicographical and Social Context of 3 John 9–10," 319 (italics hers).

68. After listing the various interpretations of ἐπιδέχομαι, she traces its history of inclusion by Baur in his earlier works of the idea of acknowledging authority and then demonstrates from extant literature that it would not have meant that, here or anywhere else ("'Diotrephes does not receive us': The Lexicographical and Social Context of 3 John 9–10," 306–17). Of note is that in the latest edition (BDAG,

sure of the nature of the problem (Akin, 248; Schnackenburg, 327).[69] This is really the best option. Obviously John and Gaius knew the real issues. John's promise to come and confront Diotrephes is clear, as well as his actions that moved John to write. However, the silences of John in this letter are as significant as what he says. It is always risky to speculate where the divine Author of Scripture chose to leave us uninformed.

10 John now turns to the solution to the problem. He will come and confront Diotrephes.[70]

διὰ τοῦτο, ἐὰν ἔλθω, "Because of this, when I come." With the anaphoric* διὰ τοῦτο, John looks back on the reason for what will follow (Burdick, 455; Culy, 164; Harris, 266). However, when John says ἐὰν, he is not saying "if" in the sense of contingency.[71] The two understandings of this use of ἐὰν are: (1) John is not certain he will visit (Brown, 718; Harris, 266). This indicates he does not want a "hostile" visit (Brown, 718). This would be similar to Paul's reluctance to visit Corinth until he had heard an encouraging report of their attitude toward him (2 Cor 1:23–2:2; 12:20). However, since Gaius is not a member of Diotrephes' church, the planned visit to Gaius need not include a visit to Diotrephes (Brown, 718). (2) Rather he is saying "when" or "whenever" (Akin, 248; Burdick, 455; Haas, de Jonge, and Swellengrebel, 184; Lenski, 586; Smalley, 357; Westcott, 240; Williamson, 214). This is the same use of ἐὰν as we find in 1 John 2:28. Thus, John has every intention of confronting Diotrephes. This "if" is more than a question of mere possibility, but a statement of anticipation.

---

370), the editors now say "the idea of 'authority' is not lexically defensible" and note her article as their authority.

69. J. Polhill, "An Analysis of II and III John," 470; J. Lieu, *Second and Third Epistles of John*, 163.

70. Painter (373), as does Lieu (275) notes the "linguistic connection" between 3 John 10 and 2 John 10–11 by the repeated terms "work" and "evil." He argues from this that Diotrephes is the false teacher to be rejected in 2 John and that John "was not simply involved in a personal power struggle with Diotrephes." However, there is no indication that John intends this connection. Rather, the points of contact are incidental and simply reflect his writing style and way of saying things. What can be seen from this is that John considers both false teaching and abuse of fellow-believers as similarly evil though they are different offenses.

71. BDAG, 268; D. B. Wallace, *Grammar*, 696–97. This would fit into the "more probable future" category of third class conditional sentences.

ὑπομνήσω αὐτοῦ τὰ ἔργα ἃ ποιεῖ λόγοις πονηροῖς φλυαρῶν ἡμᾶς, "I will call to attention his works which he does in evil words disparaging us." With the future indicative John removes any doubt of his intention of coming. Also, he states his intention with ὑπομνήσω, which means to "call to mind," "call attention to," or "bring up" (Burdick, 455; Yarbrough, 378).[72] This is a promise of public rebuke rather than some "judicial" action (discipline) (Lenski, 587; Schnackenburg, 327).[73] It is "his works" (αὐτοῦ τὰ ἃ ποιεῖ ἔργα) that will be John's focus. Diotrephes will be called to task for things he has done.

Brown (719) thinks that there is some uncertainty about how the meeting will turn out with John. Lieu (276) questions the authority of "the elder," who she does not see as John and the significance of what he says in this verse and whether his visit would be effective. She says, "Those who identify the author with the apostle John or another senior figure see this promised visit as full of foreboding and suppressed power. So, Paul's own visits to his communities could be occasions of considerable tension (2 Cor 1:23–2:3; 13:1–4). Without the assumption of such a powerful voice behind them, the elder's protestations sound somewhat less confident; it is not all clear what he can or what he hopes to achieve." Lieu (278) then suggests instead that this upcoming confrontation is intended by John to restore their relationship rather than to reject Diotrephes. This doubt and reading of the text on her part arises from the presupposition of a non-apostolic author. If the author were not John the Apostle, then there might be a chance of her reading the situation correctly. However, no sense of doubt or timidity need be read in anything John says. Marshall (91, n. 17) rightly sees loving restraint rather than weakness. Moreover, in fact, knowing John's heart as expressed in his three epistles, a gentle rebuke would be his desired means of resolution. Why? Because reconciliation is central to the heart attitude of God toward sinners (Rom 5:10–11; 2 Cor 5:18–19).

Diotrephes' "deeds" involve more than expulsion of other believes.[74] They also involve slander. He has been making senseless accusations against

---

72. BDAG, 1039.

73. Bultmann (101) interprets John's plan to visit to indicate he still has "followers" in Diotrephes' church. It would be better to say that the church's membership still recognize his apostolic authority.

74. Johnson (177), who interprets 3 John from the perspective of the Johannine school theory, approaches the problem of Diotrephes by first noting that John

the apostles. John describes his conduct as acts involving "evil words." His choice of πονηροῖς to describe what he has been saying expresses John's moral assessment of Diotrephes. This same term for evil (πονηρός) occurs in John 3:19–21 where John describes those who prefer "darkness" over Jesus, the Light.

He is not just ambitious or arrogant. His ambition has led to immorality, though in this case it is not of a sexual nature. John clarifies this with the adverbial present participle φλυαρῶν. This term, occurring only here in the New Testament as a verbal, means to disparage or talk nonsense about someone or something (Burdick, 455; Johnson, 176).[75] Its cognate noun (φλύαροι) is used by Paul of idle widows gossiping in 1 Tim 5:13. Many interpreters give this use the same sense of "gossip" (Akin, 248; Edwards, 25; Kruse, 227; Stott, 231). Here, though, it "suggests empty and unjustified charges" (Brooke, 190; Painter, 376).[76] It is speech delivered with malice. It intends harm.[77] The present tense suggests that this has been a continuing practice (Burdick, 455). Again, it is useless talk that harms another. So, Diotrephes' talk is unfounded and harmful, reflecting an immoral soul.

So, why does John not call them lies, or Diotrephes a liar? He certainly did not hesitate to brand the false teachers of 1 John "liars" and of 2 John "deceivers." His choice of "nonsense" seems to be less pejorative. It may also be designed to indicate the actual insignificance of Diotrephes. He is more like a gossipy widow than a powerful opponent.[78] This does not mean that John is not taking him seriously. Rather, he sees him in perspective. This may also indicate that his planned confrontation is intended to be admonitional more than punitive.

Who is included in "us" (ἡμᾶς) here? Following his theory, Brown (719) sees the Johannine school as the referent. However, it remains best

---

does not accuse him of doctrinal deviation. He then sees him as representing "a third alternative in the disintegrating Johannine fellowship" and he represents a " 'new wave' of the secessionists." Culpepper (281) notes, "The restraint of 3 John and the notable absence of the strident language of 1 and 2 John suggest that the differences between the elder and Diotrephes were not doctrinal."

75. BDAG, 1060.

76. C. Rogers, Jr. and C. Rogers III, *The New Linguistic and Exegetical Key to the Greek New Testament*, 603–604.

77. BDAG, 1060.

78. Since John is dealing with attitude and conduct rather than theological heresy, we might think of Diotrephes' actions as more political than doctrinal.

to see John intending himself along with his co-workers (Yarbrough, 379), which would be the rebuffed missionaries that had returned to their home church and reported their treatment to John.

καὶ μὴ ἀρκούμενος ἐπὶ τούτοις, "and not being satisfied with these." John continues to describe Diotrephes' conduct in terms of both his actions and attitude.[79] He notes that he was "not satisfied" (*μὴ ἀρκούμενος*) just with maligning John and his representatives. He targeted others as well. This dissatisfaction motivated his failure to receive or welcome others.

οὔτε αὐτὸς ἐπιδέχεται τοὺς ἀδελφοὺς, "he does not receive the brethren." This second use of ἐπιδέχεται emphasizes his refusal to show hospitality by welcoming visiting ministers (Kruse, 227).[80] It also stands in tandem with φλυαρῶν. While disparaging someone expresses malice, receiving someone expresses the opposite—love and benevolence. This is absent in Diotrephes.

καὶ τοὺς βουλομένους κωλύει καὶ ἐκ τῆς ἐκκλησίας ἐκβάλλει, "and those wishing to he hinders and throws out of the church." Along with refusing to welcome the brethren from outside his home church, Diotrephes did not "welcome" the welcoming members in his own church as well. He is described as both hindering those attempting to receive visiting brethren and throwing some out of the church. This reveals not only his power over the congregation, but also his choice to exercise that power if anyone acted contrary to his will.

Of interest is John's repeated use of present tense verbs. This indicates not only that it was a customary practice of Diotrephes, but that it was continuing at the time of writing (Akin, 249; Brooke). This was not an isolated incident. Rather, it was a pattern of conduct.[81] One thing Diotrephes did was to hinder (κωλύω) those who wished to show hospitality. This verb is often used in New Testament to describe those actively hindering.[82] The

79. This is the only occurrence of ἐπὶ τούτοις with ἀρκέω in the NT. It may be equivalent to a simple dative (BDAG, 132), or may be causal (Culy, 165).

80. "Diotrephes was prepared to treat the emissaries of the presbyter as John has urged that congregation addressed in 2 John (on doctrinal grounds) to treat the emissaries of the secessionists" (Smalley, 358). Also, Brown, *Community of the Beloved Disciple*, 133, n 260.

81. Bultmann (101) notes the present tense "indicates the customary conduct of Diotrephes, but it does not specify when and how often Diotrephes has actually acted in this manner."

82. Mark 9:38–39 (disciples stopped others from casting out demons in Jesus' name, also Luke 9:49–50), Luke 6:29 (withholding one's cloak in the sense of hindering

most notable comes from the disciples hindering children from meeting Jesus (Matt 19:14; Mark 10:14; Luke 18:16).

Painter (373–74) sees ἐκβάλλει indicating excommunication. He notes that others do not see this as excommunication but a refusal of hospitality. He responds, "But in this case the household involved a house church and the householder had the power to behave quite autocratically." Lieu concurs, but observes that John does not say Diotrephes cast John out, only members of his church.[83] Brown (720) notes the use of this same verb in John 9:34–35 for "expulsion from the synagogue." Josephus likewise used it with regard to people being thrown out of the Essene communities.[84] This also does not require that Diotrephes himself expelled them. He may have convinced the congregation to do so. Schnackenburg (328) sees his attempt against church members as unsuccessful; he just hinders, and so his church was limiting his influence.[85] He was not in absolute control. Thus this present tense may be conative, and express the idea that "he is trying to" throw people out (Westcott, 241). However, it seems better to see it as factual, "he is putting them out" (Akin, 248; Kistemaker, 397, Marshall, 91, n. 16)."

11 Using antithesis, familiar to us from his first epistle, John now contrasts two kinds of people, those who do good and those who do evil. Does he by this imply that Diotrephes is an unbeliever? A possible chiasm is formed

---

someone from taking it); Luke 11:52 (Scribes keeping people from the key of knowledge), Luke 23:2 (Jesus accused of hindering Jews from paying taxes), Acts 10:47 (keeping people from being baptized), 11:17 (keeping God from accomplishing His will), 24:23 (friends kept from helping Paul), Rom 1:13 (Paul kept from visiting the church in Rome), 1 Cor 14:39 (not allowing people to speak in tongues), 1 Thess 2:16 (keeping Paul from witnessing to Gentiles), and 1 Tim 4:3 (keeping people from getting married). There are also some non-negative uses in the NT. They include: Acts 8:36 (Ethiopian Eunuch wants to be baptized), 16:6 (the Holy Spirit forbade Paul from preaching in Asia because he was to go to Macedonia), 27:43 (Centurion kept his soldiers from killing his prisoners, including Paul), Heb 7:23 (death kept priests from having perpetual ministries), 2 Pet 2:16 (Balaam's donkey helped restrain his madness).

83. J. Lieu, *Second and Third Epistles*, 113, n. 158.

84. Josephus, *J.W.* 2.8.8 (143) reads: "But for those that are caught in any heinous sins, they cast them out of their society" (from W. Whiston, trans., *The Works of Josephus: Complete and Unabridged*).)

85. Schnackenburg (329) sees Gaius as a member of Diotrephes' church and that Diotrephes failed to excommunicate him.

by the alternation of κακὸς and ἀγαθός with ἀγαθοποιῶν and κακοποιῶν with "good" at its center (Akin, 248; Brown, 720; Smalley, 359). Thus John's point is that Gaius should "copy the example of good people" (Marshall, 92).[86]

This is the only imperative in the letter. Culy (166) sees it marking the "peak" of the letter. It is the moral purpose of the letter, even as it was written to endorse Demetrius and encourage Gaius.

Ἀγαπητέ, μὴ μιμοῦ τὸ κακὸν ἀλλὰ τὸ ἀγαθόν, "Beloved, do not imitate the evil *person*, but the good." John develops the first half of this verse with the present imperative μιμοῦ.[87] Though the present imperative might at times be translated with the idea of "stop imitating," in this case it is clear from the context that Gaius has not been conducting himself in the same manner as Diotrephes (Harris, 266). Thus it is better to see John stating a principle here once again. None of God's children should imitate evil. His use of the article with κακὸν indicates its substantival role in the sentence, whether being used conceptually or with an implied "person" or "conduct." The same is true with ἀγαθόν.[88] His choice of κακὸν over another term for evil such as πονηρός, seems to result from the nature of Diotrephes' actions. They were not immoral as such, but more harmful, reprehensible, socially unacceptable.[89] In contrast to κακὸν, John chooses its antonym ἀγαθόν which indicates the person's actions are beneficial to others and of social worth.[90] Since he is discussing Diotrephes' actions and attitudes, it seems best to understand his use of these two adjectives with the idea of a kind of person rather than evil or good in general. Furthermore, imitation is of people, not concepts. Further, John's choice of μιμοῦ focuses attention on the model being emulated and involves imitating behavior.[91] He is now ready to explain why it is important to imitate good people.

ὁ ἀγαθοποιῶν ἐκ τοῦ θεοῦ ἐστιν·, "He who does good is from God." This abrupt statement (Harris, 266, calls it "asyndetic") is emphatic by its

86. Grayston (162) describes this verse as "a stock piece of moral advice" that is "strengthened by a moralizing reference to God composed in the familiar couplet style. It underlines the religious origin of the judgments that have been recorded."
87. Other uses of μιμοῦ in the NT include 2 Thess 3:7, 9, and Heb 3:17.
88. This is the only place κακὸς and ἀγαθός occur in Johannine literature. John's normal term for "good" is καλός (Painter, 374).
89. BDAG, 501; W. Grundmann, "κακός," *TDNT* 3:479–81.
90. BDAG, 4; W. Grundmann, "ἀγαθός," *TDNT* 1:15–17.
91. BDAG, 651; W. Michaelis, "μιμέομαι," *TDNT* 4:666–74.

insertion. It is the moral point of the letter. With the use of an articular present participle (in this case ἀγαθοποιῶν)[92] characteristic of his first epistle, John again describes a kind of person. He focuses on character rather than the progressive sense with this construction and indicates by this that one characterized by doing good is "from God." This is a principle that applies to everyone and so should be the basis of Gaius' actions. With his familiar ἐκ τοῦ θεοῦ construction he describes the source of all "good" conduct, namely, it comes "from God" and God is its source (Kistemaker, 399; Lenski, 589; Strecker, 266). Thus, we prove our relationship with and commitment to God by rejecting evil life patterns and pursuing good. "Doing good flows naturally from the person born of God, just as doing evil is a calling card of 'children of the devil'" (Yarbrough, 383).

ὁ κακοποιῶν οὐχ ἑώρακεν τὸν θεόν, "he who does evil has not seen God." In contrast to the person characterized by good conduct, is the one characterized by evil conduct.[93] Though the expected adversative conjunction ἀλλὰ is absent (by asyndeton*, a figure of speech where a conjunction is left out for emphasis),[94] this absence draws attention to the contrast and thereby strengthens it further. However, does οὐχ ἑώρακεν τὸν θεόν mean the person is unregenerate? Smalley (359) is correct when he says, "Behavior is an indication of spiritual condition." Harris (267) assesses the problem raised by this statement well. He notes that this expresses a "common Johannine theme of behavior as an indication of genuine faith, found in 1 John in 3:6, 3:10, 4:7, and 4:20, and in the Gospel of John in 3:17–21. By implication the genuineness of Diotrephes' faith is called into question, because he has obviously done 'what is bad' (vv. 9–10)."[95] Most interpreters understand John to be implying by this that Diotrephes is not a believer and will refer to many of the same verses as Harris (Burdick, 458; Harris, 267; Lenski, 590; Yarbrough, 383). Thus Marshall (92) says, "It is clear that

92. This is the sole use of ἀγαθοποιέω in Johannine literature. It occurs only seven other times in the NT (Luke 6:9, 33, 35 and 1 Pet 2:15, 20; 3:6, 17).

93. This is also the sole instance of κακοποιέω being used in Johannine literature. It occurs six times in the rest of the NT, a favorite term for Peter (Mark 3:4; Luke 6:9; 1 Pet 2:12, 14; 3:17; 4:15).

94. E. W. Bullinger, *Figures of Speech*, 137.

95. Painter (377) too sees this parallel with 1 John 3:10, but without the double negatives. Rensberger (162) points to 1 John 4:12 and says that those who "see" God reveal him through love of the brethren.

the lack of Christian character is to be regarded as a mark of the absence of true Christian experience." Kistemaker (400) argues from the perfect with the negative οὐχ "signifies that the one who does evil has never seen God in the past and consequently not in the present either" (so too, Smalley, 359). Lenski (589) paraphrases John's words well. "Copy the good because doing this is evidence that one is from God, but shun the base because to do the base is evidence that one has not even gotten near enough to have as much as caught a glimpse of God" (Lenski, 589).

So, the consensus of scholarship understands John to be affirming that Diotrephes is not a believer. Taken absolutely, that is what John is saying. Also, if John 3:17–21 describes the same situation, it would be a good clarifying text. However, in John 3, the issue is justification in terms of responses to Jesus.[96] A contrast is drawn between those who do good or evil in terms of their response to "the light," Jesus. A second text that would hopefully clarify this passage is 1 John 3:4–9. There John indicates that one reflects whether they have "seen" God or not. To the extent that one "knows" him relationally, one will choose not to sin, but rather to reflect his holiness and righteousness. Just as someone might claim to know God while failing to imitate Jesus' conduct of obedience (1 John 2:3–6), here, someone might claim to have seen God (a claim to relationship) while living otherwise. The sticking point with those passages in 1 John was John's relating conduct to how one treated his or her Christian "brother."[97] One must be a "brother" to mistreat a "brother." Ultimately one has to recognize John's use of antithesis and literary dualism as a rhetorical device to emphasize proper behavior rather than to define who is "saved" and who is "lost" (in terms of his or her justification).

Having said all that, John is making an absolute statement that applies to believers and non-believers alike. This is a principle. However, as it is applied to Diotrephes, some problems arise. John is going to meet with him

96. Nonetheless, a major theme I see in John's Gospel is that believers (OT saints) believe in Jesus when they meet him because they are already believers. They are not becoming justified saints, they are confirming their justification status by their response to Jesus. That is the context and sense of John 3:17–21. Here the issue is different and so this passage is not relevant to the question raised by 3 John.

97. See my commentary on those passages for a full explanation of the problem and why I do not see them as tests of life (determining whether one is a justified saint or not).

and confront him concerning his conduct and verbiage. He promises to expose, but not excommunicate. His plan sounds more in keeping with Paul's instructions for rebuking sinning elders (1 Tim 5:19–20) than punishing sinning members (1 Cor 5:3–5). John has the testimony of more than two or three witnesses, and he plans to go to Diotrephes' church and rebuke him publically. However, if Diotrephes is a believer, then what does John mean by this?

With John "seeing" God is not experiencing a vision, but having a relationship with God that involves fellowship (Haas, de Jonge, and Swellengrebel, 185). This relationship cannot be experienced apart from obedience and loving other believers, as was made clear in his first epistle. So, here, too, seeing God must be understood relationally. However, as a principle, it can mean either a non-believer or an out-of-fellowship disobedient believer. Diotrephes is someone whose conduct fits the idea of "hate" and "murder" of a fellow-believer by failing to love him or her in 1 John. So John is not especially questioning Diotrephes' salvation as much as his walk with the Lord, and rebutting any claim he might make to fellowship with God. As noted earlier, this may explain the absence of such descriptors as "liar" or "deceiver," though his "empty talk" is certainly filled with lies, or "antichrist," though his conduct ultimately opposes Christ's work. There is not even a hint that John plans on removing him from office or whatever leadership role he has in the church. Additionally, if he was a nonbeliever, it is very doubtful that John would willingly leave him in charge of a church.

12 Now John moves to the purpose of his letter, the endorsement of Demetrius.[98] John drives home the trustworthiness of Demetrius with the testimonies of three witnesses.

Δημητρίῳ μεμαρτύρηται ὑπὸ πάντων καὶ ὑπὸ αὐτῆς τῆς ἀληθείας·, "Demetrius has received a testimony from all and from the truth itself."[99]

98. We can see an example of a similar letter of recommendation in 1 Cor 16:3. There Paul instructs the church at Corinth that they would send representatives with their gift to Jerusalem with "letters of introduction" (Harris, 267).

99. This is not the same Demetrius as the silversmith at Ephesus who opposed Paul (Acts 19:23–27) (Burdick, 458; Brown, 721). His was a common name, and so could be anybody (Moody, 133). Some see it as a lengthened form of Demas. Burdick (458) rejects this as conjecture. He is not likely to be the Demas who deserted Paul in 2 Tim 4:10 (Brown, 721–22; Burdick, 458). Brown (721) notes, "The fourth-century *Apostolic Constitutions* (7.46.9; Funk 1, 454) reports that the

Smalley (361) notes that his name means "belonging to Demeter" who was the Greek goddess of fruits and crops. He notes further that by implication "Demetrius came from a pagan family; in which case official confirmation of his good character and doctrinal orthodoxy, and of his suitability as a witness to the truth in the present struggle, would not have been out of place." At the same time, it would seem that the church was still experiencing a steady flow of new converts from paganism and having a pagan name would not cause suspicion in and of itself. From what we can see in this epistle, he is most likely the bearer of the letter and an itinerant missionary (Burdick, 458; Harris, 267; Marshall, 93), possibly even the leader of a missionary team (Brooke, 192; Harris, 267).[100]

What John tells us about Demetrius is that he has already been approved by "all." John's use of "all" is either hyperbole (Brown, 723; Burdick, 458; Williamson, 217) or, better, a synecdoche* of the whole.[101] It indicates a consistent and persistent testimony by every person who has met him and subsequently mentioned him to John and his church. Thus "all" either indicates John and the other missionaries (Lenski, 591), or everyone to whom he has ministered in this role as an itinerant messenger (Akin, 250; Marshall, 93; Smalley, 361).[102] This second option seems best.

Their testimony is expressed using the perfect passive *μεμαρτύρηται*. The perfect tense indicates he has an established reputation in his church that continues to the time of writing (Akin, 250; Brown, 722; Burdick, 458; Smalley 361). Also, John's choice of the passive form indicates that

---

Apostle John ultimately made him bishop of Philadelphia in Asia Minor ... but this information is of dubious historical value, exemplifying as it does a tendency to invent successful careers for NT worthies." I am not as quick to dismiss the testimony of the church fathers and suspect that more of what they say will be proven true over time than disproven. Unless there is substantial evidence of an intention to fabricate, we should give them the respect their testimony is due rather than read them through the same skeptical lens liberal scholarship has applied to inspired Scripture.

100. I. Lorencin ("Hospitality versus Patronage," 174) suggests that Demetrius may have been a member of Diotrephes' church and had been expelled by him rather than being an itinerant preacher.

101. E. W. Bullinger, *Figures of Speech*, 635.

102. Naturally, Brown (723) sees it referring to Johannine Christians. Painter (379) describes it as his "public *persona* outside the church."

Demetrius has received this testimony rather than making personal claims.[103] He has an established reputation among those who know him.[104] This reference to him indicates that he was the bearer of this letter (Marshall, 93) and that it was serving as his introduction as well as credential before Gaius. Thus he would likely fit into the category of the kind of "stranger" (v 5) to whom Gaius was known to show hospitality.

Demetrius has not only received testimony from people who have known him, but from "truth itself." With the article and adjective intensive αὐτῆς, truth is personified as another of the witnesses on Demetrius' behalf (Bultmann, 102; Marshall, 93; Moody, 133; Plummer, 193; Strecker, 265). Here again interpreters understand John's use of "truth" here widely. They identify it as the body of truth affirmed by all orthodox believers (Kruse, 233; Moody, 133), God's Word (Kistemaker, 400; Lenski, 591), God who is true (Burdick, 459; Yarbrough, 383), Jesus (Bruce, 155),[105] the Spirit (Brooke, 192–93; Williamson, 218), or truthful conduct which is "in accordance with God's will" (Haas, de Jonge, and Swellengrebel, 186).[106] Painter (379) sees the testimony of "the truth" as meaning "truth is self-evident in the life of Demetrius" (so too Dodd, 167 and Smalley, 361). The use of the article with "truth," along with the repeated preposition ὑπὸ, indicates that "the truth" and those who know Demetrius agree concerning him and so their testimonies can be trusted.[107] Thus this serves as a very strong endorsement of Demetrius in that he has three "witnesses" that verify his character.

---

103. Culy (166) notes that "when μαρτυρέω is modified by a dative noun phrase, it often carries the sense of providing confirming or affirming testimony," and (167) "when the verb is passivized, the one doing the affirming is introduced by ὑπὸ, and the one being affirmed remains in the dative case."

104. Painter (379) observes: "Interestingly, while a plurality of people attest the truth of a single witness (Jesus) in the Gospel, a single person attests the truth of a plurality of witnesses in 3 John!"

105. He quotes Papias of Hierapolis who refers to Jesus as "the Truth himself." (Eusebius, *Hist. eccl.* 3.39.3)

106. Burge (246) agrees, though still allows the possibility of a reference to either the Spirit or Jesus. Bultmann (102) and Plummer (193) describe it as personification of the "Christian revelation." Barker (376) sees it as personification of the gospel. J. Lieu (*The Second and Third Epistles of John,* 119) asserts that "Demetrius' approval is upheld by the very spirit and norm of Johannine Christianity."

107. Lieu (279) sees John building this imagery from Greek law courts. "The language is that of the law court, where the case for or against someone is—so it is argued—beyond questioning: Aeschines declares that the evidence stacked against

καὶ ἡμεῖς δὲ μαρτυροῦμεν, καὶ οἶδας ὅτι ἡ μαρτυρία ἡμῶν ἀληθής ἐστιν, "and we are testifying and know that our testimony is true." Next John adds his own testimony to the company. Who is "we" here?[108] (1) Brown again sees it as the Johannine school (Brown, 724) and equivalent to "us" in vv 9–10. "That would explain why 'our testimonial' is reserved to the last and most solemn place, even after testimony from the truth; for the Johannine School preserves the tradition that interprets the truth." (2) Others see this as an authorial "we" and so refers to John (Burdick, 459; Stott, 233; Yarbrough, 384) (3) It refers to John and "those allied with him" (Haas, de Jonge, and Swellengrebel, 186; Williamson, 218) or John and his home church (Akin, 251; Marshall, 93; Westcott, 242). This follows the pattern of John 21:24 (Barker, 376) and seems the best option.

The present tense μαρτυροῦμεν is either an instantaneous present, indicating that in the writing of the letter he is testifying, or that the company included in "we" continues to testify concerning Demetrius. It seems best to see this as an instantaneous present and that John is saying that the letter serves as a witness to Demetrius' character and is included for Gaius' sake. Finally, John reminds Gaius that he knows he can trust John's word.

Biblical Theology Comments

Though this is not as theological an epistle as 1 and 2 John, it still addresses ecclesiology, though from a different perspective than one might have expected. It does not detail the organizational structure of a church or the roles its members play. Rather, it describes the kind of person that should lead in terms of character and conduct by contrasting two positive (Gaius, Demetrius) and one negative (Diotrephes) example. As Paul included hospitality as a requirement for elders (1 Tim 3:2; Titus 1:8) and church supported widows (1 Tim 5:9–10), so too does John. It is how one expresses God's love toward fellow-believers.

We also are exposed to two aspects of a theology of missions. Missionaries go out for the sake of Christ to represent him to a lost and

Timarchus, 'testified against ... by his own life and by the truth,' must override any biased support he might claim (Aeschines, *Against Timarchus* 90), whereas, closer to the time of 3 John, *1 Clement* declares that those who 'have testimony borne to them ... by everyone' should not be deposed from office (*1 Clem.* 44.3)."

108. Burdick (459) describes this pronoun as "somewhat" emphatic.

dying world. They are to be supported by the church, whose support makes them participants in their ministries. Missionaries must always offer the gospel free of charge, for the gospel's sake. That can only happen when the church enables them by its generosity.

Application and Devotional Implications

Hospitality is a New Testament virtue, not a Greco-Roman cultural expression that may be ignored today. We need more of it. The hospitality shown by Gaius can still be expressed today. I have known a couple, Bill and Geri, who lived out the hospitality described in this epistle. They always kept a guest room ready in their home for visiting preachers, missionaries, or conference speakers invited to their church. They did not only entertain people they knew, but got to meet a lot of interesting servants of the Lord. However, it did not stop there. Their reputation spread. Eventually they began to have complete strangers arrived at their doorstep unannounced. They would be missionaries or "regular" Christians traveling up or down California who had been told they could find lodging and a meal with them, and to tell them so-and-so had sent them. Bill and Geri never turned anyone away, no matter how inconvenient the timing of their arrival might be. They continued this till age caught up to them and the Lord took Bill home to heaven and Geri moved into a retirement center. The church around the world needs more people like Bill and Geri.

One thing we see affirmed by Diotrephes' actions is that Christians can act very unchristian. We may even wonder about their salvation. However, when conduct does not match profession, we are better off questioning their sanctification than their justification. Just as in 1 John 3, we have every right to tell them they are acting like they belong in the devil's family rather than God's.

Selected Bibliography

Bauer, W. *Orthodoxy and Heresy in Earliest Christianity*. Edited and translated by R. A. Kraft and G. Krodel. Philadelphia Seminar on Christian Origins. Philadelphia: Fortress, 1971.

Bonsack, B."Der Presbzteros des dritten Briefs und der geliebte Jünger des Evangeliums nach Johannes." *ZNW* 79 (1988): 45–62.

Brown, R. E. *The Community of the Beloved Disciple*. Mahwah, NJ: Paulist Press, 1979.

Bullinger, E. W. *Figures of Speech Used in the Bible.* New York: Eyre & Spottiswoode, 1898. Repr., Grand Rapids: Baker, 1968.

Hengel, M. *The Johannine Question*. London: SCM, 1989.

Hiebert, D. E. "Studies in 3 John—Part 2: An Exposition of 3 John 5–10." *BSac* 144 (1987): 194–207.

Käsemann, E. "Ketzer und Zeuge: Zum johanneischen Verfasserproblem." *ZTK* 48 (1951): 292–311.

Lieu, J. *The Second and Third Epistles of John: History and Background.* Edinburgh: T & T Clark, 1986.

Lightner, R. "False Doctrine and the Child of God." *The Journal of Ministry and Theology* 10 (2006): 44–53.

Lorencin, I. "Hospitality versus Patronage: An Investigation of Social Dynamics in the Third Epistle of John." *Andrews University Seminary Studies* 46 (2008): 165–74.

Metzger, B. M., and United Bible Societies. *A Textual Commentary on the Greek New Testament.* 2nd ed. New York: United Bible Societies, 1994.

Mitchell, M. M. "'Diotrephes Does Not Receive Us': The Lexicographical and Social Context of 3 John 9–10." *JBL* 117 (1998): 299–320.

Moulton, J. H., and N. Turner. *A Grammar of New Testament Greek. Vol. 3: Syntax*. Edinburgh: T & T Clark, 1963.

Polhill, J. B. "An Analysis of II and III John." *RevExp* 67 (1970): 461–71.

Price, R. M. "The Sitz-im-Leben of Third John: A New Reconstruction." *EvQ* 61 (1989): 109–19.

Roberts, A., J. Donaldson, and A. C. Coxe. *The Ante-Nicene Fathers Vol. I : Translations of the Writings of the Fathers Down to A.D. 325*. Oak Harbor, WA: Logos Research Systems, 1997.

Rogers, C. L., Jr., and C. L. Rogers III. *The New Linguistic and Exegetical Key to the Greek New Testament.* Grand Rapids: Zondervan, 1998.

von Harnack, A. "Über den dritten Johannesbrief." TU 15 (1897): 3–27.

Wallace, D. B. *Greek Grammar beyond the Basics*. Grand Rapids: Zondervan, 1996.

Closing Remarks (13–15)

Introduction

Like 2 John, this is a fairly standard first-century closing. Yet, it still expresses John's heart and personality. Rather than dismissing his comments as standard fare, we need to see also his heart. He loves people and prefers personal interaction over that of a written correspondence. Though he writes in Greek to a Greek, John is still very Jewish. So, rather than skip over this ending, let us see one last time the heart of the disciple whom Jesus loved.

Original Text

13 *Πολλὰ εἶχον γράψαι σοι, ἀλλ' οὐ θέλω διὰ μέλανος καὶ καλάμου σοι γράφειν·*
14 *ἐλπίζω δὲ εὐθέως σε ἰδεῖν, καὶ στόμα πρὸς στόμα λαλήσομεν.* **15** *Εἰρήνη σοι.*
ἀσπάζονταί σε οἱ φίλοι. ἀσπάζου τοὺς φίλους κατ' ὄνομα.

Translation

13 I have many things to write to you but do not wish to write you through
ink and pen; **14** but I hope to see you quickly, and we will speak face-to-
face. **15** Peace to you. The friends greet you. Greet the friends by name.

Commentary

John closes this letter in much the same manner as his second epistle. Though he has much he could write, such is not the medium of communication he prefers. With regard to the similarities and differences between this ending and that of 2 John, Painter (380) notes well that the closeness of wording indicates this "must have been the way the Elder was accustomed to end his letters" and that "slight variation indicates common authorship."

13 Πολλὰ εἶχον γράψαι σοι ἀλλ' οὐ θέλω διὰ μέλανος καὶ καλάμου σοι γράφειν·, "I have many things to write to you but do not wish to write you through ink and pen;" Once more, the brevity of this letter indicates his intention to speak personally with Gaius sometime in the near future.[1] Though the wording of this closing is very similar to 2 John, one of the difference is his use of pen (reed) in place of paper (parchment). Brown (724) notes well, "The differences reflect a letter writer who has a general pattern but who shifts details unconsciously and without significance within that pattern." This "suggests" that 2 John and 3 John were written about the same time (Harris, 267).

John affirms his intention to write more.[2] Also, like the second epistle, he prefers to communicate personally and so plans to do so. That he is including this along with the promise to confront Diotrephes may indicate that Gaius' church is either in the same town or a nearby town with Diotrephes' church, and that John plans to visit both on the same trip (Harris, 267).

14 John concludes his epistle expressing his desire to come see Gaius and have a personal visit. He also conveys greetings from "friends" whom he does not identify by name.

ἐλπίζω δὲ εὐθέως σε ἰδεῖν, "but I hope to see you quickly." John expresses his desire to see Gaius. The implication of ἐλπίζω is that he fully intends to see him and so does not imply uncertainty (Lenski, 593).[3] Though ἐλπίζω carries the sense of a desire more than an intention, his addition of εὐθέως indicates that John sees this as more a matter of timing than of possibility. John's use of εὐθέως may indicate how urgent he felt it was to confront

1. Bultmann (103) responds that it "sounds formulaic and is reminiscent of Jn 20:30."
2. Burdick (459) thinks the aor. "I had" may look at a previous intention by John to write. However, it may be better seen as a reference to this letter with John in essence apologizing for its brevity before promising to say more in person.
3. Burdick (460) observes "there is no essential difference between γενέσθαι 'to come' (2 John), and ἰδεῖν, 'to see' (3 John)." This serves as another evidence of John's authorship rather than a copyist's attempt at imitation.

Diotrephes quickly (Burdick, 460).[4] Further, his addition of εὐθέως when compared to his comments in 2 John indicates he may be assuring Gaius that he will not have to wait long before John intervenes in this situation (Akin, 251).

Lenski (593) sees this indicating a plan of action in which the missionaries will arrive first, with this letter of recommendation. They will announce that John is coming, but not when. Then the next day or two he will arrive. "Thus John will suddenly appear on the scene, will have the congregation called together for a meeting, and will settle accounts with Diotrephes. This boss is not to have time to stir up and to marshal his forces."

καὶ στόμα πρὸς στόμα λαλήσομεν, "and we will speak face-to-face." With the idiomatic "mouth to mouth" John affirms his intention of a personal visit with Gaius.[5] This is equivalent to Paul's πρόσωπον πρὸς πρόσωπον ("face to face") in 1 Cor 13:12.[6] Where John used the infinitive λαλῆσαι in 2 John, here he chooses the future λαλήσομεν to communicate the same idea (Burdick, 460). Interestingly, John does not repeat "that our joy may be made complete" from 2 John. Smith (134) sees this as another evidence that 3 John was not the product of an imitator, and so this argues for common authorship of 2 and 3 John.

15 εἰρήνη σοι, "Peace to you." He closes with a blessing of peace.[7] Whereas he included this blessing at the beginning of his second epistle (2 John 3), John saves it for the end with Gaius, likely because he senses he needs such a blessing. This is a variation from 2 John and Hellenistic letters (Painter, 380). This varies from the standard greeting, ἔρρωσο ("be strong"), and may be another Johannine Semitism (Lieu, 283; Marshall, 94).[8] It "reflects the Jewish custom of using '*Shalom*' both as introductory greeting and farewell" (Brown, 725–26; Burdick, 460; Marshall, 94). It may be influenced by Jesus' greeting in John 20:19 and 26 which Brown (725–26) sees as the fulfillment

4. Lenski (592) understands John to mean "immediately" as opposed to "shortly."
5. This same Hebrew idiom can be found in Num 12:8 and Jer 39:4.
6. Kruse (234) notes that "face to face rather than by letter is typical of the friendly letter tradition of the first-century Mediterranean world."
7. Culy (168) says σοι may be dative of advantage ("peace is wished for you") or dative indirect object "("[May] peace [be given] to you")." Either makes sense and would be appropriate.
8. BDAG, 908.

of his promise of peace in John 14:27. It certainly follows the pattern of New Testament writers and is part of the Christian conceptual world.[9]

ἀσπάζονταί σε οἱ φίλοι, "The friends greet you." These unnamed friends were known to Gaius, thus the article. Just as John does not identify himself by name, so he leaves these individuals unnamed as well. This is probably not from any fear that Diotrephes will intercept the letter and expel them as well from the church. Rather, it fits the pattern of brevity with John as well as indicating that Gaius probably knew which of his personal friends were in Ephesus at that time.

This is the only place in the New Testament where fellow Christians are called "friends." Φίλοι is equivalent to "the children of your elect sister" in 2 John and may indicate personal friends, or be a reference to fellow believers. This could be a term used as equivalent to "brothers" that arose from Jesus' teaching in John 15:13–15 (Akin, 252; Burdick, 460; Harris, 268; Perkins, 100).[10] They could be either members of his household or his local church who sided with John (Marshall, 94–95). Painter (380) sees this use of "friends" to be more secular while "brothers" would have had a more Christian connotation. It was also more characteristic of Hellenistic letters. Brook (195) describes it as a standard Greek greeting and that has no special significance. Culy's (168) suggestion seems best. Φίλοι describes close friends and goes "beyond simple brotherhood in Christ." They are not just fellow Christians who love each other because they are fellow Christians. They are fellow Christians who desire to be together and enjoy each other's company as well.

ἀσπάζου τοὺς φίλους κατ' ὄνομα, "Greet the friends by name." There are those in Gaius' church viewed as friends by John. He conveys his greetings through Gaius to them as well. Again, they remain unnamed, but known to Gaius. The preposition *κατά* may have the distributive sense of "name by

9. Examples include: John 20:19, 21, 26; Rom 15:23; 16:20; 2 Cor 13:11; Gal 6:16; Eph 6:23; 1 Thess 5:23; 2 Thess 3:16; Heb 13:20; and 1 Pet 5:14.

10. Brown (726) argues for this to be translated as "beloved" because as *ἀγαπάω* and *φιλέω* are "interchangeable" in John's literature, so too should be *ἀγαπήτος* and *φίλος*. However, John has not used *φίλος* interchangeably with *γαπήτος* in this or the other epistles and so the change should be seen as intentional and "friends" is intended, and not "beloveds."

name" (Culy, 168) which means John wants him to greet each one of them individually (Bultmann, 103; Smalley, 364; Strecker, 268, n. 7).[11]

Selected Bibliography

Fanning, B. M. *Verbal Aspect in New Testament Greek*. Oxford: Clarendon, 1990.

11. B. M. Fanning (*Verbal Aspect in New Testament Greek*, 356) describes this as an example of a specific command using a generic title for those to be greeted.

Excursuses

Excursus: Eternal Life in Johannine Literature

Eternal life is a prominent theme in all three of John's major works and especially in his Gospel. Even so, with all the attention he gives the subject, it is possibly one of the least understood themes he develops. This has resulted because what John says is most often interpreted through the grid of a justification-oriented theological system. Thus, eternal life is infused with justification-salvation meaning to the detriment of its place in the sanctification experience of the believer. Yet, in both his First Epistle and Gospel, it is very often described in terms of its impact on the daily life of the believer, and so should at times be interpreted in light of its place in sanctification.[1]

Justification-Salvation View

The tendency of those who approach the Gospel of John from the perspective that its primary purpose is evangelistic, what may be called the justification-salvation view, is to see it primarily functioning in its quantitative aspect, as something possessed rather than experienced, seeing it as

1. "Eternal life" has both quantitative and qualitative aspects to its meaning, which are recognized by all (Cook, *The Theology of John*, 93–95; Dodd, *New Testament Studies*, 168; Law, 296; *Wycliffe Bible Encyclopedia,* s.v. "Eternal life," 1:552). Ζωὴ αἰώνος occurs forty-three times in the New Testament, with twenty-three of those in either John's Gospel or epistles. Additionally, "life" (ζωὴV) is used ninety-two times without "eternal" (αἰώνιος), including forty-four occurrences in Johannine literature. The quantitative aspect focuses on its unending character and possession. The qualitative aspect involves personal experience and expression in daily life. This kind of life is entered into at regeneration and is experienced in the present (Bruns, *The Art and Thought of John*, 58; Cook, *The Theology of John,* 93; Westcott, 215; Stevens, *The Theology of the New Testament*, 231–32). Though either aspect of its meaning may be emphasized at any given time, both senses are often contained in any use. This makes it difficult at times to distinguish the two senses. This is true with John as well as throughout the New Testament.

synonymous with salvation (Vanderlip, 35–36; Smalley, 10).[2] For example, Robert Law (62) says that eternal life stresses "cause, not effect; not phenomenon, but essence; not conscious experience, but that which underlies and produces experience." He describes it as "the medium of our subconscious," "the animating principle" that produces "fruits and evidences" (Law, 187). It is something received, which has an effect on a person's life, not a description of that person's experience of life (Law, 55–56, 201–203). Still, proponents of this view also say it describes the believer's present experience of life as well (Law, 188–89; Vanderlip, 37).[3]

Sanctification-Salvation View

Eternal life need not be a source of action, but may be an expression of relationship. Robert Cook reflects the sanctification-salvation view well when he recognizes the qualitative "content" of eternal life to be described in John 17:3.[4] Though Zane Hodges (114–15) sees eternal life as something possessed, he also correctly sees John expressing the contingent nature of a person's experience. The believer's experience of eternal life depends on obedience that leads to the experience of fellowship with the divine embodiment of eternal life, Jesus. The believer properly in fellowship (when sin is not producing a barrier) experiences the quality of life characterized by Jesus' unbroken relationship with the Father as he walked in obedience to him moment by moment. John's use of eternal life reflects more than the mere possession of future life or the presence of a motivating factor within the believer. It reflects a quality of life experienced by the obedient Christian in this life. A child of God can lose his or her experience of eternal life without forfeiting his or her possession of it.

Johannine Use

Eternal life is not simply another justification-salvation term in John's literature.[5] Nor is it a single-faceted theme with him. For example, his devel-

2. Lee, *The Religious Thought of St. John,* 191.
3. Dodd, "Eternal Life," 34.
4. Cook, *The Theology of John*, 91, 94.
5. Though eternal life is a sanctification term with John, it refers to more than just the present experience of divine life. The danger faced by any view that limits its meaning to just a sanctification sense is the temptation to define its meaning based on verses such as John 17:3 and 17 rather than its use throughout the Gospel. John

opment of the theme begins in the prologue of his Gospel and climaxes in Jesus' declarations that he is "the life" (John 14:6) and that life is "knowing God" relationally (John 17:3). Similarly it begins in the prologue of his epistle with the declaration that he is eternal life incarnate that was seen, heard, and handled (1:1–3). In his Gospel John traces its meaning through Jesus' ministry and description of it as something experienced in this life. Jesus' descriptions say more than how someone is to obtain it. He describes it as more than a possession. It is an experience involving present life abundance (John 7:37–39; 10:10), as well as future (John 6:51).

The water of life offered to the woman at the well (John 4:13–14), clearly not a believer before meeting Jesus, and offered to the nation on the last day of the Feast of Tabernacles (John 7:37–38) was intended to be understood as an offer of life from Jesus. However, what he offered was something to be enjoyed in this life. John makes that reality applicable to his regenerate readers by defining it as the indwelling Holy Spirit verse 39.

In his Bread of Life discourse, Jesus offers eternal life through faith in him (John 6:26–58). This offer focuses on their need for justification by faith in him. Yet, in the midst of this discussion he draws their attention to the present enjoyment of the life he is offering them (John 6:35). He points them to its immediate effect, an abundant supply for their spiritual hunger and thirst in this life that will be realized in its fullness in the life to come.

When Jesus calls himself the light of life in John 8:12, he is again pointing his listeners to a present experience and not a future hope. His promise is not limited to a possession. He is not saying they will simply become sharers in eternal life or possessors of eternal life. He is saying that they will experience life as they "walk" through life.

Though one may argue that the first eight chapters of John use the phrase more in terms of receiving salvation, in John 10:10 Jesus clearly sees it as something to be experienced by his listeners *before* they enter into eternity. The abundant life Jesus offers (John 10:7–10) involves the security of his protection in *this* life. Entrance in and out of the sheepfold describes a present benefit of his watchcare in this life, not a description of the believer's hope of a future safe haven in heaven. His statement "I am come

---

17:3 and 17 do not determine the Johannine sense of eternal life any more than do John 3, 4, 6, or 8. Each passage and use contributes to its broad meaning with the sense resident within its immediate context.

that they may have life, and that they may have it more abundantly" (John 10:10) looks at the in-this-life experience of his listeners.

Though Jesus' words in John 12:25 focused on a promise of future life for his followers who would be martyred, it serves in the Gospel as a call for present living, applicable to believers facing persecution. Then Jesus' words "I am the way, the truth, and the life. No one comes to the Father except through Me" (John 14:6) are spoken to regenerate men. All believe in him and are identified a few minutes later as belonging to him (John 17:6–19). Yet it is they who are asking him to show them the way to the Father (John 14:1–10). Additionally, in his prayer to his Father, Jesus defines eternal life relationally rather than as a possession.[6] His use of the term in John 17:3 shows that he views it as more than something one possesses.

Though the focus may not be on the future, to be experienced in heaven, aspect of eternal life in the Gospel, neither Jesus nor John ignores it. It is addressed in places such as John 6:40 and 10:27–30. However, repeatedly Jesus' emphasis is on how his listener can experience God's life in *this* life, not just the life to come. Thus, in light of the Gospel's inclusion of the present experience of eternal life in its description by Jesus, the meaning of "life" in John 20:31 should reflect more than "salvation" in the sense of justification. John is speaking of life in its entirety. It is as much sanctification truth as justification truth.

When we move to his description of Jesus in his epistle, we learn that for John, eternal life is a Person, not a possession. Yes, it is a quality of life as well as a quantity. This is evident in both John's quotations of Jesus in his Gospel and his description of his own experience of eternal life in the prologue of this epistle.

However, in the Gospel, John recorded how Jesus defined eternal life in terms of himself. When he went to raise Lazarus, he responded to Martha's grief with the promise that her brother would not remain dead. She misunderstood him and responded with "correct" theology. Her brother would certainly rise again, just in "the regeneration." In Jewish eschatology a day would come in which all the righteous would be raised in order to enter Messiah's kingdom. She took Jesus' promise as a word of comfort rather than a promise for action. Jesus corrected her misconception, but not by

6. For a full discussion of the meaning of eternal life in this context, see my discussion of this in *The Disciplemaker*, 254–65.

stating plainly what he was about to do. This was unlike the clarification he provided the disciples when they misunderstood what he meant by "Our friend Lazarus sleeps, but I go that I may wake him up" (John 11:11). He moved to the truth about himself that she was to believe. Instead of saying, "I am going to raise Lazarus from the dead today," he told her, "I am the resurrection and the life" (John 11:25). Resurrection was not an event, not something about to happen, but a person, the one who was going to make it happen. In the same way, eternal life is not a state of being, but a person, Jesus.

In the prologue and epistle proper John has the choice of three terms that can be translated as "life": ζωή, ψυχὴ, and βίος. Ζωή, John's choice here focuses attention more on the "activity" aspect of life, though "vitality" expresses the Greek cultural concept as well, where ψυχὴ (used in 3:16 and 3 John 2) focuses more on the "principle of life" as a natural force that includes desires and emotions, and βίος on the essentials of life such as possessions and occupations.[7] Haas, de Jonge, and Swellengrebel (13) describe it well: "In the Johannine writings *zōē* is often used in a pregnant sense, namely, real life, life seen as something which man does not possess by nature, but which God gives to those who believe in Christ. For John it is not an abstraction but a reality, as real as Christ himself, with whom it is equated. ... A fuller expression of the same concept is 'eternal life.'"

In the upper room, while discussing his departure from this earth with the disciples, Jesus was asked the way to the Father. His answer, once again, did not point to a path or an event, but a person, himself. He responded, "I am the way, the truth, and the life" (John 14:6). In both instances Jesus did not describe himself as the giver of life, but as that life itself.

In the prologue of John's first epistle, the key terms "we heard, ... have seen with our eyes, ... have looked upon, ... our hands have handled ..." all describe John's personal experience of the person of Jesus. He, along with the other apostles, had personally witnessed Jesus healing the sick, raising the dead, and showing compassion to the poor. Following these experiences and hearing Jesus' response to Martha, John recognized that eternal life is more than a possession or experience, but is a person—Jesus. Still, the

---

7. BDAG, 177, 430, 1099; R. Bultmann, "ζάω ... βίος," *TDNT* 2:835–37 ; R. Bultmann, "ζάω, ζωή," *TDNT* 2:832, 861–64; A. Dihle, "ψυχή," *TDNT* 637–52.

experience of that life, dependent on a relationship with eternal life incarnate, is expressed in terms of its time as well as its enjoyment.

As said earlier in this excursus, eternal life has two aspects. It is a *quality* of life as well as a *quantity* of life. Often Christians tend to think of eternal life only in terms of its quantity—unending life. Also, references to it as unending life do occur in John's writings. This quantitative aspect of eternal life is evident in places where it is described as unaffected by physical death (John 5:28, 29; 6:27, 39, 40, 51–58; 11:24–26; and 12:25).[8] Yet for John, its quality is far more significant than its quantity. In his Gospel, it is the quality of life that is John's and Jesus' focus. It is evident in those passages that focus on eternal life as a "present possession" for believers, such as John 3:36 and 5:24–26.[9] It is expressed in such quotations of Jesus as John 10:10, "I have come that they may have life, and that they may have *it* more abundantly." In John 17:3 Jesus defines eternal life relationally as knowing God. His choice of γινώσκω indicates a personal relational kind of knowledge, rather than intuitional or learned, as would be implied by οἶδα. For John, eternal life is a quality of life—a kind of life that is experienced—not merely unending future existence. This is very evident in his epistle. It is the life his readers are to experience in the present, not gain for the future. Every human ever born will exist forever. Some will exist in eternal death, denied fellowship with God throughout eternity. For believers, eternal life expressed as eternal fellowship with God begins in the present and stretches into eternity. Only those living in God's presence in the present experience his life, eternal life. Likewise, in eternity only those living in the new Jerusalem on the new earth (Rev 21:1–8) will experience his life, eternal life. However, as seen in the epistle, whereas possessing that life is the fulfilled promise for everyone who believes (John 3:16–18; 5:24; 6:40, 47), experiencing that life is contingent and can be missed in this life.[10]

Haas, de Jonge, and Swellengrebel (15) describe John's use of "eternal" to describe this life as well. "The qualification *eternal* (Greek *aiōnios*) is

8. Cook (*The Theology of John,* 93) sees John 6:52–54 reflecting the qualitative aspect of the term rather than the quantitative.

9. Other verses that use ζωή in its qualitative sense are John 3:15–16; 6:47, 68; 10:28; and 17:2–3.

10. It will not be missed in the life to come. Those hindrances will be removed with the removal of the sin nature and exchange of the mortal body for the immortal (1 Cor 15:50–54).

added in order to make explicit that this life is something of a different order, namely, the order of the coming eon or age (Greek *aiōn*), and accordingly has a quality which is superior to anything in the present age. This life of the coming age, revealed in the person of Jesus Christ, is attainable in the present age for all who believe in him." Vanderlip (33) notes well that John's attribution of eternal to life "speaks of a new quality of existence so radically different from what a man experiences without it that its opposite can be called 'death' (5:24)." Wendt describes it as "a higher Divine form of life already existing in believers, as the foundation of the life which eternally endures beyond the grave."[11]

Thus eternal life is a relational concept with John, both in his Gospel and in this epistle. This aspect is what guides his discussion as will be seen in the commentary of the text.

Selected Bibliography

Bruns, J. E. *The Art and Thought of John.* New York: Herder and Herder, 1969.

Cook, W. R. *The Theology of John.* Chicago: Moody, 1979.

Derickson, G. W., and E. D. Radmacher. *The Disciplemaker: What Matters Most to Jesus.* Salem, OR: Charis, 2001.

Dodd, C. H. "Eternal Life." *Christianity and Crisis* 10 (1950): 33–34.

Dodd, C. H. *New Testament Studies.* Manchester: Manchester University Press, 1953.

Hodges, Z. C. *The Epistles of John: Walking in the Light of God's Love.* Irving, TX: Grace Evangelical Society, 1999.

Law, R. *The Tests of Life.* Edinburgh: T & T Clark, 1909. Repr., Grand Rapids: Baker, 1969.

Lee, E. K. *The Religious Thought of St. John.* London: SPCK., 1950.

Smalley, S. *1, 2, 3 John.* WBC 51. Waco, TX: Word, 1984.

Stevens, G. B. *The Theology of the New Testament.* New York: Scribner, 1947, c1927.

Tenney, M. C. "Eternal life." *Wycliffe Bible Encyclopedia,* 1:552. Chicago: Moody, 1975.

Vanderlip, D. G. *Christianity according to John.* Philadelphia: Westminster, 1975.

Wendt, H. H. *The Teaching of Jesus.* Vol. 1. Translated by John Wilson. Edinburgh: T & T Clark, 1892.

Westcott, B. F. *The Epistles of St. John.* Grand Rapids: Eerdmans, 1966.

11. Wendt, *The Teaching of Jesus,* 1:249.

Excursus: Chiasms in Johannine Literature

Ronald Mann has noted well that "all too often chiastic structures are passed off in the scholarly literature as mere literary niceties, a structural tour de force which serves only aesthetic ends. Too little consideration has been given to the possible exegetical significance of such structures in the interpretation of biblical passages."[12] Lund notes that Greek literature is not characterized by elaborate chiasms, but scholarship has established the presence of smaller chiastic units.[13] Thus, the presence of smaller chiasms within the New Testament literature should come as no surprise, especially at the verse or paragraph level. However, in light of the presence of larger chiastic units in the Old Testament, one should expect to find more elaborate chiasms in the New Testament.

The use of elaborate structural devices is now recognized among Old and New Testament authors.[14] Traina identifies five types of structural units, which he labels "materials." These are utilized by an author to "construct" his message. The author may utilize biography (using persons), chronological material (time element plays a prominent role), geography (places), history (events), or logical arrangement (ideas) to develop his "structural units."[15] While chiasms may employ any one or more of these elements within their structure, they will invariably reflect a logical arrangement of ideas that focus the reader on the author's idea, whether it is explicitly stated or only implied.

The chiasm may be composed of as few as four lines, or encompass a complete literary work, such as the Pentateuch or Matthew. Though one important characteristic of chiasms is their repetition of similar material in reverse order, their arrangement of material accomplishes more than that.[16] The ordering of material points the reader, or ancient listener, to its center section as the focal point of the unit, whether it is large or small.[17]

---

12. R. E. Mann, "The Value of Chiasm for New Testament Interpretation," 147.
13. N. W. Lund, *Chiasmus in the New Testament,* 33, 35.
14. D. A. Dorsey, *The Literary Structure of the Old Testament*, 36.
15. R. A. Traina, *Methodical Bible Study*, 55–56.
16. S. McKnight, "Literary Criticism of the Synoptic Gospels," 68.
17. D. A. Dorsey, *The Literary Structure of the Old Testament*, 44. In his seminal work, N. W. Lund (*Chiasmus in the New Testament*, 40–41) detailed his seven "laws" of chiastic structures. "(1) *The centre is always the turning point.* ... (2) At the

The remaining pairs of units (normally sharing common terms, events, people, or other clues to their unity) help contribute to the author's message. However, normally, it is the central unit or units that communicate the author's intended message. Ronald Mann explains the role its parts play in the development of the author's message. "Two characteristics of chiasm help interpreters understand the meaning of biblical passages: (1) the presence of either a single central or of two complementary central elements in the structure, which generally highlight the major thrust of the passage encompassed by the chiasm; and (2) the presence of complementary pairs of elements, in which each member of a pair can elucidate the other member and together form a composite meaning."[18] The complementary pairs may be related through either synonymous or antithetical parallelism. Further, their parallel and opposing placement in the structure serves to "strengthen the comparison or the contrast."[19]

As stated earlier, chiasms focus the reader's attention on the central point of the chiasm, and thereby the author's message. As Mann notes well, "The point may be obvious even without recognizing the chiasm; but the chiasm serves to highlight and heighten the effect of this emphasis in the minds of the readers, even on an unconscious level."[20] It is the author's choice of a chiastic structure that serves to communicate his message "through the emphases and movements inherent in the structure."[21] The material outside the center is not insignificant, nor becomes less significant as it moves out from the center. Rather, its relationship to the center is what

---

centre there is often a change in the trend of thought, and an antithetic idea is introduced. After this the original trend is resumed and continued until the system is concluded ...*the law of the shift at the centre*. (3) Identical ideas are often distributed in such a fashion that *they occur in the extremes and at the centre* of their respective system, and nowhere else in the system. (4) There are also many instances of ideas, occurring at the centre of one system and recurring in the extremes of a corresponding system, the second system evidently having been constructed to match the first ...*the law of the shift from centre to the extremes*. (5) There is a definite tendency of certain terms to gravitate toward certain positions within a given system. ... (6) Larger units are frequently introduced and concluded by *frame-passages*. (7) There is frequently a mixture of chiastic and alternating lines within one and the same unit."

18. R. E. Mann, "The Value of Chiasm for New Testament Interpretation," 147–48.
19. Ibid., 148.
20. R. E. Mann, "The Value of Chiasm for New Testament Interpretation," 150.
21. R. E. Mann, "The Value of Chiasm for New Testament Interpretation," 153.

gives it significance. Ultimately, though, it is the central point that must govern the meaning and significance of its surrounding units, not vice versa.

A chiastic structure can be seen in the presentation of the seven churches in Revelation: the first and last are on the verge of losing their Christian identity (Rev 2:5; 3:16), though Christ still commends the first (Ephesus) for a few things. The second and sixth churches have no weaknesses, and are encouraged to continue on in their faithful witness. The third, fourth, and fifth churches, in the middle of the chiasm, are in a mixed condition. They are commended for some good things but corrected for serious problems, which if allowed to continue will rip the churches apart. In one way or another, all the problems of the churches have to do with the challenge of witnessing in the midst of temptations to compromise with idolatry.[22]

Selected Bibliography

Beale, G. K. *The Book of Revelation: A Commentary on the Greek Text.* NIGTC. Grand Rapids: Eerdmans, 1999.

Dorsey, D. A. *The Literary Structure of the Old Testament: A Commentary on Genesis-Malachi.* Grand Rapids: Baker, 1999.

Lund, N. W. *Chiasmus in the New Testament: A Study in the Form and Function of Chiastic Structures.* Peabody, MA: Hendrickson, 1942, 1970.

Mann, R. E. "The Value of Chiasm for New Testament Interpretation." *BSac* 141 (2002): 144–54.

McKnight, S. "Literary Criticism of the Synoptic Gospels." *TJ* 8 (1987): 56–79.

Traina, R. A. *Methodical Bible Study.* Grand Rapids: Francis Asbury, 1952, 1980.

Excursus: Johannine Concept of "Belief"

The concept of belief, like other themes in John's literature, has a double thrust to it. Within the tapestry of this theme are woven two aspects to faith: its place in spiritual birth and its importance in the life of the believer. It is a mistake to limit John's development of the concept to "justifying faith" alone. This misses the aspect of John's concept that involves the growth and development of the faith of Jesus' already regenerate disciples as they come to understand more fully just who it is they are believing in. This is indicated in part by the interplay of the theme of light and darkness as it relates to the theme of believing, especially in the Gospel. Jesus

22. G. K. Beale, *The Book of Revelation,* 32–33.

is the Light of the world that gives life (John 1:4–5). The unbeliever loves "darkness rather than light" and so does not come to the light while the believer, "he who does the truth," moves toward the light "that his deeds may be clearly seen, that they have been done in God" (John 3:18–21). The disciples fit this group. They come to the Light, Jesus, in the first chapters of the Gospel and remain in the light as they follow him. However, their faith still must grow as they come to understand him more fully. Carson and others are correct when they see the disciples' faith develop and grow in the Gospel. They are simply wrong to relate that faith to justifying faith. The disciples were already justified when they first came to the light. They were Old Testament saints, after all! The faith that grows is not justifying faith, but sanctifying faith.

The Johannine formula for justifying faith is defined in the prologue (John 1:12) where the right to become children of God is given "to those who believe in his name."[23] It is restated in John 3:14–16, where it is the *look of faith* on the lifted up (crucified) Jesus that gives eternal life.[24] This is the formula used by Jesus when addressing the man born blind (John 9:35) and used by that same man in confessing his faith (John 9:36). However, nothing in the Gospel or John's First Epistle requires it be a mature faith to

---

23. In the Gospel of John, justifying and sanctifying faith in Jesus is described through the use of πιστεύω εἰς or πιστεύω ἐν. These two constructions are interchangeable, as evidenced by their synonymous use in John 3:15–16. This same construction is used in 1 John 5:13 wherein the immediate context of 5:11–12 indicates that justifying faith is in view ("to have the Son" means to be justified). Thus John's use of πιστεύω εἰς and πιστεύω ἐν to describe an individual consistently implies that person's status as a true "believer," and so a justified saint.

24. Jesus' choice of the serpent lifted in the wilderness is instructive with regard to justifying faith. In the wilderness a person only had to look. Their faith could be weak. They might even experience doubts as they looked. But if they looked, they were healed regardless of how strong or weak their faith was. The promise was not "if you look and have sufficient faith." It was "when you look." In Num 21:8–9, the text says: "Then the LORD said to Moses, 'Make a fiery *serpent,* and set it on a pole; and it shall be that everyone who is bitten, when he looks at it, shall live.' So Moses made a bronze serpent, and put it on a pole; and so it was, if a serpent had bitten anyone, when he looked at the bronze serpent, he lived." Thus Jesus' allusion to this necessarily means anyone looking to him as their crucified Savior will be saved. It requires the "look of faith" and not any works or lifestyle of faith that proves the look was long enough or consistent enough. Justifying faith brings instantaneous and full justification, not progressive, conditional, or partial justification.

be justifying. Why? It is always the *object* of faith that makes it effective, not its volume or maturity.

Sanctifying faith involves a more complete understanding of the person of Jesus than that required for regeneration. Belief in Jesus is something believers *must do* in order to have fellowship with God and *experience* the eternal life they possess. Believing in Jesus' name is something Christians *must do* in order to commune with him, to abide in him. It is something believers *must do* to bear fruit. We cannot experience eternal life in this life apart from the first step of believing in Jesus, even as a believer. Failure to exercise it can cause a genuine believer to fail to abide, to fail to have communion with Christ, and therefore to fail to be fruitful. That is the sense of Jesus' instructions to his regenerate, believing, eleven apostles the night before his betrayal in John 15:4–5. There he commanded them to abide in him in order to bear fruit.[25] Would he command them to do something that is automatic for all genuine believers? No. Would he command them and us to do something that is a fruit of regeneration? No. That which is automatic need not be commanded, only that which is legitimately optional. He commanded them to do something that they as regenerate believers were capable of choosing not to do.

Can someone have genuine faith in Jesus in an immature manner? John tells us that "many believed in his name" (πολλοὶ ἐπίστευσαν εἰς τὸ ὄνομα αὐτοῦ) when they saw Jesus' signs (John 2:23). However, Jesus does not entrust himself to them (Ἰησοῦς οὐκ ἐπίστευεν αὐτὸν αὐτοῖς, John 2:24). John uses the same formula found in the prologue (τοῖς πιστεύουσιν εἰς τὸ ὄνομα αὐτοῦ, John 1:12). In such close literary proximity one would expect the author to intend a connection. Also, based on the parallel construction, it is legitimate to see the crowd as regenerate, children of God. However, for those who read Jesus' action as indicating the people were not true believers, it is given a different meaning. For example, many theologians describe the multitude's response as "spurious faith" rather than saving faith since Jesus did not entrust himself to them.[26] The point of John is that Jesus knew

25. A full discussion of this is contained in *The Disciplemaker*, 170–73.

26. D. A. Carson, *The Gospel According to John*, 184; W. Hendriksen, *The Gospel of John*, 128. A.T Robertson, *Word Pictures in the New Testament*, Jn 2:24. Terms used to describe this faith as less than saving include "spurious" (D. A. Carson, "Reflections on Christian Assurance," 17; J. F. MacArthur, Jr., "Faith According to the Apostle James," 16; and J. C. Macaulay, *Expository Commentary on John*,

they believed in him and knew the limits of their understanding and maturity, not that he questioned their salvation. Carson correctly notes that Nicodemus' place in the narrative is related to what John says at the end of chapter two. He sees him playing a role in the Johannine development of the concept of belief, describing Nicodemus as "not particularly open to the truth ... yet eventually he comes around to side with Jesus (7:45–52) and ultimately to take his place at Calvary (19:38–42)."[27] He *does* play a part in the development of the narrative. However, he does not serve as an example of what Carson considers the spuriousness, and therefore incompleteness, of the faith of the crowd that was believing in him. Rather, Nicodemus, along with the woman at the well and the invalid by the pool all serve as examples of what John meant by "he knew what was in man." All three demonstrate this aspect of Jesus' omniscience, and therefore deity.

Reflecting the light/darkness motif, we are told that Nicodemus visits Jesus at night. He comes out of the darkness, is enlightened by Jesus, and then returns to the darkness. Therefore, using the light/darkness motif, we may conclude that he was not a believer at that time. Nicodemus seems to be an example of a silent believer later in the Gospel. So, when did he become regenerate? Carson implies that he was not truly regenerate before the cross when he publicly identified with Jesus. He describes the response of the guards in 7:45–46 as not "borne of genuine faith," something John clearly does not intend (thus he does not use the term). Concerning Nicodemus' response in 7:45–52, Carson says, "Even if Nicodemus is not a genuine disciple at this point (*cf.* notes on 3:1ff.), nevertheless he, 'Israel's

---

41), "superficial" (J. G. Mitchell, *An Everlasting Love,* 49; John 2:23, *New Geneva Study Bible*, R. C. Sproul gen. ed.; M. C. Tenney, "John" in *The Expositor's Bible Commentary,* 46), "false" (B. F. Westcott, *The Gospel According to John*, 44), "shallow" (G. C. Morgan, *The Gospel According to John*, 55), "partial" (D. N. Freedman, *The Anchor Bible Dictionary*, 4: 1106), "inadequate" (D. Guthrie, *New Bible Commentary: 21st Century Edition*, John 2:23–25; R.C. H. Lenski, *St. John's Gospel,* 223). John Calvin described it as "not a true and genuine faith," though not hypocritical, but not saving (J. Calvin, *John*, John 2:24), "not real" (E. A. Blum, "John" in *The Bible Knowledge Commentary: New Testament*, 280; J. G. Mitchell, *An Everlasting Love*, 49), lacking "a profound faith" (L. Morris, *The Gospel According to John*, 205). F. F. Bruce (*The Gospel of John*, 78) concludes that "there are two levels of believing in Jesus" after acknowledging that this is the same construction used in 1:12 to describe justifying faith.

27. Carson, *The Gospel According to John*, 186.

teacher' (3:10), had addressed Jesus as 'a teacher who has come from God' (3:2). Indeed, a little farther on John will report that 'many even among the leaders believed in him' (12:42)."[28] Carson describes the leaders who were believing in, but not confessing, Jesus, as seeming "to fit the pattern of inadequate, irresolute, even spurious faith that John repeatedly describes in this Gospel.... They knew nothing of the powerful new birth that could make them children of God and enable them to enter the messianic kingdom (3:3, 5; 1:12, 13; cf. 12:26). Perhaps after the resurrection they joined other Jewish leaders in becoming true Christians."[29] However, this misses the point of John in 12:42–43. There John again uses the justified faith formula, "believe in," to describe these rulers before calling them cowardly. He describes their faith *in contrast to the unbelief* of the crowd in 12:37 in fulfillment of Isaiah's prophecy (12:40) of Israel's blindness and hardness of heart. There he clearly says, "they could not believe" in contrast to the rulers who did believe in him but did not confess him. Only by ignoring the context can one say that these men only "sort-of" believed in Jesus and that was why they were not confessing him. John's point is precisely that *they did believe*! They believed in the exact same way that everyone who gets to be a child of God (1:12) does. However, does being a child of God make someone a mature Christian? Does it make someone trustworthy?

As John develops his theme of belief, he reveals the importance of both the content of belief along with the act of believing. It is an error to focus on the act of believing and miss this first element. The disciples believe in Jesus from the beginning of his ministry within the limits of their knowledge. However, as time goes by they see more and more of Jesus and come to understand him better and better. Yet, even in the upper room they do not understand him in a mature manner, evidenced by their immature behavior. Their faith does not reach maturity or fullness until they see him resurrected. Then they fully grasp his person, evidenced by Thomas' exclamation, "My Lord and my God!"

In the upper room, Jesus continues to develop their faith and commands them to believe in him (14:1). Does this mean that they had not yet believed in him? No. It means that they must continue to believe in him as he gives them new revelation. To this extent it is correct to say that the

28. Carson, *The Gospel According to John*, 331.
29. Carson, *The Gospel According to John*, 450–51.

Gospel describes the development and growth of the faith of the apostles as they moved from being Old Testament saints to New Testament saints. Yet we must observe also that all the promises of the upper room are contingent on faith *and* obedience, are issues of sanctification and not justification. However, we must also observe that the incomplete faith of the apostles did not keep them from being regenerate, again, as evidenced by Jesus' description of them as those kept by him "while" he "was with them in the world" (17:12). Yes, it is correct to see faith grow and develop in the Gospel. However, it is wrong to read into this a faith that cannot save.

Selected Bibliography

Anchor Bible Dictionary. Edited by David N. Freedman. Vol. 4. New York: Doubleday, 1996.

Blum, E. A. "John." In *The Bible Knowledge Commentary: New Testament*. Edited by J. F. Walvoord and R. B. Zuck. Wheaton, IL: Victor, 1983–1985.

Bruce, F. F. *The Gospel of John*. Grand Rapids: Eerdmans, 1983.

Calvin, J. *John*. The Crossway Classic Commentaries. Electronic ed. Wheaton, IL: Crossway, 1994.

Carson, D. A. "Reflections on Christian Assurance." *WTJ* 54 (Spring 1992): 1–29.

——— *The Gospel according to John*. Grand Rapids: Eerdmans, 1991.

Guthrie, D. *New Bible Commentary: 21st Century Edition*. D. A. Carson, ed. Rev. ed. of *The New Bible Commentary*. 3rd ed. / D. Guthrie, J. A. Motyer, eds. 1970. 4th ed., 1994 electronic ed. Downers Grove, IL: InterVarsity, 1994.

Hendriksen, W. *The Gospel of John*. NTC. Grand Rapids: Baker, 1953.

Lenski, R. C. H. *St. John's Gospel.* Minneapolis: Augsburg, 1943.

MacArthur, J. F., Jr. "Faith according to the Apostle James." *JETS* 33 (March 1990): 11–47.

Macaulay, J. C. *Expository Commentary on John.* Chicago: Moody, 1941.

Mitchell, J. G. *An Everlasting Love.* Portland, OR: Multnomah, 1982.

Morgan, G. Cl. *The Gospel according to John.* Westwood, NJ: Revell, n.d.

Morris, L. *The Gospel according to John.* Grand Rapids: Eerdmans, 1971.

New Geneva Study Bible. R. C. Sproul, gen. ed. Electronic ed. Nashville: Thomas Nelson, 1997.

Robertson, A. T. *Word Pictures in the New Testament*. Vol. 5 c1932, vol. 6 c1933 by Sunday School Board of the Southern Baptist Convention. Jn 2:24. Oak Harbor, WA: Logos Research Systems, 1997.

Tenney, M. C. "John." In *The Expositor's Bible Commentary,* vol. 9. Edited by F. E. Gaebelein. Grand Rapids: Zondervan, 1981.

Westcott, B. F. *The Gospel According to John.* Grand Rapids: Eerdmans, 1981 repr.

Excursus: Johannine Concept of Abiding

The concept of abiding is a prominent theme within John's literature. He communicates this idea through two words: μενω, accounting for the majority of instances of "abiding," and his frequent use of the phrase εἶναι ἐν, which is essentially synonymous.[30] The term μένω, generally translated "to abide" (ASV, ESV, ISV, NASB95, NKJV, NRSV, RSV) or "to remain" (HCSB, NAB, NCV, NIV84, NLT), has a broad range of meaning throughout the New Testament, both literal and figurative. As a transitive verb, it may mean to "wait for, await," or it can also be used with the sense of "to expect someone."[31] As an intransitive verb it means "to remain in a place, to tarry, to remain, to stay still" and can be used of either persons or things.[32] The word also may have the literal sense of living, dwelling, or lodging. Figuratively it can mean someone "does not leave the realm or sphere in which he finds himself" and can be translated as "remain," "continue," or "abide."[33] It can also mean "to stand against opposition, to hold out, to stand fast," and "to remain, to last, to remain in legal force."[34]

Non-Johannine Use of Μένω

Μένω occurs 112 times in the New Testament, with sixty-six of those occurrences in the non-Johannine literature.[35] It is used with the literal sense of waiting for someone in Acts 20:5 and 23. The literal sense of tarrying, or remaining in place occurs ten times in narrative literature (Matt 26:38; Mark 14:34; Luke 19:5; 24:29; Acts 18:3, 20; 20:15; 21:7, 8; 27:31, 41) and three times with Paul (1 Cor 15:6; Phil 1:25; 2 Tim 4:20).[36] Nine times (all

30. E. Malatesta, *Interiority and Covenant*, 24–26. He notes that μένειν ἐν includes an "enduring" sense not contained in εἶναι ἐν. Further, εἶναι ἐν is more often used to describe the mutual indwelling of God and the believer, as well as among members of the Godhead, than is μένειν ἐν.
31. BDAG, 631; F. Hauck, "μένω," *TDNT* 4:574–88.
32. BDAG, 630–31.
33. BDAG., 630–31.
34. F. Hauck, "μένω," *TDNT* 4:574–88. Hauck also says, "Religiously μένειν is a mark of God and of what is commensurate with Him."
35. F. Hauck, "μένω," *TDNT* 4:575, n. 3.
36. Paul refers to people still living among the readers (1 Cor 15:6), his own expectation of still living among his readers (Phil 1:25), and Erastus' staying in Corinth rather than following him (2 Tim 4:20).

in narrative literature) it means "to live" somewhere (Matt 10:11; Mark 6:10; Luke 1:56; 8:27; 9:4; 10:7; Acts 9:43; 16:15; and 28:16).

Though μένω reflects some figurative use in narrative literature, the figurative sense is principally found in the epistles. Paul uses it seven times to refer to people with the sense of remaining "in the realm or sphere in which one finds himself" (1 Cor 7:8, 11, 20, 24, 40; 1 Tim 2:15; 2 Tim 3:14).[37] Seventeen times the term carries the figurative sense of remaining in legal force, lasting, or enduring (Matt 11:23; Acts 5:4; Rom 9:11; 1 Cor 3:14; 13:13; 2 Cor 3:11, 14; 9:9; and 2 Tim 2:13). Its use in Hebrews reflects the sense of continuing, living eternally, or lasting forever, whether it refers to a person such as Melchizedek (Heb 7:3, 24), things such as heaven (Heb 13:14), or the believer's possessions in heaven (Heb 10:34).[38] Peter uses μένω to describe God's Word as eternal (1 Pet 1:23, 25).[39] It also describes "the immutability of God and the things of God" (Rom 9:1; 1 Pet 1:23, 25; 1 Cor 13:13; 2 Cor 3:11).[40] Of note is the absence in Paul's writings of the use of μένω to communicate his concept of a believer being "in Christ," and he does not use the word to describe walking in the Spirit.[41]

Johannine Use of Μένω

John uses the verb μένω with its full range of senses throughout his literature. He uses μένω thirty-four times in the Gospel of John, twenty in 1 John, and three more in 2 John and Rev.[42] (1) He uses μένω with its *literal* sense

---

37. BDAG, 631. Widows, the single, and married are to remain in whatever marital state they find themselves (1 Cor 7:8, 11, 20, 24, 40). Women are to "continue" in the faith (1 Tim 2:15) and Timothy is to "continue" in the things he has learned (2 Tim 3:14).

38. In Heb 13:1 it occurs as an imperative addressed to believers to maintain brotherly love in their midst.

39. In 1:25, μένει is a translation of יָקוּם in Isa 40:8.

40. F. Hauck, "μένω," *TDNT* 4:574–88.

41. This is a good example of the unique character of each author of Scripture expressing himself even as the Holy Spirit bears each of them along (2 Pet 1:21) in inspiration. For example, Paul's "in Christ" includes aspects of John's mutual abiding of God and believers (John 14:18, 20, 23; 1 John 2:24; 3:24). Further, when Paul says "Let the word of Christ dwell in you richly" (ὁ λόγος τοῦ Χριστοῦ ἐνοικείτω ἐν ὑμῖν πλουσίως) in Col 3:16, he uses a different word for "dwell" to communicate the same sense as John's use of μένω with respect to Jesus' words (John 15:7) and what his readers "heard from the beginning" (1 John 2:24) "abiding."

42. Μένω in Rev 17:10 reflects the literal sense of living or dwelling.

in his Gospel (narrative literature) to describe Jesus' remaining in places, whether for a few days or extended periods of ministry (John 1:39; 2:12; 4:40; 7:9; 10:40; 11:6, 54) and with reference to his body remaining on the cross (19:31).[43] He quotes John the Baptist when he uses *μένω* with this same literal sense to describe the Holy Spirit's "remaining" on Jesus (John 1:32–33), and in a slightly more conceptual sense, to refer to God's wrath "abiding" on men (John 3:36). (2) The word also describes living or dwelling *among* people (John 8:35; 12:34; 21:22–23; Rev 17:10). For example, like Paul (1 Cor 7:8, 11, 20, 24, 40), John uses *μένω* to express the idea of a person or thing continuing "in the state in which he or it is found" (John 12:24; 1 John 2:10; 3:14). (3) Related to the previous use is the idea of staying in legal force, lasting, or remaining (1 John 2:14, 24, 27; 3:9, 15, 17).[44]

When Jesus himself is the speaker and uses *μένω* in the Gospel of John, he primarily uses it with a wide range of *figurative* senses.[45] (1) He uses *μένω* to refer to God's Word abiding in men (John 5:38), his own words abiding in men (John 15:7), and men abiding in God's Word (John 8:31).[46] (2) Jesus uses it to describe both an enduring presence and reciprocal relationship with someone. Thus he refers to the Father "abiding" in him (John 14:10), the Spirit abiding in believers (John 14:17), and he abiding in his disciples and they in him (John 15:4–5). In the context of that abiding relationship, Jesus conditions answered prayer on both "abiding" in him and letting his words "abide" in them (John 15:7). (3) Jesus describes the gift of life he offers the multitude as food given by him that "endures" (*μένουσαν*) to eternal life (John 6:27).[47] He also informs the Pharisees' of their sin "remaining" because they refuse to admit their spiritual blindness (John 9:41). He uses

43. E. A. Abbott, *Johannine Grammar*, 334.

44. Paul's use of *μένω* in 1 Cor 13:13 reflects this sense with respect to faith, hope, and love. Peter (1 Pet 1:23) uses it to describe God's word both remaining and continuing in its effect eternally.

45. Once Jesus does use it with its literal sense of living with them (14:25).

46. BDAG, 631. Bauer's example is that of God's relationship with Jesus in John 14:10. Jesus uses this sense of *μένω* to describe the disciple's relationship to himself in such places as John 6:56; 8:31; and 15:4–7. He notes that a favorite phrase of John, who is quoting Jesus in all his examples, is the use of abiding in something "to denote an inward, enduring personal communion."

47. The permanency of the possession is expressed through the use of the *ἔχειν τι μένον ἐν ἑαυτῷ*, according to Bauer (BDAG, 631). He also notes Jesus' words in John 14:17, *ὅτι παρ' ὑμῖν μένει καὶ ἐν ὑμῖν ἔσται*, describe the Spirit of truth remaining with

μένω to describe the permanence of the believer's fruit as something that continues, or "remains" (John 15:16). (4) Jesus uses μένω to express the idea of a person or thing continuing "in the state in which he or it is found" (John 12:24, 46).[48] (5) They are also to follow Jesus' example of obedience in order to abide in his love like he abides in his Father's (15:10).[49]

John's use of the term in his First and Second Epistles *always* reflects one of its figurative senses.[50] For example, in 1 John 2:10 and 3:14 he uses it to express the concept of remaining in the realm or sphere in which one finds oneself (Dodd, 83–84; King, 38; Pentecost, 89; Roberts, 44, 48, 91; Westcott, 56). In 2 John 9 this same sense carries with it the idea of obeying or living according to that realm in which one finds oneself. It also refers to remaining in legal force, lasting, enduring, or continuing to live in 1 John 2:14, 24, 27; 3:9, 15, and 17 (Dodd, 61; Stott, 103, 117–18; Brown, 355–59; Smalley, 124; Pentecost, 66).[51] In 1 John 2:17 "remaining" refers to experiencing eternal life into eternity, not possessing it (Brown, 315, 327; Dodd, 43; Ryrie, 1470; Smalley, 88–89; Stott, 106).[52] It also means to remain in fel-

---

someone. Finally, the wrath of God is described as remaining on someone (μένει ἐπ' αὐτόν).

48. W. Bauer (BDAG, 631) identifies John 8:31; 12:24; and 15:9 as examples of this. John 8:31 does not seem to relate. In John 15:9, Jesus commands us to "abide" in His love. Only John 12:24 and 46 are clear examples of this use.

49. Of note is the absence of Jesus' use of εἶναι ἐν in the Upper Room Discourse, especially at those places it would be expected. It may be implied in John 14:11, as indicated in the NKJV, although μένω could be used as the verb and make sense as well. The same is true for John 14:20. In John 17:21, Jesus' prayer for unity ("that they may be one" does use εἴναι at its beginning and end of the sentence, and so may by this imply εἴναι ἐν is intended with respect to the mutual unity of God the Father and Son, though the sense of abiding is not indicated in the context. It is again absent, but likely implied, in John 17:23, but finally used by Jesus in v 26 as a subjunctive (ἵνα ἡ ἀγάπη ἣν ἠγάπησάς με ἐν αὐτοῖς ᾖ κἀγὼ ἐν αὐτοῖς).

50. Μένω is found in 1 John 2:6, 10, 14, 17, 19, 24, 27 (twice), 28; 3:6, 9, 14, 15, 17, 24 (twice); 4:12, 13, 15, 16 (three times). Brown (195–96) sees three meanings for εἶναι ἐν which are also parallel to μένειν ἐν: (1) "indwelling pertinent to God" as in John 10:38; 14:10, 11, 17, 20, 23; 15:2; 17:21, 23, 26; 1 John 2:5; 4:4; and 5:20; (2) "indwelling of other realities in the Christian" as in John 11:10; 12:35; 15:11; 17:26; 1 John 1:8, 10; 2:4, and 15; and (3) "miscellaneous theological uses" which he did not categorize.

51. BDAG, 631.

52. Roberts (59) varies by seeing abiding in this verse as describing the believer's "fellowship with God" as a "foretaste or earnest of the life to come."

lowship (communion) with someone, such as believers in 1 John 2:19 (King, 54; Roberts, 64; Stott, 110; Westcott, 72).[53] In 2 John 2 the term refers to God's truth having an influence in our lives. In 1 John 4:12–16, it is used by John to refer to the mutual indwelling of God within the believer and the believer in God, the Pauline concept of being "in Christ" (Brown, 521–22, 524, 526; Dodd, 114; King, 96; Smalley, 247, 249, 254–55; Stott, 166, 168–70). Love for others is an evidence of "God's indwelling presence" in the believer (King, 94; Stott, 167).

Interpretive Issue

Μένω is used in two senses in Johannine writings, to express personal and impersonal relationships. The term is used by Jesus and John to describe the believer's relationship to God and other believers, as well as interrelationship (fellowship) with them. Also, its significance and use is not limited by Jesus or John to personal interrelationships with "other realities" that "indwell" the believer (Brown, 195–96). How one understands these various relationships, whether they be dynamic or static, is a key to understanding John's use of μένω, as well as how εἶναι ἐν relates to μένω.

The Test of Life understanding of John's epistles is that John uses μένω principally to convey the sense of union rather than interrelationship (fellowship or communion). Consequently, the term is equivalent to "being in" (εἶναι ἐν), which conveys a "stronger form" of the Pauline concept of "in Christ."[54] Abiding, then, reflects the condition of union that is associated with the possession of salvation resulting from the "divine indwelling" rather than the expression of relationship (Brown, 403, 447; Stott, 146). For example, Findlay (136) says abiding

> is more than communion, it is *union*. This Divine κοινωνία is not the intercourse of two separate personalities external to each other, but of the finite knowledge and love with the infinite, that is at once immanent to it and transcendent, the fellowship of the seeing eye with the light that fills the universe, of the spark of kindled

53. BDAG, 631.

54. F. Hauck, "μένω," *TDNT* 4:574–88. Also seeing the term as equivalent to Paul's ἐν Χριστῷ are B. George (*Classic Christianity*, 204) and V. Taylor (*Forgiveness and Reconciliation*, 122).

being with the eternal Source, ... which is pervaded and enfolded by the loving will of God.

Further (146), abiding "is existence in God perpetuated; it is union made restful and secure." Seifrid contrasts John and Paul's use of εἶναι ἐν similarly: "Unlike the Johannine literature, which focuses on the mutual inherence of Christ and believers, Paul does not emphasize this reciprocal aspect. The idea that Christ is in or among believers appears in his letters (e.g., Gal 2:19; Rom 8:10; Col 1:27) but is only occasionally brought into association with the thought that believers are in Christ."[55] Since Paul does not use μένω to describe the Christian's relationship with God, and John does not use ἐν Χριστῷ (though "in me" does occur with John), the commonality of meaning may be difficult to establish conclusively. However, Paul's use of "in Christ" does seem to imply some measure of mutuality of relationship that is dynamic (Acts 9:4–5; Gal 2:19–20; Eph 2:13; 3:6; Phil 1:1; 2:1; 3:10; Col 1:2; 3:3, 24). It should not be limited to a locative or spacial sense.[56]

The Test of Life view sees obedience, love, and holy living as evidence of the union of Christ and the believer (Brown, 421; Dodd, 64, 94–95; Stott, 121, 131, 154). The relational sense of the term, though an aspect of its meaning, is not viewed as paramount (Dodd, 32, 46, 58; Law, 54). The "union" (rather than relationship) definition arises from an understanding that Jesus' teachings in the Gospel of John focus primarily on justification. Thus, what he says to the disciples in the Upper Room Discourse must be viewed in that light as well. For example, Strombeck says concerning John 15 that "'Abide in me and I in you', does not mean that those who have been cleansed by a similar command on his part must keep themselves in him." Rather Jesus keeps them and they must simply "remain in continuous union with him."[57]

---

55. Seifrid, M. A. "In Christ," in *Dictionary of Paul and His Letters*. Gerald F. Hawthorne, Ralph P. Martin, and Daniel G. Reid, eds. (Downers Grove: InterVarsity, 1993) 433–36.

56. E. E. Johnson (*Expository Hermeneutics*, 24) notes well the hermeneutical principle that, since the term is used in a theologically significant manner by Jesus in the Upper Room Discourse and then by John in his epistle, those significant uses should be allowed to "set the limits on the meaning communicated" by the term in its passages.

57. J. F. Strombeck, *Shall Never Perish*, 215.

The Test of Fellowship view says that μένω need not be understood solely as a justification term, but also as a word Jesus used to describe living by faith in fellowship with God.[58] Ryrie (1468) defines *abiding* on the basis of 1 John 3:24, as "habitual fellowship maintained by keeping his commandments." Harrison notes, "Abiding is not to be confused with position. Christ stated the fact of spiritual position before he inculcated the necessity of abiding (John 14:20; 15:4). Abiding is an activity. It means communion with the person of Christ and submission to the will of Christ."[59] Jesus used μένω to describe the relationship between him and his believing disciples. As a result, its meaning and use can be seen as related to issues of sanctification without placing any stress on the text.[60] Thus, when Jesus commands his disciples to abide in him, he is instructing them concerning issues of fellowship and relationship with God. Thus, the imagery used by Jesus in the vine-branch analogy describes fellowship with God rather than union (Hodges, 82).[61] Cook defends the position well:

> *Abiding* in Christ is to be distinguished from *being* in Christ, although ideally there should be no practical difference between the two. We may observe the distinction by noting John 15:1–11, where the "in Me" branch of verse 2 is seen to be different from the "abide in Me" branch of verse 4. To *be* in Christ is to be born again, to be regenerated, to have had forgiveness of sins through Christ. Thus the disciples are in Christ (v. 2) because they have been cleansed of their sins (v. 3). To *abide* in Christ, however, is to be an obedient follower in fellowship with Christ the Savior and Lord (vv. 4–5, 9–11). An examination of 1 John 3:24 will reveal that obedience is the condition for abiding. Moreover, in John

58. This would be related more to the Pauline idea of walking and being led by the Spirit (Gal 5:16–18) or being filled with the Spirit (Eph 5:18). It is also the point at which the interrelationship sense would be understood with Paul's use of "in Christ."

59. E. F. Harrison, "A Key to the Understanding of First John," 44. J. C. Dillow (*The Reign of the Servant Kings,* 174) is an example of someone from the Test of Fellowship view that describes it as John's "word for something conditional in the believer's relationship with Christ, fellowship within the family." For him (406) it means "to continue in close relationship to" Christ.

60. W. R. Cook, *The Theology of John,* 134.

61. L. S. Chafer, "The Eternal Security of the Believer," 402–3.

> 15:10 our obeying Christ and thus abiding in him is compared to the Son's obeying the Father and thus abiding in him; the Son was already *in* the Father by virtue of his sonship, but the Son *abided* in the Father by obeying him. We see, then, that just as Christ's abiding in the Father was the maintenance of personal fellowship with the Father, so our abiding in Christ is the maintenance of personal fellowship with Christ. ... Furthermore, a study of John 15:4–11 will show that abiding is the condition for fruit bearing (vv. 4–5), that abiding brings the confidence of answered prayer (v. 7), and that abiding is commanded of Christians (v. 9).[62]

What, then, is the meaning that Jesus and John give to the figurative use of μένω, both in the Upper Room Discourse and in 1 John? What does it mean to mutually abide, whether referring to God, believers, or God's Word?

The Conceptual Meaning of Μένω

There is almost always some aspect of mutuality, or reciprocity, in the concept of abiding as Jesus and John use it. Rensberger (62) calls this use of μένω "virtually unique" to John. He notes that it is absent not only with the other New Testament authors, but is also missing from Hellenistic literature as well. Malatesta says that "all the *reciprocal personal relationships* in the Letter [1 John] are expressed by μένειν ἐν."[63] John uses this term to describe the believer experiencing a reciprocal relationship with God (2:24, 27, 28; 3:6), God with the believer (4:12), and the mutual abiding of the believer and God (3:243; 4:13, 15, 16).[64] John's use of μένω includes both a

62. W. R. Cook, *The Theology of John,* 133–34 (italics his). J. C. Dillow (*The Reign of the Servant Kings,* 174) concurs, pointing to John 15:10 as evidence of the "conditional nature of the abiding relationship with Christ" and to 1 John 3:24 as revealing that "the abiding relationship is conditioned on obedience."

63. E. Malatesta, *Interiority and Covenant*, 34 (italics his). I have also used the term "interrelationship" to describe this idea of mutuality.

64. Rensberger says further (63) that whereas "in the Gospel of John, Jesus always stands as intermediary between Christians and God ... in 1 John, however, they can abide (or simply "be") directly in God and God in them." This was promised by Jesus in John 14:16–17 and 23 and fulfilled with the coming of the Holy Spirit at Pentecost.

locative sense as well as durative (Rensberger, 62–63).[65] When used of God or his word, it focuses on the immutability of God, and thus expresses a durative sense as well.[66] Along with the relational and reciprocal sense is the understanding that all relationship presupposes God's indwelling of the person in the sense of his actual presence in the person of the Holy Spirit (John 14:17; 1 John 3:24). As Kruse (186–87) notes well:

> It is apparent that the "abiding" language of John's Gospel, as far as it relates to believers abiding in Christ, denotes continuing loyalty and obedience to Christ, but it is not exhausted by this. There is an ontological dimension to it as well. As far as it relates to Christ abiding in believers (which is closer to the notion of "having the Son"), the abiding language definitely has ontological significance. In the light of the latter, we could say that in 1 John to "have the Son" means to be indwelt by the Son, something which viewed from the human perspective is initiated when people believe in him.

Μένω is also used with a sense of contingency when applied to a believer's reciprocal relationship with God. Jesus' use of third class conditional sentences in John 15:6, 7, and 10 to describe the disciples' ability to choose whether they abide or do not abide is very significant in understanding his use of the term.[67] His use of ἐὰν emphasizes the contingency (hypothetical or more probable future sense[68]) of their choice and thereby indicates that

65. BDAG 630–31. Painter (170) sees these passages suggesting that "God abides in those who abide in God, so that even when only one aspect of abiding is mentioned, as here the claim to abide in God, mutual abiding is implied if the claim is true."

66. F. Hauck, "μένω," *TDNT* 4:574–75.

67. John 15:18–19 provides examples of Jesus' use of first and second class conditions to express certainty. In v. 18 Jesus uses the first class conditional clause (εἰ plus the indicative) to describe the certainty of the world's hatred toward believers. Then in v. 19 He chooses a second class condition (εἰ plus the indicative in the protasis and ἂν in the apodosis) to communicate the certainty of their separateness from the world. Jesus' use of the third class condition to communicate contingency is very significant in demonstrating the possibility of believers not abiding. See D. B. Wallace (*Grammar*, 689–701) for a full discussion of conditional sentences and their significances.

68. D. B. Wallace, *Grammar*, 696.

abiding is something influenced by the believer's choices.[69] Thus abiding in Christ is a relational and contingent concept rather than static (or what some refer to as "positional" truth).

This reciprocal relationship is also evident from Jesus' abiding in his Father's love, with his experience of that loving relationship being contingent on his obedience (John 15:9–10). This does not mean that Jesus' use of μένω does not include the sense of union as well. Only believers can abide in God, and only obedient believers can abide either in him (3:24) or in his love (John 14:20–21). When a believer fails to abide in God, God does not cease to remain in him or her in the person of the Holy Spirit who indwells and seals every believer (Rom 8:9; 1 Cor 12:13; Eph 1:13–14). However, though believers may grieve and quench the Holy Spirit through sin (Eph 4:30; 1 Thess 5:19), this does not mean the Spirit ceases to indwell them, only to fill them (Eph 5:18). While in a state of disobedience and before confession of sin and restoration of fellowship, a believer will not experience the reciprocal relationship (fellowship) that is available to him or her, though it remains potentially available through confession. Thus, the abiding relationship is both permanent (the durative sense implicit in the term μένω) and contingent. Its permanence results from God's faithfulness to preserve the saint. Its contingence results from God's demand of honesty about sin (1:8–10) and obedience (John 14:23; 1 John 2:3–6).

In the reciprocal relationship of love, believers love God by loving one another in response to the love of God received by them. God thereby expresses his love for his children through the actions of his children directed toward one another (1 John 4:12–16). Malatesta describes this well when he says, "the intimate relationship between Jesus, the Father and the Spirit establishes, maintains and develops the communion of the members of the Christian community with Jesus, the Spirit and the Father. Moreover, according to John, the communion of Christians with each other and their relationship to the world are grounded in their communion with

69. BDAG, 267. As noted elsewhere, the fact that Jesus commanded the Eleven to abide in him must indicate that it was possible for them not to abide and therefore to become either less fruitful than He desired or unfruitful. If it was possible for them to fail to abide, it is just as possible for other believers to fail to abide, and therefore to be less fruitful.

God."[70] Along with this sense of a dynamic reciprocal relationship, there is also an element of influence that grows out of that reciprocity.

John also uses μένω to describe the interaction of believers with other realities besides God (Father, Son, and Holy Spirit) that indwell them.[71] For example Jesus speaks of his word "abiding" in the disciples in John 15:7. Since his word, his commands and instructions, can neither be animate nor have a relationship as such, then what must this mean? The best explanation is that his word is exerting an influence on the disciples as expressed through obedience. This can be seen in Jesus' previous statement in John 14:23–24 of the disciples' need to "keep" Jesus' word as an expression of their love for him. This is more than memorizing Scripture or even meditating on it. It means that as they know God's Word, and therefore his will, they (and we) are to be motivated to obey it and act according to that word rather than according to the world's ideas (Psa 119). God's Word "abides" in them (and us) only to the extent it modifies their (and our) behavior. In response to the word's influence and their abiding in Christ, Jesus promises the disciples, and so us, answered prayer. Implied in this promise is the reality that a person who is rightly related to God through obedience and therefore experiencing a reciprocal fellowship, who is thereby being "influenced" by God through his word, will in turn "influence" God through the prayer that God responds to positively. Answered prayer results from a healthy relationship with God, a relationship that grows out of obedience.

A second "reality" that "abides" in, and thereby influences, believers is eternal life. In 3:15, the believer who "hates" and therefore "murders" his Christian brother is said not to have eternal life abiding in him. As discussed with that verse, John's use of "hates his brother," by implication, means the person "hating" is a believer and therefore possesses eternal life (Pentecost, 89). However, that life is not functioning as a motivating factor in his relationship with other believers. It is in this sense that it does not "abide." Or, consistent with the concept of fellowship being developed in the epistle, the hating believer is not experiencing a reciprocal relationship

70. E. Malatesta, *Interiority and Covenant*, 6.

71. When Jesus speaks of abiding in his love (John 15:9–10), it has more to do with experiencing His love by relating properly with him. Here the relationship is with Jesus, with the benefit being that of experiencing love from him, rather than any interaction with love. Conversely, in 4:12–16 it is God's love experienced that motivates believers to love one another.

with Christ, who is eternal life incarnate, and so is out of fellowship with God, described earlier as walking in darkness (2:9–11).

Conclusion

John's use of μένω expresses the concept of the reciprocal relationships (fellowship) that grow out of mutual indwelling (εἶναι ἐν) between God (Father, Son, and Holy Spirit) and believers. This mutual abiding is predicated on the obedience of the believer and expresses itself in terms of the loving relationships believers have with one another as an expression of their love for God as recipients of his love (4:19). One expression of this mutuality has to do with influence, in that the presence of God, his love, and his word serves to motivate the believer to action, particularly that of loving other believers. Another expression of this mutuality is that obedience to Christ and his word serves to "motivate" God to listen to the fruitful believer's prayers and respond favorably (John 15:7, 16).[72] Just as his word is to be a motivating factor in the believer's life, so too is his love and the life. Thus, when John uses μένω, he intends to communicate more than possession or presence. He speaks of relationship and effect, reciprocity and influence.

Selected Bibliography

Abbott, E. A. *Johannine Grammar.* London: Adam & Charles Black, 1906.

Brown, R. E. *The Epistles of John: A New Translation with Introduction and Commentary*. AB 30. New York: Doubleday, 1982.

Chafer, L. S. "The Eternal Security of the Believer, Part 2." *BSac* 106 (1949; 2002): 391–419.

Cook, W. R. *The Theology of John*. Chicago: Moody, 1979.

Dillow, J. C. *The Reign of the Servant Kings: A Study of Eternal Security and the Final Significance of Man*. Hayesville, NC: Schoettle, 1993.

Dodd, C. H. *The Johannine Epistles*. MNTC. New York: Harper and Brothers, 1946.

Findlay, G. G. *Fellowship in the Life Eternal.* Grand Rapids: Eerdmans, 1955.

George, B. *Classic Christianity*. Eugene, OR: Harvest House, 1989.

Harrison, E. F. "A Key to the Understanding of First John." *BSac* 111 (1954): 39–46.

Hawthorne, G. F., R. P. Martin, and D. G. Reid, eds. *Dictionary of Paul and His Letters.* Downers Grove, IL: InterVarsity Press, 1993.

72. This is with the understanding that answered prayer is limited to that which is according to God's will (5:14–15) and character (John 14:13; 15:16).

Johnson, E. E. *Expository Hermeneutics: An Introduction.* Grand Rapids: Zondervan, 1990.
King, G. H. *The Fellowship.* London: Marshall, Morgan & Scott, 1954.
Kruse, C. J. *The Letters of John.* PNTC. Grand Rapids: Eerdmans, 2000.
Malatesta, E. *Interiority and Covenant: A Study of* εἶναι ἐν *and* μένειν ἐν *in the First Letter of Saint John.* Rome: Biblical Institute Press, 1978.
Pentecost, J. D. *The Joy of Fellowship: A Study of First John.* Grand Rapids: Lamplighter Books, 1977.
Rensberger, D. *1 John, 2 John, 3 John.* ANTC. Nashville: Abingdon, 1997.
Roberts, J. W. *The Letters of John.* LW. Austin, TX: R. B. Sweet, 1968.
Ryrie, C. C. "I, II, and III John." In *The Wycliffe Bible Commentary.* Edited by C. F. Pfeiffer and E. F. Harrison. Chicago: Moody, 1962.
Smalley, S. S. *1, 2, 3 John.* WBC 51. Waco, TX: Word, 1984.
Stott, J. R. W. *The Letters of John.* Rev. ed. TNTC. Grand Rapids: Eerdmans, 1964, 1988.
Strombeck, J. F. *Shall Never Perish.* Philadelphia: American Bible Conference Association, 1936.
Taylor, V. *Forgiveness and Reconciliation: A Study in New Testament Theology.* New York: St. Martin's Press, 1956.
Wallace, D. B. *Greek Grammar beyond the Basics.* Grand Rapids: Zondervan, 1996.
Westcott, B. F. *The Epistles of St. John.* Grand Rapids: Eerdmans, 1966 ed.

Excursus: Patronage and the First-Century House Church

A central part of the Greco-Roman social structure revolved around patronage. This impacted the relationships of individuals, whether of equal or different social and economic status. This especially involved the question of reciprocity as it related to the obligations of guests in a "host-guest" relationship. It was understood that in any future encounter the guest of a host would assume the role of host and the host could expect to be treated as a guest to the same degree he had treated his guest, not host. If for some reason this reciprocity could not occur due to differences in economic or social status, then a patronage relationship occurred.[73] All of Roman culture, including their system of government was based on this system.[74] The governors were clients of the emperor and patrons of the wealthy landowners below them socially. The landowners were, in turn, patrons of the

73. I. Lorencin, "Hospitality versus Patronage," 168.
74. W. A. Simmons, *Peoples of the New Testament World*, 275.

land tenants below them.[75] Each client depended on the patron for survival while the patron benefited economically and socially from his clients. "The intention of the patron was to use his clients for the purpose of increasing his own wealth, popularity, and power."[76] The "client" did benefit from the relationship, though, including provision of food, funding, protection, occupational advancement, citizenship, freedom from taxation, and other things.[77] Thus there was a reciprocal aspect to these relationships. However, their roles were fixed, and so well defined societally. Inequality was the chief trait of these relationships.[78] "The imbalance in exchange led to a dependent relationship, which allowed the patron to begin dominating and exploiting his client."[79]

This cultural norm had its potential impact on the church as it spread throughout the Roman empire and met in homes. Campbell describes the blessing as well as potential problem that this brought to the church. "So long as the local church was confined to one household, the household provided the leadership of the church. The church in the house came with its leadership so to speak 'built-in'. The church that met in someone's house met under that person's presidency. The householder was *ex hypothesi* a person of standing, a patron of others, and the space where the church met was his space, in which he was accustomed to the obedience of slaves and the deference of his wife and children. Those who came into it will have been to a large extent constrained by the norms of hospitality to treat the host as master of ceremonies, especially if he was a person of greater social sanding or age than themselves. The table moreover was his table, and if any prayers were to be said, or bread or wine offered, the part was naturally his to play."[80]

The apostles do not address this issue directly in any of the New Testament epistles. However, Paul does mention churches in person's homes (Rom 16:3–4, 23; Col 4:15; Phlm 2) wherein this mindset could have been present, though there is no indication that Paul was aware of any problems arising from a patronal mindset. Additionally, his mention of the location of the church in that person's home never indicates that they were

75. W. A. Simmons, *Peoples of the New Testament World*, 277–82.
76. I. Lorencin, "Hospitality versus Patronage," 170.
77. I. Lorencin, "Hospitality versus Patronage," 170.
78. I. Lorencin, "Hospitality versus Patronage," 171.
79. I. Lorencin, "Hospitality versus Patronage," 172.
80. A. R. Campbell, *The Elder: Seniority within Earliest Christianity*, 126.

functioning as the head of that church. Jeffers, in fact, suggests that those patrons who hosted churches in their homes and supported it financially were not always leaders within the congregation.[81] The theory that the host of the church exercised patronal control is a deduction interpreters make.

There were, though, problems that resulted from differences in social status and wealth in the churches, as is evident from Jas 2:1–13 as well as Paul's instructions about spiritual gifts (1 Cor 12). Simmons suggests that the divisions evident in the church at Corinth, embodied in the slogans of 1 Cor 1:10–17, was characteristic of the practice of praising one's patron and supporting his political or social ambitions.[82] Paul's letter to Philemon addressed the changing relationship between the wealthy Philemon and his slave, Onesimus. Thus, between Lorencin's theory and Mitchell's thesis we may speculate that Diotrephes' failure to extend hospitality should be seen more as a rejection of John. However, though his rejection of those men was not a response to their inability to repay his hospitality, his attitude that he had the right to reject them and expel members of his church from his home likely resulted from a patronal mindset. This was not considered appropriate behavior in the churches as John's assessment of his character clearly indicates.

Selected Bibliography

Campbell, A. R. *The Elder: Seniority within Earliest Christianity*. Edinburgh: T & T Clark, 1994.

Jeffers, J. S. *The Greco-Roman World of the New Testament Era: Exploring the Background of Early Christianity*. Downers Grove, IL: InterVarsity Press, 1999.

Lorencin, I. "Hospitality versus Patronage: An Investigation of Social Dynamics in the Third Epistle of John." *Andrews University Seminary Studies* 46 (2008):) 165–74.

Mitchell, M. M. "'Diotrephes Does Not Receive Us': The Lexicographical and Social Context of 3 John 9–10." *JBL* 117 (1998):) 299–320.

Simmons, W. A. *Peoples of the New Testament World*. Peabody, MA: Hendrickson, 2008.

81. J. Jeffers, *The Greco-Roman World of the New Testament Era*, 85.

82. W. A. Simmons, *Peoples of the New Testament World*, 287.

List of Foreign and Technical Words

Actionsart: The "kind of action" contained in a verb before it is given its aspect by the author within the context of its sentence.

Anacoluthon: A figure of speech in which the initial thrust of the sentence is abruptly changed such that the following portion of the sentence does not naturally follow the first part. Often the object of the verb is missing.

Anaphoric: The adjectival form of anaphora, which means a word or phrase that refers back to a previous word or phrase.

Apodosis: The main clause of a conditional sentence wherein the consequence of the condition stated in the protasis is expressed.

Asyndeton: A figure of speech where a word is left out for emphasis.

Cataphoric: The adjectival form of cataphora, which means a word or phrase that refers forward to a following word or phrase.

Constructio ad sensum: A construction in which the third person singular pronoun lacks an antecedent, and the context makes it clear what its referent would be.

Diatribe: A rhetorical device in which an imagined opponent raises an objection that the author then refutes for pedagogical purposes.

Double entendre: A figure of speech in which a word expresses two distinct and different meanings intended by the author.

Hendiadys: A figure of speech in which two related nouns or verbs are used to communicate a single idea, often heightening its meaning.

Homoeoteleuton: A copyist's error involving the omission of words or lines from the text because, on returning to the text after writing the word or words he was copying, he mistakenly returned to a different word having the same ending. This same term can also refer to a figure of speech involving the repetition of the same letter or syllable at the end of successive words.

Inclusio: A literary device involving the repetition of a word or group of words that mark the beginning and end of a unit within the work.

Leitmotif: A recurring theme, whether a word, person, image, or event that plays a significant role in developing the message.

Litotes (meiosis): A figure of speech used for emphasis involving omission of a word's natural sense in order to lower one thing and elevate or stress another using the contrast it creates. The importance of the thing lessened is brought, thereby, into focus.

Metonymy: A figure of speech in which one noun, often a name, is used in place of another with which it is related in some manner.

Paronomasia: A figure of speech involving the combination of words with similar sounds, though not of meanings, in order to call attention to the point being made.

Pleonasm: A figure of speech in which more words are used than are necessary to communicate the idea, also known as "redundancy."

Polyptoton: A figure of speech involving the repetition of an idea using the same root word, but in a different form, whether a noun and verb, or different cases, moods, tenses, persons, or other distinguishing features.

Protasis: The conditional statement ("if" clause) of a conditional sentence.

Sitz im Leben: The German term literally means "setting in life" and refers to the circumstances, culture, and historical milieu from which an author wrote.

Synecdoche: A figure of speech in which one idea is exchanged for another: the genus for the species, the species for the genus, the whole for the part, the part for the whole.

General Bibliography

Commentaries on the Johannine Epistles

Akin, Daniel L. *1, 2, 3 John*. NAC 38. Nashville: Broadman & Holman, 2001.

Alexander, Neil. *The Epistles of John*. New York: Macmillan, 1962.

Alexander, William. *The Epistles of St. John: Twenty-one Discourses with Greek Text, Comparative Versions, and Notes Chiefly Exegetical*. 3rd ed. London: Hodder and Stoughton, 1892.

Anderson, David. *Maximum Joy: First John—Relationship or Fellowship?* Irving, TX: Grace Evangelical Society, 2005.

Barker, G. W. "1, 2, 3 John." In *Expositor's Bible Commentary*, vol. 12. Grand Rapids: Regency Reference Library, 1981.

Barrett, G. S. *The First Epistles General of St. John*. London: Religious Tract Society, 1910.

Blaiklock, E. M. *Faith is Victory*. Grand Rapids: Eerdmans, 1959.

Blair, J. Allen. *The Epistles of John*. Neptune, NJ: Loizeaux Brothers, 1982.

Boice, James M. *The Epistles of John*. Grand Rapids: Zondervan, 1979.

Bonnard, Pierre. *Les Ēpitres Johanniques*. Commentaire du Nouveau Testament. Geneva: Labor et Fides, 1983.

Brooke, A. E. *A Critical and Exegetical Commentary on the Johannine Epistles*. ICC. Edinburgh: T & T Clark, nd.

Brown, Raymond E. *The Epistles of John: A New Translation with Introduction and Commentary*. AB 30. New York: Doubleday, 1982.

Bruce, F. F. *The Epistles of John*. Grand Rapids: Eerdmans, 1970.

Bultmann, Rudolf. *The Johannine Epistles*. Translated by R. P. O'Hara, L. C. McGaughy, and R. W. Funk. Philadelphia: Fortress, 1973.

Burdick, Donald W. *The Letters of John the Apostle*. Chicago: Moody, 1985.

Burge, Gary M. *Letters of John*. NIVAC. Grand Rapids: Zondervan, 1996.

Calvin, John. *The Gospel According to St John 11–21 and The First Epistle of John*. Calvin's New Testament Commentaries. Translated by T. H. L. Parker, 1961. Grand Rapids: Eerdmans, 1959–61.

Cameron, Robert. *The First Epistle of John*. Philadelphia: A. J. Rowland, 1899.

Candlish, Robert S. *The First Epistle of John*. 2nd ed. Grand Rapids: Zondervan, n.d.

Clark, Gordon H. *First John*. Phillipsburg, NJ: Presbyterian and Reformed, n.d.

Cotton, J. *An Exposition of First John*. Evansville, IN: Sovereign Grace, 1962.

Crain, C. *Readings On The First Epistle Of John*. Garland, TX: Galaxie Software, 2004. Repr., New York: Loizeaux Brothers, n.d.

Culpepper, R. Alan. *1 John, 2 John, 3 John*. Knox Preaching Guides. Atlanta: John Knox, 1985.

Culy, M. M. *1, 2, 3 John: A Handbook on the Greek Text*. Waco, TX: Baylor University Press, 2004.

Dillow, Joseph C. *The Reign of the Servant Kings: A Study of Eternal Security and the Final Significance of Man*. Hayesville, NC: Schoettle, 1993.

Dodd, C. H. *The Johannine Epistles*. MNTC. New York: Harper and Brothers, 1946.

Edwards, Ruth B. *The Johannine Epistles*. Sheffield: Sheffield Academic Press, 2001.

Epp, Theodore H. *Studies in the General Epistles of John*. Lincoln, NE: Back to the Bible Broadcast, 1957.

Findlay, George G. *Fellowship in the Life Eternal*. Grand Rapids: Eerdmans, 1955.

Gingrich, Raymond E. *1, 2, 3 John: Fellowship with the Word of Life*. Winona Lake, IN: BMH, 1977.

———. *An Outline and Analysis of the First Epistle of John*. Grand Rapids: Zondervan, 1943.

Goodman, George. *The Epistle of Eternal Life*. London: Pickering and Inglis, 1936.

Gore, C. *The Epistles of St John*. London: John Murray, 1920.

Grayston, Kenneth. *The Johannine Epistles*. New Century Bible Commentary. Grand Rapids: Eerdmans, 1984.

Haas, C., M. de Jonge, and J. L. Swellengrebel. *A Handbook on the Letters of John*. UBS Handbook Series; Helps for Translators. New York: United Bible Societies, 1994.

Harris, W. H. *1, 2, 3 John: Comfort and Counsel for a Church in Crisis*. Dallas, TX: Biblical Studies Press, 2003.

Hauck, Friedrich. *Die Briefe des Jakobus, Petrus, Judas und Johannes (Kirchenbriefe)*. NTD 10. Göttingen: Vandenhoeck & Ruprecht, 1954.

Haupt, E. *The First Epistle of St. John*. Translated by W. B. Pope. Clark's Foreign Theological Library, n.s., 64. Edinburgh: T & T Clark, 1879.

Hiebert, D. Edmond. *The Epistles of John: An Expositional Commentary*. Greenville, SC: Bob Jones University Press, 1991.

Hobbs, Herschel H. *The Epistles of John*. Nashville: Thomas Nelson, 1983.

Hodges, Zane C. *The Epistles of John: Walking in the Light of God's Love*. Irving, TX: Grace Evangelical Society, 1999.

Houlden, J. L. *A Commentary on the Johannine Epistles*. Black's New Testament Commentaries. New York: Harper & Row, 1973.

———. *The Johannine Epistles*. Harper's New Testament Commentaries. New York: Harper & Row, 1973.

Johnson, Thomas F. *1, 2, and 3 John*. NIBCNT. Peabody, MA: Hendrickson, 1993.

Jones, Peter R. *1, 2 & 3 John*. Macon, GA: Smyth and Helwys, 2009.

Kelly, William. *An Exposition of the Epistles of John the Apostle*. London: T. Weston, 1905.

King, Guy H. *The Fellowship*. London: Marshall, Morgan & Scott, 1954.

Kistemaker, Simon J. *James and I-III John*. New Testament Commentary. Grand Rapids: Baker, 1986.

Klauck, Hans-Josef. *Der erste Johannesbrief*. EKKNT 23, no. 1; Zürich und Braunschweig: Benziger/Neukirchen-Vluyn: Neukirchener, 1991.

Kruse, Colin J. *The Letters of John*. PNTC. Grand Rapids: Eerdmans, 2000.

Kysar, Robert. *I, II, III John*. Augsburg Commentary on the New Testament. Minneapolis: Augsburg, 1986.

Laurin, Roy L. *Epistle of John: Life at its Best*. Wheaton, IL: Van Campen Press, Inc. 1946.

Law, Robert. *The Tests of Life*. Edinburgh: T & T Clark, 1909. Repr., Grand Rapids: Baker, 1969

Lenski, R. C. H. *The Interpretation of I and II Epistles of Peter, the Three Epistles of John, and the Epistle of Jude*. Minneapolis: Augsburg, 1966.

Lieu, Judith M. *I, II, & III John*. Louisville, KY: Westminster John Knox, 2008.

Lloyd-Jones, Martyn. *Children of God*. Life in Christ: Studies in 1 John, vol. 3. Wheaton, IL: Crossway, 1993.

———. *Fellowship with God*. Life in Christ: Studies in 1 John, vol. l. Wheaton, IL: Crossway, 1993.

———. *Life in God*. Life in Christ: Studies in 1 John, vol. 5. Wheaton, IL: Crossway, 1995.

———. *The Love of God*. Life in Christ: Studies in 1 John, vol. 4. Wheaton, IL: Crossway, 1994.

———. *Walking with God*. Life in Christ: Studies in 1 John, vol. 2. Wheaton, IL: Crossway, 1993.

Loisy, Alkfred. *Le Quatrième E'vangile. Les E'pîtres dites de Jean*. 2nd ed. Paris: E'mile Nourry, E'diteur, 1921.

MacArthur, John. *1, 2, 3 John: MacArthur NT Commentary*. Chicago: Moody, 2007.

Malatesta, Edward. *The Epistles of St. John*. Rome: Pontifical Gregorian University, 1973.

Marshall, I. Howard. *The Epistles of John*. NICNT. Grand Rapids: Eerdmans, 1978.

Mitchell, John G. *Fellowship*. Portland, OR: Multnomah, 1974.

Moody, Dale. *The Letters of John*. Waco, TX: Word, 1970.

Morris, Leon. "1 John, 2 John, 3 John." In *The New Bible Commentary*. Rev. ed. Grand Rapids: Eerdmans, 1970.
Painter, John. *1, 2, and 3 John*. Sacra Pagina 18. Collegeville, MN: Liturgical Press, 2002.
Pate, C. Marvin. *The Writings of John*. Grand Rapids: Zondervan, 2011.
Pentecost, J. Dwight. *The Joy of Fellowship: A Study of First John*. Grand Rapids: Lamplighter Books, 1977.
Perkins, Pheme. *The Johannine Epistles*. New Testament Message 21. Wilmington, DE: Michael Glazier, 1979.
Phillips, John. *Exploring the Epistles of John*. The John Phillips Commentary Series. Grand Rapids: Kregel, 2003.
Plummer, Alfred. *The Epistles of St. John.* CGTSC. Cambridge: Cambridge University Press, 1896.
Rensberger, David. *1 John, 2 John, 3 John.* ANTC. Nashville, TN: Abingdon, 1997.
Roberts, J. W. *The Letters of John*. LW. Austin, TX: R. B. Sweet, 1968.
Rosscup, James E. *Abiding in Christ: Studies in John 15*. Grand Rapids: Zondervan, 1973.
Ryrie, Charles C. "I, II, and III John." In *The Wycliffe Bible Commentary*. Edited by C. F. Pfeiffer and E. F. Harrison. Chicago: Moody, 1962.
Schnackenburg, Rudolf. *Die Johannesbriefe*. HTKNT. Vol. 13, no. 3. Freiburg: Herder, 1965.
Schunack, Gerd. *Die Briefe des Johannes*. Zürcher Bibelkommentare. Zürich: Theologischer Verlag, 1982.
Smalley, Stephen S. *1,2,3 John*. WBC 51. Waco, TX: Word, 1984.
Smith, D. Moody. *First, Second, and Third John*. Interpretation. Louisville, KY: John Knox, 1991.
Smith, David. "The Epistles of St. John." In *The Expositor's Greek Testament*. Edited by W. R. Nicoll. Grand Rapids: Eerdmans, 1910.
Stott, John R. W. *The Letters of John*. Rev. ed. TNTC. Grand Rapids: Eerdmans, 1964, 1988.
Strecker, Georg. *The Johannine Letters*. Translated by L. M. Maloney. Edited by H. Attridge. Hermeneia. Minneapolis: Fortress Press, 1996.
Thomas, John C. *The Pentecostal Commentary on 1 John, 2 John, 3 John*. Cleveland, OH: Pilgrim Press, 2004.
Thomas, Robert L. *Exegetical Digest of 1 John.* Self published, 1984.
Thompson, Marianne M. *1–3 John.* IVPNTC. Downers Grove, IL: InterVarsity Press, 1992.
Thüsing, Wilhelm and Akius Stöger. *The Three Epistles of St. John and the Epistle of Jude*. New Testament for Spiritual Reading. Translated by David Smith. New York: Herder and Herder, 1971.
Van Gorder, Paul R. *In the Family*. Grand Rapids: Radio Bible Class, 1978.
Vaughan, Curtis. *1, 2, 3 John*. Grand Rapids: Zondervan, 1970.

von Wahlde, U. C. *The Johannine Commandments: 1 John and the Struggle for the Johannine Tradition*. New York: Paulist Press, 1990.

Walls, David and Max Anders. *I & II Peter, I, II & III John, Jude*. Holman New Testament Commentary 11. Nashville: Broadman & Holman, 1999.

Westcott, Brooke F. *The Epistles of St. John*. Grand Rapids: Eerdmans, 1966 ed.

Williams, Ronald R. *The Letters of John and James*. Cambridge: Cambridge University Press, 1965.

Williamson, Rick. *1, 2, & 3 John*. New Beacon Bible Commentary. Kansas City, KS: Beacon Hill Press, 2010.

Windisch, Hans. *Die katholischen Briefe erklärt von Hans Windisch*. HNT 4, no. 2. Tübingen: J. C. B. Mohr, 1911.

Yarbrough, Robert W. *1–3 John*. Baker Exegetical Commentary on the New Testament. Grand Rapids: Baker, 2008.

Commentaries on Other Books of the Bible

Adamson, James. *The Epistle of James*. NICNT. Grand Rapids: Eerdmans, 1976.

Aune, David E. *Revelation 1–5:14*. WBC 52A. Dallas, TX: Word, 2002.

Barclay, William. *The Letters of James and Peter*. The Daily Study Bible Series. Rev. ed. Philadelphia: Westminster, 2000, c1976.

Barrett, C. K. *The Gospel According to St. John*. 2nd ed. London: SPCK, 1978.

Beale, G. K. and D. A. Carson. *The Book of Revelation: A Commentary on the Greek Text*. NIGTC. Grand Rapids: Eerdmans, 1999.

Beasley-Murray, George R. *John*. WBC 6. Dallas, TX: Word, 2002.

Blue, J. Ronald. "James." In *The Bible Knowledge Commentary*. Edited by John F. Walvoord, Roy B. Zuck. Wheaton, IL: Victor, 1983–1985 .

Blum, Edwin A. "John." In *The Bible Knowledge Commentary*. Edited by John F. Walvoord and Roy B. Zuck. Wheaton, IL: Victor, 1983–1985.

Boa, Kenneth and William Kruidenier. *Romans*. Holman New Testament Commentary 6. Nashville: Broadman & Holman, 2000.

Bock, Darrell L. *Luke Vol 2: 9:51–24:53*, Baker Exegetical Commentary on the New Testament. Grand Rapids: Baker, 1996.

Borchert, Gerald L. *John 1–11*. NAC 25A. Electronic ed. Nashville: Broadman & Holman, 2001.

Brown, Raymond E. *The Gospel According to John (I-XII)*. Anchor Biblbe. Garden City, NY: Doubleday, 1966.

Bruce, F. F. *The Gospel of John*. Grand Rapids: Eerdmans, 1983.

Calvin, John. *John*. The Crossway Classic Commentaries. Electronic ed. Wheaton, IL: Crossway, 1994.

Carson, D. A. *The Gospel According to John*. Grand Rapids: Eerdmans, 1991.

Colwell, Ernest C. and Eric L. Titus. *The Gospel of the Spirit*. New York: Harper & Brothers, 1953.

Cranfield, C. E. B. *A Critical and Exegetical Commentary on the Epistle to the Romans*. ICC. Edinburgh: T & T Clark, 1975.

Davids, Peter. *Commentary on James*. NIGTC. Grand Rapids: Eerdmans, 1982.

Derickson, Gary W. and Earl D. Radmacher. *The Disciplemaker: What Matters Most to Jesus*. Salem, OR: Charis, 2001.

Dodd, Charles H. *The Interpretation of the Fourth Gospel*. Cambridge: Cambridge University Press, 1968.

Dorsey David A. *The Literary Structure of the Old Testament: A Commentary on Genesis-Malachi.* Grand Rapids: Baker, 1999.

Gangel, Kenneth O. *John*. Holman New Testament Commentary 4. Nashville, TN: Broadman & Holman, 2000.

Godet, Frederic. *Commentary on the Gospel of John*. Repr., Grand Rapids: Kregel, 1979.

Guthrie, Donald. *New Bible Commentary: 21st Century Edition*. Edited by D. A. Carson. Downers Grove, IL: InterVarsity Press, 1994.

Hartley, John E. *Leviticus*. WBC 4. Dallas: Word, 2002.

Hendriksen, William, and Simon J. Kistemaker. *Exposition of the Gospel according to John*. NTC. Grand Rapids: Baker, 1953, 1954, 2001.

Hughes Robert B., and J. Carl Laney. *Tyndale Concise Bible Commentary*. Wheaton, IL: Tyndale, 2001.

Jamieson, Robert, A. R. Fausset, and David Brown. *A Commentary, Critical and Explanatory, on the Old and New Testaments.* Oak Harbor, WA: Logos Research Systems, 1997.

Käsemann, Ernst. *Commentary on Romans*. Translated and edited by Geoffrey W. Bromiley. Grand Rapids: Eerdmans, 1980.

Kistemaker Simon J., and William Hendriksen. *Exposition of the Book of Revelation.* NTC 20. Grand Rapids: Baker, 1953–2001.

Knight, George W. *The Pastoral Epistles: A Commentary on the Greek Text.* Grand Rapids: Eerdmans, 1992.

Köstenberger, Andreas J. *John*. Baker Exegetical Commentary on the New Testament. Grand Rapids: Baker Academic, 2004.

Lenski, R.C. H. *St. John's Gospel.* Minneapolis: Augsburg, 1943.

Longenecker, Richard N. *Galatians*. WBC 41. Dallas: Word, 2002.

Macaulay, J. C. *Expository Commentary on John.* Chicago: Moody, 1941.

MacDonald, William and Arthur Farstad. *Believer's Bible Commentary: Old and New Testaments.* Nashville: Thomas Nelson, 1997.

Marshall, I. Howard. *The Gospel of Luke: A Commentary on the Greek Text*, NIGTC. Exeter: Paternoster, 1978.

Martin, Ralph P. *James*. WBC 48 Dallas, TX: Word, 2002.

Metzger, Paul L. *The Gospel of John: When Love Comes to Town*. Downers Grove, IL: InterVarsity Press, 2010.

Mitchell, John G. *An Everlasting Love.* Portland, OR: Multnomah, 1982.

Moo, Douglas J. *Romans 1–8*. Wycliffe Exegetical Commentary. Chicago: Moody, 1991.
Morgan, G. Campbell. *The Gospel According to John*. Westwood, NJ: Revell, n.d.
Morris, Leon. *The Epistle to the Romans*. Grand Rapids: Eerdmans, 1988.
———. *The Gospel According to John*. Grand Rapids: Eerdmans, 1971.
Mounce, Robert H. *Romans*. NAC 27. Electronic ed. Nashville: Broadman & Holman, 2001.
Mounce, William D. *Pastoral Epistles*. WBC 46. Dallas, TX: Word, 2002.
Osborne, Grant R. *Revelation*. BECNT. Grand Rapids: Baker Academic, 2002.
Reiling J. and Swellengrebel, J. L. *A Handbook on the Gospel of Luke*. UBS. New York: United Bible Societies, 1993.
Richardson, Kurt A. *James*. NAC 36. Electronic. ed. Nashville: Broadman & Holman, 2001.
Schreiner, Thomas R. *Romans*. BECNT 6. Grand Rapids: Baker, 1998.
Silva, Moisés. *Philippians*. 2nd ed. Baker Exegetical Commentary on the New Testament. Grand Rapids: Baker, 2005.
Stevens, James D. "James." In the *KJV Bible Commentary*. Nashville: Thomas Nelson, 1997, c1994.
Tenney, Merrill C. "John." In *The Expositor's Bible Commentary*, vol. 9. Edited by Frank E. Gaebelein. Grand Rapids: Zondervan, 1981.
Wessel, Walter W. "James 2:14." *The Wycliffe Bible Commentary: New Testament*. Edited by Charles F. Pfeiffer and Everett F. Harrison. Chicago: Moody, 1962.
Westcott, Brooke F. *The Gospel According to St. John*. Repr., Grand Rapids: Eerdmans, 1981.
Wiersbe, Warren W. *The Bible Exposition Commentary*. Wheaton, IL: Victor, 1996.

Articles and Essays

Achtemeier, Elizabeth R. "Jesus Christ, the Light of the World: The Biblical Understanding of Light and Darkness." *Int* 17 (1963): 439–49.
Aldrich, Willard M. "Assurance." *BSac* 114, no. 456 (1957): 308–15.
———. "Is Salvation Probationary?" *BSac* 91 (1934): 87–100.
Apel, Dean M. "Eternal Life in the Johannine Literature, Lutheran Theology, and African Religion." *Africa Theological Journal* 28 (2005): 41–63.
Balla, Peter. "Child-Parent Imagery in the Catholic Epistles." *Southern Baptist Journal of Theology* 6 (2002): 66–77.
Batut, Jean-Pierre. "Believing in the Resurrection; or, The Logic of Love." *Communio: International Catholic Review* 37 (2010): 34–46.
Baylis, Charles P. "The Meaning of Walking 'in the Darkness' (1 John 1:6)." *BSac* 149 (1992): 214–22.

Black, C. Clifton. "Christian Ministry in Johannine Perspective." *Int* 44 (1990): 29–41.

Black, David A. "An Overlooked Stylistic Argument in Favor of πάντα in 1 John 2:20." *Filologia Neotestamentaria* 5 (1992): 205–8.

Black, Matthew. "On 1 John II.12–14." *NTS* 6 (1959): 236–41.

Boismard, Marie-Emile. "La connaissance de Dieu dans l'Alliance Nouvelle d'après 1 Jo," *RB* 50 (1949): 365–91.

Bonsack, Bernhard."Der Presbzteros des dritten Briefs und der geliebte Jünger des Evangeliums nach Johannes." *ZNW* 79 (1988): 45–62.

Borchert, Gerald L. "The Fourth Gospel and its Theological Impact." *RevExp* 78 (1981): 246–56.

Borger, R. "Das Comma Johanneum in der Peschitta." *NovT* 29 (1987): 280–84.

Boyer, James L. "A Classification of Impv.s: A Statistical Study." *GTJ* 8 (1987): 35–54.

Bradnock, W. J. "Questions and Answers." *BT* 5 (1954): 138–44.

Breck, John. "The Function of ΠΑΣ in 1 John 2:20." *St. Vladimir's Theological Quarterly* (35 (1991): 187–206.

Briggs, R. C. "Contemporary Study of the Johannine Epistles." *RevExp* 67 (1970): 411–22.

Brown, Raymond E. "The Qumran Scrolls and the Johannine Gospel and Epistles." *CBQ* 17 (1995): 403–19.

Bryant, Bob. "Confession of Sins in the Spirit-Filled Life." *JOTGES* 14 (2001): 53–62.

Bultmann, Rudolf. "Analyse des 1 Joh." In *Festgabe für A. Jülicher zum 70v*, 138–58. Tübingen: J.C.B. Mohr, 1927.

Busenitz, Irvin A. "The Sin unto Death." *MSJ* 1 (1990): 17–31.

Campbell, Barth. "Flesh and Spirit in 1 Cor 5:5: An Exercise in Rhetorical Criticism of the NT." *JETS* 36 (1993): 331–42.

Campbell, J. Y. "Koinonia and Its Cognates in the New Testament." *JBL* 60 (1932): 352–80.

Carlton, John W. "Preaching From the Johannine Epistles." *RevExp* 67 (1970): 473–83.

Carson, D. A. "'You Have No Need That Anybody Should Teach You' (1 John 2:27): An Old Testament Allusion That Determines the Interpretation." In *The New Testament in Its First Century Setting: Essays on Context and Background in Honour of B. W. Winter on His 65th Birthday*, edited by P. J. Williams, Andrew D. Clarke, Peter M. Head, and David Instone-Brewer, 269–80. Grand Rapids: Eerdmans, 2004.

———. "1–3 John." In *Commentary on the New Testament Use of the Old Testament.* Edited by G. K. Beale and D. A. Carson, 1063–67. Grand Rapids: Baker Academic, 2007.

———. "God Is Love." *BSac* 156 (1999): 131–43.

———. "Johannine Perspectives on the Doctrine of Assurance." *Explorations* 10 (1996): 59–97.
———. "John and the Johannine Epistles." In *It is Written: Scrpipture Citing Scripture. Essays in Honor of Barnabas Lindars, SSF*. Edited by D. A Carson and H. G. M. Williamson, 245–64. Cambridge: Cambridge University Press, 1988.
———. "Reflections on Christian Assurance." *WTJ* 54 (Spring 1992): 1–29.
Cassen, N. H. "A Grammatical and Contextual inventory of the use of *κόσμος* in the Johannine Corpus with some Implications for a Johannine Cosmic Theology." *NTS* 19 (1972): 81–91.
Chafer, Lewis S. "The Eternal Security of the Believer, Part 2." *BSac* 106 (1949): 391–419.
Coetzee, J. C. "Christ and the prince of this world in the Gospel and the Epistles of St. John." *Neot* 2 (1968): 104–121.
———. "The Holy Spirit in 1 John." *Neot* 13 (1979): 43–67.
Collins, Adela Y. "The Function of 'Excommunication' in Paul." *HTR* 73 (1980): 251–63.
Collins, C. John. "John 4:23- Classification of Impv.s: A 4, 'In Spirit and Truth': An Idomatic Proposal." *Presb* 21 (1995): 118–23.
Combs, William W. "Nag Hammadi, Gnosticism and New Testament Interpretation." *GTJ* 8 (1987): 195–212.
Contsoumpos, Panayotis. "The Idolatry Dilemma in 1 John 5:21." *DavarLogos* 2 (2003): 147–52.
Conybeare, F.C. "Dionysius of Alexandria, Newly discovered letters to the Popes Stephen and Xystus." *English Historical Review* 25 (1910): 112–14.
Cook, Donald E. "Interpretation of 1 John 1–5." *RevExp* 67 (1970): 445–59.
Cook, W. Robert. "Hamartiological Problems in First John." *BSac* 123 (1966): 249–60.
Cooper, Eugene J. "The Consciousness of Sin in 1 John." *LTP* 28 (1972): 237–48.
Court, John M. "Blessed Assurance?" *JTS* 33 (1982): 508–17.
Curtis, Edward M. "The 1 Pl. in 1 John 2:18–27." *EvJ* 10 (1992): 27–36.
Dahms, John V. "The Nature of Truth." *JETS* 28 (1985): 455–65.
de Boer, Martinus C. "Jesus the Baptizer: 1 John 5:5–8 and the Gospel of John." *JBL* 107 (1988): 87–106.
de Jonge, M. "An Analysis of 1 John 1.1–4." *BT* 29 (1978): 322–30.
———. "The Use of the Word ΧΡΙΣΤΟΣ in the Johannine Epistles." In *Studies in John*, 67–74. NovTSup 24. Leiden: Brill, 1970.
de la Potterie, Ignace. "L'onction du chretien par la foi." *Biblica* 40 (1959): 12–69.
———. "La connaissance de Dieu dans le dualism eschatolgique d'après 1 Jn 2, 12–14." In *Au service de la parole de Dieu,* 77–99. Gembloux, Belgium: Mélanges Andre-Marie Charue, 1969.
Derickson, Gary W. "What Is the Message of 1 John?" *BSac* 150 (1993): 89–105.

———. "Matthew's Chiastic Structure and Its Dispensational Implications." *BSac* 163, no. 652 (2006): 423.

Dodd, C. H. "Eternal Life." *Christianity and Crisis* 10 (1950): 33–34.

———. "*Hilaskesthai*, Its Cognates, Derivatives, and Synonyms, in the Septuagint." *JTS* 32 (1931): 352–60.

Drumwright, Huber. "Problem Passages in the Johannine Epistle: a Hermeneutical Approach." *SwJT* 13 (1970): 53–64.

Dryden, J. de Waal. "The Sense of ΣΠΕΡΜΑ in 1 John 3:9." *Filologia Neotestamentaria* 11 (1998): 85–100.

Du Preez, J. "'Sperma Autou' in 1 John 3:9." In *Essays of the General Epistles of the New Testament: 11th Meeting of Die Nuwe-Testamentiese Werkgemeenskap van Suid-Afrika, 1975*. Pretoria: NTWSA, 1975

Ehrman, Bart D. "The New Testament Canon of Dydymus the Blind." *Vigiliae Christianae* 37 (1983): 1–21.

Erickson, Richard J. "Oida and Ginōskō and Verbal Aspect in Pauline Usage." *WTJ* 44 (1982): 109–22.

Evans, Craig A. "Understanding the Gospel of Judas." *BBR* 20 (2010): 561–74.

Ezell, Douglas. "The Johannine Letters in Outline." *SwJT* 13 (1970): 65–66.

Fensham, F. C. "Love in the Writings of Qumrân and John." In *Essays on the Jewish Background of the 4th Gospel*, 66–77. Pretoria: University of South Africa, 1972.

Feuillet, Andre. "The Structure of First John: Comparison with the Fourth Gospel: The Pattern of Christian Life." *BTB* 3 (1973): 194–216.

Filson, Floyd V. "First John: Purpose and Message." *Int* 23 (1969): 259–76.

Foster, Paul. "Polymorphic Christology: Its Origins and Development in Early Christianity." *JTS* 57 (2007): 66–99.

Frankfurter, David. "A Historian's View of the Gospel of Judas." *Near Eastern Archaeology* 70 (2007): 174–77.

Funk, Robert W. "The Form and Structure of II and III John." *JBL* 86 (1967): 424–30.

Gathercole, Simon. "The Gospel of Judas." *ExpTim* 118 (2007): 209–15.

Giese, Ronald L. Jr. "Dualism In The LXX Of Prov 2:17: A Case Study In The LXX As Revisionary Translation." *JETS* 36 (1993): 286–95.

Gregory, Andrew. "The Non-canonical Gospels and the Historical Jesus – some reflections on issues and methods." *EvQ* 81 (2009): 3–22.

Griffith, Terry. "A Non-polemical Reading of 1 John: Sin, Christology and the Limits of Johannine Christianity." *TynBul* 49 (1998): 253–76.

Gundry, R. H. and R. W. Howell. "The Sense and Syntax of John 3:14–17 with Special Reference to the Use of Οὕτως ... ὥστε in John 3:16." NovT 41 (1999): 24–39.

Guthrie, D. "Questions of Introduction." In *New Testament Interpretation: Essays on Principles and Methods*. Edited by I. Howard Marshall, 101–14. Milton Keynes, UK: Paternoster, 1977.

Hansford, Keir L. "The Underlying Poetic Structure of 1 John." *JOTT* 5 (1992): 126–74.

Harnack, A. von, "'Das Wir' in den Johanneischen Schriften," *SPAW* (1923): 96–113.

Harrison, Everett F. "A Key to the Understanding of First John." *BSac* 111 (1954): 39–46.

Head, Peter M. "The Gospel of Judas and the Qarara Codices," *TynBul* 58 (2007): 1–23.

Heinz, Donald. "Kosmos-Men or Men for the Kosmos." *Concordia Theological Monthly* 41 (1970): 360–65.

Hercsik, Donath. "Das 'Wort Gotte' und die Christologie." *Greg* 89 (2008): 368–95.

Hiebert, D. Edmond. "An Expositional Study of 1 John—Part 1: An Exposition of 1 John 1:1–4." *BSac* 145 (1988): 197–210.

———. "An Expositional Study of 1 John—Part 2: An Exposition of 1 John 1:5–2:6." *BSac* 145 (1988): 329–42.

———. "An Expositional Study of 1 John—Part 3: An Exposition of 1 John 2:7–17." *BSac* 145 (1988): 420–35.

———. "An Expositional Study of 1 John—Part 4: An Exposition of 1 John 2:18–28." *BSac* 146 (1989): 76–93.

———. "An Expositional Study of 1 John—Part 5: An Exposition of 1 John 2:29–3:12." *BSac* 146 (1989): 198–216.

———. "An Expositional Study of 1 John—Part 6: An Exposition of 1 John 3:13–24." *BSac* 146 (1989): 301–19.

———. "An Expositional Study of 1 John—Part 7: An Exposition of 1 John 4:1–6." *BSac* 146 (1989): 420–36.

———. "An Expositional Study of 1 John—Part 8: An Exposition of 1 John 4:7–21." *BSac* 147 (1990): 69–89.

———. "An Expositional Study of 1 John—Part 9: An Exposition of 1 John 5:1–12." *BSac* 147 (1990): 216–30.

———. "An Expositional Study of 1 John—Part 10: An Exposition of 1 John 5:13–21." *BSac* 147 (1990): 309–28.

———. "Studies in 3 John—Part 1: An Exposition of 3 John 1–4." *BSac* 144 (1987): 53–65.

———. "Studies in 3 John—Part 2: An Exposition of 3 John 5–10." *BSac* 144 (1987): 194–207.

———. "Studies in 3 John—Part 3: An Exposition of 3 John 11–14." *BSac* 144 (1987): 293–304.

Hills, Julian. "'Little Children, Keep Yourselves from Idols': 1 John 5:21 Reconsidered." *CBQ* 51 (1989): 285–310.

Hodges, Zane C. "Fellowship and Confession in 1 John 1:5–10." *BSac* 129 (1972): 48–60.

———. "We Believe In: Assurance Of Salvation." *JOTGES* 3 (90): 3–17.

———. "What Do We Mean By Propitiation? Does It Only Count If We Accept It?" *JOTGES* 19 (2006): 35–42.

Horner, Jerry. "Introduction to the Johannine Epistles." *SwJT* 13 (1970): 41–51.

Houlden, J. L. "Salvation Proclaimed II. 1 John 1.5–2.6: Belief and Growth." *ExpTim* 93 (1982): 132–36.

Hunter, A. M. "Recent Trends in Johannine Studies." *ExpTim* 71 (1960): 164–67.

Inman, V. Kerry. "Distinctive Johannine Vocabulary and the Interpretation of I John 3:9," *WTJ* 40 (1977): 136–44.

Johnson, S. Lewis, Jr. "Once Saved, Always Saved?" *Etern* 3 (1952): 10–11.

Johnston, George. "'Οἰκουμένη and κόσμος' in the New Testament." *NTS* 10 (1964): 352–60.

Jones, Peter R. "A Structural Analysis of 1 John." *RevExp* 67 (1970): 433–44.

Joslin, Barry C. "Christ Bore the Sins of Many: Substitution and the Atonement In Hebrews." *SBJT* 11 (2007): 72–96.

Jung, Chang W. "Main Thrust of the Sentence(s): in 1 John 3:19–20: Encouragement or Warning?" *Neot* 41 (2007): 97–111.

Käsemann, Ernst. "Ketzer und Zeuge: Zum johanneischen Verfasserproblem." *ZTK* 48 (1951): 292–311.

Kazen, Thomas. "The Christology of Early Christian Practice." *JBL* 3 (2008): 591–614.

Kelley, P. H. "Israel's Tabernacling God." *RevExp* 67 (1970): 485–94.

Kistemaker, Simon J. "'Deliver this Man to Satan' (1 Cor 5:5): A Case Study in Church Discipline." *Masters Seminary Journal* 3 (1992): 32–46.

———. "The Theological Message of James." *JETS* 29 (1986; 2002): 54–61.

Klauck, Hans-Josef. "In the World—of the World (1 Jn 2:15–17)." *TD* 37 (1990): 209–14.

Köstenberger, Andreas J. "The Deity of Christ in John's Letters and the Book of Revelation." In *The Deity of Christ*, edited by Christopher W. Morgan and Robert A. Peterson, 151–67. Wheaton, IL: Crossway, 2011.

Kubo, Sakae. "1 John 3:9; Absolute or Habitual?" *AUSS* 7 (1969): 47–56.

Kügler, Joachim. "Die Belehrung der Unbelehrbaren: Zur Funktion des Traditionsarguments in 1 Joh." *BZ* 32 (1988): 249–54.

Lalleman, Pieter J. "The Adversaries Envisaged in the Johannine Epistles." *ThT* 53 (1999): 17–24.

Laney, J. Carl. "Abiding Is Believing: The Analogy of the Vine in John 15:1–6." *BSac* 146 (1989): 54–66.

Lieu, Judith M. "'Authority to become Children of God.' A Study of 1 John." *NovT* 23 (1981): 210–28.

———. "Us or You? Persuasion and Identity in 1 John." *JBL* 4 (2008): 805–19.

———. "What was from the Beginning: Scripture and Tradition in the Johannine Epistles." *NTS* 39 (1993): 458–77.

Lightner, Robert. "False Doctrine and the Child of God." *The Journal of Ministry and Theology* 10 (2006): 44–53.

Longenecker, Richard N. "On the Form, Function, and Authority of the New Testament Letters." In *Scripture and Truth*, edited by D. A. Carson and John D. Woodbridge, 97–114. Grand Rapids: Baker, 1992.

Lorencin, Igor. "Hospitality versus Patronage: An Investigation of Social Dynamics in the Third Epistle of John." *Andrews Uinversity Seminary Studies* 46 (2008): 165–74.

Louw, J. P. "Verbal Aspect in the First Letter of John." *Neot* 9 (1975): 98–104.

Love, D'Esta. "Love not the World." *Leaven* 14 (2006): 119–23.

Lovell, Ora D. "The Present Possession of Perfection in First John." *WesTJ* 8 (1973): 38–44.

MacArthur, John F., Jr. "Faith According to the Apostle James." *JETS* 33 (March 1990): 11–47.

Mann, Ronald E. "The Value of Chiasm for New Testament Interpretation," *BSac* 141 (2002): 144–54.

Manson, T. W. "Entry into Membership of the Early Church." *JTS* 48 (1947): 25–33.

Marrow, Stanley B. "Κόσμος in John." *CBQ* 64 (2002): 90–102.

Marulli, Luca. "A Letter of Recommendation? A Closer look at Third John's 'rhetorical' Argumentation." *Bib* 90 (2009): 203–23.

McKnight, Scot. "Literary Criticism Of The Synoptic Gospels." *TJ* 8 (1987): 56–79.

Merrill, Eugene H. "The Odes Of Solomon And The Acts Of Thomas: A Comparative Study." *JETS* 17, no. 4 (1992): 230–33.

Minear, P. "The Idea of Incarnation in 1 John." *Int* 24 (1970): 291–302.

Mitchell, Margaret M. "'Diotrephes does not receive us': The Lexicographical and Social Context of 3 John 9–10." *JBL* 117 (1998): 299–320.

Moody, Dale. "The Theology of the Johannine Letters." *SwJT* 13 (1970): 7–22.

Morris, Leon. "The Use of *hilaskesthai* etc. in Biblical Greek." *ExpTim* 62 (1950): 227–33.

———. "The Wrath of God." *ExpTim* 63 (1951): 142–45.

Moule, C. F. D. "A Neglected Factor in the Interpretation of Johannine Eschatology." In *Studies in John*, 155–160. NovTSup 24. Leiden: E. J. Brill, 1970.

Newsom, Carol A. "Knowing as Doing: The Social Symbolics of Knowledge at Qumran." In *Semeia 59*. Edited by D. Jobling and T. Pippin. Atlanta: Society of Biblical Literature, 1992.

Nichols, Stephen J. "Prophecy Makes Strange Bedfellows: On The History of Identifying the Antichrist." *JETS* 44 (2001): 75–85.

Nicole, Roger R. "The Biblical Concept of Truth." In *Scripture and Truth*, 287–302. Grand Rapids: Zondervan, 1983.

———. "'Hilaskesthai' Revisited." *EvQ* 49 (1977): 173–77.

———. "C. H. Dodd And The Doctrine Of Propitiation." *WTJ* 17 (1954): 116–57.

Nunn, H. P. V. "The First Epistle of St. John." *EvQ* 17 (1945): 296–303.

Painter, John. "The 'Opponents' in 1 John." *NTS* 32 (1986): 48–71.

Paschal, R. W., Jr. "Sacramental symbolism and physical imagery in the Gospel of John." *TynBul* 32 (1981): 151–76.

Patterson, Richard D. "Deliverance from Darkness." *SBJT* 8, no. 1 (2004): 70–85.

Perkins, Pheme. "What is a Gnostic Gospel?" *CBQ* 71 (2009): 104–29.

Peterson, Robert A. "Apostasy." *Presb* 19 (1993): 17–31.

Pettegrew, Larry D. "Teaching Methods of Christ." *Central Bible Quarterly* 15 (1972): 3–31.

Piper, Otto A. "I John and the Didache of the Primitive Church." *JBL* 66 (1947): 437–51.

Polhill, John B. "An Analysis of II and III John." *RevExp* 67 (1970): 461–71.

Posset, Franz. "John Bugenhagen and the *Comma Johanneum*." *CTQ* 49 (1985): 245–51.

Price, R. M. "The Sitz-im-Leben of Third John: A New Reconstruction." *EvQ* 61 (1989): 109–19.

Reynolds, S. M. "The Sin unto Death and Prayers for the Dead." *RefR* 20 (1973): 130–39.

Richter, G. "Blut und Wasser aus der durchgebohrten Seite Jesu (Joh 19,34b)." In *Studien zum Johannesevangelium.* Regensburg: Pustet, 1977.

Robinson, J. A. T. "The Relation of the Prologue to the Gospel of St John." *NTS* 9 (1963): 120–129.

Salom, A. P. "Some Aspects of the Grammatical Style of I John." *JBL* 74 (1955): 96–102.

Schmid, Hansjörg. "How to Read the First Epistle of John Non-Polemically." *Bib* 85 (2004): 24–41.

Schneider, herbert. "'The Word Was Made Flesh': An Analysis of the Theology of Revelation in the Fourth Gospel." *CBQ* 31(1969): 344–56.

Seifrid, Mark A. "Justified by Faith and Judged by Works: A Biblical Paradox and Its Significance." *Southern Baptist Journal of Theology* 5 (2001): 83–95.

Sevenster, G. "Remarks on the Humanity of Jesus in the Gospel and Letters of John." In *Studies in John*, 185–93. NovTSup 24. Leiden: Brill, 1970.

Sibinga, J. Smit. "A Study in I John." In *Studies in John,* 194–208. NovTSup 24. Leiden: Brill, 1970.

Smalley, Stephen S. "What about 1 John?" In *StudBib 1978, Vol. 3: Papers on Paul and Other New Testament Authors,* edited by E. A. Livingstone, 337–43. Sheffield: JSOT Press, 1980.

Smith, Charles R. "The Unfruitful Branches in John 15. " *Grace Journal* 9 (1968): 3–20.

Smith, D. M., Jr. "Johannine Christianity: Some Reflections on its Character and Delineation." *NTS* 21 (1975): 222–48.

Smit-Sibinga, J. "A Study in 1 John." In *Studies in John,* 194–208. NovTSup 24. Leiden: Brill, 1970.

Snodderly, B. and D. G. Van der Merwe. "Status Degradation in First John: Social, Scientific and Literary Perspectives." *Acta Patristica et Byzantina* 18 (2007): 179–98.

Songer, Harold S. "The Life Situation of the Johannine Epistles." *RevExp* 67 (1970): 399–409.

Stagg, Frank. "Orthodoxy and Orthopraxy in the Johannine Epistles." *RevExp* 67 (1970): 423–32.

Storm, Melvin R. "Diotrephes: A Study of Rivalry in the Apostolic Church." *ResQ* 35 (1993): 193–202.

Suggit, J. N. "1 John 5:21: ΤΕΚΝΙΑ, ΦΥΛΑΞΑΤΕ ΕΑΥΤΑ ΑΠΟ ΤΩΝ ΕΙΔΩΛΩΝ." *JTS* 36 (1985): 386–90.

Sundberg, Albert, C., Jr. "Canon Muratori: A Fourth Century List." *HTR* 66 (1973): 1–41.

Swadling, Harry C. "Sin and Sinlessness in 1 John." *SJT* 35 (1982): 205–211.

Tan, Randall K. J. "Should We Pray For Straying Brethren? John's Confidence In 1 John 5:16–17." *JETS* 45 (2002): 599–609.

Taylor, Jerry. "Marching in the Light: 1 John 1:1–10." *Leaven* 18 (2010): 32–35.

Thiselton, Anthony C. "Semantics and New Testament Interpretation." In *New Testament Interpretation: Essays on Principles and Methods*. Edited by I. Howard Marshall, 74–100. Milton Keynes, UK: Paternoster, 1977.

Thomas, John C. "The Literary Structure of 1 John." *NovT* 40 (1998): 369–81.

Townsend, Jerry. "The Sin Unto Death." *ResQ* 6 (1962): 147–50.

Trudinger, Paul. "Concerning Sins, Mortal and Otherwise. A Note on 1 John 5:16–17." *Bib* 52 (1971): 541–42.

Van der Merwe, D. G. "'Experiencing Fellowship with God' According to 1 John 1:5–2:28: Dealing with the Change in Social Behavior." *Acta Patristica et Byzantina* 18 (2007): 231–62.

———. "'Having Fellowship with God' According to 1 John: Dealing with the Intermediation and Environment through Which and in Which it is Constituted." *Acta Theologica Supplementum* 8 (2006): 165–92.

von Harnack, Adolf. "Über den dritten Johannesbrief." *TU* 15 (1897): 3–27.

Vorster, W. S. "Heterodoxy in 1 John." *Neot* 9 (1975): 87–97.

Walvoord, John F. "Christ's Olivet Discourse on the End of the Age, Part VII: The Judgment of the Nations." *BSac* 129 (1972): 306–15.

———. "Series in christology, Part 4: The Preincarnate Son of God." *BSac* 104 (1947): 414–440.

Ward, Ronald A. "Theological Pattern of the Johannine Epistles." *SwJT* 13 (1970): 23–39.

Washburn, David L. "Third Class Conditions in First John." *GTJ* 11 (1990): 221–28.

Watson, Duane F. "1 John 2.12–14 as *Distributio, Conduplicatio, and Expolitio*: A Rhetorical Understanding." *JSNT* 35 (1989): 97–110.

Wead, David W. "The Johannine Double Meaning." *ResQ* 13 (1970): 106–20.

Weiss, Harold. "Foot Washing in the Johannine Community." *NovT* 21 (1979): 298–325.

Wendland, Ernst R. "'Dear Children' Versus the 'Antichrists': The Rhetoric of Reassurance in First John." *JOTT* 11 (1998): 40–84.

———. "What is Truth? Semantic Density and the Language of the Johannine Epistles (with Special Reference to 2 John)." *Neot* 24 (1990): 301–33.

Willett, Don. "A Biblical Model of Stages of Spiritual Development: The Journey According to John." *Journal of Spiritual Formation & Soul Care* 3 (2010): 88–102.

Witherington, Ben. "The Waters of Birth: John 3:5 and 1 John 5:6–8." *NTS* 35 (1989): 155–60.

Wolter, Michael. "Der altbose Feind." *Glaube und Lernen* 12 (1997): 22–30.

Yarid, John R., Jr. "Reflections of the Upper Room Discourse in 1 John." *BSac* 160, no. 637 (January 2003): 65–76.

Yong, Amos. "'The Light Shines in the Darkness,' Johannine Dualism and the Challenge for Christian Theology of Religions Today." *JR* 89 (2009): 31–56.

Young, Norman H. "'Hilaskesthai' and Related Words in the New Testament." *EvQ* 55 (1983): 169–76.

———. "C. H. Dodd, 'Hilaskesthai' and his Critics." *EvQ* 48 (1976): 67–78.

Youngblood, Ronald. "Qoheleth's 'Dark House' (Eccl 12:5)." *JETS* 29, no. 4 (1986): 396–417.

General Books

Abbott, Edwin A. *Johannine Grammar.* London: Adam & Charles Black, 1906.

Archer, Gleason L., R. Laird Harris, and Bruce K. Waltke, eds. *Theological Wordbook of the Old Testament*. Electronic ed. Chicago: Moody, 1999.

Arndt, William F., Fredrick W. Danker and Walter Bauer. *A Greek-English Lexicon of the New Testament and Other Early Christian Literature*. 3rd ed. Chicago: University of Chicago Press, 2000.

Balz, Horst R., and Gerhard Schneider, eds. *Exegetical Dictionary of the New Testament.* Translated by P. Howard and James W. Thompson. Edinburgh: T & T Clark, 1990.

Bauer, Walter. *Orthodoxy and Heresy in Earliest Christianity.* Edited by Robert A. Kraft and Gerhard Krodel. Translated by Philadelphia Seminar on Christian Origins. Philadelphia: Fortress, 1971.

Beale, G. K. and D. A. Carson. *Commentary on the New Testament Use of the Old Testament*. Grand Rapids: Baker Academic, 2007.

Beasley-Murray, George R. *John*. Word Biblical Themes. Waco: Word, 1989.

Bengel, Johann A. *Gnomon of the New Testament.* Vol. 5. Translated by W. Flestcher. Edinburgh: T & T Clark, 1858.

Blass, F., A. Debrunner, and R. W. Funk. *A Greek Grammar of the New Testament and Other Early Christian Literature*. Chicago: University of Chicago Press, 1961.

Bock, Darrell L. and Gregory J. Herrick. eds. *Jesus in Context: Background Readings for Gospel Study.* Grand Rapids: Baker, 2005.

Bogart, John. *Orthodox and Hereticalhe Perfectionism in the Johannine Community as Evident in the First Epistle of John*. SBL Dissertation Series 33. Missoula, MT: Scholars Press, 1977.

Boice, James M. *Christ's Call to Discipleship.* Chicago: Moody, 1986.

———. *Witness and Revelation in the Gospel of John*. Grand Rapids: Zondervan, 1970.

Bonhoeffer, Dietrich. *Life Together*. Translated by John W. Doberstein. New York: Harper & Bros, 1954.

Borgen, Peder, Kåre Fuglseth, and Roald Skarsten. *The Works of Philo: Greek Text With Morphology.* Bellingham, WA: Logos Research Systems, Inc., 2005.

Brand, Chad, Charles Draper, and Archie England, eds. *Holman Illustrated Bible Dictionary.* Nashville: Holman Bible Publishers, 2003.

Braun, François-Marie. *Jean le théologien: sa théologie, le mystère de Jésus-Christ.* Paris: J. Gabalda, 1966.

Brown, Colin, ed. *New International Dictionary of New Testament Theology.* 4 vols. Grand Rapids: Zondervan, 1975–1985.

Brown, Raymond E. *The Community of the Beloved Disciple*. Mahwah, NJ: Paulist Press, 1979.

Bruce, F. F. *Paul: Apostle of the Heart Set Free*. Grand Rapids: Eerdmans, 1977.

Bruns, J. Edgar. *The Art and Thought of John*. New York: Herder and Herder, 1969.

Büchsel, Friedrich. *Johannes und der Hellenistische Synkretismus*. BFCT 2, no. 16. Gütersloh, Germany: Bertelsmann, 1928.

Bullinger, E. W. *Figures of Speech Used in the Bible.* New York: Eyre & Spottiswoode, 1898. Repr., Grand Rapids: Baker, 1968.

Burton, Ernest DeWitt. *Syntax of the Moods and Tenses in New Testament Greek.* 3rd ed. Chicago: University of Chicago, 1898.

Campbell, Alastair R. *The Elder: Seniority within Earliest Christianity.* Edinburgh: T & T Clark, 1994.

Carson D. A. and John D. Woodbridge, eds. *Scripture and Truth.* Grand Rapids: Baker, 1992.

Charles, Robert H., ed. *Pseudepigrapha of the Old Testament.* Bellingham, WA: Logos Research Systems, Inc., 2004.

Charlesworth, James H., ed. *The Old Testament Pseudepigrapha.* 2 vols. Garden City, NY: Doubleday, 1983–85.

Clark, Gordon H. *The Johannine Logos.* N.p.: Presbyterian and Reformed, 1972.

Cook, W. Robert. *The Theology of John.* Chicago: Moody, 1979.

Cross, F. L., and Elizabeth A. Livingstone, eds. *The Oxford Dictionary of the Christian Church*, 3rd ed. Oxford: Oxford University Press, 2005.

Culpepper, R. Allan. *The Johannine School: An Evaluation of the Johannine-School Hypothesis Based on an Investigation of the Nature of Ancient Schools.* SBL Dissertation Series 26. Missoula, MT: Scholars Press, 1975.

Dana, Harvey E. and Julius R. Mantey. *A Manual Grammar of the Greek New Testament.* New York: Macmillan, 1957.

Danby, Herbert. *Mishnah: Translated from the Hebrew with Introduction and Brief Explanatory Notes.* Oxford: Oxford University Press, 1933.

Deconick, April D. *The Original Gospel of Thomas in Translation: With a Commentary and New English Translation of the Complete Gospel.* Library of New Testament Studies 287. New York: Clark, 2006.

Dorsey, David A. *The Literary Structure of the Old Testament: A Commentary on Genesis-Malachi.* Grand Rapids: Baker, 1999.

Ehrman, Bart D. *The Lost Gospel of Judas Iscariot: A New Look at Betrayer and Betrayed.* Oxford: Oxford University Press, 2006.

Elwell, Walter A., ed. *Baker Encyclopedia of the Bible.* Grand Rapids: Baker, 1988.

Fanning, Buist M. *Verbal Aspect in New Testament Greek.* Oxford: Clarendon, 1990.

Ferguson, Sinclair B., and J. I. Packer, eds. *New Dictionary of Theology.* Downers Grove, IL: InterVarsity Press, 2000.

Feuillet, André. *Johannine Studies.* Staten Island, NY: Alba House, 1965.

Freedman, David Noel, ed. *Anchor Bible Dictionary.* New York: Doubleday, 1996.

Freedman, David N., Allen C. Myers, and Astrid B. Beck, eds. *Eerdmans Dictionary of the Bible.* Grand Rapids: Eerdmans, 2000.

Friberg, Timothy; Barbara Friberg; and Neva F. Miller. *Analytical Lexicon of the Greek New Testament.* BGNTL 4. Grand Rapids: Baker, 2000.

George, Bob. *Classic Christianity.* Eugene, OR: Harvest House, 1989.

Grenfell, Bernard P. and Arthur S. Hunt, eds. *The Oxyrhynchus Papyri: Part 2*. London: Egpyt Exploration Fund, 1899.

Guthrie, Donald. *New Testament Introduction*. Downers Grove, IL: InterVarsity Press, 1996.

Hahneman, Geoffrey M. *The Muratorian Fragment and the Development of the Canon*. Oxford: Clarendon, 1992.

Hanna, Robert. *A Grammatical Aid to the Greek New Testament*. Grand Rapids: Baker, 1983.

Harris, Murray J. *Jesus as God: The New Testament Use of Theos in Reference to Jesus.* Grand Rapids: Baker, 1992.

Hawthorne, Gerald F., Ralph P. Martin, and Daniel G. Reid, eds. *Dictionary of Paul and His Letters.* Downers Grove, IL: InterVarsity, 1993.

Henderson, David W. *Culture Shift: Communicating God's Truth in our Changing World* Grand Rapids: Baker, 1998.

Hengel, Martin. *The Johannine Question*. London: SCM, 1989.

Hill, David. *Greek Words and Hebrew Meanings.* Eugene, OR: Wipf & Stock, 2001.

Hodge, Charles. *Systematic Theology*. 3 vols. Oak Harbor, WA: Logos Research Systems, Inc., 1997.

Holmes, Michael W. *The Apostolic Fathers: Greek Texts and English Translations*. Updated ed. Grand Rapids: Baker, 1999.

Howard, W. F. *Christianity According to St. John*. Philadelphia: Westminster, 1946.

Hunt, Arthur S. and Campbell C. Edgar. *Select Papyri: An English Translation*. 3 Vols. Cambridge: Harvard, 1959.

Jeffers, James S. *The Greco-Roman World of the New Testament Era: Exploring the Background of Early Christianity*. Downers Grove, IL: InterVarsity Press, 1999.

Johnson, Elliot E. *Expository Hermeneutics: An Introduction.* Grand Rapids: Zondervan, 1990.

Koch, Klaus. *Die israelitische Sühneanschauung und ihre historischeen Wandlungen*. Erlangen: Habilitationsschrift, 1956.

Köstenberger, Andreas J. *A Theology of John's Gospel and Letters: The Word, the Christ, the Son of God*. Biblical Theology of the New Testament. Grand Rapids: Zondervan, 2009.

Kurian, George T., ed. *Nelson's New Christian Dictionary: The Authoritative Resource on the Christian World.* Nashville: Thomas Nelson, 2001.

Lee, Edwin K. *The Religious Thought of St. John*. London: SPCK, 1950.

Lieu, Judith. *The Second and Third Epistles of John: History and Background*. Edinburgh: T & T Clark, 1986.

Lund, Nils W. *Chiasmus in the New Testament: A Study in the Form and Function of Chiastic Structures*. Peabody, MA: Hendrickson, 1942, 1970.

MacArthur, John F., Jr. *The Gospel According to Jesus*, Grand Rapids: Academie, 1988.

Malatesta, Edward. *Interiority and Covenant: A Study of* εἶναι ἐν *and* μένειν ἐν *In the First Letter of Saint John*. Rome: Biblical Institute Press, 1978.

Martin, Ralph P., and Peter H. Davids, eds. *Dictionary of the Later New Testament and Its Developments*. Downers Grove, IL: InterVarsity Press, 2000.

Metzger, Bruce M., and United Bible Societies, *A Textual Commentary on the Greek New Testament*. 2nd ed. New York: United Bible Societies, 1994.

Moffatt, James A. R. *The Bible, A New Translation*. New York: Harper & Row, 1954.

Morris, Leon. *Jesus is the Christ: Studies in the Theology of John*. Grand Rapids: Eerdmans, 1989.

———. *The Apostolic Preaching of the Cross*. Rev. ed. Grand Rapids: Eerdmans, 1965.

Moule, C. F. D. *An Idiom-book of New Testament Greek*. 2nd ed. New York: Cambridge University Press, 1953, 1959.

Moulton, James H., and Nigel Turner. *A Grammar of New Testament Greek. Vol. 3: Syntax*. Edinburgh: T & T Clark, 1963.

Moulton, James H., and George Milligan. *The Vocabulary of the Greek Testament*. London, 1930. Repr., Peabody, MA: Hendrickson, 1982.

Nauck, Wolfgang. *Die Tradition und der Charakter des ersten Johannesbriefes, zugleich ein Beitrag zur Taufe im Urchristentum und in der alten Kirche*. WUNT, 3. Tübingen: Mohr, 1957.

Sproul, R. C., ed. *New Geneva Study Bible*. Nashville: Thomas Nelson, 1997.

O'Loughlin, Thomas. *The Didache: A Window on the Earliest Christians*. Grand Rapids: Baker, 2010.

O'Neill, John C. *The Puzzle of 1 John*. London: SPCK, 1966.

Odeberg, Hugo. *The Fourth Gospel: Interpreted in its Relation to Contemporaneous Religious Currents in Palestine and the Hellenistic-Oriental World*. Chicago: Argonaut, 1968.

Ogilvie, Lloyd John. *When God First Thought of You*. Waco, TX: Word, 1978.

Parkes, James. *The Conflict of the Church and the Synagogue: A Study of the Origins of Antisemitism*. London: Soncino, 1934. Repr., New York: Atheneum, 1969.

Perrin, Nicholas. *Thomas, the Other Gospel*. London: SPCK, 2007.

Reddish, Mitchel G. ed. *Apocalyptic Literature: A Reader*. Peabody, MA: Hendrickson, 1990.

Reymond, Robert L. *John, Beloved Disciple: A Survey of His Theology*. Geanies House, Great Britain: Christian Focus, 2001.

Roberts, Alexander, James Donaldson and A. Cleveland Coxe, *The Ante-Nicene Fathers Vol. VIII: Translations of the Writings of the Fathers Down to A.D. 325*. Electronic ed. Oak Harbor, WA: Logos Research Systems, 1997.

Roberts, Alexander, James Donaldson, and A. Cleveland Coxe. *The Ante-Nicene Fathers Vol. I : Translations of the Writings of the Fathers Down to A.D. 325*. Electronic ed. Oak Harbor, WA: Logos Research Systems, 1997.

Robertson, Archibald T. *A Grammar of the Greek New Testament in the Light of Historical Research*. Nashville: Broadman, 1931.

———. *Word Pictures in the New Testament*. Vol. 5 c1932, Vol. 6 c1933 by Sunday School Board of the Southern Baptist Convention., Jn 2:24. Electronic ed. Oak Harbor, WA: Logos Research Systems, 1997.

Robinson, Maurice A. and William G. Pierpont. *The New Testament in the Original Greek: Byzantine Textform 2005, With Morphology*. Bellingham, WA: Logos Research Systems, 2006.

Rogers, Cleon L., Jr. and Cleon L. Rogers III. *The New Linguistic and Exegetical Key to the Greek New Testament*. Grand Rapids: Zondervan, 1998.

Rosscup, James E. *Abiding in Christ*. Grand Rapids: Zondervan, 1973.

Rusam, Dietrich. *Gemeinschaft der Kinder Gottes: Das Motiv der Gotteskindschaft und die Gemeinden der johanneischen Briefe*. Stuttgart: Verlag W. Kohlhammer, 1993.

Ryrie, Charles C. *Biblical Theology of the New Testament*. Chicago: Moody, 1959.

———. *So Great Salvation*. Wheaton, IL: Victor, 1989.

Schaff, P. *The Nicene and Post-Nicene Fathers, Second Series. Vol. I.* Oak Harbor, WA: Logos Research Systems, 1997.

Simmons, William A. *Peoples of the New Testament World*. Peabody, MA: Hendrickson, 2008.

Smith, Carl B. II, *No Longer Jews*. Peabody, MA: Henrickson, 2004.

Spicq, Ceslas. *Theological Lexicon of the New Testament*. Translated and edited by J. D. Ernest. 3 vols. Peabody, MA: Hendrickson, 1994.

Stevens, George B. *The Johannine Theology*. New York: Scribner, 1908.

———. *The Theology of the New Testament*. Edinburgh: T & T Clark, 1918.

Stowers, Stanley K. *Letter Writing in Greco-Roman Antiquities*. Philadelphia : Westminster, 1986.

Strombeck, John F. *Shall Never Perish*. Philadelphia: American Bible Conference Association, 1936.

Taylor, Vincent. *Forgiveness and Reconciliation: A Study in New Testament Theology*. New York: St. Martin's, 1956

Traina, Robert A. *Methodical Bible Study*. Grand Rapids: Francis Asbury, 1952, 1980.

Turner, Nigel. *Grammatical Insights into the New Testament*. Edinburgh: T & T Clark, 1965.

Vanderlip, D. George. *Christianity According to John*. Philadelphia: Westminster, 1975.

Vanhoozer, Kevin J., Craig G. Bartholomew, Daniel J. Treier, and N. T. Wright, eds. *Dictionary for Theological Interpretation of the Bible*. Grand Rapids: Baker Academic, 2005.

Vellanickal, Matthew. *The Divine Sonship of Christians in the Johannine Writings*. Rome: Biblical Institute Press, 1977.

Virkler, Henry A. *Hermeneutics: Principles and Processes of Biblical Interpretation*. Grand Rapids: Baker, 1981.

Wallace, Daniel B. *Granville Sharp's Canon and Its Kin: Semantics and Significance*, Studies in Biblical Greek 14. New York: Lang, 2009.

———. *Greek Grammar Beyond the Basics*. Grand Rapids: Zondervan, 1996.

Wendt, Hans H. *The Teaching of Jesus*. Translated by John Wilson. Vol. 1. Edinburgh: T & T Clark, 1892.

Whiston, William, trans. *The Works of Josephus: Complete and Unabridged*. Peabody, MA: Hendrickson, 1996.

Wright, N. T. *Judas and the Gospel of Jesus: Have We Missed the Truth about Christianity?* Grand Rapids: Baker, 2006.

Yonge, Charles D. *The Works of Philo: Complete and Unabridged*. New updated ed. Peabody, MA: Hendrickson, 1996.

Zerwick, Maximilian. *Biblical Greek: Illustrated by Examples*. Scripta Pontificii Instituti Biblici ; 114. English ed. adapted from the fourth Latin ed. by Joseph Smith. Rome: Tipografia PUG, 1963.

Zodhiates, Spiros. *The Complete Word Study Dictionary: New Testament*. Electronic ed. Chattanooga, TN: AMG, 2000.

Unpublished Works

Curtis, Edward M. "The Purpose of 1 John." Th.D. diss., Dallas Theological Seminary, 1986.

Derickson, Gary W. "An Evaluation of Expository Options of 1 John." Unpublished diss., Dallas Theological Seminary, 1992.

McCabe, Clifford A. "The Use of the Present Tense in the First Epistle of John and the Interpretation of 3:6 and 9." Unpublished diss., Bob Jones University, 1988.

Potter, David R. "The Substance and Hope of Johannine Christology." Unpublished diss., Bob Jones University, 1978.

Snodderly, Mary E. C. "A Socio-Rhetorical Investigation of the Johannine Understanding of 'the Works of the Devil' in 1 John 3:8." Unpublished diss., University of South Africa, 2008.

Wetzler, Wellington. "The Doctrine of Assurance in 1 John." Unpublished thesis, Dallas Theological Seminary, 1956.

Index of Biblical Verses

Old Testament

New Testament

Mark

Luke

Acts

Romans

1 Corinthians

2 John

3 John

Revelations